PHILOSOPHY

The Quest for Truth

FIFTH EDITION

PHILOSOPHY

The Quest for Truth

FIFTH EDITION

Louis P. Pojman
United States Military Academy at West Point

New York • Oxford
OXFORD UNIVERSITY PRESS
2002

Oxford University Press

Oxford   New York
Auckland Bangkok Buenos Aires Cape Town Chennai
Dar es Salaam Delhi Hong Kong Istanbul Karachi Kolkata
Kuala Lumpur Madrid Melbourne Mexico City Mumbai Nairobi
São Paulo Shanghai Singapore Taipei Tokyo Toronto

and an associated company in Berlin

Copyright © 2002 by Oxford University Press, Inc.

Published by Oxford University Press, Inc.
198 Madison Avenue, New York, New York, 10016
http://www.oup-usa.org

Oxford is a registered trademark of Oxford University Press

ISBN 0-19-515624-2

Printing number: 9 8 7 6 5 4 3 2 1

Printed in the United States of America
on acid-free paper.

Dedicated to Teachers
who themselves are dedicated
to opening the hearts of the young
to the love of wisdom and
the quest for truth

Contents

V. Freedom of the Will and Determinism   327

VI. Ethics   359

Preface

I AM GRATEFUL FOR THE WIDE USE the first four editions of this introductory textbook received and am happy to bring forth an improved edition. Many instructors sent in constructive suggestions for this edition. I have given them serious consideration and incorporated many of them without sacrificing the central focus and methodology.

This anthology was designed for lower-division (freshen and sophomore) students in Introduction to Philosophy courses. After several years of using some of the more comprehensive anthologies, and rejecting spoon-fed introductory texts, I came to the conclusion that the more rigorous anthologies are simply too hard for the average undergraduate nonphilosophy major. There was need for an anthology with more modest ambitions—but one that concentrated on the classic texts and raised the classic issues: the nature of philosophy, the existence of God, immortality, knowledge, the mind-body question, personal identity, free will and determinism, ethics, political philosophy, and the meaning of life.

I have sought to provide such a middle way between the heavy-duty textbooks and those that seem trendy and simplistic. Although other fine anthologies are available, few are centered in classic texts, as this book is. My book raises some questions not usually covered. It provides more and different readings to discuss all the questions and, at the end of each reading, it provides reflective questions. In this way *Philosophy: The Quest for Truth* fills a need and establishes a niche of its own.

Organization

Each of the nineteen questions considered in this book has a substantial introduction; in addition, individual introductions, including biographical sketches, are provided for each of the seventy-three readings. Each reading is preceded by a set of study questions and followed by a set of reflective questions that challenge the student to analyze, critique, and develop the arguments presented in the readings. A short bibliography follows each major part of the book. There is an appendix on how to read and write a philosophy paper. A glossary appears at the end.

Teachers will use the two sets of questions in different ways. The study questions, at the beginning of the readings, center on the content of the article and highlight material important for understanding the text. Some instructors may want students to write out answers to these questions as homework assignments. Others may simply use them as informal guides, leaving the students to use them as they see fit. Not every student needs auxiliary questions to the same degree, but most seem to find them helpful. My suggestion is to use an SQ2R approach: Survey, Question, Read, Reflect. That is, first read the article quickly, not worrying about whether you grasp all the important ideas; then go over the study questions and read the article more carefully with them in mind. Finally, look at the reflective questions and try to answer them. It may help to write out your responses.

This book is organized in a traditional way. First, I introduce the question "What is Philosophy?" with an introductory essay and readings by Plato and Bertrand Russell. Next, I offer a chapter on logic, including deductive, inductive, and abductive reasoning, followed by a discussion of informal fallacies. I then move to the classic questions about which more philosophy has been written than any other: Is there a God? Can we prove—or at least provide strong arguments—that a Supreme Being exists? I follow the tradition of beginning with this question for two reasons. First, it may be the most important question that philosophy asks. This is arguable, of course, as is almost everything in philosophy, but it can be supported with plausible reasons. Second, this theme provides us with some of the clearest examples in philosophy of deductive argument, as well as some classic examples of inductive and abductive reasoning, and thus enables students to develop their reasoning skills. In this section I also consider the relation of faith to reason.

Next we turn to Part III, The Theory of Knowledge: What can we know, if anything, and how do we know? Here I treat several classical theories and then tackle the contemporary debate on truth and cognitive relativism. I regard these classic texts—especially Descartes, Locke, Berkeley, Hume—as the heart of philosophy, although they may be the hardest in the book. Part IV deals with Philosophy of Mind, considering the mind-body problem, personal identity, and the implications of the problem of personal identity for the possibility of immortality. Part V treats various responses to the question of whether we have freedom of the will.

Part VI deals with Ethics and includes such questions as "Are there any moral absolutes? Why should I be moral? Which ethical theory (if any) is the correct one?" This is followed by Part VII on political philosophy and the justification of the State. Part VIII asks, "What is the Meaning of Life?" and, finally, Part IX, on Applied Ethics, offers opposing views on abortion, capital punishment, animal rights, and affirmative action, some of the most pressing moral problems of our age.

There is nothing sacred about this order. Each part is independent of the others, and the instructor is free to treat these topics in any order desired. I seldom cover more than five major topics during a semester. The only part I invariably use and begin with is Part I "What is Philosophy?"

The Readings

The readings have been chosen for their clarity and cogency of argument, classical expression of the positions, and accessibility to intelligent college students. They are, for the most part, classical readings, raising classic questions and trying to solve them or shed light on them. There are several selections from Plato, René Descartes, John Locke, David Hume, William James, Bertrand Russell, John Hick, John Hospers, and James Rachels—as well as essays by Aristotle, Thomas Aquinas, Blaise Pascal, Thomas Hobbes, George Berkeley, Immanuel Kant, Gilbert Ryle, Albert Camus, Jean-Paul Sartre, Frederich Nietzsche, Alvin Plantinga, and other important writers.

I have striven to represent opposing views on virtually every topic in this book and to find the strongest arguments for these opposing positions. No compliment has pleased me more than those letters or comments stating that my work is fair to the various positions in the debate.

The articles are generally presented in chronological order within a given section, but sometimes this conflicts with the dialogic nature of this work, in which case I have sacrificed chronology for development of argument.

For example, Hume's critique of the teleological argument actually was written before Paley's classic defense, but it is better to have the defense before the critique.

New Material in the Fifth Edition

Responding to several users of this textbook, I have made a number of changes from the previous edition. I have improved several parts, by adding nine new articles, and revising some of the articles from the fourth edition. I have also added new study questions.

The nine new articles are:

5. Father F. C. Copleston and Bertrand Russell: A Debate on the Argument from Contingency

40. Corliss Lamont: Freedom of the Will and Human Responsibility

42. Richard Taylor: Fate

47. Louis Pojman: A Critique of Ethical Egoism

52. Robert Paul Wolff: In Defense of Anarchism

57. Brian Barry: A Cosmopolitan Theory of International Society

62. Thomas Nagel: The Absurd

67. Thurgood Marshall: The Death Penalty Is a Denial of Human Dignity

68. Buton Leiser: The Death Penalty Is Permissible

In Part VII I have included more of John Stuart Mill's defense of liberty from *On Liberty*.

Acknowledgments

I would like to thank the reviewers who prompted these improvements: Richard Gale, University of Pittsburgh; Marie Friquegnon, William Patterson College; Paul Hedengren, Brigham Young University; Thomas Senor, University of Arkansas; David Fletcher and Jay Wood, Wheaton College; Michael Eldridge, University of North Carolina, Charlotte; Sterling Harwood, Esq.; and Thomas C. Ryckman, Lawrence University. Ken King, former senior editor of Wadsworth Publishing Company, was responsible for getting me to put this work together in the first place.

I am grateful to Ruth Cottrell for doing an excellent job in bringing this edition to life. I should also note that this new edition of *Philosophy: The Quest for Truth* is now being published by Oxford University Press, and I am delighted to be working again with my editor there, Robert Miller, with whom I have published several other philosophy textbooks.

Philosophy is an exciting subject. Indeed, I start out by arguing that it has revolutionary possibilities. Every intelligent young person should be exposed to and challenged by the questions it asks and the attempts it makes to respond to these questions, searching for truth and learning to enjoy the process of growing in wisdom. In order for that challenge to be effective, it is important to have teachers dedicated to teaching philosophy, for, perhaps more than any other subject, philosophy needs a mediator for its communication. The competent, committed teacher, in a tradition going as far back as Socrates, the gadfly of the Athenian marketplace, as a catalyst for learning, is the most vital part of doing philosophy. I have sought to put together a set of readings with accompanying resources to help such dedicated teachers carry on that process in the classroom. To them this book is dedicated.

Louis P. Pojman
United States Military Academy
West Point, New York
December 3, 2001

PHILOSOPHY

The Quest for Truth

FIFTH EDITION

Part I

What Is Philosophy?

The unexamined life is not worth living.

SOCRATES

If God held all Truth in His right hand and in His left hand the eternal Quest for Truth, and said to me, "Choose!" I would with courage touch His left and say, "Father, Give me this! The pure Truth is fit for you alone."

G. E. LESSING, *Werke*, vol. X, p. 53; my translation.

PHILOSOPHY IS REVOLUTIONARY and vitally important to the good life. This book starts from an assumption that I hope you will be convinced of by the time you have completed this course: namely, that the unexamined life is not worth living and that while philosophy disturbs, it also consoles. Philosophy, as Aristotle said more than two thousand years ago, begins with wonder at the marvels and mysteries of the world. It begins in wonder, in the pursuit of truth and wisdom, and ends in life lived in passionate moral and intellectual integrity. At least this is the classical philosophical ideal and the faith—a rational faith, I hope. Of course, this thesis about the worth of philosophy is to be subject to rational scrutiny. Perhaps it is wrong, but it's one that I deeply believe. Let me expand on it.

The term "philosophy" literally means the love of wisdom (etymologically from the Greek *philos* = love and *sophia* = wisdom), but it is a wisdom that results from a pursuit of knowledge of the most important parts of reality. Hence the title of this book, the quest for truth. The quest for truth is the contemplation or study of the most important questions in existence with the goal of promoting illumination and understanding, a vision of the whole. It uses reason, sense perception, the imagination, and intuitions in its activity of analyzing and constructing arguments and theories as possible answers to these perennial questions. It is revolutionary because its deliverances often disturb our common sense or our received tradition. Philosophy usually goes against the stream or the majority because the majority opinion is often a composite of past intellectual struggles or "useful" biases. There is often deeper truth, better and new evidence that disturbs the status quo and that forces us to revise or reject some of our beliefs. This experience can be as painful as it is exciting.

The pain may lead us to give up philosophical inquiry and may require a great deal of emotional health to persevere in it. We may retreat into unreason and obey the commandment of Ignorance, "Think not, lest Thou be confounded!" Truth (or what we seem justified in believing) may not always be edifying. But in the end, the philosopher's faith is that the Truth is good and worth pursuing for its own sake and for its secondary benefits. Intelligent inquiry, which philosophy promotes, is liberating, freeing us from prejudice, self-deceptive notions, and half-truths. As Bertrand Russell says in our second reading,

> The [person] who has no tincture of philosophy goes through life imprisoned in the prejudices derived from common sense, from the habitual beliefs of his age or his nation, and from convictions which have grown up in his mind without the co-operation or consent of his deliberate reason. . . . While diminishing our feeling of certainty as to what things are, [philosophy] greatly increases our knowledge as to what they may be; it removes the somewhat arrogant dogmatism of those who have never travelled into the region of liberating doubt, and it keeps alive the sense of wonder by showing familiar things in an unfamiliar light.

Philosophy should result in a wider vision of life in which the impartial use of reason results in an appreciation of other viewpoints and other people's rights and needs. There is no guarantee that this will occur. Some become radical skeptics with accompanied behavioral patterns, and some nasty people seem to be able to do philosophy quite well without being transformed by it. But for the most part those who have had the vision of a better life and have worked through arguments on substantive issues relating to the nature and destiny of humanity have been positively affected by the perennial pilgrimage. They march to a different drummer and show in their lives the fruits of their travail. This ability to live by reflective principle in spite of and in the midst of the noise of the masses is a special virtue of philosophy. It is illustrated by one of its heroes, Socrates (470–399 B.C.), in our first reading from Plato's work, *Apology.*

The hallmark of philosophy is centered in the argument. Philosophers clarify concepts, analyze and test propositions and beliefs, but the major task is to analyze and construct arguments. At the end of Part I, I have added a section "A Little Bit of Logic" to help you understand the nature of arguments. Philosophical reasoning is closely allied to scientific reasoning in that both look for evidence and build hypotheses that are tested with the hope of coming closer to the truth. However, scientific experiments take place in laboratories and have testing procedures through which to record objective or empirically verifiable results. The laboratory of the philosopher is the domain of ideas: the mind, where imaginative thought-experiments take place; the study, where ideas are written down and examined; and wherever conversation or debate about the perennial questions takes place, where thesis and counter-example and counter-thesis are considered. A joke compares the equipment needs of the scientist, the mathematician, and the philosopher: The scientist needs an expensive laboratory with all sorts of experimental equipment. The mathematician needs only a pencil, paper, and a waste-paper basket. The philosopher needs only a pencil and paper! The truth embodied in this bit of humor is that it is not as easy to test philosophical theories as it is to test a mathematical theorem or a scientific hypothesis. Because philosophical questions are more speculative and metaphysical, one cannot prove or disprove most of the important theses. The relationship of philosophy to science is more complicated than this suggests, for some of what theoretical scientists do could with justice be called philosophy. In general, the sciences have one by one made their way out of the family fold of philosophy to independence as they systematized their decision-making procedures. In the words of Jeffrey Olen,

> The history of philosophy reads like a long family saga. In the beginning there were the great patriarch and matriarch, the searches for knowledge and wisdom, who bore a large number of children. Mathematics, physics, ethics, psychology, logic, political thought, metaphysics, . . . and epistemology . . .—all belonged to the same family. Philosophers were not *just* philosophers, but mathematicians and physicists and psychologists as well. Indeed, in the beginning of the family's history, no distinction was made between philosophy and these other disciplines. . . .
>
> In the beginning, then, all systematic search for knowledge was philosophy. This fact is still reflected in the modern university, where the highest degree granted in all of the sciences and humanities is the Ph.D.—the doctor of philosophy.
>
> But the children gradually began to leave home. First to leave were physics and astronomy, as they began to develop experimental techniques of their own. This exodus, led by Galileo (1564–1642), Isaac Newton (1642–1727), and Johannes Kepler (1571–1630), created the first of many great family crises. . . . Eventually, psychology left home. [*Persons and Their World*, Random House, 1983, p. 3f]

Although many of her children have left home, not all have, and some seem permanent residents. The major areas of philosophy today are metaphysics (regarding the nature of ultimate reality), epistemology (regarding the nature of knowledge and justification), logic, philosophy of religion, ethics, and political philosophy. But there are also secondary areas of philosophy that work on conceptual or theoretical problems arising within first-order nonphilosophical disciplines. Examples of these are philosophy of science, philosophy of psychology, philosophy of mathematics, philosophy of language, and philosophy of art. Wherever conceptual analysis or justification of a theoretical schema is needed, philosophical expertise is appropriate. More recently, as technology creates new possibilities and problems, applied ethics (for example, biomedical ethics, business ethics, environmental ethics, and legal ethics) has arisen. History plays a dialectical role relative to philosophy, for not only do philosophers do philosophy while teaching the history of philosophy, but they also critically examine the principles that underlie historical investigation itself, creating a philosophy of history.

We will touch on many of these areas in this work: philosophy of religion; epistemology; metaphysics, and within metaphysics the mind-body problem, personal identity, immortality, and free will and determinism; ethics; and political philosophy. These are more than enough for an introduction to philosophy.

Philosophical study is dialectic, proceeding as an intellectual conversation in which thesis and counter-thesis, hypothesis and counter-example continue in a way that exposes the weaknesses of proposed solutions to the puzzles of existence and leaves some answers as more or less plausible. In this conversation, all sides of an issue should receive a fair hearing, and then the reader is left to make up his or her own mind on the issue. Hence, in this work at least two opposing views are set forth on every issue.

Although a clearer understanding of the nature of philosophy will only emerge while you work through the arguments on the various issues you are going to study, I want to end this introduction with a set of guidelines for philosophical inquiry, "Ten Commandments of Philosophy," that I hope will aid you in your own pilgrimage as you build your own philosophy of life. They embody what I take to be the classical philosophical perspective, but they are set forth as hypothetical. You should test them, refine them, and possibly reject some of them or add better ones as you proceed on your own Quest for Truth.

Ten Commandments of Philosophy

BRAINSTORMING—1. *Allow the spirit of Wonder to flourish in your breast.* Philosophy begins with deep wonder about the universe and about who we are and where we came from and where we are going. What is this life all about?

2. *Doubt every claim you encounter until the evidence convinces you of its Truth.* Be reasonably cautious, a moderate skeptic, suspicious of those who claim to have the Truth. Doubt is the soul's purgative. Do not fear intellectual inquiry. As Goethe said, "The masses fear the intellectual, but it is stupidity that they should fear, if they only realized how dangerous it really is."

3. *Love the Truth.* "Philosophy is the eternal search for truth, a search which inevitably fails and yet is never defeated; which continually eludes us, but which

LET GO
of PREJUDICES

always guides us. This free, intellectual life of the mind is the noblest inheritance of the Western World; it is also the hope of our future." (W. T. Jones)

4. *Divide and Conquer.* Divide each problem and theory into its smallest essential components so you can analyze each unit carefully. This is the analytic method.

5. *Collect and Construct.* Build a coherent argument or theory from component parts. One should move from the simple, secure foundations to the complex and comprehensive. Bertrand Russell once said that the aim of philosophical argument was to move from simple propositions so obvious that no one would think of doubting them via a method of valid argument to conclusions so preposterous that no one could help but doubt them.

6. *Conjecture and Refute.* Make a complete survey of possible objections to your position, looking for counter-examples and subtle mistakes. As Karl Popper has insisted, philosophy is a system of conjecture and refutation. Seek bold hypotheses and seek to find disconfirmations of your favorite positions. In this way, by a process of elimination, you will negatively and indirectly and asymptotically approach the Truth.

7. *Revise and Rebuild.* Be willing to revise, reject, and modify your beliefs and the degree with which you hold any belief. Acknowledge that you probably have many false beliefs and be grateful to those who correct you. This is the Principle of Fallibilism, the thesis that we are very likely incorrect in many of our beliefs and have a tendency towards self-deception when considering objections to our position.

8. *Seek Simplicity.* Prefer the Simpler Explanation to the more complex, all things being equal. This is the Principle of Parsimony, sometimes known as "Occam's Razor."

9. *Live the Truth!* Appropriate your ideas in a personal way, so that even as the Objective Truth is a correspondence of the thought to the world, this Lived Truth will be a correspondence of the life to the thought. As Kierkegaard said, "Here is a definition of [subjective] truth: holding fast to an objective uncertainty in an appropriation process of the most passionate inwardness is the truth, the highest truth available for an existing individual."

10. *Live the Good!* Let the practical conclusions of a philosophical reflection on the moral life inspire and motivate you to action. Let moral Truth transform your life so that you shine like a jewel in its light amidst the darkness of global ignorance.

I hope these guides will help you think about philosophy as you read the essays in this book. As I mentioned earlier, they are intended, not as dogmatic pronouncements, but as embodying the perennial values that have guided the classic vision of the goal of philosophy in pursuing the truth. I believe in these rules of pursuit, although not every philosopher agrees with all of them. Those who see philosophy only as technique would disagree with the tenth rule, but the classic vision, reflected in our first reading, holds that the pursuit of the Truth should result in living the morally good life. Truth is intrinsically good and leads to the good life.

We turn to our three readings on the nature and task of philosophy as the Quest for Truth.

I.1   Socratic Wisdom

PLATO

Plato (427–347 B.C.) is one of the most important philosophers who ever lived and the first to write systematically on philosophical subjects. He lived in Athens, the great Greek democratic city-state, in the aftermath of its glory under its illustrious leader, Pericles. During much of Plato's life, Athens was at war with Sparta, the Greek city-state to the south. He was Socrates' disciple, the founder of the first school of philosophy (the Academy in Athens), Aristotle's teacher, and an advisor to emperors. Among his important works are the *Republic*, the *Apology, Phaedo,* and *Timaeus.* Alfred North Whitehead calls the whole history of Western philosophy "a series of footnotes to Plato."

Socrates (470–399 B.C.) is one of the most impressive human beings to have lived, and a paradigm of a philosopher. He is considered the father of moral philosophy (see Part VI). Living in Athens under Pericles, he enjoyed the freedoms of a democratic society. Socrates spent much of his life in the marketplace of Athens, questioning and arguing with his contemporaries on philosophical issues (for example, what is justice, friendship, self-control, piety, virtue? how do we teach virtue? does anyone do evil voluntarily? and so forth). He saw himself as the gadfly of the Greek city-state, serving his fellow citizens without pay, but many of its leading citizens saw him as a nuisance and, eventually, brought him to trial. Our reading is about this trial. Three Athenians —Meletus, Anytus, and Lycon—have brought charges against Socrates that he has corrupted the youth and doesn't believe in the Greek gods. The real cause of the trial is probably that Socrates had made a number of enemies in high places. He defied the authorities when they ordered him to arrest naval officers against what Socrates took to be the law. He embarrassed many of the leading citizens, politicians, artisans, poets, and orators—often before their sons—in exposing their pretenses to knowledge. The accumulated ire erupted and caused one of the most famous trials of all time, if not the most famous trial of all time. The following reading is Plato's rendition of it.

Study Questions

1. What is the message of the Oracle of Delphi to Chaerephon about Socrates?
2. What is Socrates' response and how does he go about trying to disprove the oracle? What was the effect of his probing on his fellow citizens?
3. How does Socrates finally interpret the message of the oracle?
4. What are the charges brought against Socrates? What are Socrates' responses to the charges?
5. What should be our only concern when we deliberate on what to do?
6. Why doesn't Socrates plead for his life? What does he propose as the counter-penalty?
7. What penalty does the jury decide on? Do you notice anything peculiar when comparing the numbers voting for the original verdict and the numbers voting for the penalty? What accounts for this?

8. What kind of life does Socrates think is worth living?

9. Does Socrates believe that his fellow citizens are doing him enormous harm?

FROM THE APOLOGY

HOW YOU, O ATHENIANS, have been affected by my accusers, I cannot tell; but I know that they almost made me forget who I was—so persuasively did they speak; and yet they have hardly uttered a word of truth. But of the many falsehoods told by them, there was one which quite amazed me—I mean when they said that you should be upon your guard and not allow yourselves to be deceived by the force of my eloquence. To say this, when they were certain to be detected as soon as I opened my lips and proved myself to be anything but a great speaker, did indeed appear to me most shameless—unless by the force of eloquence they mean the force of truth; for if such is their meaning, I admit that I am eloquent. But in how different a way from theirs! Well, as I was saying, they have scarcely spoken the truth at all; but from me you shall hear the whole truth: not, however, delivered after their manner in a set oration duly ornamented with words and phrases. No, by heaven! but I shall use the words and arguments which occur to me at the moment; for I am confident in the justice of my cause*: at my time of life I ought not to be appearing before you, O men of Athens, in the character of a juvenile orator—let no one expect it of me. And I must beg of you to grant me a favour: If I defend myself in my accustomed manner, and you hear me using the words which I have been in the habit of using in the [market], at the tables of the money-changers, or anywhere else, I would ask you not to be surprised, and not to interrupt me on this account. For I am more than seventy years of age, and appearing now for the first time in a court of law, I

*Or, I am certain that I am right in taking this course.

am quite a stranger to the language of the place; and therefore I would have you regard me as if I were really a stranger, whom you would excuse if he spoke in his native tongue, and after the fashion of his country: Am I making an unfair request of you? Never mind the manner, which may or may not be good; but think only of the truth of my words, and give heed to that: let the speaker speak truly and the judge decide justly. . . .

Well, then, I must make my defence, and endeavor to clear away in a short time, a slander which has lasted a long time. May I succeed, if to succeed be for my good and yours, or likely to avail me in my cause! The task is not an easy one; I quite understand the nature of it. And so leaving the event with God, in obedience to the law I will now make my defence.

I will begin at the beginning, and ask what is the accusation which has given rise to the slander of me, and in fact has encouraged Meletus to prefer this charge against me. Well, what do the slanderers say? They shall be my prosecutors, and I will sum up their words in an affidavit: 'Socrates is an evil-doer, and a curious person, who searches into things under the earth and in heaven, and he makes the worse appear the better cause; and he teaches the aforesaid doctrines to others.' Such is the nature of the accusation: it is just what you have yourselves seen in the comedy of Aristophanes, who has introduced a man whom he calls Socrates, going about and saying that he walks in air, and talking a deal of nonsense concerning matters of which I do not pretend to know either much or little—not that I mean to speak disparagingly of any one who is a student of natural philosophy. I should be very sorry if Meletus could bring so grave a charge against me. But the simple truth is, O Athenians, that I have nothing to do with physical speculations.

Reprinted from Dialogues of Plato, *trans. Benjamin Jowett, Oxford, 1896.*

Very many of those here present are witnesses to the truth of this, and to them I appeal. Speak then, you who have heard me, and tell your neighbours whether any of you have ever known me hold forth in few words or in many upon such matters. . . . You hear their answer. And from what they say of this part of the charge you will be able to judge of the truth of the rest.

As little foundation is there for the report that I am a teacher, and take money; this accusation has no more truth in it than the other. Although, if a man were really able to instruct mankind, to receive money for giving instruction would, in my opinion, be an honour to him. There is Gorgias of Leontium, and Prodicus of Ceos, and Hippias of Elis, who go the round of the cities, and are able to persuade the young men to leave their own citizens by whom they might be taught for nothing, and come to them whom they not only pay, but are thankful if they may be allowed to pay them. . . .

I dare say, Athenians, that some one among you will reply, 'Yes, Socrates, but what is the origin of these accusations which are brought against you; there must have been something strange which you have been doing? All these rumours and this talk about you would never have arisen if you had been like other men: tell us, then, what is the cause of them, for we should be sorry to judge hastily of you.' Now I regard this as a fair challenge, and I will endeavour to explain to you the reason why I am called wise and have such an evil fame. Please to attend then. And although some of you may think that I am joking, I declare that I will tell you the entire truth. Men of Athens, this reputation of mine has come of a certain sort of wisdom which I possess. If you ask me what kind of wisdom, I reply, wisdom such as may perhaps be attained by man, for to that extent I am inclined to believe that I am wise; whereas the persons of whom I was speaking have a superhuman wisdom, which I may fail to describe, because I have it not myself; and he who says that I have, speaks falsely, and is taking away my character. And here, O men of Athens, I must beg you not

to interrupt me, even if I seem to say something extravagant. For the word which I will speak is not mine. I will refer you to a witness who is worthy of credit; that witness shall be the God of Delphi—he will tell you about my wisdom, if I have any, and of what sort it is. You must have known Chaerephon; he was early a friend of mine, and also a friend of yours, for he shared in the recent exile of the people, and returned with you. Well, Chaerephon, as you know, was very impetuous in all his doings, and he went to Delphi and boldly asked the oracle to tell him whether—as I was saying, I must beg you not to interrupt—he asked the oracle to tell him whether any one was wiser than I was, and the Pythian prophetess answered, that there was no man wiser. Chaerephon is dead himself; but his brother, who is in court, will confirm the truth of what I am saying.

Why do I mention this? Because I am going to explain to you why I have such an evil name. When I heard the answer, I said to myself, What can the god mean? and what is the interpretation of his riddle? for I know that I have no wisdom, small or great. What then can he mean when he says that I am the wisest of men? And yet he is a god, and cannot lie; that would be against his nature. After long consideration, I thought of a method of trying the question. I reflected that if I could only find a man wiser than myself, then I might go to the god with a refutation in my hand. I should say to him, 'Here is a man who is wiser than I am; but you said that I was the wisest.' Accordingly I went to one who had the reputation of wisdom, and observed him—his name I need not mention; he was a politician whom I selected for examination—and the result was as follows: When I began to talk with him, I could not help thinking that he was not really wise, although he was thought wise by many, and still wiser by himself; and thereupon I tried to explain to him that he thought himself wise, but was not really wise; and the consequence was that he hated me, and his enmity was shared by several who were present and heard me. So I left him, saying to myself, as I went away: Well, although I do not suppose that either of us knows anything really beautiful and good, I am better off than he is—for he knows nothing, and thinks that he knows; I neither know nor think that I know. In this latter particular, then, I seem to have slightly the advantage of him.

Then I went to another who had still higher pretensions to wisdom, and my conclusion was exactly the same. Whereupon I made another enemy of him, and of many others besides him. Then I went to one man after another, being not unconscious of the enmity which I provoked, and I lamented and feared this: But necessity was laid upon me,—the word of God, I thought, ought to be considered first. And I said to myself, Go I must to all who appear to know, and find out the meaning of the oracle. And I swear to you, Athenians, by the dog I swear!— for I must tell you the truth—the result of my mission was just this: I found that the men most in repute were all but the most foolish; and that others less esteemed were really wiser and better. I will tell you the tale of my wanderings and of the "Herculean" labours, as I may call them, which I endured only to find at last the oracle irrefutable. After the politicians, I went to the poets; tragic, dithyrambic, and all sorts. And there, I said to myself, you will be instantly detected; now you will find out that you are more ignorant than they are. Accordingly, I took them some of the most elaborate passages in their own writings, and asked what was the meaning of them—thinking that they would teach me something. Will you believe me? I am almost ashamed to confess the truth, but I must say that there is hardly a person present who would not have talked better about their poetry than they did themselves. Then I knew that not by wisdom do poets write poetry, but by a sort of genius and inspiration; they are like diviners or soothsayers who also say many fine things, but do not understand the meaning of them. The poets appeared to me to be much in the same case; and I further observed that upon the strength of their poetry they believed themselves to be the wisest of men in other things in which they were not

wise. So I departed, conceiving myself to be superior to them for the same reason that I was superior to the politicians.

At last I went to the artisans, for I was conscious that I knew nothing at all, as I may say, and I was sure that they knew many fine things; and here I was not mistaken, for they did know many things of which I was ignorant, and in this they certainly were wiser than I was. But I observed that even the good artisans fell into the same error as the poets;—because they were good workmen they thought that they also knew all sorts of high matters, and this defect in them overshadowed their wisdom; and therefore I asked myself on behalf of the oracle, whether I would like to be as I was, neither having their knowledge nor their ignorance, or like them in both; and I made answer to myself and to the oracle that I was better off as I was.

This inquisition has led to my having many enemies of the worst and most dangerous kind, and has given occasion also to many calumnies. And I am called wise, for my hearers always imagine that I myself possess the wisdom which I find wanting in others: but the truth is, O men of Athens, that God only is wise; and by his answer he intends to show that the wisdom of men is worth little or nothing; he is not speaking of Socrates, he is only using my name by way of illustration, as if he said, He, O men, is the wisest, who, like Socrates, knows that his wisdom is in truth worth nothing. And so I go about the world, obedient to the god, and search and make enquiry into the wisdom of any one, whether citizen or stranger, who appears to be wise; and if he is not wise, then in vindication of the oracle I show him that he is not wise; and my occupation quite absorbs me, and I have no time to give either to any public matter of interest or to any concern of my own, but I am in utter poverty by reason of my devotion to the god.

There is another thing: Young men of the richer classes, who have not much to do, come about me of their own accord; they like to hear the pretenders examined, and they often imitate me, and proceed to examine others; there are plenty of persons, as they quickly discover, who think that they know something, but really know little or nothing; and then those who are examined by them instead of being angry with themselves are angry with me: This confounded Socrates, they say; this villainous misleader of youth!—and then if somebody asks them, Why, what evil does he practise or teach? they do not know, and cannot tell; but in order that they may not appear to be at a loss, they repeat the ready-made charges which are used against all philosophers about teaching things up in the clouds and under the earth, and having no gods, and making the worse appear the better cause; for they do not like to confess that their pretence of knowledge has been detected—which is the truth; and as they are numerous and ambitious and energetic, and are drawn up in battle array and have persuasive tongues, they have filled your ears with their loud and inveterate calumnies. And this is the reason why my three accusers, Meletus and Anytus and Lycon, have set upon me; Meletus, who has a quarrel with me on behalf of the poets; Anytus, on behalf of the craftsmen and politicians; Lycon, on behalf of the rhetoricians: and as I said at the beginning, I cannot expect to get rid of such a mass of calumny all in a moment. And this, O men of Athens, is the truth and the whole truth; I have concealed nothing, I have dissembled nothing. And yet, I know that my plainness of speech makes them hate me, and what is their hatred but a proof that I am speaking the truth?—Hence has arisen the prejudice against me; and this is the reason of it, as you will find out either in this or in any future enquiry.

I have said enough in my defence against the first class of my accusers; I turn to the second class. They are headed by Meletus, that good man and true lover of his country, as he calls himself. . . . He says that I am a doer of evil, and corrupt the youth; but I say, O men of Athens, that Meletus is a doer of evil, in that he pretends to be in earnest when he is only in jest, and is so eager to bring men to trial from a pretended zeal and interest about matters in which he

really never had the smallest interest. And the truth of this I will endeavour to prove to you.

Come hither, Meletus, and let me ask a question of you. You think a great deal about the improvement of youth?

Yes, I do.

Tell the judges, then, who is their improver; for you must know, as you have taken the pains to discover their corrupter, and are citing and accusing me before them. Speak, then, and tell the judges who their improver is.—Observe, Meletus, that you are silent, and have nothing to say. But is not this rather disgraceful, and a very considerable proof of what I was saying, that you have no interest in the matter? Speak up, friend, and tell us who their improver is.

The laws.

But that, my good sir, is not my meaning. I want to know who the person is, who, in the first place, knows the laws.

The judges, Socrates, who are present in court.

What, do you mean to say, Meletus, that they are able to instruct and improve youth?

Certainly they are.

What, all of them, or some only and not others?

All of them.

By the goddess Herè, that is good news! There are plenty of improvers, then. And what do you say of the audience—do they improve them?

Yes, they do.

And the senators?

Yes, the senators improve them.

But perhaps the members of the assembly corrupt them?—or do they too improve them?

They improve them.

Then every Athenian improves and elevates them; all with the exception of myself; and I alone am their corrupter? Is that what you affirm?

That is what I stoutly affirm.

I am very unfortunate if you are right. But suppose I ask you a question: How about horses? Does one man do them harm and all the world good? Is not the exact opposite the truth? One man is able to do them good, or at least not many—the trainer of horses, that is to say, does them good, and others who have to do with them rather injure them? Is not that true, Meletus, of horses, or of any other animals? Most assuredly it is; whether you and Anytus say yes or no. Happy indeed would be the condition of youth if they had one corrupter only, and all the rest of the world were their improvers. But you, Meletus, have sufficiently shown that you never had a thought about the young: your carelessness is seen in your not caring about the very things which you bring against me.

And now, Meletus, I will ask you another question—by Zeus I will: Which is better, to live among bad citizens, or among good ones? Answer, friend, I say; the question is one which may be easily answered. Do not the good do their neighbours good, and the bad do them evil?

Certainly.

And is there any one who would rather be injured than benefited by those who live with him? Answer, my good friend, the law requires you to answer—does any one like to be injured?

Certainly not.

And when you accuse me of corrupting and deteriorating the youth, do you allege that I corrupt them intentionally or unintentionally?

Intentionally, I say.

But you have just admitted that the good do their neighbours good, and evil do them evil. Now, is that a truth which your superior wisdom has recognized thus early in life, and am I, at my age, in such darkness and ignorance as not to know that if a man with whom I have to live is corrupted by me, I am very likely to be harmed by him; and yet I corrupt him, and intentionally, too—so you say, although neither I nor any other human being is ever likely to be convinced by you. But either I do not corrupt them, or I corrupt them unintentionally; and on either view of the case you lie. If my offence is unintentional, the law has no cognizance of unintentional offences: you ought to have taken me privately, and warned and admonished me; for if I had been better advised, I should have left off doing what I only did unintentionally— no doubt I should; but you would have nothing

to say to me and refused to teach me. And now you bring me up in this court, which is a place not of instruction, but of punishment.

It will be very clear to you, Athenians, as I was saying, that Meletus has no care at all, great or small, about the matter. But still I should like to know, Meletus, in what I am affirmed to corrupt the young. I suppose you mean, as I infer from your indictment, that I teach them not to acknowledge the gods which the state acknowledges, but some other new divinities or spiritual agencies in their stead. These are the lessons by which I corrupt the youth, as you say.

Yes, that I say emphatically.

Then, by the gods, Meletus, of whom we are speaking, tell me and the court, in somewhat plainer terms, what you mean! for I do not as yet understand whether you affirm that I teach other men to acknowledge some gods, and therefore that I do believe in gods, and am not an entire atheist—this you do not lay to my charge—but only you say that they are not the same gods which the city recognizes—the charge is that they are different gods. Or, do you mean that I am an atheist simply, and a teacher of atheism?

I mean the latter—that you are a complete atheist.

What an extraordinary statement! Why do you think so, Meletus? Do you mean that I do not believe in the godhead of the sun or moon, like other men?

I assure you, judges, that he does not: for he says that the sun is stone, and the moon earth.

Friend Meletus, you think that you are accusing Anaxagoras: and you have but a bad opinion of the judges, if you fancy them illiterate to such a degree as not to know that these doctrines are found in the books of Anaxagoras the Clazomenian, which are full of them. And so, forsooth, the youth are said to be taught them by Socrates, when there are not infrequently exhibitions of them at the theatre (price of admission one drachma at the most); and they might pay their money, and laugh at Socrates if he pretends to father these extraordinary views. And so, Meletus, you really think that I do not believe in any god?

I swear by Zeus that you believe absolutely in none at all.

Nobody will believe you, Meletus, and I am pretty sure that you do not believe yourself. I cannot help thinking, men of Athens, that Meletus is reckless and impudent, and that he has written this indictment in a spirit of mere wantonness and youthful bravado. Has he not compounded a riddle, thinking to try me? He said to himself: I shall see whether the wise Socrates will discover my facetious contradiction, or whether I shall be able to deceive him and the rest of them. For he certainly does appear to me to contradict himself in the indictment as much as if he said that Socrates is guilty of not believing in the gods, and yet of believing in them—but this is not like a person who is in earnest.

I should like you, O men of Athens, to join me in examining what I conceive to be his inconsistency; and do you, Meletus, answer. And I must remind the audience of my request that they would not make a disturbance if I speak in my accustomed manner:

Did ever man, Meletus, believe in the existence of human things, and not of human beings? . . . I wish, men of Athens, that he would answer, and not be always trying to get up an interruption. Did ever any man believe in horsemanship, and not in horses? or in flute-playing, and not in flute-players? No, my friend; I will answer to you and to the court, as you refuse to answer for yourself. There is no man who ever did. But now please to answer the next question: Can a man believe in spiritual and divine agencies, and not in spirits or demigods?

He cannot.

How lucky I am to have extracted that answer, by the assistance of the court! But then you swear in the indictment that I teach and believe in divine or spiritual agencies (new or old, no matter for that); at any rate, I believe in spiritual agencies—so you say and swear in the affidavit; and yet if I believe in divine beings, how can I help believing in spirits or demigods—must I not? To be sure I must; and therefore I may assume that your silence gives consent.

Now what are spirits or demigods? are they not either gods or the sons of gods?

Certainly they are.

But this is what I call the facetious riddle invented by you: the demigods or spirits are gods, and you say first that I do not believe in gods, and then again that I do believe in gods; that is, if I believe in demigods. For if the demigods are the illegitimate sons of gods, whether by the nymphs or by any other mothers, of whom they are said to be the sons—what human being will ever believe that there are no gods if they are the sons of gods? You might as well affirm the existence of mules, and deny that of horses and asses. Such nonsense, Meletus, could only have been intended by you to make trial of me. You have put this into the indictment because you had nothing real of which to accuse me. But no one who has a particle of understanding will ever be convinced by you that the same men can believe in divine and superhuman things, and yet not believe that there are gods and demigods and heroes.

I have said enough in answer to the charge of Meletus: any elaborate defence is unnecessary; but I know only too well how many are the enmities which I have incurred, and this is what will be my destruction if I am destroyed—not Meletus, nor yet Anytus, but the envy and detraction of the world, which has been the death of many good men, and will probably be the death of many more; there is no danger of my being the last of them.

Some one will say: And are you not ashamed, Socrates, of a course of life which is likely to bring you to an untimely end? To him I may fairly answer: There you are mistaken: a man who is good for anything ought not to calculate the chance of living or dying; he ought only to consider whether in doing anything he is doing right or wrong—acting the part of a good man or of a bad. . . .

Strange, indeed, would be my conduct, O men of Athens, if I who, when I was ordered by the generals whom you chose to command me at Potidaea and Amphipolis and Delium, remained where they placed me, like any other man, facing death—if now, when, as I conceive and imagine, God orders me to fulfill the philosopher's mission of searching into myself and other men, I were to desert my post through fear of death, or any other fear; that would indeed be strange, and I might justly be arraigned in court for denying the existence of the gods, if I disobeyed the oracle because I was afraid of death, fancying that I was wise when I was not wise. For the fear of death is indeed the pretence of wisdom, and not real wisdom, being a pretence of knowing the unknown; and no one knows whether death, which men in their fear apprehend to be the greatest evil, may not be the greatest good. Is not this ignorance of a disgraceful sort, the ignorance which is the conceit that man knows what he does not know? And in this respect only I believe myself to differ from men in general, and may perhaps claim to be wiser than they are— that whereas I know but little of the world below, I do not suppose that I know: but I do know that injustice and disobedience to a better, whether God or man, is evil and dishonourable, and I will never fear or avoid a possible good rather than a certain evil. And therefore if you let me go now, and are not convinced by Anytus, who said that since I had been prosecuted I must be put to death . . .—if you say to me, Socrates, this time we will not mind Anytus, and you shall be let off, but upon one condition, that you are not to enquire and speculate in this way any more, and that if you are caught doing so again you shall die—if this was the condition on which you let me go, I should reply: Men of Athens, I honour and love you; but I shall obey God rather than you, and while I have life and strength I shall never cease from the practice and teaching of philosophy, exhorting any one whom I meet and saying to him after my manner: You, my friend—a citizen of the great and mighty and wise city of Athens—are you not ashamed of heaping up the greatest amount of money and honour and reputation, and caring so little about wisdom and truth and the greatest improvement of the soul, which you never regard or heed at all? And if the person with whom I am arguing,

says: Yes, but I do care; then I do not leave him or let him go at once; but I proceed to interrogate and examine and cross-examine him, and if I think that he has no virtue in him, but only says that he has, I reproach him with undervaluing the greater, and overvaluing the less. And I shall repeat the same words to every one whom I meet, young and old, citizen and alien, but especially to the citizens, inasmuch as they are my brethren. For know that this is the command of God; and I believe that no greater good has ever happened in the state than my service to the God. For I do nothing but go about persuading you all, old and young alike, not to take thought for your persons or your properties, but first and chiefly to care about the greatest improvement of the soul. I tell you that virtue is not given by money, but that from virtue comes money and every other good of man, public as well as private. This is my teaching, and if this is the doctrine which corrupts the youth, I am a mischievous person. But if any one says that this is not my teaching, he is speaking an untruth. Wherefore, O men of Athens, I say to you, do as Anytus bids or not as Anytus bids, and either acquit me or not; but whichever you do, understand that I shall never alter my ways, not even if I have to die many times. . . .

And now, Athenians, I am not going to argue for my own sake, as you may think, but for yours, that you may not sin against the God by condemning me, who am his gift to you. For if you kill me you will not easily find a successor to me, who, if I may use such a ludicrous figure of speech, am a sort of gadfly, given to the state by God; and the state is a great and noble steed who is tardy in his motions owing to his very size, and requires to be stirred into life. I am that gadfly which God has attached to the state, and all day long and in all places am always fastening upon you, arousing and persuading and reproaching you. You will not easily find another like me, and therefore I would advise you to spare me. . . .

Perhaps it may seem strange to you that, though I go about giving this advice privately and meddling in others' affairs, yet I do not venture to come forward in the assembly and advise the state. You have often heard me speak of my reason for this, and in many places: it is that I have a certain divine sign, which is what Meletus has caricatured in his indictment. I have had it from childhood. It is a kind of voice which, whenever I hear it, always turns me back from something which I was going to do, but never urges me to act. It is this which forbids me to take part in politics. And I think it does well to forbid me. For, Athenians, it is quite certain that, if I had attempted to take part in politics, I should have perished at once and long ago without doing any good either to you or to myself. And do not be indignant with me for telling the truth. There is no man who will preserve his life for long, either in Athens or elsewhere, if he firmly opposes the multitude, and tries to prevent the commission of much injustice and illegality in the state. He who would really fight for justice must do so as a private citizen, not as an office-holder, if he is to preserve his life, even for a short time.

I will prove to you that this is so by very strong evidence, not by mere words, but by what you value highly, actions. Listen then to what has happened to me, that you may know that there is no man who could make me consent to do wrong from the fear of death, but that I would perish at once rather than give way. What I am going to tell you may be a commonplace in the law court; nevertheless it is true. The only office that I ever held in the state, Athenians, was that of Senator. When you wished to try the ten generals who did not rescue their men after the battle of Arginusae, as a group, which was illegal, as you all came to think afterwards, the tribe Antiochis, to which I belong, held the presidency. On that occasion I alone of all the presidents opposed your illegal action and gave my vote against you. The speakers were ready to suspend me and arrest me; and you were clamoring against me, and crying out to me to submit. But I thought that I ought to face the danger, with law and justice on my side, rather than join with

you in your unjust proposal, from fear of imprisonment or death. That was when the state was democratic. When the oligarchy came in, the Thirty sent for me, with four others, to the council-chamber, and ordered us to bring Leon the Salaminian from Salamis, that they might put him to death. They were in the habit of frequently giving similar orders, to many others, wishing to implicate as many as possible in their crimes. But, then, I again proved, not by mere words, but by my actions, that, if I may speak bluntly, I do not care a straw for death; but that I do care very much indeed about not doing anything unjust or impious. That government with all its powers did not terrify me into doing anything unjust; but when we left the council-chamber, the other four went over to Salamis and brought Leon across to Athens; and I went home. And if the rule of the Thirty had not been destroyed soon afterwards, I should very likely have been put to death for what I did then. Many of you will be my witnesses in this matter.

Now do you think that I could have remained alive all these years if I had taken part in public affairs, and had always maintained the cause of justice like an honest man, and had held it a paramount duty, as it is, to do so? Certainly not, Athenians, nor could any other man. But throughout my whole life, both in private and in public, whenever I have had to take part in public affairs, you will find I have always been the same and have never yielded unjustly to anyone; no, not to those whom my enemies falsely assert to have been my pupils. But I was never anyone's teacher. I have never withheld myself from anyone, young or old, who was anxious to hear me discuss while I was making my investigation; neither do I discuss for payment, and refuse to discuss without payment. I am ready to ask questions of rich and poor alike, and if any man wishes to answer me, and then listen to what I have to say, he may. . . .

I believe in the gods as no one of my accusers believes in them: and to you and to God I commit my cause to be decided as is best for you and for me.

[The vote is taken and he is found guilty by 281 votes to 220.]

There are many reasons why I am not grieved, O men of Athens, at the vote of condemnation. I expected it, and am only surprised that the votes are so nearly equal; for I had thought that the majority against me would have been far larger; but now, had thirty votes gone over to the other side, I should have been acquitted. And I may say, I think, that I have escaped Meletus. I may say more; for without the assistance of Anytus and Lycon, any one may see that he would not have had a fifth part of the votes, as the law requires, in which case he would have incurred a fine of a thousand drachmae.

And so he proposes death as the penalty. And what shall I propose on my part, O men of Athens? Clearly that which is my due. And what is my due? What return shall be made to the man who has never had the wit to be idle during his whole life; but has been careless of what the many care for—wealth, and family interests, and military offices, and speaking in the assembly, and magistracies, and plots, and parties. Reflecting that I was really too honest a man to be a politician and live, I did not go where I could do no good to you or to myself; but where I could do the greatest good privately to every one of you, thither I went, and sought to persuade every man among you that he must look to himself, and seek virtue and wisdom before he looks to his private interests, and look to the state before he looks to the interests of the state; and that this should be the order which he observes in all his actions. What shall be done to such an one? Doubtless some good thing, O men of Athens, if he has his reward; and the good should be of a kind suitable to him. What would be a reward suitable to a poor man who is your benefactor, and who desires leisure that he may instruct you? There can be no reward so fitting as maintenance in the Prytaneum, O men of Athens, a reward which he deserves far more than the citizen who has won the prize at Olympia in the horse or chariot race, whether the chariots were drawn by two horses or by many. For I am in want, and he has enough;

and he only gives you the appearance of happiness, and I give you the reality. And if I am to estimate the penalty fairly, I should say that maintenance in the Prytaneum is the just return.

Perhaps you think that I am braving you in what I am saying now, as in what I said before about the tears and prayers. But this is not so. I speak rather because I am convinced that I never intentionally wronged any one, although I cannot convince you—the time has been too short; if there were a law at Athens, as there is in other cities, that a capital cause should not be decided in one day, then I believe that I should have convinced you. But I cannot in a moment refute great slanders; and, as I am convinced that I never wronged another, I will assuredly not wrong myself. I will not say of myself that I deserve any evil, or propose any penalty. Why should I? Because I am afraid of the penalty of death which Meletus proposes? When I do not know whether death is a good or an evil, why should I propose a penalty which would certainly be an evil? Shall I say imprisonment? And why should I live in prison, and be the slave of the magistrates of the year—of the Eleven? Or shall the penalty be a fine, and imprisonment until the fine is paid? There is the same objection. I should have to lie in prison, for money I have none, and cannot pay. And if I say exile (and this may possibly be the penalty which you will affix), I must indeed be blinded by the love of life, if I am so irrational as to expect that when you, who are my own citizens, cannot endure my discourses and words, and have found them so grievous and odious that you will have no more of them, others are likely to endure me. No indeed, men of Athens, that is not very likely. And what a life should I lead, at my age, wandering from city to city, ever changing my place of exile, and always being driven out! For I am quite sure that wherever I go, there, as here, the young men will flock to me; and if I drive them away, their elders will drive me out at their request; and if I let them come, their fathers and friends will drive me out for their sakes.

Some one will say: Yes, Socrates, but cannot you hold your tongue, and then you may go into a foreign city, and no one will interfere with you? Now I have great difficulty in making you understand my answer to this. For if I tell you that to do as you say would be a disobedience to the God, and therefore that I cannot hold my tongue, you will not believe that I am serious; and if I say again that daily to discourse about virtue, and of those other things about which you hear me examining myself and others, is the greatest good of man, and that the unexamined life is not worth living, you are still less likely to believe me. Yet I say what is true, although a thing of which it is hard for me to persuade you. Also, I have never been accustomed to think that I deserve to suffer any harm. Had I money I might have estimated the offence at what I was able to pay, and not have been much the worse. But I have none, and therefore I must ask you to proportion the fine to my means. Well, perhaps I could afford a mina, and therefore I propose that penalty: Plato, Crito, Critobulus, and Apollodorus, my friends here, bid me say thirty minae, and they will be the sureties. Let thirty minae be the penalty; for which sum they will be ample security to you.

[2nd vote: The jury decides for the death penalty by a vote of 360 to 141.]

Not much time will be gained, O Athenians, in return for the evil name which you will get from the detractors of the city, who will say that you killed Socrates, a wise man; for they will call me wise, even although I am not wise, when they want to reproach you. If you had waited a little while, your desire would have been fulfilled in the course of nature. For I am far advanced in years, as you may perceive, and not far from death. . . . The difficulty, my friends, is not to avoid death, but to avoid unrighteousness; for that runs faster than death. I am old and move slowly, and the slower runner has overtaken me, and my accusers are keen and quick, and the faster runner, who is unrighteousness, has overtaken them. And now I depart hence condemned by you to suffer the penalty of death—they too go their ways condemned by the truth to suffer the penalty of villainy and

wrong; and I must abide by my award—let them abide by theirs. I suppose that these things may be regarded as fated—and I think that they are well. . . .

Friends, who would have acquitted me, I would like also to talk with you about the thing which has come to pass, while the magistrates are busy, and before I go to the place at which I must die. Stay then a little, for we may as well talk with one another while there is time. You are my friends, and I should like to show you the meaning of this event which has happened to me. O my judges—for you I may truly call judges—I should like to tell you of a wonderful circumstance. Hitherto the divine faculty of which the internal oracle is the source has constantly been in the habit of opposing me even about trifles, if I was going to make a slip or error in any matter; and now as you see there has come upon me that which may be thought, and is generally believed to be, the last and worst evil. But the oracle made no sign of opposition, either when I was leaving my house in the morning, or when I was on my way to the court, or while I was speaking, at anything which I was going to say; and yet I have often been stopped in the middle of a speech, but now in nothing I either said or did touching the matter in hand has the oracle opposed me. What do I take to be the explanation of this silence? I will tell you. It is an intimation that what has happened to me is a good, and that those of us who think that death is an evil are in error. For the customary sign would surely have opposed me had I been going to evil and not to good.

Let us reflect in another way, and we shall see that there is great reason to hope that death is a good; for one of two things—either death is a state of nothingness and utter unconsciousness, or, as men say, there is a change and migration of the soul from this world to another. Now if you suppose that there is no consciousness, but a sleep like the sleep of him who is undisturbed even by dreams, death will be an unspeakable gain. For if a person were to select the night in which his sleep was undisturbed even by dreams, and were to compare with this the other days and nights of his life, and then were to tell us how many days and nights he had passed in the course of his life better and more pleasantly than this one, I think that any man, I will not say a private man, but even the great king will not find many such days or nights, when compared with the others. Now if death be of such a nature, I say that to die is gain; for eternity is then only a single night. But if death is the journey to another place, and there, as men say, all the dead abide, what good, O my friends and judges, can be greater than this? If indeed when the pilgrim arrives in the world below, he is delivered from the professors of justice in this world, and finds the true judges who are said to give judgment there, Minos and Rhadamanthus and Aeacus and Triptolemus, and other sons of God who were righteous in their own life, that pilgrimage will be worth making. What would not a man give if he might converse with Orpheus and Musaeus and Hesiod and Homer? Nay, if this be true, let me die again and again. I myself, too, shall have a wonderful interest in there meeting and conversing with Palamedes, and Ajax the son of Telamon, and any other ancient hero who has suffered death through an unjust judgment; and there will be no small pleasure, as I think, in comparing my own sufferings with theirs. Above all, I shall then be able to continue my search into true and false knowledge; as in this world, so also in the next; and I shall find out who is wise, and who pretends to be wise, and is not. What would not a man give, O judges, to be able to examine the leader of the great Trojan expedition; or Odysseus or Sisyphus, or numberless others, men and women too! What infinite delight would there be in conversing with them and asking them questions! In another world they do not put a man to death for asking questions: assuredly not. For besides being happier than we are, they will be immortal, if what is said is true.

Wherefore, O judges, be of good cheer about death, and know of a certainty, that no evil can happen to a good man, either in life or after death. He and his are not neglected by the gods; nor has my own approaching end happened by mere chance. But I see clearly that the time had arrived when it was better for me to die and be released from trouble; wherefore the oracle gave no sign. For which reason, also, I am not angry with my condemners, or with my accusers; they have done me no harm, although they did not mean to do me any good; and for this I may gently blame them.

Still I have a favour to ask of them. When my sons are grown up, I would ask you, O my friends, to punish them; and I would have you trouble them, as I have troubled you, if they seem to care about riches, or anything, more than about virtue; or if they pretend to be something when they are really nothing,—then reprove them, as I have reproved you, for not caring about that for which they ought to care, and thinking that they are something when they are really nothing. And if you do this, both I and my sons will have received justice at your hands.

The hour of departure has arrived, and we go our ways—I to die, and you to live. Which is better God only knows.

For Further Reflection

1. Describe Socrates. What kind of man was he? What were his deepest beliefs?

2. Some have found a note of arrogance and insensitivity in Socrates and argue that he deserved what he got. Does this reading lend any support to that thesis?

3. In the dialogue *Protagoras* Socrates identifies evil with ignorance. "My own opinion is more or less this: no wise man believes that anyone errs voluntarily or willingly does evil or any base act. They know very well that every base or evil act is committed involuntarily." If

people cannot do evil voluntarily, can we hold them responsible for their actions? Do you see this thesis in the *Apology*? Discuss this thesis.

4. Can the good be harmed by the bad? How do we harm ourselves?

5. What does Socrates mean when he says that "the unexamined life is not worth living"?

We will return to Socrates in Parts IV and VI.

I.2   Of Enthusiasm and the Quest for Truth

JOHN LOCKE

John Locke (1632–1704) is considered the greatest English philosopher of the modern period. Educated at Christ Church, Oxford University, he was a tutor in Greek classics and philosophy. Later he was the administrative assistant and physician to the Earl of Shaftsbury. His work on representative government and human rights, *Two Treatises on Government* (1689, Reading VII.54 in this book), greatly influenced the founding fathers of the United States. His *Essay Concerning Human Understanding* (1689), from which this selection is taken, is considered a classic in the theory of knowledge. We will examine it more fully in Reading III.19.

Locke's value of philosophy as the search for truth is connected to his Christian faith, but the implications of his thought go beyond any particular religion. Locke held that since God was a God of Truth, he would never require that we believe anything, including in God, against or without the natural light of reason—although some mysteries (for example, immortality) are beyond our understanding. Religious people, who have ample grounds for believing in God, must beware lest they allow their imagination and passion ("enthusiasm") to run away with them. Reason and faith are compatible, so that every claim of faith must be supported with sufficient evidence. That is, we must be lovers of Truth, believing propositions in proportion to the strength of the evidence. In a letter to Anthony Collins, Locke wrote, "To love the truth for truth's sake is the principal part of human perfection in this world, and the seed-plot of all other virtues" (29 October 1703). His friend, Lady Masham, wrote of him, "Locke was always, in the greatest and in the smallest affairs of human life, as well as in speculative opinions, disposed to follow reason, whosoever suggested it; he being ever a faithful servant, I had almost said a slave, to truth; never abandoning anything else, and following her for her own sake purely."*

Locke's use of *enthusiasm* contains the negative connotations that the word held for many philosophers and theologians of his day, including Bishop Butler, Jonathan Swift, Henry More, and Bishop Warburton. Leibniz, the German philosopher and

Quoted in A.S. Pingle-Pattison's edition of Locke's An Essay Concerning Human Understanding *(Oxford University Press, 1924), p. 359.*

Locke's friend, expressed the sentiment of these intellectuals when he wrote, "Enthusiasm was originally a good term. Just as *sophism* properly indicates an exercise of wisdom, so *enthusiasm* signifies that there is divinity in us. But these men having consecrated their passions, fancies, dreams, and even their anger, as something divine, *enthusiasm* began to signify a mental disturbance attributed to the influence of some divinity. . . . Since then, we attribute it to those who believe without foundation that their impulses come from God."

Study Questions

1. What is the first requirement in searching for Truth?
2. What is the one unerring mark of loving the Truth?
3. How does Locke characterize *enthusiasm*? What is its source?
4. How do reason and enthusiasm conflict?
5. How does enthusiasm cause us to go astray in our reasoning?
6. How can people distinguish a true revelation from God from a misguided claim of revelation?
7. How did God confirm his revelations to holy men of old?

1. HE THAT WOULD SERIOUSLY set upon the search of truth, ought in the first place to prepare his mind with a love of it. For he that loves it not, will not take much pains to get it, nor be much concerned when he misses it. There is nobody in the commonwealth of learning, who does not profess himself a lover of truth; and there is not a rational creature that would not take it amiss to be thought otherwise of. And yet for all this, one may truly say, that there are very few lovers of truth for truths sake, even amongst those who persuade themselves that they are so. How a man may know whether he be so in earnest, is worth inquiry: And I think there is one unerring mark of it, viz, the not entertaining any proposition with greater assurance than the proofs it is built upon will warrant. Whoever goes beyond this measure of assent, it is plain receives not the truth in the love of it; loves not truth for truths sake, but for some other bye end. For the evidence that any proposition is true (except such as are self-evident) lying only in the proofs a man has of it, whatsoever degrees of assent he affords it beyond the degrees of that evidence, it is plain that all the surplusage of assurance is owing to some other affection, and not to the love of truth: It being as impossible, that the love of truth should carry my assent above the evidence there is to me that it is true, as that the love of truth should make me assent to any proposition for the sake of that evidence, which it has not, that it is true; which is in effect to love it as a truth, because it is possible or probable that it may not be true. In any truth that gets not possession of our minds by the irresistible light of self-evidence, or by the force of demonstration, the arguments that gain it assent are the vouchers and gage of its probability to us; and we can receive it for no other, than such as they deliver it to our understandings. Whatsoever credit or authority we give to any proposition, more than it receives from the principles and proofs it supports itself upon, is owing to our inclinations that way, and is so far a derogation from the love of truth as such: Which, as it can receive no evidence from our passions or interests, so it should receive no tincture from them.

Reprinted from An Essay Concerning Human Understanding *Book IV.19 (1689).*

2. The assuming an authority of dictating to others, and a forwardness to prescribe to their opinions, is a constant concomitant of this bias and corruption of our judgments. For how almost can it be otherwise, but that he should be ready to impose on another's belief, who has already imposed on his own? Who can reasonably expect arguments and conviction from him, in dealing with others, whose understanding is not accustomed to them in his dealing with himself? Who does violence to his own faculties, tyrannizes over his own mind, and usurps the prerogative that belongs to truth alone, which is to command assent by only its own authority, i.e., by and in proportion to that evidence which it carries with it.

3. Upon this occasion I shall take the liberty to consider a third ground of assent [the first two are reason and revelation, ed.], which with some men has the same authority, and is as confidently relied on as either faith or reason; I mean enthusiasm: Which laying by reason, would set up revelation without it. Whereby in effect it takes away both reason and revelation, and substitutes in the room of it the ungrounded fancies of a man's own brain, and assumes them for a foundation both of opinion and conduct.

4. Reason is natural revelation, whereby the eternal father of light, and fountain of all knowledge, communicates to mankind that portion of truth which he has laid within the reach of their natural faculties: Revelation is natural reason enlarged by a new set of discoveries communicated by God immediately, which reason vouches the truth of, by the testimony and proofs it gives, that they come from God. So that he that takes away reason, to make way for revelation, puts out the light of both, and does much—what the same, as if he would persuade a man to put out his eyes, the better to receive the remote light of an invisible star by a telescope.

5. Immediate revelation being a much easier way for men to establish their opinions and regulate their conduct, than the tedious and not always successful labor of strict reasoning, it is no wonder that some have been very apt to pretend to revelation, and to persuade themselves that they are under the peculiar guidance of heaven in their actions and opinions, especially in those of them which they cannot account for by the ordinary methods of knowledge and principles of reason. Hence we see that in all ages, men, in whom melancholy has mixed with devotion, or whose conceit of themselves has raised them into an opinion of a greater familiarity with God, and a nearer admittance to his favor than is afforded to others, have often flattered themselves with a persuasion of an immediate intercourse with the Deity, and frequent communications from the Divine Spirit. God, I own, cannot be denied to be able to enlighten the understanding, by a ray darted into the mind immediately from the fountain of light; this they understand he has promised to do, and who then has so good a title to expect it as those who are his peculiar people, chosen by him, and depending on him?

6. Their minds being thus prepared, whatever groundless opinion comes to settle itself strongly upon their fancies, is an illumination from the spirit of God, and presently of divine authority: And whatsoever odd action they find in themselves a strong inclination to do, that impulse is concluded to be a call or direction from heaven, and must be obeyed; it is a commission from above, and they cannot err in executing it.

7. This I take to be properly enthusiasm, which, though founded neither on reason nor divine revelation, but rising from the conceits of a warmed or over-weening brain, works yet, where it once gets footing, more powerfully on the persuasions and actions of men, than either of those two, or both together: Men being most forwardly obedient to the impulses they receive from themselves; and the whole man is sure to act more vigorously, where the whole man is carried by a natural motion. For strong conceit, like a new principle, carries all easily with it, when got above common sense, and freed from all restraint of reason, and check of reflection, it is heightened into a divine authority, in concurrence with our own temper and inclination.

8. Though the odd opinions and extravagant actions enthusiasm has run men into, were enough to warn them against this wrong principle, so apt to misguide them both in their belief and conduct; yet the love of something extraordinary, the ease and glory it is to be inspired, and be above the common and natural ways of knowledge, so flatters many men's laziness, ignorance, and vanity, that when once they are got into this way of immediate revelation, of illumination without search, and of certainty without proof, and without examination, it is a hard matter to get them out of it. Reason is lost upon them, they are above it: They see the light infused into their understandings, and cannot be mistaken; it is clear and visible there, like the light of bright sunshine; shows itself, and needs no other proof but its own evidence: They feel the hand of God moving them within, and the impulses of the spirit, and cannot be mistaken in what they feel. . . .

9. This is the way of talking of these men: They are sure, because they are sure: And their persuasions are right, because they are strong in them. For, when what they say is stripped of the metaphor of seeing and feeling, this is all it amounts to: And yet these similes so impose on them, that they serve them for certainty in themselves, and demonstration to others.

10. But to examine a little soberly this internal light, and this feeling on which they build so much. These men have, they say, clear light, and they see; they have awakened sense, and they feel; this cannot, they are sure, be disputed them. For when a man says he sees or feels, nobody can deny it him, that he does so. But here let me ask: This seeing, is it the perception of the truth of the proposition, or of this, that it is a revelation from God? This feeling, is it a perception of an inclination or fancy to do something, or of the spirit of God moving that inclination? These are two very different perceptions, and must be carefully distinguished, if we would not impose upon ourselves. I may perceive the truth of a proposition, and yet not perceive that it is an immediate revelation from God. I may perceive

the truth of a proposition in Euclid, without its being or my perceiving it to be a revelation: Nay, I may perceive I came not by this knowledge in a natural way, and so may conclude it revealed, without perceiving that it is a revelation from God; because there be spirits, which, without being divinely commissioned, may excite those ideas in me, and lay them in such order before my mind, that I may perceive their connection. So that the knowledge of any proposition coming into my mind, I know not how, is not a perception that it is from God. Much less is a strong persuasion, that it is true, a perception that it is from God, or so much as true. But however it be called light and seeing, I suppose it is at most but belief and assurance: And the proposition taken for a revelation, is not such as they know to be true, but take to be true. For where a proposition is known to be true, revelation is needless: And it is hard to conceive how there can be a revelation to any one of what he knows already. If therefore it be a proposition which they are persuaded, but do not know, to be true, whatever they may call it, it is not seeing, but believing. For these are two ways, whereby truth comes into the mind, wholly distinct, so that one is not the other. What I see I know to be so by the evidence of the thing itself: What I believe I take to be so upon the testimony of another: But this testimony I must know to be given, or else what ground have I of believing? I must see that it is God that reveals this to me, or else I see nothing. The question then here is, how do I know that God is the revealer of this to me; that this impression is made upon my mind by his Holy Spirit, and that therefore I ought to obey it? If I know not this, how great soever the assurance is that I am possessed with, it is groundless; whatever light I pretend to, it is but enthusiasm. For whether the proposition supposed to be revealed, be in itself evidently true, or visibly probable, or by the natural ways of knowledge uncertain, the proposition that must be well grounded, and manifested to be true, is this, that God is the revealer of it, and that what I take to be a revelation is certainly put into my mind by him, and is not an illusion dropped in by some other spirit, or raised by my own fancy. For if I mistake not, these men receive it for true, because they presume God revealed it. Does it not then stand them upon, to examine upon what grounds they presume it to be a revelation from God? or else all their confidence is mere presumption: And this light, they are so dazzled with, is nothing but an ignis fatuus that leads them constantly round in this circle; it is a revelation, because they firmly believe it, and they believe it, because it is a revelation.

11. In all that is of divine revelation, there is need of no other proof but that it is an inspiration from God: For he can neither deceive nor be deceived. But how shall it be known that any proposition in our minds is a truth infused by God; a truth that is revealed to us by him, which he declares to us, and therefore we ought to believe? Here it is that enthusiasm fails of the evidence it pretends to. For men thus possessed boast of a light whereby they say they are enlightened, and brought into the knowledge of this or that truth. But if they know it to be a truth, they must know it to be so, either by its own self-evidence to natural reason, or by the rational proofs that make it out to be so. If they see and know it to be a truth, either of these two ways, they in vain suppose it to be a revelation. For they know it to be true the same way, that any other man naturally may know that it is so without the help of revelation. For thus all the truths, of what kind soever, that men uninspired are enlightened with, came into their minds, and are established there. If they say they know it to be true because it is a revelation from God, the reason is good: But then it will be demanded how they know it to be a revelation from God. If they say, by the light it brings with it, which shines bright in their minds, and they cannot resist: I beseech them to consider whether this be any more than what we have taken notice of already, viz, that it is a revelation, because they strongly believe it to be true. For all the light they speak of is but a strong, though ungrounded persuasion of their own minds, that it

is a truth. For rational grounds from proofs that it is a truth, they must acknowledge to have none; for then it is not received as a revelation, but upon the ordinary grounds that other truths are received: And if they believe it to be true because it is a revelation, and have no other reason for its being a revelation, but because they are fully persuaded without any other reason that it is true; they believe it to be a revelation, only because they strongly believe it to be a revelation; which is a very unsafe ground to proceed on, either in our tenets or actions. And what readier way can there be to run ourselves into the most extravagant errors and miscarriages, than thus to set up fancy for our supreme and sole guide, and to believe any proposition to be true, any action to be right, only because we believe it to be so? The strength of our persuasions is no evidence at all of their own rectitude: Crooked things may be as stiff and inflexible as straight: And men may be as positive and peremptory in error as in truth. How come else the untractable zealots in different and opposite parties? For if the light, which every one thinks he has in his mind, which in this case is nothing but the strength of his own persuasion, be an evidence that it is from God, contrary opinions have the same title to be inspirations; and God will be not only the father of lights, but of opposite and contradictory lights, leading men contrary ways; and contradictory propositions will be divine truths, if an ungrounded strength of assurance be an evidence, that any proposition is a divine revelation.

12. This cannot be otherwise, whilst firmness of persuasion is made the cause of believing, and confidence of being in the right is made an argument of truth. St. Paul himself believed he did well, and that he had a call to it when he persecuted the Christians, whom he confidently thought in the wrong: But yet it was he, and not they, who were mistaken. Good men are men still, liable to mistakes; and are sometimes warmly engaged in errors, which they take for divine truths, shining in their minds with the clearest light.

13. Light, true light, in the mind is, or can be nothing else but the evidence of the truth of any proposition; and if it be not a self-evident proposition, all the light it has, or can have, is from the cleanness and validity of those proofs, upon which it is received. To talk of any other light in the understanding is to put ourselves in the dark, or in the power of the Prince of darkness, and by our own consent to give ourselves up to delusion to believe a lie. For if strength of persuasion be the light, which must guide us; I ask how shall any one distinguish between the delusions of Satan, and the inspirations of the Holy Ghost? He can transform himself into an angel of light. And they who are led by this son of the morning, are as fully satisfied of the illumination, i.e., are as strongly persuaded, that they are enlightened by the spirit of God, as any one who is so: They acquiesce and rejoice in it, are acted by it: And nobody can be more sure, nor more in the right (if their own strong belief may be judge) than they.

14. He therefore that will not give himself up to all the extravagancies of delusion and error, must bring this guide of his light within to the trial. God, when he makes the prophet, does not unmake the man. He leaves all his faculties in the natural state, to enable him to judge of his inspirations, whether they be of divine original or no. When he illuminates the mind with supernatural light, he does not extinguish that which is natural. If he would have us assent to the truth of any proposition, he either evidences that truth by the usual methods of natural reason, or else makes it known to be a truth which he would have us assent to, by his authority; and convinces us that it is from him, by some marks which reason cannot be mistaken in. Reason must be our last judge and guide in every thing. I do not mean that we must consult reason, and examine whether a proposition revealed from God can be made out by natural principles, and if it cannot, that then we may reject it: But consult it we must, and by it examine, whether it be a revelation from God or no. And if reason finds it to be revealed from God,

reason then declares for it, as much as for any other truth, and makes it one of her dictates. Every conceit that thoroughly warms our fancies must pass for an inspiration, if there be nothing but the strength of our persuasions, whereby to judge of our persuasions: If reason must not examine their truth by something extrinsic to the persuasions themselves, inspirations and delusions, truth and falsehood, will have the same measure, and will not be possible to be distinguished.

15. Thus we see the holy men of old, who had revelations from God, had something else besides that internal light of assurance in their own minds, to testify to them that it was from God. They were not left to their own persuasions alone, that those persuasions were from God; but had outward signs to convince them of the author of those revelations. And when they were to convince others, they had a power given them to justify the truth of their commission from heaven, and by visible signs to assert the divine authority of a message they were sent with. Moses saw the bush burn without being consumed, and heard a voice out of it. This was something besides finding an impulse upon his mind to go to Pharaoh, that he might bring his brethren out of Egypt: And yet he thought not this enough to authorize him to go with that message, till God, by another miracle of his rod turned into a serpent, had assured him of a power to testify his mission, by the same miracle repeated before them, whom he was sent to. Gideon was sent by an angel to deliver Israel from the Midianites, and yet he desired a sign to convince him that this commission was from God. These, and several the like instances to be found among the prophets of old, are enough to show that they thought not an inward seeing or persuasion of their own minds, without any other proof, a sufficient evidence that it was from God; though the scripture does not every where mention their demanding or having such proofs.

16. In what I have said I am far from denying that God can, or doth sometimes enlighten men's minds in the apprehending of certain truths, or

excite them to good actions by the immediate influence and assistance of the holy spirit, without any extraordinary signs accompanying it. But in such cases too we have reason and scripture, unerring rules to know whether it be from God or no. Where the truth embraced is consonant to the revelation in the written word of God, or the action conformable to the dictates of right reason or holy writ, we may be assured that we run no risk in entertaining it as such; because though perhaps it be not an immediate revelation from God, extraordinarily operating on our minds, yet we are sure it is warranted by that revelation which he has given us of truth. . . .

For Further Reflection

1. Examine Locke's claim that the love of truth entails "not entertaining any proposition with greater assurance than the proofs it is built upon will warrant." Do you agree with this?

2. Discuss these questions: Do most people have a strong love of the Truth? How much do you value Truth?

3. How does Locke try to reconcile reason and revelation? Note how he thinks revelation was confirmed in the past. Is this the case today? What are the implications of this feature (confirmation) for the relationship of reason and religious belief?

I.3   The Value of Philosophy

BERTRAND RUSSELL

Bertrand Russell (1872–1970) is one of the most important philosophers of the twentieth century. His works cover almost every area of philosophy, from logic and philosophy of mathematics (*Principia Mathematica* [1910], written with Alfred North Whitehead) to philosophy of religion ("Mysticism" and "Why I Am Not a Christian") and ethics ("Science and Ethics"). Russell's concern to live out his philosophy in his life led him to found a special school on his philosophy of education, become a leader in Britain's "Ban the Bomb" (the atom bomb) Movement, and speak out on moral and political issues, sometimes at personal risk.

In this reading, coming at the end of his brilliant essay *The Problems of Philosophy* (1912), Russell argues that the value of philosophy is not in any ability to produce material goods ("philosophy bakes no bread") or arrive at definitive conclusions about the nature of reality, but is its effect upon the lives of those who take it seriously. In its contemplation of the perennial questions of life, this essay enlarges our understanding of the task of philosophical reflection.

Study Questions

1. What do many scientific and practical people think of philosophy?
2. What is Russell's assessment of their views of philosophy? Why does he think that their prejudice occurs?
3. What are the aims of philosophy? Has it been successful in attaining them? Explain.
4. Where does Russell think that the value of philosophy is to be sought?
5. What effect can philosophy have on the instinctive person? What are the fruits of philosophical contemplation?
6. How does Russell define knowledge? What does he mean by this?
7. What does Russell think of the view that "man is the measure of all things"?

HAVING NOW COME TO THE END of our brief and very incomplete review of the problems of philosophy, it will be well to consider, in conclusion, what is the value of philosophy and why it ought to be studied. It is the more necessary to consider this question, in view of the fact that many men, under the influence of science or of practical affairs, are inclined to doubt whether philosophy is anything better than innocent but useless trifling, hair-splitting distinctions, and controversies on matters concerning which knowledge is impossible.

This view of philosophy appears to result, partly from a wrong conception of the ends of life, partly from a wrong conception of the kind of goods which philosophy strives to achieve. Physical science, through the medium of inventions, is useful to innumerable people who are wholly ignorant of it; thus the study of physical science is to be recommended, not only, or primarily, because of the effect on the student, but rather because of the effect on mankind in general. Thus utility does not belong to philosophy. If the study of philosophy has any value at all for others than students of philosophy, it must be only indirectly, through its effects upon the lives of those who study it. It is in these effects, therefore, if anywhere, that the value of philosophy must be primarily sought.

But further, if we are not to fail in our endeavour to determine the value of philosophy, we must first free our minds from the prejudices of what are wrongly called "practical" men. The "practical" man, as this word is often used, is one who recognizes only material needs, who realizes that men must have food for the body, but is oblivious of the necessity of providing food for the mind. If all men were well off, if poverty and disease had been reduced to their lowest possible point, there would still remain much to be done to produce a valuable society; and even in the existing world the goods of the mind are at least as important as the goods of the body. It is exclusively among the goods of the mind that the value of philosophy is to be found; and only those who are not indifferent to these goods can be persuaded that the study of philosophy is not a waste of time.

Philosophy, like all other studies, aims primarily at knowledge. The knowledge it aims at is the kind of knowledge which gives unity and system to the body of the sciences, and the kind which results from a critical examination of the grounds of our convictions, prejudices, and beliefs. But it cannot be maintained that philosophy has had any very great measure of success in its attempts to provide definite answers to its questions. If you ask a mathematician, a mineralogist, a historian, or any other man of learning, what definite body of truths has been ascertained by his science, his answer will last as long as you are willing to listen. But if you put the same question to

From Bertrand Russell, The Problems of Philosophy *(New York: Oxford University Press, 1969),* pp. 153–161.

a philosopher, he will, if he is candid, have to confess that his study has not achieved positive results such as have been achieved by other sciences. It is true that this is partly accounted for by the fact that, as soon as definite knowledge concerning any subject becomes possible, this subject ceases to be called philosophy, and becomes a separate science. The whole study of the heavens, which now belongs to astronomy, was once included in philosophy; Newton's great work was called "the mathematical principles of natural philosophy." Similarly, the study of the human mind, which was a part of philosophy, has now been separated from philosophy and has become the science of psychology. Thus, to a great extent, the uncertainty of philosophy is more apparent than real: those questions which are already capable of definite answers are placed in the sciences, while those only to which, at present, no definite answer can be given, remain to form the residue which is called philosophy.

This is, however, only a part of the truth concerning the uncertainty of philosophy. There are many questions—and among them those that are of the profoundest interest to our spiritual life—which, so far as we can see, must remain insoluble to the human intellect unless its powers become of quite a different order from what they are now. Has the universe any unity of plan or purpose, or is it a fortuitous concourse of atoms? Is consciousness a permanent part of the universe, giving hope of indefinite growth in wisdom, or is it a transitory accident on a small planet on which life must ultimately become impossible? Are good and evil of importance to the universe or only to man? Such questions are asked by philosophy, and variously answered by various philosophers. But it would seem that, whether answers be otherwise discoverable or not, the answers suggested by philosophy are none of them demonstrably true. Yet, however slight may be the hope of discovering an answer, it is part of the business of philosophy to continue the consideration of such questions, to make us aware of their impor-

tance, to examine all the approaches to them, and to keep alive that speculative interest in the universe which is apt to be killed by confining ourselves to definitely ascertainable knowledge.

Many philosophers, it is true, have held that philosophy could establish the truth of certain answers to such fundamental questions. They have supposed that what is of most importance in religious beliefs could be proved by strict demonstration to be true. In order to judge of such attempts, it is necessary to take a survey of human knowledge, and to form an opinion as to its methods and its limitations. On such a subject it would be unwise to pronounce dogmatically; but if the investigations of our previous chapters have not led us astray, we shall be compelled to renounce the hope of finding philosophical proofs of religious beliefs. We cannot, therefore, include as part of the value of philosophy any definite set of answers to such questions. Hence, once more, the value of philosophy must not depend upon any supposed body of definitely ascertainable knowledge to be acquired by those who study it.

The value of philosophy is, in fact, to be sought largely in its very uncertainty. The man who has no tincture of philosophy goes through life imprisoned in the prejudices derived from common sense, from the habitual beliefs of his age or his nation, and from convictions which have grown up in his mind without the cooperation or consent of his deliberate reason. To such a man the world tends to become definite, finite, obvious; common objects rouse no questions, and unfamiliar possibilities are contemptuously rejected. As soon as we begin to philosophize, on the contrary, we find, as we saw in our opening chapters, that even the most everyday things lead to problems to which only very incomplete answers can be given. Philosophy, though unable to tell us with certainty what is the true answer to the doubts which it raises, is able to suggest many possibilities which enlarge our thoughts and free them from the tyranny of custom. Thus, while diminishing our feeling of certainty as to what things are, it greatly increases our knowledge as to what they may be; it removes the somewhat arrogant dogmatism of those who have never travelled into the region of liberating doubt, and it keeps alive our sense of wonder by showing familiar things in an unfamiliar aspect.

Apart from its utility in showing unsuspected possibilities, philosophy has a value—perhaps its chief value—through the greatness of the objects which it contemplates, and the freedom from narrow and personal aims resulting from this contemplation. The life of the instinctive man is shut up within the circle of his private interests: family and friends may be included, but the outer world is not regarded except as it may help or hinder what comes within the circle of instinctive wishes. In such a life there is something feverish and confined, in comparison with which the philosophic life is calm and free. The private world of instinctive interests is a small one, set in the midst of a great and powerful world which must, sooner or later, lay our private world in ruins. Unless we can so enlarge our interests as to include the whole outer world, we remain like a garrison in a beleaguered fortress, knowing that the enemy prevents escape and that ultimate surrender is inevitable. In such a life there is no peace, but a constant strife between the insistence of desire and the powerlessness of will. In one way or another, if our life is to be great and free, we must escape this prison and this strife.

One way of escape is by philosophic contemplation. Philosophic contemplation does not, in its widest survey, divide the universe into two hostile camps—friends and foes, helpful and hostile, good and bad—it views the whole impartially. Philosophic contemplation, when it is unalloyed, does not aim at proving that the rest of the universe is akin to man. All acquisition of knowledge is an enlargement of the Self, but this enlargement is best attained when it is not directly sought. It is obtained when the desire for knowledge is alone operative, by a study which does not wish in advance that its objects should

have this or that character, but adapts the Self to the characters which it finds in its objects. This enlargement of Self is not obtained when, taking the Self as it is, we try to show that the world is so similar to this Self that knowledge of it is possible without any admission of what seems alien. The desire to prove this is a form of self-assertion and, like all self-assertion, it is an obstacle to the growth of Self which it desires, and of which the Self knows that it is capable. Self-assertion, in philosophic speculation as elsewhere, views the world as a means to its own ends; thus it makes the world of less account than Self, and the Self sets bounds to the greatness of its goods. In contemplation, on the contrary, we start from the not-Self, and through its greatness the boundaries of Self are enlarged; through the infinity of the universe the mind which contemplates it achieves some share in infinity.

For this reason greatness of soul is not fostered by those philosophies which assimilate the universe to Man. Knowledge is a form of union of Self and not-Self; like all union, it is impaired by dominion, and therefore by any attempt to force the universe into conformity with what we find in ourselves. There is a widespread philosophical tendency towards the view which tells us that Man is the measure of all things, that truth is manmade, that space and time and the world of universals are properties of the mind, and that, if there be anything not created by the mind, it is unknowable and of no account for us. This view, if our previous discussions were correct, is untrue; but in addition to being untrue, it has the effect of robbing philosophic contemplation of all that gives it value, since it fetters contemplation to Self. What it calls knowledge is not a union with the not-Self, but a set of prejudices, habits, and desires, making an impenetrable veil between us and the world beyond. The man who finds pleasure in such a theory of knowledge is like the man who never leaves the domestic circle for fear his word might not be law.

The true philosophic contemplation, on the contrary, finds its satisfaction in every enlargement of the not-Self, in everything that magnifies the objects contemplated, and thereby the subject contemplating. Everything, in contemplation, that is personal or private, everything that depends upon habit, self-interest, or desire, distorts the object, and hence impairs the union which the intellect seeks. By thus making a barrier between subject and object, such personal and private things become a prison to the intellect. The free intellect will see as God might see, without a *here* and *now*, without hopes and fears, without the trammels of customary beliefs and traditional prejudices, calmly, dispassionately, in the sole and exclusive desire of knowledge—knowledge as impersonal, as purely contemplative, as it is possible for man to attain. Hence also the free intellect will value more the abstract and universal knowledge into which the accidents of private history do not enter, than the knowledge brought by the senses, and dependent, as such knowledge must be, upon an exclusive and personal point of view and a body whose sense-organs distort as much as they reveal.

The mind which has become accustomed to the freedom and impartiality of philosophic contemplation will preserve something of the same freedom and impartiality in the world of action and emotion. It will view its purposes and desires as parts of the whole, with the absence of insis-

tence that results from seeing them as infinitesimal fragments in a world of which all the rest is unaffected by any one man's deeds. The impartiality which, in contemplation, is the unalloyed desire for truth, is the very same quality of mind which, in action, is justice, and in emotion is that universal love which can be given to all, and not only to those who are judged useful or admirable. Thus contemplation enlarges not only the objects of our thoughts, but also the objects of our actions and our affections: it makes us citizens of the universe, not only of one walled city at war with all the rest. In this citizenship of the universe consists man's true freedom, and his liberation from the thraldom of narrow hopes and fears.

Thus, to sum up our discussion of the value of philosophy; Philosophy is to be studied, not for the sake of any definite answers to its questions, since no definite answers can, as a rule, be known to be true, but rather for the sake of the questions themselves; because these questions enlarge our conception of what is possible, enrich our intellectual imagination and diminish the dogmatic assurance which closes the mind against speculation; but above all because, through the greatness of the universe which philosophy contemplates, the mind also is rendered great, and becomes capable of that union with the universe which constitutes its highest good.

For Further Reflection

1. Compare Russell's essay with Socrates' thought.

2. Evaluate Russell's contention: "The man who has no tincture of philosophy goes through life imprisoned in its prejudice derived from common sense, from habitual beliefs of his age or his nation, and from convictions which have grown up in his mind without the cooperation or consent of his deliberate reason. . . . Through the greatness of the universe which philosophers contemplate, the mind also is rendered great, and becomes capable of that union with the universe which constitutes the highest good."

3. A particularly poignant vignette of his view of the significance of philosophy is recorded in his autobiography, where he relates the experience of seeing Mrs. Whitehead in severe pain. (See the last article in Part VIII.) What sort of view of philosophy do you see in this experience? Is it identical with what you read in Russell's essay, or does it add a new dimension? If you think it does bring in something new, what is that?

Suggestions for Further Reading

Audi, Robert. *The Cambridge Dictionary of Philosophy*. New York: Cambridge University Press, 1996.

Copleston, F. C. *History of Philosophy*. Westminster, MD: Newman, 1966. This eight-volume set is the most comprehensive contemporary work in the history of philosophy.

Cornman, James and Keith Lehrer. *Philosophical Problems and Arguments*. New York: Macmillan, 1982. A contemporary paradigm of the analytic method.

Edwards, Paul, ed. *Encyclopedia of Philosophy*. New York: Macmillan, 1967. Many of the articles in this eight-volume set are excellent introductions to various aspects of philosophy.

Jones, W. T. *History of Western Philosophy*. New York: Harper & Row, 1976. A lucid, accessible five-volume set.

Miller, Ed. *Questions That Matter*. New York: McGraw-Hill, 1987.

Pojman, Louis. *Philosophy: The Pursuit of Wisdom*, 3rd ed. Belmont, CA: Wadsworth, 2001. A discussion of the topics included in this work.

Russell, Bertrand. *The Problems of Philosophy*. Oxford: Oxford University Press, 1912. Although the perspective is a little dated, this is a well-written, well-thought-out little book from which much can be learned.

Woodhouse, Mark. *A Preface to Philosophy*. Belmont, CA: Wadsworth, 1984. This little gem is useful in discussing the purposes and methods of philosophical inquiry. It contains lively discussions of informal logic, reading philosophy, and writing philosophical papers.

Excursus: A Little Bit of Logic

Philosophy is centered in the analysis and construction of *arguments*. We call the study of arguments *logic*. Let us devote a little time to the rudiments of logic. By argument we do not mean a verbal fight but a process of supporting a thesis (called the *conclusion*) with reasons (called *premises*). An argument consists of at least two declarative sentences (sometimes called *propositions*), one of which (the conclusion) logically follows from the others (the premises). The connection by which the conclusion follows from the premises is called an *inference*:

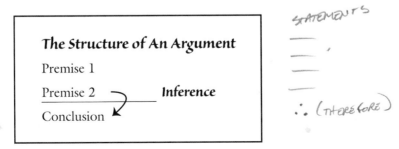

Deductive and Inductive Reasoning

Deductive Arguments

A *valid deductive argument* is one that follows a correct logical form, so that if the premises are true, the conclusion must also be true. If the form is not a good one, the argument is invalid. We say that a valid deductive argument *preserves truth*. It does so in much the same way as a good refrigerator preserves food. If the food is good, a good refrigerator will preserve it; but if the food is already spoiled, the refrigerator will not make it good. Similarly, the same is true with premises of a valid argument. If the statements are true and the form is correct, the conclusion will be true; but if the premises are not true, a valid argument will not guarantee a true conclusion.

A classic example of a valid argument is the following:

1. Socrates is a man.
2. All men are mortal.
3. ∴ Socrates is mortal.

To identify the form, let us look at the conclusion (3) and identify the two major components: a subject (S) and a predicate (P). *Socrates* is the subject term, and *mortal* is the predicate term. Now return to the two premises and identify these two terms in them. We discover that the two terms are connected by a third term, *man* (or the plural *men*). We call this the *middle term* (M).

The form of the argument is as follows:

1. S is M.
2. All M are P.
3. ∴ S is P.

This is an example of a valid deductive form. If premises 1 and 2 are true, we will always get a true conclusion by using this form. But notice how easy it would be to get an invalid form. Change the order of the second premise to read "All P are M." Let the first premise read "My roommate is a mammal" and the second premise read "All dogs are mammals." What do you get? The following:

1. My roommate, Sam Smith, is a mammal. (Premise)
2. Dogs are mammals. (Premise)
3. ∴ My roommate is a dog. (Conclusion)

Regardless of how badly you might treat your roommate, the argument has improper form and cannot yield a valid conclusion. It is *invalid*. Every argument is either valid or invalid. Like a woman who cannot be a little pregnant, an argument cannot be partly valid or invalid but must be completely one or the other. By seeking to find counterexamples for argument forms, we can discover which are the correct forms. (A full study of this would have to wait for a course in logic.)

Validity is not the only concept we need to examine. *Soundness* is also important. An argument can be valid but still unsound. An argument is sound if it has a valid form and all its premises are true. If at least one premise is false, the argument is *unsound*. Here is an example of a sound argument:

1. If Mary is a mother, she must be a woman.

2. Mary is a mother (for she has just given birth to a baby).

3. ∴ Mary is a woman.

If Mary hasn't given birth, then premise 2 is false, and the argument is unsound.

| Validity | + | All True Premises | = | Soundness |

There are four other deductive argument forms of which you should be aware: *modus ponens, modus tollens, disjunctive syllogism,* and *reductio ad absurdum.* Here are their forms:

Modus Ponens (MP)
(*Affirming the Antecedent*)

1. If *P*, then *Q*.
2. *P*.
3. ∴ *Q*.

Modus Tollens (MT)
(*Denying the Consequent*)

1. If *P*, then *Q*.
2. Not *Q*.
3. ∴ Not *P*.

✱ KNOW THESE

Note in a hypothetical proposition (if *P*, then *Q*) the first term (the proposition *P*) is called the antecedent and the second term (*Q*) the consequent. Both affirming the antecedent and denying the consequent yield valid forms:

Disjunctive Syllogism (DS)
Disjunctive Syllogism (DS) (*or Denying the Disjunct*)

1. Either *P* or *Q*.

2. Not *Q*.

3. ∴ *P*.

Reductio ad Absurdum (RAA)
(*Reduce to a Contradiction*)

1. Assume *A* (*A* is the logical opposite of the conclusion you seek to prove).
2. Logically deduce a contradiction from *A*. (This shows that *A* implies a contradiction).
3. This proves A is false, since a contradiction cannot be true. So not-*A* must be true.

We have already given an example of *modus ponens*:

1. If Mary is a mother, she must be a woman.

2. Mary is a mother.

3. ∴ Mary is a woman.

Here is an example of *modus tollens*:

1. If Leslie is a mother, she is a woman.

2. Leslie is not a woman (but a man).

3. ∴ Leslie is not a mother.

Here is an example of a *disjunctive syllogism* (sometimes called "denying the disjunct"—a *disjunct* refers to a proposition with an "or" statement in it, such as "*P* or *Q*").

1. John is either a bachelor or a married man.

2. We know for certain that John is not married.

3. ∴ John is a bachelor.

We turn to *reductio ad absurdum* (RAA). This is an indirect method of proving or establishing a thesis. You assume the opposite of what you want to prove and show that it produces an absurd conclusion. Therefore, your thesis must be true. Here is an example of a *reductio ad absurdum*. It is a little more complicated than the other forms, but it is important especially in reference to the ontological argument (see Reading II.7). Suppose that someone denies that there is such a thing as a self, and you want to refute the assertion. You might argue in the following manner:

1. Suppose that you're correct, and there is no such thing as a self (not *A*).

2. But if there is no such thing as a self, then no one ever acts (if not *A*, then not *B*).

3. But if no one ever acts, then no one can utter meaningful statements (if not *B*, then not *C*).

4. But you have purported to utter a meaningful statement in saying that there is no such thing as a self, so there is at least one meaningful statement (*C*).

5. According to your argument, there is and there is not at least one meaningful statement (*C* and not *C*).

6. ∴ It must be false that there is no such thing as a self (not, not *A*—which by double negation yields *A*). Thus, we have proved by reductio ad absurdum that there is such a thing as a self.

Before we leave the realm of deductive argument, we must point out two invalid forms that often give students trouble. To understand them, look back at forms MP and MT, which respectively argue by affirming the antecedent and denying the consequent. But notice that there are two other possible forms. You can also deny the antecedent and affirm the consequent in the following manner:

Denying the Antecedent (DA)	Affirming the Consequent (AC)
1. If *P*, then *Q*.	1. If *P*, then *Q*.
2. Not *P*.	2. *Q*.
3. ∴ Not *Q*.	3. ∴ *P*.

Are these valid forms? Remember a valid form must always yield true conclusions if the premises are true. Try to find a counterexample that will show that these two forms are invalid. You might let proposition 1 (if *P*, then *Q*) be represented by the previous proposition, "If Mary is a mother, then she is a woman." First, deny the antecedent. Does it necessarily yield a true conclusion? Not necessarily. The conclusion says that Mary is not a woman, but there are many women who are not mothers. So DA is an invalid form:

1. If Mary is a mother, she is a woman.

2. Mary is not a mother.

3. ∴ Mary is not a woman.

Take the same initial proposition and affirm the consequent "Mary is a woman." Does this in itself yield the conclusion that she is a mother? Of course not. She could be a woman without being a mother:

1. If Mary is a mother, she is a woman.

2. She is a woman.

3. ∴ Mary is a mother.

Thus, whereas MP and MT are valid forms, DA and AC are not. Be careful here. Many students slur over these distinctions. Work out your own examples of each form of argument.

These are just simple examples of deductive argument forms. Often, alas, it is difficult to state exactly what the author's premises are.

Inductive Arguments

Let us turn our attention to inductive arguments. Unlike their counterparts, valid deductive arguments, *inductive arguments* are not truth-preserving. That is, they do not guarantee that if we have true premises, we will obtain a true conclusion. They bring only *probability,* but in most of life, that is the best we can hope for. Thus, David Hume (1711–1776) said that "probability is the guide of life." The wise person guides his or her life by the best evidence available, always realizing that one could be mistaken. We usually do not speak of inductive arguments as valid/invalid or sound/unsound but as strong or weak—or as cogent or implausible. In inductive arguments, the premises are *evidence* for the conclusion or hypothesis. If the evidence for the conclusion is substantial, we call the argument a strong inductive argument; but if the evidence is weak, so is the argument as a whole. An inductive argument has the following form:

1. A_1 is a B.

2. A_2 is a B.

3. A_3 is a B.

4. So probably the next A we encounter (A_4) will also be a B.

For example, suppose that you are surrounded by four islands somewhere in the Pacific Ocean. You examine all the trees on three of the islands, but you cannot get to the fourth. Nevertheless, you might make some predictions on the basis of your experience on the first three islands. For example, you note that all the trees on islands A, B, and C are coconut trees. From this you predict that there will be coconut trees on island D and that probably only coconut trees will be found there.

We learn from experience, that is, by induction. We observe resemblances and regularities in life and generalize from them. After a few experiences of getting burned by fire (or after a few experiences with people of a certain type), we learn to avoid fire (or people of a certain type). The human race has learned by inductive experience that cooperation generally produces more benefits than noncooperation, so we advocate cooperative ventures.

Naturally, the greater the sample size of our observation, the greater the probability of our generalization. Asking 1,000 representative Americans whom they will vote for is likely to yield a more accurate prediction of who will be elected than asking only 100 Americans. Sometimes we generalize or make predictions from an inadequate sample. When we should know better, we call this type of malformed induction *prejudice*. If a child infers from his only six bad experiences with people from Podunkville that all people in Podunkville are bad, that might be acceptable. However, if an adult, who could easily have evidence that many good people live in Podunkville, still generalizes about the people of Podunkville and acts accordingly, we label this an irrational bias, a prejudice.

Inductive reasoning can lead us astray—it can be dangerous. The chicken who innately reasons that the farmer will feed her again today because he has done so twice a day for a long time, is in for a cruel shock when he wrings her neck in preparation for his meal.

A special kind of induction reasoning is called *reasoning by analogy* (see the teleological argument Readings II.5 and II.6 for its use). Reasoning by analogy allows us to reason from the similarity of two things in some relevant respects to their similarity in an unexpected respect. For example, suppose I am lost in the forest and I want to determine whether to eat a certain mushroom, which my hungry stomach craves. I note that it is similar in shape, color, and constituency with other mushrooms that turned out to be edible. Thus, I infer that probably this mushroom will be edible too.

Abductive Reasoning

We said earlier that there were two main types of argument, deductive and inductive. There is a lesser known type of reasoning, first formulated by the American philosopher Charles S. Peirce (1839–1914), called abductive reasoning or "reasoning to the best explanation." Like inductive reasoning, *abduction* yields only probable truth. Whereas induction establishes general premises or probabilities about future occurrences, abduction provides explanatory hypotheses. It answers the question, Why is such and such the case? We can illustrate abductive reasoning with the following example of Sherlock Holmes's reasoning:

> The portly client puffed out his chest with an appearance of some little pride and
> pulled a dirty and wrinkled newspaper from the inside pocket of his greatcoat. As he

glanced down the advertisement column with his head thrust forward and the paper flattened out upon his knee, I took a good look at the man and endeavored, after the fashion of my companion, to read the indications which might be presented by his dress or appearance.

I did not gain very much, however, by my inspection. Our visitor bore every mark of being an average commonplace British tradesman, obese, pompous, and slow. He wore rather baggy gray shepherd's check trousers, a not over-clean black frock-coat, unbuttoned in the front, and a drab waistcoat with a heavy brassy Albert chain, and a square pierced bit of metal dangling down as an ornament. A frayed top-hat and a faded brown overcoat with a wrinkled velvet collar lay upon a chair beside him. Altogether, look as I would, there was nothing remarkable about the man save his blazing red head and the expression of extreme chagrin and discontent upon his features.

Sherlock Holmes's quick eye took in my occupation, and he shook his head with a smile as he noticed my questioning glances. "Beyond the obvious facts that he has at some time done manual labour, that he takes snuff, that he is a Freemason, that he has been in China, and that he has done a considerable amount of writing lately, I can *deduce* nothing else." Mr. Jabez Wilson started up in his chair, with his forefinger upon the paper, but his eyes upon my companion.

"How, in the name of good-fortune did you know all that, Mr. Holmes?" he asked. "How did you know, for example, that I did manual labour? It's as true as gospel, for I began as a ship's carpenter."

"Your hands, my dear sir. Your right hand is quite a size larger than your left. You have worked with it, and the muscles are more developed."

"Well, the snuff, then, and the Freemasonry?"

"I won't insult your intelligence by telling you how I read that, especially as, rather against the strict rules of your order, you use an arc-and-compass breastpin."

"Ah, of course, I forgot that. But the writing?"

"What else can be indicated by that right cuff so very shiny for five inches, and the left one with the smooth patch near the elbow where you rest it upon the desk?"

"Well, but China?"

"The fish which you have tattooed immediately above your right wrist could only have been done in China. I have made a small study of tattoo marks and have even contributed to the literature of the subject. That trick of staining the fishes' scales of a delicate pink is quite peculiar to China. When, in addition, I see a Chinese coin hanging from your watchchain, the matter becomes even more simple."

Mr. Jabez Wilson laughed heavily. "Well, I never!" said he. "I thought at first that you had done something clever, but I see that there was nothing in it, after all."[1]

Philosophers appreciate Mr. Wilson's final remark, that Holmes's explanation makes so much sense that one wonders why one didn't think of it oneself. Holmes often chided Watson: "You see, but you do not observe." A good philosopher, like a good detective or scientist, observes while he or she sees.

There is, however, a significant inaccuracy in Holmes's description of what he does. He claims to be deducing the conclusions about Mr. Wilson from the telltale signs. Strictly speaking, he is doing no such thing. In deductive reasoning, if the form is correct and the premises are true, one cannot help but obtain a true conclusion, but such is not the case with Mr. Holmes's reasoning. For example, consider Wilson's arc-and-compass breastpin, which leads Holmes to conclude that Wilson is a Freemason. If the reasoning were deductive, the argument would go something like this:

1. Everyone wearing an arc-and-compass breastpin is a Freemason.

2. Mr. Wilson is wearing an arc-and-compass breastpin.

3. ∴ Mr. Wilson is a Freemason.

Is this a sound argument? Of course not. Imagine that Mr. Wilson, who is not a Freemason, bought a similar arc-and-compass breastpin at a pawnshop and wore it, thinking it was a beautiful bit of Moslem design. In that case, premise 1 would be false. Not everyone wearing an arc-and-compass breastpin is a Freemason. Because it is possible that non-Freemasons wear that pin, the above deductive argument is not sound.

What Holmes has really done is reason abductively, that is, reason to the best explanation of the facts. Like inductive reasoning, abduction does not guarantee the truth of the conclusions. Unlike induction it is not simply about the probability of such and such being the case based on the evidence. Abductive reasoning attempts to offer explanations of the facts, why things are the way they are. The best explanation of Mr. Wilson's wearing the arc-and-compass breastpin is his belonging to the Freemasons. The best explanation of a child's having a fever and red spots is that she has the measles. The best explanation of the puddles outside is that it has recently rained.

The notion of the best explanation is fascinating in its own right. How do we discover the best explanation? What characteristics does it have? How do we rank various virtues of a good explanation? There are no definite answers to these questions, but it is generally agreed that such traits as predictability, coherence, simplicity, and fruitfulness are among the main characteristics. If a theory helps us predict future events, that is a powerful weapon. If it coheres well with everything or nearly everything else that we hold true in the field, that lends support to it. If it is simpler than its rivals, if it demands fewer *ad hoc*, or auxiliary, hypotheses, that is a virtue. If it leads to new insight and discoveries, that is also a point in its favor. But what if explanatory theory A has more of one of these features and theory B more of another? Which should we prefer? There is no decision-making procedure to decide the matter with any finality. In a sense, abduction is educated guesswork or intuition. Counterevidence counts strongly against a hypothesis, so that if we can falsify our thesis, we have good reason to drop it; however, sometimes we can make adjustments in our hypothesis to accommodate the counterevidence.

Abduction has been neglected in philosophy, but it really is of the utmost importance. Consider the following questions: Why do you believe in God? Why do you believe in evolutionary theory? Why do you believe that there are universal moral principles? Why do you believe that all events are caused? In one way or another, the answer will probably be abductive: What you believe seems to you to be the best explanation among all the competitors of certain phenomena. We will have opportunity to use abductive reasoning at several points during our course of study.

Some Applications

Let us apply these brief lessons of logic to reading philosophy. Because the key to philosophy is the argument, you will want to concentrate and even outline the author's reasoning. Find his or her thesis or conclusion. Usually, it is stated early on. After this, identify the premises that support or lead to the conclusion. For example, Thomas Aquinas (1224–1274) holds the conclusion that God exists. He argues for this conclusion in five different ways. In the second argument, he uses the following premises to reach his conclusion: There is motion, and there cannot be motion without something initiating the motion.

It helps to outline the premises of the argument. For example, here's how we might set forth Aquinas's second argument:

1. Some things are in motion. (Premise)

2. Nothing in the world can move itself but must be moved by another. (Premise)

3. There cannot be an infinite regress of motions. (Premise)

4. There must be a First Mover who is responsible for all other motion. (Conclusion of premises 1–3, which in turn becomes a premise for the rest of the argument)

5. This First Mover is what we call God. (Explanation of the meaning of God) (Premise)

6. ∴ God exists. (Conclusion of second part of the argument, premises 4 and 5)

After you have identified the premises and conclusion, analyze them, looking for mistakes in the reasoning process. Sometimes arguments are weak or unsound, but not obviously so. Then stretch your imagination and think of possible counterexamples to the claims of the author. I found this process almost impossible at first, but gradually it became second-nature.

Because philosophical arguments are often complex and subtle (and because philosophers do not always write as clearly as they should), a full understanding of an essay is not readily available after a single reading. So read it twice or even thrice. The first time I read a philosophy essay, I read it for understanding. I want to know where the author is coming from and what he or she is trying to establish. After the first reading, I leave the essay for some time, ruminating on it. Sometimes objections to the arguments awaken me at night or while I am working at something else. Then I go back a day or so later and read the essay a second time, this time, trying to determine its soundness.

A few pointers should be mentioned along the way. Some students find it helpful to keep a notebook on their reflections on the readings. If you own the book, I suggest that you make notes in the margins—initially in pencil because you may want to revise your impressions after a second reading.

Finally, practice charity. Give the author the best possible interpretation in order to see if the argument has merit. Always try to deal with the most generous version of the argument, especially if you don't agree with its conclusion. A position has not been seriously challenged unless the best arguments for it have been refuted. That's why it is necessary to construe all arguments, including those of your opponents, as charitably as possible. The exercise will broaden your horizons and help you develop sharper reasoning skills.

Fallacies of Reasoning

Before we sum up this chapter, I would like to identify a number of common fallacies of reasoning. Good reasoning depends on justified beliefs (acceptable premises) and valid logical form. But many arguments fail to satisfy these conditions. I have listed some of the main fallacies of reasoning. See if you can illustrate them with examples of your own.

Ad Hominem Argument (or an argument against the man). This argument attacks the person instead of the position—for example, if I say to you, "You can't trust what Joan says about abortion, she is an immoral person." But, of course, her argument for or against abortion might be sound on independent grounds. Even the devil has true beliefs. The character of the person is irrelevant to the soundness of the argument.

Argument from Authority Suppose we are arguing about the death penalty, and I tell you that we should believe in the death penalty because Plato believed in it. Since you don't know Plato's reasons (I might not either), it is not sufficient grounds for either of us to believe in the death penalty. We need positive arguments, not simply authority. Advertisements are notorious for subtly and sometimes not so subtly using this device. In a beer commercial, a famous athlete (nicely remunerated for the exercise) can be seen gratifying his thirst, proclaiming the ecstasy of the beverage, as if that were proof of its quality.

Of course, authority might sometimes be the best we can get and sufficient for justified belief as when a physicist tells us the conclusions of a complicated physics research or a friend from Australia gives you pertinent information for your upcoming visit to that country. We sometimes do need to trust authority, but often it is an improper substitute for good reasoning.

Arguing in a Circle (sometimes referred to as "begging the question"). Suppose that I argue that you should believe that God exists. You ask why. I say, "Because the Bible says so." You ask, "Why should I believe what the Bible says?" I reply, "Because it's the Word of God. That is, I argue in a circle, using my conclusion as a premise to prove the conclusion. Note that all valid deductive argument can appear as arguing in a circle, since the conclusion of such an argument is contained in the premises. The difference is that in a valid argument the conclusion brings out a nontrivial feature of the premises. Essentially, arguing in a circle is not invalid, just trivial and unconvincing, having no power to convince an opponent.

Argument from Ignorance This kind of argument occurs when I claim that because you cannot prove a proposition is false, I am justified in believing it to be true. For example, because you can't prove God doesn't exist, I am free to believe that He does exist. Or because you can't prove that we do not have a soul, I am free to believe that we do.

False Dilemma This happens when we reduce several possibilities to two alternatives. I once read of two travelers facing a swamp in which traveler A said to traveler B: "Since you admit you don't know the way through the swamp and there must be a way, follow me. I must know the way." Of course, neither might know the way. Likewise, someone can argue that since your answer to a problem isn't correct, his or hers must be. But, of course, both can be wrong.

Slippery Slope Fallacy This is sometimes called the Edge of the Wedge Argument. Once you let the camel's nose under the wedge of the tent, it will collapse the entire tent. Likewise, it will be argued, once we allow act A to occur, event B, which is evil, will occur. Robert Wright has argued that "once you buy the premise that animals can experience pain and pleasure, and that their welfare therefore deserves *some* consideration, you're on the road to comparing yourself with a lobster. There may be some exit ramps along the way—plausible places to separate welfare from rights—but I can't find any." Others have argued that if we allow voluntary euthanasia, we are on the slippery slope to involuntary euthanasia, even eventually to a holocaust. Still others have argued that if we pass a National Health Care bill, it will inevitably lead to socialism and communism. The slippery slope fallacy ignores the truth that very often wise policy is a moderate stance between two extremes and that rational people can hold to a rational position without going to an extreme.

Straw Man Argument This is an instance of misrepresenting an opponent's position. It occurs when someone ignores the evidence for a position and instead attacks an inferior version of the position. In the heat of debate on whether our nation should reduce its military spending, a militarist might argue that his opponent wants to leave our nation defenseless or a willing prey to communism. I once heard of a Russian tourist guide who claimed that she knew that God didn't exist, because if He did, He would announce His presence from heaven. The straw man argument is often a distortion of the other person's position. There is a tendency in all of us to attack a weaker, less plausible version of our opponent's position. The *principle of charity* is the opposite of the straw man argument. It instructs us to give our opponent's position the very best form we can find—and then try to show it is unsound.

Genetic Fallacy Arguing against a position or argument because its origins are suspect. Suppose I tell you not to believe in the principles of chemistry because they originated in superstitious alchemy or that I tell you not to believe in an astronomical theory because it arose from astrological sources. The fact that a theory or position originated in discredited circumstances is irrelevant if the theory is supported by the evidence. Chemistry and astronomy can produce impressive evidence for their theories that is independent of the authority of alchemy and astrology. It doesn't matter where the truth comes from, as long as it is true.

Fallacy of Composition When the conclusion of an argument depends on an erroneous inference from the part to the whole. That is, because each part has an attribute, the whole is said to have the same attribute. For example sodium and chlorine are each deadly poisons, so that sodium chlorine must be a deadly poison. But it's not. It's ordinary table salt. The whole can have different properties from its parts. Here is another example: Each member of the football team is an excellent player, therefore the team must be excellent. But it might not be, for their individual excellences might not transfer into the right combination. For example, they might all be excellent half-backs and quarterbacks, but none be good at blocking. Is the following an example of this fallacy: *Because every part of the world exhibits design, the whole must exhibit design?*

Inconsistency When we argue inconsistently, we argue from contradictory premises. Politicians, when trying to win votes from one constituency, sometimes contradict what they have said to other constituencies. For an illustration of this consider some statements made by former President Ronald Reagan at different periods of his political career:

On Civil Rights
1. I favor the Civil Rights Act of 1964 and it must be enforced at the point of a bayonet, if necessary" (October 19, 1965).
2. I would have voted against the Civil Rights Act of 1964" (June 16, 1966).

On Redwood National Park
1. I believe our country can and should have a Redwood National Park in California (April 17, 1967).
2. There can be no proof given that a national park is necessary to preserve the redwoods. The state of California has already maintained a great conservation program" (April 18, 1967-the next day) .

On the Soviet Grain Embargo
1. I just don't believe the farmers should be made to pay a special price for our diplomacy, and I'm opposed to [the Soviet grain embargo]" (January 7, 1980).
2. If we are going to do such a thing to the Soviet Union as a full grain embargo, which I support, first we have to be sure our own allies would join us on this" (January 8, 1980, the next day).[2]

Of course, people change their minds and come to believe the opposite of what they formerly believed. That might show progress. But many of us are not aware of the inconsistencies in our own belief systems. For example, Fred might believe that morality entails universalizing principles (what's good for the goose is good for the gander), but fail to note that his view that premarital sex is morally permissible for men but not for women is inconsistent with that principle.

Summary

In a valid deductive argument, if the premises are true, the conclusion must be true by virtue of a logically necessary form.

In a strong inductive argument, the premises, if true, make the conclusion probable but do not guarantee the truth of the conclusion.

In a good abductive argument, the conclusion or hypothesis offers the best explanation of the data.

Logic Exercises

Show the form of the following arguments and tell whether they are valid:

1) 1. If Mary gets the job, then she will be happy.
    2. Mary will get the job.
    3. Therefore, Mary will be happy.

2) 1. If Napoleon was born in Chicago, he was Emperor of France.
    2. Napoleon was not born in Chicago.
    3. Therefore Napoleon was not Emperor of France.

3) An Environmental Argument:
    1. If I wash, I'll pollute the water.
    2. If I don't wash, I'll pollute the air.
    3. Therefore whatever I do I will be a polluter.

4) 1. All cadets at military institutions are drug-free.
    2. Timothy Leary was once a West Point cadet (a true statement).
    3. Therefore Timothy was drug free.

5) 1. If John is a bachelor, he is unmarried.
    2. John is married.
    3. Therefore [fill in blank].

6) 1. If Mary gets the job, she will be happy.
    2. If she is happy, then her husband will be happy.
    3. If her husband is happy, her mother-in-law will be happy.
    4. If her mother-in-law is happy, her mother-in-law's boss, Bob, will be happy.
    5. If Bob will be happy, his dog will be happy.
    6. Therefore [fill in the blank].

7) 1. All dogs are animals.
    2. All cats are animals.
    3. Therefore all dogs are cats.

8) 1. If the fetus is a person, abortion is immoral.
    2. Abortion is not immoral.
    3. Therefore, the fetus is not a person.

Questions for Discussion

1. What is an argument? Using the argument forms discussed in this chapter, construct an argument of your own for each form shown.

2. Explain the difference between deductive, inductive, and abductive reasoning.

3. Explain the difference between validity and soundness.

3. Get a copy of your student newspaper or your local newspaper and analyze two arguments therein. Begin to look at the claims of others in argument form.

4. Philosophy can be seen as an attempt to solve life's perennial puzzles. Taking the material at hand, it tries to unravel enigmas by thought alone. See what you can do with the puzzles and paradoxes included here.

   a. There is a barber in Barberville who shaves all and only those barbers who do not shave themselves. Does this barber shave himself?

   (Who does shave him?)

   b. You are the sole survivor of a shipwreck and are drifting in a small raft parallel to the coast of an island. You know that on this island there are only two tribes of natives: Nobles, kind folk who *always* tell the truth, and Savages, cannibals who always lie. Naturally, you want to find refuge with the Nobles. You see a man standing on the shore and call out, "Are you a Noble or a Savage?" The man answers the question, but a wave breaks on the beach at that very moment, so you don't hear the reply. The boat drifts farther down along the shore when you see another man. You ask him the same question, and he replies, pointing to the first man, "He said he was a Noble." Then he continues, "I am a Noble." Your boat drifts farther down the shore where you see a third man. You ask him the same question. The man seems very friendly as he calls out, "They are both liars. I am a Noble. They are Savages."

   The puzzle: Is the data given sufficient to tell you any man's tribe? Is it sufficient to tell you each man's tribe?

   c. Mrs. Smith, a schoolteacher, announces to her class on Friday that there will be a surprise test during the following week. She defines "surprise test" as one that no one could reasonably predict on the day of the test. Johnny, one of her students, responds that she may not give the test on pain of contradicting herself. Mrs. Smith asks, "Why not?" Johnny replies, "You cannot give the test on Friday because on Friday everyone would know that the test would take place on that day, and so it would not be a surprise. So the test must take place on a day between Monday and Thursday. But it cannot take place on Thursday, for if it hasn't taken place by then, it would not be a surprise on Thursday. So the test must take place between Monday and Wednesday. But it cannot take place on Wednesday for the same reason that we rejected Friday and Thursday. Similarly, we can use the same reason to exclude Tuesday and Monday. On no day of the week can a surprise test be given. So the test cannot be given next week."

> Mrs. Smith heard Johnny's argument and wondered what the solution was. She gave the test on Tuesday, and everyone was surprised, including Johnny. How was this possible?

d. What follows from this puzzle?

It is sometimes said that space is empty, which means presumably that there is nothing between two stars. But if there is nothing between stars, then they are not separated by anything, and, thus, they must be right up against one another, perhaps forming some peculiar sort of double star. We know this not to be the case, of course.[3]

5. A good reason to be a critical thinker is to avoid getting cheated. Occasionally, you may be in danger of being duped by an unscrupulous salesperson. Thinking clearly may save you. Here is an example of such a situation that occurred after the Loma Prieta earthquake in the California Bay area in 1989.

> Last week the 55 year old [Eva] Davis was evicted from her...home of 22 years by San Francisco sheriff's deputies. Her troubles began in 1990 when a contractor offered to repair front steps damaged in the Loma Prieta earthquake. Two hours later came a disaster worse than an earthquake, a disaster with a smile, a representative of Congress Mortgage Co. of San Jose. Convinced that she was getting a federal loan that didn't have to be repaid until the house was sold, Davis signed a 15 percent loan with a 15 percent origination fee. The 15 points meant a $23,000 fee, instead of a usual $4,000 or so. Suddenly, Davis had $1,800 monthly payments instead of $459. It was only a matter of time before the house belonged to Congress Mortgage.
>
> Congress Mortgage sold the home, valued at $225,000. The company makes some 400 loans a year and has scheduled 51 foreclosure sales in the next month alone. The bust business is booming. (Rob Morse, *San Francisco Chronicle* [Feb. 20, 1994])

Think of other examples of how critical thinking can save people from evil.

NOTES

1. Arthur Conan Doyle, *The Red-Headed League* (New York: Harper & Bros., 1892).

2. Marc Green and Gail MacCall, *There He Goes Again: Ronald Reagan's Reign of Error* (New York: Pantheon, 1983).

3. Jay Rosenberg, *The Practice of Philosophy* (Englewood Cliffs, N.J.: Prentice Hall, 1978), 99.

Suggestions for Further Reading

Copi, Irving. *Introduction to Logic,* 6th ed. New York: Macmillan, 1982. A widely used text, clear and concise.

Hurley, Patrick. *A Concise Introduction to Logic,* 4th ed. Belmont, Calif. Wadsworth, 1991.
    An excellent work, clear and accessible.
Kahane, Howard. *Logic and Contemporary Rhetoric,* 7th ed. (Wadsworth, 1995). An accessi-
    ble introduction to critical thinking. Filled with interesting illustrations and examples.
More, Brooke, and Richard Parker. *Critical Thinking.* Mountain View, Calif. Mayfield, 1992.
    A very good introduction to logical thinking.
Scriven, Michael. *Reasoning.* New York: McGraw-Hill, 1976. A rich presentation of the major
    topics in philosophical reasoning.

Part II

Philosophy of Religion

If there is no God, then God is incalculably the greatest single creation of the human imagination. No other creation of the imagination has been so fertile of ideas, so great an inspiration to philosophy, to literature, to painting, sculpture, architecture, and drama. Set beside the idea of God, the most original inventions of mathematicians and the most unforgettable characters in drama are minor products of the imagination: Hamlet and the square root of minus one pale into insignificance by comparison.

ANTHONY KENNY, *Faith and Reason*, p. 59

QUESTIONS CONNECTED WITH THE EXISTENCE OF GOD may be the most important that we can ask and try to answer. If God, an omnibenevolent, supremely powerful being who interacts with the world, exists, then it is of the utmost importance that we come to know that fact and as much as possible about God and his plan. Implications follow that affect our understanding of the world and ourselves. If God exists, the world is not accidental, a product of mere chance and necessity, but a home which has been designed for rational and sentient beings. The universe is his handiwork, a place of personal purposefulness. We are not alone in the world to struggle for justice, but are working together with one whose plan is to redeem the world from evil. Most important, there is someone to whom we are responsible and to whom we owe absolute devotion and worship. Other implications follow for our self-understanding, the way we ought to live our lives and prospects for continued life after death.

Of course, it may be false that a supreme being exists, and many people have lived well without believing in God. La Place, when asked about his faith, is reported to have replied, "I have no need of that hypothesis." But the testimony of humankind is against him. Millions have needed and been inspired by this notion. So great is the inspiration issuing from the idea of God that we could say that if God doesn't exist, the idea is the greatest invention of the human mind. What are all the world's works of literature, art, music, drama, architecture, science, and philosophy compared to this simple concept?

The field of philosophy of religion documents a significant part of the history of humanity's quest for a supreme being. Even if God does not exist, philosophy of religion retains importance for this documentation. The arguments centered around such a quest are interesting in their own right, for their ingenuity and subtlety, even apart from their possible soundness. It may be argued that the Judeo-Christian tradition has informed our self-understanding to such a degree that it is imperative for every would-be well-informed person to come to grips with the arguments and counter-arguments surrounding its claims. Hence, even if the assertions of religion are rejected as misguided or superstitious left-overs from darker ages, an understanding of what is being rejected and why it is to be rejected is important.

The readings that follow center on three questions: (1) Are there arguments that demonstrate the existence of a supreme being? (2) Does the existence of evil provide evidence against the thesis that there is a God? and (3) What is the relationship between faith and reason? Is it rational to believe in God?

II.A   Is Belief in God Rationally Justified?
Arguments for the Existence of God

Can the existence of God be demonstrated or made probable by argument? The debate between those who believe that reason can demonstrate that God exists and those who do not has an ancient lineage, going back to Protagoras (ca. 450 B.C.) and Plato (427–347 B.C.). The Roman Catholic Church has traditionally held that the existence of God is demonstrable by human reason. The strong statement of the First Vatican Council (1870) indicates that human reason is adequate to arrive at a state of knowledge of God's existence:

> If anyone says that the one and true God, our creator and Lord, cannot be known with certainty with the natural light of human reason by means of the things that have been made: Let him be anathema.

Many others—theists and nontheists, including Catholics—have denied that human reason is adequate to arrive at knowledge or demonstrate the existence of God.

Arguments for the existence of God divide into two main groups: *a priori* and *a posteriori* arguments. An *a posteriori* argument is based on premises that can be known only by means of experience of the world (for example, that there is a world, events have causes, and so forth). An *a priori* argument depends on no such premises. Rather, it rests on premises that can be known to be true independently of experience of the world: One need only clearly conceive of the proposition to see that it is true.

In this section we shall consider two types of *a posteriori* arguments for the existence of God and one *a priori* argument. The *a posteriori* arguments are the cosmological argument and the teleological argument. The *a priori* argument is the ontological argument.

The questions before us are these: What do the arguments for the existence of God establish? Do any of them demonstrate beyond reasonable doubt the existence of a supreme being or deity? Do any of them make it probable (given the evidence at hand) that such a being exists?

The Cosmological Argument

All the versions of the cosmological argument begin with the *a posteriori* assumptions that the universe exists and that something outside the universe is required to explain its existence. That is, it is *contingent,* depending on something outside of itself for its existence. That "something else" is logically before the universe. It constitutes the reason for the existence of the universe. Such a being is God.

One version of the cosmological argument is called the "First Cause Argument." The first two arguments given by St. Thomas Aquinas in our readings serve as examples of it. The general outline goes something like this :

1. Everything in the universe has a cause. That is, for everything that exists (E), there is some other thing (C), which existed before E existed, and C produced

E—that is, without C, E would not have existed. But C itself was caused by a prior cause, C_1, and C_1 by still another cause before it, C_2, and so on.

2. An infinite regress is impossible. The series of causes and effects cannot go on indefinitely but must have a beginning.

3. So there must be a first cause outside of the universe capable of producing everything besides itself (which is not produced but a necessary being).

4. Such a being must be an infinite, necessary being, that is, God.

This sort of argument can be challenged at every point, and you will find many of these challenges in Paul Edwards' article, "A Critique of the Cosmological Argument." You will decide whether the challenges are successful. First of all, we may challenge the first premise. Must everything have a cause? A significant number of physicists would deny that the principle of causality applies to some behavior of subatomic particles. These particles seem to behave randomly and can be predicted only statistically. Their noncausal thesis has been confirmed by certain experiments, though the issue is controversial. Some physicists offer other explanations. In any case, the question should be raised: How do we know that everything must have a cause?

The second premise may be challenged with the question, how do we know that an infinite regress of causes is impossible? We have infinite series in mathematics, why not in physics, too? Do we understand enough about the world to rule out such a series? If we can imagine an infinite series into the future, why not allow its possibility into the past?

Regarding the third premise, in using the notion of an infinite being to explain the world, have we really solved anything? For don't we still have to explain what an infinite being is? Isn't this simply a case of explaining the obscure with the even more obscure? And do we help our argument any by calling this unknown being God (the fourth premise)? Does the notion of a necessary being make any sense? We usually apply the notion of "necessity" to logically necessary propositions (such as that a contradiction is necessarily false or that it is necessarily true that $2 + 2 = 4$). What sense does it make to say that a being must necessarily exist?

Let us turn to Aquinas' Five Ways.

II.4   The Five Ways

THOMAS AQUINAS

The Dominican monk Thomas Aquinas (1225–1274) is considered by many to be the greatest theologian in Western religion. The five arguments given here are *a posteriori* arguments, already described in the introduction. Put simply, their strategies are as follows. The first argument begins with the fact that there is change and argues that there must be an Unmoved Mover that originates all change (or motion) but itself is not moved. The second argument is from causation and argues that there must be a first cause to explain the existence of cause. The third argument is from contingency and argues that because there are dependent beings (for example, humans), there must be an independent or necessary being on whom the dependent beings rely for their subsistence. The fourth argument is from excellence, and it argues that because there are degrees of excellence, there must be a perfect being from whence come all excellences. The final argument is from the harmony of things: There is a harmony of nature that calls for an explanation. The only sufficient explanation is that there is a divine designer who planned such harmony.

Study Questions

1. What are the two objections that people give to deny the existence of God?
2. What are Aquinas' solutions to these two objections (stated at the end of his exposition)?
3. Identify the central idea in each of the five arguments.
4. Outline the second argument in your own words and analyze it. After this, try to sum up the other arguments.

[Aquinas first identifies two objections to the thesis that God exists]

OBJECTION 1. It seems that God does not exist, because if one of two contraries be infinite, the other would be altogether destroyed. But the name *God* means that He is infinite goodness. If, therefore, God existed, there would be no evil discoverable; but there is evil in the world. Therefore God does not exist.

OBJECTION 2. Further, it is superfluous to suppose that what can be accounted for by a few principles has been produced by many. But it seems that everything we see in the world can be accounted for by other principles, supposing God did not exist. For all natural things can be reduced to one principle, which is nature; and all voluntary things can be reduced to one principle, which is human reason, or will. Therefore there is no need to suppose God's existence.

On the Contrary, It is said in the person of God: *I am Who I am* (Ex. iii.14).

I answer that, The existence of God can be proved in five ways.

THE FIRST WAY: THE ARGUMENT FROM CHANGE

The first and clearest [way] is taken from the idea of motion. (1) Now it is certain, and our senses corroborate it, that some things in this world are in motion. (2) But everything which is in motion is moved by something else. (3) For nothing is in motion except insofar as it is potentiality in relation to that towards which it is in motion. (4) Now a thing causes movement in so far as it is in actuality. For to cause movement is nothing else than to bring something from potentiality to actuality; but a thing cannot be brought from potentiality to actuality except by something which exists in actuality, as, for example, that which is hot in actuality, like fire, makes

Reprinted from Thomas Aquinas, Summa Theologica, *Laurence Shapcote (London: O. P. Benziger Brothers, 1911).*

wood, which is only hot in potentiality, to be hot in actuality, and thereby causes movement in it and alters it. (5) But it is not possible that the same thing should be at the same time in actuality and potentiality in relation to the same thing, but only in relation to different things; for what is hot in actuality cannot at the same time be hot in potentiality, though it is at the same time cold in potentiality. (6) It is impossible, therefore, that in relation to the same thing and in the same way anything should both cause movement and be caused, or that it should cause itself to move. (7) Everything therefore that is in motion must be moved by something else. If therefore the thing which causes it to move be in motion, this too must be moved by something else, and so on. (8) But we cannot proceed to infinity in this way, because in that cause there would be no first mover, and in consequence, neither would there be any other mover; for secondary movers do not cause movement except they be moved by a first mover, as, for example, a stick cannot cause movement unless it is moved by the hand. Therefore it is necessary to stop at some first mover which is moved by nothing else. And this is what we all understand God to be.

THE SECOND WAY:
THE ARGUMENT
FROM CAUSATION

The Second Way is taken from the idea of the Efficient Cause. (1) For we find that there is among material things a regular order of efficient causes. (2) But we do not find, nor indeed is it possible, that anything is the efficient cause of itself, for in that case it would be prior to itself, which is impossible. (3) Now it is not possible to proceed to infinity in efficient causes. (4) For if we arrange in order all efficient causes, the first is the cause of the intermediate, and the intermediate the cause of the last, whether the intermediate be many or only one. (5) But if we remove a cause the effect

is removed; therefore, if there is no *first* among efficient causes, neither will there be a last or an intermediate. (6) But if we proceed to infinity in efficient causes there will be no first efficient cause, and thus there will be no ultimate effect, nor any intermediate efficient causes, which is clearly false. Therefore it is necessary to suppose the existence of some first efficient cause, and this men call God.

THE THIRD WAY:
THE ARGUMENT
FROM CONTINGENCY

The Third Way rests on the idea of the "contingent" and the "necessary" and is as follows: (1) Now we find that there are certain things in the Universe which are capable of existing and of not existing, for we find that some things are brought into existence and then destroyed, and consequently are capable of being or not being. (2) But it is impossible for all things which exist to be of this kind, because anything which is capable of not existing, at some time or other does not exist. (3) If therefore *all* things are capable of not existing, there was a time when nothing existed in the Universe. (4) But if this is true there would also be nothing in existence now; because anything that does not exist cannot begin to exist except by the agency of something which has existence. If therefore there was once nothing which existed, it would have been impossible for anything to begin to exist, and so nothing would exist now. (5) This is clearly false. Therefore all things are not contingent, and there must be something which is necessary in the Universe. (6) But everything which is necessary either has or has not the cause of its necessity from an outside source. Now it is not possible to proceed to infinity in necessary things which have a cause of their necessity, as has been proved in the case of efficient causes. Therefore it is necessary to suppose the existence of something which is necessary in itself, not having the cause of its necessity from any outside source, but which is the cause of necessity in others. And this "something" we call God.

THE FOURTH WAY:
THE ARGUMENT FROM
DEGREES OF EXCELLENCE

The Fourth Way is taken from the degrees which are found in things. (1) For among different things we find that one is more or less good or true or noble; and likewise in the case of other things of this kind. (2) But the words "more" or "less" are used of different things in proportion as they approximate in their different ways to something which has the particular quality in the highest degree—e.g., we call a thing hotter when it approximates more nearly to that which is hot in the highest degree. There is therefore something which is true in the highest degree, good in the highest degree and noble in the highest degree; (3) and consequently there must be also something which has being in the highest degree. For things which are true in the highest degree also have being in the highest degree (see Aristotle, *Metaphysics*, 2). (4) But anything which has a certain quality of any kind in the highest degree is also the cause of all the things of that kind, as, for example, fire which is hot in the highest degree is the cause of all hot things (as is said in the same book). (5) Therefore there exists something which is the cause of being, and goodness, and of every perfection in all existing things; and this we call God.

THE FIFTH WAY:
THE ARGUMENT
FROM HARMONY

The Fifth Way is taken from the way in which nature is governed. (1) For we observe that certain things which lack knowledge, such as natural bodies, work for an End. This is obvious, because they always, or at any rate very frequently, operate in the same way so as to attain the best possible result. (2) Hence it is clear that they do not arrive at their goal by chance, but by purpose. (3) But those things which have no knowledge do not move towards a goal unless they are guided by someone or something which does possess knowledge and intelligence—e.g., an arrow by an archer. Therefore, there does exist something which possesses intelligence by which all natural things are directed to their goal; and this we call God.

Reply Obj. 1. As Augustine says: *Since God is the highest good, He would not allow any evil to exist in His works, unless His omnipotence and goodness were such as to bring good even out of evil.* This is part of the infinite goodness of God, that He should allow evil to exist, and out of it produce good.

Reply Obj. 2. Since nature works for a determinate end under the direction of a higher agent, whatever is done by nature must be traced back to God as to its first cause. So likewise whatever is done voluntarily must be traced back to some higher cause other than human reason and will, since these can change and fail; for all things that are changeable and capable of defect must be traced back to an immovable and self-necessary first principle, as has been shown.

For Further Reflection

1. Has Aquinas proved the existence of God? Why or why not? What do you think the value of these arguments is?

2. Do you agree that an infinite regress of causes is repugnant to reason?

3. Consider this question asked by John Stuart Mill: If God caused everything, what caused God? Is that a valid question? How would Aquinas respond to it? How would you respond to it?

II.5   A Debate on the Argument from Contingency

FATHER F. C. COPLESTON AND
BERTRAND RUSSELL

Father F. C. Copleston (1907–   ) was a professor of philosophy at Heythrop College in England and at the Gregorian University in Rome. He is famous for his multi-volume *A History of Philosophy*. Bertrand Russell (1872–1970) is one of the most important philosophers of this century and an agnostic who argued against Christian belief. In this famous BBC radio debate of 1948, Copleston defends the argument from contingency (a version of St. Thomas's Third Way), which Russell attacks.

Study Questions

1. Do Copleston and Russell agree or disagree that the issue of God's existence is of great importance to there being any purpose and absolute values in life?
2. Outline the argument from contingency. What are its premises?
3. What is the disagreement over the use of the term "necessary" in the argument? How does Copleston distinguish between *cause* and *sufficient reason*? How do the two speakers disagree in treating the word "universe"?

COPLESTON: AS WE ARE GOING to discuss the existence of God, it might perhaps be as well to come to some provisional agreement as to what we understand by the term "God." I presume that we mean a supreme personal being—distinct from the world and creator of the world. Would you agree—provisionally at least—to accept this statement as the meaning of the term "God"?

Russell: Yes, I accept this definition.

Copleston: Well, my position is the affirmative position that such a being actually exists, and that His existence can be proved philosophically. Perhaps you would tell me if your position is that of agnosticism or of atheism. I mean, would you say that the non-existence of God can be proved?

Russell: No, I should not say that: my position is agnostic.

Copleston: Would you agree with me that the problem of God is a problem of great importance? For example, would you agree that if God does not exist, human beings and human history can have no other purpose than the purpose they choose to give themselves, which—in practice—is likely to mean the purpose which those impose who have the power to impose it?

Russell: Roughly speaking, yes, though I should have to place some limitation on your last clause.

Copleston: Would you agree that if there is no God—no absolute Being—there can be no absolute values? I mean, would you agree that if there is no absolute good that the relativity of values results?

Russell: No, I think these questions are logically distinct. Take, for instance, G. E. Moore's *Principia Ethica,* where he maintains that there is a distinction of good and evil, that both of these are definite concepts. But he does not bring the idea of God to support that contention.

Copleston: Well, suppose we leave the question of good till later, till we come to the moral argument, and I give first a metaphysical argument. I'd like to put the main weight on the metaphysical argument based on Leibniz's argument from "Contingency" and then later we might discuss the moral argument. Suppose I give a brief statement on the metaphysical argument and that then we go on to discuss it?

Russell: That seems to me to be a very good plan.

Copleston: Well, for clarity's sake, I'll divide the argument into distinct stages. First of all, I should say, we know that there are at least some beings in the world which do not contain in themselves the reason for their existence. For example, I depend on my parents, and now on the air, and on food, and so on. Now, secondly, the world is simply the real or imagined totality or aggregate of individual objects, none of which contain in themselves alone the reason for their existence. There isn't any world distinct from the objects which form it, any more than the human race is something apart from the members. Therefore, I should say, since objects or events exist, and since no object of experience contains within itself the reason of its existence, this reason, the totality of objects, must have a reason external to itself. That reason must be an existent being. Well, this being is either itself the reason for its own existence, or it is not. If it is, well and good. If it is not, then we must proceed farther. But if we proceed to infinity in that sense, then there's no explanation of existence at all. So, I should say, in order to explain existence, we must come to a being which contains within itself the reason for its own existence, that is to say, which cannot not exist.

Russell: This raises a great many points and it is not altogether easy to know where to begin, but I think that, perhaps, in answering your argument, the best point at which to begin is the question of necessary being. The word "necessary," I should maintain, can only be applied significantly to propositions. And, in fact, only to such as are analytic—that is to say—such as it is self-contradictory to deny. I could only admit a necessary being if there were a being whose existence it is self-contradictory to deny. I should like to know whether you would accept Leibniz's division of propositions into truths of reason and truths of fact. The former—the truths of reason—being necessary.

Copleston: Well, I certainly should not subscribe to what seems to be Leibniz's idea of truths of reason and truths of fact, since it would appear that, for him, there are in the long run only analytic propositions. It would seem that for Leibniz truths of fact are ultimately reducible to truths of reason. That is to say, to analytic propositions, at least for an omniscient mind. Well, I couldn't agree with that. For one thing it would fail to meet the requirements of the experience of freedom. I don't want to uphold the whole philosophy of Leibniz. I have made use of his argument from contingent to necessary being, basing the argument on the principle of sufficient reason, simply because it seems to me a brief and clear formulation of what is, in my opinion, the fundamental metaphysical argument for God's existence.

Russell: But, to my mind, "a necessary proposition" has got to be analytic. I don't see what else it can mean. And analytic propositions are always complex and logically somewhat late. "Irrational animals are animals" is an analytic proposition; but a proposition such as "This is an animal" can never be analytic. In fact, all the propositions that can be analytic are somewhat late in the build-up of propositions.

Copleston: Take the proposition "If there is a contingent being then there is a necessary being." I consider that that proposition hypothetically expressed is a necessary proposition. If you are going to call every necessary proposition an analytic proposition, then—in order to avoid a dispute in terminology—I would agree to call it analytic, though I don't consider it a tautological proposition. But the proposition is a necessary proposition only on the supposition that there is a contingent being. That there is a contingent being actually existing has to be discovered by experience, and the proposition that there is a contingent being is certainly not an analytic proposition, though once you know, I should maintain, that there is a contingent being, it follows of necessity that there is a necessary being.

Russell: The difficulty of this argument is that I don't admit the idea of a necessary being and I don't admit that there is any particular meaning in calling other beings "contingent." These phrases don't for me have any significance except within a logic that I reject.

Copleston: Do you mean that you reject these terms because they won't fit in with what is called "modern logic"?

Russell: Well, I can't find anything that they could mean. The word "necessary," it seems to me, is a useless word, except as applied to analytic propositions, not to things.

Copleston: In the first place, what do you mean by "modern logic"? As far as I know, there are somewhat differing systems. In the second place, not all modern logicians surely would admit the meaninglessness of metaphysics. We both know, at any rate, one very eminent modern thinker whose knowledge of modern logic was profound, but who certainly did not think that metaphysics are meaningless or, in particular, that the problem of God is meaningless. Again, even if all modern logicians held that metaphysical terms are meaningless, it would not follow that they were right. The proposition that metaphysical terms are meaningless seems to me to be a proposition based on an assumed philosophy. The dogmatic position behind it seems to be this: What will not go into my machine is non-existent, or it is meaningless; it is the expression of emotion. I am simply trying to point out that anybody who says that a particular system of modern logic is the sole criterion of meaning is saying something that is over-dogmatic; he is dogmatically insisting that a part of philosophy is the whole of philosophy. After all, a "contingent" being is a being which has not in itself the complete reason for its existence, that's what I mean by a contingent being. You know, as well as I do, that the existence of neither of us can be explained without reference to something or somebody outside us, our parents, for example. A "necessary" being, on the other hand, means a being that must and cannot not exist. You may say that there is no such being, but you will find it hard to convince me that you do not understand the terms I am using. If you do not understand them, then how can you be entitled to say that such a being does not exist, if that is what you do say?

Russell: Well, there are points here that I don't propose to go into at length. I don't maintain the meaninglessness of metaphysics in general at all. I maintain the meaninglessness of certain particular terms—not on any general ground, but simply because I've not been able to see an interpretation of those particular terms. It's not a general dogma—it's a particular thing. But those points I will leave out for a moment. And I will say that what you have been saying brings us back, it seems to me, to the ontological argument that there is a being whose essence involves existence, so that his existence is analytic. That seems to me to be impossible, and it raises, of course, the question what one means by existence, and as to this, I think a subject named can never be significantly said to exist but only a subject described. And that existence, in fact, quite definitely is not a predicate.

Copleston: Well, you say, I believe, that it is bad grammar, or rather bad syntax to say for example "T. S. Eliot exists"; one ought to say, for example, "He, the author of *Murder in the Cathedral*, exists." Are you going to say that the proposition, "The cause of the world exists," is without meaning? You may say that the world has no cause; but I fail to see how you can say that the proposition that the "cause of the world exists" is meaningless. Put it in the form of a question: "Has the world a cause?" or "Does a cause of the world exist?" Most people surely would understand the question, even if they don't agree about the answer.

Russell: Well, certainly the question "Does the cause of the world exist?" is a question that has meaning. But if you say, "Yes, God is the cause of the world" you're using God as a proper name; then "God exists" will not be a statement that has meaning; that is the position that I'm maintaining. Because, therefore, it will follow that it cannot be an analytic proposition ever to say that this or that exists. For example, suppose you take as your subject "the existent round-square," it would look like an analytic proposition that "the existent round-square exists," but it doesn't exist.

Copleston: No, it doesn't, then surely you can't say it doesn't exist unless you have a conception of what existence is. As to the phrase "existent round-square," I should say that it has no meaning at all.

Russell: I quite agree. Then I should say the same thing in another context in reference to a "necessary being."

Copleston: Well, we seem to have arrived at an impasse. To say that a necessary being is a being that must exist and cannot not exist has for me a definite meaning. For you it has no meaning.

Russell: Well, we can press the point a little, I think. A being that must exist and cannot not exist, would surely, according to you, be a being whose essence involves existence.

Copleston: Yes, a being the essence of which is to exist. But I should not be willing to argue the existence of God simply from the idea of His essence because I don't think we have any clear intuition of God's essence as yet. I think we have to argue from the world of experience to God.

Russell: Yes, quite see the distinction. But, at the same time, for a being with sufficient knowledge, it would be true to say "Here is this being whose essence involves existence!"

Copleston: Yes, certainly, if anybody saw God, he would see that God must exist.

Russell: So that I mean there is a being whose essence involves existence although we don't know that essence. We only know there is such a being.

Copleston: Yes, I should add we don't know the essence *a priori*. It is only *a posteriori* through our experience of the world that we come to a knowledge of the existence of that being. And then one argues, the essence and existence must be identical. Because if God's essence and God's existence was not identical, then some sufficient reason for this existence would have to be found beyond God.

Russell: So it all turns on this question of sufficient reason, and I must say you haven't defined "sufficient reason" in a way that I can understand—what do you mean by sufficient reason? You don't mean cause?

Copleston: Not necessarily. Cause is a kind of sufficient reason. Only contingent being can have a cause. God is His own sufficient reason; and He is not cause of Himself. By sufficient reason in the full sense I mean an explanation adequate for the existence of some particular being.

Russell: But when is an explanation adequate? Suppose I am about to make a flame with a match. You may say that the adequate explanation of that is that I rub it on the box.

Copleston: Well, for practical purposes—but theoretically, that is only a partial explanation. An adequate explanation must ultimately be a total explanation, to which nothing further can be added.

Russell: Then I can only say that you're looking for something which can't be got, and which one ought not to expect to get.

Copleston: To say that one has not found it is one thing; to say that one should not look for it seems to me rather dogmatic.

Russell: Well, I don't know. I mean, the explanation of one thing is another thing which makes the other thing dependent on yet another, and you have to grasp this sorry scheme of things entire to do what you want, and that we can't do.

Copleston: But are you going to say that we can't, or we shouldn't even raise the question of the existence of the whole of this sorry scheme of things—of the whole universe?

Russell: Yes, I don't think there's any meaning in it at all. I think the word "universe" is a handy word in some connections, but I don't think it stands for anything that has a meaning.

Copleston: If the word is meaningless, it can't be so very handy. In any case, I don't say that the universe is something different from the objects which compose it (I indicated that in my brief summary of the proof), what I'm doing is to look for the reason, in this case the cause of the objects—the real or imagined totality of which constitute what we call the universe. You say, I think that the universe—or my existence if you prefer, or any other existence—is unintelligible?

Russell: First may I take up the point that if a word is meaningless it can't be handy. That sounds well but isn't in fact correct. Take, say, such a word as "the" or "than." You can't point to any object that those words mean, but they are very useful words; I should say the same of "universe." But leaving that point, you ask whether I consider that the universe is unintelligible. I shouldn't say unintelligible—I think it is without explanation. Intelligible, to my mind, is a different thing. Intelligible has to do with the thing itself intrinsically and not with its relations.

Copleston: Well, my point is that what we call the world is intrinsically unintelligible, apart from the existence of God. You see, I don't believe that the infinity of the series of events—I mean a horizontal series, so to speak—if such an infinity could be proved, would be in the slightest degree relevant to the situation. If you add up chocolates you get chocolates after all and not a sheep. If you add up chocolates to infinity you presumably get an infinite number of chocolates. So if you add up contingent beings to infinity, you still get contingent beings, not a necessary being. An infinite series of contingent beings will be, to my way of thinking, as unable to cause itself as one contingent being. However, you say, I think, that it is illegitimate to raise the question of what will explain the existence of any particular object?

Russell: It's quite all right if you mean by explaining it, simply finding a cause for it.

Copleston: Well, why stop at one particular object? Why shouldn't one raise the question of the cause of the existence of all particular objects?

Russell: Because I see no reason to think there is any. The whole concept of cause is one we derive from our observation of particular things; I see no reason whatsoever to suppose that the total has any cause whatsoever.

Copleston: Well, to say that there isn't any cause is not the same thing as saying that we shouldn't look for a cause. The statement that there isn't any cause should come, if it comes at all, at the end of the inquiry, not the beginning. In any case, if the total has no cause, then to my way of thinking it must be its own cause, which seems to me impossible. Moreover, the statement that the world is simply there if in answer to a question, presupposes that the question has meaning.

Russell: No, it doesn't need to be its own cause, what I'm saying is that the concept of cause is not applicable to the total.

Copleston: Then you would agree with Sartre that the universe is what he calls "gratuitous"?

Russell: Well, the word "gratuitous" suggests that it might be something else; I should say that the universe is just there, and that's all.

Copleston: Well, I can't see how you can rule out the legitimacy of asking the question how the total, or anything at all comes to be there. Why something rather than nothing, that is the question? The fact that we gain our knowledge of causality empirically, from particular causes, does not rule out the possibility of asking what the cause of the series is. If the word "cause" were meaningless or if it could be shown that Kant's view of the matter were correct, the question would be illegitimate I agree; but you don't seem to hold that the word "cause" is meaningless, and I do not suppose you are a Kantian.

Russell: I can illustrate what seems to me your fallacy. Every man who exists has a mother, and it seems to me your argument is that therefore the human race must have a mother, but obviously the human race hasn't a mother— that's a different logical sphere.

Copleston: Well, I can't really see any parity. If I were saying "every object has a phenomenal cause, therefore, the whole series has a phenomenal cause," there would be a parity; but I'm not saying that; I'm saying, every object has a phenomenal cause if you insist on the infinity of the series—but the series of phenomenal causes is an insufficient explanation of the series. Therefore, the series has not a phenomenal cause but a transcendent cause.

Russell: That's always assuming that not only every particular thing in the world, but the world as a whole must have a cause. For that assumption I see no ground whatever. If you'll give me a ground I'll listen to it.

Copleston: Well, the series of events is either caused or it's not caused. If it is caused, there must obviously be a cause outside the series. If it's not caused then it's sufficient to itself, and if it's sufficient to itself it is what I call necessary. But it can't be necessary since each member is contingent, and we've agreed that the total has no reality apart from its members, therefore, it can't be necessary. Therefore, it can't be (caused)—uncaused—therefore it must have a cause. And I should like to observe in passing that the statement "the world is simply there and is inexplicable" can't be got out of logical analysis.

Russell: I don't want to seem arrogant, but it does seem to me that I can conceive things that you say the human mind can't conceive. As for things not having a cause, the physicists assure us that individual quantum transitions in atoms have no cause.

Copleston: Well, I wonder now whether that isn't simply a temporary inference.

Russell: It may be, but it does show that physicists' minds can conceive it.

Copleston: Yes, I agree, some scientists— physicists—are willing to allow for indetermination within a restricted field. But very many scientists are not so willing. I think that Professor Dingle, of London University, maintains that the Heisenberg uncertainty principle tells us something about the success (or the lack of it) of the present atomic theory in correlating observations, but not about nature in itself, and many physicists would accept this view. In any case, I don't see how physicists can fail to accept the theory in practice, even if they don't do so in theory. I cannot see how science could be conducted on any other assumption than that of order and intelligibility in nature. The physicist presupposes, at least tacitly, that there is some sense in investigating nature and looking for the causes of events, just as the detective presupposes that there is some sense in looking for the cause of a murder. The metaphysician assumes that there is sense in looking for the reason or cause of phenomena, and, not being a Kantian, I consider that the metaphysician is as justified in his assumption as the physicist. When Sartre, for example, says that the world is gratuitous, I think that he has not sufficiently considered what is implied by "gratuitous."

Russell: I think—there seems to me a certain unwarrantable extension here; a physicist looks for causes; that does not necessarily imply that there are causes everywhere. A man may look for gold without assuming that there is gold everywhere; if he finds gold, well and good, if he doesn't he's had bad luck. The same is true when the physicists look for causes. As for Sartre, I don't profess to know what he means, and I shouldn't like to be thought to interpret him, but for my part, I do think the notion of the world having an explanation is a mistake. I don't see why one should expect it to have, and I think you say about what the scientist assumes is an over-statement.

Copleston: Well, it seems to me that the scientist does make some such assumption. When he experiments to find out some particular truth, behind that experiment lies the assumption that the universe is not simply discontinuous. There is the possibility of finding out a truth by experiment. The experiment may be a bad one, it may lead to no result, or not to the result that he wants, but that at any rate there is the possibility, through experiment, of finding out the truth that he assumes. And that seems to me to assume an ordered and intelligible universe.

Russell: I think you're generalizing more than is necessary. Undoubtedly the scientist assumes that this sort of thing is likely to be found and will often be found. He does not assume that it will be found, and that's a very important matter in modern physics.

Copleston: Well I think he does assume or is bound to assume it tacitly in practice. It may be that, to quote Professor Haldane, "when I light the gas under the kettle, some of the water molecules will fly off as vapor, and there is no way of finding out which will do so," but it doesn't follow necessarily that the idea of chance must be introduced except in relation to our knowledge.

Russell: No it doesn't—at least if I may believe what he says. He's finding out quite a lot of things—the scientist is finding out quite a lot of things that are happening in the world, which are, at first, beginnings of causal chains—first causes which haven't in themselves got causes. He does not assume that everything has a cause.

Copleston: Surely that's a first cause within a certain selected field. It's a relatively first cause.

Russell: I don't think he'd say so. If there's a world in which most events, but not all, have causes, he will then be able to depict the probabilities and uncertainties by assuming that this particular event you're interested in probably has a cause. And since in any case you won't get more than probability that's good enough.

Copleston: It may be that the scientist doesn't hope to obtain more than probability, but in raising the question he assumes that the question of explanation has a meaning. But your general point then, Lord Russell, is that it's illegitimate even to ask the question of the cause of the world?

Russell: Yes, that's my position.

Copleston: If it's a question that for you has no meaning, it's of course very difficult to discuss it, isn't it?

Russell: Yes, it is very difficult. What do you say—shall we pass on to some other issue?

For Further Reflection

1. Consider this question: Why is there something rather than nothing? Is it a meaningful question? Does it open a fruitful discussion of the possibility of the existence of a supreme being? What do Russell and Copleston think about such questions? What do you think?

2. Do Russell and Copleston shed light on the issue of God's existence or do they have too many fundamental differences to permit fruitful dialogue? Is the problem between the believer and the nonbeliever sometimes one of starting from different assumptions? What, if anything, can be done to mitigate this problem and promote a useful debate?

A Critique of the Cosmological Argument   II.6

PAUL EDWARDS

Paul Edwards (1923–) is emeritus professor of philosophy at Brooklyn College, City University of New York, and the author of several books and articles, including *The Logic of Moral Discourse*. He is the editor of the *Encyclopedia of Philosophy*. In this article he attacks the cosmological argument, specifically Aquinas' second and third arguments, at several different points, holding that the argument fails at each of these points.

Study Questions

1. Even if the cosmological argument is sound, would it show that God is all-good or all-powerful? What is Edwards' view?
2. According to Aquinas, the idea of an infinite regress of causes would imply that nothing exists. Why does Aquinas hold this view? What mistake does Edwards accuse him of making?
3. Could there be more than one first cause?
4. Distinguish between causes *in fieri* and causes *in esse*. Give an illustration of this distinction.
5. Illustrate the difference between the cause of a whole series and the cause of individuals in the series.
6. State the argument from contingency.
7. What does Edwards say about the possibility of the universe being uncaused? What is his view about the universe being a "brute fact," something that is unexplainable?

INTRODUCTION

THE SO-CALLED "cosmological proof" is one of the oldest and most popular arguments for the existence of God. It was forcibly criticized by Hume, Kant, and Mill, but it would be inaccurate to consider the argument dead or even moribund. Catholic philosophers, with hardly any exception, appear to believe that it is as solid and conclusive as ever. Thus Father F. C. Copleston confidently championed it in his Third Programme debate* with Bertrand Russell, and in

*BBC, 1948—ED.

America, where Catholic writers are more sanguine, we are told by a Jesuit professor of physics that "the existence of an intelligent being as the First Cause of the universe can be established by *rational scientific inference*."[1]

I am absolutely convinced [the same writer continues] that any one who would give the same consideration to that proof (the cosmological argument), as outlined for example in William Brosnan's *God and Reason*, as he would give to a line of argumentation found in the *Physical Review* or the *Proceedings of the Royal Society* would be forced to admit that the cogency of this argument for the existence of God far outstrips that

Reprinted from The Rationalist Annual, *1959, edited by Hector Hawton. Reprinted by permission of Paul Edwards. Notes [at end of reading] were edited.*

which is found in the reasoning which Chadwick uses to prove the existence of the neutron, which today is accepted as certain as any conclusion in the physical sciences.

Mild theists like the late Professor Dawes Hicks and Dr. [A. C.] Ewing, who concede many of Hume's and Kant's criticisms, nevertheless contend that the argument possesses a certain core of truth. In popular discussions it also crops up again and again—for example, when believers address atheists with such questions as "You tell me where the universe came from!" Even philosophers who reject the cosmological proof sometimes embody certain of its confusions in the formulation of their own position. In the light of all this, it may be worthwhile to undertake a fresh examination of the argument with special attention to the fallacies that were not emphasized by the older critics.

ANALYSIS OF THE CAUSAL ARGUMENT

The cosmological proof has taken a number of forms, the most important of which are known as the "causal argument" and "the argument from contingency," respectively. In some writers, in Samuel Clarke for example, they are combined, but it is best to keep them apart as far as possible. The causal argument is the second of the "five ways" of Aquinas and roughly proceeds as follows: We find that the things around us come into being as the result of the activity of other things. These causes are themselves the result of the activity of other things. But such a causal series cannot "go back to infinity." Hence there must be a first member, a member which is not itself caused by any preceding member—an uncaused or "first" cause.

It has frequently been pointed out that even if this argument were sound it would not establish the existence of *God*. It would not show that the first cause is all-powerful or all-good or that it is in any sense personal. Somebody believing in the eternity of atoms, or of matter generally, could quite consistently accept the conclusion. Defenders of the causal argument usually concede this and insist that the argument is not in itself meant to prove the existence of God. Supplementary arguments are required to show that the first cause must have the attributes assigned to the deity. They claim, however, that the argument, if valid, would at least be an important step towards a complete proof of the existence of God.

Does the argument succeed in proving so much as a first cause? This will depend mainly on the soundness of the premise that an infinite series of causes is impossible. Aquinas supports this premise by maintaining that the opposite belief involves a plain absurdity. To suppose that there is an infinite series of causes logically implies that nothing exists now; but we know that plenty of things do exist now; and hence any theory which implies that nothing exists now must be wrong. Let us take some causal series and refer to its members by the letters of the alphabet:

$$A \rightarrow B \ldots W \rightarrow X \rightarrow Y \rightarrow Z$$

Z stands here for something presently existing, e.g., Margaret Truman. Y represents the cause or part of the cause of Z, say Harry Truman. X designates the cause or part of the cause of Y, say Harry Truman's father, etc. Now, Aquinas reasons, whenever we take away the cause, we also take away the effect: if Harry Truman had never lived, Margaret Truman would never have been born. If Harry Truman's father had never lived, Harry Truman and Margaret Truman would never have been born. If A had never existed, none of the subsequent members of the series would have come into existence. But it is precisely A that the believer in the infinite series is "taking away." For in maintaining that the series is infinite he is denying that it has a first member; he is denying that there is such a thing as a first cause; he is in other words denying the existence of A. Since without A, Z could not have existed, his position implies that Z does not exist now; and that is plainly false. This argument fails to do justice to the supporter of the infinite series of causes. Aquinas has failed to distinguish between the two statements:

1. *A* did not exist, and

2. *A* is not uncaused.

To say that the series is infinite implies (2), but it does not imply (1). The following parallel may be helpful here: Suppose Captain Spaulding had said, "I am the greatest explorer who ever lived," and somebody replied, "No, you are not." This answer would be denying that the Captain possessed the exalted attribute he had claimed for himself, but it would not be denying his existence. It would not be "taking him away." Similarly, the believer in the infinite series is not "taking *A* away." He is taking away the privileged status of *A;* he is taking away its "first causiness." He does not deny the *existence* of *A* or of any particular member of the series. He denies that *A* or anything else *is the first member* of the series. Since he is not taking *A* away, he is not taking *B* away, and thus he is also not taking *X, Y,* or *Z* away. His view, then, does not commit him to the absurdity that nothing exists now, or more specifically, that Margaret Truman does not exist now. It may be noted in this connection that a believer in the infinite series is not necessarily denying the existence of supernatural beings. He is merely committed to denying that such a being, if it exists, is uncaused. He is committed to holding that whatever other impressive attributes a supernatural being might possess, the attribute of being a first cause is not among them.

The causal argument is open to several other objections. Thus, even if otherwise valid, the argument, would not prove a *single* first cause. For there does not seem to be any good ground for supposing that the various causal series in the universe ultimately merge. Hence even if it is granted that no series of causes can be infinite, the possibility of a plurality of first members has not been ruled out. Nor does the argument establish the *present* existence of the first cause. It

does not prove this, since experience clearly shows that an effect may exist long after its cause has been destroyed.

ORIGINATING VS. SUSTAINING CAUSES

Many defenders of the causal argument would contend that at least some of these criticisms rest on a misunderstanding. They would probably go further and contend that the argument was not quite fairly stated in the first place—or at any rate that if it was fair to some of its adherents it was not fair to others. They would in this connection distinguish between two types of causes— what they call "causes *in fieri*" and what they call "causes *in esse*." A cause *in fieri* is a factor which brought or helped to bring an effect into existence. A cause *in esse* is a factor which "sustains" or helps to sustain the effect "in being." The parents of a human being would be an example of a cause *in fieri*. If somebody puts a book in my hand and I keep holding it up, his putting it there would be the cause *in fieri*, and my holding it would be the cause *in esse* of the book's position. To quote Father [G. H.] Joyce:

> If a smith forges a horse-shoe, he is only a cause *in fieri* of the shape given to the iron. That shape persists after his action has ceased. So, too, a builder is a cause *in fieri* of the house which he builds. In both cases the substances employed act as causes *in esse* as regards the continued existence of the effect produced. Iron, in virtue of its natural rigidity, retains in being the shape which it has once received, and, similarly, the materials employed in building retain in being the order and arrangement which constitute them into a house.[2]

Using this distinction, the defender of the argument now reasons in the following way. To say that there is an infinite series of causes *in fieri* does not lead to any absurd conclusions. But Aquinas is concerned only with causes *in esse*, and an infinite series of *such* causes is impossible. In the words of the contemporary American Thomist, R. P. Phillips:

> Each member of the series of causes possesses being solely by virtue of the actual present operation of a superior cause. . . . Life is dependent, inter alia, on a certain atmospheric pressure, this again on the continual operation of physical forces, whose being and operation depends on the position of the earth in the solar system, which itself must endure relatively unchanged, a state of being which can only be continuously produced by a definite—if unknown—constitution of the material universe. This constitution, however, cannot be its own cause. That a thing should cause itself is impossible: for in order that it may cause it is necessary for it to exist, which it cannot do, on the hypothesis, until it has been caused. So it must *be* in order to cause itself. Thus, not being uncaused nor yet its own cause, it must be caused by another, which produces and preserves it. It is plain, then, that as no member of this series possesses being except in virtue of the actual present operation of a superior cause, if there *be* no first cause actually operating none of the dependent causes could operate either. We are thus irresistibly led to posit a first efficient cause which, while itself uncaused, shall impart causality to a whole series. . . .
>
> The series of cause which we are considering is not one which stretches back into the past; so that we are not demanding a beginning of the world at some definite moment reckoning back from the present, but an actual cause now operating, to account for the present being of things.[3]

Professor Phillips offers the following parallel to bring out his point:

> In a goods train each truck is moved and moves by the action of the one immediately in front of it. If then we suppose the train to be infinite, i.e., that there is no end to it, and so no engine which starts the motion, it is plain that no truck will move. To lengthen it out to infinity will not give it what no member of it possesses of itself, viz. the power of drawing the truck behind it. If then we see any truck in motion we know there must be an end to the series of trucks which gives causality to the whole.[4]

Father Joyce introduces an illustration from Aquinas to explain how the present existence of things may be compatible with an infinite series of causes *in fieri* but not with an infinite series of causes *in esse*.

> When a carpenter is at work, the series of efficient causes on which his work depends is necessarily limited. The final effect, e.g., the fastening of a nail is caused by a hammer: the hammer is moved by the arm: and the motion of his arm is determined by the motor-impulses communicated from the nerve centres of the brain. Unless the subordinate causes were limited in number, and were connected with a starting-point of motion, the hammer must remain inert, and the nail will never be driven in. If the series be supposed infinite, no work will ever take place. But if there is question of causes on which the work is not essentially dependent, we cannot draw the same conclusion. We may suppose the carpenter to have broken an infinite number of hammers, and as often to have replaced the broken tool by a fresh one. There is nothing in such a supposition which excludes the driving home of the nail.

The supporter of the infinite series of causes, Joyce also remarks, is

> . . . asking us to believe that although each link in a suspended chain is prevented from falling simply because it is attached to the one above it, yet if only the chain be long enough, it will, taken as a whole, need no support, but will hang loose in the air suspended from nothing.

This formulation of the causal argument unquestionably circumvents one of the objections mentioned previously. If Y is the cause *in esse* of an effect, Z, then it must exist as long as Z exists. If the argument were valid in this form it would therefore prove the present and not merely the past existence of a first cause. In this form the argument is, however, less convincing in another respect. To maintain that all "natural" or "phenomenal" objects—things like tables and mountains and human beings—require a cause *in fieri* is not implausible, though even here Mill and others have argued that strictly speaking only *changes* require a causal explanation. It is far from plausible, on the other hand, to claim that all natural objects require a cause *in esse*. It may be granted that the air around us is a cause *in esse* of human life and further that certain gravitational forces are among the causes *in esse* of the air being where it is. But when we come to gravitational forces or, at any rate, to material particles like atoms or electrons it is difficult to see what cause *in esse* they require. To those not already convinced of the need for a supernatural First Cause some of the remarks by Professor Phillips in this connection appear merely dogmatic and question-begging. Most people would grant that such particles as atoms did not cause themselves, since, as Professor Phillips observes, they would in that event have had to exist before they began existing. It is not at all evident, however, that these particles cannot be uncaused. Professor Phillips and all other supporters of the causal argument immediately proceed to claim that there is something else which needs no cause *in esse*. They themselves admit thus, that there is nothing self-evident about the proposition that everything must have a cause *in esse*. Their entire procedure here lends substance to Schopenhauer's gibe that supporters of the cosmological argument treat the law of universal causation like "a hired cab which we dismiss when we have reached our destination."

But waiving this and all similar objections, the restatement of the argument in terms of causes *in esse* in no way avoids the main difficulty which was previously mentioned. A believer in the infinite series would insist that his position was just as much misrepresented now as before. He is no more removing the member of the series which is supposed to be the first cause *in esse* than he was removing the member

which had been declared to be the first cause *in fieri*. He is again merely denying a privileged status to it. He is not denying the reality of the cause *in esse* labelled "*A*." He is not even necessarily denying that it possesses supernatural attributes. He is again merely taking away its "first causiness."

The advocates of the causal argument in either form seem to confuse an infinite series with one which is long but finite. If a book, *Z*, is to remain in its position, say 100 miles up in the air, there must be another object, say another book, *Y*, underneath it to serve as its support. If *Y* is to remain where it is, it will need another support, *X*, beneath it. Suppose that this series of supports, one below the other, continues for a long time, but eventually, say after 100,000 members, comes to a first book which is not resting on any other book or indeed on any other support. In that event the whole collection would come crashing down. What we seem to need is a first member of the series, a first support (such as the earth) which does not need another member as *its* support, which in other words is "self-supporting."

This is evidently the sort of picture that supporters of the First Cause argument have before their minds when they rule out the possibility of an infinite series. But such a picture is not a fair representation of the theory of the infinite series. A *finite* series of books would indeed come crashing down, since the first or lowest member would not have a predecessor on which it could be supported. If the series, however, were infinite this would not be the case. In that event every member *would* have a predecessor to support itself on and there would be no crash. That is to say: a crash can be avoided either by a finite series with a first self-supporting member or by an infinite series. Similarly, the present existence of motion is equally compatible with the theory of a first unmoved mover and with the theory of an infinite series of moving objects, and the present existence of causal activity is compatible with the theory of a first cause *in esse* as much as with the theory of an infinite series of such causes.

The illustrations given by Joyce and Phillips are hardly to the point. It is true that a carpenter would not, in a *finite* time-span, succeed in driving in a nail if he had to carry out an infinite number of movements. For that matter, he would not accomplish this goal in a finite time if he broke an infinite number of hammers. However, to make the illustrations relevant we must suppose that he has infinite time at his disposal. In that case he would succeed in driving in the nail even if he required an infinite number of movements for this purpose. As for the goods train, it may be granted that the trucks do not move unless the train has an engine. But this illustration is totally irrelevant as it stands. A relevant illustration would be that of engines, each moved by the one in front of it. Such a train would move if it were infinite. For every member of this series there would be one in front capable of drawing it along. The advocate of the infinite series of causes does not, as the original illustration suggests, believe in a series whose members are not really causally connected with one another. In the series he believes in, every member is genuinely the cause of the one that follows it.

CAUSES OF SERIES AND OF INDIVIDUALS

No staunch defender of the cosmological argument would give up at this stage. Even if there were an infinite series of causes *in fieri* or *in esse,* he would contend, this still would not do away with the need for an ultimate, a first cause. As Father Copleston put it in his debate with Bertrand Russell:

> Every object has a phenomenal cause, if you insist on the infinity of the series. But the series of phenomenal causes is an insufficient explanation of the series. Therefore, the series has not a phenomenal cause, but a transcendent cause. . . .

An infinite series of contingent beings will be, to my way of thinking, as unable to cause itself as one contingent being.

The demand to find the cause of the series as a whole rests on the erroneous assumption that the series is something over and above the members of which it is composed. It is tempting to suppose this, at least by implication, because the word "series" is a noun like "dog" or "man." Like the expression "this dog" or "this man," the phrase "this series" is easily taken to designate an individual object. But reflection shows this to be an error. If we have explained the individual members there is nothing additional left to be explained. Supposing I see a group of five Eskimos standing on the corner of Sixth Avenue and 50th Street and I wish to explain why the group came to New York. Investigation reveals the following stories:

- Eskimo No. 1 did not enjoy the extreme cold in the polar region and decided to move to a warmer climate.

- No. 2 is the husband of Eskimo No. 1. He loves her dearly and did not wish to live without her.

- No. 3 is the son of Eskimos 1 and 2. He is too small and too weak to oppose his parents.

- No. 4 saw an advertisement in the *New York Times* for an Eskimo to appear on television.

- No. 5 is a private detective engaged by the Pinkerton Agency to keep an eye on Eskimo No. 4.

Let us assume that we have now explained in the case of each of the five Eskimos why he or she is in New York. Somebody then asks: "All right, but what about the group as a whole; why is *it* in New York?" This would plainly be an absurd question. There is no group over and above the five members, and if we have explained why each of the five members is in New

York we have *ipso facto* explained why the group is there. It is just as absurd to ask for the cause of the series as a whole as distinct from asking for the causes of individual members.

THE ARGUMENT FROM CONTINGENCY

It is most unlikely that a determined defender of the cosmological line of reasoning would surrender even here. He would probably admit that the series is not a thing over and above its members and that it does not make sense to ask for the cause of the series if the cause of each member has already been found. He would insist, however, that when he asked for the explanation of the entire series, he was not asking for its *cause*. He was really saying that a series, finite or infinite, is not "intelligible" or "explained" if it consists of nothing but "contingent" members. To quote Father Copleston once more:

> What we call the world is intrinsically unintelligible apart from the existence of God. The infinity of the series of events, if such an infinity could be proved, would not be in the slightest degree relevant to the situation. If you add up chocolates, you get chocolates after all, and not a sheep. If you add up chocolates to infinity, you presumably get an infinite number of chocolates. So, if you add up contingent beings to infinity, you still get contingent beings, not a necessary being.

This last quotation is really a summary of the "contingency argument," the other main form of the cosmological proof and the third of the five ways of Aquinas. It may be stated more fully in these words: All around us we perceive contingent beings. This includes all physical objects and also all human minds. In calling them "contingent," we mean that they might not have existed. We mean that the universe can be *conceived* without this or that physical object, without this or that human being, however cer-

tain their actual existence may be. These contingent beings we can trace back to other contingent beings—e.g. a human being to his parents. However, since these other beings are also contingent, they do not provide a real or full explanation. The contingent beings we originally wanted explained have not yet become intelligible, since the beings to which they have been traced back are no more necessary than they were. It is just as true of our parents, for example, as it is of ourselves, that they might not have existed. We can then properly explain the contingent beings around us only by tracing them back ultimately to some necessary being, to something which exists necessarily, which has "the reason for its existence within itself." The existence of contingent beings, in other words, implies the existence of a necessary being.

This form of cosmological argument is even more beset with difficulties than the causal variety. In the first place, there is the objection, stated with great force by Kant, that it really commits the same error as the ontological argument in tacitly regarding existence as an attribute or characteristic. To say that there is a necessary being is to say that it would be a self-contradiction to deny its existence. This would mean that at least one existential statement is a necessary truth, and this in turn presupposes that in at least one case existence is contained in a concept. But only a characteristic can be contained in a concept and it has seemed plain to most philosophers since Kant that existence is not a characteristic, that it can hence never be contained in a concept, and that hence no existential statement can ever be a necessary truth. To talk about anything "existing necessarily" is in their view about as sensible as to talk about round squares, and they have concluded that the contingency-argument is quite absurd.

It would lead too far to discuss here the reasons for denying that existence is a characteristic. I will assume that this difficulty can somehow be surmounted and that the expression "necessary being," as it is intended by the champions of the contingency-argument, might conceivably apply to something. There remain other objections which are of great weight. I shall try to state these by first quoting again from the debate between Bertrand Russell and Father Copleston:

Russell: . . . It all turns on this question of sufficient reason, and I must say you haven't defined "sufficient reason" in a way that I can understand—what do you mean by sufficient reason? You don't mean cause?

Copleston: Not necessarily. Cause is a kind of sufficient reason. Only contingent being can have a cause. God is his own sufficient reason, and he is not cause of himself. By sufficient reason in the full sense I mean an explanation adequate for the existence of some particular being.

Russell: But when is an explanation adequate? Suppose I am about to make a flame with a match. You may say that the adequate explanation of that is that I rub it on the box.

Copleston: Well for practical purposes—but theoretically, that is only a partial explanation. An adequate explanation must ultimately be a total explanation, to which nothing further can be added.

Russell: Then I can only say that you're looking for something which can't be got, and which one ought not to expect to get.

Copleston: To say that one has not found it is one thing; to say that one should not look for it seems to me rather dogmatic.

Russell: Well, I don't know. I mean, the explanation of one thing is another thing which makes the other thing dependent on yet another, and you have to grasp this sorry scheme of things entire to do what you want, and that we can't do.

Russell's main point here may be expanded in the following way. The contingency-argument rests on a misconception of what an explanation is and does, and similarly on what it is that makes phenomena "intelligible." Or else it involves an obscure and arbitrary redefinition of "explanation," "intelligible," and related terms.

Normally, we are satisfied that we have explained a phenomenon if we have found its cause or if we have exhibited some other uniform or near-uniform connection between it and something else. Confining ourselves to the former case, which is probably the most common, we might say that a phenomenon, *Z*, has been explained if it has been traced back to a group of factors, *a, b, c, d*, etc., which are its cause. These factors are the full and real explanation of *Z*, quite regardless of whether they are pleasing or displeasing, admirable or contemptible, necessary or contingent. The explanation would not be adequate only if the factors listed are not really the cause of *Z*. If they are the cause of *Z*, the explanation would be adequate, even though each of the factors is merely a "contingent" being.

Let us suppose that we have been asked to explain why General Eisenhower won the elections of 1952. "He was an extremely popular general," we might answer, "while Stevenson was relatively little known; moreover there was a great deal of resentment over the scandals in the Truman Administration." If somebody complained that this was only a partial explanation we might mention additional antecedents, such as the widespread belief that the Democrats had allowed communist agents to infiltrate the State Department, that Eisenhower was a man with a winning smile, and that unlike Stevenson he had shown the good sense to say one thing on race relations in the North and quite another in the South. Theoretically, we might go further and list the motives of all American voters during the weeks or months preceding the elections. If we could do this we would have explained Eisenhower's victory. We would have made it intelligible. We would "understand" why he won and why Stevenson lost. Perhaps there is a sense in which we might make Eisenhower's victory even more intelligible if we went further back and discussed such matters as the origin of American views on Communism or of racial attitudes in the North and South. However, to explain the outcome of the election in any ordinary sense, loose or strict, it would not be necessary to go back to prehistoric days or to the amoeba or to a first cause, if such a first cause exists. Nor would our explanation be considered in any way defective because each of the factors mentioned was a "contingent" and not a necessary being. The only thing that matters is whether the factors were really the cause of Eisenhower's election. If they were, then it has been explained although they are contingent beings. If they were not the cause of Eisenhower's victory, we would have failed to explain it even if each of the factors were a necessary being.

If it is granted that, in order to explain a phenomenon or to make it intelligible, we need not bring in a necessary being, then the contingency-argument breaks down. For a series, as was already pointed out, is not something over and above its members, and every contingent member of it could in that case be explained by reference to other contingent beings. But I should wish to go further than this and it is evident from Russell's remarks that he would do so also. Even if it were granted, both that the phrase "necessary being" is meaningful and that all explanations are defective unless the phenomena to be explained are traced back to a necessary being, the conclusion would still not have been established. The conclusion follows from this premise together with the additional premise that *there are* explanations of phenomena in the special sense just mentioned. It is this further premise which Russell (any many other philosophers) would question. They do not merely question, as Copleston implies, whether human beings can ever obtain explanations in this sense, but whether they *exist*. To assume without further ado that phenomena have explanations or an explanation in this sense is to beg the very point at issue. The use of the same word "explanation" in two crucially different ways lends the additional premise a plausibility it does not really possess. It may indeed be highly plausible to assert that phenomena have

explanations, whether we have found them or not, in the ordinary sense in which this usually means that they have causes. It is then tempting to suppose, because of the use of the same word, that they also have explanations in a sense in which this implies dependence on a necessary thing. But this is a gross *non sequitur.*

COULD THE UNIVERSE BE UNCAUSED?

It is necessary to add a few words about the proper way of formulating the position of those who reject the main premise of the cosmological argument, in either of the forms we have considered. It is sometimes maintained in this connection that in order to reach a "self-existing" entity it is not necessary to go beyond the universe: the universe itself (or "Nature") is "self-existing." And this in turn is sometimes expanded into the statement that while all individual things "within" the universe are caused, the universe itself is uncaused. Statements of this kind are found in Büchner, Bradlaugh, Haeckel, and other freethinkers of the nineteenth and early twentieth century. Sometimes the assertion that the universe is "self-existing" is elaborated to mean that *it* is the "necessary being." Some eighteenth-century unbelievers, apparently accepting the view that there is a necessary being, asked why Nature or the material universe could not fill the bill as well or better than God.

> "Why," asks one of the characters in Hume's *Dialogues,* "may not the material universe be the necessarily existent Being? . . . We dare not affirm that we know all the qualities of matter; and for aught we can determine, it may contain some qualities, which, were they known, would make its nonexistence appear as great a contradiction as that twice two is five."

Similar remarks can be found in d'Holbach and several of the Encyclopedists.

The former of these formulations immediately invites the question why the universe, alone of all "things," is exempted from the universal sway of causation. "The strong point of the cosmological argument," writes Dr. Ewing, "is that after all it does remain incredible that the physical universe should just have happened . . . It calls out for some further explanation of some kind." The latter formulation is exposed to the criticism that there is nothing any more "necessary" about the existence of the universe or Nature as a whole than about any particular thing within the universe.

I hope some of the earlier discussions in this article have made it clear that in rejecting the cosmological argument one is not committed to either of these propositions. If I reject the view that there is a supernatural first cause, I am not thereby committed to the proposition that there is a *natural* first cause, and even less to the proposition that a mysterious "thing" called "the universe" qualifies for this title. I may hold that there is no "universe" over and above individual things of various sorts, and, accepting the causal principle, I may proceed to assert that all these things are caused by other things, and these other things by yet other things, and so on, *ad infinitum*. In this way no arbitrary exception is made to the principle of causation. Similarly, if I reject the assertion that God is a "necessary being," I am not committed to the view that the universe is such an entity. I may hold that it does not make sense to speak of anything as a "necessary being" and that even if

there were such a thing as the universe it could not be properly considered a necessary being.

However, in saying that nothing is uncaused or that there is no necessary being, one is not committed to the view that everything, or for that matter anything, is merely a "brute fact." Dr. Ewing laments that "the usual modern philosophical views opposed to theism do not try to give any rational explanation of the world at all, but just take it as a brute fact not to be explained." They thus fail to "rationalize" the universe. Theism, he concedes, cannot completely rationalize things either since it does not show "how God can be his own cause or how it is that he does not need a cause." Now, if one means by "brute fact" something for which there *exists* no explanation (as distinct from something for which no explanation is in our possession), then the theists have at least one brute fact on their hands, namely God. Those who adopt Büchner's formulation also have one brute fact on their hands, namely "the universe." Only the position I have been supporting dispenses with brute facts altogether. I don't know if this is any special virtue, but the defenders of the cosmological argument seem to think so.

NOTES

1. J. S. O'Connor, "A Scientific Approach to Religion," *The Scientific Monthly* (1940), p. 369; my italics.
2. *The Principles of Natural Theology*, p. 58.
3. *Modern Thomistic Philosophy*, Vol. II, pp. 284–285.
4. Ibid., p. 278.

For Further Reflection

1. Consider this question: "Why is there something rather than nothing?" Is it a question that we should try to answer? What would Aquinas say about this question? What does Edwards think? What do you think?

2. How successful has Edwards been in criticizing the two forms of the cosmological argument? How might a theist respond to him?

The Teleological Argument

The teleological argument for the existence of God begins with the premise that the world exhibits intelligent purpose or order and proceeds to the conclusion that there must be or probably is a divine intelligence, a supreme designer to account for the observed or perceived intelligent purpose or order. Although the argument has been cited by Plato, by St. Paul in the Epistle to the Romans (Chapter 1), and by Cicero, the clearest sustained treatment is found in William Paley's *Natural Theology* (1802), our first selection.

Paley argues that just as we infer an intelligent designer to account for the purpose-revealing watch, we must analogously infer an intelligent grand designer to account for the purpose-revealing world. "Every indication of contrivance, every manifestation of design, which existed in the watch, exists in the works of nature; with the difference, on the side of nature, of being greater and more, and that in a degree which exceeds all computation." The skeleton of the argument looks like this:

1. Human artifacts are products of intelligent design (purpose).
2. The universe resembles these human artifacts.
3. Therefore, the universe is (probably) a product of intelligent design (purpose).
4. But the universe is vastly more complex and gigantic than a human artifact.
5. Therefore, there probably is a powerful and vastly intelligent designer who designed the universe.

Ironically, Paley's argument was attacked even before Paley had set it down, for David Hume (1711–1776) had long before written his famous *Dialogues Concerning Natural Religion* (published posthumously in 1779), which constitutes the classic critique of the teleological argument. Paley seems to have been unaware of it. A selection of the *Dialogues* constitutes our second reading. In it, the natural theologian, Cleanthes, debates the orthodox believer, Demea, and the skeptic or critic, Philo, who does most of the serious arguing.

Hume, through Philo, attacks the argument from several different angles. First, he argues that the universe is not sufficiently like the productions of human design to support the argument.

Philo's second objection is that the analogy from artifact to divine designer fails because we have no other universe with which to compare this one, which would be necessary to decide if it were the kind of universe designed or simply the kind that developed on its own. As C. S. Peirce put it, "Universes are not as plentiful as blackberries." There is only one of them, so we have no standard of comparison by which to judge it. Paley's answer to this would be that if we can find one clear instance of purposeness in nature (for example, the eye), we have a sufficient instance enabling us to conclude that there is probably an intelligent designer.

A third objection is that on the analogy from artifact to designer, we should infer a grand anthropomorphic designer, a human writ large, who has all the properties that we have. "Why not become a perfect anthropomorphite? Why not assert the Deity or Deities to be corporeal, and to have eyes, a nose, mouth, ears, and so on?"

Hume makes several other points against the design argument. The universe resembles in some ways an animal and in other ways a plant, in which case the argument fails because it depends on our seeing the world as a grand machine. The world might well be the result of mere chance. And, finally, the argument is weak because the world exhibits not merely order but much disorder. The question is whether the theist can answer enough of Hume's objections to make use of this argument.

II.7   The Watch and the Watchmaker

WILLIAM PALEY

William Paley (1743–1805), archdeacon of Carlisle, was a leading evangelical apologist. His most important work is *Natural Theology, or Evidences of the Existence and Attributes of the Deity Collected from the Appearances of Nature* (1802), the first chapter of which is reprinted here. Paley argues that just as we infer an intelligent designer to account for the purpose-revealing watch, so we must infer an intelligent grand designer to account for the purpose-revealing world.

Study Questions

1. What does Paley think are the inherent differences between a stone and a watch? What inferences does each permit about its origins?
2. What is the analogy between the watch and the world, according to Paley? Describe his argument.
3. How does Paley respond to objections to the analogy?

STATEMENT OF THE ARGUMENT

IN CROSSING A HEATH, suppose I pitched my foot against a *stone*, and were asked how the stone came to be there, I might possibly answer, that, for anything I knew to the contrary, it had lain there forever; nor would it, perhaps, be very easy to show the absurdity of this answer. But suppose I found a *watch* upon the ground, and it should be inquired how the watch happened to be in that place, I should hardly think of the answer which I had given—that, for anything I knew, the watch might have always been there. Yet why should not this answer serve for the watch as well as for the stone? Why is it not as admissible in the second case as in the first? For this reason, and for no other; viz., that, when we come to inspect the watch, we perceive (what we could not discover

From William Paley, Natural Theology, or Evidences of the Existence and Attributes of the Deity Collected from the Appearances of Nature *(1801).*

in the stone) that its several parts are framed and put together for a purpose, e.g., that they are so formed and adjusted as to produce motion, and that motion so regulated as to point out the hour of the day; that, if the different parts had been differently shaped from what they are, if a different size from what they are, or placed a   fter any other manner, or in any other order than that in which they are placed, either no motion at all would have been carried on in the machine, or none which would have answered the use that is now served by it. To reckon up a few of the plainest of these parts, and of their offices, all tending to one result: We see a cylindrical box containing a coiled elastic spring, which, by its endeavor to relax itself, turns round the box. We next observe a flexible chain (artificially wrought for the sake of flexure) communicating the action of the spring from the box to the fuse. We then find a series of wheels, the teeth of which catch in, and apply to, each other, conducting the motion from the fuse to the balance, and from the balance to the pointer, and, at the same time, by the size and shape of those wheels, so regulating that motion as to terminate in causing an index, by an equable and measured progression, to pass over a given space in a given time. We take notice that the wheels are made of brass, in order to keep them from rust; the springs of steel, no other metal being so elastic; that over the face of the watch there is placed a glass, a material employed in no other part of the work, but in the room of which, if there had been any other than a transparent substance, the hour could not be seen without opening the case. This mechanism being observed, (it requires indeed an examination of the instrument, and perhaps some previous knowledge of the subject, to perceive and understand it; but being once, as we have said, observed and understood,) the inference, we think, is inevitable, that the watch must have had a maker; that there must have existed, at some time, and at some place or other, an artificer or artificers who formed it for the purpose which we find it actually to answer; who comprehended its construction, and designed its use.

I. Nor would it, I apprehend, weaken the conclusion, that we had never seen a watch made; that we had never known an artist capable of making one; that we were altogether incapable of executing such a piece of workmanship ourselves, or of understanding in what manner it was performed; all this being no more than what is true of some exquisite remains of ancient art, of some lost arts, and, to the generality of mankind, of the more curious productions of modern manufacture. Does one man in a million know how oval frames are turned? Ignorance of this kind exalts our opinion of the unseen and unknown artist's skill, if he be unseen and unknown, but raises no doubt in our minds of the existence and agency of such an artist, at some former time, and in some place or other. Nor can I perceive that it varies at all the inference, whether the question arise concerning a human agent, or concerning an agent of a different species, or an agent possessing, in some respect, a different nature.

II. Neither, secondly, would it invalidate our conclusion, that the watch sometimes went wrong, or that it seldom went exactly right. The purpose of the machinery, the design, and the designer, might be evident, and, in the case supposed, would be evident, in whatever way we accounted for the irregularity of the movement, or whether we could account for it or not. It is not necessary that a machine be perfect, in order to show with what design it was made; still less necessary, where the only question is, whether it were made with any design at all.

III. Nor, thirdly, would it bring any uncertainty into the argument, if there were a few parts of the watch, concerning which we could not discover, or had not yet discovered, in what manner they conduced to the general effect; or even some parts, concerning which we could not ascertain whether they conduced to that effect in any manner whatever. For, as to the first branch of the case, if by the loss, or disorder, or decay of the parts in question, the movement of the watch were found in fact to be stopped, or disturbed, or retarded, no doubt would remain in our minds as to the utility or intention of these parts, although we should be unable to investigate the manner according to which, or the connection by which, the ultimate effect depended upon their action or assistance; and the more complex is the machine, the more likely is this obscurity to arise. Then, as to the second thing supposed, namely, that there were parts which might be spared without prejudice to the movement of the watch, and that he had proved this by experiment, these superfluous parts, even if we were completely assured that they were such, would not vacate the reasoning which we had instituted concerning other parts. The indication of contrivance remained, with respect to them, nearly as it was before.

IV. Nor, fourthly, would any man in his senses think the existence of the watch, with its various machinery, accounted for, by being told that it was one out of possible combinations of material forms; that whatever he had found in the place where he found the watch, must have contained some internal configuration or other; and that this configuration might be the structure now exhibited, viz., of the works of a watch, as well as a different structure.

V. Nor, fifthly, would it yield his inquiry more satisfaction, to be answered, that there existed in things a principle of order, which had disposed the parts of the watch into their present form and situation. He never knew a watch made by the principle of order; nor can he even form to himself an idea of what is meant by a principle of order, distinct from the intelligence of the watchmaker.

VI. Sixthly, he would be surprised to hear that the mechanism of the watch was no proof of contrivance, only a motive to induce the mind to think so.

VII. And not less surprised to be informed, that the watch in his hand was nothing more than the result of the laws of *metallic* nature. It is a perversion of language to assign any law as the efficient, operative cause of anything. A law presupposes an

agent; for it is only the mode according to which an agent proceeds; it implies a power; for it is the order according to which that power acts. Without this agent, without this power, which are both distinct from itself, the *law* does nothing, is nothing. The expression, "the law of metallic nature," may sound strange and harsh to a philosophic ear; but it seems quite as justifiable as some others which are more familiar to him such as "the law of vegetable nature," "the law of animal nature," or, indeed, as "the law of nature" in general, when assigned as the cause of phenomena in exclusion of agency and power, or when it is substituted into the place of these.

VIII. Neither, lastly, would our observer be driven out of his conclusion, or from his confidence in its truth, by being told that he knew nothing at all about the matter. He knows enough for his argument: he knows the utility of the end: he knows the subserviency and adaptation of the means to the end. These points being known, his ignorance of other points, his doubts concerning other points, affect not the certainty of his reasoning. The consciousness of knowing little need not beget a distrust of that which he does know. . . .

APPLICATION OF THE ARGUMENT

Every indication of contrivance, every manifestation of design, which existed in the watch, exists in the works of nature; with the difference, on the side of nature, of being greater and more, and that in a degree which exceeds all computation. I mean that the contrivances of nature surpass the contrivances of art, in the complexity, subtlety, and curiosity of the mechanism; and still more, if possible, do they go beyond them in number and variety; yet in a multitude of cases, are not less evidently mechanical, not less evidently contrivances, not less evidently accommodated to their end, or suited to their office, than are the most perfect productions of human ingenuity. . . .

For Further Reflection

1. Do you think that Paley's argument is cogent? Do you think that the universe does reveal design or order? Is there a significant difference between the concepts of design and order?

2. Can you think of possible objections to Paley's argument? How might Paley respond to them?

A Critique of the Teleological Argument   II.8

DAVID HUME

The Scottish empiricist and skeptic David Hume (1711–1776) is one of the most important philosophers in the history of philosophy. The *Dialogues Concerning Natural Religion* (published posthumously in 1779) contains the classic critique of the argument from design. Our reading is from Parts 2 and 5 of this dialogue. Cleanthes, who opens our selection, is a natural theologian, the Paley of his time, who opposes both the orthodox believer, Demea, and the skeptic, Philo. Philo puts forth the major criticisms against the argument from design.

Study Questions

1. How does the natural theologian Cleanthes argue for the existence of God?
2. What are (the orthodox believer) Demea's objections to Cleanthes' way of arguing for the existence of God?
3. What does the agnostic Philo say is his chief scruple about Cleanthes' argument?
4. In Philo's second main speech, what distinction does he make between order and arrangement, on the one hand, and design, on the other? What is his purpose in this?
5. What is Philo's contention about arguing from parts to wholes?
6. Why does Philo accuse Cleanthes of anthropomorphism?
7. List six objections that Philo makes to the design argument. Are they plausible objections?
8. What is Cleanthes' response to Philo's objections?

CLEANTHES: LOOK ROUND THE WORLD: Contemplate the whole and every part of it: You will find it to be nothing but one great machine, subdivided into an infinite number of lesser machines, which again admit of subdivisions to a degree beyond what human senses and faculties can trace and explain. All these various machines, and even their most minute parts, are adjusted to each other with an accuracy which ravishes into admiration all men who have ever contemplated them. The curious adapting of means to ends, throughout all nature, resembles exactly, though

From David Hume, Dialogues Concerning Natural Religion *(1779).*

it much exceeds, the productions of human contrivance; of human design, thought, wisdom, and intelligence. Since therefore the effects resemble each other, we are led to infer, by all the rules of analogy, that the causes also resemble, and that the Author of Nature is somewhat similar to the mind of man, though possessed of much larger faculties, proportioned to the grandeur of the work which he has executed. By this argument *a posteriori*, and by this argument alone, do we prove at once the existence of a Deity and his similarity to human mind and intelligence.

Demea: I shall be so free, *Cleanthes,* said *Demea,* as to tell you that from the beginning I could not approve of your conclusion concerning the similarity of the Deity to men; still less can I approve of the mediums by which you endeavor to establish it. What! No demonstration of the Being of God! No abstract arguments! No proofs *a priori!* Are these which have hitherto been so much insisted on by philosophers all fallacy, all sophism? Can we reach no farther in this subject than experience and probability? I will say not that this is betraying the cause of a Deity; but surely, by this affected candor, you give advantages to atheists which they never could obtain by the mere dint of argument and reasoning.

Philo: What I chiefly scruple in this subject, said *Philo,* is not so much that all religious arguments are by *Cleanthes* reduced to experience, as that they appear not to be even the most certain and irrefragable of that inferior kind. That a stone will fall, that fire will burn, that the earth has solidity, we have observed a thousand and a thousand times; and when any new instance of this nature is presented, we draw without hesitation the accustomed inference. The exact similarity of the cases gives us a perfect assurance of a similar event, and a stronger evidence is never desired nor sought after. But wherever you depart, in the least, from the similarity of the cases, you diminish proportionately the evidence, and may at last bring it to a very weak *analogy,* which is confessedly liable to error and uncertainty. After having experienced the circulation of the blood in human creatures, we make no doubt that it takes place in *Titius* and *Maevius;* but from its circulation in frogs and fishes it is only a presumption, though a strong one, from analogy that it takes place in men and other animals. The analogical reasoning is much weaker when we infer the circulation of the sap in vegetables from our experience that the blood circulates in animals; and those who hastily followed that imperfect analogy are found, by more accurate experiments to have been mistaken.

If we see a house, *Cleanthes,* we conclude, with the greatest certainty, that it had an architect or builder because this is precisely that species of effect which we have experienced to proceed from that species of cause. But surely you will not affirm that the universe bears such a resemblance to a house that we can with the same certainty infer a similar cause, or that the analogy is here entire and perfect. The dissimilitude is so striking that the utmost you can here pretend to is a guess, a conjecture, a presumption concerning a similar cause; and how that pretension will be received in the world, I leave you to consider.

Cleanthes: It would surely be very ill received, replied *Cleanthes;* and I should be deservedly blamed and detested did I allow that the proofs of a Deity amounted to no more than a guess or conjecture. But is the whole adjustment of means to ends in a house and in the universe so slight a resemblance? The economy of final causes? The order, proportion, and arrangement of every part? Steps of a stair are plainly contrived that human legs may use them in mounting, and this inference is certain and infallible. Human legs are also contrived for walking and mounting; and this inference, I allow, is not altogether so certain because of the dissimilarity which you remark; but does it, therefore, deserve the name only of presumption or conjecture?

Demea: Good God! cried *Demea,* interrupting him, where are we? Zealous defenders of religion allow that the proofs of a Deity fall short of perfect evidence! And you, *Philo,* on whose assistance I depended in proving the adorable mysteriousness of the Divine Nature, do you assent to all these extravagant opinions of *Cleanthes*? For what other name can I give them? or, why spare my censure when such principles are advanced, supported by such an authority, before so young a man as *Pamphilus*?

Philo: You seem not to apprehend, replied *Philo,* that I argue with *Cleanthes* in his own way, and, by showing him the dangerous consequences of his tenets, hope at last to reduce him to our opinion. But what sticks most with you, I observe, is the representation which *Cleanthes* has made of the argument *a posteriori*; and, finding that that argument is likely to escape your hold and vanish into air, you think it so disguised that you can scarcely believe it to be set in its true light. Now, however much I may dissent, in other respects, from the dangerous principle of *Cleanthes,* I must allow that he has fairly represented that argument, and I shall endeavor so to state the matter to you that you will entertain no further scruples with regard to it.

Were a man to abstract from everything which he knows or has seen, he would be altogether incapable, merely from his own ideas, to determine what kind of scene the universe must be, or to give the preference to one state or situation of things above another. For as nothing which he clearly conceives could be esteemed impossible or implying a contradiction, every chimera of his fancy would be upon an equal footing; nor could he assign any just reason why he adheres to one idea or system, and rejects the others which are equally possible.

Again, after he opens his eyes and contemplates the world as it really is, it would be impossible for him at first to assign the cause of any one event, much less of the whole of things, or of the universe. He might set his fancy a rambling, and she might bring him in an infinite variety of reports and representations. These would all be possible; but, being all equally possible, he would never of himself give a satisfactory account for his preferring one of them to the rest. Experience alone can point out to him the true cause of any phenomenon.

Now, according to this method of reasoning, *Demea,* it follows (and is, indeed, tacitly allowed by *Cleanthes* himself) that order, arrangement, or the adjustment of final causes, is not of itself any proof of design, but only so far as it has been experienced to proceed from that principle. For aught we can know *a priori,* matter may contain the source or spring of order originally within itself, as well as mind does; and there is no more difficulty in conceiving that the several elements, from an internal unknown cause, may fall into the most exquisite arrangement, than to conceive that their ideas, in the great universal mind, from a like internal unknown cause, fall into that arrangement. The equal possibility of both these suppositions is allowed. But, by experience, we find, according to *Cleanthes,* that there is a difference between them. Throw several pieces of steel together, without shape or form; they will never arrange themselves so as to compose a watch. Stone and mortar and wood, without an architect, never erect a house. But the ideas in a human mind, we see, by an unknown, inexplicable economy, arrange themselves so as to form the plan of a watch or house. Experience, therefore, proves that there is an original principle of order in mind, not in matter. From similar effects we infer similar causes. The adjustment of means to ends is alike in the universe, as in a machine of human contrivance. The causes, therefore, must be resembling.

I was from the beginning scandalized, I must own, with this resemblance which is asserted between the Deity and human creatures, and must conceive it to imply such a degradation of the Supreme Being as no sound theist could endure. With your assistance, therefore, *Demea,* I shall endeavor to defend what you justly call the adorable mysteriousness of the Divine Nature, and shall refute this reasoning of *Cleanthes,* provided he allows that I have made a fair representation of it.

When *Cleanthes* had assented, *Philo,* after a short pause, proceeded in the following manner.

That all inferences, *Cleanthes,* concerning fact are founded on experience, and that all experimental reasonings are founded on the supposition that similar causes prove similar effects, and similar effects similar causes, I shall not at present much dispute with you. But observe, I entreat you, with what extreme caution all just reasoners proceed in the transferring of experiments to similar cases. Unless the cases be exactly similar, they repose no perfect confidence in applying their past observation to any particular phenomenon. Every alteration of circumstances occasions a doubt concerning the event; and it requires new experiments to prove certainly that the new circumstances are of no moment or importance. A change in bulk, situation, arrangement, age, disposition of the air, or surrounding bodies; any of these particulars may be attended with the most unexpected consequences. And unless the objects be quite familiar to us, it is the highest temerity to expect with assurance, after any of these changes, an event similar to that which before fell under our observation. The slow and deliberate steps of philosophers here, if anywhere, are distinguished from the precipitate march of the vulgar, who, hurried on by the smallest similitude, are incapable of all discernment or consideration.

But can you think, *Cleanthes,* that your usual phlegm and philosophy have been preserved in so wide a step as you have taken when you compared to the universe houses, ships, furniture, machines; and, from their similarity in some circumstances, inferred a similarity in their causes? Thought, design, intelligence, such as we discover in men and other animals, is no more than one of the springs and principles of the universe, as well as heat or cold, attraction or repulsion, and a hundred others which fall under daily observation. It is an active cause by which some particular parts of nature, we find, produce alterations on other parts. But can a conclusion, with any propriety, be transferred from parts to the whole? Does not the great disproportion bar all comparison and inference? From observing the growth of a hair, can we learn anything concerning the generation of a man? Would the manner of a leaf's blowing, even though perfectly known, afford us any instruction concerning the vegetation of a tree?

But allowing that we were to take the *operations* of one part of nature upon another for the foundation of our judgment concerning the *origin* of the whole (which never can be admitted), yet why select so minute, so weak, so bounded a principle as the reason and design of animals is found to be upon this planet? What peculiar privilege has this little agitation of the brain which we call "thought," that we must thus make it the model of the whole universe? Our partiality in our own favor does indeed present it on all occasions, but sound philosophy ought carefully to guard against so natural an illusion.

So far from admitting, continued *Philo,* that the operations of a part can afford us any just conclusion concerning the origin of the whole, I will not allow any one part to form a rule for another part if the latter be very remote from the former. Is there any reasonable ground to conclude that the inhabitants of other planets possess thought, intelligence, reason, or anything similar to these faculties in men? When nature has so extremely diversified her manner of operation in this small globe, can we imagine that she incessantly copies herself throughout so immense a universe? And if thought, as we may well suppose, be confined merely to this narrow corner, and has even there so limited a sphere of action, with what propriety can we assign it for the original cause of all things? The narrow views of a peasant who makes his domestic economy the rule for the government of kingdoms is in comparison a pardonable sophism.

But were we ever so much assured that a thought and reason resembling the human were to be found throughout the whole universe, and were its activity elsewhere vastly greater and more commanding than it appears in this globe; yet I cannot see why the operations of a world constituted, arranged, adjusted, can with any propriety be extended to a world which is in its embryostate, and is advancing towards that constitution and arrangement. By observation we know somewhat of the economy, action, and nourishment of a finished animal; but we must transfer with great caution that observation to the growth of a foetus in the womb, and still more to the formation of an animalcule in the loins of its male parent. Nature, we find, even from our limited experience, possesses an infinite number of springs and principles which incessantly discover themselves on every change of her position and situation. And what new and unknown principles would actuate her in so new and unknown a situation as that of the formation of a universe, we cannot, without the utmost temerity, pretend to determine.

A very small part of this great system, during a very short time, is very imperfectly discovered to us; and do we thence pronounce decisively concerning the origin of the whole?

Admirable conclusion! Stone, wood, brick, iron, brass, have not, at this time, in this minute globe of earth, an order or arrangement without human art and contrivance; therefore, the universe could not originally attain its order and arrangement without something similar to human art. But is a part of nature a rule for another part very wide of the former? Is it a rule for the whole? Is a very small part a rule for the universe? Is nature in one situation a certain rule for nature in another situation vastly different from the former?

And can you blame me, *Cleanthes,* if I here imitate the prudent reserve of *Simonides,* who, according to the noted story, being asked by *Hiero, What God was?* desired a day to think of it, and then two days more; and after that manner continually prolonged the term, without ever bringing in his definition or description? Could you even blame me if I had answered, at first, *that I did not know,* and was sensible that this subject lay vastly beyond the reach of my faculties? You might cry out skeptic and raillier, as much as you pleased; but, having found in so many other subjects much more familiar the imperfections and even contradictions of human reason, I never should expect any success from its feeble conjectures in a subject so sublime and so remote from the sphere of our observation.

When two *species* of objects have always been observed to be conjoined together, I can *infer,* by custom, the existence of one wherever I see the existence of the other; and this I call an argument from experience. But how this argument can have place where the objects, as in the present case, are single, individual, without parallel or specific resemblance, may be difficult to explain. And will any man tell me with a serious countenance that an orderly universe must arise from some thought and art like the human because we have experience of it? To ascertain this reasoning it were requisite that we had experience of the origin of worlds; and it is not sufficient, surely, that we have seen ships and cities arise from human art and contrivance. . . .

Philo: But to show you still more inconveniences, continued *Philo,* in your anthropomorphism, please to take a new survey of your principles. *Like effects prove like causes.* This is the experimental argument; and this, you say too, is the sole theological argument. Now it is certain that the liker the effects which are seen and the liker the causes which are inferred, the stronger is the argument. Every departure on either side diminishes the probability and renders the experiment less conclusive. You cannot doubt of the principle; neither ought you to reject its consequences.

All the new discoveries in astronomy which prove the immense grandeur and magnificence of the works of nature are so many additional arguments for a Deity, according to the true system of theism; but, according to your hypothesis of experimental theism, they become so many objections, by removing the effect still farther from all resemblance to the effects of human art and contrivance. For if *Lucretius,* even following the old system of the world, could exclaim:

> Who is strong enough to rule the sum, who to hold in hand and control the mighty bridle of the unfathomable deep? who to turn about all the heavens at one time, and warm the fruitful worlds with ethereal fires, or to be present in all places and at all times.[1]

If Tully[2] esteemed this reasoning so natural as to put it into the mouth of his Epicurean:

> What power of mental vision enabled your master Plato to descry the vast and elaborate architectural process which, as he makes out, the deity adopted in building the structure of the universe? What method of engineering was employed? What tools and levers and derricks? What agents carried out so vast an understanding? And how were air, fire, water, and earth enabled to obey and execute the will of the architect?

If this argument, I say, had any force in former ages, how much greater must it have at present when the bounds of nature are so infinitely enlarged and such a magnificent scene is opened to us? It is still more unreasonable to form our idea of so unlimited a cause from our experience of the narrow productions of human design and invention.

The discoveries by microscopes, as they open a new universe in miniature, are still objections, according to you; arguments, according to me. The farther we push our researches of this kind, we are still led to infer the universal cause of all to be vastly different from mankind, or from any object of human experience and observation.

And what say you to the discoveries in anatomy, chemistry, botany? . . . *Cleanthes:* These surely are no objections, replied *Cleanthes;* they only discover new instances of art and contrivance. It is still the image of mind reflected on us from innumerable objects. *Philo:* Add a mind *like the human,* said *Philo. Cleanthes:* I know of no other, replied *Cleanthes. Philo:* And the liker, the better, insisted *Philo. Cleanthes:* To be sure, said *Cleanthes.*

Philo: Now, *Cleanthes,* said *Philo,* with an air of alacrity and triumph, mark the consequences. *First,* by this method of reasoning you renounce all claim to infinity in any of the attributes of the Deity. For, as the cause ought only to be proportioned to the effect, and the effect, so far as it falls under our cognizance, is not infinite: What pretensions have we, upon your suppositions, to ascribe that attribute to the Divine Being? You will still insist that, by removing him so much from all similarity to human creatures, we give in to the most arbitrary hypothesis, and at the same time weaken all proofs of his existence.

Secondly, you have no reason, on your theory, for ascribing perfection to the Deity, even in his finite capacity; or for supposing him free from every error, mistake, or incoherence, in his undertakings. There are many inexplicable difficulties in the works of Nature which, if we allow a perfect author to be proved *a priori,* are easily solved, and become only seeming difficulties from the narrow capacity of man, who cannot trace infinite relations. But according to your method of reasoning, these difficulties become all real; and, perhaps, will be insisted on as new instances of likeness to human art and contrivance. At least, you must acknowledge that it is impossible for us to tell, from our limited views, whether this system contains any great faults or deserves any considerable praise if compared to other possible and even real systems. Could a peasant, if the *Aeneid* were read to him, pronounce that poem to be absolutely faultless, or even assign to it its proper rank among the productions of human wit, he who had never seen any other production?

But were this world ever so perfect a production, it must still remain uncertain whether all the excellences of the work can justly be ascribed to the workman. If we survey a ship, what an exalted idea must we form of the ingenuity of the carpenter who framed so complicated, useful, and beautiful a machine? And what surprise must we feel when we find him a stupid mechanic who imitated others, and copied an art which, through a long succession of ages, after multiplied trials, mistakes, corrections, deliberations, and controversies, had been gradually improving? Many worlds might have been botched and bungled, throughout an eternity, ere this system was struck out; much labor lost; many fruitless trials made; and a slow but continued improvement carried on during infinite ages in the art of world-making. In such subjects, who can determine where the truth, nay, who can conjecture where the probability lies, amidst a great number of hypotheses which may be proposed, and a still greater which may be imagined?

And what shadow of an argument, continued *Philo*, can you produce from your hypothesis to prove the unity of the Deity? A great number of men join in building a house or ship, in rearing a city, in framing a commonwealth; why may not several deities combine in contriving and framing a world? This is only so much greater similarity to human affairs. By sharing the work among several, we may so much further limit the attributes of each, and get rid of that extensive power and knowledge which must be supposed in one deity, and which, according to you, can only serve to weaken the proof of his existence. And if such foolish, such vicious creatures as man can yet often unite in framing and executing one plan, how much more those deities or demons, whom we may suppose several degrees more perfect?

To multiply causes without necessity is indeed contrary to true philosophy, but this principle applies not to the present case. Were one deity antecedently proved by your theory who were possessed of every attribute requisite to the production of the universe, it would be needless, I own (though not absurd), to suppose any other deity existent. But while it is still a question whether all these attributes are united in one subject or dispersed among several independent beings; by what phenomena in nature can we pretend to decide the controversy? Where we see a body raised in a scale, we are sure that there is in the opposite scale, however concealed from sight, some counterpoising weight equal to it; but it is still allowed to doubt whether that weight be an aggregate of several distinct bodies or one uniform united mass. And if the weight requisite very much exceeds anything which we have ever seen conjoined in any single body, the former supposition becomes still more probable and natural. An intelligent being of such vast power and capacity as is necessary to produce a universe, or, to speak in the language of ancient philosophy, so prodigious an animal, exceeds all analogy and even comprehension.

But further, *Cleanthes*, men are mortal, and renew their species by generation; and this is common to all living creatures. The two great sexes of male and female, says *Milton*, animate the world. Why must this circumstance, so universal, so essential, be excluded from those numerous and limited deities? Behold, then, the theogeny of ancient times brought back upon us.

And why not become a perfect anthropomorphite? Why not assert the deity or deities to be corporeal, and to have eyes, a nose, mouth, ears, etc.? *Epicurus* maintained that no man had ever seen reason but in a human figure; therefore, the gods must have a human figure. And this argument, which is deservedly so much ridiculed by *Cicero*, becomes, according to you, solid and philosophical.

In a word, *Cleanthes*, a man who follows your hypothesis is able, perhaps, to assert or conjecture that the universe sometime arose from something like design. But beyond that position he cannot ascertain one single circumstance and is left afterwards to fix every point of his theology by the utmost license of fancy and hypothesis. This world, for aught he knows, is very faulty and imperfect, compared to a superior standard, and was only the first rude essay of some infant deity who afterwards abandoned it, ashamed of his lame performance. It is the work only of some dependent, inferior deity, and is the object of derision to his superiors. It is the production of old age and dotage in some superannuated deity; and ever since his death has run on at adventures, from the first impulse and active force which it received from him. . . . You justly give signs of horror, *Demea*, at these strange suppositions; but these, and a thousand more of the same kind, are *Cleanthes'* suppositions, not mine. From the moment the attributes of the Deity are supposed finite, all these have place. And I cannot, for my part, think that so wild and unsettled a system of theology is, in any respect, preferable to none at all.

Cleanthes: These suppositions I absolutely disown. They strike me, however, with no horror, especially when proposed in that rambling way in which they drop from you. On the contrary, they give me pleasure when I see that, by the utmost indulgence of your imagination, you never get rid of the hypothesis of design in the universe, but are obliged at every turn to have recourse to it. To this concession I adhere steadily; and this I regard as a sufficient foundation for religion.

NOTES

1. *On the Nature of Things*, II, 1096–1099 (trans. by W. D. Rouse).

2. Tully was a common name for the Roman lawyer and philosopher Marcus Tullius Cicero, 106–43 B.C. The excerpt is from *The Nature of the Gods*, I, viii, 19 (trans. by H. Rackham).

For Further Reflection

1. The teleological argument has had a long and distinguished career, but is it plausible? How probable does it make the existence of a God?

2. How effective are Hume's criticisms? Consider his contention that we can't argue from the part to a whole. Is that always true? Can't we sometimes make valid inferences from a part to the whole? For example, if I discover that the saltwater from the Atlantic Ocean that is by my home in Long Island is undrinkable, can't I infer that the rest of the water in the Atlantic Ocean is likely undrinkable? This may be a weak argument, but doesn't the part lend some probability to conclusions about the whole?

3. Examine each of Hume's objections to determine their strength. What might Paley reply to them?

The Ontological Argument

The ontological argument for the existence of God is the most intriguing of all the arguments for theism. It is one of the most remarkable arguments ever set forth. First set forth by St. Anselm (1033–1109), in the eleventh century, the argument has continued to puzzle and fascinate philosophers ever since.

The argument is not only important because it claims to be an *a priori* proof for the existence of God, but it also is the primary locus of such philosophical problems as whether existence is a property and whether the notion of necessary existence is intelligible. Furthermore, it has special religious significance because it is the only one of the traditional arguments which clearly concludes to the necessary properties of God, that is, his omnipotence, omniscience, omnibenevolence, and so on.

Although there are many versions of the ontological argument and many interpretations of some of these, most philosophers agree on the essential form of Anselm's version in the second chapter of his *Proslogium*. Anselm believes that God's existence is absolutely certain, so that only a fool would doubt or deny it. Yet he desires understanding to fulfill his faith.

The argument that follows can be treated as a *reductio ad absurdum* argument. That is, it begins with a supposition (S: suppose that the greatest conceivable being exists in the mind alone) that is contradictory to what one desires to prove and then one goes about showing that (S) together with other certain or self-evident assumptions (A_1 and A_2) yields a contradiction, which in turn demonstrates that the contradictory of (S) must be true. A greatest possible being must exist in reality; I shall leave it to you to work out the details of the argument.

Anselm's contemporary, Gaunilo, sets forth the first objection to Anselm's argument. Accusing Anselm of pulling rabbits out of hats, he tells the story of a delectable lost island, one that is more excellent than all lands. Because it is better that such a perfect island exists in reality rather than simply in the mind alone, this Isle of the Blest must necessarily exist. Anselm's reply is that the analogy fails, for unlike the greatest possible being, the greatest possible island can be conceived as not existing. Recently, Alvin Plantinga has clarified Anselm's point. There simply are some properties that do have intrinsic maximums, and some properties that don't have them. No matter how wonderful you make the Isle of the Blest, we can conceive of a more wonderful island. The greatness of islands are like the greatness of numbers in this respect. There is no greatest natural number, for no matter how large the number you choose, we can always conceive of one twice as large. On the other hand, the properties of God have intrinsic maximums. For example, we can define perfect knowledge this way. For any proposition an omniscient being knows whether it is true or false.

The Ontological Argument   II.9

ST. ANSELM AND GAUNILO

St. Anselm (c. 1033–1109) was Abbot of Bec and later Archbishop of Canterbury. He wrote several important treatises on theological subjects, including *Cur Deus Homo* (*Why God Became Man*). In this selection from his *Proslogium*, he begins with the definition of God as "that than which nothing greater can be conceived." Today we might translate that as "the greatest possible being." From that definition he proceeds to argue for the necessary existence of God.

Gaunilo was an eleventh-century Benedictine monk who first criticized Anselm's argument. Little is known about him.

Study Questions

1. Note that St. Anselm begins his argument with a prayer to God. Is this significant for understanding the argument? What does his request show about Anselm's assumptions?
2. What is the significance of the analogy with the painter?
3. After an initial reading, attempt to outline the argument. Do you agree with Anselm that it proves the existence of God?
4. What is Gaunilo's criticism of the argument? Is it plausible?
5. Evaluate Anselm's rejoinder.

ST. ANSELM'S PRESENTATION

Truly there is a God, although the fool hath said in his heart, There is no God.

AND SO, LORD, DO THOU, who dost give understanding to faith, give me, so far as thou knowest it to be profitable, to understand that thou art as we believe; and that thou art that which we believe. And, indeed, we believe that thou art a being than which nothing greater can be conceived. Or is there no such nature, since the fool hath said in his heart, there is no God? (Psalms xiv, 1). But, at any rate, this very fool, when he hears of this being of which I speak—a being than which nothing greater can be conceived—understands what he hears, and what he understands is in his understanding; although he does not understand it to exist.

For, it is one thing for an object to be in the understanding, and another to understand that the object exists. When a painter first conceives of what he will afterwards perform, he has it in his understanding, but he does not yet understand it to be, because he has not yet performed it. But after he has made the painting, he both has it in his understanding, and he understands that it exists, because he has made it.

Hence, even the fool is convinced that something exists in the understanding, at least, than which nothing greater can be conceived. For, when he hears of this, he understands it. And whatever is understood, exists in the understanding. And assuredly that, than which nothing greater can be conceived, cannot exist in the understanding alone. For, suppose it exists in the understanding alone: then it can be conceived to exist in reality; which is greater.

Therefore, if that, than which nothing greater can be conceived, exists in the understanding alone, the very being, than which nothing greater can be conceived, is one, than which a greater can be conceived. But obviously this is impossible. Hence, there is no doubt that there exists a being than which nothing greater can be conceived, and it exists both in the understanding and in reality.

God cannot be conceived not to exist.—God is that, than which nothing greater can be conceived.—That which can be conceived not to exist is not God.

And it assuredly exists so truly, that it cannot be conceived not to exist. For, it is possible to conceive of a being which cannot be conceived not to exist; and this is greater than one which can be conceived not to exist. Hence, if that, than which nothing greater can be conceived, can be conceived not to exist, it is not that, than which nothing greater can be conceived. But this is an irreconcilable contradiction. There is, then, so truly a being than which nothing greater can be conceived to exist, that it cannot even be conceived not to exist; and this being thou art, O Lord, our God.

So truly, therefore, dost thou exist, O Lord, my God, that thou canst not be conceived not to exist; and rightly. For, if a mind could conceive of a being better than thee, the creature would rise above the Creator; and this is most absurd. And, indeed, whatever else there is, except thee alone, can be conceived not to exist. To thee alone, therefore, it belongs to exist more truly than all other beings, and hence in a higher degree than all others. For, whatever else exists does not exist so truly, and hence in a less degree it belongs to it to exist. Why, then, has the fool said in his heart, there is no God (Psalms xiv, 1), since it is so evident, to a rational mind, that thou dost exist in the highest degree of all? Why, except that he is dull and a fool?

How the fool has said in his heart what cannot be conceived.—A thing may be conceived in two

These exerpts are from Anselm's Proslogium, Gaunilo's In Bahalf of the Fool, *and Anselm's "Apologetic." Reprinted from St. Anselm,* Basic Writings, *trans. S. W. Deane, by permission of The Open Court Pubishing Company. Copyrighted by The Open Court Publishing Co. 1903. Second copyright © by The Open Court Publishing Co. 1962.*

ways: (1) when the word signifying it is conceived; (2) when the thing itself is understood. As far as the word goes, God can be conceived not to exist; in reality he cannot.

But how has the fool said in his heart what he could not conceive; or how is it that he could not conceive what he said in his heart? since it is the same to say in the heart, and to conceive.

But, if really, nay, since really, he both conceived, because he said in his heart; and did not say in his heart, because he could not conceive; there is more than one way in which a thing is said in the heart or conceived. For, in one sense, an object is conceived, when the word signifying it is conceived; and in another, when the very entity, which the object is, is understood.

In the former sense, then, God can be conceived not to exist; but in the latter, not at all. For no one who understands what fire and water are can conceive fire to be water, in accordance with the nature of the facts themselves, although this is possible according to the words. So, then, no one who understands what God is can conceive that God does not exist; although he says these words in his heart, either without any or with some foreign, signification. For, God is that than which a greater cannot be conceived. And he who thoroughly understands this, assuredly understands that this being so truly exists, that not even in concept can it be non-existent. Therefore, he who understands that God so exists, cannot conceive that he does not exist.

I thank thee, gracious Lord, I thank thee; because what I formerly believed by thy bounty, I now so understand by thine illumination, that if I were unwilling to believe that thou dost exist, I should not be able not to understand this to be true.

GAUNILO'S CRITICISM

For example: it is said that somewhere in the ocean is an island, which, because of the difficulty, or rather the impossibility, of discovering what does not exist, is called the lost island. And they say that this island has an inestimable wealth of all manner of riches and delicacies in greater abundance than is told of the Islands of the Blest; and that having no owner or inhabitant, it is more excellent than all other countries, which are inhabited by mankind, in the abundance with which it is stored.

Now if some one should tell me that there is such an island, I should easily understand his words, in which there is no difficulty. But suppose that he went on to say, as if by a logical inference: "You can no longer doubt that this island which is more excellent than all lands exists somewhere, since you have no doubt that it is in your understanding. And since it is more excellent not to be in the understanding alone, but to exist both in the understanding and in reality, for this reason it must exist. For if it does not exist, any land which really exists will be more excellent than it; and so the island already understood by you to be more excellent will not be more excellent."

If a man should try to prove to me by such reasoning that this island truly exists, and that its existence should no longer be doubted, either I should believe that he was jesting, or I know not which I ought to regard as the greater fool: myself, supposing that I should allow this proof; or him, if he should suppose that he had established with any certainty the existence of this island. For he ought to show first that the hypothetical excellence of this island exists as a real and indubitable fact, and in no wise as any unreal object, or one whose existence is uncertain, in my understanding.

ST. ANSELM'S REJOINDER

A criticism of Gaunilo's example, in which he tries to show that in this way the real existence of a lost island might be inferred from the fact of its being conceived.

But, you say, it is as if one should suppose an island in the ocean, which surpasses all lands in its fertility, and which, because of the difficulty, or rather the impossibility, of discovering what does not exist, is called a lost island; and should say that there can be no doubt that this island truly exists in reality, for this reason, that one who hears it described easily understands what he hears.

Now I promise confidently that if any man shall devise anything existing either in reality or in concept alone (except that than which a greater cannot be conceived) to which he can adapt the sequence of my reasoning, I will discover that thing, and will give him his lost island, not to be lost again.

But it now appears that this being than which a greater is inconceivable cannot be conceived not to be, because it exists on so assured a ground of truth; for otherwise it would not exist at all.

Hence, if any one says that he conceives this being not to exist, I say that at the time when he conceives of this either he conceives of a being than which a greater is inconceivable, or he does not conceive at all. If he does not conceive, he does not conceive of the non-existence of that of which he does not conceive. But if he does conceive, he certainly conceives of a being which cannot be even conceived not to exist. For if it could be conceived not to exist, it could be conceived to have a beginning and an end. But this is impossible.

He, then, who conceives of this being conceives of a being which cannot be even conceived not to exist; but he who conceives of this being does not conceive that it does not exist; else he conceives what is inconceivable. The nonexistence, then, of that than which a greater cannot be conceived is inconceivable.

For Further Reflection

1. Some philosophers have objected that Anselm misunderstands the concept of "being." Being is not an ordinary concept like "red" or "horse," but an instantiating concept which asserts that these other concepts are exemplified (for example, the concept unicorn is not exemplified, but the concept of horse is). It makes no sense, they contend, to say that being is exemplified. Are they correct?

2. Is it greater to exist than not to exist, as Anselm argues? Or is the term "greater" ambiguously or wrongly used here?

3. Could a similar argument as Anselm's be used to prove that a perfectly powerful devil exists as the supreme being and creator of all things?

II.B   Why Is There Evil?

Is he willing to prevent evil, but not able? then he is impotent. Is he able, but not willing? then he is malevolent. Is he both able and willing? whence then is evil? [Epicurus 341–270 B.C.]

We have been looking at arguments in favor of God's existence. The agnostic and atheist usually base their case on the *absence* of evidence for God's existence. But they have one arrow in their own quiver, an argument for disbelief. It is the problem of evil. From it the "atheologian" (one who argues against the existence of God, represented by Bruce Russell in our readings) hopes either to neutralize any positive evidence for God's existence based on whatever in the traditional arguments survives their criticism or to demonstrate that it is unreasonable to believe in God.

→ The problem of evil arises because of the paradox of an omnibenevolent, omnipotent deity allowing the existence of evil. The Judeo-Christian tradition has affirmed these three propositions: *(HE IS OVER ALL GOOD, STRONG)*

1. God is all-powerful (including omniscience). *ALL KNOWING*
2. God is perfectly good.
3. Evil exists.

But if God is perfectly good, why does he allow evil to exist? Why didn't he create a better world, if not with no evil, at least with substantially less evil than in this world? Many have contended that this paradox, first schematized by Epicurus, is worse than a paradox. It is an implicit contradiction for it contains premises that are inconsistent with one another. These philosophers argue something like the following:

4. If God (an all-powerful, omniscient, omnibenevolent being) exists, there would be no (or no unnecessary) evil in the world.
5. There is evil (or unnecessary evil) in the world.
6. Therefore, God does not exist.

You should examine each of these premises carefully. A few words are in order. Generally, Western thought has distinguished between two types of evil: moral and natural. "Moral evil" covers all those bad things for which humans are morally responsible. "Natural evil" or "surd evil" stands for all those terrible events that nature does of her own accord, for example, hurricanes, tornadoes, earthquakes, volcano eruptions, natural diseases, which bring on suffering to humans and animals. However, some defenses of theism affirm that all evil is essentially moral evil. Here the devil is brought in as the cause of natural evil.

The main defense of theism in the light of evil is the *free-will defense,* going back as far as St. Augustine (354–430) and receiving modern treatment in the work of John Hick, Alvin Plantinga, and Richard Swinburne. The free-will defense adds a fourth premise to Epicurus' paradox to show that premises 1–3 are consistent and not contradictory. This premise is

7. It is logically impossible for God to create free creatures and guarantee that they will never do evil.

The proponent of the free will defense claims that all moral evil derives from creature freedom of the will. But what about natural evil? How does the theist account for it? There are two different ways. The first one, suggested by Alvin Plantinga (see also bibliography), is to attribute natural evil to the work of the devil and his angels. Disease and tornadoes are caused by the devil and his minions. The second way, favored by Hick and Swinburne, argues that natural evil is part and parcel of the nature of things: a result of the combination of deterministic physical laws that are necessary for consistent action and the responsibility given to humans to exercise their freedom.

One further distinction is necessary to work through this problem. Some theists attempt to answer the charge of inconsistency by simply showing that there is no formal contradiction between propositions 1 through 3, so that the nontheist hasn't proved his point. But others want to go beyond this negative function and offer a plausible account of evil. These latter are called "theodicists," for they attempt to justify the ways of God before humankind. They endeavor to show that God allows the temporary evil to bring out greater good. In our readings, John Hick represents the theodicist position.

THEODICY —
AN ATTEMPT TO
UNDERSTAND GOD
IN THE FACE OF
EVIL.

II.10   Why Is There Evil?

FYODOR DOSTOEVSKY

Fyodor Dostoevsky (1822–1881) was one of the greatest Russian novelists. He was born in Moscow. His revolutionary sympathies and a penchant for gambling managed to keep him in constant danger. Among his famous writings are *Crime and Punishment* (1866), *The Idiot* (1868) and *The Brothers Karamazov* (1880), from which our reading is taken.

In this scene from Dostoevsky's most famous work, Ivan Karamazov is explaining to his pious brother, Alyosha, a Christian monk, why he cannot accept God.

Study Questions

1. Does Ivan believe that God exists? What does he think of the hypothesis that humanity invented the notion of God?
2. Does Ivan think that we can understand God? Why or why not?
3. What is Ivan's creed? Has he stated his position very clearly or consistently? How can he speak of God as holy and yet admit that God is the cause of children's suffering?
4. What does Ivan mean in saying that there can be solidarity with the suffering and guilt of humanity (or other adults) but not with children?
5. What is Ivan's response to the proposal that the solution of the problem of evil is to be found in an eternal harmony?
6. What does he mean when he says, "I most respectfully return Him the ticket?"

"WELL, TELL ME WHERE TO BEGIN, give your orders. The existence of God, eh?"

"Begin where you like. You declared yesterday at father's that there was no God." Alyosha looked searchingly at his brother.

"I said that yesterday at dinner on purpose to tease you and I saw your eyes glow. But now I've no objection to discussing with you, and I say so very seriously. I want to be friends with you, Alyosha, for I have no friends and want to try it.

From Fyodor Dostoevsky, The Brothers Karamazov, *trans. by Constance Garnett (London: Heinemann, 1912).*

Well, only fancy, perhaps I too accept God," laughed Ivan, "that's a surprise for you, isn't it?"

"Yes of course, if you are not joking now."

"Joking? I was told at the elder's yesterday that I was joking. You know, dear boy, there was an old sinner in the eighteenth century who declared that, if there were no God, he would have to be invented. . . . And man has actually invented God. And what's strange, what would be marvelous, is not that God should really exist; the marvel is that such an idea, the idea of the necessity of God, could enter the head of such a savage, vicious beast as man. So holy it is, so touching, so wise and so great a credit it does to man. As for me, I've long resolved not to think whether man created God or God man. . . . For what are we aiming at now? I am trying to explain as quickly as possible my essential nature, that is what manner of man I am, what I believe in, and for what I hope, that's it, isn't it? And therefore I tell you that I accept God simply. But you must note this: if God exists and if He really did create the world, then, as we all know, He created it according to the geometry of Euclid and the human mind with the conception of only three dimensions in space. Yet there have been and still are geometricians and philosophers, and even some of the most distinguished, who doubt whether the whole universe, or to speak more widely the whole of being, was only created in Euclid's geometry; they even dare to dream that two parallel lines, which according to Euclid can never meet on earth, may meet somewhere in infinity. I have come to the conclusion that, since I can't understand even that, I can't expect to understand about God. I acknowledge humbly that I have no faculty for settling such questions. I have a Euclidian earthly mind, and how could I solve problems that are not of this world? And I advise you never to think about it either, my dear Alyosha, especially about God, whether He exists or not. All such questions are utterly inappropriate for a mind created with an idea of only three dimensions. And so I accept God and am glad to, and what's more I accept His wisdom, His purpose—which are utterly beyond our ken;

I believe in the underlying order and the meaning of life; I believe in the eternal harmony in which they say we shall one day be blended. I believe in the Word to Which the universe is striving, and Which Itself was 'with God,' and Which Itself is God and so on, and so on, to infinity. There are all sorts of phrases for it. I seem to be on the right path, don't I? Yet would you believe it, in the final result I don't accept this world of God's, and, although I know it exists, I don't accept it at all. It's not that I don't accept God, you must understand, it's the world created by Him I don't and cannot accept. Let me make it plain. I believe like a child that suffering will be healed and made up for, that all the humiliating absurdity of human contradictions will vanish like a pitiful mirage, like the despicable fabrication of the impotent and infinitely small Euclidian mind of man, that in the world's finale, at the moment of eternal harmony, something so precious will come to pass that it will suffice for all hearts, for the comforting of all resentments, for the atonement of all the crimes of humanity, of all the blood they've shed; that it will make it not only possible to forgive but to justify all that has happened with men—but though all that may come to pass, I don't accept it. I won't accept it. Even if parallel lines do meet and I see it myself, I shall see it and say that they've met, but still I won't accept it. That's what's at the root of me, Alyosha; that's my creed.

". . . Do you understand why this infamy must be and is permitted? Without it, I am told, man could not have known good and evil. Why should he know that diabolical good and evil when it costs so much? Why, the whole world of knowledge is not worth that child's prayer to 'dear, Kind God'! I say nothing of the sufferings of grown-up people, they have eaten the apple, damn them, and the devil take them all! But these little ones! I am making you suffer, Alyosha, you are not yourself. I'll leave off if you like."

"Never mind. I want to suffer too," muttered Alyosha.

"One picture, only one more, because it's so curious, so characteristic, and I have only just read it in some collection of Russian antiquities. I've forgotten the name. I must look it up. It was in the darkest days of serfdom at the beginning of the century, and long live the Liberator of the People! There was in those days a general of aristocratic connections, the owner of great estates, one of these men—somewhat exceptional, I believe, even then—who, retiring from the service into a life of leisure, are convinced that they've earned absolute power over the lives of their subjects. There were such men then. So our general, settled on his property of two thousand souls, lives in pomp and domineers over his poor neighbors as though they were dependents and buffoons. He has kennels of hundreds of hounds and nearly a hundred dog-boys—all mounted, and in uniform. One day a serf boy, a little child of eight, threw a stone in play and hurt the paw of the general's favorite hound. 'Why is my favorite dog lame?' He is told that the boy threw a stone that hurt the dog's paw. 'So you did it.' The general looked the child up and down. 'Take him.' He was taken—taken from his mother and kept shut up all night. Early that morning the general comes out on horseback, with the hounds, his dependents, dog-boys, and huntsmen, all mounted around him in full hunting parade. The servants are summoned for their edification, and in front of them all stands the mother of the child. The child is brought from the lockup. It's a gloomy, cold, foggy autumn day, a capital day for hunting. The general orders the child to be undressed; the child is stripped naked. He shivers, numb with terror not daring to cry.... 'Make him run,' commands the general. 'Run! run!' shout the dog-boys. The boy runs.... 'At him!' yells the general, and he sets the whole pack of hounds on the child. The hounds catch him, and tear him to pieces before his mother's eyes! ... I believe the general was afterwards declared incapable of administering his estates. Well—what did he deserve? To be shot? to be shot for the satisfaction of our moral feelings? Speak, Alyosha!"

"To be shot," murmured Alyosha, lifting his eyes to Ivan with a pale twisted smile.

"Bravo!" cried Ivan delighted. "If even you say so ... You're a pretty monk! So there is a little devil sitting in your heart, Alyosha Karamazov!"

"What I said was absurd, but—"

"That's just the point that 'but'!" cried Ivan. "Let me tell you, novice, that the absurd is only too necessary on earth. The world stands on absurdities, and perhaps nothing would have come to pass in it without them. We know what we know!"

"What do you know?"

"I understand nothing," Ivan went on, as though in delirium. "I don't want to understand anything now. I want to stick to the fact. I made up my mind long ago not to understand. If I try to understand anything, I shall be false to the fact and I have determined to stick to the fact."

"Why are you trying me?" Alyosha cried, with sudden distress. "Will you say what you mean at last?"

"Of course, I will; that's what I've been leading up to. You are dear to me, I don't want to let you go, and I won't give you up to your Zossima."

Ivan for a minute was silent, his face became all at once very sad.

"Listen! I took the case of the children only to make my case clearer. Of the other tears of humanity with which the earth is soaked from its crust to its center, I will say nothing. I have narrowed my subject on purpose. I am a bug, and I recognize in all humility that I cannot understand why the world is arranged as it is. Men are themselves to blame, I suppose; they were given paradise, they wanted freedom, and stole fire from heaven, though they knew they would become unhappy, so there is no need to pity them. With my pitiful, earthly, Euclidian understanding, all I know is that there is suffering and that there are none guilty; that cause follows effect, simply and directly; that everything flows and finds its level—but that's only Euclidian nonsense, I know that, and I can't consent to live by it! What comfort is it to me that there are none guilty and that cause follows effect simply and directly, and that I know it—I must have justice, or I will destroy myself. And not justice in some remote infinite time and space, but here on earth, and that I could see myself. I have believed in it. I want to see it, and if I am dead by then, let me rise again, for if it all happens without me, it will be too unfair. Surely I haven't suffered, simply that I, my crimes and my sufferings, may manure the soil of the future harmony for somebody else. I want to see with my own eyes the hind lie down with the lion and the victim rise up and embrace his murderer. I want to be there when everyone suddenly understands what it has all been for. All the religions of the world are built on this longing, and I am a believer. But then there are the children, and what am I to do about them? That's a question I can't answer. For the hundredth time I repeat, there are numbers of questions, but I've only taken the children, because in their case what I mean is so unanswerably clear. Listen! If all must suffer to pay for the eternal harmony, what have children to do with it, tell me, please? It's beyond all comprehension why they should suffer, and why they should pay for the harmony. Why should they, too, furnish material to enrich the soil for the harmony of the future? I understand solidarity in sin among men. I understand solidarity in retribution, too; but there can be no such solidarity with children. And if it is really true that they must share responsibility for all their fathers' crimes, such a truth is not of this world and is beyond my comprehension. Some jester will say, perhaps, that the child would have grown up and have sinned, but you see he didn't grow up, he was torn to pieces by the dogs, at eight years old. Oh, Alyosha, I am not blaspheming! I understand, of course, what an upheaval of the universe it will be, when everything in heaven and earth blends in one hymn of praise and everything that lives and has lived cries aloud: 'Thou art just, O Lord, for Thy ways are revealed,' when the mother embraces the fiend who threw her child to the dogs, and all three cry aloud with tears, 'Thou are just, O Lord!' then, of course, the crown of knowledge will be reached and all will be made clear. But what pulls me up here is that I can't accept that harmony. And while I am on earth, I make haste to

take my own measures. You see, Alyosha, perhaps it really may happen that if I live to that moment, or rise again to see it, I, too, perhaps, may cry aloud with the rest, looking at the mother embracing the child's torturer, 'Thou art just, O Lord!' but I don't want to cry aloud then. While there is still time, I hasten to protect myself and so I renounce the higher harmony altogether. It's not worth the tears of that one tortured child who beat itself on the breast with its little fist and prayed in its stinking outhouse, with its unexpiated tears to 'dear, kind God'! It's not worth it, because those tears are unatoned for. They must be atoned for, or there can be no harmony. But how? How are you going to atone for them? Is it possible? By their being avenged? But what do I care for avenging them? What do I care for a hell for oppressors? What good can hell do, since those children have already been tortured? And what becomes of harmony, if there is hell? I want to forgive. I want to embrace. I don't want more suffering. And if the sufferings of children go to swell the sum of sufferings which was necessary to pay for truth, then I protest that the truth is not worth such a price. I don't want the mother to embrace the oppressor who threw her son to the dogs! She dare not forgive him! Let her forgive him for herself, if she will, let her forgive the torturer for the immeasurable suffering of her mother's heart. But the sufferings of her tortured child she has no right to forgive; she dare not forgive the torturer, even if the child were to forgive him! And if that is so, if they dare not forgive, what becomes of harmony? Is there in the whole world a being who would have the right to forgive and could forgive? I don't want harmony. From love for humanity I don't want it. I would rather be left with the unavenged suffering. I would rather remain with my unavenged suffering and unsatisfied indignation, *even if I were wrong*. Besides, too high a price is asked for harmony; it's beyond our means to pay so much to enter on it. And so I hasten to give back my entrance ticket, and if I am an honest man I am bound to give it back as soon as possible. And that I am doing. It's not God that I don't accept, Alyosha, only I most respectfully return Him the ticket."

"That's rebellion," murmured Alyosha, looking down.

"Rebellion? I am sorry you call it that," said Ivan earnestly. "One can hardly live in rebellion, and I want to live. Tell me yourself, I challenge you—answer. Imagine that you are creating a fabric of human destiny with the object of making men happy in the end, giving them peace and rest at last, but that it was essential and inevitable to torture to death only one tiny creature—that baby beating its breast with its fist, for instance—and to found that edifice on its unavenged tears, would you consent to be the architect on those conditions? Tell me, and tell the truth."

"No, I wouldn't consent," said Alyosha softly.

For Further Reflection

1. There are three propositions involved in the traditional formulation of the problem of evil: a. God is all-powerful (including omniscience); b. God is perfectly good; and c. Evil exists. How would Ivan deal with them?

2. Do you think that the fact of evil counts against the proposition that God exists? Explain why or why not.

3. Some people believe that we are completely causally determined, a subject that will be discussed in Part V. What will they make of the free-will defense?

II.11   Why Doesn't God Intervene to Prevent Evil?

B. C. JOHNSON

B. C. Johnson is a pen name for the author, who wishes to remain anonymous.

In this essay, Johnson compares God's behavior with that of a morally good person. If you know that a six-month-old baby is in a burning building and you have the opportunity to save it without undue risk to your life, you would no doubt save it. Of course, if you couldn't save it, you would be excused. The question is "Why doesn't God intervene to save not just babies who are caught in fires but people everywhere who are suffering and in great need of help?" Johnson considers various "excuses" the theist might claim for God and argues that they all fail. His conclusion is that if there is a God, he or she is probably either evil or both good and evil.

Study Questions

1. What, according to Johnson, are some of the bad explanations for God not intervening to prevent evil?
2. How is God like a bystander who, though he didn't start the fire, refuses to help save the baby, even when he could easily do so.
3. How does Johnson respond to the suggestion that it is best for us to face disaster without assistance?
4. What does Johnson say to the objection that God's intervention would destroy a considerable amount of moral urgency?
5. What does Johnson say about the claim that evil is a necessary by-product of the laws of nature, so that it would be irrational for God to interfere every time a disaster happens?
6. What do people mean when they say that God has a "higher morality" than we have, so that we cannot apply our standards to him? What is Johnson's response to this defense of theism?
7. What are the three possibilities concerning God's moral character? Which does Johnson argue for? Do you agree?

HERE IS A COMMON SITUATION: A house catches on fire and a six-month-old baby is painfully burned to death. Could we possibly describe as "good" any person who had the power to save this child and yet refused to do so? God undoubtedly has this power and yet in many cases of this sort he has refused to help. Can we call God "good"? Are there adequate excuses for his behavior?

First, it will not do to claim that the baby will go to heaven. It was either necessary for the baby to suffer or it was not. If it was not, then it was wrong to allow it. The child's ascent to heaven does not change this fact. If it was necessary, the fact that the baby will go to heaven does not explain why it was necessary, and we are still left without an excuse for God's inaction.

It is not enough to say that the baby's painful death would in the long run have good results and therefore should have happened, otherwise God would not have permitted it. For if we know this to be true, then we know—just as God knows—that every action successfully performed must in the end be good and therefore the right thing to do, otherwise God would not

have allowed it to happen. We could deliberately set houses ablaze to kill innocent people and if successful we would then know we had a duty to do it. A defense of God's goodness which takes as its foundation duties known only after the fact would result in a morality unworthy of the name. Furthermore, this argument does not explain why God allowed the child to burn to death. It merely claims that there is some reason discoverable in the long run. But the belief that such a reason is within our grasp must rest upon the additional belief that God is good. This is just to counter evidence against such a belief by assuming the belief to be true. It is not unlike a lawyer defending his client by claiming that the client is innocent and therefore the evidence against him must be misleading—that proof vindicating the defendant will be found in the long run. No jury of reasonable men and women would accept such a defense and the theist cannot expect a more favorable outcome.

The theist often claims that man has been given free will so that if he accidentally or purposefully causes fires, killing small children, it is his fault alone. Consider a bystander who had

Reprinted with permission of the publisher from B. C. Johnson, The Athiest Debater's Handbook. *Prometheus Books, Buffalo, New York, © 1981 by B. C. Johnson.*

nothing to do with starting the fire but who refused to help even though he could have saved the child with no harm to himself. Could such a bystander be called good? Certainly not. If we would not consider a mortal human being good under these circumstances, what grounds could we possibly have for continuing to assert the goodness of an all-powerful God?

The suggestion is sometimes made that it is best for us to face disasters without assistance, otherwise we would become dependent on an outside power for aid. Should we then abolish modern medical care or do away with efficient fire departments? Are we not dependent on their help? Is it not the case that their presence transforms us into soft, dependent creatures? The vast majority are not physicians or firemen. These people help in their capacity as professional outside sources of aid in much the same way that we would expect God to be helpful. Theists refer to aid from firemen and physicians as cases of man helping himself. In reality, it is a tiny minority of men helping a great many. We can become just as dependent on them as we can on God. Now the existence of this kind of outside help is either wrong or right. If it is right, then God should assist those areas of the world which do not have this kind of help. In fact, throughout history, such help has not been available. If aid ought to have been provided, then God should have provided it. On the other hand, if it is wrong to provide this kind of assistance, then we should abolish the aid altogether. But we obviously do not believe it is wrong.

Similar considerations apply to the claim that if God interferes in disasters, he would destroy a considerable amount of moral urgency to make things right. Once again, note that such institutions as modern medicine and fire departments are relatively recent. They function irrespective of whether we as individuals feel any moral urgency to support them. To the extent that they help others, opportunities to feel moral urgency are destroyed because they reduce the number of cases which appeal to us

for help. Since we have not always had such institutions, there must have been a time when there was greater moral urgency than there is now. If such a situation is morally desirable, then we should abolish modem medical care and fire departments. If the situation is not morally desirable, then God should have remedied it.

Besides this point, we should note that God is represented as one who tolerates disasters, such as infants burning to death, in order to create moral urgency. It follows that God approves of these disasters as a means to encourage the creation of moral urgency. Furthermore, if there were no such disasters occurring, God would have to see to it that they occur. If it so happened that we lived in a world in which babies never perished in burning houses, God would be morally obliged to take an active hand in setting fire to houses with infants in them. In fact, if the frequency of infant mortality due to fire should happen to fall below a level necessary for the creation of maximum moral urgency in our real world, God would be justified in setting a few fires of his own. This may well be happening right now, for there is no guarantee that the maximum number of infant deaths necessary for moral urgency are occurring.

All of this is of course absurd. If I see an opportunity to create otherwise nonexistent opportunities for moral urgency by burning an infant or two, then I should *not* do so. But if it is good to maximize moral urgency, then I *should* do so. Therefore, it is not good to maximize moral urgency. Plainly we do not in general believe that it is a good thing to maximize moral urgency. The fact that we approve of modern medical care and applaud medical advances is proof enough of this.

The theist may point out that in a world without suffering there would be no occasion for the production of such virtues as courage, sympathy, and the like. This may be true, but the atheist need not demand a world without suffering. He need only claim that there is suffering which is in excess of that needed for the production of various virtues. For example, God's active attempts to save six-month-old infants from fires would not in itself create a world without suffering. But no one could sincerely doubt that it would improve the world.

The two arguments against the previous theistic excuse apply here also. "Moral urgency" and "building virtue" are susceptible to the same criticisms. It is worthwhile to emphasize, however, that we encourage efforts to eliminate evils; we approve of efforts to promote peace, prevent famine, and wipe out disease. In other words, we do value a world with fewer or (if possible) no opportunities for the development of virtue (when "virtue" is understood to mean the reduction of suffering). If we produce such a world for succeeding generations, how will they develop virtues? Without war, disease, and famine, they will not be virtuous. Should we then cease our attempts to wipe out war, disease, and famine? If we do not believe that it is right to cease attempts at improving the world, then by implication we admit that virtue-building is not an excuse for God to permit disasters. For we admit that the development of virtue is no excuse for permitting disasters.

It might be said that God allows innocent people to suffer in order to deflate man's ego so that the latter will not be proud of his apparently deserved good fortune. But this excuse succumbs to the arguments used against the preceding excuses and we need discuss them no further.

Theists may claim that evil is a necessary by-product of the laws of nature and therefore it is irrational for God to interfere every time a disaster happens. Such a state of affairs would alter the whole causal order and we would then find it impossible to predict anything. But the death of a child caused by an electrical fire could have been prevented by a miracle and no one would ever have known. Only a minor alteration in electrical equipment would have been necessary. A very large disaster could have been avoided simply by producing in Hitler a miraculous heart attack— and no one would have known it was a miracle.

To argue that continued miraculous intervention by God would be wrong is like insisting that one should never use salt because ingesting five pounds of it would be fatal. No one is requesting that God interfere all of the time. He should, however, intervene to prevent especially horrible disasters. Of course, the question arises: where does one draw the line? Well, certainly the line should be drawn somewhere this side of infants burning to death. To argue that we do not know where the line should be drawn is no excuse for failing to interfere in those instances that would be called clear cases of evil.

It will not do to claim that evil exists as a necessary contrast to good so that we might know what good is. A very small amount of evil, such as a toothache, would allow that. It is not necessary to destroy innocent human beings.

The claim could be made that God has a "higher morality" by which his actions are to be judged. But it is a strange "higher morality" which claims that what we call "bad" is good and what we call "good" is bad. Such a morality can have no meaning to us. It would be like calling black "white" and white "black." In reply the theist may say that God is the wise Father and we are ignorant children. How can we judge God any more than a child is able to judge his parent? It is true that a child may be puzzled by his parents' conduct, but his basis for deciding that their conduct is nevertheless good would be the many instances of good behavior he has observed. Even so, this could be misleading. Hitler, by all accounts, loved animals and children of the proper race; but if Hitler had had a child, this offspring would hardly have been justified in arguing that his father was a good man. At any rate, God's "higher morality," being the opposite of ours, cannot offer any grounds for deciding that he is somehow good.

Perhaps the main problem with the solutions to the problem of evil we have thus far considered is that no matter how convincing they may be in the abstract, they are implausible in certain particular cases. Picture an infant dying in a burning house and then imagine God simply observing from afar. Perhaps God is reciting excuses in his own behalf. As the child succumbs to the smoke and flames, God may be pictured as saying: "Sorry, but if I helped you I would have considerable trouble deflating the ego of your parents. And don't forget I have to keep those laws of nature consistent. And anyway if you weren't dying in that fire, a lot of moral urgency would just go down the drain. Besides, I didn't start this fire, so you can't blame *me*."

It does no good to assert that God may not be all-powerful and thus not able to prevent evil. He can create a universe and yet is conveniently unable to do what the fire department can do—rescue a baby from a burning building. God should at least be as powerful as a man. A man, if he had been at the right place and time, could have killed Hitler. Was this beyond God's abilities? If God knew in 1910 how to produce polio vaccine and if he was able to communicate with somebody, he should have communicated this knowledge. He must be incredibly limited if he could not have managed this modest accomplishment. Such a God if not dead, is the next thing to it. And a person who believes in such a ghost of a God is practically an atheist. To call such a thing a god would be to strain the meaning of the word.

The theist, as usual, may retreat to faith. He may say that he has faith in God's goodness and therefore the Christian Deity's existence has not been disproved. "Faith" is here understood as being much like confidence in a friend's innocence despite the evidence against him. Now in order to have confidence in a friend one must know him well enough to justify faith in his goodness. We cannot have justifiable faith in the supreme goodness of strangers. Moreover, such confidence must come not just from a speaking acquaintance. The friend may continually assure us with his words that he is good but if he does not act like a good person, we would have no reason to trust him. A person who says he has faith in God's goodness is speaking as if he had known God for a long time and during that

time had never seen Him do any serious evil. But we know that throughout history God has allowed numerous atrocities to occur. No one can have justifiable faith in the goodness of such a God.

This faith would have to be based on a close friendship wherein God was never found to do anything wrong. But a person would have to be blind and deaf to have had such a relationship with God. Suppose a friend of yours had always claimed to be good yet refused to help people when he was in a position to render aid. Could you have justifiable faith in his goodness?

You can of course say that you trust God anyway—that no arguments can undermine your faith. But this is just a statement describing how stubborn you are; it has no bearing whatsoever on the question of God's goodness.

The various excuses theists offer for why God has allowed evil to exist have been demonstrated to be inadequate. However, the conclusive objection to these excuses does not depend on their inadequacy.

First, we should note that every possible excuse making the actual world consistent with the existence of a good God could be used in reverse to make that same world consistent with an evil God. For example, we could say that God is evil and that he allows free will so that we can freely do evil things, which would make us more truly evil than we would be if forced to perform evil acts. Or we could say that natural disasters occur in order to make people more selfish and bitter, for most people tend to have a "me-first" attitude in a disaster (note, for example, stampedes to leave burning buildings). Even though some people achieve virtue from disasters, this outcome is necessary if persons are to react freely to disaster—necessary if the development of moral degeneracy is to continue freely. But, enough; the point is made. Every excuse we could provide to make the world consistent with a good God can be paralleled by an excuse to make the world consistent with an evil God. This is so because the world is a mixture of both good and bad.

Now there are only three possibilities concerning God's moral character. Considering the world as it actually is, we may believe: (*a*) that God is more likely to be all evil than is to be all good; (*b*) that God is less likely to be all evil than he is to be all good; or (*c*) that God is equally as likely to be all evil as he is to be good. In case (*a*) it would be admitted that God is unlikely to be all good. Case (*b*) cannot be true at all, since—as we have seen—the belief that God is all evil can be justified to precisely the same extent as the belief that God is all good. Case (*c*) leaves us with no reasonable excuses for a good God to permit evil. The reason is as follows: if an excuse is to be a reasonable excuse, the circumstances it identifies as excusing conditions must be actual. For example, if I run over a pedestrian and my excuse is that the brakes failed because someone tampered with them, then the facts had better bear this out. Otherwise the excuse will not hold. Now if case (*c*) is correct and, given the facts of the actual world, God is as likely to be all evil as he is to be all good, then these facts do not support the excuses which could be made for a good God permitting evil. Consider an analogous example. If my excuse for running over the pedestrian is that my brakes were tampered with, and if the actual facts lead us to believe that it is no more likely that they were tampered with than that they were not, the excuse is no longer reasonable. To make good my excuse, I must show that it is a fact or at least highly probable that my brakes were tampered with—not that it is just a possibility. The same point holds for God. His excuse must not be a possible excuse, but an actual one. But case (*c*), in maintaining that it is just as likely that God is all evil as that he is all good, rules this out. For if case (*c*) is true, then the facts of the actual world do not make it any more likely that God is all good than that he is all evil. Therefore, they do not make it any more likely that his excuses are good than that they are not. But, as we have seen, good excuses have a higher probability of being true.

Cases (*a*) and (*c*) conclude that it is unlikely that God is all good, and case (*b*) cannot be true. Since these are the only possible cases, there is no escape from the conclusion that it is unlikely that God is all good. Thus the problem of evil triumphs over traditional theism.

For Further Reflection

UNDERSTANDABLE OR VALID

1. Do you find Johnson's arguments cogent? How might a theist reply to them?

2. Some theologians have argued that the biblical picture of God is not the same as the philosopher's. The philosopher pictures God as being all-powerful, while the Bible sees God as very powerful but still limited: He cannot prevent all evils. Would this revision of theism be an acceptable way to get around the problem of evil? Why or why not?

3. Suppose someone objects to the way the problem of evil is set forth, arguing that the problem is unjustifiably anthropomorphic. As one person wrote me, "Who put human beings at the center of the definition of evil?" Should we take a more global view of evil, considering the harm done to animals and the environment? Is it a self-serving bias (sometimes called *speciesism*) that makes humanity the ultimate object of concern here?

II.12   There Is a Reason Why God Allows Evil

JOHN HICK

John Hick (1922–   ) was for many years professor of theology at the University of Birmingham in England. He is now emeritus professor of philosophy at Claremont Graduate School. His book *Evil and the God of Love* (1966) is considered one of the most thorough treatises on the problem of evil. Our reading is a shorter version of some of the ideas presented there. Hick presents a *theodicy,* a justification of God's creation in the face of evil. Theodicies can be of two types, depending on how they justify the ways of God. The Augustinian position is that God created humans without sin and set them in a sinless, paradisical world. However, humanity fell into sin through misuse of its free will. God's grace will save some of us, but others will perish everlastingly. The second type of theodicy stems from the thinking of Irenaeus (120–202), of the Greek church. The Irenaean tradition views Adam not as a free agent rebelling against God, but as a child. The fall is humanity's first faulty step in the direction of freedom. God is still working with humanity to bring it from undeveloped life (*bios*: biological life) to a state of self-realization in divine love, spiritual life (*zoe*). This life is a vale of soul-making.

Hick accepts the soul-making view of life in this defense of God's ways in the face of evil.

Study Questions

1. Why is the problem of evil a dilemma?
2. Which solutions to the problem does Hick rule out as unacceptable?
3. Does the Hebrew-Christian view of the world judge matter to be evil?
4. What is a *negative* theodicy?
5. What does Hick mean by *moral* versus *non-moral* evil?
6. Why couldn't God create people who were both free and totally good?
7. What does Hick say about non-moral evil? Why is it here, and what is its function in human development?
8. According to Hick what is the purpose of our creation?
9. Why does Hick reject a world without suffering and harm?

TO MANY, THE MOST powerful objection to belief in God is the fact of evil. Probably for most agnostics it is the appalling depth and extent of human suffering, more than anything else, that makes the idea of a loving Creator seem too implausible and disposes them toward one or another of the various naturalistic theories of religion.

As a challenge to theism, the problem of evil has traditionally been posed in the form of a dilemma: If God is perfectly loving, he must wish to abolish evil, and if he is all-powerful, he

From *John Hick*, Philosophy of Religion, *3rd. ed.,* © *1963, pp. 40–46. Reprinted by permission of Prentice Hall, Inc., Englewod Cliffs, Nw Jersey.*

must be able to abolish evil. But evil exists; therefore God cannot be both omnipotent and perfectly loving.

Certain solutions, which at once suggest themselves, have to be ruled out so far as the Judaic-Christian faith is concerned.

To say, for example (with contemporary Christian Science), that evil is an illusion of the human mind, is impossible within a religion based upon the stark realism of the Bible. Its pages faithfully reflect the characteristic mixture of good and evil in human experience. They record every kind of sorrow and suffering, every mode of man's inhumanity to man and of his painfully insecure existence in the world. There is no attempt to regard evil as anything but dark, menacingly ugly, heartrending, and crushing. In the Christian scriptures, the climax of this history of evil is the crucifixion of Jesus, which is presented not only as a case of utterly unjust suffering, but as the violent and murderous rejection of God's Messiah. There can be no doubt, then, that for biblical faith, evil is unambiguously evil, and stands in direct opposition to God's will.

Again, to solve the problem of evil by means of the theory (sponsored for example, by the Boston "Personalist" School) of a finite deity who does the best he can with a material, intractable and coeternal with himself, is to have abandoned the basic premise of Hebrew-Christian monotheism; for the theory amounts to rejecting belief in the infinity and sovereignty of God.

Indeed, any theory which would avoid the problem of the origin of evil by depicting it as an ultimate constituent of the universe, coordinate with good, has been repudiated in advance by the classic Christian teaching, first developed by Augustine, that evil represents the going wrong of something which in itself is good. Augustine holds firmly to the Hebrew-Christian conviction that the universe is *good*—that is to say, it is the creation of a good God for a good purpose. He completely rejects the ancient prejudice, widespread in his day, that matter is evil. There are, according to Augustine, higher and lower, greater and lesser goods in immense abundance and variety, but everything which has being is good in its own way and degree, except insofar as it may have become spoiled or corrupted. Evil—whether it be an evil will, an instance of pain, or some disorder or decay in nature—has not been set there by God, but represents the distortion of something that is inherently valuable. Whatever exists is, as such, and in its proper place, good: Evil is essentially parasitic upon good, being disorder and perversion in a fundamentally good creation. This understanding of evil as something negative means that it is not willed and created by God, but it does not mean (as some have supposed) that evil is unreal and can be disregarded. On the contrary, the first effect of this doctrine is to accentuate even more the question of the origin of evil.

Theodicy,[1] as many modern Christian thinkers see it, is a modest enterprise, negative rather than positive in its conclusions. It does not claim to explain, nor to explain away, every instance of evil in human experience, but only to point to certain considerations which prevent the fact of evil (largely incomprehensible though it remains) from constituting a final and insuperable bar to rational belief in God.

In indicating these considerations it will be useful to follow the traditional division of the subject. There is the problem of *moral evil* or wickedness: why does an all-good and all-powerful God permit this? And there is the problem of the *non-moral evil* of suffering and pain, both physical and mental: Why has an all-good and all-powerful God created a world in which this occurs?

Christian thought has always considered moral evil in its relation to human freedom and responsibility. To be a person is to be a finite center of freedom, a (relatively) free and self-directing agent responsible for one's own decisions. This involves being free to act wrongly as well as to act rightly. The idea of a person who can be infallibly guaranteed always to act rightly is self-contradictory. There can be no guarantee in advance that a genuinely free moral agent will never choose amiss. Consequently, the possibility of wrongdoing or sin is logically inseparable from the creation of finite persons, and to say that God should not have created beings who might sin amounts to saying he should not have created people.

This thesis has been challenged in some recent philosophical discussions of the problem of evil, in which it is claimed that no contradiction is involved in saying that God might have made people who would be genuinely free and who could yet be guaranteed always to act rightly. A quote from one of these discussions follows:

> If there is no logical impossibility in a man's freely choosing the good on one, or on several occasions, there cannot be a logical impossibility in his freely choosing the good on every occasion. God was not, then, faced with a choice between making innocent automata and making beings who, in acting freely, would sometimes go wrong: there was open to him the obviously better possibility of making beings who would act freely but always go right. Clearly, his failure to avail himself of this possibility is inconsistent with his being both omnipotent and wholly good.[2]

A reply to this argument is suggested in another recent contribution to the discussion.[3] If by a free action we mean an action which is not externally compelled but which flows from the nature of the agent as he reacts to the circumstances in which he finds himself, there is, indeed, no contradiction between our being free and our actions being "caused" (by our own nature) and therefore being in principle predictable. There is a contradiction, however, in saying that God is the cause of our acting as we do but that we are free beings in relation to God. There is, in other words, a contradiction in saying that God has made us so that we shall of necessity act in a certain way, and that we are genuinely independent persons in relation to him. If all our thoughts and actions are divinely predestined, however free and morally responsible we may seem to be to ourselves, we cannot be free and morally responsible in the sight

of God, but must instead be his helpless puppets. Such "freedom" is like that of a patient acting out a series of post-hypnotic suggestions: he appears, even to himself, to be free, but his volitions have actually been pre-determined by another will, that of the hypnotist, in relation to whom the patient is not a free agent.

A different objector might raise the question of whether or not we deny God's omnipotence if we admit that he is unable to create persons who are free from the risks inherent in personal freedom. The answer that has always been given is that to create such beings is logically impossible. It is no limitation upon God's power that he cannot accomplish the logically impossible, since there is nothing here to accomplish, but only a meaningless conjunction of words—in this case "person who is not a person." God is able to create beings of any and every conceivable kind, but creatures who lack moral freedom, however superior they might be to human beings in other respects, would not be what we mean by persons. They would constitute a different form of life which God might have brought into existence instead of persons. When we ask why God did not create such beings in place of persons, the traditional answer is that only persons could, in any meaningful sense, become "children of God," capable of entering into a personal relationship with their Creator by a free and uncompelled response to his love.

When we turn from the possibility of moral evil as a correlate of man's personal freedom to its actuality, we face something which must remain inexplicable even when it can be seen to be possible. For we can never provide a complete causal explanation of a free act; if we could, it would not be a free act. The origin of moral evil lies forever concealed within the mystery of human freedom.

The necessary connection between moral freedom and the possibility, now actualized, of sin throws light upon a great deal of the suffering which afflicts mankind. For an enormous amount of human pain arises either from the inhumanity or the culpable incompetence of mankind. This includes such major scourges as poverty, oppression and persecution, war, and all the injustice, indignity, and inequity which occur even in the most advanced societies. These evils are manifestations of human sin. Even disease is fostered to an extent, the limits of which have not yet been determined by psychosomatic medicine, by moral and emotional factors seated both in the individual and in his social environment. To the extent that all of these evils stem from human failures and wrong decisions, their possibility is inherent in the creation of free persons inhabiting a world which presents them with real choices which are followed by real consequences.

We may now turn more directly to the problem of suffering. Even though the major bulk of actual human pain is traceable to man's misused freedom as a sole or part cause, there remain other sources of pain which are entirely independent of the human will, for example, earthquake, hurricane, storm, flood, drought, and blight. In practice it is often impossible to trace a boundary between the suffering which results from human wickedness and folly and that which falls upon mankind from without. Both kinds of suffering are inextricably mingled together in human experience. For our present purpose, however, it is important to note that the latter category does exist and that it seems to be built into the very structure of our world. In response to it, theodicy, if it is wisely conducted, follows a negative path. It is not possible to show positively that each item of human pain serves the divine purpose of good, but, on the other hand, it does seem possible to show that the divine purpose as it is understood in Judaism and Christianity could not be forwarded in a world which was designed as a permanent hedonistic paradise.

An essential premise of this argument concerns the divine purpose in creating the world. The skeptic's assumption is that man is to be viewed as a completed creation and that God's purpose in making the world was to provide a suitable dwelling-place for this fully-formed creature. Since God is good and loving, the environment which he has created for human life to inhabit is naturally as pleasant and comfortable as possible. The problem is essentially similar to that of a man who builds a cage for some pet animal. Since our world, in fact, contains sources of hardship, inconvenience, and danger of innumerable kinds, the conclusion follows that this world cannot have been created by a perfectly benevolent and all-powerful deity.

Christianity, however, has never supposed that God's purpose in the creation of the world was to construct a paradise whose inhabitants would experience a maximum of pleasure and a minimum of pain. The world is seen, instead, as a place of "soul-making" in which free beings, grappling with the tasks and challenges of their existence in a common environment, may become "children of God" and "heirs of eternal life." A way of thinking theologically of God's continuing creative purpose for man was suggested by some of the early Hellenistic Fathers of the Christian Church, especially Irenaeus. Following hints from St. Paul, Irenaeus taught that man has been made as a person in the image of God but has not yet been brought as a free and responsible agent into the finite likeness of God, which is revealed in Christ. Our world, with all its rough edges, is the sphere in which this second and harder stage of the creative process is taking place.

This conception of the world (whether or not set in Irenaeus' theological framework) can be supported by the method of negative theodicy. Suppose, contrary to fact, that his world were a paradise from which all possibility of pain and suffering were excluded. The consequences would be very far-reaching. For example, no one could ever injure anyone else; the murderer's knife would turn to paper or his bullets to thin air; the bank safe, robbed of a million dollars, would miraculously become filled with another million dollars (without this device, on however large a scale, proving inflationary); fraud, deceit, conspiracy, and treason would somehow always leave the fabric of society undamaged. Again, no one would ever be injured by accident: the mountain-climber, steeplejack, or playing child falling from a height would float unharmed to the ground; the reckless driver would never meet with disaster. There would be no need to work, since no harm could result from avoiding work; there would be no call to be concerned for others in time of need or danger, for in such a world there could be no real needs or dangers.

To make possible this continual series of individual adjustments, nature would have to work by "special providences" instead of running according to general laws which men must learn to respect on penalty of pain or death. The laws of nature would have to be extremely flexible: sometimes gravity would operate, sometimes not; sometimes an object would be hard and solid, sometimes soft. There could be no sciences, for there would be no enduring world structure to investigate. In eliminating the problems and hardships of an objective environment, with its own laws, life would become like a dream in which, delightfully but aimlessly, we would float and drift at ease.

One can at least begin to imagine such a world. It is evident that our present ethical concepts would have no meaning in it. If, for example, the notion of harming someone is an essential element in the concept of a wrong action, in our hedonistic paradise there could be no wrong actions—nor any right actions in distinction from wrong. Courage and fortitude would have no point in an environment in which there is, by definition, no danger of difficulty. Generosity, kindness, the *agape* aspect of love, prudence, unselfishness, and all other ethical notions which presuppose life in a stable environment, could not even be formed. Consequently, such a world, however well it might promote pleasure, would be very ill adapted for the development of the moral qualities of human personality. In relation to this purpose it would be the worst of all possible worlds.

It would seem, then, that an environment intended to make possible the growth in free beings of the finest characteristics of personal life, must have a good deal in common with our present world. It must operate according to general and dependable laws, and it must involve real dangers, difficulties, problems, obstacles, and possibilities of pain, failure, sorrow, frustration, and defeat. If it did not contain the particular trials and perils which—subtracting man's own very considerable contribution—our world contains, it would have to contain others instead.

To realize this is not, by any means, to be in possession of a detailed theodicy. It is to understand that this world, with all its "heartaches and the thousand natural shocks that flesh is heir to," an environment so manifestly not designed for the maximization of human pleasure and the minimization of human pain, may be rather well adapted to the quite different purpose of "soul-making."

NOTES

1. The word "theodicy," from the Greek *theos* (God) and *dike* (righteous), means the justification of God's goodness in the face of the fact of evil.

2. J. L. Mackie, "Evil and Omnipotence." *Mind* (April 1955), 209.

3. Flew, in *New Essays in Philosophical Theology.* [See Reading II.16.]

For Further Reflection

1. How convincing is Hick's argument? Does it explain natural evil (what Hick calls *non-moral evil;* that is, disease, earthquakes, famines, and floods)?

2. What would Hick say to the problem of animal suffering? How does that work toward soul-making?

3. Some have said that it is not just the existence of evil but the sheer quantity of evil in the world that makes it hard to believe that a good God exists. Why doesn't God intervene at crucial moments to prevent a holocaust or, to take Dostoevsky's example, to prevent a child from being torn to death by ferocious dogs?

II.C   Is Faith Compatible with Reason?

One of the most important areas of philosophy of religion is that of the relationship of faith to reason. Is religious belief rational? Or is faith essentially irrational? If we cannot prove the claims of religious belief, is it nevertheless reasonable to believe these claims? For example, even if we do not have a deductive proof for the existence of God, is it nevertheless reasonable to believe that God exists? In the debate over faith and reason, two opposing positions have dominated the field. The first position asserts that faith and reason are compatible (that is, it is rational to believe in God).

The second position denies this assertion. Those holding to the first position differ among themselves as to the extent of the compatibility between faith and reason; most adherents follow Thomas Aquinas in relegating the compatibility to the "preambles of faith" (for example, the existence of God and his nature) over against the "articles of faith" (for example, the doctrine of the incarnation). Few have gone as far as Immanuel Kant, who maintained complete harmony between reason and faith, that is, a religious belief within the realm of reason alone. The second position divides into two subpositions: (1) that which asserts that faith is opposed to reason (which includes such unlikely bedfellows as David Hume and Søren Kierkegaard), placing faith in the area of irrationality; and (2) that which asserts that faith is higher than reason, transcends reason. John Calvin and Karl Barth assert that a natural theology is inappropriate because it seeks to meet unbelief on its own ground (ordinary, finite reason). Revelation, however, is "self-authenticating," "carrying with it its own evidence." We may call this position the *transrational* view of faith. Faith is not against reason but above it and beyond its proper domain.

The irrationalist and transrationalist positions are sometimes hard to separate in the incompatibilist's argument. At least, it seems that faith gets such a high value that reason looks not simply inadequate but culpable. To use reason where faith claims the field is not only inappropriate but irreverent and faithless.

In the following readings, each of these positions is represented.

II.13   Yes, Faith Is a Logical Bet

BLAISE PASCAL

Blaise Pascal (1623–1662) was a French scientist, philosopher, and mathematician. He founded probability theory and made important contributions to science through his studies of barometric pressure. His conversion to a radical form of Catholicism in 1653 caused him to turn all his attention to religious matters. In this famous section from his *Pensées* (Thoughts), Pascal argues that if we do a cost-benefit analysis of the matter, it turns out that it is eminently reasonable to get ourselves to believe that God exists, regardless of whether we have good evidence for that belief. The argument goes something like this: Regarding the proposition "God exists," reason is neutral. It can neither prove nor disprove it. But we must make a choice on this matter, for not to choose for God is in effect to choose against him and lose the possible benefits that belief would bring. Since these benefits of faith promise to be infinite and the loss equally infinite, we must take a gamble on faith.

Study Questions

1. What is the relationship between our finitude and infinity? What is the infinite?
2. Why can we not know the existence or nature of God?
3. What does Pascal say regarding those who blame Christians for not producing evidence or proofs for the existence of God? Can God's existence be proved? Why or why not?
4. What is the wager Pascal advocates, and how does he calculate the cost-benefit ratio?

INFINITE—NOTHING.—Our soul is cast into a body, where it finds number, time, dimension. Thereupon it reasons, and calls this nature, necessity, and can believe nothing else.

Unity joined to infinity adds nothing to it, no more than one foot to an infinite measure. The finite is annihilated in the presence of the infinite, and becomes a pure nothing. So our spirit before God, so our justice before divine justice. There is not so great disproportion between our justice and that of God, as between unity and infinity.

The justice of God must be vast like His compassion. Now, justice to the outcast is less vast, and ought less to offend our feelings than mercy towards the elect.

We know that there is an infinite, and are ignorant of its nature. As we know it to be false that numbers are finite, it is therefore true that there is an infinity in number. But we do not know what it is. It is false that it is even, it is false that it is odd; for the addition of a unit can make no change in its nature. Yet it is a number, and every number is odd or even (this is certainly true of

Reprintd from Blaise Pascal, Thoughts, *translated by W. F. Trtter (New York: Collier & Son, 1910).*

every finite number). So we may well know that there is a God without knowing what He is. Is there not one substantial truth, seeing there are so many things which are not the truth itself?

We know then the existence and nature of the finite, because we also are finite and have extension. We know the existence of the infinite, and are ignorant of its nature, because it has extension like us, but not limits like us. But we know neither the existence nor the nature of God, because He has neither extension nor limits.

But by faith we know His existence; in glory we shall know His nature. Now, I have already shown that we may well know the existence of a thing, without knowing its nature.

Let us now speak according to natural lights.

If there is a God, He is infinitely incomprehensible, since, having neither parts nor limits, He has no affinity to us. We are then incapable of knowing either what He is or if He is. This being so, who will dare to undertake the decision of the question? Not we, who have no affinity to Him.

Who then will blame Christians for not being able to give a reason for their belief, since they profess a religion for which they cannot give a reason? They declare, in expounding it to the world, that it is a foolishness, *stultitiam;* and then you complain that they do not prove it! If they proved it, they would not keep their words; it is in lacking proofs, that they are not lacking in sense. "Yes, but although this excuses those who offer it as such, and takes away from them the blame of putting it forward without reason, it does not excuse those who receive it." Let us then examine this point, and say, "God is, or He is not." But to which side shall we incline? Reason can decide nothing here. There is an infinite chaos which separates us. A game is being played at the extremity of this infinite distance where heads or tails will turn up. What will you wager? According to reason, you can do neither the one thing nor the other; according to reason, you can defend neither of the propositions.

Do not then reprove for error those who have made a choice; for you know nothing about it. "No, but I blame them for having made, not this choice, but a choice; for again both he who chooses heads and he who chooses tails are equally at fault, they are both in the wrong. The true course is not to wager at all."

—Yes; but you must wager. It is not optional. You are embarked. Which will you choose then; Let us see. Since you must choose, let us see which interests you least. You have two things to lose, the true and the good; and two things to stake, your reason and your will, your knowledge and your happiness; and your nature has two things to shun, error and misery. Your reason is no more shocked in choosing one rather than the other, since you must of necessity choose. This is one point settled. But your happiness? Let us weigh the gain and the loss in wagering that God is. Let us estimate these two chances. If you gain, you gain all; if you lose, you lose nothing. Wager then without hesitation that He is.—"That is very fine. Yes, I must wager, but I may perhaps wager too much."—Let us see. Since there is an equal risk of gain and of loss, if you had only to gain two lives, instead of one, you might still wager. But if there were three lives to gain, you would have to play (since you are under the necessity of playing), and you would be imprudent, when you are forced to play, not to chance your life to gain three at a game where there is an equal risk of loss and gain. But there is an eternity of life and happiness. And this being so, if there were an infinity of chances, of which one only would be for you, you would still be right in wagering one to win two, and you would act stupidly, being obliged to play, by refusing to stake one life against three at a game in which you had an infinity of an infinitely happy life to gain. But there is here an infinity of an infinitely happy life to gain, a chance of gain against a finite number of chances of loss, and what you stake is finite. It is all divided; wherever the infinite is and there is not an infinity of chances of loss against that of gain, there is no time to hesitate, you must give all. And thus, when one is forced to play, he must renounce reason to preserve his life, rather than risk it for infinite gain, as likely to happen as the loss of nothingness.

For it is no use to say it is uncertain if we will gain, and it is certain that we risk, and that the infinite distance between the *certainty* of what is staked and the *uncertainty* of what will be gained, equals the finite good which is certainly staked against the uncertain infinite. It is not so, as every player stakes a certainty to gain an uncertainty, and yet he stakes a finite certainty to gain a finite uncertainty, without transgressing against reason. There is not an infinite distance between the certainty staked and the uncertainty of the gain; that is untrue. In truth, there is an infinity between the certainty of gain and the certainty of loss. But the uncertainty of the gain is proportioned to the certainty of the stake according to the proportion of the chances of gain and loss. Hence it comes that, if there are as many risks on one side as on the other, the course is to play even, and then the certainty of the stake is equal to the uncertainty of the gain, so far is it from the fact that there is an infinite distance between them. And so our proposition is of infinite force, when there is the finite to stake in a game where there are equal risks of gain and of loss, and the infinite to gain. This is demonstrable, and if men are capable of any truths, this is one.

"I confess it, I admit it. But still is there no means of seeing the faces of the cards?"—Yes, Scripture and the rest, &c.—"Yes, but I have my hands tied and my mouth closed; I am forced to wager, and am not free. I am not released, and am so made that I cannot believe. What then would you have me do?"

"True. But at least learn your inability to believe, since reason brings you to this, and yet you cannot believe. Endeavour then to convince yourself, not by increase of proofs of God, but by the abatement of your passions. You would like to attain faith, and do not know the way; you would like to cure yourself of unbelief, and ask the remedy for it. Learn of those who have been bound like you, and who now stake all their possessions. These are people who know the way which you would follow, and who are cured of an ill of which you would be cured. Follow the way by which they began; by acting as if they believe, taking the holy water, having masses said, &c. Even this will naturally make you believe, and deaden your acuteness.—"But this is what I am afraid of."—And why? What have you to lose?

But to show you that this leads you there, it is this which will lessen the passions, which are your stumbling-blocks.

The end of this discourse.—Now what harm will befall you in taking this side? You will be faithful, honest, humble, grateful, generous, a sincere friend, truthful. Certainly you will not have those poisonous pleasures, glory and luxury, but will you not have others? I will tell you that you will thereby gain in this life, and that, at each step you take on this road, you will see so great certainty of gain, so much nothingness in what you risk, that you will at last recognize that you have wagered for something certain and infinite, for which you have given nothing.

"Ah! This discourse transports me, charms me," &c.

If this discourse pleases you and seems impressive, know that it is made by a man who has knelt, both before and after it, in prayer to that Being, infinite and without parts, before whom he lays all he has, for you also to lay before Him all you have for your own good and for His glory, so that strength may be given to lowliness.

For Further Reflection

1. Do you agree with Pascal that by a cost-benefit analysis it is good common sense to wager on God?

2. Is there anything problematic with Pascal's argument? Can other religions make similar or even more striking claims and use Pascal's argument to urge us to give up our religion and join theirs?

3. Could it be that God, if there be one, disdains making faith in him an outcome of a wager and not an honest estimation of the evidence?

The Ethics of Belief   II.14

W. K. CLIFFORD

In this essay the British philosopher W. K. Clifford (1845–1879) argues against Pascalian Wagers and against all pragmatic justification for religious belief. He contends that believing involves ethical principles, so that we violate our moral duty if we obtain beliefs where the evidence is insufficient. Such acquisitions of beliefs are tantamount to theft. Clifford begins this essay by relating the story of a shipowner who sends a ship full of emigrants out to sea, knowing that the ship is old and not well-built. He stifles doubts and launches it anyway, sincerely trusting Providence to care for it. When it sinks and all passengers are drowned, he collects his insurance money without a trace of guilt. Clifford argues that sincerity in no way excuses the shipowner, because "he had no right to believe on such evidence as was before him." The rest of the essay is a discussion of the ethics of acquiring beliefs on insufficient evidence.

Study Questions

1. What, according to Clifford, did the shipowner do wrong and why was it wrong?
2. What did the accusers of the religious people on the island (the second illustration) do wrong?
3. What do these two illustrations have in common? What is the lesson Clifford seeks to bring out in discussing them?
4. What is *The Ethics of Belief*? How do moral duties apply to beliefs?
5. What is the danger to a society of becoming credulous?
6. How does Clifford set forth his principle of acquiring beliefs?
7. Does Clifford admit any exceptions to his principle?

A SHIPOWNER WAS ABOUT TO SEND to sea an emigrant ship. He knew that she was old, and not over-well built at the first; that she had seen many seas and climes, and often had needed repairs. Doubts had been suggested to him that possibly she was not seaworthy. These doubts preyed upon his mind and made him unhappy; he thought that perhaps he ought to have her thoroughly overhauled and refitted, even though this should put him to great expense. Before the ship sailed, however, he succeeded in overcoming these melancholy reflections. He said to himself that she had gone safely through so many voyages and weathered so many storms that it was idle to suppose she would not come safely home from this trip also. He would put his trust in Providence, which could hardly fail to protect all these unhappy families that were leaving their fatherland to seek for better times elsewhere. He would dismiss from his mind all ungenerous suspicions about the honesty of builders and contractors. In such ways he acquired a sincere and comfortable conviction that his vessel was thoroughly safe and seaworthy; he watched her departure with a light heart, and benevolent wishes for the success of the exiles in their strange new home that was to be; and he got his insurance money when she went down in midocean and told no tales.

What shall we say of him? Surely this, that he was verily guilty of the death of those men. It is admitted that he did sincerely believe in the soundness of his ship; but the sincerity of his conviction can in no wise help him, because *he had no right to believe on such evidence as was before him.* He had acquired his belief not by honestly earning it in patient investigation, but by stifling his doubts. And although in the end he may have felt so sure about it that he could not think otherwise, yet inasmuch as he had knowingly and willingly worked himself into that frame of mind, he must be held responsible for it.

Let us alter the case a little, and suppose that the ship was not unsound after all; that she made her voyage safely, and many others after it. Will that diminish the guilt of her owner? Not one jot. When an action is once done, it is right or wrong forever; no accidental failure of its good or evil fruits can possibly alter that. The man would not have been innocent, he would only have been not found out. The question of right or wrong has to do with the origin of his belief, not the matter of it; not what it was, but how he got it; not whether it turned out to be true or false, but whether he had a right to believe on such evidence as was before him.

There was once an island in which some of the inhabitants professed a religion teaching neither the doctrine of original sin nor that of eternal punishment. A suspicion got abroad that the professors of this religion had made use of unfair means to get their doctrines taught to children. They were accused of wresting the laws of their country in such a way as to remove children from the care of their natural and legal guardians; and even of stealing them away and keeping them concealed from their friends and relations. A certain number of men formed themselves into a society for the purpose of agitating the public about this matter. They published grave accusations against individual citizens of the highest position and character, and did all in their power to injure those citizens in the exercise of their professions. So great was the noise they made, that a Commission was appointed to investigate the facts, but after the Commission had carefully inquired into all the evidence that could be got, it appeared that the accused were innocent. Not only had they been accused on insufficient evidence, but the evidence of their innocence was such as the agitators might easily have obtained, if they had attempted a fair inquiry. After these disclosures the inhabitants of that country looked upon the members of the agitating society not only as persons whose judgment was to be distrusted, but also as no longer to be counted honorable men. For although

Reprinted from W. K. Clifford's Lectures and Essays *(London: Macmillan, 1879).*

they had sincerely and conscientiously believed in the charges they had made, *yet they had no right to believe on such evidence as was before them*. Their sincere convictions, instead of being honestly earned by patient inquiring, were stolen by listening to the voice of prejudice and passion.

Let us vary this case also, and suppose, other things remaining as before, that a still more accurate investigation proved the accused to have been really guilty. Would this make any difference in the guilt of the accusers? Clearly not; the question is not whether their belief was true or false, but whether they entertained it on wrong grounds. They would no doubt say, "Now you see that we were right after all; next time perhaps you will believe us." And they might be believed, but they would not thereby become honorable men. They would not be innocent, they would only be not found out. Every one of them, if he chose to examine himself *in foro conscientiae*, would know that he had acquired and nourished a belief, when he had no right to believe on such evidence as was before him; and therein he would know that he had done a wrong thing.

It may be said, however, that in both of these supposed cases it is not the belief which is judged to be wrong, but the action following upon it. The shipowner might say, "I am perfectly certain that my ship is sound, but still I feel it my duty to have her examined, before trusting the lives of so many people to her." And it might be said to the agitator, "However convinced you were of the justice of your cause and the truth of your convictions, you ought not to have made public attack upon any man's character until you had examined the evidence on both sides with the utmost patience and care."

In the first place, let us admit that, so far as it goes, this view of the case is right and necessary; right, because even when a man's belief is so fixed that he cannot think otherwise, he still has a choice in regard to the action suggested by it, and so cannot escape the duty of investigating on the ground of the strength of his convic-

tions; and necessary, because those who are not yet capable of controlling their feelings and thoughts must have a plain rule dealing with overt acts.

But this being premised as necessary, it becomes clear that it is not sufficient, and that our previous judgment is required to supplement it. For it is not possible so to sever the belief from the action it suggests as to condemn the one without condemning the other. No man holding a strong belief on one side of a question, or even wishing to hold a belief on one side, can investigate it with such fairness and completeness as if he were really in doubt and unbiased; so that the existence of a belief not founded on fair inquiry unfits a man for the performance of this necessary duty.

Nor is that truly a belief at all which has not some influence upon the actions of him who holds it. He who truly believes that which prompts him to an action has looked upon the action to lust after it, he has committed it already in his heart. If a belief is not realized immediately in open deeds, it is stored up for the guidance of the future. It goes to make a part of that aggregate of beliefs which is the link between sensation and action at every moment of all our lives, and which is so organized and compacted together that no part of it can be isolated from the rest, but every new addition modifies the structure of the whole. No real belief, however trifling and fragmentary it may seem, is ever truly insignificant; it prepares us to receive more of its like, confirms those which resembled it before, and weakens others; and so gradually it lays a stealthy train in our inmost thoughts, which may some day explode into overt action, and leave its stamp upon our character forever.

And no one man's belief is in any case a private matter which concerns himself alone. Our lives are guided by that general conception of the course of things which has been created by society for social purposes. Our words, our phrases, our forms and processes and modes of thought are common property, fashioned and perfected from age to age; an heirloom which every succeeding generation inherits as a precious deposit and a sacred trust to be handed on to the next one, not unchanged but enlarged and purified, with some clear marks of its proper handiwork. Into this, for good or ill, is woven every belief of every man who has speech of his fellows. An awful privilege, and an awful responsibility, that we should help to create the world in which posterity will live.

In the two supposed cases which have been considered, it has been judged wrong to believe on insufficient evidence, or to nourish belief by suppressing doubts and avoiding investigation. The reason of this judgment is not far to seek; it is that in both these cases the belief held by one man was of great importance to other men. But for as much as no belief held by one man, however seemingly trivial the belief, and however obscure the believer, is ever actually insignificant or without its effect on the fate of mankind, we have no choice but to extend our judgment to all cases of belief whatever. Belief, that sacred faculty which prompts the decisions of our will, and knits into harmonious working all the compacted energies of our being, is ours not for ourselves but for humanity. It is rightly used on truths which have been established by long experience and waiting toil, and which have stood in the fierce light of free and fearless questioning. Then it helps to bind men together, and to strengthen and direct their common action. It is desecrated when given to unproved and unquestioned statements, for the solace and private pleasure of the believer; to add a tinsel splendor to the plain straight road of our life and display a bright mirage beyond it; or even to drown the common sorrows of our kind by a self-deception which allows them not only to cast down, but also to degrade us. Whoso would deserve well of his fellows in this matter will guard the purity of his belief with a very fanaticism of jealous care, lest at any time it should rest on an unworthy object, and catch a stain which can never be wiped away.

It is not only the leader of men, statesman, philosopher, or poet, that owes this bounden duty to mankind. Every rustic who delivers in the village alehouse his slow, infrequent sentences, may help to kill or keep alive the fatal superstitions which clog his race. Every hard-worked wife of an artisan may transmit to her children beliefs which shall knit society together, or rend it in pieces. No simplicity of mind, no obscurity of station, can escape the universal duty of questioning all that we believe.

It is true that this duty is a hard one, and the doubt which comes out of it is often a very bitter thing. It leaves us bare and powerless where we thought that we were safe and strong. To know all about anything is to know how to deal with it under all circumstances. We feel much happier and more secure when we think we know precisely what to do, no matter what happens, than when we have lost our way and do not know where to turn. And if we have supposed ourselves to know all about anything, and to be capable of doing what is fit in regard to it, we naturally do not like to find that we are really ignorant and powerless, that we have to begin again at the beginning, and try to learn what the thing is and how it is to be dealt with—if indeed anything can be learned about it. It is the sense of power attached to a sense of knowledge that makes men desirous of believing, and afraid of doubting.

This sense of power is the highest and best of pleasures when the belief on which it is founded is true belief, and has been fairly earned by investigation. For then we may justly feel that it is common property, and holds good for others as well as for ourselves. Then we may be glad, not that *I* have learned secrets by which I am safer and stronger, but that *we men* have got mastery over more of the world; and we shall be strong, not for ourselves, but in the name of Man and in his strength. But if the belief has been accepted on insufficient evidence, the pleasure is a stolen one. Not only does it deceive ourselves by giving us a sense of power which we do not really possess, but it is sinful, because it is stolen in defiance of our duty to mankind. That duty is to guard ourselves from such beliefs as from a pestilence, which may shortly master our own body and then spread to the rest of the town. What would be thought of one who, for the sake of a sweet fruit, should deliberately run the risk of bringing a plague upon his family and his neighbors?

And, as in other such cases, it is not the risk only which has to be considered; for a bad action is always bad at the time when it is done, no matter what happens afterwards. Every time we let ourselves believe for unworthy reasons, we weaken our powers of self-control, of doubting, of judicially and fairly weighing evidence. We all suffer severely enough from the maintenance and support of false beliefs and the fatally wrong actions which they lead to, and the evil born when one such belief is entertained is great and wide. But a greater and wider evil arises when the credulous character is maintained and supported, when a habit of believing for unworthy reasons is fostered and made permanent. If I steal money from any person, there may be no harm done by the mere transfer of possession; he may not feel the loss, or it may prevent him from using the money badly. But I cannot help doing this great wrong towards Man, that I make myself dishonest. What hurts society is not that it should lose its property, but that it should become a den of thieves; for then it must cease to be society. This is why we ought not to do evil that good may come; for at any rate this great evil has come, that we have done evil and are made wicked thereby. In like manner, if I let myself believe anything on insufficient evidence, there may be no great harm done by the mere belief; it may be true after all, or I may never have occasion to exhibit it in outward acts. But I cannot help doing this great wrong toward Man, that I make myself credulous. The danger to society is not merely that it should believe wrong things, though that is great enough; but that it should become credulous, and lose the habit of testing things and inquiring into them; for then it must sink back into savagery.

The harm which is done by credulity in a man is not confined to the fostering of a credulous character in others, and consequent support of false beliefs. Habitual want of care about what I believe leads to habitual want of care in others about the truth of what is told to me. Men speak the truth to one another when each reveres the truth in his own mind and in the other's mind; but how shall my friend revere the truth in my mind when I myself am careless about it, when I believe things because I want to believe them, and because they are comforting and pleasant? Will he not learn to cry, "Peace," to me, when there is no peace? By such a course I shall surround myself with a thick atmosphere of falsehood and fraud, and in that I must live. It may matter little to me, in my cloud-castle of sweet illusions and darling lies; but it matters much to Man that I have made my neighbors ready to deceive. The credulous man is father to the liar and the cheat; he lives in the bosom of this his family, and it is no marvel if he should become even as they are. So closely are our duties knit together, that whoso shall keep the whole law, and yet offend in one point, he is guilty of all.

To sum up; it is wrong always, everywhere, and for anyone, to believe anything upon insufficient evidence.

If a man, holding a belief which he was taught in childhood or persuaded of afterwards, keeps down and pushes away any doubts which arise about it in his mind, purposely avoids the reading of books and the company of men that call in question or discuss it, and regards as impious those questions which cannot easily be asked without disturbing it—the life of that man is one long sin against mankind.

If this judgment seems harsh when applied to those simple souls who have never known better, who have been brought up from the cradle with a horror of doubt, and taught that their eternal welfare depends on what they believe, then it leads to the very serious question. Who hath made Israel to sin?

Inquiry into the evidence of a doctrine is not to be made once for all, and then taken as finally settled. It is never lawful to stifle a doubt; for either it can be honestly answered by means of the inquiry already made, or else it proves that the inquiry was not complete.

"But," says one, "I am a busy man; I have no time for the long course of study which would be necessary to make me in any degree a competent judge of certain questions, or even able to understand the nature of the arguments." Then he would have no time to believe....

For Further Reflection

1. Describe Clifford's ethics of belief. Does Clifford exaggerate our duty to believe exactly according to the evidence? Does he falsely suppose that we can measure the evidence? Explain your position.

2. Is Clifford's shipowner example relevant to religious belief, or are there significant dissimilarities? (If so, describe them.)

3. Is it sometimes permissible to believe some proposition without strong evidence? Consider the following situation: There is evidence that your best friend has committed a crime, but something deep inside of you tells you that he is innocent and you find yourself believing against the evidence? If it turned out that you were right, would this justify you in your confidence in your friend? Would this serve as a counterexample to Clifford's rationalism? Or can Clifford give a plausible account of this sort of situation? Explain.

II.15   The Will to Believe

WILLIAM JAMES

The classic response to Clifford's ethics of belief is William James's "The Will to Believe" (1896), in which James argues that life would be greatly impoverished if we confined our beliefs to such a Scrooge-like epistemology as Clifford proposes. In everyday life, where the evidence for important propositions is often unclear, we must live by faith or cease to act at all. Although we may not make leaps of faith just anywhere, sometimes practical considerations force us to make decisions regarding propositions that do not have their truth value written on their faces. "Belief" is defined as a live, momentous optional hypothesis on which we cannot avoid a decision, for not to choose is in effect to choose against the hypothesis. James claims that religion can be such an optional hypothesis for many people, and in this case one has the right to believe the better story rather than the worse. To do so, one must will to believe what the evidence alone is inadequate to support.

Study Questions

1. What does James mean by *live* or *dead* hypotheses?
2. What does he mean by a *genuine option*?
3. What does he think about the validity of Pascal's Wager?
4. Does James think Clifford's *Ethics of Belief* is valid? What does he think of Clifford's views?
5. How does James think our passional nature functions with regard acquiring beliefs?
6. How does James reply to Clifford's fear of being duped, that is, by having false beliefs?
7. What are the two ways of looking at our duty in matters of opinion? That is, regarding acquiring beliefs?
8. How can faith change reality?
9. What two things does religion say? What does James mean by these two things?
10. Does James think we ought to withhold belief regarding religion if we lack sufficient evidence?

LET US GIVE THE NAME of hypothesis to anything that may be proposed to our belief; and just as the electricians speak of live and dead wires, let us speak of any hypothesis as either *live* or *dead*. A live hypothesis is one which appeals as a real possibility to him to whom it is proposed. If I ask you to believe in the Mahdi [1844–1885, a Sudanese leader who led a successful revolt against Egypt in 1885), the notion makes no electric connection with your nature—it refuses to scintillate with any credibility at all. As an hypothesis it is completely dead. To an Arab, however (even if he be not one of the Mahdi's followers), the hypothesis is among the mind's possibilities: It is alive. This shows that deadness and liveness in an hypothesis are not intrinsic properties, but relations to the individual thinker. They are measured by his willingness to act. The maximum of liveness in an hypothesis means willingness to act irrevocably. Practically, that means belief; but there is some believing tendency wherever there is willingness to act at all.

Next, let us call the decision between two hypotheses an *option*. Options may be of several kinds. They may be first, *living* or *dead;* secondly, *forced* or *avoidable;* thirdly, *momentous* or *trivial;* and for our purposes we may call an op-

tion a genuine option when it is of a forced, living, and momentous kind.

1. A living option is one in which both hypotheses are live ones. If I say to you: "Be a theosophist or be a Mohammedan," it is probably a dead option, because for you neither hypothesis is likely to be alive. But if I say: "Be an agnostic or be a Christian," it is otherwise: trained as you are, each hypothesis makes some appeal, however small, to your belief.

2. Next, if I say to you: "Choose between going out with your umbrella or without it," I do not offer you a genuine option, for it is not forced. You can easily avoid it by not going out at all. Similarly, if I say, "Either love me or hate me," "Either call my theory true or call it false," your option is avoidable. You may remain indifferent to me, neither loving nor hating, and you may decline to offer any judgment as to my theory. But if I say, "Either accept this truth or go without it," I put on you a forced option, for there is no standing place outside of the alternative. Every dilemma based on a complete logical dis-

Reprinted from William James, The Will to Believe (*New York: Longmans, Gree & Co., 1897).*

junction, with no possibility of not choosing, is an option of this forced kind.

3. Finally, if I were Dr. Nansen and proposed to you to join my North Pole expedition, your option would be momentous; for this would probably be your similar opportunity, and your choice now would either exclude you from the North Pole sort of immortality altogether or put at least the chance of it into your hands. He who refuses to embrace a unique opportunity loses the prize as surely as if he tried and failed. *Per contra,* the option is trivial when the opportunity is not unique, when the stake is insignificant, or when the decision is reversible if it later prove unwise. Such trivial options abound in the scientific life. A chemist finds an hypothesis live enough to spend a year in its verification: he believes in it to that extent. But if his experiments prove inconclusive either way, he is quit for his loss of time, no vital harm being done.

It will facilitate our discussion if we keep all these distinctions well in mind.

The next matter to consider is the actual psychology of human opinion. When we look at certain facts, it seems as if our passional and volitional nature lay at the root of all our convictions. When we look at others, it seems as if they could do nothing when the intellect had once said its say. Let us take the latter facts up first.

Does it not seem preposterous on the very face of it to talk of our opinions being modifiable at will? Can our will either help or hinder our intellect in its perceptions of truth? Can we, by just willing it, believe that Abraham Lincoln's existence is a myth, and that the portraits of him in *McClure's Magazine* are all of some one else? Can we, by any effort of our will, or by any strength of wish that it were true, believe ourselves well and about when we are roaring with rheumatism in bed, or feel certain that the sum of the two one-dollar bills in our pocket must be a hundred dollars? We can say any of these things, but we are absolutely impotent to believe them; and of just such things is the whole fabric of the truths that we do believe in made up—matters of fact, immediate or remote, as Hume said, and relations between ideas, which are either there or not there for us if we see them so, and which if not there cannot be put there by any action of our own.

In Pascal's *Thoughts* there is a celebrated passage known in literature as Pascal's wager. In it he tries to force us into Christianity by reasoning as if our concern with truth resembled our concern with the stakes in a game of chance. Translated freely his words are these: You must either believe or not believe that God is—which will you do? Your human reason cannot say. A game is going on between you and the nature of things which at the day of judgment will bring out either heads or tails. Weigh what your gains and your losses would be if you should stake all you have on heads, or God's existence: if you win in such case, you gain eternal beatitude; if you lose, you lose nothing at all. If there were an infinity of chances, and only one for God in this wager, still you ought to stake your all on God; for though you surely risk a finite loss by this procedure, any finite loss is reasonable, even a certain one is reasonable, if there is but the possibility of infinite gain. Go, then, and take holy water, and have masses said; belief will come and stupefy your scruples. Why should you not? At bottom, what have you to lose?

You probably feel that when religious faith expresses itself thus, in the language of the gaming-table, it is put to its last trumps. Surely Pascal's own personal belief in masses and holy water had far other springs; and this celebrated page of his is but an argument for others, a last desperate snatch at a weapon against the hardness of the unbelieving heart. We feel that a faith in masses and holy water adopted wilfully after such a mechanical calculation would lack the inner soul of faith's reality; and if we were ourselves in the place of the Deity, we should probably take particular pleasure in cutting off believers of this pattern from their infinite reward. It is evident that unless there be some preexisting tendency to believe in masses and holy water, the option offered to the will by Pascal is not a living option. Certainly no Turk ever took to masses and holy water on its account; and even to us Protestants these means of salvation seem such foregone impossibilities that Pascal's logic, invoked for them specifically, leaves us unmoved. As well might the Mahdi write to us, saying, "I am the Expected One whom God has created in his effulgence. You shall be infinitely happy if you confess me; otherwise you shall be cut off from the light of the sun. Weigh, then, your infinite gain if I am genuine against your finite sacrifice if I am not!" His logic would be that of Pascal; but he would vainly use it on us, for the hypothesis he offers us is dead. No tendency to act on it exists in us to any degree.

The talk of believing by our volition seems, then, from one point of view, simply silly. From another point of view it is worse than silly, it is vile. When one turns to the magnificent edifice of the physical sciences, and sees how it was reared; what thousands of disinterested moral lives of men lie buried in its mere foundations; what patience and postponement, what choking down of preference, what submission to the icy laws of outer fact are wrought into its very stones and mortar; how absolutely impersonal it stands in its vast augustness—then how besotted and contemptible seems every little sentimentalist who comes blowing his voluntary smoke-wreaths, and pretending to decide things from out of his private dream! Can we wonder if those bred in the rugged and manly school of science should feel like spewing such subjectivism out of their mouths? The whole system of loyalties which grow up in the schools of science go dead against its toleration; so that it is only natural that those who have caught the scientific fever should pass over to the opposite extreme, and write sometimes as if the incor-

ruptibly truthful intellect ought positively to prefer bitterness and unacceptableness to the heart in its cup.

> It fortifies my soul to know
> That though I perish, Truth is so.

sings Clough, while Huxley exclaims: "My only consolation lies in the reflection that, however bad our posterity may become, so far as they hold by the plain rule of not pretending to believe what they have no reason to believe, because it may be to their advantage so to pretend [the word 'pretend' is surely here redundant], they will not have reached the lowest depth of immorality." And that delicious *enfant terrible* Clifford writes: "Belief is desecrated when given to unproved and unquestioned statements for the solace and private pleasure of the believer. . . . Whoso would deserve well of his fellows in this matter will guard the purity of his belief with a very fanaticism of jealous care, lest at any time it should rest on an unworthy object, and catch a stain which can never be wiped away. . . . If [a] belief has been accepted on insufficient evidence [even though the belief be true, as Clifford on the same page explains] the pleasure is a stolen one. . . . It is sinful because it is stolen in defiance of our duty to mankind. That duty is to guard ourselves from such beliefs as from a pestilence which may shortly master our own body and then spread to the rest of the town. . . . It is wrong always, everywhere, and for every one, to believe anything upon insufficient evidence."

All this strikes one as healthy, even when expressed, as by Clifford, with somewhat too much of robustious pathos in the voice. Free will and simple wishing do seem, in the matter of our credences, to be only fifth wheels to the coach. Yet if any one should thereupon assume that intellectual insight is what remains after wish and will and sentimental preference have taken wing, or that pure reason is what then settles our opinions, he would fly quite as directly in the teeth of the facts.

It is only our already dead hypotheses that our willing nature is unable to bring to life again. But what has made them dead for us is for the most part a previous action of our willing nature of an antagonistic kind. When I say "willing nature," I do not mean only such deliberate volitions as may have set up habits of belief that we cannot now escape from—I mean all such factors of belief as fear and hope, prejudice and passion, imitation and partisanship, the circumpressure of our caste and set. As a matter of fact we find ourselves believing, we hardly know how or why. Mr. Balfour gives the name of "authority" to all those influences, born of the intellectual climate, that make hypotheses possible or impossible for us, alive or dead. Here in this room, we all of us believe in molecules and the conservation of energy, in democracy and necessary progress, in Protestant Christianity and the duty of fighting for "the doctrine of the immortal Monroe," all for no reasons worthy of the name. We see into these matters with no more inner clearness, and probably with much less, than any disbeliever in them might possess. His unconventionality would probably have some grounds to show for its conclusions; but for us, not insight, but the *prestige* of the opinions, is what makes the spark shoot from them and light up our sleeping magazines of faith. Our reason is quite satisfied, in nine hundred and ninety-nine cases out of every thousand of us, if it can find a few arguments that will do to recite in case our credulity is criticized by some one else. Our faith is faith in some one else's faith, and in the greatest matters this is the most the case. . . .

Evidently, then, our non-intellectual nature does influence our convictions. There are passional tendencies and volitions which run before and others which come after belief, and it is only the latter that are too late for the fair; and they are not too late when the previous passional work has been already in their own direction. Pascal's argument, instead of being powerless, then seems a regular clincher, and is the last stroke needed to make our faith in masses and holy water complete. The state of things is evidently far from simple; and pure insight and logic, whatever they might do ideally, are not the only things that really do produce our creeds.

Our next duty, having recognized this mixedup state of affairs, is to ask whether it be simply reprehensible and pathological, or whether, on the contrary, we must treat it as a normal element in making up our minds. The thesis I defend is, briefly stated, this: *Our passional nature not only lawfully may, but must, decide an option between propositions, whenever it is a genuine option that cannot by its nature be decided on intellectual grounds; for to say, under such circumstances, "Do not decide, but leave the question open," is itself a passional decision—just like deciding yes or no—and is attended with the same risk of losing the truth.* . . .

One more point, small but important, and our preliminaries are done. There are two ways of looking at our duty in the matter of opinion—ways entirely different, and yet ways about whose difference the theory of knowledge seems hitherto to have shown very little concern. *We must know the truth;* and *we must avoid error*—these are our first and great commandments as would-be knowers; but they are not two ways of stating an identical commandment, they are two separable laws. Although it may indeed happen that when we believe the truth A, we escape as an incidental consequence from believing the falsehood B, it hardly ever happens that by merely disbelieving B we necessarily believe A. We may in escaping B fall into believing other falsehoods, C or D, just as bad as B; or we may escape B by not believing anything at all, not even A.

Believe truth! Shun error!—these, we see, are two materially different laws; and by choosing between them we may end by coloring differently our whole intellectual life. We may regard the chase for truth as paramount, and the avoidance of error as secondary; or we may, on the other hand, treat the avoidance of error as more imperative, and let truth take its chance. Clifford, in the instructive passage which I have quoted, exhorts us to the latter course. Believe nothing, he tells us, keep your mind in suspense forever, rather than by closing it on insufficient evidence incur the awful risk of believing lies. You, on the other hand, may think that the risk of being in error is a very small matter when compared with the blessings of real knowledge, and be ready to be duped many times in your investigation rather than postpone indefinitely the chance of guessing true. I myself find it impossible to go with Clifford. We must remember that these feelings of our duty about either truth or error are in any case only expressions of our passional life. Biologically considered, our minds are as ready to grind out falsehood as veracity, and he who says, "Better go without belief forever than believe a lie!" merely shows his own preponderant private horror of becoming a dupe. He may be critical of many of his desires and fears, but this fear he slavishly obeys. He cannot imagine any one questioning its binding force. For my own part, I have also a horror of being duped; but I can believe that worse things than being duped may happen to a man in this world: so Clifford's exhortation has to my ears a thoroughly fantastic sound. It is like a general informing his soldiers that it is better to keep out of battle forever than to risk a single wound. Not so are victories either over enemies or over nature gained. Our errors are surely not such awfully solemn things. In a world where we are so certain to incur them in spite of all our caution, a certain lightness of heart seems healthier than this excessive nervousness on their behalf. At any rate, it seems the fittest thing for the empiricist philosopher.

And now, after all this introduction, let us go straight at our question. I have said, and now repeat it, that not only as a matter of fact do we find our passional nature influencing us in our opinions, but that there are some options between opinions in which this influence must be regarded both as an inevitable and as a lawful determinant of our choice.

I fear here that some of you my hearers will begin to scent danger, and lend an inhospitable ear. Two first steps of passion you have indeed had to admit as necessary—we must think so as to avoid dupery, and we must think so as to gain truth; but the surest path to those ideal consummations, you will probably consider, is from now onwards to take no further passional step.

Well, of course, I agree as far as the facts will allow. Wherever the option between losing truth and gaining it is not momentous, we can throw the chance of *gaining truth* away, and at any rate save ourselves from any chance of *believing falsehood*, by not making up our minds at all till objective evidence has come. In scientific questions, this is almost always the case; and even in human affairs in general, the need of acting is seldom so urgent that a false belief to act on is better than no belief at all. Law courts, indeed, have to decide on the best evidence attainable for the moment, because a judge's duty is to make law as well as to ascertain it, and (as a learned judge once said to me) few cases are worth spending much time over: the great thing is to have them decided on *any* acceptable principle, and got out of the way. But in our dealings with objective nature we obviously are recorders, not makers, of the truth; and decisions for the mere sake of deciding promptly and getting on to the next business would be wholly out of place. Throughout the breadth of physical nature facts are what they are quite independently of us, and seldom is there any such hurry about them that the risks of being duped by believing a premature theory need be faced. The questions here are always trivial options, the hypotheses are hardly living (at any rate not living for us spectators), the choice between believing truth or falsehood is seldom forced. The attitude of sceptical balance is therefore the absolutely wise one if we would escape mistakes. What difference, indeed, does it make to most of us whether we have or have not a theory of the Röntgen rays, whether we believe or not in mind-stuff, or have a conviction about the causality of conscious states? It makes no difference. Such options are not forced on us. On every account it is better not to make them, but still keep weighing reasons *pro et contra* with an indifferent hand.

I speak, of course, here of the purely judging mind. For purposes of discovery such indifference is to be less highly recommended, and science would be far less advanced than she is if the passionate desires of individuals to get their own faiths confirmed had been kept out of the game. See for example the sagacity which Spencer and Weismann now display. On the other hand, if you want an absolute duffer in an investigation, you must, after all, take the man who has no interest whatever in its results: he is the warranted incapable, the positive fool. The most useful investigator, because the most sensitive observer, is always he whose eager interest in one side of the question is balanced by an equally keen nervousness lest he become deceived. Science has organized this nervousness into a regular *technique,* her so-called method of verification; and she has fallen so deeply in love with the method that one may even say she has ceased to care for truth by itself at all. It is only truth as technically verified that interests her. The truth of truths might come in merely affirmative form, and she would decline to touch it. Such truth as that, she might repeat with Clifford, would be stolen in defiance of her duty to mankind. Human passions, however, are stronger than technical rules. *"Le coeur a ses raisons,"* as Pascal says, *"que la raison ne connait pas"*[1]; and however indifferent to all but the bare rules of the game the umpire, the abstract intellect, may be, the concrete players who furnish him the materials to judge of are usually, each one of them, in love with some pet "live hypothesis" of his own. Let us agree, however, that wherever there is no forced option, the dispassionately judicial intellect with no pet hypothesis, saving us, as it does, from dupery at any rate, ought to be our ideal.

The question next arises: Are there not somewhere forced options in our speculative questions, and can we (as men who may be interested at least as much in positively gaining truth as in merely escaping dupery) always wait with impunity till the coercive evidence shall have arrived? It seems *a priori* improbable that the truth should be so nicely adjusted to our needs and powers as that. In the great boarding-house of nature, the cakes and the butter and the syrup seldom come out so even and leave the plates so clean. Indeed, we should view them with scientific suspicion if they did.

Moral questions immediately present themselves as questions whose solution cannot wait for sensible proof. A moral question is a question not of what sensibly exists, but of what is good, or would be good if it did exist. Science can tell us what exists; but to compare the worths, both of what exists and of what does not exist, we must consult not science, but what Pascal calls our heart. . . .

Turn now from these wide questions of good to a certain class of questions of fact, questions concerning personal relations, states of mind between one man and another. *Do you like me or not?*—for example. Whether you do or not depends, in countless instances, on whether I meet you halfway, am willing to assume that you must like me, and show you trust and expectation. The previous faith on my part in your liking's existence is in such cases what makes your liking come. But if I stand aloof, and refuse to budge an inch until I have objective evidence, until you shall have done something apt, as the absolutists say, *ad extorquendum assensum meum,* ten to one your liking never comes. How many women's hearts are vanquished by the mere sanguine insistence of some man that they *must* love him! He will not consent to the hypothesis that they cannot. The desire for a certain kind of truth here brings about that special truth's existence; and so it is in innumerable cases of other sorts. . . . *And where faith in a fact can help create the fact,* that would be an insane logic which should say that

1. "The heart has its reasons which reason does not know."

faith running ahead of scientific evidence is the "lowest kind of immorality" into which a thinking being can fall. Yet such is the logic by which our scientific absolutists pretend to regulate our lives!

In truths dependent on our personal action, then, faith based on desire is certainly a lawful and possibly an indispensable thing.

But now, it will be said, these are all childish human cases, and have nothing to do with great cosmical matters, like the question of religious faith. Let us then pass on to that. Religions differ so much in their accidents that in discussing the religious question we must make it very generic and broad. What then do we now mean by the religious hypothesis? Science says things are; morality says some things are better than other things; and religion says essentially two things.

First, she says that the best things are the more eternal things, the overlapping things, the things in the universe that throw the last stone, so to speak, and say the final word. "Perfection is eternal"—this phrase of Charles Secrétan seems a good way of putting this first affirmation of religion, an affirmation which obviously cannot yet be verified scientifically at all.

The second affirmation of religion is that we are better off even now if we believe her first affirmation to be true.

Now, let us consider what the logical elements of this situation are *in case the religious hypothesis in both its branches be really true.* (Of course, we must admit that possibility at the outset. If we are to discuss the question at all, it must involve a living option. If for any of you religion be a hypothesis that cannot, by any living possibility, be true, then you need go no farther. I speak to the "saving remnant" alone.) So proceeding, we see, first, that religion offers itself as a momentous option. We are supposed to gain, even now, by our belief, and to lose by our non-belief, a certain vital good. Secondly, religion is a *forced* option, so far as that good goes. We cannot escape the issue by remaining sceptical and waiting for more light, because, although we do avoid error in that way *if reli-gion be untrue,* we lose the good, *if it be true,* just as certainly as if we positively chose to disbelieve. It is as if a man should hesitate indefinitely to ask a certain woman to marry him because he was not perfectly sure that she would prove an angel after he brought her home. Would he not cut himself off from that particular angel-possibility as decisively as if he went and married some one else? Scepticism, then, is not avoidance of option; it is option of a certain particular kind of risk. *Better risk loss of truth than chance of error*—that is your faith-vetoer's exact position. He is actively playing his stake as much as the believer is; he is backing the field against the religious hypothesis, just as the believer is backing the religious hypothesis against the field. To preach scepticism to us as a duty until "sufficient evidence" for religion be found, is tantamount therefore to telling us, when in presence of the religious hypothesis, that to yield to our fear of its being error is wiser and better than to yield to our hope that it may be true. It is not intellect against all passions, then; it is only intellect with one passion laying down its law. And by what, forsooth, is the supreme wisdom of this passion warranted? Dupery for dupery, what proof is there that dupery through hope is so much worse than dupery through fear? I, for one, can see no proof; and I simply refuse obedience to the scientist's command to imitate his kind of option, in a case where my own stake is important enough to give me the right to choose my own form of risk. If religion be true and the evidence for it be still insufficient, I do not wish, by putting your extinguisher upon my nature (which feels to me as if it had after all some business in this matter), to forfeit my sole chance in life of getting upon the winning side—that chance depending, of course, on my willingness to run the risk of acting as if my passional need of taking the world religiously might be prophetic and right.

All this is on the supposition that it really may be prophetic and right, and that, even to us who are discussing the matter, religion is a live hypothesis which may be true. Now, to most of us religion comes in a still further way that makes a veto on our active faith even more illogical. The more perfect and more eternal aspect of the universe is represented in our religions as having personal form. The universe is no longer a mere *It* to us, but a *Thou*, if we are religious; and any relation that may be possible from person to person might be possible here. For instance, although in one sense we are passive portions of the universe, in another we show a curious autonomy, as if we were small active centers on our own account. We feel, too, as if the appeal of religion to us were made to our own active goodwill, as if evidence might be forever withheld from us unless we met the hypothesis halfway to take a trivial illustration: just as a man who in a company of gentlemen made no advances, asked a warrant for every concession, and believed no one's word without proof, would cut himself off by such churlishness from all the social rewards that a more trusting spirit would earn—so here, one who should shut himself up in snarling logicality and try to make the gods extort his recognition willy-nilly, or not get it at all, might cut himself off forever from his only opportunity of making the gods' acquaintance. This feeling, forced on us we know not whence that by obstinately believing that there are gods (although not to do so would be so easy both for our logic and our life) we are doing the universe the deepest service we can, seems part of the living essence of the religious hypothesis. If the hypothesis were true in all its parts, including this one, then pure intellectualism, with its veto on our making willing advances, would be an absurdity; and some participation of our sympathetic nature would be logically required. I, therefore, for one, cannot see my way to accepting the agnostic rules for truth-seeking, or wilfully agree to keep my willing nature out of the game. I cannot do so for this plain reason, that *a rule of thinking which would absolutely prevent me from acknowledging certain kinds of truth if those kinds of truth were really there, would be an irrational rule.* That for

me is the long and short of the formal logic of the situation, no matter what the kinds of truth might materially be.

I confess I do not see how this logic can be escaped. But sad experience makes me fear that some of you may still shrink from radically saying with me, *in abstracto,* that we have the right to believe at our own risk any hypothesis that is live enough to tempt our will. I suspect, however, that if this is so, it is because you have got away from the abstract logical point of view altogether, and are thinking (perhaps without realizing it) of some particular religious hypothesis which for you is dead. The freedom to 'believe what we will' you apply to the case of some patent superstition; and the faith you think of is the faith defined by the schoolboy when he said, "Faith is when you believe something that you know ain't true." I can only repeat that this is misapprehension. *In concreto,* the freedom to believe can only cover living options which the intellect of the individual cannot by itself resolve; and living options never seem absurdities to him who has them to consider. When I look at the religious question as it really puts itself to concrete men, and when I think of all the possibilities which both practically and theoretically it involves, then this command that we shall put a stopper on our heart, instincts, and courage, and *wait*—acting of course meanwhile more or less as if religion were *not* true—till doomsday, or till such time as our intellect and senses working together may have raked in evidence enough,—this command, I say, seems to me the queerest idol ever manufactured in the philosophic cave. Were we scholastic absolutists, there might be more excuse. If we had an infallible intellect with its objective certitudes, we might feel ourselves disloyal to such a perfect organ of knowledge in not trusting to it exclusively, in not waiting for its releasing word. But if we are empiricists, if we believe that no bell in us tolls to let us know for certain when truth is in our grasp, then it seems a piece of idle fantasticality to preach so solemnly our duty of waiting for the bell. Indeed we *may* wait if we will—I hope you do not think that I am denying that—but if we do so, we do so at our peril as much as if we believed. In either case we *act*, taking our life in our hands. No one of us ought to issue vetoes to the other, nor should we bandy words of abuse. We ought, on the contrary, delicately and profoundly to respect one another's mental freedom: then only shall we bring about the intellectual republic: then only shall we have that spirit of inner tolerance without which all our Outer tolerance is soulless, and which is empiricism's glory; then only shall we live and let live, in speculative as well as in practical things. . . .

For Further Reflection

1 Explain what James means by a "genuine" option. Is he correct in calling religious belief a genuine option? Why or why not?

2. Has James successfully met Clifford's objections to religious belief, or has he confused self-creating beliefs with wishful thinking? That is, by getting myself into the state where I believe I am capable of winning a race (although there's not enough evidence to decide the likelihood of the matter), I might actually increase my chances of winning the race; but my *believing* that God exists doesn't increase the probability that God does exist because God either exists, or does not exist, independently of my beliefs. How would James or one of his followers respond to this objection?

3. Can we obtain beliefs simply by *willing* to have them, or is this an exercise in futility? Explain your answer.

A Debate on the Rationality of Religious Belief   II.16

ANTONY FLEW, R. M. HARE, AND BASIL MITCHELL

Antony Flew was for many years professor of philosophy at the University of Reading in England. R. M. Hare and Basil Mitchell were, until their recent retirements, professors of philosophy at Oxford University. All three were educated at Oxford University, where they all began their teaching careers. In this 1948 Oxford University symposium, Flew challenges theists to state the conditions under which they would give up their faith, for, he contends, unless one can state what would falsify one's belief, one does not have a meaningful belief. If nothing could count against the belief, it does not make a serious assertion, for serious truth claims must be ready to undergo rational scrutiny. Hare responds by arguing that this is the wrong way to describe faith, for religious faith consists of a set of profoundly unfalsifiable assumptions, which he calls "bliks," which govern all of a person's other beliefs. There are insane and sane bliks, but we cannot escape having them. Even the scientist has such fundamental assumptions. Hence religion should not be subject to the kind of rational scrutiny, Flew urges. Mitchell opts for a compromise position.

Rational considerations enter into the debate on faith, but no one can say exactly when a gradual accumulation of evidence is sufficient to overthrow religious belief. Although rational considerations count against faith, the believer will not let them count decisively against it.

Study Questions

1. What is the significance of the parable of the garden? How does Flew interpret it? Do you agree with him?
2. What does Flew mean by his statement that a brash hypothesis can be "killed by inches, the death by a thousand qualifications"?
3. What is Hare's strategy in telling the story of the paranoid student who believes that all dons (teachers) intend to harm him?
4. What is a "blik"? Describe it.
5. How does Hare disagree with Flew?
6. What is the one thing that Mitchell allows to count against his faith in God? How much should it count against one's faith?
7. How does Mitchell illustrate his thesis? How does his story throw light on the relationship of faith to reason?

ANTONY FLEW

LET US BEGIN WITH A PARABLE. It is a parable developed from a tale told by John Wisdom in his haunting and revelatory article "Gods."[1] Once upon a time two explorers came upon a clearing in the jungle. In the clearing were growing many flowers and many weeds. One explorer says, "Some gardener must tend this plot." The other disagrees, "There is no gardener." So they pitch their tents and set a watch. No gardener is ever seen. "But perhaps he is an invisible gardener." So they set up a barbed-wire fence. They electrify it. They patrol with bloodhounds. (For they remember how H. G. Wells's *The Invisible Man* could be both smelt and touched though he could not be seen.) But no shrieks ever suggest that some intruder has received a shock. No movements of the wire ever betray an invisible climber. The bloodhounds never give cry. Yet still the Believer is not convinced. "But there is a gardener, invisible, in-

tangible, insensible to electric shocks, a gardener who has no scent and makes no sound, a gardener who comes secretly to look after the garden which he loves." At last the Sceptic despairs. "But what remains of your original assertion? Just how does what you call an invisible, intangible, eternally elusive gardener differ from an imaginary gardener or even from no gardener at all?"

In this parable we can see how what starts as an assertion, that something exists or that there is some analogy between certain complexes of phenomena, may be reduced step by step to an altogether different status, to an expression perhaps of a "picture preference." The Sceptic says there is no gardener. The Believer says there is a gardener (but invisible, etc.). One man talks about sexual behaviour. Another man prefers to talk of Aphrodite (but knows that there is not really a superhuman person additional to, and somehow responsible for, all sexual phenomena). The process of qualification may be

From New Essays in Philosophical Theology, *edited by Antony Flew and Alasdair MacIntyre (London: SCM Press, 1955), pp. 96–108. Copyright © 1953 by SCM Press Ltd. Reprinted by permission of Macmillan Publishing Company. Footnotes edited.*

checked at any point before the original assertion is completely withdrawn and something of
that first assertion will remain (Tautology). Mr.
Wells's invisible man could not, admittedly, be
seen, but in all other respects he was a man like
the rest of us. But though the process of qualification may be, and of course usually is, checked
in time, it is not always judiciously so halted.
Someone may dissipate his assertion completely
without noticing that he has done so. A fine
brash hypothesis may thus be killed by inches,
the death by a thousand qualifications.

And in this, it seems to me, lies the peculiar
danger, the endemic evil, of theological utterance.
Take such utterances as "God has a plan," "God
created the world," "God loves us as a father loves
his children." They look at first sight very much
like assertions, vast cosmological assertions. Of
course, this is no sure sign that they either are, or
are intended to be, assertions. But let us confine
ourselves to the cases where those who utter such
sentences intend them to express assertions.
(Merely remarking parenthetically that those who
intend or interpret such utterances as crypto-com-
mands, expressions of wishes, disguised ejacula-
tions, concealed ethics, or as anything else but
assertions, are unlikely to succeed in making them
either properly orthodox or practically effective).

Now to assert that such and such is the case is
necessarily equivalent to denying that such and
such is not the case. Suppose then that we are in
doubt as to what someone who gives vent to an
utterance is asserting, or suppose that, more radically, we are sceptical as to whether he is really
asserting anything at all, one way of trying to understand (or perhaps it will be to expose) his utterance is to attempt to find what he would regard
as counting against, or as being incompatible
with, its truth. For if the utterance is indeed an assertion, it will necessarily be equivalent to a denial
of the negation of that assertion. And anything
which would count against the assertion, or
which would induce the speaker to withdraw it
and to admit that it had been mistaken, must be
part of (or the whole of) the meaning of the negation of that assertion. And to know the meaning

of the negation of an assertion, is as near as makes
no matter, to know the meaning of that assertion.
And if there is nothing which a putative assertion
denies then there is nothing which it asserts either: and so it is not really an assertion. When the
Sceptic in the parable asked the Believer, "Just
how does what you call an invisible, intangible,
eternally elusive gardener differ from an imaginary gardener or even from no gardener at all?"
he was suggesting that the Believer's earlier statement had been eroded by qualification so that it
was no longer an assertion at all.

Now it often seems to people who are not religious as if there was no conceivable event or series
of events the occurrence of which would be admitted by sophisticated religious people to be a sufficient reason for conceding "There wasn't a God
after all" or "God does not really love us then."
Someone tells us that God loves us as a father loves
his children. We are reassured. But then we see a
child dying of inoperable cancer of the throat. His
earthly father is driven frantic in his efforts to help,
but his Heavenly Father reveals no obvious sign of
concern. Some qualification is made—God's love
is "not a merely human love" or it is "an in-
scrutable love," perhaps—and we realize that such
sufferings are quite compatible with the truth of
the assertion that "God loves us as a father (but, of
course,...)." We are reassured again. But then
perhaps we ask: What is this assurance of God's
(appropriately qualified) love worth, what is this
apparent guarantee really a guarantee against? Just
what would have to happen not merely (morally
and wrongly) to tempt but also (logically and
rightly) to entitle us to say "God does not love us"
or even "God does not exist"? I therefore put to
the succeeding symposiasts the simple central
questions, "What would have to occur or to have
occurred to constitute for you a disproof of the
love of, or of the existence of, God?"

R. M. HARE

I WISH TO MAKE IT CLEAR that I shall not try to
defend Christianity in particular, but religion in

general—not because I do not believe in Christianity, but because you cannot understand what Christianity is, until you have understood what religion is.

I must begin by confessing that, on the ground marked out by Flew, he seems to me to be completely victorious. I therefore shift my ground by relating another parable. A certain lunatic is convinced that all dons want to murder him. His friends introduce him to all the mildest and most respectable dons that they can find, and after each of them has retired, they say, "You see, he doesn't really want to murder you; he spoke to you in a most cordial manner; surely you are convinced now?" But the lunatic replies "Yes, but that was only his diabolical cunning; he's really plotting against me the whole time, like the rest of them; I know it, I tell you." However many kindly dons are produced, the reaction is still the same.

Now we say that such a person is deluded. But what is he deluded about? About the truth or falsity of an assertion? Let us apply Flew's test to him. There is no behaviour of dons that can be enacted which he will accept as counting against his theory, and therefore his theory, on this test, asserts nothing. But it does not follow that there is no difference between what he thinks about dons and what most of us think about them—otherwise we should not call him a lunatic and ourselves sane, and dons would have no reason to feel uneasy about his presence in Oxford.

Let us call that in which we differ from this lunatic, our respective *bliks*. He has an insane *blik* about dons; we have a sane one. It is important to realize that we have a sane one, not no *blik* at all; for there must be two sides to any argument—if he has a wrong *blik*, then those who are right about dons must have a right one. Flew has shown that a *blik* does not consist in an assertion or system of them, but nevertheless it is very important to have the right *blik*.

Let us try to imagine what it would be like to have different *bliks* about other things than dons. When I am driving my car, it sometimes occurs to me to wonder whether my movements of the steering-wheel will always continue to be followed by corresponding alterations in the direction of the car. I have never had a steering failure, though I have had skids, which must be similar. Moreover, I know enough about how the steering of my car is made, to know the sort of thing that would have to go wrong for the steering to fail—steel joints would have to part, or steel rods break, or something—but how do I know that this won't happen? The truth is, I don't know; I just have a *blik* about steel and its properties, so that normally I trust the steering of my car; but I find it not at all difficult to imagine what it would be like to lose this *blik* and acquire the opposite one. People would say I was silly about steel, but there would be no mistaking the reality of the difference between our respective *bliks*—for example, I should never go in a motor-car. Yet I should hesitate to say that the difference between us was the difference between contradictory assertions. No amount of safe arrivals or bench-tests will remove my *blik* and restore the normal one: for my *blik* is compatible with any finite number of such tests.

It was Hume who taught us that our whole commerce with the world depends upon our *blik* about the world, and that differences between *bliks* about the world cannot be settled by observation of what happens in the world. That was why, having performed the interesting experiment of doubting the ordinary man's *blik* about the world, and showing that no proof could be given to make us adopt one *blik* rather than another, he turned to backgammon to take his mind off the problem. It seems, indeed, to be impossible even to formulate as an assertion the normal *blik* about the world which makes me put my confidence in the future reliability of steel joints, in the continued ability of the road to support my car, and not gape beneath it revealing nothing below; in the general nonhomicidal tendencies of dons; in my own continued well-being (in some sense of that word that I may not now fully understand) if I continued to do what is right according to my lights; in the general likelihood of people like Hitler coming to a bad end. But perhaps a formulation less inadequate than most is to be found in the Psalms: "The earth is weak and all the inhabiters thereof: I bear up the pillars of it."

The mistake of the position which Flew selects for attack is to regard this kind of talk as some sort of *explanation,* as scientists are accustomed to use the word. As such, it would obviously be ludicrous. We no longer believe in God as an Atlas—*nous n'avons pas besoin de cette hypothèse.* But it is nevertheless true to say that, as Hume saw, without a *blik* there can be no explanation; for it is by our *bliks* that we decide what is and what is not an explanation. Suppose we believed that everything that happened, happened by pure chance. This would not of course be an assertion; for it is compatible with anything happening or not happening, and so, incidentally, is its contradictory. But if we had this belief, we should not be able to explain or predict or plan anything. Thus, although we should not be *asserting* anything different from those of a more normal belief, there would be a great difference between us; and this is the sort of difference that there is between those who really believe in God and those who really disbelieve in him.

The word "really" is important, and may excite suspicion. I put it in, because when people have had a good Christian upbringing, as have most of those who now profess not to believe in any sort of religion, it is very hard to discover what they really believe. The reason why they find it so easy to think that they are not religious, is that they have never got into the frame of mind of one who suffers from the doubts to which religion is the answer. Not for them the terrors of the primitive jungle. Having abandoned some of the more picturesque fringes of religion, they think that they have abandoned the whole thing—whereas in fact they still have got, and could not live without, a religion of a comfortably substantial, albeit highly sophisticated, kind, which differs from that of many "religious people" in little more than this, that "religious people" like to sing Psalms about theirs—a very

natural and proper thing to do. But nevertheless there may be a big difference lying behind—the difference between two people who, though side by side, are walking in different directions. I do not know in what direction Flew is walking; perhaps he does not know either. But we have had some examples recently of various ways in which one can walk away from Christianity, and there are any number of possibilities. After all, man has not changed biologically since primitive times; it is his religion that has changed, and it can easily change again. And if you do not think that such changes make a difference, get acquainted with some Sikhs and some Mussulmans of the same Punjabi stock; you will find them quite different sorts of people.

There is an important difference between Flew's parable and my own which we have not yet noticed. The explorers do not *mind* about their garden; they discuss it with interest, but not with concern. But my lunatic, poor fellow, minds about dons, and I mind about the steering of my car; it often has people in it that I care for. It is because I mind very much about what goes on in the garden in which I find myself, that I am unable to share the explorers' detachment.

BASIL MITCHELL

FLEW'S ARTICLE IS SEARCHING and perceptive, but there is, I think, something odd about his conduct of the theologian's case. The theologian surely would not deny that the fact of pain counts against the assertion that God loves men. This very incompatibility generates the most intractable of theological problems—the problem of evil. So the theologian *does* recognize the fact of pain as counting against Christian doctrine. But it is true that he will not allow it—or anything—to count decisively against it; for he is committed by his faith to trust in God. His attitude is not that of the detached observer, but of the believer.

Perhaps this can be brought out by yet another parable. In time of war in an occupied country, a member of the resistance meets one night a stranger who deeply impresses him. They spend that night together in conversation. The Stranger tells the partisan that he himself is on the side of the resistance—indeed that he is in command of it, and urges the partisan to have faith in him no matter what happens. The partisan is utterly convinced at that meeting of the Stranger's sincerity and constancy and undertakes to trust him.

They never meet in conditions of intimacy again. But sometimes the Stranger is seen helping members of the resistance, and the partisan is grateful and says to his friends, "He is on our side."

Sometimes he is seen in the uniform of the police handing over patriots to the occupying power. On these occasions his friends murmur against him, but the partisan still says, "He is on our side." He still believes that, in spite of appearances, the Stranger did not deceive him. Sometimes he asks the Stranger for help and receives it. He is then thankful. Sometimes he asks and does not receive it. Then he says, "The Stranger knows best." Sometimes his friends, in exasperation, say "Well, what *would* he have to do for you to admit that you were wrong and that he is not on our side?" But the partisan refuses to answer. He will not consent to put the Stranger to the test. And sometimes his friends complain, "Well, if *that's* what you mean by his being on our side, the sooner he goes over to the other side the better."

The partisan of the parable does not allow anything to count decisively against the proposition "The Stranger is on our side." This is because he has committed himself to trust the Stranger. But he of course recognizes that the Stranger's ambiguous behaviour *does* count against what he believes about him. It is precisely this situation which constitutes the trial of his faith.

When the partisan asks for help and doesn't get it, what can he do? He can (*a*) conclude that the stranger is not on our side, or (*b*) maintain that he is on our side, but that he has reasons for withholding help.

The first he will refuse to do. How long can he uphold the second position without its becoming just silly?

I don't think one can say in advance. It will depend on the nature of the impression created by the Stranger in the first place. It will depend, too, on the manner in which he takes the Stranger's behaviour. If he blandly dismisses it as of no consequence, as having no bearing upon his belief, it will be assumed that he is thoughtless or insane. And it quite obviously won't do for him to say easily, "Oh, when used of the Stranger the phrase 'is on our side' *means* ambiguous behavior of this sort." In that case he would like the religious man who says blandly of a terrible disaster "It is God's will." No, he will only be regarded as sane and reasonable in his belief, if he experiences in himself the full force of the conflict.

It is here that my parable differs from Hare's. The partisan admits that many things may and do count against his belief: whereas Hare's lunatic who has a *blik* about dons doesn't admit that anything counts against his *blik*. Nothing *can* count against *bliks*. Also the partisan has a reason for having in the first instance committed himself, viz. the character of the Stranger; whereas the lunatic has no reason for his *blik* about dons—because, of course, you can't have reasons for *bliks*.

This means that I agree with Flew that theological utterances must be assertions. The partisan is making an assertion when he says, "The Stranger is on our side."

Do I want to say that the partisan's belief about the Stranger is, in any sense, an explanation? I think I do. It explains and makes sense of the Stranger's behaviour: It helps to explain also the resistance movement in the context of which he appears. In each case it differs from the interpretation which the others put upon the same facts.

"God loves men" resembles "the Stranger is on our side" (and many other significant statements, e.g., historical ones) in not being conclusively falsifiable. They can both be treated in at least three different ways: (1) As provisional hypotheses to be discarded if experience tells against them; (2) As significant articles of faith; (3) As vacuous formulae (expressing, perhaps, a desire for reassurance) to which experience makes no difference and which make no difference to life.

The Christian, once he has committed himself, is precluded by his faith from taking up the first attitude: "Thou shalt not tempt the Lord thy God." He is in constant danger, as Flew has observed, of slipping into the third. But he need not, and, if he does, it is a failure in faith as well as in logic.

NOTE

1. *P.A.S.*, 1944–1945, reprinted as Chapter X of *Logic and Language*, Vol. I (Blackwell, 1951), and in his *Philosophy and Psychoanalysis* (Blackwell, 1953).

For Further Reflection

1. Analyze the different strategies in our three philosophers' statements. Who has made the best case?

2. Should the believer follow Flew's advice and give an account of what would count against his or her faith? Should one's faith be open to revision or rejection on the basis of arguments?

3. Does the believer need to be able to cite evidence before he or she can affirm that it is rational to believe in God?

Religious Belief Without Evidence   II.17

ALVIN PLANTINGA

Alvin Plantinga (1932–   ) is a professor of philosophy at the University of Notre Dame and has written widely in metaphysics and philosophy of religion, including *The Nature of Necessity* (1974) and *God, Freedom and Evil* (1974). In the following essay, he argues that it is rational to believe in God despite the lack of evidence for such belief. Those (like W. K. Clifford) who insist that we must have evidence for all our beliefs simply fail to make their case, because the evidentialists have not set forth clear criteria that would account for all the clear cases of justified beliefs and that would exclude the belief in God. Plantinga outlines the position of the foundationalist-evidentialist as claiming that all justified beliefs must either (1) be "properly basic" by fulfilling certain criteria, or (2) be based on other beliefs that eventually result in a treelike construction with properly basic beliefs at the bottom, or foundation. Plantinga shows that many beliefs we seem to be justified in holding do not fit into the foundationalist framework; such beliefs as memory beliefs (for example, that I ate breakfast this morning), belief in an external world, and belief in other minds. These beliefs do not depend on other beliefs, yet neither are they self-evident, incorrigible (impossible not to believe), or evident to the senses.

Having shown the looseness of what we can accept as "properly basic," Plantinga next shows that the Protestant reformers saw belief in God as "properly basic." He asks us to consider this belief as a legitimate option and examines possible objections to it.

Study Questions

1. What is the main objection many philosophers have raised against belief in God?
2. What does W. K. Clifford say about the correct or ethical way to believe?
3. How does Antony Flew think the debate between theism and atheism should begin? Where should the burden of proof lie? Does Plantinga agree with Flew?
4. What are the two premises of the evidentialist's objection to belief in God?
5. Do Reformed thinkers and theologians accept natural theology (the attempt to establish God's existence through human reason)? Why (or why not)?
6. How do Reformed theologians view belief in God?
7. What is the difference between *prima facie* obligations and *all-things-considered* obligations?
8. Plantinga links evidentialism with classical foundationalism. What is classical foundationalism?
9. What does Plantinga say is wrong with classical foundationalism?
10. What is the Great Pumpkin objection?

THE EVIDENTIALIST OBJECTION TO THEISTIC BELIEF

MANY PHILOSOPHERS—Clifford, Blanshard, Russell, Scriven, and Flew, to name a few— have argued that belief in God is irrational, or unreasonable, or not rationally acceptable, or intellectually irresponsible, or somehow noetically below par because, as they say, there is *insufficient evidence* for it.[1] Bertrand Russell was once asked what he would say if, after dying, he were brought into the presence of God and asked why he hadn't been a believer. Russell's reply: "I'd say, 'Not enough evidence, God! Not enough evidence!'"[2] I don't know just how such a response would be received, but Russell, like many others, held that theistic belief is unreasonable because there is insufficient evidence for it. We all remember W. K. Clifford, that delicious *enfant terrible,* as William

James called him, and his insistence that it is immoral, wicked, and monstrous, and maybe even impolite to accept a belief for which you don't have sufficient evidence:

> Who so would deserve well of his fellows in this matter will guard the purity of his belief with a very fanaticism of jealous care, lest at any time it should rest on an unworthy object, and catch a stain which can never be wiped away.

He adds that if a

> belief has been accepted on insufficient evidence, the pleasure is a stolen one. Not only does it deceive ourselves by giving us a sense of power which we do not really possess, but it is sinful, because it is stolen in defiance of our duty to mankind. That duty is to guard ourselves from such beliefs as from a pestilence which may shortly master our body and spread to the rest of the town.

From Religious Experience and Religious Belief, *ed. Joseph Runzo and Craig Ihara (New York: University Press of America, 1986). Reprinted with permission.*

and finally:

> To sum up: it is wrong always, everywhere, and for anyone to believe anything upon insufficient evidence.

(It is not hard to detect, in these quotations, the "tone of robustious pathos" with which James credits him.) Clifford, of course, held that one who accepts belief in God *does* accept that belief on insufficient evidence, and has indeed defied his duty to mankind. More recently, Bertrand Russell has endorsed the evidentialist injunction "Give to any hypothesis which is worth your while to consider, just that degree or credence which the evidence warrants."

More recently, Antony Flew[3] has commended what he calls Clifford's "luminous and compulsive essay" (perhaps "compulsive" here is a misprint for "compelling"), and Flew goes on to claim that there is, in his words a "presumption of atheism." What is a presumption of atheism, and why should we think there is one? Flew puts it as follows:

> The debate about the existence of God should properly begin from the presumption of atheism . . . the onus of proof must lie upon the theist. The word "atheism," however, has in this contention to be construed unusually. Whereas nowadays the usual meaning of "atheist" in English is "someone who asserts there is no such being as God," I want the word to be understood not positively but negatively. I want the original Greek prefix "a" to be read in the same way in "atheist" as it is customarily read in such other Greco-English words as "amoral," "atypical," and "asymmetrical." In this interpretation an atheist becomes not someone who positively asserts the non-existence of God, but someone who is simply not a theist.
>
> What the protagonist of my presumption of atheism wants to show is that the debate about the existence of God ought to be conducted in a particular way, and that the issue should be seen in a certain perspective. His thesis about the onus of proof involves that it is up to the theist: first to introduce and to defend his proposed concept of God, and second, to provide

sufficient reason for believing that this concept of his does in fact have an application.

How shall we understand this? What does it mean, for example, to say that the debate "should properly begin from the presumption of atheism"? What sorts of things do debates begin from, and what is it for one to begin from such a thing? Perhaps Flew means something like this: to speak of where a debate should begin is to speak of the sorts of premises to which the affirmative and negative sides can properly appeal in arguing their cases. Suppose you and I are debating the question whether, say, the United States has a right to seize Mideast oil fields if the OPEC countries refuse to sell us oil at what we think is a fair price. I take the affirmative, and produce for my conclusion an argument one premise of which is the proposition that the United States has indeed a right to seize these oil fields under those conditions. Doubtless that maneuver would earn me very few points. Similarly, a debate about the existence of God cannot sensibly start from the assumption that God does indeed exist. That is to say, the affirmative can't properly appeal, in its arguments, to such premises as that there is such a person as God; if it could, it'd have much too easy a time of it. So in this sense of "start," Flew is quite right: the debate can't start from the assumption that God exists.

Of course, it is also true that the debate can't start from the assumption that God does *not* exist; using "atheism" in its ordinary sense, there is equally a presumption of aatheism (which, by a familiar principle of logic, reduces to theism). So it looks as if there is in Flew's sense a presumption of atheism, all right, but in that same sense an equal presumption of aatheism. If this is what Flew means, then what he says is entirely correct, if something of a truism.

In another passage, however, Flew seems to understand the presumption of atheism in quite another different fashion:

> It is by reference to this inescapable demand for grounds that the presumption of atheism is justi-

fied. If it is to be established that there is a God, then we have to have good grounds for believing that this is indeed so. Until or unless some such grounds are produced we have literally no reason at all for believing; and in that situation the only reasonable posture must be that of either the negative atheist or the agnostic.

Here we have the much more substantial suggestion that it is unreasonable or irrational to accept theistic belief in the absence of sufficient grounds or reasons. And of course Flew, along with Russell, Clifford, and many others, holds that in fact there aren't sufficient grounds or evidence for belief in God. The evidentialist objection, therefore, appeals to the following two premises:

(A) It is irrational or unreasonable to accept theistic belief in the absence of sufficient evidence or reasons.

and

(B) There is no evidence, or at any rate not sufficient evidence, for the proposition that God exists.

(B), I think, is at best dubious. At present, however, I'm interested in the objector's other premise—the claim that it is irrational or unreasonable to accept theistic belief in the absence of evidence or reasons. Why suppose *that's* true? Why suppose a theist must have evidence or reason to think there *is* evidence for this belief, if he is not to be irrational? This isn't just *obvious*, after all.

Now many Reformed thinkers and theologians[4] have rejected *natural theology* (thought of as the attempt to provide proofs or arguments for the existence of God). They have held not merely that the proffered arguments are unsuccessful, but that the whole enterprise is in some way radically misguided. I have argued (1980) that the Reformed rejection of natural theology is best construed as an inchoate and unfocused rejection of (A). What these Reformed thinkers really mean to hold, I think, is that belief in God is properly basic: it need not be based on argument or evidence from other propositions at all. They mean to hold that the believer is entirely

within his intellectual right in believing as he does, even if he doesn't know of any good theistic argument (deductive or inductive), even if he doesn't believe that there is any such argument, and even if in fact no such argument exists. They hold that it is perfectly rational to accept belief in God without accepting it on the basis of any other beliefs or propositions at all. Why suppose that the believer must have evidence if he is not to be irrational? Why should anyone accept (A)? What is to be said in its favor?

Suppose we begin by asking what the objector means by describing a belief as *irrational*. What is the force of his claim that the theistic belief is irrational and how is it to be understood? The first thing to see is that this claim is rooted in a *normative* contention. It lays down conditions that must be met by anyone whose system of beliefs is *rational;* and here "rational" is to be taken as a normative or evaluative term. According to the objector, there is a right way and a wrong way with respect to belief. People have responsibilities, duties and obligations with respect to their believings just as they do with respect to their actions—or if we think believings are a kind of action, their *other* actions. Professor Brand Blanshard puts this clearly:

> everywhere and always belief has an ethical aspect. There is such a thing as a general ethics of the intellect. The main principle of that ethic I hold to be the same inside and outside religion. This principle is simple and sweeping: Equate your assent to the evidence. (*Reason and Belief,* p. 401)

and according to Michael Scriven:

> Now even belief in something for which there is no evidence, i.e., a belief which goes beyond the evidence, although a lesser sin than a belief in something which is contrary to well-established laws, is plainly irrational in that it simply amounts to attaching belief where it is not justified. So the proper alternative, when there is no evidence, is not mere suspension of belief, e.g., about Santa Claus, it is disbelief. It most certainly is not faith. (*Primary Philosophy,* p. 103)

Perhaps this sort of obligation is really a special case of a more general moral obligation; or perhaps, on the other hand, it is *sui generis*. In any event, says the objector, there are such obligations: to conform to them is to be rational and to go against them is to be irrational.

Now here the objector seems right; there are duties and obligations with respect to beliefs. One's own welfare and that of others sometimes depends on what one believes. If we're descending the Grand Teton and I'm setting the anchor for the 120-foot rappel into the Upper Saddle, I have an obligation to form such beliefs as *this anchor point is solid* only on the basis of careful scrutiny and testing. One commissioned to gather intelligence—the spies Joshua sent into Canaan, for example—has an obligation to get it right. I have an obligation with respect to the belief that Justin Martyr was a Latin apologist—an obligation arising from the fact that I teach medieval philosophy, must make a declaration on this issue, and am obliged not to mislead my students here. The precise *form* of these obligations may be hard to specify: Am I obliged to believe that J. M. was a Latin apologist if and only if J. M. *was* a Latin apologist? Or to form a belief on this topic only after the appropriate amount of checking and investigating? Or maybe just to tell the students the truth about it, whatever I myself believe in the privacy of my own study? Or to tell them what's generally thought by those who should know? In the rappel case: Do I have a duty to believe that the anchor point is solid if and only if it is? Or just to check carefully before forming the belief? Or perhaps there's no obligation to believe at all, but only to *act on* a certain belief only after appropriate investigation. In any event, it seems plausible to hold that there are obligations and norms with respect to belief, and I do not intend to contest this assumption.

The objector begins, therefore, from the plausible contention that there are duties or obligations with respect to belief: call them *intellectual duties*. These duties can be understood in several ways. First, we could construe them teleologically; we could adopt an intellectual utili-

tarianism. Here the rough idea is that our intellectual obligations arise out of a connection between our beliefs and what is intrinsically good and intrinsically bad, and our intellectual obligations are just a special case of the general obligation so to act to maximize good and minimize evil. Perhaps this is how W. K. Clifford thinks of the matter. If people accepted such propositions as *this DC-10 is airworthy* when the evidence is insufficient, the consequences could be disastrous; so perhaps some of us, at any rate, have an obligation to believe that proposition only in the presence of adequate evidence. The intellectual utilitarian could be an ideal utilitarian; he could hold that certain epistemic states are intrinsically valuable—knowledge, perhaps, or believing the truth, or a skeptical and judicial temper that is not blown about by every wind of doctrine. Among our duties, then, is a duty to try to bring about these valuable states of affairs. Perhaps this is how Professor Roderick Chisholm is to be understood when he says

> Let us consider the concept of what might be called an "intellectual requirement." We may assume that every person is subject to a purely intellectual requirement: that of trying his best to bring it about that, for every proposition that he considers, he accepts it if and only if it is true. (*Theory of Knowledge*, 2nd ed., p. 9)

Secondly, we could construe intellectual obligations *aretetically*; we could adopt what Professor Frankena calls a "mixed ethics of virtue" with respect to the intellect. There are valuable noetic or intellectual states (whether intrinsically or extrinsically valuable); there are also the corresponding intellectual virtues, the habits of acting so as to produce or promote or enhance those valuable states. One's intellectual obligations, then, are to try to produce and enhance these intellectual virtues in oneself and others.

Thirdly, we could construe intellectual obligations *deontologically*; we could adopt a *pure* ethics of obligation with respect to the intellect. Perhaps there are intellectual obligations that do not arise from any connection with good or evil, but attach to us just by virtue of our having the sorts of noetic powers human beings do in fact display. The quotation from Chisholm could also be understood along these lines.

Intellectual obligations, therefore, can be understood teleologically or aretetically or deontologically. And perhaps there are purely intellectual obligations of the following sorts. Perhaps I have a duty not to take as basic a proposition whose denial seems self-evident. Perhaps I have a duty to take as basic the proposition *I seem to see a tree* under certain conditions. With respect to certain kinds of propositions, perhaps I have a duty to believe them only if I have evidence for them, and a duty to proportion the strength of my belief to the strength of my evidence.

Of course, these would be *prima facie* obligations. One presumably has an obligation not to take bread from the grocery store without permission and another to tell the truth. Both can be overridden, in specific circumstances, by other obligations—in the first case, perhaps, an obligation to feed my starving children and in the second, an obligation to protect a human life. So we must distinguish *prima facie* duties or obligations from *all-things-considered* or *on-balance (ultima facie?)* obligations. I have a *prima facie* obligation to tell the truth; in a given situation, however, that obligation may be overridden by others, so that my duty, all things considered, is to tell a lie. This is the grain of truth contained in situation ethics and the ill-named "new morality."

And *prima facie* intellectual obligations can conflict, just as obligations of other sorts. Perhaps I have a *prima facie* obligation to believe what seems to me self-evident, and what seems to me to follow self-evidently from what seems to me self-evident. But what if, as in the Russell paradoxes, something that seems self-evidently false apparently follows, self-evidently, from what seems self-evidently true? Here *prima facie* intellectual obligations conflict, and no matter what I do I will violate a *prima facie* obligation. Another example: in reporting the Grand Teton rappel, I neglected to mention the violent electrical storm coming in from the southwest; to escape it we must get off in a hurry, so that I have a *prima facie* obligation to inspect the anchor point carefully, but anchor to set up the rappel rapidly, which means I can't spend a lot of time inspecting the anchor point.

Thus lightly armed, suppose we return to the evidential objector. Does he mean to hold that the theist without evidence is violating some intellectual obligation? If so, which one? Does he claim, for example, that the theist is violating his *ultima facie* intellectual obligation in thus believing? Perhaps he thinks anyone who believes in God without evidence is violating his all-things-considered intellectual duty. This, however, seems unduly harsh. What about the fourteen-year-old theist brought up to believe in God in a community where everyone believes? This fourteen-year-old theist, we may suppose, doesn't believe on the basis of evidence. He doesn't argue thus: everyone around here says God loves us and cares for us; most of what everyone around here says is true; so probably *that's* true. Instead, he simply believes what he's taught. Is he violating an all-things-considered intellectual duty? Surely not. And what about the mature theist—Thomas Aquinas, let's say—who thinks he *does* have adequate evidence? Let's suppose he's wrong; let's suppose all of his arguments are failures. Nevertheless, he has reflected long, hard, and conscientiously on the matter and thinks he *does* have adequate evidence. Shall we suppose he's violating an all-things-considered intellectual duty here? I should think not. So construed, the objector's contention is totally implausible.

Perhaps, then, he is to be understood as claiming that there is a *prima facie* intellectual duty not to believe in God without evidence. This duty can be overridden by circumstances, of course, but there is a *prima facie* obligation to believe propositions of this sort only on the basis of evidence. But here too there are problems. The suggestion is that I now have the *prima facie* obligation to believe propositions of this sort only on the basis of evidence. I have a *prima facie* duty to comply with the following command: either have evidence or don't believe.

But this may be a command I can't comply with. The objector thinks there *isn't* adequate evidence for this belief, so presumably I can't *have* adequate evidence for it, unless we suppose I could create some. And it is also not within my power to refrain from believing this proposition. My beliefs aren't for the most part directly within my control. If you order me now, for example, to cease believing that the earth is very old, there's no way I can comply with your order. But in the same way it isn't within my power to cease believing in God now. So this alleged *prima facie* duty is one it isn't within my power to comply with. But how can I have a *prima facie* duty to do what isn't within my power to do?

Presumably, then, the objector means to be understood in still another fashion. Although it is not within my power now to cease believing now, there may be a series of actions now, such that I can now take the first, and after taking the first, will be able to take the second, and so on, and after taking the whole series of actions, I will no longer believe in God. Perhaps the objector thinks it is my *prima facie* duty to undertake whatever sort of regimen will at some time in the future result in my not believing without evidence. Perhaps I should attend a Universalist Unitarian Church, for example, and consort with members of the Rationalist Society of America. Perhaps I should read a lot of Voltaire and Bertrand Russell. Even if I can't now stop believing without evidence, perhaps there are other actions I can now take, such that if I do take them, then at some time in the future I won't be in this deplorable condition.

There is still another option available to the objector. He need not hold that the theist without evidence is violating some duty, *prima facie*, *ultima facie* or otherwise. Consider someone who believes that Venus is smaller than Mercury, not because he has evidence, but because he finds it amusing to believe what everyone disbelieves— or consider someone who holds this belief on the basis of an outrageously bad argument. Perhaps there is no obligation he has failed to meet; nevertheless his intellectual condition is defective in

some way; or perhaps alternatively there is a commonly achieved excellence he fails to display. Perhaps he is like someone who is easily gulled, or walks with a limp, or has a serious astigmatism, or is unduly clumsy. And perhaps the evidentialist objection is to be understood, not as the claim that the theist without evidence has failed to meet some obligation, but that he suffers from a certain sort of intellectual deficiency. If this is the objector's view, then his proper attitude towards the theist would be one of sympathy rather than censure.

These are some of the ways, then, in which the evidentialist objection could be developed, and of course there are still other possibilities. For ease of exposition, let us take the claim deontologically; what I shall say will apply *mutatis mutandis* if we take it one of the other ways. The evidentialist objector, then, holds that it is irrational to believe in God without evidence. He doesn't typically hold, however, that the same goes for *every* proposition; for given certain plausible conditions on the evidence relation it would follow that if we believe anything, then we are under obligation to believe infinitely many propositions. Let's say that proposition p is *basic* for a person S if S believes p but does not have evidence for p; and let's say that p is *properly basic* for S if S is within his epistemic rights in taking p as basic. The evidentialist objection, therefore, presupposes some view about what sorts of propositions are correctly or rightly or justifiably taken as basic; it presupposes a view about what is properly basic. And the minimally relevant claim for the evidentialist objector is that belief in God is *not* properly basic. Typically this objection has been rooted in some form of *classical foundationalism*, an enormously popular picture or total way of looking at faith, knowledge, justified belief, rationality and allied topics. This picture has been widely accepted ever since the days of Plato and Aristotle; its near relatives, perhaps, remain the dominant ways of thinking about these topics. According to the classical foundationalist, some propositions are *properly* or *rightly* basic for a person and some are not. Those that are not are rationally accepted only on the basis of *evidence* where the evidence must trace back, ultimately, to what is properly basic. Now there are two varieties of classical foundationalism. According to the ancient and medieval variety, a proposition is properly basic for a person *S* if and only if it is either self-evident to *S* or "evident to the senses," to use Aquinas' term, for *S*; according to the modern variety, a proposition is properly basic for *S* if and only if it is either self- evident to *S* or incorrigible for him. For ease of exposition, let's say that classical foundationalism is the disjunction of ancient and medieval with modern foundationalism; according to the classical foundationalist, then, a proposition is properly basic for a person *S* if and only if it is either self-evident to *S* or incorrigible for *S* or evident to the senses for *S*.

Now I said that the evidentialist objection to theistic belief is typically rooted in classical foundationalism. Insofar as it is so rooted, it is *poorly* rooted. For classical foundationalism is self-referentially incoherent. Consider the main tenet of classical foundationalism:

(C)   *p* is properly basic for *S* if and only if *p* is self-evident, incorrigible, or evident to the senses for *S*.

Now of course the classical foundationalist accepts (C) and proposes that we do so as well. And either he takes (C) as basic or he doesn't. If he doesn't, then if he is rational in accepting it, he must by his own claims have an argument for it from propositions that are properly basic, by argument forms whose corresponding conditionals are properly basic. Classical foundationalists do not, so far as I know, offer such arguments for (C). I suspect the reason is that they don't know of any arguments of that sort for (C). It is certainly hard to see what such an argument would be. Accordingly, classical foundationalists probably take (C) as basic. But then according to (C) itself, if (C) is properly taken as basic, it must be either self-evident, incorrigible, or evident to the senses for the foundationalist, and clearly it isn't any of those. If the founda-

tionalist takes (C) as basic, therefore, he is self-referentially inconsistent. We must conclude, I think, that the classical foundationalist is in self-referential hot water—his own acceptance of the central tenet of his view is irrational by his own standards.

OBJECTIONS TO TAKING BELIEF IN GOD AS BASIC

Insofar as the evidentialist objection is rooted in classical foundationalism, it is poorly rooted indeed; and so far as I know, no one has developed and articulated any other reason for supporting that belief in God is not properly basic. Of course it doesn't follow that it *is* properly basic; perhaps the class of properly basic propositions is broader than classical foundationalists think, but still not broad enough to admit belief in God. But why think so? What might be the objections to the Reformed view that belief in God is properly basic?

I've heard it argued that if I have no evidence for the existence of God, then if I accept that proposition, my belief will be *groundless*, or *gratuitous*, or *arbitrary*. I think this is an error; let me explain.

Suppose we consider perceptual beliefs, memory beliefs, and beliefs ascribing mental states to other persons; such beliefs as

(1) I see a tree.

(2) I had breakfast this morning.

(3) That person is angry.

Although beliefs of this sort are typically and properly taken as basic, it would be a mistake to describe them as *groundless*. Upon having experience of a certain sort, I believe that I am perceiving a tree. In the typical case I do not hold this belief on the basis of other beliefs; it is nonetheless not groundless. My having that characteristic sort of experience—to use Professor Chisholm's language, my being appeared freely to—plays a crucial role in the formation and justification of that belief. We might say this experience, together, perhaps, with other circumstances, is what *justifies* me in holding it; this is the *ground* of my justification, and, by extension, the ground of the belief itself.

If I see someone displaying typical pain behavior, I take it that he or she is in pain. Again, I don't take the displayed behavior as *evidence* for that belief; I don't infer that belief from others I hold; I don't accept it on the basis of other beliefs. Still, my perceiving the pain behavior plays a unique role in the formation and justification of that belief; as in the previous case, it forms the ground of my justification for the belief in question. The same holds for memory beliefs. I seem to remember having breakfast this morning; that is, I have an inclination to believe the proposition that I had breakfast, along with a certain past-tinged experience that is familiar to all but hard to describe. Perhaps we should say that I am appeared to pastly, but perhaps that insufficiently distinguishes the experience in question from that accompanying beliefs about the past not grounded in my own memory. The phenomenology of memory is a rich and unexplored realm; here I have no time to explore it. In this case as in the others, however, there is a justifying circumstance present, a condition that forms the ground of my justification for accepting the memory belief in question.

In each of these cases, a belief is taken as basic, and in each case properly taken as basic. In each case there is some circumstance or condition that confers justification; there is a circumstance that serves as the *ground* of justification. So in each case there will be some true proposition of the sort:

(4) In condition *C*, *S* is justified in taking *p* as basic. Of course *C* will vary with *p*.

For a perceptual judgment such as

(5) I see a rose-colored wall before me,

C will include my being appeared to in a certain fashion. No doubt *C* will include more. If I'm appeared to in the familiar fashion but know that I am wearing rose-colored glasses, or that I am suffering from a disease that causes me to be thus appeared to, no matter what the color of the nearby objects, then I am not justified in taking (5) as basic. Similarly for memory. Suppose I know that my memory is unreliable; it often plays me tricks. In particular, when I seem to remember having breakfast, then, more often than not, I *haven't* had breakfast. Under these conditions I am not justified in taking it as basic that I had breakfast, even though I seem to remember that I did.

So being appropriately appeared to, in the perceptual case, is not sufficient for justification; some further condition—a condition hard to state in detail—is clearly necessary. The central point, here, however, is that a belief is properly basic only in certain conditions; these conditions are, we might say, the ground of its justification and, by extension, the ground of the belief itself. In this sense, basic beliefs are not, or are not necessarily, *groundless* beliefs.

Now similar things may be said about belief in God. When the Reformers claim that this belief is properly basic, they do not mean to say, of course, that there are no justifying circumstances for it, or that it is in that sense groundless or gratuitous. Quite the contrary. Calvin holds that God "reveals and daily discloses himself in the whole workmanship of the universe," and the divine art "reveals itself in the innumerable and yet distinct and well-ordered variety of the heavenly host." God has so created us that we have a tendency or disposition to see his hand in the world about us. More precisely, there is in us a disposition to believe propositions of the sort *this flower was created by God* or *this vast and intricate universe was created by God* when we contemplate the flower or behold the starry heavens or think about the vast reaches of the universe.

Calvin recognizes, at least implicitly, that other sorts of conditions may trigger this disposition. Upon reading the Bible, one may be impressed with a deep sense that God is speaking to one. Upon having done what I know is cheap, or wrong, or wicked, I may feel guilty in God's sight and form the belief *God disapproves of what I've done.* Upon confession and repentance, I may feel forgiven, forming the belief *God forgives me for what I've done.* A person in grave danger may turn to God, asking for His protection and help, and of course he or she then forms the belief that God is indeed able to hear and help if He sees fit. When life is sweet and satisfying, a spontaneous sense of gratitude may well up within the soul; someone in this condition may thank and praise the Lord for His goodness, and will of course form the accompanying belief that indeed the Lord is to be thanked and praised.

There are therefore many conditions and circumstances that call forth belief in God: guilt, gratitude, danger, a sense of God's presence, a sense that He speaks, perception of various parts of the universe. A complete job would explore the phenomenology of all these conditions and of more besides. This is a large and important topic, but here I can only point to the existence of these conditions.

Of course, none of the beliefs I mentioned a moment ago is the simple belief that God exists. What we have instead are such beliefs as

(6) God is speaking to me.

(7) God has created all this.

(8) God disapproves of what I have done.

(9) God forgives me.

(10) God is to be thanked and praised.

These propositions are properly basic in the right circumstances. But it is quite consistent with this to suppose that the proposition *there is such a person as God* is neither properly basic nor taken as basic by those who believe in God. Perhaps what they take as basic are such propositions as (6)–(10), believing in the existence of God on the basis of such propositions. From this point of view, it isn't exactly right to say that belief in God is properly basic; more exactly, what are properly basic are such propositions (6)–(10), each of which self-evidently entails that God exists. It isn't the rela-

tively high level and general proposition *God exists* that is properly basic, but instead propositions detailing some of His attributes or actions.

Suppose we return to the analogy between belief in God and belief in the existence of perceptual objects, other persons, and the past. Here too it is relatively specific and concrete propositions rather than their more general and abstract colleagues that are properly basic. Perhaps such items as

(11) There are trees.

(12) There are other persons.

(13) The world has existed for more than 5 minutes

are not properly basic; it is instead such propositions as

(14) I see a tree.

(15) That person is pleased.

(16) I had breakfast more than an hour ago

that deserve the accolade. Of course, propositions of the latter sort immediately and self-evidently entail propositions of the former sort, and perhaps there is thus no harm in speaking of the former as properly basic, even though so to speak is to speak a bit loosely.

The same must be said about belief in God. We may say, speaking loosely, that belief in God is properly basic; strictly speaking, however, it is probably not that proposition but such propositions as (6)–(10) that enjoy that status. But the main point, here, is this: belief in God or (6)–(10) are properly basic; to say so, however, is not to deny that there are justifying conditions for these beliefs, or conditions that confer justification on one who accepts them as basic. They are therefore not groundless or gratuitous.

A second objection I've often heard: If belief in God is properly basic, why can't *just any* belief be properly basic? What about voodoo or astrology? What about the belief that the Great Pumpkin returns every Halloween? Could I properly take *that* as basic? And if I can't, why can I properly take belief in God as basic? Suppose I believe that if I flap my arms with sufficient vigor, I can take off and fly about the room; could I defend myself against the charge of irrationality by claiming this belief is basic? If we say that belief in God is properly basic, won't we be committed to holding that just anything, or nearly anything, can properly be taken as basic, thus throwing wide the gates to irrationalism and superstition?

Certainly not. What might lead one to think the Reformed epistemologist is in this kind of trouble? The fact that he rejects the criteria for proper basicality purveyed by classical foundationalism? But why should *that* be thought to commit him to such tolerance or irrationality? Consider an analogy. In the palmy days of positivism, the positivists went about confidently wielding their verifiability criterion and declaring meaningless much that was obviously meaningful. Now suppose someone rejected a formulation of that criterion—the one to be found in the second edition of A. J. Ayer's *Language, Truth and Logic,* for example. Would that mean she was committed to holding that

(17) 'Twas brillig; and the slithy toves did
          gyre and gimble in the wabe

contrary to appearances, makes good sense? Of course not. But then the same goes for the Reformed epistemologist; the fact that he rejects the Classical Foundationalist's criterion of proper basicality does not mean that he is committed to supposing just anything is properly basic.

But what then is the problem? Is it that the Reformed epistemologist not only rejects those criteria for proper basicality, but seems in no hurry to produce what he takes to be a better substitute? If he has no such criterion, how can he fairly reject belief in the Great Pumpkin as properly basic?

This objection betrays an important misconception. How do we rightly arrive at or develop criteria for meaningfulness, or justified belief, or proper basicality? Where do they come from? Must one have such a criterion before one can sensibly make any judgments—positive or negative—about proper basicality? Surely not. Suppose I don't know of a satisfactory substitute for the criteria proposed by Classical Foundationalism; I am

nevertheless entirely within my rights in holding that certain propositions are not properly basic in certain conditions. Some propositions seem self-evident when in fact they are not; that is the lesson of some of the Russell paradoxes. Nevertheless it would be irrational to take as basic the denial of a proposition that seems self-evident to you. Similarly, suppose it seems to you that you see a tree; you would then be irrational in taking as basic the proposition that you don't see a tree, or that there aren't any trees. In the same way, even if I don't know of some illuminating criterion of meaning, I can quite properly declare (17) meaningless.

And this raises an important question—one Roderick Chisholm has taught us to ask. What is the status of the criteria for knowledge, or proper basicality, or justified belief? Typically, these are universal statements. The modern foundationalist's criterion for proper basicality, for example, is doubly universal:

(18) For any proposition *A* and person *S*, *A*
          is properly basic for *S* if and only if *A* is
          incorrigible for *S* or self-evident to *S*.

But how could one know a thing like that? What are its credentials? Clearly enough, (18) isn't self-evident or just obviously true. But if it isn't, how does one arrive at it? What sorts of arguments would be appropriate? Of course, a foundationalist might find (18) so appealing, he simply takes it to be true, neither offering argument for it, nor accepting it on the basis of other things he believes. If he does so, however, his noetic structure will be self-referentially incoherent. (18) itself is neither self-evident nor incorrigible; hence in accepting (18) as basic, the modern foundationalist violates the condition of proper basicality he himself lays down in accepting it. On the other hand, perhaps the foundationalist will try to produce some argument for it from premises that are self-evident or incorrigible: it is exceedingly hard to see, however, what such an argument might be like. And until he has produced such arguments, what shall the rest of us do—we who do not find (18) at all obvious or compelling? How could he use (18) to show us that belief in God, for example, is not properly basic? Why should we believe (18), or pay it any attention?

The fact is, I think, that neither (18) nor any other revealing necessary and sufficient condition for proper basicality follows from clearly self-evident premises by clearly acceptable arguments. And hence the proper way to arrive at such a criterion is, broadly speaking, *inductive*. We must assemble examples of beliefs and conditions such that the former are obviously properly basic in the latter, and examples of beliefs and conditions such that the former are obviously *not* properly basic in the latter. We must then frame hypotheses on the necessary and sufficient conditions of proper basicality and test these hypotheses by reference to those examples. Under the right conditions, for example, it is clearly rational to believe that you see a human person before you: a being who has thoughts and feelings, who knows and believes things, who makes decisions and acts. It is clear, furthermore, that you are under no obligation to reason to this belief from others you hold; under those conditions that belief is properly basic for you. But then (18) must be mistaken; the belief in question, under those circumstances, is properly basic, though neither self-evident nor incorrigible for you. Similarly, you may seem to remember that you had breakfast this morning, and perhaps you know of no reason to suppose your memory is playing you tricks. If so, you are entirely justified in taking that belief as basic. Of course it isn't properly basic on the criteria offered by classical foundationalists, but that fact counts not against you but against those criteria.

Accordingly, criteria for proper basicality must be reached from below rather than above; they should not be presented as *obiter dicta*, but argued to and tested by a relevant set of examples. But there is no reason to assume, in advance, that everyone will agree on the examples. The Christian will of course suppose that belief in God is entirely proper and rational; if he doesn't accept this belief on the basis of other propositions, he will conclude that it is basic for him and quite properly so. Followers of Bertrand Russell and

Madelyn Murray O'Hare may disagree, but how is that relevant? Must my criteria, or those of the Christian community, conform to their examples? Surely not. The Christian community is responsible to *its* set of examples, not to theirs.

Accordingly, the Reformed epistemologist can properly hold that belief in the Great Pumpkin is not properly basic, even though he holds that belief in God *is* properly basic and even if he has no full-fledged criterion of proper basicality. Of course he is committed to supposing that there is a relevant *difference* between belief in God and belief in the Great Pumpkin, if he holds that the former, but not the latter, is properly basic. But this should prove no great embarrassment; there are plenty of candidates. These candidates are to be found in the neighborhood of the conditions I mentioned in the last section that justify and ground belief in God. Thus, for example, the Reformed epistemologist may concur with Calvin in holding that God has implanted in us a natural tendency to see his hand in the world around us; the same cannot be said for the Great Pumpkin, there being no Great Pumpkin and no natural tendency to accept beliefs about the Great Pumpkin.

By way of conclusion, then: being self-evident, or incorrigible, or evident to the senses is not a necessary condition of proper basicality. Furthermore, one who holds that belief in God *is* properly basic is not thereby committed to the idea that belief in God is groundless or gratuitous or without justifying circumstances. And even if he lacks a general criterion of proper basicality, he is not obliged to suppose that just any, or nearly any, belief—belief in the Great Pumpkin, for example—is properly basic. Like everyone should, he begins with examples, and he may take belief in the Great Pumpkin, in certain circumstances, as a paradigm of irrational basic belief.

NOTES

1. See, for example, Blanshard, *Reason and Belief,* pp. 400ff; Clifford, "The Ethics of Belief," pp. 345ff;

Flew, *The Presumption of Atheism*, p. 22; Russell, "Why I Am Not a Christian," pp. 3ff; and Scriven, *Primary Philosophy*, pp. 87ff. In Plantinga, "Is Belief in God Rational?"

2. W. Salmon, "Religion and Science: A New Look at Hume's Dialogues," *Philosophical Studies* 33 (1978), p. 176.

3. A. G. N. Flew, *The Presumption of Atheism* (London: Pemberton Publishing Co., 1976).

4. A Reformed thinker or theologian is one whose intellectual sympathies lie with the Protestant tradition going back to John Calvin (not someone who was formerly a theologian and has since seen the light).

For Further Reflection

1. Has Plantinga successfully defended the view that one has no rational obligation to support one's belief in God with evidence? Explain. Compare Plantinga's view with the argument that anyone who claims that something exists must be able to give good reasons for its existence.

2. Is there a relevant difference between believing in the Great Pumpkin and believing in God? Could a worshiper of a devil use Plantinga's argument to claim that there is a natural human tendency to believe in a Creator Devil?

Suggestions for Further Reading

GENERAL

Davies, Brian. *An Introduction to the Philosophy of Religion*. Oxford: Oxford University Press, 1982. Readable, reliable, written from a distinctive theistic framework.

Harrison, Jonathan. *God, Freedom and Immortality*. London: Aylesbury, 1999.

Hick, John. *Arguments for the Existence of God*. London: Macmillan, 1971. A clearly written, insightful examination.

Mackie, J. L. *The Miracle of Theism*. Oxford: Oxford University Press, 1982. A lively discussion of the proofs by one of the ablest atheist philosophers of our time, but uneven.

Matson, Wallace. *The Existence of God*. Ithaca, NY: Cornell University Press, 1965. A cogent attack on the traditional arguments.

Moreland, J. P. and Nielsen, Kay. *Does God Exist? The Great Debate*. Buffalo, NY: Prometheus, 1995.

Pojman, Louis. *Philosophy of Religion: An Anthology*, 3rd ed. Belmont, CA: Wadsworth, 1998.

Rowe, William. *Philosophy of Religion: An Introduction*. Belmont, CA: Dickenson, 1978. A very readable and reliable introduction for beginners.

Swinburne, Richard. *The Existence of God*. Oxford: Clarendon, 1979. Perhaps the most sustained, if not the overall best, defense of the traditional arguments since the Middle Ages.

Yandell, Keith. *Christianity and Philosophy*. Grand Rapids, MI: Eerdmans, 1984. A rigorously analytic approach, crammed full of outlines of arguments without as much discussion as one might like.

THE COSMOLOGICAL ARGUMENT

Craig, William. *The Cosmological Argument from Plato to Leibniz*. New York: Barnes & Noble, 1980. A good survey of the history of the argument.

Rowe, William. *The Cosmological Argument*. Princeton, NJ: Princeton University Press, 1975. A very thorough and penetrating study of the classic formulations (especially Aquinas, Scotus, and Clark).

THE TELEOLOGICAL ARGUMENT

McPherson, Thomas. *The Argument from Design*. London: Macmillan, 1972. A good introduction to the various forms of the argument.

Salmon, Wesley. "Religion and Science: A New Look at Hume's Dialogue." *Philosophical Studies* 33 (1978), 145.

Swinburne, Richard. "The Argument from Design—A Defence." *Religious Studies* 8 (1972), 193–205.

Swinburne, Richard. "The Argument from Design." *Philosophy* 43 (1968). A detailed response to Hume.

Tennant, R. R. *Philosophical Theology*. Cambridge, England: Cambridge University Press, 1928–30. A classic post-Humean version of the teleological argument.

THE ONTOLOGICAL ARGUMENT

Barnes, Jonathan. *The Ontological Argument*. London: Macmillan, 1972. A good general discussion of the argument.

Plantinga, Alvin, ed. *The Ontological Argument from St. Anselm to Contemporary Philosophers*. Garden City, NY: Doubleday, 1965.

THE PROBLEM OF EVIL

Lewis, C. S. *The Problem of Pain*. London: Geoffrey Bles, 1940. Clear and cogent.

Mackie, J. L. "Evil and Omnipotence." *Mind* 64 (1955), 200–212. One of the earlier contemporary attacks on the existence of God from the argument from evil, used in many anthologies.

Mackie, J. L. *The Miracle of Theism*. Oxford: Oxford University Press, 1982. Chapter 9 is insightful and well-argued from an atheist's point of view.

McCloskey, H. J. "God and Evil." *The Philosophical Quarterly* 10 (1960). A sharp attack on theism, arguing that given the problem of evil, theism is indefensible.

Pike, Nelson. "Hume on Evil." *The Philosophical Review* LXXII (1963), 180–97. A trenchant criticism of Hume's position.

Plantinga, Alvin. *The Nature of Necessity*. Oxford: Clarendon, 1974. Chapter 9 is an excellent article developing in detail a version of the free will defense. A more accessible version of his argument is found in Plantinga's *God, Freedom and Evil* (New York: Harper & Row, 1974).

Rowe, William. "The Problem of Evil and Some Varieties of Atheism." *APQ* 16 (1970), 335–41.

Swinburne, Richard. *The Existence of God*. Oxford: Oxford University Press, 1978. Chapter 11 contains a fuller defense than is in the article included in this volume.

Wainwright, William J. "God and the Necessity of Physical Evils." *Sophia* 11 (1972), 16–19.

FAITH AND REASON

Delaney, C. F., ed. *Rationality and Religious Belief*. Notre Dame, IN: University of Notre Dame Press, 1978. A good collection of essays on faith and reason.

Flew, Antony. *The Presumption of Atheism*. New York: Harper & Row, 1976. Part I, Chapters 1, 2, and 5 are relevant to the discussion.

Mackie, J. L. *The Miracle of Theism: Arguments for and against the Existence of God*. Oxford: Clarendon, 1982. Probably the best defense of atheism in recent years, taking into consideration every major argument in the field.

Mavrodes, George. *Belief in God*. New York: Random House, 1970. A clear presentation of religious epistemology.

Mitchell, Basil. *The Justification of Religious Belief*. London: Macmillan, 1973. A good discussion of the cumulative case for theism.

Phillips, D. Z. *Religion Without Explanation*. Oxford: Basil Blackwell, 1976. A valuable study by one of the foremost Wittgensteinian philosophers.

Plantinga, Alvin and Wolterstorff, Nicholas, eds. *Faith and Rationality*. Notre Dame, IN: University of Notre Dame Press, 1983.

Plantinga, Alvin. *Warranted Christian Belief*. New York: Oxford University Press, 2000.

Pojman, Louis. *Religious Belief and the Will*. London: Routledge & Kegan Paul, 1986.

Swinburne, Richard. *Faith and Reason*. Oxford: Clarendon, 1981. One of the best studies of the subject in recent years.

Part III

Knowledge

I am the wisest man alive, for I know one thing, and that is that I know nothing.

SOCRATES in Plato's *Apology*

III.A What Can We Know?
Classical Theories of Knowledge

WHAT DO WE REALLY KNOW? How can we be certain that we have the truth?

The theory of knowledge, or epistemology (from the Greek "the science of knowledge"), inquires into the nature of knowledge and justification of our beliefs. Many philosophers believe that it is the central area of philosophy, for if philosophy is the quest for truth, then we need to know how we obtain the truth and justify our beliefs, how we judge propositions as true. The first issue that arises is whether we can possess any truth at all.

To claim to know something is to claim to possess the truth. But can we ever be certain that we do possess the truth? People make knowledge claims everyday that turn out to be false. We often misremember and misperceive. Sometimes we make knowledge claims that are contradicted by those of others. For example, you and your sister each claim to have washed the dishes last night. A Moslem priest and a Roman Catholic theologian each claims that his is the true religion. While hiking in the forest, you feel sure that the campsite is to the right, while your friend is equally convinced that it is to the left. You are absolutely sure that Communism is evil, and your roommate is equally convinced that it is the only hope for a better world.

In these contrary cases, both parties cannot be correct, but it could turn out that neither is. It could be that both you and your sister are misremembering that you washed the dishes last night, and that your mother did. It is logically possible that neither Islam nor Catholicism is the truth. Both you and your friend could be wrong about the whereabouts of the campsite, for it could be in front of or behind you. And it could turn out that Communism is neither completely evil nor the only hope for a better world.

What do we really know? And how can we know when indeed we really *do* know something? Could it be that we know nothing at all? Could it be that we do not even know that we know nothing at all? *Skepticism* is the theory that we do not have any knowledge; that we cannot be completely certain of any of our beliefs, not even the belief that we cannot be completely certain of any of our beliefs. For all we know, the universe and everything in it could have doubled in size last night while we were sleeping. We cannot check this by measuring our height with a ruler because the ruler has also doubled in size. How could we prove that the world didn't double in size or become 27 percent smaller? How can we prove that the world and ourselves were not created seven minutes ago with all our apparent memories of the past built into our minds, fossils built into the stones, and buildings artificially aged? Could the world all be an illusion? How can we prove there are indeed other minds, that the other beings in our classroom are not just cleverly constructed robots programmed to speak and smile and write exams? How do you know that you are not the only person who exists and that everything else is merely part of a long dream you are dreaming? Soon you will awaken and be surprised to discover that what you thought were dreams were really mini-dreams within one grand and glorious maxi-dream. Or perhaps you are simply a brain suspended in a tub full of a chemical solution in a laboratory and wired to a computer that is causing you to have your apparent present experiences? If you are under the control of an ingenious scientist (me, the author of this introduction), you will never discover it, for I have arranged it that you will only be able to compare your beliefs to the experiences I simulate. Your tub is your destiny!

Can you defeat the skeptic? In our first reading, the French philosopher René Descartes (1596–1650), the father of modern philosophy, attempts to use skepticism to defeat skepticism. He doubted in such a way that, he hoped, would pave the way for the end of doubt and the beginning of absolute certainty. Like many perceptive young people, Descartes had been disillusioned by the discovery that many of the so-called "truths" which he had been taught in home and school turned out to be false. Having a healthy hatred of deception and an equally healthy love of truth, he endeavored to find a method that would guarantee truth and ensure against error.

Descartes was a *rationalist* who believed that all truth can be known by the mind alone by inquiring within itself. He held to the doctrine of innate ideas (that the mind possesses knowledge at birth) which we know *a priori*—that is, prior to experience, though experience may be necessary to stimulate awareness of this knowledge.

Our next three readings, by John Locke (1632–1704), George Berkeley (1685–1753), and David Hume (1711–1776), represent an opposite tradition, called *empiricism*. This school of philosophy asserts that the source of all knowledge is experience. John Locke stated that our minds were like blank slates (*tabula rasa*) on which experience writes her messages. There are no innate ideas. There is no *a priori* knowledge; all knowledge is known *a posteriori,* on the basis of experience. Berkeley rejects Locke's commonsense notion of a material world that is the object of perception and claims that matter doesn't exist. Only perceivers and perceptions exist. Hume sets forth an empirical version of skepticism. The final reading is John Hospers' rebuttal of skepticism.

In the following section, we examine four essays on the questions of truth, rationality, and cognitive relativism.

Cartesian Doubt and the Search for Foundational Knowledge   III.18

RENÉ DESCARTES

René Descartes (1596–1650) was born in France and educated by the Jesuits at the College of La Fleche. After a three-year career as a professional soldier, he traveled through Europe, trying to complete his education by reading the "great book of the world." Finally, he settled in Holland and began to write philosophical treatises. These were radically innovative because instead of starting with the accumulated authority of the medieval tradition, Descartes began with his own experience and philosophized from there. The self becomes the center of authority instead of the tradition. His two major works are *Discourse on Method* (1637) and *Meditations on First Philosophy* (1641), from which our present selection is taken.

Descartes writes philosophy in the first person singular. He desires to know the truth, and he realizes that this will be an arduous enterprise because he has discovered by painful experience that much of what he has been taught and has taken for granted is false. He must destroy his tottering house of "knowledge" and lay a new foundation on which to construct an indestructible edifice. The method consists of doubting everything that can be doubted, and then, on the pure remainder of certain truth, beginning the process of constructing an indubitable system of knowledge. The result is a type of rationalism in which the only certainties are discovered by the mind through self-evident insight or reason.

Study Questions

1. What caused Descartes to begin the process of doubting everything?
2. Why does he not examine all of his beliefs separately?
3. Why does he doubt his senses?
4. Why does he posit the idea of an evil genius who always deceives him?
5. What is the first thing that Descartes comes to know with certainty?

MEDITATION ONE: CONCERNING THOSE THINGS THAT CAN BE CALLED INTO DOUBT

SEVERAL YEARS HAVE NOW PASSED since I first realized how many were the false opinions that in my youth I took to be true, and thus how doubtful were all the things that I subsequently built upon these opinions. From the time I became aware of this, I realized that for once I had to raze everything in my life, down to the very bottom, so as to begin again from the first foundations, if I wanted to establish anything firm and lasting in the sciences. But the task seemed so enormous that I waited for a point in my life that was so ripe that no more suitable a time for laying hold of these disciplines would come to pass. For this reason, I have delayed so long that I would be at fault were I to waste on deliberation the time that is left for action. Therefore, now that I have liberated my mind from all cares, and I have secured for myself some leisurely and carefree time, I withdraw in solitude. I will, in short, apply myself earnestly and openly to the general destruction of my former opinions.

Yet to this end it will not be necessary that I show that all my opinions are false, which perhaps I could never accomplish anyway. But because reason now persuades me that I should withhold my assent no less carefully from things which are not plainly certain and indubitable than I would to what is patently false, it will be sufficient justification for rejecting them all, if I find a reason for doubting even the least of them.

Reprinted from Descartes' Meditations on First Philosophy, *trans. Donald A. Cress (Cambridge University Press, 1931).*

Nor therefore need one survey each opinion one after the other, a task of endless proportion. Rather—because undermining the foundations will cause whatever has been built upon them to fall down of its own accord—I will at once attack those principles which supported everything that I once believed.

Whatever I had admitted until now as most true I took in either from the senses or through the senses; however, I noticed that they sometimes deceived me. And it is a mark of prudence never to trust wholly in those things which have once deceived us.

But perhaps, although the senses sometimes deceive us when it is a question of very small and distant things, still there are many other matters which one certainly cannot doubt, although they are derived from the very same senses: that I am sitting here before the fireplace wearing my dressing gown, that I feel this sheet of paper in my hands, and so on. But how could one deny that these hands and that my whole body exist? Unless perhaps I should compare myself to insane people whose brains are so impaired by a stubborn vapor from a black bile that they continually insist that they are kings when they are in utter poverty, or that they are wearing purple robes when they are naked, or that they have a head made of clay, or that they are gourds, or that they are made of glass. But they are all demented, and I would appear no less demented if I were to take their conduct as a model for myself.

All of this would be well and good, were I not a man who is accustomed to sleeping at night, and to undergoing in my sleep the very same things—or now and then even less likely ones— as do these insane people when they are awake. How often has my evening slumber persuaded me of such customary things as these: that I am here, clothed in my dressing gown, seated at the fireplace, when in fact I am lying undressed between the blankets! But right now I certainly am gazing upon this piece of paper with eyes wide awake. This head which I am moving is not heavy with sleep. I extend this hand consciously and deliberately and I feel it. These things would

not be so distinct for one who is asleep. But this all seems as if I do not recall having been deceived by similar thoughts on other occasions in my dreams. As I consider these cases more intently, I see so plainly that there are no definite signs to distinguish being awake from being asleep that I am quite astonished, and this astonishment almost convinces me that I am sleeping.

Let us say, then, for the sake of argument, that we are sleeping and that such particulars as these are not true: that we open our eyes, move our heads, extend our hands. Perhaps we do not even have these hands, or any such body at all. Nevertheless, it really must be admitted that things seen in sleep are, as it were, like painted images, which could have been produced only in the likeness of true things. Therefore at least these general things (eyes, head, hands, the whole body) are not imaginary things, but are true and exist. For indeed when painters wish to represent sirens and satyrs by means of bizarre and unusual forms, they surely cannot ascribe utterly new natures to these creatures. Rather, they simply intermingle the members of various animals. And even if they concoct something so utterly novel that its likes have never been seen before (being utterly fictitious and false), certainly at the very minimum the colors from which the painters compose the thing ought to be true. And for the same reason, although even these general things (eyes, head, hands, and the like) can be imaginary, still one must necessarily admit that at least other things that are even more simple and universal are true, from which, as from true colors, all these things—be they true or false—which in our thought are images of things, are constructed.

To this class seems to belong corporeal nature in general, together with its extension; likewise the shape of extended things, their quantity or size, their number; as well as the place where they exist, the time of their duration, and other such things.

Hence perhaps we do not conclude improperly that physics, astronomy, medicine, and all the other disciplines that are dependent upon the consideration of composite things are all doubtful. But arithmetic, geometry, and other such disciplines—which treat of nothing but the simplest and most general things and which are indifferent as to whether these composite things do or do not exist—contain something certain and indubitable. For whether I be awake or asleep, two plus three makes five, and a square does not have more than four sides; nor does it seem possible that such obvious truths can fall under the suspicion of falsity.

All the same, a certain opinion of long standing has been fixed in my mind, namely that there exists a God who is able to do anything and by whom I, such as I am, have been created. How do I know that he did not bring it about that there be no earth at all, no heavens, no extended thing, no figure, no size, no place, and yet all these things should seem to me to exist precisely as they appear to do now? Moreover—for I judge that others sometimes make mistakes in matters that they believe they know most perfectly—how do I know that I am not deceived every time I add two and three or count the sides of a square or perform an even simpler operation, if such can be imagined? But perhaps God has not willed that I be thus deceived, for it is said that he is good in the highest degree. Nonetheless, if it were repugnant to his goodness that he should have created me such that I be deceived all the time, it would seem, from this same consideration, to be foreign to him to permit me to be deceived occasionally. But we cannot make this last assertion.

Perhaps there are some who would rather deny such a powerful God, than believe that all other matters are uncertain. Let us not put these people off just yet; rather, let us grant that everything said here about God is fictitious. Now they suppose that I came to be what I am either by fate or by chance or by a continuous series of events or by some other way. But because being deceived and being mistaken seem to be imperfections, the less powerful they take the author of my being to be, the more probable it will be that I would be so imperfect as to

be deceived perpetually. I have nothing to say in response to these arguments. At length I am forced to admit that there is nothing, among the things I once believed to be true, which it is not permissible to doubt—not for reasons of frivolity or a lack of forethought, but because of valid and considered arguments. Thus I must carefully withhold assent no less from these things than from the patently false, if I wish to find anything certain.

But it is not enough simply to have made a note of this; I must take care to keep it before my mind. For long-standing opinions keep coming back again and again, almost against my will; they seize upon my credulity, as if it were bound over to them by long use and the claims of intimacy. Nor will I get out of the habit of assenting to them and believing in them, so long as I take them to be exactly what they are, namely, in some respects doubtful as by now is obvious, but nevertheless highly probable, so that it is much more consonant with reason to believe them than to deny them. Hence, it seems to me, I would do well to turn my will in the opposite direction, to deceive myself and pretend for a considerable period that they are wholly false and imaginary, until finally, as if with equal weight of prejudice* on both sides, no bad habit should turn my judgment from the correct perception of things. For indeed I know that no danger or error will follow and that it is impossible for me to indulge in too much distrust, since I now am concentrating only on knowledge, not on action.

Thus I will suppose not a supremely good God, the source of truth, but rather an evil genius, as clever and deceitful as he is powerful, who has directed his entire effort to misleading me. I will regard the heavens, the air, the earth, colors, shapes, sounds, and all external things as nothing but the deceptive games of my dreams, with which he lays snares for my credulity. I will regard myself as having no hands, no eyes, no

---

*A "prejudice" is a prejudgement, that is, an adjudication of an issue without having first reviewed the appropriate evidence.

flesh, no blood, no senses, but as nevertheless falsely believing that I possess all these things. I will remain resolutely fixed in this meditation, and, even if it be out of my power to know anything true, certainly it is within my power to take care resolutely to withhold my assent to what is false, lest this deceiver, powerful and clever as he is, have an effect on me. But this undertaking is arduous, and laziness brings me back to my customary way of living. I am not unlike a prisoner who might enjoy an imaginary freedom in his sleep. When he later begins to suspect that he is sleeping, he fears being awakened and conspires slowly with these pleasant illusions. In just this way, I spontaneously fall back into my old beliefs, and dread being awakened, lest the toilsome wakefulness which follows upon a peaceful rest, have to be spent thenceforward not in the light but among the inextricable shadows of the difficulties now brought forward.

MEDITATION TWO: CONCERNING THE NATURE OF THE HUMAN MIND: THAT THE MIND IS MORE KNOWN THAN THE BODY

Yesterday's meditation filled my mind with so many doubts that I can no longer forget about them—nor yet do I see how they are to be resolved. But, as if I had suddenly fallen into a deep whirlpool, I am so disturbed that I can neither touch my foot to the bottom, nor swim up to the top. Nevertheless I will work my way up, and I will follow the same path I took yesterday, putting aside everything which admits of the least doubt, as if I had discovered it to be absolutely false. I will go forward until I know something certain—or, if nothing else, until I at least know for certain that nothing is certain. Archimedes sought only a firm and immovable point in order to move the entire earth from one place to another. Surely great things are to be hoped for if I am lucky enough to find at least one thing that is certain and indubitable.

Therefore I will suppose that all I see is false. I will believe that none of those things that my deceitful memory brings before my eyes ever existed. I thus have no senses: body, shape, extension, movement, and place are all figments of my imagination. What then will count as true? Perhaps only this one thing: that nothing is certain.

But on what grounds do I know that there is nothing over and above all those which I have just reviewed, concerning which there is not even the least cause for doubt? Is there not a God (or whatever name I might call him) who instills these thoughts in me? But why should I think that, since perhaps I myself could be the author of these things? Therefore am I not at least something? But I have already denied that I have any senses and any body. Still, I hesitate; for what follows from that? Am I so tied to the body and to the senses that I cannot exist without them? But I have persuaded myself that there is nothing at all in the world: no heaven, no earth, no minds, no bodies. Is it not then true that I do not exist? But certainly I should exist, if I were to persuade myself of something. But there is a deceiver (I know not who he is) powerful and sly in the highest degree, who is always purposely deceiving me. Then there is no doubt that I exist, if he deceives me. And deceive me as he will, he can never bring it about that I am nothing so long as I shall think that I am something. Thus it must be granted that, after weighing carefully and sufficiently everything, one must come to the considered judgment that the statement "I am, I exist" is necessarily true every time it is uttered by me or conceived in my mind.

But I do not yet understand well enough who I am—I, who now necessarily exist. And from this point on, I must take care lest I imprudently substitute something else in place of myself; and thus be mistaken even in that knowledge which I claim to be the most certain and evident of all. To this end, I shall meditate once more on what I once believed myself to be before having embarked upon these deliberations. For this reason, then, I will set aside whatever can be refuted even to a slight degree by the arguments brought forward, so that at length there shall remain precisely nothing but what is certain and unshaken.

What therefore did I formerly think I was? A man, of course. But what is a man? Might I not say a rational animal? No, because then one would have to inquire what an "animal" is and what "rational" means. And then from only one question we slide into many more difficult ones. Nor do I now have enough free time that I want to waste it on subtleties of this sort. But rather here I pay attention to what spontaneously and by my own nature came into my thought beforehand whenever I pondered what I was. Namely, it occurred to me first that I have a face, hands, arms, and this entire mechanism of bodily members, the very same as are discerned in a corpse—which I referred to by the name "body." It also occurred to me that I eat, walk, feel and think; these actions I used to assign to the soul as their cause. But what this soul was I either did not think about or I imagined it was something terribly insubstantial—after the fashion of a wind, fire, or ether—which has been poured into my coarser parts. I truly was not in doubt regarding the body; rather I believed that I distinctly knew its nature, which, were I perhaps tempted to describe it such as I mentally conceived it, I would explain it thus: by "body," I understand all that is suitable for being bounded by some shape, for being enclosed in some place, and thus for filling up space, so that it excludes every other body from that space; for being perceived by touch, sight, hearing, taste, or smell; for being moved in several ways, not surely by itself, but by whatever else that touches it. For I judged that the power of self-motion, and likewise of sensing or of thinking, in no way pertains to the nature of the body. Nonetheless, I used to marvel especially that such faculties were found in certain bodies.

But now what am I, when I suppose that some deceiver—omnipotent and, if I may be allowed to say it, malicious—takes all the pains he can in order to deceive me? Can I not affirm that I possess at least a small measure of all those traits which I already have said pertain to the nature of the body? I pay attention, I think, I deliberate—but nothing happens. I am wearied of repeating this in vain. But which of these am I to ascribe to the soul? How about eating or walking? These are surely nothing but illusions, because I do not have a body. How about sensing? Again, this also does not happen without a body, and I judge that I really did not sense those many things I seemed to have sensed in my dreams. How about thinking? Here I discover that thought is an attribute that really does belong to me. This alone cannot be detached from me. I am; I exist; this is certain. But for how long? For as long as I think. Because perhaps it could also come to pass that if I should cease from all thinking I would then utterly cease to exist. I now admit nothing that is not necessarily true. I am therefore precisely only a thing that thinks; that is, a mind, or soul, or intellect, or reason—words the meaning of which I was ignorant before. Now, I am a true thing, and truly existing, but what kind of thing? I have said it already: a thing that thinks.

What then? I will set my imagination going to see if I am not something more. I am not that connection of members which is called the human body. Neither am I some subtle air infused into these members, not a wind, not a fire, not a vapor, not a breath—nothing that I imagine to myself, for I have supposed all these to be nothing. The assertion stands: the fact still remains that I am something. But perhaps it is the case that nevertheless, these very things which I take to be nothing (because I am ignorant of them) in reality do not differ from that self which I know. This I do not know. I shall not quarrel about it right now; I can make a judgment only regarding things which are known to me. I know that I exist; I ask now who is this "I" whom I know. Most certainly the knowledge of this matter, thus precisely understood, does not depend upon things that I do not yet know to exist. Therefore, it is not dependent upon any of those things that I feign in my imagination. But this word "feign" warns me of my error. For I would be feigning if I should "imagine" that I am something, because imagining is merely the contemplation of the shape or image of a corporeal thing. But I know now with certainty that I am, and at the same time it could happen that all these images—and, generally, everything that pertains to the nature of the body—are nothing but dreams. When these things are taken into account, I would speak no less foolishly were I to say: "I will imagine so that I might recognize more distinctly who I am," than were I to say: "Now I surely am awake, and I see something true, but because I do not yet see it with sufficient evidence, I will take the trouble of going to sleep so that my dreams might show this to me more truly and more evidently." Thus I know that none of what I can comprehend by means of the imagination pertains to this understanding that I have of myself. Moreover, I know that I must be most diligent about withdrawing my mind from these things so that it can perceive its nature as distinctly as possible.

But what then am I? A thing that thinks. What is that? A thing that doubts, understands, affirms, denies, wills, refuses, and which also imagines and knows.

For Further Reflection

1. Are you convinced by Descartes' argument? Is the self the most certain of objects?

2. Is Descartes' argument against trusting the senses a valid one? Why should we always distrust the senses? Discuss this issue and compare it with what Locke says when you get to the next reading. Descartes is a *rationalist,* believing that unaided reason can discover all truth, whereas Locke and Hume are *empiricists,* believing that sense perception is the only way to knowledge. Keep this in mind as you continue in this section.

3. Does Descartes convince you that the mind is more certain than matter?

The Empiricist Theory of Knowledge   III.19

JOHN LOCKE

A biographical sketch of John Locke (1632–1704) precedes Reading I.2.

Locke's work in the theory of knowledge, *An Essay Concerning Human Understanding* (1689), is the first systematic assault on Cartesian rationalism, the view that reason alone guarantees knowledge. Locke argues that if our claims to knowledge make any sense, they must be derived from the world. He rejects the rationalist notion that we have innate ideas (actual knowledge of metaphysical truths, such as mathematical truths, universals, and the laws of nature) because (1) there is no good deductive argument establishing the existence of such entities, (2) children and idiots do not seem to possess them, and (3) an empirical way of knowing, which seems far more reasonable, has no place for such entities. Locke does believe that we have intuitive knowledge of our own existence and that the existence of God can be demonstrated by reason (see Book IV, Chapter XI in this selection). Scholars are puzzled at this apparent inconsistency, but Locke would respond that it is no inconsistency. We know that we exist on immediate reflection because of the nature of consciousness, not because of any poor knowledge hidden within us. Nor do we have innate knowledge of God. It is simply that we can reason from empirical truths about the world to the existence of God (using such arguments as the cosmological and teleological arguments we discussed in Part II).

According to Locke, the mind at birth is a *tabula rasa*, a blank slate. It is like white paper, devoid of characteristics until it receives sense perceptions. All knowledge begins with sensory experience on which the powers of the mind operate, developing complex ideas, abstractions, and the like. In place of the absolute certainty that the rationalists sought to find, Locke says that apart from the knowledge of the self, most of what we know we know in degrees of certainty derived from inductive generalizations. For example, we see the sun rise every morning and infer that it is highly probable that it will rise tomorrow, but we cannot be absolutely certain.

Study Questions

1. Why is it important to inquire into the structure of human understanding?
2. Describe Locke's design of purpose. Which ideas does he plan to treat and which to omit?
3. What is his method?
4. What does he mean by the word "idea"?
5. What are so-called "innate principles" (or "ideas")? What is Locke's view of them?
6. What does Locke argue is the origin of our ideas?
7. What is the difference between primary and secondary qualities?
8. Describe Locke's view of the degrees of knowledge. What are the highest degrees of knowledge and what do we know to lesser degrees?
9. What is Locke's view of probability?

INTRODUCTION

1. AN INQUIRY INTO THE UNDERSTANDING *pleasant and useful.*—Since it is the *understanding* that sets man above the rest of sensible beings, and gives him all the advantage and dominion which he has over them; it is certainly a subject, even for its nobleness, worth our labour to inquire into. The understanding, like the eye, whilst it makes us see and perceive all other things, takes no notice of itself; and it requires art and pains to set it at a distance and make it its own object. But whatever be the difficulties that lie in the way of this inquiry; whatever it be that keeps us so much in the dark to ourselves; sure I am that all the light we can let in upon our minds, all the acquaintance we can make with our own understandings, will not only be very pleasant, but bring us great advantage, in directing our thoughts in the search of other things.

2. *Design.*—This, therefore, being my purpose—to inquire into the origin, certainty, and extent of *human knowledge,* together with the grounds and degrees of *belief, opinion,* and *assent*—I shall not at present meddle with the physical consideration of the mind; or trouble myself to examine wherein its essence consists; or by what motions of our spirits or alterations of our bodies we come to have any *sensation* by

From An Essay Concerning Human Understanding *(London: E. Holt, 1689).*

our organs, or any *ideas* in our understandings, and whether those ideas do in their formation, any or all of them, depend on matter or not. These are speculations which, however curious and entertaining, I shall decline, as lying out of my way in the design I am now upon. It shall suffice to my present purpose, to consider the discerning faculties of a man, as they are employed about the objects which they have to do with. And I shall imagine I have not wholly misemployed myself in the thoughts I shall have on this occasion, if, in this historical, plain method, I can give any account of the ways whereby our understandings come to attain those notions of things we have; and can set down any measures of the certainty of our knowledge; or the grounds of those persuasions which are to be found amongst men, so various, different, and wholly contradictory; and yet asserted somewhere or other with such assurance and confidence, that he that shall take a view of the opinions of mankind, observe their opposition, and at the same time consider the fondness and devotion wherewith they are embraced, the resolution and eagerness wherewith they are maintained, may perhaps have reason to suspect, that either there is no such thing as truth at all, or that mankind hath no sufficient means to attain a certain knowledge of it.

3. *Method.*—It is therefore worth while to search out the bounds between opinion and knowledge, and examine by what measures, in things whereof we have no certain knowledge, we ought to regulate our assent and moderate our persuasion. In order whereunto I shall pursue this following method:

First, I shall inquire into the original of those *ideas,* notions, or whatever else you please to call them, which a man observes, and is conscious to himself he has in his mind, and the ways whereby the understanding comes to be furnished with them.

Secondly, I shall endeavour to show what *knowledge* the understanding hath by those ideas; and the certainty, evidence, and extent of it. Thirdly, I shall make some inquiry into the

nature and grounds of *faith* or *opinion:* whereby I mean that assent which we give to any proposition as true, of whose truth yet we have no certain knowledge. And here we shall have occasion to examine the reasons and degrees of *assent.*

BOOK I

Chapter I

1. It is an established opinion amongst some men, that there are in the understanding certain *innate principles,* some primary notions, κοιναὶ ἔννοιαι, characters, as it were stamped upon the mind of man, which the soul receives in its very first being, and brings into the world with it. It would be sufficient to convince unprejudiced readers of the falseness of this supposition, if I should only show (as I hope I shall in the following parts of this Discourse) how men, barely by the use of their natural faculties, may attain to all the knowledge they have, without the help of any innate impressions, and may arrive at certainty, without any such original notions or principles. For I imagine any one will easily grant that it would be impertinent to suppose the ideas of colours innate in a creature to whom god hath given sight, and a power to receive them by the eyes from external objects: and no less unreasonable would it be to attribute several truths to the impressions of nature, and innate characters, when we may observe in ourselves faculties fit to attain as easy and certain knowledge of them as if they were originally imprinted on the mind.

But because a man is not permitted without censure to follow his own thoughts in the search of truth, when they lead him ever so little out of the common road, I shall set down the reasons that made me doubt of the truth of that opinion, as an excuse for my mistake, if I be in one, which I leave to be considered by those who, with me, dispose themselves to embrace truth wherever they find it.

2. There is nothing more commonly taken for granted than that there are certain *principles,* both *speculative* and *practical* (for they speak of

both), universally agreed upon by all mankind, which therefore, they argue, must needs be the constant impressions which the souls of men receive in their first beings, and which they bring into the world with them, as necessarily and really as they do any of their inherent faculties.

3. This argument, drawn from universal consent, has this misfortune in it, that if it were true in matter of fact, that there were certain truths wherein all mankind agreed, it would not prove them innate, if there can be any other way shown how men may come to that universal agreement, in the things they do consent in, which I presume may be done.

4. But, which is worse, this argument of universal consent, which is made use of to prove innate principles, seems to me a demonstration that there are none such because there are none to which all mankind give an universal assent. I shall begin with the speculative, and instance in those magnified principles of demonstration, "Whatsoever is, is," and "It is impossible for the same thing to be and not to be," which, of all others, I think have the most allowed title to innate. These have so settled a reputation of maxims universally received, that it will no doubt be thought strange if any one should seem to question it. But yet I take liberty to say, that these propositions are so far from having an universal assent, that there are a great part of mankind to whom they are not so much as known.

5. For, first, it is evident, that all children and idiots have not the least apprehension or thought of them. And the want of that is enough to destroy that universal assent which must needs be the necessary concomitant of all innate truths: it seeming to me near a contradiction to say, that there are truths imprinted on the soul, which it perceives or understands not: imprinting, if it signify anything, being nothing else but the making certain truths to be perceived. For to imprint anything on the mind without the mind's perceiving it, seems to me hardly intelligible. If therefore children and idiots have souls, have minds, with those impressions upon them, *they* must unavoidably perceive them, and necessarily

know and assent to these truths; which since they do not, it is evident that there are no such impressions. For if they are not notions naturally imprinted, how can they be innate? and if they are notions imprinted, how can they be unknown? To say a notion is imprinted on the mind, and yet at the same time to say that the mind is ignorant of it, and never yet took notice of it, is to make this impression nothing. No proposition can be said to be in the mind which it never yet knew, which it was never yet conscious of. For if any one may, then, by the same reason, all propositions that are true, and the mind is capable ever of assenting to, may be said to be in the mind, and to be imprinted: since, if any one can be said to be in the mind, which it never yet knew, it must be only because it is capable of knowing it, and so the mind is of all truths it ever shall know. Nay, thus truths may be imprinted on the mind which it never did, nor ever shall know; for a man may live long, and die at last in ignorance of many truths which his mind was capable of knowing, and that with certainty. So that if the capacity of knowing be the natural impression contended for, all the truths a man ever comes to know will, by this account, be every one of them innate; and this great point will amount to no more, but only to a very improper way of speaking; which, whilst it pretends to assert the contrary, says nothing different from those who deny innate principles. For nobody, I think, ever denied that the mind was capable of knowing several truths. The capacity, they say, is innate; the knowledge acquired. But then to what end such contest for certain innate maxims? If truths can be imprinted on the understanding without being perceived, I can see no difference there can be between any truths the mind is *capable* of knowing in respect of their original: they must all be innate or all adventitious: in vain shall a man go about to distinguish them. He therefore that talks of innate notions in the understanding, cannot (if he intend thereby any distinct sort of truths) mean such truths to be in the understanding as it never perceived, and is yet wholly ignorant of. For if these words "to be in the understanding" have any propriety, they signify to be understood. So that to be in the understanding, and not to be understood; to be in the mind and never to be perceived, is all one as to say anything is and is not in the mind or understanding. If therefore these two propositions, "Whatsoever is, is," and "It is impossible for the same thing to be and not to be," are by nature imprinted, children cannot be ignorant of them: infants, and all that have souls, must necessarily have them in their understandings, know the truth of them, and assent to it. . . .

BOOK II

Chapter I

1. Every man being conscious to himself that he thinks and that which his mind is applied about whilst thinking being the *ideas* that are there, it is past doubt that men have in their minds several ideas—such as are those expressed by the words *whiteness, hardness, sweetness, thinking, motion, man, elephant, army, drunkenness,* and others; it is in the first place then to be inquired, *How he comes by them?*

I know it is a received doctrine, that men have native ideas, and original characters, stamped upon their minds in their very first being. This opinion I have at large examined already; and, I suppose what I have said in the foregoing Book will be much more easily admitted, when I have shown whence the understanding may get all the ideas it has; and by what ways and degrees they may come into the mind—for which I shall appeal to every one's own observation and experience.

2. Let us then suppose the mind to be, as we say, white paper, void of all characters, without any ideas:—How comes it to be furnished? Whence comes it by that vast store which the busy and boundless fancy of man has painted on it with an almost endless variety? Whence has it all the *materials* of reason and knowledge? To this I answer, in one word, from EXPERIENCE. In that all our knowledge is founded, and from that it ultimately derives itself. Our observation

employed either, about external sensible objects, or about the internal operations of our minds perceived and reflected on by ourselves, is that which supplies our understandings with all the *materials* of thinking. These two are the fountains of knowledge, from whence all the ideas we have, or can naturally have, do spring.

3. First, our Senses, conversant about particular sensible objects, do convey into the mind several distinct perceptions of things, according to those various ways wherein those objects do affect them. And thus we come by those *ideas* we have of *yellow, white, heat, cold, soft, hard, bitter, sweet,* and all those which we call sensible qualities, which when I say the senses convey into the mind, I mean, they from external objects convey into the mind what produces there those perceptions. This great source of most of the ideas we have, depending wholly upon our senses, and derived by them to the understanding, I call SENSATION.

4. Secondly, the other fountain from which experience furnisheth the understanding with ideas is—the perception of the operations of our own mind within us, as it is employed about the ideas it has got—which operations, when the soul comes to reflect on and consider, do furnish the understanding with another set of ideas, which could not be had from things without. And such are *perception, thinking, doubting, believing, reasoning, knowing, willing,* and all the different actings of our own minds, which we being conscious of, and observing in ourselves, do from these receive into our understandings as distinct ideas as we do from bodies affecting our senses. This source of ideas every man has wholly in himself, and though it be not sense, as having nothing to do with external objects, yet it is very like it, and might properly enough be called *internal sense.* But as I call the other Sensation, so I call this REFLECTION, the ideas it affords being such only as the mind gets by reflecting on its own operations within itself. By reflection then, in the following part of this discourse, I would be understood to mean, that notice which the mind takes of its own opera-

tions, and the manner of them, by reason whereof there come to be ideas of these operations in the understanding. These two, I say, viz. external material things, as the objects of SENSATION, and the operations of our own minds within, as the objects of REFLECTION, are to me the only originals from whence all our ideas take their beginnings. The term *operations* here I use in a large sense, as comprehending not barely the actions of the mind about its ideas, but some sort of passions arising sometimes from them, such as is the satisfaction or uneasiness arising from any thought.

5. The understanding seems to me not to have the least glimmering of any ideas which it doth not receive from one of these two. *External objects* furnish the mind with the ideas of sensible qualities, which are all those different perceptions they produce in us, and *the mind* furnishes the understanding with ideas of its own operations.

These, when we have taken a full survey of them, and their several modes, combinations, and relations, we shall find to contain all our whole stock of ideas, and that we have nothing in our minds which did not come in one of these two ways. Let any one examine his own thoughts, and thoroughly search into his understanding, and then let him tell me, whether all the original ideas he has there, are any other than of the objects of his senses, or of the operations of his mind, considered as objects of his reflection. And how great a mass of knowledge soever he imagines to be lodged there, he will, upon taking a strict view, see that he has not any idea in his mind but what one of these two have imprinted—though perhaps, with infinite variety compounded and enlarged by the understanding, as we shall see hereafter.

6. He that attentively considers the state of a child, at his first coming into the world, will have little reason to think him stored with plenty of ideas, that are to be the matter of his future knowledge. It is *by degrees* he comes to be furnished with them. And though the ideas of obvious and familiar qualities imprint themselves before the memory begins to keep a register of time or order, yet it is often so late before some unusual qualities come in the way, that there are few men that cannot recollect the beginning of their acquaintance with them. And if it were worth while, no doubt a child might be so ordered as to have but a very few, even of the ordinary ideas, till he were grown up to a man. But all that are born into the world, being surrounded with bodies that perpetually and diversely affect them, variety of ideas, whether care be taken of it or not, are imprinted on the minds of children. Light and colours are busy at hand everywhere, when the eye is but open; sounds and some tangible qualities fail not to solicit their proper senses, and force an entrance to the mind—but yet, I think, it will be granted easily, that if a child were kept in a place where he never saw any other but black and white till he were a man, he would have no more ideas of scarlet or green, than he that from his childhood never tasted an oyster, or a pineapple, has of those particular relishes. . . .

Chapter VIII

8. Whatsoever the mind perceives *in itself*, or is the immediate object of perception, thought, or understanding, that I call *idea*, and the power to produce any idea in our mind, I call *quality* of the subject wherein that power is. Thus a snowball having the power to produce in us the ideas of white, cold, and round,—the power to produce those ideas in us, as they are in the snowball, I call qualities, and as they are sensations or perceptions in our understandings, I call them ideas, which *ideas*, if I speak of sometimes as in the things themselves, I would be understood to mean those qualities in the objects which produce them in us.

9. Qualities thus considered in bodies are, *First*, such as are utterly inseparable from the body, in what state soever it be, and such as in all the alterations and changes it suffers, all the force can be used upon it, it constantly keeps; and such as sense constantly finds in every particle of matter which has bulk enough to be perceived; and

the mind finds inseparable from every particle of matter, though less than to make itself singly be perceived by our senses: v.g. Take a grain of wheat, divide it into two parts; each part has still solidity, extension, figure, and mobility. Divide it again, and it retains still the same qualities, and so divide it on, till the parts become insensible; they must retain still each of them all those qualities. For division (which is all that a mill, or pestle, or any other body, does upon another, in reducing it to insensible parts) can never take away either solidity, extension, figure, or mobility from any body, but only makes two or more distinct separate masses of matter, of that which was but one before; all which distinct masses, reckoned as so many distinct bodies, after division, make a certain number.

These I call *original* or *primary qualities* of body, which I think we may observe to produce simple ideas in us, viz. solidity, extension, figure, motion or rest, and number.

10. *Secondly,* such qualities which in truth are nothing in the objects themselves but powers to produce various sensations in us by their primary qualities, i.e., by the bulk, figure, texture, and motion of their insensible parts, as colours, sounds, tastes, etc. These I call *secondary qualities.* To these might be added a *third* sort, which are allowed to be barely powers; though they are as much real qualities in the subject as those which I, to comply with the common way of speaking, call qualities, but for distinction, secondary qualities. For the power in fire to produce a new colour, or consistency, in *wax* or *clay,*—by its primary qualities, is as much a quality in fire, as the power it has to produce in *me* a new idea or sensation of warmth or burning, which I felt not before—by the same primary qualities, viz. the bulk, texture, and motion of its insensible parts. . . .

13. . . . let us suppose at present that the different motions and figures, bulk and number, of such particles, affecting the several organs of our senses, produce in us those different sensations which we have from the colours and smells of bodies; v.g. that a violet, by the impulse of such insensible particles of matter, of peculiar figures and bulks, and in different degrees and modifications of their motions, causes the ideas of the blue colour, and sweet scent of that flower to be produced in our minds. It being no more impossible to conceive that God should annex such ideas to such motions, with which they have no similitude, than that he should annex the idea of pain to the motion of a piece of steel dividing our flesh, with which that idea hath no resemblance.

14. What I have said concerning colours and smells may be understood also of tastes and sounds, and other the like sensible qualities, which, whatever reality we by mistake attribute to them, are in truth nothing in the objects themselves, but powers to produce various sensations in us; and depend on those primary qualities, viz. bulk, figure, texture, and motion of parts as I have said.

15. From whence I think it easy to draw this observation—that the ideas of primary qualities of bodies are resemblances of them, and their patterns do really exist in the bodies themselves, but the ideas produced in us by these secondary qualities have no resemblance of them at all. There is nothing like our ideas, existing in the bodies themselves. They are, in the bodies we denominate from them, only a power to produce those sensations in us, and what is sweet, blue, or warm in idea, is but the certain bulk, figure, and motion of the insensible parts, in the bodies themselves, which we call so.

16. Flame is denominated hot and light; snow, white and cold; and manna, white and sweet, from the ideas they produce in us. Which qualities are commonly thought to be the same in those bodies that those ideas are in us, the one the perfect resemblance of the other, as they are in a mirror, and it would by most men be judged very extravagant if one should say otherwise. And yet he that will consider that the same fire that, at one distance produces in us the sensation of warmth, does, at a nearer approach, produce in us the far different sensation of pain, ought to bethink himself what reason he has to say—that this idea of warmth, which was produced in him

by the fire, is *actually in the fire,* and his idea of pain, which the same fire produced in him the same way, is *not* in the fire. Why are whiteness and coldness in snow, and pain not, when it produces the one and the other idea in us, and can do neither, but by the bulk, figure, number, and motion of its solid parts? . . .

21. Ideas being thus distinguished and understood, we may be able to give an account how the same water, at the same time, may produce the idea of cold by one hand and of heat by the other; whereas it is impossible that the same water, if those ideas were really in it, should at the same time be both hot and cold. For, if we imagine *warmth,* as it is in our hands, to be nothing but a certain sort and degree of motion in the minute particles of our nerves or animal spirits, we may understand how it is possible that the same water may, at the same time, produce the sensations of heat in one hand and cold in the other, which yet *figure* never does, that never producing the idea of a square by one hand which has produced the idea of a globe by another. But if the sensation of heat and cold be nothing but the increase or diminution of the motion of the minute parts of our bodies, caused by the corpuscles of any other body, it is easy to be understood, that if that motion be greater in one hand than in the other; if a body be applied to the two hands, which has in its minute particles a greater motion than in those of one of the hands, and a less than in those of the other, it will increase the motion of the one hand and lessen it in the other, and so cause the different sensations of heat and cold that depend thereon. . . .

When children have, by repeated sensations, got ideas fixed in their memories, they begin by degrees to learn the use of signs. And when they have got the skill to apply the organs of speech to the framing of articulate sounds, they begin to make use of words, to signify their ideas to others. These verbal signs they sometimes borrow from others, and sometimes make themselves, as one may observe among the new and unusual names children often give to things in the first use of language.

The use of words then being to stand as outward marks of our internal ideas, and those ideas being taken from particular things, if every particular idea that we take in should have a distinct name, names must be endless. To prevent this, the mind makes the particular ideas received from particular objects to become general, which is done by considering them as they are in the mind such appearances—separate from all other existences, and the circumstances of real existence, as time, place, or any other concomitant ideas. This is called ABSTRACTION, whereby ideas taken from particular beings become general representatives of all of the same kind; and their names general names, applicable to whatever exists conformable to such abstract ideas. Such precise, naked appearances in the mind, without considering how, whence, or with what others they came there, the understanding lays up (with names commonly annexed to them) as the standards to rank real existences into sorts, as they agree with these patterns, and to denominate them accordingly. Thus the same colour being observed today in chalk or snow, which the mind yesterday received from milk, it considers that appearance alone, makes it a representative of all of that kind; and having given it the name *whiteness,* it by that sound signifies the same quality wheresoever to be imagined or met with; and thus universals, whether ideas or terms, are made. . . .

BOOK IV

Chapter II

1. All our knowledge consisting, as I have said, in the view the mind has of its own ideas, which is the utmost light and greatest certainty we, with our faculties, and in our way of knowledge, are capable of, it may not be amiss to consider a little the degrees of its evidence. The different clearness of our knowledge seems to

me to lie in the different way of perception the mind has of the agreement or disagreement of any of its ideas. For if we will reflect on our own ways of thinking, we will find, that sometimes the mind perceives the agreement or disagreement of two ideas *immediately by themselves,* without the intervention of any other: and this I think we may call *intuitive knowledge.* For in this the mind is at no pains of proving or examining, but perceives the truth as the eye doth light, only by being directed towards it. Thus the mind perceives that *white* is not *black,* that a *circle* is not a *triangle,* that *three* are more than *two* and equal to *one and two.* Such kinds of truths the mind perceives at the first sight of the ideas together, by bare intuition, without the intervention of any other idea; and this kind of knowledge is the clearest and most certain that human frailty is capable of. This part of knowledge is irresistible, and, like bright sunshine, forces itself immediately to be perceived, as soon as ever the mind turns its view that way, and leaves no room for hesitation, doubt, or examination, but the mind is presently filled with the clear light of it. *It is on this intuition that depends all the certainty and evidence of all our knowledge;* which certainty every one finds to be so great, that he cannot imagine, and therefore not require a greater: for a man cannot conceive himself capable of a greater certainty than to know that any idea in his mind is such as he perceives it to be, and that two ideas, wherein he perceives a difference, are different and not precisely the same. He that demands a greater certainty than this, demands he knows not what, and shows only that he has a mind to be a sceptic, without being able to be so. Certainty depends so wholly on this intuition, that, in the next degree of knowledge which I call demonstrative, this intuition is necessary in all the connexions of the intermediate ideas, without which we cannot attain knowledge and certainty.

2. The next degree of knowledge is, where the mind perceives the agreement or disagreement of any ideas, but not immediately. Though wherever the mind perceives the agreement or disagreement of any of its ideas, there be certain knowledge; yet it does not always happen, that the mind sees that agreement or disagreement, which there is between them, even where it is discoverable; and in that case remains in ignorance, and at most gets no further than a probable conjecture. The reason why the mind cannot always perceive presently the agreement or disagreement of two ideas, is, because those ideas, concerning whose agreement or disagreement the inquiry is made, cannot by the mind be so put together as to show it. In this case then, when the mind cannot so bring its ideas together as by their immediate comparison, and as it were juxtaposition or application one to another, to perceive their agreement or disagreement, it is fain, *by the intervention of other ideas* (one or more, as it happens) to discover the agreement or disagreement which it searches; and this is that which we call *reasoning.* Thus, the mind being willing to know the agreement or disagreement in bigness between the three angles of a triangle and two right ones, cannot by an immediate view and comparing them do it: because the three angles of a triangle cannot be brought at once, and be compared with any other one, or two, angles; and so of this the mind has no immediate, no intuitive knowledge. In this case the mind is fain to find out some other angles, to which the three angles of a triangle have an equality; and, finding those equal to two right ones, comes to know their equality to two right ones.

3. Those intervening ideas, which serve to show the agreement of any two others, are called *proofs;* and where the agreement and disagreement is by this means plainly and clearly perceived, it is called *demonstration;* it being *shown* to the understanding, and the mind made to see that it is so. A quickness in the mind to find out these intermediate ideas (that shall discover the agreement or disagreement of any other), and to apply them right, is, I suppose, that which is called *sagacity.*

4. This knowledge, by intervening proofs, though it be certain, yet the evidence of it is not altogether so clear and bright, nor the assent so ready, as in intuitive knowledge. For, though in demonstration the mind does at last perceive the agreement or disagreement of the ideas it considers; yet it is not without pains and attention: There must be more than one transient view to find it. A steady application and pursuit are required to this discovery, and there must be a progression by steps and degrees, before the mind can in this way arrive at certainty, and come to perceive the agreement or repugnancy between two ideas that need proofs and the use of reason to show it.

5. Another difference between intuitive and demonstrative knowledge is, that, though in the latter all doubt be removed when, by the intervention of the intermediate ideas, the agreement or disagreement is perceived, yet before the demonstration there was a doubt; which in intuitive knowledge cannot happen to the mind that has its faculty of perception left to a degree capable of distinct ideas; no more than it can be a doubt to the eye (that can distinctly see white and black), whether this ink and this paper be all of a colour. If there be sight in the eyes, it will, at first glimpse, without hesitation, perceive the words printed on this paper different from the colour of the paper, and so if the mind have the faculty of distinct perception, it will perceive the agreement or disagreement of those ideas that produce intuitive knowledge. If the eyes have lost the faculty of seeing, or the mind of perceiving, we in vain inquire after the quickness of sight in one, or clearness of perception in the other. . . .

14. These two, viz. intuition and demonstration, are the degrees of our *knowledge;* whatever comes short of one of these, with what assurance soever embraced, is but *faith* or *opinion,* but not knowledge, at least in all general truths. There is, indeed, another perception of the mind, employed about *the particular existence of finite beings without us,* which, going beyond bare probability, and yet not reaching perfectly to ei-

ther of the foregoing degrees of certainty, passes under the name of *knowledge.* There can be nothing more certain than that the idea we receive from an external object is in our minds: this is intuitive knowledge. But whether there be anything more than barely that idea in our minds; whether we can thence certainly infer the existence of anything without us, which corresponds to that idea, is that whereof some men think there may be a question made; because men may have such ideas in their minds, when no such thing exists, no such object affects their senses. But yet here I think we are provided with an evidence that puts us past doubting. For I ask any one, Whether he be not invincibly conscious to himself of a different perception, when he looks on the sun by day, and thinks on it by night; when he actually tastes wormwood, or smells a rose, or only thinks on that savour or odour? We as plainly find the difference there is between any idea revived in our minds by our own memory, and actually coming into our minds by our senses, as we do between any two distinct ideas. If any one says, a dream may do the same thing, and all these ideas may be produced in us without any external objects, he may please to dream that I make him this answer: 1. That it is no great matter, whether I remove his scruple or no; where all is but dream, reasoning and arguments are of no use, truth and knowledge nothing. 2. That I believe he will allow a very manifest difference between dreaming of being in the fire, and being actually in it. But yet if he be resolved to appear so sceptical as to maintain, that what I call being actually in the fire is nothing but a dream; and that we cannot thereby certainly know, that any such thing as fire actually exists without us: I answer, That we certainly finding that pleasure or pain follows upon the application of certain objects to us, whose existence we perceive, or dream that we perceive, by our senses; this certainty is as great as our happiness or misery, beyond which we have no concernment to know or to be. So that, I think, we may add to the two former sorts of knowledge this also, of the existence of particular external objects, by that perception and consciousness we have of the actual entrance of ideas from them, and allow these three degrees of knowledge, viz. *intuitive, demonstrative,* and *sensitive:* in each of which there are different degrees and ways of evidence and certainty. . . .

Chapter XI   Of Our Knowledge of the Existence of Other Things

1. The knowledge of our own being we have by intuition. The existence of a God, reason clearly makes known to us, as has been shown.

The knowledge of the existence of *any other thing* we can have only by *sensation:* for there being no necessary connexion of real existence with any *idea* a man hath in his memory; nor of any other existence but that of God with the existence of any particular man: no particular man can know the existence of any other being, but only when, by actual operating upon him, it makes itself perceived by him. For, the having the idea of anything in our mind, no more proves the existence of that thing, than the picture of a man evidences his being in the world, or the visions of a dream make thereby a true history.

2. It is therefore the *actual receiving* of ideas from without that gives us notice of the existence of other things, and makes us know, that something doth exist at that time without us, which causes that idea in us; though perhaps we neither know nor consider how it does it. For it takes not from the certainty of our senses, and the ideas we receive by them, that we know not the manner wherein they are produced: v.g. whilst I write this, I have, by the paper affecting my eyes, that idea produced in my mind, which, whatever object causes, I call *white;* by which I know that that quality or accident (i.e., whose appearance before my eyes always causes that idea) doth really exist, and hath a being without me. And of this, the greatest assurance I can possibly have, and to which my faculties can attain, is the testimony of my eyes, which are the proper and sole judges of this thing; whose testimony I have reason to rely on as so certain, that I can no more doubt, whilst I write this, that I see white and black, and that

something really exists that causes that sensation in me, than that I write or move my hand; which is a certainty as great as human nature is capable of, concerning the existence of anything, but a man's self alone, and of God.

3. The notice we have by our senses of the existing of things without us, though it be not altogether so certain as our intuitive knowledge, or the deductions of our reason employed about the clear abstract ideas of our own minds; yet it is an assurance that deserves the name of *knowledge.* If we persuade ourselves that our faculties act and inform us right concerning the existence of those objects that affect them, it cannot pass for an ill-grounded confidence; for I think nobody can, in earnest, be so sceptical as to be uncertain of the existence of those things which he sees and feels. At least, he that can doubt so far (whatever he may have with his own thoughts), will never have any controversy with me; since he can never be sure I say anything contrary to his own opinion. As to myself, I think God has given me assurance enough of the existence of things without me: Since, by their different application, I can produce in myself both pleasure and pain, which is one great concernment of my present state. This is certain: The confidence that our faculties do not herein deceive us, is the greatest assurance we are capable of concerning the existence of material beings. For we cannot act anything but by our faculties; nor talk of knowledge itself, but by the help of those faculties which are fitted to apprehend even what knowledge is. But besides the assurance we have from our senses themselves, that they do not err in the information they give us of the existence of things without us, when they are affected by them, we are further confirmed in this assurance by other concurrent reasons:

4. I. It is plain those perceptions are produced in us by exterior causes affecting our senses: because those that want the *organs* of any sense, never can have the ideas belonging to that sense produced in their minds. This is too evident to be doubted, and therefore we cannot but be assured that they come in by the organs of

that sense, and no other way. The organs themselves, it is plain, do not produce them: for then the eyes of a man in the dark would produce colours, and his nose smell roses in the winter. But we see nobody gets the relish of a pineapple, till he goes to the Indies, where it is, and tastes it.

5. II. Because sometimes I find that *I cannot avoid the having those ideas produced in my mind*. For though, when my eyes are shut, or windows fast, I can at pleasure recall to my mind the ideas of light, or the sun, which former sensations had lodged in my memory; so I can at pleasure lay by *that* idea, and take into my view that of the smell of a rose, or taste of sugar. But, if I turn my eyes at noon towards the sun, I cannot avoid the ideas which the light or sun then produces in me. So that there is a manifest difference between the ideas laid up in my memory (over which, if they were there only, I should have constantly the same power to dispose of them, and lay them by at pleasure), and those which force themselves upon me, and I cannot avoid having. And therefore it must needs be some exterior cause, and the brisk acting of some objects without me, whose efficacy I cannot resist, that produces those ideas in my mind, whether I will or no. Besides, there is nobody who doth not perceive the difference in himself between contemplating the sun, as he hath the idea of it in his memory, and actually looking upon it, of which two, his perception is so distinct, that few of his ideas are more distinguishable one from another. And therefore he hath certain knowledge that they are not *both* memory, or the actions of his mind, and fancies only within him, but that actual seeing hath a cause without. . . .

Chapter XV   Of Probability

1. As *demonstration* is the showing the agreement or disagreement of two ideas, by the intervention of one or more proofs, which have a constant, immutable, and visible connexion one with another; so *probability* is nothing but the appearance of such an agreement or disagreement, by the intervention of proofs, whose connexion is not constant and immutable, or at least is not perceived to be so, but is, or appears for the most part to be so, and is enough to induce the mind to judge the proposition to be true or false, rather than the contrary. For example: in the demonstration of it a man perceives the certain, immutable connexion there is of equality between the three angles of a triangle, and those intermediate ones which are made use of to show their equality to two right ones; and so, by an intuitive knowledge of the agreement or disagreement of the intermediate ideas in each step of the progress, the whole series is continued with an evidence, which clearly shows the agreement or disagreement of those three angles in equality to two right ones, and thus he has certain knowledge that it is so. But another man, who never took the pains to observe the demonstration, hearing a mathematician, a man of credit, affirm the three angles of a triangle to be equal to two right ones, assents to it, i.e., receives it for true, in which case the foundation of his assent is the probability of the thing; the proof being such as for the most part carries truth with it: The man on whose testimony he receives it, not being wont to affirm anything contrary to or besides his knowledge, especially in matters of this kind, so that that which causes his assent to this proposition, that the three angles of a triangle are equal to two right ones, that which makes him take these ideas to agree, without knowing them to do so, is the wonted veracity of the speaker in other cases, or his supposed veracity in this.

2. Our knowledge, as has been shown, being very narrow, and we not happy enough to find certain truth in everything which we have occasion to consider; most of the propositions we think, reason, discourse—nay, act upon, are such as we cannot have undoubted knowledge of their truth, yet some of them border so near upon certainty, that we make no doubt at all about them, but assent to them as firmly, and act, according to that assent, as resolutely as if they were infallibly demonstrated, and that our knowledge of them was perfect and certain. But

there being degrees herein, from the very neighbourhood of certainty and demonstration, quite down to improbability and unlikeness, even to the confines of impossibility; and also degrees of assent from full assurance and confidence, quite down to conjecture, doubt, and distrust. I shall come now (having, as I think, found out *the bounds of human knowledge and certainty*), in the next place, to consider *the several degrees and grounds of probability, and assent or faith. . . .*

5. Probability wanting that intuitive evidence which infallibly determines the understanding and produces certain knowledge, the mind, if it *will proceed rationally*, ought to examine all the grounds of probability, and see how they make more or less for or against any proposition, before it assents to or dissents from it; and, upon a due balancing the whole, reject or receive it, with a more or less firm assent, proportionably to the preponderancy of the greater grounds of probability on one side or the other.

For Further Reflection

1. Has Locke successfully refuted the theory of innate ideas? How does he account for our intuitive certainty of the laws of logic or the reality of the self, two items which the rationalists consider innate knowledge?

2. Is Lockean empiricism plausible? Are our minds like empty paper until experience writes its message upon them? Note, Locke is not denying that the mind has capabilities and that some humans have greater capabilities to learn than others.

3. How does Locke deal with the problem of skepticism about sensory experience, which is so prominent in Descartes? Is he successful? Hume will disagree with him, as you will see in a later reading.

An Idealist Theory of Knowledge   III.20

GEORGE BERKELEY

George Berkeley (1685–1753), an Irish philosopher and Anglican bishop, was educated at Trinity College, Dublin, where he subsequently taught. A deeply committed Christian, he sought to reconcile science with his faith by proving that although matter does not exist, the laws of physics, being God's laws, govern a universe made up of ideas. To exist is to be perceived, and God is that being who, perceiving all, causes them to exist as ideas in his mind. This position is called *philosophical idealism*. Berkeley's principal works are *A Treatise on the Principles of Knowledge* (1710) and *Three Dialogues between Hylas and Philonous* (1713), from which the present selection is taken.

In this dialogue, Berkeley defends his idealism, that is, his belief that only ideas exist. "To be is to be perceived"—to be is to be an idea in a mind—and hence matter existing apart from the mind does not exist. In this dialogue Hylas (from the Greek word for "matter") debates with Philonous (from the Greek "love of mind").

The unique thing about Berkeley's idealism is that unlike traditional idealism (for example, Plato's), it is not rationalistic. Berkeley does not propose that ideas exist independently, but rather assumes an empirical foundation. He agrees with Locke that all ideas originate in sense experience, and proceeds to show that all we ever experience is ideas. The only reality that exists to be known is perceivers and perceptions. To hold all of this ideal reality together one must posit a Divine mind who perceives us and hence causes our existence as ideas in his mind.

Study Questions

1. What is the most "extravagant opinion that ever entered into the mind of man"?
2. What is Philonous' response to Hylas' surprise at his views? How does he attempt to rebut the charge of skepticism?
3. What are sensible things according to Hylas and Philonous?
4. How does Philonous convince Hylas that heat and pain are ideas in the mind? Go through the argument step by step.
5. What is the point Philonous makes with the experiment of putting a cold and a warm hand into the same vessel of water?
6. What does Hylas mean by "to exist is one thing and to be perceived is another"?
7. Why does Philonous reject the notion of a material substratum, that is, matter that exists independently of our perceptions?
8. What conclusion does Philonous eventually force Hylas to accept regarding perceptions?
9. Why does the world continue to exist when we are not perceiving it, for example, when we are asleep?

HYLAS: YOU WERE REPRESENTED in last night's conversation as one who maintained the most extravagant opinion that ever entered into the mind of man, to wit, that there is no such thing as "material substance" in the world.

PHILONOUS: That there is no such thing as what philosophers call "material substance," I am seriously persuaded, but if I were made to see anything absurd or skeptical in this, I should then have the same reason to renounce this that I imagine I have now to reject the contrary opinion.

HYL.: What! Can anything be more fantastical, more repugnant to common sense or a more manifest piece of skepticism than to believe there is no such thing as matter?

PHIL.: Softly, good Hylas. What if it should prove that you, who hold there is, are, by virtue of that opinion, a greater skeptic and maintain more paradoxes and repugnances to common sense than I who believe no such thing? . . .

How comes it to pass then, Hylas, that you pronounce me a skeptic because I deny what you affirm, to wit, the existence of matter? Since, for aught you can tell, I am as peremptory in my denial as you in your affirmation.

HYL.: Hold, Philonous, I have been a little out in my definition; but every false step a man makes in discourse is not to be insisted on. I said indeed that a "skeptic" was one who doubted of everything, but I should have added: or who denies the reality and truth of things.

PHIL.: What things? Do you mean the principles and theorems of sciences? But these you know are universal intellectual notions, and conse-

---

From George Berkeley, Three Dialogues between Hylas and Philonous, 1713.

quently independent of matter; the denial therefore of this does not imply the denying them.

HYL.: I grant it. But are there no other things? What think you of distrusting the senses, of denying the real existence of sensible things, or pretending to know nothing of them. Is not this sufficient to denominate a man a skeptic?

PHIL.: Shall we therefore examine which of us it is that denies the reality of sensible things or professes the greatest ignorance of them, since, if I take you rightly, he is to be esteemed the greatest skeptic?

HYL.: That is what I desire.

PHIL.: What mean you by "sensible things"?

HYL.: Those things which are perceived by the senses. Can you imagine that I mean anything else?

PHIL.: Pardon me, Hylas, if I am desirous clearly to apprehend your notions, since this may much shorten our inquiry. Suffer me then to ask you this further question. Are those things only perceived by the senses which are perceived immediately? Or may those things properly be said to be "sensible" which are perceived immediately, or not without the intervention of others?

HYL.: I do not sufficiently understand you.

PHIL.: In reading a book, what I immediately perceive are the letters, but mediately, or by means of these, are suggested to my mind the notions of God, virtue, truth, etc. Now, that the letters are truly sensible things, or perceived by sense, there is no doubt; but I would know whether you take the things suggested by them to be so too.

HYL.: No, certainly; it were absurd to think God or virtue sensible things, though they may be signified and suggested to the mind by sensible marks with which they have an arbitrary connection.

PHIL.: It seems, then, that by "sensible things" you mean those only which can be perceived immediately by sense.

HYL.: Right.

PHIL.: Does it not follow from this that, though I see one part of the sky red, and another blue, and that my reason does thence evidently conclude there must be some cause of that diversity of colors, yet that cause cannot be said to be a sensible thing or perceived by the sense of seeing?

HYL.: It does.

PHIL.: In like manner, though I hear variety of sounds, yet I cannot be said to hear the causes of those sounds.

HYL.: You cannot.

PHIL.: And when by my touch I perceive a thing to be hot and heavy, I cannot say, with any truth or propriety, that I feel the cause of its heat or weight.

HYL.: To prevent any more questions of this kind, I tell you once for all that by "sensible things" I mean those only which are perceived by sense, and that in truth the senses perceive nothing which they do not perceive immediately, for they make no inferences. The deducing therefore of causes or occasions from effects and appearances, which alone are perceived by sense, entirely relates to reason.

PHIL.: This point then is agreed between us— that *sensible things are those only which are immediately perceived by sense.* You will further inform me whether we immediately perceive by sight anything besides light and colors and figures; or by hearing, anything but sounds; by the palate, anything besides tastes; by the smell, besides odors; or by the touch, more than tangible qualities.

HYL.: We do not.

PHIL.: It seems, therefore, that if you take away all sensible qualities, there remains nothing sensible?

HYL.: I grant it.

PHIL.: Sensible things therefore are nothing else but so many sensible qualities or combinations of sensible qualities?

HYL.: Nothing else.

PHIL.: Heat is then a sensible thing?

HYL.: Certainly.

PHIL.: Does the reality of sensible things consist in being perceived, or is it something distinct from their being perceived, and that bears no relation to the mind?

HYL.: To *exist* is one thing, and to be *perceived* is another.

PHIL.: I speak with regard to sensible things only; and of these I ask, whether by their real existence you mean a subsistence exterior to the mind and distinct from their being perceived?

HYL.: I mean a real absolute being, distinct from and without any relation to their being perceived.

PHIL.: Heat therefore, if it be allowed a real being, must exist without the mind?

HYL.: It must.

PHIL.: Tell me, Hylas, is this real existence equally compatible to all degrees of heat, which we perceive, or is there any reason why we should attribute it to some and deny it to others? And if there be, pray, let me know that reason.

HYL.: Whatever degree of heat we perceive by sense, we may be sure the same exists in the object that occasions it.

PHIL.: What! the greatest as well as the least?

HYL.: I tell you, the reason is plainly the same in respect of both: They are both perceived by sense; nay, the greater degree of heat is more sensibly perceived; and consequently, if there is any difference, we are more certain of its real existence than we can be of the reality of a lesser degree.

PHIL.: But is not the most vehement and intense degree of heat a very great pain?

HYL.: No one can deny it.

PHIL.: And is any unperceiving thing capable of pain or pleasure?

HYL.: No, certainly.

PHIL.: Is your material substance a senseless being or a being endowed with sense and perception?

HYL.: It is senseless, without doubt.

PHIL.: It cannot, therefore, be the subject of pain?

HYL.: By no means.

PHIL.: Nor, consequently, of the greatest heat perceived by sense, since you acknowledge this to be no small pain?

HYL.: I grant it.

PHIL.: What shall we say then of your external object: is it a material substance, or no?

HYL.: It is a material substance with the sensible qualities inhering in it.

PHIL.: How then can a great heat exist in it, since you own it cannot in a material substance? I desire you would clear this point.

HYL.: Hold, Philonous, I fear I was out in yielding intense heat to be a pain. It should seem rather that pain is something distinct from heat, and the consequence or effect of it.

PHIL.: Upon putting your hand near the fire, do you perceive one simple uniform sensation or two distinct sensations?

HYL.: But one simple sensation.

PHIL.: Is not the heat immediately perceived?

HYL.: It is.

PHIL.: And the pain?

HYL.: True.

PHIL.: Seeing therefore they are both immediately perceived at the same time, and the fire affects you only with one simple or uncompounded idea, it follows that this same simple idea is both the intense heat immediately perceived and the pain; and, consequently, that the intense heat immediately perceived is nothing distinct from a particular sort of pain.

HYL.: It seems so.

PHIL.: Again, try in your thoughts, Hylas, if you can conceive a vehement sensation to be without pain or pleasure.

HYL.: I cannot.

PHIL.: Or can you frame to yourself an idea of sensible pain or pleasure, in general, abstracted from every particular idea of heat, cold, tastes, smells, etc.?

HYL.: I do not find that I can.

PHIL.: Does it not therefore follow that sensible pain is nothing distinct from those sensations or ideas—in an intense degree?

HYL.: It is undeniable; and, to speak the truth, I begin to suspect a very great heat cannot exist but in a mind perceiving it.

PHIL.: What! Are you then in that *skeptical* state of suspense, between affirming and denying?

HYL.: I think I may be positive in the point. A very violent and painful heat cannot exist without the mind.

PHIL.: It has not therefore, according to you, any real being?

HYL.: I own it.

PHIL.: Is it therefore certain that there is no body in nature really hot?

HYL.: I have not denied there is any real heat in bodies. I only say there is no such thing as an intense real heat.

PHIL.: But did you not say before that all degrees of heat were equally real, or, if there was any difference, that the greater were more undoubtedly real than the lesser?

HYL.: True, but it was because I did not then consider the ground there is for distinguishing between them, which I now plainly see. And it is this: because intense heat is nothing else but a particular kind of painful sensation, and pain cannot exist but in a perceiving being, it follows that no intense heat can really exist in an unperceiving corporeal substance. But this is no reason why we should deny heat in an inferior degree to exist in such a substance.

PHIL.: But how shall we be able to discern those degrees of heat which exist only in the mind from those which exist without it?

HYL.: That is no difficult matter. You know the least pain cannot exist unperceived; whatever, therefore, degree of heat is a pain exists only in the mind. But as for all other degrees of heat nothing obliges us to think the same of them.

PHIL.: I think you granted before that no unperceiving being was capable of pleasure any more than of pain.

HYL.: I did.

PHIL.: And is not warmth, or a more gentle degree of heat than what causes uneasiness, a pleasure?

HYL.: What then?

PHIL.: Consequently, it cannot exist without the mind in an unperceiving substance, or body.

HYL.: So it seems.

PHIL.: Since, therefore, as well those degrees of heat that are not painful, as those that are, can exist only in a thinking substance, may we not conclude that external bodies are absolutely incapable of any degree of heat whatsoever?

HYL.: On second thoughts, I do not think it is so evident that warmth is a pleasure as that a great degree of heat is pain.

PHIL.: I do not pretend that warmth is as great a pleasure as heat is a pain. But if you grant it to be even a small pleasure, it serves to make good my conclusion.

HYL.: I could rather call it an "indolence." It seems to be nothing more than a privation of both pain and pleasure. And that such a quality or state as this may agree to an unthinking substance, I hope you will not deny.

PHIL.: If you are resolved to maintain that warmth, or a gentle degree of heat, is no pleasure, I know not how to convince you otherwise than by appealing to your own sense. But what think you of cold?

HYL.: The same that I do of heat. An intense degree of cold is a pain; for to feel a very great cold is to perceive a great uneasiness; it cannot therefore exist without the mind, but a lesser degree of cold may, as well as a lesser degree of heat.

PHIL.: Those bodies, therefore, upon whose application to our own we perceive a moderate degree of heat must be concluded to have a moderate degree of heat or warmth in them; and those upon whose application we feel a like degree of cold must be thought to have cold in them.

HYL.: They must.

PHIL.: Can any doctrine be true that necessarily leads a man into an absurdity?

HYL.: Without doubt it cannot.

PHIL.: Is it not an absurdity to think that the same thing should be at the same time both cold and warm?

HYL.: It is.

PHIL.: Suppose now one of your hands is hot, and the other cold, and that they are both at once put into the same vessel of water, in an intermediate state, will not the water seem cold to one hand, and warm to the other?

HYL.: It will.

PHIL.: Ought we not therefore, by your principles, to conclude it is really both cold and warm at the same time, that is, according to your own concession, to believe an absurdity?

HYL.: I confess it seems so.

PHIL.: Consequently, the principles themselves are false, since you have granted that no true principle leads to an absurdity.

HYL.: But, after all, can anything be more absurd than to say, *there is no heat in the fire?*

PHIL.: To make the point still clearer; tell me whether, in two cases exactly alike, we ought not to make the same judgment?

HYL.: We ought.

PHIL.: When a pin pricks your finger, does it not rend and divide the fibres of your flesh?

HYL.: It does.

PHIL.: And when a coal burns your finger, does it any more?

HYL.: It does not.

PHIL.: Since, therefore, you neither judge the sensation itself occasioned by the pin, nor anything like it to be in the pin, you should not, conformably to what you have now granted, judge the sensation occasioned by the fire, or anything like it, to be in the fire.

HYL.: Well, since it must be so, I am content to yield this point and acknowledge that heat and cold are only sensations existing in our minds. But there still remain qualities enough to secure the reality of external things.

PHIL.: But what will you say, Hylas, if it shall appear that the case is the same with regard to all other sensible qualities, and that they can no more be supposed to exist without the mind than heat and cold?

HYL.: Then, indeed, you will have done something to the purpose; but this is what I despair of seeing proved.

PHIL.: Let us examine them in order. What think you of tastes—do they exist without the mind, or no?

HYL.: Can any man in his senses doubt whether sugar is sweet or wormwood bitter?

PHIL.: Inform me, Hylas. Is a sweet taste a particular kind of pleasure or pleasant sensation, or is it not?

HYL.: It is.

PHIL.: And is not bitterness some kind of uneasiness or pain?

HYL.: I grant it.

PHIL.: If therefore sugar and wormwood are unthinking corporeal substances existing without the mind, how can sweetness and bitterness, that is, pleasure and pain, agree to them? . . .

HYL.: I see it is to no purpose to hold out, so I give up the cause as to those mentioned qualities, though I profess it sounds oddly to say that sugar is not sweet.

PHIL.: But, for your further satisfaction, take this along with you: that which at other times seems sweet shall, to a distempered palate, appear bitter, and nothing can be plainer than that divers persons perceive different tastes in the same food, since that which one man delights in, another abhors. And how could this be if the taste was something really inherent in the food?

HYL.: I acknowledge I know not how.

PHIL.: In the next place, odors are to be considered. And with regard to these I would fain know whether what has been said of tastes does not exactly agree to them? Are they not so many pleasing or displeasing sensations?

HYL.: They are.

PHIL.: Can you then conceive it possible that they should exist in an unperceiving thing?

HYL.: I cannot.

PHIL.: Or can you imagine that filth and ordure affect those brute animals that feed on them out of choice with the same smells which we perceive in them?

HYL.: By no means.

PHIL.: May we not therefore conclude of smells, as of the other forementioned qualities, that they cannot exist in any but a perceiving substance or mind?

HYL.: I think so.

PHIL.: Then as to sounds, what must we think of them, are they accidents really inherent in external bodies or not?

HYL.: That they inhere not in the sonorous bodies is plain from hence; because a bell struck in the exhausted receiver of an air-pump sends forth no sound. The air, therefore, must be thought the subject of sound.

PHIL.: What reason is there for that, Hylas?

HYL.: Because, when any motion is raised in the air, we perceive a sound greater or less, in proportion to the air's motion; but without some motion in the air we never hear any sound at all.

PHIL.: And granting that we never hear a sound but when some motion is produced in the air, yet I do not see how you can infer from thence that the sound itself is in the air.

HYL.: It is this very motion in the external air that produces in the mind the sensation of sound. For, striking on the drum of the ear, it causes a vibration which by the auditory nerves being communicated to the brain, the soul is thereupon affected with the sensation called "sound."

PHIL.: What! is sound then a sensation?

HYL.: I tell you, as perceived by us, it is a particular sensation in the mind.

PHIL.: And can any sensation exist without the mind?

HYL.: No, certainly.

PHIL.: How then can sound, being a sensation, exist in the air if by the "air" you mean a senseless substance existing without the mind?

HYL.: You must distinguish, Philonous, between sound as it is perceived by us, and as it is in itself; or (which is the same thing) between the sound we immediately perceive and that which exists without us. The former, indeed, is a particular kind of sensation, but the latter is merely a vibrative or undulatory motion in the air.

PHIL.: I thought I had already obviated that distinction by the answer I gave when you were applying it in a like case before. But, to say no more of that, are you sure then that sound is really nothing but motion?

HYL.: I am.

PHIL.: Whatever, therefore, agrees to real sound may with truth be attributed to motion?

HYL.: It may.

PHIL.: It is then good sense to speak of "motion" as of a thing that is *loud, sweet, acute,* or *grave.*

HYL.: I see you are resolved not to understand me. Is it not evident those accidents or modes belong only to sensible sound, or sound in the common acceptation of the word, but not to sound in the real and philosophic sense, which, as I just now told you, is nothing but a certain motion of the air?

PHIL.: It seems then there are two sorts of sound—the one vulgar, or that which is heard, the other philosophical and real?

HYL.: Even so.

PHIL.: And the latter consists in motion?

HYL.: I told you so before.

PHIL.: Tell me, Hylas, to which of the senses, think you, the idea of motion belongs? To the hearing?

HYL.: No, certainly, but to the sight and touch.

PHIL.: It should follow then that, according to you, real sounds may possibly be *seen* or *felt,* but never *heard.*

HYL.: Look you, Philonous, you may, if you please, make a jest of my opinion, but that will not alter the truth of things. I own, indeed, the inferences you draw me into sound something oddly, but common language, you know, is framed by, and for the use of, the vulgar. We must not therefore wonder if expressions adapted to exact philosophic notions seem uncouth and out of the way.

PHIL.: Is it come to that? I assure you I imagine myself to have gained no small point since you make so light of departing from common phrases and opinions, it being a main part of our inquiry to examine whose notions are widest of the common road and most repugnant to the general sense of the world. But can you think it no more than a philosophical paradox to say that "real sounds are never heard," and that the idea of them is obtained by some other sense? And is there nothing in this contrary to nature and the truth of things?

HYL.: To deal ingenuously, I do not like it. And, after the concessions already made, I had as well grant that sounds, too, have no real being without the mind. . . .

I frankly own, Philonous, that it is in vain to stand out any longer. Colors, sounds, tastes, in a word, all those termed "secondary qualities," have certainly no existence without the mind. But by this acknowledgment I must not be supposed to derogate anything from the reality of matter or external objects; seeing it is no more than several philosophers maintain, who nevertheless are the farthest imaginable from denying matter. For the clearer understanding of this you must know sensible qualities are by philosophers divided into "primary" and "secondary." The former are extension, figure, solidity, gravity, motion, and rest. And these they hold exist really in bodies. The latter are those above enumerated, or, briefly, all sensible qualities besides the primary, which they assert are only so many sensations or ideas existing nowhere but in the mind. But all this, I doubt not, you are already apprised of. For my part I have been a long time sensible there was such an opinion current among philosophers, but was never thoroughly convinced of its truth till now.

PHIL.: You are still then of opinion that *extension* and *figures* are inherent in external unthinking substances?

HYL.: I am.

PHIL.: But what if the same arguments which are brought against secondary qualities will hold good against these also?

HYL.: Why then I shall be obliged to think they too exist only in the mind. . . .

I acknowledge, Philonous, that, upon a fair observation of what passes in my mind, I can discover nothing else but that I am a thinking being affected with variety of sensations; neither is it possible to conceive how a sensation should exist in an unperceiving substance. But then, on the other hand, when I look on sensible things in a different view, considering them as so many modes and qualities, I find it neces-

sary to suppose a material *substratum,* without which they cannot be conceived to exist.

PHIL.: "Material substratum" call you it? Pray, by which of your senses came you acquainted with that being?

HYL.: It is not itself sensible; its modes and qualities only being perceived by the senses.

PHIL.: I presume then it was by reflection and reason you obtained the idea of it?

HYL.: I do not pretend to any proper positive idea of it. However, I conclude it exists because qualities cannot be conceived to exist without a support.

PHIL.: It seems then you have only a relative notion of it, or that you conceive it not otherwise than by conceiving the relation it bears to sensible qualities? . . .

HYL.: Right.

PHIL.: Be pleased, therefore, to let me know wherein that relation consists.

HYL.: Is it not sufficiently expressed in the term "substratum" or "substance"?

PHIL.: If so, the word "substratum" should import that it is spread under the sensible qualities or accidents?

HYL.: True.

PHIL.: And consequently under extension?

HYL.: I own it.

PHIL.: It is therefore somewhat in its own nature distinct from extension?

HYL.: I tell you extension is only a mode, and matter is something that supports modes. And is it not evident the thing supported is different from the thing supporting?

PHIL.: So that something distinct from, and exclusive of, extension is supposed to be the *substratum* of extension?

HYL.: Just so.

PHIL.: Answer me, Hylas, can a thing be spread without extension, or is not the idea of extension necessarily included in *spreading*?

HYL.: It is.

PHIL.: Whatsoever therefore you suppose spread under anything must have in itself an extension distinct from the extension of that thing under which it is spread?

HYL.: It must.

PHIL.: Consequently, every corporeal substance being the *substratum* of extension must have in itself another extension by which it is qualified to be a *substratum*, and so on to infinity? And I ask whether this be not absurd in itself and repugnant to what you granted just now, to wit, that the *substratum* was something distinct from and exclusive of extension?

HYL.: Aye, but, Philonous, you take me wrong. I do not mean that matter is *spread* in a gross literal sense under extension. The word "substratum" is used only to express in general the same thing with "substance."

PHIL.: Well then, let us examine the relation implied in the term "substance." Is it not that it stands under accidents?

HYL.: The very same.

PHIL.: But that one thing may stand under or support another, must it not be extended?

HYL.: It must.

PHIL.: Is not therefore this supposition liable to the same absurdity with the former?

HYL.: You still take things in a strict literal sense; that is not fair, Philonous.

PHIL.: I am not for imposing any sense on your words; you are at liberty to explain them as you please. Only, I beseech you, make me understand something by them. You tell me matter supports or stands under accidents. How! Is it as your legs support your body?

HYL.: No, that is the literal sense.

PHIL.: Pray let me know any sense, literal or not literal, that you understand it in—How long must I wait for an answer, Hylas?

HYL.: I declare I know not what to say. I once thought I understood well enough what was meant by matter's supporting accidents. But now, the more I think on it, the less can I comprehend it; in short, I find that I know nothing of it.

PHIL.: It seems then you have no idea at all, neither relative nor positive, of matter? You know neither what it is in itself nor what relation it bears to accidents?

HYL.: I acknowledge it…

Other men may think as they please, but for your part you have nothing to reproach me with. My comfort is you are as much a skeptic as I am.

PHIL.: There, Hylas, I must beg leave to differ from you.

HYL.: What! Have you all along agreed to the premises, and do you now deny the conclusion and leave me to maintain those paradoxes by myself which you led me into? This surely is not fair.

PHIL.: I deny that I agreed with you in those notions that led to skepticism. You indeed said the *reality* of sensible things consisted in an *absolute existence* out of the minds of spirits, or distinct from their being perceived. And, pursuant to this notion of reality, you are obliged to deny sensible things any real existence; that is, according to your own definition, you profess yourself a skeptic. But I neither said nor thought the reality of sensible things was to be defined after that manner. To me it is evident, for the reasons you allow of, that sensible things cannot exist otherwise than in a mind or spirit. Whence I conclude, not that they have no real existence, but that, seeing they depend not on my thought and have an existence distinct from being perceived by me, *there must be some other mind wherein they exist.* As sure, therefore, as the sensible world really exists, so sure is there an infinite omnipresent Spirit, who contains and supports it.

HYL.: What! this is no more than I and all Christians hold; nay, and all others, too, who believe there is a God and that He knows and comprehends all things.

PHIL.: Aye, but here lies the difference. Men commonly believe that all things are known or perceived by God, because they believe the being of a God; whereas I, on the other side, immediately and necessarily conclude the being of a God, because all sensible things must be perceived by him.

HYL.: But so long as we all believe the same thing, what matter is it how we come by that belief?

PHIL.: But neither do we agree in the same opinion. For philosophers, though they acknowledge all corporeal beings to be perceived by God, yet they attribute to them an absolute subsistence distinct from their being perceived by any mind whatever, which I do not. Besides, is there no difference between saying, *there is a God, therefore He perceives all things*, and saying, *sensible things do really exist; and if they really exist, they are necessarily perceived by an infinite mind: therefore there is an infinite mind, or God?* This furnishes you with a direct and immediate demonstration, from a most evident principle, of the *being of a God*. Divines and philosophers had proved beyond all controversy, from the beauty and useful-ness of the several parts of the creation, that it was the workmanship of God. But that—setting aside all help of astronomy and natural philosophy, all contemplation of the contrivance, order and adjustment of things—an infinite mind should be necessarily inferred from the bare *existence* of the sensible world is an advantage peculiar to them only who have made this easy reflection, that the sensible world is that which we perceive by our several senses; and that nothing is perceived by the senses besides ideas; and that no idea or archetype of an idea can exist otherwise than in a mind.

For Further Reflection

1. Do you agree with Berkeley that only ideas exist? Does it seem obvious to you that matter really does exist? If you disagree with Berkeley, can you show where he has made an error in his argument?

2. According to Berkeley there is no sound independent of our hearing it and no reality but our experiencing it. Does this mean that when we leave our rooms, they disappear? There is an old Oxford limerick on this point:

> There was a young man who said, "God
> Must think it exceedingly odd
> If he finds that this tree
> Continues to be,
> When there's no one about in the quad."

> Dear Sir, your astonishment's odd
> I'm always about in the quad,
> And that's why the tree
> Continues to be,
> Since observed by,
>
>   Yours faithfully,
>
>   God

The question is, in whose mind does God exist? Does the notion of God fit into Berkeley's system?

The Origin of Our Ideas and Skepticism about Causal Reasoning III.21

DAVID HUME

In this selection from *An Enquiry Concerning Human Understanding* (1748) we have an extension of the empiricism begun with Locke. Like Locke, Hume locates the foundation of all our ideas in sensory experience. But Hume moves even further away from the possibility of absolute certainty of knowledge toward the view that we can justly only have relative certainty. We can only be certain of analytic truths ("relations of ideas"), namely, mathematics and tautologies. With regard to synthetic truths ("matters of fact") we, at best, can have a high degree of probability. But even the notion of probability is dubious and leads to a certain skepticism because the notion of cause and effect on which experiential knowledge is based is itself not an impression but an idea.

(A biographical note on Hume is found in Reading II.8.)

Study Questions

1. What is the origin of our ideas? How does Hume distinguish ideas from impressions?
2. What does Hume say about the reputed "unbounded liberty" of thought? How free is it?
3. What are Hume's two proofs for his thesis about ideas and impressions?
4. What are the practical implications of Hume's empiricism? What effect would it have on metaphysical speculation?
5. What sort of knowledge is certain? What kind lacks certainty?
6. Why is causal reasoning doubtful? What does Hume mean by saying causal relations can never be discovered by *a priori* argument?
7. What is Hume's solution to the problem of doubt? What is the principle or cause that leads us to rely on experience despite the inherent difficulties of justifying the procedure?

OF THE ORIGIN OF IDEAS

EVERY ONE WILL READILY ALLOW, that there is a considerable difference between the perceptions of the mind, when a man feels the pain of excessive heat, or the pleasure of moderate warmth, and when he afterwards recalls to his memory this sensation, or anticipates it by his imagination. These faculties may mimic or copy the perceptions of the senses; but they never can entirely reach the force and vivacity of the original sentiment. The utmost we say of them, even when they operate with greatest vigor, is, that they represent their object in so lively a manner, that we could *almost* say we feel or see it: But, except the mind be disordered by disease or madness, they never can arrive at such a pitch of vivacity, as to render these perceptions altogether undistinguishable. All the colors of poetry, however splendid, can never paint natural objects in

Reprinted from David Hume, An Enquiry Concerning Human Understanding *(Oxford: Clarendon Press, 1748).*

such a manner as to make the description be taken for a real landscape. The most lively thought is still inferior to the dullest sensation.

We may observe a like distinction to run through all the other perceptions of the mind. A man in a fit of anger, is actuated in a very different manner from one who only thinks of that emotion. If you tell me, that any person is in love, I easily understand your meaning, and form a just conception of his situation, but never can mistake that conception for the real disorders and agitations of the passion. When we reflect on our past sentiments and affections, our thought is a faithful mirror, and copies its objects truly; but the colors which it employs are faint and dull, in comparison of those in which our original perceptions were clothed. It requires no nice discernment or metaphysical head to mark the distinction between them.

Here therefore we may divide all the perceptions of the mind into two classes or species, which are distinguished by their different degrees of force and vivacity. The less forcible and lively are commonly denominated *Thoughts* or *Ideas.* The other species want a name in our language, and in most others; I suppose, because it was not requisite for any, but philosophical purposes, to rank them under a general term or appellation. Let us, therefore, use a little freedom, and call them *Impressions;* employing that word in a sense somewhat different from the usual. By the term *impression,* then, I mean all our more lively perceptions, when we hear, or see, or feel, or love, or hate, or desire, or will. And impressions are distinguished from ideas, which are the less lively perceptions, of which we are conscious, when we reflect on any of those sensations or movements above mentioned.

Nothing, at first view, may seem more unbounded than the thought of man, which not only escapes all human power and authority, but is not even restrained within the limits of nature and reality. To form monsters, and join incongruous shapes and appearances, costs the imagination no more trouble than to conceive the most natural and familiar objects. And while the body is confined to one planet, along which it creeps with pain and difficulty, the thought can in an instant transport us into the most distant regions of the universe, or even beyond the universe, into the unbounded chaos, where nature is supposed to lie in total confusion. What never was seen, or heard of, may yet be conceived; nor is any thing beyond the power of thought, except what implies an absolute contradiction.

But though our thought seems to possess this unbounded liberty, we shall find, upon a nearer examination, that it is really confined within very narrow limits, and that all this creative power of the mind amounts to no more than the faculty of compounding, transposing, augmenting, or diminishing the materials afforded us by the senses and experience. When we think of a golden mountain, we only join two consistent ideas, *gold,* and *mountain,* with which we were formerly acquainted. A virtuous horse we can conceive; because, from our own feeling, we can conceive virtue; and this we may unite to the figure and shape of a horse, which is an animal familiar to us. In short, all the materials of thinking are derived either from our outward or inward sentiment: The mixture and composition of these belongs alone to the mind and will. Or, to express myself in philosophical language, all our ideas or more feeble perceptions are copies of our impressions or more lively ones.

To prove this, the two following arguments will, I hope, be sufficient. First, when we analyze our thoughts or ideas, however compounded or sublime, we always find that they resolve themselves into such simple ideas as were copied from a precedent feeling or sentiment. Even those ideas, which, at first view, seem the most wide of this origin, are found, upon a nearer scrutiny, to be derived from it. The idea of God, as meaning an infinitely intelligent, wise, and good Being, arises from reflecting on the operations of our own mind, and augmenting, without limit, those qualities of goodness and wisdom. We may prosecute this enquiry to what length we please, where we shall always find that every idea which we examine is copied from a similar impression. Those who would assert that this position is not universally true nor without exception, have only one, and that an easy method of refuting it; by producing that idea, which, in their opinion, is not derived from this source. It will then be incumbent on us, if we would maintain our doctrine, to produce the impression, or lively perception, which corresponds to it.

Secondly. If it happen, from a defect of the organ, that a man is not susceptible of any species of sensation, we always find that he is as little susceptible of the correspondent ideas. A blind man can form no notion of colors; a deaf man of sounds. Restore either of them that sense in which he is deficient; by opening this new inlet for his sensations, you also open an inlet for the ideas; and he finds no difficulty in conceiving these objects. . . .

Here, therefore, is a proposition, which not only seems, in itself, simple and intelligible, but, if a proper use were made of it, might render every dispute equally intelligible, and banish all that jargon, which has so long taken possession of metaphysical reasonings, and drawn disgrace upon them. All ideas, especially abstract ones, are naturally faint and obscure: the mind has but a slender hold of them: they are apt to be confounded with other resembling ideas; and when we have often employed any term, though without a distinct meaning, we are apt to imagine it has a determinate idea annexed to it. On the contrary, all impressions, that is, all sensations, either outward or inward, are strong and determined, nor is it easy to fall into any error or mistake with regard to them. When we entertain, therefore, any suspicion that a philosophical term is employed without any meaning or idea (as is but too frequent), we need but enquire, *from what impression is that supposed idea derived?* And if it be impossible to assign any, this will serve to confirm our suspicion. By bringing ideas into so clear a light we may reasonably hope to remove all dispute, which may arise, concerning their nature and reality.

SCEPTICAL DOUBTS CONCERNING THE OPERATIONS OF THE UNDERSTANDING

Part I

All the objects of human reason or enquiry may naturally be divided into two kinds, to wit, *Relations of Ideas,* and *Matters of Fact.* Of the first kind are the sciences of Geometry, Algebra, and Arithmetic, and in short, every affirmation which is either intuitively or demonstratively certain. *That the square of the hypotenuse is equal to the squares of the two sides,* is a proposition which expresses a relation between these figures. *That three times five is equal to the half of thirty,* expresses a relation between these numbers. Propositions of this kind are discoverable by the mere operation of thought, without dependence on what is anywhere existent in the universe. Though there never were a circle or triangle in nature, the truths demonstrated by Euclid would for ever retain their certainty and evidence.

Matters of fact, which are the second objects of human reason, are not ascertained in the same manner; nor is our evidence of their truth, however great, of a like nature with the foregoing. The contrary of every matter of fact is still possible; because it can never imply a contradiction, and is conceived by the mind with the same facility and distinctness, as if ever so conformable to reality. *That the sun will not rise tomorrow* is no less intelligible a proposition, and implies no more contradiction than the affirmation, *that it will rise.* We should in vain, therefore, attempt to demonstrate its falsehood. Were it demonstratively false, it would imply a contradiction, and could never be distinctly conceived by the mind.

It may, therefore, be a subject worthy of curiosity, to enquire what is the nature of that evidence which assures us of any real existence and matter of fact, beyond the present testimony of our senses, or the records of our memory. This part of philosophy, it is observable, has been little cultivated, either by the ancients or moderns; and therefore our doubts and errors, in the prosecution of so important an enquiry, may be the more excusable, while we march through such difficult paths without any guide or direction. They may even prove useful, by exciting curiosity, and destroying that implicit faith and security, which is the bane of all reasoning and free enquiry. The discovery of defects in the common philosophy, if any such there be, will not, I presume, be a discouragement, but rather an incitement, as is usual, to attempt something more full and satisfactory than has yet been proposed to the public.

All reasonings concerning matter of fact seem to be founded on the relation of *Cause and Effect*. By means of that relation alone we can go beyond the evidence of our memory and senses. If you were to ask a man, why he believes any matter of fact, which is absent; for instance, that his friend is in the country, or in France; he would give you a reason; and this reason would be some other fact; as a letter received from him, or the knowledge of his former resolutions and promises. A man finding a watch or any other machine in a desert island would conclude that there had once been men in that island. All our reasonings concerning fact are of the same nature. And here it is constantly supposed that there is a connection between the present fact and that which is inferred from it. Were there nothing to bind them together, the inference would be entirely precarious. The hearing of an articulate voice and rational discourse in the dark assures us of the presence of some person: Why? because these are the effects of the human make and fabric, and closely connected with it. If we anatomize all the other reasonings of this nature, we shall find that they are founded on the relation of cause and effect, and that this relation is either near or remote, direct or collateral. Heat and light are collateral effects of fire, and the one effect may justly be inferred from the other.

If we would satisfy ourselves, therefore, concerning the nature of that evidence, which assures us of matters of fact, we must enquire how we arrive at the knowledge of cause and effect. . . .

This proposition, *that causes and effects are discoverable, not by reason but by experience,* will readily be admitted with regard to such objects, as we remember to have once been altogether unknown to us, since we must be conscious of the utter inability, which we then lay under, of foretelling what would arise from them. Present two smooth pieces of marble to a man who has no tincture of natural philosophy; he will never discover that they will adhere together in such a manner as to require great force to separate them in a direct line, while they make so small a resistance to a lateral pressure. Such events, as bear little analogy to the common course of nature, are also readily confessed to be known only by experience; nor does any man imagine that the explosion of gunpowder, or the attraction of a loadstone, could ever be discovered by arguments *a priori*. In like manner, when an effect is supposed to depend upon an intricate machinery or secret structure of parts, we make no difficulty in attributing all our knowledge of it to experience. Who will assert that he can give the ultimate reason why milk or bread is proper nourishment for a man, not for a lion or a tiger?

But the same truth may not appear, at first sight, to have the same evidence with regard to events, which have become familiar to us from our first appearance in the world, which bear a close analogy to the whole course of nature, and which are supposed to depend on the simple qualities of objects, without any secret structure of parts. We are apt to imagine that we could discover these effects by the mere operation of our reason, without experience. We fancy, that were we brought on a sudden into this world, we could at first have inferred that one Billiard-ball would communicate motion to another upon impulse, and that we needed not to have waited for the event, in order to pronounce with certainty concerning it. Such is the influence of custom, that, where it is strongest, it not only covers our natural ignorance, but even conceals itself, and seems not to take place, merely because it is found in the highest degree.

But to convince us that all the laws of nature, and all the operations of bodies without exception, are known only by experience, the following reflections may, perhaps, suffice. Were any object presented to us, and were we required to pronounce concerning the effect, which will result from it, without consulting past observation, after what manner, I beseech you, must the mind proceed in this operation? It must invent or imagine some event, which it ascribes to the object as its effect; and it is plain that this invention must be entirely arbitrary. The mind can never possibly find the effect in the supposed cause, by the most accurate scrutiny and examination. For the effect is totally different from the cause, and consequently can never be discovered in it. Motion in the second Billiard-ball is a quite distinct event from motion in the first; nor is there anything in the one to suggest the smallest hint of the other. A stone or piece of metal raised into the air, and left without any support, immediately falls, but to consider the matter *a priori*, is there anything we discover in this situation which can beget the idea of a downward, rather than an upward, or any other motion, in the stone or metal?

And as the first imagination or invention of a particular effect, in all natural operations, is arbitrary, where we consult not experience, so must we also esteem the supposed tie or connection between the cause and effect, which binds them together, and renders it impossible that any other effect could result from the operation of that cause. When I see, for instance, a Billiard-ball moving in a straight line towards another, even suppose motion in the second ball should by accident be suggested to me, as the result of their contact or impulse, may I not conceive, that a hundred different events might as well follow from that cause? May not both these balls remain at absolute rest? May not the first ball return in a straight line, or leap off from the second in any line or direction? All

these suppositions are consistent and conceivable. Why then should we give the preference to one, which is no more consistent or conceivable than the rest? All our reasonings *a priori* will never be able to show us any foundation for this preference.

In a word, then, every effect is a distinct event from its cause. It could not, therefore, be discovered in the cause, and the first invention or conception of it, *a priori*, must be entirely arbitrary. And even after it is suggested, the conjunction of it with the cause must appear equally arbitrary, since there are always many other effects, which, to reason, must seem fully as consistent and natural. In vain, therefore, should we pretend to determine any single event, or infer any cause of effect, without the assistance of observation and experience. . . .

Part II

But we have not yet attained any tolerable satisfaction with regard to the question first proposed. Each solution still gives rise to a new question as difficult as the foregoing, and leads us on to farther enquiries. When it is asked, *What is the nature of all our reasonings concerning matter of fact?* the proper answer seems to be, that they are founded on the relation of cause and effect. When again it is asked, *What is the foundation of all our reasonings and conclusions concerning that relation?* it may be replied in one word, Experience. But if we still carry on our sifting humor, and ask, *What is the foundation of all conclusions from experience?* this implies a new question, which may be of more difficult solution and explication. Philosophers, that give themselves airs of superior wisdom and sufficiency, have a hard task when they encounter persons of inquisitive dispositions, who push them from every corner to which they retreat, and who are sure at last to bring them to some dangerous dilemma. The best expedient to prevent this confusion is to be modest in our pretensions, and even to discover the difficulty ourselves before it is objected to us. By this means, we may make a kind of merit of our very ignorance.

I shall content myself, in this section, with an easy task, and shall pretend only to give a negative answer to the question here proposed. I say then, that, even after we have experience of the operations of cause and effect, our conclusions from that experience are *not* founded on reasoning, or any process of the understanding. This answer we must endeavor both to explain and to defend. . . .

In reality, all arguments from experience are founded on the similarity which we discover among natural objects, and by which we are induced to expect effects similar to those which we have found to follow from such objects. And though none but a fool or madman will ever pretend to dispute the authority of experience, or to reject that great guide of human life, it may surely be allowed a philosopher to have so much curiosity at least as to examine the principle of human nature, which gives this mighty authority to experience, and makes us draw advantage from that similarity which nature has placed among different objects. From causes which appear *similar* we expect similar effects. This is the sum of all our experimental conclusions. Now it seems evident that, if this conclusion were formed by reason, it would be as perfect at first, and upon one instance, as after ever so long a course of experience. But the case is far otherwise. Nothing so like as eggs; yet no one, on account of this appearing similarity, expects the same taste and relish in all of them. It is only after a long course of uniform experiments in any kind, that we attain a firm reliance and security with regard to a particular event. Now where is that process of reasoning which, from one instance, draws a conclusion, so different from that which it infers from a hundred instances that are nowise different from that single one? This question I propose as much for the sake of information, as with an intention of raising difficulties. I cannot find, I cannot imagine any such reasoning. But I keep my mind still open to instruction, if any one will vouchsafe to bestow it on me.

Should it be said that, from a number of uniform experiments, we *infer* a connection between the sensible qualities and the secret powers; this, I must confess, seems the same difficulty, couched in different terms. The question still recurs, on what process of argument this *inference* is founded? Where is the medium, the interposing ideas, which join propositions so very wide of each other? It is confessed that the color, consistence, and other sensible qualities of bread appear not, of themselves, to have any connection with the secret powers of nourishment and support. For otherwise we could infer these secret powers from the first appearance of these sensible qualities, without the aid of experience, contrary to the sentiment of all philosophers, and contrary to plain matter of fact. Here, then, is our natural state of ignorance with regard to the powers and influence of all objects. How is this remedied by experience? It only shows us a number of uniform effects, resulting from certain objects, and teaches us that those particular objects, at that particular time, were endowed with such powers and forces. When a new object, endowed with similar sensible qualities, is produced, we expect similar powers and forces, and look for a like effect. From a body of like color and consistence with bread we expect like nourishment and support. But this surely is a step or progress of the mind, which wants to be explained. When a man says, *I have found, in all past instances, such sensible qualities conjoined with such secret powers:* And when he says, *Similar sensible qualities will always be conjoined with similar secret powers,* he is not guilty of a tautology, nor are these propositions in any respect the same. You say that the one proposition is an inference from the other. But you must confess that the inference is not intuitive; neither is it demonstrative. Of what nature is it, then? To say it is experimental, is begging the question. For all inferences from experience suppose, as their foundation, that the future will resemble the past, and that similar powers will be conjoined with similar sensible qualities. If there be any suspicion that the course of nature may change, and that the past may be no rule for the future, all experience becomes useless, and can give rise to no inference or conclusion. It is impossible, therefore, that any arguments from experience can prove this resemblance of the past to the future, since all these arguments are founded on the supposition of that resemblance. Let the course of things be allowed hitherto ever so regular; that alone, without some new argument or inference, proves not that, for the future, it will continue so. In vain do you pretend to have learned the nature of bodies from your past experience. Their secret nature, and consequently all their effects and influence, may change, without any change in their sensible qualities. This happens sometimes, and with regard to some objects: Why may it [not] happen always, and with regard to all objects? What logic, what process of argument secures you against this supposition? My practice, you say, refutes my doubts. But you mistake the purport of my question. As an agent, I am quite satisfied in the point; but as a philosopher, who has some share of curiosity, I will not say scepticism, I want to learn the foundation of this inference. No reading, no enquiry has yet been able to remove my difficulty, or give me satisfaction in a matter of such importance. Can I do better than propose the difficulty to the public, even though, perhaps, I have small hopes of obtaining a solution? We shall, at least, by this means, be sensible of our ignorance, if we do not augment our knowledge.

I must confess that a man is guilty of unpardonable arrogance who concludes, because an argument has escaped his own investigation, that therefore it does not really exist. I must also confess that, though all the learned, for several ages, should have employed themselves in fruitless search upon any subject, it may still, perhaps, be rash to conclude positively that the subject must, therefore, pass all human comprehension. Even though we examine all the sources of our knowledge, and conclude them unfit for such a subject, there may still remain a suspicion, that the enumeration is not complete, or the examination not accurate. But with regard to the present subject, there are some considerations which seem to remove all this accusation of arrogance or suspicion of mistake.

It is certain that the most ignorant and stupid peasants—nay infants, nay even brute beasts—improve by experience, and learn the qualities of natural objects, by observing the effects which result from them. When a child has felt the sensation of pain from touching the flame of a candle, he will be careful not to put his hand near any candle, but will expect a similar effect from a cause which is similar in its sensible qualities and appearance. If you assert, therefore, that the understanding of the child is led into this conclusion by any process of argument or ratiocination, I may justly require you to produce that argument; nor have you any pretense to refuse so equitable a demand. You cannot say that the argument is abstruse, and may possibly escape your enquiry, since you confess that it is obvious to the capacity of a mere infant. If you hesitate, therefore, a moment, or if, after reflection, you produce any intricate or profound argument, you, in a manner, give up the question, and confess that it is not reasoning which engages us to suppose the past resembling the future, and to expect similar effects from causes which are, to appearance, similar. This is the proposition which I intended to enforce in the present section. If I be right, I pretend not to have made any mighty discovery. And if I be wrong, I must acknowledge myself to be indeed a very backward scholar, since I cannot now discover an argument which, it seems, was perfectly familiar to me long before I was out of my cradle.

SCEPTICAL SOLUTION OF THESE DOUBTS

Part I

... Nature will always maintain her rights, and prevail in the end over any abstract reasoning whatsoever. Though we should conclude, for instance, as in the foregoing section, that, in all reasonings from experience, there is a step taken by the mind which is not supported by any argument or process of the understanding, there is no danger that these reasonings, on which almost all knowledge depends, will ever be affected by such a discovery. If the mind be not engaged by argument to make this step, it must be induced by some other principle of equal weight and authority, and that principle will preserve its influence as long as human nature remains the same. What that principle is may well be worth the pains of enquiry.

Suppose a person, though endowed with the strongest faculties of reason and reflection, to be brought on a sudden into this world; he would, indeed, immediately observe a continual succession of objects, and one event following another, but he would not be able to discover anything farther. He would not, at first, by any reasoning, be able to reach the idea of cause and effect, since the particular powers, by which all natural operations are performed, never appear to the senses; nor is it reasonable to conclude, merely because one event, in one instance, precedes another, that therefore the one is the cause, the other the effect. Their conjunction may be arbitrary and casual. There may be no reason to infer the existence of one from the appearance of the other. And in a word, such a person, without more experience, could never employ his conjecture or reasoning concerning any matter of fact, or be assured of anything beyond what was immediately present to his memory and senses.

Suppose, again, that he has acquired more experience, and has lived so long in the world as to have observed familiar objects or events to be constantly conjoined together; what is the consequence of this experience? He immediately infers the existence of one object from the appearance of the other. Yet he has not, by all his experience, acquired any idea or knowledge of the secret power by which the one object produces the other; nor is it, by any process of reasoning, he is engaged to draw this inference. But still he finds himself determined to draw it:

And though he should be convinced that his understanding has no part in the operation, he would nevertheless continue in the same course of thinking. There is some other principle which determines him to form such a conclusion.

This principle is Custom or Habit. For wherever the repetition of any particular act or operation produces a propensity to renew the same act or operation, without being impelled by any reasoning or process of the understanding, we always say, that this propensity is the effect of *Custom*. By employing that word, we pretend not to have given the ultimate reason of such a propensity. We only point out a principle of human nature, which is universally acknowledged, and which is well known by its effects. Perhaps we can push our enquiries no farther, or pretend to give the cause of this cause, but must rest contented with it as the ultimate principle, which we can assign, of all our conclusions from experience. It is sufficient satisfaction, that we can go so far, without repining at the narrowness of our faculties because they will carry us no farther. And it is certain we here advance a very intelligible proposition at least, if not a true one, when we assert that, after the constant conjunction of two objects—heat and flame, for instance, weight and solidity—we are determined by custom alone to expect the one from the appearance of the other. This hypothesis seems even the only one which explains the difficulty, why we draw, from a thousand instances, an inference which we are not able to draw from one instance, that is, in no respect, different from them. Reason is incapable of any such variation. The conclusions which it draws from considering one circle are the same which it would form upon surveying all the circles in the universe. But no man, having seen only one body move after being impelled by another, could infer that every other body will move after a like impulse. All inferences from experience, therefore, are effects of custom, not of reasoning.

Custom, then, is the great guide of human life. It is that principle alone which renders our experience useful to us, and makes us expect, for the future, a similar train of events with those which have appeared in the past. Without the influence of custom, we should be entirely ignorant of every matter of fact beyond what is immediately present to the memory and senses. We should never know how to adjust means to ends, or to employ our natural powers in the production of any effect. There would be an end at once of all action, as well as of the chief part of speculation.

But here it may be proper to remark, that though our conclusions from experience carry us beyond our memory and senses, and assure us of matters of fact which happened in the most distant places and most remote ages, yet some fact must always be present to the senses or memory, from which we may first proceed in drawing these conclusions. A man, who should find in a desert country the remains of pompous buildings, would conclude that the country had, in ancient times, been cultivated by civilized inhabitants; but did nothing of this nature occur to him, he could never form such an inference. We learn the events of former ages from history; but then we must peruse the volumes in which this instruction is contained, and thence carry up our inferences from one testimony to another, till we arrive at the eyewitnesses and spectators of these distant events. In a word, if we proceed not upon some fact, present to the memory or senses, our reasonings would be merely hypothetical; and however the particular links might be connected with each other, the whole chain of inferences would have nothing to support it,

nor could we ever, by its means, arrive at the knowledge of any real existence. If I ask why you believe any particular matter of fact, which you relate, you must tell me some reason; and this reason will be some other fact, connected with it. But as you cannot proceed after this manner, *in infinitum,* you must at last terminate in some fact, which is present to your memory or senses, or must allow that your belief is entirely without foundation.

What, then, is the conclusion of the whole matter? A simple one; though, it must be confessed, pretty remote from the common theories of philosophy. All belief of matter of fact or real existence is derived merely from some object, present to the memory or senses, and a customary conjunction between that and some other object. Or in other words, having found in many instances, that any two kinds of objects—flame and heat, snow and cold—have always been conjoined together; if flame or snow be presented anew to the senses, the mind is carried by custom to expect heat or cold, and to *believe* that such a quality does exist, and will discover itself upon a nearer approach. This belief is the necessary result of placing the mind in such circumstances. It is an operation of the soul, when we are so situated, as unavoidable as to feel the passion of love, when we receive benefits, or hatred, when we meet with injuries. All these operations are a species of natural instincts, which no reasoning or process of the thought and understanding is able either to produce or to prevent.

For Further Reflection

1. Hume's empiricism is more radical than Locke's because it leads to skepticism over metaphysical issues which Locke thought safe (for example, the nature of the self, causality, the existence of God). Hume closes the book from which our selection comes with these words: "By way of conclusion to these reflections on diverse questions: When we run over libraries, persuaded of the principles here expounded, what havoc must we make? If we take in hand any volume, of divinity or metaphysics, for instance, let us ask: Does it contain any reasoning concerning quantity or number? No. Does it contain any experimental (probable) reasoning concerning matter of fact? No. Commit it then to the flames: for it can contain

nothing but sophistry and illusion." Are you convinced by Hume's reasoning? If not, how would you go about arguing against him?

2. Do you understand Hume's argument against justifying our belief that the future will resemble the past? Note that (1) the foundation of reasoning regarding matters of fact is the idea of causation, (2) the foundation of reasoning concerning causation is *experience,* and (3) the foundation of all conclusions regarding trust in experience is the principle of the uniformity of nature (for example, bread will continue to nourish us in the future as it has in the past and the sun will rise tomorrow because it always has in the past). But why should we accept (3) the uniformity of nature? There is no contradiction in supposing its opposite (for example, that bread will cease to nourish us or that the sun will not rise tomorrow). We cannot reason that it will continue to do so because it has always done so in the past, for that is begging the question. It seems that the foundation of (3) is our trust in causation of which (3) is supposed to be the foundation. Do you see the circularity? Can you find anything wrong in Hume's reasoning?

III.22   An Argument Against Skepticism

JOHN HOSPERS

John Hospers is professor of philosophy at the University of Southern California and editor of the *Pacific Journal of Philosophy.* He is the founder of the Libertarian party and was that party's candidate for president of the United States in 1972. He is the author of several textbooks as well as *Libertarianism: A Political Philosophy for Tomorrow* (1971). In this essay, Hospers first analyzes the different uses of the word "know" and then sets forth the conditions of descriptive knowledge. After that he distinguishes a weak sense of knowledge from a strong sense and uses this distinction to argue against the claims of skepticism.

Study Questions

1. What are the three senses of "know" that Hospers describes? Which is the most important philosophically?
2. What are the three conditions for propositional knowledge?
3. Why is it important to have good evidence before one can rightly be said to know?
4. What are the weak and strong senses of knowledge?
5. How does this distinction bear on the claims of skepticism?

I. REQUIREMENTS FOR KNOWING

THE WORD "KNOW" IS SLIPPERY. It is not always used in the same way. Here are some of its principal uses:

[*Senses of "know"*] 1. Sometimes when we talk about knowing, we are referring to *acquaintance* of some kind. For example, "Do you know Richard Smith?" means approximately the same as "Are you acquainted with Richard Smith? (have you met him? etc.) . . ."

2. Sometimes we speak of knowing *how:* Do you know how to ride a horse, do you know how to use a soldering iron? We even use a colloquial noun, "know-how," in talking about this. Knowing how is an *ability*—we know how to ride a horse if we have the ability to ride a horse, and the test of whether we have the ability is whether in the appropriate situation we can perform the activity in question. . . .

3. But by far the most frequent use of the word "know"—and the one with which we shall be primarily concerned—is the *propositional* sense: "I know that . . ." where the word "that" is followed by a proposition: "I know that I am now reading a book," "I know that I am an American citizen," and so on. There is some relation between this last sense of "know" and the earlier ones. We cannot be acquainted with Smith without knowing some things about him (without knowing *that* certain propositions about him are true), and it is difficult to see how one can know *how* to swim without knowing some true propositions about swimming, concerning what you must do with your arms and legs when in the water. (But the dog knows how to swim, though presumably he knows no propositions about swimming.) . . .

[*Conditions for knowing that*] Now, what is required for us to know in this third and most important sense? Taking the letter p to stand for any proposition, what requirements must be met

in order for one to assert truly that he knows p? There are, after all, many people who claim to know something when they don't; so how can one separate the rightful claims to know from the mistaken ones?

a. *p must be true.* The moment you have some reason to believe that a proposition is not true, this immediately negates a person's claim to know it: You can't know p if p isn't true. If I say, "I know p, but p is not true," my statement is self-contradictory, for part of what is involved in knowing p is that p is true. Similarly, if I say, "He knows p, but p is not true," this too is self-contradictory. It may be that I *thought* I knew p; but if p is false, I didn't really know it. I only thought I did. If I nevertheless claim to know p, while admitting that p is false, my hearers may rightly conclude that I have not yet learned how to use the word "know." This is already implicit in our previous discussion, for what is it that you know about p when you know p? You know *that p is true,* of course; the very formulation gives away the case: Knowing p is knowing that p is true. . . .

But the truth-requirement, though necessary, is not sufficient. There are plenty of true propositions, for example in nuclear physics, that you and I do not know to be true unless we happen to be specialists in that area. But the fact that they are true does not imply that we know them to be true. . . .

b. *Not only must p be true: We must believe that p is true.* This may be called the "subjective requirement": We must have a certain attitude toward p—not merely that of wondering or speculating about p, but positively *believing* that p is true. "I know that p is true, but I don't believe that it is" would not only be a very peculiar thing to say, it would entitle our hearers to conclude that we had not learned in what circumstances to use the word "know." There may be numerous statements that you believe but do not know to be true, but there can be none which you know to be true but don't believe,

From John Hospers, An Introduction to Philosophical Analysis, *2/e © 1967, pp. 143–145, 148–155. Reprinted by permission of Prentice Hall, Inc., Englewood Cliffs, NJ.*

since believing is a part (a defining characteristic) of knowing.

"I know p" implies "I believe p," and "He knows p" implies "He believes p," for believing is a defining characteristic of knowing. But believing p is *not* a defining characteristic of p's *being true*: p can be true even though neither he nor I nor anyone else believes it. (The earth was round even before anyone believed that it was.) There is no contradiction whatever in saying, "He believed p (that is, believed it to be true), but p is not true." Indeed, we say things of this kind all the time: "He believes that people are persecuting him, but of course it isn't true." . . .

We have now discussed two requirements for knowing, an "objective" one (p must be true) and a "subjective" one (one must believe p). Are these sufficient? Can you be said to know something if you believe it and if what you believe is true? If so, we can simply define knowledge as true belief, and that will be the end of the matter.

Unfortunately, however, the situation is not so simple. True belief is not yet knowledge. A proposition may be true, and you may believe it to be true, and yet you may not *know* it to be true. Suppose you believe that there are sentient beings on Mars, and suppose that in the course of time, after space-travelers from the earth have landed there, your belief turns out to be true. The statement was true at the time you uttered it, and you also believed it at the time you uttered it—but did you *know* it to be true at the time you uttered it? Certainly not, we would be inclined to say; you were not in a position to know. It was a lucky guess. Even if you had *some* evidence that it was true, you didn't *know* that it was true at the time you said it. Some further condition, therefore, is required to prevent a lucky guess from passing as knowledge. . . .

c. *You must have evidence for p (reason to believe p).* When you guessed which tosses of the coin would be heads, you had no reason to believe that your guesses would be correct, so you did not *know*. But after you watched all the tosses and carefully observed which way the coin tossed each time, then you knew. You had the evidence of your senses—as well as of people around you, and photographs if you wished to take them—that this throw was heads, that one tails, and so on. Similarly, when you predict on the basis of tonight's red sunset that tomorrow's weather will be fair, you don't yet *know* that your prediction will be borne out by the facts; you have some reason (perhaps) to believe it, but you cannot be sure. But tomorrow when you go outdoors and see for yourself what the weather is like, you do know for sure; when tomorrow comes you have the full evidence before you, which you do not yet have tonight. Tomorrow "the evidence is in"; tonight, it is not knowledge but only an "educated guess."

[*Problem*] This, then, is our third requirement—evidence. But at this point our troubles begin. How much evidence must there be? "Some evidence" won't suffice as an answer: there may be *some* evidence that tomorrow will be sunny, but you don't yet know it. How about "all the evidence that is available"? But this won't do either; all the evidence that is now available may not be enough. All the evidence that is now available is far from sufficient to enable us to know whether there are conscious beings on other planets. We just don't know, even after we have examined all the evidence at our disposal.

How about "enough evidence to give us *good reason* to believe it"? But how much evidence is this? I may have known someone for years and found him to be scrupulously honest during all that time; by virtually any criterion, this would constitute good evidence that he will be honest the next time—and yet he may not be; suppose that the next time he steals someone's wallet. I had good reason to believe that he would remain honest, but nevertheless I didn't *know* that he would remain honest, for it was not true. We are all familiar with cases in which someone had good reason to believe a proposition that nevertheless turned out to be false.

What then *is* sufficient? We are now tempted to say, "Complete evidence—all the evidence there could ever be—the works, everything." But if we say this, let us notice at once that there are very few propositions whose truth we can claim to know. Most of those propositions that in daily life we claim to know without the slightest hesitation we would *not* know according to this criterion. For example, we say, "I know that if I were to let go of this pencil, it would fall," and we don't have the slightest hesitation about it; but although we may have excellent evidence (pencils and other objects have always fallen when let go), we don't have *complete* evidence, for we have not yet observed the outcome of letting go of it *this* time. To take an even more obvious case, we say, "I know that there is a book before me now," but we have not engaged in every possible observation that would be relevant to determining the truth of this statement: We have not examined the object (the one we take to be a book) from *all* angles (and since there are an infinite number of angles, who could?), and even if we have looked at it steadily for half an hour, we have not done so for a hundred hours, or a million; and yet it would *seem* (though some have disputed this, as we shall see) that if one observation provides evidence, a thousand observations should provide more evidence—and when could the accumulation of evidence end? . . .

We might, nevertheless, stick to our definition and say that we really do *not* know most of the propositions that in daily life we claim to know: Perhaps I don't *know* that this is a book before me, that I am now indoors and not outdoors, that I am now reading sentences written in the English language, or that there are any other people in the world. But this is a rather astounding claim and needs to be justified. We are all convinced that we know these things: We act on them every day of our lives, and if we were asked outside a philosophy classroom whether we knew them, we would say "yes" without hesitation. Surely we cannot accept a definition of "know" that would practically define knowledge out of existence? But if not, what alternative have we?

"Perhaps we don't have to go so far as to say '*all* the evidence,' '*complete* evidence,' and so on. All we have to say is that we must have "*ad-*

equate evidence." But when is the evidence adequate? Is anything less than "all the evidence there could ever be" adequate? "Well, adequate for enabling us to know." But this little addition to our definition lands us in a circle. We are trying to define "know," and we cannot in doing so employ the convenient phrase "enough to enable us to know"—for the last word in this definition is the very one we are trying to define. But once we have dropped the phrase "to know," we are left with our problem once more: How much evidence is adequate evidence? Is it adequate when anything less than *all* the evidence is in? If not all the evidence is in, but only 99.99 percent of it, couldn't that .01 percent go contrary to the rest of it and require us to conclude that the proposition might not be true after all, and that therefore we didn't know it? Surely it has happened often enough that a statement that we thought we knew, perhaps even would have staked our lives on, turned out in the end to be false, or just doubtful. But in that case we didn't really *know* it after all: The evidence was good, even overwhelming, but yet not good enough, not really adequate, for it was not enough to guarantee the truth of the proposition. Can we know *p* with anything less than *all* the evidence there ever could be for *p*?

II. STRONG AND WEAK SENSES OF "KNOW"

[*Disputes About Knowing*] In daily life we say we know—not just believe or surmise, but *know*—that heavier-than-air objects fall, that snow is white, that we can read and write, and countless other things. If someone denies this, and no fact cited by the one disputant suffices to convince the other, we may well suspect that there is a verbal issue involved: In this case, that they are operating on two different meanings of "know," because they construe the third requirement—the evidence requirement—differently.

[*Case 1*] Suppose I say, "There is a bookcase in my office," and someone challenges this assertion. I reply, "I *know* that there is a bookcase in my office. I put it there myself, and I've seen it there for years. In fact, I saw it there just two minutes ago when I took a book out of it and left the office to go into the classroom." Now suppose we both go to my office, take a look, and there is the bookcase, exactly as before. "See, I *knew* it was here," I say. "Oh no," he replies, "you *believed with good reason* that it was still there, because you had seen it there often before and you didn't see or hear anyone removing it. But you didn't *know* it was there when you said it, for at that moment you were in the classroom and not in your office."

At this point, I may reply, "But I did know it was there, even when I said it. I knew it because *(1) I believed it, (2) I had good grounds on which to base the belief, and (3) the belief was true.* And I would call it knowledge whenever these three conditions are fulfilled. This is the way we use the word 'know' every day of our lives. One knows those true propositions that one believes with good reason. And when I said the bookcase was still in my office, I was uttering one of those propositions."

But now my opponent may reply, "But you still didn't know it. You had good reason to say it, I admit, for you had not seen or heard anyone removing it. You had good reason, but not *sufficient* reason. The evidence you gave was still compatible with your statement being false—and if it was false, you of course did not *know* that it was true. [*Case 2*] Suppose that you had made your claim to knowledge, and I had denied your claim, and we had both gone into your office, and to your great surprise (and mine too) the bookcase was no longer there. Could you *then* have claimed to know that it was still there?"

"Of course not. The falsity of a statement always invalidates the claim to know it. If the bookcase had not been there, I would not have been entitled to say that I knew it was there; my claim would have been mistaken."

"Right—it would have been mistaken. But now please note that the only difference between the two cases is that in the first case the bookcase

was there and in the second case it wasn't. *The evidence in the two cases was exactly the same.* You had exactly the same reason for saying that the bookcase was still there in the *second* case (when we found it missing) that you did in the *first* case (when we found it still there). And since you—as you yourself admit—didn't know it in the second case, you couldn't have known it in the first case either. You believed it with good reason, but you didn't *know* it."

[*Solution*] Here my opponent may have scored an important point; he may have convinced me that since I admittedly didn't know in the second case I couldn't have known in the first case either. But here I may make an important point in return: "My belief was the same in the two cases; the evidence was the same in the two cases (I had seen the bookcase two minutes before, had heard or seen no one removing it). The only difference was that in the first case the bookcase was there and in the second case it wasn't (*p* was true in the first case, false in the second). But *this doesn't show that I didn't know* in the first case. What it does show is that *although I might have been mistaken, I wasn't mistaken.* Had the bookcase not been there, I couldn't have claimed to know that it was; but since the bookcase in fact *was* still there, I *did* know, although (on the basis of the evidence I had) I *might* have been mistaken."

"Yes, it turned out to be true—you were lucky. But as we both agree, a lucky guess isn't the same as knowledge."

"But this wasn't just a lucky guess. I had excellent reasons for believing that the bookcase was still there. So the evidence requirement was fulfilled."

"No, it wasn't. You had good reason, excellent reason, but not *sufficient* reason—both times—for believing that the bookcase was still there. But in the second case it wasn't there, so you didn't know; therefore, in the first case where your evidence was *exactly the same,* you didn't know either; you just believed it with good reason, but that wasn't enough: Your reason wasn't sufficient, and so you didn't *know.*"

Now the difference in the criterion of knowing between the two disputants begins to emerge. According to me, I did know *p* in the first case because my belief was based on excellent evidence and was also true. According to my opponent, I did not know *p* in the first case because my evidence was still less than complete—I wasn't in the room seeing or touching the bookcase when I made the statement. It seems, then, that I am operating with a less demanding definition of "know" than he is. I am using "know" in the *weak* sense, in which I know a proposition when I believe it, have good reason for believing it, and it is true. But he is using "know" in a more demanding sense: He is using it in the *strong* sense, which requires that in order to know a proposition, it must be true, I must believe it, and I must have absolutely *conclusive* evidence in favor of it.

[*Examples*] Let us contrast these two cases:

Suppose that after a routine medical examination the excited doctor reports to me that the X-ray photographs show that I have no heart. I should tell him to get a new machine. I should be inclined to say that the fact that I have a heart is one of the few things that I can count on as absolutely certain. I can feel it beat. I know it's there. Furthermore, how could my blood circulate if I didn't have one? Suppose that later on I suffer a chest injury and undergo a surgical operation. Afterwards the astonished surgeons solemnly declare that they searched my chest cavity and found no heart, and that they made incisions and looked about in other likely places but found it not. They are convinced that I am without a heart. They are unable to understand how circulation can occur or what accounts for the thumping in my chest. But they are in agreement and obviously sincere, and they have clear photographs of my interior spaces. What would be my attitude? Would it be to insist that they were all mistaken? I think not. I believe that I should eventually accept their testimony and the evidence of the photographs. I should consider to be false what I now regard as an absolute certainty. [When I say I know I have a heart, I know it in the weak sense.]

Suppose that as I write this paper someone in the next room were to call out to me, "I can't find an ink-bottle; is there one in the house?" I should reply, "Here is an ink-bottle." If he said in a doubtful tone, "Are you sure? I looked there before," I should reply, "Yes, I know there is; come and get it."

Now could it turn out to be false that there is an ink-bottle directly in front of me on this desk? Many philosophers have thought so. They would say that many things could happen of such a nature that if they did happen it would be proved that I am deceived. I agree that many extraordinary things could happen, in the sense that there is no logical absurdity in the supposition. It could happen that when I next reach for this ink-bottle my hand should seem to pass *through* it and I should not feel the contact of any object. It could happen that in the next moment the ink-bottle will suddenly vanish from sight; or that I should find myself under a tree in the garden with no ink-bottle about; or that one or more persons should enter this room and declare with apparent sincerity that they see no ink-bottle on this desk; or that a photograph taken now of the top of the desk should clearly show all of the objects on it except the ink-bottle. Having admitted that these things *could happen*, am I compelled to admit that if they did happen, then it would be proved that there is no ink-bottle here *now*? Not at all. I could say that when my hand seemed to pass through the ink-bottle I should *then* be suffering from hallucination; that if the ink-bottle suddenly vanished, it would have miraculously ceased to exist; that the other persons were conspiring to drive me mad, or were themselves victims of remarkable concurrent hallucinations; that the camera possessed some strange flaw or that there was trickery in developing the negative: . . . Not only do I not *have* to admit that those extraordinary occurrences would be evidence that there is no ink-bottle here; the fact is that I *do not* admit it. There is nothing whatever that could happen in the next moment or the next year that would by me be called *evidence* that there is not an ink-bottle here now. No future experience or investigation could prove to me that I am mistaken.

Therefore, if I were to say, "I know that there is an ink-bottle here," I should be using "know" in the strong sense.[1]

It is in the weak sense that we use the word "know" in daily life, as when I say I know that I have a heart, that if I let go of this piece of chalk it will fall, that the sun will rise tomorrow, and so on. I have excellent reason (evidence) to believe all these things, evidence so strong that (so we say) it amounts to certainty. And yet there are events that could conceivably occur which, if they did occur, would cast doubt on the beliefs or even show them to be false. . . .

III. ARGUMENT AGAINST SKEPTICISM

[*Skepticism*] But the philosopher is apt to be more concerned with "know" in the strong sense. He wants to inquire whether there are any propositions that we can know without the shadow of a doubt will never be proved false, or even rendered dubious to the smallest degree. "You can say," he will argue, "and I admit that it would be good English usage to say, that you know that you have a heart and that the sun is more than 90 million miles from the earth. But you don't know it until you have absolutely conclusive evidence, and you must admit that the evidence you have, while very strong, is not conclusive. So I shall say, using 'know' in the strong sense, that you do not know these propositions. I want then to ask what propositions can be known in the strong sense, the sense that puts the proposition forever past the possibility of doubt."

And on this point many philosophers have been quite skeptical; they have granted few if any propositions whose truth we could know in the strong sense. . . . Such a person is a *skeptic*. We claim (he says) to know many things about the world, but in fact none of these propositions can be known for certain. What are we to say of the skeptic's position?

[*Criticism*] Let us first note that in the phrase "know for certain" the "for certain" is redundant—how can we know except for certain? If it is less than certain, how can it be knowledge? We do, however, use the word "certain" ambiguously: (1) Sometimes we say "I am certain," which just means that I have a feeling of certainty about it— "I feel certain that I locked the door of the apartment"—and of course the feeling of certainty is no guarantee that the statement is true. People have very strong feelings of certainty about many propositions that they have no evidence for at all, particularly if they want to believe them or are consoled by believing them. The phrase "feeling certain," then, refers simply to a psychological state, whose existence in no way guarantees that what the person feels certain about is true. But (2) sometimes when we say "I am certain" we mean that it *is* certain—in other words, that we *do* know the proposition in question to be true. This, of course, is the sense of "certain" that is of interest to philosophers (the first sense is of more interest to psychiatrists in dealing with patients). Thus we could reformulate our question, "Is anything certain?" or "Are any propositions certain?"

"I can well understand," one might argue, "how you could question some statements, even most statements. But if you carry on this merry game until you have covered *all* statements, you are simply mistaken, and I think I can show you why. You may see someone in a fog or in a bad light and not know (not be certain) whether he has a right hand. But don't you know that *you* have a right hand? There it is! Suppose I now raise my hand and say, 'Here is a hand.' Now you say to me, 'I doubt that there's a hand.' But what evidence do you want? What does your doubt consist of? You don't believe your eyes, perhaps? Very well, then come up and touch the hand. You still aren't satisfied? Then keep on looking at it steadily and touching it, photograph it, call in other people for testimony if you like. If after all this you still say it isn't certain, what more do you want? Under what conditions would you admit that it *is* certain, that you *do* know it? I can understand your doubt when there is some condition left unfulfilled, some test left uncompleted. At the beginning, perhaps you doubted that *if* you tried to touch my hand you would find anything there to touch; but then you did touch, and so you resolved *that* doubt. You resolved further doubts by calling in other people and so on. You performed all the relevant tests, and they turned out favorably. So now, at the end of the process, what is it that you doubt? Oh, I know what you *say:* 'I still doubt that that's a hand.' But isn't this saying 'I doubt' now an empty formula? I can no longer attach any content to that so-called doubt, for there is nothing left to doubt; you yourself *cannot specify any further test that, if performed, would resolve your doubt.* 'Doubt' now becomes an empty word. You're not doubting now that *if* you raised your hand to touch mine, you would touch it, or that *if* Smith and others were brought in, they would also testify that this is a hand—we've already gone through all that. So what is it specifically that you doubt? What possible test is there the negative result of which you fear? I submit that there isn't any. You are confusing a situation in which doubt is understandable (*before* you made the tests) with the later situation in which it isn't, for it has all been dispelled. . . .

"But your so-called doubt becomes meaningless when there is nothing left to doubt—when the tests have been carried out and their results are all favorable. Suppose a physician examines a patient and says, 'It's probable that you have an inflamed appendix.' Here one can still doubt, for the signs may be misleading. So the physician operates on the patient, finds an inflamed appendix and removes it, and the patient recovers. *Now* what would be the sense of the physician's saying, 'It's *probable* that he had an inflamed appendix'? If seeing it and removing it made it only *probable,* what would make it certain? Or you are driving along and you hear a rapid regular thumping sound and you say, 'It's probable that I have a flat tire.' So far you're right; it's only probable—the thumping might be caused by something else. So you go out and have a look, and there is the tire, flat. You find a nail embedded in it, change the tire, and then resume your ride with no more thumping. Are you *now* going to say, 'It's merely *probable* that the car had a flat tire'? But if given all those conditions it would be merely probable, what in the world would make it certain? Can you describe to me the circumstances in which you would say it's certain? If you can't, then the phrase 'being certain' has no meaning as you are using it. You are simply using it in such a special way that it has no application at all, and there is no reason at all why anyone else should follow your usage. In daily life we have a very convenient and useful distinction between the application of the words 'probable' and 'certain.' We say appendicitis is probable *before* the operation, but when the physician has the patient's appendix visible before him on the operating table, now it's certain—that's just the kind of situation in which we apply the word 'certain,' as opposed to 'probable.' Now you, for some reason, are so fond of the word 'probable' that you want to use it for everything—you use it to describe *both* the preoperative and postoperative situations, and the word 'certain' is left without any application at all. But this is nothing but a *verbal manipulation* on your part. You have changed nothing; you have only taken, as it were, two bottles with different contents, and instead of labeling them differently ('probable' and 'certain'), as the rest of us do, you put the same label ('probable') on both of them! What possible advantage is there in this? It's just verbal contrariness. And since you have pre-empted the word 'probable' to cover *both* the situations, we now have to devise a *different* pair of words to mark the perfectly obvious distinction between the situation *before* the surgery and the situation *during* the surgery—the same difference we previously marked by the words 'probable' and 'certain' until you used the word 'probable' to apply to both of them. What gain is there in this *verbal manipulation* of yours?" . . .

NOTE

1. Norman Malcolm, "Knowledge and Belief," in *Knowledge and Certainty,* pp. 66–68.

For Further Reflection

1. Do you think that Hospers' conditions for knowing are adequate? Do you see how they differ from Descartes, who would only allow absolute certainty to count as knowledge? Who is right?

2. Is Hospers correct in saying that the skeptic holds up an unrealistic standard (too strong a sense) of knowledge?

3. In Hospers' sense of knowledge can we ever "know that we know"? Or can we be justified only in believing that we know? If this is so, then should the focus of discussion be on the adequacy of justified belief?

III.B   Truth, Rationality, and Cognitive Relativism

To say that what is, is not, or that what is not is, is false; but to say that what is, is, and what is not, is not, is true. (Aristotle 384–322 B.C.)

Man is the measure of all things,
Both of things that are,
Man is the measure that they are,
And of the things that are not,
Man is the measure that they are not.
(Protagoras the Sophist, 5th century B.C.)

In the 1990s a professor, call him D, from the English department at a major university, gave a talk on political biases in university curriculum, arguing that curricula are oppressive to women and minorities. After the speech, a philosopher came up to D and pointed out that he, D, had contradicted himself in his speech. The English professor responded, saying, "So, what's wrong with that? Look young man, I'm sure you know more logic than I do, but I know more about logic than you do! I know that it's a phallologocentric instrument for the oppression of minorities."

Two diametrically opposed views on truth exist in contemporary culture, especially, among intellectuals in academia. One position, call it "cognitive realism," accepts one or another version of the correspondence theory of truth and holds the classical view that some things exist independently of whether anyone thinks about them. Some propositions are true whether or not anyone believes them. There are mind-independent facts, and they exist whether or not anyone believes them. Examples of this are the propositions "2 + 2 = 4," "the solar system has more than one planet," and "pigs can't fly."

The other position, which is called "cognitive relativism," or "anti-realism," holds that there are no mind-independent facts or truths. Cognitive relativists generally combine anti-realism with a pragmatic notion of truth. A pragmatic theory of truth defines truth in terms of usefulness or workability. The proposition "2 + 2 = 4" is part of a human mathematical invention and the proposition that "the solar system has more than one planet" can be analyzed into specific concepts, which are human inventions: The idea of a "planet," a "sun," a "system," and "more." Similarly, "pigs can't fly" depends on the way we divide up reality. A culture might not have a concept of "pig" or "fly," or it might have several "pig-concepts" or "fly-concepts." We invent reality via our conceptual-linguistic systems. Many cognitive relativists would not go as far as our English professor (D) who believes even the laws of logic are inventions, for they might agree that there are formal constraints on what can be intelligibly said to be within a system of thought and that contradictions are formal criteria of exclusion. But other intellectuals would bite the bullet, as it were, and deny that contradictions need be false. The classic expression of the pragmatic theory of truth is given by William James in our second reading.

The realists trace their lineage back to Plato, who distinguished reality from appearance, and Aristotle, who (see the earlier quotation) defined truth as a *correspondence* between statements and facts. In our readings, Bertrand Russell explains and defends the correspondence theory of truth and Margarita Levin accepts it along with realism in her critique of cognitive relativism.

The new cognitive relativists can trace their roots back to Protagoras, who said "Man is the measure of all things"—that is, what we think is true is so. Their beliefs are also reminiscent of Berkeley's Idealism (see Reading III.20), with the important difference that they reject Idealism, as well as Berkeley's God. They agree with Berkeley, against Locke, that we cannot build a bridge from our conceptual schemes to the world itself, but they reject a God's-eye perspective wherein reality is unified ideally. Instead, we have many worlds, many realities, many perspectives. In the words of Nietzsche, who is quoted approvingly:

> Truth is a mobile army of metaphors, metonyms, and anthropomorphisms—in short a sum of human relations, which have been enhanced, transposed, and embellished poetically and rhetorically and which after long use seem firm, canonical, and obligatory to a people.

In our third reading, Richard Rorty identifies his version of this anti-realism with the pragmatism of the American philosophers William James (1842–1910)—Reading III.24—and John Dewey (1859–1952). Rorty characterizes it as a civilized ethnocentrism, one which chooses social solidarity over objectivity and rejects the notion that truth is the correspondence between our ideas and an independent reality. There is no privileged perspective and no unifying reality, so there is no absolute knowledge, no Truth (with a capital "T"). These ideas must be deconstructed. What is left is our ways of justifying our beliefs, "warranted assertibility," as Dewey would say. So the division between truth and opinion collapses and truth becomes what our peers will let us get away with. For a fuller defense of Rorty's epistemological pragmatism you should see his *Philosophy and the Mirror of Nature* (1979), where he develops his thesis that truth, rather than being a correspondence between our ideas and the world, is what we agree on, what it is better to believe. In the present selection, "Dismantling Truth: Solidarity versus Objectivity," Rorty applies his thesis to the idea that science seeks to secure objectivity, arguing that science, objectivity, and truth need to be replaced or reinterpreted by more pragmatic, ethnocentric notions.

In our fourth reading, "Upholding Truth: Objectivity versus Solidarity," Margarita Levin defends the idea of objectivity against detractors, such as Rorty, Duhem, and Quine.

III.23   The Correspondence Theory of Truth

BERTRAND RUSSELL

In this selection, Russell first distinguishes between knowledge by acquaintance (for example, knowledge by appearances, such as "I seem to see a red book" or "I am in pain" or "I think therefore I am") and knowledge by description (knowledge of truths, such as your knowing that you are really seeing a red book or that your pain is caused by having twisted your ankle). Knowledge by acquaintance is infallible, for believing it makes the proposition true. But the same is not the case for descriptive knowledge claims, for your beliefs could be false. Thus, descriptive knowledge is dualistic—it has the properties of truth and falsity as opposites— whereas knowledge by acquaintance is monistic and does not admit such opposites.

Russell goes on to specify the conditions for an adequate theory of truth and shows how the correspondence theory meets these conditions, whereas the coherence theory does not.

(A biographical sketch of Russell precedes Reading I.3.)

Study Questions

1. How is knowledge of truths unlike knowledge of things?
2. What are the three conditions a theory of truth must meet?
3. What are the two major difficulties with the coherence theory of truth?
4. What is the proper role for coherence in a theory of truth?
5. What is Russell's theory of belief as relational? How does this fit into his theory of truth?
6. What does Russell mean by saying, "Minds do not create truth or falsehood"?

OUR KNOWLEDGE OF TRUTHS, unlike our knowledge of things, has an opposite, namely *error*. So far as things are concerned, we may know them or not know them, but there is no positive state of mind which can be described as erroneous knowledge of things, so long, at any rate, as we confine ourselves to knowledge by acquaintance. Whatever we are acquainted with must be something: We may draw wrong inference from our acquaintance, but the acquaintance itself cannot be deceptive. Thus there is no dualism as regards acquaintance. But as regards knowledge of truths, there is a dualism. We may believe what is false as well as what is true. We know that on very many subjects different people hold different and incompatible opinions: Hence some beliefs must be erroneous. Since erroneous beliefs are often held just as strongly as true beliefs, it becomes a difficult question how they are to be distinguished from true beliefs. How are we to know, in a given case, that our belief is not erroneous? That is a question of the very greatest difficulty, to which no completely satisfactory answer is possible. There is, however, a preliminary question which is rather less difficult, and that is: What do we *mean* by truth and falsehood? It is this preliminary question which is to be considered in this chapter. . . .

. . . We are not asking how we can know whether a belief is true or false: We are asking what is meant by the question whether a belief is true or false. It is to be hoped that a clear answer to this question may help us to obtain an answer to the question what beliefs are true, but for the present we ask only "What is truth?" and "What is falsehood?" not "What beliefs are true?" and "What beliefs are false?" It is very important to keep these different questions entirely separate, since any confusion between them is sure to produce an answer which is not really applicable to either.

There are three points to observe in the attempt to discover the nature of truth, three requisites which any theory must fulfill.

(1) Our theory of truth must be such as to admit of its opposite, falsehood. A good many philosophers have failed adequately to satisfy this condition: they have constructed theories according to which all our thinking ought to have been true and have then had the greatest difficulty in finding a place for falsehood. In this respect our theory of belief must differ from our theory of acquaintance, since in the case of acquaintance it was not necessary to take account of any opposite.

(2) It seems fairly evident that if there were no beliefs there could be no falsehood, and no truth either, in the sense in which truth is correlative to falsehood. If we imagine a world of mere matter, there would be no room for falsehood in such a world, and although it would contain what may be called "facts," it would not contain any truths, in the sense in which truths are things of the same kind as falsehoods. In fact, truth and falsehood are properties of beliefs and statements: hence a world of mere matter, since it would contain no beliefs or statements, would also contain no truth or falsehood.

(3) But, as against what we have just said, it is to be observed that the truth or falsehood of a belief always depends upon something which lies outside the belief itself. If I believe that Charles I died on the scaffold, I believe truly, not because of any intrinsic quality of my belief, which could be discovered by merely examining the belief, but because of an historical event which happened two and a half centuries ago. If I believe that Charles I died in his bed, I believe falsely: no degree of vividness in my belief, or of care in arriving at it, prevents it from being false, again because of what happened long ago, and not because of any intrinsic property of my belief. Hence, although truth and falsehood are proper-

From Bertrand Russell, The Problems of Philosophy *(Oxford: Oxford University Press, 1912).*
Reprinted by permission of Oxford University Press.

ties of beliefs, they are properties dependent upon the relations of the beliefs to other things, not upon any internal quality of the beliefs.

The third of the above requisites leads us to adopt the view—which has on the whole been commonest among philosophers—that truth consists in some form of correspondence between belief and fact. It is, however, by no means an easy matter to discover a form of correspondence to which there are no irrefutable objections. By this partly—and partly by the feeling that, if truth consists in a correspondence of thought with something outside thought, thought can never know when truth has been attained—many philosophers have been led to try to find some definition of truth which shall not consist in relation to something wholly outside belief. The most important attempt at a definition of this sort is the theory that truth consists in *coherence*. It is said that the mark of falsehood is failure to cohere in the body of our beliefs, and that it is the essence of a truth to form part of the completely rounded system which is The Truth.

There is, however, a great difficulty in this view, or rather two great difficulties. The first is that there is no reason to suppose that only *one* coherent body of beliefs is possible. It may be that, with sufficient imagination, a novelist might invent a past for the world that would perfectly fit on to what we know, and yet be quite different from the real past. In more scientific matters, it is certain that there are often two or more hypotheses which account for all the known facts on some subject, and although, in such cases, men of science endeavor to find facts which will rule out all the hypotheses except one, there is no reason why they should always succeed.

In philosophy, again, it seems not uncommon for two rival hypotheses to be both able to account for all the facts. Thus, for example, it is possible that life is one long dream, and that the outer world has only that degree of reality that the objects of dreams have; but although such a view does not seem inconsistent with known facts, there is no reason to prefer it to the com-

monsense view, according to which other people and things do really exist. Thus coherence as the definition of truth fails because there is no proof that there can be only one coherent system.

The other objection to this definition of truth is that it assumes the meaning of "coherence" known, whereas, in fact, "coherence" presupposes the truth of the laws of logic. Two propositions are coherent when both may be true and are incoherent when one at least must be false. Now in order to know whether two propositions can both be true, we must know such truths as the law of contradiction. For example, the two propositions "this tree is a beech" and "this tree is not a beech," are not coherent, because of the law of contradiction. But if the law of contradiction itself were subjected to the test of coherence, we should find that, if we choose to suppose it false, nothing will any longer be incoherent with anything else. Thus the laws of logic supply the skeleton or framework within which the test of coherence applies, and they themselves cannot be established by this test.

For the above two reasons, coherence cannot be accepted as giving the *meaning* of truth, though it is often a most important *test* of truth after a certain amount of truth has become known.

Hence we are driven back to *correspondence with fact* as constituting the nature of truth. It remains to define precisely what we mean by "fact," and what is the nature of the correspondence which must subsist between belief and fact, in order that belief may be true.

In accordance with our three requisites, we have to seek a theory of truth which (1) allows truth to have an opposite, namely falsehood, (2) makes truth a property of beliefs, but (3) makes it a property wholly dependent upon the relation of the beliefs to outside things.

The necessity of allowing for falsehood makes it impossible to regard belief as a relation of the mind to a single object, which could be said to be what is believed. If belief were so regarded, we should find that, like acquaintance, it would not admit of the opposition of truth and falsehood, but would have to be always true. This may be made clear by examples. Othello believes falsely that Desdemona loves Cassio. We cannot say that this belief consists in a relation to a single object, "Desdemona's love for Cassio," for if there were such an object, the belief would be true. There is in fact no such object, and therefore Othello cannot have any relation to such an object. Hence his belief cannot possibly consist in a relation to this object.

It might be said that his belief is a relation to a different object, namely "that Desdemona loves Cassio"; but it is almost as difficult to suppose that there is such an object as this, when Desdemona does not love Cassio, as it was to suppose that there is "Desdemona's love for Cassio." Hence it will be better to seek for a theory of belief which does not make it consist in a relation of the mind to a single object.

It is common to think of relations as though they always held between *two* terms, but in fact this is not always the case. Some relations demand three terms, some four, and so on. Take, for instance, the relation "between." So long as only two terms come in, the relation "between" is impossible: three terms are the smallest number that render it possible. York is between London and Edinburgh; but if London and Edinburgh were the only places in the world, there could be nothing which was between one place and another. Similarly *jealousy* requires three people: there can be no such relation that does not involve three at least. Such a position as "A wishes B to promote C's marriage with D" involves a relation of four terms; that is to say, A and B and C and D all come in, and the relation involved cannot be expressed otherwise than in a form involving all four. Instances might be multiplied indefinitely, but enough has been said to show that there are relations which require more than two terms before they can occur.

The relation involved in *judging* or *believing* must, if falsehood is to be duly allowed for, be taken to be a relation between several terms, not between two. When Othello believes that Desdemona loves Cassio, he must not have before his mind a single object, "Desdemona's love for Cassio," or "that Desdemona loves Cassio," for that would require that there should be objective falsehoods, which subsist independently of any minds; and this, though not logically refutable, is a theory to be avoided if possible. Thus it is easier to account for falsehood if we take judgment to be a relation in which the mind and the various objects concerned all occur severally; that is to say, Desdemona and loving and Cassio must all be terms in the relation which subsists when Othello believes that Desdemona loves Cassio. This relation, therefore, is a relation of four terms, since Othello also is one of the terms of the relation. When we say that it is a relation of four terms, we do not mean that Othello has a certain relation to Desdemona, and has the same relation to loving and also to Cassio. This may be true of some other relation than believing; but believing, plainly, is not a relation which Othello has to *each* of the three terms concerned, but to *all* of them together: there is only one example of the relation of believing involved, but this one example knits together four terms. Thus the actual occurrence, at the moment when Othello is entertaining his belief, is that the relation called "believing" is knitting together into one complex whole the four terms Othello, Desdemona, loving, and Cassio. What is called belief or judgment is nothing but this relation of believing or judging, which relates a mind to several things other than itself. An *act* of belief or of judgment is the occurrence between certain terms at some particular time, of the relation of believing or judging.

We are now in a position to understand what it is that distinguishes a true judgment from a false one. For this purpose we will adopt certain definitions. In every act of judgment there is a mind which judges, and there are terms concerning which it judges. We will call the mind the *subject* in the judgment, and the remaining terms the *objects*. Thus, when Othello judges that Desdemona loves Cassio, Othello is the subject, while the objects are Desdemona and loving and Cassio. The subject and the objects together are called the *constituents* of the judgment. It will be observed that the relation of judging has what is called a "sense" or "direction." We may say, metaphorically, that it puts its objects in a certain *order*, which we may indicate by means of the order of the words in the sentence. (In an inflected language, the same thing will be indicated by inflections, e.g., by the difference between nominative and accusative.) Othello's judgment that Cassio loves Desdemona differs from his judgment that Desdemona loves Cassio, in spite of the fact that it consists of the same constituents, because the relation of judging places the constituents in a different order in the two cases. Similarly, if Cassio judges that Desdemona loves Othello, the constituents of the judgment are still the same, but their order is different. This property of having a "sense" or "direction" is one which the relation of judging shares with all other relations. The "sense" of relations is the ultimate source of order and series and a host of mathematical concepts; but we need not concern ourselves further with this aspect.

We spoke of the relation called "judging" or "believing" as knitting together into one complex whole the subject and the objects. In this respect, judging is exactly like every other relation. Whenever a relation holds between two or more terms, it unites the terms into a complex whole. If Othello loves Desdemona, there is such a complex whole as "Othello's love for Desdemona." The terms united by the relation may be themselves complex, or may be simple, but the whole which results from their being united must be complex. Wherever there is a relation which relates certain terms, there is a complex object formed of the union of those terms; and conversely, wherever there is a complex object, there is a relation which relates its constituents. When an act of believing occurs, there is a complex, in which "believing" is the uniting relation, and subject and objects are arranged in a certain order by the "sense" of the relation of believing. Among the objects, as we saw in considering "Othello believes that Desdemona loves Cassio,"

one must be a relation—in this instance, the relation "loving." But this relation, as it occurs in the act of believing, is not the relation which creates the unity of the complex whole consisting of the subject and the objects. The relation "loving," as it occurs in the act of believing, is one of the objects—it is a brick in the structure, not the cement. The cement is the relation "believing." When the belief is *true*, there is another complex unity, in which the relation which was one of the objects of the belief relates the other objects. Thus, e.g., if Othello believes *truly* that Desdemona loves Cassio, then there is a complex unity, "Desdemona's love for Cassio," which is composed exclusively of the *objects* of the belief, in the same order as they had in the belief, with the relation which was one of the objects occurring now as the cement that binds together the other objects of the belief. On the other hand, when a belief is *false*, there is no such complex unity composed only of the objects of the belief. If Othello believes *falsely* that Desdemona loves Cassio, then there is no such complex unity as "Desdemona's love for Cassio."

Thus a belief is *true* when it *corresponds* to a certain associated complex, and *false* when it does not. Assuming, for the sake of definiteness, that the objects of the belief are two terms and a relation, the terms being put in a certain order by the "sense" of the believing, then if the two terms in that order are united by the relation into a complex, the belief is true; if not, it is false. This constitutes the definition of truth and falsehood that we were in search of. Judging or believing is a certain complex unity of which a mind is a constituent; if the remaining constituents, taken in the order which they have in the belief, form a complex unity, then the belief is true; if not, it is false.

Thus although truth and falsehood are properties of beliefs, yet they are in a sense extrinsic properties, for the condition of the truth of a belief is something not involving beliefs, or (in general) any mind at all, but only the *objects* of the belief. A mind, which believes, believes truly when there is a *corresponding* complex not involving the mind, but only its objects. This correspondence ensures truth, and its absence entails falsehood. Hence we account simultaneously for the two facts that beliefs (*a*) depend on mind for their *existence*, (*b*) do not depend on minds for their *truth*.

We may restate our theory as follows: If we take such a belief as "Othello believes that Desdemona loves Cassio," we will call Desdemona and Cassio the *object-terms*, and loving the *object-relation*. If there is a complex unity "Desdemona's love for Cassio," consisting of the object-terms related by the object-relation in the same order as they have

in the belief, then this complex unity is called the *fact corresponding to the belief*. Thus a belief is true when there is a corresponding fact and is false when there is no corresponding fact. . . .

. . . Minds do not *create* truth or falsehood. They create beliefs, but when once the beliefs are created, the mind cannot make them true or false, except in the special case where they concern future things which are within the power of the person believing, such as catching trains. What makes a belief true is a *fact*, and this fact does not (except in exceptional cases) in any way involve the mind of the person who has the belief.

For Further Reflection

1. Is the correspondence theory of truth plausible? Do you think that it adequately conveys what we mean by "truth," or is something missing?

2. Some opponents of the correspondence theory say it has a certain usefulness for trivial statements like "the cat is on the mat," where correspondence between words and things is plausible, but it loses its appeal when applied to more complex matters such as "there is no such thing as natural motion" or "the universe is infinite" (examples of Richard Rorty). How would a defender of the correspondence theory respond to this criticism?

The Pragmatic Theory of Truth   III.24

WILLIAM JAMES

William James (1842–1910), an American philosopher and psychologist, was born in New York City and educated at Harvard. He was the brother of Henry James the novelist. William James struggled through much of his life with ill health. He was assailed by doubts over freedom of the will and the existence of God, and he developed the philosophy of pragmatism in part as a response to these difficulties. Pragmatism originated with James' friend Charles Peirce but underwent crucial changes and popularization in the hands of James. His principal works are *The Principles of Psychology* (1890), *The Will to Believe* (1897), *The Varieties of Religious Experience* (1902), and *Pragmatism, A New Name for Some Old Ways of Thinking* (1907), from which this selection is taken.

After a brief introduction to pragmatism by way of a fascinating example of resolving a dispute about the correct characterization of a squirrel's behavior, James sets forth his view of truth. He holds that truth is dynamic rather than static and is to be defined in terms of beliefs that are useful or satisfying. Unlike the "intellectualists" (James' characterization of the traditional static approaches to the question of truth, viz., the correspondence theorists) truth is in process—still becoming and changing. Yesterday's truth is today's falsehood, and today's truth is tomorrow's half-truth. What really matters is what you can *do* with an idea, what difference it makes to your life, its (in James' term) "cash-value."

Study Questions

1. What is the dispute regarding the squirrel's behavior?
2. How does James' solution illustrate the meaning of pragmatism?
3. What is the problem with the dictionary definition of truth?
4. What is James' argument against the "intellectualists" (that is, i.e., philosophers who believe in the correspondence theory)?
5. How does James define true and false ideas?
6. What does he mean by "Truth lives . . . for the most part on a credit system"? Does this make truth relative to the beholder?
7. How does James interpret the idea that truth is an agreement with reality?
8. What does James mean by, "'The true' . . . is only the expedient in the way of our thinking, just as 'the right' is only the expedient in the way of our behaving" (by "expedient" James means prudent or suitable to achieve success)? What is the significance of the phrase that it is expedient "in the long run and on the whole"?
9. How does an idea become retrospectively true?
10. What is the relationship between the good and the true?

WHAT PRAGMATISM MEANS

SOME YEARS AGO, being with a camping party in the mountains, I returned from a solitary ramble to find every one engaged in a ferocious metaphysical dispute. The *corpus* of the dispute was a squirrel—a live squirrel supposed to be clinging to one side of a tree-trunk; while over against the tree's opposite side a human being was imagined to stand. This human witness tries to get sight of the squirrel by moving rapidly round the tree, but no matter how fast he goes, the squirrel moves as fast in the same direction, and always keeps the tree between himself and the man, so that never a glimpse of him is caught. The resultant metaphysical problem now is this: *Does the man go round the squirrel or not?* He goes round the tree, sure

enough, and the squirrel is on the tree; but does he go round the squirrel? In the unlimited leisure of the wilderness, discussion had been worn threadbare. Every one had taken sides, and was obstinate; and the numbers on both sides were even. Each side, when I appeared, therefore appealed to me to make it a majority. Mindful of the scholastic adage that whenever you meet a contradiction you must make a distinction, I immediately sought and found one, as follows: "Which party is right," I said, "depends on what you *practically mean* by 'going round' the squirrel. If you mean passing from the north of him to the east, then to the south, then to the west, and then to the north of him again, obviously the man does go round him, for he occupies these successive positions. But if on the contrary you mean being

From William James, Pragmatism, A New Name for Some Old Ways of Thinking *(Lectures II and VI), New York, 1907.*

first in front of him, then on the right of him, then behind him, then on his left, and finally in front again, it is quite as obvious that the man fails to go round him, for by the compensating movements the squirrel makes, he keeps his belly turned towards the man all the time, and his back turned away. Make the distinction, and there is no occasion for any further dispute. You are both right and both wrong according as you conceive the verb 'to go round' in one practical fashion or the other."

Although one or two of the hotter disputants called my speech a shuffling evasion, saying they wanted no quibbling or scholastic hair-splitting, but meant just plain honest English "round," the majority seemed to think that the distinction had assuaged the dispute.

I tell this trivial anecdote because it is a peculiarly simple example of what I wish now to speak of as *the pragmatic method*. The pragmatic method is primarily a method of settling metaphysical disputes that otherwise might be interminable. Is the world one or many?—fated or free?—material or spiritual?—here are notions either of which may or may not hold good of the world; and disputes over such notions are unending. The pragmatic method in such cases is to try to interpret each notion by tracing its respective practical consequences. What difference would it practically make to any one if this notion rather than that notion were true? If no practical difference whatever can be traced, then the alternatives mean practically the same thing, and all dispute is idle. Whenever a dispute is serious, we ought to be able to show some practical difference that must follow from one side or the other's being right.

A glance at the history of the idea will show you still better what pragmatism means. The term is derived from the same Greek word pragma, meaning action, from which our words "practice" and "practical" come. It was first introduced into philosophy by Mr. Charles Peirce in 1878. In an article entitled "How to Make Our Ideas Clear," in the *Popular Science Monthly* for January of that year. Mr. Peirce, after pointing out that our beliefs are really rules

for action, said that, to develop a thought's meaning, we need only determine what conduct it is fitted to produce: that conduct is for us its sole significance. And the tangible fact at the root of all our thought-distinctions, however subtle, is that there is no one of them so fine as to consist in anything but a possible difference of practice. To attain perfect clearness in our thoughts of an object, then, we need only consider what conceivable effects of a practical kind the object may involve—what sensations we are to expect from it, and what reactions we must prepare. Our conception of these effects, whether immediate or remote, is then for us the whole of our conception of the object, so far as that conception has positive significance at all. . . .

[Next James turns to the pragmatist theory of truth.]

PRAGMATISM'S CONCEPTION OF TRUTH

I fully expect to see the pragmatist view of truth run through the classic stages of a theory's career. First, you know, a new theory is attacked as absurd; then it is admitted to be true, but obvious and insignificant; finally it is seen to be so important that its adversaries claim that they themselves discovered it. Our doctrine of truth is at present in the first of these three stages, with symptoms of the second stage having begun in certain quarters. I wish that this lecture might help it beyond the first stage in the eyes of many of you.

Truth, as any dictionary will tell you, is a property of certain of our ideas. It means their "agreement," as falsity means their "disagreement," with "reality." Pragmatists and intellectualists both accept this definition as a matter of course. They begin to quarrel only after the question is raised as to what may precisely be meant by the term "agreement," and what by the term "reality," when reality is taken as something for our ideas to agree with.

In answering these questions the pragmatists are more analytic and painstaking, the intellectualists more offhand and irreflective. The popular notion is that a true idea must copy its reality. Like other popular views, this one follows the analogy of the most usual experience. Our true ideas of sensible things do indeed copy them. Shut your eyes and think of yonder clock on the wall, and you get just such a true picture or copy of its dial. But your idea of its "works" (unless you are a clockmaker) is much less of a copy, yet it passes muster, for it in no way clashes with the reality. Even though it should shrink to the mere word "works," that word still serves you truly; and when you speak of the "time-keeping function" of the clock, or of its spring's "elasticity," it is hard to see exactly what your ideas can copy.

You perceive that there is a problem here. Where our ideas cannot copy definitely their object, what does agreement with that object mean? Some idealists seem to say that they are true whenever they are what God means that we ought to think about that subject. Others hold the copy-view all through, and speak as if our ideas possessed truth just in proportion as they approach to being copies of the Absolute's eternal way of thinking.

These views, you see, invite pragmatistic discussion. But the great assumption of the intellectualists is that truth means essentially an inert static relation. When you've got your true idea of anything, there's an end of the matter. You're in possession; you *know;* you have fulfilled your thinking destiny. You are where you ought to be mentally; you have obeyed your categorical imperative; and nothing more need follow on that climax of your rational destiny. Epistemologically you are in stable equilibrium.

Pragmatism, on the other hand, asks its usual question. "Grant an idea or belief to be true," it says, "what concrete difference will its being true make in any one's actual life? How will the truth be realized? What experiences will be different from those which would obtain if the be-lief were false? What, in short, is the truth's cash-value in experiential terms?"

The moment pragmatism asks this question, it sees the answer: *True ideas are those that we can assimilate, validate, corroborate and verify. False ideas are those that we cannot.* That is the practical difference it makes to us to have true ideas; that, therefore, is the meaning of truth, for it is all that truth is known-as.

This thesis is what I have to defend. The truth of an idea is not a stagnant property inherent in it. Truth *happens* to an idea. It *becomes* true, is *made* true by events. Its verity *is* in fact an event, a process: the process namely of its verifying itself, its veri-*fication.* Its validity is the process of its valid-*ation.*

But what do the words verification and validation themselves pragmatically mean? They again signify certain practical consequences of the verified and validated idea. It is hard to find any one phrase that characterizes these consequences better than the ordinary agreement-formula—just such consequences being what we have in mind whenever we say that our ideas "agree" with reality. They lead us, namely, through the acts and other ideas which they instigate, into or up to, or towards, other parts of experience with which we feel all the while—such feeling being among our potentialities—that the original ideas remain in agreement. The connexions and transitions come to us from point to point as being progressive, harmonious, satisfactory. This function of agreeable leading is what we mean by an idea's verification. . . .

. . . The possession of true thoughts means everywhere the possession of invaluable instruments of action; and that our duty to gain truth, so far from being a blank command from out of the blue, or a "stunt" self-imposed by our intellect, can account for itself by excellent practical reasons.

The importance to human life of having true beliefs about matters of fact is a thing too notorious. We live in a world of realities that can be infinitely useful or infinitely harmful. Ideas that tell us which of them to expect count as the true ideas in all this primary sphere of verification, and the pursuit of such ideas is a primary human duty. The possession of truth, so far from being here an end in itself, is only a preliminary means towards other vital satisfactions. If I am lost in the woods and starved, and find what looks like a cow-path, it is of the utmost importance that I should think of a human habitation at the end of it, for if I do so and follow it, I save myself. The true thought is useful here because the house which is its object is useful. The practical value of true ideas is thus primarily derived from the practical importance of their objects to us. Their objects are, indeed, not important at all times. I may on another occasion have no use for the house; and then my idea of it, however verifiable, will be practically irrelevant, and had better remain latent. Yet since almost any object may some day become temporarily important, the advantage of having a general stock of *extra* truths, of ideas that shall be true of merely possible situations, is obvious. We store such extra truths away in our memories, and with the overflow we fill our books of reference. Whenever such an extra truth becomes practically relevant to one of our emergencies, it passes from cold-storage to do work in the world and our belief in it grows active. You can say of it then either that "it is useful because it is true" or that "it is true because it is useful." Both these phrases mean exactly the same thing, namely that here is an idea that gets fulfilled and can be verified. True is the name for whatever idea starts the verification-process, useful is the name for its completed function in experience. True ideas would never have been singled out as such, would never have acquired a class-name, least of all a name suggesting value, unless they had been useful from the outset in this way.

From this simple cue pragmatism gets her general notion of truth as something essentially bound up with the way in which one moment in our experience may lead us towards other moments which it will be worth while to have been led to. Primarily, and on the common-sense level, the truth of a state of mind means this function of *a leading that is worth while*. When a moment in our experience, of any kind whatever, inspires us with a thought that is true, that means that sooner or later we dip by that thought's guidance into the particulars of experience again and make advantageous connexion with them. This is a vague enough statement, but I beg you to retain it, for it is essential.

Our experience meanwhile is all shot through with regularities. One bit of it can warn us to get ready for another bit, can "intend" or be "significant of" that remoter object. The object's advent is the significance's verification. Truth, in these cases, meaning nothing but eventual verification, is manifestly incompatible with waywardness on our part. Woe to him whose beliefs play fast and loose with the order which realities follow in his experience; they will lead him nowhere or else make false connexions.

By "realities" or "objects" here, we mean either things of common sense, sensibly present, or else common-sense relations, such as dates, places, distances, kinds, activities. Following our mental image of a house along the cow-path, we actually come to see the house; we get the image's full verification. *Such simply and fully verified leadings are certainly the originals and prototypes of the truth-process.* Experience offers indeed other forms of truth-process, but they are all conceivable as being primary verifications arrested, multiplied or substituted one for another.

Take, for instance, yonder object on the wall. You and I consider it to be a "clock," altho no one of us has seen the hidden works that make it one. We let our notion pass for true without attempting to verify. If truths mean verification-process essentially, ought we then to call such unverified truths as this abortive? No, for they form the overwhelmingly large number of the truths we live by. Indirect as well as direct verifications pass muster. Where circumstantial evidence is sufficient, we can go without eye-witnessing. Just as we here assume Japan to exist without ever having been there, because it *works* to do so, everything we know conspiring with the belief, and nothing interfering, so we assume that thing to be a clock. We *use* it as a clock, regulating the length of our lecture by it. The verification of the assumption here means its leading to no frustration or contradiction. Verifi*ability* of wheels and weights and pendulum is as good as verification. For one truth-process completed there are a million in our lives that function in this state of nascency. They turn us *towards* direct verification; lead us into the *surroundings* of the objects they envisage; and then, if everything runs on harmoniously, we are so sure that verification is possible that we omit it, and are usually justified by all that happens.

Truth lives, in fact, for the most part on a credit system. Our thoughts and beliefs "pass," so long as nothing challenges them, just as bank-notes pass so long as nobody refuses them. But this all points to direct face-to-face verifications somewhere, without which the fabric of truth collapses like a financial system with no cash-basis whatever. You accept my verification of one thing, I yours of another. We trade on each other's truth. But beliefs verified concretely by *somebody* are the posts of the whole superstructure.

Another great reason—beside economy of time—for waiving complete verification in the usual business of life is that all things exist in kinds and not singly. Our world is found once for all to have that peculiarity. So that when we have once directly verified our ideas about one specimen of a kind, we consider ourselves free to apply them to other specimens without verification. A mind that habitually discerns the kind of thing before it, and acts by the law of the kind immediately, without pausing to verify, will be a "true" mind in ninety-nine out of a hundred emergencies, proved so by its conduct fitting everything it meets, and getting no refutation.

Indirectly or only potentially verifying processes may thus be true as well as full verification-processes. They work as true processes would work, give us the same advantages, and claim our recognition for the same reasons. . . .

[James returns to the notion that truth is an agreement with reality.]

Here it is that pragmatism and intellectualism begin to part company. Primarily, no doubt, to agree means to copy, but we saw that the mere word "clock" would do instead of a mental picture of its works, and that of many realities our ideas can only be symbols and not copies. "Past time," "power," "spontaneity"—how can our mind copy such realities?

To "agree" in the widest sense with a reality *can only mean to be guided either straight up to it or into its surroundings, or to be put into such working touch with it as to handle either it or something connected with it better than if we disagreed*. Better either intellectually or practically! And often agreement will only mean the negative fact that nothing contradictory from the quarter of that reality comes to interfere with the way in which our ideas guide us elsewhere. To copy a reality is, indeed, one very important way of agreeing with it, but it is far from being essential. The essential thing is the process of being guided. Any idea that helps us to *deal*, whether practically or intellectually, with either the reality or its belongings, that doesn't entangle our progress in frustrations, that *fits*, in fact, and adapts our life to the reality's whole setting, will agree sufficiently to meet the requirement. It will hold true of that reality.

Thus, *names* are just as "true" or "false" as definite mental pictures are. They set up similar verification-processes, and lead to fully equivalent practical results.

All human thinking gets discursified; we exchange ideas; we lend and borrow verifications, get them from one another by means of social intercourse. All truth thus gets verbally built out, stored up, and made available for every one. Hence, we must *talk* consistently just as we must *think* consistently: for both in talk and thought we deal with kinds. Names are arbitrary, but once understood they must be kept to. We mustn't now call Abel "Cain" or Cain "Abel." If we do, we ungear ourselves from the whole book of Genesis, and from all its connexions with the universe of speech and fact down to the present time. We throw ourselves out of whatever truth that entire system of speech and fact may embody.

The overwhelming majority of our true ideas admit of no direct or face-to-face verification—those of past history, for example, as of Cain and Abel. The stream of time can be remounted only verbally, or verified directly by the present prolongations or effects of what the past harbored. Yet if they agree with these verbalities and effects, we can know that our ideas of the past are true. *As true as past time itself was,* so true was Julius Caesar, so true were antediluvian monsters all in their proper dates and settings. That past time itself was, is guaranteed by its coherence with everything that's present. True as the present *is,* the past *was* also.

Agreement thus turns out to be essentially an affair of leading—leading that is useful because it is into quarters that contain objects that are important. True ideas lead us into useful verbal and conceptual quarters as well as directly up to useful sensible termini. They lead to consistency, stability and flowing human intercourse. They lead away from excentricity and isolation, from foiled and barren thinking. The untrammelled flowing of the leading-process, its general freedom from clash and contradiction, passes for its indirect verification; but all roads lead to Rome, and in the end and eventually, all true processes must lead to the face of directly verifying sensible experiences *somewhere,* which somebody's ideas have copied.

Such is the large loose way in which the pragmatist interprets the word agreement. He treats it altogether practically. He lets it cover any process of conduction from a present idea to a future terminus, provided only it run prosperously. It is only thus that "scientific" ideas, flying as they do beyond common sense, can be said to agree with their realities. It is, as I have already said, *as if* reality were made of ether, atoms or electrons, but we mustn't think so literally. The term "energy" doesn't even pretend to stand for anything "objective." It is only a way of measuring the surface of phenomena so as to string their changes on a simple formula.

Yet in the choice of these man-made formulas we cannot be capricious with impunity any more than we can be capricious on the common-sense practical level. We must find a theory that will *work;* and that means something extremely difficult; for our theory must mediate between all previous truths and certain new experiences. It must derange common sense and previous belief as little as possible, and it must lead to some sensible terminus or other that can be verified exactly. To "work" means both these things; and the squeeze is so tight that there is little loose play for any hypothesis. Our theories are wedged and controlled as nothing else is. Yet sometimes alternative theoretic formulas are equally compatible with all the truths we know, and then we choose between them for subjective reasons. We choose the kind of theory to which we are already partial; we follow "elegance" or "economy." Clerk-Maxwell somewhere says it would be "poor scientific taste" to choose the more complicated of two equally well-evidenced conceptions; and you will all agree with him. Truth in science is what gives us the maximum possible sum of satisfactions, taste included, but consistency both with previous truth and with novel fact is always the most imperious claimant. . . .

Our account of truth is an account of truths in the plural, of processes of leading, realized *in rebus,** and having only this quality in common, that they *pay.* They pay by guiding us into or towards some part of a system that dips at numerous points into sense-percepts, which we may copy mentally or not, but with which at any rate we are now in the kind of commerce vaguely designated as verification. Truth for us is simply a collective name for verification-processes, just as health, wealth, strength, etc., are names for other processes connected with life, and also pursued because it pays to pursue them. Truth is *made,* just as health, wealth and strength are made, in the course of experience.

*[in things]

Here rationalism is instantaneously up in arms against us. I can imagine a rationalist to talk as follows:

"Truth is not made," he will say; "it absolutely obtains, being a unique relation that does not wait upon any process, but shoots straight over the head of experience, and hits its reality every time. Our belief that yon thing on the wall is a clock is true already, altho no one in the whole history of the world should verify it. The bare quality of standing in that transcendent relation is what makes any thought true that possesses it, whether or not there be verification. You pragmatists put the cart before the horse in making truth's being reside in verification-processes. These are merely signs of its being, merely our lame ways of ascertaining after the fact, which of our ideas already has possessed the wondrous quality. The quality itself is timeless, like all essences and natures. Thoughts partake of it directly, as they partake of falsity or of irrelevancy. It can't be analyzed away into pragmatic consequences."

The whole plausibility of this rationalist tirade is due to the fact to which we have already paid so much attention. In our world, namely, abounding as it does in things of similar kinds and similarly associated, one verification serves for others of its kind, and one great use of knowing things is to be led not so much to them as to their associates, especially to human talk about them. The quality of truth, obtaining *ante rem,** pragmatically means, then, the fact that in such a world innumerable ideas work better by their indirect or possible than by their direct and actual verification. Truth *ante rem* means only verifiability, then; or else it is a case of the stock rationalist trick of treating the *name* of a concrete phenomenal reality as an independent prior entity, and placing it behind the reality as its explanation. . . .

In the case of "wealth" we all see the fallacy. We know that wealth is but a name for concrete processes that certain men's lives play a part in,

and not a natural excellence found in Messrs. Rockefeller and Carnegie, but not in the rest of us.

Like wealth, "health" also lives *in rebus*. It is a name for processes, as digestion, circulation, sleep, etc., that go on happily, tho in this instance we are more inclined to think of it as a principle and to say the man digests and sleeps so well *because* he is so healthy.

With "strength" we are, I think, more rationalistic still, and decidedly inclined to treat it as an excellence preexisting in the man and explanatory of the herculean performances of his muscles.

With "truth" most people go over the border entirely, and treat the rationalistic account as self-evident. But really all these words in *th* are exactly similar. Truth exists *ante rem* just as much and as little as the other things do.

The scholastics, following Aristotle, made much of the distinction between habit and act. Health *in actu* means, among other things, good sleeping and digesting. But a healthy man need not always be sleeping, or always digesting, any more than a wealthy man need be always handling money, or a strong man always lifting weights. All such qualities sink to the status of "habits" between their times of exercise; and similarly truth becomes a habit of certain of our ideas and beliefs in their intervals of rest from their verifying activities. But those activities are the root of the whole matter, and the condition of there being any habit to exist in the intervals.

"The true," to put it very briefly, *is only the expedient in the way of our thinking, just as "the right" is only the expedient in the way of our behaving.* Expedient in almost any fashion; and expedient in the long run and on the whole of course; for what meets expediently all the experience in sight won't necessarily meet all further experiences equally satisfactorily. Experience, as we know, has ways of *boiling over*, and making us correct our present formulas.

The "absolutely" true, meaning what no further experience will ever alter, is that ideal vanishing-point towards which we imagine that all our temporary truths will some day converge. It runs on all fours with the perfectly wise man, and with

*[before the thing]

the absolutely complete experience; and, if these ideals are ever realized, they will all be realized together. Meanwhile we have to live today by what truth we can get today, and be ready tomorrow to call it falsehood. Ptolemaic astronomy, Euclidean space, Aristotelian logic, Scholastic metaphysics, were expedient for centuries, but human experience has boiled over those limits, and we now call these things only relatively true, or true within those borders of experience. "Absolutely" they are false; for we know that those limits were casual, and might have been transcended by past theorists just as they are by present thinkers.

When new experiences lead to retrospective judgments, using the past tense, what these judgments utter *was* true, even tho no past thinker had been led there. We live forwards, a Danish thinker [Kierkegaard] has said, but we understand backwards. The present sheds a backward light on the world's previous processes. They may have been truth-processes for the actors in them. They are not so for one who knows the latter revelations of the story.

This regulative notion of a potential better truth to be established later, possibly to be established some day absolutely, and having powers of retroactive legislation, turns its face, like all pragmatist notions, towards concreteness of fact, and towards the future. Like the half-truths, the absolute truth will have to be *made*, made as a relation incidental to the growth of a mass of verification-experience, to which the half-true ideas are all along contributing their quota.

I have already insisted on the fact that truth is made largely out of previous truths. Men's beliefs at any time are so much experience *funded*. But the beliefs are themselves parts of the sum total of the world's experience, and become matter, therefore, for the next day's funding operations. So far as reality means experienceable reality, both it and the truths men gain about it are everlastingly in process of mutation—mutation towards a definite goal, it may be—but still mutation.

Mathematicians can solve problems with two variables. On the Newtonian theory, for instance, acceleration varies with distance, but distance also varies with acceleration. In the realm of truth-processes facts come independently and determine our beliefs provisionally. But these beliefs make us act, and as fast as they do so, they bring into sight or into existence new facts which re-determine the beliefs accordingly. So the whole coil and ball of truth, as it rolls up, is the product of a double influence. Truths emerge from facts; but they dip forward into facts again and add to them; which facts again create or reveal new truth (the word is indifferent) and so on indefinitely. The "facts" themselves meanwhile are not *true*. They simply *are*. Truth is the function of the beliefs that start and terminate among them. . . .

The case is like a snowball's growth, due as it is to the distribution of the snow on the one hand, and to the successive pushes of the boys on the other, with these factors co-determining each other incessantly. . . .

I am well aware how odd it must seem to some of you to hear me say that an idea is "true" so long as to believe it is profitable to our lives. That it is *good*, for as much as it profits, you will gladly admit. If what we do by its aid is good, you will allow the idea itself to be good in so far forth, for we are the better for possessing it. But is it not a strange misuse of the word "truth," you will say, to call ideas also "true" for this reason? . . .

. . . Let me now say only this, that truth is *one species of good*, and not, as is usually supposed, a category distinct from good, and co-ordinate with it. *The true is the name of whatever proves itself to be good in the way of belief, and good, too, for definite, assignable reasons.* Surely you must admit this, that if there were *no* good for life in true ideas, or if the knowledge of them were positively disadvantageous and false ideas the only useful ones, then the current notion that truth is divine and precious, and its pursuit a duty, could never have grown up or become a dogma. In a world like that, our duty would be to *shun* truth, rather. But in this world, just as certain foods are not only agreeable to our taste, but good for our teeth, our stomach, and our tissues; so certain ideas are not only agreeable to think about, or agreeable as supporting other ideas that we are fond of, but they are also helpful in life's practical struggles. If there be any life that it is really better we should lead, and if there be any idea which, if believed in, would help us to lead that life, then it would be really *better for us* to believe in that idea, *unless, indeed, belief in it incidentally clashed with other greater vital benefits.*

"What would be better for us to believe!" This sounds very like a definition of truth. It comes very near to saying "what we *ought* to believe"; and in *that* definition none of you would find any oddity. Ought we ever not to believe what it is *better for us* to believe? And can we then keep the notion of what is better for us, and what is true for us, permanently apart?

Pragmatism says no, and I fully agree with her. Probably you also agree, so far as the abstract statement goes, but with a suspicion that if we practically did believe everything that made

for good in our own personal lives, we should be found indulging all kinds of fancies about this world's affairs, and all kinds of sentimental superstitions about a world hereafter. Your suspicion here is undoubtedly well founded, and it is evident that something happens when you pass from the abstract to the concrete that complicates the situation.

I said just now that what is better for us to believe is true *unless the belief incidentally clashes with some other vital benefit.* Now in real life what vital benefits is any particular belief of ours most liable to clash with? What indeed except the vital benefits yielded by *other beliefs* when these prove incompatible with the first ones? In other words, the greatest enemy of any one of our truths may be the rest of our truths. Truths have once for all this desperate instinct of self-preservation and of desire to extinguish whatever contradicts them.

For Further Reflection

1. Does James' dynamic idea of truth appeal to you? What are its strengths?

2. Is James' criterion of truth as the success of an idea in practice clear? What problems, if any, do you see with it? Suppose that the Nazis had been successful in winning the Second World War; would their theories be "true"? Is success or usefulness the correct criterion of the true?

3. James elsewhere applied his ideas to religion and maintained that since religious beliefs were inspiring, we ought to believe them and make them true for ourselves. Do you agree with this? What if it turned out that the truth was bad news, not a gospel (literally, "good news") but a badspel (or "bad news"). Would you still rather know it than believe a falsehood that was expedient or inspiring? Is truth in the neutral, nonpragmatic sense, good in itself?

III.25   Dismantling Truth: Solidarity versus Objectivity

RICHARD RORTY

Richard Rorty is Professor of Comparative Literature at Stanford University and the author of several works, including *Philosophy and the Mirror of Nature* (1979).

In this selection, Rorty attacks the distinction between objectivity and subjectivity as well as the correspondence theory of truth. He sides with Thomas Kuhn in arguing that we can have no theory-independent notion of reality and proposes to erase the essential difference between science and the humanities and arts. Embracing the title of "the new fuzzies," Rorty proposes that a notion of social solidarity replace the enlightenment notion of objective truth.

Study Questions

1. What is the present relationship in our culture between science and the humanities? Which receives greater respect and why?
2. What are the two meanings of "rational" which Rorty discusses? Which does he think superior to the other?
3. What are the criteria of scientific rationality? How do the humanities measure up to those criteria?
4. What does Rorty think should be done about the idea of objective truth?
5. What is Rorty's criticism of the correspondence theory of truth?
6. What role does Thomas Kuhn's work play in the debate between science and the humanities? Why does Rorty congratulate Kuhn?
7. What is the central idea of Rorty's "pragmatism"? Why is it called by its critics "the new fuzziness"?
8. What would be a pragmatist's paradise? What was the charge against John Dewey in proposing such a paradise?

IN OUR CULTURE, the notions of "science," "rationality," "objectivity" and "truth" are bound up with one another. Science is thought of as offering "hard," "objective" truth—truth as correspondence to reality, the only sort of truth worthy of the name. Humanists—philosophers, theologians, historians, literary critics—have to worry about whether they are being "scientific"—whether they are entitled to think of their conclusions, no matter how carefully argued, as worthy of the term "true." We tend to identify seeking "objective truth" with "using reason," and so we think of the natural sciences as paradigms of rationality. We also think of rationality as a matter of following procedures laid down in advance, of being "methodical." So we tend to use "methodical," "rational," "scientific" and "objective" as synonyms.

Worries about "cognitive status" and "objectivity" are characteristic of a secularized culture in which the scientist replaces the priest. The scientist is now seen as the person who keeps humanity in touch with something beyond itself. As the universe was depersonalized, beauty (and, in time, even moral goodness) came to be thought of as "subjective." So truth is now thought of as the only point at which human beings are responsible to something non-human. A commitment to "rationality" and to "method" is thought to be a recognition of this responsibility. The scientist becomes a moral exemplar, one who selflessly exposes himself again and again to the hardness of facts.

One result of this way of thinking is that any academic discipline which wants a place at the trough, but is unable to offer the predictions

From Richard Rorty, "Science and Solidarity," in Rhetoric of the Human Sciences: Language and Arguments in Scholarship and Public Affairs *edited by Nelson et al. (Madison: University of Wisconsin Press, 1987). Reprinted with permission of the University of Wisconsin Press.*

and the technology provided by the natural sciences, must either pretend to imitate science or find some way of obtaining "cognitive status" without the necessity of discovering facts. Practitioners of these disciplines must either affiliate themselves with this quasi-priestly order by using terms like "behavioral sciences" or else find something other than "fact" to be concerned with. People in the humanities typically choose the latter strategy. They describe themselves either as concerned with "values" as opposed to facts, or as developing and inculcating habits of "critical reflection."

Neither sort of rhetoric is very satisfactory. No matter how much humanists talk about "objective values," the phrase always sounds vaguely confused. It gives with one hand what it takes back with the other. The distinction between the objective and the subjective was designed to parallel that between fact and value, so an objective value sounds vaguely mythological as a winged horse. Talk about the humanists' special skill at critical reflection fares no better. Nobody really believes that philosophers or literary critics are better at critical thinking, or at taking big broad views of things, than theoretical physicists or microbiologists. So society tends to ignore both these kinds of rhetoric. It treats humanities as on a par with the arts, and thinks of both as providing pleasure rather than truth. Both are, to be sure, thought of as providing "high" rather than "low" pleasure. But an elevated and spiritual sort of pleasure is still a long way from the grasp of a truth.

These distinctions between hard facts and soft values, truth and pleasure, and objectivity and subjectivity are awkward and clumsy instruments. They are not suited to divide up culture; they create more difficulties than they resolve. It would be best to find another vocabulary, to start afresh. But in order to do so we first have to find a new way of describing the natural sciences. It is not a question of debunking or downgrading the natural sciences, but simply of ceasing to see them on the model of the priest. We need to stop thinking of science as the place where the human mind confronts the world. We need a way of explaining why scientists are, and deserve to be, moral exemplars which does not depend on a distinction between objective fact and something softer, squishier and more dubious.

To get to such a way of thinking we can start by distinguishing two senses of the term "rationality." In one sense, the one I have already discussed, to be rational is to be methodical: that is, to have criteria for success laid down in advance. We think of poets and painters as using some other faculty than "reason" in their work because, by their own confession, they are not sure of what they want to do before they have done it. They make up new standards of achievement as they go along. By contrast, we think of judges as knowing in advance what criteria a brief will have to satisfy in order to invoke a favorable decision, and of businessmen as setting well-defined goals and being judged by their success in achieving them. Law and business are good examples of rationality, but the scientist, knowing in advance what would count as disconfirming his hypothesis and prepared to abandon that hypothesis as a result of the unfavorable outcome of a single experiment, seems a truly heroic example. Further, we seem to have a clear criterion of the success of a scientific theory—namely, its ability to predict, and thereby to enable us to control some portion of the world. If to be rational means to be able to lay down criteria in advance, then it is plausible to take natural science as the paradigm of rationality.

The trouble is that in this sense of "rational" the humanities are never going to qualify as rational activities. If the humanities are concerned with ends rather than means, then there is no way to evaluate their success in terms of antecedently specified criteria. If we already knew what criteria we wanted to satisfy, we would not worry about whether we were pursuing the right ends. If we thought we knew the goals of culture and society in advance, we would have no use for the humanities—as totalitarian societies in fact do not. It is characteristic of democracies and pluralistic societies to redefine their goals continually. But if to be rational means to satisfy criteria, then this process of redefinition will be bound to be non-rational. So if the humanities are to be viewed as rational activities, rationality will have to be thought of as something other than the satisfaction of criteria which are statable in advance.

[The second] meaning of "rational" is, in fact, available. In this sense, the word means something like "sane" or "reasonable" rather than "methodical." It names a set of moral virtues: tolerance, respect for the opinion of those around one, willingness to listen, reliance on persuasion rather than force. These are the virtues which members of a civilized society must possess if the society is to endure. In this sense of "rational," the word means something more like "civilized" than like "methodical." When so construed, the distinction between the rational and the irrational has nothing in particular to do with the difference between the arts and the sciences. On this construction, to be rational is simply to discuss any topic—religious, literary, or scientific—in a way which eschews dogmatism, defensiveness, and righteous indignation.

There is no problem about whether, in this latter, weaker sense the humanities are "rational disciplines." Usually humanists display the moral virtues in question. Sometimes they do not, but then sometimes scientists don't either. Yet these moral virtues are felt to be not enough. Both humanists and the public hanker after rationality in the first, stronger sense of the term: a sense which is associated with objective truth, correspondence to reality, method and criteria.

We should not try to satisfy this hankering, but rather try to eradicate it. No matter what one's opinion of the secularization of culture, it was a mistake to try to make the natural scientist into a new sort of priest, a link between the human and the non-human. So was the idea that some sorts of truths are "objective" whereas others are merely "subjective" or "relative"—the attempt to divide up the set of true sentences into "genuine knowledge" and "mere opinion," or into the "factual" and the "judgmental." So was the idea

that the scientist has a special method which, if only the humanists would apply it to ultimate values, would give us the same kind of self-confidence about moral ends as we now have about technological means. I think that we should content ourselves with the second, "weaker" conception of rationality and avoid the first, "stronger" conception. We should avoid the idea that there is some special virtue in knowing in advance what criteria you are going to satisfy, in having standards by which to measure progress.

[IS SCIENCE RATIONAL?]

One can make these issues somewhat more concrete by taking up the current controversy among philosophers about the "rationality of science." For some twenty years, ever since the publication of Thomas Kuhn's book, *The Structure of Scientific Revolutions* philosophers have been debating the question of "whether science is rational." Attacks on Kuhn for being "irrational" are now as frequent and urgent as, in the 1930s and 1940s, were attacks on the logical positivists for saying that moral judgments were "meaningless." We are constantly being warned of the danger of "relativism" which will beset us if we give up our attachment to objectivity and to the idea of rationality as obedience to criteria.

Whereas Kuhn's enemies routinely accuse him of reducing science to "mob psychology," and pride themselves on having (by a new theory of meaning or reference or verisimilitude) vindicated the "rationality of science," his pragmatic friends (such as myself) routinely congratulate him on having softened the distinction between science and non-science. . . . [H]e has said that "there is no theory-independent way to reconstruct phrases like "really there." He has asked whether it really helps "to imagine that there is some one full, objective, true account of nature and that the proper measure of scientific achievement is the extent to which it brings us closer to the ultimate goal." We pragmatists quote these passages incessantly in the course of our effort to enlist Kuhn in our campaign to drop the objective-subjective distinction altogether.

What I am calling "pragmatism" might also be called "left-wing Kuhnianism." It has also been rather endearingly called (by one of its critics, Clark Glymour) "the new fuzziness," because it is an attempt to blur just those distinctions between the objective and the subjective and between fact and value which the criterial conception of rationality has developed. We fuzzies would like to substitute the idea of "unforced agreement" for that of "objectivity." We should like to put all culture on an epistemological level (or get rid of the idea of "epistemological level"). . . . On our view, "truth" is a univocal term. It applies equally to the judgments of lawyers, anthropologists, physicists, philologists and literary critics. There is point in assigning degrees of "objectivity" or "hardness" to such disciplines. For the presence of unforced agreement in all of them gives us everything in the way of "objective truth" which one could possibly want: namely, intersubjective agreement.

As soon as one says that all there is to objectivity is intersubjectivity, one is likely to be accused of being a relativist. That is the epithet traditionally applied to pragmatists. But this epithet is ambiguous. It can name any of three different views:

1. The silly and self-refuting view that every belief is as good as every other.

2. The wrong-headed view that "true" is an equivocal term, having as many meanings as there are contexts of justification.

3. The ethnocentric view that there is nothing to be said about either truth or rationality apart from descriptions of the familiar procedures of justification which a given society—*ours*—uses in one or another area of inquiry.

The pragmatist does hold this third, ethnocentric view. But he does not hold the first or the second view of relativism.

But "relativism" is not an appropriate term to describe this sort of ethnocentrism. For we pragmatists are not holding a positive theory which says that something is relative to something else. Instead, we are making the purely *negative* point that we would be better off without the traditional distinctions between knowledge and opinion, construed as the distinction between truth as correspondence to reality and truth as a commendatory term for well-justified beliefs. Our opponents call this negative claim "relativistic" because they cannot imagine that anybody would seriously deny that truth has an intrinsic nature. So when we say that there is nothing to be said about truth save that each of us will commend as true those beliefs which he or she finds good to believe, the realist is inclined to interpret this as one more positive theory about the nature of truth: a theory according to which truth is simply the contemporary opinion of a chosen individual or group. Such a theory would, of course, be self-refuting. But we pragmatists do not have a theory of truth, much less a relativistic one. As partisans of solidarity, our account of the value of cooperative human enquiry has only an ethical base, not an epistemological or metaphysical one.

To say that we must be ethnocentric may sound suspicious, but this will only happen if we identify ethnocentrism with pigheaded refusal to talk to representatives of other communities. In my sense of ethnocentrism, to be ethnocentric is simply to work by our own lights. The defense of ethnocentrism is simply that there are no other lights to work by. Beliefs suggested by another individual or another culture must be tested by trying to weave them together with beliefs which we already have. . . .

This way of thinking runs counter to the attempts, familiar since the eighteenth century, to think of political liberalism as based on a conception of the nature of man. To most thinkers of the Enlightenment, it seemed clear that the access to Nature which physical science had provided should now be followed by the establishment of social, political and economic institutions which were "in accordance with Nature." Ever since, liberal social thought has centered around social reform as made possible by objective knowledge of what human beings are like—not knowledge of what Greeks or Frenchmen or Chinese are like, but of humanity as such. This tradition dreams of a universal human community which will exhibit a non-parochial solidarity because it is the expression of an ahistorical human nature.

Philosophers who belong to this tradition, who wish to ground solidarity in objectivity, have to construe truth as correspondence to reality. So they must construct an epistemology which has room for a kind of justification which is not merely social but natural, springing from human nature itself, and made possible by a link between that part of nature and the rest of nature. By contrast we pragmatists, who wish to reduce objectivity to solidarity, do not require either a metaphysics or an epistemology. . . . We see the gap between truth and justification not as something to be bridged by isolating a natural and transcultural sort of rationality which can be used to criticize certain cultures and praise others, but simply as the gap between the actual good and the possible better. From a pragmatist point of view, to say that what is rational for us now to believe may not be *true,* is simply to say that somebody may come up with a better idea. . . .

Another reason for describing us as "relativistic" is that we pragmatists drop the idea that enquiry is destined to converge to a single point—that Truth is "out there" waiting for human beings to arrive at it. This idea seems to us an unfortunate attempt to carry a religious conception over into a secular culture. All that is worth preserving of the claim that rational inquiry will converge to a single point is the claim that we must be able to explain why past false views were held in the past, and thus explain how we go about re-educating our benighted ancestors. To say that we think we're heading in the right direction is just to say, with Kuhn, that we can, by hindsight, tell the story of the past as a story of progress.

But the fact that we can trace such a direction and tell such a story does not mean that we have come closer to a goal which is out there waiting for us. We cannot, I think, imagine a moment at which the human race could settle back and say, "Well, now that we've finally arrived at the Truth we can relax." Paul Feyerabend is right in suggesting that we should discard the metaphor of inquiry, and human activity generally, as converging rather than proliferating, becoming more unified rather than more diverse. On the contrary, we should *relish* that thought that the sciences as well as the arts will *always* provide a spectacle of fierce competition between alternative theories, movements and schools. The end of human activity is not rest, but rather richer and better human activity. We should think of human progress as making it possible for human beings to do more interesting things and be more interesting people, not as heading toward a place which has somehow been prepared for us in advance. To drop the criterial conception of rationality in favor of the pragmatist conception would be to give up the idea of Truth as something to which we were responsible. Instead we should think of "true" as a word which applies to those beliefs upon which we are able to agree, as roughly synonymous with "justified." . . .

. . . Pragmatists would like to replace the desire for objectivity—the desire to be in touch with a reality which is more than some community with which we identify ourselves—with the desire for solidarity with that community. They think that the habits of relying on persuasion rather than force, of respect for opinions of colleagues, of curiosity and eagerness for new data and ideas, are the *only* virtues which scientists have. They do not think that there is an intellectual virtue called "rationality" over and above these moral virtues. . . .

Pragmatists interpret the goal of inquiry (in any sphere of culture) as the attainment of an appropriate mixture of unforced agreement with tolerant disagreement (where what counts as appropriate is determined, within that sphere, by trial and error). Such a reinterpretation of our sense of responsibility would, if carried through, gradually make unintelligible the subject-object model of enquiry, the child-parent model of moral obligation, and the correspondence theory of truth. A world in which those models, and that theory, no longer had any intuitive appeal would be a pragmatist's paradise.

When Dewey urged that we try to create such a paradise he was said to be irresponsible. For, it was said, he left us bereft of weapons to use against our enemies; he gave us nothing with which to "answer the Nazis." When we new fuzzies try to revive Dewey's repudiation of criteriology we are said to be "relativistic." We must, people say, believe that every coherent view is as good as every other, since we have no "outside" touchstone for choice among such views. We are said to leave the general public defenseless against the witch doctor, the defender of creationism, or anyone else who is clever and patient enough to deduce a consistent and wide-ranging set of theorems from his "alternative first principles."

Nobody is convinced when we fuzzies say that we can be just as morally indignant as the next philosopher. We are suspected of being contritely fallibilist when righteous fury is called for. Even when we actually display appropriate emotions we get nowhere, for we are told that we have no *right* to these emotions. When we suggest that one of the few things we know (or need to know) about truth is that it is what wins in a free and open encounter, we are told that we have defined "true" as "satisfies the standards of our community." But we pragmatists do not hold this relativist view. We do not infer from "There is no way to step outside communities to a neutral standpoint" to "There is no rational way to justify liberal communities over totalitarian communities." For that inference involves just the notion of "rationality" as a set of ahistorical principles which pragmatists abjure. What we in fact infer is that there is no way to beat totalitarians in argument by appealing to shared common premises, and no point in pretending

that a common human nature makes the totalitarians unconsciously hold such premises.

The claim that we fuzzies have no right to be furious at moral evil, no right to commend our views as true unless we simultaneously refute ourselves by claiming that there are objects out there which *make* those views true, begs all the theoretical questions. But it gets to the practical and moral heart of the matter. This is the question of whether notions like "unforced agreement" and "free and open encounter'—descriptions of social situations—can take the place in our moral lives of notions like "the world," "the will of God," "the moral law," "what our beliefs are trying to represent accurately" and "what makes our beliefs true." All the philosophical presuppositions which make Hume's fork seem inevitable are ways of suggesting that human communities must justify their existence by striving to attain a non-human goal. To suggest that we can forget about Hume's fork [the radical separation of facts from values], forget about being responsible to what is "out there," is to suggest that human communities can justify their existence only by comparisons with other actual and possible human communities . . . .

Imagine . . . that a few years from now you open your copy of the *New York Times* and read that the philosophers, in convention assembled, have unanimously agreed that values are objective, science rational, truth a matter of correspondence to reality, etc. Recent breakthroughs in semantics and meta-ethics, the report goes on, have caused the last remaining non-cognitivists in ethics to recant. Similarly breakthroughs in the philosophy of science have led Kuhn formally to abjure his claim that there is no theory-independent way to reconstruct statements about what is "really there." All the new fuzzies have repudiated all their former views. By way of making amends for the intellectual confusion which the philosophical profession has recently caused, the philosophers have adopted a short, crisp set of standards of rationality and morality. Next year the convention is expected to adopt the report of the committee charged with formulating a standard of aesthetic taste.

Surely the public reaction to this would not be "Saved!" but rather "Who on earth do these philosophers think they *are?*" It is one of the best things about the form of intellectual life we Western liberals lead that this *would* be our reaction. No matter how much we moan about the disorder and confusion of the current philosophical scene, about the treason of the clerks, we do not really want things any other way. What prevents us from relaxing and enjoying the new fuzziness is perhaps no more than cultural lag, the fact that the rhetoric of the Enlightenment praised the emerging natural sciences in a vocabulary which was left over from a less liberal and tolerant era. This rhetoric enshrined all the old philosophical opposition between mind and world, appearance and reality, subject and object, truth and pleasure. Dewey thought that it was the continued prevalence of such opposition which prevented us from seeing that modern science was a new and promising invention, a way of life which had not existed before and which ought to be encouraged and imitated, something which required a new rhetoric rather than justification by an old one.

Suppose that Dewey were right about this, and that eventually we learn to find the fuzziness which results from breaking down such opposition spiritually comforting rather than morally offensive. What would the rhetoric of the culture, and in particular of the humanities, sound like? Presumably it would be more Kuhnian, in the sense that it would mention particular concrete achievements—paradigms—more, and "method" less. There would be less talk about rigor and more about originality. The image of the great scientist would not be of somebody who got it right but of somebody who made it new. The new rhetoric would draw more on the vocabulary of Romantic poetry and socialist pol-

itics, and less on that of Greek metaphysics, religious morality or Enlightenment scientism. A scientist would rely on a sense of solidarity with the rest of her profession, rather than a picture of herself as battling through the veils of illusion, guided by the light of reason.

If all this happened, the term "science," and thus the opposition between the humanities, the arts and the sciences might gradually fade away. Once "science" was deprived of an honorific sense, we might not need it for taxonomy. . . . The people now called "scientists" would no longer think of themselves as members of a quasi-priestly order, nor would the public think of themselves as in the care of such an order.

In this situation, the "humanities" would no longer think of themselves as such, nor would they share a common rhetoric. Each of the disciplines which now fall under that rubric would worry as little about its method, cognitive status or "philosophical foundations" as do mathematics, civil engineering or sculpture. For terms which denoted disciplines would not be thought to divide "subject matter," chunks of the world which had "interfaces" with each other. Rather, they would be thought to denote communities whose boundaries were as fluid as the interests of their members. In this heyday of the fuzzies, there would be as little reason to be self-conscious about the nature and status of one's discipline as, in the ideal democratic community, about the nature and status of one's race or sex. For one's ultimate loyalty would be to the larger community which permitted and encouraged this kind of freedom and insouciance. This community would serve no higher end than its own preservation and self-improvement, the preservation and enhancement of civilization. It would identify rationality with that effort, rather than with the desire for objectivity. So it would feel no need for a foundation more solid than reciprocal loyalty.

For Further Reflection

1. What are the major motivations of Rorty in rejecting the correspondence theory of truth and the object-subject distinction? Why does he think that the notion of intersubjective agreement (or unforced agreement) is a better idea? What are the strengths and weaknesses of Rorty's proposal?

2. Rorty distinguishes three types of relativism. What are they and which does he choose? Do you agree with his argument here? Explain your answer.

3. What does Rorty mean by saying that pragmatic truth has only an ethical base, not an epistemological or metaphysical one? What is his argument for this? Is it sound?

4. Has Rorty successfully eliminated metaphysical and epistemological notions? Has he argued successfully against the distinction between the ideas of objectivity and subjectivity and against the correspondence theory of truth? Critique his argument.

5. Do you detect any hidden assumptions in this article? Who is in the community with which Rorty identifies? What are its values? Does it include religious people? conservatives? socialists? Explain your answer.

6. Elsewhere in *Philosophy and the Mirror of Nature* (p. 176), Rorty describes "truth" as "what you can defend against all comers, . . . what our peers will *ceteris paribus* let us get away with saying." Analyze this characterization of truth.

III.26　　Upholding Truth: Objectivity versus Solidarity

MARGARITA R. LEVIN

Margarita R. Levin teaches philosophy at Stern College in New York and is the author of several essays in Philosophy of Science and Environmental Ethics. In this essay she defends the idea of objectivity against detractors, such as Rorty, Duhem, and Quine. She defines "objectivity" as "intersubjectively accessible knowledge," and holds that we can arrive at such truth that is "independent of bias, tradition, wishes or other influences." She examines three objections to objectivity that she argues against.

Study Questions

1. What does Levin mean by *objectivity*?
2. What does she mean by *nihilism*?
3. What is one of the hallmarks of objective theory making? Why is it important and how does it support Levin's thesis?
4. What is the Quine-Duhem Thesis?
5. What two themes does the argument for the Quine-Duhem thesis contain?
6. What is the significance of the comparison between the Ptolemaic, Tycho Brahe and the Copernican, Johannes Kepler?

7. How does Levin respond to those who point to the experiments, such as asking people to compare two objects of different length, and argue that beliefs are a product of social pressure, not objective judgment?

8. How does Levin respond to Rorty's "fuzzies" thesis that we should substitute "unforced agreement" for "objectivity"?

9. What are Levin's criticisms of those who say that unless we have experienced something, we cannot understand it (the thesis of *verstehen* = understanding)?

10. What does Levin say about those who argue that we cannot objectively examine the behavior of other cultures because we cannot separate our judgment from our own biases or values?

11. What contradictions, according to Levin in her *Conclusion*, are anti-objectivists involved in?

IT IS A PARADOX that the twentieth century, which has witnessed the greatest triumphs of science and technology, should also be the century in which the ideal of objectivity has been subjected to the most severe challenges. By "objectivity" I mean inter-subjectively accessible knowledge, by definition truly independent of anyone's biases, traditions, wishes, or other influences. The idea that objectivity is not only possible but regularly realized continues to underpin modern natural science. This same objectivity was a goal that initially inspired the social sciences.[1]

Just *why* the denial of objectivity is so alluring to modern thinkers is perhaps best left to future psychologists and historians. I confine myself to classifying, analyzing and replying to the various arguments purporting to establish nihilism—the thesis that there is no fixed reality—or skepticism—the thesis that we can't know what that reality is. I claim no great originality or completeness. What follows is meant as a representative sample of current positions.

The order I have chosen sorts arguments against objectivity into four (somewhat artificial) categories that descend in degree of generality. I begin by examining *general* philosophical arguments against the possibility of objectivity in the construction of theories. Then I turn to arguments with similar conclusions but which are grounded in the *history and sociology of science*. Since the social sciences seem particularly vulnerable to charges of bias, I conclude with arguments that single them out.

I. GENERAL SKEPTICAL AND NIHILIST ARGUMENTS

One of the hallmarks of objective theory-making is testability. A theory must be tested; if it fails its test, if its predictions turn out false or it is somehow incompatible with the evidence it must be rejected. But W.v.O. Quine and Pierre Duhem have separately pointed out that it is never *logically* necessary to discard a hypothesis or theory because of disconfirming evidence. Their position, generally referred to as the Quine-Duhem thesis, is that one can always consistently alter one's "auxiliary assumptions" to accommodate the new evidence. Such assumptions are inevitable: the factors mentioned in one's hypotheses always connect with other factors. There is no getting around this; you can't test everything at once. But it does mean that the seeming failure of a hypothesis to pass its test could, *in principle,* be attributed to an erroneous auxiliary assumption. For example,

This article was commissioned for The Theory of Knowledge, *ed. Louis Pojman, 2nd edition (Wadsworth Publishing Company, 1999) and appears here in a slightly revised form with the author's permission.*

when testing whether a new medicine will lower high fevers we must make certain assumptions about how thermometers work. If after administering the medicine we find thermometers inserted in treated patients continue to register high fevers, we *could* argue that the medicine has impaired the ability of the thermometers to record body temperature.[2] There is no logical absurdity in this. If A and B together imply C but C turns out to be false, all that follows is that *either* A or B (or possibly both) is false.

The relevance of this point to objectivity is that if we can always save any theory in the face of conflicting evidence, then we can never know any theory to be true. If you *know* A you can not believe or reasonably assert not-A, no matter what the evidence. Since, given the Quine-Duhem thesis, you can *always* believe or assert not-A, you never know A. To put the point intuitively, the world never forces acceptance or rejection of theories. Within very wide limits we can believe what we want.

This argument contains two themes that will recur. The first is the implicit use of mathematical certainty as a paradigm: If the data do not *entail* some one theory, then either there is no objective "fact of the matter" or (a weaker conclusion) we can never know what that fact is. The second theme is revealed when it is asked how the theorizer, or the Quinean himself, *knows* that an experiment requires some adjustment to his theory. The situation is evidently one in which it must be assumed to be *objectively true* that evidence and theory conflict. Hence the second theme: appeal to the concept of objective knowledge in arguments which purport to dispose of it. Even the enemies of objectivity rely on it.

This latter point might be blunted if one could strongly distinguish theory from data—perhaps we can know the *data* are true, e.g., that the mercury in a thermometer has reached a certain level, but we cannot know that any *theory* is true. But even if this distinction is drawn, surely the knowledge that data conflict with theory would be located on the *theoretical* side of such a line.

However that may be, and whatever the merits of the Quine-Duhem thesis as such, it cannot justify doubts about objectivity. Quine's point, it must be remembered, is a *logical* one—that it is always logically possible to preserve any theory. Another way of saying this is that the language of theories is not definable in terms of the data language. But this observation does not show that there are no objective truths beyond the data; it does not even address that question. Nor does Quine's thesis entail that we cannot *know* that one interpretation of the data is right—unless, again, it is assumed that knowledge requires mathematical certainty. Just because you can *believe* not-A doesn't mean you can *rationally* believe it. When you look at any concrete case you realize how irrational it is, after a certain point, to continue to "make changes elsewhere" rather than accept the failure of a hypothesis. For example, we were not compelled to accept Copernicus' heliocentric account of planetary motion. We could have kept Ptolemy's geocentric model by assuming the other planets followed strange orbits that circled back on themselves (epicycles) and that would have accounted for the observations of their motion in the night skies. But that would have required assuming far more complexity than expected and only for the purpose of saving a particular theory, not for any independent reason. The accepted position since Copernicus has been that heliocentrism is the simplest theory that fits the data. Data need not entail a theory to compel acceptance.

As noted, skepticism based on Quine's thesis works best with a sharp line between theory and data. The next argument rests on the opposite claim: "theory informs observation." This is the view that theory influences observation to such an extent that the two cannot be distinguished. Two observers with different theories will allegedly disagree on what is supposed to be a common data base. Furthermore, on this view, it is impossible to even experience data without unconsciously interpreting them according to some theory. It is therefore impossible to achieve a neutral perspective from which to judge competing theories.

The *locus classicus* of this position is a passage from *Patterns of Discovery* in which Norwood Hanson imagines the dawn as viewed by Tycho Brahe, a Ptolemaic, and Johannes Kepler, a Copernican:

> Tycho sees the sun beginning its journey from horizon to horizon. He sees that from some celestial vantage point the sun . . . could be watched circling our fixed earth . . . Kepler will see the horizon dipping, or turning away, from our local fixed star. The shift from sunrise to horizon-turn is . . . occasioned by differences between what Tycho and Kepler think they know.[3]

We are supposed to conclude that two observers with different theories *see* differently, and therefore lack common ground. Fortunately, this thought experiment is one we can all perform ourselves. Modern Americans have assimilated more thoroughly than Kepler the idea that the earth goes around the sun, yet we do not summon our children to view the dawn by saying "come see this beautiful earth-turn." Sunrise looks to us just as it did to Brahe. The difference between ourselves and him is that we know that the sun's apparent motion is deceptive.

So the argument in this particular case fails because one of its premises is false. In spite of holding different theories, observers will see the same thing. Nor is the fault in the example. Consider the series of experiments in which several people around a table were asked to compare two objects that were clearly of different lengths. All but one person had been secretly instructed to insist that the objects were the same length. The test subject was therefore under social pressure to deny the evidence of his senses and quite often succumbed and agreed with the rest. This experiment makes no sense and establishes nothing about the influence of non-perceptual factors on perception unless

there is an objective fact of the matter as to how the objects appeared to the participants and what their true lengths were. Furthermore, critics of objectivity can get no mileage from this example unless they claim that it actually happened. Once again the critics of objectivity must rely on it for their arguments.

A different version of nihilism is encapsulated in the phrase "we make the world." Many distinguished contemporary philosophers—Nelson Goodman, Richard Rorty, Hilary Putnam—defend some version of it. I will first discuss the fairly accessible version presented by Robert Schwartz in "Let Me Make You a Star." Schwartz argues that human beings, through the order they impose by their thinking, somehow determine what the world is. (What they impose the order *on* is not made clear.) This is reminiscent of Kant's theory of knowledge but it differs in that the mind's categories are not seen as fixed and *a priori*. Here is Schwartz:

> Whether there are stars, and what they are like, are facts that can emerge only in our attempts to describe and organize the world. The world is not given to us ready-made with stars . . . [T]he property of being a star would lack definitive character and boundaries until fashioned in the course of describing the heavens and accounting for its doings.[4]

To the natural objection that surely people don't *literally* make stars, he responds "Of course they don't! . . . We never compressed huge quantities of gas and set them aglow in the heavens above . . . *It*, the sun, was in the ready-made world all along. Yet, independent of our fashioning the relevant properties and kinds, questions about what *it* is really like *have neither any force nor any answers*." (pp. 437–438)

Schwartz seems to be confusing our freedom to *talk* about something—we can call the Missouri River a separate river or an arm of the Mississippi—with our inability to change the facts of what we're talking about—e.g., the Missouri is wet and cold. However much we theorize about it, if we fall in it and can't swim, we will drown.

He does grant that "there are constraints on our scientific schemes of classification and organization," although these are not spelled out. They are *not* a function of an independently existing world because the idea of "[an] external ready-made version of the world—untinged by our cognitive efforts—is not a notion we can have much confidence in making sense of." [5]

Well, if someone insists that he doesn't understand an idea you can't force him to admit he does. The most you can do is compare it to another idea that he does understand. So consider a newborn baby lying in his crib, lacking a theoretical framework to make sense of those enduring entities we know to be mother, lights, walls, etc. It hardly makes sense to speak of his knowledge of them, yet the world contains those things anyway. Everything Schwartz says about us can be said of the baby, and that is quite consistent with a definite world existing independently of our knowledge.

Schwartz' promise to "make" a star is most plausible when seen as a promise to remake classification schemes. Most would say that Jupiter is not a star because, unlike our sun, it is not a burning globe of gas. But one could classify Jupiter as a star because it is a gas giant and just say it is non-burning. In this sense we "make" Jupiter a star when we so classify it. But it is trivial to switch from one scheme to the other. There is no real disagreement between someone who says there are nine planets and someone who says there are eight planets and one non-burning star, just alternate ways of describing the same facts. So Schwartz' point is the triviality that the world can be described in several ways, not that there is no fixed world until we get around to describing it.

Another opponent of objectivity with a preference for words over facts is Rorty. In *Philosophy and the Mirror of Nature* he rejects all metaphors about knowledge that suggest that true statements about the world accurately reflect an independent reality, that reality needs to be uncovered or illuminated. He also repudiates any sharp distinction between the sciences and the humanities, between knowledge and opinion, between fact and value.[6] Adopting the term "fuzziness" for his position he writes:

> We fuzzies would like to substitute the idea of "unforced agreement " for that of "objectivity." We should like to put all culture on an epistemological level . . . [Truth] applies equally to the judgments of lawyers, anthropologists, physicists, philologists and literary critics. There is no point in assigning degrees of "objectivity" or "hardness" to such disciplines. For the presence of unforced agreement in all of them gives us everything in the way of "objective truth" which one could possibly want: namely, intersubjective agreement.[7]

Rorty gives no specific examples of *how* people arrive at "unforced agreement" other than by pointing to evidence. We can certainly imagine fashions in literary criticism as arising from "unforced agreement." If there are several incompatible theories about whether Hamlet's madness is real or feigned no one will much care. But how do we handle the case of a significant fraction of our population coming to "unforced agreement" to give up the germ theory of disease and adopt the view that illness is due to negative thoughts? Suppose they act on their agreement and refuse immunizations, knowingly sell contaminated meat, and let animals foul the water supply. Does Rorty really think there's no objective truth here, that agreement is the end of the matter? Won't *reality* force them to change their minds?

He does anticipate that critics will misread him:

> [W]hen we say that there is nothing to be said about truth save that each of us will commend as true those beliefs which he or she finds good to believe, the realist is inclined to interpret this as one more positive theory about the nature of truth: a theory according to which truth is simply the contemporary opinion of a chosen individual's group. Such a theory would, of course, be self-refuting. But pragmatists do not have a theory of truth, much less a

relativistic one. As partisans of solidarity, our account of the value of cooperative human enquiry has only an ethical base, not an epistemological or metaphysical one.[8]

Well, Rorty can *say* he doesn't have a theory—but if you declare that talk of X is meaningless, that opposing views of X are wrong, that X does not exist, then you certainly *do* have a theory of X.

Rorty keeps mocking the picture of human knowledge as seeking to come *closer* to the truth, of progress in reaching "a place which has somehow been prepared in advance." Michael Devitt[9] has an apt response: belief in objective truth, realism about the world, is *not* the thesis that people *will* know everything. Realism has nothing to do with human activity. To say that there is life on planets in other solar systems is not to say that we will ever contact them, that they have ever visited here, or that some other group is responsible for seeding life both here and there. It is to say that there is life on other planets, period.

Finally, when Rorty says that "from a pragmatist point of view, to say that what is rational for us now to believe may not be *true*, is simply to say that somebody *may come up with a better idea*."[10] one has to ask how it can be better if it isn't true or truer. How does one sort out the unpleasant truth from the delightful delusion? This is an old objection to pragmatism, and Rorty does not avoid it.

II. MORE SPECIFIC SKEPTICAL AND NIHILISTIC ARGUMENTS

Even if unbiased investigation is theoretically possible, it is sometimes argued, in practice, investigators are human. They have blindspots, pre- conceptions, and unconscious motives. You cannot expect objectivity from an investigator even if he sincerely believes he has rid himself of bias.

This is an argument that feminists stress: because of their male gender and their socialization,

men are unreliable about any area where gender plays a role. (Feminists are inconsistent—sometimes they attack objectivity *in toto*, at other times they only question the possibility of male objectivity.) At a minimum this includes research in animal and human behavior; more extreme feminists extend this claim to the physical sciences. Feminists cite as an example the work of early male entomologists who erroneously assumed that the large insects that seemed to dominate hives and anthills were "kings."

Now this example clearly has no force unless one can go on to say that further research showed that the "ruling" insects were more properly labeled "queens." Speaking generally, one cannot present an example of investigator bias without also presenting the objective fact that the investigator has missed. So it is unnecessary to examine in detail any instances of bias from the history of science that are produced to support skepticism or nihilism. All such instances self-destruct in the same way.

Perhaps the most promising of the skeptical responses to the success of science is to hark back to the Quine-Duhem thesis and argue that the success of a scientific theory does not logically entail its truth. This is correct. It is also true that many theories can be consistent with a narrow set of observations. But as a theory is tested, refined, and reconfirmed under many different circumstances, it becomes less and less likely that a wildly different theory will do a better job. It is safe to say that we know that certain diseases are caused by germs even though the data do not entail this, and many questions about how germs do this remain open. To demand that knowledge have the certainty of mathematics is to use the word "knowledge" in a non-standard way. You know you are reading this article even though it is theoretically possible that you are under a hypnotically induced illusion. Indeed, the demand for absolute certainty is unsatisfiable even in mathematics, since it is always possible that we are systematically confused about some basic rule of inference.

It appears to be rhetorically effective to label the position just stated "naive" realism. One is evidently expected to retract one's views rather than admit to naiveté, but I, for one, will not back off. I won't buy the Brooklyn Bridge, but I will buy the idea that the simplest explanation is the likeliest and the simplest explanation for the success of science is that we are indeed coming nearer to understanding some external reality. Rather than calling my opponents names ("decadent"?), let me challenge them to provide a positive alternative account of the success of science, one that scientists themselves will accept.

III. GENERAL ARGUMENTS FOR SKEPTICISM AND NIHILISM IN THE SOCIAL SCIENCES

The arguments in this category are variations on a single theme: you cannot be objective about what is subjective in nature. The social sciences involve people, and people attach values to their activities, so the social sciences have a normative dimension. Far from seeing it as a problem for social science some see it as an inevitable, even welcome, aspect of dealing with human beings. Thus, William Outhwaite:

> The fact that we are ourselves human beings makes it possible for us to understand what it is like to be another human being, what it is (probably) like to hold the beliefs which other human beings hold, and so on. But this also means that we cannot simply record, in an objective and value-free way, the practices and beliefs of other human beings. The social scientist does not go out into the field as a *tabula rasa* and return with an account of what it is like to be a European carworker or an African peasant; it is precisely the encounter between the social scientist's own beliefs and practices and those of the people he . . . is studying which makes up whatever understanding we can have of another social reality.[11]

Indeed, as Outhwaite observes, people and their values are involved on both sides of any in-

quiry in social science. It is therefore convenient to divide the arguments in this section into those which focus on the values of the human *objects* of social inquiry, and those that focus on the values of the inquirer himself.

So let us first ask whether values can be neutrally identified, and neutrally attributed to others. It seems to me that such attribution is indeed possible. Wittgenstein's celebrated attacks on private languages apply with full force to a private language of values. If evaluating were a private act, people could not learn—as they obviously do learn—what someone means when he says that he "admires" something or "despises" it. There are public indicators of valuing; most clearly, what a culture encourages and discourages—which it is possible to determine at least in principle—is a good sign of what it values. Of course, the values an individual will publicly assent to may not be the values he secretly holds, and ferreting out his true preferences may require considerable ingenuity, but again this is not *in principle* impossible. On the whole, determining values poses no less but no more difficulty than detecting the presence of a shy nocturnal animal.

But people aren't raccoons, it will be said; detecting guilt is not like detecting leaf eaters in your garden. Two equally remorseful individuals may differ in how much of their feelings they let show and how they show them. Surely there is something here inaccessible to ordinary observation. In reply, we must focus again on how we ordinarily spot, e.g., guilt. Regret over some past action or inaction typically leads to reluctance to discuss it, expressions of desire that it not be generally known, and possibly the wish that it had never been committed, as well as a desire to be punished for it. These are the sorts of clues that lead us to conclude that a person is experiencing guilt.

To be sure, establishing the same fact about a subject from a different culture requires certain preliminaries, such as acquiring a working knowledge of his language. Aha, says the skeptic, a working knowledge of another language means being able to translate such terms as "guilt" in the first place, and how are we to know on the basis of sheer behavior that we are correctly translating such words? Once again, it must be insisted that observable behavior is, in the end, all we *ever* have to go on. No child at his mother's knee has access to his mother's inner states. He knows only what she says and does when she corrects his speech, and if this is sufficient to allow the child to learn his mother's words for emotions, it suffices for penetrating an alien one.

However—the skeptic now urges—the problem isn't as simple as just finding the alien's word for "guilt." Correctly identifying his values means, in addition, finding out the sorts of things his culture thinks *ought* to be regretted, the ways in which his culture understands personal responsibility, the culturally approved forms of public displays of emotion—a whole "system of meanings" which must be grasped before guilt can be properly understood. The Irish at a wake behave differently than Jews sitting shiva, yet both are presumably "distressed." In fact, the whole issue of judging foreign values is a special case of *verstehen*. This phrase encapsulates the view that at least some types of behavior are incomprehensible without a certain sympathetic understanding ("verstehen") from the inside of what the behavior means to the participants. Peter Winch had this requirement in mind when he wrote:

> A historian or sociologist of religion must himself have some religious feeling if he is to make sense of the religious movement he is studying and understand the considerations which govern the lives of its participants.[12]

Thus, Winch might say, you cannot understand why a born-again Christian might quit his job unless you yourself have experienced a comparable spiritual rebirth. Only then will you realize how even the most pressing material concerns might come to seem unimportant.

Plausible as this may seem, it is simply not true. One need not oneself believe in a world to come to reason that someone who does believe might well lose interest in this world. One need

not know what it feels like to have such a belief to make and test predictions about his actions. A great many people understand *Othello* without having endured irrational jealousy. We would do well to remember a quip by Albert Einstein, often cited in this context: It is not the job of science "to *give* the taste of the soup." It *is* the job of science to describe and account for the taste of the soup. Similarly, it is not the job of social science to give the feeling of guilt or "reproduce"[13] the feeling of someone acting within a normative tradition. Its job is to describe the mental state of the agent by the behavior it evokes and its relation to other phenomena.

What do we expect of a social science? Is it information, lawlike statements, predictions, correlations and unification of seemingly disparate data? Or are social scientists expected to be professional empaths who feel and act like the people they study? Social science should not be conceived so narrowly that one questions whether there has ever been a successful study of human behavior.

The fact is that we *do* understand certain alien "forms of life." Consider the treaties between the various Indian tribes and European settlers. The Indians did not have the concept of land ownership or, consequently, any idea of the significance that the signing of treaties had for the Europeans. Many of us, accustomed to talk of selling air rights, buying lots, and the distinction between public and private land, find it hard to put ourselves in the Indians' frame of mind. Yet we can grasp their "system of meanings" enough to see how its conflict with that of the European system would have led to trouble on the frontier. You might say that it is not difficult to see the Indians' point of view (many environmentalists do say this) and that is why we think we understand them. Well then, consider the focus of the ancient Egyptians on the afterlife, their custom of preserving the body through mummification, filling the tomb with actual goods (food) and representations of goods (statuettes of slaves) needed in the next world. Today's theology is not so literal-minded, and those who expect an afterlife imagine that they will take purely spiritual forms. We can nonetheless discuss and interpret ancient Egyptian finds, and even make predictions about future discoveries.

Indeed, it is possible to predict and even influence the behavior of beings whose view of the world we cannot experience, namely non-humans. None of us, except possibly the blind, have an inkling of what it is like to navigate by echolocation as bats do. Scientists have nevertheless analyzed echolocation thoroughly enough to convince bats to try to land on a ledge that isn't there by sending the sort of signals the bat would receive from a genuine ledge.

Having considered the values of the investigated, let us consider the values of the investigator. Neutrally describing behavior to which one is indifferent is hard enough, runs the argument; it is impossible to do justice to practices one considers inhumane, depraved, or unjust. Well, that all depends on what is meant by "doing justice." It certainly seems possible in actual practice to separate fact from values and establish the concrete facts about such institutions as slavery in the antebellum South and Nazi concentration camps. One can deplore these institutions, yet ask how they were run and what beliefs sustained them. Did different kinds of plantation workers enjoy different social status? Did German farmers think they would gain anything from the elimination of the Jews?

Let us remember that facts normally *precede* judgments of value and changes in awareness of facts can and do lead to changes in evaluations. Two recent controversies show at least an intuitive awareness of this on the part of partisans of what might seem like purely normative positions. Opponents of the death penalty, even those who say their opposition is not based on questions of deterrence, almost always deny that capital punishment deters. They thus recognize that how people assess capital punishment depends in large part on what they believe to be its empirical effects. Similarly, those who criticize Harry Truman for dropping the atomic bomb on Japan commonly argue that Japan was on the point of surrender, and they often try to produce documentary evidence for this factual claim. Revisionist historians realize that it is difficult to dispute the decision once it is admitted that it saved millions of lives.

"But," the skeptic asks, "what about the 'big picture'? What caused the Civil War? Did the New Deal hasten the end of the Depression? The facts may not be in dispute, little facts anyway—it's the interpretation of the facts that allows personal values to enter. Values may wait upon facts, but this only tempts historians to shade the facts to reinforce their own values."

The quick answer to this is "speak for yourself." A more careful answer begins by admitting that, indeed, we may never have enough data to definitely establish what factors caused the Civil War or even to rank several possible causes in order of importance. And since (for instance) we may never know all of Lincoln's motives for declaring war on the Confederacy, those who approve Lincoln's decision are free to believe that he was acting as he thought his oath of office required, while his critics are free to attribute less flattering motives. The sensible response to the selectivity forced on us by the gaps in the record is not that we can't know *anything*, but that there is a difference between uncovering some truths and uncovering them *all*. That we can't know the whole truth does not mean that we can't know any of it. What is more, our inability to find out about something in the past doesn't imply that nothing definite ever happened. Unavoidable ignorance does not justify nihilism, and it is worth noting that ignorance can never be known to be irremediable. A Lincoln diary might turn up tomorrow in some forgotten closet that would help us determine what Lincoln was thinking.

The skeptic is apt to retreat another step and claim that it is the choice of problems and interests that is dictated by values. While true to some extent—although it ignores the contribution of pure curiosity—this is logically irrelevant to the issue of objectivity. Why you become interested in something has no bearing on the quality or validity of your research. A study of driving habits sponsored by General Motors may have merit; a study commissioned by Kelloggs' that determines that women prefer Rice Krispies while men prefer Corn Flakes can be as trustworthy as any other study of cereal preferences. To think otherwise is to commit a particularly blatant form of the genetic fallacy. Indeed, a commercially sponsored survey might be *more* reliable since Kellogg's needs accurate data and doesn't want to be lied to.

It is an *empirical* question whether choice of a topic implies a desire for certain conclusions and, more significantly, whether that desire will blind the investigator to contrary evidence. A relevant experiment involved the submission of papers with identical protocols but different results to social work journals.[14] The version reporting social work intervention in children's environments to be ineffective was rejected significantly more often than the version reporting such intervention to be effective. Interestingly, the negative paper was criticized on methodological grounds when it was identical in that respect to the positive paper. Yet, while this experiment does show something—that social work journals are biased toward reports of the effectiveness of environmental intervention—it *cannot* show that the evaluation of research is always subject to bias. Anyone accepting that strong conclusion would have to think that he accepted it because he was biased (in favor of finding bias everywhere) and not because the conclusion was supported by the evidence. As usual, skepticism defeats itself. There *can't* be evidence that all investigation is biased.

Social scientists are quite aware of the problem of wishes and commitments swaying the critical eye. It is precisely to neutralize such factors that "double-blind" experiments are routinely deployed in experiments. This is especially true for such emotionally charged subjects as beauty and intelligence, or any placebo effect. For instance, a psychologist studying the connection between attractiveness and perceived intelligence would not rely on his own opinion of who was attractive. He—or, better, an assistant unaware of the purpose of the experiment—would show an assortment of photos to a panel of respondents to establish which were generally seen as attractive. Another panel would then be asked for estimates of intelligence based on the photos.

Because investigators, like anyone else, sometimes let their emotions or predilections cloud their judgments, science must be not done in a vacuum. This is why results must be replicable, why raw data must be published so that others may evaluate the arguments and the statistical analyses. It is why people should not be discouraged from engaging in research about those whose background is significantly different from theirs. Failure to appreciate this is *the* error in the often heard remark that only blacks should study blacks, only women should study women, and the like. Far from its being the case that you need to be an X to study X's, non-X's are needed to check and correct blindspots that X's may have about their own group.

The final objection in this group concerns the reality of social constructs. Personality traits, social forces and institutions, and morale have no obvious physical embodiments. Hence they might seem more like the impositions of our minds on reality than are the constructs of physics. Proponents of such skepticism generally view the constructs of social theory as vehicles for prejudices and hidden values.

Is there really a problem here? So long as talk about social forces and institutions can be appropriately anchored in talk about observable traits of individuals, there is no *new* objectivity problem. Thus, "socioeconomic status" is epistemologically acceptable because it can be measured in terms of individuals' income, health and occupation. A more interesting example is the concept of general intelligence, a theoretical construct which is applied to individuals rather than groups, but which has drawn criticism for allegedly being arbitrary and value-laden. "Intelligent" is sometimes said to be no more than a label for the middle-class cognitive style, or for members of an economic elite that wishes to preserve itself. In fact, while neither a structure nor a process in the brain has been identified as "intelligence," there are a number of tests of information processing which are found to correlate highly with each other, with independent indicators such as academic achievement, and with what people have in mind when they use the word "intelligent." So talk of intelligence can be anchored in such observables as reaction speed and memorization ability. This is no more suspect than talk of magnetism....

V. CONCLUSION

We have found that virtually all critics of objectivity say something like the following:

1. It is an objective fact that there are no objective facts.

2. It is absolutely true that everything is relative to a framework.

3. No one can divorce himself from his social milieu to examine his society with a critical eye, and that conclusion is the result of my having done so.

4. There is evidence for the position that there is no such thing as evidence.

In each case the skeptic states a position that cannot possibly be substantiated or rationally believed. In each case he is, in effect, asking that you not apply his assertion to his own position, without giving any reason for exempting his words from his own general claim. His position is futile and self-refuting; it can be stated, but it cannot convince anyone who recognizes its implications.

It might be argued that, strictly speaking, these arguments are not literally contradictory. Consider "theory always influences perception; therefore, there is no objective verification of any claim." The conclusion of this argument (being about theories) does not contradict its premise (which is about observation). To defend skepticism this way, however, overlooks the point of

presenting an argument. If we are supposed to accept a conclusion on the basis of a premise, then there must be a reason for accepting the premise. The skeptic must be claiming that we can verify his premise that theory influences perception if he thinks his argument proves that there is no such thing as verification. Merely observing that a premise entails a conclusion accomplishes nothing; I display valid but unsound arguments in logic class every semester. The skeptic must claim that there is some reason to accept his premise as true, in which case his argument really does lead him to contradict himself. If it is replied that the skeptic does not think that his premises are rationally compelling, but only "relatively compelling" to those who share his biases, then his argument loses any point. It can only persuade those who already accept its conclusion, and cannot persuade non-skeptics.

Ironically, what the skeptic is attempting is one of the few instances in which inherent contradiction a la Derrida does make a hash out of the whole enterprise. You can't use reason to attack the very idea of reason, you can't use arguments to convince anyone that arguments are useless. In fact, the ultimate source of Derrida's theory may lie here. Having grasped at some level that the skeptical project is doomed, undermined from within, he may have unconsciously sought to disguise the futility of his own argument by asserting that *all* argument, *all* writing, *all* thinking suffers from this instability, so that skeptics are no more misguided than anyone else.

That the self-refuting character of skepticism and nihilism has long been noted makes the persistence of arguments against objectivity curious—like influenza they reappear periodically in slightly different forms and must be attacked with adjusted medications. I suspect that nihilism survives because it resembles a somewhat more benign claim—not that there are no truths or that there is no knowledge, but that we can never be certain which of our beliefs amount to knowledge. The idea that we might know things but not know which ones we know is reminiscent of a paradox about belief. Each of us will grant that, being fallible, not everything we believe is true. But of no particular belief p can we say both that p is false and that we believe p. From this it does not follow that we really are infallible, any more than the impossibility of being aware that we are dreamlessly asleep shows that we are always awake.[15] Similarly, those of us who hold out for objective knowledge will argue that we can come to know some truths, but alas, may never be in a position to state positively of any given belief that it is one that we know.

NOTES

1. What drew my attention to this topic were recent feminist attacks on traditional science. Their particular spin is that objectivity is a male contrivance, engendered—pun intended—by the male propensity for domination and psychological distancing. Having discussed these views elsewhere, I refer to them only briefly here. See "Caring New World: Feminism and Science," *American Scholar*, Winter 1988.

2. The same maneuver occurs when someone who claims paranormal powers but can't perform in a controlled laboratory setting argues that the presence of doubters diminishes the power. Here the auxiliary assumption being challenged is that perception is independent of the opinions of witnesses.

3. Norwood Russell Hanson, *Patterns of Discovery* (London: Cambridge University Press), pp. 23–24.

4. Robert Schwartz, "Let Me Make You a Star," *Midwest Studies in Philosophy*, XII, 1986, p. 435.

5. Schwartz, ibid, p. 437.

6. It has been argued that science is laden with value words, as when we speak of a "good" fit between hypothesis and data, or what an experiment's outcome "should" be. This almost pre-Socratic argument would show that every activity is value laden, from selling cars ("it gets good mileage") to folding laundry ("you should sort the socks first"). But in each case we can substitute non-normative words that refer to some standard being met, e.g., that a hypothesis is probable given specified antecedents.

7. Richard Rorty, this volume, p. 208.

8. Rorty, p. 208

9. *Realism and Truth*, 2nd ed. (Blackwell, Cambridge, 1991).

10. Rorty, p. 209.

11. William Outhwaite, "Gadamer," in *The Return of Grand Theory in the Human Sciences*, ed. Quentin Skinner, Cambridge University Press, 1985, p.29.

12. Peter Winch, *The Idea of a Social Science*, Routledge & Kegan Paul, 1965, p. 88.

13. Richard Rudner's phrase.

14. Peters, D., and Ceci, S., "Peer-review Practices of Psychological Journals," *The Behavioral and Brain Sciences*, June 1982.

15. The whole topic of impossible mental states is discussed in Roy Sorensen, *Blindspots* (New York: Oxford University Press, 1989).

For Further Reflection

1. Compare Rorty and Levin's arguments and evaluate the strengths and weaknesses in each.

2. What do you make of Levin's "paradox of the twentieth century" which juxtaposes the greatest triumphs of science and technology with the most severe challenges to the ideal of objectivity which underlies these triumphs? Why should the reaction occur?

3. Consider Levin's comparison between the Ptolemaic, Tycho Brahe and the Copernican, Johannes Kepler. Here is another quotation from N. R. Hanson:

> Let us consider Johannes Kepler; imagine him on a hill watching the dawn. With him is Tycho Brahe. Kepler regarded the sun as fixed: it was the earth that moved. But Tycho followed Ptolemy and Aristotle in this much at least: the earth was fixed and the other celestial bodies moved around it. *Do Kepler and Tycho see the same thing in the east at dawn?* (Hanson, *Pattern of Discovery* [Cambridge University Press, 1958], p. 5.)

How does Levin answer it? How would you answer this question?

4. Review Levin's response the subjectivist thesis that our beliefs are the product of social pressure. Recall her citation of such experiments as asking people to compare two objects of different length. A similar experiment has to do with flashing lights. Ten people are in a room who are told to lie about how many times a light flashes. You are brought into the room and see the light flash 10 times and say so. But then everyone else says it flashed 11 times. The flashing is repeated and each time the audience says they saw it flash 11 times, while the subject says 10. Eventually, the data is said to show that almost everyone breaks down and claims to see the light flashing 11 times. Discuss what this tells us about objectivity and subjectivity? Would the experiment work if the light flashed only once or twice and the audience said they saw it flash 10 or 20 or 30 times?

5. Review the "self-refuting" statements which Levin accuses the anti-objectivists of making (in her *Conclusion*). Is she fair to their position? How might they respond to her accusations? What do you think about the value of objectivity and the opposing of the objectivists and the anti-objectivists?

Suggestions for Further Reading

Audi, Robert. *Belief, Justification and Knowledge*. Belmont, CA: Wadsworth, 1988. The best short introduction to the subject.

Audi, Robert. *Epistemology*. Routledge, 1998.

Blanshard, Brand. *The Nature of Thought*. 2 vols. London: George Allen & Unwin, 1940.

BonJour, Laurence. *In Defense of Pure Reason*. Cambridge University Press, 1998.

Chisholm, R. M. *Theory of knowledge*, 2nd. ed. Englewood Cliffs, NJ: Prentice Hall, 1977. A rich outline of a foundational approach to epistemology.

Dancy, Jonathan. *Introduction to Contemporary Epistemology*. Oxford: Blackwell, 1985. A penetrating analysis of contemporary problems, though not always clear.

Horwich, Paul. *Truth*. Oxford: Basil Blackwell, 1990.

James, William. *Pragmatism*. London: Longman's, Green & Co., 1907.

Johnson, Lawrence E. *Focusing on Truth*. London: Routledge, 1992.

Landsman, Charles. *An Introduction to Epistemology*. Oxford, Eng.: Blackwell's 1997.

Lawson, Hilary, and Lisa Applignanesi, eds. *Dismantling Truth*. London: Weidenfield and Nicolson, 1989.

Lehrer, Keith. *Theory of Knowledge*. Boulder, CO: Westview Press, 1990.

Moser, Paul, and Arnold Vander Nat, eds. *Human Knowledge*. Oxford: Oxford University Press, 1987. A recent comprehensive anthology.

Pojman, Louis, ed. *The Theory of Knowledge*. Belmont, CA: Wadsworth, 1999.

Pojman, Louis. *What Can We Know?* 2nd ed., Belmont, CA: Wadsworth, 2001.

Pollock, John. *Knowledge and Justification*. Totowa, NJ: Rowman and Littlefield, 1986. Innovative and well argued.

Quine, W. V., and Joseph Ullian. *The Web of Belief*, 2nd ed. New York: Random House, 1978. A very useful book for beginners.

Rorty, Richard. *Philosophy and the Mirror of Nature*. Princeton, NJ: Princeton University Press, 1979.

Russell, Bertrand. *The Problems of Philosophy*. Oxford: Oxford University Press, 1912.

Woozley, A. D. *Theory of Knowledge*. London: George Allen & Unwin, 1949.

Part IV

Philosophy of Mind: The Mind-Body Problem

The curiosity of Man, and the cunning of his Reason, have revealed much of what Nature held hidden. The structure of space-time, the constitution of matter, the many forms of energy, the nature of life itself; all of these mysteries have become open books to us. To be sure, deep questions remain unanswered and revolutions await us still, but it is difficult to exaggerate the explosion in scientific understanding we humans have fashioned over the past 500 years. Despite this general advance, a central mystery remains largely a mystery: the nature of conscious intelligence.

PAUL CHURCHLAND, *Matter and Consciousness*

FOR MILLENNIA, from biblical times until very recently, human beings thought of themselves as standing midway between the ape and the angel. The Psalmist praised God for our essential dignity:

> When I consider Thy heavens, the work of Thy fingers, the moon and the stars, which Thou hast ordained; What is man, that Thou art mindful of him? and the son of man, that Thou hast visitest him? For Thou hast made him a little lower than the angels, and hast crowned him with glory and honor. Thou madest him to have dominion over the works of Thy hands; Thou hast put all things under his feet. (Ps. 8 : 3–6)

Today there is a tendency to see humans as standing somewhere between the ape and the computer. It was never seriously denied that we were animals or had an animal aspect in behaving like animals in eating, excreting, procreating, breathing, sleeping, and dying. But there was something more. We were esteemed as rational, spiritual, deliberative beings, made in the image of God, a little lower than the angels. The biblical image of humanity is noble and inspiring. The contemporary model of homo-computer is less inspiring. Being mechanistic, we are seen as lacking a free will, hence as lacking responsibility and intrinsic value altogether. Indeed, all that marks us off from a moderately reliable computer is the animal in us, the nonrational elements of sensation, emotions, and consciousness. If the latter model is closer to the truth, we will have to make the best of it. But the question of our essential nature is worth asking and pursuing: Is there something special about us, a soul or mind which perdures through change and survives our death, something that constitutes our true identity and is the locus of eternal value? Or is the mind simply a function of the body, in particular, of the brain? The theory that there is a mind (or soul) separate from the body is called *dualism*. The theory that the mind (or soul) is really an aspect or function of the brain is called *materialism* (or *physicalism*). In this part of our book we will examine arguments for and against these two theses.

IV.A   What Am I? A Mind or a Body?

Intuitively, there seem to be two different types of reality: mind and body, that is, mental and physical (material).

Bodies are solid, material entities, extended in three-dimensional space, publicly observable, measurable, capable of causing things to happen in accordance with invariant laws of mechanics.

A mind, on the other hand, has none of these properties. Consciousness is not solid or material, is not extended in three-dimensional space, does not occupy space at

226

all, is directly observable only by the person who owns it, cannot be measured, and seems incapable of causing things to happen in accordance with invariant laws of mechanics. Only the person him- or herself can think his thoughts, feel his emotions, and suffer his pain. Although neurosurgeons can open your skull and observe your brain, they cannot observe your mind or your beliefs, sensations, emotions, or desires.

Unlike physical bodies, mental entities have no shape, weight, length, width, height, color, mass, velocity, or temperature. It would sound odd, indeed, to speak of a belief weighing 16 ounces like a cut of beef, or a feeling of love measuring 4″ × 4″ × 10′ like a piece of lumber, or a pain being as heavy as a cement bag, or a desire that was green and had a temperature of 102 degrees.

Yet common sense tells us that these two entities somehow interact. We step on a nail, and it pierces our skin, sending a message through our nervous system which results in something altogether different from the shape or size of the nail or skin, something that does not possess size or shape and which cannot be seen, smelt, tasted, or heard—a feeling of distress or pain. Whereas the nail is public, the pain is private.

On the other hand, our mind informs us that it would be a good thing to get a bandage to put over the cut that has resulted (maybe a tetanus shot, too)—so the mind causes us to move our body. Our legs carry us to the medicine cabinet, where we stop, raise our arms, and with our hands take hold of the cabinet door, open it, take the bandage out, then apply it dexterously to the wound.

Here we have an instance where the body affects the mind and the mind, in turn, affects the body. So common sense shows that there is an interaction between the two radically different entities. But how exactly does this transaction occur? And where does it occur? Or could it be that the mind is really simply a function of the body, not a separate substance at all? Or that the body is really an illusion and that there is only one substance, the mind alone? The following schema may help you through the readings in this part of the work.

Theory	Dualist interactionism	Ideal monism	Material monism
Nature of Substance	Mental and physical	Mental	Physical
Philosophers	Plato	Berkeley	Hume
	Descartes	Hinduism	Russell
	Locke	Christian Science	Taylor
	Moreland		Churchland

Idealism was represented in the last part (III.20) by George Berkeley. *Dualist Interactionism* is represented by Descartes and J. P. Moreland in this part (Readings IV.27 and IV.29, respectively). Gilbert Ryle, in Reading IV.28, attacks all versions of dualism. Materialism is represented in Reading IV.30 by Paul Churchland.

These are the three classic theories, but there are many other lesser-known theories. *Epiphenomenalism* is a dualism that holds to one-way causality: The body causes mental states but not vice versa. Mental events are like babbling brooks or the smoke from trains' chimneys. They are effects of physical processes, but do not themselves cause motion in the water or train. Another view is called *panpsychism*, which holds that everything in nature has a mind or a soul. Panpsychism is a correlate of pantheism, which holds that everything is God or contains God. According to panpsychism, there is soul or mind in the ultimate particles of physics and only because there is can we experience consciousness. Thomas Nagel has defended this view.[1]

There are also several versions of materialism. Paul Churchland discusses two of them: *reductive materialism* and *eliminative materialism*. Reductive materialism (sometimes called "the identity theory") holds to a one-to-one correlation between mental states and brain states, identifying mental states as brain states. Eliminative materialism attempts, ideally, to eliminate all talk of mental states, claiming that the language of mental events is part of folk mythology, called *folk psychology,* and includes our concepts of belief, desire, emotions, and intentions. As we learn more about our brains and the way they work, we will be able to replace this subjectivist speech with a more scientific discourse. For example, instead of talking about a headache in your forehead, you might talk about certain C-fibers firing in your brain.

Our thirty-first reading, Thomas Nagel's, "What Is It Like to Be a Bat?" is a critique of this kind of objectivism, the view that we can give a complete and accurate description of the world by omitting the subjective point of view. Subjectivity, conscious awareness and experience, is an integral part of the truth.

Another view that is widely held by philosophers of mind is *functionalism,* which denies that any one type of brain state can always be correlated with a type of mental state. For example, I might feel pain in my hand on two different occasions, but may have two *different* areas of my brain might be activated. Actually, functionalism need not be materialist at all. It could be agnostic on the mind-body problem, confining itself to outputs of human activity. Churchland critiques functionalism in his essay.

Finally, we turn to a problem of whether computers can think. If materialists are correct, mental states are really physical states. If so, then why can't we say that sophisticated computers or highly developed robots think? In our final reading in this section, John Searle argues that computers can't think because they can't have intentional states. Through an ingenious thought experiment, he argues that strong AI (artificial intelligence) is misguided because computers lack the requisite conditions for understanding.

Let us turn to our readings.

NOTE

1. Thomas Nagel, *Mortal Questions* (Cambridge: Cambridge University Press, 1979), pp. 181–195.

Dualistic Interactionism   **IV.27**

RENÉ DESCARTES

According to René Descartes there are three kinds of objects or substances in the universe: (1) the eternal substance, God; (2) his creation in terms of mind; (3) his creation in terms of matter: "We may thus easily have two clear and distinct notions or ideas, the one of created substance which thinks, and the other of corporeal substances, provided we carefully separate all the attributes of thought from those of extension."

We are thinking substances or embodied minds, "for I am not only lodged in my body as a pilot in a ship, but I am very closely united to it, and so to speak so intermingled with it that I seem to compose with it one whole. For if that were not the case, when my body hurt, I, who am merely a thinking thing, should perceive this wound by the understanding only, just as the sailor perceives by sight when something is damaged in his vessel."

The two kinds of substances which make us each a person intermingle in such a way that they causally act upon each other. Although it might be that a mind interacts with each part of its body separately, Descartes' view is that mind interacts only with the brain. The material event that causally stimulates one of our five senses (for example, light hitting the retina of the eye) results in a chain of physical causation that leads to a certain brain process from which a certain sensation results. Then, in turn, being affected by the brain, the mind through mental events acts on the brain, which in turn affects the body. Descartes thought he could pinpoint the place in the brain where the interaction between mind and brain took place. "The part of the body in which the soul exercises its function immediately is in nowise the heart, nor the whole of the brain, but merely the most inward of all its parts, to wit, a certain very small gland which is situated in the middle of its substance."

Descartes identified this seat of consciousness with the pineal gland. It functions, according to Descartes, as the intermediary that transmits the effects of the mind to the brain and the effects of the brain to the mind. Modern neurophysiology has shown Descartes was wrong about this, but that doesn't affect the central thesis of Descartes' theory. Even if he was wrong about the precise details of the interaction, dualist interactionism could still be the correct account of mental activity.

With this introduction we turn to our reading. We pick up the discussion where we left off toward the end of the second meditation (Reading III.18), where Descartes has discovered his self as the only indubitable piece of knowledge and begins to realize that all knowledge is a mental experience.

(A biographical sketch of Descartes precedes Reading III.18.)

Study Questions

1. How does Descartes characterize the self? What characteristics does it have? Can you recall the argument that led him to his conclusion about the nature of the self?

2. Why is Descartes tempted to regard the material as more certain than the mental? What is his explanation of this phenomenon?
3. How does the illustration of the piece of wax illustrate his thesis about the priority of the mental over the material?
4. What reason does Descartes give for believing that he has a body?
5. Why does he believe that there are other bodies besides his own?
6. What is the difference between the body and the mind?
7. What is the relationship of the body to the mind?
8. Where do the body and mind interact?

I SHALL EXERCISE MY IMAGINATION [in order to see if I am not something more]. I am not a collection of members which we call the human body: I am not a subtle air distributed through these members, I am not a wind, a fire, a vapour, a breath, nor anything at all which I can imagine or conceive; because I have assumed that all these were nothing. Without changing that supposition I find that I only leave myself certain of the fact that I am somewhat. But perhaps it is true that these same things which I supposed were non-existent because they are unknown to me, are really not different from the self which I know. I am not sure about this, I shall not dispute about it now; I can only give judgment on things that are known to me. I know that I exist, and I inquire what I am, I whom I know to exist. But it is very certain that the knowledge of my existence taken in its precise significance does not depend on things whose existence is not yet known to me; consequently it does not depend on those which I can feign in imagination. And indeed the very term *feign* in imagination proves to me my error, for I really do this if I image myself a something, since to imagine is nothing else than to contemplate the figure or image of a corporeal thing. But I already know for certain that I am, and that it may be that all these images, and, speaking generally, all things that relate to the nature of body are nothing but dreams [and chimeras]. For this reason I see clearly that I have as little reason to say, "I shall stimulate my imagination in order to know more distinctly what I am," than if I were to say, "I am now awake, and I perceive somewhat that is real and true: but because I do not yet perceive it distinctly enough, I shall go to sleep of express purpose, so that my dreams may represent the perception with greatest truth and evidence." And, thus, I know for certain that nothing of all that I can understand by means of my imagination belongs to this knowledge which I have of myself, and that it is necessary to recall the mind from this mode of thought with the utmost diligence in order that it may be able to know its own nature with perfect distinctness.

But what then am I? A thing which thinks. What is a thing which thinks? It is a thing which doubts, understands, [conceives], affirms, denies, wills, refuses, which also imagines and feels.

Certainly it is no small matter if all these things pertain to my nature. But why should they not so pertain? Am I not that being who now doubts nearly everything, who nevertheless understands certain things, who affirms that one only is true, who denies all the others, who desires to know more, is averse from being deceived, who imagines many things, sometimes indeed despite his will, and who perceives many likewise, as by the intervention of the bodily organs? Is there nothing in all this which is as true as it is certain that I exist, even though I should always sleep and though he who has given me being employed all his ingenuity in deceiving

Reprinted from the Philosophical Works of Descartes, *trans. Elizabeth Haldane and G. Ross, vol. I (Cambridge University Press, 1931).*

me? Is there likewise any one of these attributes which can be distinguished from my thought, or which might be said to be separated from myself? For it is so evident of itself that it is I who doubts, who understands, and who desires, that there is no reason here to add anything to explain it. And I have certainly the power of imagining likewise; for although it may happen (as I formerly supposed) that none of the things which I imagine are true, nevertheless this power of imagining does not cease to be really in use, and it forms part of my thought. Finally, I am the same who feels, that is to say, who perceives certain things, as by the organs of sense, since in truth I see light, I hear noise, I feel heat. But it will be said that these phenomena are false and that I am dreaming. Let it be so; still it is at least quite certain that it seems to me that I see light, that I hear noise and that I feel heat. That cannot be false; properly speaking it is what is in me called feeling, and used in this precise sense that is no other thing than thinking.

From this time I begin to know what I am with a little more clearness and distinction than before; but nevertheless it still seems to me, and I cannot prevent myself from thinking, that corporeal things, whose images are framed by thought, which are tested by the senses, are much more distinctly known than that obscure part of me which does not come under the imagination. Although really it is very strange to say that I know and understand more distinctly these things whose existence seems to me dubious, which are unknown to me, and which do not belong to me, than others of the truth of which I am convinced, which are known to me and which pertain to my real nature, in a word, than myself. But I see clearly how the case stands: My mind loves to wander, and cannot yet suffer itself to be retained within the just limits of truth. Very good, let us once more give it the freest rein, so that, when afterwards we seize the proper occasion for pulling up, it may the more easily be regulated and controlled.

Let us begin by considering the commonest matters, those which we believe to be the most distinctly comprehended, to wit, the bodies which we touch and see; not indeed bodies in general, for these general ideas are usually a little more confused, but let us consider one body in particular. Let us take, for example, this piece of wax: It has been taken quite freshly from the hive, and it has not yet lost the sweetness of the honey which it contains; it still retains somewhat of the odour of the flowers from which it has been culled; its colour, its figure, its size are apparent; it is hard, cold, easily handled, and if you strike it with the finger, it will emit a sound. Finally all the things which are requisite to cause us distinctly to recognise a body, are met with in it. But notice that while I speak and approach the fire what remained of the taste is exhaled, the smell evaporates, the colour alters, the figure is destroyed, the size increases, it becomes liquid, it heats, scarcely can one handle it, and when one strikes it, no sound is emitted. Does the same wax remain after this change? We must confess that it remains; none would judge otherwise. What then did I know so distinctly in this piece of wax? It could certainly be nothing of all that the senses brought to my notice, since all these things which fall under taste, smell, sight, touch, and hearing, are found to be changed, and yet the same wax remains.

Perhaps it was what I now think, viz. that this wax was not that sweetness of honey, nor that agreeable scent of flowers, nor that particular whiteness, nor that figure, nor that sound, but simply a body which a little while before appeared to me as perceptible under these forms, and which is now perceptible under others. But what, precisely, is it that I imagine when I form such conceptions? Let us attentively consider this, and, abstracting from all that does not belong to the wax, let us see what remains. Certainly nothing remains excepting a certain extended thing which is flexible and movable. But what is the meaning of flexible and movable? Is it not that I imagine that this piece of wax being round is capable of becoming square and of passing from a square to a triangular figure? No, certainly it is not that, since I imagine it admits of an infinitude of similar changes, and I nevertheless do not know how to compass the infinitude by my imagination, and consequently this conception which I have of the wax is not brought about by the faculty of imagination. What now is this extension? Is it not also unknown? For it becomes greater when the wax is melted, greater when it is boiled, and greater still when the heat increases; and I should not conceive [clearly] according to truth what wax is, if I did not think that even this piece that we are considering is capable of receiving more variations in extension than I have ever imagined. We must then grant that I could not even understand through the imagination what this piece of wax is, and that it is my mind alone which perceives it. I say this piece of wax in particular, for as to wax in general it is yet clearer. But what is this piece of wax which cannot be understood excepting by the [understanding or] mind? It is certainly the same that I see, touch, imagine, and finally it is the same which I have always believed it to be from the beginning. But what must particularly be observed is that its perception is neither an act of vision, nor of touch, nor of imagination, and has never been such, although it may have appeared formerly to be so, but only an intuition of the mind, which may be imperfect and confused as it was formerly, or clear and distinct as it is at present, according as my attention is more or less directed to the elements which are found in it, and of which it is composed.

Yet in the meantime I am greatly astonished when I consider [the great feebleness of mind] and its proneness to fall [insensibly] into error; for although without giving expression to my thoughts I consider all this in my own mind, words often impede me and I am almost deceived by the terms of ordinary language. For we say that we see the same wax, if it is present, and not that we simply judge that it is the same from its having the same colour and figure. From this I should conclude that I knew the wax by means of vision and not simply by the intuition of the mind; unless by chance I remember that, when looking from a window and saying I see men who pass in the street, I really do not

see them, but infer that what I see is men, just as I say that I see wax. And yet what do I see from the window but hats and coats which may cover automatic machines? Yet I judge these to be men. And similarly solely by the faculty of judgment which rests in my mind, I comprehend that which I believed I saw with my eyes.

A man who makes it his aim to raise his knowledge above the common should be ashamed to derive the occasion for doubting from the forms of speech invented by the vulgar; I prefer to pass on and consider whether I had a more evident and perfect conception of what the wax was when I first perceived it, and when I believed I knew it by means of the external senses or at least by the common sense as it is called, that is to say by the imaginative faculty, or whether my present conception is clearer now that I have most carefully examined what it is, and in what way it can be known. It would certainly be absurd to doubt as to this. For what was there in this first perception which was distinct? What was there which might not as well have been perceived by any of the animals? But when I distinguish the wax from its external forms, and when, just as if I had taken from it its vestments, I consider it quite naked, it is certain that although some error may still be found in my judgment, I can nevertheless not perceive it thus without a human mind.

But finally what shall I say of this mind, that is, of myself, for up to this point I do not admit in myself anything but mind? What then, I who seem to perceive this piece of wax so distinctly, do I not know myself, not only with much more truth and certainty, but also with much more distinctness and clearness? For if I judge that the wax is or exists from the fact that I see it, it certainly follows much more clearly that I am or that I exist myself from the fact that I see it. For it may be that what I see is not really wax, it may also be that I do not possess eyes with which to see anything; but it cannot be that when I see, or (for I no longer take account of the distinction) when I think I see, that I myself who think am nought. So if I judge that the wax exists from the fact that I touch it, the same thing will follow, to wit, that I am; and if I judge that my imagination, or some other cause, whatever it is, persuades me that the wax exists, I shall still conclude the same. And what I have here remarked of wax may be applied to all other things which are external to me [and which are met with outside of me]. And further, if the [notion or] perception of wax has seemed to me clearer and more distinct, not only after the sight or the touch, but also after many other causes have rendered it quite manifest to me, with how much more [evidence] and distinctness must it be said that I now know myself, since all the reasons which contribute to the knowledge of wax, or any other body whatever, are yet better proofs of the nature of my mind! And there are so many other things in the mind itself which may contribute to the elucidation of its nature, that those which depend on body such as these just mentioned, hardly merit being taken into account.

But finally here I am, having insensibly reverted to the point I desired, for, since it is now manifest to me that even bodies are not properly speaking known by the senses or by the faculty of imagination, but by the understanding only, and since they are not known from the fact that they are seen or touched, but only because they are understood, I see clearly that there is nothing which is easier for me to know than my mind. But because it is difficult to rid oneself so promptly of an opinion to which one was accustomed for so long, it will be well that I should halt a little at this point, so that by the length of my meditation I may more deeply imprint on my memory this new knowledge.

MEDITATION III:
OF GOD: THAT HE EXISTS

I shall now close my eyes, I shall stop my ears, I shall call away all my senses, I shall efface even from my thoughts all the images of corporeal things, or at least (for that is hardly possible) I

shall esteem them as vain and false; and thus holding converse only with myself and considering my own nature, I shall try little by little to reach a better knowledge of and a more familiar acquaintanceship with myself. I am a thing that thinks, that is to say, that doubts, affirms, denies, that knows a few things, that is ignorant of many [that loves, that hates], that wills, that desires, that also imagines and perceives; for as I remarked before, although the things which I perceive and imagine are perhaps nothing at all apart from me and in themselves, I am nevertheless assured that these modes of thought that I call perceptions and imaginations, inasmuch only as they are modes of thought, certainly reside [and are met with] in me. . . .

ON THE SEPARATION
OF THE MIND FROM THE BODY

But now that I begin to know myself better, and to discover more clearly the author of my being, I do not in truth think that I should rashly admit all the matters which the senses seem to teach us, but, on the other hand, I do not think that I should doubt them all universally.

And first of all, because I know that all things which I apprehend clearly and distinctly can be created by God as I apprehend them, it suffices that I am able to apprehend one thing apart from another clearly and distinctly in order to be certain that the one is different from the other, since they may be made to exist in separation at least by the omnipotence of God; and it does not signify by what power this separation is made in order to compel me to judge them to be different: and, therefore, just because I know certainly that I exist, and that meanwhile I do not notice that any other thing necessarily pertains to my nature or essence, excepting that I am a thinking thing, I rightly conclude that my essence consists solely in the fact that I am a thinking thing [or a substance whose whole essence or nature is to think]. And although possibly (or rather certainly, as I shall say in a moment) I possess a body with which I am very intimately conjoined, yet because, on the one side, I have a clear and distinct idea of myself inasmuch as I am only a thinking and unextended thing, and as, on the other, I possess a distinct idea of body, inasmuch as it is only an extended and unthinking thing, it is certain that this I [that is to say, my soul by which I am what I am], is entirely and absolutely distinct from my body, and can exist without it.

I further find in myself faculties employing modes of thinking peculiar to themselves, to wit, the faculties of imagination and feeling, without which I can easily conceive myself clearly and distinctly as a complete being; while, on the other hand, they cannot be so conceived apart from me, that is without an intelligent substance in which they reside, for [in the notion we have of these faculties, or, to use the language of the Schools] in their formal concept, some kind of intellection is comprised, from which I infer that they are distinct from me as its modes are from a thing. I observe also in me some other faculties such as that of change of position, the assumption of different figures and such like, which cannot be conceived, any more than can the preceding, apart from some substance to which they are attached, and consequently cannot exist without it; but it is very clear that these faculties, if it be true that they exist, must be attached to some corporeal or extended substance, and not to an intelligent substance, since in the clear and distinct conception of these there is some sort of extension found to be present, but no intellection at all. There is certainly further in me a certain passive faculty of perception, that is, of receiving and recognising the ideas of sensible things, but this would be useless to me [and I could in no way avail myself of it], if there were not either in me or in some other thing another active faculty capable of forming and producing these ideas. But this active faculty cannot exist in me [inasmuch as I am a thing that thinks] seeing that it does not presuppose thought, and also that those ideas are often produced in me without my contributing in any way to the same, and

often even against my will; it is thus necessarily the case that the faculty resides in some substance different from me in which all the reality which is objectively in the ideas that are produced by this faculty is formally or eminently contained, as I remarked before. And this substance is either a body, that is, a corporeal nature in which there is contained formally [and really] all that which is objectively [and by representation] in those ideas, or it is God Himself, or some other creature more noble than body in which that same is contained eminently. But, since God is no deceiver, it is very manifest that He does not communicate to me these ideas immediately and by Himself, nor yet by the intervention of some creature in which their reality is not formally, but only eminently, contained. For since He has given me no faculty to recognise that this is the case, but, on the other hand, a very great inclination to believe [that they are sent to me or] that they are conveyed to me by corporeal objects, I do not see how He could be defended from the accusation of deceit if these ideas were produced by causes other than corporeal objects. Hence we must allow that corporeal things exist. However, they are perhaps not exactly what we perceive by the senses, since this comprehension by the senses is in many instances very obscure and confused; but we must at least admit that all things which I conceive in them clearly and distinctly, that is to say, all things which, speaking generally, are comprehended in the object of pure mathematics, are truly to be recognised as external objects.

As to other things, however, which are either particular only, as, for example, that the sun is of such and such a figure, etc., or which are less clearly and distinctly conceived, such as light, sound, pain and the like, it is certain that although they are very dubious and uncertain, yet on the sole ground that God is not a deceiver, and that consequently He has not permitted any falsity to exist in my opinion which He has not likewise given me the faculty of correcting, I may assuredly hope to conclude that I have within me the means of arriving at the truth even here. And first of all there is no doubt that in all things which nature teaches me there is some truth contained; for by nature, considered in general, I now understand no other thing than either God Himself or else the order and disposition which God has established in created things; and by my nature in particular I understand no other thing than the complexus of all the things which God has given me.

But there is nothing which this nature teaches me more expressly [nor more sensibly] than that I have a body which is adversely affected when I feel pain, which has need of food or drink when I experience the feelings of hunger and thirst, and so on; nor can I doubt there being some truth in all this.

Nature also teaches me by these sensations of pain, hunger, thirst, etc., that I am not only lodged in my body as a pilot in a vessel, but that I am very closely united to it, and so to speak so intermingled with it that I seem to compose with it one whole. For if that were not the case, when my body is hurt, I, who am merely a thinking thing, should not feel pain, for I should perceive this wound by the understanding only, just as the sailor perceives by sight when something is damaged in his vessel; and when my body has need of drink or food, I should clearly understand the fact without being warned of it by confused feelings of hunger and thirst. For all these sensations of hunger, thirst, pain, etc. are in truth none other than certain confused modes of thought which are produced by the union and apparent intermingling of mind and body. . . .

. . . It still remains to inquire how the goodness of God does not prevent the nature of man so regarded from being fallacious.

In order to begin this examination, then, I here say, in the first place, that there is a great difference between mind and body, inasmuch as body is by nature always divisible, and the mind is entirely indivisible. For, as a matter of fact, when I consider the mind, that is to say, myself inasmuch as I am only a thinking thing, I cannot distinguish in myself any parts, but apprehend myself to be clearly one and entire; and

although the whole mind seems to be united to the whole body, yet if a foot, or an arm, or some other part, is separated from my body, I am aware that nothing has been taken away from my mind. And the faculties of willing, feeling, conceiving, etc. cannot be properly speaking said to be its parts, for it is one and the same mind which employs itself in willing and in feeling and understanding. But it is quite otherwise with corporeal or extended objects, for there is not one of these imaginable by me which my mind cannot easily divide into parts, and which consequently I do not recognise as being divisible; this would be sufficient to teach me that the mind or soul of man is entirely different from the body, if I had not already learned it from other sources.

I further notice that the mind does not receive the impressions from all parts of the body immediately, but only from the brain, or perhaps even from one of its smallest parts, to wit, from that in which the common sense is said to reside, which, whenever it is disposed in the same particular way, conveys the same thing to the mind, although meanwhile the other portions of the body may be differently disposed, as is testified by innumerable experiments which it is unnecessary here to recount. . . .

[From *The Passions of the Souls*]

The small gland which is the main seat of the souls is so suspended between the cavities which contain the spirits that it can be moved by them in as many ways as there are sensible diversities in the object, but that it may also be moved in diverse ways by the soul, whose nature is such that it receives in itself as many diverse impressions, that is to say, that it possesses as many diverse perceptions, as there are diverse movements in this gland. Reciprocally, likewise, the machine of the body is so formed that from the simple fact that this gland is diversely moved by the soul, or by such other cause, whatever it is, it thrusts the spirits which surround it towards the pores of the brain, which conducts them by the nerves into the muscles, by which means it causes them to move the limbs.

For Further Reflection

Here is a summary of Descartes' argument. Examine it and see whether you agree with his premises and his reasoning.

1. We can know the mind better than anything else (except possibly God's existence).

2. We can know the mind as distinct from the body (waking up in the morning, I do not need to open my eyes to see that I exist in order to know that I do).

3. It makes more sense to suppose that the mind and the body interact and face the difficulties of interactionist dualism than to say that they are one and struggle to explain the phenomena of consciousness.

4. The mind is in the pineal gland within the brain. At least it is clear that consciousness must reside in the brain since (a) sleep and disease which affect only the brain interrupt the operations of the senses; (b) if the nerves between external sense organs and the brain are cut, no sensations occur; and (c) it is possible to have sensations when the apparent place of sensation no longer exists (e.g., the phantom limb syndrome wherein an amputee imagines pain in his arm—even though he has none).

IV.28   Exorcising Descartes' "Ghost in the Machine"

GILBERT RYLE

Gilbert Ryle (1900–1976), an English philosopher, was educated at Oxford University, where he taught and greatly influenced a generation of students until his death in 1976. He was the editor of *Mind*, one of the most important philosophy journals, from 1948–1971. His principal works are *The Concept of Mind*, from which the present selection is taken, and *Dilemmas* (1954).

In this selection Ryle criticizes Cartesian dualism, which he labels "the Ghost in the Machine," as involving a category mistake. A category mistake is a confusion one slips into when something that belongs to one category or context is mistakenly taken to belong to another. Jokes intentionally thrive on this. For example, "The average woman in the United States has 2.5 children" would be an example of such a mistake if one went looking for the .5 child, treating a functional term "average woman" as a proper noun.

Ryle attempts to show that Descartes' dualism commits a similar category confusion. That is, just because we speak of bodily functions and mental functions as different in no way entails that they are two entirely separate entities. Ryle believes that this functional language can be reduced to observation language.

Study Questions

1. What is the official doctrine? Describe it.
2. What are the person's private and public histories? What does Ryle say about them?
3. What is Ryle's estimation of the official doctrine?
4. What is a category mistake? How does Ryle illustrate this concept?
5. What is the origin of the Cartesian category mistake?

THE ABSURDITY OF THE OFFICIAL DOCTRINE OF "THE GHOST IN THE MACHINE"

The Official Doctrine

THERE IS A DOCTRINE about the nature and place of minds which is so prevalent among theorists and even among laymen that it deserves to be described as the official theory. Most philosophers, psychologists and religious teachers subscribe, with minor reservations, to its main articles and, although they admit certain theoretical difficulties in it, they tend to assume that these can be overcome without serious modifications being made to the architecture of the theory. It will be argued here that the central principles of the doctrine are unsound and conflict with the whole body of what we know about minds when we are not speculating about them.

The official doctrine, which hails chiefly from Descartes, is something like this. With the doubtful exceptions of idiots and infants in arms, every human being has both a body and a mind. Some would prefer to say that every human being is both a body and a mind. His body and his mind are ordinarily harnessed together, but after the death of the body, his mind may continue to exist and function.

Human bodies are in space and are subject to the mechanical laws which govern all other bodies in space. Bodily processes and states can be inspected by external observers. So a man's bodily life is as much a public affair as are the lives of animals and reptiles and even as the careers of trees, crystals and planets.

But minds are not in space, nor are their operations subject to mechanical laws. The workings of one mind are not witnessable by other observers; its career is private. Only I can take direct cognisance of the states and processes of my own mind. A person therefore lives through two collateral histories, one consisting of what happens in and to his body, the other consisting of what happens in and to his mind. The first is public, the second private. The events in the first history are events in the physical world, those in the second are events in the mental world.

It has been disputed whether a person does or can directly monitor all or only some of the episodes of his own private history, but, according to the official doctrine, of at least some of these episodes he has direct and unchallengeable cognisance. In consciousness, self-consciousness and introspection he is directly and authentically apprised of the present states and operations of his mind. He may have great or small uncertainties about concurrent and adjacent episodes in the physical world, but he can have none about at least part of what is momentarily occupying his mind.

It is customary to express this bifurcation of his two lives and of his two worlds by saying that the things and events which belong to the physical world, including his own body, are external, while the workings of his own mind are internal. This antithesis of outer and inner is of course meant to be construed as a metaphor, since minds, not being in space, could not be described as being spatially inside anything else, or as having things going on spatially inside themselves. But relapses from this good intention are common and theorists are found speculating how stimuli, the physical sources of which are yards or miles outside a person's skin, can generate mental responses inside his skull, or how decisions framed inside his cranium can set going movements of his extremities.

Even when "inner" and "outer" are construed as metaphors, the problem of how a person's mind and body influence one another is notoriously charged with theoretical difficulties. What the mind wills, the legs, arms and the tongue execute; what affects the ear and the eye has something to do with what the mind perceives; grimaces and smiles betray the mind's moods and bodily castigations lead, it is hoped, to moral improvement. But the actual transactions between the episodes of the private history and those of the public history remain mysterious, since by definition they can belong to neither series. They could not be reported among the happenings described in a person's autobiography of his inner life, nor could they be reported among those described in some one else's biography of that person's overt career. They can be inspected neither by introspection nor by laboratory experiment. They are theoretical shuttlecocks which are forever being bandied from the physiologist back to the psychologist and from the psychologist back to the physiologist.

Underlying this partly metaphorical representation of the bifurcation of a person's two lives there is a seemingly more profound and philosophical assumption. It is assumed that there are two different kinds of existence or status. What exists or happens may have the status of physical existence, or it may have the status of mental existence. Somewhat as the faces of coins are either heads or tails, or somewhat as living creatures are either male or female, so, it is supposed, some existing is physical existing, other existing is mental existing. It is a necessary feature of what has physical existence that it is in space and time; it is a necessary feature of what has mental existence that it is in time but not in space. What has physical existence is composed of matter, or else is a function of matter; what has mental existence consists of consciousness, or else is a function of consciousness.

There is thus a polar opposition between mind and matter, an opposition which is often brought out as follows. Material objects are situated in a common field, known as "space," and what happens to one body in one part of space is mechanically connected with what happens to other bodies in other parts of space. But mental happenings occur in insulated fields, known as "minds," and there is, apart maybe from telepathy, no direct causal connection between what happens in one mind and what happens in another. Only through the medium of the public physical world can the mind of one person make a difference to the mind of another. The mind is its own place and in his inner life each of us lives the life of a ghostly Robinson Crusoe. People can see, hear and jolt one another's bodies, but they are irremediably blind and deaf to the workings of one another's minds and inoperative upon them.

What sort of knowledge can be secured of the workings of a mind? On the one side, according to the official theory, a person has direct knowledge of the best imaginable kind of the workings of his own mind. Mental states and processes are (or are normally) conscious states and processes, and the consciousness which irradiates them can engender no illusions and leaves the door open for no doubts. A person's present thinkings, feelings and willings, his perceivings, rememberings and imaginings are intrinsically "phosphorescent"; their existence and their nature are inevitably betrayed to their owner. The inner life is a stream of consciousness of such a sort that it would be absurd to suggest that the mind whose life is that stream might be unaware of what is passing down it.

True, the evidence adduced recently by Freud seems to show that there exist channels tributary to this stream, which run hidden from their owner. People are actuated by impulses the existence of which they vigorously disavow; some of their thoughts differ from the thoughts which they acknowledge; and some of the actions which they think they will to perform they do not really will. They are thoroughly gulled by some of their own hypocrisies, and they successfully ignore facts about their mental lives, which, on the official theory, ought to be patent to them. Holders of the official theory tend, however, to maintain that anyhow in normal circumstances a person must be directly and authentically seized of the present state and workings of his own mind.

Besides being currently supplied with these alleged immediate data of consciousness, a person is also generally supposed to be able to exercise from time to time a special kind of perception, namely inner perception, or introspection. He can take a (non-optical) "look" at what is passing in his mind. Not only can he view and scrutinize a flower through his sense of sight and listen to and discriminate the notes of a bell through his sense of hearing; he can also reflectively or introspectively watch, without any bodily organ of sense, the current episodes of his inner life. This self-observation is also commonly supposed to be immune from illusion, confusion or doubt. A mind's reports of its own affairs have a certainty superior to the best that is possessed by its reports of matters in the physical world. Sense-perceptions can, but consciousness and introspection cannot, be mistaken or confused.

On the other side, one person has no direct access of any sort to the events of the inner life of another. He cannot do better than make problematic inferences from the observed behaviour of the other person's body to the states of mind which, by analogy from his own conduct, he supposes to be signalised by that behaviour. Direct access to the workings of a mind is the privilege of that mind itself; in default of such privileged access, the workings of one mind are inevitably occult to everyone else. For the supposed arguments from bodily movements similar to their own, to mental workings similar to their own, would lack any possibility of observational corroboration. Not unnaturally, therefore, an adherent of the official theory finds it difficult to resist this consequence of his premisses, that he has no good reason to believe that there do exist minds other than his own. Even if he prefers to believe that to other human bodies there are harnessed minds not unlike his own, he cannot claim to be able to discover their individual characteristics, or the particular things that they undergo and do. Absolute solitude is on this showing the ineluctable destiny of the soul. Only our bodies can meet.

As a necessary corollary of this general scheme there is implicitly prescribed a special way of construing our ordinary concepts of mental powers and operations. The verbs, nouns and adjectives, with which in ordinary life we describe the wits, characters and higher-grade performances of the people with whom we have to do, are required to be construed as signifying special episodes in their secret histories, or else as signifying tendencies for such episodes to occur. When someone is described as knowing, believing or guessing something, as hoping, dreading, intending or shirking something, as designing this or being amused at that, these verbs are supposed to denote the occurrence of specific modifications in his (to us) occult stream of consciousness. Only his own privileged access to this stream in direct awareness and introspection could provide authentic testimony that these mental-conduct verbs were correctly or incorrectly applied. The onlooker, be he teacher, critic, biographer or friend, can never assure himself that his comments have any vestige of truth. Yet it was just because we do in fact all know how to make such comments, make them with general correctness and correct them when they turn out to be confused or mistaken, that philosophers found it necessary to construct their theories of the nature and place of minds. Finding mental-conduct concepts being regularly and effectively used, they properly sought to fix their logical geography. But the logical geography officially recommended would entail that there could be no regular or effective use of these mental-conduct concepts in our descriptions of, and prescriptions for, other people's minds.

The Absurdity of the Official Doctrine

Such in outline is the official theory. I shall often speak of it, with deliberate abusiveness, as "the dogma of the Ghost in the Machine." I hope to prove that it is entirely false, and false not in detail but in principle. It is not merely an assemblage of particular mistakes. It is one big mistake and a mistake of a special kind. It is, namely, a category-mistake. It represents the facts of mental life as if they belonged to one logical type or category (or range of types or categories), when they actually belong to another. The dogma is therefore a philosopher's myth. In attempting to explode the myth I shall probably be taken to be denying well-known facts about the mental life of human beings, and my plea that I aim at doing nothing more than rectify the logic of mental-conduct concepts will probably be disallowed as mere subterfuge.

I must first indicate what is meant by the phrase "Category-mistake." This I do in a series of illustrations.

A foreigner visiting Oxford or Cambridge for the first time is shown a number of colleges, libraries, playing fields, museums, scientific departments and administrative offices. He then asks "But where is the University? I have seen where the members of the Colleges live, where the Registrar works, where the scientists experiment and the rest. But I have not yet seen the University in which reside and work the members of your University." It has then to be explained to him that the University is not another collateral institution, some ulterior counterpart to the colleges, laboratories and offices which he has seen. The university is just the way in which all that he has already seen is organized. When they are seen and when their co-ordination is understood, the University has been seen. His mistake lay in his innocent assumption that it was correct to speak of Christ Church, the Bodleian Library, the Ashmolean Museum *and* the University, to speak, that is, as if "the University" stood for an extra member of the class of which these other units are members. He was mistakenly allocating the University to the same category as that to which the other institutions belong.

The same mistake would be made by a child witnessing the march-past of a division who, having had pointed out to him such and such battalions, batteries, squadrons, etc., asked when the division was going to appear. He would be supposing that a division was a counterpart to the units already seen, partly similar to them and partly unlike them. He would be shown his mistake by being told that in watching the battalions, batteries and squadrons marching past he had been watching the division marching past. The march-past was not a parade of battalions, batteries, squadrons *and* a division; it was a parade of the battalions, batteries and squadrons *of* a division.

One more illustration. A foreigner watching his first game of cricket learns what are the functions of the bowlers, the batsmen, the fielders, the umpires and the scorers. He then says, "But there is no one left on the field to contribute the famous element of team-spirit. I see who does the bowling, the batting and the wicket-keeping, but I do not see whose role it is to exercise *esprit de corps*. "Once more, it would have to be explained that he was looking for the wrong type of thing. Team-spirit is not another cricketing-operation supplementary to all of the other special tasks. It is, roughly, the keenness with which each of the special tasks is performed, and performing a task keenly is not performing two tasks. Certainly exhibiting team-spirit is not the same thing as bowling or catching, but nor is it a third thing such that we can say that the bowler first bowls *and* then exhibits team-spirit or that a fielder is at a given moment *either* catching *or* displaying *esprit de corps*.

These illustrations of category-mistakes have a common feature which must be noticed. The mistakes were made by people who did not know how to wield the concepts *University, division* and *team-spirit*. Their puzzles arose from inability to use certain items in the English vocabulary.

The theoretically interesting category-mistakes are those made by people who are perfectly competent to apply concepts, at least in the situations with which they are familiar, but are still liable in their abstract thinking to allocate those concepts to logical types to which they do not belong. An instance of a mistake of this sort would be the following story. A student of politics has learned the main differences between the British, the French and the American Constitutions, and has learned also the differences and connections between the Cabinet, Parliament, the various Ministries, the Judicature and the Church of England. But he still becomes embarrassed when asked questions about the connections between the Church of England, the Home Office and the British Constitution. For while the Church and the Home Office are institutions, the British Constitution is not another institution in the same sense of that noun. So inter-institutional relations which can be asserted or denied to hold between the Church and the Home Office cannot be asserted or denied to hold between either of them and the British Constitution. "The British Constitution" is not a term of the same logical type as "the Home Office" and "the Church of England." In a partially similar way, John Doe may be a relative, a friend, an enemy or a stranger to Richard Roe; but he cannot be any of these things to the Average Taxpayer. He knows how to talk sense in certain sorts of discussions about the Average Taxpayer, but he is baffled to say why he could not come across him in the street as he can come across Richard Roe.

It is pertinent to our main subject to notice that, so long as the student of politics continues to think of the British Constitution as a counterpart to the other institutions, he will tend to describe it as a mysteriously occult institution; and so long as John Doe continues to think of the Average Taxpayer as a fellow-citizen, he will tend to think of him as an elusive insubstantial man, a ghost who is everywhere yet nowhere.

My destructive purpose is to show that a family of radical category-mistakes is the source of the double-life theory. The representation of a person as a ghost mysteriously ensconced in a machine derives from this argument. Because, as is true, a person's thinking, feeling and purposive doing cannot be described solely in the idioms of physics, chemistry and physiology, therefore they must be described in counterpart idioms. As the human body is a complex organised unit, so the human mind must be another complex organised unit, though one made of a different sort of stuff and with a different sort of structure. Or, again, as the human body, like any other parcel of matter, is a field of causes and effects, so the mind must be another field of causes and effects, though not (Heaven be praised) mechanical causes and effects.

The Origin of the Category-Mistake

One of the chief intellectual origins of what I have yet to prove to be the Cartesian category-mistake seems to be this. When Galileo showed that his methods of scientific discovery were competent to provide a mechanical theory which should cover every occupant of space, Descartes found in himself two conflicting motives. As a man of scientific genius he could not but endorse the claims of mechanics, yet as a religious and moral man he could not accept, as Hobbes accepted, the discouraging rider to those claims, namely that human nature differs only in degree of complexity from clockwork. The mental could not be just a variety of the mechanical.

[Descartes] and subsequent philosophers naturally but erroneously availed themselves of the following escape-route. Since mental-conduct words are not to be construed as signifying the occurrence of mechanical processes, they must be construed as signifying the occurrence of non-mechanical processes; since mechanical laws explain movements in space as the effects of other movements in space, other laws must explain some of the non-spatial workings of minds as the effects of other non-spatial workings of minds.

The difference between the human behaviours which we describe as intelligent and those which we describe as unintelligent must be a difference in their causation; so, while some movements of human tongues and limbs are the effects of mechanical causes, others must be the effects of non-mechanical causes, i.e., some issue from movements of particles of matter, others from workings of the mind. The differences between the physical and the mental were thus represented as differences inside the common framework of the categories of "thing," "stuff," "attribute," "state," "process," "change," "cause" and "effect." Minds are things, but different sorts of things from bodies; mental processes are causes and effects, but different sorts of causes and effects from bodily movements. And so on. Somewhat as the foreigner expected the University to be an extra edifice, rather like a college but also considerably different, so the repudiators of mechanism represented minds as extra centres of causal processes, rather like machines but also considerably different from them. Their theory was a para-mechanical hypothesis. . . .

If my argument is successful, there will follow some interesting consequences. First, the hallowed contrast between mind and matter will be dissipated, but dissipated not by either of the equally hallowed absorptions of mind by matter or of matter by mind, but in quite a different way. For the seeming contrast of the two will be shown to be as illegitimate as would be the contrast of "she came home in a flood of tears" and "she came home in a sedan-chair." The belief that there is a polar opposition between mind and matter is the belief that they are terms of the same logical type.

For Further Reflection

1. What is the value of Ryle's essay? Does it severely undermine Cartesian dualism? Does it argue directly against dualism or does it try to suggest another way of looking at the problem?

2. Do you think that Descartes has committed a category mistake as Ryle charges? Is there something missing, unaccounted for, in Ryle's portrayal of dualism? Can a functional monism successfully escape the problems of the mind-body controversy?

IV.29   A Contemporary Defense of Dualism

J. P. MORELAND

J. P. Moreland (1948–) teaches philosophy at Talbot School of Theology at Biola University in California. He is the author of *Scaling the Secular City* and *Christianity and the Nature of Science*. In this selection, Moreland defends dualist interactionism, arguing that the mind is distinct from the brain. He compares physicalism, the view that the only thing that exists in the universe is matter, with substance dualism, the view that mind is separate from matter. He gives several reasons for rejecting physicalism and accepting dualism. Moreland claims that the idea of dualism is best understood from within a wider metaphysic, such as theism.

Study Questions

1. What are the two primary issues involved in the mind-body dispute?
2. What is the name for the view that holds that matter is the only thing that exists?
3. Identify the two varieties of dualism. Which has been the historic Christian view?
4. What are some problems with physicalism?
5. Moreland contends that the physicalist must show that mental and brain phenomena are not only inseparable (like the redness and roundness of an apple) but also that they are _____ [fill in blank].
6. What are examples of mental events?

7. What are some of Moreland's reasons for believing in the distinction between physical and mental events?
8. How does Moreland describe *intentionality*? How does it support a dualist view?
9. How do dualists and physicalists differ regarding personal identity?
10. What is Quine's view on personal identity?
11. What is the emergent property view (EPV)?
12. Why does Moreland reject the EPV?

ARGUMENTS FOR DUALISM: DUALISM DEFINED

THE MIND-BODY PROBLEM focuses on two main issues. First, is a human being composed of just one ultimate component or two? Second, if the answer is two, how do these two relate to one another? Physicalism is one solution to the problem. As a general worldview, physicalism holds that the only thing which exists is matter (where matter is defined by an ideal, completed form of physics). Applied to the mind-body problem, physicalism asserts that a human being is just a physical system. There is no mind or soul, just a brain and central nervous system. Dualism is the opponent of physicalism, and it asserts that in addition to the body, a human being also has a nonphysical component called a soul, mind, or self (words which will be used interchangeably for our purposes).

There are two main varieties of dualism—property dualism and substance dualism. In order to understand the difference, we must first spell out the distinction between a property and a substance. A property is an entity: redness, hardness, wisdom, triangularity, or painfulness. A property has at least four characteristics which distinguish it from a substance. First, a property is a universal, not a particular. It can be in more than one thing or at more than one place at the same time. Redness can be in my coat and your flag at the same time. Second, a property is immutable and does not contain opposites (hot and cold, red and green) within it. When a leaf goes from green to

red, the *leaf* changes. Greenness does not become redness. Greenness leaves the leaf and redness replaces it. Greenness and redness remain the same. Third, properties can be had by something else. They can be in another thing which has them. Redness is in the apple. The apple *has* the redness. Fourth, properties do not have causal powers. They do not act as efficient causes. Properties are not agents which act on other agents in the world.

A substance is an entity like an apple, my dog Fido, a carbon atom, a leaf, or an angel. Substances contrast with properties in the four characteristics listed. First, substances are particulars. For example, my dog Fido cannot be in more than one place at the same time. Second, a substance can change and have opposites. A leaf can go from green to red or hot to cold by gaining or losing properties. During the process of change, the substance gains and loses properties, but it is still the same substance. The same leaf which was green is now red. Third, substances are basic, fundamental existents. They are not *in* other things or *had by* other things. Fido is not a property of some more basic entity. Rather, Fido *has* properties. Fido is a unity of properties (dogness, brownness, shape), parts (paws, teeth, ears), and dispositions or capacities (law-like tendencies to realize certain properties in the process of growth if certain conditions obtain; for instance, the capacity to grow teeth if the fetus is nourished). They are all united into the substance Fido and possessed by him. Finally, a substance has causal powers. It can act as a causal

From J. P. Moreland, Scaling the Secular City *(Baker Books, 1987). Reprinted by permission of the author and the publisher.*

agent in the world. A carbon atom can act on another atom. A dog can bark or pick up a bone. A leaf can hit the ground.

Property dualists hold that the mind is a property of the body. As Richard Taylor puts it, "A person is a living physical body having mind, the mind consisting, however, of nothing but a more or less continuous series of conscious or unconscious states and events . . . which are the effects but never the causes of bodily activity." This view is called *epiphenomenalism*. The mind is to the body as smoke is to fire. Smoke is different from fire, but smoke does not cause anything. Smoke is a byproduct of fire. Similarly, mind is a byproduct of the body which does not cause anything. It just "rides" on top of the events in the body. Body events cause mind as a byproduct. The mind is a property of the body which ceases to exist when the body ceases to function. Though some theists have denied it recently, the historic Christian view has been substance dualism. The mind, distinct from the body, is a real substance which can cause things to happen by acting and which can exist when the body ceases to function.

DUALISM DEFENDED

Problems with Physicalism as a General Worldview

Physicalism as a worldview holds that everything that exists is nothing but a single spatio-temporal system which can be completely described in terms of some ideal form of physics. Matter/energy is all that exists. God, souls, and nonphysical abstract entities do not exist. If physicalism is true at the worldview level, then obviously, mind-body physicalism would follow. But is physicalism adequate as a worldview? Several factors indicate that it is not.

First, if theism is true, then physicalism as a worldview is false. God is not a physical being. Second, a number of people have argued that numbers exist and that they are abstract, non-

physical entities (e.g., sets, substances, or properties). Several arguments can be offered for the existence of numbers, but two appear frequently. For one thing, mathematics claims to give us knowledge. But if this is so, there must be something that mathematics is about. Just as the biologist *discovers* biological truths about biological objects (organisms), so the mathematician often *discovers* mathematical truths (he does not invent them all the time) and these truths are about mathematical objects. If one denies the existence of numbers, then it is hard to rescue mathematics as a field which conveys knowledge about something. Without numbers, mathematics becomes merely an internally consistent game which is invented.

A second argument is often given for holding to the existence of numbers. Scientific laws and theories seem to assert their existence. For example, a calcium ion has a positive charge of two which is expressed in the formula Ca^{+2}. The number two here seems to be more than a mere formula for calculating relative amounts of compounds in laboratory reactions. Two expresses a property of the calcium ion itself. The property of twoness is just as much a real property of the charge of the calcium as the property of positiveness. If one denies that numbers exist, it is hard to continue to maintain that science gives us a real description of the world rather than a set of operations that work in the laboratory. In sum, without numbers, mathematical and scientific knowledge is hard to maintain. But if numbers exist, physicalism as a worldview is false because numbers are not physical entities.

Some have argued that values, in addition to God and numbers, exist and are not physical. Certain objects (persons, animals) and certain events (helping a stranger, for example) have a nonphysical property of worth or goodness. Furthermore, moral laws are often held to be absolute, objective realities (e.g., one should not torture babies). But if certain objects possess goodness, and if certain moral laws are objective realities, then physicalism must be false, because the property of goodness and the nature of moral laws are not physical. For example, it makes no sense to ask how much goodness weighs, or to ask where a moral law exists. Such realities are not physical.

Fourth, if physicalism is true, it is hard to see what one should make of the existence and nature of theories, meanings, concepts, propositions, the laws of logic, and truth itself. It would seem that theories themselves exist and can be discovered. The laws of logic seem to be real laws that govern the relationships between propositions. Propositions seem to exist and be the content of thoughts which become associated with the physical scratchings of a given language called sentences. Sentences may be made of black ink, be on a page, and be four inches long. But it is hard to see how the *content* of the sentence (i.e., the proposition or thought expressed by the sentence) could be on the page. Such entities seem to be nonphysical entities which can be in the mind. Truth appears to be a relation of correspondence between a thought and the world. If a thought really describes the world accurately, it is true. It stands to the world in a relation of correspondence. But whatever else one wants to say about the relation of correspondence, it does not seem to be a physical relation like cause and effect.

Finally, universals seem to exist and they are not material. A universal is an entity that can be in more than one place at the same time. Some universals are properties (redness, hardness, triangularity); others are relations (larger than, to the left of). Whatever else one may use to characterize the nature of matter, it is clear that a clump of matter is a particular. A piece of matter cannot be in more than one place at the same time. Physicalists deny the existence of universals at the level of general worldview, because universals are not physical entities.

The entities listed have caused a lot of difficulty for physicalists. They have spent a good deal of time trying to do away with numbers, values, propositions, laws of logic, and universals

by reducing them to notions compatible with physicalism. But these reductionist attempts have failed and physicalism as a worldview cannot adequately handle the existence of these entities. Theism can embrace them, however, by holding that God created these nonphysical entities and sustains them in existence. The falsity of physicalism as a worldview does not refute mind-body physicalism. One could hold to the existence of numbers and values but deny the existence of the soul. But much of the motivation for mind-body physicalism has been the desire to argue for physicalism at the worldview level. If physicalism at that level is false, then part of the reason for holding to mind-body physicalism is removed. For example, just because one cannot see the soul, weigh it, or say where it is, it does not follow that the soul does not exist. One cannot see, weigh, or locate numbers or values, but they still exist.

Problems with Mind-Body Physicalism

In order to facilitate an understanding of some of the arguments against mind-body physicalism, we must first examine the nature of identity. Suppose you know that someone named J. P. Moreland exists and that the author of this book exists. Assume further that you do not know that J. P. Moreland wrote this book. If someone asked you whether J. P. Moreland is identical to the author of this book, how would you decide? How would you determine that the "two" individuals are identical instead of being two different people? If you could find something true of J. P. Moreland which is not true of the author of this book or vice versa, then they would be different people. They could not be identical. For example, if J. P. Moreland is married to Hope Moreland but the author of this book is not, they would be different people. On the other hand, if everything true of one is true of the other, "they" would be one person. In general, if "two" things are identical, then whatever is true of the one is true of the other, since in reality only one thing is being discussed. However, if something is true of the one which is not true of the other, then they are two things and not one. This is sometimes called the indiscernibility of identicals and is expressed as follows:

$$(x)(y)[(x = y) \rightarrow (P)(Px \leftrightarrow Py)]$$

For any entities x and y, if x and y are really the same thing, then for any property P, P is true of x if and only if P is true of y.[1] If x is the mind or one of its states and y is a body or part or state of the body (e.g., the brain), then if physicalism is true, x must be identical to y. On the other hand, if something is true of the mind which is not true of the body, then the mind is not identical to the body and physicalism is false. This would be true even if the mind and body are inseparable. The roundness of an apple cannot be separated from its redness. One does not find redness sitting on a table by itself and roundness sitting next to it. But the redness of an apple is not identical to the roundness of the apple. One is a color and one is a shape.

Every time something happens in the mind (someone has a thought of an ice cream cone), some event may be going on in the brain which could be described by a neurophysiologist. In general, brain events may always have mental events that correlate with them and vice versa. They may be inseparable in that one does not occur without the other in an embodied person. But this does not mean that the mental thought is identical to the brain event. The redness and roundness of an apple, though inseparable, are not identical. The property of having three sides (trilaterality) and the property of having three angles (triangularity) always go together. They are inseparable. But they are not identical. Physicalists must not only show that mental and brain phenomena are inseparable to make their case. They must also show that they are identical. With this in mind let us turn to some arguments for dualism.

The Distinctiveness of Mental and Physical Properties.   Mental events include episodes of thoughts, feelings of pain, the experience of being a person, or episodes of having sensory experience, e.g., a picture of a ball in my mind. Physical events are events in the brain or central nervous system which can be described exhaustively using terms of chemistry, physics, and (for now) biology. The difficulty for physicalism is that mental events do not seem to have properties that hold for physical events. My thought of Kansas City is not ten centimeters long, it does not weigh anything, it is not located anywhere (it is not two inches from my left ear). Nor is it identical to any behavior or tendency to behave in a certain way (shouting "Kansas City" when I hear the name *George Brett*). But the brain event associated with having this thought may be located inside my head, it may have a certain chemical composition and electrical current, and so forth. My afterimage of a ball (the impression of the ball present to my consciousness when I close my eyes after seeing the ball) may be pink, but nothing in my brain is pink.[2] Mental events and properties have different attributes and therefore they are not identical.[3]

Private Access and Incorrigibility.   Mental events are self-presenting. I seem to be in a position to know my own thoughts and mental processes in a way not available to anyone else. I am in a privileged position with regard to my own mental life. I have private access to my own thoughts in a way not open to anyone else. Furthermore, my mental states seem to be incorrigible, at least some of the time. That is, I cannot be mistaken about them. Suppose I am experiencing what I take to be a green rug. It is possible that the rug is not there or that the light is poor and the rug is really gray. I could be mistaken about the rug itself. But it does not seem to be possible for me to be mistaken that I am experiencing what I take to be a green rug right now. That is, my mental state is directly present to me and I know my own mental states immediately.

It would be possible for a brain surgeon to know more about my brain than I do. He may be looking into my brain, seeing it better than I, and knowing its operations better than I. But he does not—indeed, he cannot—know my mental life as well as I. I have private, privileged access to that. Further, it seems that one could always be wrong about his knowledge of some physical state of affairs in the world. The brain surgeon could be wrong about what is happening in my brain. But I cannot be wrong about what is currently happening in my mind. It would seem then that I have privileged, private access to my mental states which is sometimes incorrigible. But neither I nor anyone else has private access to my brain states, and whatever access someone has is irreducibly third-person access (described from a standpoint outside of me) and is not incorrigible.[4]

The Experience of First-Person Subjectivity. The subjective character of experience is hard to capture in physicalist terms. The simple fact of consciousness is a serious difficulty for physicalism. To see this, consider the following. Suppose a deaf scientist became the world's leading expert on the neurology of hearing. It would be possible for him to know and describe everything there is to the physical processes involved in hearing. However, something would still be left out of such a description—the experience of what it is like to be a human who hears. As Howard Robinson puts it:

> The notion of *having something as an object of experience* is not, *prima facie,* a physical notion; it does not figure in any physical science. *Having something as an object of experience* is the same as the subjective feel or the *what it is like* of experience (*Matter and Sense,* p. 7).

Subjective states of experiences exist. My experience of what it is like to be me, to hear a bird or see a tree, exists, and I have a first-person awareness of it. Such first-person experiences of my own self or "I" which has experiences cannot be reduced to a third-person "he" or "it," because the latter do not describe the experience itself or its first-person standpoint. A physicalist, scientific description of the world leaves out this character of subjective awareness. Such a description characterizes the world in impersonal, third-person terms (e.g., "there exists an object with such and such properties and states") and leaves out the first-person, subjective experience itself (e.g., "I feel sad and food tastes sour to me").

Speaking of the character of subjective awareness, Thomas Nagel has this to say:

> If physicalism is to be defended, the phenomenological features [the sounds, colors, smells, tastes of experience that make the experience what it is] must themselves be given a physical account. But when we examine their subjective character it seems that such a result is impossible. The reason is that every subjective phenomenon is essentially connected with a single point of view, and it seems inevitable that an objective, physical theory will abandon that point of view (*Mortal Questions,* p. 167).

Secondary Qualities. Secondary qualities are qualities such as colors, tastes, sounds, smells, and textures. Physicalism seems to imply that such qualities do not exist in the external world. But we do sense such qualities, so where are they, if they are not in the external world? They must exist as sense data (mental objects or images) in the mind. Frank Jackson has put the point this way:

> It is a commonplace that there is an apparent clash between the picture Science gives of the world around us and the picture our senses give us. We *sense* the world as made up of coloured, materially continuous, macroscopic, stable objects; Science and, in particular, Physics, tells us that the material world is constituted of clouds of minute, colourless, highly-mobile particles.... Science forces us to acknowledge that physical or material things are not coloured.... This will enable us to conclude that sense-data are all mental, for they are coloured (*Perception,* p. 121).

In other words, science does away with secondary qualities, but since we know they do exist—we see them—they must exist in our minds as sense data. This shows that there must be minds, and sense data must be little images or pictures which exist as mental objects in minds.

I do not accept this understanding of secondary qualities, because it implies that I do not see the world when I use my senses. Rather, it implies that I see my sense images of the world. But if this view is correct, then it would seem that some form of dualism is correct. If, on the other hand, one holds (as I do) that secondary qualities are real properties of objects in the world, physicalism as a worldview may still be in trouble. If macroscopic objects (regular-sized tables, apples, dogs) do have properties of color, odor, stability, continuous surfaces, and the like, then there must be more to them than what physics tells us. Physics tends to reduce objects to mere heaps of colorless, odorless, rapid-moving packets of matter/energy. But if objects have macroproperties which escape description in these terms, then these properties, call them metaphysical properties, are not physical. That does not mean that they are mental. But it does show that a full treatment of objects must appeal to metaphysical properties which deal with the objects as wholes. If physicalism reduces objects to the mere heaps of microphysics, then physicalism is incomplete as a worldview. On the other hand, if secondary qualities are in fact mental sense data, then physicalism is inadequate as a mind-body theory. Either way, physicalism as a general theory is in trouble.

Intentionality. Some have argued that the mark of the mental is intentionality. Intentionality is the mind's aboutness or ofness. Mental states point beyond themselves to other objects even if those objects do not exist. I have a thought *about* my wife, I hope *for* a new car, I dream *of* a unicorn. The mind has the ability to transcend itself and be of or about something else. This aboutness is not a property of anything physical. Some physicalists have tried to reduce intentionality to the mere ability to receive input, give output, and advance to some other internal state. A computer receives input from a keyboard, gives output on a printer, and advances to a new internal state where it is ready to receive new input. But the computer still has no awareness of or about anything. It seems, then, that physical states do not have intentionality and thus the fact of intentionality is evidence that the self is not physical but mental.

Personal Identity. Imagine a wooden table which had all its parts removed one by one and replaced by metal parts. When the top and all the legs were replaced would it still be the same table? The answer would seem to be no. In fact, it would be possible to take all the original wooden parts and rearrange them into the original table. Even when the table had just one leg replaced, it would not literally be the same table. It would be a table similar to the original.

Losing old parts and gaining new ones changes the identity of the object in question. But now a question arises regarding persons. Am I literally the same self that I was a moment ago? Are my baby pictures really pictures of *me* or are they pictures of an ancestor of me who resembles me? I am constantly losing physical parts. I lose hair and fingernails; atoms are constantly being replaced, and every seven years my cells are almost entirely replaced. Do I maintain literal, absolute identity through change or not?

Substance dualists argue that persons do maintain absolute identity through change, because they have, in addition to their bodies, a soul that remains constant through change, and personal identity is constituted by sameness of soul, not sameness of body.

Physicalists have no alternative but to hold that personal identity is not absolute. Usually they argue that persons are really ancestral chains of successive "selves" which are connected with one another in some way. At each moment a new self exists (since the self or physical organism is constantly in flux, losing and gaining parts) and this self resembles the self prior to and after it. The relation of resemblance between selves plus the fact that later selves have the same memories as earlier selves and the body of each self traces a continuous path through space when the whole chain of selves is put together, constitute a relative sense of personal identity.

So substance dualists hold to a literal, absolute sense of personal identity and physicalists hold to a loose, relative sense of personal identity which amounts to a stream of successive selves held together into "one" person by resemblance between each self (also called a person stage), similarity of memory, and spatial continuity. For the physicalist, a person becomes a space-time worm (i.e., a path traced through space and time). The person is the entire path marked off at the time and place of his birth and death. At any given moment and location where "I" happen to be, "I" am not a person, just a person stage. The person is the whole path. So there is no literal sameness through change.

But now certain problems arise for physicalism. First, why should "I" ever fear the future? When it gets here, "I" will not be present; rather, another self who looks like me will be there but "I" will have ceased to exist. Second, why should anyone be punished? The self who did the crime in the past is not literally the same self who is present at the time of punishment. Physicalism seems to require a radical readjustment of our common-sense notions of future expectations and past actions because both presuppose a literal identity of the same self present in past, present, and future.

Third, physicalists not only have difficulty handling the unity of the self through time, but also cannot explain the unity of the self at a given time. As Harvard philosopher W. V. O. Quine puts it, according to physicalism, the self becomes a sum or heap of scattered physical parts. The unity of the self is like the unity of an assembly of building blocks. If I have a pain in my foot while I am thinking about baseball, each is a distinct experience involving different physical parts. There is no self which *has* each experience. The self is merely a bundle or heap of parts and experiences. It has no real unity. The dualist says that the soul is diffused throughout the body and it is present before each experience. The soul has each experience. The unity of consciousness is due to the fact that the same soul is the possessor of each and every experience of consciousness. But the physicalist must say that each experience is possessed by different parts of the body and there is no real unity. However, my own experience of the unity of my consciousness shows this unity to be genuine and not arbitrary. *I* have my experiences. They are all *mine*. Physicalism does not adequately explain this fact.

THE ORIGIN OF MIND: THE EMERGENT PROPERTY VIEW

We have seen that there are good reasons for holding that strict physicalism is false. But most physicalists are recalcitrant. If they embrace dualism at all, they embrace epiphenomenalism because, as I will show later, it is more compatible with physicalism than is substance dualism. Mind is not matter, but it comes from matter through evolution when matter reaches a suitable structural arrangement for mind to emerge.... There are serious difficulties with epiphenomenalism. To see these we must first clarify what epiphenomenalism involves. The view is also called holism, and when mind is seen to emerge through the coming together of matter in a certain way (for instance, through the evolution of the central nervous system and brain) the position is called the emergent property view (EPV). Here are four main features of the EPV.

Wholes and Parts. In nature, wholes are often greater than the sum of their parts. Nature exhibits a hierarchy of systems—subatomic particles, atoms, molecules, cells, organs, whole organisms. Each level has properties of the wholes at that level which are not properties of their constituent parts. For example, water has the property of being wet, but this property is not true of either hydrogen or oxygen. Similarly, the mind is a property of the brain.

Levels of Explanation and Complementarity. Each level in a hierarchy can be explained by using concepts appropriate at that level. Further, all the levels are complementary. For example, an explanation of a person's behavior could be given at a psychological level which used the concepts *beliefs, desires,* or *fears.* The same behavior could be given an explanation at the neurophysiological level using the concepts *neurons, synapses,* and so forth. These two levels of explanation are not in competition; they complement one another by offering descriptions of the same behavior at different levels.

Causation Between Levels.   Lower levels in the hierarchy cause things to happen at higher levels but not vice versa. When it comes to persons, events at the physical level can be characterized in terms of physical laws which make no reference to the causal efficaciousness of future events (e.g., the purposes of the agent) or higher levels of organization. The events at the physical level obey deterministic physical laws and mental events are mere byproducts.

Resultant View of the Self.   The self is not some mental substance added to the brain from the "outside" when the brain reaches a certain level of complexity. It is an emergent property which supervenes upon the brain. The self becomes a discontinuous series of mental events when mental properties are instanced in different brain events. The self is a series of events which "ride" on top of the brain. Consider the following diagram:

$$M_1 \quad M_2 \quad M_3 \quad M_4$$
$$\nearrow \quad \nearrow \quad \nearrow \quad \nearrow$$
$$B_1 \rightarrow B_2 \rightarrow B_3 \rightarrow B_4$$

Suppose M_1 is the mental state of seeing an apple from a distance of five feet. It is a *mental* state since it involves the conscious awareness of seeing the apple, and conscious awareness is something true of minds and not matter. Now suppose M_2 is the mental state of seeing the apple from one foot, M_3 the state of feeling a pain on the toe, and M_4 the state of hearing a plane fly overhead. B_1 through B_4 are brain states which are associated with each mental state.

Three things stand out immediately. First, B_1 through B_4 stand in rigid physical, causal relations with one another. B_1 causes B_2 and so on. There is no room for a rational agent to intervene in this causal sequence. Mental agents do not act here. The physical level determines all the action. Mental states are mere byproducts of their physical states as smoke is a byproduct of fire.

Second, there is no unified, enduring self at the mental level. According to substance dualism, the self is not identical to its states; it *has* its states. The mind *has* its thoughts and experiences, and the same mind can have two experiences at the same time (hearing a plane and seeing an apple) or it can have one experience followed by another. The *self* is present at both experiences and underlies the change of experiences.

When a leaf goes from green to red, green does not become red. Rather, green leaves and is replaced by red *in* the leaf. The leaf is the same substance present at both ends of the process. When a substance gains or loses properties, *it* remains the same while the properties come and go. They are replaced. Red replaces green. The EPV says that M_1 through M_4 are properties of the body. There is no enduring mental substance which has them. There is just one mental property at one time which leaves and is replaced by another mental property at another time. The "self" is a series of mental events where mental properties are had by physical states.

Third, it is hard to see what sense can be given to intentionality. How is it that M_1 is of or about an apple? M_1 is just a dummy, a free rider on B_1. At best, B_1 would just be a state caused by light waves from the apple but it is hard to see how this would cause M_1 to be really a state *about* that apple. Even if it were, what difference would it make? Any further body states (the act of touching the apple or eating it) would be caused totally by brain states and make no reference to mental states at all.

It should now be clear why epiphenomenalism was ruled out as an inadequate account of the necessary features of rationality. It cannot account for the existence of intentionality, it leaves no room for genuine rational agency to freely choose mental beliefs, and there is no enduring "I" to be present through the process of thought.

But let us waive these problems for the moment. Where would the mind as an emergent property come from? How can mind, the capacity to know truth, and so forth, emerge from mindless, nonrational matter? Remember, mind here is not identical to the brain's structure. If it were, then the view would be some form of crude materialism or, perhaps, some unclear intermediate view between dualism and physicalism. But in either case, the position would be worse than epiphenomenalism, for it would suffer from the same deficiencies as the latter, as well as those raised earlier against physicalism in its pure form.

The EPV holds that mind is a genuine mental property (or series of properties) which supervenes on top of matter. Consider water again. Wetness emerges when hydrogen and oxygen come together into a structure known as H_2O. Wetness is not identical to that structure. Wetness is a simple quality; the structure is a set of relationships which can be quantified (spatial relations, relations of force, which can be given numerical values). So the structure is not the same thing as the wetness. Similarly, the mind is not the same thing as the brain's structure; it supervenes over that structure in the EPV view. So it is a genuinely new entity which must come into being somehow or other.

It does not seem that it could come into being from nothing. For one thing, that would violate a generally accepted principle that something does not come from nothing. Some have disputed this principle, but it still seems reasonable, especially at the macroscopic level and not the level of the microparticles of physics (though I believe it to hold at that level as well). And it is the macroscopic level that is involved when mind emerges, since it emerges over an object the size of a structured brain.

One could respond that the mind is not itself a macroscopic entity—perhaps by saying that

the macro/micro distinction does not hold for minds. But if the EPV view means that mind emerges over a structured brain out of nothing and that this fact is not anchored to the nature of that brain, then it is hard to see why mind emerges time and again over just this type of structured matter and not over a nickel or a bowling pin. The defender of the EPV cannot appeal to the causal efficacy of the mind itself and argue that the mind of a child comes from the mind of its parents, for this allows minds to cause something, and this is not allowed according to the EPV.

At the level of normal-sized macroscopic objects (objects visible to normal sight) things just do not pop in and out of existence. Even if mind is not such an object, its emergence seems to be tied to the brain. And the brain is such an object. So it is not very promising to account for the emergence of mind by saying it comes from nothing.

There is, however, a more promising view. Aristotle taught us long ago that when something new emerges, it does not come from nothing but from potentiality. When a leaf turns from green to red, the red does not simply come into existence; it was already in the leaf potentially. When an apple seed produces apples, the apples were in the seed potentially. In general, when a property emerges in a substance, it comes to actuality from potentiality, not from pure nonbeing. The property was in the substance potentially and when it emerges, it becomes actual.

Mind must somehow be in matter potentially such that when matter reaches a certain stage of development, mind becomes actual. This is a more plausible version of the EPV, but it still has serious difficulties.

First, it is hard to see how this is compatible with the doctrines and motives of physicalism. Physicalism is embraced in part out of a desire to promote science as the ultimate, perhaps only, kind of knowledge. So physicalists often assert that the world is a network of physical causes wherein only physical causality does anything. Further, the world for a physicalist is in principle describable in strictly physical laws. But if mind is potential in matter, then physicalism seems to become some form of panpsychism, the view that mind is ultimate. Matter no longer is describable in terms of familiar physical properties and laws alone. Now it contains elusive mental potentialities.

After wrestling with this problem, Nobel Prize–winning scientist Max Delbruck argued that "our ideas about the objective character of the physical world, and hence of the nature of truth have been revised. In other words, mind looks less psychic and matter looks less materialistic. . . ." So if one admits that mind is potential in matter, then one can no longer hold that reality is exhausted by the spatiotemporal physical universe.

Second, this emergent property view could not rule out the future existence of God. If mind can emerge from matter when a high-level system reaches a certain point of complexity, why is it not possible for a large-scale Mind to emerge at a later period in evolutionary development? In other words, the EPV cannot rule out Hegelianism, the view that mind emerges from matter all the way up to the emergence of God himself. This may sound far-fetched. But the point is that the EPV cannot rule it out, for the emergence of mind over brains is a startling fact which could hardly have been predicted from the properties of matter alone. So why should one think the process of emergence should stop with finite, human minds? Why could not some form of deity emerge, since mind is in some sense a basic constituent of the universe? Christian philosopher Richard Purtill has called this the God-not-yet view. And it should come as no comfort to an atheist, who is trying to save some form of minimal physicalism, to be told that his view seems to imply some form of emergent theism. At the very least, emergent theism cannot be ruled out.

Finally, Clark points out that it is hard to specify just what these potential mental properties

are. Are these potential properties conscious? If so, then why do we have no memory from them when they emerge to form our own minds? Does it really make sense to say that my mind is composed of several particles of mind dust (i.e., little selves which came together to form my own mental life)? If these potential properties are not conscious, how are they still mental? These questions may have an answer, but they are certainly puzzling, and the EPV seems to commit one to the existence of rather odd potential mental properties, odd at least from the standpoint of one who wants to maintain some form of respectable physicalism.

The simple fact is that the existence of mind has always been a problem for the physicalist. As physicalist Paul M. Churchland argues,

> The important point about the standard evolutionary story is that the human species and all of its features are the wholly physical outcome of a purely physical process. . . . If this is the correct account of our origins, then there seems neither need, nor room, to fit any nonphysical substances or properties into our theoretical account of ourselves. We are creatures of matter (*Matter and Consciousness*, p. 21).

Physicalism is false because it fails to adequately handle several general arguments raised against it. And it is self-refuting, for it undercuts the very prerequisites of rational thought itself. Once one grants the existence of mind, then the question arises as to where it came from. The emergent property view is one answer to this question. But it fails as an adequate theory of mind itself, and it postulates either the origin of mind from nothing or its emergence from potentiality in matter. Both options are problematic. Mind appears to be a basic feature of the cosmos, and its origin at a finite level of persons is best explained by postulating a fundamental Mind who gave finite minds being and design. As Calvin put it, the endowments which we possess cannot possibly be from ourselves. They point to the ultimate Mind and ground of rationality himself.

NOTES

1. The identity relation is necessary. That is, for all *x* and all *y*, if *x* is identical to *y*, then, *necessarily, x* is identical to *y*. There is no possible world where one obtains without the other.

2. Again, pains are natural kinds whose essential nature is a conscious feeling, but a conscious feeling is not an essential part of anything physical.

3. An individual pain or type of pain could exist without the presence of any individual physical state existing. Indeed, it is logically possible for a person to exist and have a pain in a completely disembodied state. Thus, persons and their states are not identical to bodies and their states, given that the identity relation is necessary.

4. Private access and incorrigibility are two pieces of evidence for the claim that mental entities are self-presenting. But no physical entity is self presenting.

For Further Reflection

1. Do you accept Moreland's analysis of the mind-body problem? Can you find weaknesses in his rejection of physicalism or acceptance of dualism? Can you think of other alternatives? What do you make of the *panpsychism* hinted at by the view of the physicist Max Delbruck, mentioned in the article? Could matter itself already contain mind?

2. He lists two issues: (1) "Is a human being composed of just one ultimate component or two?" and (2) "If the answer is two, how do these two relate to one another?" Has Moreland given a clear explanation of how dualism solves the second problem? Is physicalism more plausible on this problem?

3. Is Moreland's argument for mathematical entities relevant to the mind-body problem? Explain.

On Functionalism and Materialism   IV.30

PAUL CHURCHLAND

Paul Churchland is a professor of philosophy at the University of California at San Diego. He has written a number of books and articles in philosophy of mind, including *Scientific Realism and the Plasticity of Mind* (1979) and *Matter and Consciousness* (1984) from which this selection is taken. His work has won him a reputation for clarity, fairness, and insight.

In this selection Churchland examines functionalism and the two prominent versions of materialism in philosophy of mind. Reductivism claims that there is an identity of mental states with brain states. Functionalism rejects any one-to-one correlation between mental types and physical types, and concentrates on the relationship between inputs and outputs. For example, the mental event of pain could be similar in two beings that have altogether different types of bodies and brains. Most functionalists are materialists but someone could be a functionalist *and* be a nonmaterialist. Eliminative materialism is more radical than either of these other theories and seeks to eliminate "folk psychology"—talk of beliefs, feelings, and perceptions—in favor of more scientific descriptions of what is going on in the brain. Churchland concludes that the truth may be a combination of the two materialist theories, although the evidence points more in the direction of eliminativism.

Study Questions

1. Why is reductive materialism referred to as the "identity theory"?
2. What is intertheoretic reduction?
3. What are the four arguments for the identity theory?
4. What are the arguments against the identity theory?
5. What is Leibniz's law? Is it always valid?
6. Explain functionalism.
7. What are the main arguments against functionalism?
8. What is eliminative materialism?
9. What does Churchland say are the historical parallels to it?
10. What are the main arguments for eliminativism?
11. What are the main arguments against eliminativism?

I. REDUCTIVE MATERIALISM (THE IDENTITY THEORY)

REDUCTIVE MATERIALISM, more commonly known as *the identity theory,* is the most straight-forward of the several materialist theories of mind. Its central claim is simplicity itself: Mental states *are* physical states of the brain. That is, each type of mental state or process is *numerically identical with* (is one and the very same thing as) some type of physical state or process within the brain or central nervous system. At present we do not know enough about the intricate functionings of the brain actually to state the relevant identities, but the identity theory is committed to the idea that brain research will eventually reveal them. . . .

Historical Parallels

As the identity theorist sees it, the result here predicted has familiar parallels elsewhere in our scientific history. Consider sound. We now know that sound is just a train of compression waves traveling through the air, and that the property of being high pitched is identical with the property of having a high oscillatory frequency. We have learned that light is just electromagnetic waves, and our best current theory says that the color of an object is identical with a triplet of reflectance efficiencies the object has, rather like a musical chord that it strikes, though the "notes" are struck in electromagnetic waves instead of in sound waves. We now appreciate that the warmth or coolness of a body is just the energy of motion of the molecules that make it up: Warmth is identical with high average molecular kinetic energy, and coolness is identical with low average molecular kinetic energy. We know that lightning is identical with a sudden large-scale discharge of electrons between clouds, or between the atmosphere and the ground. What we now think of as "mental states," argues the identity theorist, are identical with brain states in exactly the same way.

Intertheoretic Reduction

These illustrative parallels are all cases of successful *intertheoretic reduction.* That is, they are all

Reprinted from Matter and Consciousness *(Cambridge, MA: MIT Press, 1984) by permission of the author and publisher.*

cases where a new and very powerful theory turns out to entail a set of propositions and principles that mirror perfectly (or almost perfectly) the propositions and principles of some older theory or conceptual framework. The relevant principles entailed by the new theory have the same structure as the corresponding principles of the old framework, and they apply in exactly the same cases. The only difference is that where the old principles contained (for example) the notions of "heat," "is hot," and "is cold," the new principles contain instead the notions of "total molecular kinetic energy," "has a high mean molecular kinetic energy," and "has a low mean molecular kinetic energy."

If the new framework is far better than the old at explaining and predicting phenomena, then we have excellent reason for believing that the theoretical terms of the *new* framework are the terms that describe reality correctly. But if the old framework worked adequately, so far as it went, and if it parallels a portion of the new theory in the systematic way described, then we may properly conclude that the old terms and the new terms refer to the very same things, or express the very same properties. We conclude that we have apprehended the very same reality that is incompletely described by the old framework, but with a new and more penetrating conceptual framework. And we announce what philosophers of science call "intertheoretic identities": light *is* electromagnetic waves, temperature *is* mean molecular kinetic energy, and so forth.

The examples of the preceding two paragraphs share one more important feature in common. They are all cases where the things or properties on the receiving end of the reduction are *observable* things and properties within our *common-sense* conceptual framework. They show that intertheoretic reduction occurs not only between conceptual frameworks in the theoretical stratosphere: common-sense observables can also be reduced. There would therefore be nothing particularly surprising about a reduction of our familiar introspectible mental states to physical states of the brain. All that would be required

would be that an explanatorily successful neuroscience develop to the point where it entails a suitable "mirror image" of the assumptions and principles that constitute our common-sense conceptual framework for mental states, an image where brain-state terms occupy the positions held by mental-state terms in the assumptions and principles of common sense. If this (rather demanding) condition were indeed met, then, as in the historical cases cited, we would be justified in announcing a reduction, and in asserting the identity of mental states with brain states.

Arguments for the Identity Theory

What reasons does the identity theorist have for believing that neuroscience will eventually achieve the strong conditions necessary for the reduction of our "folk" psychology? There are at least four reasons, all directed at the conclusion that the correct account of human-behavior-and-its-causes must reside in the physical neurosciences.

We can point first to the purely physical origins and ostensibly physical constitution of each individual human. One begins as a genetically programmed monocellular organization of molecules (a fertilized ovum), and one develops from there by the accretion of further molecules whose structure and integration is controlled by the information coded in the DNA molecules of the cell nucleus. The result of such a process would be a purely physical system whose behavior arises from its internal operations and its interactions with the rest of the physical world. And those behavior-controlling internal operations are precisely what the neurosciences are about.

This argument coheres with a second argument. The origins of each *type* of animal also appear exhaustively physical in nature. The argument from evolutionary history discussed earlier . . . lends further support to the identity theorist's claim, since evolutionary theory provides the only serious explanation we have for the behavior-controlling capacities of the brain and central nervous system. Those systems were selected for because of the many advantages (ultimately, the reproductive advantage) held by creatures whose behavior was thus controlled. Again our behavior appears to have its basic causes in neural activity.

The identity theorist finds further support in the argument, discussed earlier, from the neural dependence of all known mental phenomena. . . . This is precisely what one should expect, if the identity theory is true. Of course, systematic neural dependence is also a consequence of property dualism, but here the identity theorist will appeal to considerations of simplicity. Why admit two radically different classes of properties and operations if the explanatory job can be done by one?

A final argument derives from the growing success of the neurosciences in unraveling the nervous systems of many creatures and in explaining their behavioral capacities and deficits in terms of the structures discovered. The preceding arguments all suggest that neuroscience should be successful in this endeavor, and the fact is that the continuing history of neuroscience bears them out. Especially in the case of very simple creatures (as one would expect), progress has been rapid. And progress has also been made with humans, though for obvious moral reasons exploration must be more cautious and circumspect. In sum, the neurosciences have a long way to go, but progress to date provides substantial encouragement to the identity theorist.

Even so, these arguments are far from decisive in favor of the identity theory. No doubt they do provide an overwhelming case for the idea that the causes of human and animal behavior are essentially physical in nature, but the identity theory claims more than just this. It claims that neuroscience will discover a taxonomy of neural states that stand in a one-to-one correspondence with the mental states of our common-sense taxonomy. Claims for intertheoretic identity will be justified only if such a match-up can be found. But nothing in the preceding arguments guarantees that the old and new frameworks will match up in this way, even if the new framework is a roaring success at explaining and predicting our behavior. Furthermore, there are arguments from other positions within the materialist camp to the effect that such convenient match-ups are rather unlikely. Before exploring those, however, let us look at some more traditional objections to the identity theory.

Arguments Against the Identity Theory

We may begin with the argument from introspection discussed. Introspection reveals a domain of thoughts, sensations, and emotions, not a domain of electrochemical impulses in a neural network. Mental states and properties, as revealed in introspection, appear radically different from any neurophysiological states and properties. How could they possibly be the very same things?

The answer, as we have already seen, is, "Easily." In discriminating red from blue, sweet from sour, and hot from cold, our external senses are actually discriminating between subtle differences in intricate electromagnetic, stereochemical, and micromechanical properties of physical objects. But our senses are not sufficiently penetrating to reveal on their own the detailed nature of those intricate properties. That requires theoretical research and experimental exploration with specially designed instruments. The same is presumably true of our "inner" sense: introspection. It may discriminate efficiently between a great variety of neural states, without being able to reveal on its own the detailed nature of the states being discriminated. Indeed, it would be faintly miraculous if it did reveal them, just as miraculous as if unaided sight were to reveal the existence of interacting electric and magnetic fields whizzing by with an oscillatory frequency of a million billion hertz and a wavelength of less than a millionth of a meter. For despite "appearances," that is what light is. The argument from introspection, therefore, is quite without force.

The next objection argues that the identification of mental states with brain states would commit us to statements that are literally unintelligible, to what philosophers have called "category errors," and that the identification is therefore a case of sheer conceptual confusion. We may begin the discussion by noting a most important law concerning numerical identity. Leibniz's Law states that two items are numerically identical just in case any property had by either one of them is also had by the other: in logical notation,

$$(x)(y)[(x = y) \equiv (F)(Fx \equiv Fy)]$$

This law suggests a way of refuting the identity theory: find some property that is true of brain states, but not of mental states (or vice versa), and the theory would be exploded.

Spatial properties were often cited to this end. Brain states and processes must of course have some specific spatial location: in the brain as a whole, or in some part of it. And if mental states are identical with brain states, then they must have the very same spatial location. But it is literally meaningless, runs the argument, to say that my feeling-of-pain is located in my ventral thalamus, or that my belief-that-the-sun-is-a-star is located in the temporal lobe of my left cerebral hemisphere. Such claims are as meaningless as the claim that the number 5 is green, or that love weighs twenty grams.

Trying the same move from the other direction, some have argued that it is senseless to ascribe the various *semantic* properties to brain states. Our thoughts and beliefs, for example, have a meaning, a specific propositional content; they are either true or false; and they can enjoy relations such as consistency and entailment. If thoughts and beliefs were brain states, then all these semantic properties would have to be true of brain states. But it is senseless, runs the argument, to say that some resonance in my association cortex is true, or logically entails some other resonance close by, or has the meaning that *P*.

Neither of these moves has the same bite it did twenty years ago, since familiarity with the identity theory and growing awareness of the brain's role have tended to reduce the feelings of semantic oddity produced by the claims at issue. But even if they still struck all of us as semantically confused, this would carry little weight. The claim that sound has a wavelength, or that light has a frequency, must have seemed equally unintelligible in advance of the conviction that both sound and light are wave phenomena. (See, for example, Bishop Berkeley's eighteenth-century dismissal of the idea that sound is a vibratory motion of the air, in Dialogue I of his *Three Dialogues*. The objections are voiced by Philonous.)* The claim that warmth is measured in kilogram • meters^2/seconds^2 would have seemed semantically perverse before we understood that temperature is mean molecular kinetic energy. And Copernicus' sixteenth-century claim that the earth *moves* also struck people as absurd to the point of perversity. It is not difficult to appreciate why. Consider the following argument.

> Copernicus' claim that the earth moves is sheer conceptual confusion. For consider what it *means* to say that something moves: "*x* moves" means "*x* changes position relative to the earth." Thus, to say that the earth moves is to say that the earth changes position relative to itself! Which is absurd. Copernicus' position is therefore an abuse of language.

The *meaning analysis* here invoked might well have been correct, but all that would have meant is that the speaker should have set about changing his meanings. The fact is, any language involves a rich network of assumptions about the structure of the world, and if a sentence *S* provokes intuitions of semantic oddness, that is usually because *S* violates one or more of those background assumptions. But one cannot always reject *S* for that reason alone, since the overthrow of those background assumptions may be precisely what the facts require. The "abuse" of accepted modes of speech is often an essential feature of real scientific progress! Perhaps we shall just have to get used to the idea that mental states have anatomical locations and brain states have semantic properties.

While the charge of sheer senselessness can be put aside, the identity theorist does owe us some account of exactly how physical brain

*Part of this dialogue is reprinted in Reading III.20.

states can have semantic properties. The account currently being explored can be outlined as follows. Let us begin by asking how it is that a particular *sentence* (= utterance type) has the specific propositional content it has: the sentence "La pomme est rouge," for example. Note first that a sentence is always an integrated part of an entire system of sentences: a language. Any given sentence enjoys many relations with countless other sentences: it entails many sentences, is entailed by many others, is consistent with some, is inconsistent with others, provides confirming evidence for yet others, and so forth. And speakers who use that sentence within that language draw inferences in accordance with those relations. Evidently, each sentence (or each set of equivalent sentences) enjoys a unique pattern of such entailment relations: It plays a distinct inferential role in a complex linguistic economy. Accordingly, we say that the sentence "La pomme est rouge" has the propositional content, *the apple is red*, because the sentence "La pomme est rouge" plays *the same role* in French that the sentence "The apple is red" plays in English. To have the relevant propositional content is just to play the relevant inferential role in a cognitive economy.

Returning now to types of brain states, there is no problem in principle in assuming that one's brain is the seat of a complex inferential economy in which types of brain states are the role-playing elements. According to the theory of meaning just sketched, such states would then have propositional content, since having content is not a matter of whether the contentful item is a pattern of sound, a pattern of letters on paper, a set of raised Braille bumps, or a pattern of neural activity. What matters is the inferential role the item plays. Propositional content, therefore, seems within the reach of brain states after all. We began this subsection with an argument against materialism that appealed to the qualitative *nature* of our mental states, as revealed in introspection. The next argument appeals to the simple fact that they are introspectible at all.

1. My mental states are introspectively known by me as states of my conscious self.
2. My brain states are *not* introspectively known by me as states of my conscious self.

Therefore, by Leibniz's Law (that numerically identical things must have exactly the same properties),

3. My mental states are not identical with my brain states.

This, in my experience, is the most beguiling form of the argument from introspection, seductive of freshmen and faculty alike. But it is a straightforward instance of a well-known fallacy, which is clearly illustrated in the following parallel arguments:

1. Muhammad Ali is widely known as a heavyweight champion.
2. Cassius Clay is *not* widely known as a heavyweight champion.

Therefore, by Leibniz's Law,

3. Muhammad Ali is not identical with Cassius Clay.

or,

1. Aspirin is recognized by John to be a pain reliever.
2. Acetylsalicylic acid is *not* recognized by John to be a pain reliever.

Therefore, by Leibniz's Law,

3. Aspirin is not identical with acetylsalicylic acid.

Despite the truth of the relevant premises, both conclusions are false: the identities are wholly genuine. Which means that both arguments are invalid. The problem is that the "property" ascribed in premise (1), and withheld in premise (2), consists only in the subject item's being *recognized, perceived,* or *known* as something-or-other. But such apprehension is not a genuine property of the item itself, fit for divining identities, since one and the same subject may be successfully recognized under one name or description, and yet fail to be recognized under another (accurate, coreferential) description. Bluntly, Leibniz's Law is not valid for these bogus "properties." The attempt to use them as above commits what logicians call an *intensional* fallacy. The premises may reflect, not the failure of certain objective identities, but only our continuing failure to appreciate them.

A different version of the preceding argument must also be considered, since it may be urged that one's brain states are more than merely not (yet) known by introspection: they are not know *able* by introspection under any circumstances. Thus,

1. My mental states are knowable by introspection.
2. My brain states are *not* knowable by introspection.

Therefore, by Leibniz's Law,

3. My mental states are not identical with my brain states.

Here the critic will insist that being know *able* by introspection *is* a genuine property of a thing, and that this modified version of the argument is free of the "intensional fallacy" discussed above.

And so it is. But now the materialist is in a position to insist that the argument contains a false premise—premise (2). For if mental states are indeed brain states, then it is really brain states we have been introspecting all along, though without fully appreciating what they are. And if we can learn to think of and recognize those states under mentalistic descriptions, as we all have, then we can certainly learn to think of and recognize them under their more penetrating neurophysiological descriptions. At the very least, premise (2) simply begs the question against the identity theorist. The mistake is amply illustrated in the following parallel argument:

1. Temperature is knowable by feeling.
2. Mean molecular kinetic energy is *not* knowable by feeling.

Therefore, by Leibniz's Law,

3. Temperature is not identical with mean molecular kinetic energy.

This identity, at least, is long established, and this argument is certainly unsound: premise (2) is false. Just as one can learn to feel that the summer air is about 70° F, or 21° C, so one can learn to feel that the mean KE of its molecules is about 6.2×10^{-21} joules, for whether we realize it or not, that is what our discriminatory mechanisms are keyed to. Perhaps our brain states are similarly accessible. . . .

Consider now a final argument, again based on the introspectible qualities of our sensations. Imagine a future neuroscientist who comes to know everything there is to know about the physical structure and activity of the brain and its visual system, of its actual and possible states. If for some reason she has never actually *had* a sensation-of-red (because of color blindness, say, or an unusual environment), then there will remain something she does *not* know about certain sensations: *what it is like to have a sensation-of-red.* Therefore, complete knowledge of the physical facts of visual perception and its related brain activity still leaves something out. Accordingly, materialism cannot give an adequate account of all mental phenomena, and the identity theory must be false.

The identity theorist can reply that this argument exploits an unwitting equivocation on the term "know." Concerning our neuroscientist's utopian knowledge of the brain, "knows" means something like "has mastered the relevant set of neuroscientific propositions." Concerning her (missing) knowledge of what it is like to have a sensation-of-red, "knows" means something like "has a prelinguistic representation of redness in her mechanisms for noninferential discrimination." It is true that one might have the former without the latter, but the materialist is not committed to the idea that having knowledge in the former sense automatically constitutes having knowledge in the second sense. The identity theorist can admit a duality, or even a plurality, of different *types of knowledge* without thereby committing himself to a duality in *types of things known*. The difference between a person who knows all about the visual cortex but has never enjoyed the sensation-of-red, and a person who knows no neuroscience but knows well the sensation-of-red, may reside not in *what* is respectively known by each (brain states by the former, nonphysical *qualia* by the latter), but rather in the different *type*, or *medium*, or *level* of representation each has of exactly the same thing: brain states.

In sum, there are pretty clearly more ways of "having knowledge" than just having mastered a set of sentences, and the materialist can freely admit that one has "knowledge" of one's sensations in a way that is independent of the neuroscience one may have learned. Animals, including humans, presumably have a prelinguistic mode of sensory representation. This does not mean that sensations are beyond the reach of physical science. *It just means that the brain uses more modes and media of representation than the mere storage of sentences.* All the identity theorist needs to claim is that those other modes of representation will also yield to neuroscientific explanation.

The identity theory has proved to be very resilient in the face of these predominantly antimaterialist objections. But further objections, rooted in competing forms of materialism, constitute a much more serious threat, as the following sections will show.

II. FUNCTIONALISM

According to *functionalism*, the essential or defining feature of any type of mental state is the set of causal relations it bears to (1) environmental effects on the body, (2) other types of mental states, and (3) bodily behavior. Pain, for example, characteristically results from some bodily damage or trauma; it causes distress, annoyance, and practical reasoning aimed at relief; and it causes wincing, blanching, and nursing of the traumatized area. Any state that plays exactly that functional role is a pain, according to functionalism. Similarly, other types of mental states (sensations, fears, beliefs, and so on) are also defined by their unique causal roles in a complex economy of internal states mediating sensory inputs and behavioral outputs.

This view may remind the reader of behaviorism, and indeed it is the heir to behaviorism, but there is one fundamental difference between the two theories. Where the behaviorist hoped to define each type of mental state solely in terms of environmental input and behavioral output, the functionalist denies that this is possible. As he sees it, the adequate characterization of almost any mental state involves an ineliminable reference to a variety of other mental states with which it is causally connected, and so a reductive definition solely in terms of publicly observable inputs and outputs is quite impossible. Functionalism is therefore immune to one of the main objections against behaviorism.

Thus the difference between functionalism and behaviorism. The difference between functionalism and the identity theory will emerge from the following argument raised against the identity theory.

Imagine a being from another planet, says the functionalist, a being with an alien physiological constitution, a constitution based on the chemical element silicon, for example, instead of on the element carbon, as ours is. The chemistry and even the physical structure of the alien's brain would have to be systematically different from ours. But even so, that alien brain could well sustain a functional economy of internal states whose mutual *relations* parallel perfectly the mutual relations that define our own mental states. The alien may have an internal state that meets all the conditions for being a pain state, as outlined earlier. That state, considered from a purely physical point of view, would have a very different makeup from a human pain state, but it could nevertheless be identical to a human pain state from a purely functional point of view. And so for all of his functional states.

If the alien's functional economy of internal states were indeed *functionally isomorphic* with our own internal economy—if those states were causally connected to inputs, to one another, and to behavior in ways that parallel our own internal connections—then the alien would have pains, and desires, and hopes, and fears just as fully as we, despite the differences in the physical system that sustains or realizes those functional states. What is important for mentality is not the matter of which the creature is made, but the structure of the internal activities which that matter sustains.

If we can think of one alien constitution, we can think of many, and the point just made can also be made with an artificial system. Were we to create an electronic system—a computer of some kind—whose internal economy were functionally isomorphic with our own in all the relevant ways, then it too would be the subject of mental states.

What this illustrates is that there are almost certainly many more ways than one for nature, and perhaps even for man, to put together a thinking, feeling, perceiving creature. And this raises a problem for the identity theory, for it seems that there is no single type of physical state to which a given type of mental state must always correspond. Ironically, there are *too many* different kinds of physical systems that can realize the functional economy characteristic of conscious intelligence. If we consider the universe at large, therefore, and the future as well as the present, it seems quite unlikely that the identity theorist is going to find the one-to-one match-ups between the concepts of our common-sense mental taxonomy and the concepts of an overarching theory that encompasses all of the relevant physical systems. But that is what intertheoretic reduction is standardly said to require. The prospects for universal identities, between types of mental states and types of brain states, are therefore slim.

If the functionalists reject the traditional "mental-type = physical type" identity theory, virtually all of them remain committed to a weaker "mental token = physical token" identity theory, for they still maintain that each *instance* of a given type of mental state is numerically identical with some specific physical state in some physical system or other. It is only universal (type/type) identities that are rejected. Even so, this rejection is typically taken to support the claim that the science of psychology is or should be *methodologically autonomous* from the various physical sciences such as physics, biology, and even neurophysiology. Psychology, it is claimed, has its own irreducible laws and its own abstract subject matter.

As this book is written, functionalism is probably the most widely held theory of mind among philosophers, cognitive psychologists, and artificial intelligence researchers. Some of the reasons are apparent from the preceding discussion, and there are further reasons as well. In characterizing mental states as essentially functional states, functionalism places the concerns of psychology at a level that abstracts from the teeming detail of a brain's neurophysiological (or crystallographic, or microelectronic) structure. The science of psychology, it is occasionally said, is methodologically autonomous from those other sciences (biology, neuroscience, circuit theory) whose concerns are with what amount to engineering details. This provides a rationale for a great deal of work in cognitive psychology and artificial intelligence, where researchers postulate a system of abstract functional states and then test the postulated system, often by way of its computer simulation, against human behavior in similar circumstances. The aim of such work is to discover in detail the functional organization that makes us what we are.

Arguments Against Functionalism

Current popularity aside, functionalism also faces difficulties. The most commonly posed objection cites an old friend: sensory qualia. Functionalism may escape one of behaviorism's fatal flaws, it is said, but it still falls prey to the other. By attempting to make its *relational* properties the definitive feature of any mental state, functionalism ignores the "inner" or qualitative nature of our mental states. But their qualitative nature is the essential feature of a great many types of mental state (pain, sensations of color, of temperature, of pitch, and so on), runs the objection, and functionalism is therefore false.

The standard illustration of this apparent failing is called "the inverted spectrum thought-experiment." It is entirely conceivable, runs the story, that the range of color sensations that I enjoy upon viewing standard objects is simply inverted relative to the color sensations that you enjoy. When viewing a tomato, I may have what is really a sensation-of-green where you have the normal sensation-of-red; when viewing a banana, I may have what is really sensation-of-blue where you have the normal sensation-of- yellow; and so forth. But since we have no way of comparing our inner qualia, and since I shall make all the same observational discriminations among objects that you will, there is no way to tell whether my spectrum is inverted relative to yours.

The problem for functionalism arises as follows. Even if my spectrum is inverted relative to yours, we remain functionally isomorphic with one another. My visual sensation upon viewing a tomato is *functionally* identical with your visual sensation upon viewing a tomato. According to functionalism, therefore, they are the very same type of state, and it does not even make sense to suppose that my sensation is "really" a sensation- of-green. If it meets the functional conditions for being a sensation-of-red, then by definition it is a sensation-of-red. According to functionalism, apparently, a spectrum inversion of the kind described is ruled out by definition. But such inversions are entirely conceivable, concludes the objection, and if functionalism entails that they are not conceivable, then functionalism is false.

Another qualia-related worry for functionalism is the so-called "absent qualia problem." The functional organization characteristic of

conscious intelligence can be instantiated (= realized or instanced) in a considerable variety of physical systems, some of them radically different from a normal human. For example, a giant electronic computer might instantiate it, and there are more radical possibilities still. One writer asks us to imagine the people of China—all 10^9 of them— organized into an intricate game of mutual interactions so that collectively they constitute a giant brain which exchanges inputs and outputs with a single robot body. That system of the robot-plus-10^9-unit-brain could presumably instantiate the relevant functional organization (though no doubt it would be much slower in its activities than a human or a computer), and would therefore be the subject of mental states, according to functionalism. But surely, it is urged, the complex states that there play the functional roles of pain, pleasure, and sensations-of-color would not have intrinsic qualia as ours do, and would therefore fail to be genuine mental states. Again, functionalism seems at best an incomplete account of the nature of mental states.

It has recently been argued that both the inverted-qualia and the absent-qualia objections can be met, without violence to functionalism and without significant violence to our common-sense intuitions about qualia. Consider the inversion problem first. I think the functionalist is right to insist that the type-identity of our visual sensations be reckoned according to their functional role. But the objector is also right in insisting that a relative inversion of two people's qualia, without functional inversion, is entirely conceivable. The apparent inconsistency between these positions can be dissolved by insisting that (1) our functional states (or rather, their physical realizations) do indeed have an intrinsic nature on which our introspective identification of those states depends, while also insisting that (2) such intrinsic natures are nevertheless not essential to the type-identity of a given mental state, and may indeed *vary* from instance to instance of the same type of mental state.

What this means is that the qualitative character of your sensation-of-red might be different from the qualitative character of my sensation-of-red, slightly or substantially, and a third person's sensation-of-red might be different again. But so long as all three states are standardly caused by red objects and standardly cause all three of us to believe that something is red, then all three states are sensations-of-red, whatever their intrinsic qualitative character. Such intrinsic qualia merely serve as salient features that permit the quick introspective identification of sensations, as black-on-orange stripes serve as a salient feature for the quick visual identification of tigers. But specific qualia are not essential to the type-identity of mental states, any more than black-on-orange stripes are essential to the type-identity of tigers.

Plainly, this solution requires the functionalist to admit the *reality* of qualia, and we may wonder how there can be room for qualia in his materialist world-picture. Perhaps they can be fit in as follows: *identify* them with physical properties of whatever physical states instantiate the mental (functional) states that display them. For example, identify the qualitative nature of your sensations-of-red with that physical feature (of the brain state that instantiates it) to which your mechanisms of introspective discrimination are in fact responding when you judge that you have a sensation-of-red. If materialism is true, then there must *be* some internal physical feature or other to which your discrimination of sensations-of-red is keyed: *that* is the quale of your sensations-of-red. If the pitch of a sound can turn out to be the frequency of an oscillation in air pressure, there is no reason why the quale of a sensation cannot turn out to be, say, a spiking frequency in a certain neural pathway. ("Spikes" are the tiny electrochemical pulses by which our brain cells communicate.)

This entails that creatures with a constitution different from ours may have qualia different from ours, despite being psychologically isomorphic with us. It does not entail that they *must* have different qualia, however. If the qualitative character of my sensation-of-red is really a spiking frequency of 90 hertz in a certain neural pathway, it is possible that an electromechanical robot might enjoy the very same qualitative character if, in reporting sensations-of-red, the robot were responding to a spiking frequency of 90 hertz in a corresponding *copper* pathway. It might be the spiking frequency that matters to our respective mechanisms of discrimination, not the nature of the medium that carries it. This proposal also suggests a solution to the absent qualia problem. So long as the physical system at issue is functionally isomorphic with us, to the last detail, then it will be equally capable of subtle introspective discriminations among its sensations. Those discriminations must be made on some systematic physical basis, that is, on some characteristic physical features of the states being discriminated. Those features at the objective focus of the system's discriminatory mechanisms, *those* are its sensory qualia—though the alien system is no more likely to appreciate their true physical nature than we appreciate the true physical nature of our own qualia. Sensory qualia are therefore an inevitable concomitant of any system with the kind of functional organization at issue. It may be difficult or impossible to "see" the qualia in an alien system, but it is equally difficult to "see" them even when looking into a human brain.

I leave it to the reader to judge the adequacy of these responses. If they are adequate, then, given its other virtues, functionalism must be conceded a very strong position among the competing contemporary theories of mind. It is interesting, however, that the defense offered in the last paragraph found it necessary to take a leaf from the identity theorist's book (types of quale are reduced to or identified with types of physical state), since the final objection we shall consider also tends to blur the distinction between functionalism and reductive materialism.

Consider the property of *temperature*, runs the objection. Here we have a paradigm of a physical property, one that has also been cited as the paradigm of a successfully *reduced* property, as expressed in the intertheoretic identity

"temperature = mean kinetic energy of constituent molecules."

Strictly speaking, however, this identity is true only for the temperature of a gas, where simple particles are free to move in ballistic fashion. In a *solid*, temperature is realized differently, since the interconnected molecules are confined to a variety of vibrational motions. In a *plasma*, temperature is something else again, since a plasma has no constituent molecules; they, and their constituent atoms, have been ripped to pieces. And even a *vacuum* has a so-called "blackbody" temperature—in the distribution of electromagnetic waves coursing through it. Here temperature has nothing to do with the kinetic energy of particles.

It is plain that the physical property of temperature enjoys "multiple instantiations" no less than do psychological properties. Does this mean that thermodynamics (the theory of heat and temperature) is an "autonomous science," separable from the rest of physics, with its own irreducible laws and its own abstract nonphysical subject matter?

Presumably not. What it means, concludes the objection, is that *reductions are domain-specific:*

temperature-in-a-gas
    = mean kinetic energy of
        the gas's molecules,

whereas

temperature-in-a-vacuum
    = blackbody distribution of the vacuum's
        transient radiation.

Similarly, perhaps

joy-in-a-human = resonances in the lateral
                hypothalamus,

whereas

joy-in-a-Martian = something else entirely.

This means that we may expect some type/type reductions of mental states to physical states after all, though they will be much narrower than was first suggested. Furthermore, it means that functionalist claims concerning the radical autonomy of psychology cannot be sustained. And last, it suggests that functionalism is not so profoundly different from the identity theory as was first made out.

As with the defense of functionalism outlined earlier, I leave the evaluation of this criticism to the reader. We shall have occasion for further discussion of functionalism in later chapters. At this point, let us turn to the final materialist theory of mind, for functionalism is not the only major reaction against the identity theory.

III. ELIMINATIVE MATERIALISM

The identity theory was called into doubt not because the prospects for a materialist account of our mental capacities were thought to be poor, but because it seemed unlikely that the arrival of an adequate materialist theory would bring with it the nice one-to-one match-ups, between the concepts of folk psychology and the concepts of theoretical neuroscience, that intertheoretic reduction requires. The reason for that doubt was the great variety of quite different physical systems that could instantiate the required functional organization. *Eliminative materialism* also doubts that the correct neuroscientific account of human capacities will produce a neat reduction of our commonsense framework, but here the doubts arise from a quite different source.

As the eliminative materialists see it, the one-to-one match-ups will not be found, and our common-sense psychological framework will not enjoy an intertheoretic reduction, *because our common-sense psychological framework is a false and radically misleading conception of the causes of human behavior and the nature of cognitive activity.* On this view, folk psychology is not just an incomplete representation of our inner natures; it is an outright *mis*representation of our internal states and activities. Consequently, we cannot expect a truly adequate neuroscientific account of our inner lives to provide theoretical categories that match up nicely with the categories of our common-sense framework. Accordingly, we must expect that the older framework will simply be eliminated, rather than be reduced, by a matured neuroscience.

Historical Parallels

As the identity theorist can point to historical cases of successful intertheoretic reduction, so the eliminative materialist can point to historical cases of the outright elimination of the ontology of an older theory in favor of the ontology of a new and superior theory. For most of the eighteenth and nineteenth centuries, learned people believed that heat was a subtle *fluid* held in bodies, much in the way water is held in a sponge. A fair body of moderately successful theory described the way this fluid substance—called "caloric"—flowed within a body, or from one body to another, and how it produced thermal expansion, melting, boiling, and so forth. But by the end of the last century it had become abundantly clear that heat was not a substance at all, but just the energy of motion of the trillions of jostling molecules that make up the heated body itself. The new theory—the "corpuscular/kinetic theory of matter and heat"—was much more successful than the old in explaining and predicting the thermal behavior of bodies. And since we were unable to *identify* caloric fluid with kinetic energy (according to the old theory, caloric is a material *substance;* according to the new theory, kinetic energy is a form of *motion*), it was finally agreed that there is *no such thing* as caloric. Caloric was simply eliminated from our accepted ontology.

A second example. It used to be thought that when a piece of wood burns, or a piece of metal rusts, a spiritlike substance called "phlogiston" was being released: briskly, in the former case, slowly in the latter. Once gone, that "noble" substance left only a base pile of ash or rust. It later came to be appreciated that both processes involve, not the loss of something, but the *gaining* of a substance taken from the atmosphere: oxygen. Phlogiston emerged, not as an incomplete description of what was going on, but as a radical misdescription. Phlogiston was therefore not suitable for reduction to or identification with some notion from within the new oxygen chemistry, and it was simply eliminated from science. Admittedly, both of these examples concern the elimination of something nonobservable, but our history also includes the elimination of certain widely accepted "observables." Before Copernicus' views became available, almost any human who ventured out at night could look up at *the starry sphere of the heavens,* and if he stayed for more than a few minutes he could also see that it *turned,* around an axis through Polaris. What the sphere was made of (crystal?) and what made it turn (the gods?) were theoretical questions that exercised us for over two millennia. But hardly anyone doubted the existence of what everyone could observe with their own eyes. In the end, however, we learned to reinterpret our visual experience of the night sky within a very different conceptual framework, and the turning sphere evaporated.

Witches provide another example. Psychosis is a fairly common affliction among humans, and in earlier centuries its victims were standardly seen as cases of demonic possession, as instances of Satan's spirit itself, glaring malevolently out at us from behind the victims' eyes. That witches exist was not a matter of any controversy. One would occasionally see them, in any city or hamlet, engaged in incoherent, paranoid, or even murderous behavior. But observable or not, we eventually decided that witches simply do not exist. We concluded that the concept of a witch is an element in a conceptual framework that misrepresents so badly the phenomena to which it was standardly applied that literal application of the notion should be permanently withdrawn. Modern theories of mental dysfunction led to the elimination of witches from our serious ontology.

The concepts of folk psychology—belief, desire, fear, sensation, pain, joy, and so on—await a similar fate, according to the view at issue. And when neuroscience has matured to the point where the poverty of our current conceptions is apparent to everyone, and the superiority of the new framework is established, we shall then be able to set about *re*conceiving our internal states and activities, within a truly adequate conceptual framework at last. Our explanations of one another's behavior will appeal to such things as our neuropharmacological states, the neural activity in specialized anatomical areas, and whatever other states are deemed relevant by the new theory. Our private introspection will also be transformed, and may be profoundly enhanced by reason of the more accurate and penetrating framework it will have to work with—just as the astronomer's perception of the night sky is much enhanced by the detailed knowledge of modern astronomical theory that he or she possesses.

The magnitude of the conceptual revolution here suggested should not be minimized: it would be enormous. And the benefits to humanity might be equally great. If each of us possessed an accurate neuroscientific understanding of (what we now conceive dimly as) the varieties and causes of mental illness, the factors involved in learning, the neural basis of emotions, intelligence, and socialization, then the sum total of human misery might be much reduced. The simple increase in mutual understanding that the new framework made possible could contribute substantially toward a more peaceful and humane society. Of course, there would be dangers as well: increased knowledge means increased power, and power can always be misused.

Arguments for Eliminative Materialism

The arguments for eliminative materialism are diffuse and less than decisive, but they are stronger than is widely supposed. The distinguishing feature of this position is its denial that a smooth intertheoretic reduction is to be expected—even a species-specific reduction—of the framework of folk psychology to the framework of a matured neuroscience. The reason for this denial is the eliminative materialist's conviction that folk psychology is a hopelessly primitive and deeply confused conception of our internal activities. But why this low opinion of our common-sense conceptions?

There are at least three reasons. First, the eliminative materialist will point to the widespread ex-

planatory, predictive, and manipulative failures of folk psychology. So much of what is central and familiar to us remains a complete mystery from within folk psychology. We do not know what *sleep* is, or why we have to have it, despite spending a full third of our lives in that condition. (The answer, "For rest," is mistaken. Even if people are allowed to rest continuously, their need for sleep is undiminished. Apparently, sleep serves some deeper functions, but we do not yet know what they are.) We do not understand how *learning* transforms each of us from a gaping infant to a cunning adult, or how differences in *intelligence* are grounded. We have not the slightest idea how *memory* works, or how we manage to retrieve relevant bits of information instantly from the awesome mass we have stored. We do not know what *mental illness* is, nor how to cure it.

In sum, the most central things about us remain almost entirely mysterious from within folk psychology. And the defects noted cannot be blamed on inadequate time allowed for their correction, for folk psychology has enjoyed no significant changes or advances in well over 2,000 years, despite its manifest failures. Truly successful theories may be expected to reduce, but significantly unsuccessful theories merit no such expectation.

This argument from explanatory poverty has a further aspect. So long as one sticks to normal brains, the poverty of folk psychology is perhaps not strikingly evident. But as soon as one examines the many perplexing behavioral and cognitive deficits suffered by people with *damaged* brains, one's descriptive and explanatory resources start to claw the air. . . . As with other humble theories asked to operate successfully in unexplored extensions of their old domain (for example, Newtonian mechanics in the domain of velocities close to the velocity of light, and the classical gas law in the domain of high pressures or temperatures), the descriptive and explanatory inadequacies of folk psychology become starkly evident.

The second argument tries to draw an inductive lesson from our conceptual history. Our early folk theories of motion were profoundly confused, and were eventually displaced entirely by more sophisticated theories. Our early folk theories of the structure and activity of the heavens were wildly off the mark, and survive only as historical lessons in how wrong we can be. Our folk theories of the nature of fire, and the nature of life, were similarly cockeyed. And one could go on, since the vast majority of our past folk conceptions have been similarly exploded. All except folk psychology, which survives to this day and has only recently begun to feel pressure. But the phenomenon of conscious intelligence is surely a more complex and difficult phenomenon than any of those just listed. So far as accurate understanding is concerned, it would be a *miracle* if we had got *that* one right the very first time, when we fell down so badly on all the others. Folk psychology has survived for so very long, presumably, not because it is basically correct in its representations, but because the phenomena addressed are so surpassingly difficult that any useful handle on them, no matter how feeble, is unlikely to be displaced in a hurry.

A third argument attempts to find an a priori advantage for eliminative materialism over the identity theory and functionalism. It attempts to counter the common intuition that eliminative materialism is distantly possible, perhaps, but is much less probable than either the identity theory or functionalism. The focus again is on whether the concepts of folk psychology will find vindicating match-ups in a matured neuroscience. The eliminativist bets no; the other two bet yes. (Even the functionalist bets yes, but expects the match-ups to be only species-specific, or only person-specific. Functionalism, recall, denies the existence of *universal* type/type identities.)

The eliminativist will point out that the requirements on a reduction are rather demanding. The new theory must entail a set of principles and embedded concepts that mirrors very closely the specific conceptual structure to be reduced. And the fact is, there are vastly many more ways of being an explanatorily successful neuroscience while *not* mirroring the structure of folk psychology, than there are ways of being an explanatorily successful neuroscience while also *mirroring* the

very specific structure of folk psychology. Accordingly, the a priori probability of eliminative materialism is not lower, but substantially *higher* than that of either of its competitors. One's initial intuitions here are simply mistaken.

Granted, this initial a priori advantage could be reduced if there were a very strong presumption in favor of the truth of folk psychology—true theories are better bets to win reduction. But according to the first two arguments, the presumptions on this point should run in precisely the opposite direction.

Arguments Against Eliminative Materialism

The initial plausibility of this rather radical view is low for almost everyone, since it denies deeply entrenched assumptions. That is at best a question-begging complaint, of course, since those assumptions are precisely what is at issue. But the following line of thought does attempt to mount a real argument.

Eliminative materialism is false, runs the argument, because one's introspection reveals directly the existence of pains, beliefs, desires, fears, and so forth. Their existence is as obvious as anything could be.

The eliminative materialist will reply that this argument makes the same mistake that an ancient or medieval person would be making if he insisted that he could just see with his own eyes that the heavens form a turning sphere, or that witches exist. The fact is, all observation occurs within some system of concepts, and our observation judgments are only as good as the conceptual framework in which they are expressed. In all three cases—the starry sphere, witches, and the familiar mental states—precisely what is challenged is the integrity of the background conceptual frameworks in which the observation judgments are expressed. To insist on the validity of one's experiences, *traditionally interpreted*, is therefore to beg the very question at issue. For in all three cases, the question is whether we should *re*conceive the nature of some familiar observational domain.

A second criticism attempts to find an incoherence in the eliminative materialist's position. The bald statement of eliminative materialism is that the familiar mental states do not really exist. But that statement is meaningful, runs the argument, only if it is the expression of a certain *belief,* and an *intention* to communicate, and a *knowledge* of the language, and so forth. But if the statement is true, then no such mental states exist, and the statement is therefore a meaningless string of marks or noises, and cannot be true. Evidently, the assumption that eliminative materialism is true entails that it cannot be true.

The hole in this argument is the premise concerning the conditions necessary for a statement to be meaningful. It begs the question. If eliminative materialism is true, then meaningfulness must have some different source. To insist on the "old" source is to insist on the validity of the very framework at issue. Again, an historical parallel may be helpful here. Consider the medieval theory that being biologically *alive* is a matter of being ensouled by an immaterial *vital spirit.* And consider the following response to someone who has expressed disbelief in that theory.

> My learned friend has stated that there is no such thing as vital spirit. But this statement is incoherent. For if it is true, then my friend does not have vital spirit, and must therefore be *dead.* But if he is dead, then his statement is just a string of noises, devoid of meaning or truth. Evidently, the assumption that antivitalism is true entails that it cannot be true! Q.E.D.

This second argument is now a joke, but the first argument begs the question in exactly the same way.

A final criticism draws a much weaker conclusion, but makes a rather stronger case. Eliminative materialism, it has been said, is making mountains out of molehills. It exaggerates the defects in folk psychology, and underplays its real successes. Perhaps the arrival of a matured neuroscience will require the elimination of the occasional folk-psychological concept, continues the criticism, and a minor adjustment in certain folk-psychological principles may have to be endured. But the large-scale elimination forecast by the eliminative materialist is just an alarmist worry or a romantic enthusiasm.

Perhaps this complain is correct. And perhaps it is merely complacent. Whichever, it does bring out the important point that we do not confront two simple and mutually exclusive possibilities here: pure reduction versus pure elimination. Rather, these are the end points of a smooth spectrum of possible outcomes, between which there are mixed cases of partial elimination and partial reduction. Only empirical research . . . can tell us where on that spectrum our own case will fall. Perhaps we should speak here, more liberally, of "revisionary materialism," instead of concentrating on the more radical possibility of an across-the-board elimination. Perhaps we should. But it has been my aim in this section to make it at least intelligible to you that our collective conceptual destiny lies substantially toward the revolutionary end of the spectrum.

For Further Reflection

1. Evaluate the arguments for and against reductive and eliminative materialism. Do you agree with Churchland's assessment? Explain.

2. Try to imagine how we would describe our beliefs, perceptions, feelings, and desires within an eliminative framework. Describe two people talking to each other who have just fallen in love. Eliminative materialism does sound revolutionary, but the question is, is it true?

3. Evaluate functionalism. Why is it attractive to many philosophers of mind?

4. Compare the three theories discussed in this article with dualism. What are the strengths and weaknesses of each?

What Is It Like to Be a Bat?   IV.31

THOMAS NAGEL

Thomas Nagel is professor of philosophy at New York University and the author of several works in ethics and philosophy of mind, including *The View from Nowhere* (1986). Much of Nagel's work involves showing the incongruities between objective and subjective perspectives, especially between the scientific explanation of humanness and our subjective experience of it. Something vital is lost in the reduction of mental states to brain states.

In this article Nagel argues against the view that the objective perspective is the correct one. He contends that the peculiarity of the subjective character experience is that increased objectivity actually takes us further from its real nature.

Study Questions

1. What is Nagel's main concern in this article?
2. What is the "subjective character of experience," according to Nagel?
3. How does the bat serve as an example of Nagel's thesis? Why does he choose a bat to illustrate his thesis?
4. Does Nagel think we can be aware of facts without being able to express or comprehend them? Give some examples.
5. What is Nagel's speculative proposal regarding bridging the gap between the subjective and the objective?

CONSCIOUSNESS IS WHAT MAKES the mind-body problem really intractable. Perhaps that is why current discussions of the problem give it little attention or get it obviously wrong. The recent wave of reductionist euphoria has produced several analyses of mental phenomena and mental concepts designed to explain the possibility of some variety of materialism, psychophysical identification, or reduction. But the problems dealt with are those common to this type of reduction and other types, and what makes the mind-body problem unique, and unlike the water–H_2O problem or the Turing machine–IBM machine problem or the lightning–electrical discharge problem or the gene-DNA problem or the oak tree–hydrocarbon problem, is ignored. Every reductionist has his favorite analogy from modern science. It is most unlikely that any of these unrelated examples of successful reduction will shed light on the relation of mind to brain. But philosophers share the general human weakness for explanations of what is incomprehensible in terms suited for what is familiar and well understood, though entirely different. This has led to the acceptance of implausible accounts of the mental largely because they would permit familiar kinds of reduction. I shall try to explain why the usual examples do not help us to understand the relation between mind and body—why, indeed, we have at present no conception of what an explanation of the physical

From Thomas Nagel, *"What Is It Like to Be a Bat,"* in Philosophical Review *(October 1974)*. *Reprinted by permission of the author. Footnotes edited.*

nature of a mental phenomenon would be. Without consciousness the mind-body problem would be much less interesting. With consciousness it seems hopeless. The most important and characteristic feature of conscious mental phenomena is very poorly understood. Most reductionist theories do not even try to explain it. And careful examination will show that no currently available concept of reduction is applicable to it. Perhaps a new theoretical form can be devised for the purpose, but such a solution, if it exists, lies in the distant intellectual future.

Conscious experience is a widespread phenomenon. It occurs at many levels of animal life, though we cannot be sure of its presence in the simpler organisms, and it is very difficult to say in general what provides evidence of it. (Some extremists have been prepared to deny it even of mammals other than man.) No doubt it occurs in countless forms totally unimaginable to us, on other planets in other solar systems throughout the universe. But no matter how the form may vary, the fact that an organism has conscious experience *at all* means, basically, that there is something it is like to *be* that organism. There may be further implications about the form of the experience; there may even (though I doubt it) be implications about the behavior of the organism. But fundamentally an organism has conscious mental states if and only if there is something that it is like to *be* that organism—something it is like *for* the organism.

We may call this the subjective character of experience. It is not captured by any of the familiar, recently devised reductive analyses of the mental, for all of them are logically compatible with its absence. It is not analyzable in terms of any explanatory system of functional states, or intentional states, since these could be ascribed to robots or automata that behaved like people though they experienced nothing. It is not analyzable in terms of the causal role of experiences in relation to typical human behavior—for similar reasons. I do not deny that conscious mental states and events cause behavior, nor that they may be given functional characterizations. I deny

only that this kind of thing exhausts their analysis. Any reductionist program has to be based on an analysis of what is to be reduced. If the analysis leaves something out, the problem will be falsely posed. It is useless to base the defense of materialism on any analysis of mental phenomena that fails to deal explicitly with their subjective character. For there is no reason to suppose that a reduction which seems plausible when no attempt is made to account for consciousness can be extended to include consciousness. Without some idea, therefore, of what the subjective character of experience is, we cannot know what is required of physicalist theory.

While an account of the physical basis of mind must explain many things, this appears to be the most difficult. It is impossible to exclude the phenomenological features of experience from a reduction in the same way that one excludes the phenomenal features of an ordinary substance from a physical or chemical reduction of it—namely, by explaining them as effects on the minds of human observers. If physicalism is to be defended, the phenomenological features must themselves be given a physical account. But when we examine their subjective character it seems that such a result is impossible. The reason is that every subjective phenomenon is essentially connected with a single point of view, and it seems inevitable that an objective, physical theory will abandon that point of view.

Let me first try to state the issue somewhat more fully than by referring to the relation between the subjective and the objective. This is far from easy. Facts about what it is like to be an X are very peculiar, so peculiar that some may be inclined to doubt their reality, or the significance of claims about them. To illustrate the connexion between subjectivity and a point of view, and to make evident the importance of subjective features, it will help to explore the matter in relation to an example that brings out clearly the divergence between the two types of conception, subjective and objective.

I assume we all believe that bats have experience. After all, they are mammals, and there is no more doubt that they have experience than that mice or pigeons or whales have experience. I have chosen bats instead of wasps or flounders because if one travels too far down the phylogenetic tree, people gradually shed their faith that there is experience there at all. Bats, although more closely related to us than those other species, nevertheless present a range of activity and a sensory apparatus so different from ours that the problem I want to pose is exceptionally vivid (though it certainly could be raised with other species). Even without the benefit of philosophical reflection, anyone who has spent some time in an enclosed space with an excited bat knows what it is to encounter a fundamentally *alien* form of life.

I have said that the essence of the belief that bats have experience is that there is something that it is like to be a bat. Now we know that most bats (the microchiroptera, to be precise) perceive the external world primarily by sonar, or echolocation, detecting the reflections, from objects within range, of their own rapid, subtly modulated, high-frequency shrieks. Their brains are designed to correlate the outgoing impulses with the subsequent echoes, and the information thus acquired enables bats to make precise discrimination of distance, size, shape, motion, and texture comparable to those we make by vision. But bat sonar, though clearly a form of perception, is not similar in its operation to any sense that we possess, and there is no reason to suppose that it is subjectively like anything we can experience or imagine. This appears to create difficulties for the notion of what it is like to be a bat. We must consider whether any method will permit us to extrapolate to the inner life of the bat from our own case,[1] and if not, what alternative methods there may be for understanding the notion.

Our own experience provides the basic material for our imagination, whose range is therefore limited. It will not help to try to imagine that one has webbing on one's arms, which enables one to fly around at dusk and dawn catching insects in one's mouth; that one has very poor

vision, and perceives the surrounding world by a system of reflected high-frequency sound signals; and that one spends the day hanging upside down by one's feet in an attic. Insofar as I can imagine this (which is not very far), it tells me only what it would be like for *me* to behave as a bat behaves. But that is not the question. I want to know what it is like for a *bat* to be a bat. Yet if I try to imagine this, I am restricted to the resources of my own mind, and those resources are inadequate to the task. I cannot perform it either by imagining additions to my present experience, or by imagining segments gradually subtracted from it, or by imagining some combination of additions, subtractions, and modifications.

To the extent that I could look and behave like a wasp or a bat without changing my fundamental structure, my experiences would not be anything like the experiences of those animals. On the other hand, it is doubtful that any meaning can be attached to the supposition that I should possess the internal neurophysiological constitution of a bat. Even if I could by gradual degrees be transformed into a bat, nothing in my present constitution enables me to imagine what the experiences of such a future stage of myself thus metamorphosed would be like. The best evidence would come from the experiences of bats, if we only knew what they were like.

So if extrapolation from our own case is involved in the idea of what it is like to be a bat, the extrapolation must be incompletable. We cannot form more than a schematic conception of what it *is* like. For example, we may ascribe general *types* of experience on the basis of the animal's structure and behavior. Thus we describe bat sonar as a form of three-dimensional forward perception; we believe that bats feel some versions of pain, fear, hunger, and lust, and that they have other, more familiar types of perception besides sonar. But we believe that these experiences also have in each case a specific subjective character, which it is beyond our ability to conceive. And if there is conscious life elsewhere in the universe, it is likely that some of it will not be describable even in the most general experiential terms available to us.[2] (The problem is not confined to exotic cases, however, for it exists between one person and another. The subjective character of the experience of a person deaf and blind from birth is not accessible to me, for example, nor presumably is mine to him. This does not prevent us each from believing that the other's experience has such a subjective character.)

If anyone is inclined to deny that we can believe in the existence of facts like this whose exact nature we cannot possibly conceive, he should reflect that in contemplating the bats we are in much the same position that intelligent bats or Martians[3] would occupy if they tried to form a conception of what it was like to be us. The structure of their own minds might make it impossible for them to succeed, but we know they would be wrong to conclude that there is not anything precise that it is like to be us: that only certain general types of mental state could be ascribed to us (perhaps perception and appetite would be concepts common to us both; perhaps not). We know they would be wrong to draw such a skeptical conclusion because we know what it is like to be us. And we know that while it includes an enormous amount of variation and complexity, and while we do not possess the vocabulary to describe it adequately, its subjective character is highly specific, and in some respects describable in terms that can be understood only by creatures like us. The fact that we cannot expect ever to accommodate in our language a detailed description of Martian or bat phenomenology should not lead us to dismiss as meaningless the claim that bats and Martians have experiences fully comparable in richness of detail to our own. It would be fine if someone were to develop concepts and a theory that enabled us to think about those things, but such an understanding may be permanently denied to us by the limits of our nature. And to deny the reality or logical significance of what we can never describe or understand is the crudest form of cognitive dissonance.

This brings us to the edge of a topic that requires much more discussion than I can give it here: namely, the relation between facts on the one hand and conceptual schemes or systems of representation on the other. My realism about the subjective domain in all its forms implies a belief in the existence of facts beyond the reach of human concepts. Certainly it is possible for a human being to believe that there are facts which humans never *will* possess the requisite concepts to represent or comprehend. Indeed, it would be foolish to doubt this, given the finiteness of humanity's expectations. After all, there would have been transfinite numbers even if everyone had been wiped out by the Black Death before Cantor discovered them. But one might also believe that there are facts which *could* not ever be represented or comprehended by human beings, even if the species lasted for ever—simply because our structure does not permit us to operate with concepts of the requisite type. This impossibility might even be observed by other beings, but it is not clear that the existence of such beings, or the possibility of their existence, is a precondition of the significance of the hypothesis that there are humanly inaccessible facts. (After all, the nature of beings with access to humanly inaccessible facts is presumably itself a humanly inaccessible fact.) Reflection on what it is like to be a bat seems to lead us, therefore, to the conclusion that there are facts that do not consist in the truth of propositions expressible in a human language. We can be compelled to recognize the existence of such facts without being able to state or comprehend them.

I shall not pursue this subject, however. Its bearing on the topic before us (namely, the mind-body problem) is that it enables us to make a general observation about the subjective character of experience. Whatever may be the status of facts about what it is like to be a human being, or a bat, or a Martian, these appear to be facts that embody a particular point of view.

I am not adverting here to the alleged privacy of experience to its possessor. The point of view in question is not one accessible only to a single individual. Rather it is a *type*. It is often possible to take up a point of view other than one's own, so the comprehension of such facts is not limited to one's own case. There is a sense in which phenomenological facts are perfectly objective: One person can know or say of another what the quality of the other's experience is. They are subjective, however, in the sense that even this objective ascription of experience is possible only for someone sufficiently similar to the object of ascription to be able to adopt his point of view— to understand the ascription in the first person as well as in the third, so to speak. The more different from oneself the other experiencer is, the less success one can expect with this enterprise. In our own case we occupy the relevant point of view, but we will have as much difficulty understanding our own experience properly if we approach it from another point of view as we would if we tried to understand the experience of another species without taking up *its* point of view.

This bears directly on the mind-body problem. For if the facts of experience—facts about what it is like *for* the experiencing organism— are accessible only from one point of view, then it is a mystery how the true character of experiences could be revealed in the physical operation of that organism. The latter is a domain of objective facts *par excellence*—the kind that can be observed and understood from many points of view and by individuals with differing perceptual systems. There are no comparable imaginative obstacles to the acquisition of knowledge about bat neurophysiology by human scientists, and intelligent bats or Martians might learn more about the human brain than we ever will.

This is not by itself an argument against reduction. A Martian scientist with no understanding of visual perception could understand the rainbow, or lightning, or clouds as physical phenomena, though he would never be able to understand the human concepts of rainbow, lightning, or cloud, or the place these things occupy in our phenomenal world. The objective nature of the things picked out by these concepts could be apprehended by him because, although the concepts themselves are connected

with a particular point of view and a particular visual phenomenology, the things apprehended from that point of view are not: They are observable from the point of view but external to it; hence they can be comprehended from other points of view also, either by the same organisms or by others. Lightning has an objective character that is not exhausted by its visual appearance, and this can be investigated by a Martian without vision. To be precise, it has a *more* objective character than is revealed in its visual appearance. In speaking of the move from subjective characterization, I wish to remain noncommittal about the existence of an end point, the completely objective intrinsic nature of the thing, which one might or might not be able to reach. It may be more accurate to think of objectivity as a direction in which the understanding can travel. And in understanding a phenomenon like lightning, it is legitimate to go as far away as one can from a strictly human viewpoint.

In the case of experience, on the other hand, the connexion with a particular point of view seems much closer. It is difficult to understand what could be meant by the *objective* character of an experience, apart from the particular point of view from which its subject apprehends it. After all, what would be left of what it was like to be a bat if one removed the viewpoint of the bat? But if experience does not have, in addition to its subjective character, an objective nature that can be apprehended from many different points of view, then how can it be supposed that a Martian investigating my brain might be observing physical processes which were my mental processes (as he might observe physical processes which were bolts of lightning), only from a different point of view? How, for that matter, could a human physiologist observe them from another point of view?[4]

We appear to be faced with a general difficulty about psychophysical reduction. In other areas the process of reduction is a move in the direction of greater objectivity, toward a more accurate view of the real nature of things. This is accomplished by reducing our dependence on individual or species-specific points of view toward the object of investigation. We describe it not in terms of the impressions it makes on our senses, but in terms of its more general effects and of properties detectable by means other than the human senses. The less it depends on a specifically human viewpoint, the more objective is our description. It is possible to follow this path because although the concepts and ideas we employ in thinking about the external world are initially applied from a point of view that involves our perceptual apparatus, they are used by us to refer to things beyond themselves—toward which we *have* the phenomenal point of view. Therefore we can abandon it in favor of another, and still be thinking about the same things.

Experience itself, however, does not seem to fit the pattern. The idea of moving from appearance to reality seems to make no sense here. What is the analogue in this case to pursuing a more objective understanding of the same phenomena by abandoning the initial subjective viewpoint toward them in favour of another that is more objective but concerns the same thing? Certainly it *appears* unlikely that we will get closer to the real nature of human experience by leaving behind the particularity of our human point of view and striving for a description in terms accessible to beings that could not imagine what it was like to be us. If the subjective character of experience is fully comprehensible only from one point of view, then any shift to greater objectivity—that is, less attachment to a specific viewpoint—does not take us nearer to the real nature of the phenomenon: It takes us farther away from it.

In a sense, the seeds of this objection to the reducibility of experience are already detectable in successful cases of reduction; for in discovering sound to be, in reality, a wave phenomenon in air or other media, we leave behind one viewpoint to take up another, and the auditory, human or animal viewpoint that we leave behind remains unreduced. Members of radically different species may both understand the same physical events in objective terms, and this does not require that they understand the phenomenal forms in which those events appear to the senses of members of the other species. Thus it is a condition of their referring to a common reality that their more particular viewpoints are not part of the common reality that they both apprehend. The reduction can succeed only if the species-specific viewpoint is omitted from what is to be reduced.

But while we are right to leave this point of view aside in seeking a fuller understanding of the external world, we cannot ignore it permanently, since it is the essence of the internal world, and not merely a point of view on it. Most of the neobehaviorism of recent philosophical psychology results from the effort to substitute an objective concept of mind for the real thing, in order to have nothing left over which cannot be reduced. If we acknowledge that a physical theory of mind must account for the subjective character of experience, we must admit that no presently available conception gives us a clue how this could be done. The problem is unique. If mental processes are indeed physical processes, then there is something it is like, intrinsically, to undergo certain physical processes. What it is for such a thing to be the case remains a mystery.

What moral should be drawn from these reflections, and what should be done next? It would be a mistake to conclude that physicalism must be false. Nothing is proved by the inadequacy of physicalist hypotheses that assume a faulty objective analysis of mind. It would be truer to say that physicalism is a position we cannot understand because we do not at present have any conception of how it might be true. Perhaps it will be thought unreasonable to require such a conception as a condition of understanding. After all, it might be said, the meaning of physicalism is clear enough: Mental states are states of the body; mental events are physical events. We do not know *which* physical states and events they are, but that should not prevent us from understanding the hypothesis. What could be clearer than the words "is" and "are"?

But I believe it is precisely this apparent clarity of the word "is" that is deceptive. Usually, when we are told that X is Y we know *how* it is supposed to be true, but that depends on a conceptual or theoretical background and is not conveyed by the "is" alone. We know how both "X" and "Y" refer, and the kinds of things to which they refer, and we have a rough idea how the two referential paths might converge on a single thing, be it an object, a person, a process, an event or whatever. But when the two terms of the identification are very disparate it may not be so clear how it could be true. We may not have even a rough idea of how the two referential paths could converge, or what kind of things they might converge on, and a theoretical framework may have to be supplied to enable us to understand this. Without the framework, an air of mysticism surrounds the identification.

This explains the magical flavor of popular presentations of fundamental scientific discoveries, given out as propositions to which one must subscribe without really understanding them. For example, people are now told at an early age that all matter is really energy. But despite the fact that they know what "is" means, most of them never form a conception of what makes this claim true, because they lack the theoretical background.

At the present time the status of physicalism is similar to that which the hypothesis that matter is energy would have had if uttered by a pre-Socratic philosopher. We do not have the beginnings of a conception of how it might be true. In order to understand the hypothesis that a mental event is a physical event, we require more than an understanding of the word "is." The idea of how a mental and a physical term might refer to the same thing is lacking, and the usual analogies with theoretical identification in other fields fail to supply it. They fail because if we construe the reference of mental terms to physical events on the usual model, we either get a reappearance of separate subjective events as the effects through which mental reference to physical events is secured, or else we get a false

account of how mental terms refer (for example, a causal behaviorist one).

Strangely enough, we may have evidence for the truth of something we cannot really understand. Suppose a caterpillar is locked in a sterile safe by someone unfamiliar with insect metamorphosis, and weeks later the safe is reopened, revealing a butterfly. If the person knows that the safe has been shut the whole time, he has reason to believe that the butterfly is or was once the caterpillar, without having any idea in what sense this might be so. (One possibility is that the caterpillar contained a tiny winged parasite that devoured it and grew into the butterfly.) It is conceivable that we are in such a position with regard to physicalism. Donald Davidson has argued that if mental events have physical causes and effects, they must have physical descriptions. He holds that we have reason to believe this even though we do not—and in fact *could* not—have a general psychophysical theory. His argument applies to intentional mental events, but I think we also have some reason to believe that sensations are physical processes, without being in a position to understand how. Davidson's position is that certain physical events have irreducibly mental properties, and perhaps some view describable in this way is correct. But nothing of which we can now form a conception corresponds to it; nor have we any idea what a theory would be like that enabled us to conceive of it. Very little work has been done on the basic question (from which mention of the brain can be entirely omitted) whether any sense can be made of experiences' having an objective character at all. Does it make sense, in other words, to ask what my experiences are *really* like, as opposed to how they appear to me? We cannot genuinely understand the hypothesis that their nature is captured in a physical description unless we understand the more fundamental idea that they *have* an objective nature (or that objective processes can have a subjective nature).

I should like to close with a speculative proposal. It may be possible to approach the gap between subjective and objective from another direction. Setting aside temporarily the relation between the mind and the brain, we can pursue a more objective understanding of the mental in its own right. At present we are completely un-equipped to think about the subjective character of experience without relying on the imagination—without taking up the point of view of the experiential subject. This should be regarded as a challenge to form new concepts and devise a new method—an objective phe-nomenology not dependent on empathy or the imagination. Though presumably it would not capture everything, its goal would be to de-scribe, at least in part, the subjective character of experiences in a form comprehensible to be-ings incapable of having those experiences.

We would have to develop such a phenome-nology to describe the sonar experiences of bats; but it would also be possible to begin with humans. One might try, for example, to develop concepts that could be used to explain to a per-son blind from birth what it was like to see. One would reach a blank wall eventually, but it should be possible to devise a method of ex-pressing in objective terms much more than we can at present, and with much greater precision. The loose intermodal analogies—for example, 'Red is like the sound of a trumpet'—which crop up in discussions of this subject are of little use. That should be clear to anyone who has both heard a trumpet and seen red. But struc-tural features of perception might be more ac-cessible to objective description, even though something would be left out. And concepts al-ternative to those we learn in the first person

may enable us to arrive at a kind of understand-ing even of our own experience which is denied us by the very ease of description and lack of distance that subjective concepts afford.

Apart from its own interest, a phenomenol-ogy that is in this sense objective may permit questions about the physical basis of experience to assume a more intelligible form. Aspects of subjective experience that admitted this kind of objective description might be better candidates for objective explanations of a more familiar sort. But whether or not this guess is correct, it seems unlikely that any physical theory of mind can be contemplated until more thought has been given to the general problem of subjective and objective. Otherwise we cannot even pose the mind-body problem without sidestepping it.

NOTES

1. By "our own case," I do not mean just "my own case," but rather the mentalistic ideas that we apply un-problematically to ourselves and other human beings.

2. Therefore the analogical form of the English ex-pression 'what it is *like*' is misleading. It does not mean 'what (in our experience) it *resembles*,' but rather 'how it is for the subject himself.'

3. Any intelligent extraterrestrial beings totally dif-ferent from us.

4. The problem is not just that when I look at the *Mona Lisa*, my visual experience has a certain quality, no trace of which is to be found by someone looking into my brain. For even if he did observe there a tiny image of the *Mona Lisa*, he would have no reason to identify it with the experience.

For Further Reflection

1. Explain Nagel's case against reductionism. How strong is it? What would Churchland be likely to say in response to Nagel's arguments?

2. In another place Nagel states his thesis this way:

There are things about the world and life and ourselves that cannot be adequately un-derstood from a maximally objective standpoint, however much it may extend our un-derstanding beyond the point from which we started. A great deal is essentially connected to a particular point of view, and the attempt to give a complete account of the world in objective terms detached from these perspectives inevitably leads to false reductions or to outright denials that certain patently real phenomena exist at all. To the extent that such no-nonsense theories have an effect, they merely threaten to impoverish the intellectual landscape for a while by inhibiting the serious expression of certain questions. In the name of liberation, these movements have offered us intellectual repression (*A View from Nowhere* [Oxford: Oxford University Press, 1986], pp. 7, 11).

Do you agree with Nagel? Or is the objective perspective really the true perspective? Or is the objective compatible with the subjective? Explain your answer.

Minds, Brains, and Computers   IV.32

JOHN SEARLE

John Searle is professor of philosophy at the University of California, Berkeley, and the author of several works in the philosophy of language and the philosophy of mind, including *Intentionality* (1983) and *The Rediscovery of the Mind* (1992). In this essay, Searle argues that although weak AI (artificial intelligence), which states that the mind functions somewhat like a computer, might be correct, strong AI, which states the appropriately programmed computer *is* mind and has intentions, is false.

Study Questions

1. What is the difference between weak and strong AI?
2. What two claims do partisans of strong AI make?
3. What does the example of correlating sets of Chinese symbols illustrate?
4. How does Searle address the two claims of strong AI?
5. Does Searle believe that a man-made machine could be made to think?

WHAT PSYCHOLOGICAL AND PHILOSOPHICAL significance should we attach to recent efforts at computer simulations of human cognitive capacities? In answering this question, I find it useful to distinguish what I will call "strong" AI from "weak" or "cautious" AI (artificial intelligence). According to weak AI, the principal value of the computer in the study of the mind is that it gives us a very powerful tool. For example, it enables us to formulate and test hypotheses in a more rigorous and precise fashion. But according to strong AI, the computer is not merely a tool in the study of the mind; rather, the appropriately programmed computer really *is* a mind, in the sense that computers given the right programs can be literally said to *understand* and have other cognitive states. In strong AI, because the programmed computer has cognitive states, the programs are not mere tools that enable us to test psychological explanations; rather, the programs are themselves the explanations.

I have no objection to the claims of weak AI, at least as far as this article is concerned. My discussion here will be directed at the claims I have defined as those of strong AI, specifically the claim that the appropriately programmed computer literally has cognitive states and that the programs thereby explain human cognition. When I hereafter refer to AI, I have in mind the strong version, as expressed by these two claims.

I will consider the work of Roger Schank and his colleagues at Yale (Schank and Abelson 1977), because I am more familiar with it than I am with any other similar claims, and because it provides a very clear example of the sort of work I wish to examine. But nothing that follows depends upon the details of Schank's programs. The same arguments would apply to Winograd's SHRDLU (Winograd 1973), Weizenbaum's ELIZA (Weizenbaum 1965), and indeed any Turing machine simulation of human mental phenomena. . . .

Very briefly, and leaving out the various details, one can describe Schank's program as follows: The aim of the program is to simulate the human ability to understand stories. It is characteristic of human beings' story-understanding capacity that they can answer questions about the story even though the information that they give was never explicitly stated in the story. Thus, for example, suppose you are given the following story: "A man went into a restaurant and ordered a hamburger. When the hamburger arrived it was burned to a crisp, and the man stormed out of the restaurant angrily, without paying for the hamburger or leaving a tip." Now, if you are asked "Did the man eat the hamburger?" you will presumably answer, "No, he did not." Similarly, if you are given the following story: "A man went into a restaurant and ordered a hamburger; when the hamburger

came he was very pleased with it; and as he left the restaurant he gave the waitress a large tip before paying his bill," and you are asked the question, "Did the man eat the hamburger?" you will presumably answer, "Yes, he ate the hamburger." Now Schank's machines can similarly answer questions about restaurants in this fashion. To do this, they have a "representation" of the sort of information that human beings have about restaurants, which enables them to answer such questions as those above, given these sorts of stories. When the machine is given the story and then asked the question, the machine will print out answers of the sort that we would expect human beings to give if told similar stories. Partisans of strong AI claim that in this question and answer sequence the machine is not only simulating a human ability but also (1) that the machine can literally be said to *understand* the story and provide the answers to questions, and (2) that what the machine and its programs do *explains* the human ability to understand the story and answer questions about it.

Both claims seem to me to be totally unsupported by Schank's work, as I will attempt to show in what follows. I am not, of course, saying that Schank himself is committed to these claims. One way to test any theory of the mind is to ask oneself what it would be like if my mind actually worked on the principles that the theory says all minds work on. Let us apply this test to the Schank program with the following thought experiment. Suppose that I'm locked in a room and given a large batch of Chinese writing. Suppose furthermore (as is indeed the case) that I know no Chinese, either written or spoken, and that I'm not even confident that I could recognize Chinese writing as Chinese writing distinct from, say, Japanese writing or meaningless squiggles. To me, Chinese writing is just so many meaningless squiggles. Now suppose further that after this first batch of Chinese writing I am given a second batch of Chinese script together with a set of rules for correlating the second batch with the first batch. The rules are in English, and I understand these rules as well as any other native speaker of English. They enable me to correlate one set of formal symbols with another set of formal symbols, and all that "formal" means here is that I can identify the symbols entirely by their shapes. Now suppose also that I am given a third batch of Chinese symbols together with some instructions, again in English, that enable me to correlate elements of this third batch with the first two batches, and these rules instruct me how to give back certain Chinese symbols with certain sorts of shapes in response to certain sorts of shapes given me in the third batch. Unknown to me, the people who are giving me all of these symbols call the first batch a "script," they call the second batch a "story," and they call the third batch "questions." Furthermore, they call the symbols I give them back in response to the third batch "answers to the questions," and the set of rules in English that they gave me, they call the "program." Now just to complicate the story a little, imagine that these people also give me stories in English, which I understand, and they then ask me questions in English about these stories, and I give them back answers in English. Suppose also that after a while I get so good at following the instructions for manipulating the Chinese symbols and the programmers get so good at writing the programs that from the external point of view—that is, from the point of view of somebody outside the room in which I am locked—my answers to the questions are absolutely indistinguishable from those of native Chinese speakers. Nobody just looking at my answers can tell that I don't speak a word of Chinese. Let us also suppose that my answers to the English questions are, as they no doubt would be, indistinguishable from those of other native English speakers, for the simple reason that I am a native English speaker. From the external point of view—from the point of view of someone reading my "answers"—the answers to the Chinese questions and the English questions are equally good. But in the Chinese case, unlike the English case, I produce the answers by manipulating uninterpreted formal symbols. As far as the Chinese is concerned, I simply behave like a computer; I perform computational operations on formally specified elements. For the purposes of the Chinese, I am simply an instantiation of the computer program.

Now the claims made by strong AI are that the programmed computer understands the stories and that the program in some sense explains human understanding. But we are now in a position to examine these claims in light of our thought experiment.

1. As regards the first claim, it seems to me quite obvious in the example that I do not understand a word of the Chinese stories. I have in-puts and outputs that are indistinguishable from those of the native Chinese speaker, and I can have any formal program you like, but I still understand nothing. For the same reasons, Schank's computer understands nothing of any stories, whether in Chinese, English, or whatever, since in the Chinese case the computer is me, and in cases where the computer is not me, the computer has nothing more than I have in the case where I understand nothing.

2. As regards the second claim, that the program explains human understanding, we can see that the computer and its program do not provide sufficient conditions of understanding since the computer and the program are functioning, and there is no understanding. But does it even provide a necessary condition or a significant contribution to understanding? One of the claims made by the supporters of strong AI is that when I understand a story in English, what I am doing is exactly the same—or perhaps more of the same—as what I was doing in manipulating the Chinese symbols. It is simply more formal symbol manipulation that distinguishes the case in English, where I do understand, from the case in Chinese, where I don't. I have not demonstrated that this claim is false, but it would certainly appear an incredible claim in the example. Such plausibility as the claim has derives from the supposition that we can construct a program that will have the same inputs and outputs as native speakers, and in addition we assume that speakers have some level of description where they are

also instantiations of a program. On the basis of these two assumptions we assume that even if Schank's program isn't the whole story about understanding, it may be part of the story. Well, I suppose that is an empirical possibility, but not the slightest reason has so far been given to believe that it is true, since what is suggested—though certainly not demonstrated—by the example is that the computer program is simply irrelevant to my understanding of the story. In the Chinese case I have everything that artificial intelligence can put into me by way of a program, and I understand nothing; in the English case I understand everything, and there is so far no reason at all to suppose that my understanding has anything to do with computer programs, that is, with computational operations on purely formally specified elements. As long as the program is defined in terms of computational operations on purely formally defined elements, what the example suggests is that these by themselves have no interesting connection with understanding. They are certainly not sufficient conditions, and not the slightest reason has been given to suppose that they are necessary conditions or even that they make a significant contribution to understanding. Notice that the force of the argument is not simply that different machines can have the same input and output while operating on different formal principles—that is not the point at all. Rather, whatever purely formal principles you put into the computer, they will not be sufficient for understanding, since a human will be able to follow the formal principles without understanding anything. No reason whatever has been offered to suppose that such principles are necessary or even contributory, since no reason has been given to suppose that when I understand English I am operating with any formal program at all.

Well, then, what is it that I have in the case of the English sentences that I do not have in the case of the Chinese sentences? The obvious answer is that I know what the former mean, while I haven't the faintest idea what the latter mean.

But in what does this consist and why couldn't we give it to a machine, whatever it is? . . .

I have had the occasions to present this example to several workers in artificial intelligence, and, interestingly, they do not seem to agree on what the proper reply to it is. . . .

. . . I want to block some common misunderstandings about "understanding": In many of these discussions one finds a lot of fancy footwork about the word "understanding." My critics point out that there are many different degrees of understanding; that "understanding" is not a simple two-place predicate; that there are even different kinds and levels of understanding, and often the law of excluded middle doesn't even apply in a straightforward way to statements of the form "x understands y"; that in many cases it is a matter for decision and not a simple matter of fact whether x understands y; and so on. To all of these points I want to say: of course, of course. But they have nothing to do with the points at issue. There are clear cases in which "understanding" literally applies and clear cases in which it does not apply; and these two sorts of cases are all I need for this argument. I understand stories in English; to a lesser degree I can understand stories in French; to a still lesser degree, stories in German; and in Chinese, not at all. My car and my adding machine, on the other hand, understand nothing: they are not in that line of business.* We often attribute "understanding" and other cognitive predicates by metaphor and analogy to cars, adding machines, and other artifacts, but nothing is proved by such attributions. We say, "The door *knows* when to open because of its photoelectric cell," "The adding machine *knows how* (*understands how*, is *able*) to do addition and subtraction but not division," and "The thermostat *perceives* changes in the temperature." The reason we make these attributions is quite interesting, and

---

*Also, "understanding" implies both the possession of mental (intentional) states and the truth (validity, success) of these states. For the purposes of this discussion we are concerned only with the possession of the states.

it has to do with the fact that in artifacts we extend our own intentionality;* our tools are extensions of our purposes, and so we find it natural to make metaphorical attributions of intentionality to them; but I take it no philosophical ice is cut by such examples. The sense in which an automatic door "understands instructions" from its photoelectric cell is not at all the sense in which I understand English. If the sense in which Schank's programmed computers understand stories is supposed to be the metaphorical sense in which the door understands, and not the sense in which I understand English, the issue would not be worth discussing. But Newell and Simon (1963) write that the kind of cognition they claim for computers is exactly the same as for human beings. I like the straightforwardness of this claim, and it is the sort of claim I will be considering. I will argue that in the literal sense the programmed computer understands what the car and the adding machine understand, namely, exactly nothing. The computer's understanding is not just (like my understanding of German) partial or incomplete; it is zero. . . .

By way of concluding I want to try to state some of the general philosophical points implicit in the argument. For clarity I will try to do it in a question-and-answer fashion, and begin with that old chestnut of a question:

"Could a machine think?"

The answer is, obviously, yes. We are precisely such machines.

"Yes, but could an artificial, a man-made machine, think?"

Assuming it is possible to produce artificially a machine with a nervous system, neurons, with axons and dendrites, and all the rest of it, sufficiently like ours, again the answer to the question seems to be obviously, yes. If you can exactly duplicate the causes, you could duplicate the effects. And indeed it might be possible to produce con-

*Intentionality is by definition that feature of certain mental states by which they are directed at or about objects and states of affairs in the world. Thus, beliefs, desires, and intentions are intentional states; undirected forms of anxiety and depression are not.

sciousness, intentionality, and all the rest of it using some other sorts of chemical principles than those that human beings use. It is, as I said, an empirical question.

"OK, but could a digital computer think?"

If by "digital computer" we mean anything at all that has a level of description where it can correctly be described as the instantiation of a computer program, then again the answer is, of course, yes, since we are the instantiations of any number of computer programs, and we can think.

"But could something think, understand, and so on *solely* by virtue of being a computer with the right sort of program? Could instantiating a program, the right program of course, by itself be a sufficient condition of understanding?" This I think is the right question to ask, though it is usually confused with one or more of the earlier questions, and the answer to it is no.

"Why not?"

Because the formal symbol manipulations by themselves don't have any intentionality; they are quite meaningless; they aren't even *symbol* manipulations, since the symbols don't symbolize anything. In the linguistic jargon, they have only a syntax but no semantics. Such intentionality as computers appear to have is solely in the minds of those who program them and those who use them, those who send in the input and those who interpret the output.

The aim of the Chinese room example was to try to show this by showing that as soon as we put something into the system that really does have intentionality (a man), and we program him with the formal program, you can see that the formal program carries no additional intentionality. It adds nothing, for example, to a man's ability to understand Chinese.

Precisely that feature of AI that seemed so appealing—the distinction between the program and the realization—proves fatal to the claim that simulation could be duplication. The distinction between the program and its realization in the hardware seems to be parallel to the distinction between the level of mental operations and the level of brain operations. And if we could describe the level of mental operations as a formal program, then it seems we could describe what was essential about the mind without doing either introspective psychology or neurophysiology of the brain. But the equation "mind is to brain as program is to hardware" breaks down at several points, among them the following three:

First, the distinction between program and realization has the consequence that the same program could have all sorts of crazy realizations that had no form of intentionality. Weizenbaum (1976, Ch. 2), for example, shows in detail how to construct a computer using a roll of toilet paper and a pile of small stones. Similarly, the Chinese story understanding-program can be programmed into a sequence of water pipes, a set of wind machines, or a monolingual English speaker, none of which thereby acquires an understanding of Chinese. Stones, toilet paper, wind, and water pipes are the wrong kind of stuff to have intentionality in the first place—only something that has the same causal powers as brains can have intentionality—and though the English speaker has the right kind of stuff for intentionality you can easily see that he doesn't get any extra intentionality by memorizing the program, since memorizing it won't teach him Chinese.

Second, the program is purely formal, but the intentional states are not in that way formal. They are defined in terms of their content, not their form. The belief that it is raining, for example, is not defined as a certain formal shape, but as a certain mental content with conditions of satisfaction, a direction of fit (see Searle 1979), and the like. Indeed the belief as such hasn't even got a formal shape in this syntactic sense, since one and the same belief can be given an indefinite number of different syntactic expressions in different linguistic systems.

Third, as I mentioned before, mental states and events are literally a product of the operation of the brain, but the program is not in that way a product of the computer.

"Well if programs are in no way constitutive of mental processes, why have so many people believed the converse? That at least needs some explanation."

I don't really know the answer to that one. The idea that computer simulations could be the real thing ought to have seemed suspicious in the first place because the computer isn't confined to simulating mental operations, by any means. No one supposes that computer simulations of a five-alarm fire will burn the neighborhood down or that a computer simulation of a rainstorm will leave us all drenched. Why on earth would anyone suppose that a computer simulation of understanding actually understood anything? It is sometimes said that it would be frightfully hard to get computers to feel pain or fall in love, but love and pain are neither harder nor easier than cognition or anything else. For simulation, all you need is the right input and output and a program in the middle that transforms the former into the latter. That is all the computer has for anything it does. To confuse simulation with duplication is the same mistake, whether it is pain, love, cognition, fires, or rainstorms.

Still, there are several reasons why AI must have seemed—and to many people perhaps still does seem—in some way to reproduce and thereby explain mental phenomena, and I believe we will not succeed in removing these illusions until we have fully exposed the reasons that give rise to them.

First, and perhaps most important, is a confusion about the notion of "information processing": Many people in cognitive science believe that the human brain, with its mind, does something called "information processing," and analogously the computer with its program does information processing; but fires and rainstorms, on the other hand, don't do information processing at all. Thus, though the computer can simulate the formal features of any process whatever, it stands in a special relation to the mind and brain because when the computer is properly programmed, ideally with the same program as the brain, the information processing is identical in the two cases, and this information processing is really the essence of the mental. But the trouble with this argument is that it rests on an ambiguity in the notion of "information." In the sense in which people "process information" when they reflect, say, on problems in arithmetic or when they read and answer questions about stories, the programmed computer does not do "information processing." Rather, what it does is manipulate formal symbols. The fact that the programmer and the interpreter of the computer output use the symbols to stand for objects in the world is totally beyond the scope of the computer. The computer, to repeat, has a syntax but no semantics. Thus, if you type into the computer "2 plus 2 equals?" it will type out "4." But it has no idea that "4" means 4 or that it means anything at all. And the point is not that it lacks some second-order information about the interpretation of its first-order symbols, but rather that its first-order symbols don't have any interpretations as far as the computer is concerned. All the computer has is more symbols. The introduction of the notion of "information processing" therefore produces a dilemma: Either we construe the notion of "information processing" in such a way that it implies intentionality as part of the process or we don't. If the former, then the programmed computer does not do information processing: it only manipulates formal symbols. If the latter, then, though the computer does information processing, it is only doing so in the sense in which adding machines, typewriters, stomachs, thermostats, rainstorms, and hurricanes do information processing; namely, they have a level of description at which we can describe them as taking information in at one end, transforming it, and producing information as output. But in this case it is up to outside observers to interpret the input and output as information in the ordinary sense. And no similarity is established between the computer and the brain in terms of any similarity of information processing.

Second, in much of AI there is a residual behaviorism or operationalism. Since appropriately programmed computers can have input-output patterns similar to those of human beings, we are tempted to postulate mental states in the computer similar to human mental states. But once we see that it is both conceptually and empirically possible for a system to have human capacities in some realm without having any intentionality at all, we should be able to overcome this impulse. My desk adding machine has calculating capacities, but no intentionality, and in this paper I have tried to show that a system could have input and output capabilities that duplicated those of a native Chinese speaker and still not understand Chinese, regardless of how it was programmed. The Turing test is typical of the tradition in being unashamedly behavioristic and operationalistic, and I believe that if AI workers totally repudiated behaviorism and operationalism much of the confusion between simulation and duplication would be eliminated.

Third, this residual operationalism is joined to a residual form of dualism; indeed strong AI only makes sense given the dualistic assumption that, where the mind is concerned, the brain doesn't matter. In strong AI (and in functionalism, as well) what matters are programs, and programs are independent of their realization in machines; indeed, as far as AI is concerned, the same program could be realized by an electronic machine, a Cartesian mental substance, or a Hegelian world spirit. The single most surprising discovery that I have made in discussing these issues is that many AI workers are quite shocked by my idea that actual human mental phenomena might be dependent on actual physical-chemical properties of actual human brains. But if you think about it a minute you can see that I should not have been surprised; for unless you accept some form of dualism, the strong AI project hasn't got a chance. The project is to reproduce and explain the mental by designing programs, but unless the mind is not only conceptually but empirically independent of the brain you couldn't carry out the project, for the program is completely independent of any realization. Unless you believe that the mind is separable from the brain both conceptually and empirically—dualism in a strong form—you cannot hope to reproduce the mental by writing and running programs since programs must be independent of brains or any other particular forms of instantiation. If mental operations consist in computational operations on formal symbols, then it follows that they have no interesting connection with the brain; the only connection would be that the brain just happens to be one of the indefinitely many types of machines capable of instantiating the program. This form of dualism is not the traditional Cartesian variety that claims there are two sorts of *substances,* but it is Cartesian in the sense that it insists that what is specifically mental about the mind has no intrinsic connection with the actual properties of the brain. This underlying dualism is masked from us by the fact that AI literature contains frequent fulminations against "dualism"; what the authors seem to be unaware of is that their position presupposes a strong version of dualism.

"Could a machine think?" My own view is that *only* a machine could think, and indeed only very special kinds of machines, namely brains and machines that had the same causal powers as brains. And that is the main reason strong AI has had little to tell us about thinking, since it has nothing to tell us about machines. By its own definition, it is about programs, and programs are not machines. Whatever else intentionality is, it is a biological phenomenon, and it is as likely to be as causally dependent on the specific biochemistry of its origins as lactation, photosynthesis, or any other biological phenomena. No one would suppose that we could produce milk and sugar by running a computer simulation of the formal sequences in lactation and photosynthesis, but where the mind is concerned many people are willing to believe in such a miracle because of a deep and abiding dualism: The mind they suppose is a matter of formal processes and is independent of quite specific material causes in the way that milk and sugar are not.

In defense of this dualism the hope is often expressed that the brain is a digital computer (early computers, by the way, were often called "electronic brains"). But that is no help. Of course the brain is a digital computer. Since everything is a digital computer, brains are too. The point is that the brain's causal capacity to produce intentionality cannot consist in its instantiating a computer program, since for any program you like it is possible for something to instantiate that program and still not have any mental states. Whatever it is that the brain does to produce intentionality, it cannot consist in instantiating a program since no program, by itself, is sufficient for intentionality.

For Further Reflection

1. Evaluate Searle's argument against strong AI. Can you see any weaknesses in it? How might a proponent of strong AI defend his or her position?

2. Suppose we could devise a robot with a television camera inside enabling it to see and a voice machine to utter meaningful sentences in response to its environmental input. Would this be an advance on the Schank program that would meet Searle's objections?

3. Here is one reply of an AI proponent discussed in Searle's original essay:

Your whole argument presupposes that AI is only about analog and digital computers. But that just happens to be the present state of technology. Whatever these causal processes are that you say are essential for intentionality, eventually we will be able to build devices that have these causal processes, and that will be artificial intelligence. So your arguments are in no way directed at the ability of artificial intelligence to produce and explain cognition (*The Many Mansions Reply* (Berkeley)).

Evaluate this response. Does it show that artificial intelligence could eventually become conscious, have intentional states, and understand language?

IV.B   *Who Am I? Do We Have Personal Identity?*

Suppose you wake up tomorrow in a strange room. There are pictures of unfamiliar people on the light blue walls. The furniture in the room is very odd. You wonder how you got here. You remember being in the hospital where you were dying of cancer. Your body was wasting away, and your death was thought to be a few days away. Dr. Thomas had kindly given you an extra dose of morphine to kill the pain. That's all you can remember. You notice a calendar on the wall in front of you. The date is April 1, 1992. "This can't be," you think, "for yesterday was December 2nd, 1991. Where have I been all this time?" Suddenly, you see a mirror. In horror you reel back, for it's not your body that you spy in the glass, but a large woman's body. You have more than doubled your previous weight and look 20 years older. You feel tired and confused and frightened and start to cry. Soon a strange man, about 45 years of age, comes into your room. "I was wondering when you would waken, Maria. The doctor said that I should let you sleep as long as possible, but I didn't think that you would be asleep two whole days. Anyway, the operation was a success. We had feared that the accident had ended your life. The children and I are so grateful. Juanita and Caesar will be home in an hour and will be so happy to see you awake. How do you feel?"

"Can this be a bad joke?" you wonder. "Who is this strange man and who am I?" Unbeknownst to you, your doctor, Dr. Thomas, needed a living brain to implant in the head of Mrs. Maria Garcia, mother of four children. She had been in a car accident and arrived at the hospital on a ventilator but brain dead. Your brain was in excellent shape but lacked a healthy body. Maria Garcia's body was intact but needed a brain. Being an enterprising brain surgeon, Dr. Thomas saw his chance of performing the first successful brain transplant. Frightened and confused, you wonder if this fate is worse than death. The fact that the operation was a success was of little comfort to you, for you're not sure whether you are *you*!

The problem of personal identity is one of the most fascinating in the history of philosophy. It is especially complicated because it involves not one but three, and possibly four, philosophical questions: (1) What is it to be a person? (2) What is identity? (3) What is personal identity? and (4) How is survival possible given the problems of personal identity? Let us look briefly at the first three questions with reference to the readings in this section of our book. We will discuss the fourth question in the next section of this part.

1. What is it to be a person?

In our first reading, John Locke (1632–1704) says that a person is defined by having a soul, and the criterion of having a soul is the ability to reflect and reason. That is, our ability to introspect and survey our memories and intentions sets us apart from the animals as being of greater value. The view might be challenged by the materialist who says that it is really our brain (or our brain and our body) that defines our personhood; it is the fact that we have a more developed brain that sets us apart from other animals. Of course, we are conscious beings. Although we do not understand how consciousness works, the physicalist believes that consciousness is a function of the brain.

In our second reading, David Hume (1711–1776) argues that the notion of a self or soul is very likely a fiction. "I" am merely a bundle of perceptions. There is consciousness of a continuing succession of experiences, but not of a continuing experiencer. This view is compatible with the physicalist view of personhood.

2. What is identity?

This sounds like an absurdly simple question. Identity is the fact that everything is itself and not another. In logic, the Law of Identity (A = A) formally states the definition of identity. But we are not interested in a formal definition of mere identity but identity *over time*, or *reidentification* (sometimes this is referred to as "numerical identity"). What is it to be the *same* thing over time? Suppose that you go to an automobile dealership to buy a new car. You see several blue Fords parked side by side. They resemble each other so much that you cannot tell them apart. They are the same type of car and are exactly similar to each other. Suppose you pick one out at random and buy it. Your car is a different car than the other blue Fords even though you couldn't tell the difference between them. A year passes and your blue Ford now has 20,000 miles on it and a few scratches. Is it the same car that you originally bought? Most of us would probably agree that it is. The changes have altered it but not destroyed its identity as the blue car that you bought and have driven 20,000 miles.

What does your blue Ford have that causes it to be the same car over the period of one year? A common history, continuity over time. The car is linked by a succession of spatial-temporal events from its origins in Detroit to its present place in your parking lot. This distinguishes it from all the other Fords that were ever built, no matter how similar they appear. So we might conclude that *continuity over time* is the criterion of identity.

But immediately we find problems with this criterion. The Rio Grande dries up in places in New Mexico every summer, only to reappear as a running river in the early spring. Is the Rio Grande the same river this year as it was the last? There isn't any continuity over time of water flowing over the riverbed. Perhaps we can escape the problem by saying that by "river" we really mean the riverbed, which must hold running water sometimes but need not always convey it. Does this solve the problem?

Consider another counter-example: The Chicago White Sox are playing the New York Yankees in Yankee Stadium in late April. The game is called in the fifth inning with the Yankees leading 3–2. Shortly afterwards there is a baseball strike and all the players take to the picket lines while a new set of players come up from the minor leagues to fill their positions. The "game" is continued in Chicago in August with a whole new set of players on both sides. The White Sox win, and the game decides who wins the division. Suppose a Yankee player who has studied some philosophy argues that this latter game was not part of the original game played in April. There was no *continuity* between them. He demands that a new game be played from the start since it is impossible to play the same game as was played four months ago or even four days ago. Would he have a point? Should the commissioner of baseball call for a make-up game?

The most perplexing problem regarding the notion of "sameness" or identity over time is illustrated by the ancient tale of Theseus' ship. Suppose you have a small ship that is in need of some repairs. You begin (at time t) to replace the old planks and material with new planks and material until after one year (time t_1) the ship is completely composed of different material. Do you have the same ship at t_1 as you had at t? If so, at what point did it (call it *Theseus 2*) become a different ship?

People disagree whether Theseus' ship has changed its identity. Suppose that you argue that it has not changed its identity, for it had a continuous history over time and therefore is the same ship. But now suppose that your friend takes the material discarded from the original *Theseus* and reconstructs "that" ship (call it *Theseus 3*). Which ship is now Theseus' ship? There is continuity of the ship between *Theseus 1* and *2* but continuity of material between *Theseus 1* and *3*. If it worries you that there was a time when the material of *Theseus 1* was not functioning as a ship, we could alter the example and suppose that as the planks were taken from *Theseus 1*, they were transformed to another ship, *Argos*, where they replaced the *Argos'* planks, ending up with a ship that contained every board and nail from the original *Theseus* (call this transformed Argos, *Theseus 4*). Which is now the original *Theseus*?

Does there seem something peculiar about the notion of identity?

3. What is personal identity?

What is it to be the same person over time? Are you the same person that you were when you were one year old or even sixteen years old? We recall Locke's idea of personhood. The mental characteristics (ability to reflect or introspect) constituted personhood. Personal identity was indicated by the successive memories that the person had, the continuity over time of a set of experiences which were remembered. We can call this the *psychological states criterion of personal identity*. The main competitor of this view is the *brain criterion*, though some philosophers hold to a *body criterion*. Let us examine each of these briefly.

The psychological states criterion holds that our memories constitute our identity over time. You are the same person you were at ten years of age because you have a continuous set of memories that contains all those that you had at ten plus others that continued after that year. There are several problems with this view. In the first place, our memories are not continuous in our consciousness. When we sleep, we cease to have memories at all. In partial amnesia, do we cease to be who we were? Thomas Reid suggests a problem of transitivity in memories. Suppose there is a gallant officer who at age twenty-five is a hero in a battle and who remembers getting a flogging in his childhood. Later, at age sixty-five, he recalls the heroic deed done at twenty-five but cannot recall the flogging. Since he cannot remember the earlier deed, is he the same person he was when he did remember it? Can Locke answer Reid?

What about the phenomenon of split personalities and multiple personalities—the most famous of which is Sybil, who allegedly expressed sixteen different personalities with sixteen different sets of memories? On a psychological states account, would we have to say that one body contains sixteen persons? Are there different persons inside each of us, expressed by different "sides" of our personalities?

Sometimes a person expresses apparent memories of events that occurred in distant times and to different "persons." Is the body of the contemporary being possessed by another person? If your friend suddenly starts reminiscing about the Battle of Waterloo and the beautiful Empress Josephine, has Napoleon suddenly come alive in your friend's body? This would truly be a case of reincarnation. But what if two of your friends came to you with the same "foreign" memories? And what is to prohibit complete soul flow, a different person inside you each day? How do you know that the soul that is remembering today is the same soul that remembered yesterday? You might object that this couldn't be the case because you have the same body, but that objection won't work since the body has nothing to do with the psychological states criterion. If you think that the body is important, this might be an indication that the memory criterion is inadequate on its own and depends on a physical body for continuity.

The body criterion has difficulties, one of which is the fact that the body can undergo radical changes and we would still want to call the person the same person. Almost all of the cells of our body change every seven years. Do we become a new person every seven years? Or think of the story at the beginning of this section in which Dr. Thomas transplants your brain into Maria Garcia's body. Wouldn't you still be you?

This suggests the third criterion, the brain criterion of personal identity. Our memories are contained within our brains, so we might want to say that having the same brain constitutes the same person. But this has difficulties, as are brought out in our third reading by Derek Parfit. It is well known that if the corpus callosum, the great band of fibers that unites the two hemispheres of the brain, is cut, two different centers of consciousness can be created. When either side of the brain's cerebral cortex is destroyed, the person can live on as a conscious being. It is also possible in principle to transplant brains. Suppose that your body is destroyed and neurologists transplant each half of your brain into a different body. Dr. Thomas transplants one half of your brain into Maria Garcia and the other half into the head of Kareem Abdul Jabbar's look-alike. "You" wake up with two personalities. Do you survive the operation? There seems to be just three possible answers: (1) you do not survive; (2) you survive as one of the two; and (3) you survive as two people.

All these options seem unsatisfactory. It seems absurd to say (1) that you don't survive, for there is continuity of consciousness (in the Lockean sense) as though you had gone to sleep and awakened. If you had experienced the destruction of one half of your brain, we would still say you survived with half a brain, so why not say so now when each half is autonomous? The logic of this thesis would seem to say that double life equals death.

But (2) seems arbitrary. Why say that you only survive as one of the two, and which one is it? And (3) that you survive as both is not satisfactory either since it gives up the notion of identity. You cannot be numerically one with two centers of consciousness and two spatial-temporal bodies. Otherwise we might say when we wreck our new Ford that the other one left in the automobile dealer's parking lot (the blue Ford which was exactly like yours) was indeed yours.

If this is an accurate analysis of the personal identity problem, what sense can we make of the concept? Not much, according to Parfit. We should speak of survival of the person, not the identity of the person. Persons, as psychological states, survive and gradually merge (like Theseus' rebuilt ship) into descendent persons. Your memories and personality gradually emerged from the sixteen-year-old who gradually developed from the ten-year-old who bore your name. These were your ancestor selves. But you too will merge with future or descendent selves as you have different experiences, take on new memories, and forget old ones. Suppose every year neurologists could transplant half of your brain into another body, in which a new half would duplicate the present state of the transferred half. In this way a tree-like operation would continue to spread successors of yourself as though by psychological parthenogenesis. You would survive in a sense, but it would make no sense to speak of personal identity, a concept which Parfit wants to get rid of. We could also imagine a neurological game of musical hemispheres as half of your brain was merged with half of someone else's brain in a third person's head. You could continue the hemisphere moving game every six months so that you might even get re-merged with your own other half at some future time—kind of like meeting your spouse again after other adventures. You'd have a lot to talk about through the medium of the corpus callosum!

Of course, Parfit's point is that we are going through significant changes all the time, so that as we have new experiences, we take on new selfhood. Something in us survives but with a difference. If Parfit is right about the relativity of identity in survival, then we might be less interested in our long-term future than our immediate future. After all, that person ten years down the line is less like us than the person we'll be tomorrow. This might encourage a sort of general utilitarianism— since our distant interests really are not as pressing, we would be free to work for the total greater good. On the other hand, it could have the opposite effect of making us indifferent to the future of society. This notion of proximate identity also raises the question of whether we should be concerned about our distant death fifty years down the line that one of our successor selves will have to face. This view might also cause us to prohibit long-term prison sentences for criminal actions, for why punish a descendent for what one of his or her ancestors did? Finally, it could be used to argue against exorbitant awards in malpractice litigation. Often a jury is asked to award a sum of money (as high as $12 million) to a severely retarded child whose damage has been incurred through medical malpractice. The justification for the large sum is the expectation that the child could have become, for example, a physician or lawyer and made an enormous sum of money in his or her lifetime. But if we were to take the notion of proximate identity seriously, we could only sue the physician for the damages done to the immediate person, not to his or her descendent selves.

What is the truth about personal identity? Are you the same person that you were at sixteen? And will you be still the same person at sixty?

Our Psychological Properties Define the Self   IV.33

JOHN LOCKE

In this selection Locke sets forth his psychological state theory of personal identity, locating the criterion of personal identity in terms of consciousness, especially memory. The soul or essence of the person, defined as a reflective being, could take on different bodily forms and still preserve the same identity.

(A biographical sketch of Locke precedes Reading III.19.)

Study Questions

1. What is Locke's definition of a person?
2. In what does personal identity consist?
3. Is it necessary that consciousness be the same identical substance?
4. Can we be the same persons though we have different bodies?
5. How is Locke's view relevant to the question of life after death?
6. What is the lesson of the story of the prince and the cobbler?

. . . IF THE IDENTITY OF *soul alone* makes the same *man,* and there be nothing in the nature of matter why the same individual spirit may not be united to different bodies, it will be possible that those men, living in distant ages, and of different tempers, may have been the same man: which way of speaking must be from a very strange use of the word man, applied to an idea out of which body and shape are excluded. . . .

An animal is a living organized body; and consequently the same animal, as we have observed, is the same continued *life* communicated to different particles of matter, as they happen successively to be united to that organized living body. And whatever is talked of other definitions, ingenious observation puts it past doubt, that the idea in our minds, of which the sound "man" in our mouths is the sign, is nothing else but of an animal of such a certain form. . . .

I presume it is not the idea of a thinking or rational being alone that makes the *idea of a man* in most people's sense: but of a body, so and so shaped, joined to it; and if that be the idea of a man, the same successive body not shifted all at once, must, as well as the same immaterial spirit, go to the making of the same man.

This being premised, to find wherein personal identity consists, we must consider what *person* stands for—which, I think, is a thinking intelligent being, that has reason and reflection, and can consider itself as itself, the same thinking thing, in different times and places; which it does only by that consciousness which is inseparable

from thinking, and, as it seems to me, essential to it: it being impossible for any one to perceive without *perceiving* that he does perceive. When we see, hear, smell, taste, feel, meditate, or will anything, we know that we do so. Thus it is always as to our present sensations and perceptions: and by this every one is to himself that which he calls self—it not being considered, in this case, whether the same self be continued in the same or divers substances. For, since consciousness always accompanies thinking, and it is that which makes every one to be what he calls self, and thereby distinguishes himself from all other thinking things, in this alone consists personal identity, i.e., the sameness of a rational being: and as far as this consciousness can be extended backwards to any past action or thought, so far reaches the identity of that person; it is the same self now it was then; and it is by the same self with this present one that now reflects on it, that that action was done.

But it is further inquired, whether it be the same identical substance. This few would think they had reason to doubt of, if these perceptions, with their consciousness, always remained present in the mind, whereby the same thinking thing would be always consciously present, and, as would be thought, evidently the same to itself. But that which seems to make the difficulty is this, that this consciousness being interrupted always by forgetfulness, there being no moment of our lives wherein we have the whole train of all our past actions before our eyes in one view,

---

From John Locke, An Essay Concerning Human Understanding, *Book II, Chapter 27, "Of Ideas of Identity and Diversity." First published in 1690.*

but even the best memories losing the sight of one part whilst they are viewing another; and we sometimes, and that the greatest part of our lives, not reflecting on our past selves, being intent on our present thoughts, and in sound sleep having no thoughts at all, or at least none with that consciousness which remarks our waking thoughts—I say, in all these cases, our consciousness being interrupted, and we losing the sight of our past selves, doubts are raised whether we are the same thinking thing, i.e., the same *substance* or no. Which, however reasonable or unreasonable, concerns not *personal* identity at all. The question being what makes the same person; and not whether it be the same identical substance, which always thinks in the same person, which, in this case, matters not at all: different substances, by the same consciousness (where they do partake in it) being united into one person, as well as different bodies by the same life are united into one animal, whose identity is perceived in that change of substances by the unity of one continued life. For, it being the same consciousness that makes a man be himself to himself, personal identity depends on that only, whether it be annexed solely to one individual substance, or can be continued in a succession of several substances. For as far as any intelligent being *can* repeat the idea of any past action with the same consciousness it had of it at first, and with the same consciousness it has of any present action; so far it is the same personal self. For it is by the consciousness it has of its present thoughts and actions, that it is *self to itself* now, and so will be the same self, as far as the same consciousness can extend to actions past or to come; and would be by distance of time, or change of substance, no more two persons, than a man be two men by wearing other clothes today than he did yesterday, with a long or a short sleep between: the same consciousness uniting those distant actions in the same person, whatever substances contributed to their production.

That this is so, we have some kind of evidence in our very bodies, all whose particles, whilst vitally united to this same thinking conscious self, so that *we feel* when they are touched, and are affected by, and conscious of good or harm that happens to them, are a part of ourselves; i.e., of our thinking conscious self. Thus, the limbs of his body are to every one a part of himself; he sympathizes and is concerned for them. Cut off a hand, and thereby separate it from that consciousness he had of its heat, cold, and other affections, and it is then no longer a part of that which is himself, any more than the remotest part of matter. Thus, we see the *substance* whereof personal self consisted at one time may be varied at another, without the change of personal identity; there being no question about the same person, though the limbs which but now were a part of it, be cut off. . . .

And thus may we be able, without any difficulty, to conceive the same person at the resurrection, though in a body not exactly in make or parts the same which he had here,—the same consciousness going along with the soul that inhabits it. But yet the soul alone, in the change of bodies, would scarce to any one but to him that makes the soul the man, be enough to make the same man. For should the soul of a prince, carrying with it the consciousness of the prince's past life, enter and inform the body of a cobbler, as soon as deserted by his own soul, every one sees he would be the same *person* with the prince, accountable only for the prince's actions: but who would say it was the same *man?* The body too goes to the making the man, and would, I guess, to everybody determine the man in this case, wherein the soul, with all its princely thoughts about it, would not make another man: but he would be the same cobbler to every one besides himself. I know that, in the ordinary way of speaking, the same person, and the same man, stand for one and the same thing. And indeed every one will always have a liberty to speak as he pleases, and to apply what articulate sounds to what ideas he thinks fit, and change them as often as he pleases. But yet, when we will inquire what makes the same *spirit, man,* or *person,* we must fix the ideas of spirit, man, or person in our minds; and having resolved with ourselves what we mean by them, it will not be hard to determine in either of them, or the like, when it is the same, and when not.

But though the immaterial substance or soul does not alone, wherever it be, and in whatsoever state, make the same *man;* yet it is plain, consciousness, as far as ever it can be extended—should it be to ages past—unites existences and actions very remote in time into the same *person,* as well as it does the existences and actions of the immediately preceding moment: so that whatever has the consciousness of present and past actions, is the same person to whom they both belong. Had I the same consciousness that I saw the ark and Noah's flood, as that I saw an overflowing of the Thames last winter, or as that I write now, I could no more doubt that I who write this now, that saw the Thames overflowed last winter, and that viewed the flood at the general deluge, was the same *self*—place that self in what *substance* you please—than that I who write this am the same *myself* now whilst I write (whether I consist of all the same substance, material or immaterial, or no) that I was yesterday. For as to this point of being the same self, it matters not whether this present self be made up of the same or other substances—I being as much concerned, and as justly accountable for any action that was done a thousand years since, appropriated to me now by this self-consciousness, as I am for what I did the last moment. . . .

But yet possibly it will still be objected—Suppose I wholly lose the memory of some parts of my life, beyond a possibility of retrieving them, so that perhaps I shall never be conscious of them again; yet am I not the same person that did those actions, had those thoughts that I once was conscious of, though I have now forgot them? To which I answer, that we must here take notice what the word *I* is applied to; which, in this case, is the *man* only. And the same man being presumed to be the same person, *I* is easily here supposed to stand also for the same person. But if it be possible for the same man to have distinct incommunicable consciousness at different times, it is past doubt the same man would at different times make different persons; which, we see, is the sense of mankind in the solemnest declaration of their opinions, human laws not punishing the mad man for the sober man's actions, nor the sober man for what the mad man did,—thereby making them two persons: which is somewhat explained by our way of speaking in English when we say such an one is "not himself," or is "beside himself"; in which phrases it is insinuated, as if those who now, or at least first used them, thought that self was changed; the selfsame person was no longer in that man.

But yet it is hard to conceive that Socrates, the same individual man, should be two persons. To help us a little in this, we must consider what is meant by Socrates, or the same individual *man.*

First, it must be either the same individual, immaterial, thinking substance; in short, the same numerical soul, and nothing else.

Secondly, or the same animal, without any regard to the immaterial soul.

Thirdly, or the same immaterial spirit united to the same animal.

Now, take which of these suppositions you please, it is impossible to make personal identity to consist in anything but consciousness; or reach any further than that does.

For Further Reflection

1. How would Locke respond to the objection that memories are not continuous in our consciousness? When we sleep, we cease to have memories at all. In partial amnesia do we cease to be who we were? Recall Thomas Reid's suggestion in the introduction to IV.B, of the problem of transitivity in memories. Suppose there is a gallant officer who at age twenty-five is a hero in a battle and who remembers getting a flogging in his childhood. Later, at age sixty-five, he recalls the heroic deed done at twenty-five but cannot recall the flogging. Since

he cannot remember the earlier deed, is he the same person he was when he did remember it? Can Locke answer Reid?

2. What about the phenomenon of split personalities and multiple personalities, also discussed in the introduction to this section, the most famous of which is Sybil, who allegedly expressed sixteen different personalities with sixteen different sets of memories? On a psychological states account, would we have to say that one body contains sixteen persons? Are there different persons inside each of us, expressed by different "sides" of our personalities?

We Have No Substantial Self with Which We Are Identical

IV.34

DAVID HUME

Hume does not believe that we have a self. For Hume, you might recall from Reading III.21, all learning comes from sensory impressions. There does not seem to be a separate impression of the self which we experience, so there is no reason to believe that we have a self. The most we can identify ourselves with is our consciousness and that constantly changes. There is no separate, permanent self which endures over time. Hence, personal identity is a fiction.

(A biographical sketch of Hume precedes Reading III.21.)

Study Questions

1. What does Hume mean by saying that the self is not any one impression, and what significance does this have for him?
2. What does Hume say of people who differ with him?
3. What is the "self"?
4. What does Hume say about the problem of identity?

THERE ARE SOME PHILOSOPHERS, who imagine we are every moment intimately conscious of what we call our Self; that we feel its existence and its continuance in existence; and are certain, beyond the evidence of a demonstration, both of its perfect identity and simplicity. . . .

Unluckily all these positive assertions are contrary to that very experience, which is pleaded for them, nor have we any idea of *self*, after the manner it is here explained. For from what impression could this idea be derived? This question 'tis impossible to answer without a manifest contradiction and absurdity; and yet 'tis a question, which must necessarily be answered, if we would have the idea of self pass for clear and intelligible. It must be some one impression, that gives rise to every real idea. But self or person is not any one impression, but that to which our

From David Hume, A Treatise of Human Nature. *First published in England in 1738.*

several impressions and ideas are supposed to have a reference. If any impression gives rise to the idea of self, that impression must continue invariably the same, through the whole course of our lives; since self is supposed to exist after that manner. But there is no impression constant and invariable. Pain and pleasure, grief and joy, passions and sensations succeed each other, and never all exist at the same time. It cannot, therefore, be from any of these impressions, or from any other, that the idea of self is derived; and consequently there is no such idea.

But farther, what must become of all our particular perceptions upon this hypothesis? All these are different, and distinguishable, and separable from each other, and may be separately considered, and may exist separately, and have no need of any thing to support their existence. After what manner, therefore, do they belong to self; and how are they connected with it? For my part, when I enter most intimately into what I call *myself*, I always stumble on some particular perception or other, of heat or cold, light or shade, love or hatred, pain or pleasure. I never can catch *myself* at any time without a perception, and never can observe any thing but the perception. When my perceptions are removed for any time, as by sound sleep; so long am I insensible of *myself*, and may truly be said not to exist. And were all my perceptions removed by death, and could I neither think, nor feel, nor see, nor love, nor hate after the dissolution of my body, I should be entirely annihilated, nor do I conceive what is farther requisite to make me a perfect nonentity. If any one upon serious and unprejudiced reflection, thinks he has a different notion of *himself*, I must confess I can reason no longer with him. All I can allow him is, that he may be in the right as well as I, and that we are essentially different in this particular. He may, perhaps, perceive something simple and continued, which he calls *himself*; though I am certain there is no such principle in me.

But setting aside some metaphysicians of this kind, I may venture to affirm of the rest of mankind, that they are nothing but a bundle or collection of different perceptions, which succeed each other with an inconceivable rapidity, and are in a perpetual flux and movement. Our eyes cannot turn in their sockets without varying our perceptions. Our thought is still more variable than our sight; and all our other senses and faculties contribute to this change; nor is there any single power of the soul, which remains unalterably the same, perhaps for one moment. The mind is a kind of theatre, where several perceptions successively make their appearance; pass, repass, glide away, and mingle in an infinite variety of postures and situations. There is properly no *simplicity* in it at one time, nor *identity* in different; whatever natural propension we may have to imagine that simplicity and identity. The comparison of the theatre must not mislead us. They are the successive perceptions only, that constitute the mind; nor have we the most distant notion of the place, where these scenes are represented, or of the materials, of which it is composed.

What then gives us so great a propension to ascribe an identity to these successive perceptions, and to suppose ourselves possessed of an invariable and uninterrupted existence through the whole course of our lives? . . .

We have a distinct idea of an object, that remains invariable and uninterrupted through a supposed variation of time; and this idea we call that of *identity* or *sameness*. We have also a distinct idea of several different objects existing in succession, and connected together by a close relation; and this to an accurate view affords as perfect a notion of *diversity*, as if there was no manner of relation among the objects. But though these two ideas of identity, and a succession of related objects be in themselves perfectly distinct, and even contrary, yet 'tis certain, that in our common way of thinking they are generally confounded with each other. That action of the imagination, by which we consider the uninterrupted and invariable object, and that by which we reflect on the succession of related objects, are almost the same to the feeling, nor is there much more effort of thought required in the latter case than in the former. The relation facilitates the transition of the mind from one object to another, and renders its passage as smooth as if it contemplated one continued object. This resemblance is the cause of the confusion and mistake, and makes us substitute the notion of identity, instead of that of related objects. . . .

Thus we feign the continued existence of the perceptions of our senses, to remove the interruption; and run into the notion of a *soul*, and *self*, and *substance*, to disguise the variation. But we may farther observe, that where we do not give rise to such a fiction, our propension to confound identity with relation is so great, that we are apt to imagine something unknown and mysterious, connecting the parts, beside their relation; and this I take to be the case with regard to the identity we ascribe to plants and vegetables. And even when this does not take place, we still feel a propensity to confound these ideas, though we are not able fully to satisfy ourselves in that particular, nor find any thing invariable and uninterrupted to justify our notion of identity.

Thus the controversy concerning identity is not merely a dispute of words. For when we attribute identity, in an improper sense, to variable or interrupted objects, our mistake is not confined to the expression, but is commonly attended with a fiction, either of something invariable and uninterrupted, or of something mysterious and inexplicable, or at least with a propensity to such fictions. What will suffice to prove this hypothesis to the satisfaction of every fair enquirer, is to show from daily experience and observation, that the objects, which are variable or interrupted, and yet are supposed to continue the same, are such only as consist of a succession of parts, connected together by resemblance, contiguity, or causation. . . .

A ship, of which a considerable part has been changed by frequent reparations, is still considered as the same; nor does the difference of the materials hinder us from ascribing an identity to it. The common end, in which the parts conspire, is the same under all their variations, and affords an easy transition of the imagination from one situation of the body to another. . . .

Though every one must allow, that in a very few years both vegetables and animals endure a *total* change, yet we still attribute identity to them, while their form, size, and substance are entirely altered. An oak, that grows from a small plant to a large tree, is still the same oak; though there be not one particle of matter, or figure of its parts the same. An infant becomes a man, and is sometimes fat, sometimes lean, without any change in his identity. . . . A man, who hears a noise, that is frequently interrupted and renewed, says, it is still the same noise; though 'tis evident the sounds have only a specific identity or resemblance, and there is nothing numerically the same, but the cause, which produced them. In like manner it may be said without breach of the propriety of language, that such a church, which was formerly of brick, fell to ruin, and that the parish rebuilt the same church of free-stone, and according to modern architecture. Here neither the form nor materials are the same, nor is there any thing common to the two objects, but their relation to the inhabitants of the parish; and yet this alone is sufficient to make us denominate them the same. . . .

From thence it evidently follows, that identity is nothing really belonging to these different perceptions, and uniting them together; but is merely a quality, which we attribute to them, because of the union of their ideas in the imagination, when we reflect upon them. . . .

The only question, therefore, which remains, is, by what relations this uninterrupted progress of our thought is produced, when we consider the successive existence of a mind or thinking person. And here 'tis evident we must confine ourselves to resemblance and causation. . . . Also, as memory alone acquaints us with the continuance and extent of this succession of perceptions, 'tis to be considered, upon that account chiefly, as the source of personal identity. Had we no memory, we never should have any notion of causation, nor consequently of that chain of causes and effects, which constitute our self or person.

For Further Reflection

Kant criticized Hume for reducing the mind to a stream of consciousness. The fact to be explained, says Kant, is not the succession of awarenesses, but an awareness of succession. If that which is aware passed with the awareness, there would be no awareness of succession, but it *doesn't* pass with it. This suggests that there is a transcendent self beyond the stream of consciousness of which Hume speaks. What do you make of this as an objection to Hume?

IV.35   Brain Transplants and Personal Identity: A Dialogue

DEREK PARFIT AND GODFREY VESEY

Derek Parfit is an English philosopher who was educated and now teaches at Oxford University. He has made outstanding contributions to the subjects of ethical theory and the problem of personal identity. His major work is *Reasons and Persons* (1984). Godfrey Vesey was educated at Cambridge University and is a professor of philosophy at the Open University. His principal works are *Perception* (1971) and *Personal Identity* (1974).

In this dialogue Vesey introduces the problem of split-brain transplants. That is, a brain is divided in two, and half is put into each of two other people's brainless heads. What do we say about this situation? Does the original person survive? Parfit then responds by developing his ideas of personal identity as psychological identity.

Study Questions

1. Describe the imaginary situation of Mr. Brown and Mr. Robinson's brain transplant.
2. What is a "*q*-memory"?
3. What does Parfit think of the "all-or-nothing" view of personal identity? Why does he hold to his position?
4. What are the three possible answers to the question "What's going to happen to me?" in the split-brain case and how does Parfit treat them?
5. What is Parfit's solution to the problem?

BRAIN TRANSPLANTS

In 1973 in the *Sunday Times* there was a report of how a team from the Metropolitan Hospital in Cleveland under Dr. R. J. White had successfully transplanted a monkey's head on to another monkey's body.[1] Dr. White was reported as having said, "Technically a human head transplant is pos-

From Godfrey Vesey, Philosophy in the Open, *1974, reprinted by permission of Open University Press.*

sible," and as hoping that "it may be possible eventually to transplant *parts* of the brain or other organs inside the head."

The possibility of brain transplants gives rise to a fascinating philosophical problem. Imagine the following situation:

> Two men, a Mr. Brown and a Mr. Robinson, had been operated on for brain tumours and brain extractions had been performed on both of them. At the end of the operations, however, the assistant inadvertently put Brown's brain in Robinson's head, and Robinson's brain in Brown's head. One of these men immediately dies, but the other, the one with Robinson's body and Brown's brain, eventually regains consciousness. Let us call the latter "Brownson." Upon regaining consciousness Brownson exhibits great shock and surprise at the appearance of his body. Then, upon seeing Brown's body, he exclaims incredulously, "That's me lying there!" Pointing to himself he says, "This isn't my body; the one over there is!" When asked his name he automatically replies "Brown." He recognizes Brown's wife and family (whom Robinson had never met), and is able to describe in detail events in Brown's life, always describing them as events in his own life. Of Robinson's past life he evinces no knowledge at all. Over a period of time he is observed to display all of the personality traits, mannerisms, interests, likes and dislikes, and so on, that had previously characterized Brown, and to act and talk in ways completely alien to the old Robinson.[2]

The next step is to suppose that Brown's brain is not simply transplanted whole into someone else's brainless head, but is divided in two and half put into each of *two* other people's brainless heads. The same memory having been coded in many parts of the cortex, they *both* then say they are Brown, are able to describe events in Brown's life as if they are events in their own lives, etc. What should we say now?

The implications of this case for what we should say about personal identity are considered by Derek Parfit in a paper entitled "Personal Identity." Parfit's own view is expressed in terms of a relationship he calls "psychological

continuity." He analyses this relationship partly in terms of what he calls "*q*-memory" ("*q*" stands for "quasi"). He sketches a definition of "*q*-memory" as follows:

> I am *q*-remembering an experience if (1) I have a belief about a past experience which seems in itself like a memory belief, (2) someone did have such an experience, and (3) my belief is dependent upon this experience in the same way (whatever that is) in which a memory of an experience is dependent upon it.[3]

The significance of this definition of *q*-memory is that *two* people can, in theory, *q*-remember doing what only one person did. So two people can, in theory, be psychologically continuous with one person.

Parfit's thesis is that there is nothing more to personal identity than this "psychological continuity." This is *not* to say that whenever there is a sufficient degree of psychological continuity there is personal identity, for psychological continuity could be a one-two, or "branching," relationship, and we are able to speak of "identity" only when there is a one-one relationship. It *is* to say that a common belief—in the special nature of personal identity—is mistaken.

In the discussion that follows I began by asking Parfit what he thinks of this common belief.

PERSONAL IDENTITY

Vesey: Derek, can we begin with the belief that you claim most of us have about personal identity? It's this: whatever happens between now and some future time either I shall still exist or I shan't. And any future experience will either be my experience or it won't. In other words, personal identity is an all or nothing matter: either I survive or I don't. Now what do you want to say about that?

Parfit: It seems to me just false. I think the true view is that we can easily describe and imagine large numbers of cases in which the question, "Will that future person be me—or someone else?," is both a question which doesn't have any answer at all, and there's no puzzle that there's no answer.

Vesey: Will you describe one such case.

Parfit: One of them is the case discussed in the correspondence material, the case of division in which we suppose that each half of my brain is to be transplanted into a new body and the two resulting people will both seem to remember the whole of my life, have my character and be psychologically continuous with me in every way. Now in this case of division there were only three possible answers to the question, "What's going to happen to *me?*" And all three of them seem to me open to very serious objections. So the conclusion to be drawn from the case is that the question of what's going to happen to me, just doesn't have an answer. I think the case also shows that that's not mysterious at all.

Vesey: Right, let's deal with these three possibilities in turn.

Parfit: Well, the first is that I'm going to be both of the resulting people. What's wrong with that answer is that it leads very quickly to a contradiction.

Vesey: How?

Parfit: The two resulting people are going to be different people from each other. They're going to live completely different lives. They're going to be as different as any two people are. But if they're different people from each other it can't be the case that I'm going to be both of them. Because if I'm both of them, then one of the resulting people is going to be the same person as the other.

Vesey: Yes. They can't be different people and be the same person, namely me.

Parfit: Exactly. So the first answer leads to a contradiction.

Vesey: Yes. And the second?

Parfit: Well, the second possible answer is that I'm not going to be both of them but just one of them. This doesn't lead to a contradiction, it's just wildly implausible. It's implausible because my relation to each of the resulting people is exactly similar.

Vesey: Yes, so there's no reason to say that I'm one rather than the other?

Parfit: It just seems absurd to suppose that, when you've got exactly the same relation, one of them is identity and the other is nothing at all.

Vesey: It does seem absurd, but there are philosophers who would say that sort of thing. Let's go on to the third.

Parfit: Well, the only remaining answer, if I'm not going to be both of them or only one of them, is that I'm going to be neither of them. What's wrong with this answer is that it's grossly misleading.

Vesey: Why?

Parfit: If I'm going to be neither of them, then there's not going to be anyone in the world after the operation who's going to be me. And that implies, given the way we now think, that the operation is as bad as death. Because if there's going to be no one who's going to be me, then I cease to exist. But it's obvious on reflection that the operation isn't as bad as death. It isn't bad in any way at all. That this is obvious can be shown by supposing that when they do the operation only one of the transplants succeeds and only one of the resulting people ever comes to consciousness again.

Vesey: Then I think we would say that this person is me. I mean we'd have no reason to say that he wasn't.

Parfit: On reflection I'm sure we would all think that I would survive as that one person.

Vesey: Yes.

Parfit: Yes. Well, if we now go back to the case where both operations succeed . . .

Vesey: Where there's a double success. . . .

Parfit: It's clearly absurd to suppose that a double success is a failure.

Vesey: Yes.

Parfit: So the conclusion that I would draw from this case is firstly, that to the question, "What's going to happen to me?," there's no true answer.

Vesey: Yes.

Parfit: Secondly, that if we decide to say one of the three possible answers, what we say is going to obscure the true nature of the case.

Vesey: Yes.

Parfit: And, thirdly, the case isn't in any way puzzling. And the reason for that is this. My relation to each of the resulting people is the relation of full psychological continuity. When I'm psychologically continuous with only one person, we call it identity. But if I'm psychologically continuous with two future people, we can't call it identity. It's not puzzling because we know exactly what's going to happen.

Vesey: Yes, could I see if I've got this straight? Where there is psychological continuity in a one—one case, this is the sort of case which we'd ordinarily talk of in terms of a person having survived the operation, or something like that.

Parfit: Yes.

Vesey: Now what about when there is what you call psychological continuity—that's to say, where the people seem to remember having been me and so on—in a one-two case? Is this survival or not?

Parfit: Well, I think it's just as good as survival, but the block we have to get over is that we can't say that anyone in the world after the operation is going to be me.

Vesey: No.

Parfit: Well, we can say it but it's very implausible. And we're inclined to think that if there's not going to be anyone who is me tomorrow, then I don't survive. What we need to realize is that my relation to each of those two people is just as good as survival. Nothing is missing at all in my relation to both of them, as compared with my relation to myself tomorrow.

Vesey: Yes.

Parfit: So here we've got survival without identity. And that only seems puzzling if we think that identity is a further fact over and above psychological continuity.

Vesey: It is very hard not to think of identity being a further fact, isn't it?

Parfit: Yes, I think it is. I think that the only way to get rid of our temptation to believe this is to consider many more cases than this one case of division. Perhaps I should give you another one. Suppose that the following is going to happen to

me. When I die in a normal way, scientists are going to map the states of all the cells in my brain and body and after a few months they will have constructed a perfect duplicate of me out of organic matter. And this duplicate will wake up fully psychologically continuous with me, seeming to remember my life with my character, etc.

Vesey: Yes.

Parfit: Now in this case, which is a secular version of the Resurrection, we're very inclined to think that the following question arises and is very real and very important. The question is, "Will that person who wakes up in three months be me or will he be some quite other person who's merely artificially made to be exactly like me?"

Vesey: It does seem to be a real question. I mean in the one case, if it is going to be me, then I have expectations and so on, and in the other case, where it isn't me, I don't.

Parfit: I agree, it seems as if there couldn't be a bigger difference between it being me and it being someone else.

Vesey: But you want to say that the two possibilities are in fact the same?

Parfit: I want to say that those two descriptions, "It's going to be me" and "It's going to be someone who is merely exactly like me" don't describe different outcomes, different courses of events, only one of which can happen. They are two ways of describing one and the same course of events. What I mean by that perhaps could be shown if we take an exactly comparable case involving not a person but something about which I think we're not inclined to have a false view.

Vesey: Yes.

Parfit: Something like a club. Suppose there's some club in the nineteenth century. . . .

Vesey: The Sherlock Holmes Club or something like that?

Parfit: Yes, perhaps. And after several years of meeting it ceases to meet. The club dies.

Vesey: Right.

Parfit: And then two of its members, let's say, have emigrated to America, and after about fifteen years they get together and they start up a club. It has exactly the same rules, completely new membership except for the first two people, and they give it the same name. Now suppose someone came along and said: "There's a real mystery here, because the following question is one that must have an answer. But how can we answer it?" The question is, "Have they started up the very same club—is it the same club as the one they belonged to in England—or is it a completely new club that's just exactly similar?"

Vesey: Yes.

Parfit: Well, in that case we all think that this man's remark is absurd; there's no difference at all. Now that's my model for the true view about the case where they make a duplicate of me. It seems that there's all the difference in the world between its being me and its being this other person who's exactly like me. But if we think there's no difference at all in the case of the clubs, why do we think there's a difference in the case of personal identity, and how can we defend the view that there's a difference?

Vesey: I can see how some people would defend it. I mean, a dualist would defend it in terms of a soul being a simple thing, but. . . .

Parfit: Let me try another case which I think helps to ease us out of this belief we're very strongly inclined to hold.

Vesey: Go on.

Parfit: Well, this isn't a single case, this is a whole range of cases. A whole smooth spectrum of different cases which are all very similar to the next one in the range. At the start of this range of cases you suppose that the scientists are going to replace one per cent of the cells in your brain and body with exact duplicates.

Vesey: Yes.

Parfit: Now if that were to be done, no one has any doubt that you'd survive. I think that's obvious because after all you can *lose* one per cent of the cells and survive. As we get further along the range they replace a larger and larger percentage of cells with exact duplicates, and of course at the far end of this range, where they replace a hundred per cent, then we've got my case where they just make a duplicate out of wholly fresh matter.

Vesey: Yes.

Parfit: Now on the view that there's all the difference in the world between its being me and its being this other person who is exactly like me, we ought in consistency to think that in some case in the middle of that range, where, say, they're going to replace fifty per cent, the same question arises: is it going to be me or this completely different character? I think that even the most convinced dualist who believes in the soul is going to find this range of cases very embarrassing, because he seems committed to the view that there's some crucial percentage up to which it's going to be him and after which it suddenly ceases to be him. But I find that wholly unbelievable.

Vesey: Yes. He's going to have to invent some sort of theory about the relation of mind and body to get round this one. I'm not quite sure how he would do it. Derek, could we go on to a related question? Suppose that I accepted what you said, that is, that there isn't anything more to identity than what you call psychological continuity in a one-one case. Suppose I accept that, then I would want to go on and ask you, well, what's the philosophical importance of this?

Parfit: The philosophical importance is, I think, that psychological continuity is obviously, when we think about it, a matter of degree. So long as we think that identity is a further fact, one of the things we're inclined to think is that it's all or nothing, as you said earlier. Well, if we give up that belief and if we realize that what matters in my continued existence is a matter of degree, then this does make a difference in actual cases. All the cases that I've considered so far are of course bizarre science fiction cases. But I think that in actual life it's obvious on reflection that, to give an example, the relations between me now and me next year are much closer in every way than the relations between me now and me in twenty years. And the sorts of relations that I'm thinking of are relations of memory, character, ambition, intention—all of those. Next year I shall remember much more of this year than I will in twenty years. I shall have a much more similar character. I shall be carrying out more of the same plans, ambitions and, if that is so, I think there are various plausible implications for our moral beliefs and various possible effects on our emotions.

Vesey: For our moral beliefs? What have you in mind?

Parfit: Let's take one very simple example. On the view which I'm sketching it seems to me much more plausible to claim that people deserve much less punishment, or even perhaps no punishment, for what they did many years ago as compared with what they did very recently. Plausible because the relations between them now and them many years ago when they committed the crime are so much weaker.

Vesey: But they are still the people who are responsible for the crime.

Parfit: I think you say that because even if they've changed in many ways, after all it was just as much they who committed the crime. I think that's true, but on the view for which I'm arguing, we would come to think that it's a completely trivial truth. It's like the following truth: it's like the truth that all of my relatives are just as much my relatives. Suppose I in my will left more money to my close relatives and less to my distant relatives; a mere pittance to my second cousin twenty-nine times removed. If you said, "But that's clearly unreasonable because all of your relatives are just as much your relatives," there's a sense in which that's true but it's obviously too trivial to make my will an unreasonable will. And that's because what's involved in kinship is a matter of degree.

Vesey: Yes.

Parfit: Now, if we think that what's involved in its being the same person now as the person who committed the crime is a matter of degree, then the truth that it was just as much him who committed the crime, will seem to us trivial in the way in which the truth that all my relatives are equally my relatives is trivial.

Vesey: Yes. So you think that I should regard myself in twenty years' time as like a fairly distant relative of myself?

Parfit: Well, I don't want to exaggerate; I think the connections are much closer.

Vesey: Suppose I said that this point about psychological continuity being a matter of degree—suppose I said that this isn't anything that anybody denies?

Parfit: I don't think anybody does on reflection deny that psychological continuity is a matter of degree. But I think what they may deny, and I think what may make a difference to their view, if they come over to the view for which I'm arguing—what they may deny is that psychological continuity is all there is to identity. Because what I'm arguing against is this further belief which I think we're all inclined to hold even if we don't realize it. The belief that however much we change, there's a profound sense in which the changed us is going to be just as much us. That even if some magic wand turned me into a completely different sort of person—a prince with totally different character, mental powers—it would be just as much me. That's what I'm denying.

Vesey: Yes. This is the belief which I began by stating, and I think that if we did lose that belief that would be a change indeed.

NOTES

1. *Sunday Times,* 9 December, 1973, p. 13.
2. Shoemaker (1963) pp. 23–24.
3. Parfit (1971) p. 15.

For Further Reflection

1. Is Parfit's analysis of the problem of the split-brain case plausible? Do you think that he correctly construes the issue or does he already presuppose controversial premises?

2. Do you think that there is another solution to the problem of personal identity?

IV.C   Is There Life After Death? Am I Immortal?

Suppose the ingenious neurologist Dr. Thomas were to design a brain just like yours in his laboratory, and suppose he were to design a body like yours but virtually indestructible (well, a nuclear bomb could destroy it, but failing that it would be impervious to alteration). The brain is now dormant, but at your death, Dr. Thomas will activate it and bring it to life within the prosthetic body. Now Thomas tells you that he needs to kill you to allow your alter ego to exist. You complain, but Thomas assures you that one exactly similar to you will live again with all your memories (or copies of them, but Alter Ego won't know the difference). Would you be comforted by that news? Would you take comfort in the fact that you will live again?

Where does all of this leave us with regard to survival after death? If there is no continuity of consciousness, is it the same person who would be resurrected or reconstituted by God at some future time? Or is the reconstituted person like Thomas' replica of you? A different token of the same generic type? Could God make several tokens of your type—say, five of you—that could be reconstituted and go on to live a new and eternal life? Quintuple resurrection!

Are the disembodied memories of a person enough to constitute survival? The question is perplexing. On the one hand, it seems that our identity is somehow tied to our psychological states (for example, memories and personality traits), which don't seem to depend on a body. But, then, if this is so, would our survival occur if a computer stored much of the information about our personalities and memory states?

We do seem to need a body and brain to instantiate our consciousness and personalities. It is hard to imagine any learning or experiencing or communication with others without a recognizable body. And the brain seems to be the locus of conscious experience. But our bodies and brains die and disintegrate. What happens to our consciousness and our personal identity? Is the gap between the present conscious life and the next simply like a long sleep during which God prepares a new and glorified body for our personality? Or does the fact that there will have to be a new creation rule out the possibility of personal survival altogether? Or can it be that there is an intrinsically spiritual character to our selves that both survives the death of the body and perdures in a life beyond this one?

The issue is as difficult as it is important to us. In this section, our first reading from Plato's *Phaedo* sets forth a view of the soul that is separate and of infinitely higher value than the body. The soul is good and the body evil. The body is really an encumbrance of the soul, which longs to be liberated from it. Death releases the soul from the body so that it can attain a wholly spiritual existence devoid of evil. In our second reading, Paul Edwards challenges the notion of survival after death and argues that it is essentially incoherent. In our third reading, John Hick responds to those who say that personal immortality is impossible. He sets forth conditions for justifying our belief in survival and shows that those conditions could be met. According to Hick, there is nothing incoherent about the notion of immortality.

Arguments for the Immortality of the Soul IV.36

PLATO

Plato (427–347 B.C.) believed that human beings were composed of two substances, a body and a soul. Of these, the true self is the soul, which lives on after the death of the body. All Plato's writings are in the form of dialogues. In the first dialogue (from *Alcibiades I*) Socrates argues with Alcibiades about the true self. The second dialogue (from *Phaedo*) takes place in prison, where Socrates has been condemned to die. He is offered a way of escape but rejects it, arguing that it would be immoral to flee such a fate at this time and that he is certain of a better life after death. He is speaking with Simmias and Cebes.

Study Questions

1. How does Socrates argue in *Alcibiades I* for the reality of the soul?
2. In the *Phaedo,* what is the role of the body with regard to attaining knowledge? What should the philosopher do about the body?
3. What is the significance in the argument of ideas such as absolute justice and beauty?
4. What is the attitude of the true philosopher toward death, and why?
5. How does Plato describe the process that leads to the attainment of wisdom?
6. How does the soul resemble the divine?

FROM ALCIBIADES I

SOCRATES: And is self-knowledge an easy thing, and was he to be lightly esteemed who inscribed the text on the temple at Delphi? ["Know Thyself"] Or is self-knowledge a difficult thing, which few are able to attain?

ALCIBIADES: At times, I fancy, Socrates, that anybody can know himself; at other times, the task appears to be very difficult.

Soc.: But whether easy or difficult, Alcibiades, still there is no other way; knowing what we are, we shall know how to take care of ourselves, and if we are ignorant we shall not know.

Al.: That is true.

Soc.: Well, then, let us see in what way the self-existent can be discovered by us; that will give us a chance to discover our own existence, which without that we can never know.

Al.: You say truly.

Soc.: Come, now, I beseech you, tell me with whom you are conversing?—with whom but with me?

Al.: Yes.

Soc.: As I am with you?

Al.: Yes.

Soc.: That is to say, I, Socrates, am talking?

Al.: Yes.

Soc.: And I in talking use words?

Al.: Certainly.

Soc.: And talking and using words are, as you would say, the same?

Al.: Very true.

From Plato, Alcibiades I *and the* Phaedo, *translated by William Jowett (New York: Charles Scribner's Sons, 1889).*

Soc.: And the user is not the same as the thing which he uses?

Al.: What do you mean?

Soc.: I will explain: the shoemaker, for example, uses a square tool, and a circular tool, and other tools for cutting?

Al.: Yes.

Soc.: But the tool is not the same as the cutter and user of the tool?

Al.: Of course not.

Soc.: And in the same way the instrument of the harper is to be distinguished from the harper himself?

Al.: He is.

Soc.: Now the question which I asked was whether you conceive the user to be always different from that which he uses?

Al.: I do.

Soc.: Then what shall we say of the shoemaker? Does he cut with his tools only or with his hands?

Al.: With his hands as well.

Soc.: He uses his hands too?

Al.: Yes.

Soc.: And does he use his eyes in cutting leather?

Al.: He does.

Soc.: And we admit that the user is not the same with the things which he uses?

Al.: Yes.

Soc.: Then the shoemaker and the harper are to be distinguished from the hands and feet which they use?

Al.: That is clear.

Soc.: And does not a man use the whole body?

Al.: Certainly.

Soc.: And that which uses is different from that which is used?

Al.: True.

Soc.: Then a man is not the same as his own body?

Al.: That is the inference.

Soc.: What is he, then?

Al.: I cannot say.

Soc.: Nay, you can say that he is the user of the body.

Al.: Yes.

Soc.: And the user of the body is the soul?

Al.: Yes, the soul.

Soc.: And the soul rules?

Al.: Yes.

Soc.: Let me make an assertion which will, I think, be universally admitted.

Al.: What is that?

Soc.: That man is one of three things.

Al.: What are they?

Soc.: Soul, body, or the union of the two.

Al.: Certainly.

Soc.: But did we not say that the actual ruling principle of the body is man?

Al.: Yes, we did.

Soc.: And does the body rule over itself?

Al.: Certainly not.

Soc.: It is subject, as we were saying?

Al.: Yes.

Soc.: Then that is not what we are seeking?

Al.: It would seem not.

Soc.: But may we say that the union of the two rules over the body, and consequently that this is man?

Al.: Very likely.

Soc.: The most unlikely of all things: for if one of the members is subject, the two united cannot possibly rule.

Al.: True.

Soc.: But since neither the body, nor the union of the two, is man, either man has no real existence, or the soul is man?

Al.: Just so.

Soc.: Would you have a more precise proof that the soul is man?

Al.: No; I think that the proof is sufficient.

Soc.: If the proof, although not quite precise, is fair, that is enough for us; more precise proof will be supplied when we have discovered that which we were led to omit, from a fear that the inquiry would be too much protracted.

Al.: What was that?

Soc.: What I meant, when I said that absolute existence must be first considered; but now, instead of absolute existence, we have been considering the nature of individual existence, and that may be sufficient; for surely there is nothing belonging to us which has more absolute existence than the soul?

Al.: There is nothing.

Soc.: Then we may truly conceive that you and I are conversing with one another, soul to soul?

Al.: Very true.

Soc.: And that is just what I was saying—that I, Socrates, am not arguing or talking with the face of Alcibiades, but with the real Alcibiades; and that is with his soul.

Al.: True. . . .

FROM PHAEDO

Socrates: What again shall we say of the actual acquirement of knowledge?—is the body, if invited to share in the inquiry, a hinderer or a helper? I mean to say, have sight and hearing any truth in them? Are they not, as the poets are always telling us, inaccurate witnesses? and yet, if even they are inaccurate and indistinct, what is to be said of the other senses?—for you will allow that they are the best of them?

Certainly, he [Simmias] replied.

Then when does the soul attain truth?—for in attempting to consider anything in company with the body she is obviously deceived.

Yes, that is true.

Then must not existence be revealed to her in thought, if at all?

Yes.

And thought is best when the mind is gathered into herself and none of these things trouble her—neither sounds nor sights nor pain nor any pleasure,—when she has as little as possible to do with the body, and has no bodily sense of feeling, but is aspiring after being?

That is true.

And in this the philosopher dishonors the body; his soul runs away from the body and desires to be alone and by herself?

That is true.

Well, but there is another thing, Simmias: Is there or is there not an absolute justice?

Assuredly there is.

And an absolute beauty and absolute good?

Of course.

But did you ever behold any of them with your eyes?

Certainly not.

Or did you ever reach them with any other bodily sense? (and I speak not of these alone, but of absolute greatness, and health, and strength, and of the essence of true nature of everything). Has the reality of them ever been perceived by you through the bodily organs? or rather, is not the nearest approach to the knowledge of their several natures made by him who so orders his intellectual vision as to have the most exact conception of the essence of that which he considers?

Certainly.

And he attains to the knowledge of them in their highest purity who goes to each of them with the mind alone, not allowing when in the act of thought the intrusion or introduction of sight or any other sense in the company of reason, but with the very light of the mind in her clearness penetrates into the very light of truth in each; he has got rid, as far as he can, of eyes and ears and of the whole body, which he conceives of only as a disturbing element, hindering the soul from the acquisition of knowledge when in company with her—is not this the sort of man who, if ever man did, is likely to attain the knowledge of existence?

There is admirable truth in that, Socrates, replied Simmias.

And when they consider all this, must not true philosophers make a reflection, of which they will speak to one another in such words as these: We have found, they will say, a path of speculation which seems to bring us and the argument to the conclusion, that while we are in the body, and while the soul is mingled with this mass of evil, our desire will not be satisfied, and our desire is of the truth. For the body is a source of endless trouble to us by reason of the mere requirement of food; and also is liable to diseases which overtake and impede us in the search after truth: and by filling us so full of loves, and lusts, and fears, and fancies, and idols, and every sort of folly, prevents our ever having, as people say, so much as a thought. From whence come wars, and fightings, and factions? whence but from the body and the lusts of the body? For wars are occasioned by the love of money, and money has to be acquired for the sake and in the service of the body; and in consequence of all these things the time which ought to be given to philosophy is lost. Moreover, if there is time and an inclination toward philosophy, yet the body introduces a turmoil and confusion and fear into the course of speculation, and hinders us from seeing the truth, and all experience shows that if we would have pure knowledge of anything we must be quit of the body, and the soul in herself must behold all things in themselves: then I suppose that we shall attain that which we desire, and of which we say that we are lovers, and that is wisdom; not while we live, but after death, as the argument shows; for if while in company with the body, the soul cannot have pure knowledge, one of two things seems to follow—either knowledge is not to be attained at all, or, if at all, after death. For then, and not till then, the soul will be in herself alone and without the body. In this present life, I reckon that we make the nearest approach to knowledge when we have the least possible concern or interest in the body, and are not saturated with the bodily nature, but remain pure until the hour when God himself is pleased to release us. And then the foolishness of the body will be cleared away and we shall be pure and hold converse with other pure souls, and know of ourselves the clear light everywhere; and this is surely the light of truth. For no impure thing is allowed to approach the pure. These are the sort of words, Simmias, which the true lovers of wisdom cannot help saying to one another, and thinking. You will agree with me in that?

Certainly, Socrates.

But if this is true, O my friend, then there is great hope that, going whither I go, I shall

there be satisfied with that which has been the chief concern of you and me in our past lives. And now that the hour of departure is appointed to me, this is the hope with which I depart, and not I only, but every man who believes that he has his mind purified.

Certainly, replied Simmias.

And what is purification but the separation of the soul from the body, as I was saying before; the habit of the soul gathering and collecting herself into herself, out of all the courses of the body; the dwelling in her own place alone, as in another life, so also in this, as far as she can; the release of the soul from the chains of the body?

Very true, he said.

And what is that which is termed death, but this very separation and release of the soul from the body?

To be sure, he said.

And the true philosophers, and they only, study and are eager to release the soul. Is not the separation and release of the soul from the body their especial study?

That is true.

And as I was saying at first, there would be a ridiculous contradiction in men studying to live as nearly as they can in a state of death, and yet repining when death comes.

Certainly.

Then Simmias, as the true philosophers are ever studying death, to them, of all men, death is the least terrible. Look at the matter in this way: how inconsistent of them to have been always enemies of the body, and wanting to have the soul alone, and when this is granted to them, to be trembling and repining; instead of rejoicing at their departing to that place where, when they arrive, they hope to gain that which in life they loved (and this was wisdom), and at the same time to be rid of the company of their enemy. Many a man has been willing to go to the world below in the hope of seeing there an earthly love, or wife, or son, and conversing with them. And will he who is a true lover of wisdom, and is persuaded in like manner that only in the world below he can worthily enjoy her, still repine at death? Will he not depart with joy? Surely, he will, my friend, if he be a true philosopher. For he will have a firm conviction that there only, and nowhere else, he can find wisdom in her purity. And if this be true, he would be very absurd, as I was saying, if he were to fear death. . . .

Socrates: And were we not saying long ago that the soul when using the body as an instrument of perception, that is to say, when using the sense of sight or hearing or some other sense (for the meaning of perceiving through the body is perceiving through the senses)— were we not saying that the soul too is then dragged by the body into the region of the changeable, and wanders and is confused; the world spins round her, and she is like a drunkard when under their influence?

Very true.

But when returning into herself she reflects; then she passes into the realm of purity, and eternity, and immortality, and unchangeableness, which are her kindred, and with them she ever lives, when she is by herself and is not let or hindered; then she ceases from her erring ways, and being in communion with the unchanging, is unchanging. And this state of the soul is called wisdom?

That is well and truly said, Socrates, he replied.

And to which class is the soul more nearly alike and akin, as far as may be inferred from this argument, as well as from the preceding one?

I think, Socrates, that, in the opinion of every one who follows the argument, the soul will be infinitely more like the unchangeable—even the most stupid person will not deny that.

And the body is more like the changing?

Yes.

Yet once more consider the matter in this light: When the soul and the body are united, then nature orders the soul to rule and govern, and the body to obey and serve. Now which of these two functions is akin to the divine? and which to the mortal? Does not the divine appear to you to be that which naturally orders and rules, and the mortal that which is subject and servant?

True.

And which does the soul resemble?

The soul resembles the divine, and the body the mortal—there can be no doubt of that, Socrates.

Then reflect, Cebes: is not the conclusion of the whole matter this—that the soul is in the very likeness of the divine, and immortal, and intelligible, and uniform, and indissoluble, and unchangeable; and the body is in the very likeness of the human, and mortal, and unintelligible, and multiform, and dissoluble, and changeable. Can this, my dear Cebes, be denied?

No indeed.

But if this is true, then is not the body liable to speedy dissolution? and is not the soul almost or altogether indissoluble?

Certainly.

And do you further observe, that after a man is dead, the body, which is the visible part of man, and has a visible framework, which is called a corpse, and which would naturally be dissolved and decomposed and dissipated, is not dissolved or decomposed at once, but may remain for a good while, if the constitution be sound at the time of death, and the season of the year favorable? For the body when shrunk and embalmed, as is the custom in Egypt, may remain almost entire through infinite ages; and even in decay, still there are some portions, such as the bones and ligaments, which are practically indestructible. You allow that?

Yes.

And are we to suppose that the soul, which is invisible, in passing to the true Hades, which like her is invisible, and pure, and noble, and on her way to the good and wise God, whither, if God will, my soul is also soon to go—that the soul, I repeat, if this be her nature and origin, is blown away and perishes immediately on quitting the body, as the many say? That can never be, my dear Simmias and Cebes. The truth rather is, that the soul which is pure at departing draws after her no bodily taint, having never voluntarily had connection with the body, which she is ever avoiding, herself gathered into herself (for such abstraction has been the study of her life). And what does this mean but that she has been a true disciple of philosophy, and has practiced how to die easily? And is not philosophy the practice of death?

Certainly.

That soul, I say, herself invisible, departs to the invisible world—to the divine and immortal and rational: thither arriving, she lives in bliss and is released from the error and folly of men, their fears and wild passions and all other human ills, and forever dwells, as they say of the initiated, in company with the gods? Is not this true, Cebes?

Yes, said Cebes, beyond a doubt.

For Further Reflection

1. Are Plato's arguments in these two dialogues persuasive? Do the arguments depend overly much on his theory of the forms, which gives ideas separate existence?

2. Is Plato correct in thinking that the body always hinders pure thought? How might a contemporary materialist respond to Plato?

IV.37   An Argument Against Survival: The Dependence of Consciousness on the Brain

PAUL EDWARDS

A biographical sketch of Paul Edwards precedes Reading II.6. In this essay Edwards argues that a powerful case against survival after death can be made from what we know about the dependence of consciousness on the brain. Edwards grants his opponent dualist assumptions, that is, that the mind cannot be identified with the brain and that corporealism (the doctrine that we are wholly material beings) is false. He argues that, even with these generous concessions, the case against survival is overwhelming.

Study Questions

1. What is Hume's argument against immortality?
2. How does J. J. C. Smart differ from Hume?
3. To which versions of survival does Edwards' argument apply? What is the "literal resurrection" view?
4. How does Edwards use the nature of Alzheimer's Disease in his argument?
5. What does Edwards say about the view that the body is an instrument of the mind?
6. How does Stevenson argue for reincarnation against Cohen and Taylor?
7. What is Mill's argument for complete agnosticism over survival?
8. At the end of his essay Edwards offers two final objections to the idea that our self or soul is a spiritual substance. What are they?

IN THIS ARTICLE I will discuss the case against survival after death based on what is known about the dependence of consciousness on the brain. This may be called the body-mind dependence argument. I shall try to bring out what a formidable argument it is. Among other things I shall try to show that the various replies to it by philosophers and theologians are unsound.

I will make two assumptions which are favorable to the case for survival. By this I mean that without them one of the major forms of survival-belief would be ruled out from the start. I will assume, first, that some form of dualism is true, i.e., that a person is a body and a mind in a sense in which the mind cannot be identified with any bodily processes or behavior. I will also assume that when we talk about personal identity, bodily continuity is not an essential ingredient in what we mean. The view that bodily continuity is an essential ingredient in personal identity has sometimes been referred to as "corporealism" and I will here assume that corporealism is false.

THE SCOPE OF THE ARGUMENT

In a rudimentary form the argument can already be found in Lucretius and Pomponazzi and, since Bishop Butler expressly argued against it in the first chapter of his *Analogy of Religion* we may infer that it was current among English free-thinkers in the early years of the eighteenth century. However, the first full statement with which I am familiar occurs in Hume's posthumous essay on immortality:

> Where any two objects are so closely connected that all alterations which we have ever seen in the one are attended with proportionable alterations in the other, we ought to conclude, by all rules of analogy, that, when there are still greater alterations produced in the former, and it is totally dissolved, there follows a total dissolution of the

latter. . . . The weakness of the body and that of the mind in infancy are exactly proportioned; their vigour in manhood, their sympathetic disorder in sickness; their common gradual decay in old age. The step further seems unavoidable; their common dissolution in death. The last symptoms which the mind discovers, are disorder, weakness, insensibility, and stupidity; the forerunners of its annihilation. The further progress of the same causes increasing, the same effects totally extinguish it.

Some of Hume's detailed observations are of course quite indefensible. There is surely no "exact" proportionality between physical and mental development or between bodily and mental "decay." Nor is it true that all human beings are "insensible" and "stupid" immediately before their death. Hume was also handicapped by the undeveloped state of brain physiology in the eighteenth century. Nevertheless his statement conveys very vividly the basic idea of the argument.

More recent defenders have placed heavy emphasis on information about the relation between the brain and our mental states and processes. Unlike Hume Professor J. J. C. Smart rejects dualism. As a materialist he maintains that mental states are identical with brain states, but he nevertheless endorses the body-mind dependence argument as valid within a dualistic framework:

> Even if some form of philosophical dualism is accepted and the mind is thought of as something over and above the body, the empirical evidence in favor of an invariable correlation between mental states and brain states is extremely strong: that is, the mind may be thought of as in some sense distinct from the body but also as fundamentally dependent upon physical states. Without oxygen or under the influence of anesthetics or soporific drugs, we rapidly lose consciousness. Moreover, the quality of our consciousness can be influenced in spectacular ways by appropriate drugs or by

From Paul Edwards, "The Dependence of Consciousness on the Brain" in Immortality *by Paul Edwards (ed.) (Amherst, NY: Prometheus Books). © 1997. Reprinted by permission of the publisher.*

mechanical stimulation of different areas of the brain. In the face of all the evidence that is being accumulated by modern research in neurology, it is hard to believe that after the dissolution of the brain there could be any thought or conscious experience whatever.

I will add one other recent formulation which states the argument simply and forcefully and is based on the most recent evidence from neurology. "What we call 'the mind,'" writes Colin McGinn,

> is in fact made up of a great number of subcapacities, and each of these depends upon the functioning of the brain.

Now, the facts of neurology

> compellingly demonstrate . . . that everything about the mind, from the sensory-motor periphery to the inner sense of self, is minutely controlled by the brain: if your brain lacks certain chemicals or gets locally damaged, your mind is apt to fall apart at the seams. . . . If parts of the mind depend for their existence upon parts of the brain, then the whole of the mind must so depend too. Hence the soul dies with the brain, which is to say it is mortal.[1]

It should be emphasized that the argument does *not* start from the premise that after a person is dead he never again acts in the world. A correspondent in the *London Review* replied to McGinn by observing that we do not need his or the neuropathologist's "assistance to learn that all behavior stops at death." Similarly, John Stuart Mill in his chapter on "Immortality" in *Three Essays on Religion* thought the argument inconclusive on the ground that the absence of any acts by an individual after his death is as consistent with the view that he will "recommence" his existence "elsewhere" as it is with the assumption that he has been extinguished forever. Such remarks are due to a misunderstanding. The absence of any actions by the dead is certainly not irrelevant, but the argument is primarily based on the observed dependence of our

mental states and processes on what goes on in the brain.

At first sight it may seem that, if valid, the argument merely rules out the survival of the disembodied mind and leaves other forms of survival untouched. In fact, however, it equally rules out reincarnation and the more sophisticated or replica-version of resurrectionism. This is so because the conclusion of the argument is that my mind depends on *my* brain. It does not merely support the less specific conclusion that my mind needs *some* brain as its foundation. If my mind is finished when my brain dies, then it cannot transmigrate to any other body. Similarly, if God created a duplicate of my body containing a duplicate of my brain, *my* mind would not be able to make use of it since it stopped existing with the death of my original body. The argument does not refute belief in the literal resurrection of the body. For on this view God will reconstitute our *original* bodies and hence also our original brains on the Day of Judgment. There are indeed vast numbers of fundamentalists and also a few pious philosophers who believe or say that they believe in resurrection in this literal sense, but to the great majority of scientists and philosophers and of educated persons generally it seems totally incredible. However, if anybody does believe in survival in *this* sense our argument has no bearing on his view.

ALZHEIMER'S DISEASE AND COMAS

The literature on survival contains a number of standard rejoinders to the body-mind dependence argument. Before turning to them, I will consider two concrete instances of body-mind dependence which will help to bring out the full force of the argument. The first is Alzheimer's disease, a dreadful affliction that ruins the last years of a sizable percentage of the world's population. Almost everybody above the age of thirty has known some elderly relative or friend afflicted with this illness. I can therefore be brief

1. *London Review of Books,* January 23, 1986, pp. 24–25.

in my description of what happens to Alzheimer patients. In the early stages the person misses appointments, he constantly loses and mislays objects, and he frequently cannot recall events in the recent past. As the illness progresses he can no longer read or write and his speech tends to be incoherent. In nursing homes Alzheimer patients commonly watch television, but there is no evidence that they understand what is happening on the screen. The decline in intellectual function is generally accompanied by severe emotional symptoms, such as extreme irritability and violent reactions to persons in the environment, as well as hallucinations and paranoid fears. In the final stages the patient is totally confused, frequently incontinent, and quite unable to recognize anybody, including the closest relatives and friends. At present Alzheimer's is incurable and, unlike in the case of Parkinson's disease, there are no known means of slowing down the deterioration. It is also as yet a mystery why Alzheimer's strikes certain individuals while sparing the majority of old people. However, a great deal is known about what goes on in the brains of Alzheimer patients. Alois Alzheimer, the neurologist after whom the disease is named, found in 1906 that the cerebral cortex and the hippocampus of his patients contained twisted tangles and filaments as well as abnormal neurites known as "neuritic" or "senile plaques." It has since been determined that the density of these abnormal components is directly proportional to the severity of the disorder. Autopsies have shown that Alzheimer victims have a vastly reduced level of an enzyme called "choline acetyltransferase," which is needed for producing the neurotransmitter acetylcholine. Although the reduced level of the enzyme and the neurotransmitter appear in the cortex, the origin of the trouble lies in another region of the brain, the nucleus basalis, which is situated just above the place where the optic nerves meet and cross. Autopsies have revealed a dramatic loss of neurons from the nucleus basalis in Alzheimer victims, and this explains why so little of the enzyme is manufactured in their brains.

The information just summarized has been culled from articles about Alzheimer's that have appeared in magazines and popular science monthlies in recent years. The authors of these articles are evidently not concerned with the question of survival after death, but they invariably use such phrases as "destruction of the mind" in describing what happens to the victims. In an article in *Science 84* entitled "The Clouded Mind," the author, Michael Shodell, speaks of Alzheimer's as "an illness that destroys the mind, leaving the body behind as a grim reminder of the person who once was there." Similarly, the cover story in *Newsweek* of December 3, 1984, which contained many heart-rending illustrations and listed some of the famous men and women who are suffering from Alzheimer's, was entitled "A Slow Death of the Mind." I think that these descriptions are entirely appropriate: A person who can no longer read or write, whose memory has largely disappeared, whose speech is incoherent, and who is totally indifferent to his environment has in effect lost all or most of what we normally call his mind. The relevance of this to our discussion is obvious. While still alive, an Alzheimer patient's brain is severely damaged and most of his mind has disappeared. After his death his brain is not merely damaged but completely destroyed. It is surely logical to conclude that now his mind is also gone. It seems preposterous to assert that, when the brain is completely destroyed, the mind suddenly returns intact, with its emotional and intellectual capacities, including its memory, restored. How does the *complete* destruction of the brain bring about a cure that has so far totally eluded medical science?

The same obviously applies to people in irreversible comas. Karen Ann Quinlan lay in a coma for over ten years before she finally died. The damage to her brain had made her, in the phrase used by the newspapers, nothing more than a "vegetable." Her E.E.G. was flat; she was unable to speak or write; visits by her foster parents did not register the slightest response. A more recent widely publicized case was that of the great

American tenor Jan Peerce. Peerce had amazed the musical public by singing right into his seventies with only a slight decline in his vocal powers. In the end, however, he was felled by two severe strokes, and he spent the last year of his life in an irreversible coma. Relatives and friends could get no response of any kind. Peerce died in December 1984, and Karen Ann Quinlan in June 1985. Did the total destruction of the bodies of these individuals suddenly bring back their emotional and intellectual capacities? If so, where were these during the intervening periods?

THE BODY AS THE INSTRUMENT OF THE MIND

The first of the rejoinders I will consider does not dispute the manifold dependence of mental functions on brain processes. It is claimed, however, that these facts are not inconsistent with survival. They are indeed compatible with the view that the mind is annihilated at death, but they are also compatible with the very different position that the mind continues to exist but has lost its "instrument" for acting in the world, and more specifically, for communicating with people who are still alive. An excellent illustration of what the supporters of this rejoinder have in mind is supplied by Father John A. O'Brien in his pamphlet: *The Soul—What Is It?* In order to carve a statue, Father O'Brien writes, a sculptor needs his tools, his hammer and chisel. If the tools are seriously damaged, the quality of his work will be correspondingly impaired, but this does not mean that the sculptor cannot exist if the tools are completely destroyed.

Variants of this argument are found in numerous Protestant theologians, in Catholic philosophers who have frequently relied on the distinction between what they call "extrinsic" and "intrinsic" dependence, and in several secular philosophers, including Descartes, Kant, James, Schiller and McTaggart. "I do not agree with you," writes Descartes to Gassendi in his "Reply to the Fifth Objection" to his *Meditations,*

that the mind waxes and wanes with the body; for from the fact that it does not work equally well in the body of a child and in that of a grown man, and that its actions are often impeded by wine and other bodily things, it follows merely that while it is united to the body it uses the body as an instrument in its normal operations.

Have we any reason, asks McTaggart, to suppose that "a body is essential to a self"? Not at all. The facts support the very different proposition that "while a self has a body, that body is essentially connected with the self's mental life." A self needs "sufficient data" for its mental activity. In this life the material is given in the form of sensations, and these can only be obtained by means of a body. It does not follow, however, that "it would be impossible for a self without a body to get data in some other way." McTaggart then offers an analogy which has frequently been quoted by believers in survival:

> If a man is shut up in a house, the transparency of the windows is an essential condition of his seeing the sky. But it would not be prudent to infer that, if he walked out of the house, he could not see the sky because there was no longer any glass through which he might see it.

McTaggart is totally unimpressed by the evidence from brain physiology which, it is safe to say, he did not study in detail and which was very extensive even in 1906 when his book was published. He does not dispute that "diseases or mutilations of the brain affect the course of thought," but "the fact that an abnormal state of the brain may affect our thought does not prove that the normal states of the brain are necessary for thought."

It may be instructive at this stage to consider some of the exchanges between Professor Ian Stevenson, the well-known champion of reincarnation, and two of his skeptical interrogators in the course of a BBC program that took place in the spring of 1976. The program dealt with the claims of Edward Ryall, an elderly Englishman who in May 1970 had written a letter to the *Daily Express* in which he mentioned his clear and extensive memories of a life in the seventeenth century as a West Country farmer by the name of John Fletcher. Stevenson corresponded with Ryall and became convinced of the authenticity of his recollections. He encouraged Ryall to write a book about his previous life. *Second Time Around* appeared in 1974, with an introduction and supplementary notes by Stevenson. Besides Stevenson and Ryall, the participants in the BBC program were John Taylor, professor of mathematics at London University, and John Cohen, professor of psychology at Manchester. Here are some of the exchanges that are relevant to our discussion.

Cohen: . . . memories are tied to a particular brain tissue. If you take away the brain, there is no memory.

Stevenson: I think that's an assumption. Memories may exist in the brain and exist elsewhere also.

Cohen: But we have not the slightest evidence, even a single case, of a memory existing without a brain. We have plenty of slight damage to a brain which destroys memory, but not the other way around.

Stevenson: I feel that's one of the issues here—whether memories can, in fact, survive the destruction of the brain.

Taylor: Professor Stevenson, do you have any evidence, other than these reincarnation cases, that memories can survive the destruction of physical tissue?

Stevenson: No. I think the best evidence comes from the reincarnation cases.

Taylor then brought up the well-known case of people who lose all or most of their memories as a result of brain injuries. Stevenson was not fazed.[2]

Stevenson: Well, it's possible that what is affected is his ability to express memories that he may still have.

Taylor: But are you suggesting, in fact, that memories themselves are in some way nonphysically bound up, and can be stored in a nonphysical manner?

2. *The Listener*, June 3, 1976, p. 698.

Stevenson: Yes, I'm suggesting that there might be a nonphysical process of storage.

Taylor: What does that mean? Nonphysical storage of what?

Stevenson: The potentiality for the reproduction of an image memory.

Taylor: But information itself involves energy. Is there such a thing as nonphysical energy?

Stevenson: I think there may be, yes.

Taylor: How can you define it? Nonphysical energy, to me, is a complete contradiction in terms. I can't conceive how on earth you could ever conceive of such a quantity.

Stevenson: Well, it might be in some dimension of which we are just beginning to form crude ideas, through the study of what we parapsychologists call paranormal phenomena. We are making an assumption of some kind of process that is not, and maybe cannot be, understood in terms of current physical concepts. That is a jump, a gap, I freely admit.

These exchanges bring out very clearly what is at issue between those who accept the body—mind dependence argument and the supporters of the instrument theory.

It has on occasion been suggested that we have no way of deciding between these two rival explanations of the relevant facts. I see no reason to accept such an agnostic conclusion. It seems to me that by retrodictive extrapolation to cases like Alzheimer patients or people in comas we can see that the alternative to annihilation proposed by the instrument theory is absurd. Let us consider the behavior of Alzheimer patients in the later stages of their affliction. The more specific the case, the clearer the implications of the rival views will appear. The mother of a close friend of mine, Mrs. D., recently died from Alzheimer's after suffering from the disease for about eight years. Mrs. D. was a prosperous lady from Virginia, the widow of a banker. In her pre-Alzheimer days she was a courteous and well-behaved person, and she had of course no difficulty recognizing her daughter or any of her other relatives or friends. I do not know what her feelings were about paralyzed people, but my guess is that she pitied them and certainly had no wish to beat them up. As her illness progressed she was put into a nursing home run by nuns who were renowned for their gentle and compassionate ways. She shared a room with an older lady who was paralyzed. For the first year or so Mrs. D. did not become violent. Then she started hitting the nurses. At about the time when she could no longer recognize her daughter, she beat up the paralyzed lady on two or three occasions. From then on she had to be confined to the "seventh floor," which was reserved for violent and exceptionally difficult patients.

Let us now see what the survival theorists would have to say about Mrs. D.'s behavior. It should be remembered that on this view Mrs. D., after her death, will exist with her mind intact and will only lack the means of communicating with people on earth. This view implies that throughout her affliction with Alzheimer's Mrs. D.'s mind *was* intact. She recognized her daughter but had lost her ability to express this recognition. She had no wish to beat up an inoffensive paralyzed old woman. On the contrary, "inside" she was the same considerate person as before the onset of the illness. It is simply that her brain disease prevented her from acting in accordance with her true emotions. I must insist that these *are* the implications of the theory that the mind survives the death of the brain and that the brain is only an instrument for communication. Surely these consequences are absurd: The facts are that Mrs. D. no longer recognized her daughter and that she no longer had any compassionate feelings about paralyzed old women. At any rate, we have the same grounds for saying this as we do in any number of undisputed cases in which people do not suffer from Alzheimer's and fail to recognize other human beings or fail to feel compassion.

The guards in Argentine dungeons who tortured and killed liberals had no compassion for their victims, and neither of course did the Nazis who rounded up and then shot Jews in Poland and elsewhere. We have exactly the same kind of evidence for concluding that Mrs. D., who probably did feel compassion for paralyzed peo-

ple before she suffered from Alzheimer's, no longer felt compassion when beating up her paralyzed roommate. As for memories, all of us sometimes cannot place a familiar tune or remember the name of a person we know well; and in such cases it makes good sense to say that the memories are still there. Even when the name never comes back there is a suspicion that the memory may not have been lost: it is entirely possible that one could bring it back under hypnosis. However, the memory loss in Alzheimer's is totally different, and the same of course applies to people in irreversible comas. It is surely fantastic to maintain that during his last months Jan Peerce did recognize his wife and children and simply could not express his recognition. If anybody makes such a claim it can only be for ulterior metaphysical reasons and not because it is supported by the slightest evidence.

MILL, BUTLER, EWING— THE ABSENSE OF DIRECT NEGATIVE EVIDENCE

Mill's posthumously published essay on "Theism" contains a chapter on immortality in which he surveys and evaluates all the major arguments on both sides that were known to him. Mill finds all of them defective and concludes on a note of complete agnosticism. We have here, he writes, "one of those very rare cases in which there is really a total absence of evidence on either side" and "in which the absence of evidence for the affirmative does not, as in so many other cases, create a strong presumption in favor of the negative."[3]

Mill discusses in some detail the evidence from brain physiology. It supplies us with "sufficient evidence that cerebral action is, if not the cause, at least, in our present state of existence, a condition *sine qua non* of mental operations." We are entitled to conclude that the death of the

3. *Three Essays on Religion* (London: Longman's Green, Reader and Dyer, 1876), p. 203.

brain would put a stop to all mental function and "remand it [the mind] to unconsciousness unless and until some other set of conditions supervenes, capable of recalling it into activity." The facts of brain physiology most emphatically do not prove that the mind cannot exist after death. "The same thoughts, emotions, volitions, and even sensations which we have here" may, for all we can tell, "persist or recommence somewhere else under other conditions." This is no less possible than that "other thoughts and sensations may exist under other conditions in other parts of the universe." What Mill evidently seems to require in order to establish the negative case is that we observe the nonexistence of the thoughts, volitions, and sensations of the dead person; and this the body-mind dependence argument does not give us.

Independently of this argument, Bishop Butler insists on the same requirement and regards its nonfulfillment as a fatal flaw in the unbeliever's position. Not only do we never directly observe the nonexistence of human minds, but the same is also true of animals. We never "find anything throughout the whole analogy of nature" that could afford us "even the slightest presumption, that animals ever lose their living powers." This is so because we have "no faculties wherewith to trace any beyond or through death to see what becomes of them." In the case of human beings and animals alike death only destroys "the sensible proof which we had before their death of their being possessed of living powers," but it does not "afford the least reason" for supposing that death causes the extinction of their minds.

A much more recent philosopher, the late A. C. Ewing, used the same kind of reasoning to rebut the unbeliever's argument. Ewing first observes that there is no logically necessary connection between bodily and mental events, something that all dualists would endorse. This means that no deductive argument is available to the unbeliever. At the same time he is also unable to mount an inductive argument. He cannot do this because "we have never observed

a mind being annihilated at death." The only one who could do this is the person himself. "No one could observe this," Ewing writes, "but the mind in question itself, and even that could not because it was annihilated, so, if a phenomenon, it is certainly an unobservable one." Ewing is happy to note that once we have disposed of the argument from the connection between body and mind the field is left open "for any empirical evidence drawn from psychical research and any arguments for survival there may be based on ethics and religion."

Butler deserves credit for realizing that his reasoning applies to animals and not only to human beings. It is not clear that either Mill or Ewing saw this. However, not even Butler carried the argument far enough. What reason do we have for denying that purely inanimate objects have an "inner" psychic life? What evidence do I have that the chocolate cream puff I am about to eat does not bitterly resent this murderous activity on my part and how do I know that a tennis ball I am about to serve does not acutely suffer as a result of being hit? For that matter how do I know that the tennis ball does not enjoy the experience of being hit? Since we have no access to the inner life of tennis balls, if they have any, we cannot know either that the tennis ball does or does not like being hit. Not only cannot we know that tennis balls do not have an inner life. We also cannot know that they, or any other inanimate objects, do not continue to have an inner, psychical life after the death of their bodies, whether as disembodied minds or in conjunction with replicas that will be produced in a resurrection world. It is true that we have no evidence that such an inner life will continue after the death of their bodies, but we equally have none that it will not. A complete suspense of judgment is the only defensible attitude.

All who regard *panpsychism* as either false or meaningless will surely regard the fact that the rejoinder here under discussion can be extended to inanimate objects as its *reductio ad absurdum*. Others will go further and treat the entire rejoinder as a *reductio ad absurdum* of dualism. For clearly we do know that tennis balls and cream puffs do not have an inner life and we can and do know that human beings and animals have certain feelings or sensations. However, we have agreed to accept dualism throughout this article, and it can be shown that the rejoinder is invalid even within a dualistic framework. After all, dualists allow that although we cannot inspect the minds of others we can frequently know that they have certain experiences. We can know that another person is in pain or that he is angry, and we can at least have strong evidence that he has certain thoughts. Now, the same *kind* of evidence is available to us that other people do *not* have these experiences. We can know that somebody has ceased to be in pain, that his anger is gone, or that he no longer thinks about a certain subject. I do not have to *be* the other person to know that he is no longer in pain or angry. By the same token I do not have to be Mrs. D., the Alzheimer patient herself, to know that her memory is gone and I equally do not have to be Jan Peerce in his coma to know that he no longer recognizes his family. In such cases we surely have the right to assert more than that the memories and thoughts have been "remanded to unconsciousness." This description fits a person under general anesthesia or during dreamless sleep who may very well return to full consciousness, but it is highly misleading about people in a coma or with advanced Alzheimer's. The only description that is fitting in such cases is that the thoughts and memories have been destroyed; and if they have been destroyed then they cannot be "recalled into activity" when a "different set of conditions supervenes."

THE MIND AND THE SOUL

The last rejoinder to be considered involves a distinction between the mind, which is identical with the phenomenal or empirical self whose existence is not disputed by Hume and other empiricists, and another nonphysical entity to which various labels have been applied. It is the immaterial or spiritual substance of Clarke, Butler, and Reid and numerous other philosophers, past and present, it is the Atman of the Hindu version of reincarnation, the noumenal self of Kant, and the soul (in one of its senses) of the Christian and Jewish traditions. It is argued that, although the mind may indeed so closely depend on the body that it must cease with the body's death, the same is not true of the soul. The soul is the "I" that "owns" both the body and the mind. I am five feet seven inches tall, I weigh one hundred and fifty pounds, I have blue eyes and brown hair; but I also have certain sensations and feelings and thoughts. I have various physical skills and I also possess certain emotional and intellectual dispositions. It is this underlying "I"—the subject of both the body and the mind—that has not been shown to require a body for its existence.

There are two objections to this rejoinder, each of them fatal. In the first place, although the way we speak in certain contexts suggests an underlying subject of both body and mind, there is no reason to suppose that it exists. Hume's theory that human beings are nothing but "bundles of impressions and ideas" is seriously inadequate. Each of us, at least while he is sane, has a sense of himself, more specifically, a sense of himself as continuing the same person from moment to moment. However, what this consists in is not the totally unchanging metaphysical entity that Hume rightly rebelled against. It is a sense of continuity in certain bodily sensations (especially of our limbs and certain muscle groups) and of our various tastes, opinions, and habits—more generally of our emotional and intellectual dispositions. These, together with our bodies, make us the kinds of persons we are. Although our emotional and intellectual dispositions are subject to change, unlike our moods and sensations, they are relatively stable. If this is what is meant by "soul," there is no reason to deny that we have a soul; but the soul in this sense is just as dependent on the body and the brain as any particular sensations, feelings, and thoughts.

The second objection to this rejoinder is that if there were such a thing as the spiritual substance or the metaphysical soul, it would not be what anybody means by "I." Human beings who are afraid of death dread the annihilation of their *empirical* selves and it is these empirical selves which they would like to survive. This is true of Western and Eastern believers alike. The great seventeenth-century philosopher Pierre Cassendi, who was both a Catholic priest and an atomistic materialist, professed belief in the metaphysical soul. He also believed that insanity was a brain disease. Since the soul or reason (Gassendi preferred the latter word) did not depend on the body, he concluded quite consistently that the soul or reason remained sane even when the individual had become insane. Gassendi's consistency led to a *reductio ad absurdum* of his position. If I go mad and if at the same time my soul remains sane then I and my soul are not the same thing.

For Further Reflection

1. Outline Edwards' argument against survival. How successful is he in defending his conclusion that we don't survive death?
2. Examine Edwards' criticism of Mill's agnosticism. How strong is his objection to Mill?

In Defense of Immortality   IV.38

JOHN HICK

John Hick, a British philosopher who retired from Claremont Graduate School in California, examines the Platonic notion of the immortality of the soul and argues that it is filled with problems. In its place, he argues for the New Testament view of the recreation of the psychophysical person, a holistic person who is body-soul in one. He then offers a thought experiment of "John Smith" reappearances to show that recreation is conceivable and worthy of rational belief. In the last part of this essay, Hick considers whether parapsychology can provide evidence for our survival after death.

Study Questions

1. How old is the idea of a soul separate from the body?
2. How, according to Hick, is the biblical view of human nature different from the Greek view?
3. What is the significance of the story of John Smith?
4. What does Hick take to be the significance of data obtained through parapsychology?

THE IMMORTALITY OF THE SOUL

SOME KIND OF DISTINCTION between physical body and immaterial or semimaterial soul seems to be as old as human culture; the existence of such a distinction has been indicated by the manner of burial of the earliest human skeletons yet discovered. Anthropologists offer various conjectures about the origin of the distinction: perhaps it was first suggested by memories of dead persons; by dreams of them; by the sight of reflections of oneself in water and on other bright surfaces; or by meditation upon the significance of religious rites which grew up spontaneously in face of the fact of death.

It was Plato (428–348 B.C.), the philosopher who has most deeply and lastingly influenced Western culture, who systematically developed the body-mind dichotomy and first attempted to prove the immortality of the soul.[1]

Plato argues that although the body belongs to the sensible world,[2] and shares its changing and impermanent nature, the intellect is related to the unchanging realities of which we are aware when we think not of particular good things but of Goodness itself, not of specific just acts but of Justice itself, and of the other "universals" or eternal Ideas in virtue of which physical things and events have their own specific characteristics. Being related to this higher and abiding realm, rather than to the evanescent world of sense, reason or the soul is immortal. Hence, one who devotes his life to the contemplation of eternal realities rather than to the gratification of the fleeting desires of the body will find at death that whereas his body turns to dust, his soul gravitates to the realm of the unchanging, there to live forever. Plato painted an awe-inspiring picture, of haunting beauty and persuasiveness, which has moved and elevated the minds of men in many different centuries and lands. Nevertheless, it is not today (as it was during the first centuries of the Christian era) the common philosophy of the West; and a demonstration of immortality which presupposes Plato's metaphysical system cannot claim to constitute a proof for the twentieth-century disbeliever.

Plato used the further argument that the only things that can suffer destruction are those that are composite, since to destroy something means to disintegrate it into its constituent parts. All material bodies are composite; the soul, however, is simple and therefore imperishable. This argument was adopted by Aquinas and has become standard in Roman Catholic theology, as in the following passage from the modern Catholic philosopher, Jacques Maritain:

> A spiritual soul cannot be corrupted, since it possesses no matter; it cannot be disintegrated, since it has no substantial parts; it cannot lose its individual unity, since it is self-subsisting, nor its internal energy, since it contains within itself all the sources of its energies. The human soul cannot die. Once it exists, it cannot disappear; it will necessarily exist for ever, endure without end. Thus, philosophic reason, put to work by a great metaphysician like Thomas Aquinas, is able to prove the immortality of the human soul in a demonstrative manner.[3]

This type of reasoning has been criticized on several grounds. Kant pointed out that although it is true that a simple substance cannot disintegrate, consciousness may nevertheless cease to exist through the diminution of its intensity to zero.[4] Modern psychology has also questioned the basic premise that the mind is a simple entity. It seems instead to be a structure of only relative unity, normally fairly stable and tightly integrated but capable under stress of various degrees of division and dissolution. This comment from psychology makes it clear that the assumption that the soul is a simple substance is not an empirical observation but a metaphysical theory. As such, it cannot provide the basis for a general proof of immortality.

From John H. Hick, Philosophy of Religion, *3d ed., copyright © 1983, pp. 122–132. Reprinted by permission of Prentice Hall, Englewood Cliffs, N.J. Footnotes edited.*

The body-soul distinction, first formulated as a philosophical doctrine in ancient Greece, was baptized into Christianity, ran through the medieval period, and entered the modern world with the public status of a self-evident truth when it was redefined in the seventeenth century by Descartes. Since World War II, however, the Cartesian mind-matter dualism, having been taken for granted for many centuries, has been strongly criticized by philosophers of the contemporary analytical school.[5] It is argued that the words that describe mental characteristics and operations—such as "intelligent," "thoughtful," "carefree," "happy," "calculating" and the like—apply in practice to types of human behavior and to behavioral dispositions. They refer to the empirical individual, the observable human being who is born and grows and acts and feels and dies, and not to the shadowy proceedings of a mysterious "ghost in the machine." Man is thus very much what he appears to be—a creature of flesh and blood, who behaves and is capable of behaving in a characteristic range of ways—rather than a nonphysical soul incomprehensibly interacting with a physical body.

As a result of this development much mid-twentieth-century philosophy has come to see man in the way he is seen in the biblical writings, not as an eternal soul temporarily attached to a mortal body, but as a form of finite, mortal, psychophysical life. Thus, the Old Testament scholar, J. Pedersen, says of the Hebrews that for them "... the body is the soul in its outward form."[6] This way of thinking has led to quite a different conception of death from that found in Plato and the neo-Platonic strand of European thought.

THE RE-CREATION OF THE PSYCHOPHYSICAL PERSON

Only toward the end of the Old Testament period did after-life beliefs come to have any real importance in Judaism. Previously, Hebrew religious insight had focused so fully upon God's covenant with the nation, as an organism that continued through the centuries while successive generations lived and died, that the thought of a divine purpose for the individual, a purpose that transcended this present life, developed only when the breakdown of the nation as a political entity threw into prominence the individual and the problem of his personal destiny.

When a positive conviction arose of God's purpose holding the individual in being beyond the crisis of death, this conviction took the non-Platonic form of belief in the resurrection of the body. By the turn of the eras, this had become an article of faith for one Jewish sect, the Pharisees, although it was still rejected as an innovation by the more conservative Sadducees.

The religious difference between the Platonic belief in the immortality of the soul, and the Judaic-Christian belief in the resurrection of the body is that the latter postulates a special divine act of re-creation. This produces a sense of utter dependence upon God in the hour of death, a feeling that is in accordance with the biblical understanding of man as having been formed out of "the dust of the earth,"[7] a product (as we say today) of the slow evolution of life from its lowly beginnings in the primeval slime. Hence, in the Jewish and Christian conception, death is something real and fearful. It is not thought to be like walking from one room to another, or taking off an old coat and putting on a new one. It means sheer unqualified extinction—passing out from the lighted circle of life into "death's dateless night." Only through the sovereign creative love of God can there be a new existence beyond the grave.

What does "the resurrection of the dead" mean? Saint Paul's discussion provides the basic Christian answer to this question.[8] His conception of the general resurrection (distinguished from the unique resurrection of Jesus) has nothing to do with the resuscitation of corpses in a cemetery. It concerns God's re-creation or re-constitution of the human psychophysical individual, not as the organism that has died but as a *soma pneumatikon*, a "spiritual body," inhabiting a spiritual world as the physical body inhabits our present physical world.

A major problem confronting any such doctrine is that of providing criteria of personal identity to link the earthly life and the resurrection life. Paul does not specifically consider this question, but one may, perhaps, develop his thought along lines such as the following.[9]

Suppose, first, that someone—John Smith—living in the USA were suddenly and inexplicably to disappear from before the eyes of his friends, and that at the same moment an exact replica of him were inexplicably to appear in India. The person who appears in India is exactly similar in both physical and mental characteristics to the person who disappeared in America. There is continuity of memory, complete similarity of bodily features including fingerprints, hair and eye coloration, and stomach contents, and also of beliefs, habits, emotions, and mental dispositions. Further, the "John Smith" replica thinks of himself as being the John Smith who disappeared in the USA. After all possible tests have been made and have proved positive, the factors leading his friends to accept "John Smith" as John Smith would surely prevail and would cause them to overlook even his mysterious transference from one continent to another, rather than treat "John Smith," with all John Smith's memories and other characteristics, as someone other than John Smith.

Suppose, second, that our John Smith, instead of inexplicably disappearing, dies, but that at the moment of his death a "John Smith" replica, again complete with memories and all other characteristics, appears in India. Even with the corpse on our hands we would, I think, still have to accept this "John Smith" as the John Smith who died. We would have to say that he had been miraculously re-created in another place.

Now suppose, third, that on John Smith's death the "John Smith" replica appears, not in India, but as a resurrection replica in a different world altogether, a resurrection world inhabited only by resurrected persons. This world occupies its own space distinct from that with which we are now familiar. That is to say, an object in the resurrection world is not situated at any distance or in any direction from the objects in our present world, although each object in either world is spatially related to every other object in the same world.

This supposition provides a model by which one may conceive of the divine re-creation of the embodied human personality. In this model, the element of the strange and the mysterious has been reduced to a minimum by following the view of some of the early Church Fathers that the resurrection body has the same shape as the physical body,[10] and ignoring Paul's own hint that it may be as unlike the physical body as a full grain of wheat differs from the wheat seed.[11]

What is the basis for this Judaic-Christian belief in the divine recreation or reconstitution of the human personality after death? There is, of course, an argument from authority, in that life after death is taught throughout the New Testament (although very rarely in the Old Testament). But, more basically, belief in the resurrection arises as a corollary of faith in the sovereign purpose of God, which is not restricted by death and which holds man in being beyond his natural mortality. In the words of Martin Luther, "Anyone with whom God speaks, whether in wrath or in mercy, the same is certainly immortal. The Person of God who speaks, and the Word, show that we are creatures with whom God wills to speak, right into eternity, and in an immortal manner."[12] In a similar vein it is argued that if it be God's plan to create finite persons to exist in fellowship with himself, then it contradicts both his own intention and his love for the creatures made in his image if he allows men to pass out of existence when his purpose for them remains largely unfulfilled.

It is this promised fulfillment of God's purpose for man, in which the full possibilities of human nature will be realized, that constitutes the "heaven" symbolized in the New Testament as a joyous banquet in which all and sundry rejoice together. As we saw when discussing the problem of evil, no theodicy can succeed without drawing into itself this eschatological[13] faith in an eternal, and therefore infinite, good which thus outweighs all the pains and sorrows that have been endured on the way to it.

Balancing the idea of heaven in Christian tradition is the idea of *hell*. This, too, is relevant to the problem of theodicy. For just as the reconciling of God's goodness and power with the fact of evil requires that out of the travail of history there shall come in the end an eternal good for man, so likewise it would seem to preclude man's eternal misery. The only kind of evil that is finally incompatible with God's unlimited power and love would be utterly pointless and wasted suffering, pain which is never redeemed and worked into the fulfilling of God's good purpose. Unending torment would constitute precisely such suffering; for being eternal, it could never lead to a good end beyond itself. Thus, hell as conceived by its enthusiasts, such as Augustine or Calvin, is a major part of the problem of evil! If hell is construed as eternal torment, the theological motive behind the idea is directly at variance with the urge to seek a theodicy. However, it is by no means clear that the doctrine of eternal punishment can claim a secure New Testament basis.[14] If, on the other hand, "hell" means a continuation of the purgatorial suffering often experienced in this life, and leading eventually to the high good of heaven, it no longer stands in conflict with the needs of theodicy. Again, the idea of hell may be deliteralized and valued as a *mythos*, as a powerful and pregnant symbol of the grave responsibility inherent in man's freedom in relation to his Maker.

DOES PARAPSYCHOLOGY HELP?

The spiritualist movement claims that life after death has been proved by well-attested cases of communication between the living and the "dead." During the closing quarter of the nineteenth century and the decades of the present century this claim has been made the subject of careful and prolonged study by a number of responsible and competent persons.[15] This work, which may be approximately dated from the founding in London of the Society for Psychical Research in 1882, is known either by the name adopted by that society or in the United States by the name parapsychology.

Approaching the subject from the standpoint of our interest in this chapter, we may initially divide the phenomena studied by the parapsychologist into two groups. There are those phenomena that involve no reference to the idea of a life after death, chief among these being psychokinesis and extrasensory perception (ESP) in its various forms (such as telepathy, clairvoyance, and precognition). And there are those phenomena that raise the question of personal survival after death, such as the apparitions and other sensory manifestations of dead persons and the "spirit messages" received through mediums. This division is, however, only of preliminary use, for ESP has emerged as a clue to the understanding of much that occurs in the second group. We shall begin with a brief outline of the reasons that have induced the majority of workers in this field to be willing to postulate so strange an occurrence as telepathy.

Telepathy is a name for the mysterious fact that sometimes a thought in the mind of one person apparently causes a similar thought to occur to someone else when there are no normal means of communication between them, and under circumstances such that mere coincidence seems to be excluded.

For example, one person may draw a series of pictures or diagrams on paper and somehow transmit an impression of these to someone else in another room who then draws recognizable reproductions of them. This might well be a coincidence in the case of a single successful reproduction; but can a series consist entirely of coincidences?

Experiments have been devised to measure the probability of chance coincidence in supposed cases of telepathy. In the simplest of these, cards printed in turn with five different symbols are used. A pack of fifty, consisting of ten bearing each symbol, is then thoroughly shuffled, and the sender concentrates on the cards one at a time while the receiver (who of course can see neither sender nor cards) tries to write down the correct order of symbols. This procedure is repeated, with constant reshuffling, hundreds or thousands of times. Since there are only five different symbols, a random guess would stand one chance in five of being correct. Consequently, on the assumption that only "chance" is operating, the receiver should be right in about 20 per cent of his tries, and wrong in about 80 per cent; and the longer the series, the closer should be the approach to this proportion. However, good telepathic subjects are right in a far larger number of cases than can be reconciled with random guessing. The deviation from chance expectation can be converted mathematically into "odds against chance" (increasing as the proportion of hits is maintained over a longer and longer series of tries). In this way, odds of over a million to one have been recorded. J. B. Rhine (Duke University) has reported results showing "antichance" values ranging from seven (which equals odds against chance of 100,000 to one) to eighty-two (which converts the odds against chance to billions).[16] S. G. Soal (London University) has reported positive results for precognitive telepathy with odds against chance of $10^{35} \times 5$, or of billions to one.[17] Other researchers have also recorded confirming results. In the light of these reports, it is difficult to deny that some positive factor, and not merely "chance," is operating. "Telepathy" is simply a name for this unknown positive factor.

How does telepathy operate? Only negative conclusions seem to be justified to date. It can, for example, be said with reasonable certainty that telepathy does not consist in any kind of physical radiation, analogous to radio waves. For, first, telepathy is not delayed or weakened in proportion to distance, as are all known forms of radiation; and, second, there is no organ in the brain or elsewhere that can plausibly be regarded as its sending or receiving center. Telepathy appears to be a purely mental occurrence.

It is not, however, a matter of transferring or transporting a thought out of one mind into another—if, indeed, such an idea makes sense at all. The telepathized thought does not leave the sender's consciousness in order to enter that of the receiver. What happens would be better described by saying that the sender's thought gives rise to a mental "echo" in the mind of the receiver. This "echo" occurs at the unconscious level, and consequently the version of it that rises into the receiver's consciousness may be only fragmentary and may be distorted or symbolized in various ways, as in dreams.

According to one theory that has been tentatively suggested to explain telepathy, our minds are separate and mutually insulated only at the conscious (and preconscious) level. But at the deepest level of the unconscious, we are constantly influencing one another, and it is at this level that telepathy takes place.

How is a telepathized thought directed to one particular receiver among so many? Apparently the thoughts are directed by some link of emotion or common interest. For example, two friends are sometimes telepathically aware of any grave crisis or shock experienced by the other, even though they are at opposite ends of the earth.

We shall turn now to the other branch of parapsychology, which has more obvious bearing upon our subject. The *Proceedings of the Society for Psychical Research* contains a large number of carefully recorded and satisfactorily attested cases of the appearance of the figure of someone who has recently died to living people (in rare instances to more than one at a time) who were, in many cases, at a distance and unaware of the death. The S.P.R. reports also establish beyond reasonable doubt that the minds that operate in the mediumistic trance, purporting to be spirits of the departed, sometimes give personal information the medium could not have acquired by normal means and at times even give information, later verified, which had not been known to any living person.

On the other hand, physical happenings, such as the "materializations" of spirit forms in a visible and tangible form, are much more doubtful. But even if we discount the entire range of physical phenomena, it remains true that the best cases of trance utterance are impressive and puzzling, and taken at face value are indicative of survival and communication after death. If, through a medium, one talks with an intelligence that gives a coherent impression of being an intimately known friend who has died and establishes identity by a wealth of private information and indefinable personal characteristics—as has occasionally happened—then we cannot dismiss without careful trial the theory that what is taking place is the return of a consciousness from the spirit world.

However, the advance of knowledge in the other branch of parapsychology, centering upon the study of extrasensory perception, has thrown unexpected light upon this apparent commerce with the departed. For it suggests that unconscious telepathic contact between the medium and his or her client is an important and possibly a sufficient explanatory factor. This was vividly illustrated by the experience of two women who decided to test the spirits by taking into their minds, over a period of weeks, the personality and atmosphere of an entirely imaginary character in an unpublished novel written by one of the women. After thus filling their minds with the characteristics of this fictitious person, they went to a reputable medium, who proceeded to describe accurately their imaginary friend as a visitant from beyond the grave and to deliver appropriate messages from him.

An even more striking case is that of the "direct voice" medium (i.e., a medium in whose séances the voice of the communicating "spirit" is heard apparently speaking out of the air) who produced the spirit of one "Gordon Davis" who spoke in his own recognizable voice, displayed considerable knowledge about Gordon Davis, and remembered his death. This was extremely impressive until it was discovered that Gordon Davis was still alive; he was, of all ghostly occupations, a real-estate agent, and had been trying to sell a house at the time when the séance took place!

Such cases suggest that genuine mediums are simply persons of exceptional telepathic sensitiveness who unconsciously derive the "spirits" from their clients' minds.

In connection with "ghosts," in the sense of apparitions of the dead, it has been established that there can be "meaningful hallucinations," the source of which is almost certainly telepathic. To quote a classic and somewhat dramatic example: a woman sitting by a lake sees the figure of a man running toward the lake and throwing himself in. A few days later a man commits suicide by throwing himself into this same lake. Presumably, the explanation of the vision is that the man's thought while he was contemplating suicide had been telepathically projected onto the scene via the woman's mind.

In many of the cases recorded there is delayed action. The telepathically projected thought lingers in the recipient's unconscious mind until a suitable state of inattention to the outside world enables it to appear to his conscious mind in a dramatized form—for example, by a hallucinatory voice or vision—by means of the same mechanism that operates in dreams.

If phantoms of the living can be created by previously experienced thoughts and emotions of the person whom they represent, the parallel possibility arises that phantoms of the dead are caused by thoughts and emotions that were experienced by the person represented when he was alive. In other words, ghosts may be "psychic footprints," a kind of mental trace left behind by the dead, but not involving the presence or even the continued existence of those whom they represent.

These considerations tend away from the hopeful view that parapsychology will open a window onto another world. However, it is too early for a final verdict; and in the meantime one should be careful not to confuse absence of knowledge with knowledge of absence.

NOTES

1. *Phaedo.*

2. The world known to us through our physical senses.

3. Jacques Maritain, *The Range of Reason* (London: Geoffrey Bles Ltd. and New York: Charles Scribner's Sons, 1953), p. 60.

4. Kant, *Critique of Pure Reason, Transcendental Dialectic,* "Refutation of Mendelssohn's Proof of the Permanence of the Soul."

5. Gilbert Ryle's *The Concept of Mind* (London: Hutchinson & Co., Ltd., 1949) is a classic statement of this critique.

6. *Israel* (London: Oxford University Press, 1926), I, 170.

7. Genesis, 2 : 7; Psalm 103 : 14.

8. I Corinthians 15.

9. The following paragraphs are adapted, with permission, from a section of my article, "Theology and Verification," published in *Theology Today* (April, 1960) and reprinted in *The Existence of God* (New York: The Macmillan Company, 1964).

10. For example, Irenaeus, *Against Heresies,* Book II, Chap. 34, para. 1.

11. 1 Corinthians 15 : 37.

12. Quoted by Emil Brunner, *Dogmatics,* II, 69.

13. From the Greek *eschaton,* end.

14. The Greek word *aionios,* which is used in the New Testament and which is usually translated as "eternal" or "everlasting," can bear either this meaning or the more limited meaning of "for the aeon, or age."

15. The list of past presidents of the Society for Psychical Research includes the philosophers Henri Bergson, William James, Hans Driesch, Henry Sidgwick, F. C. S. Schiller, C. D. Broad, and H. H. Price; the psychologists William McDougall, Gardner Murphy, Franklin Prince, and R. H. Thouless; the physicists Sir William Crookes, Sir Oliver Lodge, Sir William Barrett, and Lord Rayleigh; and the classicist Gilbert Murray.

16. J. B. Rhine, *Extrasensory Perception* (Boston: Society for Psychical Research, 1935), Table XLIII, p. 162. See also Rhine, *New Frontiers of the Mind* (New York: Farrar and Rinehart, Inc., 1937), pp. 69 f.

17. S. G. Soal, *Proceedings of the Society for Psychical Research,* XLVI, 152–98 and XLVII, 21–150. See also S. G. Soal's *The Experimental Situation in Psychical Research* (London: The Society for Psychical Research, 1947).

For Further Reflection

1. Has Hick successfully shown the plausibility of survival after death? Has he made the Judeo-Christian view intelligible in the light of modern psychology?

Suggestions for Further Reading

Borst, C. V., ed. *The Mind /Brain Identity Theory.* New York: St. Martin's, 1970. Contains the best overall collection on the identity theory.

Campbell, Keith. *Body and Mind.* New York: Doubleday, 1970.

Churchland, Paul. *Matter and Consciousness.* Cambridge, MA: MIT Press, 1984.

Cornman, James and Keith Lehrer. *Philosophical Problems and Arguments.* New York: Macmillan, 1982. Chapter 4, "The Mind-Body Problem," is excellent and accessible to lower-division college students.

Dennett, Daniel. *Brainstorms.* Cambridge, MA: MIT Press, 1978.

Ducasse, Curt J. *A Critical Examination of the Belief in Life after Death.* Thomas, 1961.

Flew, Antony, ed. *Body, Mind and Death.* New York: Macmillan, 1974. Contains the classic readings.

Hofstadter, Douglas and Daniel Dennett, eds. *The Mind's I.* New York: Bantam, 1982. A scintillating set of articles on the idea of the self.

McGinn, Colin. *The Character of Mind.* Oxford: Oxford University Press, 1982. A good, concise introduction to the subject.

Penelhum, Terrence. *Survival and Disembodied Existence*. London: Routledge & Kegan Paul, 1970.

Perry, John. *Personal Identity*. Berkeley: University of California, 1975. A very fine set of articles.

Quinton, Anthony. "The Soul." *Journal of Philosophy,* 1962.

Ryle, Gilbert. *The Concept of Mind*. New York: Barnes and Noble, 1949. A classic in logical behaviorism.

Shaffer, Jerome. *Philosophy of Mind*. Englewood Cliffs, NJ: Prentice Hall, 1963. Almost a classic summary of the problems.

Swinburne, Richard. *The Evolution of the Soul*. Oxford: Clarendon Press, 1986. This contains Swinburne's 1983–1984 Gifford's Lectures. It treats the subject from a theistic perspective.

Part V

Freedom of the Will and Determinism

*If I were capable of correct reasoning, and if, at the same time, I had a
complete knowledge both of his disposition and of all the events by which
he was surrounded, I should be able to foresee the line of conduct which, in
consequence of those events, [any person] would adopt.*

H. T. BUCKLE in his *History of Civilization in England (1857)*

THE PROBLEM OF FREEDOM OF THE WILL and determinism is one of the most intriguing and difficult in the whole of philosophy. It constitutes a paradox. If we look at ourselves, at our ability to deliberate and make choices, it seems obvious that we are free. On the other hand, if we look at what we believe about causality (that is, that every event and thing must have a cause), then it appears that we do not have free wills but are determined. So we seem to have inconsistent beliefs.

Let us look closer at the two theses involved in order to see how they work and what support there is for each of them.

1. *Determinism*: The theory that everything in the universe (or at least the macroscopic universe) is entirely determined by causal laws, so that whatever happens at any given moment is the effect of some antecedent cause.

2. *Libertarianism*: The theory that there are some actions which are exempt from the causal laws, in which the individual is the sole (or decisive) cause of the act, the act originating ex nihilo, cut off from all other causes but the self's origination.

There is a third position which tries to combine the best of the two positions. Called *compatibilism* or *soft determinism,* it admits that while everything is determined, we can still be free insofar as we can still act voluntarily.

Determinism (Sometimes Called "Hard Determinism")

Determinism is the theory that everything in the universe is governed by causal laws. That is, everything in the universe is entirely determined so that whatever happens at any given moment is the effect of some antecedent cause. If we were omniscient, we could predict exactly everything that would happen for the rest of this hour, for the rest of our life time, for the rest of time itself, simply because we know how everything hitherto is causally related. This theory, which, it is claimed, is the basic presupposition of science, implies that there is no such thing as an uncaused event (sometimes this is modified to include only the macrocosmic world, leaving the microcosmic world in doubt). Hence, since all human actions are events, human actions are not undetermined, are not *free* in a radical sense but are the product of a causal process. Hence, while we may self-importantly imagine that we are autonomous and possess free will, in reality we are totally conditioned by heredity and environment.

The outline of the argument for determinism goes something like this:

1. Every event (or state of affairs) must have a cause.
2. Human actions (as well as the agent who gives rise to those actions) are events (or state of affairs).
3. Therefore, every human action (including the agent himself) is caused.
4. Hence determinism is true.

Although the hypothesis of universal causality cannot be proved, it is something we all assume—either because of considerable inductive evidence or as an *a priori* truth which seems to make sense of the world. We cannot easily imagine an uncaused event taking place in ordinary life. For example, imagine how you would feel if, on visiting your dentist for relief of a toothache, he were to conclude his oral examination with the remark, "I certainly can see that you are in great pain because of your toothache, but I'm afraid that I can't help you, for there is no cause of this toothache." Perhaps he calls his partner over to confirm his judgment. "Sure enough," she says, "this is one of those interesting noncausal cases. Sorry, there's nothing we can do for you. Even medicine and pain-relievers won't help these noncausal types."

Why do we believe that everything has a cause? Most philosophers have echoed John Stuart Mill's answer that the doctrine of universal causality is a conclusion of inductive reasoning. We have had an enormous range of experience wherein we have found causal explanations to individual events, which in turn seem to participate in a further causal chain. The problem with this answer, however, is that we have only experienced a very small part of the universe, not enough of it to warrant the conclusion that every event must have a cause.

David Hume (see also Reading III.21) pointed out that the idea of causality was not a logical truth (like the notion that all triangles have three sides). The hypothesis that every event has a cause arises from the observation of regular conjunctions. "When many uniform instances appear, and the same object is always followed by the same event; we then begin to entertain the notion of cause and connexion" (*Enquiry,* p. 78). So after a number of successful tries at putting water over a fire and seeing it disappear, we conclude that heat (or fire) causes water to disappear (or vaporize). But we cannot prove causality. We never see it. All we see are two events in constant spatio-temporal order and infer from this constant conjunction a binding relation between them. For example, we see one billiard ball (a) hit another (b), and we see (b) move away from (a), and we conclude that (a's) hitting (b) at a certain velocity is the cause of (b's) moving away as it did. However, we cannot prove that it is the sufficient cause of the movement.

Immanuel Kant first suggested that the principle of universal causality is a synthetic *a priori*—that is, an assumption that we cannot prove by experience but simply cannot conceive not to be the case. Our mental construction demands that we read all experience in the light of universal causation. We have no knowledge of what the world is in itself, or whether there really is universal causation, but we cannot understand experience except by means of causal explanation. The necessary idea of causality is part and parcel of our noetic structure. We are programmed to read our experience in the causal script.

Kant saw that there was a powerful incentive to believe in determinism, but he also thought that the notion of morality provided a powerful incentive to believe in freedom of the will. Hence, Kant's dilemma.

The man who used the idea of determinism more effectively for practical purposes than anyone before him was the great American criminal lawyer Clarence Darrow. In the 1920s, two teenage geniuses from the University of Chicago, Leopold and Loeb, committed what they regarded as the perfect murder. They grotesquely dismembered a child and buried the parts in a prairie. Caught, they faced an outraged public who demanded the death penalty. The defense attorney was Clarence Darrow, champion of lost causes. He conceded that the boys committed the deed, but argued that they were, nevertheless, "innocent." His argument was based on the theory of determinism. It is worth reading part of the plea:

> We are all helpless. . . . This weary world goes on, begetting, with birth and with living and with death; and all of it is blind from the beginning to the end. I do not know what it was that made these boys do this mad act, but I do know there is a reason for it. I know they did not beget themselves. I know that anyone of an infinite number of causes reaching back to the beginning might be working out in these boys' minds, whom you are asked to hang in malice and in hatred and injustice. . . .
>
> Nature is strong and she is pitiless. She works in her own mysterious way, and we are her victims. We have not much to do with it ourselves. Nature takes this job in hand, and we play our part. In the words of old Omar Khayam, we are:
>
> *But helpless pieces in the game He plays*
> *Upon the chess board of nights and days;*
> *Hither and thither moves, and checks and slays,*
> *And one by one back in the closet lays.*
>
> What had this boy to do with it? He was not his own father, he was not his own mother; he was not his own grandparents. All of this was handed to him. He did not surround himself with governesses and wealth. He did not make himself. And yet he is to be compelled to pay. (Clarence Darrow, *Attorney for the Damned*. New York: Simon and Schuster, 1957.)

This was sufficient to convince the jury to go against public opinion and recommend a life sentence in lieu of the death penalty. If Leopold and Loeb were determined by antecedent causes to do the deed, we cannot blame them for what they did, any more than we can blame a cow for not being able to fly.

Determinism has received new attention and respect because of modern neurological studies that suggest the hypothesis that there is a one-to-one correlation between mental states and brain states, so that every conscious action can be traced back to a causally sufficient brain state. In other words, the laws of physics deterministically produce mental states.

Libertarianism

Libertarianism is the theory that we do have free wills. It contends that given the same antecedent conditions at time t_1, an agent S could do either act A1 or A2. That is, it is up to S what the world will look like after t_1, and that his act is causally underdetermined, the self making the unexplained difference. Libertarians do not contend that all our actions are free, only some of them. Neither do they offer an explanatory theory of free will. Their arguments are indirect. They offer two main arguments for their position: the argument from deliberation and the argument from moral responsibility.

The Argument from Deliberation

The position is nicely summed up in the words of Corliss Lamont: "[There] is the unmistakable intuition of virtually every human being that he is free to make the choices he does and that the deliberations leading to those choices are also free flowing. The normal man feels too, after he has made a decision, that he could have decided differently. That is why regret or remorse for a past choice can be so disturbing."

There is a difference between a knee jerk and purposefully kicking a football. In the first case, the behavior is involuntary, a reflex action. In the second case, we deliberate, notice that we have an alternative (namely, not kicking the ball), consciously choose to kick the ball, and, if successful, we find our body moving in the requisite manner, so that the ball is kicked.

Deliberation can take a short or long time, be foolish or wise, but the process is a conscious one wherein we believe that we really can do either of the actions (or any of many possible actions). That is, in deliberating we assume we are free to choose between alternatives and that we are not determined to do simply one action. Otherwise, why deliberate?

Furthermore, there seems to be something psychologically lethal about accepting determinism in human relations; it tends to curtail deliberation and paralyze actions. If people really believe themselves totally determined, the tendency is for them to excuse their behavior. Human effort seems pointless. As Arthur Eddington put it, "What significance is there to my mental struggle tonight whether I shall or shall not give up smoking, if the laws which govern the matter of the physical universe already preordain for the morrow a configuration of matter consisting of pipe, tobacco, and smoke connected to my lips?" The determinist has an objection to this argument, which you will encounter in d'Holbach's and Hospers' essays. And the libertarian has a counter-response in agent causation, a version of which will be found in Richard Taylor's article.

The Argument from Moral Responsibility

Determinism seems to conflict with the thesis that we have moral responsibilities, for responsibility implies that we could have done otherwise than we did. We do not hold a dog responsible for chewing up our philosophy book or a one-month-old baby responsible for crying, because they could not help it, but we do hold a twenty-year-old student responsible for her cheating because (we believe) she could have done otherwise. Blackbacked sea gulls will tear apart a stray baby herring gull without the slightest suspicion that their act may be immoral, but if humans lack this sense, we judge them as pathological, as substandard.

Moral responsibility is something that we take very seriously. We believe that we do have duties, oughts, over which we feel rational guilt at failure to perform. But there can be no such things as duties, oughts, praise, blame or rational guilt, if we are not essentially free. The argument form is the following.

1. If determinism is true, and our actions are merely the product of the laws of nature and antecedent states of affairs, then it is not up to us to choose what we do.

2. But if it is not up to us to choose what we do, we cannot be said to be responsible for what we do.

3. So if determinism is true, we are not responsible for what we do.

4. But our belief in moral responsibility is self-evident,   at least as strong as our belief in universal causality.

5. So if we believe that we have moral responsibilities, determinism cannot be accepted.

We must reject the notion of determinism even if we cannot give a full explanatory account of how agents choose.

Here the determinist usually bites the bullet and admits that we do not have moral responsibilities, and that it is just an illusion that we do. But we are determined to have such an illusion, so there is nothing we can do about it. We cannot consciously live as determinists, but why should we think that we can? We are finite and fallible creatures, driven by causal laws, but with self-consciousness that makes us aware of part (but only a part) of the process that governs our behavior.

Compatibilism (How to Have Your Cake and Eat It Too)

However, there is another response to the problem of free will and determinism, one similar to Kant but perhaps more subtle. It can be called reconciling determinism or soft-determinism or compatibilism. It argues that although we are determined, we still have moral responsibilities, that the distinction is between *voluntary* and *involuntary* behavior.

The language of freedom and the language of determinism are but two different ways of talking about certain human or rational events, both necessary for mankind (one is necessary for science and the other is necessary for morality and personal relationships). The compatibilist argues that the fact that we are determined does not affect our interpersonal relations. We will still have feelings that we must deal with, using internalist insights. We will still feel resentment when someone hurts us "on purpose." We will still feel grateful for services rendered and hold people responsible for their actions. Only we will still acknowledge that from the external perspective the determinist's account of all of this is valid.

Along these lines, Walter T. Stace (in our third reading in this section) argues that the problem of freedom and determinism is really only a semantic one, a dispute about the meanings of words. Freedom has to do with acts done voluntarily and determinism with the causal processes that underlie all behavior and events. These need not be incompatible. Gandhi's fasting because he wanted to free India was a voluntary or free act, whereas a man starving in the desert is not doing so voluntarily or as a free act. A thief purposefully and voluntarily steals, whereas a kleptomaniac cannot help stealing. In both cases each act or event has causal antecedents, but the former in each set are free, whereas the latter are unfree. According to Stace, "Acts freely done are those whose immediate causes are psychological states in the agent. Acts not freely done are those whose immediate causes are states of affairs external to the agent."

We Are Completely Determined   V.39

BARON D'HOLBACH

Baron Paul Henri d'Holbach (1723–1789), born in Edesheim, Germany, and growing up in France, was one of the leading philosophers of the French Enlightenment. He was a materialist who believed that nature is one grand machine, and humans are particular machines within this grand machine—a machine which needs no machinist. He was a significant contributor to the *Encyclopedie* and a friend of Diderot, Hume, and Rousseau. His principal writings are *Christianity Unveiled* (1767), *The System of Nature* (1770), from which the present selection is taken, and *Common Sense, or Natural Ideas Opposed to Supernatural Ideas* (1772).

d'Holbach is one of the first philosophers to provide a sustained systematic critique of the doctrine of free will. According to him, if we accept science, which he equates with a system of material particles operating according to fixed laws of motion, then we will see that free will is an illusion. There is no such entity as a soul, but we are simply material objects in motion, having very complicated brains that lead the unreflective to believe that they are free.

Study Questions

1. What is the result of dualism, which separates soul from body?
2. What does d'Holbach believe has been proved about the relation of the soul to body?
3. How does he characterize human life?
4. What is the role that the doctrine of free will plays in religion and our system of punishment?
5. Deliberation between alternative courses of action has often been used by libertarians as evidence of free will. What does d'Holbach say about this psychological activity?
6. What are the causes of our belief in free will?

THOSE WHO HAVE AFFIRMED that the *soul* is distinguished from the body, is immaterial, draws its ideas from its own peculiar source, acts by its own energies, without the aid of any exterior object, have, by a consequence of their own system, enfranchised [liberated] it from those physical laws according to which all beings of which we have a knowledge are obliged to act. They have believed that the soul is mistress of its own conduct, is able to regulate its own peculiar operations, has the faculty to determine its will by its own natural energy; in a word, they have pretended that man is a *free agent.*

It has been already sufficiently proved that the soul is nothing more than the body considered relatively to some of its functions more concealed than others: it has been shown that this soul, even when it shall be supposed immaterial, is continually modified conjointly with the body, is submitted to all its motion, and that without this it would remain inert and dead; that, consequently, it is subjected to the influence of those material and physical causes which give impulse to the body; of which the mode of existence, whether habitual or transitory, depends upon the material elements by which it is surrounded, that form its texture, constitute its temperament, enter into it by means of the aliments, and penetrate it by their subtility. The faculties which are called *intellectual,* and those qualities which are styled *moral,* have been explained in a manner purely physical and natural. In the last place it has been demonstrated that all the ideas, all the systems, all the affections, all the opinions, whether true or false, which man forms to himself, are to be attributed to his physical and material senses. Thus man is a being purely physical; in whatever manner he is considered, he is connected to universal nature, and submitted to the necessary and immutable laws that she imposes on all the beings she contains, according to their peculiar essences or to the respective properties with which, without consulting them,

she endows each particular species. Man's life is a line that nature commands him to describe upon the surface of the earth, without his ever being able to swerve from it, even for an instant. He is born without his own consent; his organization does in nowise depend upon himself; his ideas come to him involuntarily; his habits are in the power of those who cause him to contract them; he is unceasingly modified by causes, whether visible or concealed, over which he has no control, which necessarily regulate his mode of existence, give the hue to his way of thinking, and determine his manner of acting. He is good or bad, happy or miserable, wise or foolish, reasonable or irrational, without his will being for any thing in these various states. Nevertheless, in despite of the shackles by which he is bound, it is pretended he is a free agent, or that independent of the causes by which he is moved, he determines his own will, and regulates his own condition.

However slender the foundation of this opinion, of which every thing ought to point out to him the error, it is current at this day and passes for an incontestable truth with a great number of people, otherwise extremely enlightened; it is the basis of religion, which, supposing relations between man and the unknown being she has placed above nature, has been incapable of imagining how man could either merit reward or deserve punishment from this being, if he was not a free agent. Society has been believed interested in this system; because an idea has gone abroad, that if all the actions of man were to be contemplated as necessary, the right of punishing those who injure their associates would no longer exist. At length human vanity accommodated itself to a hypothesis which, unquestionably, appears to distinguish man from all other physical beings, by assigning to him the special privilege of a total independence of all other causes, but of which a very little reflection would have shown him the impossibility. . . .

From Chapter XI, "Of the System of Man's Free Agency," of The System of Nature *(1770). The translation is by H. D. Robinson.*

The will . . . is a modification of the brain, by which it is disposed to action, or prepared to give play to the organs. This will is necessarily determined by the qualities, good or bad, agreeable or painful, of the object or the motive that acts upon his senses, or of which the idea remains with him, and is resuscitated by his memory. In consequence, he acts necessarily, his action is the result of the impulse he receives either from the motive, from the object, or from the idea which has modified his brain, or disposed his will. When he does not act according to this impulse, it is because there comes some new cause, some new motive, some new idea, which modifies his brain in a different manner, gives him a new impulse, determines his will in another way, by which the action of the former impulse is suspended: thus, the sight of an agreeable object, or its idea, determines his will to set him in action to procure it; but if a new object or a new idea more powerfully attracts him, it gives a new direction to his will, annihilates the effect of the former, and prevents the action by which it was to be procured. This is the mode in which reflection, experience, reason, necessarily arrests or suspends the action of man's will: without this he would of necessity have followed the anterior impulse which carried him towards a then desirable object. In all this he always acts according to necessary laws, from which he has no means of emancipating himself.

If when tormented with violent thirst, he figures to himself in idea, or really perceives a fountain, whose limpid streams might cool his feverish want, is he sufficient master of himself to desire or not to desire the object competent to satisfy so lively a want? It will no doubt be conceded, that it is impossible he should not be desirous to satisfy it; but it will be said—if at this moment it is announced to him that the water he so ardently desires is poisoned, he will, notwithstanding his vehement thirst, abstain from drinking it: and it has, therefore, been falsely concluded that he is a free agent. The fact, however, is, that the motive in either case is exactly the same: his own conservation. The same necessity that determined him to drink before he knew the water was deleterious, upon this new discovery equally determines him not to drink; the desire of conserving himself either annihilates or suspends the former impulse; the second motive becomes stronger than the preceding, that is, the fear of death, or the desire of preserving himself, necessarily prevails over the painful sensation caused by his eagerness to drink; but, it will be said, if the thirst is very parching, an inconsiderate man without regarding the danger will risk swallowing the water. Nothing is gained by this remark: in this case the anterior impulse only regains the ascendency; he is persuaded that life may possibly be longer preserved, or that he shall derive a greater good by drinking the poisoned water than by enduring the torment, which, to his mind, threatens instant dissolution: thus the first becomes the strongest and necessarily urges him on to action. Nevertheless, in either case, whether he partakes of the water, or whether he does not, the two actions will be equally necessary; they will be the effect of that motive which finds itself most puissant; which consequently acts in the most coercive manner upon his will.

This example will serve to explain the whole phenomena of the human will. This will, or rather the brain, finds itself in the same situation as a ball, which, although it has received an impulse that drives it forward in a straight line, is deranged in its course whenever a force superior to the first obliges it to change its direction. The man who drinks the poisoned water appears a madman; but the actions of fools are as necessary as those of the most prudent individuals. The motives that determine the voluptuary and the debauchee to risk their health, are as powerful, and their actions are as necessary, as those which decide the wise man to manage his. But, it will be insisted, the debauchee may be prevailed on to change his conduct: this does not imply that he is a free agent; but that motives may be found sufficiently powerful to annihilate the effect of those that previously acted upon him; then these new motives determine his will to the new mode of conduct he may adopt as necessarily as the former did to the old mode.

Man is said to *deliberate*, when the action of the will is suspended; this happens when two opposite motives act alternately upon him. *To deliberate,* is to hate and to love in succession; it is to be alternately attracted and repelled; it is to be moved, sometimes by one motive, sometimes by another. Man only deliberates when he does not distinctly understand the quality of the objects from which he receives impulse, or when experience has not sufficiently apprised him of the effects, more or less remote, which his actions will produce. He would take the air, but the weather is uncertain; he deliberates in consequence; he weighs the various motives that urge his will to go out or to stay at home; he is at length determined by that motive which is most probable; this removes his indecision, which necessarily settles his will, either to remain within or to go abroad: his motive is always either the immediate or ultimate advantage he finds, or thinks he finds, in the action to which he is persuaded.

Man's will frequently fluctuates between two objects, of which either the presence or the ideas move him alternately: he waits until he has contemplated the objects, or the ideas they have left in his brain which solicit him to different actions; he then compares these objects or ideas; but even in the time of deliberation, during the comparison, pending these alternatives of love and hatred which succeed each other, sometimes with the utmost rapidity, he is not a free agent for a single instant; the good or the evil which he believes he finds successively in the objects, are the necessary motives of these momentary wills; of the rapid motion of desire or fear, that he experiences as long as his uncertainty continues. From this it will be obvious that deliberation is necessary; that uncertainty is necessary; that whatever part he takes, in consequence of this deliberation, it will always necessarily be that which he has judged, whether well or ill, is most probable to turn to his advantage.

When the soul is assailed by two motives that act alternately upon it, or modify it successively, it deliberates; the brain is in a sort of equilibrium, accompanied with perpetual oscillations, sometimes towards one object, sometimes towards the other, until the most forcible carries the point, and thereby extricates it from this state of suspense, in which consists the indecision of his will. But when the brain is simultaneously assailed by causes equally strong that move it in opposite directions, agreeable to the general law of all bodies when they are struck equally by contrary powers, it stops . . . it is neither capable to will nor to act; it waits until one of the two causes has obtained sufficient force to overpower the other; to determine its will; to attract it in such a manner that it may prevail over the efforts of the other cause.

This mechanism, so simple, so natural, suffices to demonstrate why uncertainty is painful, and why suspense is always a violent state for man. The brain, an organ so delicate and so mobile, experiences such rapid modifications that it is fatigued; or when it is urged in contrary directions, by causes equally powerful, it suffers a kind of compression, that prevents the activity which is suitable to the preservation of the whole, and which is necessary to procure what is advantageous to its existence. This mechanism will also explain the irregularity, the indecision, the inconstancy of man, and account for that conduct which frequently appears an inexplicable mystery, and which is, indeed, the effect of the received systems. In consulting experience, it will be found that the soul is submitted to precisely the same physical laws as the material body. If the will of each individual, during a given time, was only moved by a single cause or passion, nothing would be more easy than to foresee his actions; but his heart is frequently assailed by contrary powers, by adverse motives, which either act on him simultaneously or in succession; then his brain, attracted in opposite directions, is either fatigued, or else tormented by a state of compression, which deprives it of activity. Sometimes it is in a state of incommodious inaction; sometimes it is the sport of the alternate shocks it undergoes. Such, no doubt, is the state in which man finds himself when a lively passion solicits him to the commission of crime, whilst fear points out to him the danger by which it is attended; such, also, is the condition of him whom remorse, by the continued labour of his distracted soul, prevents from enjoying the objects he has criminally obtained.

Choice by no means proves the free agency of man: he only deliberates when he does not yet know which to choose of the many objects that move him; he is then in an embarrassment, which does not terminate until his will is decided by the greater advantage he believes he shall find in the object he chooses, or the action he undertakes. From whence it may be seen, that choice is necessary, because he would not determine for an object, or for an action, if he did not believe that he should find in it some direct advantage. That man should have free agency it were needful that he should be able to will or choose without motive, or that he could prevent motives coercing his will. Action always being the effect of his will once determined, and as his will cannot be determined but by a motive which is not in his own power, it follows that he is never the master of the determination of his own peculiar will; that consequently he never acts as a free agent. It has been believed that man was a free agent because he had a will with the power of choosing; but attention has not been paid to the fact that even his will is moved by causes independent of himself; is owing to that which is inherent in his own organization, or which belongs to the nature of the beings acting on him. Is he the master of willing not to withdraw his hand from the fire when he fears it will be burnt? Or has he the power to take away from fire the property which makes him fear it? Is he the master of not choosing a dish of meat, which he knows to be agreeable or analogous to his palate; of not preferring it to that which he knows to be disagreeable or dangerous? It is always according to his sensations, to his own peculiar experience, or to his suppositions, that he judges of things, either well or ill; but whatever may be his judgment, it depends necessarily on his mode of feeling, whether habitual or accidental, and the qualities he finds in the causes that move him, which exist in despite of himself. . . .

When it is said, that man is not a free agent, it is not pretended to compare him to a body moved by a simple impulsive cause: he contains within himself causes inherent to his existence; he is moved by an interior organ, which has its own peculiar laws, and is itself necessarily determined in consequence of ideas formed from perceptions resulting from sensations which it receives from exterior objects. As the mechanism of these sensations, of these perceptions, and the manner they engrave ideas on the brain of man, are not known to him; because he is unable to unravel all these motions; because he cannot perceive the chain of operations in his soul, or the motive principle that acts within him, he supposes himself a free agent; which, literally translated, signifies, that he moves himself by himself; that he determines himself without cause: when he rather ought to say, that he is ignorant how or for why he acts in the manner he does. It is true the soul enjoys an activity peculiar to itself; but it is equally certain that this activity would never be displayed, if some motive or some cause did not put it in a condition to exercise itself: at least it will not be pretended that the soul is able either to love or to hate without being moved, without knowing the objects, without having some idea of their qualities. Gunpowder has unquestionably a particular activity, but this activity will never display itself, unless fire be applied to it; this, however, immediately sets it in motion.

It is the great complication of motion in man, it is the variety of his action, it is the multiplicity of causes that move him, whether simultaneously or in continual succession, that persuades him he is a free agent: if all his motions were simple, if the causes that move him did not confound themselves with each other, if they were distinct, if his machine were less complicated, he would perceive that all his actions were necessary, because he would be enabled to recur instantly to the cause that made him act. A man who should be always obliged to go towards the west, would always go on that side; but he would feel that, in so going, he was not a free agent: if he had another sense, as his actions or his motion, augmented by a sixth, would be still more varied and much more complicated, he would believe himself still more a free agent than he does with his five senses.

It is, then, for want of recurring to the causes that move him; for want of being able to analyze, from not being competent to decompose the complicated motion of his machine, that man believes himself a free agent; it is only upon his own ignorance that he founds the profound yet deceitful notion he has of his free agency; that he builds those opinions which he brings forward as a striking proof of his pretended freedom of action. If, for a short time, each man was willing to examine his own peculiar actions, search out their true motives to discover their concatenation, he would remain convinced that the sentiment he has of his natural free agency, is a chimera that must speedily be destroyed by experience.

Nevertheless it must be acknowledged that the multiplicity and diversity of the causes which continually act upon man, frequently without even his knowledge, render it impossible, or at least extremely difficult for him to recur to the true principles of his own peculiar actions, much less the actions of others: they frequently depend upon causes so fugitive, so remote from their effects, and which, superficially examined, appear to have so little analogy, so slender a relation with them, that it requires singular sagacity to bring them into light. This is what renders the study of the moral man a task of such difficulty; this is the reason why his heart is an abyss, of which it is frequently impossible for him to fathom the depth. He is then obliged to content himself with a knowledge of the general and necessary laws by which the human heart is regulated: for the individuals of his own species these laws are pretty nearly the same; they vary only in consequence of the organization that is peculiar to each, and of the modification it undergoes: This, however, cannot be rigorously the same in any two. It suffices to know, that by his essence, man tends to conserve himself, and to render his existence happy: this granted, whatever may be his actions, if he recur back to this first principle, to this general, this necessary tendency of his will, he never can be deceived with regard to his motives.

For Further Reflection

1. Has d'Holbach proved that we do not have free will? Is his argument that science precludes such a notion convincing?

2. d'Holbach points out that without the doctrine of free will, the notion of just punishment crumbles: that religion could not justify God's sending people to hell for their sins, and the Law could not justify its system of punishments without the doctrine. Do you agree with d'Holbach?

3. Could we go even farther and say that we would not have any place for moral praise or blame without a notion of free will? What would d'Holbach make of moral responsibility?

4. J. B. S. Haldane has written, "If my mental processes are determined wholly by the motion of atoms in my brain, I have no reason to suppose that my beliefs are true . . . and hence I have no reason for supposing my brain to be composed of atoms." Does this show that determinism is self-refuting?

Freedom of the Will and Human Responsibility   V.40

CORLISS LAMONT

Corliss Lamont (1902–1995) was a leading humanist philosopher, the chairman of the national emergency of Civil Liberties Committee, and one of the most ardent supporters of metaphysical and political liberty.

Lamont briefly sets forth several reasons why he thinks we have free will. He qualifies his arguments and shows how free will relates to moral responsibility.

Study Questions

1. What is Lamont's thesis?
2. What does he say about classic determinism?
3. What are Lamont's eight reasons for believing in free will?
4. How does Lamont qualify his thesis that we have free will and are not determined?
5. How does the reality of chance show that determinism is only relative?
6. What does Jean Paul Sartre say about freedom?

IT IS MY THESIS that a man who is convinced he possesses freedom of choice or free will has a greater sense of responsibility than a person who thinks that total determinism rules the universe and human life. Determinism in the classic sense means that the flow of history, including all human choices and actions, is completely predetermined from the beginning of time. He who believes that "whatever is, was to be" can try to escape moral responsibility for wrongdoing by claiming that he was compelled to act as he did because it was predestined by the iron laws of cause and effect.

But if free choice truly exists at the moment of choosing, men clearly have full moral responsibility in deciding between two or more genuine alternatives, and the deterministic alibi has no weight. The heart of our discussion, then, lies in the question of whether free choice or universal determinism represents the truth. I

shall try to summarize briefly the main reasons that point to the existence of free will.

First, there is the immediate, powerful, common-sense intuition shared by virtually all human beings that freedom of choice is real. This intuition seems as strong to me as the sensation of pleasure or pain; and the attempt of the determinists to explain the intuition away is as artificial as the Christian Scientist claim that pain is not real. The intuition of free choice does not, of course, in itself prove that such freedom exists, but that intuition is so strong that the burden of proof is on the determinists to show that it is based on an illusion.

Second, we can defuse the determinist argument by admitting, and indeed insisting, that a great deal of determinism exists in the world. Determinism in the form of if-then causal laws governs much of the human body's functioning and much of the universe as a whole. We can be glad

Reprinted from Religious Humanism, *Summer, 1969.*

that the automatic system of breathing, digestion, circulation of the blood, and beating of the heart operate deterministically—until they get out of order. Determinism *versus* free choice is a false issue; what we always have is *relative* determinism and *relative* free choice. Free will is ever limited by the past and by the vast range of if-then laws. At the same time, human beings utilize free choice to take advantage of those deterministic laws embodied in science and man-made machines. Most of us drive cars, but it is we and not the autos that decide when and where they are to go. Determinism wisely used and controlled—which is by no means always the case—can make us freer and happier.

Third, determinism is a relative thing, not only because human free choice exists, but also because contingency or chance is an ultimate trait of the cosmos. Contingency is best seen in the intersection of mutually independent event-streams between which there was no previous causal connection. My favorite example here is the collision of the steamship *Titanic* with an iceberg off Newfoundland, in the middle of the night on April 14, 1912. It was a terrible accident, with more than 1,500 persons lost. The drifting of the iceberg down from the north and the steaming of the *Titanic* west from England clearly represented two causal streams independent of each other.

Even if a team of scientific experts had been able, *per impossible*, to trace back the two causal streams and ascertain that the catastrophe had been predestined from the moment the steamship left Southampton, that would not upset my thesis. For the space-time relation of the iceberg and the *Titanic*, as the ship started on its voyage, would have been itself a matter of contingency, since there was no relevant cause to account for that precise relation.

The pervasive presence of contingency in the world is also proved by the fact that all natural laws, as I have observed, take the form of if-then sequences or relations. The *if* factor is obviously conditional and demonstrates the continual coexistence of contingency with determinism. The actuality of contingency negates the idea of total and all-inclusive necessity operating throughout the universe. As regards human choice, contingency ensures that at the outset the alternatives one faces are indeterminate in relation to the act of choosing, which proceeds to make one of them determinate.

My fourth point is that the accepted meaning of *potentiality*, namely, that every object and event in the cosmos possesses plural possibilities of behavior, interaction, and development, knocks out the determinist thesis. From the determinist viewpoint, multiple potentialities are an illusion. If you want to take a vacation trip next summer, you will no doubt think over a number of possibilities before you make a final decision. Determinism logically implies that such deliberation is mere playacting, because you were destined all the time to choose the trip you did choose. When we relate the causal pattern to potentiality, we find that causation as mediated through free choice can have its appropriate effect in the actualization of any one of various possibilities.

Fifth, the normal processes of human thought are tied in with potentiality as I have just described it, and likewise tend to show that freedom of choice is real. Thinking constantly involves general conceptions, universals, or abstractions under which are classified many varying particulars. In the case that I discussed under my fourth point, "vacation travel" was the general conception and the different places that might be visited were the particulars, the alternatives, the potentialities, among which one could freely choose. Unless there is free choice, the function of human thought in solving problems becomes superfluous and a mask of make-believe.

Sixth, it is clarifying for the problem of free choice to realize that only the present exists, and that it is always some present activity that builds up the past, as a skier leaves a trail behind him in the snow as he weaves down the hill. Everything that exists—the whole vast aggregate of inanimate matter, the swarming profusion of earthly life, man in his every aspect—exists only as an event or events taking place at this instant moment, which is now. The past is dead and gone; it is efficacious only as it is embodied in present structures and activities.

The activity of former presents establishes the foundations upon which the immediate present operates. What happened in the past creates both limitations and potentialities, always conditioning the present. But conditioning in this sense is not the same as determining; and each day sweeps onward under its own momentum, actualizing fresh patterns of existence, maintaining other patterns and destroying still others. Thus a man choosing and acting in the present is not wholly controlled by the past, but is part of the unending forward surge of cosmic power. He is an active, initiating agent, riding the wave of the present, as it were, and deliberating among open alternatives to reach decisions regarding the many different phases of his life.

My seventh point is that the doctrine of universal and eternal determinism is seen to be self-refuting when we work out its full implications in the cases of *reductio ad absurdum* implied. If our choices and actions today were all predestined yesterday, then they were equally predestined yesteryear, at the day of our birth, and at the birth of our solar system and earth some five billion years ago. To take another instance: for determinism, the so-called *irresistible impulse* that the law recognizes in assessing crimes by the insane must hold with equal force for the actions of the sane and virtuous. In the determinist philosophy, the good man has an irresistible impulse to tell the truth, to be kind to animals, and to expose the graft in City Hall.

Eighth, in the novel dialect of determinism many words lose their normal meaning. I refer to such words as *refraining, forbearance, self-restraint,* and *regret.* If determinism turns out to be true, we shall have to scrap a great deal in existing dictionaries and do a vast amount of re-defining. What meaning, for example, is to be assigned to *forbearance* when it is determined in advance that you are going to refuse that second Martini cocktail? You can truly forbear only when you refrain from doing something that it is possible for you to do. But under the determinist dispensation it is not possible for you to accept the second cocktail because fate has already dictated your "No." I am not saying that nature necessarily conforms to our linguistic usages, but human language habits that have evolved over aeons of time cannot be neglected in the analysis of free choice and determinism.

Finally, I do not think that the term *moral responsibility* can retain its traditional meaning unless freedom of choice exists. From the viewpoint of ethics, law, and criminal law, it is difficult to understand how a consistent determinist would have a sufficient sense of personal responsibility for the development of decent ethical standards. But the question remains whether there have ever been or can be any consistent determinists or whether free choice runs so deep in human nature as an innate characteristic that, as Jean Paul Sartre suggests, "We are not free to cease being free."

For Further Reflection

1. Describe and evaluate Lamont's argument for free will. How convincing is it?

2. Explain the relationship between free will and moral responsibility. Is Lamont correct about the relationship?

3. Discuss the eight reasons for supporting the thesis of free will. Which ones are the most cogent? Which are the least cogent?

4. Examine and evaluate Sartre's dictum, "We are not free to cease being free." What does that mean? Is it true?

V.41   Compatibilism

W. T. STACE

W. T. Stace (1886–1967) was born in Britain, educated at Trinity College, Dublin, and served in the British Civil Service in Ceylon. In 1932 he came to the United States to teach at Princeton University. One of his chief goals was to reconcile empiricism with mysticism. Among his works are *The Concept of Morals* (1952), *Time and Eternity* (1952), and *Mysticism and Philosophy* (1960).

Stace attempts to reconcile free will with causal determinism. He takes the position that William James labeled "soft determinism," what is sometimes called compatibilism. We must have free will to be held morally responsible, and yet it seems plausible that all our actions are caused. How can these two apparently inconsistent ideas be brought together? Stace argues that the problem is merely a verbal dispute, and that, rightly understood, there is no inconsistency in holding to both doctrines. Free actions are those we do voluntarily, whereas unfree actions are those that we do involuntarily.

Study Questions

1. Why is it important to discover whether we have free will? Explain Stace's argument.
2. In practice, by what doctrine do even determinists live?
3. How does Stace characterize the dispute between free will and determinism?
4. What is Stace's strategy in consulting common language usage to show that free will is compatible with determinism?
5. What is the difference between a free and an unfree act?
6. What is Stace's general conclusion?
7. How does moral responsibility actually require determinism, according to Stace?

I SHALL FIRST DISCUSS the problem of free will, for it is certain that if there is no free will there can be no morality. Morality is concerned with what men ought and ought not to do. But if a man has no freedom to choose what he will do, if whatever he does is done under compulsion, then it does not make sense to tell him that he ought not to have done what he did and

that he ought to do something different. All moral precepts would in such case be meaningless. Also if he acts always under compulsion, how can he be held morally responsible for his actions? How can he, for example, be punished for what he could not help doing?

It is to be observed that those learned professors of philosophy or psychology who deny the

Specified excerpts (pp. 248–258) from W. T. Stace, Religion and the Modern Mind *(J. B. Lippincott Company). Copyright 1952 by W. T. Stace. Reprinted by Permission of HarperCollins Publishers.*

existence of free will do so only in their professional moments and in their studies and lecture rooms. For when it comes to doing anything practical, even of the most trivial kind, they invariably behave as if they and others were free. They inquire from you at dinner whether you will choose this dish or that dish. They will ask a child why he told a lie, and will punish him for not having chosen the way of truthfulness. All of which is inconsistent with a disbelief in free will. This should cause us to suspect that the problem is not a real one; and this, I believe, is the case. The dispute is merely verbal, and is due to nothing but a confusion about the meanings of words. It is what is now fashionably called a semantic problem.

How does a verbal dispute arise? Let us consider a case which, although it is absurd in the sense that no one would ever make the mistake which is involved in it, yet illustrates the principle which we shall have to use in the solution of the problem. Suppose that someone believed that the word "man" means a certain sort of five-legged animal; in short that "five-legged animal" is the correct *definition* of man. He might then look around the world, and rightly observing that there are no five-legged animals in it, he might proceed to deny the existence of men. This preposterous conclusion would have been reached because he was using an incorrect definition of "man." All you would have to do to show him his mistake would be to give him the correct definition; or at least show him that his definition was wrong. Both the problem and its solution would, of course, be entirely verbal. The problem of free will, and its solution, I shall maintain, is verbal in exactly the same way. The problem has been created by the fact that learned men, especially philosophers, have assumed an incorrect definition of free will, and then finding that there is nothing in the world which answers to their definition, have denied its existence. As far as logic is concerned, their conclusion is just as absurd as that of the man who denies the existence of men. The only difference is that the mistake in the latter case is obvious

and crude, while the mistake which the deniers of free will have made is rather subtle and difficult to detect.

Throughout the modern period, until quite recently, it was assumed, both by the philosophers who denied free will and by those who defended it, that *determinism is inconsistent with free will*. If a man's actions were wholly determined by chains of causes stretching back into the remote past, so that they could be predicted beforehand by a mind which knew all the causes, it was assumed that they could not in that case be free. This implies that a certain definition of actions done from free will was assumed, namely that they are actions *not* wholly determined by causes or predictable beforehand. Let us shorten this by saying that free will was defined as meaning indeterminism. This is the incorrect definition which has led to the denial of free will. As soon as we see what the true definition is we shall find that the question whether the world is deterministic, as Newtonian science implied, or in a measure indeterministic, as current physics teaches, is wholly irrelevant to the problem.

Of course there is a sense in which one can define a word arbitrarily in any way one pleases. But a definition may nevertheless be called correct or incorrect. It is correct if it accords with a *common usage* of the word defined. It is incorrect if it does not. And if you give an incorrect definition, absurd and untrue results are likely to follow. For instance, there is nothing to prevent you from arbitrarily defining a man as a five-legged animal, but this is incorrect in the sense that it does not accord with the ordinary meaning of the word. Also it has the absurd result of leading to a denial of the existence of men. This shows that *common usage is the criterion for deciding whether a definition is correct or not*. And this is the principle which I shall apply to free will. I shall show that indeterminism is not what is meant by the phrase "free will" *as it is commonly used*. And I shall attempt to discover the correct definition by inquiring how the phrase is used in ordinary conversation.

Here are a few samples of how the phrase might be used in ordinary conversation. It will be noticed that they include cases in which the question whether a man acted with free will is asked in order to determine whether he was morally and legally responsible for his acts.

Jones: I once went without food for a week.
Smith: Did you do that of your own free will?
Jones: No. I did it because I was lost in a desert and could find no food.

But suppose that the man who had fasted was Mahatma Gandhi. The conversation might then have gone:

Gandhi: I once fasted for a week.
Smith: Did you do that of your own free will?
Gandhi: Yes. I did it because I wanted to compel the British Government to give India its independence.

Take another case. Suppose that I had stolen some bread, but that I was as truthful as George Washington. Then, if I were charged with the crime in court, some exchange of the following sort might take place:

Judge: Did you steal the bread of your own free will?
Stace: Yes. I stole it because I was hungry.

Or in different circumstances the conversation might run:

Judge: Did you steal of your own free will?
Stace: No. I stole because my employer threatened to beat me if I did not.

At a recent murder trial in Trenton some of the accused had signed confessions, but afterwards asserted that they had done so under police duress. The following exchange might have occurred:

Judge: Did you sign the confession of your own free will?
Prisoner: No. I signed it because the police beat me up.

Now suppose that a philosopher had been a member of the jury. We could imagine this conversation taking place in the jury room:

Foreman of the Jury: The prisoner says he signed the confession because he was beaten, and not of his own free will.
Philosopher: This is quite irrelevant to the case. There is no such thing as free will.
Foreman: Do you mean to say that it makes no difference whether he signed because his conscience made him want to tell the truth or because he was beaten?
Philosopher: None at all. Whether he was caused to sign by a beating or by some desire of his own—the desire to tell the truth, for example—in either case his signing was causally determined, and therefore in neither case did he act of his own free will. Since there is no such thing as free will, the question whether he signed of his own free will ought not to be discussed by us.

The foreman and the rest of the jury would rightly conclude that the philosopher must be making some mistake. What sort of a mistake could it be? There is only one possible answer. The philosopher must be using the phrase "free will" in some peculiar way of his own which is not the way in which men usually use it when they wish to determine a question of moral responsibility. That is, he must be using an incorrect definition of it as implying action not determined by causes.

Suppose a man left his office at noon, and were questioned about it. Then we might hear this:

Jones: Did you go out of your own free will?
Smith: Yes. I went out to get my lunch.

But we might hear:

Jones: Did you leave your office of your own free will?

Smith: No. I was forcibly removed by the police.

We have now collected a number of cases of actions which, in the ordinary usage of the English language, would be called cases in which people have acted of their own free will. We should also say in all these cases that they *chose* to act as they did. We should also say that they could have acted otherwise, if they had chosen. For instance, Mahatma Gandhi was not compelled to fast; he chose to do so. He could have eaten if he had wanted to. When Smith went out to get his lunch, he chose to do so. He could have stayed and done some work, if he had wanted to. We have also collected a number of cases of the opposite kind. They are cases in which men were not able to exercise their free will. They had no choice. They were compelled to do as they did. The man in the desert did not fast of his own free will. He had no choice in the matter. He was compelled to fast because there was nothing for him to eat. And so with the other cases. It ought to be quite easy, by an inspection of these cases, to tell what we ordinarily mean when we say that a man did or did not exercise free will. We ought therefore to be able to extract from them the proper definition of the term. Let us put the cases in a table:

Free Acts	Unfree Acts
Gandhi fasting because he wanted to free India.	The man fasting in the desert because there was no food.
Stealing bread because one is hungry.	Stealing because one's employer threatened to beat one.
Signing a confession because one wanted to tell the truth.	Signing because the police beat one.
Leaving the office because one wanted one's lunch.	Leaving because forcibly removed.

It is obvious that to find the correct definition of free acts we must discover what characteristic is common to all the acts in the left-hand column, and is, at the same time, absent from all the acts in the right-hand column. This characteristic which all free acts have, and which no unfree acts have, will be the defining characteristic of free will.

Is being uncaused, or not being determined by causes, the characteristic of which we are in search? It cannot be, because although it is true that all the acts in the right-hand column have causes, such as the beating by the police or the absence of food in the desert, so also do the acts in the left-hand column. Mr. Gandhi's fasting was caused by his desire to free India, the man leaving his office by his hunger, and so on. Moreover there is no reason to doubt that these causes of the free acts were in turn caused by prior conditions, and that these were again the results of causes, and so on back indefinitely into the past. Any physiologist can tell us the causes of hunger. What caused Mr. Gandhi's tremendously powerful desire to free India is no doubt more difficult to discover. But it must have had causes. Some of them may have lain in peculiarities of his glands or brain, others in his past experiences, others in his heredity, others in his education. Defenders of free will have usually tended to deny such facts. But to do so is plainly a case of special pleading, which is unsupported by any scrap of evidence. The only reasonable view is that all human actions, both those which are freely done and those which are not, are either wholly determined by causes, or at least as much determined as other events in nature. It may be true, as the physicists tell us, that nature is not as deterministic as was once thought. But whatever degree of determinism prevails in the world, human actions appear to be as much determined as anything else. And if this is so, it cannot be the case that what distinguishes actions freely chosen from those which are not free is that the latter are determined by causes while the former are not. Therefore, being uncaused or being undetermined by causes, must be an incorrect definition of free will.

What, then, is the difference between acts which are freely done and those which are not? What is the characteristic which is present to all the acts in the left-hand column and absent from all those in the right-hand column? Is it not obvious that, although both sets of actions have causes, the causes of those in the left-hand column are *of a different kind* from the causes of those in the right-hand column? The free acts are all caused by desires, or motives, or by some sort of internal psychological states of the agent's mind. The unfree acts, on the other hand, are all caused by physical forces or physical conditions, outside the agent. Police arrest means physical force exerted from the outside; the absence of food in the desert is a physical condition of the outside world. We may therefore frame the following rough definitions. *Acts freely done are those whose immediate causes are psychological states in the agent. Acts not freely done are those whose immediate causes are states of affairs external to the agent.*

It is plain that if we define free will in this way, then free will certainly exists, and the philosopher's denial of its existence is seen to be what it is—nonsense. For it is obvious that all those actions of men which we should ordinarily attribute to the exercise of their free will, or of which we should say that they freely chose to do them, are in fact actions which have been caused by their own desires, wishes, thoughts, emotions, impulses, or other psychological states.

In applying our definition we shall find that it usually works well, but that there are some puzzling cases which it does not seem exactly to fit. These puzzles can always be solved by paying careful attention to the ways in which words are used, and remembering that they are not always used consistently. I have space for only one example. Suppose that a thug threatens to shoot you unless you give him your wallet, and suppose that you do so. Do you, in giving him your wallet, do so of your own free will or not? If we apply our definition, we find that you acted freely, since the immediate cause of the action was not an actual outside force but the fear of death, which is a psychological cause. Most people, however, would say that you did not act of your own free will but under compulsion. Does this show that our definition is wrong? I do not think so. Aristotle, who gave a solution of the problem of free will substantially the same as ours (though he did not use the term "free will") admitted that there are what he called "mixed" or borderline cases in which it is difficult to know whether we ought to call the acts free or compelled. In the case under discussion, though no actual force was used, the gun at your forehead so nearly approximated to actual force that we tend to say the case was one of compulsion. It is a borderline case.

Here is what may seem like another kind of puzzle. According to our view an action may be free though it could have been predicted beforehand with certainty. But suppose you told a lie, and it was certain beforehand that you would tell it. How could one then say, "You could have told the truth"? The answer is that it is perfectly true that you could have told the truth *if* you had wanted to. In fact you would have done so, for in that case the causes producing your action, namely your desires, would have been different, and would therefore have produced different effects. It is a delusion that predictability and free will are incompatible. This agrees with common sense. For if, knowing your character, I predict that you will act honorably, no one would say when you do act honorably, that this shows you did not do so of your own free will.

Since free will is a condition of moral responsibility, we must be sure that our theory of free will gives a sufficient basis for it. To be held morally responsible for one's actions means that one may be justly punished or rewarded, blamed or praised, for them. But it is not just to punish a man for what he cannot help doing. How can it be just to punish him for an action which it was certain beforehand that he would do? We have not attempted to decide whether, as a matter of fact, all events, including human actions, are completely determined. For that question is irrelevant to the problem of free will. But if we assume for the purposes of argument that complete determinism is true, but that we are nevertheless free, it may then be asked whether such a deterministic free will is compatible with moral responsibility. For it may seem unjust to punish a man for an action which it could have been predicted with certainty beforehand that he would do.

But that determinism is incompatible with moral responsibility is as much a delusion as that it is incompatible with free will. You do not excuse a man for doing a wrong act because, knowing his character, you felt certain beforehand that he would do it. Nor do you deprive a man of a reward or prize because, knowing his goodness or his capabilities, you felt certain beforehand that he would win it.

Volumes have been written on the justification of punishment. But so far as it affects the question of free will, the essential principles involved are quite simple. The punishment of a man for doing a wrong act is justified, either on the ground that it will correct his own character, or that it will deter other people from doing similar acts. The instrument of punishment has been in the past, and no doubt still is, often unwisely used; so that it may often have done more harm than good. But that is not relevant to our present problem. Punishment, if and when it is justified, is justified only on one or both of the grounds just mentioned. The question then is how, if we assume determinism, punishment can correct character or deter people from evil actions.

Suppose that your child develops a habit of telling lies. You give him a mild beating. Why? Because you believe that his personality is such that the usual motives for telling the truth do not cause him to do so. You therefore supply the missing cause, or motive, in the shape of pain and the fear of future pain if he repeats his untrustful behavior. And you hope that a few treatments of this kind will condition him to the habit of truth-telling, so that he will come to tell the truth without the infliction of pain. You assume that his actions are determined by causes, but that the usual causes of truth-telling do not in him produce their usual effects. You therefore supply him with an artificially injected motive, pain and fear, which you think will in the future cause him to speak truthfully.

The principle is exactly the same where you hope, by punishing one man, to deter others from wrong actions. You believe that the fear of punishment will cause those who might otherwise do evil to do well.

We act on the same principle with non-human, and even with inanimate, things, if they do not behave in the way we think they ought to behave. The rose bushes in the garden produce only small and poor blooms, whereas we want large and rich ones. We supply a cause which will produce large blooms, namely fertilizer. Our automobile does not go properly. We supply a cause which will make it go better, namely oil in the works. The punishment for the man, the fertilizer for the plant, and the oil for the car, are all justified by the same principle and in the same way. The only difference is that different kinds of things require different kinds of causes to make them do what they should. Pain may be the appropriate remedy to apply, in certain cases, to human beings, and oil to the machine. It is, of course, of no use to inject motor oil into the boy or to beat the machine.

Thus we see that moral responsibility is not only consistent with determinism, but requires it. The assumption on which punishment is based is that human behavior is causally determined. If pain could not be a cause of truth-telling there would be no justification at all for punishing lies. If human actions and volitions were uncaused, it would be useless either to punish or reward, or indeed to do anything else to correct people's bad behavior. For nothing that you could do would in any way influence them. Thus moral responsibility would entirely disappear. If there were no determinism of human beings at all, their actions would be completely unpredictable and capricious, and therefore irresponsible. And this is in itself a strong argument against the common view of philosophers that free will means being undetermined by causes.

For Further Reflection

1. Has Stace successfully reconciled free will with determinism? Does his analysis of ordinary language settle the matter?

2. Do you think one can accept determinism and still hold people responsible for their voluntary actions? Can we really help holding people responsible for their purposive actions?

V.42   Fate

RICHARD TAYLOR

Richard Taylor (1919–   ) was for many years a professor of philosophy at Brown University, Rochester University, and Union College. He is the author of several books, including *Metaphysics,* from which this selection is taken.

Taylor defines fatalism as the thesis that the future is unavoidable, that the course of our lives is fixed regardless of what we do. He illustrates his thesis with the story of Osmo who discovers a book, *The Life of Osmo, as Given by God,* detailing his entire life, including his death, which Osmo cannot falsify, try as he might.

Study Questions

1. What is fatalism?
2. How is determinism related to fatalism?
3. What are the sources of fatalism?
4. What is the story of Osmo?
5. What are the four questions Taylor considers at the end of the story of Osmo?
6. What does Taylor say about the law of excluded middle?
7. What objections to his thesis does Taylor discuss at the end of the article?

WE ARE ALL, at certain moments of pain, threat, or bereavement, apt to entertain the idea of fatalism, the thought that what is happening at a particular moment is unavoidable, that we are powerless to prevent it. Sometimes we find ourselves in circumstances not of our own making, in which our very being and destinies are so thoroughly anchored that the thought of fatalism can be quite overwhelming, and sometimes consoling. One feels that whatever then happens, however good or ill, will be what those circumstances yield, and we are helpless. Soldiers, it is said, are sometimes possessed by such thoughts. Perhaps everyone would feel more inclined to them if they paused once in a while to think of how little they ever had to do with bringing themselves to wherever they have arrived in life, how much of their fortunes and

Reprinted from Metaphysics, *3rd ed. (Prentice-Hall, 1983) by permission.*

destinies were decided for them by sheer circumstance, and how the entire course of their lives is often set, once and for all, by the most trivial incidents, which they did not produce and could not even have foreseen. If we are free to work on our destinies at all, which is doubtful, we have freedom that is at best exercised within exceedingly narrow paths. All the important things—when we are born, of what parents, into what culture, whether we are loved or rejected, whether we are male or female, our temperament, our intelligence or stupidity, indeed everything that makes for the bulk of our happiness and misery—all these are decided for us by the most casual and indifferent circumstances, by sheer coincidences, chance encounters, and seemingly insignificant fortuities. One can see this in retrospect if he searches, but few search. The fate that has given us our very being has given us also our pride and conceit, and has thereby formed us so that, being human, we congratulate ourselves on our blessings, which we call our achievements; blame the world for our blunders, which we call our misfortunes; and scarcely give a thought to that impersonal fate that arbitrarily dispenses both.

FATALISM AND DETERMINISM

Determinism, it will be recalled, is the theory that all events are rendered unavoidable by their causes. The attempt is sometimes made to distinguish this from fatalism by saying that, according to the fatalist, certain events are going to happen *no matter what,* or in other words, regardless of causes. But this is enormously contrived. It would be hard to find in the whole history of thought a single fatalist, on that conception of it.

Fatalism is the belief that whatever happens is unavoidable. That is the clearest expression of the doctrine, and it provides the basis of the attitude of calm acceptance that the fatalist is thought, quite correctly, to embody. One who endorses the claim of universal causation, then,

and the theory of the causal determination of an human behavior, is a kind of fatalist—or at least he should be, if he is consistent. For that theory, as we have seen, once it is clearly spelled out and not hedged about with unresolved "ifs," does entail that whatever happens is rendered inevitable by the causal conditions preceding it, and is therefore unavoidable. One can indeed think of verbal formulas for distinguishing the two theories, but if we think of a fatalist as one who has a certain attitude, we find it to be the attitude that a thoroughgoing determinist should, in consistency, assume. That some philosophical determinists are not fatalists does not so much illustrate a great difference between fatalism and determinism but rather the humiliation to one's pride that a fatalist position can deliver, and the comfort that can sometimes be found in evasion.

FATALISM WITH RESPECT TO THE FUTURE AND THE PAST

A fatalist, then, is someone who believes that whatever happens is and always was unavoidable. He thinks it is not up to him what will happen a thousand years hence, next year, tomorrow, or the very next moment. Of course he does not pretend always to *know* what is going to happen. Hence, he might try sometimes to read signs and portents, as meteorologists and astrologers do, or to contemplate the effects upon him of the various things that might, for all he knows, be fated to occur. But he does not suppose that whatever happens could ever have really been avoidable.

A fatalist thus thinks of the future in the way we all think of the past, for everyone is a fatalist as he looks *back* on things. To a large extent we know what has happened—some of it we can even remember—whereas the future is still obscure to us, and we are therefore tempted to imbue it, in our imagination, with all sorts of "possibilities." The fatalist resists this temptation, knowing that mere ignorance can hardly give rise to any genuine possibility in things. He thinks of both past and future "under the aspect of eternity," the way God is supposed to view them. We all think of the past this way, as something settled and fixed, to be taken for what it is. We are never in the least tempted to try to modify it. It is not in the least up to us what happened last year, yesterday, or even a moment ago, any more than are the motions of the heavens or the political developments in Tibet. If we are not fatalists, then we might think that past things once *were* up to us, to bring about or prevent, as long as they were still future, but this expresses our attitude toward the future, not the past.

Such is surely our conception of the whole past, whether near or remote. But the consistent fatalist thinks of the future in the same way. We say of past things that they are no longer within our power. The fatalist says they never were.

THE SOURCES OF FATALISM

A fatalistic way of thinking most often arises from theological ideas, or from what are generally thought to be certain presuppositions of science and logic. Thus, if God is really all-knowing and all-powerful, it is not hard to suppose that He has arranged for everything to happen just as it is going to happen, that He already knows every detail of the whole future course of the world, and there is nothing left for you and me to do except watch things unfold, in the here or the hereafter. But without bringing God into the picture, it is not hard to suppose, as we have seen, that everything that happens is wholly determined by what went before it, and hence that whatever happens at any future time is the only thing that can then happen, given what precedes it. Or even disregarding that, it seems natural to suppose that there is a body of truth concerning what the future holds, just as there is such truth concerning what is contained in the past, whether or not it

is known to any person or even to God, and hence, that everything asserted in that body of truth will assuredly happen, in the fullness of time, precisely as it is described therein.

No one needs to be convinced that fatalism is the only proper way to view the past. That it is also the proper way to view the future is less obvious, due in part, perhaps, to our vastly greater ignorance of what the future holds. The consequences of holding such fatalism are obviously momentous. To say nothing of the consolation of fatalism, which enables a person to view all things as they arise with the same undisturbed mind with which he contemplates even the most revolting of history's horrors, the fatalist teaching also relieves one of all tendency towards both blame and approbation of others and of both guilt and conceit in himself. It promises that a perfect understanding is possible and removes the temptation to view things in terms of human wickedness and moral responsibility. This thought alone, once firmly grasped, yields a sublime acceptance of all that life and nature offer, whether to oneself or one's fellows; and although it thereby reduces one's pride, it simultaneously enhances the feelings, opens the heart, and expands the understanding.

DIVINE OMNISCIENCE

Suppose for the moment, just for the purpose of this discussion, that God exists and is omniscient. To say that God is omniscient means that He knows everything that is true. He cannot, of course, know that which is false. Concerning any falsehood, an omniscient being can know that it is false; but then it is a truth that is known, namely, the truth that the thing in question *is* a falsehood. So if it is false that the moon is a cube, then God can, like you or me, know that this is false; but He cannot know the falsehood itself, that the moon is a cube.

Thus, if God is omniscient He knows, as you probably do, the date of your birth. He also knows, as you may not, the hour of your birth.

Furthermore, God knows, as you assuredly do not, the date of your conception—for there is such a truth, and we are supposing that God knows every truth. Moreover, He knows, as you surely do not, the date of your death, and the circumstances thereof—whether at that moment, known already to Him, you die as the result of accident, a fatal malady, suicide, murder, whatever. And, still assuming God exists and knows everything, He knows whether any ant walked across my desk last night, and if so, what ant it was, where it came from, how long it was on the desk, how it came to be there, and so on, to every truth about this insect that there is. Similarly, of course, He knows when some ant will again appear on my desk, if ever. He knows the number of hairs on my head, notes the fall of every sparrow, knows why it fell, and why it was going to fall. These are simply a few of the consequences of the omniscience that we are for the moment assuming. A more precise way of expressing all this is to say that God knows, concerning any statement whatever that anyone could formulate, that it is true, in case it is, and otherwise, that it is false. And let us suppose that God, at some time or other, or perhaps from time to time, vouchsafes some of his knowledge to people, or perhaps to certain chosen persons. Thus prophets arise, proclaiming the coming of certain events, and things do then happen as they have foretold. Of course it is not surprising that they should, on the supposition we are making; namely, that the foreknowledge of these things comes from God, who is omniscient.

THE STORY OF OSMO

Now, then, let us make one further supposition, which will get us squarely into the philosophical issue these ideas are intended to introduce. Let us suppose that God has revealed a particular set of facts to a chosen scribe who, believing (correctly) that they came from God, wrote them all down. The facts in question then turned out to be all the more or less significant episodes in the life of some perfectly ordinary man named Osmo. Osmo was entirely unknown to the scribe, and in fact to just about everyone, but there was no doubt concerning whom all these facts were about, for the very first thing received by the scribe from God, was: "He of whom I speak is called Osmo." When the revelations reached a fairly voluminous bulk and appeared to be completed, the scribe arranged them in chronological order and assembled them into a book. He at first gave it the title *The Life of Osmo, as Given by God,* but thinking that people would take this to be some sort of joke, he dropped the reference to God.

The book was published but attracted no attention whatsoever, because it appeared to be nothing more than a record of the dull life of a very plain man named Osmo. The scribe wondered, in fact, why God had chosen to convey such a mass of seemingly pointless trivia.

The book eventually found its way into various libraries, where it gathered dust until one day a high school teacher in Indiana, who rejoiced under the name of Osmo, saw a copy on the shelf. The title caught his eye. Curiously picking it up and blowing the dust off, he was thunderstruck by the opening sentence: "Osmo is born in Mercy Hospital in Auburn, Indiana, on June 6, 1942, of Finnish parentage, and after nearly losing his life from an attack of pneumonia at the age of five, he is enrolled in the St. James school there." Osmo turned pale. The book nearly fell from his hands. He thumbed back in excitement to discover who had written it. Nothing was given of its authorship nor, for that matter, of its publisher. His questions of the librarian produced no further information, he being as ignorant as Osmo of how the book came to be there.

So Osmo, with the book pressed tightly under his arm, dashed across the street for some coffee, thinking to compose himself and then examine this book with care. Meanwhile he glanced at a few more of its opening remarks, at the things said there about his difficulties with his younger sister, how he was slow in learning to read, of the summer on Mackinac Island, and so on. His emotions now somewhat quieted, Osmo began a close reading. He noted that everything was expressed in the present tense, the way newspaper headlines are written. For example, the text read, "Osmo is born in Mercy Hospital," instead of saying he *was* born there, and is recorded that he quarrels with his sister, is a slow student, is fitted with dental braces at age eight, and so on, all in the journalistic present tense. But the text itself made quite clear approximately when all these various things happened, for everything was in chronological order, and in any case each year of its subject's life constituted a separate chapter and was so titled—"Osmo's Seventh Year," "Osmo's Eighth Year," and so on through the book.

Osmo became absolutely engrossed, to the extent that he forgot his original astonishment, bordering on panic, and for a while even lost his curiosity concerning authorship. He sat drinking coffee and reliving his childhood, much of which he had all but forgotten until the memories were revived by the book now before him. He had almost forgotten about the kitten, for example, and had entirely forgotten its name, until he read, in the chapter called "Osmo's Seventh Year," this observation: "Sobbing, Osmo takes Fluffy, now quite dead, to the garden, and buries her next to the rose bush." Ah yes! And then there was Louise, who sat next to him in the eighth grade—it was all right there. And how he got caught smoking one day. And how he felt when his father died. On and on. Osmo became so absorbed that he quite forgot the business of the day, until it occurred to him to turn to Chapter 26, to see what might be said there, he having just recently turned twenty-six. He had no sooner done so than his panic returned, for lo! what the book said was *true!* That it rains on his birthday for example, that his wife fails to give him the binoculars he had hinted he would like, that he receives a raise in salary shortly thereafter, and so on. Now how in God's name, Osmo pondered, could anyone

know that apparently before it had happened? For these were quite recent events, and the book had dust on it. Quickly moving on, Osmo came to this: "Sitting and reading in the coffee shop across from the library, Osmo, perspiring copiously, entirely forgets, until it is too late, that he is supposed to collect his wife at the hairdresser's at four." Oh my god! He had forgotten all about that. Yanking out his watch, Osmo discovered that it was nearly five o'clock—too late. She would be on her way home by now, and in a very sour mood.

Osmo's anguish at this discovery was nothing, though, compared with what the rest of the day held for him. He poured more coffee, and it now occurred to him to check the number of chapters in this amazing book: only twenty-nine! But surely, he thought, that doesn't mean anything. How anyone could have gotten all this stuff down so far was puzzling enough, to be sure, but no one on God's earth could possibly know in advance how long this or that person is going to live. (Only God could know that sort of thing, Osmo reflected.) So he read along; though not without considerable uneasiness and even depression, for the remaining three chapters were on the whole discouraging. He thought he had gotten that ulcer under control, for example. And he didn't see any reason to suppose his job was going to turn out that badly, or that he was really going to break a leg skiing; after all, he could just give up skiing. But then the book took on a terribly dismal note. It said: "And Osmo, having taken Northwest flight 569 from O'Hare, perishes when the aircraft crashes on the runway at Fort Wayne, with considerable loss of life, a tragedy rendered the far more calamitous by the fact that Osmo had neglected to renew his life insurance before the expiration of the grace period." And that was all. That was the end of the book.

So *that's* why it had only twenty-nine chapters. Some idiot thought he was going to get killed in a plane crash. But, Osmo thought, he just wouldn't get on that plane. And this would also remind him to keep his insurance in force.

(About three years later our hero, having boarded a flight for St. Paul, went berserk when the pilot announced they were going to land at Fort Wayne instead. According to one of the flight attendants, he tried to hijack the aircraft and divert it to another airfield. The Civil Aeronautics Board cited the resulting disruptions as contributing to the crash that followed as the plane tried to land.)

FOUR QUESTIONS

Osmo's extraordinary circumstances led him to embrace the doctrine of fatalism. Not quite completely, perhaps, for there he was, right up to the end, trying vainly to buck his fate—trying, in effect, to make a fool of God, though he did not know this, because he had no idea of the book's source. Still, he had the overwhelming evidence of his whole past life to make him think that everything was going to work out exactly as described in the book. It always had. It was, in fact, precisely this conviction that terrified him so.

But now let us ask these questions, in order to make Osmo's experiences more relevant to our own. First, why did he become, or nearly become, a fatalist? Second, just what did his fatalism amount to? Third, was his belief justified in terms of the evidence he had? And finally, is that belief justified in terms of the evidence *we* have—or in other words, should we be fatalists too?

This last, of course, is the important metaphysical question, but we have to approach it through the others.

Why did Osmo become a fatalist? Osmo became a fatalist because there existed a set of true statements about the details of his life, both past and future, and he came to know what some of these statements were and to believe them, including many concerning his future. That is the whole of it.

No theological ideas entered into his conviction, nor any presuppositions about causal de-terminism, the coercion of his actions by causes, or anything of this sort. The foundations of Osmo's fatalism were entirely in logic and epistemology, having to do only with truth and knowledge. Ideas about God did not enter in, for he never suspected that God was the ultimate source of those statements. And at no point did he think God was *making* him do what he did. All he was concerned about was that someone seemed somehow to *know* what he had done and was going to do.

What, then, did Osmo believe? He did not, it should be noted, believe that certain things were going to happen to him *no matter what.* That does not express a logically coherent belief. He did not think he was in danger of perishing in an airplane crash even in case he did not get into any airplane, for example, or that he was going to break his leg skiing, whether he went skiing or not. No one believes what he considers to be plainly impossible. If anyone believes that a given event is going to happen, he does not doubt that those things necessary for its occurrence are going to happen too. The expression "no matter what," by means of which some philosophers have sought an easy and even childish refutation of fatalism, is accordingly highly inappropriate in any description of the fatalist conviction.

Osmo's fatalism was simply the realization that the things described in the book were unavoidable.

Of course we are all fatalists in this sense about some things, and the metaphysical question is whether this familiar attitude should not be extended to everything. We know the sun will rise tomorrow, for example, and there is nothing we can do about it. Each of us knows he is sooner or later going to die, too, and there is nothing to be done about that either. We normally do not know just when, of course, but it is mercifully so! For otherwise we would sit simply checking off the days as they passed, with growing despair, like a man condemned to the gallows and knowing the hour set for his execution. The tides ebb and flow, and heavens revolve, the seasons follow in order, generations arise and pass, and no one speaks of taking preventive measures. With respect to those things each of us recognizes as beyond his control, we are of necessity fatalists.

The question of fatalism is simply: Of all the things that happen in the world, which, if any, are avoidable? And the philosophical fatalist replies: None of them. They never were. Some of them only seemed so.

Was Osmo's fatalism justified? Of course it was. When he could sit right there and read a true description of those parts of his life that had not yet been lived, it would be idle to suggest to him that his future might, nonetheless, contain alternative possibilities. The only doubts Osmo had were whether those statements could really be true. But here he had the proof of his own experience, as one by one they were tested. Whenever he tried to prevent what was set forth, he of course failed. Such failure, over and over, of even the most Herculean efforts, with never a single success, must surely suggest, sooner or later, that he was *destined* to fail. Even to the end, when Osmo tried so desperately to save himself from the destruction described in the book, his effort was totally in vain—as he should have realized it was going to be had he really known that what was said there was true. No power in heaven or earth can render false a statement that is true. It has never been done, and never will be.

Is the doctrine of fatalism, then, true? This amounts to asking whether our circumstances are significantly different from Osmo's. Of course we cannot read our own biographies the way he could. Only people who become famous ever have their lives recorded, and even so, it is always in retrospect. This is unfortunate. It is too bad that someone with sufficient knowledge—God, for example—cannot set down the lives of great men in advance, so that their achievements can be appreciated better by their contemporaries, and indeed, by their predecessors—their parents, for instance. But mortals do not have the requisite knowledge, and if there are any gods who do, they seem to keep it to themselves.

None of this matters, as far as our own fatalism is concerned. For the important thing to note is that, of the two considerations that explain Osmo's fatalism, only one of them was philosophically relevant, and that one applies to us no less than to him. The two considerations were: (1) there existed a set of true statements about his life, both past and future, and (2) he came to know what those statements were and to believe them. Now the second of these two considerations explains why, as a matter of psychological fact, Osmo became fatalistic, but it has nothing to do with the validity of that point of view. Its validity is assured by (1) alone. It was not the fact that the statements happened to be written down that rendered the things they described unavoidable; that had nothing to do with it at all. Nor was it the fact that, because they had been written, Osmo could read them. His reading them and coming to believe them likewise had nothing to do with the inevitability of what they described. This was ensured simply by there being such a set of statements, whether written or not, whether read by anyone or not, and whether or not known to be true. All that is required is that they should *be* true.

Each of us has but one possible past, described by that totality of statements about us in the past tense, each of which happens to be true. No one ever thinks of rearranging things there; it is simply accepted as given. But so also, each of us has but one possible future, described by that totality of statements about oneself in the future tense, each of which happens to be true. The sum of these constitutes one's biography. Part of it has been lived. The main outlines of it can still be seen, in retrospect, though most of its details are obscure. The other part has not been lived, though it most assuredly is going to be, in exact accordance with that set of statements just referred to. Some of its outlines can already be seen, in prospect, but it is on the whole more obscure than the part belonging to the past. We have at best only premonitory glimpses of it. It is no doubt for this reason that not all of this part, the part that awaits us, is perceived as given, and people do sometimes speak absurdly of altering it—as though what the future holds, as identified by any true statement in the future tense, might after all *not* hold.

Osmo's biography was all expressed in the present tense because all that mattered was that the things referred to were real events, it did not matter to what part of time they belonged. His past consisted of those things that preceded his reading of the book, and he simply accepted it as given. He was not tempted to revise what was said there, for he was sure it was true. But it took the book to make him realize that his future was also something given. It was equally pointless for him to try to revise what was said there, for it, too, was true. As the past contains what has happened, the future contains what will happen, and neither contains, in addition to these things, various other things that did not and will not happen.

Of course we know relatively little of what the future contains. Some things we know. We know the sun will go on rising and setting, for example, that taxes will be levied and wars will rage, that people will continue to be callous and greedy, and that people will be murdered and robbed. It is only the details that remain to be discovered. But the same is true of the past; it is only a matter of degree. When I meet a total stranger, I do not know, and will probably never know, what his past has been, beyond certain obvious things—that he had a mother, and things of this sort. I know nothing of the particulars of that vast realm of fact that is unique to his past. And the same for his future, with only this difference—that *all* people are strangers to me as far as their futures are concerned, and here I am even a stranger to myself.

Yet there is one thing I know concerning any stranger's past and the past of everything under the sun; namely, that whatever it might hold, there is nothing anyone can do about it now. What has happened cannot be undone. The mere fact that it has happened guarantees this.

And so it is, by the same token, of the future of everything under the sun. Whatever the future might hold, there is nothing anyone can do about it now. What will happen cannot be altered. The mere fact that it is going to happen guarantees this.

THE LAW OF EXCLUDED MIDDLE

The presupposition of fatalism is therefore nothing but the commonest presupposition of all logic and inquiry; namely, that there is such a thing as truth, and that this has nothing at all to do with the passage of time. Nothing *becomes* true or *ceases* to be true; whatever is truth at all simply *is* true.

It comes to the same thing, and is perhaps more precise, to say that every meaningful statement, whether about oneself or anything else, is either true or else it is false; that is, its denial is true. There is no middle ground. The principle is thus appropriately called *the law of excluded middle*. It has nothing to do with what tense a statement happens to express, nor with the question for whether anyone, man or god, happens to know whether it is true or false.

Thus no one knows whether there was an ant on my desk last night, and no one ever will. But we do know that either this statement is true or else its denial is true—there is no third alternative. If we say it *might* be true, we mean only that we do not happen to know. Similarly, no one knows whether or not there is going to be an ant there tonight, but we know that either it will or else it will not be there.

In a similar way we can distinguish two mutually exclusive but exhaustive classes of statements about any person; namely, the class of all those that are true, and the class of all that are false. There are no others in addition to these. Included in each are statements never asserted or even considered by anyone, but such that, if anyone were to formulate one of them, it would either be a true statement or else a false one.

Consider, then, that class of statements about some particular person—you, let us suppose—each of which happens to be true. Their totality constitutes your biography. One combination of such statements describes the time, place, and circumstances of your birth. Another combination describes the time, place, and circumstances of your death. Others describe in detail the rises and falls of your fortunes, your achievements and failures, your joys and sorrows—absolutely everything that is true of you.

Some of these things you have already experienced, others await you. But the entire biography is there. It is not written, and probably never will be; but it is nevertheless there, all of it. If, like Osmo, you had some way of discovering those statements in advance, then like him you could hardly help becoming a fatalist. But foreknowledge of the truth would not create any truth, nor invest your philosophy with truth, nor add anything to the philosophical foundations of the fatalism that would then be so apparent to you. It would only serve to make it apparent.

OBJECTIONS

This thought, and the sense of its force, have tormented and frightened people from the beginning, and thinkers whose pride sometimes exceeds their acumen and their reverence for truth have attempted every means imaginable to demolish it. There are few articles of faith upon which virtually everyone can agree, but one of them is certainly the belief in their cherished free will. Any argument in opposition to the doctrine of fate, however feeble, is immediately and uncritically embraced, as though the refutation of fatalism required only the denial of it, supported by reasons that would hardly do credit to a child. It will be worthwhile, therefore, to look briefly at some of the arguments most commonly heard.

1. One can neither foresee the future nor prove that there is any god, or even if there is, that he could know in advance the free actions of men.

    The reply to this is that it is irrelevant. The thesis of fatalism rests on no theory of divination and on no theology. These ideas were introduced only illustratively.

2. True statements are not the causes of anything. Statements only entail; they do not cause, and hence threaten no man's freedom.

    But this, too, is irrelevant, for the claim here denied is not one that has been made,

3. The whole argument just conflates fact and necessity into one and the same thing, treating as unavoidable that which is merely true. The fact that a given thing is *going* to happen implies only that it is going to happen, not that it *has* to. Someone might still be able to prevent it—though of course no one will. For example, President Kennedy was murdered. This means it was true that he was going to be murdered. But it does not mean his death at that time and place was unavoidable. Someone *could* have rendered that statement false; though of course no one did.

    That is probably the commonest "refutation" of fatalism ever offered. But how strong is the claim that something *can* be done, when in fact it never *has* been done in the whole history of the universe, in spite, sometimes, of the most strenuous efforts? No one has ever rendered false a statement that was true, however hard some have tried. When an attempt, perhaps a heroic attempt, is made to avoid a given calamity, and the thing in question happens anyway, at just the moment and in just the way it was going to happen, we have reason to doubt that it could have been avoided. And in fact great effort was made to save President Kennedy, for example, from the destruction toward which he was heading on that fatal day, a whole legion of bodyguards having no other mission. And it failed. True, we can say that *if* more strenuous precautions had been taken, the event would not have happened. But to this we must add *true*, they were not taken, and hence *true*, they were not going to be taken—and we have on our hands again a true statement of the kind that no man has ever had the slightest degree of success in rendering false.

For Further Reflection

1. Describe and evaluate Taylor's argument for fatalism. How convincing is it?
2. How does the story of Osmo illustrate Taylor's thesis?
3. Discuss the four questions that Taylor raises at the end of the story of Osmo.
4. Examine the objections raised against fatalism at the end of the article.

Suggestions for Further Reading

Dennett, Daniel. *Elbow Room: Varieties of Free Will Worth Wanting*. Cambridge, MA: MIT Press, 1985. The best defense of compatibilism.

Feinberg, Joel, ed. *Reason and Responsibility*. Belmont, CA: Wadsworth, 1985. Part 4 contains a very good selection of readings, including four readings on the implications for justifying punishment.

Honderich, Ted, ed. *Essays on Freedom of Action*. London: Routledge & Kegan Paul, 1973. A good collection of essays.

Lehrer, Keith, and Cornman, James. *Philosophical Problems and Arguments*, 3rd ed. New York: Macmillan, 1982. Lehrer's essay (Chapter 3) is excellent.

MacKay, Donald M. *Freedom of Action in a Mechanistic Universe*. Cambridge: Cambridge University Press, 1967.

Morgenbesser, Sidney, and Walsh, James, eds. *Free Will*. Englewood Cliffs, NJ: Prentice Hall, 1962. This contains many of the classic readings.

Stace, Walter. *Religion and the Modern Mind*. New York: Lippincott, 1952.

Trusted, Jennifer. *Free Will and Responsibility*. Oxford: Oxford University Press, 1984. One of the clearest introductions to the subject. Accessible to beginners and reliable.

van Inwagen, Peter. *An Essay on Free Will*. Oxford: Oxford University Press, 1983. This is the best critique of compatibilism available.

Watson, Gary. *Free Will*. Oxford: Oxford University Press, 1982. This volume contains the best collections of recent articles on the subject, especially those of Frankfurt, van Inwagen, and Watson. It also contains two clear discussions of the problem of mechanism and freedom of the will: Norman Malcolm's "The Conceivability of Mechanism" and Daniel Dennett's "Mechanism and Responsibility."

Part VI

Ethics

We are discussing no small matter, but how we ought to live.

SOCRATES in Plato's *Republic*

Some years ago the nation was stunned by a report from Kew Gardens, Queens in New York City. A young woman, Kitty Genovese, was brutally stabbed in her neighborhood while thirty-eight respectable, law-abiding citizens watched a killer stalk and stab her in three separate attacks. Her neighbors looked on from their bedroom windows for some thirty-five minutes as the assailant beat her, stabbed her, left her, and returned to repeat the process two more times until she died. No one lifted a phone to call the police, no one shouted at the criminal, let alone went to the aid of Kitty. Finally, a 70-year-old woman called the police. It took them two minutes to arrive, but by that time Kitty was dead. Only one other woman came out to testify until the ambulance came an hour later. Then the whole neighborhood poured out. Asked why they didn't do anything, the responses ranged from "I don't know" and "I was tired" to "Frankly, we were afraid."

Who is my neighbor? What should these respectable citizens have done? What would you have done? What kinds of generalizations can we make from this episode about contemporary culture in America? Is it an anomaly or quite indicative of something deeply disturbing?

What is it to be a moral person in contemporary North America? What is the nature of morality? Why should I be moral? What is the good and how shall I know it? Are moral principles absolute or simply relative to social group or culture? Is morality, like beauty, in the eye of the beholder? Is it in my interest to be moral or to be moral when it calls for personal sacrifice? How does one justify one's moral beliefs? What is the relationship between morality and religion? What is the basis of morality? Why do we need morality anyway?

These are some of the questions that we shall be looking at in this part of our work. We want to know how we should live.

What Is Ethics?

The terms "moral" and "ethics" come from Latin and Greek, respectively (*mores* and *ethos*), deriving their meaning from the idea of custom. I shall follow the custom of using "morality" and "ethics" synonymously to refer to actual or ideal moralities. Sometimes, however, we use the term *ethics* to refer to the philosophical analysis of morality, the systematic endeavor to understand moral concepts and justify moral principles and theories. It undertakes to analyze such concepts as "right," "wrong," "permissible," "ought," "good," and "evil" in their moral contexts. Moral philosophy seeks to establish principles of right behavior that can serve as action guides for individuals and groups. It investigates which values and virtues are paramount to the worthwhile life or society. It builds and scrutinizes arguments in ethical theories, and it seeks to discover valid principles (for example, "Never kill innocent human beings") and the relationship between those principles (for example, Does saving a life in some situations constitute a valid reason for breaking a promise?).

Ethics is concerned with values—not with what is, but what ought to be. How should I live my life? What is the right thing to do in this situation? Should I always tell the truth? Do I have a duty to report a coworker whom I have seen cheating our company? Should I tell my friend that his spouse is having an affair? Is premarital sex morally permissible? Ought a woman ever to have an abortion? Ethics has a distinct action-guiding aspect and, as such, belongs to the group of practical institutions that include religion, law, and etiquette.

Ethics can be closely allied to religion, but it need not be. There are both religious and secular ethical systems. Secular or purely philosophical ethics are grounded in reason and common human experience. To use a spatial metaphor, secular ethics are horizontal, lacking a vertical or transcendental dimension. Religious ethics has a vertical dimension, being grounded in revelation or divine authority. These two differing orientations will often generate different moral principles and standards of evaluation, but they need not. Some versions of religious ethics, which posit God's revelation of the moral law in nature or conscience, hold that reason can discover what is right or wrong even apart from divine revelation.

Ethics is also closely related to law, and in some societies (such as that depicted in the Hebrew Bible) the two are seen as the same—as a single reality. Many laws are instituted to promote well-being, resolve conflicts of interest or promote social harmony, just as morality does, but ethics can judge that some laws are immoral without denying that they are valid laws: for example, laws permitting slavery or irrelevant discrimination against people on the basis of race or sex. A Catholic or antiabortion advocate might believe that the laws permitting abortion are immoral.

In a 1989 PBS television series, *Ethics in America,* James Neal, a trial lawyer, was asked what he would do if he discovered that his client, some years back, had committed a murder for which another man had been convicted and was going to die for in a few days. Mr. Neal said that he had a legal obligation to keep this information confidential and that if he divulged it he would be disbarred. Some would argue that he has a moral obligation that overrides his legal obligation and that demands that he take action to protect the innocent man from being executed.

Furthermore, there are some aspects of morality that are not covered by law. For example, although it is generally agreed that lying is usually immoral, there is no law against it. College newspapers publish advertisements for phony research papers, which students use in lieu of their own work. Publication of such ads is legal, but it is not moral. Likewise, Kitty Genovese's neighbors were not guilty of any legal wrongdoing, but they were very likely morally culpable for not calling the police or shouting at the assailant.

There is one other major difference between law and morality. In 1351 King Edward III of England promulgated a law against treason that made it a crime merely to think homicidal thoughts about the king. But, alas, the law could not be enforced, for no tribunal can search the heart and fathom the intentions of the mind. But there are other problems. If malicious intentions (called in law *mens rea*) were criminally illegal, would we not all deserve imprisonment? Even if it were possible to detect intentions, when should the punishment be administered? As soon as the subject has the intention? But how do we know that he will not change his mind? Furthermore, is there not a continuum between imagining some harm to X, wishing a harm to X, desiring a harm to X, and intending a harm to X?

Even though it is impractical to have laws against bad intentions, these intentions are still bad, still morally wrong. Suppose I buy a gun with the intention of killing Uncle Charlie to inherit his wealth, but never get a chance to fire it (for example, Uncle Charlie moves to Australia). Although I have not committed a crime, I have committed a moral wrong.

Finally, law differs from morality in that there are physical sanctions enforcing the law but only the sanctions of conscience and reputation enforcing morality. Etiquette also differs from morality in that it concerns form and style rather than the essence of social existence.

Etiquette determines what is polite behavior rather than what is *right* behavior in a deeper sense. Etiquette represents society's decision about how we are to dress, greet one another, eat, celebrate festivals, dispose of the dead, and carry out social transactions. Whether we greet each other with a handshake, a bow, a hug, or a kiss on the cheek will differ in different social systems, but none of these rituals has any moral superiority.

People in England hold their forks in their left hands when they eat (and sometimes look at Americans with wonder when they see us holding forks in our right hands), whereas people in other countries hold forks in their right hands or in whichever hand they feel like holding it, and people in India typically eat without a fork at all, using the fingers of the right hand to convey food from plate to mouth.

Although Americans pride themselves on tolerance and awareness of other cultures, custom and etiquette can be a bone of contention. A friend of mine relates an incident that took place early in his marriage. John and his wife were hosting their first Thanksgiving meal. He had been used to small celebrations with his immediate family, whereas his wife had been used to grand celebrations. He writes, "I had been asked to carve, something I had never done before, but I was willing. I put on an apron, entered the kitchen, attacked the bird with as much artistry as I could muster. And what reward did I get? [My wife] burst into tears. In *her* family the turkey is brought to the *table*, laid before [the father], grace is said, and *then* he carves! 'So I fail patriarchy,' I hollered later. 'What do you expect?'"

Etiquette is a spice of life. Polite manners grace our social existence but they are not what social existence is about. They help social transactions to flow smoothly, but are not the substance of those transactions.

At the same time, it can be immoral to disregard or flout etiquette. A cultural crisis recently developed in India when Americans went to the beaches clad in bikini bathing suits. This was highly offensive to the Indians and an uproar erupted.

There is nothing intrinsically wrong with wearing skimpy bathing suits, or with wearing nothing at all, for that matter, but people get used to certain behavioral patterns and it's terribly insensitive to flout those customs—especially when you are a guest in someone else's home or country. Not the bathing suits themselves; the *insensitivity* is morally offensive.

Law, etiquette, and religion are all important institutions, but each has limitations. The limitation of the law is that you can't have a law against every social malady nor can you enforce every desirable rule. The limitation of etiquette is that it doesn't get to the heart of what is of vital importance for personal and social existence. Whether or not one eats with one's fingers pales in significance compared with being honest or trustworthy or just. Etiquette is a cultural invention, but morality claims to be a discovery.

The limitation of the religious injunction is that it rests on authority, and we are not always sure of or in agreement about the credentials of the authority, nor on how the authority would rule in ambiguous or new cases. Religion is founded not on reason but on revelation, so there is no way to convince someone who does not share your religious views that your view is the right one.

Ethics, as the analysis of morality, distinguishes itself from law and etiquette by going deeper into the essence of rational existence. Ethics distinguishes itself from religion in that it seeks reasons, rather than authority, to justify its principles. Its central purpose is to secure valid principles of conduct and values that can be instrumental in guiding human actions and producing good character. As such ethics is the most important activity known to humans, for it has to do with how we are to live.

We turn now to a discussion of one of the most pressing issues of our time, moral relativism.

VI.A   Are There Any Moral Absolutes or Is Morality Completely Relative?

Ethical relativism is the notion that there are no universally valid moral principles, but that all moral principles are valid relative to cultural or individual choice. Ethical relativism is to be distinguished from *moral skepticism,* the view that there are no valid moral principles at all (or at least none that we can be confident about). There are two forms of ethical relativism: (1) *subjectivism,* which views morality as a personal decision ("Morality is in the eye of the beholder"), and (2) *conventionalism,* which views moral validity by social acceptance. Opposed to ethical relativism are various theories of *ethical objectivism.* All forms of objectivism affirm the universal validity of some moral principles. The strongest form, *moral absolutism,* holds that there is exactly one right answer to every "What should I do in situation *X?*" question, whatever that situation be, and that a moral principle can never be overridden—even by another moral principle. A weaker form of objectivism sees moral principles as universally valid but not always applicable. That is, moral principle A could be overridden by moral principle B in a given situation, and in other situations, there might be no right answer.

We turn now to our readings. First we have a defense of moral relativism, and after that an attack on moral relativism that defends moral objectivism.

VI.43   Morality Is Relative

RUTH BENEDICT

Ruth Benedict (1887–1948) was a foremost American anthropologist who taught at Columbia University and is best known for her book *Patterns of Culture* (1934). Benedict views social systems as communities with common beliefs and practices that have become more or less well-integrated patterns of ideas and practices. Like a work of art, the social system chooses which theme of its repertoire of basic tendencies to emphasize and then goes about to produce a holistic grand design favoring those tendencies. The final systems differ from one another in striking ways, but there is no reason to say that one system is better than another. What is considered normal or abnormal behavior will depend on the choices of these social systems, or what Benedict calls the "idea-practice pattern of the culture."

Benedict views morality as dependent on the varying histories and environments of different cultures. In this essay, she assembles an impressive amount of data from her anthropological research of tribal behavior on an island in northwest Melanesia from which she draws her conclusion that moral relativism is the correct view of moral principles.

Study Questions

1. What does Benedict see as the purpose of modern social anthropology?
2. What is her thesis about normalcy and abnormalcy?
3. How does Benedict illustrate her thesis? Are the examples sufficient to make her case?
4. What is the point of her illustration of homosexual behavior? Do you find her point plausible?
5. How does Benedict characterize morality? With what phrase is the sentence "It is morally good" synonymous?
6. What is the significance of her final comments on the range of human behavioral tendencies? What does she mean by the phrase "the proportion in which behavior types stand to one another in different societies is not universal"?

MODERN SOCIAL ANTHROPOLOGY has become more and more a study of the varieties and common elements of cultural environment and the consequences of these in human behavior. For such a study of diverse social orders primitive peoples fortunately provide a laboratory not yet entirely vitiated by the spread of a standardized worldwide civilization. Dyaks and Hopis, Fijians and Yakuts are significant for psychological and sociological study because only among these simpler peoples has there been sufficient isolation to give opportunity for the development of localized social forms. In the higher cultures the standardization of custom and belief over a cou-

From "Anthropology and the Abnormal," by Ruth Benedict, in The Journal of General Psychology 10 (1934): 59–82, a publication of the Helen Dwight Reid Educational Foundation. Reprinted by permission of Heldref Publications.

ple of continents has given a false sense of the inevitability of the particular forms that have gained currency, and we need to turn to a wider survey in order to check the conclusions we hastily base upon this near-universality of familiar customs. Most of the simpler cultures did not gain the wide currency of the one which, out of our experience, we identify with human nature, but this was for various historical reasons, and certainly not for any that gives us as its carriers a monopoly of social good or of social sanity. Modern civilization, from this point of view, becomes not a necessary pinnacle of human achievement but one entry in a long series of possible adjustments.

These adjustments, whether they are in mannerisms like the ways of showing anger, or joy, or grief in any society, or in major human drives like those of sex, prove to be far more variable than experience in any one culture would suggest. In certain fields, such as that of religion or of formal marriage arrangements, these wide limits of variability are well known and can be fairly described. In others it is not yet possible to give a generalized account, but that does not absolve us of the task of indicating the significance of the work that has been done and of the problems that have arisen.

One of these problems relates to the customary modern normal-abnormal categories and our conclusions regarding them. In how far are such categories culturally determined, or in how far can we with assurance regard them as absolute? In how far can we regard inability to function socially as diagnostic of abnormality, or in how far is it necessary to regard this as a function of the culture?

As a matter of fact, one of the most striking facts that emerge from a study of widely varying cultures is the ease with which our abnormals function in other cultures. It does not matter what kind of "abnormality" we choose for illustration, those which indicate extreme instability, or those which are more in the nature of character traits like sadism or delusions of grandeur or of persecution, there are well-described cultures in which these abnormals function at ease and with honor, and apparently without danger or difficulty to the society. . . .

The most notorious of these is trance and catalepsy. Even a very mild mystic is aberrant in our culture. But most peoples have regarded even extreme psychic manifestations not only as normal and desirable, but even as characteristic of highly valued and gifted individuals. This was true even in our own cultural background in that period when Catholicism made the ecstatic experience the mark of sainthood. It is hard for us, born and brought up in a culture that makes no use of the experience, to realize how important a role it may play and how many individuals are capable of it, once it has been given an honorable place in any society. . . .

Cataleptic and trance phenomena are, of course, only one illustration of the fact that those whom we regard as abnormals may function adequately in other cultures. Many of our culturally discarded traits are selected for elaboration in different societies. Homosexuality is an excellent example, for in this case our attention is not constantly diverted, as in the consideration of trance, to the interruption of routine activity which it implies. Homosexuality poses the problem very simply. A tendency toward this trait in our culture exposes an individual to all the conflicts to which all aberrants are always exposed, and we tend to identify the consequences of this conflict with homosexuality. But these consequences are obviously local and cultural. Homosexuals in many societies are not incompetent, but they may be such if the culture asks adjustments of them that would strain any man's vitality. Wherever homosexuality has been given an honorable place in any society, those to whom it is congenial have filled adequately the honorable roles society assigns to them. Plato's *Republic* is, of course, the most convincing statement of such a reading of homosexuality. It is presented as one of the major means to the good life, and it was generally so regarded in Greece at that time.

The cultural attitude toward homosexuals has not always been on such a high ethical plane, but it has been very varied. Among many American Indian tribes there exists the institution of the berdache, as the French called them. These men-women were men who at puberty or thereafter took the dress and the occupations of women. Sometimes they married other men and lived with them. Sometimes they were men with no inversion, persons of weak sexual endowment who chose this role to avoid the jeers of the women. The berdaches were never regarded as of first-rate supernatural power, as similar men-women were in Siberia, but rather as leaders in women's occupations, good healers in certain diseases, or, among certain tribes, as the genial organizers of social affairs. In any case, they were socially placed. They were not left exposed to the conflicts that visit the deviant who is excluded from participation in the recognized patterns of his society.

The most spectacular illustrations of the extent to which normality may be culturally defined are those cultures where an abnormality of our culture is the cornerstone of their social structure. It is not possible to do justice to these possibilities in a short discussion. A recent study of an island of northwest Melanesia by Fortune describes a society built upon traits which we regard as beyond the border of paranoia. In this tribe the exogamic groups look upon each other as prime manipulators of black magic, so that one marries always into an enemy group which remains for life one's deadly and unappeasable foes. They look upon a good garden crop as a confession of theft, for everyone is engaged in making magic to induce into his garden the productiveness of his neighbors'; therefore no secrecy in the island is so rigidly insisted upon as the secrecy of a man's harvesting of his yams. Their polite phrase at the acceptance of a gift is, "And if you now poison me, how shall I repay you this present?" Their preoccupation with poisoning is constant; no woman ever leaves her cooking pot for a moment untended. Even the great affinal economic exchanges that are characteristic of this Melanesian culture area are quite altered in Dobu since they are incompatible with this fear

and distrust that pervades the culture. They go farther and people the whole world outside their own quarters with such malignant spirits that all-night feasts and ceremonials simply do not occur here. They have even rigorous religiously enforced customs that forbid the sharing of seed even in one family group. Anyone else's food is deadly poison to you, so that communality of stores is out of the question. For some months before harvest the whole society is on the verge of starvation, but if one falls to the temptation and eats up one's seed yams, one is an outcast and a beachcomber for life. There is no coming back. It involves, as a matter of course, divorce and the breaking of all social ties.

Now in this society where no one may work with another and no one may share with another, Fortune describes the individual who was regarded by all his fellows as crazy. He was not one of those who periodically ran amok and, beside himself and frothing at the mouth, fell with a knife upon anyone he could reach. Such behavior they did not regard as putting anyone outside the pale. They did not even put the individuals who were known to be liable to these attacks under any kind of control. They merely fled when they saw the attack coming on and kept out of the way. "He would be all right tomorrow." But there was one man of sunny, kindly disposition who liked work and liked to be helpful. The compulsion was too strong for him to repress it in favor of the opposite tendencies of his culture. Men and women never spoke of him without laughing; he was silly and simple and definitely crazy. Nevertheless, to the ethnologist used to a culture that has, in Christianity, made his type the model of all virtue, he seemed a pleasant fellow. . . .

. . . Among the Kwakiutl it did not matter whether a relative had died in bed of disease, or by the hand of an enemy; in either case death was an affront to be wiped out by the death of another person. The fact that one had been caused to mourn was proof that one had been put upon. A chief's sister and her daughter had gone up to Victoria, and either because they drank bad whiskey or because their boat capsized they never came back. The chief called together his warriors, "Now I ask you, tribes, who shall wail? Shall I do it or shall another?" The spokesman answered, of course, "Not you, Chief. Let some other of the tribes." Immediately they set up the war pole to announce their intention of wiping out the injury, and gathered a war party. They set out, and found seven men and two children asleep and killed them. "Then they felt good when they arrived at Sebaa in the evening."

The point which is of interest to us is that in our society those who on that occasion would feel good when they arrived at Sebaa that evening would be the definitely abnormal. There would be some, even in our society, but it is not a recognized and approved mood under the circumstances. On the Northwest Coast those are favored and fortunate to whom that mood under those circumstances is congenial, and those to whom it is repugnant are unlucky. This latter minority can register in their own culture only by doing violence to their congenial responses and acquiring others that are difficult for them. The person, for instance, who, like a Plains Indian whose wife has been taken from him, is too proud to fight, can deal with the Northwest Coast civilization only by ignoring its strongest bents. If he cannot achieve it, he is the deviant in that culture, their instance of abnormality.

This head-hunting that takes place on the Northwest Coast after a death is no matter of blood revenge or of organized vengeance. There is no effort to tie up the subsequent killing with any responsibility on the part of the victim for the death of the person who is being mourned. A chief whose son has died goes visiting wherever his fancy dictates, and he says to his host, "My prince has died today, and you go with him." Then he kills him. In this, according to their interpretation, he acts nobly because he has not been downed. He has thrust back in return. The whole procedure is meaningless without the fundamental paranoid reading of bereavement. Death, like all the other untoward accidents of existence, confounds man's pride and can only be handled in the category of insults.

Behavior honored upon the Northwest Coast is one which is recognized as abnormal in our civilization, and yet it is sufficiently close to the attitudes of our own culture to be intelligible to us and to have a definite vocabulary with which we may discuss it. The megalomaniac paranoid trend is a definite danger in our society. It is encouraged by some of our major preoccupations, and it confronts us with a choice of two possible attitudes. One is to brand it as abnormal and reprehensible, and is the attitude we have chosen in our civilization. The other is to make it an essential attribute of ideal man, and this is the solution in the culture of the Northwest Coast.

These illustrations, which it has been possible to indicate only in the briefest manner, force upon us the fact that normality is culturally defined. An adult shaped to the drives and standards of either of these cultures, if he were transported into our civilization, would fall into our categories of abnormality. He would be faced with the psychic dilemmas of the socially unavailable. In his own culture, however, he is the pillar of society, the end result of socially inculcated mores, and the problem of personal instability in his case simply does not arise.

No one civilization can possibly utilize in its mores the whole potential range of human behavior. Just as there are great numbers of possible phonetic articulations, and the possibility of language depends on a selection and standardization of a few of these in order that speech communication may be possible at all, so the possibility of organized behavior of every sort, from the fashions of local dress and houses to the dicta of a people's ethics and religion, depends upon a similar selection among the possible behavior traits. In the field of recognized economic obligations or sex taboos this selection is as nonrational and subconscious a process as it is in the field of phonetics. It is a process which goes on in the group for long periods of time and is historically conditioned by innumerable accidents of isolation or of contact of peoples. In any comprehensive study of psychology, the selection that different cultures have made in the course of history within the great circumference of potential behavior is of great significance.

Every society, beginning with some slight inclination in one direction or another, carries its preference farther and farther, integrating itself more and more completely upon its chosen basis, and discarding those types of behavior that are uncongenial. Most of those organizations of personality that seem to us most uncontrovertibly abnormal have been used by different civilizations in the very foundations of their institutional life. Conversely the most valued traits of our normal individuals have been looked on in differently organized cultures as aberrant. Normality, in short, within a very wide range, is culturally defined. It is primarily a term for the socially elaborated segment of human behavior in any culture; and abnormality, a term for the segment that that particular civilization does not use. The very eyes with which we see the problem are conditioned by the long traditional habits of our own society.

It is a point that has been made more often in relation to ethics than in relation to psychiatry. We do not any longer make the mistake of deriving the morality of our locality and decade directly from the inevitable constitution of human nature. We do not elevate it to the dignity of a first principle. We recognize that morality differs in every society, and is a convenient term for socially approved habits. Mankind has always preferred to say, "It is morally good," rather than "It is habitual," and the fact of this preference is matter enough for a critical science of ethics. But historically the two phrases are synonymous.

The concept of the normal is properly a variant of the concept of the good. It is that which society has approved. A normal action is one which falls well within the limits of expected behavior for a particular society. Its variability among different peoples is essentially a function of the variability of the behavior patterns that different societies have created for themselves, and can never be wholly divorced from a consideration of culturally institutionalized types of behavior.

Each culture is a more or less elaborate working-out of the potentialities of the segment it has chosen. In so far as a civilization is well integrated and consistent within itself, it will tend to carry farther and farther, according to its nature, its initial impulse toward a particular type of action, and from the point of view of any other culture those elaborations will include more and more extreme and aberrant traits.

Each of these traits, in proportion as it reinforces the chosen behavior patterns of that culture, is for that culture normal. Those individuals to whom it is congenial either congenitally, or as the result of childhood sets, are accorded prestige in that culture, and are not visited with the social contempt or disapproval which their traits would call down upon them in a society that was differently organized. On the other hand, those individuals whose characteristics are not congenial to the selected type of human behavior in that community are the deviants, no matter how valued their personality traits may be in a contrasted civilization.

The Dobuan who is not easily susceptible to fear of treachery, who enjoys work and likes to be helpful, is their neurotic and regarded as silly. On the Northwest Coast the person who finds it difficult to read life in terms of an insult contest will be the person upon whom fall all the difficulties of the culturally unprovided for. The person who does not find it easy to humiliate a neighbor, nor to see humiliation in his own experience, who is genial and loving, may, of course, find some unstandardized way of achieving satisfactions in his society, but not in the major patterned responses that his culture requires of him. If he is born to play an important role in a family with many hereditary privileges, he can succeed only by doing violence to his whole personality. If he does not succeed, he has betrayed his culture; that is, he is abnormal.

I have spoken of individuals as having sets toward certain types of behavior, and of these sets as running sometimes counter to the types of behavior which are institutionalized in the culture to which they belong. From all that we know of contrasting cultures it seems clear that differences of temperament occur in every society. The matter has never been made the subject of investigation, but from the available material it would appear that these temperament types are very likely of universal recurrence. That is, there is an ascertainable range of human behavior that is found wherever a sufficiently large series of individuals is observed. But the proportion in which behavior types stand to one another in different societies is not universal. The vast majority of individuals in any group are shaped to the fashion of that culture. In other words, most individuals are plastic to the moulding force of the society into which they are born. In a society that values trance, as in India, they will have supernormal experience. In a society that institutionalizes homosexuality, they will be homosexual. In a society that sets the gathering of possessions as the chief human objective, they will amass property. The deviants, whatever the type of behavior the culture has institutionalized, will remain few in number, and there seems no more difficulty in moulding the vast malleable majority to the "normality" of what we consider an aberrant trait, such as delusions of reference, than to the normality of such accepted behavior patterns as acquisitiveness. The small proportion of the number of the deviants in any culture is not a function of the sure instinct with which that society has built itself upon the fundamental sanities, but of the universal fact that, happily, the majority of mankind quite readily take any shape that is presented to them. . . .

For Further Reflection

1. Is Benedict correct in saying that our culture is "but one entry in a long series of possible adjustments"? What are the implications of this statement?

2. Can we separate the descriptive (or fact-stating) aspect of anthropological study from the prescriptive (evaluative) aspect of evaluating cultures? Are there some independent criteria by which we can say that some cultures are better than others? Can you think how this project might be begun?

3. What are the implications of Benedict's claim that morality is simply whatever a culture deems normal behavior? Is this a satisfactory equation? Can you apply it to the institution of slavery or the Nazi policy of anti-Semitism?

4. What is the significance of Benedict's statement, "The very eyes with which we see the problem are conditioned by the long traditional habits of our own society"? Can we apply the conceptual relativism embodied in this statement to her own position?

Morality Is Not Relative   VI.44

JAMES RACHELS

James Rachels is a professor of philosophy at the University of Alabama. He has written books and articles in the areas of philosophy of religion and ethics. Among his important works are his articles "Active and Passive Euthanasia" and "Can Ethics Provide Answers?"

Rachels analyzes the structure of ethical relativism, which he calls "cultural relativism," to show that the claims made by its proponents go beyond what the facts or arguments can establish. He contends that the central argument, "the cultural difference argument," is invalid, for even if there is broad cultural disagreement over morality, it doesn't prove that there is no truth in the matter, any more than the fact that flat-earthers disagree with round-earthers proves that there is no independent truth of that matter. Rachels goes on to point out three unfavorable consequences of cultural relativism that make it implausible. Finally, he points out two virtues in the doctrine.

Study Questions

1. What is the significance of Herodotus' story of the Callatians and Greeks comparing funerary practices?
2. How do Eskimo practices seem to lend support to the thesis of cultural relativism? Note what Rachels says later about the reasons for these practices.
3. What is Graham Sumner's thesis about morality?
4. What is the basic idea behind the cultural difference argument? Is it a sound argument?
5. What are the three consequences for ethics of cultural relativism?
6. Why does the author believe that the ethical relativist is unable to offer moral criticism of cruel behavior in another culture?
7. Why, according to Rachels, is there really less moral disagreement than there seems at first sight?
8. What is the argument for universal shared values or an objective morality?
9. What does the author think are the two lessons of cultural relativism?

Morality differs in every society, and is a convenient term for socially approved habits.

RUTH BENEDICT, *Patterns of Culture*, 1934

1. HOW DIFFERENT CULTURES HAVE DIFFERENT MORAL CODES

DARIUS, A KING OF ANCIENT PERSIA, was intrigued by the variety of cultures he encountered in his travels. He had found, for example, that the Callatians (a tribe of Indians) customarily ate the bodies of their dead fathers. The Greeks, of course, did not do that—the Greeks practiced cremation and regarded the funeral pyre as the natural and fitting way to dispose of the dead. Darius thought that a sophisticated understanding of the world must include an appreciation of such differences between cultures. One day, to teach this lesson, he summoned some Greeks who happened to be present at his court and asked them what they would take to eat the bodies of their dead fathers. They were shocked, as Darius knew they would be, and replied that no amount of money could persuade them to do such a thing. Then Darius called in some Callatians, and while the Greeks listened asked them what they would take to burn their dead fathers' bodies. The Callatians were horrified and told Darius not even to mention such a dreadful thing.

This story, recounted by Herodotus in his *History,* illustrates a recurring theme in the literature of social science: different cultures have different moral codes. What is thought right within one group may be utterly abhorrent to the members of another group, and vice versa. Should we eat the bodies of the dead or burn them? If you were a Greek, one answer would seem obviously correct; but if you were a Callatian, the opposite would seem equally certain.

It is easy to give additional examples of the same kind. Consider the Eskimos. They are a remote and inaccessible people. Numbering only about 25,000, they live in small, isolated settlements scattered mostly along the northern fringes of North America and Greenland. Until the beginning of this century, the outside world knew little about them. Then explorers began to bring back strange tales.

Eskimo customs turned out to be very different from our own. The men often had more than one wife, and they would share their wives with guests, lending them for the night as a sign of hospitality. Moreover, within a community, a dominant male might demand—and get—regular sexual access to other men's wives. The women, however, were free to break these arrangements simply by leaving their husbands and taking up with new partners—free, that is, so long as their former husbands chose not to make trouble. All in all, the Eskimo practice was a volatile scheme that bore little resemblance to what we call marriage.

But it was not only their marriage and sexual practices that were different. The Eskimos also seemed to have less regard for human life. Infanticide, for example, was common. Knud Rasmussen, one of the most famous early explorers, reported that he met one woman who had borne twenty children but had killed ten of them at birth. Female babies, he found, were especially liable to be destroyed, and this was permitted simply at the parents' discretion, with no social stigma attached to it. Old people also, when they became too feeble to contribute to the family, were left out in the snow to die. So there seemed to be, in this society, remarkably little respect for life.

To the general public, these were disturbing revelations. Our own way of living seems so natural and right that for many of us it is hard to conceive of others living so differently. And when we do hear of such things, we tend immediately to categorize those other peoples as "backward" or "primitive." But to anthropologists and sociologists, there was nothing particularly surprising about the Eskimos. Since the time of Herodotus, enlightened observers have been accustomed to the idea that conceptions of right and wrong differ from culture to culture. If we assume that *our* ideas of right and wrong will be shared by all peoples at all times, we are merely naive.

2. CULTURAL RELATIVISM

To many thinkers, this observation—"Different cultures have different moral codes"—has seemed to be the key to understanding morality. The idea of universal truth in ethics, they say, is a myth. The customs of different societies are all that exist. These customs cannot be said to be "correct" or "incorrect," for that implies we have an independent standard of right and wrong by which they may be judged. But there is no such independent standard; every standard is culture-bound. The great pioneering sociologist William Graham Sumner, writing in 1906, put the point like this:

> The "right" way is the way which the ancestors used and which has been handed down. The tradition is its own warrant. It is not held subject to verification by experience. The notion of right is in the folkways. It is not outside of them, of independent origin, and brought to test them. In the folkways, whatever is, is right. This is because they are traditional, and therefore contain in themselves the authority of the ancestral ghosts. When we come to the folkways we are at the end of our analysis.

This line of thought has probably persuaded more people to be skeptical about ethics than any other single thing. *Cultural Relativism*, as it has been called, challenges our ordinary belief in the objectivity and universality of moral truth. It says, in effect, that there is no such thing as universal truth in ethics; there are only the various cultural codes, and nothing more. Moreover, our own code has no special status; it is merely one among many. As we shall see, this basic idea is really a compound of several different thoughts. It is important to separate the various elements of the theory because, on analysis, some parts of the theory turn out to be correct, whereas others seem to be mistaken. As a beginning, we may distinguish the following claims, all of which have been made by cultural relativists:

1. Different societies have different moral codes.

2. There is no objective standard that can be used to judge one societal code better than another.

3. The moral code of our own society has no special status; it is merely one among many.

4. There is no "universal truth" in ethics— that is, there are no moral truths that hold for all peoples at all times.

5. The moral code of a society determines what is right within that society; that is, if the moral code of a society says that a certain action is right, then that action *is* right, at least within that society.

6. It is mere arrogance for us to try to judge the conduct of other peoples. We should adopt an attitude of tolerance toward the practices of other cultures.

Although it may seem that these six propositions go naturally together, they are independent of one another, in the sense that some of them might be true even if others are false. In what follows, we will try to identify what is correct in Cultural Relativism, but we will also be concerned to expose what is mistaken about it.

3. THE CULTURAL DIFFERENCES ARGUMENT

Cultural Relativism is a theory about the nature of morality. At first blush it seems quite plausible. However, like all such theories, it may be evaluated by subjecting it to rational analysis; and when we analyze Cultural Relativism we find that it is not so plausible as it first appears to be.

The first thing we need to notice is that at the heart of Cultural Relativism there is a certain *form of argument*. The strategy used by cultural relativists is to argue from facts about the differences between cultural outlooks to a conclusion about the status of morality. Thus we are invited to accept this reasoning:

(1) The Greeks believed it was wrong to eat the dead, whereas the Callatians believed it was right to eat the dead.

(2) Therefore, eating the dead is neither objectively right nor objectively wrong. It is merely a matter of opinion, which varies from culture to culture.

Or, alternatively:

(1) The Eskimos see nothing wrong with infanticide, whereas Americans believe infanticide is immoral.

(2) Therefore, infanticide is neither objectively right nor objectively wrong. It is merely a matter of opinion, which varies from culture to culture.

Clearly, these arguments are variations of one fundamental idea. They are both special cases of a more general argument, which says:

(1) Different cultures have different moral codes.

(2) Therefore, there is no objective "truth" in morality. Right and wrong are only matters of opinion, and opinions vary from culture to culture.

We may call this the *Cultural Differences Argument*. To many people, it is very persuasive.

But from a logical point of view, is it a *sound* argument?

It is not sound. The trouble is that the conclusion does not really follow from the premise—that is, even if the premise is true, the conclusion still might be false. The premise concerns what people *believe:* in some societies, people believe one thing; in other societies, people believe differently. The conclusion, however, concerns *what really is the case.* The trouble is that this sort of conclusion does not follow logically from this sort of premise.

Consider again the example of the Greeks and Callatians. The Greeks believed it was wrong to eat the dead; the Callatians believed it was right. Does it follow, *from the mere fact that they disagreed,* that there is no objective truth in the matter? No, it does not follow; for it *could* be that the practice was objectively right (or wrong) and that one or the other of them was simply mistaken.

To make the point clearer, consider a very different matter. In some societies, people believe the earth is flat. In other societies, such as our own, people believe the earth is (roughly) spherical. Does it follow, *from the mere fact that they disagree,* that there is no "objective truth" in geography? Of course not; we would never draw such a conclusion because we realize that, in their beliefs about the world, the members of some societies might simply be wrong. There is no reason to think that if the world is round everyone must know it. Similarly, there is no reason to think that if there is moral truth everyone must know it. The fundamental mistake in the Cultural Differences Argument is that it attempts to derive a substantive conclusion about a subject (morality) from the mere fact that people disagree about it.

It is important to understand the nature of the point that is being made here. We are *not* saying (not yet, anyway) that the conclusion of the argument is false. Insofar as anything being said here is concerned, it is still an open question whether the conclusion is true. We *are* making a purely logical point and saying that the conclu-

sion does not *follow from* the premise. This is important, because in order to determine whether the conclusion is true, we need arguments in its support. Cultural Relativism proposes this argument, but unfortunately the argument turns out to be fallacious. So it proves nothing.

4. THE CONSEQUENCES OF TAKING CULTURAL RELATIVISM SERIOUSLY

Even if the Cultural Differences Argument is invalid, Cultural Relativism might still be true. What would it be like if it were true?

In the passage quoted above, William Graham Sumner summarizes the essence of Cultural Relativism. He says that there is no measure of right and wrong other than the standards of one's society: "The notion of right is in the folkways. It is not outside of them, of independent origin, and brought to test them. In the folkways, whatever is, is right."

Suppose we took this seriously. What would be some of the consequences?

1. *We could no longer say that the customs of other societies are morally inferior to our own.* This, of course, is one of the main points stressed by Cultural Relativism. We would have to stop condemning other societies merely because they are "different." So long as we concentrate on certain examples, such as the funerary practices of the Greeks and Callatians, this may seem to be a sophisticated, enlightened attitude.

However, we would also be stopped from criticizing other, less benign practices. Suppose a society waged war on its neighbors for the purpose of taking slaves. Or suppose a society was violently anti-Semitic and its leaders set out to destroy the Jews. Cultural Relativism would preclude us from saying that either of these practices was wrong. We would not even be able to say that a society tolerant of Jews is *better* than the anti-Semitic society, for that would imply some sort of transcultural standard of comparison. The failure to condemn *these* practices does not seem "enlightened"; on the contrary, slavery and anti-Semitism seem wrong *wherever* they occur. Nevertheless, if we took Cultural Relativism seriously, we would have to admit that these social practices also are immune from criticism.

2. *We could decide whether actions are right or wrong just by consulting the standards of our society.* Cultural Relativism suggests a simple test for determining what is right and what is wrong: all one has to do is ask whether the action is in accordance with the code of one's society. Suppose a resident of South Africa is wondering whether his country's policy of *apartheid*—rigid racial segregation—is morally correct. All he has to do is ask whether this policy conforms to his society's moral code. If it does, there is nothing to worry about, at least from a moral point of view. This implication of Cultural Relativism is disturbing because few of us think that our society's code is perfect—we can think of ways it might be improved. Yet Cultural Relativism would not only forbid us from criticizing the codes of *other* societies; it would stop us from criticizing our *own*. After all, if right and wrong are relative to culture, this must be true for our own culture just as much as for others.

3. *The idea of moral progress is called into doubt.* Usually, we think that at least some changes in our society have been for the better. (Some, of course, may have been changes for the worse.) Consider this example: Throughout most of Western history the place of women in society was very narrowly circumscribed. They could not own property; they could not vote or hold political office; with a few exceptions, they were not permitted to have paying jobs; and generally they were under the almost absolute control of their husbands. Recently much of this has changed, and most people think of it as progress.

If Cultural Relativism is correct, can we legitimately think of this as progress? Progress means replacing a way of doing things with a *better* way. But by what standard do we judge the new ways as better? If the old ways were in accordance with the social standards of their time, then Cultural Relativism would say it is a mistake to judge them by the standards of a different time. Eighteenth-century society was, in effect, a different society from the one we have now. To say that we have made progress implies a judgment that present-day society is better, and that is just the sort of transcultural judgment that, according to Cultural Relativism, is impermissible.

Our idea of social *reform* will also have to be reconsidered. A reformer such as Martin Luther King, Jr., seeks to change his society for the better. Within the constraints imposed by Cultural Relativism, there is one way this might be done. If a society is not living up to its own ideals, the reformer may be regarded as acting for the best: the ideals of the society are the standard by which we judge his or her proposals as worthwhile. But the "reformer" may not challenge the ideals themselves, for those ideals are by definition correct. According to Cultural Relativism, then, the idea of social reform makes sense only in this very limited way.

These three consequences of Cultural Relativism have led many thinkers to reject it as implausible on its face. It does make sense, they say, to condemn some practices, such as slavery and anti-Semitism, wherever they occur. It makes sense to think that our own society has made some moral progress, while admitting that it is still imperfect and in need of reform. Because Cultural Relativism says that these judgments make no sense, the argument goes, it cannot be right.

5. WHY THERE IS LESS DISAGREEMENT THAN IT SEEMS

The original impetus for Cultural Relativism comes from the observation that cultures differ dramatically in their views of right and wrong. But just how much do they differ? It is true that there are differences. However, it is easy to overestimate the extent of those differences. Often, when we examine what *seems* to be a dramatic difference, we find that the cultures do not differ nearly as much as it appears.

Consider a culture in which people believe it is wrong to eat cows. This may even be a poor culture, in which there is not enough food; still, the cows are not to be touched. Such a society would *appear* to have values very different from our own. But does it? We have not yet asked why these people will not eat cows. Suppose it is because they believe that after death the souls of humans inhabit the bodies of animals, especially cows, so that a cow may be someone's grandmother. Now do we want to say that their values are different from ours? No; the difference lies elsewhere. The difference is in our belief systems, not in our values. We agree that we shouldn't eat Grandma; we simply disagree about whether the cow *is* (or could be) Grandma.

The general point is this. Many factors work together to produce the customs of a society. The society's values are only one of them. Other matters, such as the religious and factual beliefs held by its members and the physical circumstances in which they must live, are also important. We cannot conclude, then, merely because customs differ, that there is a disagreement about *values*. The difference in customs may be attributable to some other aspect of social life. Thus there may be less disagreement about values than there appears to be.

Consider the Eskimos again. They often kill perfectly normal infants, especially girls. We do not approve of this at all; a parent who did this in our society would be locked up. Thus there appears to be a great difference in the values of our two cultures. But suppose we ask *why* the Eskimos do this. The explanation is not that they have less affection for their children or less respect for human life. An Eskimo family will always protect its babies if conditions permit. But they live in a harsh environment, where food is often in short supply. A fundamental postulate of Eskimo thought is: "Life is hard, and the margin of safety small." A family may want to nourish its babies but be unable to do so.

As in many "primitive" societies, Eskimo mothers will nurse their infants over a much longer period of time than mothers in our culture. The child will take nourishment from its mother's breast for four years, perhaps even longer. So even in the best of times there are limits to the number of infants that one mother can sustain. Moreover, the Eskimos are a nomadic people—unable to farm, they must move about in search of food. Infants must be carried, and a mother can carry only one baby in her parka as she travels and goes about her outdoor work. Other family members can help, but this is not always possible.

Infant girls are more readily disposed of because, first, in this society the males are the primary food providers—they are the hunters, according to the traditional division of labor—and it is obviously important to maintain a sufficient number of food gatherers. But there is an important second reason as well. Because the hunters suffer a high casualty rate, the adult men who die prematurely far outnumber the women who die early. Thus if male and female infants survived in equal numbers, the female adult population would greatly outnumber the male adult population. Examining the available statistics, one writer concluded that "were it not for female infanticide . . . there would be approximately one-and-a-half times as many females in the average Eskimo local group as there are food-producing males."

So among the Eskimos, infanticide does not signal a fundamentally different attitude toward children. Instead, it is a recognition that drastic measures are sometimes needed to ensure the family's survival. Even then, however, killing the baby is not the first option considered. Adoption is common; childless couples are especially happy to take a more fertile couple's "surplus." Killing is only the last resort. I emphasize this in order to show that the raw data of the anthropologists can be misleading; it can make the differences in values between cultures appear greater than they are. The Eskimos' values are not all that different from our values. It is only that life forces upon them choices that we do not have to make.

6. HOW ALL CULTURES HAVE SOME VALUES IN COMMON

It should not be surprising that, despite appearances, the Eskimos are protective of their children. How could it be otherwise? How could a group survive that did *not* value its young? This suggests a certain argument, one which shows that all cultural groups must be protective of their infants:

(1) Human infants are helpless and cannot survive if they are not given extensive care for a period of years.

(2) Therefore, if a group did not care for its young, the young would not survive, and the older members of the group would not be replaced. After a while the group would die out.

(3) Therefore, any cultural group that continues to exist must care for its young. Infants that are *not* cared for must be the exception rather than the rule.

Similar reasoning shows that other values must be more or less universal. Imagine what it would be like for a society to place no value at all on truth telling. When one person spoke to another, there would be no presumption at all that he was telling the truth—for he could just as easily be speaking falsely. Within that society, there would be no reason to pay attention to what anyone says. (I ask you what time it is, and you say "Four o'clock." But there is no presumption that you are speaking truly; you could just as easily have said the first thing that came into your head. So I have no reason to pay attention to your answer—in fact, there was no point in my asking you in the first place!) Communication would then be extremely difficult, if not impossible. And because complex societies cannot exist without regular communication among their members, society would become impossible. It follows that in any complex society there *must* be a presumption in favor of truthfulness. There may of course be exceptions to this rule: there may be situations in which it is thought to be permissible to lie. Nevertheless, these will be exceptions to a rule that *is* in force in the society.

Let me give one further example of the same type. Could a society exist in which there was no prohibition on murder? What would this be like? Suppose people were free to kill other people at will, and no one thought there was anything wrong with it. In such a "society," no one could feel secure. Everyone would have to be constantly on guard. People who wanted to survive would have to avoid other people as much as possible. This would inevitably result in individuals trying to become as self-sufficient as possible—after all, associating with others would be dangerous. Society on any large scale would collapse. Of course, people might band together in smaller groups with others that they *could* trust not to harm them. But notice what this means: they would be forming smaller societies that *did* acknowledge a rule against murder. The prohibition of murder, then, is a necessary feature of all societies.

There is a general theoretical point here, namely, that *there are some moral rules that all societies will have in common, because those rules are necessary for society to exist.* The rules against lying and murder are two examples. And in fact, we do find these rules in force in all viable cultures. Cultures may differ in what they regard as legitimate exceptions to the rules, but this disagreement exists against a background of agreement on the larger issues. Therefore, it is a mistake to overestimate the amount of difference between cultures. Not *every* moral rule can vary from society to society.

7. WHAT CAN BE LEARNED FROM CULTURAL RELATIVISM

At the outset, I said that we were going to identify both what is right and what is wrong in

Cultural Relativism. Thus far I have mentioned only its mistakes: I have said that it rests on an invalid argument, that it has consequences that make it implausible on its face, and that the extent of cultural disagreement is far less than it implies. This all adds up to a pretty thorough repudiation of the theory. Nevertheless, it is still a very appealing idea, and the reader may have the feeling that all this is a little unfair. The theory *must* have something going for it, or else why has it been so influential? In fact, I think there *is* something right about Cultural Relativism, and now I want to say what that is. There are two lessons we should learn from the theory, even if we ultimately reject it.

1. Cultural Relativism warns us, quite rightly, about the danger of assuming that all our preferences are based on some absolute rational standard. They are not. Many (but not all) of our practices are merely peculiar to our society, and it is easy to lose sight of that fact. In reminding us of it, the theory does a service.

Funerary practices are one example. The Callatians, according to Herodotus, were "men who eat their fathers"—a shocking idea, to us at least. But eating the flesh of the dead could be understood as a sign of respect. It could be taken as a symbolic act that says: We wish this person's spirit to dwell within us. Perhaps this was the understanding of the Callatians. On such a way of thinking, burying the dead could be seen as an act of rejection, and burning the corpse as positively scornful. If this is hard to imagine, then we may need to have our imaginations stretched. Of course we may feel a visceral repugnance at the idea of eating human flesh in any circumstances. But what of it? This repugnance may be, as the relativists say, only a matter of what is customary in our particular society.

There are many other matters that we tend to think of in terms of objective right and wrong, but that are really nothing more than social conventions. Should women cover their breasts? A publicly exposed breast is scandalous in our society, whereas in other cultures it is unremarkable. Objectively speaking, it is neither right nor wrong—there is no objective reason why either custom is better. Cultural Relativism begins with the valuable insight that many of our practices are like this—they are only cultural products. Then it goes wrong by concluding that, because *some* practices are like this, *all* must be.

2. The second lesson has to do with keeping an open mind. In the course of growing up, each of us has acquired some strong feelings: we have learned to think of some types of conduct as acceptable, and others we have learned to regard as simply unacceptable. Occasionally, we may find those feelings challenged. We may encounter someone who claims that our feelings are mistaken. For example, we may have been taught that homosexuality is immoral, and we may feel quite uncomfortable around gay people and see them as alien and "different." Now someone suggests that this may be a mere prejudice; that there is nothing evil about homosexuality; that gay people are just people, like anyone else, who happen, through no choice of their own, to be attracted to others of the same sex. But because we feel so strongly about the matter, we may find it hard to take this seriously. Even after we listen to the arguments, we may still have the unshakable feeling that homosexuals *must*, somehow, be an unsavory lot.

Cultural Relativism, by stressing that our moral views can reflect the prejudices of our society, provides an antidote for this kind of dogmatism. When he tells the story of the Greeks and Callatians, Herodotus adds:

> For if anyone, no matter who, were given the opportunity of choosing from amongst all the nations of the world the set of beliefs which he thought best, he would inevitably, after careful consideration of their relative merits, choose that of his own country. Everyone without exception believes his own native customs, and the religion he was brought up in, to be the best.

Realizing this can result in our having more open minds. We can come to understand that our feelings are not necessarily perceptions of the truth—they may be nothing more than the result of cultural conditioning. Thus when we hear it suggested that some element of our social code is *not* really the best and we find ourselves instinctively resisting the suggestion, we might stop and remember this. Then we may be more open to discovering the truth, whatever that might be.

We can understand the appeal of Cultural Relativism, then, even though the theory has serious shortcomings. It is an attractive theory because it is based on a genuine insight—that many of the practices and attitudes we think so natural are really only cultural products. Moreover, keeping this insight firmly in view is important if we want to avoid arrogance and have open minds. These are important points, not to be taken lightly. But we can accept these points without going on to accept the whole theory.

For Further Reflection

1. On balance, which position is the stronger: some form of ethical relativism or some version of ethical objectivism? Could both theories be partly true? Explain.

2. Could Benedict respond to the objectivist that "the very eyes with which we see the problem are conditioned by the long traditional habits of our own society"? What are the implications of that view and does it rule out objectivism?

3. How would you go about building a suitable morality? What considerations are of most importance? Do you think that morality has a purpose? If so, what is it?

VI.B   Ethics and Egoism: Why Should We Be Moral?

Why should we be moral? That is, why should we do what morality requires even when it might not be in our best interest? Is it really in our best interest after all, even if we don't realize it? Or is morality only generally in our best interest, so that we should consider breaking its rules whenever they become too burdensome? Or is there some other answer?

In this section we look at various responses to this question. We begin with Glaucon's question to Socrates: Whether justice (what we would call morality) was really only a compromise relationship between the better but unattainable state of exploiting others with impunity (like the shepherd Gyges, who can become invisible) and the worst situation of being exploited by others. Socrates rejects this way of looking at the problem and argues that justice is intrinsically valuable and brings about a healthy soul, so that it is never in our interest to be immoral.

But many reject Socrates' way of viewing the matter. They accuse Socrates of supposing an objective world of values or a divine law which ensures that those who act selfishly will be punished. But take away the notion of a God or a transcendent moral order that affects us and the Socratic picture breaks down. Self-interest can involve exploiting others; treating them "unjustly."

In our second reading, Ayn Rand's "In Defense of Ethical Egoism" (VI.46), morality is made to coincide with prudence or self-interest. Rand sets forth a version of Universal Ethical Egoism, which states that everyone ought always to serve his or her own self-interest. That is, everyone ought to do what will maximize one's own expected utility or bring about one's own happiness, even when it means harming others. In our final reading, I offer several arguments against ethical egoism and conclude that these invalidate the theory.

Why Should I Be Moral?
Gyges' Ring and Socrates' Dilemma   VI.45

PLATO

Plato (427–347 B.C.) lived in Athens and is the earliest philosopher for whom extensive works still remain today. In a series of dialogues he immortalized his teacher, Socrates. Perhaps his greatest dialogue is the *Republic,* from which this present reading is taken. The *Republic* is a classic treatise on political philosophy, centering on the concept of justice or moral rightness. In this work, Plato through his idealization of Socrates, argues there will only be justice when reason rules and the people are obedient to its commands. This Utopia is only possible in an aristocracy in which the rulers are philosophers—philosopher-kings. In our selection, Glaucon, who is Plato's older brother, asks Socrates whether justice is good in itself or only a necessary evil. Playing the devil's advocate, Glaucon puts forth the hypothesis that egotistic power-seeking in which we have complete freedom to indulge ourselves might be the ideal state of existence. However, the hypothesis continues, reason quickly shows us that others might seek to have the same power, which would interfere with our freedom and cause a state of chaos in which no one was likely to have any of one's desires fulfilled. So we compromise and limit our acquisitive instincts. Justice or a system of morality is simply the result of that compromise. It has no intrinsic value but is better than chaos but worse than undisturbed power. It is better to compromise and limit our acquisitive instincts.

To illustrate his point Glaucon tells the story of a shepherd named Gyges who comes upon a ring, which at his behest makes him invisible. He uses it to escape the external sanctions of society—its laws and censure—and to serve his greed to the fullest. Glaucon asks whether it is not plausible to suppose that we all would do likewise? Then he offers a thought experiment that compares the life of the seemingly just (but unjust) man who is incredibly successful with the life of the seemingly unjust (but just) man who is incredibly unsuccessful. Which would we choose?

We enter the dialogue in the second book of the *Republic.* Socrates has just shown that the type of egoism advocated by Thrasymachus is contradictory. Socrates is speaking.

Study Questions

1. Note the distinction between different kinds of goods: (1) things desirable in themselves, (2) things not desirable in themselves but instrumental to other goods, and (3) things both intrinsically and instrumentally good. Which kind of good is justice, according to Socrates, and why?
2. What is the popular view of justice, according to Glaucon?
3. What is the lesson to be drawn from the story of Gyges' ring? Do you agree with Glaucon's conclusion about human nature?
4. What is Glaucon's point in comparing the completely just-but-seemingly-unjust man with the completely unjust-but-seemingly-just man? Which would you choose?

GYGES' RING

WITH THESE WORDS I was thinking that I had made an end of the discussion; but the end, in truth, proved to be only a beginning. For Glaucon, who is always the most pugnacious of men, was dissatisfied at Thrasymachus' retirement; he wanted to have the battle out. So he said to me: Socrates, do you wish really to persuade us, or only to seem to have persuaded us, that to be just is always better than to be unjust?

I should wish really to persuade you, I replied, if I could.

Then you certainly have not succeeded. Let me ask you now:—How would you arrange goods—are there not some which we welcome for their own sakes, and independently of their consequences, as, for example, harmless pleasures and enjoyments, which delight us at the time, although nothing follows from them?

I agree in thinking that there is such a class, I replied.

Is there not also a second class of goods, such as knowledge, sight, health, which are desirable not only in themselves, but also for their results?

Certainly, I said.

And would you not recognize a third class, such as gymnastic, and the care of the sick, and the physician's art; also the various ways of money-making—these do us good but we regard them as disagreeable; and no one would choose them for their own sakes, but only for the sake of some reward or result which flows from them?

There is, I said, this third class also. But why do you ask?

Because I want to know in which of the three classes you would place justice?

In the highest class, I replied, among those goods which he who would be happy desires both for their own sake and for the sake of their results.

Then the many are of another mind; they think that justice is to be reckoned in the troublesome class, among goods which are to be pursued for the sake of rewards and of reputation, but in themselves are disagreeable and rather to be avoided.

I know, I said, that this is their manner of thinking, and that this was the thesis which Thrasymachus was maintaining just now, when he censured justice and praised injustice. But I am too stupid to be convinced by him.

I wish, he said, that you would hear me as well as him, and then I shall see whether you and I agree. For Thrasymachus seems to me, like a snake, to have been charmed by your voice sooner than he ought to have been; but to my mind the nature of justice and injustice have not yet been made clear. Setting aside their rewards and results, I want to know what they are in themselves, and how they inwardly work in the

Reprinted from The Dialogues of Plato, translated by Benjamin Jowett (Charles Scribner's, 1889).

soul. If you please, then, I will revive the argument of Thrasymachus. And first I will speak of the nature and origin of justice according to the common view of them. Secondly, I will show that all men who practice justice do so against their will, of necessity, but not as a good. And thirdly, I will argue that there is reason in this view, for the life of the unjust is after all better far than the life of the just—if what they say is true, Socrates, since I myself am not of their opinion. But still I acknowledge that I am perplexed when I hear the voices of Thrasymachus and myriads of others dinning in my ears; and, on the other hand, I have never yet heard the superiority of justice to injustice maintained by any one in a satisfactory way. I want to hear justice praised in respect of itself; then I shall be satisfied, and you are the person from whom I think that I am most likely to hear this; and therefore I will praise the unjust life to the utmost of my power, and my manner of speaking will indicate the manner in which I desire to hear you too praising justice and censuring injustice. Will you say whether you approve of my proposal?

Indeed I do; nor can I imagine any theme about which a man of sense would oftener wish to converse.

I am delighted, he replied, to hear you say so, and shall begin by speaking, as I proposed, of the nature and origin of justice.

They say that to do injustice is, by nature, good; to suffer injustice, evil; but that the evil is greater than the good. And so when men have both done and suffered injustice and have had experience of both, not being able to avoid the one and obtain the other, they think that they had better agree among themselves to have neither; hence there arise laws and mutual covenants; and that which is ordained by law is termed by them lawful and just. This they affirm to be the origin and nature of justice:—it is a mean or compromise, between the best of all, which is to do injustice and not be punished, and the worst of all, which is to suffer injustice without the power of retaliation; and justice, being at a middle point between the two, is tolerated not as a good, but as the lesser

evil, and honoured by reason of the inability of men to do injustice. For no man who is worthy to be called a man would ever submit to such an agreement if he were able to resist; he would be mad if he did. Such is the received account, Socrates, of the nature and origin of justice.

Now that those who practice justice do so involuntarily and because they have not the power to be unjust will best appear if we imagine something of this kind: having given both to the just and the unjust power to do what they will, let us watch and see whither desire will lead them; then we shall discover in the very act the just and unjust man to be proceeding along the same road, following their interest, which all natures deem to be their good, and are only diverted into the path of justice by the force of law. The liberty which we are supposing may be most completely given to them in the form of such a power as is said to have been possessed by Gyges the ancestor of Croesus the Lydian. According to the tradition, Gyges was a shepherd in the service of the king of Lydia; there was a great storm, and an earthquake made an opening in the earth at the place where he was feeding his flock. Amazed at the sight, he descended into the opening, where, among other marvels, he beheld a hollow brazen horse, having doors, at which he stooping and looking in saw a dead body of stature, as appeared to him, more than human, and having nothing on but a gold ring; this he took from the finger of the dead and reascended. Now the shepherds met together, according to custom, that they might send their monthly report about the flocks to the king; into their assembly he came having the ring on his finger, and as he was sitting among them he chanced to turn the collet of the ring inside his hand, when instantly he became invisible to the rest of the company and they began to speak of him as if he were no longer present. He was astonished at this, and again touching the ring he turned the collet outwards and reappeared; he made several trials of the ring, and always with the same result—when he turned the collet inwards he became invisible, when outwards he reappeared. Whereupon he contrived to be chosen one of the messengers who were sent to the court; where as soon as he arrived he seduced the queen, and with her help conspired against the king and slew him, and took the kingdom. Suppose now that there were two such magic rings, and the just put on one of them and the unjust the other; no man can be imagined to be of such an iron nature that he would stand fast in justice. No man would keep his hands off what was not his own when he could safely take what he liked out of the market, or go into houses and lie with any one at his pleasure, or kill or release from prison whom he would, and in all respects be like a God among men. Then the actions of the just would be as the actions of the unjust; they would both come at last to the same point. And this we may truly affirm to be a great proof that a man is just, not willingly or because he thinks that justice is any good to him individually, but of necessity, for wherever any one thinks that he can safely be unjust, there he is unjust. For all men believe in their hearts that injustice is far more profitable to the individual than justice, and he who argues as I have been supposing, will say that they are right. If you could imagine any one obtaining this power of becoming invisible, and never doing any wrong or touching what was another's, he would be thought by the lookers-on to be a most wretched idiot, although they would praise him to one another's faces, and keep up appearances with one another from a fear that they too might suffer injustice. Enough of this.

Now, if we are to form a real judgment of the life of the just and unjust, we must isolate them; there is no other way; and how is the isolation to be effected? I answer: Let the unjust man be entirely unjust, and the just man entirely just; nothing is to be taken away from either of them, and both are to be perfectly furnished for the work of their respective lives. First, let the unjust be like other distinguished masters of craft; like the skillful pilot or physician, who knows intuitively his own powers and keeps within their limits, and who, if he fails at any point, is able to recover himself. So let the unjust make his unjust attempts in the right way, and lie hidden if he means to be great in his injustice (he who is found out is nobody): for the highest reach of injustice is: to be deemed just when you are not. Therefore I say that in the perfectly unjust man we must assume the most perfect injustice; there is to be no deduction, but we must allow him, while doing the most unjust acts, to have acquired the greatest reputation for justice. If he have taken a false step he must be able to recover himself; he must be one who can speak with effect, if any of his deeds come to light, and who can force his way where force is required by his courage and strength, and command of money and friends. And at his side let us place the just man in his nobleness and simplicity, wishing, as Aeschylus says, to be and not to seem good. There must be no seeming, for if he seem to be just he will be honoured and rewarded, and then we shall not know whether he is just for the sake of justice or for the sake of honours and rewards; therefore, let him be clothed in justice only, and have no other covering; and he must be imagined in a state of life the opposite of the former. Let him be the best of men, and let him be thought the worst; then he will have been put to the proof; and we shall see whether he will be affected by the fear of infamy and its consequences. And let him continue thus to the hour of death; being just and seeming to be unjust. When both have reached the uttermost extreme, the one of justice and the other of injustice, let judgment be given which of them is the happier of the two.

Heavens! my dear Glaucon, I said, how energetically you polish them up for the decision, first one and then the other, as if they were two statues.

I do my best, he said. And now that we know what they are like there is no difficulty in tracing out the sort of life which awaits either of them. This I will proceed to describe; but as you may think the description a little too coarse, I ask you to suppose, Socrates, that the words which follow are not mine.—Let me put them into the mouths of the eulogists of injustice: they will tell you that the just man who is thought unjust will be scourged, racked, bound—will have his eyes burnt out; and, at last, after suffering every kind of evil, he will be impaled: Then he will understand that he ought to seem only, and not to be, just; the words of Aeschylus may be more truly spoken of the unjust than of the just. For the unjust is pursuing a reality; he does not live with a view to appearances—he wants to be really unjust and not to seem only:—

> His mind has a soil deep and fertile.
> Out of which spring his prudent counsels.

In the first place, he is thought just, and therefore bears rule in the city; he can marry whom he will, and give in marriage to whom he will; also he can trade and deal where he likes, and always to his own advantage, because he has no misgivings about injustice; and at every contest, whether in public or private, he gets the better of his antagonists, and gains at their expense, and is rich, and out of his gains he can benefit his friends, and harm his enemies; moreover, he can offer sacrifices, and dedicate gifts to the gods abundantly and magnificently, and can honour the gods or any man whom he wants to honour in a far better style than the just, and therefore he is likely to be dearer than they are to the gods. And thus, Socrates, gods and men are said to unite in making the life of the unjust better than the life of the just. . . .

[We pick up the discussion in Book 9.]

BOOK 9

"Now that we've gotten this far," I said, "let's go back to that statement made at the beginning, which brought us here: that it pays for a man to be perfectly unjust if he appears to be just. Isn't that what someone said?"

"Yes."

"Then since we've agreed what power justice and injustice each have, let's have a discussion with him."

"How?"

"By molding in words an image of the soul, so that the one who said that will realize what he was saying."

"What kind of image?"

"Oh, something like those natures the myths tell us were born in ancient times—the Chimaera, Scylla, Cerberus, and others in which many different shapes were supposed to have grown into one."

"So they tell us," he said.

"Then mold one figure of a colorful, many-headed beast with heads of wild and tame animals growing in a circle all around it; one that can change and grow all of them out of itself."

"That's a job for a skilled artist. Still, words mold easier than wax or clay, so consider it done."

"And another of a lion, and one of a man. Make the first by far the biggest, the second second largest."

"That's easier, and already done."

"Now join the three together so that they somehow grow."

"All right."

"Next mold the image of one, the man, around them all, so that to someone who can't see what's inside but looks only at the container it appears to be a single animal, man."

"I have."

"Then shall we inform the gentleman that when he says it pays for this man to be unjust, he's saying that it profits him to feast his multifarious beast and his lion and make them grow strong, but to starve and enfeeble the man in him so that he gets dragged wherever the animals lead him, and instead of making them friends and used to each other, to let them bite and fight and eat each other?"

"That's just what he's saying by praising injustice."

"The one who says justice pays, however, would be saying that he should practice and say whatever will give the most mastery to his inner man, who should care for the many-headed beast like a farmer, raising and domesticating its tame heads and preventing the wild ones from growing, making the lion's nature his partner and ally, and so raise them both to be friends to each other and to him."

"That's exactly what he means by praising justice."

"So in every way the commender of justice is telling the truth, the other a lie. Whether we examine pleasure, reputation, or profit, we find that the man who praises justice speaks truly, the one who disparages it disparages sickly and knows nothing of what he disparages."

"I don't think he does at all."

"Then let's gently persuade him—his error wasn't intended—by asking him a question: 'Shouldn't we say that the traditions of the beautiful and the ugly have come about like this: Beautiful things are those that make our bestial parts subservient to the human—or rather, perhaps, to the divine—part of our nature, while ugly ones are those that enslave the tame to the wild?' Won't he agree?"

"If he takes my advice."

"On this argument then, can it pay for a man to take money unjustly if that means making his best part a slave to the worst? If it wouldn't profit a man to sell his son or his daughter into slavery—to wild and evil men at that—even if he got a fortune for it, then if he has no pity on himself and enslaves the most godlike thing in him to the most godless and polluted, isn't he a wretch who gets bribed for gold into a destruction more horrible than Euriphyle's, who sold her husband's life for a necklace?"

"Much more horrible," said Glaucon.

". . . everyone is better off being ruled by the godlike and intelligent; preferably if he has it inside, but if not, it should be imposed on him from without so that we may all be friends and as nearly alike as possible, all steered by the same thing."

"Yes, and we're right," he said.

"Law, the ally of everyone in the city, clearly intends the same thing, as does the rule of children, which forbids us to let them be free until we've instituted a regime in them as in a city. We serve their best part with a similar part in us, install a like guardian and ruler in them, and only then set them free."

"Clearly."

"Then how, by what argument, Glaucon, can we say that it pays for a man to be unjust or self-indulgent or to do something shameful to get more money or power if by doing so he makes himself worse?"

"We can't," he said.

"And how can it pay to commit injustice without getting caught and being punished? Doesn't getting away with it make a man even worse? Whereas if a man gets caught and punished, his beastlike part is taken in and tamed, his tame part is set free, and his whole soul acquires justice and temperance and knowledge. Therefore his soul recovers its best nature and attains a state more honorable than the state the body attains when it acquires health and strength and beauty, by as much as the soul is more honorable than the body."

"Absolutely."

"Then won't a sensible man spend his life directing all his efforts to this end?"

For Further Reflection

1. Which would you choose to be, Glaucon's good but suffering person or his bad but successful person? Is there a third alternative?

2. Socrates' answer to Glaucon and Adeimantus is that, despite appearances, we should choose the life of the "unsuccessful" just person because it is to our advantage to be moral. Socrates' answer depends on a notion of mental health. He contends that immorality corrupts the inner person, so that one is happy or unhappy in exact proportion to one's moral integrity. Is this a plausible reply?

3. Is the good always good for you?

In Defense of Ethical Egoism   VI.46

AYN RAND

Ayn Rand (1908–1982) wrote several philosophical novels, including *We the Living* (1936), *The Fountainhead* (1943), and *Atlas Shrugged* (1959), from which the present selection is taken. Her works set forth a form of ethical egoism that is called *objectivism*, the philosophy that the proper life for rational beings is the pursuit of their happiness and that altruism and self-sacrifice are incompatible with rational morality. In this passage, she criticizes conventional altruistic morality ("the morality of sacrifice") and praises the morality of selfishness.

Study Questions

1. What is on trial in this age of moral crisis?
2. What has conventional morality taught us about the way to live? What, according to it, is evil and immoral?
3. What is the only fundamental alternative in the universe?
4. What is the difference between animals and human beings?
5. What does Rand call a "metaphysical monstrosity"?
6. What is properly our highest moral purpose?
7. What is the "most *selfish* of all things"?
8. What are the twin ideals of the morality of sacrifice?
9. What does Rand say about the duty to serve others? Is it proper to help others? Why or why not?

VALUE YOURSELF

"...YES, THIS *IS* AN AGE OF moral crisis. Yes, you *are* bearing punishment for your evil. But it is not man who is now on trial and it is not human nature that will take the blame. It is your moral code that's through, this time. Your moral code has reached its climax, the blind alley at the end of its course. And if you wish to go on living, what you now need is not to *return* to morality—you who have never known any—but to *discover* it.

"You have heard no concepts of morality but the mystical or the social. You have been taught that morality is a code of behavior imposed on you by whim, the whim of a supernatural power or the whim of society, to serve God's purpose or your neighbor's welfare, to please an authority beyond the grave or else next door—but not to serve *your* life or pleasure. Your pleasure, you have been taught, is to be found in immorality, your interests would best be served by evil, and any moral code must be designed not *for* you, but *against* you, not to further your life, but to drain it.

"For centuries, the battle of morality was fought between those who claimed that your life belongs to God and those who claimed that it belongs to your neighbors—between those who preached that the good is self-sacrifice for the sake of ghosts in heaven and those who preached that the good is self-sacrifice for the sake of incompetents on earth. And no one came to say that your life belongs to you and that the good is to live it.

"Both sides agreed that morality demands the surrender of your self-interest and of your mind, that the moral and the practical are opposites, that morality is not the province of reason, but the province of faith and force. Both sides agreed that no rational morality is possible, that there is no right or wrong in reason—that in reason there's no reason to be moral.

"Whatever else they fought about, it was against man's mind that all your moralists have stood united. It was man's mind that all their schemes and systems were intended to despoil and destroy. Now choose to perish or to learn that the anti-mind is the anti-life.

"Man's mind is his basic tool of survival. Life is given to him, survival is not. His body is given to him, its sustenance is not. His mind is given to him, its content is not. To remain alive, he must act, and before he can act he must know the nature and purpose of his action. He cannot obtain his food without a knowledge of food and of the way to obtain it. He cannot dig a ditch—or build a cyclotron—without a knowledge of his aim and of the means to achieve it. To remain alive, he must think.

"But to think is an act of choice. The key to what you so recklessly call 'human nature,' the open secret you live with, yet dread to name, is the fact that *man is a being of volitional consciousness*. Reason does not work automatically; thinking is not a mechanical process; the connections of logic are not made by instinct. The function of your stomach, lungs, or heart is automatic; the function of your mind is not. In any hour and issue of your life, you are free to think or to evade that effort. But you are not free to escape from your nature, from the fact that *reason* is your means of survival—so that

for *you*, who are a human being, the question 'to be or not to be' is the question 'to think or not to think.'

"A being of volitional consciousness has no automatic course of behavior. He needs a code of values to guide his actions. 'Value' is that which one acts to gain and keep, 'virtue' is the action by which one gains and keeps it. 'Value' presupposes an answer to the question: of value to whom and for what? 'Value' presupposes a standard, a purpose and the necessity of action in the face of an alternative. Where there are no alternatives, no values are possible.

"There is only one fundamental alternative in the universe: existence or non-existence—and it pertains to a single class of entities: to living organisms. The existence of inanimate matter is unconditional, the existence of life is not: it depends on a specific course of action. Matter is indestructible, it changes its forms, but it cannot cease to exist. It is only a living organism that faces a constant alternative: the issue of life or death. Life is a process of self-sustaining and self-generated action. If an organism fails in that action, it dies; its chemical elements remain, but its life goes out of existence. It is only the concept of 'Life' that makes the concept of 'Value' possible. It is only to a living entity that things can be good or evil.

"A plant must feed itself in order to live; the sunlight, the water, the chemicals it needs are the values its nature has set it to pursue; its life is the standard of value directing its actions. But a plant has no choice of action; there are alternatives in the conditions it encounters, but there is no alternative in its function; it acts automatically to further its life, it cannot act for its own destruction.

"An animal is equipped for sustaining its life; its senses provide it with an automatic code of action, an automatic knowledge of what is good for it or evil. It has no power to extend its knowledge or to evade it. In conditions where its knowledge proves inadequate, it dies. But so long as it lives, it acts on its knowledge, with automatic safety and no power of choice, it is unable to ignore its own good, unable to decide to choose the evil and act as its own destroyer.

"Man has no automatic code of survival. His particular distinction from all other living species is the necessity to act in the face of alternatives by means of *volitional choice*. He has no automatic knowledge of what is good for him or evil, what values his life depends on, what course of action it requires. Are you prattling about an instinct of self-preservation? An *instinct* of self-preservation is precisely what man does not possess. An 'instinct' is an unerring and automatic form of knowledge. A desire is not an instinct. A desire to live does not give you the knowledge required for living. And even man's desire to live is not automatic: your secret evil today is that *that* is the desire you do not hold. Your fear of death is not a love for life and will not give you the knowledge needed to keep it. Man must obtain his knowledge and choose his actions by a process of thinking, which nature will not force him to perform. Man has the power to act as his own destroyer—and that is the way he has acted through most of his history.

"A living entity that regarded its means of survival as evil, would not survive. A plant that struggled to mangle its roots, a bird that fought to break its wings would not remain for long in the existence they affronted. But the history of man has been a struggle to deny and to destroy his mind.

"Man has been called a rational being, but rationality is a matter of choice—and the alternative his nature offers him is: rational being or suicidal animal. Man has to be man—by choice; he has to hold his life as a value—by choice; he has to learn to sustain it—by choice; he has to discover the values it requires and practice his virtues—by choice.

"A code of values accepted by choice is a code of morality.

"Whoever you are, you who are hearing me now, I am speaking to whatever living remnant is left uncorrupted within you, to the remnant of the human, to your *mind*, and I say: There *is*

a morality of reason, a morality proper to man, and *Man's Life* is its standard of value.

"All that which is proper to the life of a rational being is the good; all that which destroys it is the evil.

"Man's life, as required by his nature, is not the life of a mindless brute, of a looting thug or a mooching mystic, but the life of a thinking being—not life by means of force or fraud, but life by means of achievement—not survival at any price, since there's only one price that pays for man's survival: reason.

"Man's life is the *standard* of morality, but your own life is its *purpose*. If existence on earth is your goal, you must choose your actions and values by the standard of that which is proper to man—for the purpose of preserving, fulfilling and enjoying the irreplaceable value which is your life.

"Since life requires a specific course of action, any other course will destroy it. A being who does not hold his own life as the motive and goal of his actions, is acting on the motive and standard of *death*. Such a being is a metaphysical monstrosity, struggling to oppose, negate and contradict the fact of his own existence, running blindly amuck on a trail of destruction, capable of nothing but pain.

"Happiness is the successful state of life, pain is an agent of death. Happiness is that state of unconsciousness which proceeds from the achievement of one's values. A morality that dares to tell you to find happiness in the renunciation of your happiness—to value the failure of your values—is an insolent negation of morality. A doctrine that gives you, as an ideal, the role of a sacrificial animal seeking slaughter on the altars of others, is giving you *death* as your standard. By the grace of reality and the nature of life, man—every man—is an end in himself, he exists for his own sake, and the achievement of his own happiness is his highest moral purpose.

"But neither life nor happiness can be achieved by the pursuit of irrational whims. Just as man is free to attempt to survive in any random manner, but will perish unless he lives as his nature requires, so he is free to seek his happiness in any mindless fraud, but the torture of frustration is all he will find, unless he seeks the happiness proper to man. The purpose of morality is to teach you, not to suffer and die, but to enjoy yourself and live.

"Sweep aside those parasites of subsidized classrooms, who live on the profits of the minds of others and proclaim that man needs no morality, no values, no code of behavior. They, who pose as scientists and claim that man is only an animal, do not grant him inclusion in the law of existence they have granted to the lowest of insects. They recognize that every living species has a way of survival demanded by its nature, they do not claim that a fish can live out of water or that a dog can live without its sense of smell—but man, they claim, the most complex of beings, man can survive in any way whatever, man has no identity, no nature, and there's no practical reason why he cannot live with his means of survival destroyed, with his mind throttled and placed at the disposal of any orders *they* might care to issue.

"Sweep aside those hatred-eaten mystics, who pose as friends of humanity and preach that the highest virtue man can practice is to hold his own life as of no value. Do they tell you that the purpose of morality is to curb man's instinct of self-preservation? It is for the purpose of self-preservation that man needs a code of morality. The only man who desires to be moral is the man who desires to live.

"No, you do not have to live; it is your basic act of choice; but if you choose to live, you must live as a man—by the work and the judgment of your mind.

"No, you do not have to live as a man: it is an act of moral choice. But you cannot live as anything else—and the alternative is that state of living death which you now see within you and around you, the state of a thing unfit for existence, no longer human and less than animal, a thing that knows nothing but pain and drags itself

through its span of years in the agony of unthinking self-destruction.

"No, you do not have to think; it is an act of moral choice. But someone had to think to keep you alive; if you choose to default, you default on existence and you pass the deficit to some moral man, expecting him to sacrifice his good for the sake of letting you survive by your evil. . . .

"This much is true: the most *selfish* of all things is the independent mind that recognizes no authority higher than its own and no value higher than its judgment of truth. You are asked to sacrifice your intellectual integrity, your logic, your reason, your standard of truth—in favor of becoming a prostitute whose standard is the greatest good for the greatest number.

"If you search your code for guidance, for an answer to the question: 'What *is* the good?'—the only answer you will find is '*The good of others*.' The good is whatever others wish, whatever you feel they feel they wish, or whatever you feel they ought to feel. 'The good of others' is a magic formula that transforms anything into gold, a formula to be recited as a guarantee of moral glory and as a fumigator for any action, even the slaughter of a continent. Your standard of virtue is not an object, not an act, nor a principle, but an *intention*. You need no proof, no reasons, no success, you need not achieve *in fact* the good of others—all you need to know is that your motive was the good of others, *not* your own. Your only definition of the good is a negation: the good is the 'non-good for me.'

"Your code—which boasts that it upholds eternal, absolute, objective moral values and scorns the conditional, the relative and the subjective—your code hands out, as its version of the absolute, the following rule of moral conduct: If *you* wish it, it's evil; if others wish it, it's good; if the motive of your action is *your* welfare, don't do it; if the motive is the welfare of others, then anything goes.

"As this double-jointed, double-standard morality splits you in half, so it splits mankind into two enemy camps: one is *you*, the other is all the rest of humanity. *You* are the only outcast who has no right to wish or live. *You* are the only servant, the rest are the masters, *you* are the only giver, the rest are the takers, *you* are the eternal debtor, the rest are the creditors never to be paid off. You must not question their right to your sacrifice, or the nature of their wishes and their needs: their right is conferred upon them by a negative, by the fact that they are 'non-you.'

"For those of you who might ask questions, your code provides a consolation prize and booby-trap: it is for your own happiness, it says, that you must serve the happiness of others, the only way to achieve your joy is to give it up to others, the only way to achieve your prosperity is to surrender your wealth to others, the only way to protect your life is to protect all men except yourself—and if you find no joy in this procedure, it is your own fault and the proof of your evil; if you were good, you would find your happiness in providing a banquet for others, and your dignity in existing on such crumbs as *they* might care to toss you.

"You who have no standard of self-esteem, accept the guilt and dare not ask the questions. But you know the unadmitted answer, refusing to acknowledge what you see, what hidden premise moves your world. You know it, not in honest statement, but as a dark uneasiness within you, while you flounder between guiltily cheating and grudgingly practicing a principle too vicious to name.

"I, who do not accept the unearned, neither in values nor in *guilt,* am here to ask the questions you evaded. Why is it moral to serve the happiness of others, but not your own? If enjoyment is a value, why is it moral when experienced by others, but immoral when experienced by you? If the sensation of eating a cake is a value, why is it an immoral indulgence in your stomach, but a moral goal for you to achieve in the stomach of others? Why is it immoral for you to desire, but moral for others to do so? Why is it immoral to produce a value and keep it, but moral to give it away? And if it is not

moral for you to keep a value, why is it moral for others to accept it? If you are selfless and virtuous when you give it, are they not selfish and vicious when they take it? Does virtue consist of serving vice? Is the moral purpose of those who are good, self-immolation for the sake of those who are evil? . . .

"Under a morality of sacrifice, the first value you sacrifice is morality; the next is self-esteem. When need is the standard, every man is both victim and parasite. As a victim, he must labor to fill the needs of others, leaving himself in the position of a parasite whose needs must be filled by others. He cannot approach his fellow men except in one of two disgraceful roles: he is both a beggar and a sucker.

"You fear the man who has a dollar less than you, that dollar is rightfully his, he makes you feel like a moral defrauder. You hate the man who has a dollar more than you, that dollar is rightfully yours, he makes you feel that you are morally defrauded. The man below is a source of your guilt, the man above is a source of your frustration. You do not know what to surrender or demand, when to give and when to grab, what pleasure in life is rightfully yours and what debt is still unpaid to others—you struggle to evade, as 'theory,' the knowledge that by the moral standard you've accepted you are guilty every moment of your life, there is no mouthful of food you swallow that is not *needed* by someone somewhere on earth—and you give up the problem in blind resentment, you conclude that moral perfection is not to be achieved *or desired,* that you will muddle through by snatching as snatch can and by avoiding the eyes of the young, of those who look at you as if self-esteem were possible and they expected you to have it. Guilt is all that you retain within your soul—and so does every other man, as he goes past, avoiding *your* eyes. Do you wonder why your morality has not achieved brotherhood on earth or the good will of man to man?

"The justification of sacrifice, that your morality propounds, is more corrupt than the corruption it purports to justify. The motive of your sacrifice, it tells you, should be *love*—the love you ought to feel for every man. A morality that professes the belief that the values of the spirit are more precious than matter, a morality that teaches you to scorn a whore who gives her body indiscriminately to all men—this same morality demands that you surrender your soul to promiscuous love for all comers.

"As there can be no causeless wealth, so there can be no causeless love or any sort of causeless emotion. An emotion is a response to a fact of reality, an estimate dictated by your standards. To love is to *value*. The man who tells you that it is possible to value without values, to love those whom you appraise as worthless, is the man who tells you that it is possible to grow rich by consuming without producing and that paper money is as valuable as gold.

"Observe that he does not expect you to feel a causeless fear. When his kind get into power, they are expert at contriving means of terror, at giving you ample cause to feel the fear by which they desire to rule you. But when it comes to love, the highest of emotions, you permit them to shriek at you accusingly that you are a moral delinquent if you're incapable of feeling causeless love. When a man feels fear without reason, you call him to the attention of a psychiatrist; you are not so careful to protect the meaning, the nature and the dignity of love.

"Love is the expression of one's values, the greatest reward you can earn for the moral qualities you have achieved in your character and person, the emotional price paid by one man for the joy he receives from the virtues of another. Your morality demands that you divorce your love from values and hand it down to any vagrant, not as response to his worth, but as response to his *need*, not as reward, but as alms, not as a payment for virtues, but as a blank check on vices. Your morality tells you that the purpose of love is to set you free of the bonds of morality, that love is superior to moral judgment, that true love transcends, forgives and survives every manner of evil in its object, and the greater the love the greater the depravity it permits to the

loved. To love a man for his virtues is paltry and human, it tells you; to love him for his flaws is divine. To love those who are worthy of it is self-interest; to love the unworthy is sacrifice. You owe your love to those who don't deserve it, and the less they deserve it, the more love you owe them—the more loathsome the object, the nobler your love—the more unfastidious your love, the greater your virtue—and if you can bring your soul to the state of a dump heap that welcomes anything on equal terms, if you can cease to value moral values, you have achieved the state of moral perfection.

"Such is your morality of sacrifice and such are the twin ideals it offers: to refashion the life of your body in the image of a human stockyard, and the life of your spirit in the image of a dump. . . .

"Since childhood, you have been hiding the guilty secret that you feel no desire to be moral, no desire to seek self-immolation, that you dread and hate your code, but dare not say it even to yourself, that you're devoid of those moral 'instincts' which others profess to feel. The less you felt, the louder you proclaimed your selfless love and servitude to others, in dread of ever letting them discover your own self, the self that you betrayed, the self that you kept in concealment, like a skeleton in the closet of your body. And they, who were at once your dupes and your deceivers, they listened and voiced their loud approval, in dread of ever letting you discover that they were harboring the same unspoken secret. Existence among you is a giant pretense, an act you all perform for one another, each feeling that he is the only guilty freak, each placing his moral authority in the unknowable known only to others, each faking the reality he feels they expect him to fake, none having the courage to break the vicious circle.

"No matter what dishonorable compromise you've made with your impracticable creed, no matter what miserable balance, half-cynicism, half-superstition, you now manage to maintain, you still preserve the root, the lethal tenet: the belief that the moral and the practical are opposites.

Since childhood, you have been running from the terror of a choice you have never dared fully to identify: If the *practical,* whatever you must practice to exist, whatever works, succeeds, achieves your purpose, whatever brings you food and joy, whatever profits you is evil—and if the good, the moral is the *impractical,* whatever fails, destroys, frustrates, whatever injures you and brings you loss or pain—then your choice is to be moral or to live.

"The sole result of that murderous doctrine was to remove morality from life. You grew up to believe that moral laws bear no relation to the job of living, except as an impediment and threat, that man's existence is an amoral jungle where anything goes and anything works. And in that fog of switching definitions which descends upon a frozen mind, you have forgotten that the evils damned by your creed were the virtues required for living, and you have come to believe that actual evils are the *practical* means of existence. Forgetting that the impractical 'good' was self-sacrifice, you believe that self-esteem is impractical; forgetting that the practical 'evil' was production, you believe that robbery is practical. . . .

"Accept the fact that the achievement of your happiness is the only *moral* purpose of your life, and that *happiness*—not pain or mindless self-indulgence—is the proof of your moral integrity, since it is the proof and the result of your loyalty to the achievement of your values. Happiness was the responsibility you dreaded, it required the kind of rational discipline you did not value yourself enough to assume—and the anxious staleness of your days is the monument to your evasion of the knowledge that there is no moral substitute for happiness, that there is no more despicable coward than the man who deserted the battle for his joy, fearing to assert his right to existence, lacking the courage and the loyalty to life of a bird or a flower reaching for the sun. Discard the protective rags of that vice which you called a virtue: humility—learn to value yourself, which means: to fight for your happiness—and when you learn that *pride* is the sum of all virtues, you will learn to live like a man.

"As a basic step of self-esteem, learn to treat as the mark of a cannibal any man's *demand* for your help. To demand it is to claim that your life is *his* property—and loathsome as such claim might be, there's something still more loathsome: your agreement. Do you ask if it's ever proper to help another man? No—if he claims it as his right or as a moral duty that you owe him. Yes—if such is your own desire based on your own selfish pleasure in the value of his person and his struggle."

For Further Reflection

1. Has Rand successfully defended her theory of ethical egoism? How does it relate to Socrates' idea that one ought never to harm anyone else? Could one reconcile Socrates' idea with Rand's theory? Socrates believes that one should never harm anyone else because doing so is never in one's own interest. What would be needed to get Rand's theory to agree with that conclusion?

2. Can the ethical egoist make his or her views public? If you follow Rand, should you let others know where you stand? Should you persuade them to be egoists? If the egoist cannot make his theory public, does this disqualify it as a genuine ethical theory?

3. Can the ethical egoist be a consistent egoist and have friends? If friendship entails loving another in such a way as to sacrifice one's own interest for the friend's, does this give the egoist difficulty?

VI.47   A Critique of Ethical Egoism

LOUIS POJMAN

Louis Pojman is professor of philosophy at the United States Military Academy at West Point and the author and editor of several books in ethics, philosophy of religion, and epistemology, including this book. In this essay Pojman makes a case against the kind of ethical egoism defended by such thinkers as Thomas Hobbes and Ayn Rand. Appealing to the paradox of egoism, he distinguishes between two levels of thinking about the self. On a higher (tier 2) level a person does legitimately concern oneself with prospects for one's happiness, but, in so reflecting, one rationally concludes that the best way to realize happiness on an everyday (tier 1) level is to develop a strong (non-egoistic) disposition toward altruism. Limited, reciprocal altruism offers us the best chance for happiness.

Study Questions

1. What are the three kinds of egoism that Pojman discusses? Define each one.
2. What is the economist argument for ethical egoism?
3. What is Thomas Hobbes's argument for ethical egoism?
4. What is Ayn Rand's argument for ethical egoism?
5. What criticisms can be brought against the theories of Hobbes and Rand?
6. What is the paradox of egoism?
7. What is the argument from counterintuitive consequences?
8. How does the field of sociobiology provide a possible basis for altruism?

AN OVERVIEW OF THE PROBLEM

Nice guys finish last.

(Leo Durocher, former manager of the Brooklyn Dodgers)

CHILDREN ARE SOMETIMES brought up to feel guilty for being concerned about their own good. They are taught that self-love is selfishness, a sinful attitude. To do things for oneself is evil. Indeed, I was brought up in a strict religious community in which children were made to feel they were sinful. The proper attitude toward oneself was one of humility ("Blessed are the poor in spirit, for theirs is the kingdom of heaven") and self-effacement ("Unless a person hate his own life, he cannot enter the kingdom of God").[1]

Sometimes such an upbringing results in self-hatred, low self-esteem, a lack of self-confidence, masochism, and pervasive, irrational guilt. Let's call this attitude the *morality of self-effacement.*

In Dostoevsky's *The Brothers Karamazov* Lise breaks her engagement with the saintly Alyosha, explaining to him that he is too gentle for her needs:

This essay appeared in an earlier form in my book Ethics: Discovering Right and Wrong *(Wadsworth, 1995).*

I was just thinking for the thirtieth time what a good thing it is that I broke off our engagement and decided not to become your wife. You wouldn't be much of a husband, you know. . . . I want someone to marry me, tear me to pieces, betray me, and then desert me. I don't want to be happy.

Shortly afterwards we read:

Lise unlocked the door, opened it a little, put her finger in the crack, and slammed the door as hard as she could. Ten seconds later she released her hand, went slowly to her chair, sat down, and looked intently at her blackened, swollen finger and the blood that was oozing out from under the nail. Her lips quivered. "I'm vile, vile, vile, a despicable creature."[2]

At the opposite extreme is the *morality of self-exaltation*, or the *morality of me-ism*, by which we are to love ourselves first. Ayn Rand's *The Virtue of Selfishness*, Robert Ringer's *Looking Out for Number One*, and David Seabury's *The Art of Selfishness* advise us to love ourselves first even if it means hurting others. Perhaps no one was more candid about the legitimacy of egoism than Friedrich Nietzsche (1844–1900), who taught that we should strive to satisfy our own will to power, even to the extent of exploiting and dominating others before they dominated us:

What is strong wins. That is the universal law. To speak of right and wrong per se makes no sense at all. No act of violence, rape, exploitation, destruction, is intrinsically "unjust," since life itself is violent, rapacious, exploitative, and destructive and cannot be conceived otherwise.[3]

But Nietzsche's version of egoism is an extreme one. A less virulent form is found in Thomas Hobbes's (1588–1679) classic, *Leviathan* (1651). Hobbes believed that egoism is the proper foundation for the moral and political life. Human nature is basically self-interested, so it makes no sense to ask people to be altruistic. All apparently altruistic acts are, if you look deeply into the heart of people, merely dis-

guised acts of selfishness. Nevertheless, Hobbes was no relativist. Out of enlightened egoism arise objective moral norms and a legitimate political system, the Leviathan.

Hobbes's argument goes like this: Suppose we existed outside of any society, without laws or agreed-upon morality, in a "state of nature." There are no common ways of life, no means of settling conflicts of interest except violence, no reliable expectations of how other people will behave—except that, as psychological egoists, people will follow their own inclinations and perceived interests, tending to act and react and overreact in fearful, capricious, and violent ways.

The result of life in the state of nature is chaotic anarchy. Reason advises us not to depend on anyone except ourselves, for others will let us down if it is in their interests to do so. I must always be on my guard, protecting my vital interests. But I see that others are thinking the same thing; perhaps they are ganging up on me. This increases my fear of others and leads in turn to preventive or preemptive aggression, which leads to "a war of all against all":

During the time men live without a common Power to keep them all in awe they are in that condition called War; and such a war, as is of every man against every other man. . . . To this war every man against every man, this is consequent; that nothing can be Unjust. The notions of Right and Wrong, Justice and Injustice have no place.[4]

In such a state, life is "solitary, poor, nasty, brutish, and short."

But reason tells us that a war of all against all is really in no one's interest. It would be better for all of us, individually and collectively, if we adopted certain minimal rules that would override immediate self-interest whenever one's own self-interest was a threat to others. Thus the notion of a mutually agreed-upon moral code arises from a situation of rational self-interest.

Of course, the moral code will not work if only some obey it. Those who do obey will be slaughtered like sheep before waiting wolves. Reason can support morality only when the presumption about other people's behavior is reversed. Hobbes thought that this reversal could be achieved only by the creation of a Leviathan, an absolute ruler with absolute power to enforce his laws. But this is incorrect. A minimal moral society can be achieved democratically by a people if there are common rules or ways of life that are taught to all members of the society—inculcated in them early in life—and enforced by the group.

The members must be able to count on one another to obey these rules even when it is not in their immediate self-interest. Nonetheless, it is still rational to violate the rules whenever two conditions obtain: You calculate that you can get away with it, and your infraction will not seriously threaten the stability of the social system as a whole, sending you back toward the state of nature.

To prevent such violations Hobbes proposed a strong central government with a powerful police force and a sure and effective system of punishment. The threat of being caught and punished would function as a deterrent to crime. People must believe that offenses against the law are not in their overall interest. Is Hobbes correct in his account of human nature? Is he correct in his view that ethical egoism is the correct moral theory?

What place do self-regard, self-interest, and self-love have in the moral life? Is everything we do really done out of the motive of self-interest, so that morality is necessarily egoistic? Is some form of egoism the best moral theory? Or is egoism really diametrically opposed to true morality? Is altruism possible, and, if so, is it rational? These are the questions we shall discuss, but before we can consider them, we need to make some careful distinctions and define our terms. First of all, there are at least three different types of egoism: personal egoism, individual ethical egoism, and universal ethical egoism. These may be roughly defined in the following way:

1. **Personal egoism** is the state of being selfish by choice. I always choose to serve my own best interest, regardless of what happens to anyone else. This is not a reflective judgment about what is right or wrong or what ought to be the case. As such it is not an ethical theory at all, but a phenomenal state of exclusive self-love. We might call this form of egoism "phenomenal *egotism*," or just plain selfishness.

2. **Individual ethical egoism** is the view that *everyone* ought to serve *my* best interest. Unlike personal egoism or phenomenal egotism, this doctrine prescribes that others serve me (the speaker). This claims to be a moral theory, obligating others to look after my interests before everything else. It is also a version of selfishness, a version that claims moral authority.

3. **Universal ethical egoism** is the view that *everyone* ought always to do those acts that will best serve his or her own best self-interest, even when it conflicts with the interests of others.

ETHICAL EGOISM

In this section we consider three forms of egoism: personal egoism, individual ethical egoism, and universal ethical egoism. Personal egoism does not claim to be an ethical theory, although some people live by it. Individual ethical egoism and universal ethical egoism are ethical theories.

Personal egoism is not a description of human nature, but merely a description of a type of personality. It has no moral prescriptive force. It does not imply any of the other theories and is neutral between egoist and nonegoist ethical theories. Although psychological egoism is false, there seem to be many personal egoists. Personal egoism may be equated with selfishness, and it comes closest to *egotism*, the behavioral pattern in which one constantly draws attention to oneself. Egoists need not be egotists and may be more subtle about their self-interestedness.

Individual ethical egoism is the view that everyone ought to serve *my* self-interest. That is, moral rightness is defined solely in terms of what is good for *me*, whether or not it is good for anyone else. Of course, each one of us could put his or her own name in the place of "me." Say, for example, that Aunt Ruth is a personal egoist, so then all moral rightness defines itself in terms of what is good for Aunt Ruth. It would follow that whether or not a mother in India loves her child is morally irrelevant, for it has no effect on Aunt Ruth. Once Aunt Ruth is dead, morality is dead, for it no longer has an object. Interestingly enough, whereas individual ethical egoism seems implausible, it may be the central position of many religious people who define ethics as "that which serves God's interests and pleases Him." Be that as it may, as far as mere mortals are concerned, individual ethical egoism seems a partial and absurd theory. What makes any one person so special that everyone else is obligated to serve that person's interests as our primary concern?

Universal ethical egoism is the theory that everyone ought always to serve his or her own self-interest. That is, everyone ought to do whatever will maximize one's own expected utility or bring about one's own happiness, even when it means harming others. This has all the earmarks of a legitimate ethical theory. It is a universal theory, which individual ethical egoism is not. It is not egotistical; rather, it is prudential and favors long-term interests over short-term interests. In its most sophisticated form it urges everyone to *try* to win in the game of life, and it recognizes that in order to do this, some compromises are necessary. Indeed, universal egoists admit that to some extent we must all give up a certain freedom and cooperate with others to achieve our ends.

What are the arguments for ethical egoism? There are three that should be considered: (1) the economist argument, (2) the Ayn Rand argument for the virtue of selfishness, and (3) the Hobbesian argument. Let's examine each of these in turn. After expositing them, I will offer a critical assessment of each.

The Economist Argument

Economists in the mold of Adam Smith often argue that individual self-interest in a competitive marketplace produces a state of optimal goodness for society at large, because the peculiar nature of self-interested competition causes each individual to produce a better product and sell it at a lower price than its competitors. Thus, enlightened self-interest leads, as if by an invisible hand, to the best overall situation.

The Ayn Rand Argument for the Virtue of Selfishness

In her book, *The Virtue of Selfishness*, Ayn Rand argues that selfishness is a virtue and altruism a vice, a totally destructive idea that leads to the undermining of individual worth. In her novel *The Fountainhead*, Rand paints the hero Howard Roark as an egoist who succeeds in life by the single-minded pursuit of his own happiness. Ellsworth Toohey, the 'altruist,' turns out to be a consummate hypocrite, a failed egoist, who deceives himself and others about his selfish motives. Rand defines *altruism* as the view that

> any action taken for the benefit of others is good, and any action taken for one's own benefit is evil. Thus, the *beneficiary* of an action is the only criterion of moral value—and so long as the beneficiary is anybody other than oneself, anything goes.

As such, altruism is suicidal:

> If a man accepts the ethics of altruism, his first concern is not how to live his life, but how to sacrifice it. . . . Altruism erodes men's capacity to grasp the value of an individual life; it reveals a mind from which the reality of a human being has been wiped out. . . . Altruism holds death as its ultimate goal and standard of value—and it is logical that renunciation, resig-

nation, self-denial, and every other form of suffering, including self-destruction, are the virtue of its advocates.[5]

But a person ought to profit from his own action.

> Man's proper values and interests, that concern with his own interests, is the essence of a moral existence, and that man must be the beneficiary of his own moral actions.

We all really want to be the beneficiary, but society, through the Ellsworth Tooheys, has deceived us into thinking egoism is evil and altruism good.

Because finding happiness is the highest goal and good in life, altruism, which calls on us to sacrifice our happiness for the good of others, is contrary to our highest good. Rand's argument seems to go something like this:

1. The perfection of one's abilities in a state of happiness is the highest goal for humans. We have a moral duty to attempt to reach this goal.

2. The ethics of altruism prescribes that we sacrifice our interests and lives for the good of others.

3. Therefore the ethics of altruism is incompatible with the goal of happiness.

4. Ethical egoism prescribes that we seek our own happiness exclusively, and as such it is consistent with the happiness goal.

5. Therefore ethical egoism is the correct moral theory.

Rand seems to hold that every individual has a duty to seek his or her own good first, regardless of how it affects others. Of course, sometimes it is in our interest to cooperate with others. Fine. But where it is in our interest to harm another person, it's not simply permissible, but our duty to do so. Ultimately, each of us should take care of number One, letting the devil take care of anyone not strong enough to look after himself.

The Hobbesian Argument

According to some interpretations of Hobbes, we are not pure psychological egoists, but simply *predominantly* psychological egoists, having a powerful tendency in this direction.[6] Human action is generally predominantly motivated by self-interest. Because we cannot do otherwise without unreasonable effort, it follows that it is morally permissible for us to act entirely out of self-interest. However, enlightened common sense tells us that we should aim at fulfilling our long-term versus our short-term interests, and so we need to refrain from immediate gratification of our senses, from doing those things that would break down the social conditions that enable us to reach our goals. We should even, perhaps, generally obey the Golden Rule, "Do unto others as you would have them do unto you," for doing good unto others will help ensure that they do good unto us. However, sometimes we should cheat, when doing so will maximize agent utility, and sometimes we should harm others, when it is in our overall self-interest to do so.

Sometimes this version of egoism is based on the notion of agent-relative values, which states that all values are essentially owned by an agent and that each of us has our own hierarchy and specific set of values. Thus each of us has different reasons for acting in a certain way. No agent-neutral values are identical in all persons. Naturally, we have to cooperate with others in the pursuit of our goals, but ultimately we are alone in the world. I am the only person who knows exactly what my values are. Sometimes I may have to harm others in order to realize my goals.[7]

A Critique of Ethical Egoism

Essentially, the economist argument is not an argument for ethical egoism. It is really an argument for utilitarianism, which makes use of self-interest to attain (paradoxically) the good of all. Adam Smith himself was a utilitarian. The goal of this theory is social utility, but it places its faith in an invisible hand inherent in the free enterprise system that guides enlightened self-interest to reach that goal. We might say that it is a two-tier system: On the highest level it is utilitarian, but on a lower level of day-to-day action, it is practical egoism.

| Tier 2 | General goal: Social utility |
| Tier 1 | Individual motivation: Egoistic |

The economist argument via the two-tier system suggests that we not worry about the social good but only about our own good, and in that way we will attain the highest social good possible.

There may be some truth in such a two-tier system, but in the first place, it is unclear (at best) whether you can transpose the methods of economics (which are debatable) into the realm of personal relations. Personal relations may have a different logic than economic relations. The best way to maximize utility in an ethical sense may be to give one's life for others rather than to kill another person, as an egoist might enjoin. Secondly, it is not clear that classical laissez-faire capitalism works. Since the 1929 depression, most economists have altered their faith in classical capitalism, and most Western nations have supplemented capitalism with some governmental intervention. Likewise, although self-interest often leads to greater social utility, it may get out of hand and need to be supplemented by a concern for others. Just as classical capitalism has been altered to allow governmental intervention—resulting in a welfare system for the worst-off people, public education, Social Security, and Medicare—an adequate moral system may need to draw attention to the needs of others and direct us to meeting those needs even when we do not consider it to be in our immediate self-interest.

The Ayn Rand argument for the virtue of selfishness appears to be flawed by the fallacy of a false dilemma. It simplistically assumes that absolute altruism and absolute egoism are the only alternatives, but this is an extreme view of the matter. There are plenty of options between these two positions. Even a predominant egoist would admit that (analogous to the paradox of hedonism) sometimes the best way to reach self-fulfillment is for us to forget about ourselves and strive to live for goals, causes, or other persons. Even if altruism is not required (as a duty), it may be permissible in many cases. Furthermore, self-interest may not be incompatible with other-regarding motivation. Even the Second Great Commandment set forth by Moses and Jesus states *not* that you must always sacrifice yourself for the other person, but that you ought to love your neighbor *as* yourself (Lev. 19:19; Matt. 23). Self-interest and self-love are morally good things, but not at the expense of other people's legitimate interests. When there is a moral conflict of interests, a fair process of adjudication needs to take place.

Actually, in her books, Rand ambiguously slides back and forth between advocating self-interest and selfishness. But these are different concepts. *Self-interest* means we are concerned to promote our own good, though not necessarily at any cost. I want to succeed, but I recognize that sometimes I will justly fail to do so. I accept the just outcome even though it is frustrating. But *selfishness* entails that I sacrifice the good of others, even when it is unjust to do so, for my own good. Self-interest is a legitimate part of our nature, whereas selfishness is an aberration, a failure to accept the moral point of view.

Regarding the Hobbesian argument, which is the most plausible of the three arguments for ethical egoism, we can say that it seems to rest too heavily on psychological egoism. It assumes that we cannot do any better than be egoists, so we should be as enlightened about our egoism as possible. But if, as we argued earlier, psychological egoism is false, there is no reason to rule out the possibility of nonegoistic behavior. If Hobbesians qualify their position to embrace predominant psychological egoism—the theory that human nature causes us to be heavily biased toward our own self-interest over that of others' interest—then we need not of necessity become ethical egoists. However, the modified Hobbesian argument may make ethical egoism plausible.

Next we turn our attention to attempts to refute egoism in order to assess just how plausible it is as an ethical theory.

ATTEMPTED REFUTATIONS OF EGOISM

The Inconsistent Outcomes Argument

Brian Medlin argues that ethical egoism cannot be true because it fails to meet a necessary condition of morality, that of being a guide to action. He claims that it will be like advising people to do inconsistent things based on incompatible desires.[8] His argument goes like this:

1. Moral principles must be universal and categorical.

2. I must universalize my egoist desire to come out on top over Tom, Dick, and Harry.

3. But I must also prescribe Tom's egoist desire to come out on top over Dick, Harry, and me (and so on).

4. Therefore I have prescribed incompatible outcomes and have not provided a way of adjudicating conflicts of desire. In effect, I have said nothing.

The proper response to this is that of Jesse Kalin, who argues that we can separate our beliefs about ethical situations from our desires.[9] He likens the situation to a competitive sports event, in which you believe that your opponent has a right to try to win as much as you, but you desire that you, not he, will in fact win. An even better example is that of the chess game in which you recognize that your opponent ought to move her bishop to prepare for checkmate, but you hope she won't see the move. Belief that *A* ought to do *Y* does not commit you to wanting *A* to do *Y*.

The Publicity Argument

On the one hand, in order for something to be a moral theory it seems necessary that its moral principles be publicized. Unless principles are put forth as universal prescriptions that are accessible to the public, they cannot serve as guides to action or as aids in resolving conflicts of interest. But on the other hand, it is not in the egoist's self-interest to publicize principles. Egoists would rather that the rest of us be altruists. (Why did Nietzsche and Rand write books announcing their positions? Were the royalties garnered by announcing ethical egoism worth the price of letting the cat out of the bag?)

Thus it would be self-defeating for the egoist to argue for her position, and even worse that she should convince others of it. But it is perfectly possible to have a private morality that does not resolve conflicts of interest. Thus the egoist should publicly advocate standard principles of traditional morality—so that society doesn't break down—while adhering to a private, nonstandard, solely self-regarding morality. If you're willing to pay the price, you can accept the solipsistic-directed norms of egoism.

If the egoist is prepared to pay the price, egoism can be a consistent system that has some limitations. Although the egoist can cooperate with others in limited ways and perhaps even have friends—as long as their interests don't conflict with his—he has to be very careful about preserving his isolation. The egoist can't give advice or argue about his position—not sincerely at least. He must act alone, atomistically or solipsistically in moral isolation, for to announce his adherence to the principle of egoism would be dangerous to his project. He can't teach his children the true morality or justify himself to others or forgive others.

The Paradox of Egoism

The situation may be even worse than the sophisticated, self-conscious egoist supposes.

Could the egoist have friends? If limited friendship is possible, could he or she ever be in love or experience deep friendship? Suppose the egoist discovers that in the pursuit of the happiness goal, deep friendship is in his best interest. Can he become a friend? What is necessary to form a deep friendship? A true friend is one who is not always preoccupied about his or her own interest in the relationship but who forgets about himself altogether, at least sometimes, to serve or enhance the other person's interest. "Love seeketh not its own." It is an altruistic disposition, the very opposite of egoism. And yet we recognize that it is in our self-interest to have friends and loving relations, without which life lacks the highest joy and meaning. So the *paradox of egoism* is that in order to reach the goal of egoism, one must give up egoism and become (to some extent) an altruist, the very antithesis of egoism.

We may once again appeal to a level distinction. On the *highest, reflective* (tier 2) level, I conclude that I want to be happy. But I also conclude that the best way to find happiness is to have friends and good relations in a community where we all act justly and lovingly. Because having friends and acting justly requires having dispositions to act justly and altruistically, I determine on a *lower* or *first-order* (tier 1) level to live *justly* and *altruistically*, rather than *egoistically*.

Tier 2   Self-interest concern for happiness
Tier 1   Altruistic dispositions

The Argument from Counterintuitive Consequences

The final argument against ethical egoism is that it is an absolute ethics that not only permits egoistic behavior but demands it. Helping others at one's own expense is not only not required, it is morally wrong. Whenever I do not have good evidence that my helping you will end up to my advantage, I must refrain from helping you. If I can save the whole of Europe and Africa from destruction by pressing a button, then as long as there is nothing for me to gain by it, it is wrong for me to press that button. The Good Samaritan was, by this logic, morally wrong in helping the injured victim and not collecting payment for his troubles. It is certainly hard to see why the egoist should be concerned about environmental matters if he or she is profiting from polluting the environment. (For example, if the egoist gains 40 hedons in producing *P*, which produces pollution that in turn causes others 1,000 dolors—units of suffering—but suffers only 10 of those dolors himself, then by an agent-maximizing calculus he is morally obligated to produce *P*.) There is certainly no obligation to preserve scarce natural resources for future generations. "Why should I do anything for posterity?" the egoist asks. "What has posterity ever done for me?"

In conclusion, we see that ethical egoism has a number of serious problems. It cannot consistently publicize itself, nor often argue its case. It tends toward solipsism and the exclusion of many of the deepest human values, such as love and deep friendship. It violates the principle of fairness, and, most of all, it entails an absolute prohibition on altruistic behavior, which we intuitively sense as morally required (or, at least, permissible).

EVOLUTION AND ALTRUISM

If sheer unadulterated egoism is an inadequate moral theory, does that mean we ought to aim at complete altruism, total self-effacement for the sake of others? What is the role of self-love in morality? An interesting place to start answering these queries is with the new field of sociobiology, which theorizes that social structures and behavioral patterns, including morality, have a biological base, explained by evolutionary theory.

In the past, linking ethics to evolution meant justifying exploitation. Social Darwinism justified imperialism and the principle that "might makes right" by saying that survival of the fittest is a law of nature. This philosophy lent itself to a promotion of ruthless egoism. This is nature's law, "nature red in tooth and claw." Against this view ethologists such as Robert Ardrey and Konrad Lorenz argued for a more benign view of the animal kingdom—one reminiscent of Rudyard Kipling's, in which the animal kingdom survives by cooperation, which is at least as important as competition. On Ardrey's and Lorenz's view it is the group or the species, not the individual, that is of primary importance.

With the development of sociobiology—in the work of E. O. Wilson but particularly the work of Robert Trivers, J. Maynard Smith, and Richard Dawkins—a theory that combines radical individualism with limited altruism has come to the fore. It is not the group or the species that is of evolutionary importance but the gene, or, more precisely, the gene type. Genes—the parts of the chromosomes that carry the blueprints for all our natural traits (e.g., height, hair color, skin color, intelligence)—copy themselves as they divide and multiply. At conception they combine with the genes of a member of the opposite sex to form a new individual.

In his fascinating sociobiological study, Richard Dawkins describes human behavior as determined evolutionarily by stable strategies set to replicate the gene.[10] This is not done consciously, of course, but by the invisible hand that drives consciousness. We are essentially gene machines.

Morality—that is, successful morality—can be seen as an evolutionary strategy for gene replication. Here's an example: Birds are afflicted with life-endangering parasites. Because they lack limbs to enable them to pick the parasites off their heads, they—like many in the animal kingdom—depend on the ritual of mutual grooming. It turns out that nature has evolved two basic types of birds in this regard: those who are disposed to groom anyone (the non-prejudiced type?) and those who refuse to groom anyone but who present themselves for grooming. The former type of bird Dawkins calls "Suckers" and the latter "Cheaters."

In a geographical area containing harmful parasites where there are only Suckers or Cheaters, Suckers will do fairly well, but Cheaters will not survive, for want of cooperation. However, in a Sucker population in which a mutant Cheater arises, the Cheater will prosper, and the Cheater gene-type will multiply. As the Suckers are exploited, they will gradually die out. If and when they become too few to groom the Cheaters, the Cheaters will start to die off too and eventually become extinct.

Why don't birds all die off, then? Well, somehow nature has come up with a third type—call them "Grudgers." Grudgers groom all and only those who reciprocate in grooming them. They groom each other and Suckers, but not Cheaters. In fact, once caught, a Cheater is marked forever. There is no forgiveness. It turns out then that unless there are a lot of Suckers around, Cheaters have a hard time of it—harder even than Suckers. However, it is the Grudgers that prosper. Unlike Suckers, they don't waste time messing with unappreciative Cheaters, so they are not exploited and have ample energy to gather food and build better nests for their loved ones.

J. L. Mackie argues that the real name for Suckers is "Christian," one who believes in complete altruism, even turning the other cheek to one's assailant and loving one's enemy. Cheaters are ruthless egoists who can survive only if there are enough naive altruists around. Whereas Grudgers are *reciprocal* altruists who have a rational morality based on cooperative self-interest, Suckers, such as Socrates and Jesus, advocate "turning the other cheek and repaying evil with good."[11] Instead of a Rule of Reciprocity, "I'll scratch your back if you'll scratch mine," the extreme altruist substitutes the Golden Rule, "If you want the other fellow to scratch your back, you scratch his—even if he won't reciprocate."

The moral of the story is this: Altruist morality (so interpreted) is only rational given the payoff of eternal life (with a scorekeeper, as Woody Allen says). Take that away, and it looks like a Sucker system. What replaces the "Christian" vision of submission and saintliness is the reciprocal altruist with a tit-for-tat morality, someone who is willing to share with those willing to cooperate.

In a recent ground-breaking work, Elliott Sober and David Sloan Wilson illustrate this point about reciprocal altruism via the system of distributing socially beneficial rewards and punishments. They take the case of the hunter, who spends an enormous time hunting at great risk to himself, and distributes food to all of the group—hunters and nonhunters alike. This seemingly altruistic, group-enhancing behavior is rewarded by the group.

> It turns out that women think that good hunters are sexy and have more children with them, both in and out of marriage. Good hunters also enjoy a high status among men, which leads to additional benefits. Finally, individuals do not share meat the way Mr. Rogers and Barney, and Dinosaur would, out of the goodness of their heart. Refusing to share is a serious breach of etiquette that provokes punishment. In this way sharing merges with taking. These new discoveries make you feel better, because the apparently altruistic behavior of sharing meat that would have been difficult to explain now seems to fit comfortably within the framework of individual selection theory. [12]

So, whereas hunting might, at first sight, appear to be an example of pure altruism, the rule of reciprocity comes into play, rewarding the hunter for his sacrifice and contribution to the group. Sober and Wilson call activities like hunting, which increase the relative fitness of the hunter, primary behavior, and the rewards and punishment that others confer on the hunters, secondary behavior. "By itself, the primary behavior increases the fitness of the group and decreases the relative fitness of the hunters within the group. But the secondary behaviors off-set the sacrifice and promote altruistic behavior, so that they may be called the amplification of altruism."

This primitive notion of reciprocity seems to be necessary in a world like ours. One good deed deserves another (and *mutatis mutandis* with bad deeds). Reciprocity is the basis of desert—good deeds should be rewarded and bad deeds punished. We are grateful for favors rendered and thereby have an impulse to return the favor; we resent harmful deeds and seek to pay the culprit back in kind ("an eye for an eye, a tooth for a tooth, a life for a life"). To summarize, positive desert is gratitude universalized and punishment (negative desert) is resentment over harmful deeds universalized.

To be sure, there is a difference between high altruism and reciprocal altruism, which may simply be enlightened self-interest. The lesson to be drawn is that we should provide moral training so that children grow up to be spontaneously altruistic in a society that rewards such socially useful behavior. In this way what is legitimate about egoism can be merged with altruism in a manner that produces deep individual flourishing.

Mackie may caricature the position of the religious altruist, but he misses the subtleties of wisdom involved (Jesus said, "Be as wise as serpents but as harmless as doves"). Nevertheless, Mackie does remind us that there is a difference between core morality and complete altruism. We have duties to cooperate and reciprocate, but no duty to serve those who manipulate us nor an obvious duty to sacrifice ourselves for people outside our domain of special responsibility. We have a special duty of high altruism toward those in the close circle of our concern—namely, our family and friends—but we have a duty to expand the circle of our moral concerns, wider and wider, eventually reaching all humanity, and, possibly, the animal kingdom.

CONCLUSION

Martin Luther once said that humanity is like a man who, when mounting a horse, always falls off on the opposite side, especially when he tries to overcompensate for his previous exaggerations. So it is with ethical egoism. Trying to compensate for an irrational, guilt-ridden, Sucker altruism of the morality of self-effacement, one falls off the horse on the other side, embracing a Cheater's preoccupation with self-exaltation that robs the self of the deepest joys in life. Only the person who mounts properly, avoiding both extremes, is likely to ride the horse of happiness to its goal.

NOTES

1. Luke 14:26: "If any man come to me and hate not his father and his mother and his wife and children and brethren and sisters, yea and his own life also, he cannot be my disciple." Some interpretations of this difficult passage argue that Jesus is saying that *in comparison* to one's devotion to God, which should be absolute, other relationships should be quite secondary or nonabsolute.

2. Fyodor Dostoevsky, *The Brothers Karamazov*, trans. Andrew MacAndrews (Bantam Books, 1970), pp. 697, 703.

3. Friedrich Nietzsche, *Genealogy of Morals*, trans. Walter Kaufmann (Random House, 1966), p. 208. Some may accuse Nietzsche of "nihilism," of undermining ethics altogether, but I think that Nietzsche believed in an elitist morality in which the "superior" egoists cooperated with one another in their struggle against the herd, the mediocre masses of mankind.

4. Thomas Hobbes, *Leviathan*, Ch. 13.

5. Ayn Rand, *The Virtue of Selfishness* (New American Library, 1964), pp. vii and 27–32; 80ff.

6. See Gregory S. Kavka, *Hobbesian Moral and Political Theory* (Princeton University Press, 1986), pp. 64–82, where the "predominant" interpretation is set forth. I think Hobbes is unclear regarding the matter, but I am willing to call Kavka's position "revised Hobbesianism." It is a more charitable position.

7. See Jesse Kalin, "In Defense of Egoism," in *Ethical Theory*, 4th edition, ed. Louis Pojman (Wadsworth, 2002), p. 95–107.

8. Brian Medlin, "Ultimate Principles and Ethical Egoism," *Australasian Journal of Philosophy* (1957), pp. 111–118; reprinted in Louis Pojman, *Ethical Theory*, pp. 90–95.

9. Kalin, "In Defense of Egoism."

10. Richard Dawkins, *The Selfish Gene* (Oxford University Press, 1976), Ch. 10.

11. J. L. Mackie, "The Law of the Jungle: Moral Alternatives and Principles of Evolution," *Philosophy* 53 (1978).

12. Elliott Sober and David Sloan Wilson, *Unto Others: The Evolution and Psychology of Unselfish Behavior* (Harvard University Press, 1998), pp. 142–43.

For Further Reflection

1. Evaluate whether this statement, which I first encountered in a student paper, is true or false:

> "Everyone is an egoist, for everyone always tries to do what will bring them satisfaction."

2. Distinguish between individual and universal ethical egoism. Which theory appeals to you more? Does either constitute an adequate ethical theory? Explain your answer.

3. The introduction of this part of our book began with the story of the killing of Kitty Genovese. Review that story, and discuss how an ethical egoist would respond to the plight of Kitty Genovese. Would egoists admit that they had a duty to come to her aid?

4. Discuss the three arguments in favor of ethical egoism and the four against it. Which side has the best arguments? Why?

5. Does the egoist have a point in believing that most moral systems fail to recognize adequately that morality should be in our best interest? In this light, ethical egoism could be seen as an attempt to compensate for the inadequacies of other ethical views that emphasize doing duty for duty's sake or for the sake of others.

6. Some philosophers, beginning with Plato, have argued that ethical egoism is irrational, since it precludes psychological health. In an article entitled "Ethical Egoism and Psychological Dispositions" (*American Philosophical Quarterly* 17(1), 1980), Laurence Thomas sets forth the following argument:

P1. A true friend could never, as a matter of course, be disposed to harm or to exploit anyone with whom he is a friend [definition of a friend].

P2. An egoist could never be a true friend to anyone [for the egoist must be ready to exploit others whenever it is in his or her interest].

P3. Only someone with an unhealthy personality could never be a true friend to anyone [definition of a healthy personality; that is, friendship is a necessary condition for a healthy personality].

P4. Ethical egoism requires that we have a kind of disposition which is incompatible with our having a healthy personality [from P1–P3].

Conclusion: Therefore, from the standpoint of our psychological makeup, ethical egoism is unacceptable as a moral theory.

Do you agree with Thomas? How might the ethical egoist respond?

7. What is the relationship between ethics and evolution? How does this relationship throw light on egoism? What is the significance of reciprocity for ethics?

VI.C   *Which Is the Correct Ethical Theory?*

There are three major types of moral theories in Western philosophy:

1. *Virtue ethics,* which state that the emphasis in ethics should be put not on rules, but on character—on the virtues and vices people exhibit in their lives. Ethical goodness is primarily a state of being, and only secondarily a doing.

2. *Deontological ethics,* which views moral value as inherent in certain acts or types of acts (for example, "killing innocents is just wrong [period]."). The main form of deontological ethics holds that we ought to follow principles of action, for these principles of action have inherent value. In every moral act we are acting in accordance with an appropriate principle. A second type of deontological ethics (set forth by Bishop Joseph Butler [1692–1752]) holds that the criterion of right and wrong is the voice of conscience.

3. *Teleological ethics,* which assert that the rightness or wrongness of an act is determined by some nonmoral value. Teleological ethical systems can be subdivided into two major forms. *Ethical egoism* is the view that each person ought to do what will promote his or her own greatest good, and *utilitarianism* is the view that persons ought to do the act that will produce the greatest

total (or average) good (for example, "The greatest happiness for the greatest number"—Francis Hutcheson [1694–1746]).

Our first three readings in this section represent each of these three types of theories. We begin with Aristotle's virtue theory, one of the oldest accounts of ethics in the history of philosophy. Next we examine the most famous deontological theory, Kantian ethics, followed by a section from John Stuart Mill's classic *Utilitarianism*. These are followed by a type of ethics that defies systemization, yet is not in the virtue tradition, existentialist ethics, which leaves each decision to the individual in the moment. Jean-Paul Sartre's "Existentialist Ethics" represents this position.

IV.48   The Ethics of Virtue

ARISTOTLE

Aristotle (384–322 B.C.), Greek physician, Plato's prize pupil, tutor to Alexander the Great, and one of the most important philosophers who ever lived, wrote importantly on every major subject in philosophy: metaphysics, philosophy of science, philosophical psychology, aesthetics, ethics, and politics. He is the father of formal logic. Although deeply indebted to his teacher, Plato, Aristotle broke with him over the idea of Forms (Plato thought that the Forms had independent existence whereas Aristotle thought that they were in things). Aristotle tended to be more empirical than Plato. The break with the master led to the formation of the second major school of philosophy in Athens, Aristotle's Lyceum.

In this selection from the *Nicomachean Ethics*, Aristotle first discusses the nature of ethics and its relationship to human existence. He next turns to the nature of virtue, which he characterizes as traits that enable individuals to live well in communities. To achieve a state of well being (*eudaimonia*, happiness), proper social institutions are necessary. Thus the moral person cannot really exist apart from a flourishing political setting that enables the individual to develop the requisite virtues for the good life. For this reason Aristotle considers ethics to be a branch of politics.

After locating ethics as a part of politics, Aristotle explains that the moral virtues are different from the intellectual ones. Although the intellectual virtues can be taught directly, the moral ones must be lived in order to be learned. By living well, we acquire the right habits. These habits are in fact the virtues. The virtues are to be sought as the best guarantee to the happy life. But, again, happiness requires that one be lucky enough to live in a flourishing state. The morally virtuous life consists in living in moderation, according to the "Golden Mean."

Study Questions

1. How does Aristotle define politics and ethics? What is the relationship between them?
2. What is the good at which political science and ethics aim?
3. What are the characteristics of the good?
4. What is the function of human beings? How does Aristotle build his case for our having a function and how does this relate to ethics?
5. What is the relationship between habit and ethics? What does Aristotle mean by the statement, "A just man becomes just by doing what is just"? How can one do just things if one isn't already just? How does Aristotle solve this problem?
6. Does every action and emotion have a proper mean (Book II.6)?

BOOK I

All Human Activities Aim at Some Good

Chapter 1. EVERY ART AND EVERY scientific inquiry, and similarly every action and purpose, may be said to aim at some good. Hence the good has been well defined as that at which all things aim. But it is clear that there is a difference in ends; for the ends are sometimes activities, and sometimes results beyond the mere activities. Where there are ends beyond the action, the results are naturally superior to the action.

As there are various actions, arts, and sciences, it follows that the ends are also various. Thus health is the end of the medical art, a ship of shipbuilding, victory of strategy, and wealth of economics. It often happens that a number of such arts or sciences combine for a single enterprise, as the art of making bridles and all such other arts as furnish the implements of horsemanship combine for horsemanship, and horsemanship and every military action for strategy; and in the same way, other arts or sciences combine for others. In all these cases, the ends of the master arts or sciences, whatever they may be, are more desirable than those of the subordinate arts or sciences, as it is for the sake of the former that the latter are pursued. It makes no difference to the argument whether the activities themselves

are the ends of the action, or something beyond the activities, as in the above-mentioned sciences.

If it is true that in the sphere of action there is some end which we wish for its own sake, and for the sake of which we wish everything else, and if we do not desire everything for the sake of something else (for, if that is so, the process will go on *ad infinitum,* and our desire will be idle and futile), clearly this end will be good and the supreme good. Does it not follow then that the knowledge of this good is of great importance for the conduct of life? Like archers who have a mark at which to aim, shall we not have a better chance of attaining what we want? If this is so, we must endeavor to comprehend, at least in outline, what this good is, and what science or faculty makes it its object.

It would seem that this is the most authoritative science. Such a kind is evidently the political, for it is that which determines what sciences are necessary in states, and what kinds should be studied, and how far they should be studied by each class of inhabitant. We see too that even the faculties held in highest esteem, such as strategy, economics, and rhetoric, are subordinate to it. Then since politics makes use of the other sciences and also rules what people may do and what they may not do, it follows that its end will comprehend the ends of the other sciences, and will therefore be the good of

Reprinted from Aristotle's Nicomachean Ethics, *translated by James E. C. Weldon* (*Macmillan, 1897*).

mankind. For even if the good of an individual is identical with the good of a state, yet the good of the state is evidently greater and more perfect to attain or to preserve. For though the good of an individual by himself is something worth working for, to ensure the good of a nation or a state is nobler and more divine.

These then are the objects at which the present inquiry aims, and it is in a sense a political inquiry. . . .

The Science of the Good for Man Is Politics

Chapter 2. As every science and undertaking aims at some good, what is in our view the good at which political science aims, and what is the highest of all practical goods? As to its name there is, I may say, a general agreement. The masses and the cultured classes agree in calling it happiness, and conceive that "to live well" or "to do well" is the same thing as "to be happy." But as to what happiness is they do not agree, nor do the masses give the same account of it as the philosophers. The former take it to be something visible and palpable, such as pleasure, wealth, or honor; different people, however, give different definitions of it, and often even the same man gives different definitions at different times. When he is ill, it is health, when he is poor, it is wealth; if he is conscious of his own ignorance, he envies people who use grand language above his own comprehension. Some philosophers, on the other hand, have held that, besides these various goods, there is an absolute good which is the cause of goodness in them all.* It would perhaps be a waste of time to examine all these opinions; it will be enough to examine such as are most popular or as seem to be more or less reasonable.

Chapter 3. Men's conception of the good or of happiness may be read in the lives they lead. Ordinary or vulgar people conceive it to be a pleasure, and accordingly choose a life of enjoyment. For there are, we may say, three conspicuous types of life, the sensual, the political, and, thirdly, the life of thought. Now the mass of men present an absolutely slavish appearance, choosing the life of brute beasts, but they have ground for so doing because so many persons in authority share the tastes of Sardanapalus.† Cultivated and energetic people, on the other hand, identify happiness with honor, as honor is the general end of political life. But this seems too superficial an idea for our present purpose; for honor depends more upon the people who pay it than upon the person to whom it is paid, and the good we feel is something which is proper to a man himself and cannot be easily taken away from him. Men too appear to seek honor in order to be assured of their own goodness. Accordingly, they seek it at the hands of the sage and of those who know them well, and they seek it on the ground of their virtue; clearly then, in their judgment at any rate, virtue is better than honor. Perhaps then we might look on virtue rather than honor as the end of political life. Yet even this idea appears not quite complete; for a man may possess virtue and yet be asleep or inactive throughout life, and not only so, but he may experience the greatest calamities and misfortunes. Yet no one would call such a life a life of happiness, unless he were maintaining a paradox. But we need not dwell further on this subject, since it is sufficiently discussed in popular philosophical treatises. The third life is the life of thought, which we will discuss later.

The life of money making is a life of constraint; and wealth is obviously not the good of which we are in quest; for it is useful merely as a means to something else. It would be more reasonable to take the things mentioned before—sensual pleasure, honor, and virtue—as ends than wealth, since they are things desired on their own account. Yet these too are evidently not ends, although much argument has been employed to show that they are. . . .

* Plato

†A half-legendary ruler whose name to the Greeks stood for extreme mental luxury and extravagance.

Characteristics of the Good

Chapter 5. But leaving this subject for the present, let us revert to the good of which we are in quest and consider what it may be. For it seems different in different activities or arts; it is one thing in medicine, another in strategy, and so on. What is the good in each of these instances? It is presumably that for the sake of which all else is done. In medicine this is health, in strategy victory, in architecture a house, and so on. In every activity and undertaking it is the end, since it is for the sake of the end that all people do whatever else they do. If then there is an end for all our activity, this will be the good to be accomplished; and if there are several such ends, it will be these.

Our argument has arrived by a different path at the same point as before; but we must endeavor to make it still plainer. Since there are more ends than one, and some of these ends— for example, wealth, flutes, and instruments generally—we desire as means to something else, it is evident that not all are final ends. But the highest good is clearly something final. Hence if there is only one final end, this will be the object of which we are in search; and if there are more than one, it will be the most final. We call that which is sought after for its own sake more final than that which is sought after as a means to something else; we call that which is never desired as a means to something else more final than things that are desired both for themselves and as means to something else. Therefore, we call absolutely final that which is always desired for itself and never as a means to something else. Now happiness more than anything else answers to this description. For happiness we always desire for its own sake and never as a means to something else, whereas honor, pleasure, intelligence, and every virtue we desire partly for their own sakes (for we should desire them independently of what might result from them), but partly also as means to happiness, because we suppose they will prove instruments of happiness. Happiness, on the other hand, nobody de-sires for the sake of these things, nor indeed as a means to anything else at all.

If we start from the point of view of self-sufficiency, we reach the same conclusion; for we assume that the final good is self-sufficient. By self-sufficiency we do not mean that a person leads a solitary life all by himself, but that he has parents, children, wife and friends and fellow citizens in general, as man is naturally a social being. Yet here it is necessary to set some limit; for if the circle must be extended to include ancestors, descendants, and friends' friends, it will go on indefinitely. Leaving this point, however, for future investigation, we call the self-sufficient that which, taken even by itself, makes life desirable and wanting nothing at all; and this is what we mean by happiness.

Again, we think happiness the most desirable of all things, and that not merely as one good thing among others. If it were only that, the addition of the smallest more good would increase its desirableness; for the addition would make an increase of goods, and the greater of two goods is always the more desirable. Happiness is something final and self-sufficient and the end of all action.

Chapter 6. Perhaps, however, it seems a commonplace to say that happiness is the supreme good; what is wanted is to define its nature a little more clearly. The best way of arriving at such a definition will probably be to ascertain the function of man. For, as with a flute player, a sculptor, or any artist, or in fact anybody who has a special function or activity, his goodness and excellence seem to lie in his function, so it would seem to be with man, if indeed he has a special function. Can it be said that, while a carpenter and a cobbler have special functions and activities, man, unlike them, is naturally functionless? Or, as the eye, the hand, the foot, and similarly each part of the body has a special function, so may man be regarded as having a special function apart from all these? What, then, can this function be? It is not life; for life is apparently something that man shares with plants; and we are looking for something peculiar to him. We must exclude therefore the life of nutrition and growth. There is next what may be called the life of sensation. But this too, apparently, is shared by man with horses, cattle, and all other animals. There remains what I may call the active life of the rational part of man's being. Now this rational part is twofold; one part is rational in the sense of being obedient to reason, and the other in the sense of possessing and exercising reason and intelligence. The active life too may be conceived of in two ways, either as a state of character, or as an activity; but we mean by it the life of activity, as this seems to be the truer form of the conception.

The function of man then is activity of soul in accordance with reason, or not apart from reason. Now, the function of a man of a certain kind, and of a man who is good of that kind—for example, of a harpist and a good harpist—are in our view the same in kind. This is true of all people of all kinds without exception, the superior excellence being only an addition to the function; for it is the function of a harpist to play the harp, and of a good harpist to play the harp well. This being so, if we define the function of man as a kind of life, and this life as an activity of the soul or a course of action in accordance with reason, and if the function of a good man is such activity of a good and noble kind, and if everything is well done when it is done in accordance with its proper excellence, it follows that the good of man is activity of soul in accordance with virtue, or, if there are more virtues than one, in accordance with the best and most complete virtue. But we must add the words "in a complete life." For as one swallow or one day does not make a spring, so one day or a short time does not make a man blessed or happy. . . .

Inasmuch as happiness is an activity of soul in accordance with perfect virtue, we must now consider virtue, as this will perhaps be the best way of studying happiness. . . . Clearly it is human virtue we have to consider; for the good of which we are in search is, as we said, human

good, and the happiness, human happiness. By human virtue or excellence we mean not that of the body, but that of the soul, and by happiness we mean an activity of the soul. . . .

BOOK II

Moral virtues can best be acquired by practice and habit. They imply a right attitude toward pleasures and pains. A good man deliberately chooses to do what is noble and right for its own sake. What is right in matters of moral conduct is usually a mean between two extremes.

Chapter 1. Virtue then is twofold, partly intellectual and partly moral, and intellectual virtue is originated and fostered mainly by teaching; it demands therefore experience and time. Moral virtue on the other hand is the outcome of habit, and accordingly its name, *ethike,* is derived by a slight variation from *ethos,* habit. From this fact it is clear that moral virtue is not implanted in us by nature; for nothing that exists by nature can be transformed by habit. Thus a stone, that naturally tends to fall downwards, cannot be habituated or trained to rise upwards, even if we tried to train it by throwing it up ten thousand times. Nor again can fire be trained to sink downwards, nor anything else that follows one natural law be habituated or trained to follow another. It is neither by nature then nor in defiance of nature that virtues grow in us. Nature gives us the capacity to receive them, and that capacity is perfected by habit.

Again, if we take the various natural powers which belong to us, we first possess the proper faculties and afterwards display the activities. It is obviously so with the senses. Not by seeing frequently or hearing frequently do we acquire the sense of seeing or hearing; on the contrary, because we have the senses we make use of them; we do not get them by making use of them. But the virtues we get by first practicing them, as we do in the arts. For it is by doing what we ought to do when we study the arts that we learn the arts themselves; we become builders by building and harpists by playing the harp. Similarly, it is by doing just acts that we become just, by doing temperate acts that we become temperate, by doing brave acts that we become brave. The experience of states confirms this statement, for it is by training in good habits that lawmakers make the citizens good. This is the object all lawmakers have at heart; if they do not succeed in it, they fail of their purpose; and it makes the distinction between a good constitution and a bad one.

Again, the causes and means by which any virtue is produced and destroyed are the same; and equally so in any part. For it is by playing the harp that both good and bad harpists are produced; and the case of builders and others is similar, for it is by building well that they become good builders and by building badly that they become bad builders. If it were not so, there would be no need of anybody to teach them; they would all be born good or bad in their several crafts. The case of the virtues is the same. It is by our actions in dealings between man and man that we become either just or unjust. It is by our actions in the face of danger and by our training ourselves to fear or to courage that we become either cowardly or courageous. It is much the same with our appetites and angry passions. People become temperate and gentle, others licentious and passionate, by behaving in one or the other way in particular circumstances. In a word, moral states are the results of activities like the states themselves. It is our duty therefore to keep a certain character in our activities, since our moral states depend on the differences in our activities. So the difference between one and another training in habits in our childhood is not a light matter, but important, or rather, all-important.

Chapter 2. Our present study is not, like other studies, purely theoretical in intention; for the object of our inquiry is not to know what virtue is but how to become good, and that is the sole benefit of it. We must, therefore, consider the right way of performing actions, for it is acts, as we have said, that determine the character of the resulting moral states.

That we should act in accordance with right reason is a common general principle, which may here be taken for granted. The nature of right reason, and its relation to the virtues generally, will be discussed later. But first of all it must be admitted that all reasoning on matters of conduct must be like a sketch in outline; it cannot be scientifically exact. We began by laying down the principle that the kind of reasoning demanded in any subject must be such as the subject matter itself allows; and questions of conduct and expediency no more admit of hard and fast rules than questions of health.

If this is true of general reasoning on ethics, still more true is it that scientific exactitude is impossible in treating of particular ethical cases. They do not fall under any art or law, but the actors themselves have always to take account of circumstances, as much as in medicine or navigation. Still, although such is the nature of our present argument, we must try to make the best of it.

The first point to be observed is that in the matters we are now considering, deficiency and excess are both fatal. It is so, we see, in questions of health and strength. (We must judge of what we cannot see by the evidence of what we do see.) Too much or too little gymnastic exercise is fatal to strength. Similarly, too much or too little meat and drink is fatal to health, whereas a suitable amount produces, increases, and sustains it. It is the same with temperance, courage, and other moral virtues. A person who avoids and is afraid of everything and faces nothing becomes a coward; a person who is not afraid of anything but is ready to face everything becomes foolhardy. Similarly, he who enjoys every pleasure and abstains from none is licentious; he who refuses all pleasures, like a boor, is an insensible sort of person. For temperance and courage are destroyed by excess and deficiency but preserved by the mean.

Again, not only are the causes and agencies of production, increase, and destruction in moral states the same, but the field of their activity is the same also. It is so in other more obvious instances, as, for example, strength; for strength is produced by taking a great deal of food and undergoing a great deal of exertion, and it is the strong man who is able to take most food and undergo most exertion. So too with the virtues. By abstaining from pleasures we become temperate, and, when we have become temperate, we are best able to abstain from them. So again with courage; it is by training ourselves to despise and face terrifying things that we become brave, and when we have become brave, we shall be best able to face them.

The pleasure or pain which accompanies actions may be regarded as a test of a person's moral state. He who abstains from physical pleasures and feels pleasure in so doing is temperate; but he who feels pain at so doing is licentious. He who faces dangers with pleasure, or at least without pain, is brave; but he who feels pain at facing them is a coward. For moral virtue is concerned with pleasures and pains. It is pleasure which makes us do what is base, and pain which makes us abstain from doing what is noble. Hence the importance of having a certain training from very early days, as Plato says, so that we may feel pleasure and pain at the right objects; for this is true education. . . .

Chapter 3. But we may be asked what we mean by saying that people must become just by doing what is just and temperate by doing what is temperate. For, it will be said, if they do what is just and temperate they are already just and temperate themselves, in the same way as, if they practice grammar and music, they are grammarians and musicians.

But is this true even in the case of the arts? For a person may speak grammatically either by chance or at the suggestion of somebody else; hence he will not be a grammarian unless he not only speaks grammatically but does so in a grammatical manner, that is, because of the grammatical knowledge which he possesses.

There is a point of difference too between the arts and the virtues. The productions of art have their excellence in themselves. It is enough then that, when they are produced, they themselves should possess a certain character. But acts in accordance with virtue are not justly or temperately performed simply because they are in themselves just or temperate. The doer at the time of performing them must satisfy certain conditions; in the first place, he must know what he is doing; secondly, he must deliberately choose to do it and do it for his own sake; and thirdly, he must do it as part of his own firm and immutable character. If it be a question of art, these conditions, except only the condition of knowledge, are not raised; but if it be a question of virtue, mere knowledge is of little or no avail; it is the other conditions, which are the results of frequently performing just and temperate acts, that are not slightly but all-important. Accordingly, deeds are called just and temperate when they are such as a just and temperate person would do; and a just and temperate person is not merely one who does these deeds but one who does them in the spirit of the just and the temperate.

It may fairly be said that a just man becomes just by doing what is just, and a temperate man becomes temperate by doing what is temperate, and if a man did not so act, he would not have much chance of becoming good. But most people, instead of acting, take refuge in theorizing; they imagine that they are philosophers and that philosophy will make them virtuous; in fact, they behave like people who listen attentively to their doctors but never do anything that their doctors tell them. But a healthy state of the soul will no more be produced by this kind of philosophizing than a healthy state of the body by this kind of medical treatment.

Chapter 4. We have next to consider the nature of virtue. Now, as the properties of the soul are three, namely, emotions, faculties, and moral states, it follows that virtue must be one of the three. By emotions I mean desire, anger, fear, pride, envy, joy, love, hatred, regret, ambition, pity—in a word, whatever feeling is attended by pleasure or pain. I call those faculties through which we are said to be capable of experiencing these emotions, for instance, capable of getting angry or being pained or feeling pity. And I call those moral states through which we are well or ill disposed in our emotions, ill disposed, for instance, in anger, if our anger be too violent or too feeble, and well disposed, if it be rightly moderate; and similarly in our other emotions.

Now neither the virtues nor the vices are emotions; for we are not called good or bad for our emotions but for our virtues or vices. We are not praised or blamed simply for being angry, but only for being angry in a certain way; but we are praised or blamed for our virtues or vices. Again, whereas we are angry or afraid without deliberate purpose, the virtues are matters of deliberate purpose, or require deliberate purpose. Moreover, we are said to be moved by our emotions, but by our virtues or vices we are not said to be moved but to have a certain disposition.

For these reasons the virtues are not faculties. For we are not called either good or bad, nor are we praised or blamed for having simple capacity for emotion. Also while Nature gives us our faculties, it is not Nature that makes us good or bad; but this point we have already discussed. If then the virtues are neither emotions nor faculties, all that remains is that they must be moral states.

Chapter 5. The nature of virtue has been now described in kind. But it is not enough to say merely that virtue is a moral state; we must also describe the character of that moral state.

We may assert then that every virtue or excellence puts into good condition that of which it is a virtue or excellence, and enables it to perform its work well. Thus excellence in the eye makes the eye good and its function good, for by excellence in the eye we see well. Similarly, excellence of the horse makes a horse excellent himself and good at racing, at carrying its rider and at facing the enemy. If then this rule is universally true, the virtue or excellence of a man will be such a moral state as makes a man good and able to perform his proper function well. How this will be the case we have already explained, but another way of making it clear will be to study the nature or character of virtue.

Now of everything, whether it be continuous or divisible, it is possible to take a greater, a smaller, or an equal amount, and this either in terms of the thing itself or in relation to ourselves, the equal being a mean between too much and too little. By the mean in terms of the thing itself, I understand that which is equally distinct from both its extremes, which is one and the same for every man. By the mean relatively to ourselves, I understand that which is neither too much nor too little for us; but this is not one nor the same for everybody. Thus if 10 be too much and 2 too little, we take 6 as a mean in terms of the thing itself; for 6 is as much greater than 2 as it is less than 10, and this is a mean in arithmetical proportion. But the mean considered relatively to ourselves may not be ascertained in that way. It does not follow that if 10 pounds of meat is too much and 2 too little for a man to eat, the trainer will order him 6 pounds, since this also may be too much or too little for him who is to take it; it will be too little, for example, for Milo but too much for a beginner in gymnastics. The same with running and wrestling; the right amount will vary with the individual. This being so, the skillful in any art avoids alike excess and deficiency; he seeks and chooses the mean, not the absolute mean, but the mean considered relatively to himself.

Every art then does its work well, if it regards the mean and judges the works it produces by the mean. For this reason we often say of successful works of art that it is impossible to take anything from them or to add anything to them, which implies that excess or deficiency is fatal to excellence but that the mean state ensures it. Good artists too, as we say, have an eye to the mean in their works. Now virtue, like Nature herself, is more accurate and better than any art; virtue, therefore, will aim at the mean. I speak of moral virtue, since it is moral virtue which is concerned with emotions and actions, and it is in these we have excess and deficiency and the mean. Thus it is possible to go too far, or not far enough in fear, pride, desire, anger, pity, and pleasure and pain generally, and the excess and the deficiency are alike wrong; but to feel these emotions at the right times, for the right objects, towards the right persons, for the right motives, and in the right manner, is the mean or the best good, which signifies virtue. Similarly, there may be excess, deficiency, or the mean, in acts. Virtue is concerned with both emotions and actions, wherein excess is an error and deficiency a fault, while the mean is successful and praised, and success and praise are both characteristics of virtue.

It appears then that virtue is a kind of mean because it aims at the mean.

On the other hand, there are many different ways of going wrong; for evil is in its nature infinite, to use the Pythagorean phrase, but good is finite and there is only one possible way of going right. So the former is easy and the latter is difficult; it is easy to miss the mark but difficult to hit it. And so by our reasoning excess and deficiency are characteristics of vice and the mean is a characteristic of virtue.

"For good is simple, evil manifold."

Chapter 6. Virtue then is a state of deliberate moral purpose, consisting in a mean relative to ourselves, the mean being determined by reason, or as a prudent man would determine it. It is a mean, firstly, as lying between two vices, the vice of excess on the one hand, the vice of deficiency on the other, and, secondly, because, whereas the vices either fall short of or go beyond what is right in emotion and action, virtue discovers and chooses the mean. Accordingly, virtue, if regarded in its essence or theoretical definition, is a mean, though, if regarded from the point of view of what is best and most excellent, it is an extreme.

But not every action or every emotion admits of a mean. There are some whose very name implies wickedness, as, for example, malice, shamelessness, and envy among the emotions, and

adultery, theft, and murder among the actions. All these and others like them are marked as intrinsically wicked, not merely the excesses or deficiencies of them. It is never possible then to be right in them; they are always sinful. Right or wrong in such acts as adultery does not depend on our committing it with the right woman, at the right time, or in the right manner; on the contrary, it is wrong to do it at all. It would be equally false to suppose that there can be a mean or an excess or deficiency in unjust, cowardly or licentious conduct; for, if that were so, it would be a mean of excess and deficiency, an excess of excess and a deficiency of deficiency. But as in temperance and courage there can be no excess or deficiency, because the mean there is in a sense an extreme, so too in these other cases there cannot be a mean or an excess or a deficiency, but however the acts are done, they are wrong. For in general an excess or deficiency does not have a mean, nor a mean an excess or deficiency. . . .

Chapter 8. There are then three dispositions, two being vices, namely, excess and deficiency, and one virtue, which is the mean between them; and they are all in a sense mutually opposed. The extremes are opposed both to the mean and to each other, and the mean is opposed to the extremes. For as the equal if compared with the less is greater, but if compared with the greater is less, so the mean state, whether in emotion or action, if compared with deficiency is excessive, but if compared with excess is deficient. Thus the brave man appears foolhardy compared with the coward, but cowardly compared with the foolhardy. Similarly, the temperate man appears licentious compared with the insensible man but insensible compared with the licentious; and the liberal man appears extravagant compared with the stingy man but stingy compared with the spendthrift. The result is that the extremes each denounce the mean as belonging to the other extreme; the coward calls the brave man foolhardy, and the foolhardy man calls him cowardly; and so on in other cases.

But while there is mutual opposition between the extremes and the mean, there is greater opposition between the two extremes than between extreme and the mean; for they are further removed from each other than from the mean, as the great is further from the small and the small from the great than either from the equal. Again, while some extremes show some likeness to the mean, as foolhardiness to courage and extravagance to liberality, there is the greatest possible dissimilarity between extremes. But things furthest removed from each other are called opposites; hence the further things are removed, the greater is the opposition between them.

In some cases it is deficiency and in others excess which is more opposed to the mean. Thus it is not foolhardiness, an excess, but cowardice, a deficiency, which is more opposed to courage, nor is it insensibility, a deficiency, but licentiousness, an excess, which is more opposed to temperance. There are two reasons why this should be so. One lies in the nature of the matter itself; for when one of two extremes is nearer and more like the mean, it is not this extreme but its opposite that we chiefly contrast with the mean. For instance, as foolhardiness seems more like and nearer to courage than cowardice, it is cowardice that we chiefly contrast with courage; for things further removed from the mean seem to be more opposite to it. This reason lies in the nature of the matter itself; there is a second which lies in our own nature. The things to which we ourselves are naturally more inclined we think more opposed to the mean. Thus we are ourselves naturally more inclined to pleasures than to their opposites, and are more prone therefore to self-indulgence than to moderation. Accordingly we speak of those things in which we are more likely to run to great lengths as more opposed to the mean. Hence licentiousness, which is an excess, seems more opposed to temperance than insensibility.

Chapter 9. We have now sufficiently shown that moral virtue is a mean, and in what sense it is so; that it is a mean as lying between two vices, a vice of excess on the one side and a vice of deficiency on the other, and as aiming at the mean in emotion and action.

That is why it is so hard to be good; for it is always hard to find the mean in anything; it is not everyone but only a man of science who can find the mean or center of a circle. So too anybody can get angry—that is easy—and anybody can give or spend money, but to give it to the right person, to give the right amount of it, at the right time, for the right cause and in the right way, this is not what anybody can do, nor is it easy. That is why goodness is rare and praise worthy and noble. One then who aims at a mean must begin by departing from the extreme that is more contrary to the mean; he must act in the spirit of Calypso's advice,

"Far from this spray and swell hold thou thy ship,"

for of the two extremes one is more wrong than the other. As it is difficult to hit the mean exactly, we should take the second best course, as the saying is, and choose the lesser of two evils. This we shall best do in the way described, that is, steering clear of the evil which is further from the mean. We must also note the weaknesses to which we are ourselves particularly prone, since different natures tend in different ways; and we may ascertain what our tendency is by observing our feelings of pleasure and pain. Then we must drag ourselves away towards the opposite extreme; for by pulling ourselves as far as possible from what is wrong we shall arrive at the mean, as we do when we pull a crooked stick straight.

In all cases we must especially be on our guard against the pleasant, or pleasure, for we are not impartial judges of pleasure. Hence our attitude towards pleasure must be like that of the elders of the people in the *Iliad* towards Helen, and we must constantly apply the words they use; for if we dismiss pleasure as they dismissed Helen, we shall be less likely to go wrong. By action of this kind, to put it summarily, we shall best succeed in hitting the mean.

Undoubtedly this is a difficult task, especially in individual cases. It is not easy to determine the right manner, objects, occasion and duration of anger. Sometimes we praise people who are deficient in anger, and call them gentle, and at other times we praise people who exhibit a fierce temper as high spirited. It is not however a man who deviates a little from goodness, but one who deviates a great deal, whether on the side of excess or of deficiency, that is blamed; for he is sure to call attention to himself. It is not easy to decide in theory how far and to what extent a man may go before he becomes blameworthy, but neither is it easy to define in theory anything else in the region of the senses; such things depend on circumstances, and our judgment of them depends on our perception.

So much then is plain, that the mean is everywhere praiseworthy, but that we ought to aim at one time towards an excess and at another towards a deficiency; for thus we shall most easily hit the mean, or in other words reach excellence.

For Further Reflection

1. Is Aristotle's concept of happiness clear? Is it a subjective or objective notion? That is, is it subjective, in the mind of the beholder, so one is just as happy as one feels oneself to be; or is it objective, defined by a state of being, and having certain characteristics regardless of how one feels? According to Aristotle, could a criminal be happy?

2. Is Aristotle's ethics sufficiently action guiding? Does it help us make decisions? If I ask what should I do in situation *X*, Aristotle would seem to say, "Do what the virtuous person would do." But if I ask how I am to recognize the virtuous person, he would seem to say, "He is one who acts justly." Is there something circular about this reasoning? Does virtue ethics need supplementation from other ethical systems or can it solve this problem?

VI.49   The Moral Law

IMMANUEL KANT

Immanuel Kant (1724–1804) was born into a deeply pietistic Lutheran family in Königsberg, Germany, lived in that town his entire life, and taught at the University of Königsberg. He lived a duty-bound, methodical life, so regular that citizens were said to have set their clocks by his walks. Kant is one of the premier philosophers in the Western tradition. In his monumental work *The Critique of Pure Reason* (1781) he inaugurated a Copernican-like revolution in the theory of knowledge.

Our reading is from Kant's classic work *The Foundations of the Metaphysic of Morals,* written in 1785, in which he outlines his ethical system. Kant rejects those ethical theories, such as the theory of moral sentiments set forth by the Scottish moralists Francis Hutcheson (1694) and David Hume (1711–1776), in which morality is contingent and hypothetical. The moral sentiment view is contingent in that it is based on human nature and, in particular, on our feelings or sentiments. Had we been created differently, we would have a different nature and, hence, different moral duties. Moral duties or imperatives are hypothetical in that they depend on our desires for their realization. For example, we should obey the law because we want a peaceful, orderly society.

Kant rejects this naturalistic account of ethics. Ethics is not contingent but absolute, he argues, and its duties or imperatives are not hypothetical but categorical (nonconditional). Ethics is based not on feeling but on reason. Because we are rational beings we are valuable and capable of discovering moral laws binding on all persons at all times. As such, our moral duties are not dependent on feelings but on reason. They are unconditional, universally valid, and necessary, regardless of the possible consequences or opposition to our inclinations.

Kant's first formulation of his *categorical imperative* is, "Act only on that maxim whereby thou canst at the same time will that it would become a universal law." This imperative is given as the criterion (or second-order principle) by which to judge all other principles. If we could consistently will that everyone would do some type of action, then there is an application of the categorical imperative enjoining that type of action. If we cannot consistently will that everyone would do some type of action, then that type of action is morally wrong. Kant argues, for example, that we cannot consistently will that everyone make lying promises, for the very institution of promising entails or depends on general adherence to keeping the promise or having an intention to do so.

Kant offers a second formulation of the categorical imperative: "So act as to treat humanity, whether in your own person or in that of any other, in every case as an end and never as merely a means only." Each person by virtue of his or her reason has dignity and profound worth, which entails that he or she must never be exploited or manipulated or merely used as a means to our idea of what is for the general good. Kant thought that this formulation was substantively identical with the first, but his view is controversial.

Study Questions

1. What is the aim of Kant's work? Why does he want to reject empirical (for example, sociological and anthropological) data in constructing a "pure moral philosophy"?
2. What is the only quality which is good without qualification? Analyze Kant's reasoning here. Is it cogent?
3. Why does Kant deprecate the role of reason in producing happiness? Is his view of the purposive function of a faculty (for example, our rational capacity, our will) in line with standard evolutionary theory?
4. What is the relationship between duty and inclination? Do acts done out of good inclination have any moral worth?
5. What is the role of consequences in moral reasoning? According to Kant, should we ask ourselves what are the likely consequences before we decide what to do?
6. What is the categorical imperative?
7. What is the difference between a maxim and a principle of universal law?
8. How does Kant illustrate the moral law? Do you see any problems with his examples? Is it clear that none of them could be universalized?
9. What is Kant's second formulation of the moral law? Is it equivalent, as Kant thought, to the first formulation?

PREFACE

AS MY CONCERN HERE is with moral philosophy, I limit the question suggested to this: Whether it is not of the utmost necessity to construct a pure moral philosophy, perfectly cleared of everything which is only empirical, and which belongs to anthropology? for that such a philosophy must be possible is evident from the common idea of duty and of the moral laws. Everyone must admit that if a law is to have moral force, i.e. to be the basis of an obligation, it must carry with it absolute necessity; that, for example, the precept, "Thou shall not lie," is not valid for men alone, as if other rational beings had no need to observe it; and so with all the other moral laws properly so called; that, therefore, the basis of obligation must not be sought in the nature of man, or in the circumstances in the world in which he is placed, but *a priori* simply in the conception of pure reason; and although any other precept which is founded on principles of mere experience may be in certain respects universal, yet in as far as it rests even in the least degree on an empirical basis, perhaps only as to a motive, such a precept, while it may be a practical rule, can never be called a moral law. . . .

THE GOOD WILL

Nothing can possibly be conceived in the world, or even out of it, which can be called good, without qualification, except a Good Will. Intelligence, wit, judgment, and the other *talents* of the mind, however they may be named, or courage, resolution, perseverance, as qualities of temperament, are undoubtedly good and desirable in many respects; but these gifts of nature may also become extremely bad and mischievous if the will which is to make use of them, and which, therefore, constitutes what is called *character,* is not good. It is the same with the *gifts of fortune.* Power, riches, honour, even health, and the general well-being and contentment with one's conditions which is called *happiness,* inspire pride, and often presumption, if there is not a good will to correct the influence of these on the mind, and with this also to rectify the whole principle of acting, and adapt it to its end. The sight of a being who is not adorned with a single feature of a pure and good will, enjoying unbroken prosperity, can never give pleasure to an imperial rational spectator. Thus a good will appears to constitute the indispensable condition even of being worthy of happiness.

There are even some qualities which are of service to this good will itself, and may facilitate its action, yet which have no intrinsic unconditional value, but always presuppose a good will, and this qualifies the esteem that we justly have for them, and does not permit us to regard them as absolutely good. Moderation in the affections and passions, self-control, and calm deliberation are not only good in many respects, but even seem to constitute part of the intrinsic worth of the person; but they are far from deserving to be called good without qualification, although they have been so unconditionally praised by the ancients. For without the principles of a good will, they may become extremely bad; and the coolness of a villain not only makes him far more dangerous, but also directly makes him more abominable in our eyes than he would have been without it.

A good will is good not because of what it performs or effects, not by its aptness for the attainment of some proposed end, but simply by virtue of the volition, that is, it is good in itself, and considered by itself to be esteemed much higher than all that can be brought about by it in favour of any inclination, nay, even of the sum-total of all inclinations. Even if it should happen that, owing to special disfavour of fortune, or the niggardly provision of a step-motherly nature, this will should wholly lack

Reprinted from The Foundations of the Metaphysic of Morals, *translated by T. K. Abbott (this translation first published in 1873).*

power to accomplish its purpose, if with its greatest efforts it should yet achieve nothing, and there should remain only the good will (not, to be sure, a mere wish, but the summoning of all means in our power), then, like a jewel, it would still shine by its own light, as a thing which has its whole value in itself. Its usefulness or fruitlessness can neither add to nor take away anything from this value. It would be, as it were, only the setting to enable us to handle it the more conveniently in common commerce, or to attract to it the attention of those who are not yet connoisseurs, but not to recommend it to true connoisseurs, or to determine its value.

WHY REASON WAS MADE TO GUIDE THE WILL

There is, however, something so strange in this idea of the absolute value of the mere will, in which no account is taken of its utility, that notwithstanding the thorough assent of even common reason to the idea, yet a suspicion must arise that it may perhaps really be the product of mere high-blown fancy, and that we may have misunderstood the purpose of nature in assigning reason as the governor of our will. Therefore we will examine this idea from this point of view.

In the physical constitution of an organized being, that is, a being adapted suitably to the purposes of life, we assume it as a fundamental principle that no organ for any purpose will be found but what is also the fittest and best adapted for that purpose. Now in a being which has reason and a will, if the proper object of nature were its *conservatism*, its *welfare*, in a word, its *happiness*, then nature would have hit upon a very bad arrangement in selecting the reason of the creature to carry out this purpose. For all the actions which the creature has to perform with a view to this purpose, and the whole rule of its conduct, would be far more surely pre-scribed to it by instinct, and that end would have been attained thereby much more certainly than it ever can be by reason. Should reason

have been communicated to this favoured crea-ture over and above, it must only have served it to contemplate the happy constitution of its na-ture, to admire it, to congratulate itself thereon, and to feel thankful for it to the beneficent cause, but not that it should subject its desires to that weak and delusive guidance, and meddle bunglingly with the purpose of nature. In a word, nature would have taken care that reason should not break forth into *practical exercise*, nor have the presumption, with its weak insight, to think out for itself the plan of happiness, and of the means of attaining it. Nature would not only have taken on herself the choice of the ends, but also of the means, and with wise fore-sight would have entrusted both to instinct.

And, in fact, we find that the more a culti-vated reason applies itself with deliberate pur-pose to the enjoyment of life and happiness, so much the more does the man fail of true satis-faction. And from this circumstance there arises in many, if they are candid enough to confess it, a certain degree of *misology*, that is, hatred of reason, especially in the case of those who are most experienced in the use of it, because after calculating all the advantages they derive, I do not say from the invention of all the arts of common luxury, but even from the sciences (which seem to them to be after all only a lux-ury of the understanding), they find that they have, in fact, only brought more trouble on their shoulders, rather than gained in happi-ness; and they end by envying, rather than de-spising, the more common stamp of men who keep closer to the guidance of mere instinct, and do not allow their reason much influence on their conduct. And this we must admit, that the judgment of those who would very much lower the lofty eulogies of the advantages which reason gives us in regard to the happi-ness and satisfaction of life, or who would even reduce them below zero, is by no means mo-rose or ungrateful to the goodness with which the world is governed, but that there lies at the root of these judgments the idea that our exis-tence has a different and far nobler end, for which, and not for happiness, reason is properly intended, and which must, therefore, be regarded as the supreme condition to which the private ends of man must, for the most part, be postponed.

For as reason is not competent to guide the will with certainty in regard to its objects and the satisfaction of all our wants (which it to some extent even multiplies), this being an end to which an implanted instinct would have led with much greater certainty; and since, nevertheless, reason is imparted to us as a practical faculty, i.e. as one which is to have influence on the *will*, therefore, admitting that nature generally in the distribution of her capacities has adapted the means to the end, its true destination must be to produce a *will*, not merely good as a *means* to something else, but *good in itself*, for which reason was absolutely necessary. This will then, though not indeed the sole and complete good, must be the supreme good and the condition of every other, even of the desire of happiness. Under these circumstances, there is nothing inconsistent with the wisdom of nature in the fact that the cultivation of the reason, which is requisite for the first and unconditional purpose, does in many ways interfere, at least in this life, with the attainment of the second, which is always conditional, namely, happiness. Nay, it may even reduce it to nothing, without nature thereby failing in her purpose. For reason recognizes the establishment of a good will as its highest practical destination, and in attaining this purpose is capable only of a satisfaction of its own proper kind, namely, that from the attainment of an end, which end again is determined by reason only, notwithstanding that this may involve many a disappointment to the ends of inclination.

THE FIRST PROPOSITION OF MORALITY

[An action must be done from a sense of duty, if it is to have moral worth]

We have then to develop the notion of a will which deserves to be highly esteemed for itself, and is good without a view to anything further, a notion which exists already in the sound natural understanding, requiring rather to be cleared up than to be taught, and which in estimating the value of our actions always takes the first place, and constitutes the condition of all the rest. In order to do this, we will take the notion of duty, which includes that of a good will, although implying certain subjective restrictions and hindrances. These, however, far from concealing it, or rendering it unrecognizable, rather bring it out by contrast, and make it shine forth so much the brighter.

I omit here all actions which are already recognized as inconsistent with duty although they may be useful for this or that purpose, for with these the question whether they are done *from duty* cannot arise at all, since they even conflict with it. I also set aside those actions which really conform to duty, but to which men have *no direct inclination*, performing them because they are impelled thereto by some other inclination. For in this case we can readily distinguish whether the action which agrees with duty is done *from duty*, or from a selfish view. It is much harder to make this distinction when the action accords with duty, and the subject has besides a *direct* inclination to it. For example, it is always a matter of duty that a dealer should not overcharge an inexperienced purchaser; and wherever there is much commerce the prudent tradesman does not overcharge, but keeps a fixed price for everyone, so that a child buys of him as well as any other. Men are thus *honestly* served; but this is not enough to make us believe that the tradesman has so acted from duty and from principles of honesty: his own advantage required it; it is out of the question in this case to suppose that he might besides have a direct inclination in favour of the buyers, so that, as it were, from love he should give no advantage to one over another. Accordingly the action was done neither from duty nor from direct inclination, but merely with a selfish view.

On the other hand, it is a duty to maintain one's life; and, in addition, everyone has also a direct inclination to do so. But on this account the often anxious care which most men take for it has no intrinsic worth, and their maxim has no moral import. They preserve their life *as duty requires,* no doubt, but not *because duty requires.* On the other hand, if adversity and hopeless sorrow have completely taken away the relish for life; if the unfortunate one, strong in mind, indignant at his fate rather than desponding or dejected, wishes for death, and yet preserves his life without loving it—not from inclination or fear, but from duty—then his maxim has a moral worth.

To be beneficent when we can is a duty; and besides this, there are many minds so sympathetically constituted that, without any other motive of vanity or self-interest, they find a pleasure in spreading joy around them, and can take delight in the satisfaction of others so far as it is their own work. But I maintain that in such a case an action of this kind, however proper, however amiable it may be, has nevertheless no true moral worth, but is on a level with other inclinations, e.g. the inclination to honour, which, if it is happily directed to that which is in fact of public utility and accordant with duty, and consequently honourable, deserves praise and encouragement, but not esteem. For the maxim lacks the moral import, namely, that such actions be done *from duty,* not from inclination. Put the case that the mind of that philanthropist was clouded by sorrow of his own, extinguishing all sympathy with the lot of others, and that while he still has the power to benefit others in distress, he is not touched by their trouble because he is absorbed with his own; and now suppose that he tears himself out of this dead insensibility, and performs the action without any inclination to it, but simply from duty, then first has his action its genuine moral worth. Further still; if nature has put little sympathy in the heart of this or that man; if he, supposed to be an upright man, is by temperament cold and indifferent to the sufferings of others, perhaps because in respect of his own he is provided with the special gift of patience and fortitude, and supposes, or even requires, that others should have the same—and such a man would certainly not be the meanest product of nature—but if nature had not specially framed him for a philanthropist, would he not still find in himself a source from whence to give himself a far higher worth than that of a good-natured temperament could be? Unquestionably. It is just in this that the moral worth of the character is brought out which is incomparably the highest of all, namely, that he is beneficent, not from inclination, but from duty.

To secure one's own happiness is a duty, at least indirectly; for discontent with one's condition, under a pressure of many anxieties and amidst unsatisfied wants, might easily become a great *temptation to transgression of duty.* But here again, without looking to duty, all men have already the strongest and most intimate inclination to happiness, because it is just in this idea that all inclinations are combined in one total. But the precept of happiness is often of such a sort that it greatly interferes with some inclinations, and yet a man cannot form any definite and certain conception of the sum of satisfaction of all of them which is called happiness. It is not then to be wondered at that a single inclination, definite both as to what it promises and as to the time within which it can be gratified, is often able to overcome such a fluctuating idea, and that a gouty patient, for instance, can choose to enjoy what he likes, and to suffer what he may, since, according to his calculation, on this occasion at least, he has [only] not sacrificed the enjoyment of the present moment to a possibly mistaken expectation of a happiness which is supposed to be found in health. But even in this case, if the general desire for happiness did not influence his will, and supposing that in his particular case health was not a necessary element in this calculation, there yet remains in this, as in all other cases, this law, namely, that he should promote his happiness not from inclination but from duty, and by this would his conduct first acquire true moral worth.

It is in this manner, undoubtedly, that we are to understand those passages of Scripture also in which we are commanded to love our neighbour, even our enemy. For love, as an affection, cannot be commanded, but beneficence for duty's sake may; even though we are not impelled to it by any inclination—nay, are even repelled by a natural and unconquerable aversion. This is *practical* love, and not *pathological**—a love which is seated in the will, and not in the propensions of sense—in principles of action and not of tender sympathy; and it is this love alone which can be commanded.

THE SECOND PROPOSITION OF MORALITY

The second proposition is: That an action done from duty derives its moral worth, *not from the purpose* which is to be attained by it, but from the maxim by which it is determined, and therefore does not depend on the realization of the object of the action, but merely on the *principle of volition* by which the action has taken place, without regard to any object of desire. It is clear from what precedes that the purposes which we may have in view in our actions, or their effects regarded as ends and springs of the will, cannot give to actions any unconditional or moral worth. In what, then, can their worth lie, if it is not to consist in the will and in reference to its expected effect? It cannot lie anywhere but in the *principle of the will* without regard to the ends which can be attained by the action. For the will stands between its *a priori principle*, which is formal, and its *a posteriori* spring, which is material, as between two roads, and as it must be determined by something, it follows that it must be determined by the formal principle of volition when an action is done from duty, in which case every material principle has been withdrawn from it.

*passional or emotional

THE THIRD PROPOSITION OF MORALITY

The third proposition, which is a consequence of the two preceding, I would express thus: *Duty is the necessity of acting from respect for the law.* I may have *inclination* for an object as the effect of my proposed action, but I cannot have *respect* for it, just for this reason, that it is an effect and not an energy of will. Similarly, I cannot have respect for inclination, whether my own or another's; I can at most, if my own, approve it; if another's, sometimes even love it; i.e. look on it as favourable to my own interest. It is only what is connected with my will as a principle, by no means as an effect—what does not subserve my inclination, but overpowers it, or at least in case of choice excludes it from its calculation—in other words, simply the law of itself, which can be an object of respect, and hence a command. Now an action done from duty must wholly exclude the influence of inclination, and with it every object of the will, so that nothing remains which can determine the will except objectively the *law*, and subjectively *pure respect* for this practical law, and consequently the maxim that I should follow this law even to the thwarting of all my inclinations. Thus the moral worth of an action does not lie in the effect expected from it, nor in any principle of action which requires to borrow its motive from this expected effect. For all these effects—agreeableness of one's condition, and even the promotion of the happiness of others—could have been also brought about by other causes, so that for this there would have been no need of the will of a rational being; whereas it is in this alone that the supreme and unconditional good can be found. The pre-eminent good which we call moral can therefore consist in nothing else than *the conception of law* in itself, *which certainly is only possible in a rational being*, in so far as this conception, and not the expected effect, determines the will. This is a good which is already present in the person who acts accordingly, and we have not to wait for it to appear first in the result.

THE SUPREME PRINCIPLE OF MORALITY: THE CATEGORICAL IMPERATIVE

But what sort of law can that be, the conception of which must determine the will, even without paying any regard to the effect expected from it, in order that this will may be called good absolutely and without qualification? As I have deprived the will of every impulse which could arise to it from obedience to any law, there remains nothing but the universal conformity of its actions to law in general, which alone is to serve the will as a principle, i.e. I am never to act otherwise than so *that I could also will that my maxim should become a universal law*. Here, now, it is the simple conformity to law in general, without assuming any particular law applicable to certain actions, that serves the will as its principle, and must so serve it, if duty is not to be a vain delusion and a chimerical notion. The common reason of men in its practical judgments perfectly coincides with this, and always has in view the principle here suggested. Let the question be, for example: May I when in distress make a promise with the intention not to keep it? I readily distinguish here between the two significations which the question may have: Whether it is prudent, or whether it is right, to make a false promise? The former may undoubtedly often be the case. I see clearly indeed that it is not enough to extricate myself from a present difficulty by means of this subterfuge, but it must be well considered whether there may not hereafter spring from this lie much greater inconvenience than that from which I now free myself, and as, with all my supposed *cunning*, the consequences cannot be so easily foreseen but that credit once lost may be much more injurious to me than any mischief which I seek to avoid at present, it should be considered whether it would not be more *prudent* to act herein according to a universal maxim, and to make it a habit to promise nothing except with the intention of keeping it. But it is soon clear to me that such a maxim will still only be based on the fear of consequences. Now it is a wholly different thing to be truthful from duty, and to be so from apprehension of injurious consequences. In the first case, the very notion of the action already implies a law for me; in the second case, I must first look about elsewhere to see what results may be combined with it which would affect myself. For to deviate from the principle of duty is beyond all doubt wicked; but to be unfaithful to my maxim of prudence may often be very advantageous to me, although to abide by it is certainly safer. The shortest way, however, and an unerring one, to discover the answer to this question whether a lying promise is consistent with duty, is to ask myself, Should I be content that my maxim (to extricate myself from difficulty by a false promise) should hold good as a universal law, for myself as well as for others? and should I be able to say to myself, "Every one may make a deceitful promise when he finds himself in a difficulty from which he cannot otherwise extricate himself"? Then I presently become aware that while I can will the lie, I can by no means will that lying should be a universal law. For with such a law there would be no promises at all, since it would be in vain to allege my intention in regard to my future actions to those who would not believe this allegation, or if they over-hastily did so, would pay me back in my own coin. Hence my maxim, as soon as it should be made a universal law, would necessarily destroy itself.

I do not, therefore, need any far-reaching penetration to discern what I have to do in order that my will may be morally good. Inexperienced in the course of the world, incapable of being prepared for all its contingencies, I only ask myself: Canst thou also will that thy maxim should be a universal law? If not, then it must be rejected, and that not because of a disadvantage accruing from myself or even to others, but because it cannot enter as a principle into a possible universal legislation, and reason extorts from me immediate respect for such legislation. I do not indeed as yet *discern* on what this respect is based (this the philosopher may inquire), but at least I understand this, that it is an estimation of the worth which far outweighs all worth of what is recommended by inclination, and that the necessity of acting from *pure* respect for the practical law is what constitutes duty, to which every other motive must give place, because it is the condition of a will being good *in itself,* and the worth of such a will is above everything.

Thus, then, without quitting the moral knowledge of common human reason, we have arrived at its principle. And although, no doubt, common men do not conceive it in such an abstract and universal form, yet they always have it really before their eyes, and use it as the standard of their decision. . . .

Nor could anything be more fatal to morality than that we should wish to derive it from examples. For every example of it that is set before me must be first itself tested by principles of morality, whether it is worthy to serve as an original example, i.e. as a pattern, but by no means can it authoritatively furnish the conception of morality. Even the Holy One of the Gospels must first be compared with our ideal of moral perfection before we can recognize Him as such; and so He says of Himself, "Why call ye Me [whom you see] good; none is good [the model of good] but God only [whom ye do not see]." But whence have we the conception of God as the supreme good? Simply from the *idea* of moral perfection, which reason frames *a priori,* and connects inseparably with the notion of a free will. Imitation finds no place at all in morality, and examples serve only for encouragement, i.e. they put beyond doubt the feasibility of what the law commands, they make visible that which the practical rule expresses more generally, but they can never authorize us to set aside the true original which lies in reason, and to guide ourselves by examples.

From what has been said, it is clear that all moral conceptions have their seat and origin completely *a priori* in the reason, and that, moreover, in the commonest reason just as truly as in that which is in the highest degree speculative; that they cannot be obtained by abstraction from

any empirical, and therefore merely contingent knowledge; that it is just this purity of their origin that makes them worthy to serve as our supreme practical principle, and that just in proportion as we add anything empirical, we detract from their genuine influence, and from the absolute value of actions; that it is not only of the greatest necessity, in a purely speculative point of view, but is also of the greatest practical importance, to derive these notions and laws from pure reason, to present them pure and unmixed, and even to determine the compass of this practical or pure rational knowledge, i.e. to determine the whole faculty of pure practical reason; and, in doing so, we must not make its principles dependent on the particular nature of human reason, though in speculative philosophy this may be permitted, or may even at times be necessary; but since moral laws ought to hold good for every rational creature, we must derive them from the general concept of a rational being. In this way, although for its *application* to man morality has need of anthropology, yet, in the first instance, we must treat it independently as pure philosophy, i.e. as metaphysic, complete in itself (a thing which in such distinct branches of science is easily done); knowing well that unless we are in possession of this, it would not only be vain to determine the moral element of duty in right actions for purposes of speculative criticism, but it would be impossible to base morals on their genuine principles, even for common practical purposes, especially of moral instruction, so as to produce pure moral dispositions, and to engraft them on men's minds to the promotion of the greatest possible good in the world. . . .

THE RATIONAL GROUND OF THE CATEGORICAL IMPERATIVE

. . . the question, how the imperative of *morality* is possible, is undoubtedly one, the only one, demanding a solution, as this is not at all hypothetical, and the objective necessity which it presents cannot rest on any hypothesis, as is the case with the hypothetical imperatives. Only here we must never leave out of consideration that we *cannot* make out *by any example,* in other words empirically, whether there is such an imperative at all; but it is rather to be feared that all those which seem to be categorical may yet be at bottom hypothetical. For instance, when the precept is: Thou shalt not promise deceitfully; and it is assumed that the necessity of this is not a mere counsel to avoid some other evil, so that it should mean: Thou shalt not make a lying promise, lest if it become known thou shouldst destroy thy credit, but that an action of this kind must be regarded as evil in itself, so that the imperative of the prohibition is categorical; then we cannot show with certainty in any example that the will was determined merely by the law, without any other spring of action, although it may appear to be so. For it is always possible that fear of disgrace, perhaps also obscure dread of other dangers, may have a secret influence on the will. Who can prove by experience the nonexistence of a cause when all that experience tells us is that we do not perceive it? But in such a case the so-called moral imperative, which as such appears to be categorical and unconditional, would in reality be only a pragmatic precept, drawing our attention to our own interests, and merely teaching us to take these into consideration.

We shall therefore have to investigate *a priori* the possibility of a categorical imperative, as we have not in this case the advantage of its reality being given in experience, so that [the elucidation of] its possibility should be requisite only for its explanation, not for its establishment. In the meantime it may be discerned beforehand that the categorical imperative alone has the purport of a practical law: all the rest may indeed be called *principles* of the will but not laws, since whatever is only necessary for the attainment of some arbitrary purpose may be considered as in itself contingent, and we can at any time be free from the precept if we give up the purpose: on the contrary, the unconditional command leaves

the will no liberty to choose the opposite; consequently it alone carries with it that necessity which we require in a law.

Secondly, in the case of this categorical imperative or law of morality, the difficulty (of discerning its possibility) is a very profound one. It is an *a priori* synthetical practical proposition; and as there is so much difficulty in discerning the possibility of speculative propositions of this kind, it may readily be supposed that the difficulty will be no less with the practical.

FIRST FORMULATION OF THE CATEGORICAL IMPERATIVE: UNIVERSAL LAW

In this problem we will first inquire whether the mere conception of a categorical imperative may not perhaps supply us also with the formula of it, containing the proposition which alone can be a categorical imperative; for even if we know the tenor of such an absolute command, yet how it is possible will require further special and laborious study, which we postpone to the last section. When I conceive a hypothetical imperative, in general I do not know beforehand what it will contain until I am given the condition. But when I conceive a categorical imperative, I know at once what it contains. For as the imperative contains besides the law only the necessity that the maxims shall conform to this law, while the law contain no conditions restricting it, there remains nothing but the general statement that the maxim of the action should conform to a universal law, and it is this conformity alone that the imperative properly represents as necessary.

There is therefore but one categorical imperative, namely, this: *Act only on that maxim whereby thou canst at the same time will that it should become a universal law.*

Now if all imperatives of duty can be deduced from this one imperative as from their principle, then, although it should remain undecided whether what is called duty is not merely a vain notion, yet at least we shall be able to show what we understand by it and what this notion means.

Since the universality of the law according to which effects are produced constitutes what is properly called *nature* in the most general sense (as to form), that is the existence of things so far as it is determined by general laws, the imperative of duty may be expressed thus: *Act as if the maxim of thy action were to become by thy will a universal law of nature.*

FOUR ILLUSTRATIONS

We will now enumerate a few duties, adopting the usual division of them into duties to ourselves and to others, and into perfect and imperfect duties.

1. A man reduced to despair by a series of misfortunes feels wearied of life, but is still so far in possession of his reason that he can ask himself whether it would not be contrary to his duty to himself to take his own life. Now he inquires whether the maxim of his action could become a universal law of nature. His maxim is: From self-love I adopt it as a principle to shorten my life when its longer duration is likely to bring more evil than satisfaction. It is asked then simply whether this principle founded on self-love can become a universal law of nature. Now we see at once that a system of nature of which it should be a law to destroy life by means of the very feeling whose special nature it is to impel to the improvement of life would contradict itself, and therefore could not exist as a system of nature; hence that maxim cannot possibly exist as a universal law of nature, and consequently would be wholly inconsistent with the supreme principle of all duty.

2. Another finds himself forced by necessity to borrow money. He knows that he will not be able to repay it, but sees also that nothing will be lent to him, unless he promises stoutly to repay it in a definite time. He desires to make this promise, but he has still so much con-science as to ask himself: Is it not unlawful and inconsistent with duty to get out of a difficulty in this way? Suppose, however, that he resolves to do so, then the maxim of his action would be expressed thus: When I think myself in want of money, I will borrow money and promise to repay it, although I know that I never can do so. Now this principle of self-love or of one's own advantage may perhaps be consistent with my whole future welfare; but the question is, Is it right? I change then the suggestion of self-love into a universal law, and state the question thus: How would it be if my maxim were a universal law? Then I see at once that it could never hold as a universal law of nature, but would necessarily contradict itself. For supposing it to be a universal law that everyone when he thinks himself in a difficulty should be able to promise whatever he pleases, with the purpose of not keeping his promise, the promise itself would become impossible, as well as the end that one might have in view in it, since no one would consider that anything was promised to him, but would ridicule all such statements as vain pretenses.

3. A third finds in himself a talent which with the help of some culture might make him a useful man in many respects. But he finds himself in comfortable circumstances, and prefers to indulge in pleasure rather than to take pains in enlarging and improving his happy natural capacities. He asks, however, whether his maxim of neglect of his natural gifts, besides agreeing with his inclination to indulgence, agrees also with what is called duty. He sees then that a system of nature could indeed subsist with such a universal law although men (like the South Sea islanders) should let their talents rest, and resolve to devote their lives merely to idleness, amusement, and propagation of their species—in a word, to enjoyment; but he cannot possibly *will* that this should be a universal law of nature, or be implanted in us as such by a natural instinct. For, as a rational being, he necessarily wills that his faculties be developed, since they serve him, and have been given him, for all sorts of possible purposes.

4. A fourth, who is in prosperity, while he sees that others have to contend with great wretchedness and that he could help them, thinks: What concern is it of mine? Let everyone be as happy as Heaven pleases, or as he can make himself; I will take nothing from him nor even envy him, only I do not wish to contribute anything to his welfare or to his assistance in distress! Now no doubt if such a mode of thinking were a universal law, the human race might very well subsist, and doubtless even better than in a state in which everyone talks of sympathy and good-will, or even takes care occasionally to put it into practice, but, on the other side, also cheats when he can, betrays the rights of men, or otherwise violates them. But although it is possible that a universal law of nature might exist in accordance with that maxim, it is impossible to *will* that such a principle should have the universal validity of a law of nature. For a will which resolved this would contradict itself, inasmuch as many cases might occur in which one would have need of the love and sympathy of others, and in which, by such a law of nature, sprung from his own will, he would deprive himself of all hope of the aid he desires.

These are a few of the many actual duties, or at least what we regard as such, which obviously fall into two classes on the one principle that we have laid down. We must be *able to will* that a maxim of our action should be a universal law. This is the canon of the moral appreciation of the action generally. Some actions are of such a character that their maxim cannot without contradiction be even *conceived* as a universal law of nature, far from it being possible that we should *will* that it *should* be so. In others this intrinsic impossibility is not found, but still it is impossible to *will* that their maxim should be raised to the universality of a law of nature, since such a will would contradict itself. It is easily seen that the former violate strict or rigorous (inflexible) duty; the latter only laxer (meritorious) duty. Thus it has been completely shown by these examples how all duties depend as regards the na-

ture of the obligation (not the object of the action) on the same principle.

SECOND FORMULATION OF THE CATEGORICAL IMPERATIVE: HUMANITY AS AN END IN ITSELF

. . . Now I say: man and generally any rational being *exists* as an end in himself, *not merely as a means* to be arbitrarily used by this or that will, but in all his actions, whether they concern himself or other rational beings, must be always regarded at the same time as an end. All objects of the inclinations have only a conditional worth; for if the inclinations and the wants founded on them did not exist, then their object would be without value. But the inclinations themselves being sources of want are so far from having an absolute worth for which they should be desired, that, on the contrary, it must be the universal wish of every rational being to be wholly free from them. Thus the worth of any object which is *to be acquired* by our action is always conditional. Beings whose existence depends not on our will but on nature's, have nevertheless, if they are nonrational beings, only a relative value as means, and are therefore called *things;* rational beings, on the contrary, are called *persons,* because their very nature points them out as ends in themselves, that is as something which must not be used merely as means, and so far therefore restricts freedom of action (and is an object of respect). These, therefore, are not merely subjective ends whose existence has a worth *for us* as an effect of our action, but *objective ends,* that is things whose existence is an end in itself: an end moreover for which no other can be substituted, which they should subserve *merely* as means, for otherwise nothing whatever would possess *absolute worth;* but if all worth were conditioned and therefore contingent, then there would be no supreme practical principle of reason whatever.

If then there is a supreme practical principle or, in respect of the human will, a categorical imperative, it must be one which, being drawn from the conception of that which is necessarily an end for everyone because it is *an end in itself*, constitutes an *objective* principle of will, and can therefore serve as a universal practical law. The foundation of this principle is: *rational nature exists as an end in itself.* Man necessarily conceives his own existence as being so: so far then this is a *subjective* principle of human actions. But every other rational being regards its existence similarly, just on the same rational principle that holds for me: so that it is at the same time an objective principle, from which as a supreme practical law all laws of the will must be capable of being deduced. Accordingly the practical imperative will be as follows: *So act as to treat humanity, whether in thine own person or in that of any other, in every case as an end withal, never as means only.* . . .

. . . Looking back now on all previous attempts to discover the principle of morality, we need not wonder why they all failed. It was seen that man was bound to laws by duty, but it was not observed that the laws to which he is subject are *only those of his own giving*, though at the same time they are *universal*, and that he is only bound to act in conformity with his own will; a will, however, which is designed by nature to give universal laws. For when one has conceived man only as subject to a law (no matter what), then this law required some interest, either by way of attraction or constraint, since it did not originate as a law from *his own* will, but his will was according to a law obliged by *something else* to act in a certain manner. Now by this necessary consequence all the labour spent in finding a supreme principle of *duty* was irrevocably lost. For men never elicited duty, but only a necessity of acting from a certain interest.

Whether this interest was private or otherwise, in any case the imperative must be conditional, and could not by any means be capable of being a moral command. I will therefore call this the principle of *Autonomy* of the will, in contrast with every other which I accordingly reckon as *Heteronomy.*

THE KINGDOM OF ENDS

The conception of every rational being as one which must consider itself as giving in all the maxims of its will universal laws, so as to judge itself and its actions from this point of view—this conception leads to another which depends on it and is very fruitful, that of a *kingdom of ends.*

By a *kingdom* I understand the union of different rational beings in a system by common laws. Now since it is by laws that ends are determined as regards their universal validity, hence, if we abstract from the personal differences of rational beings, and likewise from all the content of their private ends, we shall be able to conceive all ends combined in a systematic whole (including both rational beings as ends in themselves, and also the special ends which each may propose to himself), that is to say, we can conceive a kingdom of ends, which on the preceding principles is possible.

For all rational beings come under the *law* that each of them must treat itself and all others *never merely as means*, but in every case *at the same time as ends in themselves.* Hence results a systematic union of rational beings by common objective laws, i.e., a kingdom which may be called a kingdom of ends, since what these laws have in view is just the relation of these beings to one another as ends and means. . . .

For Further Reflection

1. Is Kant's philosophy merely a development of the Golden Rule: "Do unto others what you would have them do unto you"? If it is equivalent, does it make Kant's system more intuitively plausible? But does it also lead to problems with what Kant thought to be the implications of his system? For example, on the basis of the Golden Rule one might endorse certain instances of euthanasia, but Kant's discussion of suicide seems to rule this out.

2. Kant's ethics are called deontological (from the Greek word for "duty") because he believes that the value of an act is in the act itself rather than in its consequences (as teleologists hold). Deontological ethics have been criticized as being too rigid. Do you think that this is true? Should the notion of consequences be taken into consideration?

3. How would Kant deal with moral conflicts? When two universal principles conflict, how would Kant resolve the dilemma?

4. Kant's categorical imperative has also been criticized for being more wide open than he realized, for it doesn't limit what could be universalized. How would Kant respond to these counter-examples: (1) Everyone should tie his right shoe before his left shoe; (2) All retarded or senile people should be executed by the government (adding, if I should become retarded or senile, I should also undergo this fate).

Utilitarianism   VI.50

JOHN STUART MILL

John Stuart Mill (1806–1873), one of the most important British philosophers of the nineteenth century, was born in London and educated by his father, learning Greek at the age of three and Latin at the age of eight. By the time he was fourteen he had received a thorough classical education at home. He began work as a clerk for the East India Company at the age of seventeen and eventually became director of the company. He was elected to Parliament in 1865. A man of liberal ideas and a penetrating mind, he made significant contributions to logic, philosophy of science, philosophy of religion, political theory, and ethics. His principal works are *A System of Logic* (1843), *Utilitarianism* (1863), *On Liberty* (1859), and *The Subjection of Women* (1869).

Mill defends utilitarianism, a form of teleological ethics, against more rule-bound deontological systems, the sort of system we considered in the last selection, Kant's categorical imperative. *Teleological* is from the Greek "telos," which means "end" or "goal." That is, the standard of right or wrong action for the teleologists is the comparative consequences of the available actions. That act is right that produces the best consequences. Whereas the deontologist is concerned only with the rightness of the act itself, the teleologist asserts that there is no such thing as an act having intrinsic worth. Although there is something intrinsically bad about lying for the deontologist, the only thing wrong with lying for the teleologist is the bad consequences it produces. If you can reasonably calculate that a lie will do even slightly more good than telling the truth, you have an obligation to lie.

The present selection was written against the background of a debate over Jeremy Bentham's hedonistic version of utilitarianism, which failed to differentiate between kinds and qualities of pleasure, and so received the name of "pig philosophy." Mill meets this charge by substituting a more complex theory of happiness for Bentham's undifferentiated pleasure.

Study Questions

1. How does Mill define utilitarianism?
2. How does Mill reply to the charge that utilitarianism is a pig philosophy?
3. What test is there to distinguish the higher pleasures from the lower?
4. What is meant by "Better to be Socrates dissatisfied than a pig satisfied"?
5. Why do some people prefer the lower pleasures?
6. How can utilitarianism attain its end?
7. Why do some critics say that utilitarianism sets too high a standard for humanity?
8. What is Mill's "proof" of the truth of utilitarianism? Is it a clear and cogent argument?

WHAT UTILITARIANISM IS

... THE CREED WHICH ACCEPTS as the foundation of morals, Utility, or the Greatest Happiness Principle, holds that actions are right in proportion as they tend to promote happiness, wrong as they tend to produce the reverse of happiness. By happiness is intended pleasure, and the absence of pain; by unhappiness, pain, and the privation of pleasure. To give a clear view of the moral standard set up by the theory, much more requires to be said; in particular, what things it includes in the ideas of pain and pleasure; and to what extent this is left an open question. But these supplementary explanations do not affect the theory of life on which this theory of morality is grounded—namely, that pleasure, and freedom from pain, are the only things desirable as ends; and that all desirable things (which are as numerous in the utilitarian as in any other scheme) are desirable either for the pleasure inherent in themselves, or as a means to the promotion of pleasure and the prevention of pain.

Now, such a theory of life excites in many minds, and among them in some of the most estimable in feeling and purpose, inveterate dislike. To suppose that life has (as they express it) no higher end than pleasure—no better and nobler object of desire and pursuit—they designate as utterly mean and grovelling; as a doctrine worthy only of swine, to whom the followers of Epicurus were, at a very early period, contemptuously likened; and modern holders of the doctrine are occasionally made the subject of equally polite comparisons by its German, French, and English assailants.

When thus attacked, the Epicureans have always answered, that it is not they, but their accusers, who represent human nature in a degrading light; since the accusation supposes human beings to be capable of no pleasures except those of which swine are capable. If this supposition were true, the charge could not be gainsaid, but would then be no longer an imputation; for if the sources of pleasure were precisely the same to human beings and to swine, the rule of life which is good enough for the one would be good

From John Stuart Mill, Utilitarianism *(1861), Chapters 2 and 4.*

enough for the other. The comparison of the Epicurean life to that of beasts is felt as degrading, precisely because a beast's pleasures do not satisfy a human being's conception of happiness. Human beings have faculties more elevated than the animal appetites, and when once made conscious of them, do not regard anything as happiness which does not include their gratification. I do not, indeed, consider the Epicureans to have been by any means faultless in drawing out their scheme of consequences from the utilitarian principle. To do this in any sufficient manner, many Stoic, as well as Christian elements require to be included. But there is no known Epicurean theory of life which does not assign to the pleasures of the intellect, of the feelings and imagination, and of the moral sentiments, a much higher value as pleasures than to those of mere sensation. It must be admitted, however, that utilitarian writers in general have placed the superiority of mental over bodily pleasures chiefly in the greater permanency, safety, uncostliness, etc., of the former—that is, in their circumstantial advantages rather than in their intrinsic nature. And on all these points utilitarians have fully proved their case; but they might have taken the other, and, as it may be called, higher ground, with entire consistency. It is quite compatible with the principle of utility to recognise the fact, that some *kinds* of pleasure are more desirable and more valuable than others. It would be absurd that while, in estimating all other things, quality is considered as well as quantity, the estimation of pleasures should be supposed to depend on quantity alone.

If I am asked, what I mean by difference of quality in pleasures, or what makes one pleasure more valuable than another, merely as a pleasure, except its being greater in amount, there is but one possible answer. Of two pleasures, if there be one which all or almost all who have experience of both give a decided preference, irrespective of any feeling of moral obligation to prefer it, that is the more desirable pleasure. If one of the two is, by those who are competently acquainted with both, placed so far above the other that they prefer it, even though knowing it to be attended with a great amount of discontent, and would not resign it for any quantity of the other pleasure which their nature is capable of, we are justified in ascribing to the preferred enjoyment a superiority in quality, so far outweighing quantity as to render it, in comparison, of small account.

Now it is an unquestionable fact that those who are equally acquainted with, and equally capable of appreciating and enjoying, both, do give a most marked preference to the manner of existence which employs their higher faculties. Few human creatures would consent to be changed into any of the lower animals, for a promise of the fullest allowance of a beast's pleasures; no intelligent human being would consent to be a fool, no instructed person would be an ignoramus, no person of feeling and conscience would be selfish and base, even though they should be persuaded that the fool, the dunce, or the rascal is better satisfied with his lot than they are with theirs. They would not resign what they possess more than he for the most complete satisfaction of all the desires which they have in common with him. If they ever fancy they would, it is only in cases of unhappiness so extreme, that to escape from it they would exchange their lot for almost any other, however undesirable in their own eyes. A being of higher faculties requires more to make him happy, is capable probably of more acute suffering, and certainly accessible to it at more points, than one of an inferior type; but in spite of these liabilities, he can never really wish to sink into what he feels to be a lower grade of existence. We may give what explanation we please of this unwillingness; we may attribute it to pride, a name which is given indiscriminately to some of the most and to some of the least estimable feelings of which mankind are capable; we may refer it to the love of liberty and personal independence, an appeal to which was with the Stoics one of the most effective means for the inculcation of it; to the love of power, or to the love of excitement, both of which do really enter into and contribute to it: but its most appropriate appellation is a sense of dignity, which all human beings possess in one form or another, and in some, though by no means in exact, proportion to their higher faculties, and which is so essential a part of the happiness of those in whom it is strong, that nothing which conflicts with it could be, otherwise than momentarily, an object of desire to them. Whoever supposes that this preference takes place at a sacrifice of happiness—that the superior being, in anything like equal circumstances, is not happier than the inferior—confounds the two very different ideas, of happiness, and content. It is indisputable that the being whose capacities of enjoyment are low, has the greatest chance of having them fully satisfied; and a highly endowed being will always feel that any happiness which he can look for, as the world is constituted, is imperfect. But he can learn to bear its imperfections, if they are at all bearable; and they will not make him envy the being who is indeed unconscious of the imperfections, but only because he feels not at all the good which those imperfections qualify. It is better to be a human being dissatisfied than a pig satisfied; better to be Socrates dissatisfied than a fool satisfied. And if the fool, or the pig, are of a different opinion, it is because they only know their own side of the question. The other party to the comparison knows both sides.

It may be objected, that many who are capable of the higher pleasures, occasionally, under the influence of temptation, postpone them to the lower. But this is quite compatible with a full appreciation of the intrinsic superiority of the higher. Men often, from infirmity of character, make their election for the nearer good, though they know it to be the less valuable; and this no less when the choice is between two bodily pleasures, than when it is between bodily and mental. They pursue sensual indulgences to the injury of health, though perfectly aware that health is the greater good. It may be further objected, that many who begin with youthful enthusiasm for everything noble, as they advance in years sink into indolence and selfishness. But I do not believe that those who undergo this very common change, voluntarily choose the lower description of pleasures in preference to the higher. I believe that before they devote themselves exclusively to the one, they have already become incapable of the other. Capacity for the nobler feelings is in most natures a very tender plant, easily killed, not only by hostile influences, but by mere want of sustenance; and in the majority of young persons it speedily dies away if the occupations to which their position in life has devoted them, and the society into which it has thrown them, are not favourable to keeping that higher capacity in exercise. Men lose their high aspirations as they lose their intellectual tastes, because they have not time or opportunity for indulging them; and they addict themselves to inferior pleasures, not because they deliberately prefer them, but because they are either the only ones to which they have access, or the only ones which they are any longer capable of enjoying. It may be questioned whether any one who has remained equally susceptible to both classes of pleasures, ever knowingly and calmly preferred the lower; though many, in all ages, have broken down in an ineffectual attempt to combine both.

From this verdict of the only competent judges, I apprehend there can be no appeal. On a question which is the best worth having of two pleasures, or which of two modes of existence is the most grateful to the feelings, apart from its moral attributes and from its consequences, the judgment of those who are qualified by knowledge of both, or, if they differ, that of the majority among them, must be admitted as final. And there needs to be the less hesitation to accept this judgment respecting the quality of pleasures, since there is no other tribunal to be referred to even on the question of quantity. What means are there of determining which is the acutest of two pains, or the intensest of two pleasurable sensations, except the general suffrage of those who are familiar with both? Neither pains nor pleasures are homogeneous, and pain is always heterogeneous with pleasure.

What is there to decide whether a particular pleasure is worth purchasing at the cost of a particular pain, except the feelings and judgment of the experienced? When, therefore, those feelings and judgment declare the pleasures derived from the higher faculties to be preferable *in kind,* apart from the question of intensity, to those of which the animal nature, disjoined from the higher faculties, is susceptible, they are entitled on this subject to the same regard.

I have dwelt on this point, as being a necessary part of a perfectly just conception of Utility or Happiness, considered as the directive rule of human conduct. But it is by no means an indispensable condition to the acceptance of the utilitarian standard; for that standard is not the agent's own greatest happiness, but the greatest amount of happiness altogether; and if it may possibly be doubted whether a noble character is always the happier for its nobleness, there can be no doubt that it makes other people happier, and that the world in general is immensely a gainer by it. Utilitarianism, therefore, could only attain its end by the general cultivation of nobleness of character, even if each individual were only benefited by the nobleness of others, and his own, so far as happiness is concerned, were a sheer deduction from the benefit. But the bare enunciation of such an absurdity as this last, renders refutation superfluous.

According to the Greatest Happiness Principle, as above explained, the ultimate end, with reference to and for the sake of which all other things are desirable (whether we are considering our own good or that of other people), is an existence exempt as far as possible from pain, and as rich as possible in enjoyments, both in point of quantity and quality; the test of quality, and the rule for measuring it against quantity, being the preference felt by those who in their opportunities of experience, to which must be added their habits of self-consciousness and self-observation, are best furnished with the means of comparison. This, being, according to the utilitarian opinion, the end of human action, is necessarily also the standard of morality; which may

accordingly be defined, the rules and precepts for human conduct, by the observance of which an existence such as has been described might be, to the greatest extent possible, secured to all mankind; and not to them only, but, so far as the nature of things admits, to the whole sentient creation. . . .

The objectors to utilitarianism cannot always be charged with representing it in a discreditable light. On the contrary, those among them who entertain anything like a just idea of its disinterested character, sometimes find fault with its standard as being too high for humanity. They say it is exacting too much to require that people shall always act from the inducement of promoting the general interests of society. But this is to mistake the very meaning of a standard of morals, and confound the rule of action with the motive of it. It is the business of ethics to tell us what are our duties, or by what test we may know them; but no system of ethics requires that the sole motive of all we do shall be a feeling of duty; on the contrary, ninety-nine hundredths of all our actions are done from other motives, and rightly so done, if the rule of duty does not condemn them. It is the more unjust to utilitarianism that this particular misapprehension should be made a ground of objection to it, inasmuch as utilitarian moralists have gone beyond almost all others in affirming that the motive has nothing to do with the morality of the action, though much with the worth of the agent. He who saves a fellow-creature from drowning does what is morally right, whether his motive be duty, or the hope of being paid for his trouble; he who betrays the friend that trusts him, is guilty of a crime, even if his object be to serve another friend to whom he is under greater obligation. But to speak only of actions done from the motive of duty, and in direct obedience to principle: it is a misapprehension of the utilitarian mode of thought, to conceive it as implying that people should fix their minds upon so wide a generality as the world, or society at large. The great majority of good actions are intended not for the benefit of the world, but for that of individuals, of which the good of the world is made up; and the thoughts of the most virtuous man need not on these occasions travel beyond the particular persons concerned, except so far as is necessary to assure himself that in benefiting them he is not violating the rights, that is, the legitimate and authorised expectations, of any one else. The multiplication of happiness is, according to the utilitarian ethics, the object of virtue: the occasions on which any person (except one in a thousand) has it in his power to do this on an extended scale, in other words to be a public benefactor, are but exceptional; and on these occasions alone is he called on to consider public utility; in every other case, private utility, the interest or happiness of some few persons, is all he has to attend to. Those alone the influence of whose actions extends to society in general, need concern themselves habitually about so large an object. In the case of abstinences indeed—of things which people forbear to do from moral considerations, though the consequences in the particular case might be beneficial—it would be unworthy of an intelligent agent not to be consciously aware that the action is of a class which, if practised generally, would be generally injurious, and that this is the ground of the obligation to abstain from it. The amount of regard for the public interest implied in this recognition, is no greater than is demanded by every system of morals, for they all enjoin to abstain from whatever is manifestly pernicious to society. . . .

CHAPTER IV OF WHAT SORT OF PROOF THE PRINCIPLE OF UTILITY IS SUSCEPTIBLE

It has already been remarked, that questions of ultimate ends do not admit of proof, in the ordinary acceptation of the term. To be incapable of proof by reasoning is common to all first principles; to the first premises of our knowledge, as well as to those of our conduct. But the former, being matters of fact, may be the subject of a direct appeal to the faculties which judge of fact—namely, our senses, and our internal consciousness. Can an appeal be made to the same faculties on questions of practical ends? Or by what other faculty is cognisance taken of them?

Questions about ends are, in other words, questions about what things are desirable. The utilitarian doctrine is, that happiness is desirable, and the only thing desirable, as an end; all other things being only desirable as means to that end. What ought to be required of this doctrine—what conditions is it requisite that the doctrine should fulfill—to make good its claim to be believed? The only proof capable of being given that an object is visible, is that people actually see it.

The only proof that a sound is audible, is that people hear it: and so of the other sources of our experience. In like manner, I apprehend, the sole evidence it is possible to produce that anything is desirable, is that people do actually desire it. If the end which the utilitarian doctrine proposes to itself were not, in theory and in practice, acknowledged to be an end, nothing could ever convince any person that it was so. No reason can be given why the general happiness is desirable, except that each person, so far as he believes it to be attainable, desires his own happiness. This, however, being a fact, we have not only all the proof which the case admits of, but all which it is possible to require, that happiness is a good: that each person's happiness is a good to that person, and the general happiness, therefore, a good to the aggregate of all persons. Happiness has made out its title as *one* of the ends of conduct, and consequently one of the criteria of morality.

But it has not, by this alone, proved itself to be the sole criterion. To do that, it would seem, by the same rule, necessary to show, not only that people desire happiness, but that they never desire anything else. . . .

We have now, then, an answer to the question, of what sort of proof the principle of utility is susceptible. If the opinion which I have now stated is psychologically true—if human nature is so constituted as to desire nothing which is not either a part of happiness or a means of happiness, we can have no other proof, and we require no other, that these are the only things desirable. If so, happiness is the sole end of human action, and the promotion of it the test by which to judge of all human conduct; from whence it necessarily follows that it must be the criterion of morality, since a part is included in the whole.

And now to decide whether this is really so; whether mankind does desire nothing for itself but that which is a pleasure to them, or of which the absence is a pain; we have evidently arrived at a question of fact and experience, dependent, like all similar questions, upon evidence. It can only

be determined by practised self-consciousness and self-observation, assisted by observation of others. I believe that these sources of evidence, impartially consulted, will declare that desiring a thing and finding it pleasant, aversion to it and thinking of it as painful, are phenomena entirely inseparable, or rather two parts of the same phenomenon; in strictness of language, two different modes of naming the same psychological fact: that to think of an object as desirable (unless for the sake of its consequences), and to think of it as pleasant, are one and the same thing; and that to desire anything, except in proportion as the idea of it is pleasant, is a physical and metaphysical impossibility.

For Further Reflection

1. To better grasp the difference between utilitarianism and deontological ethics, consider this example. Suppose a raft is floating in the Pacific Ocean. On the raft are two men starving to death. One day they discover some food in an inner compartment of a box on the raft. They have reason to believe that the food will be sufficient to keep one of them alive until the raft reaches a certain island where help is available, but if they share the food, both will most likely die. Now, one of these men is a brilliant scientist who has in his mind the cure for cancer. The other man is undistinguished. Otherwise there is no relevant difference between the two. What is the morally right thing to do? Share the food and hope against the odds for a miracle? Flip a coin to see which man gets the food? Give the food to the scientist? If you voted to flip a coin or share the food, you sided with the deontologist, but if you voted to give the food to the scientist, you sided with the teleologist, the utilitarian, who would calculate that there would be greater good accomplished as a result of the scientist getting the food and living than in any of the other likely outcomes. It has often been admitted that utilitarianism could easily be misused. If people tried to "play God" and decide each case on the basis of what they thought would be the "best" consequences, chaos might result, so that some utilitarians have advocated keeping their doctrine a secret. What do you think of both the prediction of the anti-utilitarian consequences of widespread utilitarianism and the prescription of keeping the doctrine a secret?

2. John Rawls has argued that the fault of utilitarianism is that it makes a false inference from what one is allowed to do with one's own life to what one is allowed to do with other people's lives. We often have a right to forego some present enjoyment for the sake of a future personal higher goal, but, he argues, we have not the same right to restrict some other person from a present enjoyment for what you deem to be his higher future goal. That is, utilitarianism is a paternalistic violator of human rights. It treats rights as expendable. Do you agree with this criticism?

3. What do you see as the overall merits and liabilities of deontological and utilitarian systems? Where do you stand at this juncture?

4. Nietzsche wrote, "If we possess our *why* of life we can put up with almost any *how*— Man does not strive after happiness; only the Englishman does that" (Friedrich Nietzsche,

Twilight of the Idols). Do you agree or disagree with Nietzsche on the unimportance of the search for happiness?

VI.51   Existentialist Ethics

JEAN-PAUL SARTRE

Jean-Paul Sartre (1905–1980), born in Paris, was a teacher in a French high school. He served in the French army during World War II, was captured by the Germans, and spent his time in a prison camp reading German philosophers (especially Hegel, Husserl, and Heidegger). After the war, Sartre's plays, novels, and philosophical work, especially *Being and Nothingness* (1943), set him apart as Europe's premier existentialist. Later he combined existentialism with Marxism, though he never joined the Communist party.

Here is Paul Johnson's description of Sartre's impact, and the essay we are about to read, on French society:

[On October 29, 1945 shortly after the end of the war], at the Club Maintenant, Jean-Paul Sartre delivered a lecture, "Existentialism is a Humanism." Here was the new Paris. This occasion . . . was packed. Men and women fainted, fought for chairs, smashing thirty of them, shouted and barracked. It coincided with the launching of Sartre's new review, *Les Temps Modernes,* in which he argued that literary culture, plus the haute couture of the fashion shops, were the only things France now had left—a symbol of Europe, really—and he produced Existentialism to give people a bit of dignity and to preserve their individuality in the midst of degradation and absurdity. The response was overwhelming. As his consort, Simone de Beauvoir, put it, "We were astounded by the furore we caused." Existentialism was remarkably un-Gallic; hence perhaps, its attractiveness. Sartre was half-Alsacian (Albert Schweitzer was his cousin) and he was brought up in the house of his grandfather, Karl Schweitzer. His culture was as much German as French. He was essentially a product of the Berlin school and especially Heidegger, from whom most of his ideas derived. . . . Thus Existentialism was a French cultural import, which Paris then re-exported to Germany, its country of origin, in a sophisticated and vastly more attractive guise. (Paul Johnson, *Modern Times,* Harper & Row, 1983, p. 575f)

In this essay Sartre sets forth the principles of atheistic existentialism: that we are completely free; that since there is no God to give us an essence, we must create our own essence; that we are completely responsible for our actions and are responsible for everyone else too; that because of the death of God and the human predicament, which leaves us totally free to create our values and our world, we must exist in anguish, forlornness, and despair. Yet there is a certain celebration and optimism in knowing that we are creators of our own values.

In this essay you will come across Sartre's notion that "essence precedes existence." This is a difficult idea, but he seems to mean something like the following.

If you have an idea of something in your mind first and then create it, we would say that the idea (essence) of the thing preceded the actuality or existence of the thing. But if the thing existed before any idea of it, then its existence preceded its essence. If there were a God who created us, who had us in mind, we would have an essence (in terms of a function or purpose) and our existence would succeed our essence, but since, according to Sartre, there is no God to create us, we simply find ourselves existing and must create our own essence (that is, give ourselves a function or purpose). This is a start at getting at the meaning of this difficult phrase. Perhaps you can improve on this explanation.

Study Questions

1. What are the two meanings of "subjectivism" in this essay?
2. What does Sartre mean by saying that responsibility for our actions involves being responsible for everyone? How does he answer those who deny this thesis? Has Sartre begged the question against them?
3. Describe Sartre's notion of anguish. Why must we experience it? Is his argument cogent?
4. Describe Sartre's notion of forlornness. Why must we experience it? Is his argument clear and plausible?
5. What does Sartre mean by saying that we are "condemned to be free"?
6. Examine the case of the student who finds himself in a moral dilemma. Is Sartre correct, that there are no objective principles to help him make his decision, but he must make a leap of faith?

WHAT IS MEANT by the term *existentialism?*

Most people who use the word would be rather embarrassed if they had to explain it, since, now that the word is all the rage, even the work of a musician or painter is being called existentialist. . . . It seems that for want of an advance-guard doctrine analogous to surrealism, the kind of people who are eager for scandal and flurry turn to this philosophy which in other respects does not at all serve their purposes in this sphere.

Actually, it is the least scandalous, the most austere of doctrines. It is intended strictly for specialists and philosophers. Yet it can be defined easily. What complicates matters is that there are two kinds of existentialists; first, those who are Christian, among whom I would include Jaspers and Gabriel Marcel, both Catholic;

and on the other hand, the atheistic existentialists, among whom I class Heidegger, and then the French existentialists and myself. What they have in common is that they think that existence precedes essence, or, if you prefer, that subjectivity must be the starting point.

Just what does that mean? Let us consider some object that is manufactured, for example, a book or a paper-cutter: here is an object which has been made by an artisan whose inspiration came from a concept. He referred to the concept of what a paper-cutter is and likewise to a known method of production, which is part of the concept, something which is, by and large, a routine. Thus, the paper-cutter is at once an object produced in a certain way and, on the other hand, one having a specific use; and one cannot postu-

Source: Jean-Paul Sartre, Existentialism, *trans. by Bernard Frechtman (New York, 1947).*
Reprinted by permission of the Philosophical Library, Inc.

late a man who produces a paper-cutter but does not know what it is used for. Therefore, let us say that, for the paper-cutter, essence—that is, the ensemble of both the production routines and the properties which enable it to be both produced and defined—precedes existence. Thus, the presence of the paper-cutter or book in front of me is determined. Therefore, we have here a technical view of the world whereby it can be said that production precedes existence.

When we conceive God as the Creator, He is generally thought of as a superior sort of artisan. Whatever doctrine we may be considering, whether one like that of Descartes or that of Leibnitz, we always grant that will more or less follows understanding or, at the very least, accompanies it, and that when God creates He knows exactly what He is creating. Thus, the concept of man in the mind of God is comparable to the concept of paper-cutter in the mind of the manufacturer, and, following certain techniques and a conception, God produces man, just as the artisan, following a definition and a technique, makes a paper-cutter. Thus, the individual man is the realization of a certain concept in the divine intelligence.

In the eighteenth century, the atheism of the *philosophes* discarded the idea of God, but not so much for the notion that essence precedes existence. To a certain extent, this idea is found everywhere; we find it in Diderot, in Voltaire, and even in Kant. Man has a human nature; this human nature, which is the concept of the human, is found in all men, which means that each man is a particular example of a universal concept, man. In Kant, the result of this universality is that the wild-man, the natural man, as well as the bourgeois, are circumscribed by the same definition and have the same basic qualities. Thus, here too the essence of man precedes the historical existence that we find in nature.

Atheistic existentialism, which I represent, is more coherent. It states that if God does not exist, there is at least one being in whom existence precedes essence, a being who exists before he can be defined by any concept, and that

this being is man, or, as Heidegger says, human reality. What is meant here by saying that existence precedes essence? It means that, first of all, man exists, turns up, appears on the scene, and, only afterwards, defines himself. If man, as the existentialist conceives him, is indefinable, it is because at first he is nothing. Only afterward will he be something, and he himself will have made what he will be. Thus, there is no human nature, since there is no God to conceive it. Not only is man what he conceives himself to be, but he is also only what he wills himself to be after this thrust toward existence.

Man is nothing else but what he makes of himself. Such is the first principle of existentialism. It is also what is called subjectivity, the name we are labeled with when charges are brought against us. But what do we mean by this, if not that man has a greater dignity than a stone or table? For we mean that man first exists, that is, that man first of all is the being in the future. Man is at the start a plan which is aware of itself, rather than a patch of moss, a piece of garbage, or a cauliflower; nothing exists prior to this plan; there is nothing in heaven; man will be what he will have planned to be. Not what he will want to be. Because by the word "will" we generally mean a conscious decision, which is subsequent to what we have already made of ourselves. I may want to belong to a political party, write a book, get married; but all that is only a manifestation of an earlier, more spontaneous choice that is called "will." But if existence really does precede essence, man is responsible for what he is. Thus, existentialism's first move is to make every man aware of what he is and to make the full responsibility of his existence rest on him. And when we say that a man is responsible for himself, we do not only mean that he is responsible for his own individuality, but that he is responsible for all men.

The word subjectivism has two meanings, and our opponents play on the two. Subjectivism means, on the one hand, that an individual chooses and makes himself; and, on the other, that it is impossible for man to transcend human subjectivity. The second of these is the essential meaning of existentialism. When we say that man chooses his own self, we mean that every one of us does likewise; but we also mean by that that in making this choice he also chooses all men. In fact, in creating the man that we want to be, there is not a single one of our acts which does not at the same time create an image of man as we think he ought to be. To choose to be this or that is to affirm at the same time the value of what we choose, because we can never choose evil. We always choose the good, and nothing can be good for us without being good for all.

If, on the other hand, existence precedes essence, and if we grant that we exist and fashion our image at one and the same time, the image is valid for everybody and for our whole age. Thus, our responsibility is much greater than we might have supposed, because it involves all mankind. If I am a workingman and choose to join a Christian trade-union rather than be a communist, and if by being a member I want to show that the best thing for man is resignation, that the kingdom of man is not of this world, I am not only involving my own case—I want to be resigned for everyone. As a result, my action has involved all humanity. To take a more individual matter, if I want to marry, to have children; even if this marriage depends solely on my own circumstances or passion or wish, I am involving all humanity in monogamy and not merely myself. Therefore, I am responsible for myself and for everyone else. I am creating a certain image of man of my own choosing. In choosing myself, I choose man.

This helps us understand what the actual content is of such rather grandiloquent words as anguish, forlornness, despair. As you will see, it's all quite simple.

First, what is meant by anguish? The existentialists say at once that man is anguish. What that means is this: the man who involves himself and who realizes that he is not only the person he chooses to be, but also a law-maker who is, at the same time, choosing all mankind as well as himself, cannot help escape the feeling of his total

and deep responsibility. Of course, there are many people who are not anxious; but we claim that they are hiding their anxiety, that they are fleeing from it. Certainly, many people believe that when they do something, they themselves are the only ones involved, and when someone says to them, "What if everyone acted that way?" they shrug their shoulders and answer, "Everyone doesn't act that way." But really, one should always ask himself, "What would happen if everybody looked at things that way?" There is no escaping this disturbing thought except by a kind of double-dealing. A man who lies and makes excuses for himself by saying "not everybody does that," is someone with an uneasy conscience, because the act of lying implies that a universal value is conferred upon the lie.

Anguish is evident even when it conceals itself. This is the anguish that Kierkegaard called the anguish of Abraham. You know the story: an angel has ordered Abraham to sacrifice his son; if it really were an angel who has come and said, "You are Abraham, you shall sacrifice your son," everything would be all right. But everyone might first wonder, "Is it really an angel, and am I really Abraham? What proof do I have?" . . .

Now, I'm not being singled out as an Abraham, and yet at every moment I'm obliged to perform exemplary acts. For every man, everything happens as if all mankind had its eyes fixed on him and were guiding itself by what he does. And every man ought to say to himself, "Am I really the kind of man who has the right to act in such a way that humanity might guide itself by my actions?" And if he does not say that to himself, he is masking his anguish.

There is no question here of the kind of anguish which would lead to quietism, to inaction. It is a matter of a simple sort of anguish that anybody who has had responsibilities is familiar with. For example, when a military officer takes the responsibility for an attack and sends a certain number of men to death, he chooses to do so, and in the main he alone makes the choice. Doubtless, orders come from above, but they are too broad; he interprets them, and on this interpretation depend the lives of ten or fourteen or twenty men. In making a decision he cannot help having a certain anguish. All leaders know this anguish. That doesn't keep them from acting; on the contrary, it is the very condition of their action. For it implies that they envisage a number of possibilities, and when they choose one, they realize that it has value only because it is chosen. We shall see that this kind of anguish, which is the kind that existentialism describes, is explained, in addition, by a direct responsibility to the other men whom it involves. It is not a curtain separating us from action, but is part of action itself.

When we speak of forlornness, a term Heidegger was fond of, we mean only that God does not exist and that we have to face all the consequences of this. The existentialist is strongly opposed to a certain kind of secular ethics which would like to abolish God with the least possible expense. About 1880, some French teachers tried to set up a secular ethics which went something like this: God is a useless and costly hypothesis; we are discarding it; but meanwhile, in order for there to be an ethics, a society, a civilization, it is essential that certain values be taken seriously and that they be considered as having an *a priori* existence. It must be obligatory, *a priori,* to be honest, not to lie, not to beat your wife, to have children, etc., etc. So we're going to try a little device which will make it possible to show that values exist all the same, inscribed in a heaven of ideas, though otherwise God does not exist. In other words—and this, I believe, is the tendency of everything called reformism in France—nothing will be changed if God does not exist. We shall find ourselves with the same norms of honesty, progress, and humanism, and we shall have made of God an outdated hypothesis which will peacefully die off by itself.

The existentialist, on the contrary, thinks it very distressing that God does not exist, because all possibility of finding values in a heaven of ideas disappears along with Him; there can be no longer an *a priori* Good, since there is no infinite and perfect consciousness to think it.

Nowhere is it written that the Good exists, that we must be honest, that we must not lie; because the fact is we are on a plane where there are only men. Dostoievsky said, "If God didn't exist, everything would be possible." That is the very starting point of existentialism. Indeed, everything is permissible if God does not exist, and as a result man is forlorn, because neither within him nor without does he find anything to cling to. He can't start making excuses for himself.

If existence really does precede essence, there is no explaining things away by reference to a fixed and given human nature. In other words, there is no determinism, man is free, man is freedom. On the other hand, if God does not exist, we find no values or commands to turn to which legitimize our conduct. So, in the bright realm of values, we have no excuse behind us, no justification before us. We are alone, with no excuses.

That is the idea I shall try to convey when I say that man is condemned to be free. Condemned, because he did not create himself, yet, in other respects is free; because, once thrown into the world, he is responsible for everything he does.

The existentialist does not believe in the power of passion. He will never agree that a sweeping passion is a ravaging torrent which fatally leads a man to certain acts and is therefore an excuse. He thinks that man is responsible for his passion.

The existentialist does not think that man is going to help himself by finding in the world some omen by which to orient himself, because he thinks that man will interpret the omen to suit himself. Therefore, he thinks that man, with no support and no aid, is condemned every moment to invent man. Ponge, in a very fine article, has said, "Man is the future of man." That's exactly it. But if it is taken to mean that this future is recorded in heaven, that God sees it, then it is false, because it would really no longer be a future. If it is taken to mean that, whatever a man may be, there is a future to be forged, a virgin future before him, then this remark is sound. But then we are forlorn.

To give you an example which will enable you to understand forlornness better, I shall cite the case of one of my students who came to see me under the following circumstances: his father was on bad terms with his mother, and, moreover, was inclined to be a collaborationist; his older brother had been killed in the German offensive of 1940, and the young man, with somewhat immature but generous feelings, wanted to avenge him. His mother lived alone with him, very much upset by the half-treason of her husband and the death of her older son; the boy was her only consolation.

The boy was faced with the choice of leaving for England and joining the Free French Forces—that is, leaving his mother behind—or remaining with his mother and helping her to carry on. He was fully aware that the woman lived only for him and that his going-off—and perhaps his death—would plunge her into despair. He was also aware that every act that he did for his mother's sake was a sure thing, in the sense that it was helping her to carry on, whereas every effort he made toward going off and fighting was an uncertain move which might run aground and prove completely useless; for example, on his way to England he might, while passing through Spain, be detained indefinitely in a Spanish camp; he might reach England or Algiers and be stuck in an office at a desk job. As a result, he was faced with two very different kinds of action: one, concrete, immediate, but concerning only one individual; the other concerned an incomparably vaster group, a national collectivity, but for that very reason was dubious, and might be interrupted en route. And, at the same time, he was wavering between two kinds of ethics. On the one hand, an ethics of sympathy, of personal devotion; on the other, a broader ethics, but one whose efficacy was more dubious. He had to choose between the two.

Who could help him choose? Christian doctrine? No. Christian doctrine says, "Be charitable, love your neighbor, take the more rugged path, etc., etc." But which is the more rugged path? Whom should he love as a brother? The

fighting man or his mother? Which does the greater good, the vague act of fighting in a group, or the concrete one of helping a particular human being to go on living? Who can decide *a priori*? Nobody. No book of ethics can tell him. The Kantian ethics says, "Never treat any person as a means, but as an end." Very well, if I stay with my mother, I'll treat her as an end and not as a means; but by virtue of this very fact, I'm running the risk of treating the people around me who are fighting, as means; and, conversely, if I go to join those who are fighting, I'll be treating them as an end, and, by doing that, I run the risk of treating my mother as a means.

If values are vague, and if they are always too broad for the concrete and specific case that we are considering, the only thing left for us is to trust our instincts. That's what this young man tried to do; and when I saw him, he said, "In the end, feeling is what counts. I ought to choose whichever pushes me in one direction. If I feel that I love my mother enough to sacrifice everything else for her—my desire for vengeance, for action, for adventure—then I'll stay with her. If, on the contrary, I feel that my love for my mother isn't enough, I'll leave."

But how is the value of a feeling determined? What gives his feeling for his mother value? Precisely the fact that he remained with her. I may say that I like so-and-so well enough to sacrifice a certain amount of money for him, but I may say so only if I've done it. I may say, "I love my mother well enough to remain with her" if I have remained with her. The only way to determine the value of this affection is, precisely, to perform an act which confirms and defines it. But, since I require this affection to justify my act, I find myself caught in a vicious circle. . . .

As for despair, the term has a very simple meaning. It means that we shall confine ourselves to reckoning only with what depends upon our will, or on the ensemble of probabilities which make our action possible. When we want something, we always have to reckon with probabilities. I may be counting on the arrival of a friend. The friend is coming by rail or streetcar; this supposes that the train will arrive on schedule, or that the street-car will not jump the track. I am left in the realm of possibility; but possibilities are to be reckoned with only to the point where my action comports with the ensemble of these possibilities, and no further. The moment the possibilities I am considering are not rigorously involved by my action, I ought to disengage myself from them, because no God, no scheme, can adapt the world and its possibilities to my will. When Descartes said, "Conquer yourself rather than the world," he meant essentially the same thing.

The Marxists to whom I have spoken reply, "You can rely on the support of others in your action, which obviously has certain limits because you're not going to live forever. That means: rely on both what others are doing elsewhere to help you, in China, in Russia, and what they will do later on, after your death, to carry on the action and lead it to its fulfillment, which will be the revolution. You even *have* to rely upon that, otherwise you're immortal." I reply at once that I will always rely on fellow fighters insofar as these comrades are involved with me in a common struggle, in the unity of a party or a group in which I can more or less make my weight felt; that is, one whose ranks I am in as a fighter and whose movements I am aware of at every moment. In such a situation, relying on the unity and will of the party is exactly like counting on the fact that the train will arrive on time or that the car won't jump the track. But, given that man is free and that there is no human nature for me to depend on, I cannot count on men whom I do not know by relying on human goodness or man's concern for the good of society. I don't

know what will become of the Russian revolution; I may make an example of it to the extent that at the present time it is apparent that the proletariat plays a part in Russia that it plays in no other nation. But I can't swear that this will inevitably lead to a triumph of the proletariat. I've got to limit myself to what I see.

Given that men are free, and that tomorrow they will freely decide what man will be, I cannot be sure that, after my death, fellow fighters will carry on my work to bring it to its maximum perfection. Tomorrow, after my death, some men may decide to set up Fascism, and the others may be cowardly and muddled enough to let them do it. Fascism will then be the human reality, so much the worse for us.

Actually, things will be as man will have decided they are to be. Does that mean that I should abandon myself to quietism? No. First, I should involve myself; then, act on the old saw, "Nothing ventured, nothing gained." Nor does it mean that I shouldn't belong to a party, but rather that I shall have no illusions and shall do what I can. For example, suppose I ask myself, "Will socialization, as such, ever come about?" I know nothing about it. All I know is that I'm going to do everything in my power to bring it about. Beyond that, I can't count on anything. Quietism is the attitude of people who say, "Let others do what I can't do." The doctrine I am presenting is the very opposite of quietism, since it declares, "There is no reality except in action." Moreover, it goes further, since it adds, "Man is nothing else than his plan; he exists only to the extent that he fulfills himself; he is, therefore, nothing else than the ensemble of his acts, nothing else than his life."

For Further Reflection

1. How are existentialist ethics different from other theories we have studied? What are its strengths and weaknesses?

2. Has Sartre gotten to the heart of the matter with his example of the student who must choose between his mother and the war effort? Could we object that he is making an exception to the norm? In normal situations we know perfectly well the right thing to do.

For example, suppose that there was no war; then, wouldn't it be automatically right to take care of the mother? Does existentialism have a response to this criticism?

3. Sartre believes that it makes all the difference in the world whether God exists. If God does not exist, all things are morally permissible, there is no right or wrong, but thinking makes it so. Is this correct?

Suggestions for Further Reading

GENERAL WORKS

Baier, Kurt. *The Moral Point of View.* Ithaca, NY: Cornell University Press, 1958.

Beauchamp, Tom L. *Philosophical Ethics.* New York: McGraw-Hill, 1982. A good blend of analysis with readings.

Brandt, Richard. *Ethical Theory.* Englewood Cliffs, NJ: Prentice Hall, 1959. A solid, comprehensive work on ethical theory.

Feldman, Fred. *Introductory Ethics.* Englewood Cliffs, NJ: Prentice Hall, 1978. An excellent expression of analytic method applied to ethical theory.

Harris, C. E. *Applying Moral Theories.* Belmont, CA: Wadsworth, 1986.

MacIntyre, A. *A Short History of Ethics.* New York: Macmillan, 1966.

Mackie, J. L. *Ethics: Inventing Right and Wrong.* New York: Penguin, 1977.

Pojman, Louis, ed. *Ethical Theory: Classic and Contemporary Readings.* 4th edition. Belmont, CA: Wadsworth, 2002.

Rachels, James. *The Elements of Moral Philosophy.* New York: Random House, 1986. An elementary, succinct introduction.

Taylor, Paul. *Principles of Ethics.* Belmont, CA: Dickenson, 1975.

ETHICAL RELATIVISM

Copp, David and David Zimmerman, eds. *Morality, Reason and Truth: New Essays on the Foundations of Ethics.* Totowa, NJ: Rowman & Allanheld, 1984.

Gewirth, Alan. *Reason and Morality.* Chicago: University of Chicago Press, 1978.

Gillispie, Norman, ed. *Moral Realism (Southern Journal of Philosophy,* vol. XXIV, Supplement), 1986. This volume contains an excellent collection of essays on moral realism, including a bibliography on the subject by Geoffrey Sayre-McCord.

Ladd, John, ed. *Ethical Relativism.* Belmont, CA: Wadsworth, 1973.

Stace, W. T. *The Concept of Morals.* New York: Macmillan, 1937.

Wellman, Carl. "The Ethical Implications of Cultural Relativity." *Journal of Philosophy,* LX, 1963.

Werner, Richard. "Ethical Realism." *Ethics,* vol. 93, 1983.

Westermarck, Edward. *Ethical Relativity.* Humanities Press, 1960.

Williams, Bernard. *Morality.* Harper Torchbooks, 1972.

Wong, David. *Moral Relativity.* Berkeley: University of California Press, 1985.

MORALITY AND SELF-INTEREST

Gauthier, David, ed. *Morality and Rational Self-Interest.* Englewood Cliffs, NJ: Prentice Hall, 1970.

Gauthier, David. *Morality by Agreement.* Oxford: Clarendon Press, 1986.

MacIntyre, Alasdair. "Egoism and Altruism" in *The Encyclopedia of Philosophy,* ed. Paul Edwards. New York: Macmillan, 1967.

Sidgwick, Henry. *The Methods of Ethics.* 7th ed. Indianapolis: Hackett, 1981.

Slote, Michael. "An Empirical Basis for Psychological Egoism." *Journal of Philosophy,* vol. 61.

ETHICAL THEORIES

Aristotle. *Nicomachean Ethics,* trans. Terence Irwin. Indianapolis: Hackett, 1985.

Becker, Lawrence. *On Justifying Moral Arguments,* chap. 19. London: Routledge & Kegan Paul, 1973.

Cooper, John. *Reason and the Human Good in Aristotle.* Cambridge: Harvard University Press, 1975.

Donagan, Alan. *The Theory of Morality.* Chicago: University of Chicago Press, 1977.

Hare, Richard. *Reason and Freedom.* Oxford: Oxford University Press, 1961.

Kant, Immanuel. *Fundamental Principles of the Metaphysics of Morals,* trans. Lewis Beck. Indianapolis: Bobbs-Merrill, 1949.

Kruschwitz, Robert and Robert Roberts, eds. *The Virtues.* Belmont, CA: Wadsworth, 1987. An excellent up-to-date anthology.

MacIntyre, Alasdair. *After Virtue.* Notre Dame: University of Notre Dame Press, 1981.

Mill, John Stuart. *Utilitarianism.* Indianapolis: Bobbs-Merrill, 1957.

Singer, Peter. *The Expanding Circle.* Oxford: Oxford University Press, 1983. A nice job of integrating sociobiology with moral theory.

Smart, J. J. C. and Bernard Williams. *Utilitarianism: For and Against.* Cambridge: Cambridge University Press, 1973. A classic debate.

Sommers, Christina Hoff, ed. *Vice and Virtues in Everyday Life.* New York: Harcourt Brace Jovanovich, 1985.

Taylor, Richard. *Good and Evil.* New York: Macmillan, 1970.

Taylor, Richard. *Ethics, Faith and Reason.* Englewood Cliffs, NJ: Prentice Hall, 1985.

Warnock, G. J. *The Object of Morality.* London: Methuen, 1971.

Part VII

Political Philosophy

*In heaven, there is laid up a pattern of the Ideal City, methinks, which he
who desires may behold, and beholding, may set his own house in order. But
whether such an one exists, or ever will exist in fact, is no matter: for he will
live after the manner of that city, having nothing to do with any other.*

PLATO, *Republic* IX, 592, trans. Jowett

What Is The Justification of Political Authority?

YOU ARE FILLING OUT your yearly federal income tax forms and become irritated at the large sum of money that you are going to have to pay, $5000. If that weren't bad enough, you don't believe in the programs for which most of the money will be spent. You ask yourself, what right does the government have to demand payment of me? But you don't like the probable consequences of not paying—a prison sentence—so you very reluctantly write out a check for $5000, realizing that you will not be able to afford needed house repairs nor a vacation this year.

So you put your tax forms with a check inside an envelope and go out to mail it at the nearest mailbox. On your way home, a man accosts you with a gun. "Your money or your life," he roughly demands. You open your wallet and hand him the $100 therein. You continue home, beaten in spirit, feeling twice robbed, and wondering which is the greater robber, the gunman or the government?

You ask yourself if that feeling is justified. Is the government with its laws only a gunman who observes reliable rituals and procedures and, unlike the robber, warns you in advance that a percentage of your money will be taken at a certain time every year? You've always been a law-abiding citizen, but now you wonder, by what right does the government demand my obedience? Why should I obey the state? What is the justification of government?

In this part, we examine six different answers to these questions:

1. The anarchist answer: The state is not justified in imposing its wishes on you, for your autonomy is a fundamental moral absolute, and the state has no right to violate it. The state is without moral authority. We begin this Part with Robert Paul Wolff's *In Defense of Anarchy* (Reading 52).

2. The Hobbesian (absolutist) answer: Anarchy—the state of nature without political security—is so dangerous, barbarous, and impoverished that it is rational to give up significant freedom to the state in order to obtain peace and security (Reading 53).

3. The Lockean (classical liberal) answer: Government is based on the consent of the governed (Reading 54). Locke agrees with Hobbes that we contract with the state to give up some freedom for security, but he disagrees on the degree of the surrender. In consenting to obey the state, we do not give up our natural rights to life, property, representation, and other goods—better a state of nature, which is not as bad as Hobbes makes out, than slavery to the state!

4. The libertarian answer: Represented in our readings by John Stuart Mill (Reading 55), the libertarian answer goes further than the Lockean answer in honoring freedom, especially our right to do whatever we want as long as we are not unjustly harming others.

5. The Marxist answer: Diametrically opposed to the libertarian position, the Marxist answer argues that property should belong to the state so that the state may use it for human good, taking from each as he or she is able to give and giving to each as he or she needs. In other words, the function that justi-

fies political authority is that of justice, of justly distributing the goods of the society in a radical egalitarian manner. Because capitalist societies fail to promote this state of justice, the proletariat is justified in overthrowing the State by revolutionary means (Reading 56).

6. The cosmopolitan answer: represented by Brian Barry (Reading 57). In an ever shrinking world with a global economy and telecommunications, as well as increased mass weapons of destruction, we must resolve conflicts of interest amicably and distribute wealth more justly. This requires that nations relinquish some national sovereignty in favor of an international government committed to peace and international justice and cooperation.

Political philosophy includes many related questions, which are touched on in this part of our book, including: What is the best form of government? Why should individuals obey the law? Is taxation legitimate? What exactly grounds the state's authority, making it legitimate?

Before we turn to our readings we should say a word about political anarchism, because it raises the question of political obligation and authority in a most striking manner.

Political anarchism is the philosophy that the state itself is unjustified because it improperly infringes on human autonomy. Human freedom is treated as a paramount moral value that no amount of efficiency, utility, or stability may justly override. All forms of government are bad in that they restrict the free exercise of human reason that is necessary for the attainment of perfection. The French philosopher Pierre Joseph Proudhon (1809–1865) is regarded as the father of anarchism. He rejected all forms of authority from society in favor of complete individualism. One of his famous statements is "property is theft."*

In the selection that follows, the American philosopher Robert Paul Wolff sets forth a version of anarchism, holding that all forms of government violate our overriding duty to act autonomously.

In Defense of Anarchism   VII.52

ROBERT PAUL WOLFF

Robert Paul Wolff was for many years professor of philosophy at Columbia University and is presently professor of philosophy at the University of Massachusetts at Amherst. He is the author of many articles and books but is best known for his *In Defense of Anarchism* from which the present selection is taken.

---

*P. J. Proudhon, What Is Property? *(1840)*

Wolff sets forth a version of anarchism, holding that all forms of government violate our overriding duty to act autonomously. Wolff's argument (and essay) can be divided into two parts. In the first, he describes the meaning of political authority, distinguishing it from mere power. In the second part, he defines autonomy and argues that it is incompatible with accepting authority. I have edited the selection with minor annotations to aid your study.

Study Questions

1. How does Wolff define political philosophy?
2. How does Wolff define the state?
3. How does he define authority?
4. What is the difference between *de facto* and *de jure* authority?
5. What is the basis of our responsibility?
6. How do authority and autonomy conflict? How does this conflict, according to Wolff, result in anarchism?
7. What is the relationship of the anarchist to his own country and government?

THE CONCEPT OF AUTHORITY

POLITICS IS THE EXERCISE of the power of the state, or the attempt to influence that exercise. Political philosophy is therefore, strictly speaking, the philosophy of the state. If we are to determine the content of political philosophy, and whether indeed it exists, we must begin with the concept of the state.

The state is a group of persons who have and exercise supreme authority within a given territory. Strictly, we should say that a state is a group of persons who have supreme authority within a given territory or *over a certain population*. A nomadic tribe may exhibit the authority structure of a state, so long as its subjects do not fall under the superior authority of a territorial state. The state may include all the persons who fall under its authority, as does the democratic state according to its theorists; it may also consist of a single individual to whom all the rest are subject. We may doubt whether the one-person state has ever actually existed, although Louis XIV evidently thought so when he announced, "L'etat c'est moi" [I am the State]. The distinctive characteristic of the state is supreme authority.

Authority is the right to command, and correlatively, the right to be obeyed. *It must be distinguished from power,* which is the ability to compel compliance, either through the use or threat of force. When I turn over my wallet to a thief who is holding me at gunpoint, I do so because the fate with which he threatens me is worse than the loss of money which I am made to suffer. I grant that he has power over me, but I would hardly suppose that he has *authority*, that is, that he has a right to demand my money and that I have an obligation to give it to him. When the government presents me with a bill for taxes, on the other hand, I pay it (normally) even though I do not wish to and even if I think I can get away with not paying. It is after all, the duly constituted government, and hence it has a *right* to tax me. It has *authority* over me. Sometimes, of course, I cheat the government, but even so, I acknowledge its authority, for who would speak of "cheating" a thief?

From *Robert Paul Wolff,* In Defense of Anarchism *(New York: Harper and Row, 1970).*

To claim authority is to claim the right to be obeyed. To *have* authority is then—what? It may mean to have that right, or it may mean to have one's claim acknowledged and accepted by those at whom it is directed. The term "authority" is ambiguous, having both a descriptive and a normative sense. Even the descriptive sense refers to norms or obligations, of course, but it does so by *describing* what men believe they ought to do rather than by *asserting* that they ought to do it. . . .

What is meant by *supreme* authority? Some political philosophers have held that the true state has ultimate authority over all matters whatsoever that occur within its venue. Jean Jacques Rousseau, for example, asserted that the social contract by which a just political community is formed

> gives to the body absolute command over the members of which it is formed; and it is this power, when directed by the general will, that bears . . . the name of 'sovereign.'

John Locke, on the other hand, held that the supreme authority of the just state extends only to those matters which it is proper for a state to control. The state is, to be sure, the highest authority, but its right to command is less than absolute. One of the questions which political philosophy must answer is whether there is any limit to the range of affairs over which a just state has authority.

[Wolff next distinguishes an authoritative command from a persuasive argument. I may choose to do exactly as a sovereign commands because I see it as my moral duty, but the commanding or arguing party has no authority in himself. Ed.]

The person who issues the command functions merely as the *occasion* for my becoming aware of my duty, and his role might in other instances be filled by an admonishing friend, or even by my own conscience. But this is different from the notion that a government has a right to command and the correlative obligation to obey the person who gives the command:

"Obedience is not a matter of doing what someone tells you to do. It is a matter of doing what he tells you to do *because he tells you to do it.*"

What can be inferred from the existence of de facto [actually existing] states is that men *believe* in the existence of legitimate authority, for of course a *de facto* state is simply a state whose subjects believe it to be legitimate (i.e., really to have the authority which it claims for itself). They may be wrong. Indeed, *all* beliefs in authority may be wrong—there may be not a single state in the history of mankind which has now or ever has had a right to be obeyed. It might even be impossible for such a state to exist; that is the question we must try to settle. But so long as men believe in the authority of states, we can conclude that they possess the concept of *de jure* [legitimate] authority.

[Having clarified the concept of authority and left it an open question whether any state qualifies as a legitimate authority, Wolff turns to the second part of his argument, the concept of autonomy. Ed.]

THE CONCEPT OF AUTONOMY

The fundamental assumption of moral philosophy is that men are responsible for their actions. From this assumption it follows necessarily, as Kant pointed out, that men are metaphysically free, which is to say that in some sense they are capable of choosing how they shall act. Being able to choose how he acts makes a man responsible, but merely choosing is not in itself to constitute *taking* responsibility for one's actions. Taking responsibility involves attempting to determine what one ought to do, and that, as philosophers since Aristotle have recognized, lays upon one the additional burdens of gaining knowledge, reflecting on motives, predicting outcomes, criticizing principles, and so forth.

The obligation to take responsibility for one's actions does not derive from man's freedom of will alone, for more is required in taking responsibility than freedom of choice. Only because man has the capacity to reason about his choices can he be said to stand under a continuing obligation to take responsibility for them. It is quite appropriate that moral philosophers should group together children and madmen as being not fully responsible for their actions, for as madmen are thought to lack freedom of choice, so children do not yet possess the power of reason in a developed form. It is even just that we should assign a greater degree of responsibility to children, for madmen, by virtue of their lack of free will, are completely without responsibility, while children, insofar as they possess reason in a partially developed form, can be held responsible to a corresponding degree.

Every man who possesses both free will and reason has an obligation to take responsibility for his actions, even though he may not be actively engaged in a continuing process of reflection, investigation, and deliberation about how he ought to act. A man will sometimes announce his willingness to take responsibility for the consequences of his actions, even though he has not deliberated about them, or does not intend to do so in the future. Such a declaration is, of course, an advance over the refusal to take responsibility; it at least acknowledges the existence of the obligation. But it does not relieve the man of the duty to engage in the reflective process which he has thus far shunned.

The responsible man is not capricious or anarchic, for he does acknowledge himself bound by moral constraints. But he insists that he alone is the judge of those constraints. He may listen to the advice of others, but he makes it his own by determining for himself whether it is good advice. He may learn from others about his moral obligations, but only in the sense that a mathematician learns from other mathematicians—namely by hearing from them arguments whose validity he recognizes even though he did not think of them himself. He does not learn in the sense that one learns from an explorer, by accepting as true his account of things one cannot see for oneself.

Since the responsible man arrives at moral decisions which he expresses to himself in the form of imperatives, we may say that he gives laws to himself, or is self-legislating. In short, he is *autonomous*. As Kant argued, moral autonomy is a combination of freedom and responsibility; it is a submission to laws which one has made for oneself. The autonomous man, insofar as he is autonomous, is not subject to the will of another. He may do what another tells him, but not *because* he has been told to do it. He is therefore, in the political sense of the word, *free*.

[Wolff explains that we can neglect or forfeit our autonomy either by failing to take responsibility for our actions or by voluntarily putting ourselves in a position of servitude.

Finally, Wolff brings the conflict between authority and autonomy to full focus. Ed.]

The defining mark of the state is authority, the right to rule. The primary obligation of man is autonomy, the refusal to be ruled. It would seem, then, that there can be no resolution of the conflict between the autonomy of the individual and the putative authority of the state. Insofar as a man fulfills his obligation to make himself the author of his decisions, he will resist the state's claim to have authority over him. That is to say, he will deny that he has a duty to obey the laws of the state *simply because they are laws*. In that sense, it would seem that anarchism is the only political doctrine consistent with the virtue of autonomy.

Now, of course, an anarchist may grant the necessity of *complying* with the law under certain circumstances or for the time being. He may even doubt that there is any real prospect of eliminating the state as a human institution. But he will never view the commands of the state as *legitimate*, as having a binding moral force. In a sense, we might characterize the anarchist as a man without a country, for despite the ties which bind him to the land of his childhood, he stands in precisely the same moral relationship to "his" government as he does to the government of any other country in which he might happen to be staying for a time. When

I take a vacation to Great Britain, I obey its laws, both because of prudential self-interest and because of the obvious moral considerations concerning the value of order, the general good consequences of preserving a system of property, and so forth. On my return to the United States, I have a sense of reentering *my* country, and if I think about the matter at all, I imagine myself to stand in a different and more intimate relation to American laws. They have been promulgated by *my* government, and I therefore have a special obligation to obey them. But the anarchist tells me that my feeling is purely sentimental and has no objective moral basis. All authority is equally illegitimate, although of course not therefore equally worthy or unworthy of support, and my obedience to American laws, if I am to be morally autonomous, must proceed from the same considerations which determine me abroad.

The dilemma which we have posed can be succinctly expressed in terms of the concept of a *de jure* state. If all men have a continuing obligation to achieve the highest degree of auton-

omy possible, then there would appear to be no state whose subjects have a moral obligation to obey its commands. Hence, the concept of a *de jure* legitimate state would appear to be vacuous, and philosophical anarchism would seem to be the only reasonable political belief for an enlightened man.

SUMMARY

Autonomy, for the anarchist, is the highest value and generates an absolute duty to act only from reasons the person regards as good. The state, on the other hand, claims authority over citizens, creating obligations for them even when they disagree with these obligations. Since moral autonomy is a higher obligation than obedience to the state, the state can have no moral authority over the individual. People may not forfeit or transfer their authority to the state. Hence, the state has no moral force. It is unjustified.

For Further Reflection

1. Go over the argument for anarchy. Do you see any problems with it? Is autonomy as high a value as the anarchist supposes?

2. Do you agree with Wolff regarding his anarchist argument? Is our obedience to the state unjustified and immoral? Can you find any weaknesses in Wolff's argument? Can political authority be justified?

3. Anarchism claims to offer hope for a sick world. Here is the definition of anarchism given by the Russian anarchist Peter Kropotkin:

The name given to a principle or theory of life and conduct under which society is conceived without government—harmony in such a society being obtained, not by submission to law, or by obedience to any authority, but by free agreements concluded between various groups, territorial and professional, freely constituted for the sake of production and consumption, as also for the satisfaction of the infinite variety of needs and aspiration of civilized beings.

Evaluate this definition. How realistic is it?

The Absolutist Answer:
The Justification of the State Is the Security It Affords

THOMAS HOBBES

Thomas Hobbes (1588–1679), the greatest English political philosopher, gave classic expression to the idea that morality and politics arise out of a social contract. He was born in the year of the Spanish Armada, was educated at Oxford University, and lived through an era of political revolutions as a scholar and tutor (he was tutor to Prince Charles, later King Charles II, of England). He was widely traveled and in communication with most of the intellectual luminaries of his day, both on the continent (Galileo, Gassendi, and Descartes) and in England (Francis Bacon, Ben Johnson, and William Harvey), and was regarded as a brilliant, if somewhat unorthodox and controversial, intellectual.

Hobbes is known today primarily for his masterpiece in political theory, *Leviathan* (1651), a book that was suppressed in his own day for its controversial ideas. In this book, from which our selection is taken, he develops a moral and political theory based on psychological egoism. Hobbes argues that people are all egoists who always act in their own self-interest, to obtain gratification and avoid harm. However, we cannot obtain any of the basic goods because of the inherent fear and insecurity in an unregulated "state of nature," in which life is "solitary, poor, nasty, brutish, and short." We cannot relax our guard, for everyone is constantly in fear of everyone else. In this state of anarchy the prudent person concludes that it really is in everyone's self-interest to make a contract to keep to a minimal morality of respecting human life, keeping covenants made, and obeying the society's laws. This minimal morality, which Hobbes refers to as "the laws of nature," is nothing more than a set of maxims of prudence. To ensure that we all obey this covenant Hobbes proposes a strong sovereign or "Leviathan" to impose severe penalties on those who disobey the laws, for "covenants without the sword are but words."

Study Questions

1. According to Hobbes, in what sense are all persons equal?
2. What is the natural relationship between people in the state of nature? Describe the state of nature. Are Hobbes' examples appropriate?
3. Does the notion of justice have any application in the state of nature? Why or why not?
4. What is necessary to establish morality and law?
5. What is the difference between the right of nature and the law of nature?
6. What is a contract, according to Hobbes?
7. How does Hobbes define good and evil?
8. What is the solution to the horrible state of nature?
9. What is the Leviathan? Why does Hobbes use this image?

OF THE NATURAL CONDITION OF MANKIND AS CONCERNING THEIR FELICITY, AND MISERY

NATURE HATH MADE men so equal, in the faculties of the body, and mind; as that though there be found one man sometimes manifestly stronger in body, or of quicker mind than another; yet when all is reckoned together, the difference between man, and man, is not so considerable, as that one man can thereupon claim to himself any benefit, to which another may not pretend, as well as he. For as to the strength of body, the weakest has strength enough to kill the strongest, either by secret machination, or by confederacy with others, that are in the same danger with himself.

And as to the faculties of the mind, setting aside the arts grounded upon words, and especially that skill of proceeding upon general, and infallible rules, called science; which very few have, and but in few things; as being not a native faculty, born with us; nor attained, as prudence, while we look after somewhat else, I find yet a greater equality amongst men, than that of strength. For prudence, is but experience; which equal time, equally bestows on all men, in those things they equally apply themselves unto. That which may perhaps make such equality incredible, is but a vain conceit of one's own wisdom, which almost all men think they have in a greater degree, than the vulgar; that is, than all men but themselves, and a few others, whom by fame, or for concurring with themselves, they approve. For such is the nature of men, that howsoever they may acknowledge many others to be more witty, or more eloquent, or more learned; yet they will hardly believe there be many so wise as themselves; for they see their own wit at hand, and other men's at a distance. But this proveth rather that men are in that point equal, than unequal. For there is not ordinarily a greater sign of the equal distribution of

any thing, than that every man is contented with his share.

From this equality of ability, ariseth equality of hope in the attaining of our ends. And therefore if any two men desire the same thing, which nevertheless they cannot both enjoy, they become enemies; and in the way to their end, which is principally their own conservation, and sometimes their delectation only, endeavour to destroy, or subdue one another. And from hence it comes to pass, that where an invader hath no more to fear, than another man's single power; if one plant, sow, build, or possess a convenient seat, others may probably be expected to come prepared with forces united, to dispossess, and deprive him, not only of the fruit of his labour, but also of his life, or liberty. And the invader again is in the like danger of another.

And from this diffidence of one another, there is no way for any man to secure himself, so reasonable, as anticipation; that is, by force, or wiles, to master the persons of all men he can, so long, till he see no other power great enough to endanger him: and this is no more than his own conservation requireth, and is generally allowed. Also because there be some, that taking pleasure in contemplating their own power in the acts of conquest, which they pursue farther than their security requires; if others, that otherwise would be glad to be at ease within modest bounds, should not by invasion increase their power, they would not be able, long time, by standing only on their defence, to subsist. And by consequence, such augmentation of dominion over men being necessary to a man's conservation, it ought to be allowed him.

Again, men have no pleasure, but on the contrary a great deal of grief, in keeping company, where there is no power able to over-awe them all. For every man looketh that his companion should value him, at the same rate he sets upon himself: and upon all signs of contempt, or undervaluing, naturally endeavours, as far as he dares, (which amongst them that have no com-

---

From Thomas Hobbes, Leviathan, *1651.*

mon power to keep them in quiet, is far enough to make them destroy each other), to extort a greater value from his contemners, by damage; and from others, by the example.

So that in the nature of man, we find three principal causes of quarrel. First, competition; secondly, diffidence; thirdly, glory.

The first, maketh men invade for gain; the second, for safety; and the third, for reputation. The first use violence, to make themselves masters of other men's persons, wives, children, and cattle; the second, defend them; the third, for trifles, as a word, a smile, a different option, and any other sign of undervalue, either direct in their persons, or by reflection in their kindred, their friends, their nation, their profession, or their name.

Hereby it is manifest, that during the time men live without a common power to keep them all in awe, they are in that condition which is called war; and such a war, as is of every man, against every man. For war, consisteth not in battle only, or the act of fighting; but in a tract of time, wherein the will to contend by battle is sufficiently known: and therefore the notion of *time,* is to be considered in the nature of war; as it is in the nature of weather. For as the nature of foul weather, lieth not in the shower or two of rain; but in an inclination thereto of many days together: so the nature of war, consisteth not in actual fighting; but in the known disposition thereto, during all the time there is no assurance to the contrary. All other time is PEACE.

Whatsoever therefore is consequent to a time of war, where every man is enemy to every man; the same is consequent to the time, wherein men live without other security, than what their own strength, and their own invention shall furnish them withal. In such condition, there is no place for industry; because the fruit thereof is uncertain: and consequently no culture of the earth; no navigation, nor use of the commodities that may be imported by sea; no commodious building; no instruments of moving, and removing, such things as require much force;

no knowledge of the face of the earth; no account of time; no arts; no letters; no society; and which is worst of all, continual fear, and danger of violent death; and the life of man, solitary, poor, nasty, brutish, and short.

It may seem strange to some man, that has not well weighed these things; that nature should thus dissociate, and render men apt to invade, and destroy one another: and he may therefore, not trusting to this inference, made from the passions, desire perhaps to have the same confirmed by experience. Let him therefore consider with himself, when taking a journey, he arms himself, and seeks to go well accompanied; when going to sleep, he locks his doors; when even in his house he locks his chests; and this when he knows there be laws, and public officers, armed, to revenge all injuries shall be done him; what opinion he has of his fellow-subjects, when he rides armed; of his fellow citizens, when he locks his doors; and of his children, and servants, when he locks his chests. Does he not there as much accuse mankind by his actions, as I do by my words? But neither of us accuse man's nature in it. The desires, and other passions of man, are in themselves no sin. No more are the actions, that proceed from those passions, till they know a law that forbids them: which till laws be made they cannot know: nor can any law be made, till they have agreed upon the person that shall make it.

It may peradventure be thought, there was never such a time, nor condition of war as this; and I believe it was never generally so, over all the world: but there are many places, where they live so now. For the savage people in many places of America, except the government of small families, the concord whereof dependeth on natural lust, have no government at all; and live at this day in that brutish manner, as I said before. Howsoever, it may be perceived what manner of life there would be, where there were no common power to fear, by the manner of life, which men that have formerly lived under a peaceful government, use to degenerate into, in a civil war.

But though there had never been any time, wherein particular men were in a condition of war one against another; yet in all times, kings, and persons of sovereign authority, because of their independency, are in continual jealousies, and in the state and posture of gladiators; having their weapons pointing, and their eyes fixed on one another; that is, their forts, garrisons, and guns upon the frontiers of their kingdoms; and continual spies upon their neighbours; which is a posture of war. But because they uphold thereby, the industry of their subjects; there does not follow from it, that misery, which accompanies the liberty of particular men.

To this war of every man, against every man, this also is consequent; that nothing can be unjust. The notions of right and wrong, justice and injustice have there no place. Where there is no common power, there is no law: where no law, no injustice. Force, and fraud, are in war the two cardinal virtues. Justice, and injustice are none of the faculties neither of the body, nor mind. If they were, they might be in a man that were alone in the world, as well as his senses, and passions. They are qualities, that relate to men in society, not in solitude. It is consequent also to the same condition, that there be no propriety, no dominion, no *mine* and *thine* distinct; but only that to be every man's, that he can get; and for so long, as he can keep it. And thus much for the ill condition, which man by mere nature is actually placed in; though with a possibility to come out of it, consisting partly in the passions, partly in his reason.

The passions that incline men to peace, are fear of death; desire of such things as are necessary to commodious living; and a hope by their industry to obtain them. And reason suggesteth convenient articles of peace, upon which men may be drawn to agreement. These articles, are they, which otherwise are called the Laws of Nature: whereof I shall speak more particularly, in the two following chapters.

OF THE FIRST AND SECOND NATURAL LAWS, AND OF CONTRACTS

The right of nature, which writers commonly call *jus naturale,* is the liberty each man hath, to use his own power, as he will himself, for the preservation of his own nature; that is to say, of his own life; and consequently, of doing any thing, which in his own judgment, and reason, he shall conceive to be the aptest means thereunto.

By LIBERTY, is understood, according to the proper signification of the word, the absence of external impediments: which impediments, may oft take away part of a man's power to do what he would; but cannot hinder him from using the power left him, according as his judgment, and reason shall dictate to him.

A LAW OF NATURE, *lex naturalis,* is a precept or general rule, found out by reason, by which a man is forbidden to do that, which is destructive of his life, or taketh away the means of preserving the same; and to omit that, by which he thinketh it may be best preserved. For though they that speak of this subject, use to confound *jus,* and *lex, right* and *law:* yet they ought to be distinguished; because RIGHT, consisteth in liberty to do, or to forbear; whereas LAW, determineth, and bindeth to one of them: so that law, and right, differ as much, as obligation, and liberty; which in one and the same matter are inconsistent.

And because the condition of man, as hath been declared in the precedent chapter, is a condition of war of every one against every one; in which case every one is governed by his own reason; and there is nothing he can make use of, that may not be a help unto him, in preserving his life against his enemies; it followeth, that in such a condition, every man has a right to every thing; even to one another's body. And therefore, as long as this natural right of every man to every thing endureth, there can be no security to any man, how strong or wise soever he be, of living out the time, which nature ordinarily alloweth men to live. And consequently it is a precept, or general rule of reason, *that every man, ought to endeavour peace, as far as he has hope of obtaining it; and when he cannot obtain it, that he may seek, and use, all helps, and advantages of war.* The first branch of which rule, containeth the first, and fundamental law of nature; which is, *to seek peace, and follow it.* The second, the sum of the right of nature; which is, *by all means we can, to defend ourselves.*

From this fundamental law of nature, by which men are commanded to endeavour peace, is derived this second law; *that a man be willing, when others are so too, as far-forth, as for peace, and defence of himself he shall think it necessary, to lay down this right to all things; and be contented with so much liberty against other men, as he would allow other men against himself.* For as long as every man holdeth this right, of doing any thing he liketh; so long are all men in the condition of war. But if other men will not lay down their right, as well as he; then there is no reason for any one, to divest himself of his: for that were to expose himself to prey, which no man is bound to, rather than to dispose himself to peace. This is that law of the Gospel; *whatsoever you require that others should do to you, that do ye to them.* And that law of all men, *quod tibi fieri non vis, alteri ne feceris.**

To *lay down* a man's *right* to any thing, is to *divest* himself of the *liberty,* of hindering another of the benefit of his own right to the same. For he that renounceth, or passeth away his right, giveth not to any other man a right which he had not before; because there is nothing to which every man had not right by nature: but only standeth out of his way, that he may enjoy his own original right, without hindrance from him; not without hindrance from another. So that the effect which redoundeth to one man, by another man's defect of right, is but so much diminution of impediments to the use of his own right original.

Right is laid aside, either by simply renouncing it; or by transferring it to another. By *simply* RENOUNCING; when he cares not to whom the benefit thereof redoundeth. By TRANSFERRING; when he intendeth the benefit thereof to some certain person, or persons. And when a man hath in either manner abandoned, or granted away his right; then is he said to be OBLIGED, or BOUND, not to hinder those, to whom such right is granted, or abandoned, from the benefit of it: and that he *ought,* and it is his DUTY, not to make void that voluntary act of his own: and that such hindrance is INJUSTICE, and INJURY, as being *sine jure,*† the right being before renounced, or transferred. So that *injury,* or *injustice,* in the controversies of the world, is somewhat like to that, which in the disputations of scholars is called *absurdity.* For as it is there called an absurdity, to contradict what one maintained in the beginning: so in the world, it is called injustice, and injury, voluntarily to undo that, which from the beginning he had voluntarily done. The way by which a man either simply renounceth, or transferreth his right, is a declaration, or signification, by some voluntary and sufficient sign, or signs, that he doth so renounce, or transfer; or hath so renounced, or transferred the same, to him that accepteth it. And these signs are either words only, or actions only; or, as it happeneth most often, both words, and actions. And the same are the BONDS, by which men are bound, and obliged: bonds, that have their strength, not from their own nature, for nothing is more easily broken than a man's word, but from fear of some evil consequence upon the rupture.

Whensoever a man transferreth his right, or renounceth it; it is either in consideration of some right reciprocally transferred to himself; or for some other good he hopeth for thereby. For it is a voluntary act: and of the voluntary acts of every man, the object is some *good to himself.* And therefore there be some rights, which no man can be understood by any

---

*["What you do not want done to you, do not do to others."—ed. note]

†[That is, without right.—ed. note]

words, or other signs, to have abandoned, or transferred. At first a man cannot lay down the right of resisting them, that assault him by force, to take away his life; because he cannot be understood to aim thereby, at any good to himself. The same may be said of wounds, and chains, and imprisonment; both because there is no benefit consequent to such patience; as there is to the patience of suffering another to be wounded, or imprisoned: as also because a man cannot tell, when he seeth men proceed against him by violence, whether they intend his death or not. And lastly the motive, and end for which this renouncing, and transferring of right is introduced, is nothing else but the security of a man's person, in his life, and in the means of so preserving life, as not to be weary of it. And therefore if a man by words, or other signs, seem to despoil himself of the end, for which those signs were intended; he is not to be understood as if he meant it, or that it was his will; but that he was ignorant of how such words and actions were to be interpreted.

The mutual transferring of right, is that which men call CONTRACT.

There is a difference between transferring of right to the thing; and transferring, or tradition, that is delivery of the thing itself. For the thing may be delivered together with the translation of the right; as in buying and selling with ready-money; or exchange of goods, or lands: and it may be delivered some time after.

Again, one of the contractors, may deliver the thing contracted for on his part, and leave the other to perform his part as some determinate time after, and in the mean time be trusted; and then the contract on his part, is called PACT, or COVENANT: or both parts may contract now, to perform hereafter: in which cases, he that is to perform in time to come, being trusted, his performance is called *keeping of promise*, or faith; and the failing of performance, if it be voluntary, *violation of faith*.

When the transferring of right, is not mutual: but one of the parties transferreth, in hope to gain thereby friendship, or service from an-other, or from his friends; or in hope to gain the reputation of charity, or magnanimity; or to deliver his mind from the pain of compassion; or in hope of reward in heaven, this is not contract, but GIFT, FREE-GIFT, GRACE: which words signify one and the same thing.

Signs of contract, are either *express*, or *by inference*. Express, are words spoken with understanding of what they signify: and such words are either of the time *present*, or *past*; as, *I give, I grant, I have given, I have granted, I will that this be yours*: or of the future; as, *I will give, I will grant*: which words of the future are called PROMISE.

If a covenant be made, wherein neither of the parties perform presently, but trust one another; in the condition of mere nature, which is a condition of war of every man against every man, upon any reasonable suspicion, it is void: but if there be a common power set over them both, with right and force sufficient to compel performance, it is not void. For he that performeth first, has no assurance the other will perform after; because the bonds of words are too weak to bridle men's ambition, avarice, anger, and other passions, without the fear of some coercive power; which in the condition of mere nature, where all men are equal, and judges of the justness of their own fears, cannot possibly be supposed. And therefore he which performeth first, does but betray himself to his enemy; contrary to the right, he can never abandon, of defending his life, and means of living.

But in a civil estate, where there is a power set up to constrain those that would otherwise violate their faith, that fear is no more reasonable: and for that cause, he which by the covenant is to perform first, is obliged so to do.

The cause of fear, which maketh such a covenant invalid, must be always something arising after the covenant made; as some new fact, or other sign of the will not to perform: else it cannot make the covenant void. For that which could not hinder a man from promising, ought not to be admitted as a hindrance of performing.

OF OTHER LAWS OF NATURE

From that law of nature, by which we are obliged to transfer to another, such rights, as being retained, hinder the peace of mankind, there followeth a third; which is this, *that men perform their covenants made:* without which, covenants are in vain, and but empty words; and the right of all men to all things remaining, we are still in the condition of war.

And in this law of nature, consisteth the fountain and original of JUSTICE. For where no covenant hath preceded, there hath no right been transferred, and every man has right to every thing; and consequently, no action can be unjust. But when a covenant is made, then to break it is *unjust:* and the definition of INJUSTICE, is no other than *the not performance of covenant.* And whatsoever is not unjust, is *just.*

But because covenants of mutual trust, where there is a fear of no performance on either part, as hath been said in the former chapter, are invalid; though the original of justice be the making of covenants; yet injustice actually there can be none, till the cause of such fear be taken away; which while men are in the natural condition of war, cannot be done. Therefore before the names of just, and unjust can have place, there must be some coercive power, to compel men equally to the performance of their covenants, by the terror of some punishment, greater than the benefit they expect by the breach of their covenant; and to make good that propriety, which by mutual contract men acquire, in recompense of the universal right they abandon: and such power there is none before the erection of a commonwealth. And this is also to be gathered out of the ordinary definition of justice in the Schools: for they say, that *justice is the constant will of giving to every man his own,* and therefore where there is no *own,* that is, no propriety, there is no injustice; and where there is no coercive power erected, that is, where there is no commonwealth, there is no propriety; all men having right to all things: therefore where there is no commonwealth, there nothing is unjust. So that the nature of justice, consisteth in keeping of valid covenants: but the validity of covenants begins not but with the constitution of a civil power, sufficient to compel men to keep them: and then it is also that propriety begins. . . .

And because, though men be never so willing to observe these laws, there may nevertheless arise questions concerning a man's action; first, whether it were done, or not done; secondly, if done, whether against the law, or not against the law; the former whereof, is called a question *of fact;* the latter a question *of right,* therefore unless the parties to the question, covenant mutually to stand to the sentence of another, they are as far from peace as ever. This other to whose sentence they submit is called an ARBITRATOR. And therefore it is of the law of nature, *that they that are at controversy, submit their right to the judgment of an arbitrator.*

And seeing every man is presumed to do all things in order to his own benefit, no man is a fit arbitrator in his own cause; and if he were never so fit; yet equity allowing to each party equal benefit, if one be admitted to the judge, the other is to be admitted also; and so the controversy, that is, the cause of war, remains, against the law of nature.

For the same reason no man in any cause ought to be received for arbitrator, to whom greater profit, or honour, or pleasure apparently ariseth out of the victory of one party, than of the other: for he hath taken, though an unavoidable bribe, yet a bribe; and no man can be obliged to trust him. And thus also the controversy, and the condition of war remaineth, contrary to the law of nature.

And in a controversy of *fact,* the judge being to give no more credit to one, than to the other, if there be no other arguments, must give credit to a third; or to a third and fourth; or more: for else the question is undecided, and left to force, contrary to the law of nature.

These are the laws of nature, dictating peace, for a means of the conservation of men in multitudes; and which only concern the doctrine of civil society. There be other things tending to the destruction of particular men; as drunkenness, and all other parts of intemperance; which may therefore also be reckoned amongst those things which the law of nature hath forbidden; but are not necessary to be mentioned, nor are pertinent enough to this place.

And though this may seem too subtle a deduction of the laws of nature, to be taken notice of by all men; whereof the most part are too busy in getting food, and the rest too negligent to understand; yet to leave all men inexcusable, they have been contracted into one easy sum, intelligible even to the meanest capacity; and that is, *Do not that to another, which thou wouldest not have done to thyself;* which sheweth him, that he has no more to do in learning the laws of nature, but, when weighing the actions of other men with his own, they seem too heavy, to put them into the other part of the balance, and his own into their place, that his own passions, and self-love, may add nothing to the weight; and then there is none of these laws of nature that will not appear unto him very reasonable.

The laws of nature oblige *in foro interno;** that is to say, they bind to a desire they should take place: but *in foro externo,†* that is, to the putting them in act, not always. For he that should be modest, and tractable, and perform all he promises, in such time, and place, where no man else should do so, should but make himself a prey to others, and procure his own certain ruin, contrary to the ground of all laws of nature, which tend to nature's preservation. And again, he that having sufficient security, that others shall observe the same laws towards him, observes them not himself, seeketh not peace, but war; and consequently the destruction of his nature by violence.

And whatsoever laws bind *in foro interno,* may be broken, not only by a fact contrary to the law, but also by a fact according to it, in case a man think it contrary. For though his action in this case, be according to the law; yet his purpose was against the law; which, where the obligation is *in foro interno,* is a breach.

The laws of nature are immutable and eternal; for injustice, ingratitude, arrogance, pride, iniquity, acception of persons, and the rest, can never be made lawful. For it can never be that war shall preserve life, and peace destroy it.

The same laws, because they oblige only to a desire, and endeavour, I mean an unfeigned and constant endeavour, are easy to be observed. For in that they require nothing but endeavour, he that endeavoureth their performance, fulfilleth them; and he that fulfilleth the law, is just.

And the science of them, is the true and only moral philosophy. For moral philosophy is nothing else but the science of what is *good,* and *evil,* in the conversation, and society of mankind. *Good,* and *evil,* are names that signify our appetites, and aversions; which in different tempers, customs, and doctrines of men, are different: and divers men, differ not only in their judgment, on the sense of what is pleasant, and unpleasant to the taste, smell, hearing, touch, and sight; but also of what is conformable, or disagreeable to reason, in the actions of common life. Nay, the same man, in divers times, differs from himself; and one time praiseth, that is, calleth good, what another time he dispraiseth, and called evil: from whence arise disputes, controversies, and at last war. And therefore so long as a man is in the condition of mere nature, which is a condition of war, as private appetite is the measure of good, and evil: and consequently all men agree on this, that peace is good, and therefore also the way, or means of peace, which, as I have shewed before, are *justice, gratitude, modesty, equity, mercy,* and the rest of the laws of nature, are good; that is to say; *moral virtues;* and their contrary *vices,* evil. Now the science of virtue and vice, is moral philosophy; and therefore the true doctrine of the laws of nature, is the true moral philosophy. But the writers of moral philosophy, though they acknowledge the same virtues and

---

*[Literally, "in the internal forum"—that is, in a person's mind or conscience.—ed. note]

†[Literally, "in the external forum"—that is, in the public world of action.—ed. note]

vices; yet not seeing wherein consisted their goodness; nor that they come to be praised, as the means of peaceable, sociable, and comfortable living, place them in a mediocrity of passions: as if not the cause, but the degree of daring, made fortitude; or not the cause, but the quantity of a gift, made liberality.

These dictates of reason, men used to call by the name of laws, but improperly: for they are but conclusions, of theorems concerning what conduceth to the conservation and defence of themselves; whereas law, properly, is the word of him, that by right hath command over others. But yet if we consider the same theorems, as delivered in the word of God, that by right commandeth all things; then are they properly called laws.

OF THE CAUSES, GENERATION, AND DEFINITION OF A COMMONWEALTH

The final cause, end, or design of men, who naturally love liberty, and dominion over others, in the introduction of that restraint upon themselves, in which we see them live in commonwealths, is the foresight of their own preservation, and of a more contented life thereby; that is to say, of getting themselves out from that miserable condition of war, which is necessarily consequent, as hath been shown in chapter XIII, to the natural passions of men, when there is no visible power to keep them in awe, and tie them by fear of punishment to the performance of their covenants, and observation of those laws of nature set down in the fourteenth and fifteenth chapters.

For the laws of nature, as *justice, equity, modesty, mercy,* and, in sum, *doing to others, as we would be done to,* of themselves, without the terror of some power, to cause them to be observed, are contrary to our natural passions, that carry us to partiality, pride, revenge, and the like. And covenants, without the sword, are but words, and of no strength to secure a man at all. Therefore notwithstanding the laws of nature, which every one hath then kept, when he has the will to keep them, when he can do it safely, if there be no power erected, or not great enough for our security; every man will, and may lawfully rely on his own strength and art, for caution against all other men. And in all places, where men have lived by small families, to rob and spoil one another, has been a trade, and so far from being reputed against the law of nature, that the greater spoils they gained, the greater was their honour; and men observed no other laws therein, but the laws of honour; that is, to abstain from cruelty, leaving to men their lives, and instruments of husbandry. And as small families did then; so now do cities and kingdoms which are but greater families, for their own security, enlarge their dominions, upon all pretences of danger, and fear of invasion, or assistance that may be given to invaders, and endeavour as much as they can, to subdue, or weaken their neighbours, by open force, and secret arts, for want of other caution, justly; and are remembered for it in after ages with honour.

It is true, that certain living creatures, as bees, and ants, live sociably one with another, which are therefore by Aristotle numbered amongst political creatures; and yet have no other direction, than their particular judgments and appetites; nor speech, whereby one of them can signify to another, what he thinks expedient for the common benefit: and therefore some man may perhaps desire to know, why mankind cannot do the same. To which I answer,

First, that men are continually in competition for honour and dignity, which these creatures are not; and consequently amongst men there ariseth on that ground, envy and hatred, and finally war; but amongst these not so.

Secondly, that amongst these creatures, the common good differeth not from the private; and being by nature inclined to their private, they procure thereby the common benefit. But man, whose joy consisteth in comparing himself with other men, can relish nothing but what is eminent.

Thirdly, that these creatures, having not, as man, the use of reason, do not see, nor think they see any fault, in the administration of their common business; whereas amongst men, there are very many, that think themselves wiser, and abler to govern the public, better than the rest; and these strive to reform and innovate, one this way, another that way; and thereby bring it into distraction and civil war.

Fourthly, that these creatures, though they have some use of voice, in making known to one another their desires, and other affections; yet they want that art of words, by which some men can represent to others, that which is good, in the likeness of evil; and evil, in the likeness of good; and augment, or diminish the apparent greatness of good and evil; discontenting men, and troubling their peace at their pleasure.

Fifthly, irrational creatures cannot distinguish between *injury,* and *damage;* and therefore as long as they be at ease, they are not offended with their fellows: whereas man is then most troublesome, when he is most at ease: for then it is that he loves to shew his wisdom, and control the actions of them that govern the commonwealth.

Lastly, the agreement of these creatures is natural; that of men, is by covenant only, which is artificial: and therefore it is no wonder if there be somewhat else required, besides covenant, to make their agreement constant and lasting; which is a common power, to keep them in awe, and to direct their actions to the common benefit.

The only way to erect such a common power, as may be able to defend them from the invasion of foreigners, and the injuries of one another, and thereby to secure them in such sort, as that by their own industry, and by the fruits of the earth, they may nourish themselves and live contentedly; is, to confer all their power and strength upon one man, or upon one assembly of men, that may reduce all their wills, by plurality of voices, unto one will: which is as much as to say, to appoint one man, or assembly of men, to bear their person; and every one to own, and acknowledge himself to be author of whatsoever he that so beareth their person, shall act, or cause to be acted, in those things which concern the common peace and safety; and therein to submit their wills, every one to his will, and their judgments, to his judgment. This is more than consent, or concord; it is a real unity of them all, in one and the same person, made by covenant of every man with every man, in such manner, as if every man should say to every man, *I authorize and give up my right of governing myself, to this man, or to this assembly of men, on this condition, that thou give up thy right to him, and authorize all his actions in like manner.* This done, the multitude so united in one person, is called a COMMONWEALTH, in Latin CIVITAS. This is the generation of that great LEVIATHAN, or rather, to speak more reverently, of that *mortal god,* to which we owe under the *immortal God,* our peace and defence. For by this authority, given him by every particular man in the commonwealth, he hath the use of so much power and strength conferred on him, that by terror thereof, he is enabled to perform the wills of them all, to peace at home, and mutual aid against their enemies abroad. And in him consisteth the essence of the commonwealth; which, to define it, is *one person, of whose acts a great multitude, by mutual covenants one with another, have made themselves every one the author, to the end he may use the strength and means of them all, as he shall think expedient, for their peace and common defence.*

And he that carrieth this person, is called SOVEREIGN, and said to have *sovereign* power; and every one besides, his SUBJECT.

For Further Reflection

1. Hobbes wrote, "The utility of morality and civil philosophy is to be estimated, not so much by the commodities we have by knowing these sciences, as by the calamities we receive from not knowing them." What does he mean by this, and does the selection illustrate it?

2. Is Hobbes' view of human nature accurate? Do we always act out of the motivations of fear and distrust? Are people entirely self-interested egoists? Is psychological egoism, the view that we always do what we perceive to be in our best interest, too bleak and one-sided?

3. Hobbes thought that only an absolute sovereign could establish or ensure peace and civil society. Is he correct? What would his estimation of democracy be? Could democratic society make use of his analysis? How would democrats modify Hobbes' theory?

4. David Hume criticized the idea that contract theories provide a justification of political authority. First, there is no evidence of an original contract ever being made and, secondly, even if our ancestors did sign an original contract, why should that give us any reason for obeying the laws of the state? Even as we are not bound by the marriage or business contracts of our ancestors, why should we be obligated by their political contracts?

VII.54   The Democratic Answer:
The Justification of the State Is Its Promotion
of Security and Natural Human Rights

JOHN LOCKE

With the Restoration of the Catholic royalty in 1660, after the English Civil War, Locke joined those who sought to limit the power of the King and give greater power to Parliament. After the Glorious Revolution of 1688, in which Locke's hopes were realized, he published two long essays on the justification of political authority. The second of these essays, the *Second Treatise of Civil Government,* is the most important single work on constitutional democracy and greatly influenced the formation of the United States Constitution.

Regarding human nature and the state of nature, Locke is not so pessimistic as Hobbes. Whereas Hobbes saw the state of nature as one in which life was "solitary, poor, nasty, brutish, and short," "a war of all against all," Locke sees it as an inferior state caused by lack of adequate cooperation and common laws, but still one in which our natural rights are enjoyed. Humans are not all as egoistic or innately cruel as Hobbes would make out. Government arises through a social contract in which individuals agree to be bound by the laws of a central authority that represents the will of the majority. The will of the majority and natural rights to life, liberty, and property limit the government. The government loses its legitimacy if it ceases to represent the will of the people and becomes tyrannical. In that case revolution is warranted.

There were those in Locke's day who rejected the contract theory of government (as set forth by Hobbes and others) on the basis that there was no record of an original social contract and that even if there were, it would not be binding on us. To this charge Locke responds that each of us upon reaching adulthood *implicitly* subscribes to the social contract by remaining in the country, living under its laws, and benefiting from its structure and security.

(A biographical note on Locke precedes Reading III.19.)

Study Questions

1. What is the natural state of human beings?
2. How does government come into existence?
3. How should decisions be made within the State?
4. How do we dissolve our relation to the State as individuals?
5. Why will people surrender some of their freedom to join the State? What do they gain thereby?
6. What two powers in the state of nature do we give up in joining the State?
7. When are we justified in dissolving the government? How do we dissolve the government?
8. What is the purpose of government?

OF THE BEGINNING OF POLITICAL SOCIETIES

MEN BEING BY NATURE ALL FREE, equal, and independent, no one can be put out of his estate and subjected to the political power of another without his own consent, which is done by agreeing with other men, to join and unite into a community for their comfortable, safe, and peaceful living, one amongst another, in a secure enjoyment of their properties, and a greater security against any that are not of it. This any number of men may do, because it injures not the freedom of the rest; they are left, as they were, in the liberty of the state of nature. When any number of men have so consented to make one community or government, they are thereby presently incorporated, and make one body politic, wherein the majority have a right to act and [include] the rest.

For, when any number of men have, by the consent of every individual, made a community, they have thereby made that community one body, with a power to act as one body, which is only by the will and determination of the majority. . . .

And thus every man, by consenting with others to make one body politic under one government, puts himself under an obligation to everyone of that society to submit to the determination of the majority, and to be [included] by it; or else this original compact, whereby he with others incorporates into one society, would signify nothing, and be no compact if he be left free and under no other ties than he was in before in the state of nature. For what appearance would there be of any compact? . . . For where the majority cannot include the rest, there they cannot act as one

From John Locke, Second Treatise on Civil Government *(1690).*

body, and consequently will be immediately dissolved again.

Whosoever therefore out of a state of nature unite into a community, must be understood to give up all the power necessary to the ends for which they unite society to the majority of the community, unless they expressly agreed in any number greater than the majority. And this is done by barely agreeing to unite into one political society, which is all the compact that is, or needs be, between the individuals that enter into or make up a commonwealth. And thus, that which begins and actually constitutes any political society is nothing but the consent of any number of freemen capable of a majority, to unite and incorporate into such a society. And this is that, and that only, which did or could give beginning to any lawful government in the world. . . .

Every man that hath any possession of enjoyment of any part of the dominions of any government doth thereby give his tacit consent, and is as far forth obliged to obedience to the laws of that government, during such enjoyment, as any one under it, whether this his possession be of land to him and his heirs for ever, or a lodging only for a week; or whether it be barely travelling freely on the highway; and, in effect, it reaches as far as the very being of anyone within the territories of that government.

To understand this better, it is fit to consider that every man when he at first incorporates himself into any commonwealth, he, by his uniting himself thereunto, annexes also, and submits to the community those possessions which he has, or shall acquire, that do not already belong to any other government. For it would be a direct contradiction for anyone to enter into society with others for the securing and regulating of property, and yet to suppose his land, whose property is to be regulated by the laws of the society, should be exempt from the jurisdiction of that government to which he himself, the proprietor of the land, is subject. By the same act, therefore, whereby anyone unites his person, which was before free, to any commonwealth, by the same he unites his possessions, which were before free, to it also; and they become, both of them, person and possession, subject to the government and dominion of that commonwealth as long as it hath a being. Whoever therefore from thenceforth, by inheritance, purchase, permission, or otherwise enjoys any part of the land so annexed to, and under the government of that commonwealth, must take it with the condition it is under; that is, of submitting to the government of the commonwealth, under whose jurisdiction it is, as far forth as any subject of it.

But since the government has a direct jurisdiction only over the land and reaches the possessor of it (before he has actually incorporated himself in the society) only as he dwells upon and enjoys that, the obligation anyone is under by virtue of such enjoyment to submit to the government begins and ends with the enjoyment; so that whenever the owner, who has given nothing but such a tacit consent to the government, will, by donation, sale or otherwise, quit the said possession, he is at liberty to go and incorporate himself into any other commonwealth, or agree with others to begin a new one in any part of the world they can find free and unpossessed; whereas he that has once, by actual agreement and any express declaration, given his consent to be of any commonwealth, is perpetually and indispensably obliged to be, and remain unalterably a subject to it, and can never be again in the liberty of the state of nature, unless by any calamity the government he was under comes to be dissolved; or else by some public act cuts him off from being any longer a member of it.

But submitting to the laws of any country, living quietly, and enjoying privileges and protection under them makes not a man a member of that society; this is only a local protection and homage due to and from all those who, not being in a state of war, come within the territories belonging to any government, to all parts whereof the force of its law extends. But this no more makes a man a member of that society than it would make a man a subject to another in whose family he found it convenient to abide for some time. . . . Nothing can make any man [a citizen] but his actually entering into it by positive engagement and express promise and compact.

OF THE ENDS OF POLITICAL SOCIETY AND GOVERNMENT

If man in the state of nature be so free as has been said; if he be absolute lord of his own person and possessions; equal to the greatest and subject to no body, why will he part with his freedom? Why will he give up this empire, and subject himself to the dominion and control of any other power? To which 'tis obvious to answer, that though in the state of nature he hath such a right, yet the enjoyment of it is very uncertain and constantly exposed to the invasion of others; for all being kings as much as he, every man his equal, and the greater part no strict observers of equity and justice, the enjoyment of the property he has in this state is very unsafe, very unsecure. This makes him willing to quit this condition which, however free, is full of fears and continual dangers; and 'tis not without reason that he seeks out and is willing to join in society with others who are already united, or have a mind to unite for the mutual preservation of their lives, liberties, and estates, which I call by the general name, property.

The great and chief end therefore, of men's uniting into commonwealths, and putting themselves under government, is the preservation of their property; to which in the state of nature there are many things wanting.

First, There wants an established, settled, known law, received and allowed by common consent to be the standard of right and wrong, and the common measure to decide all controversies between them. For though the law of nature be plain and intelligible to all rational creatures, yet men, being biased by their interest, as well as ignorant for want of study of it, are

not apt to allow of it as a law binding to them in the application of it to their particular cases.

Secondly, In the state of nature there wants a known and indifferent judge, with authority to determine all differences according to the established law. For everyone in that state being both judge and executioner of the law of nature, men being partial to themselves, passion and revenge is very apt to carry them too far, and with too much heat in their own cases, as well as negligence and unconcernedness, make them too remiss in other men's.

Thirdly, In the state of nature there often wants power to back and support the sentence when right, and to give it due execution. They who by any injustice offended, will seldom fail where they are able by force to make good their injustice. Such resistance many times makes the punishment dangerous, and frequently destructive to those who attempt it.

Thus mankind, notwithstanding all the privileges of the state of nature, being but in an ill condition while they remain in it, are quickly driven into society. Hence it comes to pass, that we seldom find any number of men live any time together in this state. The inconveniences that they are therein exposed to by the irregular and uncertain exercise of the power every man has of punishing the transgressions of others, make them take sanctuary under the established laws of government, and therein seek the preservation of their property. 'Tis this makes them so willingly give up every one his single power of punishing to be exercised by such alone as shall be appointed to it amongst them, and by such rules as the community, or those authorized by them to that purpose, shall agree on. And in this we have the original right and rise of both the legislative and executive power as well as of the governments and societies themselves.

For in the state of nature to omit the liberty he has of innocent delights, a man has two powers.

The first is to do whatsoever he thinks fit for the preservation of himself and others within the permission of the law of nature; by which law, common to them all, he and all the rest of mankind are one community, make up one society distinct from all other creatures and were it not for the corruption and viciousness of degenerate men, there would be no need of any other, no necessity that men should separate from this great and natural community, and associate into less combinations.

The other power a man has in the state of nature is the power to punish the crimes committed against that law. Both these he gives up when he joins in a private, if I may so call it, or particular political society, and incorporates into any commonwealth separate from the rest of mankind.

The first power, *viz.* of doing whatsoever he thought fit for the preservation of himself and the rest of mankind, he gives up to be regulated by laws made by the society, so far forth as the preservation of himself and the rest of that society shall require; which laws of the society in many things confine the liberty he had by the law of nature.

Secondly, the power of punishing he wholly gives up, and engages his natural force (which he might before employ in the execution of the law of nature, by his own single authority, as he thought fit) to assist the executive power of the society as the law thereof shall require. For being now in a new state, wherein he is to enjoy many conveniences from the labour, assistance, and society of others in the same community, as well as protection from its whole strength, he is to part also with as much of his natural liberty, in providing for himself, as the good, prosperity, and safety of the society shall require, which is not only necessary but just, since the other members of the society do the like.

But though men when they enter into society give up the equality, liberty, and executive power they had in the state of nature into the hands of the society, to be so far disposed of by the legislative as the good of the society shall require, yet it being only with an intention in everyone the better to preserve himself, his liberty and property (for no rational creature can

be supposed to change his condition with an intention to be worse), the power of the society or legislative constituted by them can never be supposed to extend farther than the common good, but is obliged to secure everyone's property by providing against those three defects above-mentioned that made the state of nature so unsafe and uneasy. And so, whoever has the legislative or supreme power of any commonwealth, is bound to govern by established standing laws, promulgated and known to the people, and not by extemporary decrees, by indifferent and upright judges, who are to decide controversies by those laws; and to employ the force of the community at home only in the execution of such laws, or abroad to prevent or redress foreign injuries and secure the community from inroads and invasion. And all this to be directed to no other end but the peace, safety, and public good of the people. . . .

OF THE EXTENT OF THE LEGISLATIVE POWER

These are the bounds which the trust that is put in them by the society and the law of God and nature have set to the legislative power of every commonwealth, in all forms of government.

First, They are to govern by promulgated established laws, not to be varied in particular cases, but to have one rule for rich and poor, for the favourite at Court, and the countryman at plough.

Secondly, These laws also ought to be designed for no other end ultimately but the good of the people.

Thirdly, They must not raise taxes on the property of the people without the consent of the people given by themselves or their deputies. And this properly concerns only such governments where the legislative is always in being, or at least where the people have not reserved any part of the legislative to deputies, to be from time to time chosen by themselves.

Fourthly, The legislative neither must nor can transfer the power of making laws to anybody else, or place it anywhere but where the people have. . . .

THE LEGITIMACY OF REVOLUTION

The reason why men enter into society is the preservation of their property; and the end why they choose and authorize a legislative is that there may be laws made and rules set as guards and fences to the properties of all the members of the society to limit the power and moderate the dominion of every part and member of the society; for since it can never be supposed to be the will of the society that the legislative should have a power to destroy that which every one designs to secure by entering into society, and for which the people submitted themselves to legislators of their own making. Whenever the legislators endeavour to take away and destroy the property of the people, or to reduce them to slavery under arbitrary power, they put themselves into a state of war with the people who are thereupon absolved from any further obedience, and are left to the common refuge which God has provided for all men against force and violence. Whensoever, therefore, the legislative shall transgress this fundamental rule of society, and either by ambition, fear, folly, or corruption, endeavour to grasp themselves, or put into the hands of any other, an absolute power over the lives, liberties, and estates of the people, by this breach of trust they forfeit the power the people had put into their hands for quite contrary ends, and it devolves to the people, who have a right to resume their original liberty and, by the establishment of a new legislative, such as they shall think fit, provide for their own safety and security, which is the end for which they are in society. What I have said here concerning the legislative in general holds true also concerning the supreme executor, who having a double trust put in him—both to have a part in the legislative and the supreme execution of the law—acts against both when he goes about to set up his own arbitrary will as the law of the society. . . .

Here, it is like, the common question will be made: Who shall be judge whether the prince or legislative act contrary to their trust? This, perhaps, ill-affected and factious men may spread amongst the people, when the prince only makes use of his due prerogative. To this I reply: The people shall be judge; for who shall be judge whether his trustee or deputy acts well and according to the trust reposed in him but he who deputes him and must, by having deputed him, have still a power to discard him when he fails in his trust? If this be reasonable in particular cases of private men, why should it be otherwise in that of the greatest moment where the welfare of millions is concerned, and also where the evil, if not prevented, is greater and the redress very difficult, dear, and dangerous? . . .

To conclude, the power that every individual gave the society when he entered into it, can never revert to the individuals again as long as the society lasts, but will always remain in the community, because without this there can be no community, no commonwealth, which is contrary to the original agreement; so also when the society hath placed the legislative in any assembly of men to continue in them and their successors, with direction and authority for providing such successors, the legislative can never revert to the people whilst that government lasts, because having provided a legislative with power to continue for ever, they have given up their political power to the legislative and cannot resume it. But if they have set limits to the duration of their legislative, and made this supreme power in any person or assembly only temporary; or else when by the miscarriages of those in authority it is forfeited; upon the forfeiture, or at the determination of the time set, it reverts to the society, and the people have a right to act as supreme, and continue the legislative in themselves; or place it in a new form, or new hands as they think good.

For Further Reflection

1. Locke justifies his notion of obedience to the State as a Social Contract, saying that it is implicit and binding because we can leave the country if we don't like it. Is this a realistic solution?

2. Compare Hobbes' account of the social contract with Locke's account. Which do you think is more accurate?

3. What would Locke say about the rights of unpopular minorities? What if a majority of a community voted that pornography should not be allowed into the community, so that it was illegal for individuals to view certain forms of art in the privacy of their homes? Would Locke's theory permit the community to limit individual liberty in this way?

VII.55   A Classical Liberal Answer: Government Must Promote Freedom

JOHN STUART MILL

Although Mill (1806–1873) agrees with Locke in favoring representational democracy, he does not accept the notion of natural rights. Typically utilitarians such as Mill follow Jeremy Bentham in viewing the idea of natural rights as "nonsense on stilts." We should promote a democracy dedicated to individual liberty because that will maximize happiness. Furthermore, Mill disagrees with Locke's majoritarian emphasis and warns of a new form of tyranny, the "tyranny of the majority." Every educated adult must be free to do what he or she desires. The only grounds for interfering with individuals is to protect others from harm.

(A biographical sketch of John Stuart Mill precedes Reading VI.50.)

Study Questions

1. What is the subject of this essay?
2. How did the concern of the patriots to set limits to power arise in society?
3. In what two ways was this limiting of political power attempted in the past?
4. What is the main problem which popular government conceals from observation?
5. What sorts of tyrannies must the individual be protected against?
6. What is the sole justification of society's interfering in the lives of its members? What are some unjustified reasons?
7. Does the principle of liberty apply to all people everywhere? Explain.
8. Does Mill base his principle of liberty on a basic natural right to liberty? If so, why? If not, why not?
9. What are the areas of life covered by the principle of liberty?
10. What is the peculiar evil of silencing unpopular expressions of opinion?
11. What does Mill say about different life styles?

CHAPTER I. INTRODUCTORY

THE SUBJECT OF THIS ESSAY is not the so-called Liberty of the Will, so unfortunately opposed to the misnamed doctrine of Philosophical Necessity, but Civil, or Social Liberty: the nature and limits of the power which can be legitimately exercised by society over the individual. A question seldom stated, and hardly ever discussed, in general terms, but which profoundly influences the practical controversies of the age by its latent presence, and is likely soon to make itself recognised as the vital question of the future. It is so far from being new, that, in a certain sense, it has divided mankind, almost from the remotest ages; but in the stage of progress into which the more civilised portions of the species have now entered, it presents itself under new conditions, and requires a different and more fundamental treatment.

The struggle between Liberty and Authority is the most conspicuous feature in the portions of history with which we are earliest familiar, particularly in that of Greece, Rome, and England. But in old times this contest was between subjects, or some classes of subjects, and the Government. By liberty, was meant protection against the tyranny of the political rulers. The rulers were conceived (except in some of the popular governments of Greece) as in a necessarily antagonistic position to the people whom they ruled. They consisted of a governing One, or a governing tribe or caste, who derived their authority from inheritance or conquest, who, at all events, did not hold it at the pleasure of the governed, and whose supremacy men did not venture, perhaps did not desire, to contest, whatever precautions might be taken against its oppressive exercise. Their power was regarded as necessary, but also as highly dangerous; as a weapon which they would attempt to use against their subjects, no less than against external enemies. To prevent the weaker members of the community from being preyed upon by innumerable vultures, it was needful that there should be an animal of prey stronger than the rest, commissioned to keep them down. But as the king of the vultures would be no less bent upon preying on the flock than any of the minor harpies, it was indispensable to be in a perpetual attitude of defence against his beak and claws. The aim, therefore, of patriots was to set limits to the power which the ruler should be suffered to exercise over the community; and this limitation was what they meant by liberty. It was attempted in two ways. First, by obtaining a recognition of certain immunities, called political liberties or rights, which it was to be regarded as a breach of duty in the ruler to infringe, and which if he did infringe, specific resistance, or general rebellion, was held to be justifiable. A second, and generally a later expedient, was the establishment of constitutional checks, by which the consent of the community, or of a body of some sort, supposed to represent its interests, was made a necessary condition to some of the more important acts of the governing power. To the first of these modes of limitation, the ruling power, in most European countries, was compelled, more or less, to submit. It was not so-with the second; and, to attain this, or when already in some degree possessed, to attain it more completely, became everywhere the principal object of the lovers of liberty. And so long as mankind were content to combat one enemy by another, and to be ruled by a master, on condition of being guaranteed more or less efficaciously against his tyranny, they did not carry their aspirations beyond this point.

A time, however, came, in the progress of human affairs, when men ceased to think it a necessity of nature that their governors should be an independent power, opposed in interest to themselves. It appeared to them much better that the various magistrates of the State should be their tenants or delegates, revocable at their pleasure. In that way alone, it seemed, could they have complete security that the powers of government would never be abused to their dis-

From On Liberty *(1859)*

advantage. By degrees this new demand for elective and temporary rulers became the prominent object of the exertions of the popular party, wherever any such party existed; and superseded, to a considerable extent, the previous efforts to limit the power of rulers. As the struggle proceeded for making the ruling power emanate from the periodical choice of the ruled, some persons began to think that too much importance had been attached to the limitation of the power itself. That (it might seem) was a resource against rulers whose interests were habitually opposed to those of the people. What was now wanted was, that the rulers should be identified with the people; that their interest and will should be the interest and will of the nation. The nation did not need to be protected against its own will. There was no fear of its tyrannising over itself. Let the rulers be effectually responsible to it, promptly removable by it, and it could afford to trust them with power of which it could itself dictate the use to be made. Their power was but the nation's own power, concentrated, and in a form convenient for exercise. This mode of thought, or rather perhaps of feeling, was common among the last generation of European liberalism, in the Continental section of which it still apparently predominates. Those who admit any limit to what a government may do, except in the case of such governments as they think ought not to exist, stand out as brilliant exceptions among the political thinkers of the Continent. A similar tone of sentiment might by this time have been prevalent in our own country, if the circumstances which for a time encouraged it, had continued unaltered.

But, in political and philosophical theories, as well as in persons, success discloses faults and infirmities which failure might have concealed from observation. The notion, that the people have no need to limit their power over themselves, might seem axiomatic, when popular government was a thing only dreamed about, or read of as having existed at some distant period of the past. Neither was that notion necessarily disturbed by such temporary aberrations as those of the French Revolution, the worst of which were the work of a usurping few, and which, in any case, belonged, not to the permanent working of popular institutions, but to a sudden and convulsive outbreak against monarchical and aristocratic despotism. In time, however, a democratic republic came to occupy a large portion of the earth's surface, and made itself felt as one of the most powerful members of the community of nations; and elective and responsible government became subject to the observations and criticisms which wait upon a great existing fact. It was now perceived that such phrases as 'self-government,' and 'the power of the people over themselves,' do not express the true state of the case. The 'people' who exercise the power are not always the same people with those over whom it is exercised; and the 'self-government' spoken of is not the government of each by himself, but of each by all the rest. The will of the people, moreover, practically means the will of the most numerous or the most active part of the people; the majority, or those who succeed in making themselves accepted as the majority; the people, consequently may desire to oppress a part of their number; and precautions are as much needed against this as against any other abuse of power. The limitation, therefore, of the power of government over individuals loses none of its importance when the holders of power are regularly accountable to the community, that is, to the strongest party therein. This view of things, recommending itself equally to the intelligence of thinkers and to the inclination of those important classes in European society to whose real or supposed interests democracy is adverse, has had no difficulty in establishing itself, and in political speculations 'the tyranny of the majority' is now generally included among the evils against which society requires to be on its guard.

Like other tyrannies, the tyranny of the majority was at first, and is still vulgarly, held in dread, chiefly as operating through the acts of the public authorities. But reflecting persons perceived that when society is itself the tyrant—society collectively over the separate individuals who compose it—its means of tyrannising are not restricted to the acts which it may do by the hands of its political functionaries. Society can and does execute its own mandates: and if it issues wrong mandates instead of right, or any mandates at all in things with which it ought not to meddle, it practises a social tyranny more formidable than many kinds of political oppression, since, though not usually upheld by such extreme penalties, it leaves fewer means of escape, penetrating much more deeply into the details of life, and enslaving the soul itself. Protection, therefore, against the tyranny of the magistrate is not enough: there needs protection also against the tyranny of the prevailing opinion and feeling; against the tendency of society to impose, by other means than civil penalties, its own ideas and practices as rules of conduct on those who dissent from them; to fetter the development, and, if possible, prevent the formation, of any individuality not in harmony with its ways, and compels all characters to fashion themselves upon the model of its own. There is a limit to the legitimate interference of collective opinion with individual independence: and to find that limit, and maintain it against encroachment, is as indispensable to a good condition of human affairs, as protection against political despotism.

The object of this Essay is to assert one very simple principle, as entitled to govern absolutely the dealings of society with the individual in the way of compulsion and control, whether the means used be physical force in the form of legal penalties, or the moral coercion of public opinion. That principle is, that the sole end for which mankind are warranted, individually or collectively, in interfering with the liberty of action of any of their number, is self-protection. That the only purpose for which power can be rightfully exercised over any member of a civilised community, against his will, is to prevent harm to others. His own good, either physical or moral, is not a sufficient warrant. He cannot rightfully be compelled to do or forbear because it will be better for him to do so, be-

cause it will make him happier, because, in the opinions of others, to do so would be wise, or even right. These are good reasons for remonstrating with him, or reasoning with him, or persuading him, or entreating him, but not for compelling him, or visiting him with any evil in case he do otherwise. To justify that, the conduct from which it is desired to deter him must be calculated to produce evil to some one else. The only part of the conduct of any one, for which he is amenable to society, is that which concerns others. In the part which merely concerns himself, his independence is, of right, absolute. Over himself, over his own body and mind, the individual is sovereign.

It is, perhaps, hardly necessary to say that this doctrine is meant to apply to human beings in the maturity of their faculties. We are not speaking of children, or of young persons below the age which the law may fix as that of manhood or womanhood. Those who are still in a state to require being taken care of by others, must be protected against their own actions as well as against external injury. For the same reason, we may leave out of consideration those backward states of society in which the race itself may be considered as in its nonage. The early difficulties in the way of spontaneous progress are so great, that there is seldom any choice of means for overcoming them; and a ruler full of the spirit of improvement is warranted in the use of any expedients that will attain an end, perhaps otherwise unattainable. Despotism is a legitimate mode of government in dealing with barbarians, provided the end be their improvement, and the means justified by actually effecting that end.

Liberty, as a principle, has no application to any state of things anterior to the time when mankind became capable of being improved by free and equal discussion. Until then, there is nothing for them but implicit obedience to an Akbar or a Charlemagne, if they are so fortunate as to find one. But as soon as mankind have attained the capacity of being guided to their own improvement by conviction or persuasion (a period long since reached in all nations with whom we need here concern ourselves), compulsion, either in the direct form or in that of pains and penalties for noncompliance, is no longer admissible as a means to their own good, and justifiable only in the security of others.

It is proper to state that I forego any advantage which could be derived to my argument from the idea of abstract right as a thing independent of utility. I regard utility as the ultimate appeal on all ethical questions; but it must be utility in the largest sense, grounded on the permanent interests of man as a progressive being. Those interests, I contend, authorize the subjection of individual spontaneity to external control, only in respect to those actions of each, which concern the interest of other people. If any one does an act hurtful to others, there is a prima facie case for punishing him, by law, or, where legal penalties are not safely applicable, by general disapprobation. There are also many positive acts for the benefit of others, which he may rightfully be compelled to perform; such as, to give evidence in a court of justice; to bear his fair share in the common defense, or in any other joint work necessary to the interest of the society of which he enjoys the protection; and to perform certain acts of individual beneficence, such as saving a fellow-creature's life, or interposing to protect the defenseless against ill-usage, things which whenever it is obviously a man's duty to do, he may rightfully be made responsible to society for not doing. A person may cause evil to others not only by his actions but by his inaction, and in neither case he is justly accountable to them for the injury. The latter case, it is true, requires a much more cautious exercise of compulsion than the former. To make any one answerable for doing evil to others, is the rule; to make him answerable for not preventing evil, is, comparatively speaking, the exception. Yet there are many cases clear enough and grave enough to justify that exception. In all things which regard the external relations of the individual, he is *de jure* amenable to those whose interests are concerned, and if need be, to society as their protector. There are often good reasons for not holding him to the responsibility; but these reasons must arise from the special expediencies of the case: either because it is a kind of case in which he is on the whole likely to act better, when left to his own discretion, than when controlled in any way in which society have it in their power to control him; or because the attempt to exercise control would produce other evils, greater than those which it would prevent. When such reasons as these preclude the enforcement of responsibility, the conscience of the agent himself should step into the vacant judgment-seat, and protect those interests of others which have no external protection; judging himself all the more rigidly, because the case does not admit of his being made accountable to the judgment of his fellow creatures.

But there is a sphere of action in which society, as distinguished from the individual, has, if any, only an indirect interest; comprehending all that portion of a person's life and conduct which affects only himself, or, if it also affects others, only with their free, voluntary, and undeceived consent and participation. When I say only himself, I mean directly, and in the first instance: for whatever affects himself, may affect others through himself, and the objection which may be grounded on this contingency, will receive consideration in the sequel. This, then, is the appropriate region of human liberty. It comprises, first, the inward domain of consciousness; demanding liberty of conscience, in the most comprehensive sense; liberty of thought and feeling; absolute freedom of opinion and sentiment on all subjects, practical or speculative, scientific, moral, or theological. The liberty of expressing and publishing opinions may seem to fall under a different principle, since it belongs to that part of the conduct of an individual which concerns other people; but, being almost of as much importance as the liberty of thought itself, and resting in great part on the same reasons, is practically inseparable from it. Secondly, the principle requires liberty of tastes and pursuits; of framing the plan of our life to suit our own character; of doing as we like, subject to such consequences as may follow; without impediment from our fellow-creatures, so long as what we do does not harm them, even though they should think our conduct foolish, perverse, or wrong. Thirdly, from this liberty of each individual, follows the liberty, within the same limits, of combination among individuals; freedom to unite, for any purpose not involving harm to others: the persons combining being supposed to be of full age, and not forced or deceived.

No society in which these liberties are not, on the whole, respected, is free, whatever may be its form of government; and none is completely free in which they do not exist absolute and unqualified. The only freedom which deserves the name, is that of pursuing our own good in our own way, so long as we do not attempt to deprive others of theirs, or impede their efforts to obtain it. Each is the proper guardian of his own health, whether bodily, or mental and spiritual. Mankind are greater gainers by suffering each other to live as seems good to themselves, than by compelling each to live as seems good to the rest.

Though this doctrine is anything but new, and, to some persons, may have the air of a truism, there is no doctrine which stands more directly opposed to the general tendency of existing opinion and practice. Society has expended fully as much effort in the attempt (according to its lights) to compel people to conform to its notions of personal as of social excellence.

CHAPTER II. OF THE LIBERTY OF THOUGHT AND DISCUSSION

The time, it is to be hoped, is gone by, when any defence would be necessary of the 'liberty of the press' as one of the securities against corrupt or tyrannical government. No argument, we may suppose, can now be needed, against permitting a legislature or an executive, not identified in interest with the people, to prescribe opinions to them, and determine what doctrines or what arguments they shall be allowed to hear. This aspect of the question, besides, has been so often and so triumphantly enforced by preceding writers, that it needs not be specially insisted on in this place. Though the law of England, on the subject of the press, is as servile to this day as it was in the time of the Tudors, there is little danger of its being actually put in force against political discussion, except during some temporary panic, when fear of insurrection drives ministers and judges from their propriety; and, speaking generally, it is not, in constitutional countries, to be apprehended, that the government, whether completely responsible to the people or not, will often attempt to control the expression of opinion, except when in doing so it makes itself the organ of the general intolerance of the public. Let us suppose, therefore, that the government is entirely at one with the people, and never thinks of exerting any power of coercion unless in agreement with what it conceives to be their voice. But I deny the right of the people to exercise such coercion, either by themselves or by their government. The power itself is illegitimate. The best government has no more title to it than the worst. It is as noxious, or more noxious, when exerted in accordance with public opinion, than when in opposition to it. If all mankind minus one were of one opinion, and only one person were of the contrary opinion, mankind would be no more justified in silencing that one person, than he, if he had the power, would be justified in silencing mankind. Were an opinion a personal possession of no value except to the owner; if to be obstructed in the enjoyment of it were simply a private injury, it would make some difference whether the injury was inflicted only on a few persons or on many. But the peculiar evil of silencing the expression of an opinion is, that it is robbing the human race; posterity as well as the existing generation; those who dissent from the opinion, still more than those who hold it. If the opinion is right, they are deprived of the opportunity of exchanging error for truth: If wrong, they lose, what is almost as great a benefit, the clearer perception and livelier impression of truth, produced by its collision with error.

As it is useful that while mankind are imperfect there should be different opinions, so is it that there should be different experiments of living; that free scope should be given to varieties of character, short of injury to others; and that the worth of different modes of life should be proved practically, when any one thinks fit to try them. It is desirable, in short, that in things which do not primarily concern others, individuality should assert itself. Where, not the person's own character, but the traditions or customs of other people are the rule of conduct, there is wanting one of the principal ingredients of human happiness, and quite the chief ingredient of individual and social progress.

In maintaining this principle, the greatest difficulty to be encountered does not lie in the appreciation of means towards an acknowledged end, but in the indifference of persons in general to the end itself. If it were felt that the free development of individuality is one of the leading essentials of well-being; that it is not only a coordinate element with all like that is designated by the terms civilization, instruction, education, culture, but is itself a necessary part and condition of all those things; there would be no danger that liberty should be undervalued, and the adjustment of the boundaries between it and social control would present no extraordinary difficulty. But the evil is, that individual spontaneity is hardly recognized by the common modes of thinking, as having any intrinsic worth, or deserving any regard on its own account.

He who lets the world, or his own portion of it, choose his plan of life for him, has no need of any other faculty than the ape-like one of imitation. He who chooses his plan for himself, employs all his faculties. He must use observation to see, reasoning and judgment to foresee activity to gather materials for decision, discrimination to decide, and when he has decided, firmness and self-control to hold to his deliberate decision. And these qualities he requires and exercises exactly in proportion as the part of his conduct which he determines according to his own judgment and feelings is a large one. It is possible that he might be guided in some good path, and kept out of harm's way, without any of these things. But what will be his comparative worth as a human being? It really is of importance, not only what men do, but also what manner of men they are that do it. Among the works of man, which human life is rightly employed in perfecting and beautifying, the first in importance surely is man himself. Supposing it were possible to get houses built, corn grown. battles fought, causes tried, and even churches erected and prayers said, by machinery—by automatons in human form—it would be a considerable loss to exchange for these automatons even the men and women who at present inhabit the more civilized parts of the world, and who assuredly are but starved specimens of what nature can and will produce. Human nature is not a machine to be built after a model, and set to do exactly the work prescribed for it, but a tree, which requires to grow and develop itself on all sides, according to the tendency of the inward forces which make it a living thing. . . .

For Further Reflection

1. Do you agree with Mill that the principle of liberty can be justified only by utilitarian considerations? Is he correct in rejecting the notion of natural rights?

2. Do you agree with Mill's formulation of the principle of liberty? Should we sometimes act paternalistically, even with educated adults? How would Mill's principle apply to someone using drugs? Should we intervene? Would Mill advocate legalizing drugs—and thereby taking the criminal and profit motive out of the drug abuse?

3. Mill wrote, "It is not useful, but hurtful, that the constitution of the country should declare ignorance to be entitled to as much political power as knowledge," and called for weighted voting rights in which the votes of higher intelligence would count for more than the uninformed and less intelligent. Do you agree with Mill

The Communist Answer: The Justification of the State Is Its Promotion of Radical Equality   VII.56

KARL MARX AND FRIEDRICH ENGELS

Friedrich Engels (1820–1895) was born the son of a German industrialist who moved to Manchester, England. He had considerable experience in the workings of British industry during the Industrial Revolution and was able to provide Marx with a first-hand insight of industrial realities. Harold Laski describes the co-founder of the Marxist movement as "always friendly, usually optimistic, with great gifts both for practical action and for getting on with others. . . . Widely read, with a very real talent for moving rapidly through a great mass of material, he was facile rather than profound. He was utterly devoid of jealousy or vanity. He had a happy nature which never agonised over the difficulty of thought. . . . It never occurred to him, during the friendship of forty years, marked only by one brief misunderstanding, to question his duty to serve Marx in every way he could." (Introduction to *The Communist Manifesto*, Random House, 1967)

Karl Marx (1818–1883) was born in Trier and educated in Catholic schools and at the University of Berlin, where he received his doctorate. He began his career in 1842 as a journalist for the liberal *Rheinische Zeitung* and soon distinguished himself as a brilliant and radical thinker. He was described as follows: "He combines the deepest philosophical seriousness with the most biting wit. Imagine Rousseau, Voltaire, d'Holbach, Lessing, Heine, and Hegel fused into one person—I say fused, not juxtaposed—and you have Dr. Marx." (cited in David McClellen's *Karl Marx,* Viking Press, 1975, p. 3) He played the dominant role in founding the Marxist movement. His principal works are *Economic and Philosophical Manuscripts of 1844,* the *Communist Manifesto* (with Friedrich Engels, 1848), and *Capital* (3 volumes, 1867, 1885, 1895).

Marx wrote as a young man, "Hitherto, the various philosophies have only interpreted the world in various ways; the point is to change it." The message of our selection from the *Communist Manifesto* embodies that thesis. It combines socioeconomic analysis of the class struggle with a plan of action for overthrowing the existing oppressive conditions. It argues that the struggle between classes is the essential catalyst of historical change, but whereas in earlier times the structure of society was a complicated arrangement of hierarchical classes, in the present period of the bourgeoisie the social structure is developing towards a simple division of two classes: the bourgeoisie, owners of the means of production and ruling class, and the proletariat, the worker-slaves. The proletariat are fast becoming self-conscious of their exploited state and an international drama is unfolding in which they will create a violent revolution, throwing off their chains and, as new dictators, inaugurating a new era of justice, a classless society in which everyone freely and equally participates, "in which the free development of each is the condition for the free development of all."

Study Questions

1. How do Marx and Engels divide all previous societies?
2. How do they characterize their own epoch? How is it different from previous times?
3. Describe the bourgeoisie. How is it in the process of self-destruction?
4. Who are the proletariat? What is their condition?
5. What do Marx and Engels predict as the future course of the class struggle?
6. What is the relationship between the Communist party and the proletariat?
7. What will be the result of the proletariat revolution?
8. What are some of the specific social changes that will occur in the most advanced countries? To what degree have their predictions been realized?

I. BOURGEOIS AND PROLETARIANS

THE HISTORY OF ALL hitherto existing society is the history of class struggles.

Freeman and slave, patrician and plebeian, lord and serf, guildmaster and journeyman, in a word, oppressor and oppressed, stood in constant opposition to one another, carried on an uninterrupted, now hidden, now open fight, a fight that each time ended, either in a revolutionary re-constitution of society at large, or in the common ruin of the contending classes.

In the earlier epochs of history, we find almost everywhere a complicated arrangement of society into various orders, a manifold gradation of social rank. In ancient Rome we have patri-cians, knights, plebeians, slaves; in the Middle Ages, feudal lords, vassals, guild-masters, journeymen, apprentices, serfs; in almost all of these classes, again, subordinate gradations.

The modern bourgeois society that has sprouted from the ruins of feudal society has not done away with class antagonisms. It has but established new classes, new conditions of oppression, new forms of struggle in place of the old ones.

Our epoch, the epoch of the bourgeoisie, possesses, however, this distinctive feature: it has simplified the class antagonisms. Society as a whole is more and more splitting up into two great hostile camps, into two great classes directly facing each other: Bourgeoisie and Proletariat.

From the serfs of the Middle Ages sprang the chartered burghers of the earliest towns. From

From Karl Marx and Friedrich Engels, Manifesto of the Communist Party, trans. by Samuel Moore in 1888 from the original German text of 1848 and edited by Frederick Engels (Progress Publishers, Moscow).

the burgesses the first elements of the bourgeoisie were developed.

The discovery of America, the rounding of the Cape, opened up fresh ground for the rising bourgeoisie. The East-Indian and Chinese markets, the colonisation of America, trade with the colonies, the increase in the means of exchange and in commodities generally, gave to commerce, to navigation, to industry, an impulse never before known, and thereby, to the revolutionary element in the tottering feudal society, a rapid development.

The feudal system of industry, under which industrial production was monopolised by closed guilds, now no longer sufficed for the growing wants of the new markets. The manufacturing system took its place. The guild-masters were pushed on one side by the manufacturing middle class; division of labour between the different corporate guilds vanished in the face of division of labour in each single workshop.

Meantime the markets kept ever growing, the demand ever rising. Even manufacture no longer sufficed. Thereupon, steam and machinery revolutionised industrial production. The place of manufacture was taken by the giant, Modern Industry, the place of the industrial middle class, by industrial millionaires, the leaders of whole industrial armies, the modern bourgeois.

Modern industry has established the world market, for which the discovery of America paved the way. This market has given an immense development to commerce, to navigation, to communication by land. This development has, in its turn, reacted on the extension of industry; and in proportion as industry, commerce, navigation, railways extended, in the same proportion the bourgeoisie developed, increased its capital, and pushed into the background every class handed down from the Middle Ages.

We see, therefore, how the modern bourgeoisie is itself the product of a long course of development, of a series of revolutions in the modes of production and of exchange. . . .

The bourgeoisie, wherever it has got the upper hand, has put an end to all feudal, patriarchal, idyllic relations. It has pitilessly torn asunder the motley feudal ties that bound man to his "natural superiors," and has left remaining no other nexus between man and man than naked self-interest, than callous "cash payment." It has drowned the most heavenly ecstasies of religious fervour, of chivalrous enthusiasm, of philistine sentimentalism, in the icy water of egotistical calculation. It has resolved personal worth into exchange value, and in place of the numberless indefeasible chartered freedoms, has set up that single, unconscionable freedom—Free Trade. In one word, for exploitation, veiled by religious and political illusions, it has substituted naked, shameless, direct, brutal exploitation.

The bourgeoisie has stripped of its halo every occupation hitherto honoured and looked up to with reverent awe. It has converted the physician, the lawyer, the priest, the poet, the man of science, into its paid wage-labourers.

The bourgeoisie has torn away from the family its sentimental zeal and has reduced the family relation to a mere money relation. . . .

The bourgeoisie cannot exist without constantly revolutionising the instruments of production, and thereby the relations of production, and with them the whole relations of society. Conservation of the old modes of production in unaltered form, was, on the contrary, the first condition of existence for all earlier industrial classes. Constant revolutionising of production, uninterrupted disturbance of all social conditions, everlasting uncertainty and agitation distinguished the bourgeois epoch from all earlier ones. All fixed, fast-frozen relations, with their train of ancient and venerable prejudices and opinions are swept away, all new-formed ones become antiquated before they can ossify. All that is solid melts into air, all that is holy is profaned, and man is at last compelled to face with sober senses, his real conditions of life, and his relations with his kind.

The need of a constantly expanding market for its products chases the bourgeoisie over the whole surface of the globe. It must nestle everywhere, settle everywhere, establish connexions everywhere.

The bourgeoisie has through its exploitation of the world market given a cosmopolitan character to production and consumption in every country. To the great chagrin of Reactionists, it has drawn from under the feet of industry the national ground on which it stood. All old-established national industries have been destroyed or are daily being destroyed. They are dislodged by new industries, whose introduction becomes a life and death question for all civilized nations, by industries that no longer work up indigenous raw material, but raw material drawn from the remotest zones; industries whose products are consumed, not only at home, but in every quarter of the globe. In place of the old wants, satisfied by the productions of the country, we find new wants, requiring for their satisfaction the products of distant lands and climes. In place of the old local and national seclusion and self-sufficiency, we have intercourse in every direction, universal inter-dependence of nations. And as in material, so also in intellectual production. The intellectual creations of individual nations become common property. National one-sidedness and narrow-mindedness become more and more impossible, and from the numerous national and local literatures there arises a world literature.

The bourgeoisie, by the rapid improvement of all instruments of production, by the immensely facilitated means of communication, draws all, even the most barbarian, nations into civilization. The cheap prices of its commodities are the heavy artillery with which it batters down all Chinese walls, with which it forces the barbarians' intensely obstinate hatred of foreigners to capitulate. It compels all nations, on pain of extinction, to adopt the bourgeois mode of production; it compels them to introduce what it calls civilization into their midst, *i.e.*, to become bourgeois themselves. In one word, it creates a world after its own image.

The bourgeoisie has subjected the country to the rule of the towns. It has created enormous cities, has greatly increased the urban population as compared with the rural, and has thus rescued a considerable part of the population from the idiocy of rural life. Just as it has made the country dependent on the towns, so it has made barbarian and semi-barbarian countries dependent on the civilized ones, nations of peasants on nations of bourgeois, the East on the West.

The bourgeoisie keeps more and more doing away with the scattered state of the population, of the means of production, and of property. It has agglomerated population, centralized means of production, and has concentrated property in a few hands. The necessary consequence of this was political centralization. Independent, or but loosely connected, provinces with separate interests, laws, governments and systems of taxation, became lumped together into one nation, with one government, one code of laws, one national class-interest, one frontier and one customs-tariff.

The bourgeoisie, during its rule of scarce one hundred years, has created more massive and more colossal productive forces than have all preceding generations together. Subjection of Nature's forces to man, machinery, application of chemistry to industry and agriculture, steam-navigation, railways, electric telegraphs, clearing of whole continents for cultivation, canalization of rivers, whole populations conjured out of the ground—what earlier century had even a presentiment that such productive forces slumbered in the lap of social labour?

We see then: the means of production and of exchange, on whose foundation the bourgeoisie built itself up, were generated in feudal society. At a certain stage in the development of these means of production and of exchange, the conditions under which feudal society produced and exchanged, the feudal organization of agriculture and manufacturing industry, in one word, the feudal relations of property became no longer compatible with the already developed productive forces; they became so many fetters. They had to be burst asunder; they were burst asunder.

Into their place stepped free competition, accompanied by a social and political constitution adapted to it, and by the economical and political sway of the bourgeois class.

A similar movement is going on before our own eyes. Modern bourgeois society with its relations of production, of exchange and of property, a society that has conjured up such gigantic means of production and of exchange, is like the sorcerer, who is no longer able to control the powers of the nether world whom he has called up by his spells. For many a decade past the history of industry and commerce is but the history of the revolt of modern productive forces against modern conditions of production, against the property relations that are the conditions for the existence of the bourgeoisie and of its rule. It is enough to mention the commercial crises that by their periodical return put on its trial, each time more threateningly, the existence of the entire bourgeois society. In these crises a great part not only of the existing products, but also of the previously created productive forces, are periodically destroyed. In these crises there breaks out an epidemic that, in all earlier epochs, would have seemed an absurdity—the epidemic of overproduction. Society suddenly finds itself put back into a state of momentary barbarism; it appears as if a famine, a universal war of devastation had cut off the supply of every means of subsistence; industry and commerce seem to be destroyed; and why? Because there is too much civilization, too much means of subsistence, too much industry, too much commerce. The productive forces at the disposal of society no longer tend to further the development of the conditions of bourgeois property; on the contrary, they have become too powerful for these conditions, by which they are fettered, and so soon as they overcome these fetters, they bring disorder into the whole of bourgeois society, endanger the existence of bourgeois property. The conditions of bourgeois society are too narrow to compromise the wealth created by them. And how does the bourgeoisie get over these crises? On the one hand by enforced destruction of a

mass of productive forces; on the other, by the conquest of new markets, and by the more thorough exploitation of the old ones. That is to say, by paving the way for more extensive and more destructive crises, and by diminishing the means whereby crises are prevented.

The weapons with which the bourgeoisie felled feudalism to the ground are now turned against the bourgeoisie itself.

But not only has the bourgeoisie forged the weapons that bring death to itself; it has also called into existence the men who are to wield those weapons—the modern working class—the proletarians.

In proportion as the bourgeoisie, *i.e.,* capital, is developed, in the same proportion is the proletariat, the modern working class, developed—a class of labourers who live only so long as they find work, and who find work only so long as their labour increases capital. The labourers, who must sell themselves piecemeal, are a commodity, like every other article of commerce, and are consequently exposed to all the vicissitudes of competition, to all the fluctuations of the market.

Owing to the extensive use of machinery and to division of labour, the work of the proletarians has lost all individual character, and, consequently, all charm for the workman. He becomes an appendage of the machine, and it is only the most simple, most monotonous, and most easily acquired knack, that is required of him. Hence, the cost of production of a workman is restricted, almost entirely, to the means of subsistence that he requires for his maintenance, and for the propagation of his race. But the price of a commodity, and therefore also of labour, is equal to its cost of production. In proportion, therefore, as the repulsiveness of the work increases, the wage decreases. Nay more, in proportion as the use of machinery and division of labour increases, in the same proportion the burden of toil also increases, whether by prolongation of the working hours, by increase of the work exacted in a given time or by increased speed of the machinery, etc.

Modern industry has converted the little workshop of the patriarchal master into the great factory of the industrial capitalist. Masses of labourers, crowded into the factory, are organized like soldiers. As privates of the industrial army they are placed under the command of a perfect hierarchy of officers and sergeants. Not only are they slaves of the bourgeois class, and of the bourgeois State; they are daily and hourly enslaved by the machine, by the overlooker, and, above all, by the individual bourgeois manufacturer himself. The more openly this despotism proclaims gain to be its end and aim, the more petty, the more hateful and more embittering it is.

The less the skill and exertion of strength implied in manual labour, in other words, the more modern industry becomes developed, the more is the labour of men superseded by that of women. Differences of age and sex have no longer any distinctive social validity for the working class. All are instruments of labour, more or less expensive to use, according to their age and sex. No sooner is the exploitation of the labourer by the manufacturer, so far, at an end, that he receives his wages in cash, than he is set upon by the other portions of the bourgeoisie, the landlord, the storekeeper, the pawnbroker, etc.

The lower strata of the middle class—the small tradespeople, shopkeepers, and retired tradesmen generally, the handicraftsmen and peasants—all these sink gradually into the proletariat, partly because their diminutive capital does not suffice for the scale on which Modern Industry is carried on, and is swamped in the competition with the large capitalists, partly because their specialized skill is rendered worthless by new methods of production. Thus the proletariat is recruited from all classes of the population.

The proletariat goes through various stages of development. With its birth begins its struggle with the bourgeoisie. At first the contest is carried on by individual labourers, then by the workpeople of a factory, then by the operatives of one trade, in one locality, against the individual bourgeois who directly exploits them. They direct their attacks not against the bourgeois conditions of production, but against the instruments of production themselves; they destroy imported wares that compete with their labour, they smash to pieces machinery, they set factories ablaze, they seek to restore by force the vanished status of the workman of the Middle Ages.

At this stage the labourers still form an incoherent mass scattered over the whole country, and broken up by their mutual competition. If anywhere they unite to form more compact bodies, this is not yet the consequence of their own active union, but of the union of the bourgeoisie, which class, in order to attain its own political ends, is compelled to set the whole proletariat in motion, and is moreover yet, for a time, able to do so. At this stage, therefore, the proletarians do not fight their enemies, but the enemies of their enemies, the remnants of absolute monarchy, the landowners, the nonindustrial bourgeois, the petty bourgeoisie. Thus the whole historical movement is concentrated in the hands of the bourgeoisie; every victory so obtained is a victory for the bourgeoisie.

But with the development of industry the proletariat not only increases in number; it becomes concentrated in greater masses, its strength grows, and it feels that strength more. The various interests and conditions of life within the ranks of the proletariat are more and more equalized, in proportion as machinery obliterates all distinctions of labour, and nearly everywhere reduces wages to the same low level. The growing competition among the bourgeois, and the resulting commercial crises, make the wages of the workers ever more fluctuating. The unceasing improvement of machinery, ever more rapidly developing, makes their livelihood more and more precarious; the collisions between individual workmen and individual bourgeois take more and more the character of collisions between two classes. Thereupon the workers begin to form combinations (Trades' Unions) against the bourgeois; they club together in order to keep up the rate of wages; they found permanent associations in order to make provision beforehand for these occasional revolts. Here and there the contest breaks out into riots.

Now and then the workers are victorious, but only for a time. The real fruit of their battles lies, not in the immediate result, but in the ever-expanding union of the workers. This union is helped on by the improved means of communication that are created by modern industry and that place the workers of different localities in contact with one another. It was just this contact that was needed to centralize the numerous local struggles, all of the same character, into one national struggle between classes. But every class struggle is a political struggle. . . .

This organization of the proletarians into a class, and consequently into a political party, is continually being upset again by the competition between the workers themselves. But it ever rises up again, stronger, firmer, mightier. It compels legislative recognition of particular interests of the workers, by taking advantage of the divisions among the bourgeoisie itself. . . .

Altogether, collisions between the classes of the old society further, in many ways, the course of development of the proletariat. The bourgeoisie finds itself involved in a constant battle. At first with the aristocracy; later on, with those portions of the bourgeoisie itself, whose interests have become antagonistic to the progress of industry; at all times, with the bourgeoisie of foreign countries. In all these battles it sees itself compelled to appeal to the proletariat, to ask for its help, and thus, to drag it into the political arena. The bourgeoisie itself, therefore, supplies the proletariat with its own elements of political and general education, in other words, it furnishes the proletariat with weapons for fighting the bourgeoisie.

Further, as we have already seen, entire sections of the ruling classes are, by the advance of industry, precipitated into the proletariat, or are at least threatened in their conditions of existence. These also supply the proletariat with fresh elements of enlightenment and progress.

Finally, in times when the class struggle nears the decisive hour, the process of dissolution going on within the ruling class, in fact within the whole range of old society, assumes such a violent, glaring character, that a small section of the ruling class cuts itself adrift, and joins the revolutionary class, the class that holds the future in its hands. Just as, therefore, at an earlier period, a section of the nobility went over to the bourgeoisie, so now a portion of the bourgeoisie goes over to the proletariat, and in particular, a portion of the bourgeoisie ideologists, who have raised themselves to the level of comprehending theoretically the historical movement as a whole.

Of all the classes that stand face to face with the bourgeoisie today, the proletariat alone is a really revolutionary class. The other classes decay and finally disappear in the face of modern industry; the proletariat is its special and essential product.

The lower middle class, the small manufacturer, the shopkeeper, the artisan, the peasant, all these fight against the bourgeoisie, to save from extinction their existence as fractions of the middle class. They are therefore not revolutionary, but conservative. Nay more, they are reactionary, for they try to roll back the wheel of history. If by chance they are revolutionary, they are so only in view of their impending transfer into the proletariat, they thus defend not their present, but their future interests, they desert their own standpoint to place themselves at that of the proletariat. . . .

In the conditions of the proletariat, those of old society at large are already virtually swamped. The proletarian is without property; his relation to his wife and children has no longer anything in common with the bourgeoisie family relations; modern industrial labour, modern subjection to capital, the same in England as in France, in America as in Germany, has stripped him of every trace of national character. Law, morality, religion, are to him so many bourgeois prejudices, behind which lurk in ambush just as many bourgeois interests.

All the preceding classes that got the upper hand, sought to fortify their already acquired status by subjecting society at large to their conditions of appropriation. The proletarians cannot become masters of the productive forces of society, except by abolishing their own previous mode of appropriation, and thereby also every other previous mode of appropriation. They have nothing of their own to secure and to fortify; their mission is to destroy all previous securities for, and insurances of, individual property. All previous historical movements were movements of minorities, or in the interest of minorities. The proletarian movement is the self-conscious, independent movement of the immense majority, in the interest of the immense majority. The proletariat, the lowest stratum of our present society, cannot stir, cannot raise itself up, without the whole superincumbent strata of official society being sprung into the air.

Though not in substance, yet in form, the struggle of the proletariat with the bourgeoisie is at first a national struggle. The proletariat of each country must, of course, first of all settle matters with its own bourgeoisie.

In depicting the most general phases of the development of the proletariat, we traced the more or less veiled civil war, raging within existing society, up to the point where that war breaks out into open revolution, and where the violent overthrow of the bourgeoisie lays the foundation for the sway of the proletariat.

Hitherto, every form of society has been based, as we have already seen, on the antagonism of oppressing and oppressed classes. But in order to oppress a class, certain conditions must be assured to it under which it can, at least, continue its slavish existence. The serf, in the period of serfdom, raised himself to membership in the commune, just as the petty bourgeois, under the yoke of feudal absolutism, managed to develop into a bourgeois. The modern labourer, on the contrary, instead of rising with the progress of industry, sinks deeper and deeper below the conditions of existence of his own class. He becomes a pauper, and pauperism develops more rapidly than population and wealth. And here it becomes evident that the bourgeoisie is unfit any longer to be

the ruling class in society, and to impose its conditions of existence upon society as an over- riding law. It is unfit to rule because it is incompetent to assure an existence to its slave within his slavery, because it cannot help letting him sink into such a state, that it has to feed him, instead of being fed by him. Society can no longer live under this bourgeoisie, in other words, its existence is no longer compatible with society.

The essential condition for the existence, and for the sway of the bourgeois class, is the formation and augmentation of capital; the condition for capital is wage labour. Wage labour rests exclusively on competition between the labourers. The advance of industry, whose involuntary promoter is the bourgeoisie, replaces the isolation of the labourers, due to competition, by their revolutionary combination, due to association. The development of Modern Industry, therefore, cuts from under its feet the very foundation on which the bourgeoisie produces and appropriates products. What the bourgeoisie, therefore, produces, above all, is its own gravediggers. Its fall and the victory of the proletariat are equally inevitable.

II. PROLETARIANS AND COMMUNISTS

In what relation do the Communists stand to the proletarians as a whole?

The Communists do not form a separate party opposed to other working-class parties.

They have no interests separate and apart from those of the proletariat as a whole.

They do not set up any sectarian principles of their own, by which to shape and mould the proletarian movement.

The Communists are distinguished from the other working-class parties by this only: 1. In the national struggles of the proletarians of the different countries, they point out and bring to the front the common interests of the entire proletariat, independently of all nationality. 2. In the various stages of development which the struggle of the working class against the bourgeoisie has to pass through, they always and everywhere represent the interests of the movement as a whole.

The Communists, therefore, are on the one hand, practically, the most advanced and resolute section of the working-class parties of every country, that section which pushes forward all others; on the other hand, theoretically, they have over the great mass of the proletariat the advantage of clearly understanding the line of march, the conditions, and the ultimate general results of the proletarian government.

The immediate aim of the Communists is the same as that of all the other proletarian parties: formation of the proletariat into a class, overthrow of the bourgeois supremacy, conquest of political power by the proletariat. . . .

The proletariat will use its political supremacy to wrest, by degrees, all capital from the bourgeoisie, to centralize all instruments of production in the hands of the State, *i.e.,* of the proletariat organized as the ruling class; and to increase the total of productive forces as rapidly as possible.

Of course, in the beginning, this cannot be effected except by means of despotic inroads on the rights of property, and on the conditions of bourgeois production; by means of measures, therefore, which appear economically insufficient and untenable, but which, in the course of the movement, outstrip themselves, necessitate further inroads upon the old social order, and are unavoidable as a means of entirely revolutionizing the mode of production.

These measures will of course be different in different countries.

Nevertheless in the most advanced countries, the following will be pretty generally applicable.

1. Abolition of property in land and application of all rents of land to public purposes.
2. A heavy progressive or graduated income tax.
3. Abolition of all right of inheritance.
4. Confiscation of the property of all emigrants and rebels.
5. Centralization of credit in the hands of the State by means of a national bank with State capital and an exclusive monopoly.
6. Centralization of the means of communication and transport in the hands of the State.
7. Extension of factories and instruments of production owned by the State; the bringing into cultivation of waste-lands, and the improvement of the soil generally in accordance with a common plan.
8. Equal liability of all to labour. Establishment of industrial armies, especially for agriculture.
9. Combination of agriculture with manufacturing industries; gradual abolition of the distinction between town and country, by a more equable distribution of the population over the country.
10. Free education for all children in public schools. Abolition of children's factory labour in its present form. Combination of education with industrial production. . . .

When, in the course of development, class distinctions have disappeared, and all production has been concentrated in the hands of a vast association of the whole nation, the public power will lose its political character. Political power, properly so called, is merely the organized power of one class for oppressing another. If the proletariat during its contest with the bourgeoisie is compelled, by the force of circumstances, to organize itself as a class, if, by means of a revolution, it makes itself the ruling class, and, as such, sweeps away by force the old conditions of production, then it will, along with these conditions, have swept away the conditions for the existence of class antagonisms and of classes generally, and will thereby have abolished its own supremacy as a class.

In place of the old bourgeois society, with its classes and class antagonisms, we shall have an association, in which the free development of each is the condition for the free development of all. . . .

The Communists disdain to conceal their views and aims. They openly declare that their ends can be attained only by the forcible overthrow of all existing social conditions. Let the ruling classes tremble at a Communistic revolution. The proletarians have nothing to lose but their chains. They have a world to win.

WORKING MEN OF ALL COUNTRIES, UNITE!

For Further Reflection

1. Do you aree with Engles and Marx that cultural values, including ideals and laws, of a society are always the reflection of the ruling class? Does this make values relative?
2. What are the strengths and weaknesses of Marxist political philosophy?

VII.57   A Cosmopolitan Theory of International Society

BRIAN BARRY

Brian Barry is professor of political science at the London School of Economics and the former editor of *Ethics*. He is the author of several works, including *Political Arguments* and *The Liberal Theory of Justice*.

Barry sets forth the basic ideas or a hypothetical contractarian view of moral cosmopolitanism. It is impartial and universal, based on principles that people could not reasonably reject. It allows for special obligations to family, friends, and country, but not *because* they are your family, friends, or country. It rules out discrimination on the basis of class, race, or nations that are not reducible to the rights, interests, and welfare of individuals, and he includes the interests of future people.

Study Questions

1. What are Barry's four principles of cosmopolitan justice?
2. What does Barry mean by human equality? What does it entail?
3. What does he say regarding the difference between the priority of basic over nonbasic needs?
4. What is the utilitarian component in Barry's system?
5. What does he advocate with regard to taxation and the redistribution of wealth?

THE COSMOPOLITAN IDEA

NOW THAT THE ETHIKON ENTERPRISE has been going for some time, we can begin to reap the rewards of continuity. Instead of offering my own definition of cosmopolitanism, I shall therefore take over the definition put forward by Charles Beitz in an earlier Ethikon book, *Political Restructuring in Europe*. According to Beitz, the two essential elements defining a cosmopolitan view are that it is inclusive and nonperspectival. "If local viewpoints can be said to be partial, then a cosmopolitan viewpoint is impartial."[1] What I am concerned with here is what Beitz calls "moral cosmopolitanism," of which he says that "it applies to the whole world the maxim that answers to questions about what we should do, or what institutions we should establish, should be based on an impartial consideration of the claims of each person who would be affected by our choices."[2]

Beitz distinguishes this moral cosmopolitanism from what he calls "institutional cosmopolitanism." It is important to recognize that moral cosmopolitanism leaves open the question of the ideal constitution of international society. Institutional cosmopolitanism is one answer to that question, or more precisely a family of answers. Thus, institutional cosmopolitanism "pertains to the way political institutions should be set up—to the political constitution of the world, so to speak. . . . Although the details may vary, the distinctive common feature is some ideal of world political organization in which states and state-like units have significantly diminished authority in comparison with the status quo and supranational institutions have more."[3]

As Beitz says, "there is no necessary link between moral and institutional cosmopolitanism."' Thus, one may be a moral cosmopolitan without believing that its precepts would best be satisfied by institutions of the kind commended by institutional cosmopolitanism.

At the level of domestic politics, it is quite consistent to start from a utilitarian position and then argue for a minimum state. Similarly, there is no inconsistency in counting the interests of everyone in the world equally and concluding that those interests will tend to be best advanced by a state-centered system with only weak international authority. Whether or not this is thought to be so will depend on what one takes the main interests of human beings to be and on the way in which one thinks the world works.

Conversely, one may support the policy conclusions embodied in institutional cosmopolitanism on a basis other than that of moral cosmopolitanism. Beitz himself says that "it is hard to think of anyone who has defended institutional cosmopolitanism on other than cosmopolitan moral grounds."[5] But it is easy to see that the case for a strengthening of international authority vis-à-vis states can plausibly be derived from Hobbesian premises under contemporary conditions. Warfare between countries now has a potential for almost unlimited destruction, and only concerted action can address global problems such as ozone depletion, the "greenhouse effect," and pollution of the oceans. I believe, therefore, that universal self-interest would support a shift toward institutional cosmopolitanism, as Beitz defines it. In addition, I believe that moral cosmopolitanism leads to the endorsement of international redistribution of a kind that Hobbesian premises do not appear to underwrite. My reasons for thinking this will appear later.

The general point I have made about moral cosmopolitanism is also made . . . for all the other approaches surveyed. That is to say, there is no automatic move from the ethical premises to any particular conclusion about the ideal world constitution. Where moral cosmopolitanism shows itself to be more distinctive is in its denial that membership of a society is of deep moral significance when the claims that people

Reprinted by permission from International Society, *edited by David Mapel and Terry Nardin (Princeton University Press, 1999).*

can legitimately make on one another are assessed. This differentiates it sharply from, for example, the kind of contractarian view advanced . . . by John Charvet, within which the bounds of society are also the bounds of justice.[6]

I should explain what I mean by saying that membership of a society does not have *deep* moral significance. We can in a variety of ways acquire obligations that we owe to some people and not to others. There is no reason for doubting that the members of a politically constituted society can acquire obligations to one another that they do not owe to others. What moral cosmopolitanism insists on, however, is that it should be possible to justify this special treatment on grounds that can in principle be accepted by those excluded. A standard way of doing this is, of course, to point out that those who are excluded can and do acquire special obligations to members of their own societies in exactly the same way. The point has been put well by Thomas Hill, Jr., in the following way:

> All the impartiality thesis says is that, if and when one raises questions regarding fundamental moral standards, the court of appeal that one addresses is a court in which no particular individual, group, or country has *special* standing. Before that court, declaring "I like it," "It serves *my* country," and the like, is not decisive; principles must be defensible to anyone looking at the matter apart from his or her special attachments, from a larger, human perspective. [7]

At the heart of moral cosmopolitanism is the idea that human beings are in some fundamental sense equal. All claims are to be weighed in the same balance. But how is this balancing to be carried out? An answer that naturally presents itself is that we reduce all claims to interests and then resolve conflicts of interest by saying that the outcome that most satisfies interests (the one in which the greatest sum of interest satisfaction obtains) is the best. If "interests" are given a subjective interpretation this is the utilitarian prescription. It is objec-

tionable on two grounds. First, it is not true that all claims can be expressed in a single currency: claims are irreducibly heterogeneous in their nature. And, second, the formula is indifferent to issues of distribution. Nobody has any good reason for accepting that he or she should do very badly merely because this is the most effective means of maximizing some aggregate good, however defined.

Rather than canvassing a number of alternatives, let me simply present what seems to me the best way of giving content to the idea of impartial treatment that underlies moral cosmopolitanism. Following an idea put forward by T. M. Scanlon, I propose that we should ask of any rule or principle whether or not it could reasonably be rejected by somebody who was motivated by "the desire to find principles which others similarly motivated could not reasonably reject."[8] We thus posit a hypothetical negotiating situation marked by equality (since everybody stands on an equal footing and is equipped with a veto to protect interests that cannot reasonably be denied) and freedom (since nobody can coerce anybody else into accepting an agreement by the exercise of superior power). Principles of justice are those principles that would emerge from a process taking this form.

We may envisage a variety of different sets of people making choices in such a hypothetical situation. By far the most effort has gone into the case in which the choice is made by people who are members of the same politically organized society. But for the present purpose I want to focus on the case in which the choice is made by all the people in the world, since it is quite possible to imagine a world in which each country is internally just but the system as a whole is extremely unjust. On the criterion of justice proposed here, this would be so if the rules governing relations between countries could reasonably be rejected by some people.

It seems clear that the premise of fundamental human equality applies without regard to time as well as without regard to place. There is no good moral reason for saying that the interests of people who will live in the future should be given less (or more) weight than the interests of those alive now simply because they come later in time. I do not, however, believe that it is useful to extend the idea of a hypothetical choosing situation to encompass relations between generations, mainly because asking how we would negotiate with people as yet unborn (especially those in the distant future) creates gratuitous problems. The point here is that, where the parties are contemporaries, the problem posed is closely related to a kind of which we have experience. Indeed, we can hope to learn from actual cases of agreement (relatively consensual policies in countries, or payment schemes in large organizations, for example), making adjustments to compensate for deviations from equal power relations. It does not follow, however, that we are without recourse to anything except a direct appeal to the idea of fundamental equality in regard to future generations. We can take the principles that would be agreed upon by contemporaries and ask if there is any reason why they should not be extrapolated to relations between different generations, perhaps being appropriately modified to cope with the special features of those relations. My belief is that this procedure will provide all we need in the way of guidance beyond the idea of fundamental equality itself.

Following Rawls, I shall take justice to be the highest-order organizing concept within political philosophy.[9] The following are, I wish to maintain, four principles of justice. I shall say a little (but only a little) in defense of each as I go along. A point to be made about all of them together is that they meet the two objections to utilitarianism: their subject-matter is heterogeneous and they are sensitive to questions of distribution.

First principle: the presumption of equality. All inequalities of rights, opportunities, and resources have to be justifiable in ways that cannot reasonably be rejected by those who get least.

This principle does not immediately generate specific conclusions. But it is important in directing attention toward those who have the best prima facie reasons for rejecting some proposal. It emphasizes that any inequality must make sense to them. As it stands, it may appear a very weak principle, and it is undeniably lacking in content. In spite of this, what impresses me is how many relations of inequality at all levels cannot meet its demands. These relations are maintained by unequal power relationships, or (not quite the same thing) by inertia, forming part of a pattern which it would not be advantageous to anyone acting alone to disturb. Thus, those disadvantaged by an inequality may well choose to act in ways that sustain it, even though they would reject it in a hypothetical ideal-choice situation.

There is a temptation (succumbed to by Rawls in some contexts) to drive the principle of the presumption of equality toward closure by specifying that the *only* justification for an inequality is that the minimum is as high as is feasible. I do not accept this because it would be inconsistent with the second principle. For this, as will be seen, has the implication that those who do worst from an inequality may under certain conditions accept reasonably that those who do better deserve to do better.

At the same time, I wish to ensure that the idea of the priority of the worst-off retains some critical force. I therefore add an *anti-aggregation* rider: aggregate gains by "winners" do not constitute a justification to "losers." This simply makes explicit the point that, from the perspective of the losers, the argument that there will be a net gain is not a sufficient ground for withdrawing a veto.

Second principle: personal responsibility and compensation. It is prima facie acceptable for people to fare differently if the difference arises from a voluntary choice on their part; conversely, victims of misfortunes that they could not have prevented have a prima facie valid claim for compensation or redress.

The first clause embodies the basic idea that human agency must be respected. It is an essential aspect of a fully human life that one's decisions should have some impact on the world, and that can happen only if what they do makes a difference to what actually happens. There is a great deal of evidence, both from surveys of opinion and from studies of freely accepted inequalities, to support the notion that the first clause would emerge from a hypothetical choice situation. What the formulation leaves open is, of course, the conditions under which a choice counts as being voluntary. The clause about personal responsibility sets the terms of the debate, however, and, I believe, imposes definite limits on the range of reasonable disagreement.[10]

The second clause is the obverse of the first. It may be said to embody what Richard Arneson has described as "the intuition that when people's lives go badly through no fault or voluntary choice of their own, it is morally incumbent on others to offer aid to the disadvantaged so long as the cost of providing aid is not excessive."[11] I should, however, wish to approach the proviso at the end of this statement with some care. What makes the cost "excessive"? Not, I think, simply that the cost is high: if the loss is great, the cost is liable to be high, but that does not affect the force of the claim. The valid form of the proviso is, I suggest, that the obligation is weakened or in extreme cases extinguished altogether if the cost of providing the aid is greatly disproportional to the benefit gained by the recipient(s).

We may combine the two parts of this principle to obtain a somewhat more precise version of the doctrine of compensation. Suppose that people fare badly not as a result of their voluntary choices but as a result of unpreventable misfortune. Then, we may say, they can legitimately demand that (1) where "nature" is the cause, the more fortunate should contribute to a scheme of compensation; and (2) where the voluntary act of some person (or persons) is the cause, redress should be looked for in the first instance from that source.

Third principle: priority of vital interests. In the absence of some compelling consideration to the contrary, the vital interests of each person should be protected in preference to the nonvital interests of anyone. Vital interests include security from physical harm, nutrition adequate for the maintenance of health, clean drinking water and sanitary arrangements, clothing and shelter appropriate to the climate, medical care, and education to a level sufficient to function effectively within one's society.

It should be observed that this principle expresses priorities not in terms of persons (as the first principle did) but in terms of types of claim. The idea underlying it is that there are certain minimum requirements of living a good life that can be acknowledged to be such by almost everyone, whatever his or her own particular conception of the good may be.[12] If the second principle is related to the idea of desert, this third principle is related to that of need. Thus, the second and third principles capture what are the commonly accepted bases for moral claims. The first principle is concerned with a third basis—the allocation of rights.

Fourth principle: mutual advantage. Whenever it would be to the prospective advantage of everyone to depart from the application of the above principles (compared with the results of applying them), it is permisable to do so. Where more than one arrangement has this property, the one to be preferred is that which maximizes the gain of those who gain least from the departure.

This principle is one of collective rationality: it endorses Pareto improvements over the baseline set by the operation of the other three principles. The second half of it provides a way of choosing between potential Pareto improvements and incorporates the idea of "the priority of the worst off." It should be observed, however, that the identity of the "worst off" here is not the same as it was in the anti-aggregation proviso. Here the worst off are defined in relation to the baseline created by applying the other principles. Those who stand to gain least by applying the fourth one may not be those who were the worst off from the application of the other three.

Read carelessly, the fourth principle may look as if it renders the others nugatory and simply gets us back to utilitarianism. It is important to recognize that this is not so. The other three principles retain their integrity. They can be supplemented by the fourth principle but they cannot be displaced by it. For those who like the vocabulary, we may say that the first three principles jointly have lexicographic priority over the fourth. This, of course, leaves us without a formula for resolving conflicts among the first three principles, but who said that ethical problems should be easy?

JUSTICE DENIED

The principles of justice I have put forward are intended to function as guides to debate: they should be capable of specifying kinds of argument that can be accepted as valid while ruling out other considerations that might be put forward. This structuring of moral discourse is what I believe principles should do. Clearly, for the full development of a theory of justice we would need to see how the principles put forward here work together to produce some conclusions about the kinds of institution they underwrite. In the space at my disposal, I have no hope of doing that. What I shall focus on, in keeping with the topic . . . are the largest-scale global implications, extended into the distant future.

The most striking feature of the world as it exists at present, if we line it up against the principles of justice, is the extent to which the third principle is violated. Probably half the total world population lacks the material conditions that are necessary for the satisfaction of their vital interests. Even in Latin America, which is on the average considerably wealthier than Africa, the Indian subcontinent, and China, half the total population was estimated by a United Nations agency to have "unmet basic needs" in 1986.[13]

These conditions coexist—in contravention of the principle of the priority of vital interests—with over a quarter of the world's population living at material standards vastly in excess of anything required to meet their basic needs.

A second observation is that there is no tendency toward an equalization of average incomes between rich and poor countries. On the contrary, the richest countries are continuing to increase their affluence (if slowly), while many poor countries have actually become poorer in the past decade, especially as a result of debt repayments. (On balance, poor countries now make net transfers to rich ones.) Moreover, within poor countries, the burden of the "adjustment" imposed by the IMF and the World Bank falls mainly on the poor, who are hit by increased unemployment and the disappearance of basic public services.

It is, of course, conceivable that the prima facie injustice arising from the wholesale violation of the third principle is nullified by the application of one or more of the other principles. There are two candidates: the second and the fourth. Under the second, it might be argued that the plight of those whose vital interests are not being met is entirely their own fault. This is immensely implausible. Insofar as natural resources make some countries better off than others, this is clearly a matter of pure good fortune. The inhabitants of the wealthier countries can claim some credit for maintaining their economic capital, social capital (institutions that work to provide a framework for prosperity), and human capital (a well-educated workforce). But even then much is inherited from previous generations. Within poor countries it is pure fantasy to suppose that the children of landless laborers in the country or dwellers in *favelas* or shanty-towns round the cities could all by sheer personal effort raise themselves in one generation to a position in which their vital interests would be fulfilled.

The other weapon of the apologists for the justice of the status quo is the fourth principle:

any attempt to improve the lot of the worst off by redistributive measures, it is sometimes claimed, would have such an inhibiting effect on the efforts of the better off that in the end everybody would be worse off than they would be under a policy of leaving the outcome to market forces. Looking at the inequalities in many poor countries and in the world as a whole, this would be hard to believe, even if indefinite increases in global production were feasible. But they are not, and this has profound implications for the fourth principle. Recall that in the previous section I said that the interests of those who live in the future must be given as much weight as the interests of those who live in the present. This means (under principle two) that we cannot justly leave them worse off than we are, since this would not reflect a voluntary choice on their part. It also implies (under principle three) that we cannot give our own pursuit of our goals priority over their vital interests.

There is, manifestly, a range of views about what this would entail. But the general form of the question is clear: unless it blows itself up or destroys its environment, there is no reason why the human race should not continue to inhabit the globe for hundreds of thousands of years to come (as against about ten thousand since the beginnings of civilization). We cannot know how people in the future will live or what inventions and discoveries they will make. But we know that they will need an inhabitable planet, with such amenities as an ozone layer, land that is neither desert nor eroded, relative freedom from air and water pollution, and a diversity of species. This requires that the current generation should not leave its successors with conditions that are worse in these respects, or if this is impossible that the current generation at least moves as far toward "substainability" as is feasible. What is crucial is that the capacity of the planet to regenerate depleted natural resources and render toxic wastes harmless (metals such as mercury, lead, and cadmium, and nuclear waste, for example) is strictly limited. Some people say

that we need not worry about any of this because people in the future *may* come up with some "technological fix" that will solve all the problems. This, however, is scarcely consistent with taking seriously the interests of future generations, since if we acted on the optimistic assumption and it turned out to be wrong the consequences would be catastrophic.[14]

There is apparently little disagreement among those who accept this general diagnosis that current production levels globally are unsustainable. The only question is how far they would have to be reduced to become sustainable. A widely held view is that the world left the path of sustainability in the early 1950s. To the extent that processes of production are modified to use fewer natural resources and create less pollution, we can avoid the conclusion that production levels must go back to those prevalent in the early 1950s, but they would still have to be reduced substantially. Even if sustainability entails only freezing total production, this is enough to demand a fundamental reorientation of virtually all thinking in the last fifty years (and most of that in the preceding hundred) about distributive justice. For a common theme running through the work of thinkers on both the left and the right of the political spectrum has been that production is not a zero-sum game. What unites these thinkers is the "productivist" premise that "a rising tide lifts all boats." Inequalities of income are therefore of no moment in themselves. Only simple-minded people, according to the conventional wisdom, believe that the poor are poor because the rich are rich; on the contrary, the poor are as well off as they are only because the rich are rich. Inequality increases the size of the cake, so that even those with the smallest slices get more.

If we drop the presupposition of an indefinitely expandable cake, the older idea that the poor are poor because the rich are rich comes into its own again. Let us suppose that we are at the sustainable maximum, and that it would be possible to stay at this maximum while shifting income from rich to poor. Then it does become true that anyone with a large slice of the cake is directly responsible for somebody else having a small one. Internationally it means that poor countries can expand production (within the limits of global sustainability) only if the rich countries cut back to make room.

This would be true even if sustainability demanded only that total production level out at its current volume. Now suppose (as seems to me more plausible) that long-run sustainability entails a substantial overall reduction in what is produced. Then further implications can be derived. Thus, the rationale (widely acted on in all western European countries in the past decade) for cutting high marginal rates of taxation—that the incentive effect of letting high earners keep more increases economic growth—has to go into reverse. Since, however, the evidence suggests that reducing marginal tax rates from their previous levels has had negligible effects on effort, it seems likely that post-tax earnings could be almost equalized before production fell by a substantial amount. The limits on equalization would perhaps lie rather in those imposed by the second principle, which permits the consequences of voluntary choice to be reflected in outcomes. People who are particularly keen to make more money should be able to do so by working at a job within their capabilities involving longer or less convenient hours or more unpleasant conditions than other jobs open to people with their capabilities. It should be observed, however, that the second principle does not legitimize inequalities that do not result from choice, and I believe that it would not therefore underwrite the vast majority of existing earned income inequalities. The only ones it would support would be of an essentially compensatory nature.

A parallel argument may be made about transfers from one country to another. Even if unlimited expansion of production were feasible, it would be grossly implausible to maintain that even a low level of transfer from rich to poor countries would hamper production in the rich countries so much that in the long run everyone would lose. There seems to me no real case for thinking that production in rich countries would necessarily be reduced at all by some modest level of transfer. Even if it were, poor countries would still be better off with transfers. For unless some of the increased wealth of the rich countries is deliberately channeled to poor countries, there does not appear to be any mechanism that automatically results in the increased wealth of the rich countries creating more in the poor ones. There is certainly one force moving in the other direction, which is that technological progress tends to make the rich countries less and less dependent on the raw materials (jute and sisal, for example) that are the export staples of some poor countries.

Now suppose that global production will have to be reduced if pollution and resource depletion are not to place an unfair burden on future generations. In this case, any inhibiting effect on production of the extra taxation imposed on rich countries by international redistribution becomes a positive advantage. Assuming that aggregate global output needs to come down substantially, I should be very surprised if that goal could be accomplished solely through the drag on production in the rich countries imposed by international transfers. Governments in rich countries would still have to introduce deliberate measures to curb the propensity of their economies to produce more than is compatible with long-run sustainability.

MORAL COSMOPOLITANISM AND INTERNATIONAL REDISTRIBUTION

Moral cosmopolitanism is, in essence, an individualistic doctrine in that it focuses on how individuals fare. This does not mean that it slights the importance of families, communities, and countries. But it treats their value as derivative: they are of value to exactly the extent that they contribute to the welfare of individuals (both those within the group and those outside it, weighting their interests equally).

This moral individualism, taken together with the considerations advanced in the previous section, leads to a radical conclusion. The demands of cosmopolitanism would, I suggest, be best satisfied in a world in which rich people wherever they lived would be taxed for the benefit of poor people wherever they lived. On the revenue-raising side, the model would be that of the United States, where the federal government imposes a federal income tax, leaving the states to raise whatever taxes (including income taxes) they like. The expenditure side is rather more messy. I believe that a large proportion of the payout would have to be to individuals, either in the form of a universal unconditional basic income or an income dependent on status (youth, age, sickness and disability, unemployment). But it would clearly be advantageous for some of the resources to go to the improvement of communal facilities in areas where the most deprived people are concentrated.

As I have already said, the units within the federation (states in the US, countries within a world federation) would be able to raise their own taxes in addition and spend them as they wished. Nevertheless, it is clear that any such system would constitute a considerable derogation of state sovereignty. (It may be recalled that in the US the introduction of a federal income tax required a constitutional amendment.) It seems to me that the least one can say is that any such scheme would be unimaginable unless it had been preceded by a long period in which transfers of a systematic kind between countries had become a well-established practice. On this alternative understanding, "international redistribution" means redistribution among countries. This immediately raises problems, since an unconditional transfer to a poor country may not benefit any poor people within that country. If, for example, the money having been raised by a broad-based tax in a relatively wealthy country goes straight into the Swiss bank accounts of the ruling elite, the net result will be

predominantly a shift of resources from those in the middle to the very wealthy. Any system open to such abuse would fail to generate support from the contributors, and reasonably enough.

I do not wish to slight the importance of these problems. They are, however, best regarded as falling within the scope of a more general issue. This can be stated as follows: given a world that is made up of states, what is the morally permissible range of diversity among them? I shall postpone the discussion of this question of diversity. . . . I shall leave on one side the question of the way in which the money is to be spent within countries and focus on the mechanism of transfer between countries.

We are looking for an alternative to a system in which an international authority levies taxes directly on individuals. The simplest alternative is to assess countries for contributions according to their gross national product at some standard rate (for example, one percent) provided their average income per head is above some level (roughly, that of the OECD countries). One percent is an amount that would scarcely be noticed, but it is vastly in excess of the amounts currently transferred and would make a large difference. I do not doubt that moral cosmopolitanism calls for more, but the point is that even that amount would represent a real transformation in the level of international transfers.

A scheme in which the levy is proportional to GNP, above some cutoff point of average income, is the simplest, as I have said. It would, obviously, be possible to make it more fancy by introducing an element of progressivity, so that (within the set of contributors) richer countries paid a larger amount in proportion to their GNP. There is no need to pursue such refinements here. The essential feature common to all is that each state would be assessed by some international authority according to some schedule and it would then be up to the state to determine how the money was to be raised—

whether by direct or indirect taxes, for example. An example of such a system that is effective is the system prevailing within the European Union whereby constituent countries have to provide a sum each year, part of which is disbursed (as "solidarity" funds) to the poorer regions.

The case for taking something like income per head as the basis of assessment is twofold. The first is that if you want to raise money you had better go where the money is. In terms of classical taxation theory, the criterion is "ability to pay." In terms of the principles of justice set out earlier, it is that a rich country can afford to collect the money demanded without jeopardizing the vital interests of anybody in it. (Of course, this says only that it has the ability to do so. It may actually raise the money in a way that is detrimental to the interests of the worst-off members of the society. This is the obverse of the problem that the proceeds may go to the rich in the recipient society.) There is a second argument as well, and this is that income per head is a proxy for the use of natural resources and the degradation of the global environment. It is not, it must be admitted, precise: the United States, for example, is much more profligate in the resources it expends for a given unit of production than other countries at a roughly similar economic level. Nevertheless, there is enough of a correlation to add support to the case derived from ability to pay.

This argument, however, suggests an alternative way of raising money for an international redistributive authority: a system of user fees (as an alternative to a rationing scheme that would create windfall gains) and taxes on the infliction of global environmental damage. The object here would be twofold. In part it would be driven by considerations of equity: those who make use of inherently limited facilities should pay, and those who impose burdens on the rest of the world should compensate for the damage they cause. But it would also work to modify behavior by providing an incentive to economize on scarce resources, and to reduce pollution.

Some recently proposed ideas are a surcharge on air tickets, a charge on ocean maritime transport, a special fee for maritime dumping of waste, parking fees for geostationary satellites, charges for the use of the electromagnetic spectrum, and charges for fishing rights in certain areas.[15] A more ambitious extension would include a "carbon tax" on emissions contributing to global warming, and a tax on the production of the CFCs that deplete the ozone layer. The author of this proposal does not discuss how the charges would actually be collected. Ideally, they would be gathered directly from the users or polluters. Only this would ensure that the cost entered into their calculations. It appearsto me, however, that many charges would, as a practical matter, have to be levied against governments. The alternative would require an international corps of collectors of fees and taxes that would constitute the same infringement of sovereignty as a corps of international income tax inspectors. The result of assessing governments is that it would be possible for a country to pay its "carbon tax" by, in turn, assessing taxpayers at large rather than by imposing, say, a levy on the burning of coal and petroleum. There is, however, no way in which such slippage can be prevented. What can at least be said is that the system of fees and taxes would put some pressure on governments to reduce their liability.

It is worth noticing that this kind of indirect taxation has a different status vis-à-vis the taxation of individual incomes from a levy based on GNP per head. Both of the rationales for taxing national income would be better served by taxing individual income: ability to pay would be more sensitively captured by taxing individuals, and individual income acts as a proxy for resource use wherever the person with the income lives. The fees and taxes I have just been proposing, however, would be desirable regardless of the way in which the direct tax element might be collected. How much it could be expected to raise would depend entirely on the rates set and the scope of the tax net. Adding a "carbon tax" could make it substantial. I believe, though, that direct taxation based on "ability to pay" is inevitably going to be required. For the indirect taxes would fall on poor countries as well as rich ones. No doubt by the nature of the case rich countries will pay the bulk, but poor countries pursuing "dirty" industrialization (for example China) will also have to pay. So they should: the whole point is to attach a realistic cost to their conduct. But the scheme as a whole can be acceptable only if there is also an element of straight transfer from rich to poor countries.

It may well be said that it is slightly absurd for me to pass over the idea of an international tax-collecting corps on the ground that it is politically infeasible when everything else I am advocating is politically infeasible. Let me begin a response by saying that it still makes good sense to say that one proposal is much *more* politically infeasible than another, even if both seem a long way off adoption. Turning to the question of feasibility head on, I suggest that we should divide it into two. What is commonly seen as the major problem is that of coercing recalcitrant states to play their part. I think the seriousness of this problem can be exaggerated. The European Union collects from its member states because that is the price of staying in, and there are perceived to be advantages in not being excluded. There is no suggestion that troops would be sent to storm the treasury of a nonpaying member. Similarly, the World Trade Organization has the authority to rule on violations, and has at its disposal the sanctions of expulsion or, short of that, denial of certain advantages available to adherents. Generalizing from this, the relatively wealthy countries (the only ones that concern us in this context) belong to a whole network of international agreements, and if the assessed contribution to the fund for international redistribution were the price for remaining a member in good standing, it would be worth paying.

The real problem is not so much coercing backsliders as setting up the scheme in the first place. I do not underestimate the scale of this problem, but I want to emphasize that the kind of political will required to create such a scheme will have to stem from moral motivation. Hobbesian reasoning, as suggested at the beginning of this chapter, will go quite a way, but it will not underwrite international redistribution. Attempts are, of course, made regularly to argue that it is in the self-interest of rich countries to transfer resources to poor ones. I have the strong impression, however, that those who make such arguments are themselves led to the conclusion by cosmopolitan moral considerations. It is therefore hardly surprising that their arguments fail to convince. All I can suggest here, then, is that, unless the moral case is made, we can be sure nothing good will happen. The more the case is made, the better the chance....

My primary focus ... is on the distribution of income, and I want ... to return to it. Here, the range of legitimate variation is inherently limited, since the principles of justice bear directly on the distribution of income. The great majority of existing countries have a degree of inequality greatly in excess of that which could reasonably be justified under the principles of justice set out here. How does this affect the case for international redistribution, whether conceived as transfers from rich to poor individuals (regardless of location) or as transfers from rich to poor countries?

The answer is perhaps surprising. Take first a scheme in which an international authority collected income taxes from relatively wealthy individuals and gave money to relatively poor individuals. (Some proportion of the money might go to such things as schools and hospitals or water and sewerage systems designed to benefit poor people collectively.) The contributors to the scheme could afford to take a quite relaxed attitude to the distribution of income within recipient countries both before and after the transfers had been made. So long as governments in the recipient countries did not use their taxing powers to take away the benefits gained by the poor, it could be said that at any rate the scheme was working in that resources were being transferred from rich to poor individuals.

Now think about a scheme in which the governments of relatively rich countries transfer resources in some systematic way to the governments of relatively poor countries. Here the distribution of income within the recipient countries becomes a matter of legitimate concern. There are two reasons for this. The first is that the whole notion of the transferred resources going to the poor is now less than transparent. The only way of determining that the results of whatever the government does can be said to constitute a transfer of the money to the poor is to ask if the poor have collectively benefited to the extent of the money provided. This requires close attention to the actual distribution of income and a comparison between it and what the distribution might be hypothesized to have been in its absence.

The second point is rather more subtle. We can best approach it by observing that the individualistic scheme treats national boundaries as having no significance (for this purpose, anyway). In contrast to this, any scheme that makes countries the units of redistribution immediately throws an emphasis on the internal distribution of income. Suppose that the distribution of income in a poor country is extremely unjust (as it actually is in virtually all cases). What implications, if any, does this have for the obligations of those in rich countries to pay taxes in order to provide the resources for transfers to be made to poor countries?

I have already mentioned one case: that in which not only is the distribution of internally generated income unjust but also any additional income from outside would be appropriated by the ruling elite. Here there can be no morally compelling reason for making transfers. There is, instead, a case for international intervention to displace the government and, if necessary, place the country under international trusteeship until more adequate institutions can be created. This intervention will have to be military rather than taking the form of economic sanctions. For (as the examples of Haiti and Iraq illustrate) a government can ensure that the worst burden of economic sanctions falls upon the poorest, and there is no reason to suppose that a government that had already proved itself indifferent to the suffering of its poorest citizens would be motivated to reform by the prospect of their plight becoming even worse as a result of economic sanctions.

The wisdom of military intervention can be challenged, and recent United Nations efforts (in the Horn of Africa, for example) are scarcely encouraging. I cannot here enter into that argument. I assert only the principle that cosmopolitan morality cannot object to intervention under the circumstances I have outlined except on grounds of inefficacy or counterproductiveness. For whatever can be said in favor of state autonomy as a contribution to the well-being of the citizens holds only contingently. Any government which is little more than a gang of looters (as in much of sub-Saharan Africa) forfeits any respect for its independence. If it can be toppled without making things worse, that has to be a (relatively) just outcome.

Bypassing cases in which the poor gain some from international transfers but less than by the amount of the transfers, let us consider now a case in which all the benefit of the transfers goes to those who should justly receive it. It might be suggested that this still does not create an obligation to make the transfer. To put the case in its strongest form, suppose that many people in the country are failing to have their vital needs met, but that there is an economically (though not politically) feasible internal redistribution of income that would enable everybody's vital needs to be met. (This is, in the nature of the case, going to be true only if the average income per capita of countries entitled to be recipients is set quite high. Brazil might then be a candidate.) It could be said then that justice begins at home: why should people elsewhere make sacrifices that would not be called for if the rich in the poor country were to behave justly?

We are here, as so often in matters of justice, confronted with the problem of the second best. If some people are not doing their bit, does that mean that others do not have to step in? If they do not, the vital needs of the poor in poor countries will continue to go unmet. If they act, vital needs will be met and the cost will be spread over hundreds of millions of people. It seems an inescapable conclusion that justice will be advanced by making the transfer. This is especially clear in the (normal) case in which even a just internal distribution would leave a need for international transfers. It would surely be unconscionable to use the lack of internal redistribution as an excuse for not acting. This is not to say that efforts should not be made to provide the government of the recipient country with strong incentives to do its bit for its poorer citizens. It would be reasonable to deny the country any development aid, for example, and this might well have some effect on the willingness of the better-off members of society to accept a measure of internal redistribution.

The obligation on rich countries to transfer resources to internally unjust poor countries might under certain conditions be challenged in another way. Imagine a country in which everyone accepts the unjust internal inequality. Can the victims of this injustice reasonably demand that their material position be improved by transfers from outside the country if they have no complaint against it themselves? This is obviously a variant of the argument from consent whose strength and scope I assessed in the previous section.

The best case would be a democracy in which a majority persistently voted for parties that did little or nothing when in government to make the distribution of income more just. The electoral success in India since independence of either the Congress Party or parties economically to its right might be advanced as a case in point, given that neither has done anything significant to tackle the maldistribution of wealth and income that the new state inherited. The argument is weak, however, even in this most favorable case. Suppose we were to accept that majority support for the status quo implied majority acceptance of the justice of status quo, a majority is far from the consensus that the argument needs. But there is no reason to make that deduction. As Gunnar Myrdal observed many years ago, India is a "soft state," marked by lack of administrative effectiveness, and in particular the cooptation of officials by the wealthy and powerful in each locality.[16] An attitude of passive resignation on the part of the poor in the face of the failure and subversion of tax and land reform legislation is therefore scarcely to be wondered at. It cannot plausibly be deduced from passivity that they accept the moral legitimacy of the status quo.

This reply, of course, brings us back to the question of the efficacy of international transfers. If the administration of a state is so liable to derailment by powerful interests that its internal efforts at reform are hijacked, what are the prospects of external funds going to the poor rather than being misappropriated? I can only repeat in conclusion that there is no case from cosmopolitan justice for making transfers unless they do get to the people for whom they are intended. But in a second-best world, that does not provide any reason for not making transfers in the remaining cases. The outcome is more just if that is done than it would otherwise be. Needless to say, it is a question of immense practical importance how great a limitation on the scope of international redistribution this proviso imposes. But the answer to that question does not affect the validity of the idea that transfers should be made where they are called for by the principles of justice and will be efficacious in making the situation more just.

NOTES

1. Charles R. Beitz, "Cosmopolitan Liberalism and the States System," in Chris Brown, ed., *Political Restructuring in Europe: Ethical Perspectives* (London: Routledge, 1994), 123–36, quotation at 124.

2. Beitz, "Cosmopolitan Liberalism," 124–25. Thomas Pogge, in the same volume, claims that all cosmopolitan positions are marked by three features: individual human beings are what ultimately matter; they matter equally; and nobody is exempted by distance or lack of a shared community from potential demands arising out of the counting of everybody equally. Thomas W. Pogge, "Cosmopolitanism and Sovereignty," in *Political Restructuring in Europe*, 89–112 at 89. There is no conflict between this and the Beitz formulation in the text, on the definitions of impartiality and equal concern that I give here.

3. Beitz, "Cosmopolitan Liberalism," 124.

4. Beitz, "Cosmopolitan Liberalism," 125.

5. Beitz, "Cosmopolitan Liberalism," 126.

6. John Charvet, Chapter 7 above.

7. Thomas E. Hill, Jr., "The Importance of Autonomy," in Eva Kittay and Diane Meyers, eds., *Women and Moral Theory* (Totowa, NJ: Rowman and Allanheld, 1987), 132.

8. T. M. Scanlon, "Contractualism and Utilitarianism," in Amartya Sen and Bernard Williams, eds., *Utilitarianism and Beyond* (Cambridge: Cambridge University Press, 1982), 103–28, quotation at 116, n. 2. For an elaborated exposition of this idea, see my *Justice as Impartiality*, Vol. 2 of *A Treatise on Social Justice* (Oxford: Oxford University Press, 1995), esp. 67–72.

9. John Rawls, *A Theory of Justice* (Cambridge, MA: Harvard University Press, 1971).

10. This conclusion is arrived at in an article whose general line I endorse: Arthur Ripstein, "Equality, Luck, and Responsibility," *Philosophy & Public Affairs* 23 (1994): 3–23.

11. Richard Arneson, "Property Rights in Persons," *Social Philosophy and Policy* 9 (1992): 201–30, at 209.

12. See T. M. Scanlon, "Preference and Urgency," *Journal of Philosophy* 72 (1975): 655–69.

13. Eduardo S. Bustelo, "Social Policies in Times of Cholera," paper presented to the IPSA World Congress, Buenos Aires, August 1991, 25, table 3.

14. See Stein Hansen, "Entropy Implications for Global Development," Centre for the Study of Global Governance, London School of Economics, 1993.

15. I. G. Patel, "Global Economic Governance: Some Thoughts on Our Current Discontents," Centre for the Study of Global Governance, London School of Economics, 1994.

16. Gunnar Myrdal, "The 'Soft State' in Underdeveloped Countries," in P. Streeten, ed., *Unfashionable Economics: Essays in Honour of Lord Balogh* (London: Weidenfeld and Nicolson, 1970), 227–43; cited and discussed (and its contemporary relevance affirmed) in Adrian Leftwich, "States of Underdevelopment," *Journal of Theoretical Politics* 6 (1994): 55–73.

For Further Reflection

1. Evaluate Barry's program for cosmopolitan justice. What do you see as its strengths and weaknesses?

2. How does Barry apply his four principles to International Society? What is the role of taxation? How feasible is such a proposal?

3. Do you think we should be moving toward limiting the power of the nation state in favor of a world government? What, if anything, is the value of nationalism? Explain your answer.

Suggestions for Further Reading

Barry, Brian. *Political Argument*. Routledge & Kegan Paul. 1965.

Bedau, Hugo, ed. *Justice and Equality*. Prentice Hall, 1971.

Benn, S. I. and R. S. Peters, *The Principles of Political Thought*. Free Press, 1995.

Benn, Stanley. "Justice," in *The Encyclopedia of Philosophy*. Macmillan, 1967.

Bowie, Norman, and Robert Simon. *The Individual and the Political Order*. Englewood Cliffs, NJ: Prentice Hall, 1977.

Daniels, Norman, ed. *Reading Rawls*. Basic Books, 1975.

Nagel, Thomas. *Equality and Partiality*. Oxford University Press, 1991.

Nielsen, Kai. "Radical Egalitarian Justice: Justice as Equality," *Social Theory and Practice*, vol. 5, no. 2, 1979.

Nozick, Robert. *Anarchy, State, and Utopia*. Basic Books, 1974.

Okin, Susan Moller. *Justice, Gender, and the Family*. Basic Books, 1989.

Pojman, Louis P. *Political Philosophy*. McGraw-Hill, 2003.

Rawls, John. *A Theory of Justice*. Harvard University Press, 1971.

Rawls, John. *Political Liberalism*. Columbia University Press, 1993.

Reiman, Jeffrey. *Justice and Modern Moral Philosophy*. Yale University Press, 1990.

Rescher, Nicholas. *Distributive Justice*. Bobbs-Merrill, 1966.

Sandel, Michael. *Liberalism and the Limits of Justice*. Cambridge University Press, 1988.

Sterba, James. *The Demands of Justice*. University of Notre Dame Press, 1980.

Sterba, James. *How to Make People Just*. Rowman and Littlefield, 1988.

Sterba, James P., ed., *Justice: Alternative Political Perspectives*. Wadsworth, 1992.

Sterba, James P., *Contemporary Social and Political Philosophy*. Wadsworth, 1995.

Taylor, Richard, *Freedom, Anarchy, and Law*, 2nd ed. Prometheus Books, 1982.

Veatch, Robert M. *The Foundations of Justice*. Oxford University Press, 1986.

Walzer, Michael. *Spheres of Justice*. Oxford University Press, 1983.

Wolgast, Elizabeth. *The Grammar of Justice*. Cornell University Press, 1987.

Part VIII

What Is the Meaning of Life?

To lose one's life is a little thing and I shall have the courage to do so if it is necessary; but to see the meaning of this life dissipated, to see our reason for existing disappear, that is what is unbearable. One cannot live without meaning.

ALBERT CAMUS

What is missing in my life is an understanding of what I must do, *not what I must know*—except, of course, that a certain amount of knowledge is presupposed in every action. *I need to understand the purpose of my life, and this means that I must find a truth which is true for me, that I must discover* that Idea for which I can live and die. *For what is truth but to live and die for an Idea?*

SØREN KIERKEGAARD as a twenty-two-year-old university student.
An entry in his journal August 1, 1835.

I N HIS AUTOBIOGRAPHY TOLSTOY tells the story of a traveler fleeing an infuriated animal. Attempting to save himself from the beast, the man runs towards a well and begins to climb down, when to his distress he spies a dragon at the bottom. The dragon is waiting for him with open jaws, ready to eat him. The poor fellow is caught in a dilemma. He dare not drop into the well for fear of the dragon, but he dare not climb out of the well for fear of the beast. So he clutches a branch of a bush growing in the cleft of the well and hangs onto it for dear life. His hands grow weak, and he feels that soon he shall have to give into his grim fate, but he still holds on desperately. As he grasps the branch for his salvation, he notices that two mice, one white and one black, are nibbling away at the main trunk of the branch onto which he is clinging. Soon they will dislodge the branch, and he will fall into the waiting jaws of the dragon.

The traveler knows that he will soon perish, but while clinging to the branch, he sees some drops of honey hanging on the leaves of the bush, and so sticks out his tongue and licks the leaves.

The traveler is you and I, and his plight is your plight and mine, the danger of our demise on every hand. The white mouse represents our days and the black our nights. Together they are nibbling away at the three score years and ten which make up our branch of life. Inevitably all will be over, and what have we to show for it? Is our brief distraction of the taste of honey all we get out of life? Is this life all there is? Can this brief moment in the history of the universe have significance? What gives life importance?

The certainty of death heightens the question of the meaning of life. Like a prisoner sentenced to death or a patient with terminal illness, we know that, in a sense, we are all sentenced to death and are terminally ill, but we flee the thought in a thousand ways. What is the purpose of life?

Our readings represent some of the classic responses to this question. Epicurus advises moderate pleasure in a life that accepts mortality without tears. Camus argues that life is meaningless and, to illustrate his view, he tells the story of Sisyphus rolling a stone up a hill for eternity. Walker finds the essence of a purposeful life in religion. Thomas Nagel argues that our sense of the absurd is what contributes to our greatness as self-conscious beings. Bertrand Russell argues that three things make life worth living: love, knowledge, and pity.

Moderate Hedonism   VIII.58

EPICURUS

Epicurus (341–271 B.C.) was a Greek philosopher who was born on the isle of Samos but lived much of his life in Athens, where he founded his very successful school of philosophy. He was influenced by the materialist Democritus (460–370 B.C.), who is the first philosopher known to believe that the world is made up of atoms. Only a few fragments of Epicurus' writings are extant.

Epicurus identified good with pleasure and evil with pain. This doctrine (repeated later in Bentham) is called *hedonism* (from the Greek word for pleasure). But contrary to popular opinion, Epicurus was not proposing what "Epicureanism" sometimes has been taken to mean: a sensuous, profligate life. He believed that the true life of pleasure consisted in an attitude of imperturbable emotional calm which needed only simple pleasures, a good diet, health, a prudent moral life, and good friends. Only good or bad sensations (pleasure or pain) should concern us, and death is not a sensation, so we should not fear death.

Study Questions

1. Does Epicurus believe in God? What sort of theology does he have?
2. What counsel does he give about death? What is his argument? Is it plausible?
3. What should the wise person seek? That is, what is the good?
4. What is the relationship between pleasure and pain? Describe his philosophy of life. What does he mean by the complete life?
5. What is his view of morality (justice)?

LETTER TO MENOECEUS

LET NO ONE WHEN YOUNG delay to study philosophy, nor when he is old grow weary of his study. For no one can come too early or too late to secure the health of his soul. And the man who says that the age for philosophy has either not yet come or has gone by is like the man who says that the age for happiness is not yet come to him, or has passed away. Wherefore both when young and old a man must study philosophy, that as he grows old he may be young in blessings through the grateful recollection of what has been, and that in youth he may be old as well, since he will know no fear of what is to come. We must then meditate on the things that make our happiness, seeing that when that is with us we have all, but when it is absent we do all to win it.

The things which I used unceasingly to commend to you, these do and practise, considering them to be the first principles of the good life. First of all believe that god is a being immortal and blessed, even as the common idea of a god is

Reprinted by permission of Oxford University Press. From Epicurus: The Extant Remains, *translated by Cyril Bailey, 1926.*

engraved on men's minds, and do not assign to him anything alien to his immortality or ill-suited to his blessedness: but believe about him everything that can uphold his blessedness and immortality. For gods there are, since the knowledge of them is by clear vision. But they are not such as the many believe them to be: for indeed they do not consistently represent them as they believe them to be. And the impious man is not he who denies the gods of the many, but he who attaches to the gods the beliefs of the many. For the statements of the many about the gods are not conceptions derived from sensation, but false suppositions, according to which the greatest misfortunes befall the wicked and the greatest blessings the good by the gift of the gods. For men being accustomed always to their own virtues welcome those like themselves, but regard all that is not of their nature as alien.

Become accustomed to the belief that death is nothing to us. For all good and evil consists in sensation, but death is deprivation of sensation. And therefore a right understanding that death is nothing to us makes the mortality of life enjoyable, not because it adds to it an infinite span of time, but because it takes away the craving for immortality. For there is nothing terrible in life for the man who has truly comprehended that there is nothing terrible in not living. So that the man speaks but idly who says that he fears death not because it will be painful when it comes, but because it is painful in anticipation. For that which gives no trouble when it comes, is but an empty pain in anticipation. So death, the most terrifying of ills, is nothing to us, since so long as we exist, death is not with us; but when death comes, then we do not exist. It does not then concern either the living or the dead, since for the former it is not, and the latter are no more.

But the many at one moment shun death as the greatest of evils, at another yearn for it as a respite from the evils in life. But the wise man neither seeks to escape life nor fears the cessation of life, for neither does life offend him nor does the absence of life seem to be any evil. And just as with food he does not seek simply the larger share and nothing else, but rather the most pleasant, so he seeks to enjoy not the longest period of time, but the most pleasant.

And he who counsels the young man to live well, but the old man to make a good end, is foolish, not merely because of the desirability of life, but also because it is the same training which teaches to live well and to die well. Yet much worse still is the man who says it is good not to be born, but

> once born make haste to pass the gates of Death.

For if he says this from conviction why does he not pass away out of life? For it is open to him to do so, if he had firmly made up his mind to this. But if he speaks in jest, his words are idle among men who cannot receive them.

We must then bear in mind that the future is neither ours, nor yet wholly not ours, so that we may not altogether expect it as sure to come, nor abandon hope of it, as if it will certainly not come.

We must consider that of desires some are natural, others vain, and of the natural some are necessary and others merely natural; and of the necessary some are necessary for happiness, others for the repose of the body, and others for very life. The right understanding of these facts enables us to refer all choice and avoidance to the health of the body and the soul's freedom from disturbance, since this is the aim of the life of blessedness. For it is to obtain this end that we always act, namely, to avoid pain and fear. And when this is once secured for us, all the tempest of the soul is dispersed, since the living creature has not to wander as though in search of something that is missing, and to look for some other thing by which he can fulfil the good of the soul and the good of the body. For it is then that we have need of pleasure, when we feel pain owing to the absence of pleasure; but when we do not feel pain, we no longer need pleasure. And for this cause we call pleasure the beginning and end of the blessed life. For we recognize pleasure as the first good innate in us, and from pleasure we begin every act of choice and avoidance, and to pleasure we return again, using the feeling as the standard by which we judge every good.

And since pleasure is the first good and natural to us, for this very reason we do not choose every pleasure, but sometimes we pass over many pleasures, when greater discomfort accrues to us as the result of them: and similarly we think many pains better than pleasures, since a greater pleasure comes to us when we have endured pains for a long time. Every pleasure then because of its natural kinship to us is good, yet not every pleasure is to be chosen: even as every pain also is an evil, yet not all are always of a nature to be avoided. Yet by a scale of comparison and by the consideration of advantages and disadvantages we must form our judgment on all these matters. For the good on certain occasions we treat as bad, and conversely the bad as good.

And again independence of desire we think a great good—not that we may at all times enjoy but a few things, but that, if we do not possess many, we may enjoy the few in the genuine persuasion that those have the sweetest pleasure in luxury who least need it, and that all that is natural is easy to be obtained, but that which is superfluous is hard. And so plain savours bring us pleasure equal to a luxurious diet, when all the pain due to want is removed; and bread and water produce the highest pleasure, when one who needs them puts them to his lips. To grow accustomed therefore to simple and not luxurious diet gives us health to the full, and makes a man alert for the needful employments of life, and when after long intervals we approach luxuries, disposes us better towards them, and fits us to be fearless of fortune.

When, therefore, we maintain that pleasure is the end, we do not mean the pleasures of profligates and those that consist in sensuality, as is supposed by some who are either ignorant or disagree with us or do not understand, but freedom from pain in the body and from trouble in the mind. For it is not continuous drinkings and revellings, nor the satisfaction of lusts, nor the enjoyment of fish and other luxuries of the wealthy table, which produce a pleasant life, but sober reasoning, searching out the motives for all choice and avoidance, and banishing mere opinions, to which are due the greatest disturbance of the spirit.

Of all this the beginning and the greatest good is prudence. Wherefore prudence is a more precious thing even than philosophy: for from prudence are sprung all the other virtues, and it teaches us that it is not possible to live pleasantly without living prudently and honourably and justly, nor, again, to live a life of prudence, honour, and justice without living pleasantly. For the virtues are by nature bound up with the pleasant life, and the pleasant life is inseparable from them. For indeed who, think you, is a better man than he who holds reverent opinions concerning the gods, and is at all times free from fear of death, and has reasoned out the end ordained by nature? He understands that the limit of good things is easy to fulfil and easy to attain, whereas the course of ills is either short in time or slight in pain: he laughs at destiny, whom some have introduced as the mistress of all things. He thinks that with us lies the chief power in determining events, some of which happen by necessity and some by chance, and some are within our control; for while necessity cannot be called to account, he sees that chance is inconstant, but that which is in our control is subject to no master, and to it are naturally attached praise and blame. For, indeed, it were better to follow the myths about the gods than to become a slave to the destiny of the natural philosophers: for the former suggests a hope of placating the gods by worship, whereas the latter involves a necessity which knows no placation. As to chance, he does not regard it as a god as most men do (for in a god's acts there is no disorder), nor as an uncertain cause of all things: for he does not believe that good and evil are given by chance to man for the framing of a blessed life, but that opportunities for great good and great evil are afforded by it. He therefore thinks it better to be unfortunate in reasonable action than to prosper in unreason. For it is better in a man's actions that what is well chosen should fail, rather than that what is ill chosen should be successful owing to chance.

Meditate therefore on these things and things akin to them night and day by yourself, and with a companion like to yourself, and never shall you be disturbed waking or asleep, but you shall live like a god among men. For a man who lives among immortal blessings is not like to a mortal being.

PRINCIPAL DOCTRINES

I. The blessed and immortal nature knows no trouble itself nor causes trouble to any other, so that it is never constrained by anger or favour. For all such things exist only in the weak.

II. Death is nothing to us: for that which is dissolved is without sensation; and that which lacks sensation is nothing to us.

III. The limit of quantity in pleasures is the removal of all that is painful. Wherever pleasure is present, as long as it is there, there is neither pain of body nor of mind, nor of both at once.

IV. Pain does not last continuously in the flesh, but the acutest pain is there for a very short time, and even that which just exceeds the pleasure in the flesh does not continue for many days at once. But chronic illnesses permit a predominance of pleasure over pain in the flesh.

V. It is not possible to live pleasantly without living prudently and honourably and justly, nor again to live a life of prudence, honour, and justice without living pleasantly. And the man who does not possess the pleasant life, is not living prudently and honourably and justly, and the man who does not possess the virtuous life, cannot possibly live pleasantly.

VI. To secure protection from men anything is a natural good, by which you may be able to attain this end.

VII. Some men wished to become famous and conspicuous, thinking that they would thus win for themselves safety from other men. Wherefore if the life of such men is safe, they have obtained the good which nature craves; but if it is not safe, they do not possess that for which they strove at first by the instinct of nature.

VIII. No pleasure is a bad thing in itself: but the means which produce some pleasures bring with them disturbances many times greater than the pleasures.

IX. If every pleasure could be intensified so that it lasted and influenced the whole organism or the most essential parts of our nature, pleasures would never differ from one another.

X. If the things that produce the pleasures of profligates could dispel the fears of the mind about the phenomena of the sky and death and its pains, and also teach the limits of desires and of pains, we should never have cause to blame them: for they would be filling themselves full with pleasures from every source and never have pain of body or mind, which is the evil of life.

XI. If we were not troubled by our suspicions of the phenomena of the sky and about death, fearing that it concerns us, and also by our failure to grasp the limits of pains and desires, we should have no need of natural science.

XII. A man cannot dispel his fear about the most important matters if he does not know what is the nature of the universe but suspects the truth of some mythical story. So that without natural science it is not possible to attain our pleasures unalloyed.

XIII. There is no profit in securing protection in relation to men, if things above and things beneath the earth and indeed all in the boundless universe remain matters of suspicion.

XIV. The most unalloyed source of protection from men, which is secured to some extent by a certain force of expulsion, is in fact the immunity which results from a quiet life and the retirement from the world.

XV. The wealth demanded by nature is both limited and easily procured; that demanded by idle imaginings stretches on to infinity.

XVI. In but few things chance hinders a wise man, but the greatest and most important matters reason has ordained and throughout the whole period of life does and will ordain.

XVII. The just man is most free from trouble, the unjust most full of trouble.

XVIII. The pleasure in the flesh is not increased, when once the pain due to want is removed, but is only varied: and the limit as regards pleasure in the mind is begotten by the reasoned understanding of these very pleasures and of the emotions akin to them, which used to cause the greatest fear to the mind.

XIX. Infinite time contains no greater pleasure than limited time, if one measures by reason the limits of pleasure.

XX. The flesh perceives the limits of pleasure as unlimited and unlimited time is required to supply it. But the mind, having attained a reasoned understanding of the ultimate good of the flesh and its limits and having dissipated the fears concerning the time to come, supplies us with the complete life, and we have no further need of infinite time: but neither does the mind shun pleasure, nor, when circumstances begin to bring about the departure from life, does it approach its end as though it fell short in any way of the best life.

XXI. He who has learned the limits of life knows that that which removes the pain due to want and makes the whole of life complete is easy to obtain; so that there is no need of actions which involve competition.

XXII. We must consider both the real purpose and all the evidence of direct perception, to which we always refer the conclusions of opinion; otherwise, all will be full of doubt and confusion.

XXIII. If you fight against all sensations, you will have no standard by which to judge even those of them which you say are false.

XXIV. If you reject any single sensation and fail to distinguish between the conclusion of opinion as to the appearance awaiting confirmation and that which is actually given by the sensation or feeling, or each intuitive apprehension of the mind, you will confound all other sensations as well with the same groundless opinion, so that you will reject every standard of judgment. And if among the mental images created by your opinion you affirm both that which awaits confirmation and that which does not, you will not escape error, since you will have preserved the whole cause of doubt in every judgment between what is right and what is wrong.

XXV. If on each occasion instead of referring your actions to the end of nature, you turn to some other nearer standard when you are making a choice or an avoidance, your actions will not be consistent with your principles.

XXVI. Of desires, all that do not lead to a sense of pain, if they are not satisfied, are not necessary, but involve a craving which is easily dispelled, when the object is hard to procure or they seem likely to produce harm.

XXVII. Of all the things which wisdom acquires to produce the blessedness of the complete life, far the greatest is the possession of friendship.

XXVIII. The same conviction which has given us confidence that there is nothing terrible that lasts for ever or even for long, has also seen the protection of friendship most fully completed in the limited evils of this life.

XXIX. Among desires some are natural and necessary, some natural but not necessary, and others neither natural nor necessary, but due to idle imagination.

XXX. Wherever in the case of desires which are physical, but do not lead to a sense of pain, if they are not fulfilled, the effort is intense, such pleasures are due to idle imagination, and it is not owing to their own nature that they fail to be dispelled, but owing to the empty imaginings of the man.

XXXI. The justice which arises from nature is a pledge of mutual advantage to restrain men from harming one another and save them from being harmed.

XXXII. For all living things which have not been able to make contracts not to harm one another or be harmed, nothing ever is either just or unjust; and likewise too for all tribes of men which have been unable or unwilling to make contracts not to harm or be harmed.

XXXIII. Justice never is anything in itself, but in the dealings of men with one another in any place whatever and at any time it is a kind of contract not to harm or be harmed.

XXXIV. Injustice is not an evil in itself, but only in consequence of the fear which attaches to the apprehension of being unable to escape those appointed to punish such actions.

XXXV. It is not possible for one who acts in secret contravention of the terms of the compact not to harm or be harmed, to be confident that he will escape detection, even if at present he escapes a thousand times. For up to the time of death it cannot be certain that he will indeed escape.

XXXVI. In its general aspect justice is the same for all, for it is a kind of mutual advantage in the dealings of men with one another: but with reference to the individual peculiarities of a country or any other circumstances the same thing does not turn out to be just for all.

XXXVII. Among actions which are sanctioned as just by law, that which is proved on examination to be of advantage in the requirements of men's dealings with one another, has the guarantee of justice, whether it is the same for all or not. But if a man makes a law and it does not turn out to lead to advantage in men's dealings with each other, then it no longer has the essential nature of justice. And even if the advantage in the matter of justice shifts from one side to the other, but for a while accords with the general concept, it is none the less just for that period in the eyes of those who do not confound themselves with empty sounds but look to the actual facts.

XXXVIII. Where, provided the circumstances have not been altered, actions which were considered just, have been shown not to accord with the general concept in actual practice, then they are not just. But where, when circumstances have changed, the same actions which were sanctioned as just no longer lead to advantage, there they were just at the time when they were of advantage for the dealings of fellow-citizens with one another; but subsequently they are no longer just, when no longer of advantage.

XXXIX. The man who has best ordered the element of disquiet arising from external circumstances has made those things that he could akin to himself and the rest at least not alien: but with all to which he could not do even this, he has refrained from mixing, and has expelled from his life all which it was of advantage to treat thus.

XL. As many as possess the power to procure complete immunity from their neighbours, these also live most pleasantly with one another, since they have the most certain pledge of security, and after they have enjoyed the fullest intimacy, they do not lament the previous departure of a dead friend, as though he were to be pitied.

For Further Reflection

1. Epicureanism is often thought of as a shallow, gluttonous, profligate life of undifferentiated pleasure, whose motto has been "Eat, drink, and be merry, for tomorrow we die" ("the pig philosophy"). Does one get this impression from Epicurus' writings?

2. Consider his view toward the fact of death: You ought not fear what never touches you. Death never touches you, for when you are, it is not; and when it is, you are not. Is this a reasonable argument against the fear of death? Why do we consider death an evil? What is the proper attitude toward death and why?

3. In the Hindu scripture *Bhagavad Gita,* Dharma, the personification of Duty, asks the young prince Yudhistira, "Of all the world's wonders, which is the most wonderful?" Yudhistira replies, "That no man, though he sees others dying all around him, believes that he himself will die." Is this applicable to Epicureanism? Is it a telling criticism?

4. How important is pleasure for the good life? What makes the "complete life" that Epicurus wrote about?

Stoicism: Enchiridion VIII.59

EPICTETUS

Epictetus (c. 50–130 AD), was born a Greek slave in Asia Minor and was freed sometime after the death of Nero in 68 CE. Epictetus was expelled from Rome by the Emperor Domitian in 90 CE and died in Northern Greece about 130. He was known as a kindly man, humble and charitable, especially to children. He was crippled in slavery which might have influenced his motto: "Bear and forbear." He embraced Stoicism and taught that we should submit to our fate as God's sacred gift and design. Epictetus did not publish anything, but his pupil Flavius Arrianus has recorded his teachings, the most famous of which is the *Enchiridion* (a handbook).

Stoicism was a Greek school of philosophy founded in 108 B.C. in Athens by Zeno of Citium and developed into the dominant philosophy of the Roman Empire. The word "stoa" from which "Stoic" derives is the Greek word for porch. Apparently Zeno lectured from his porch. The Stoics believed that we should resign ourselves to our fate, do our duty faithfully, and thereby acquire tranquillity of mind. The world is transient and unstable. We cannot change very much, but we can master our souls so that we attain tranquillity amidst the chaos all around us. The Stoics were the first world citizens, "cosmopolitans," holding that a divine spark dwelt in every human being. Chrysippus (c. 280–206 B.C.), referred to in the text, was the third leader of the Stoics and credited with more than 700 treatises. The Stoics believed that all human beings were brothers and sisters under one Father, God.

The first short selection on Duty is from the Stoic Roman Emperor Marcus Aurelius (121–180 A.D.). The second short selection on Suicide is from the Stoic Seneca (3–65 A.D.). The third, long selection is from Epictetus's teachings.

Study Questions

1. What is Marcus Aurelius's attitude toward duty?
2. What is Seneca's attitude toward death and suicide?
3. According to Epictetus, which things are and are not up to us?
4. Why should we destroy desire altogether? Is Epictetus consistent on this point?
5. Should we be upset when our loved ones die? What should our attitude toward them be?
6. Should we seek for things to happen as we wish? How should we wish them?
7. What does illness impede? What does it not impede?
8. What does Epictetus mean when he says we ought to conduct ourselves as we would at a banquet?
9. Why shouldn't you be upset by the thought that you shall live without honor, a complete nobody?
10. Is there anything intrinsically evil?
11. What are Epictetus's views on laughter, oaths, luxury, and sex?
12. What role does Socrates play in Epictetus's philosophy?

1. MARCUS AURELIUS
DEDICATION TO DUTY

Hour by hour resolve to do the task of the hour carefully, with unaffected dignity, affectionately, freely and justly. You can avoid distractions that might interfere with such performance if every act is done as though it were the last act of your life. Free yourself from random aims and curb any tendency to let the passions of emotion, hypocrisy, self-love and dissatisfaction with your allotted share cause you to ignore the commands of reason.

2. SENECA *DEATH AND SUICIDE*

Life has carried some men with the greatest rapidity to the harbor, the harbor they were bound to reach if they tarried on the way, while others it has fretted and harassed. To such a life, as you are aware, one should not always cling. *For mere living is not a good, but living well.* Accordingly, the wise man will live as long as he ought, not as long as he can. He will mark in what place, with whom, and how he is to conduct his existence, and what he is about to do. He always reflects concerning the quality, and not the quantity of his life. As soon as there are many events in his life that give him trouble and disturb his peace of mind, he sets himself free. And this privilege is his, not only when the crisis is upon him, but as soon as Fortune seems to be playing him false; then he looks about carefully and sees whether he ought, or ought not, to end his life on that account . . . He does not regard death with fear, as if it were a great loss; for no man can lose very much when but a driblet remains. It is not a question of dying earlier or later, but of dying well or ill. And dying well means escape from the danger of living ill.

3. EPICTETUS *ENCHIRIDION*

1. Some things are up to us, some are not up to us. Up to us are perception, intention, desire, aversion, and in sum, whatever are our own doings; not up to us are body, property, reputation, political office and in sum, whatever are not our own doings. And the things that are up to us are naturally free, unforbidding, unimpeding, while those not up to us are weak, slavish, forbidding, alien. Remember, then, that if you think naturally slavish things are free and that alien things are your own, you will be impeded, grieved, troubled, you will blame gods and men; but if you think that what is yours is yours and what is alien is alien, as it really is, nobody will ever compel you, nobody will forbid you, you will not blame anyone, you will not complain about anything, you will not do a single thing unwillingly, you will have no enemy, no one will hurt you; for you will not suffer anything harmful.

If you are aiming for such great things, remember that you must not be moderate in exerting yourself to attain them: you must avoid some things altogether and postpone others for the time being. For if you want both to accomplish these aims, and also to achieve eminence and riches, it may come about that you will not get the latter because you were trying for the former, and certainly you will not get the former, which are the only things that produce freedom and well-being.

So take rigorous care to say to every menacing impression, "You are just an impression, not the real thing at all." Then test it and consider it according to your rules-first and foremost this: whether it belongs among the things that are up to us or to those not up to us. And if it is something not up to us, be ready to say "It is nothing to me."

2. Remember that the aim of desire is to get what arouses the desire, the aim of aversion is to

Epictetus, Enchiridion, *translation by Wallace I. Matson. Copyright © Wallace Matson 1996. Used by permission.*

avoid that to which you are averse; and he who fails to get what he desires is miserable, and so is he who gets what he is averse to. So then, if you are averse only to things contrary to nature that are up to you, you will not get anything to which you are averse; but if you are averse to sickness or death or poverty, you will be miserable. So take your aversion away from everything that is not up to you and transfer it to things contrary to nature that are up to you. But for the time being, destroy desire altogether; for if you desire something not up to you, necessarily you will be unfortunate; as for things that are up to us, and would be good to desire, none of them is yet within your grasp. But only make use of selection and rejection, and these lightly, discreetly, and tentatively.

3. As for every thing that delights your mind or is useful or beloved, remember to describe it as it really is, starting with the smallest thing. If you are fond of a pot, say "It is a pot that I am fond of." For then, if it breaks, you will not be upset. If you kiss your child or your wife, say that you are kissing a human being. Then if they die you will not be upset.

5. It is not things that upset people but rather ideas about things. For example, death is nothing terrible, else it would have seemed so even to Socrates; rather it is the idea that death is terrible that is terrible. So whenever we are frustrated or upset or grieved, let us not blame others, but ourselves-that is, our ideas. It is the act of a philosophically ignorant person to blame others for his own troubles. One who is beginning to learn blames himself. An educated person blames neither anyone else nor himself.

6. Do not pride yourself on superiority that is not your own. If a horse in its pride should say, "I am a fine horse," that could be tolerated. You however, when you boast "I have a fine horse," should realize that you are boasting about the excellence of a horse. What then is your own? The use of impressions. So, make use of your impressions in accord with nature, and then take pride; for your pride will be in a good thing that is your own.

8. Don't seek for things to happen as you wish, but wish for things to happen as they do, and you will get on well.

9. Illness is an impediment of the body, but not of the will, as long as the will itself does not so wish. Lameness is an impediment of the leg, not of the will. And say this to yourself of every accident that befalls you; for you will find it an impediment to something else, not to yourself.

10. Whatever occasion befalls you, remember to turn around and look into yourself to see what power you have to make use of it. If you see a handsome boy or a beautiful girl, you will find the relevant power to be self-control. If labor is heaped on you, endurance is what you need; if abuse, forbearance. And thus habituating yourself, you will not be carried away by impressions.

11. Never say about anything that you have "lost it," but that you have "given it back." Your child has died? It has been given back. Your wife has died? She has been given back. "I have been deprived of my estate." This too has been given back. "But the usurper is wicked." What concern is it of yours, through whom the gift was returned to the giver? For the time it is given to you, treat it as someone else's, as travellers do an inn.

12. If you want to make progress, shun these sorts of reasonings: "If I neglect my affairs, I shall have nothing to live on"; "if I don't punish my slave, he will be good for nothing." For it is better to attain freedom from sorrow and fear and then die of hunger than to live lavishly in vexation. It is better for your slave to be bad than for you to be unhappy. Begin with little things. A little oil has been spilled, a little wine has been swiped: say to yourself, "This is the price of peace, that of serenity." Nothing is gratis. When you call for your slave, consider that maybe he won't hear you, and even if he does he still won't do what you want him to do. But he is not so well off that your tranquillity should depend on him.

13. If you want to make progress, be content to appear stupid and foolish about externals, and don't wish to seem to know anything. And whenever you seem to be somebody to someone,

distrust yourself. For be aware that it is not easy both to have your will in accordance with nature and to be on your guard about externals also, if you are to take care of the one it is absolutely necessary to neglect the other.

14. If you want your children and your wife and friends to live forever, you are a fool; for you want what is not up to you to be up to you, and what is not yours to be yours. Thus also if you want your slave not to do anything wrong, you are stupid; for you want badness not to be badness but something else. But if what you want is not to fail in getting what you desire, that you can bring about. So practise what you are capable of. Every person's master is the one who controls whether that person shall get what he wants and avoid what he doesn't want. Thus whoever wishes to be free should neither seek nor avoid anything that is up to others; otherwise he will necessarily be a slave.

15. Remember that you ought to conduct yourself as you do at a banquet. When something passed around reaches you, extend your hand and take it politely. If it is passing you by, don't grab. If it has not yet reached you, don't crave for it, but wait until it gets to you. Thus toward children, thus toward women, thus toward jobs, thus toward riches; and in due time you will be worthy to dine with the gods. But if you do not take even the things set out for you, but despise them, then not only will you be a banquet companion of the gods, you will even be a co-ruler. By thus acting, Diogenes and Heraclitus and like men came to be called divine, and deservedly

16. Whenever you see someone weeping in grief because his child is going away or he has lost his property, be careful not to be misled by the impression that he is in a bad way because of external things, but be ready to say at once "It is not the circumstances that distress him (for someone else would not be distressed), but the idea he has about them." Don't, of course, hesitate to condole with him in words, and, if there is occasion, even to groan with him; but take care not to groan inwardly.

17. Remember that you are an actor in a drama such as the playwright wishes it to be. If he wants it short, it will be short; if long, long. If he wants you to play a beggar, play even that capably; or a lame man, or a ruler, or a private person. For this is yours, to play the assigned role well. Casting is the business of another.

19. You can be unbeatable if you never enter a contest in which it is not up to you who wins. Beware lest ever, seeing someone else preferred in honor or having great power or otherwise esteemed, you get carried away by impressions and deem him blessed. For since the essence of the good lies in the things up to us, neither jealousy nor envy has a place; and you yourself will not wish to be a praetor[1] or a senator or a consul, but a free man. There is but one way to this: contempt for things not up to us.

20. Remember that it is not the man who curses you or the man who hits you that insults you, but the idea you have of them as insulting. So, whenever someone irritates you, realize that it is your own opinion that has irritated you. First of all, try not to be carried away by impressions; if you succeed just once in gaining time and avoiding hastiness, you will easily control yourself.

21. Let death and exile and all dreadful appearances be before your eyes every day, and most of all, death; and you will never deem anything trivial, nor desire anything excessively.

22. If you are eager for philosophy, be prepared from the beginning to be ridiculed and sneered at by the mob, who will say things like "All of a sudden he has come back to us a philosopher!" and "Where did he get that high brow?" But don't be a highbrow; hold fast to what seems best for you, as one who has been assigned to this territory by the god. And remember this: if you stay with it, the ones who ridicule you at first will admire you afterwards; but if they get the better of you, it will be your lot to be laughed at twice.

23. If ever it happens that you turn to externals because you want to please someone, realize

1. Roman magistrate

that you have lost your bearings. It suffices to *be* a philosopher in all things; but if you also want to *appear* to be one, appear so to yourself and that will be enough.

24. Don't let reflections like this upset you: "I shall live without honor, a complete nobody." For suppose not being honored is an evil: you cannot be subjected to evil by another, any more than to shamefulness. Is it your business to acquire power or an invitation to a banquet? By no means. How then is this being without honor? How then will you be a complete nobody, when you ought to be somebody only with respect to those things that are up to you-the domain wherein it is given to you to be of the greatest worth? But your friends will get no help from you? What do you mean by help? They won't have a penny from you; nor will you make them Roman citizens. So who told you that these things are up to you, and not the business of others? Who can give to another things that he does not have himself? "Then get them," one says, "so that we can have them." If I can get them while preserving my self-respect and trust-worthiness and high-mindedness, show me the way and I'll get them. But if you require me to be one who will lose my proper goods in order to produce worthless things for you, just look, how partial and unfair you are. Which do you want more? Money, or a faithful and upright friend? Then you had better help me to acquire the characteristics of one and not require me to do the things that would ruin them.

"But my country, as far as its fate is up to me," one says, "will be helpless." Again, what kind of help do you mean? She will not get arcades or baths from you. So what? Neither does she get shoes from smiths nor weapons from shoemakers. It is enough if everyone fulfills his own task. If you make someone else into a faithful and upright citizen, have you done something for the state? "Yes." Then you yourself are not unhelpful if you are that one. "Then what status," one asks, "will I have in the city?" Whatever you are capable of, while conserving your faithfulness and uprightness. If in wishing to aid

her you throw them away, what advantage will accrue to her when you have ended up shameless and faithless?

26. We can learn the will of nature by considering the matters about which we don't disagree with one another. For instance, when somebody else's miserable slave breaks a cup, you are ready right away to say "So it goes." But realize that when it is yours that gets broken, you ought to behave the same way you did when it was someone else's. Apply this to more important matters as well. Somebody else's child or wife has died; there is no one who would not say "That's life." But when his own child or wife dies, it is "Alas, woe is me!" We ought to remember what we feel when we hear the same thing about other people.

27. As a target is not set up for the purpose of being missed, so nothing in the world is intrinsically evil.

28. If someone were to hand over your body to just whomever happened along, you would be outraged. Why aren't you outraged at the fact that *you* turn over your own mind to whomever happens along—if he insults you and you let it upset and trouble you?

29. In every work examine the things that have to be done first and what is to follow, and only then get started on it. If you don't, you will go along eagerly at first, because you have given no consideration to what is coming next; later when difficulties appear the work will come to an ignoble halt. You want to win at Olympia? I do too, by the gods; for it is a fine thing. But look at what comes first, and what comes next, and then take on the work. You must keep discipline, diet, give up pastries, do the compulsory exercises at the set time in heat or in cold, never drink anything cold, take wine only with meals, completely submit yourself to your trainer as to your doctor, and then when the contest starts you have to wallow around in the mud, maybe dislocate your wrist or turn your ankle, swallow quantities of sand, perhaps sometimes be flogged, and after all this you still lose. Taking it all into consideration, go ahead and be an athlete, if you still want to. Otherwise

you will be turning from one thing to another like children, who now play wrestlers, now gladiators, now trumpeters, then tragic actors; you too would be now athlete, now gladiator, then orator, then philosopher, nothing with your whole soul; but like a monkey you mimic every sight that you see as one thing after another intrigues you. For you have never proceeded with something in accord with investigation, after looking at it from all sides; but just at random and out of frivolous enthusiasm.

Thus some people, when they have seen a philosopher and have heard someone speaking the way Euphrates speaks (but who can speak like him?), wish to philosophize themselves. Man, consider first what kind of business this is. And then learn what your own nature is; can you bear it? Do you want to be a pentathlete or a wrestler? Look at your arms, your thighs, learn about your hips. One man is naturally fitted for one thing, another for another. Do you suppose you can do these things and keep on eating and drinking and enthusing and sulking just as you do now? You will have to go without sleep, labor, leave home, be despised by a slave, have everyone laugh at you, get the worse in everything, in honors, in jobs, in lawsuits, in every trifle. Look these things over and decide whether you want to exchange them for tranquillity, freedom, and peace; if not, don't go ahead, don't be, like a child, now philosopher, afterwards tax collector, then orator, finally Caesar's procurator. These things do not go together. You ought to be one man, good or evil; you must cultivate either your own guiding principle or externals; that is, apply yourself either to the inner man or to outward things: assume either the role of philosopher or of layman.

30. What is proper for us to do is for the most part defined by our social relationships. He is your father: this means that it is for you to look after him, to defer to him in all things, to put up with his abuse and his beatings. "But he is a bad father." Did nature then assign you to a *good* father? No, just to a father. "My brother is wronging me." Then keep up your relationship

toward him; don't look at what he may be doing, but at what you should do to keep your will in accord with nature. No other person will hurt you unless *you* will it; you will be hurt to the extent that you think you are hurt. Thus if you will make a habit of contemplating social relationships, you will discover what it is fitting to do as a neighbor, as a citizen, as a consul.

31. Concerning piety toward the gods, know that this is the main thing: have right beliefs about them-that they exist, that they run the world well and justly; and you have been appointed to obey them and to resign yourself to whatever happens and to follow willingly because you are led by the best judgment. Thus you will never blame the gods nor accuse them of unconcern. However, this can never come about unless you withdraw yourself from things not up to us and place good and evil exclusively in the class of things up to us. Thus, if you consider anything else to be good or evil, inevitably, when you fail to get what you want and stumble in to what you don't want, you will assign blame and hate those responsible. For it is natural for every creature to flee and avert itself from hurtful appearances and their causes, and on the other hand to go after and to admire the beneficial and their causes. So it is impossible for anyone who thinks he is being hurt to enjoy what he thinks is hurting him, just as enjoying harm itself is impossible. Consequently even a father is abused by his son, insofar as he does not give the child things that seem to be good; and Polyneices and Eteocles were made enemies of each other by the idea that having the tyranny would be a good thing. On this account also the farmer curses the gods, as do the sailor, the merchant, and those who have lost their wives and children. For wherever one's interest is, there also is one's piety. So, whoever concerns himself with desire and aversion as he ought, concerns himself in the same way with piety too. But libations and sacrifices and rites according to the traditions of the country are always appropriate, and they should be done with purity and not in a slovenly manner nor carelessly; neither stingily nor extravagantly.

33. Prescribe a certain character and type for yourself, and guard it both when you are by yourself and when you meet people. And be silent about most things, or chat only when necessary and about few matters. On rare occasions, when the time is ripe and you are called on to talk, talk-but not about banal topics; not about gladiators, or athletes, or horse races, or food and drink, such as you hear everywhere; and above all, not about blaming or praising or comparing people. If you can, lead the conversation around to something proper. But if you happen to be alone with strange people, be silent.

Laugh seldom and about few things and with restraint.

Totally abstain from taking oaths, if you can; if not, then refuse whenever circumstances allow.

Avoid celebrations, both public and private; but if the occasion calls you, be alert not to lapse into vulgarity. For know that if a companion is defiled, necessarily also one who keeps company with him will be defiled, even if he himself happens to be pure.

Partake of things having to do with the body only as far as bare need goes: such things as food, drink, clothing, housing, slaves. Dispense altogether with whatever has to do with reputation or luxury.

As to sex, be as pure as you can before marriage; but if you are aroused, indulge only to the extent that is customary. However, don't by any means be troublesome to those who do indulge, or censorious; and don't keep mentioning that you yourself can get along without it.

If someone tells you that somebody else is saying awful things about you, don't defend yourself against the accusations, but reply, "He must not know about the other faults that I have, if these are the only ones he mentioned."

It isn't necessary to attend shows for the most part. But if there is a proper occasion, do not appear to be more enthusiastic for anyone else than for yourself, that is, wish only that those things should happen that do happen and that only the winner should win; that way you will not be frustrated. Abstain altogether from shouting and ridiculing anyone or getting emotionally involved. And after the performance don't talk much about what happened, if it does not tend toward your improvement. For it would be evident from this that you were dazzled by the spectacle. . . .

Whenever you are going to meet someone, especially one reputed to be important, consider what Socrates or Zeno would have done in the circumstances, and you will not be puzzled about how to use the occasion properly. When you are going to visit a powerful personage, propose to yourself that you will not find him at home, that you will be shut out, that the gates will be slammed in your face, that he will not notice you. And if nevertheless it is your duty to go, when you arrive bear with what happens and by no means say to yourself "It wasn't worth it." For it is unphilosophical to be troubled by externals.

In conversation avoid overmuch talk about your own deeds and dangers. For although it is pleasant for you to recall your own adventures, it may not be so for others to hear about what happened to you.

Also avoid raising laughter; for this is a slippery slope to vulgarity and at the same time sufficient to cancel the respect that others have for you. It is also dangerous to get into dirty talk. Whenever anything of this sort begins, if you get the opportunity, you might rebuke the person who starts it; or if not, make it clear by being silent or blushing and scowling that you are displeased by the talk.

34. When you receive an impression of a certain pleasure, be on your guard, just as you are with other impressions, lest you get carried away by it. Take your time with the thing, wait a while. Next call to mind both times-the time when you will enjoy the pleasure, and the time when, after enjoying it, you will change your mind and scold yourself; and set against these the thought of how, if you abstain, you will rejoice and praise yourself. But if it still seems to you to be the proper occasion to indulge, consider, lest you be overcome by the gentleness

and sweetness of it and its seductiveness; set against it, how much better it will be to be conscious of yourself as having won this victory.

35. When you do something because you have recognized that it ought to be done, never go out of your way not to be seen doing it, not even if public opinion takes a different view of it. For if it isn't right for you to do, shun the deed itself; if it is right, why are you afraid of people who would be censuring you wrongly?

37. If you take on a role that is too much for you, you both disgrace yourself in it and neglect the one that you might have filled.

38. Just as in walking you pay attention not to step on a nail or to turn your ankle, pay attention not to hurt your ruling principle. And if we look out for this in all of our activities, we will take them on more securely.

40. Women, soon after they have reached the age of fourteen, are called "ladies" by men. Accordingly when they see how there is going to be nothing else for them but sleeping with men, they start in to adorn themselves and they put all their hopes in that. So it is worth thinking about: how they can be brought to sense that they are honored for no other reason than that they appear chaste and modest?

41. It is the sign of a weak mind to spend too much time on things having to do with the body, such as exercising a lot, eating a lot, drinking a lot, excreting, sex. Such things should be done incidentally; let all your attention be concentrated on your mind.

42. Whenever someone treats you badly or says bad things about you, remember that he does it or says it thinking that he is doing the right thing. Now it is not possible for him to adhere to *your* conception of the right, but only his own. Whence it follows that if he has a wrong view of things, he, being deceived, is the one who is hurt. For if someone believes that a true proposition is false, it is not the proposition that suffers but the deceived believer. If you consider these things you will deal gently with the slanderer. On each occasion just say, "So it seemed to him."

43. Every thing has two handles, one by which it may be borne, one by which it cannot be borne. If your brother has done wrong, don't grasp this by the "wrongdoing" handle-it can't be borne by that one-but by the "brother," the "brought-uptogether" handle, and thereby you will be able to bear it.

44. These sorts of arguments are invalid: "I am richer than you are, therefore I am better than you"; "I am more eloquent than you are, therefore I am better than you." But these are valid: "I am richer than you are, therefore my possessions are better than yours"; "I am more eloquent than you are, therefore my speech is better than yours." *You*, however, are neither your possessions nor your speech.

46. Never refer to yourself as a philosopher or chatter much with laymen about philosophical principles, but do what the principles prescribe. For example, at a banquet do not talk about how one ought to eat, but eat as you ought. Remember that Socrates altogether eschewed ostentation. When people came to him who wanted him to introduce them to philosophers, he did so, being quite content to be over looked. And if an argument about some philosophical principle gets started among laymen, you should in most instances be silent; for there is great danger of straightway vomiting up what you have not digested. And if someone says to you that you know nothing, and you aren't hurt by the remark, you may then be sure that you are making a beginning at your task. Sheep brought to pasture don't show off to the shepherd how much they have eaten, but rather they digest their fodder internally and produce wool and milk on the outside. Likewise you should not show off your principles to laymen, but digest them and display the results.

48. Position and character of a vulgar person: he never expects help or harm from himself, but only from outside. Position and character of a philosopher: he expects all help and harm to come from himself.

Marks of one making progress: he blames nobody, he praises nobody, he complains about nobody, he accuses nobody, he never speaks of himself as if he were anybody or knew anything. If he is impeded or frustrated he blames himself. And if someone praises him, he smiles to himself at the person giving the praise; but if he is blamed, he offers no defense. He comports himself as invalids do, taking care not to move a damaged limb before it has healed. He has purged himself of all desire; he has concentrated aversion solely on things that are against nature but up to us. He takes things as they come. If he appears stupid or ignorant, he doesn't care. In sum, he guards against himself as against an enemy lying in wait.

50. Whatever principles are set before you, follow them as laws, the dishonoring of which would be impious. But don't worry about what anyone says about you; for this is not at all up to you.

51. How much time will you take yet before you judge yourself worthy of the best, and never step over the bounds discriminated by reason? You have been apprised of the philosophical principles to which you ought to subscribe, and you have subscribed. So what sort of teacher are you still waiting for, that you put off your own reformation until he gets here? You are no longer a child, but a grown man. If now you take no care and loaf and always keep putting things off and set one day after another on which to start attending to your own affairs, you will lose yourself, making no progress but going on being a layman in life and in death. Right now, then, deem yourself worthy of living as an adult making progress. And let all that appears best to you be your inviolable law. And if some task is set for you, whether pleasant or glorious or inglorious, remember, that right now you are the contestant and here are the Olympic games, and there can't be any more delay, and that one day and one deed will determine whether progress is lost or saved. That is how Socrates became what he was: by attending in all things that he encountered to nothing other than reason. But you-even if you are not yet a Socrates, at least you ought to live as someone wishing to be like Socrates.

52. The primary and most essential topic in philosophy is that of the use of philosophical principles, for instance, not to lie. The secondary is that of proofs, for instance why one ought not to lie. Tertiary is of what gives certainty and consequence to the first two, for instance, why is this a proof? what indeed is a proof? implication? inconsistency? truth? falsity? The tertiary topic is required because of the secondary, the secondary because of the primary; but the one that is most necessary and that ought never to be neglected is the primary. But we turn them around: for we wrangle about the tertiary topics and bestow all our interest on them, while we altogether neglect the primary. And so we tell lies, and at the same time we are prepared to prove why lying is wrong.

53. On every occasion you ought to have the following ready for use:

> Lead thou me on O Zeus, and Destiny
> Wherever has been fixed by thy decree.
> I shall come willingly; though if I fall
> Into corruption, no less, come I shall.
>
> —CLEANTHES

> Whoever yields with grace to what must be,
> We deem him wise: he knows divinity.
>
> —EURIPIDES

> Well, Crito, if so it pleases the gods,
>   let it be so.
>
> —SOCRATES

> Anytus and Meletus can kill me, but they
>   cannot harm me.
>
> —SOCRATES

In the things are true which are said by the philosophers about the kinship between God and man, what else remains for men to do than what Socrates did? Never in reply to the question, to what country you belong, say that you are an Athenian or a Corinthian, but that you are a citizen of the world. . . . He then who has observed with intelligence the administration of the world, and has learned that the greatest and supreme and the most comprehensive community is that which is composed of men and God, and that from God have descended the seeds not only to my father and grandfather, but to all beings which are generated on the earth and are produced, and particularly to rational beings—for these only are by their nature formed to have communion with God, being by means of reason conjoined with him—why should not such a man call himself a citizen of the world, why not a son of God, and why should he be afraid of any-thing which happens among men? Is kinship with Caesar or with any other of the powerful in Rome sufficient to enable us to live in safety, and above contempt and without any fear at all? and to have God for your maker and father and guardian, shall not this release us from sorrows and fears? (*Discourses* Bk I, 9)

If the room is smoky, if only moderately, I will stay; if there is too much smoke, I will go. Remember this, keep firm hold on it, the door is always open.

For Further Reflection

1. Compare the Stoics with Epicurus's philosophy. How different are the two philoso-phies? In what ways, if any, do they differ? For example, compare what they say about death?

2. What are the main tenets of the Stoic philosophy? Is it really possible to live according to their principles? Which are the most plausible, and which the least plausible?

3. How strongly do Stoics value friendship and loyalty? Discuss and evaluate their views.

4. Consider the following questions: Is Stoicism an optimistic or pessimistic philosophy? What does it imply about human free will?

VIII.60   Life Is Absurd

ALBERT CAMUS

Albert Camus (1913–1960) was born in French colonial Algeria, into a poor work-ing-class family. He was a French journalist, novelist, and philosopher who fought in the French underground during World War II and fought for courage and in-tegrity in public life. He is most famous for his novels *The Stranger* (1942), *The Plague* (1947), and *The Fall* (1957), for which he received a Nobel Prize for litera-ture. He was killed in a car crash in 1960. His rival existentialist, Jean-Paul Sartre, fittingly called it "an absurd death."

In this selection we see Camus' overall assessment that life is absurd, meaningless. The only important philosophical question is, why not commit suicide? Life is com-pared to the myth of Sisyphus, wherein that man is condemned by the gods to roll a huge stone up a mountain, watch it roll back down, and retrieve it, only to repeat the process again, endlessly.

Study Questions

1. What is the only important philosophical question and why is it important?
2. What is the "Absurd"? What does it mean to say that life is absurd? How does this feeling arise?
3. What is the only important thing in life? Is Camus' notion of value clear?
4. What does Camus mean by living "without appeal"?
5. Why do the gods condemn Sisyphus to his awful fate?
6. What does Sisyphus symbolize?

ABSURDITY AND SUICIDE

THERE IS BUT ONE TRULY SERIOUS philosophical problem, and that is suicide. Judging whether life is or is not worth living amounts to answering the fundamental question of philosophy. All the rest—whether or not the world has three dimensions, whether the mind has nine or twelve categories—comes afterwards. These are games; one must first answer. And if it is true, as Nietzsche claims, that a philosopher, to deserve our respect, must preach by example, you can appreciate the importance of that reply, for it will precede the definitive act. These are facts the heart can feel; yet they call for careful study before they become clear to the intellect.

If I ask myself how to judge that this question is more urgent than that, I reply that one judges by the actions it entails. I have never seen anyone die for the ontological argument. Galileo, who held a scientific truth of great importance, abjured it with the greatest of ease as soon as it endangered his life. In a certain sense, he did right.* That truth was not worth the stake. Whether the earth or the sun revolves around the other is a matter of profound indifference. To tell the truth, it is a futile question.

*From the point of view of the relative value of truth. On the other hand, from the point of view of virile behavior, this scholar's fragility may well make us smile.

On the other hand, I see many people die because they judge that life is not worth living. I see others paradoxically getting killed for the ideas or illusions that give them a reason for living (what is called a reason for living is also an excellent reason for dying). I therefore conclude that the meaning of life is the most urgent of questions. How to answer it? On all essential problems (I mean thereby those that run the risk of leading to death or those that intensify the passion of living) there are probably but two methods of thought: the method of La Palisse and the method of Don Quixote. Solely the balance between evidence and lyricism can allow us to achieve simultaneously emotion and lucidity. In a subject at once so humble and so heavy with emotion, the learned and classical dialectic must yield, one can see, to a more modest attitude of mind deriving at one and the same time from common sense and understanding.

Suicide has never been dealt with except as a social phenomenon. On the contrary, we are concerned here, at the outset, with the relationship between individual thought and suicide. An act like this is prepared within the silence of the heart, as is a great work of art. The man himself is ignorant of it. One evening he pulls the trigger or jumps. Of an apartment-building manager who had killed himself I was told that he had lost his daughter five years before, that he had changed greatly since, and that that experience had "undermined" him. A more exact word cannot be imagined. Beginning to think is beginning to be undermined. Society has but little connection with such beginnings. The worm is in man's heart. That is where it must be sought. One must follow and understand this fatal game that leads from lucidity in the face of existence to flight from light. . . .

But it is hard to fix the precise instant, the subtle step when the mind opted for death; it is easier to deduce from the act itself the consequences it implies. In a sense, and as in melodrama, killing yourself amounts to confessing. It is confessing that life is too much for you or that you do not understand it. Let's not go too far in such analogies, however, but rather return to everyday words. It is merely confessing that that "is not worth the trouble." Living, naturally, is never easy. You continue making the gestures commanded by existence for many reasons, the first of which is habit. Dying voluntarily implies that you have recognized, even instinctively, the ridiculous character of that habit, the absence of any profound reason for living, the insane character of that daily agitation, and the uselessness of suffering.

What, then, is that incalculable feeling that deprives the mind of the sleep necessary to life? A world that can be explained even with bad reasons is a familiar world. But, on the other hand, in a universe suddenly divested of illusions and lights, man feels an alien, a stranger. His exile is without remedy since he is deprived of the memory of a lost home or the hope of a promised land. This divorce between man and his life, the actor and his setting, is properly the feeling of absurdity. All healthy men having thought of their own suicide, it can be seen, without further explanation, that there is a direct connection between this feeling and the longing for death.

The subject of this essay is precisely this relationship between the absurd and suicide, the exact degree to which suicide is a solution to the absurd. The principle can be established that for a man who does not cheat, what he believes to be true must determine his action. Belief in the absurdity of existence must then dictate his conduct. It is legitimate to wonder, clearly and without false pathos, whether a conclusion of this importance requires forsaking as rapidly as possible an incomprehensible condition. I am speaking, of course, of men inclined to be in harmony with themselves. . . .

All great deeds and all great thoughts have a ridiculous beginning. Great works are often born on a street-corner or in a restaurant's revolving door. So it is with absurdity. The absurd world more than others derives its nobility from that abject birth. In certain situations, replying "nothing" when asked what one is thinking about may be pretense in a man. Those who are loved are well aware of this. But if that reply is sincere, if it symbolizes that odd state of soul in which the void becomes eloquent, in which the chain of daily gestures is broken, in which the heart vainly seeks the link that will connect it again, then it is as it were the first sign of absurdity.

It happens that the stage sets collapse. Rising, streetcar, four hours in the office or the factory, meal, streetcar, four hours of work, meal, sleep, and Monday Tuesday Wednesday Thursday Friday and Saturday according to the same rhythm—this path is easily followed most of the time. But one day the "why" arises and everything begins in that weariness tinged with amazement. "Begins"—this is important. Weariness comes at the end of the acts of a mechanical life, but at the same time it inaugurates the impulse of consciousness. It awakens consciousness and provokes what follows. What follows is the gradual return into the chain or it is the definitive awakening. At the end of the awakening comes, in time, the consequence: suicide or recovery. In itself weariness has something sickening about it. Here, I must conclude that it is good. For everything begins with consciousness and nothing is worth anything except through it. . . .

But what does life mean in such a universe? Nothing else for the moment but indifference to the future and a desire to use up everything that is given. Belief in the meaning of life always implies a scale of values, a choice, our preferences. Belief in the absurd, according to our definitions, teaches the contrary. But this is worth examining.

Knowing whether or not one can live *without appeal* is all that interests me. I do not want to get out of my depth. This aspect of life being given me, can I adapt myself to it? Now, faced with this particular concern, belief in the absurd is tantamount to substituting the quantity of experiences for the quality. If I convince myself that this life has no other aspect than that of the absurd, if I feel that its whole equilibrium depends on that perpetual opposition between my conscious revolt and the darkness in which it struggles, if I admit that my freedom has no meaning except in relation to its limited fate, then I must say that what counts is not the best of living but the most living. . . .

On the one hand the absurd teaches that all experiences are unimportant, and on the other it urges toward the greatest quantity of experiences. How, then, can one fail to do as so many of those men I was speaking of earlier—choose the form of life that brings us the most possible of that human matter, thereby introducing a scale of values that on the other hand one claims to reject?

But again it is the absurd and its contradictory life that teaches us. For the mistake is thinking that that quantity of experiences depends on the circumstances of our life when it depends solely on us. Here we have to be oversimple. To two men living the same number of years, the world always provides the same sum of experiences. It is up to us to be conscious of them. Being aware of one's life, one's revolt, one's freedom, and to the maximum, is living, and to the maximum. Where lucidity dominates, the scale of values becomes useless. . . .

THE MYTH OF SISYPHUS

The gods had condemned Sisyphus to ceaselessly rolling a rock to the top of a mountain, whence the stone would fall back of its own weight. They had thought with some reason that there is no more dreadful punishment than futile and hopeless labor.

If one believes Homer, Sisyphus was the wisest and most prudent of mortals. According to another tradition, however, he was disposed to practice the profession of highwayman. I see no contradiction in this. Opinions differ as to the reasons why he became the futile laborer of the underworld. To begin with, he is accused of a certain levity in regard to the gods. He stole their secrets. Ægina, the daughter of Æsopus, was carried off by Jupiter. The father was shocked by that disappearance and complained to Sisyphus. He, who knew of the abduction, offered to tell about it on condition that Æsopus would give water to the citadel of Corinth. To the celestial thunderbolts he preferred the benediction of water. He was punished for this in the underworld. Homer tells us also that Sisyphus had put Death in chains. Pluto could not endure the sight of his deserted, silent empire. He dispatched the god of war, who liberated Death from the hands of her conqueror.

It is said also that Sisyphus, being near to death, rashly wanted to test his wife's love. He ordered her to cast his unburied body into the middle of the public square. Sisyphus woke up in the underworld. And there, annoyed by an obedience so contrary to human love, he obtained from Pluto permission to return to earth in order to chastise his wife. But when he had seen again the face of this world, enjoyed water and sun, warm stones and the sea, he no longer wanted to go back to the infernal darkness. Recalls, signs of anger, warnings were of no avail. Many years more he lived facing the curve of the gulf, the sparkling sea, and the smiles of earth. A decree of the gods was necessary. Mercury came and seized the impudent man by the collar and, snatching him from his joys, led him forcibly back to the underworld, where his rock was ready for him.

You have already grasped that Sisyphus is the absurd hero. He *is*, as much through his passions as through his torture. His scorn of the gods, his hatred of death, and his passion for life won him that unspeakable penalty in which the whole being is exerted toward accomplishing nothing. This is the price that must be paid for the passions of this earth. Nothing is told us about Sisyphus in the underworld. Myths are made for the imagination to breathe life into them. As for this myth, one sees merely the whole effort of a body straining to raise the huge stone, to roll it and push it up a slope a hundred times over; one sees the face screwed up, the cheek tight against the stone, the shoulder bracing the clay-covered mass, the foot wedging it, the fresh start with arms outstretched, the wholly human security of two earth-clotted hands. At the very end of his long effort measured by skyless space and time without depth, the purpose is achieved. Then Sisyphus watches the stone rush down in a few moments toward that lower world whence he will have to push it up again toward the summit. He goes back down to the plain.

It is during that return, that pause, that Sisyphus interests me. A face that toils so close to stones is already stone itself ! I see that man going back down with a heavy yet measured step toward the torment of which he will never know the end. That hour like a breathing-space which returns as surely as his suffering, that is the hour of consciousness. At each of those moments when he leaves the heights and gradually sinks toward the lairs of the gods, he is superior to his fate. He is stronger than his rock.

If this myth is tragic, that is because its hero is conscious. Where would his torture be, indeed, if at every step the hope of succeeding upheld him? The workman of today works every day in his life at the same tasks, and this fate is no less absurd. But it is tragic only at the rare moments when it becomes conscious. Sisyphus, proletarian of the gods, powerless and rebellious, knows the whole extent of his wretched condition: it is what he thinks of during his descent. The lucidity that was to constitute his torture at the same time crowns his victory. There is no fate that cannot be surmounted by scorn.

If the descent is thus sometimes performed in sorrow, it can also take place in joy. This word is

not too much. Again I fancy Sisyphus returning toward his rock, and the sorrow was in the beginning. When the images of earth cling too tightly to memory, when the call of happiness becomes too insistent, it happens that melancholy rises in man's heart: this is the rock's victory, this is the rock itself. The boundless grief is too heavy to bear. These are our nights of Gethsemane. But crushing truths perish from being acknowledged. Thus, Œdipus at the outset obeys fate without knowing it. But from the moment he knows, his tragedy begins. Yet at the same moment, blind and desperate, he realizes that the only bond linking him to the world is the cool hand of a girl. Then a tremendous remark rings out: "Despite so many ordeals, my advanced age and the nobility of my soul make me conclude that all is well." Sophocles' Œdipus, like Dostoevsky's Kirilov, thus gives the recipe for the absurd victory. Ancient wisdom confirms modern heroism.

One does not discover the absurd without being tempted to write a manual of happiness. "What! by such narrow ways—?" There is but one world, however. Happiness and the absurd are two sons of the same earth. They are inseparable. It would be a mistake to say that happiness necessarily springs from the absurd discovery. It happens as well that the feeling of the absurd springs from happiness. "I conclude that all is well," says Œdipus, and that remark is sacred. It echoes in the wild and limited universe of man. It teaches that all is not, has not been, exhausted. It drives out of this world a god who had come into it with dissatisfaction and a preference for futile sufferings. It makes of fate a human matter, which must be settled among men.

All Sisyphus' silent joy is contained therein. His fate belongs to him. His rock is his thing. Likewise, the absurd man, when he contemplates his torment, silences all the idols. In the universe suddenly restored to its silence, the myriad wondering little voices of the earth rise up. Unconscious, secret calls, invitations from all the faces, they are the necessary reverse and price of victory. There is no sun without shadow, and it is essential to know the night. The absurd man says yes and his effort will henceforth be unceasing. If there is a personal fate, there is no higher destiny, or at least there is but one which he concludes is inevitable and despicable. For the rest, he knows himself to be the master of his days. At that subtle moment when man glances backward over his life, Sisyphus returning toward his rock, in that slight pivoting he contemplates that series of unrelated actions which becomes his fate, created by him, combined under his memory's eye and soon sealed by his death. Thus, convinced of the wholly human origin of all that is human, a blind man eager to see who knows that the night has no end, he is still on the go. The rock is still rolling.

I leave Sisyphus at the foot of the mountain! One always finds one's burden again. But Sisyphus teaches the higher fidelity that negates the gods and raises rocks. He too concludes that all is well. This universe henceforth without a master seems to him neither sterile nor futile. Each atom of that stone, each mineral flake of that night-filled mountain, in itself forms a world. The struggle itself toward the heights is enough to fill a man's heart. One must imagine Sisyphus happy.

For Further Reflection

1. Is life absurd, as Camus insists? Does Camus give good reasons for this claim? What leads him to this pessimistic conclusion?

2. Is Camus being irreverent in asking the question as "Why not commit suicide"?

3. Why does Camus say that Sisyphus must be imagined to be happy?

4. Compare Camus with Epicurus. In what ways are their views similar? In what ways different?

Religion Gives Meaning to Life   VIII.61

LOIS HOPE WALKER

Lois Hope Walker is the pen name for an author who wishes to remain anonymous. In this essay Walker argues that religion, specifically theistic religion, gives special meaning to life, unavailable in secular world views. Furthermore, the autonomy that secularists prize (sometimes value it beyond its worth) is not significantly diminished by religious faith.

Study Questions

1. What are the two theses that the atheist holds, and how does Walker argue against them?

2. What are her definitions of "meaning" and "autonomy"?

3. What is the relationship of meaning to freedom or autonomy?

4. Which of Walker's eight theses on the value of religious faith do you agree with and which do you disagree with?

SEVERAL YEARS AGO during a class break, I was discussing the significance of religion in our society with a few students in the college lounge. I, at that time an agnostic, was conceding to a devout Christian that it would be nice if theism were true, for then the world would not be simply a matter of chance and necessity, a sad tale with a sadder ending. Instead, "the world would be personal, a gift from our heavenly Father, who provides a basis for meaning and purpose." A mature woman from another class, whom I knew to be an atheist, overheard my remarks, charged through a group of coffee drinkers and angrily snapped at me, "That is the most disgusting thing I've ever heard!" I inquired why she thought this, and she replied, "Religion keeps humans from growing up. We don't need a big Daddy in the sky. We need to grow up and become our own parents."

I recalled Nietzsche's dictum that now that "God is dead," now that we have killed the Holy One, we must ourselves become gods to seem worthy of the deed. The atheist woman was prizing autonomy over meaning and claiming that religion did just the opposite.

In other words, she held two theses:

(1) It is more important to be free or autonomous than to have a grand meaning or purpose to life.

(2) Religion provides a grand meaning or purpose to life, but it does not allow humans to be free or autonomous.

I've thought a lot about that woman's response over the years. I think that she is wrong on both counts. In this essay I will defend religion against her two theses and try to show that meaning and autonomy are both necessary or important ingredients for an ideal existence and that they are compatible within a religious framework.

Let me begin with the first thesis, that it is more important to be free than that there be meaning in life. First let us define our terms. By

"autonomy" I mean self-governing, the ability to make choices on the basis of good reasons rather than being coerced by threats or forces from without.

By "meaning" in life I mean that life has a purpose. There is some intrinsic rationale or plan to it. Now this purpose can be good, bad, or indifferent. An example of something with a bad purpose is the activity of poisoning a reservoir on which a community depends for its sustenance. An example of something with an indifferent purpose might be pacing back and forth to pass the time of day (it is arguable that this is bad or good depending on the options and context, and if you think that then either choose your own example or dismiss the category of indifferent purpose). An example of a good purpose is digging a well in order to provide water to a community in need of water.

Now it seems to be the case that, as a value, autonomy is superior to indifferent and bad purposes, since it has positive value while these other two categories do not. Autonomy may be more valuable to us than some good purposes, but it does not seem to be superior to *all* good purposes. While it may be more valuable to be free than to have this or that incidental purpose in life, freedom cannot really be understood apart from the notion of purposiveness. To be free is to be able to do some act *A*, when you want to, in order to reach some goal *G*. So the two ideas are related.

But the atheist woman meant more than this. She meant that if she had to choose whether to have free will or to live in a world that had a governing providential hand, she would choose the former. But this seems to make two mistakes. (1) It makes autonomy into an unjustified absolute and (2) it creates a false dilemma.

(1) Consider two situations: In situation A you are as free as you are now (say you have 100 units of autonomy—call these units "autonotoms") but are deeply miserable because you

are locked in a large and interesting room which is being slowly filled with poisonous gas. You can do what ever you want for five more minutes but then you will be dead. In situation B, however, you have only 95 autonotoms (that is, there are a few things that you are unable to do in this world—say commit adultery or kill your neighbor) but the room is being filled with sunshine and fresh air. Which world would you choose? I would choose situation B, for autonomy, it seems to me, is not the only value in the universe, nor is it always the overriding value. I think most of us would be willing to give up a few autonotoms for an enormous increase in happiness. And I think that a world with a good purpose would be one in which we would be willing to give up a few bits of freedom. If we were told that we could eliminate poverty, crime, and great suffering in the world by each sacrificing one autonotom, wouldn't we do this? If so, then autonomy is not an absolute which always overrides every other value. It is one important value among others.

I turn to the atheist's second thesis, that religion always holds purpose, as superior to autonomy. I think that this is a misunderstanding of what the best types of religion try to do. As Jesus said in John 8 : 32, "Ye shall know the truth and the truth shall set you free." Rather than seeing freedom and meaning as opposites, theism sees them as inextricably bound together. Since it claims to offer us the truth about the world, and since having true beliefs is important in reaching one's goals, it follows that our autonomy is actually heightened in having the truth about the purpose of life. If we know why we are here and what the options in our destiny really are, we will be able to choose more intelligently than the blind who lead the blind in ignorance.

Indeed theistic religion (I have in mind Judaism, Christianity, and Islam, but this could apply to many forms of Hinduism and African religions as well) claims to place before us options of the greatest importance, so that if it is true the world is far better (infinitely better?) than if it is not.

Let me elaborate on this point. If theism is true and there is a benevolent supreme being governing the universe, the following eight theses are true:

1. We have a satisfying explanation of the origin and sustenance of the universe. We are the product not of chance and necessity or an impersonal Big Bang, but of a Heavenly Being who cares about us. As William James says, if religion is true, "the universe is no longer a mere *It* to us, but a *Thou* . . . and any relation that may be possible from person to person might be possible here." We can take comfort in knowing that the visible world is part of a more spiritual universe from which it draws its meaning and that there is, in spite of evil, an essential harmonious relationship between our world and the transcendent reality.

2. Good will win out over evil—we're not fighting alone, but God is on our side in the battle. So, you and I are not fighting in vain—we'll win eventually. This thought of the ultimate victory of Goodness gives us confidence to go on in the fight against injustice and cruelty when others calculate that the odds against righteousness are too great to fight against.

3. God loves and cares for us—His love compels us (II Corinthians 5 : 7), so that we have a deeper motive for morally good actions, including high altruism. We live deeply moral lives because of deep gratitude to One who loves us and whom we love. Secularism lacks this sense of cosmic love, and it is, therefore, no accident that it fails to produce moral saints like Jesus, St. Francis, Gandhi, Martin Luther King, and Mother Teresa. You need special love to leave a world of comfort in order to go to a desolate island to minister to lepers, as Father Damian did.

4. We have an answer to the problem why be moral—it's clearly in your interest. Secular ethics has a severe problem with the question, Why be moral when it is not in your best interest, when you can profitably advance yourself by an egoistic act? But such a dilemma does not arise in religious ethics, for Evil really is bad for you and the Good good for you.

5. Cosmic Justice reigns in the universe. The scales are perfectly balanced so that everyone will get what he or she deserves, according to their moral merit. There is no moral luck (unless you interpret the grace which will finally prevail as a type of "luck"), but each will be judged according to how one has used one's talents (Matthew, chapter 25).

6. All persons are of equal worth. Since we have all been created in the image of God and are His children, we are all brothers and sisters. We are family and ought to treat each other benevolently as we would family members of equal worth. Indeed, modern secular moral and political systems often assume this equal worth of the individual without justifying it. But without the Parenthood of God it makes no sense to say that all persons are innately of equal value. From a perspective of intelligence and utility, Aristotle and Nietzsche are right: there are enormous inequalities, and why shouldn't the superior persons use the baser types to their advantage? In this regard, secularism, in rejecting inegalitarianism, seems to be living off of the interest of a religious capital which it has relinquished.

7. Grace and forgiveness—a happy ending for all. All's well that ends well (the divine comedy). The moral guilt which we experience, even for the most heinous acts, can be removed, and we can be redeemed and given a new start. This is true moral liberation.

8. There is life after death. Death is not the end of the matter, but we shall live on, recognizing each other in a better world. We have eternity in our souls and are destined for a higher existence. (Of course, hell is a problem here—which vitiates the whole idea somewhat, but many variations of theism [e.g., varieties of theistic Hinduism and the Christian theologians Origen (in the second century), F. Maurice, and Karl Barth] hold to universal salvation in the end. Hell is only a temporary school in moral education—I think that this is a plausible view.) So if Hebraic-Christian theism is true,

the world is a friendly home in which we are all related as siblings in one family, destined to live forever in cosmic bliss in a reality in which good defeats evil.

If theism is false and secularism is true, then there is no obvious basis for human equality, no reason to treat all people with equal respect, no simple and clear answer to the question, Why be moral even when it is not in my best interest? no sense of harmony and purpose in the universe, but "Whirl has replaced Zeus and is king" (Sophocles).

Add to this the fact that theism doesn't deprive us of any autonomy that we have in non-theistic systems. If we are equally free to choose the good or the evil whether or not God exists (assuming that the notions of good and evil make sense in a non-theistic universe)—then it seems clear that the world of the theist is far better and more satisfying to us than one in which God does not exist.

Of course, the problem is that we probably do not know if theism, let alone our particular religious version of it, is true. Here I must use a Pascalean argument to press my third point that we may have an obligation or, at least, it may be a good thing, to live as if theism is true. That is, unless you think that theism is so improbable that we should not even consider it as a candidate for truth, we should live in such a way as to allow the virtues of theism to inspire our lives and our culture. The theistic world view is so far superior to the secular that—even though we might be agnostics or weak atheists—it is in our interest to live as though it were true, to consider each person as a child of God, of high value, to work as though God is working with us in the battle of Good over evil, and to build a society based on these ideas. It is good then to gamble on God. Religion gives us a purpose to life and a basis for morality that is too valuable to dismiss lightly. It is a heritage that we may use to build a better civilization and one which we neglect at our own peril.

For Further Reflection

1. Does Walker exaggerate the importance of religion for a meaningful life? How would a secularist respond?

2. Karl Marx said that religion was the opium of the people. Religion deludes people into thinking that all will be well with the world, leading to passive acceptance of evil and injustice. Is there some truth in Marx's dictum? How would Walker respond to this?

The Absurd   VIII.62

THOMAS NAGEL

A biographical sketch of Thomas Nagel precedes Reading IV.31. In this essay Nagel reflects on the sense of absurdity that most of us feel from time to time. He considers the experience from several perspectives and eventually concludes that it is a function of our advanced self-consciousness which marks us off from less reflective beings.

Study Questions

1. What are some reasons for feeling nothing matters?
2. What are some ordinary absurd situations in life and how do they relate to our sense of absurdity?
3. What two perspectives, by colliding, result in the sense that life is absurd?
4. What is the value of stepping back and viewing our lives *sub specie aeternitatis*? [from the view of eternity]
5. How does our perception of absurdity resemble epistemological skepticism?
6. What would we have to do to avoid the sense of absurdity?
7. What is the final escape from absurdity?

MOST PEOPLE FEEL ON OCCASION that life is absurd, and some feel it vividly and continually. Yet the reasons usually offered in defense of this conviction are patently inadequate: they *could* not really explain why life is absurd. Why then do they provide a natural expression for the sense that it is?

I

Consider some examples. It is often remarked that nothing we do now will matter in a million years. But if that is true, then by the same token, nothing that will be the case in a million years matters now. In particular, it does not matter now that in a million years nothing we do now will matter. Moreover, even if what we did now *were* going to matter in a million years, how could that keep our present concerns from being absurd? If their mattering now is not enough to accomplish that, how would it help if they mattered a million years from now?

Whether what we do now will matter in a million years could make the crucial difference only if its mattering in a million years depended on its mattering, period. But then to deny that whatever happens now will matter in a million years is to beg the question against its mattering, period; for in that sense one cannot know that it will not matter in a million years whether (for example) someone now is happy or miserable, without knowing that it does not matter, period.

What we say to convey the absurdity of our lives often has to do with space or time: we are tiny specks in the infinite vastness of the universe; our lives are mere instants even on a geological time scale, let alone a cosmic one; we will all be dead any minute. But of course none of these evident facts can be what *makes* life absurd, if it is absurd. For suppose we lived forever; would not a life that is absurd if it lasts seventy years be infinitely absurd if it lasted through eternity? And if our lives are absurd given our present size, why would they be any less absurd if we filled the universe (either because we were larger or because the universe was smaller)? Reflection on our minuteness and brevity appears to be intimately connected with the sense that life is meaningless; but it is not clear what the connection is.

Another inadequate argument is that because we are going to die, all chains of justification must leave off in mid-air: one studies and works to earn money to pay for clothing, housing, entertainment, food, to sustain oneself from year to year, perhaps to support a family and pursue a career—but to what final end? All of it is an elaborate journey leading nowhere. (One will also have some effect on other people's lives, but that simply reproduces the problem, for they will die too.)

There are several replies to this argument. First, life does not consist of a sequence of activities each of which has as its purpose some later member of the sequence. Chains of justification come repeatedly to an end within life, and whether the process as a whole can be justified has no bearing on the finality of these end-points. No further justification is needed to make it reasonable to take aspirin for a headache, attend an exhibition of the work of a painter one admires, or stop a child from putting his hand on a hot stove. No larger context or further purpose is needed to prevent these acts from being pointless.

Even if someone wished to supply a further justification for pursuing all the things in life that are commonly regarded as self-justifying, that justification would have to end somewhere too. If *nothing* can justify unless it is justified in terms of something outside itself, which is also justified, then an infinite regress results, and no chain of justification can be complete. Moreover, if a finite chain of reasons cannot justify anything, what could be accomplished by an infinite chain, each link of which must be justified by something outside itself?

Since justifications must come to an end somewhere, nothing is gained by denying that they end where they appear to, within life—or by trying to subsume the multiple, often trivial ordinary justifications of action under a single, controlling life scheme. We can be satisfied more easily than that. In fact, through its misrepresentation of the process of justification, the argument makes a vacuous demand. It insists that the reasons available within life are incomplete, but suggests thereby that all reasons that come to an end are incomplete. This makes it impossible to supply any reasons at all.

The standard arguments for absurdity appear therefore to fail as arguments. Yet I believe they attempt to express something that is difficult to state, but fundamentally correct.

II

In ordinary life a situation is absurd when it includes a conspicuous discrepancy between pretension or aspiration and reality: someone gives a complicated speech in support of a motion that has already been passed; a notorious criminal is made president of a major philanthropic foundation; you declare your love over the telephone to a recorded announcement; as you are being knighted, your pants fall down.

When a person finds himself in an absurd situation, he will usually attempt to change it, by modifying his aspirations, or by trying to bring reality into better accord with them, or by removing himself from the situation entirely. We are not always willing or able to extricate ourselves from a position whose absurdity has become clear to us. Nevertheless, it is usually possible to imagine some change that would remove the absurdity—whether or not we can or will implement it. The sense that life as a whole is absurd arises when we perceive, perhaps dimly, an inflated pretension or aspiration which is inseparable from the continuation of human life and which makes its absurdity inescapable, short of escape from life itself.

Many people's lives are absurd, temporarily or permanently, for conventional reasons having to do with their particular ambitions, circumstances, and personal relations. If there is a philosophical sense of absurdity, however, it must arise from the perception of something universal—some respect in which pretension and reality inevitably clash for us all. This condition is supplied, I shall argue, by the collison between the seriousness with which we take our lives and the perpetual possibility of regarding everything about which we are serious as arbitrary, or open to doubt.

We cannot live human lives without energy and attention, nor without making choices which show that we take some things more seriously than others. Yet we have always available a point of view outside the particular form of our lives, from which the seriousness appears gratuitous. These two inescapable viewpoints collide in us, and that is what makes life absurd. It is absurd because we ignore the doubts that we know cannot be settled, continuing to live with nearly undiminished seriousness in spite of them.

This analysis requires defense in two respects: first as regards the unavoidability of seriousness; second as regards the inescapability of doubt.

We take ourselves seriously whether we lead serious lives or not and whether we are concerned primarily with fame, pleasure, virtues, luxury, triumph, beauty, justice, knowledge, salvation, or mere survival. If we take other people seriously and devote ourselves to them, that only multiplies the problem. Human life is full of effort, plans, calculation, success and failure: we *pursue* our lives, with varying degrees of sloth and energy.

It would be different if we could not step back and reflect on the process, but were merely led from impulse to impulse without self-consciousness. But human beings do not act solely on impulse. They are prudent, they reflect, they weigh consequences, they ask whether what they are doing is worthwhile. Not only are their lives full of particular choices that hang together in larger activities with temporal structure: they also decide in the broadest terms what to pursue and what to avoid, what the priorities among their various aims should be, and what kind of people they want to be or become. Some men are faced with such choices by the large decisions they make from time to time; some merely by reflection on the course their lives are taking as the product of countless small decisions. They decide whom to marry, what profession to follow, whether to join the Country Club, or the Resistance; or they may just wonder why they go on being salesmen or academics or taxi drivers, and then stop thinking about it after a certain period of inconclusive reflection.

Although they may be motivated from act to act by those immediate needs with which life presents them, they allow the process to continue by adhering to the general system of habits and the form of life in which such motives have their place—or perhaps only by clinging to life itself. They spend enormous quantities of energy, risk, and calculation on the details. Think of how an ordinary individual sweats over his appearance, his health, his sex life, his emotional honesty, his social utility, his self-knowledge, the quality of his ties with family, colleagues, and friends, how well he does his job, whether he understands the world and what is going on in it. Leading a human life is a full-time occupation, to which everyone devotes decades of intense concern.

This fact is so obvious that it is hard to find it extraordinary and important. Each of us lives his own life—lives with himself twenty-four hours a day. What else is he supposed to do—live someone else's life? Yet humans have the special capacity to step back and survey themselves, and the lives to which they are committed, with that detached amazement which comes from watching an ant struggle up a heap of sand. Without developing the illusion that they are able to escape from their highly specific and idiosyncratic position, they can view it *sub specie aeternitatis*—and the view is at once sobering and comical.

The crucial backward step is not taken by asking for still another justification in the chain, and failing to get it. The objections to that line of attack have already been stated; justifications come to an end. But this is precisely what provides universal doubt with its object. We step back to find that the whole system of justification and criticism, which controls our choices and supports our claims to rationality, rests on responses and habits that we never question, that we should not know how to defend without circularity, and to which we shall continue to adhere even after they are called into question.

The things we do or want without reasons, and without requiring reasons—the things that define what is a reason for us and what is not—are the starting points of our skepticism.

We see ourselves from outside, and all the contingency and specificity of our aims and pursuits become clear. Yet when we take this view and recognize what we do as arbitrary, it does not disengage us from life, and there lies our absurdity: not in the fact that such an external view can be taken of us, but in the fact that we ourselves can take it, without ceasing to be the persons whose ultimate concerns are so coolly regarded.

III

One may try to escape the position by seeking broader ultimate concerns, from which it is impossible to step back—the idea being that absurdity results because what we take seriously is something small and insignificant and individual. Those seeking to supply their lives with meaning usually envision a role or function in something larger than themselves. They therefore seek fulfillment in service to society, the state, the revolution, the progress of history, the advance of science, or religion and the glory of God.

But a role in some larger enterprise cannot confer significance unless that enterprise is itself significant. And its significance must come back to what we can understand, or it will not even appear to give us what we are seeking. If we learned that we were being raised to provide food for other creatures fond of human flesh, who planned to turn us into cutlets before we got too stringy—even if we learned that the human race had been developed by animal breeders precisely for this purpose—that would still not give our lives meaning, for two reasons. First, we would still be in the dark as to the significance of the lives of those other beings; second, although we might acknowledge that this culinary role would make our lives meaningful to them, it is not clear how it would make them meaningful to us.

Admittedly, the usual form of service to a higher being is different from this. One is supposed to behold and partake of the glory of God, for example, in a way in which chickens do not share in the glory of coq au vin. The same is true of service to a state, a movement, or a revolution. People can come to feel, when they are part of something bigger, that it is part of them too. They worry less about what is peculiar to themselves, but identify enough with the larger enterprise to find their role in it fulfilling.

However, any such larger purpose can be put in doubt in the same way that the aims of an individual life can be, and for the same reasons. It is as legitimate to find ultimate justification there as to find it earlier, among the details of individual life. But this does not alter the fact that justifications come to an end when we are content to have them end—when we do not find it necessary to look any further. If we can step back from the purposes of individual life and doubt their point, we can step back also from the progress of human history, or of science, or the success of a society, or the kingdom, power, and glory of God, and put all these things into question in the same way. What seems to us to confer meaning, justification, significance, does so in virtue of the fact that we need no more reasons after a certain point.

What makes doubt inescapable with regard to the limited aims of individual life also makes it inescapable with regard to any larger purpose that encourages the sense that life is meaningful. Once the fundamental doubt has begun, it cannot be laid to rest.

Camus maintains in *The Myth of Sisyphus* that the absurd arises because the world fails to meet our demands for meaning. This suggests that the world might satisfy those demands if it were different. But now we can see that this is not the case. There does not appear to be any conceivable world (containing us) about which unsettlable doubts could not arise. Consequently the absurdity of our situation derives not from a collison between our expectations and the world, but from a collision within ourselves.

IV

It may be objected that the standpoint from which these doubts are supposed to be felt does not exist—that if we take the recommended backward step we will land on thin air, without any basis for judgment about the natural responses we are supposed to be surveying. If we retain our usual standards of what is important, then questions about the significance of what we are doing with our lives will be answerable in the usual way. But if we do not, then those questions can mean nothing to us, since there is no longer any content to the idea of what matters, and hence no content to the idea that nothing does.

But this objection misconceives the nature of the backward step. It is not supposed to give us an understanding of what is *really* important, so that we see by contrast that our lives are insignificant. We never, in the course of these reflections, abandon the ordinary standards that guide our lives. We merely observe them in operation, and recognize that if they are called into question we can justify them only by reference to themselves, uselessly. We adhere to them because of the way we are put together; what seems to us important or serious or valuable would not seem so if we were differently constituted.

In ordinary life, to be sure, we do not judge a situation absurd unless we have in mind some standards of seriousness, significance, or harmony with which the absurd can be contrasted. This contrast is not implied by the philosophical judgment of absurdity, and that might be thought to make the concept unsuitable for the expression of such judgments. This is not so, however, for the philosophical judgment depends on another contrast which makes it a natural extension from more ordinary cases. It departs from them only in contrasting the pretensions of life with a larger context in which *no* standards can be discovered, rather than with a context from which alternative, overriding standards may be applied.

V

In this respect, as in others, philosophical perception of the absurd resembles epistemological skepticism. In both cases the final, philosophical doubt is not contrasted with any unchallenged certainties, though it is arrived at by extrapolation from examples of doubt within the system of evidence or justification, where a contrast with other certainties *is* implied. In both cases our limitedness joins with a capacity to transcend those limitations in thought (thus seeing them as limitations, and as inescapable).

Skepticism begins when we include ourselves in the world about which we claim knowledge. We notice that certain types of evidence convince us, that we are content to allow justifications of belief to come to an end at certain points, that we feel we know many things even without knowing or having grounds for believing the denial of others which, if true, would make what we claim to know false.

For example, I know that I am looking at a piece of paper, although I have no adequate grounds for claiming I know that I am not dreaming; and if I am dreaming then I am not looking at a piece of paper. Here an ordinary conception of how appearance may diverge from reality is employed to show that we take our world largely for granted; the certainty that we are not dreaming cannot be justified except circularly, in terms of those very appearances which are being put in doubt. It is somewhat farfetched to suggest I may be dreaming; but the possibility is only illustrative. It reveals that our claims to knowledge depend on our not feeling it necessary to exclude certain incompatible alternatives, and the dreaming possibility or the total-hallucination possibility are just representatives for limitless possibilities most of which we cannot even conceive.[1]

Once we have taken the backward step to an abstract view of our whole system of beliefs, evidence, and justification, and seen that it works only, despite its pretensions, by taking the world largely for granted, we are *not* in a position to contrast all these appearances with an alternative reality. We cannot shed our ordinary responses, and if we could it would leave us with no means of conceiving a reality of any kind.

It is the same in the practical domain. We do not step outside our lives to a new vantage point from which we see what is really, objectively significant. We continue to take life largely for granted while seeing that all our decisions and certainties are possible only because there is a great deal we do not bother to rule out.

Both epistemological skepticism and a sense of the absurd can be reached via initial doubts posed within systems of evidence and justification that we accept, and can be stated without violence to our ordinary concepts. We can ask not only why we should believe there is a floor under us, but also why we should believe the evidence of our senses at all—and at some point the framable questions will have outlasted the answers. Similarly, we can ask not only why we should take aspirin, but why we should take trouble over our own comfort at all. The fact that we shall take the aspirin without waiting for an answer to this last question does not show that it is an unreal question. We shall also continue to believe there is a floor under us without waiting for an answer to the other question. In both cases it is this unsupported natural confidence that generates skeptical doubts; so it cannot be used to settle them.

Philosophical skepticism does not cause us to abandon our ordinary beliefs, but it lends them a peculiar flavor. After acknowledging that their truth is incompatible with possibilities that we have no grounds for believing do not obtain—apart from grounds in those very beliefs which we have called into question—we return to our familiar convictions with a certain irony and resignation. Unable to abandon the natural responses on which they depend, we take them back, like a spouse who has run off with someone else and then decided to return; but we regard them differently (not that the new attitude is necessarily inferior to the old, in either case).

The same situation obtains after we have put in question the seriousness with which we take our lives and human life in general and have looked at ourselves without presuppositions. We then return to our lives, as we must, but our seriousness is laced with irony. Not that irony enables us to escape the absurd. It is useless to mutter: "Life is meaningless; life is meaningless . . ." as an accompaniment to everything we do. In continuing to live and work and strive, we take ourselves seriously in action no matter what we say.

What sustains us, in belief as in action, is not reason for justification, but something more basic than these—for we go on in the same way even after we are convinced that the reasons have given out.[2] If we tried to rely entirely on reason, and pressed it hard, our lives and beliefs would collapse—a form of madness that may actually occur if the inertial force of taking the world and life for granted is somehow lost. If we lose our grip on that, reason will not give it back to us.

VI

In viewing ourselves from a perspective broader than we can occupy in the flesh, we become spectators of our own lives. We cannot do very much as pure spectators of our own lives, so we continue to lead them, and devote ourselves to what we are able at the same time to view as no more than a curiosity, like the ritual of an alien religion.

This explains why the sense of absurdity finds its natural expression in those bad arguments with which the discussion began. References to our small size and short lifespan and to the fact that all of mankind will eventually vanish without a trace are metaphors for the backward step which permits us to regard ourselves from without and to find the particular form of our lives curious and slightly surprising. By feigning a nebula's-eye view, we illustrate the capacity to see ourselves without presuppositions, as arbitrary, idiosyncratic, highly specific occupants of the world, one of countless possible forms of life.

Before turning to the question whether the absurdity of our lives is something to be regretted and if possible escaped, let me consider what would have to be given up in order to avoid it.

Why is the life of a mouse not absurd? The orbit of the moon is not absurd either, but that involves no strivings or aims at all. A mouse, however, has to work to stay alive. Yet he is not absurd, because he lacks the capacities for self-consciousness and self-transcendence that would enable him to see that he is only a mouse. If that *did* happen, his life would become absurd, since self-awareness would not make him cease to be a mouse and would not enable him to rise above his mousely strivings. Bringing his new-found self-consciousness with him, he would have to return to his meager yet frantic life, full of doubts that he was unable to answer, but also full of purposes that he was unable to abandon.

Given that the transcendental step is natural to us humans, can we avoid absurdity by refusing to take that step and remaining entirely within our sublunar lives? Well, we cannot refuse consciously, for to do that we would have to be aware of the viewpoint we were refusing to adopt. The only way to avoid the relevant self-consciousness would be either never to attain it or to forget it—neither of which can be achieved by the will.

On the other hand, it is possible to expend effort on an attempt to destroy the other component of the absurd—abandoning one's earthly, individual, human life in order to identify as completely as possible with that universal viewpoint from which human life seems arbitrary and trivial. (This appears to be the ideal of certain Oriental religions.) If one succeeds, then one will not have to drag the superior awareness through a strenuous mundane life, and absurdity will be diminished.

However, insofar as this self-etiolation is the result of effort, will-power, aceticism, and so forth, it requires that one take oneself seriously as an individual—that one be willing to take considerable trouble to avoid being creaturely and absurd. Thus one may undermine the aim of unworldliness by pursuing it too vigorously. Still, if someone simply allowed his individual, animal nature to drift and respond to impulse, without making the pursuit of its needs a central conscious aim, then he might, at considerable dissociative cost, achieve a life that was less absurd than most. It would not be a meaningful life either, of course; but it would not involve the engagement of a transcendent awareness in the assiduous pursuit of mundane goals. And that is the main condition of absurdity—the dragooning of an unconvinced transcendent consciousness into the service of an immanent, limited enterprise like a human life.

The final escape is suicide; but before adopting any hasty solutions, it would be wise to consider carefully whether the absurdity of our existence truly presents us with *a problem*, to which some solution must be found—a way of dealing with prima facie disaster. That is certainly the attitude with which Camus approaches the issue, and it gains support from the fact that we are all eager to escape from absurd situations on a smaller scale.

Camus—not on uniformly good grounds—rejects suicide and the other solutions he regards as escapist. What he recommends is defiance or scorn. We can salvage our dignity, he appears to believe, by shaking a fist at the world which is deaf to our pleas, and continuing to live in spite of it. This will not make our lives un-absurd, but it will lend them a certain nobility.[3]

This seems to me romantic and slightly self-pitying. Our absurdity warrants neither that much distress nor that much defiance. At the risk of falling into romanticism by a different route, I would argue that absurdity is one of the most human things about us: a manifestation of our most advanced and interesting characteristics. Like skepticism in epistemology, it is possible only because we possess a certain kind of insight—the capacity to transcend ourselves in thought.

If a sense of the absurd is a way of perceiving our true situation (even though the situation is not absurd until the perception arises), then what reason can we have to resent or escape it? Like the capacity for epistemological skepticism, it results from the ability to understand our human limitations. It need not be a matter for agony unless we make it so. Nor need it evoke a defiant contempt of fate that allows us to feel brave or proud. Such dramatics, even if carried on in private, betray a failure to appreciate the cosmic unimportance of the situation. If *sub specie aeternitatis* there is no reason to believe that anything matters, then that does not matter either, and we can approach our absurd lives with irony instead of heroism or despair.

NOTES

1. I am aware that skepticism about the external world is widely thought to have been refuted, but I have remained convinced of its irrefutability since being exposed at Berkeley to Thompson Clarke's largely unpublished ideas on the subject.

2. As Hume says in a famous passage of the *Treatise:* 'Most fortunately it happens, that since reason is incapable of dispelling these clouds, nature herself suffices to that purpose, and cures me of this philosophical melancholy and delirium, either by relaxing this bent of mind, or by some avocation, and lively impression of my senses, which obliterate all these chimeras. I dine, I play a game of backgammon, I converse, and am merry with my friends; and when after three or four hours' amusement, I would return to these speculations, they appear so cold, and strain'd, and ridiculous, that I cannot find in my heart to enter into them any farther' (bk. 1, pt. iv, sect. 7; Selby-Bigge edition, p. 269).

3. "Sisyphus, proletarian of the gods, powerless and rebellious, knows the whole extent of his wretched condition: it is what he thinks of during his descent. The lucidity that was to constitute his torture at the same time crowns his victory. There is no fate that cannot be surmounted by scorn" (*The Myth of Sisyphus*, trans. Justin O'Brien [New York: Vintage, 1959], p. 90; first published, Paris: Gallimard, 1942).

For Further Reflection

1. Evaluate Nagel's claim that the sense of absurdity derives not from a collision between our expectations and the world, but from a collision within ourselves. Is he correct? Explain.
2. How, according to Nagel, can we escape the absurd? How can the universal viewpoint free us from the absurd?
3. How should we respond to our absurdity? Why is it something noble?
4. Do you agree that life is absurd? Explain.

Reflections on Suffering   VIII.63

BERTRAND RUSSELL

A philosopher whom we have studied at length in this work is Bertrand Russell, someone who thought deeply about the question of the meaning of life. Russell says in his *Autobiography* that his youth was very unhappy and only the love of mathematics kept him from committing suicide. Gradually, he learned to find happiness. In these two short selections from his *Autobiography*, Russell first tells of an experience that greatly affected his life and then goes on to summarize what gives him meaning in life.

(A biographical sketch of Russell precedes Reading I.3.)

Study Questions

1. Describe the situation in the first part of this essay.
2. What sort of feelings and thoughts did Russell experience in the face of the suffering he witnessed?
3. What are the three passions that have dominated Russell's life?

SPRING 1901

WHEN WE CAME HOME, we found Mrs. W undergoing an unusually severe bout of pain. She seemed cut off from everyone and everything by walls of agony, and the sense of the solitude of each human soul suddenly overwhelmed me. Ever since my marriage, my emotional life had been calm and superficial. I had forgotten all the deeper issues, and had been content with flippant cleverness. Suddenly the ground seemed to give way beneath me, and I found myself in quite another region. Within five minutes I went thru some such reflections

From The Autobiography of Bertrand Russell, *v. I, p. 146, 1951. Reprinted by permission of* Unwin Hyman Ltd.

as the following: the loneliness of the human soul is unendurable; nothing can penetrate it except the highest intensity of the sort of love that religious teachers have preached; whatever does not spring from this motive is harmful, or at best useless; it follows that war is wrong, that a public school education is abominable, that the use of force is to be deprecated, and that in human relations one should penetrate to the core of loneliness in each person and speak to that. [The writer then describes his sudden awareness of Mrs. W's three year old son with whom he then and there found an affinity.] . . . At the end of those five minutes, I had become a completely different person. For a time, a sort of mystic illumination possessed me. I felt that I knew the inmost thoughts of everybody that I met in the street, and though this was, no doubt, a delusion, I did in actual fact find myself in *far closer* touch than previously with all my friends, and many of my acquaintances. Having been an Imperialist, I became during those five minutes . . . a Pacificist. Having for years cared only for exactness and analysis, I found myself filled with semi-mystical feelings about beauty, and with an intense interest in children and with a desire almost as profound as that of the Buddha to find some philosophy which should make human life endurable. A strange excitement possessed me, containing intense pain but also some element of triumph through the fact that I could dominate pain, and make it, as I thought, a gateway to wisdom. The mystic insight which I then imagined myself to possess has largely faded, and the habit of analysis has reasserted itself. But something of what I thought I saw in that moment has remained always with me, *causing* my attitude during the first war, my interest in my children, my indifference to minor misfortunes and a certain emotional tone in all my human relations.

That man is the product of causes which had no prevision of the end they were achieving; that his origin, his growth, his hopes and fears, his loves and his beliefs are but the outcome of accidental colocations of atoms; that no fire, no heroism, no intensity of thought and feeling, can preserve an individual life beyond the grave; that all the labors of the ages, all the devotion, all the inspiration, all the noonday brightness of human genius, are destined to extinction in the vast death of the solar system, and that the whole temple of man's achievement must inevitably be buried beneath the debris of a universe in ruins— all these things, if not quite beyond dispute, are yet so nearly certain that no philosophy which rejects them can hope to stand. Only within the scaffolding of these truths, only on the firm foundation of unyielding despair, can the soul's habitation henceforth be safely built.

EPILOGUE

Love, Knowledge, and Pity

Three passions, simple but overwhelmingly strong, have governed my life: the longing for love, the search for knowledge, and unbearable pity for the suffering of mankind. These passions, like great winds, have blown me hither and thither, in a wayward course, over a deep ocean of anguish, reaching to the very verge of despair.

I have sought love, first, because it brings ecstasy—ecstasy so great that I would often have sacrificed all the rest of life for a few hours of this joy. I have sought it, next, because it relieves loneliness—that terrible loneliness in which one shivering consciousness looks over the rim of the world into the cold unfathomable lifeless abyss. I have sought it, finally, because in the union of love I have seen, in a mystic miniature, the prefiguring vision of the heaven that saints and poets have imagined. This is what I sought, and though it might seem too good for human life, this is what—at last—I have found.

With equal passion I have sought knowledge. I have wished to understand the hearts of men. I have wished to know why the stars shine. And I have tried to apprehend the Pythagorean power by which number holds sway above the flux. A little of this, but not much, I have achieved.

Love and knowledge, so far as they were possible, led upward toward the heavens. But always pity brought me back to earth. Echoes of cries of pain reverberate in my heart. Children in famine, victims tortured by oppressors, helpless old people a hated burden to their sons, and the whole world of loneliness, poverty, and pain make a mockery of what human life should be. I long to alleviate the evil, but I cannot, and I too suffer.

This has been my life. I have found it worth living, and would gladly live it again if the chance were offered me.

For Further Reflection

1. Compare the first selection with the second. Do you see any differences?

2. How does your set of values compare with Russell's? Do you think that Russell's philosophy of life is adequate for happiness and the good life? Compare it with the other readings in this part.

Suggestions for Further Reading

Barrett, William. *Irrational Man.* New York: Doubleday, 1958.

Bretall, Robert, ed. *A Kierkegaard Anthology.* Princeton, NJ: Princeton University Press, 1946.

Camus, Albert. *The Myth of Sisyphus and Other Essays,* trans. J. O. O'Brien. New York: Random House, 1955.

Camus, Albert. *The Plague.* New York: Random House, 1948.

Frankl, Victor. *Man's Search for Meaning.* New York: Beacon Press, 1963.

Kaufmann, Walter. *Existentialism from Dostoevsky to Sartre.* New American Library, 1975.

Kaufmann, Walter, ed. and trans. *A Portable Nietzsche.* New York: Viking, 1954.

Kierkegaard, Søren. *Fear and Trembling,* trans. Walter Lowrie. Princeton, NJ: Princeton University Press, 1954.

Klemke, E. D. *The Meaning of Life.* Oxford: Oxford University Press, 1981.

Nietzsche, Friedrich. *The Will to Power.* New York: Random House, 1967.

Russell, Bertrand. *The Conquest of Happiness.* New American Library, 1930.

Sanders, Steven and David Cheney, eds. *The Meaning of Life.* Englewood Cliffs, NJ: Prentice Hall, 1980.

Sartre, Jean-Paul. *Existentialism and Human Emotions.* Philosophical Library, 1948.

Schopenhauer, Arthur. *The Will to Live: Selected Writings of Arthur Schopenhauer,* ed. Richard Taylor. Ungar, 1967.

Tolstoy, Leo. *My Confessions,* trans. Leo Wiener. Dent, 1905.

Part IX

Philosophy in Action

What is the use of studying philosophy if all that it does for you is enable you to talk with some plausibility about some abstruse questions of logic, and so on and if it does not improve your thinking about the important questions of everyday life?

LUDWIG WITTGENSTEIN

Several moral issues are tearing our society apart; among the most prominent are abortion, euthanasia, racism, reverse discrimination, the death penalty, and the status of animals. Can philosophical analysis throw light on these issues? Can philosophy have practical implications?

Although this introduction to philosophy concentrates on the classical problems of philosophy, the topics covered in Parts I through VIII, this short section will provide examples of how philosophical reasoning can illuminate contemporary issues. I have chosen four that have special interest to students: abortion, capital punishment, affirmative action, and animal rights.

IX.A   Is Abortion Morally Permissible?

Abortion during the first two or three months of gestation is morally equivalent to removal of a piece of tissue from the woman's body. (philosopher Thomas Szasz)

Every unborn child must be regarded as a human person with all the rights of a human person, from the moment of conception. (Ethical and Religious Directives for Catholic Hospitals)

One of the major social issues before us today, one that divides our nation as no other issue does, is that of the moral and legal status of the human fetus and the corresponding question of the moral permissibility of abortion. On the one hand, such organizations as the Roman Catholic Church and the Right to Life movement, appalled by the more than 1.5 million abortions that take place in this country each year, have exerted significant political pressure toward introducing a constitutional amendment that would grant full legal rights to fetuses. These movements have in some cases made the abortion issue the single issue in political campaigns. On the other hand, pro-choice groups such as the National Organization of Women (NOW), the National Abortion Rights Action League (NARAL), and feminist organizations have exerted enormous pressure on politicians to support pro-abortion legislation. The Republican and Democratic political platforms of the last two elections took diametrically opposite sides on this issue.

Why is abortion a moral issue? Take a fertilized egg, a zygote, a tiny diploid cell. By itself, it is hard to see what is so important about such an inconspicuous piece of matter. It is virtually indistinguishable from other clusters of cells, or the zygotes of other animals. On the other hand, take an adult human being, a class of beings that we all intuitively feel to be worthy of high respect, having rights, including the right to life. To kill an innocent human being is an act of murder and universally condemned. However, no obvious line of division separates that single-cell zygote from the adult it will become. Hence, the problem of abortion.

It is with this sort of analysis that John Noonan begins his argument against abortion. He argues that since it is always wrong to kill innocent human beings and since fetuses are innocent human beings, it is wrong to kill fetuses. He makes an exception when the mother's life is in danger, since something of comparable worth is at stake. Noonan argues that conception is the only nonarbitrary cut-off place between nonpersonhood and personhood.

Mary Anne Warren argues against Noonan that fetuses are not persons since persons must have such characteristics as self-consciousness and rationality and fetuses do not have these. Finally, Jane English argues for a moderate position. Most early abortions are permissible, most late ones immoral.

Abortion Is Not Morally Permissible   IX.64

JOHN T. NOONAN, JR.

John T. Noonan, Jr., is professor of law at the University of California, Berkeley. He is a Roman Catholic philosopher who has written several works on moral issues, including *Contraception: A History of Its Treatment by the Catholic Theologians and Canonists* (1965) and *A Private Choice: Abortion in America in the Seventies* (1979). In this selection Noonan defends the conservative view that an entity becomes a person at conception and that abortion, except to save the mother's life, is morally wrong. He uses an argument from probabilities to show that his criterion of humanity is objectively based.

Study Questions

1. What is the most fundamental question in the history of thought on abortion?
2. How did theologians answer that question?
3. What are four rival answers to the question, When does a fetus become a human being? Why does Noonan reject each of them?
4. What does Noonan say about the relevance of probabilities in the assessment of whether a fetus will become a fully formed human being?

THE MOST FUNDAMENTAL QUESTION involved in the long history of thought on abortion is: How do you determine the humanity of a being? To phrase the question that way is to put in comprehensive humanistic terms what the theologians either dealt with as an explicitly theological question under the heading of "ensoulment" or dealt with implicitly in their treatment of abortion. The Christian position as it originated did not depend on a narrow theological or philosophical concept. It had no relation to theories of infant baptism. It appealed to no special theory of instantaneous ensoulment. It took the world's view on ensoulment as that view changed from Aristotle to Zacchia. There was, indeed, theological influence affecting the theory of ensoulment finally adopted, and, of course, ensoulment itself was a theological concept, so that the position was always explained in theological terms. But the theological notion of ensoulment could easily be translated into humanistic language by substituting "human" for "rational soul"; the problem of knowing when a man is a man is common to theology and humanism.

If one steps outside the specific categories used by the theologians, the answer they gave can be analyzed as a refusal to discriminate among human beings on the basis of their varying potentialities. Once conceived, the being was recognized as man because he had man's potential. The criterion for humanity, thus, was simple and all-embracing: if you are conceived by human parents, you are human.

The strength of this position may be tested by a review of some of the other distinctions offered in the contemporary controversy over legalizing abortion. Perhaps the most popular distinction is in terms of viability. Before an age of so many months, the fetus is not viable, that is, it cannot be removed from the mother's womb and live apart from her. To that extent, the life of the fetus is absolutely dependent on the life of the mother. This dependence is made the basis of denying recognition to its humanity.

There are difficulties with this distinction. One is that the perfection of artificial incubation may make the fetus viable at any time: it may be removed and artificially sustained. Experiments with animals already show that such a procedure is possible. This hypothetical extreme case relates to an actual difficulty: there is considerable elasticity to the idea of viability. Mere length of life is not an exact measure. The viability of the fetus depends on the extent of its anatomical and functional development. The weight and length of the fetus are better guides to the state of its development than age, but weight and length vary. Moreover, different racial groups have different ages at which their fetuses are viable. Some evidence, for example, suggests that Negro fetuses mature more quickly than white fetuses. If viability is the norm, the standard would vary with race and with many individual circumstances.

The most important objection to this approach is that dependence is not ended by viability. The fetus is still absolutely dependent on someone's care in order to continue existence; indeed a child of one or three or even five years of age is absolutely dependent on another's care for existence; uncared for, the older fetus or the younger child will die as surely as the early fetus detached from the mother. The unsubstantial lessening in dependence at viability does not seem to signify any special acquisition of humanity.

A second distinction has been attempted in terms of experience. A being who has had experience, has lived and suffered, who possesses memories, is more human than one who has not. Humanity depends on formation by experience. The fetus is thus "unformed" in the most basic human sense.

This distinction is not serviceable for the embryo which is already experiencing and reacting. The embryo is responsive to touch after eight weeks and at least at that point is experiencing. At an earlier stage the zygote is certainly alive and responding to its environment. The distinction may also be challenged by the rare case where aphasia has erased adult memory: has it erased humanity? More fundamentally, this distinction leaves even the older fetus or the younger child to be treated as an unformed inhuman thing. Finally, it is not clear why experience as such confers humanity. It could be argued that certain central experiences such as loving or learning are necessary to make a man human. But then human beings who have failed to love or to learn might be excluded from the class called man.

A third distinction is made by appeal to the sentiments of adults. If a fetus dies, the grief of the parents is not the grief they would have for a living child. The fetus is an unnamed "it" till birth, and is not perceived as personality until at least the fourth month of existence when movements in the womb manifest a vigorous presence demanding joyful recognition by the parents.

Yet feeling is notoriously an unsure guide to the humanity of others. Many groups of humans have had difficulty in feeling that persons of another tongue, color, religion, sex, are as human as they. Apart from reactions to alien groups, we mourn the loss of a 10-year-old boy more than the loss of his one-day-old brother or his 90-year-old grandfather. The difference felt and the grief expressed vary with the potentialities extinguished, or the experience wiped out; they do not seem to point to any substantial difference in the humanity of baby, boy, or grandfather.

Distinctions are also made in terms of sensation by the parents. The embryo is felt within the womb only after about the fourth month. The embryo is seen only at birth. What can be neither seen nor felt is different from what is tangible. If the fetus cannot be seen or touched at all, it cannot be perceived as man.

Yet experience shows that sight is even more untrustworthy than feeling in determining humanity. By sight, color became an appropriate index for saying who was a man, and the evil of racial discrimination was given foundation. Nor can touch provide the test; a being confined by sickness, "out of touch" with others, does not thereby seem to lose his humanity. To the extent that touch still has appeal as a criterion, it appears to be a survival of the old English idea of "quickening"—a possible mistranslation of the Latin *animatus* used in the canon law. To that extent touch as a criterion seems to be dependent on the Aristotelian notion of ensoulment, and to fail when this notion is discarded.

Finally, a distinction is sought in social visibility. The fetus is not socially perceived as human. It cannot communicate with others. Thus, both subjectively and objectively, it is not a member of society. As moral rules are rules for the behavior of members of society to each other, they cannot be made for behavior toward what is not yet a member. Excluded from the society of men, the fetus is excluded from the humanity of men.

By force of the argument from the consequences, this distinction is to be rejected. It is more subtle than that founded on an appeal to physical sensation, but it is equally dangerous in its implications. If humanity depends on social recognition, individuals or whole groups may be dehumanized by being denied any status in their society. Such a fate is fictionally portrayed in *1984* and has actually been the lot of many men in many societies. In the Roman empire, for example, condemnation to slavery meant the practical denial of most human rights; in the Chinese Communist world, landlords have been classified as enemies of the people and so treated as nonpersons by the state. Humanity does not depend on social recognition, though often the failure of society to recognize the prisoner, the alien, the heterodox as human has led to the destruction of human beings. Anyone conceived by a man and a woman is human. Recognition of this condition by society follows a real event in the objective order, however imperfect and halting the recognition. Any attempt to limit humanity to exclude some group runs the risk of furnishing authority and precedent for excluding other groups in the name of the consciousness or perception of the controlling group in the society.

A philosopher may reject the appeal to the humanity of the fetus because he views "humanity" as a secular view of the soul and because he doubts the existence of anything real and objective which can be identified as humanity. One answer to such a philosopher is to ask how he reasons about moral questions without supposing that there is a sense in which he and the others of whom he speaks are human. Whatever group is taken as the society which determines who may be killed is thereby taken as human. A second answer is to ask if he does not believe that there is a right and wrong way of deciding moral questions. If there is such a difference, experience may be appealed to: to decide who is human on the basis of the sentiment of a given society has led to consequences which rational men would characterize as monstrous.

The rejection of the attempted distinctions based on viability and visibility, experience and feeling, may be buttressed by the following considerations: Moral judgments often rest on distinctions, but if the distinctions are not to appear arbitrary fiat, they should relate to some real difference in probabilities. There is a kind of continuity in all life, but the earlier stages of the elements of human life possess tiny probabilities of development. Consider for example, the spermatozoa in any normal ejaculate: There are about 200,000,000 in any single ejaculate, of which one has a chance of developing into a zygote. Consider the oocytes which may become ova: There are 100,000 to 1,000,000 oocytes in a female infant, of which a maximum of 390 are ovulated. But once spermatozoon and ovum meet and the conceptus is formed, such studies as have been made show that roughly in only 20 percent of the cases will spontaneous abortion occur. In other words, the chances are about 4 out of 5 that this new being will develop. At this stage in the life of the being there is a sharp shift in probabilities, an immense jump in potentialities. To make a distinction between the rights of spermatozoa and the rights of the fertilized ovum is to respond to an enormous shift in possibilities. For about twenty days after conception the egg may split to form twins or combine with another egg to form a chimera, but the probability of either event happening is very small.

It may be asked, What does a change in biological probabilities have to do with establishing humanity? The argument from probabilities is not aimed at establishing humanity but at establishing an objective discontinuity which may be taken into account in moral discourse. As life itself is a matter of probabilities, as most moral reasoning is an estimate of probabilities, so it seems in accord with the structure of reality and the nature of moral thought to found a moral judgment on the change in probabilities at conception. The appeal

to probabilities is the most commonsensical of arguments, to a greater or smaller degree all of us base our actions on probabilities, and in morals, as in law, prudence and negligence are often measured by the account one has taken of the probabilities. If the chance is 200,000,000 to 1 that the movement in the bushes into which you shoot is a man's, I doubt if many persons would hold you careless in shooting; but if the chances are 4 out of 5 that the movement is a human being's, few would acquit you of blame. Would the argument be different if only one out of ten children conceived came to term? Of course this argument would be different. This argument is an appeal to probabilities that actually exist, not to any and all states of affairs which may be imagined.

The probabilities as they do exist do not show the humanity of the embryo in the sense of a demonstration in logic any more than the probabilities of the movement in the bush being a man demonstrate beyond all doubt that the being is a man. The appeal is a "buttressing" consideration, showing the plausibility of the standard adopted. The argument focuses on the decisional factor in any moral judgment and assumes that part of the business of a moralist is drawing lines. One evidence of the nonarbitrary character of the line drawn is the difference of probabilities on either side of it. If a spermatozoon is destroyed, one destroys a being which had a chance of far less than 1 in 200 million of developing into a reasoning being, possessed of the genetic code, a heart and other organs, and capable of pain. If a fetus is destroyed, one destroys a being already possessed of the genetic code, organs, and sensitivity to pain, and one which had an 80 percent chance of developing further into a baby outside the womb who, in time, would reason.

The positive argument for conception as the decisive moment of humanization is that at conception the new being receives the genetic code. It is this genetic information which determines his characteristics, which is the biological carrier of the possibility of human wisdom, which makes him a self-evolving being. A being with a human genetic code is man.

This review of current controversy over the humanity of the fetus emphasizes what a fundamental question the theologians resolved in asserting the inviolability of the fetus. To regard the fetus as possessed of equal rights with other humans was not, however, to decide every case where abortion might be employed. It did decide the case where the argument was that the fetus should be aborted for its own good. To say a being was human was to say it had a destiny to decide for itself which could not be taken from it by another man's decision. But human beings with equal rights often come in conflict with each other, and some decision must be made as whose claims are to prevail. Cases of conflict involving the fetus are different only in two respects: the total inability of the fetus to speak for itself and the fact that the right of the fetus regularly at stake is the right to life itself.

The approach taken by the theologians to these conflicts was articulated in terms of "direct" and "indirect." Again, to look at what they were doing from outside their categories, they may be said to have been drawing lines or "balancing values." "Direct" and "indirect" are spatial metaphors; "line-drawing" is another. "To weigh" or "to balance" values is a metaphor of a more complicated mathematical sort hinting at the process which goes on in moral judgments. All the metaphors suggest that, in the moral judgments made, comparisons were necessary, that no value completely controlled. The principle of double effect was no doctrine fallen from heaven, but a method of analysis appropriate where two relative values were being compared. In Catholic moral theology, as it developed, life even of the innocent was not taken as an absolute. Judgments on acts affecting life issued from a process of weighing. In the weighing, the fetus was always given a value greater than zero, always a value separate and independent from its parents. This valuation was crucial and fundamental in all Christian thought on the subject and marked it off from any approach which considered that only the parents' interests needed to be considered.

Even with the fetus weighed as human, one interest could be weighed as equal or superior: that of the mother in her own life. The casuists between 1450 and 1895 were willing to weigh this interest as superior. Since 1895, that interest was given decisive weight only in the two special cases of the cancerous uterus and the ectopic pregnancy. In both of these cases the fetus itself had little chance of survival even if the abortion were not performed. As the balance was once struck in favor of the mother whenever her life was endangered, it could be so struck again. The balance reached between 1895 and 1930 attempted prudentially and pastorally to forestall a multitude of exceptions for interests less than life.

The perception of the humanity of the fetus and the weighing of fetal rights against other human rights constituted the work of the moral analysts. But what spirit animated their abstract judgments? For the Christian community it was the injunction of Scripture to love your neighbor as yourself. The fetus as human was a neighbor; his life had parity with one's own. The commandment gave life to what otherwise would have been only rational calculation.

The commandment could be put in humanistic as well as theological terms: Do not injure your fellow man without reason. In these terms, once the humanity of the fetus is perceived, abortion is never right except in self-defense. When life must be taken to save life, reason alone cannot say that a mother must prefer a child's life to her own. With this exception, now of great rarity, abortion violates the rational humanist tenet of the equality of human lives.

For Christians the commandment to love had received a special imprint in that the exemplar proposed of love was the love of the Lord for his disciples. In the light given by this example, self-sacrifice carried to the point of death seemed in the extreme situations not without meaning. In the less extreme cases, preference for one's own interests to the life of another seemed to express cruelty or selfishness irreconcilable with the demands of love.

For Further Reflection

1. Do you agree with Noonan in drawing the line between the human and nonhuman at conception? Explain your answer.

2. Has Noonan successfully argued that abortion is almost always immoral? Should he consider cases of rape and incest? What would Noonan say to the suggestion that a rape victim should be allowed to have an abortion?

3. Some have compared our practice of abortion to Hitler's Holocaust. A friend wrote, "With reference to abortion the world is upside down. When a criminal is sentenced to death, the whole world is dismayed because it goes against human rights. But when an unborn baby is sentenced to death, the world approves of it because the 'rights' of the mother take precedence over the rights of the child. But how is this different from the Nazi Holocaust, where Mother Germany sent 12 million innocent lives to the gas chamber? Haven't we sent over 30 million innocent lives to their death?" Do you agree with this comparison? Explain.

IX.65   Abortion Is Morally Permissible

MARY ANNE WARREN

Mary Anne Warren teaches philosophy at San Francisco State University and has written in the area of feminism, including *The Nature of Woman: An Encyclopedia and Guide to the Literature* (1980). In this paper she defends the liberal view that abortion is always morally permissible. She attacks Noonan's argument on the basis of an ambiguity in the use of the term *human being*, showing that the term has both a biological and moral sense. What is important is the moral sense, which presupposes certain characteristics, such as self-consciousness and rationality, which a fetus does not have. At the end of her article, she addresses the issue of infanticide.

Study Questions

1. What is the question which we must answer in order to solve the problem of whether abortion is morally permissible?
2. How is the term *human being* ambiguous?
3. How does this ambiguity undermine the conservative argument for the humanity of the fetus?
4. According to Warren, what characteristics make an entity a person? Which are the most important characteristics in this set?
5. Does potentiality for personhood grant a fetus a right to life? How does Warren illustrate her answer?
6. According to Warren, when does a woman have a right to an abortion?
7. What are Warren's views on infanticide?

THE QUESTION WHICH WE MUST answer in order to produce a satisfactory solution to the problem of the moral status of abortion is this: How are we to define the moral community, the set of beings with full and equal moral rights, such that we can decide whether a human fetus is a member of this community or not? What sort of entity, exactly, has the inalienable rights to life, liberty, and the pursuit of happiness? Jefferson attributed these rights to all *men*, and it may or may not be fair to suggest that he intended to attribute them *only* to men. Perhaps he ought to have attributed them to all human beings. If so, then we arrive, first, at Noonan's problem of defining what makes a being human, and, second, at the equally vital question which Noonan does not consider, namely, What reason is there for identifying the moral community with the set of all human beings, in whatever way we have chosen to define that term?

1. ON THE DEFINITION OF "HUMAN"

One reason why this vital second question is so frequently overlooked in the debate over the moral status of abortion is that the term "human" has two distinct, but not often distinguished, senses. This fact results in a slide of meaning, which serves to conceal the fallaciousness of the traditional argument that since (1) it is wrong to kill innocent human beings, and (2) fetuses are innocent human beings, then (3) it is wrong to kill fetuses. For if "human" is used in the same sense in both (1) and (2) then, whichever of the two senses is meant, one of these premises is question-begging. And if it is used in two different senses then of course the conclusion doesn't follow.

Thus, (1) is a self-evident moral truth, and avoids begging the question about abortion, only if "human being" is used to mean something like "a full-fledged member of the moral community."

(It may or may not also be meant to refer exclusively to members of the species *Homo sapiens.*) We may call this the *moral* sense of "human." It is not to be confused with what we will call the *genetic* sense, i.e., the sense in which *any* member of the species is a human being, and no member of any other species could be. If (1) is acceptable only if the moral sense is intended, (2) is nonquestion-begging only if what is intended is the genetic sense.

In "Deciding Who Is Human," Noonan argues for the classification of fetuses with human beings by pointing to the presence of the full genetic code, and the potential capacity for rational thought. It is clear that what he needs to show, for his version of the traditional argument to be valid, is that fetuses are human in the moral sense, the sense in which it is analytically true that all human beings have full moral rights. But, in the absence of any argument showing that whatever is genetically human is also morally human, and he gives none, nothing more than genetic humanity can be demonstrated by the presence of the human genetic code. And, as we will see, the *potential* capacity for rational thought can at most show that an entity has the potential for *becoming* human in the moral sense.

2. DEFINING THE MORAL COMMUNITY

Can it be established that genetic humanity is sufficient for moral humanity? I think that there are very good reasons for not defining the moral community in this way. I would like to suggest an alternative way of defining the moral community, which I will argue for only to the extent of explaining why it is, or should be, self-evident. The suggestion is simply that the moral community consists of all and only *people*, rather than all and only human beings; and probably the best way of demonstrating its self-evidence

Reprinted from The Monist, *vol. 57, no. 1 (January 1973), with the permission of the author and the publisher. Endnotes deleted.*

is by considering the concept of personhood, to see what sorts of entity are and are not persons, and what the decision that a being is or is not a person implies about its moral rights.

What characteristics entitle an entity to be considered a person? This is obviously not the place to attempt a complete analysis of the concept of personhood, but we do not need such a fully adequate analysis just to determine whether and why a fetus is or isn't a person. All we need is a rough and approximate list of the most basic criteria of personhood, and some idea of which, or how many, of these an entity must satisfy in order to properly be considered a person.

In searching for such criteria, it is useful to look beyond the set of people with whom we are acquainted, and ask how we would decide whether a totally alien being was a person or not. (For we have no right to assume that genetic humanity is necessary for personhood.) Imagine a space traveler who lands on an unknown planet and encounters a race of beings utterly unlike any he has ever seen or heard of. If he wants to be sure of behaving morally toward these beings, he has to somehow decide whether they are people, and hence have full moral rights, or whether they are the sort of thing which he need not feel guilty about treating as, for example, a source of food.

How should he go about making this decision? If he has some anthropological background, he might look for such things as religion, art, and the manufacturing of tools, weapons, or shelters, since these factors have been used to distinguish our human from our prehuman ancestors, in what seems to be closer to the moral than the genetic sense of "human." And no doubt he would be right to consider the presence of such factors as good evidence that the alien beings were people, and morally human. It would, however, be overly anthropocentric of him to take the absence of these things as adequate evidence that they were not, since we can imagine people who have progressed beyond, or evolved without ever developing, these cultural characteristics.

I suggest that the traits which are most central to the concept of personhood, or humanity in the moral sense, are, very roughly, the following:

1. Consciousness (of objects and events external and/or internal to the being), and in particular the capacity to feel pain;
2. Reasoning (the *developed* capacity to solve new and relatively complex problems);
3. Self-motivated activity (activity which is relatively independent of either genetic or direct external control);
4. The capacity to communicate, by whatever means, messages of an indefinite variety of types, that is, not just with an indefinite number of possible contents, but on indefinitely many possible topics;
5. The presence of self-concepts, and self-awareness, either individual or racial, or both.

Admittedly, there are apt to be a great many problems involved in formulating precise definitions of these criteria, let alone in developing universally valid behavioral criteria for deciding when they apply. But I will assume that both we and our explorer know approximately what (1)–(5) mean, and that he is also able to determine whether or not they apply. How, then, should he use his findings to decide whether or not the alien beings are people? We needn't suppose that an entity must have *all* of these attributes to be properly considered a person; (1) and (2) alone may well be sufficient for personhood, and quite probably (1)–(3) are sufficient. Neither do we need to insist that any one of these criteria is *necessary* for personhood, although once again (1) and (2) look like fairly good candidates for necessary conditions, as does (3), if "activity" is construed so as to include the activity of reasoning.

All we need to claim, to demonstrate that a fetus is not a person, is that any being which satisfies *none* of (1)–(5) is certainly not a person. I consider this claim to be so obvious that I think anyone who denied it, and claimed that a being which satisfied none of (1)–(5) was a person all the same, would thereby demonstrate that he had no notion at all of what a person is—perhaps because he had confused the concept of a person with that of genetic humanity. If the opponents of abortion were to deny the appropriateness of these five criteria, I do not know what further arguments would convince them. We would probably have to admit that our conceptual schemes were indeed irreconcilably different, and that our dispute could not be settled objectively.

I do not expect this to happen, however, since I think that the concept of a person is one which is very nearly universal (to people), and that it is common to both proabortionists and antiabortionists, even though neither group has fully realized the relevance of this concept to the resolution of their dispute. Furthermore, I think that on reflection even the antiabortionists ought to agree not only that (1)–(5) are central to the concept of personhood, but also that it is a part of this concept that all and only people have full moral rights. The concept of a person is in part a moral concept; once we have admitted that *x* is a person we have recognized, even if we have not agreed to respect, *x*'s right to be treated as a member of the moral community. It is true that the claim that *x is a human being* is more commonly voiced as part of an appeal to treat *x* decently than is the claim that *x* is a person, but this is either because "human being" is here used in the sense which implies personhood, or because the genetic and moral senses of "human" have been confused.

Now if (1)–(5) are indeed the primary criteria of personhood, then it is clear that genetic humanity is neither necessary nor sufficient for establishing that an entity is a person. Some human beings are not people, and there may well be people who are not human beings. A man or woman whose consciousness has been permanently obliterated but who remains alive is a human being which is no longer a person; defective human beings, with no appreciable mental capacity, are not and presumably never will be people; and a fetus is a human being which is not yet a person, and which therefore cannot coherently be said to have full moral rights. Citizens of the next century should be prepared to recognize highly advanced, self-aware robots or computers, should such be developed, and intelligent inhabitants of other worlds, should such be found, as people in the fullest sense, and to respect their moral rights. But to ascribe full moral rights to an entity which is not a person is as absurd as to ascribe moral obligations and responsibilities to such an entity.

3. FETAL DEVELOPMENT AND THE RIGHT TO LIFE

Two problems arise in the application of these suggestions for the definition of the moral community to the determination of the precise moral status of a human fetus. Given that the paradigm example of a person is a normal adult human being, then (1) How like this paradigm, in particular how far advanced since conception, does a human being need to be before it begins to have a right to life by virtue, not of being fully a person as of yet, but of being *like* a person? and (2) To what extent, if any, does the fact that a fetus has the *potential* for becoming a person endow it with some of the same rights? Each of these questions requires some comment.

In answering the first question, we need not attempt a detailed consideration of the moral rights of organisms which are not developed enough, aware enough, intelligent enough, etc., to be considered people, but which resemble people in some respects. It does seem reasonable to suggest that the more like a person, in the relevant respects, a being is, the stronger is the case for regarding it as having a right to life, and indeed the stronger its right to life is. Thus we ought to take seriously the suggestion that, insofar as "the human individual develops biologically in a continuous fashion . . . the rights of a human person might develop in the same way." But we must keep in mind that the attributes which are relevant in determining whether or not an entity is enough like a person to be regarded as having some of the same moral rights are no different from those which are relevant to determining whether or not it is fully a person—i.e., are no different from (1)–(5)—and that being genetically human, or having recognizably human facial and other physical features, or detectable brain activity, or the capacity to survive outside the uterus, are simply not among these relevant attributes.

Thus it is clear that even though a seven- or eight-month fetus has features which make it apt to arouse in us almost the same powerful protective instinct as is commonly aroused by a small infant, nevertheless it is not significantly more personlike than is a very small embryo. It is *somewhat* more personlike; it can apparently feel and respond to pain, and it may even have a rudimentary form of consciousness, insofar as its brain is quite active. Nevertheless, it seems safe to say that it is not fully conscious, in the way that an infant of a few months is, and that it cannot reason, or communicate messages of indefinitely many sorts, does not engage in self-motivated activity, and has no self-awareness. Thus, in the *relevant* respects, a fetus, even a fully developed one, is considerably less personlike than is the average mature mammal, indeed the average fish. And I think that a rational person must conclude that if the right to life of a fetus is to be based upon its resemblance to a person, then it cannot be said to have any more right to life than, let us say, a newborn guppy (which also seems to be capable of feeling pain), and that a right of that magnitude could never override a woman's right to obtain an abortion, at any stage of her pregnancy.

There may, of course, be other arguments in favor of placing legal limits upon the stage of pregnancy in which an abortion may be performed. Given the relative safety of the new techniques of artificially inducing labor during the third trimester, the danger to the woman's life or health is no longer such an argument. Neither is the fact that people tend to respond to the thought of abortion in the later stages of pregnancy with emotional repulsion, since mere emotional responses cannot take the place of moral reasoning in determining what ought to be permitted. Nor, finally, is the frequently heard argument that legalizing abortion, especially late in

the pregnancy, may erode the level of respect for human life, leading, perhaps, to an increase in unjustified euthanasia and other crimes. For this threat, if it is a threat, can be better met by educating people to the kinds of moral distinctions which we are making here than by limiting access to abortion (which limitation may, in its disregard for the rights of women, be just as damaging to the level of respect for human rights).

Thus, since the fact that even a fully developed fetus is not personlike enough to have any significant right to life on the basis of its personlikeness shows that no legal restrictions upon the stage of pregnancy in which an abortion may be performed can be justified on the grounds that we should protect the rights of the older fetus, and since there is no other apparent justification for such restrictions, we may conclude that they are entirely unjustified. Whether or not it would be *indecent* (whatever that means) for a woman in her seventh month to obtain an abortion just to avoid having to postpone a trip to Europe, it would not, in itself, be *immoral,* and therefore it ought to be permitted.

4. POTENTIAL PERSONHOOD AND THE RIGHT TO LIFE

We have seen that a fetus does not resemble a person in any way which can support the claim that it has even some of the same rights. But what about its *potential*, the fact that if nurtured and allowed to develop naturally it will very probably become a person? Doesn't that alone give it at least some right to life? It is hard to deny that the fact that an entity is a potential person is a strong prima facie reason for not destroying it; but we need not conclude from this that a potential person has a right to life, by virtue of that potential. It may be that our feeling that it is better, other things being equal, not to destroy a potential person is better explained by the fact that potential people are still (felt to be) an invaluable resource, not to be lightly squandered. Surely, if every speck of dust were a potential person, we would be much less apt to conclude that every potential person has a right to become actual.

Still, we do not need to insist that a potential person has no right to life whatever. There may well be something immoral, and not just imprudent, about wantonly destroying potential people, when doing so isn't necessary to protect anyone's rights. But even if a potential person does have some *prima facie* right to life, such a right could not possibly outweigh the right of a woman to obtain an abortion, since the rights of any actual person invariably outweigh those of any potential person, whenever the two conflict. Since this may not be immediately obvious in the case of a human fetus, let us look at another case.

Suppose that our space explorer falls into the hands of an alien culture, whose scientists decide to create a few hundred thousand or more human beings, by breaking his body into its component cells, and using these to create fully developed human beings, with, of course, his genetic code. We may imagine that each of these newly created men will have all of the original man's abilities, skills, knowledge, and so on, and also have an individual self-concept, in short that each of them will be a bona fide (though hardly unique) person. Imagine that the whole project will take only seconds, and that its chances of success are extremely high, and that our explorer knows all of this, and also knows that these people will be treated fairly. I maintain that in such a situation he would have every right to escape if he could, and thus to deprive all of these potential people of their potential lives; for his right to life outweighs all of theirs together, in spite of the fact that they are all genetically human, all innocent, and all have a very high probability of becoming people very soon, if only he refrains from acting.

Indeed, I think he would have a right to escape even if it were not his life which the alien scientists planned to take, but only a year of his freedom, or, indeed, only a day. Nor would he be obligated to stay if he had gotten captured (thus bringing all these people-potentials into existence) because of his own carelessness, or even if he had done so deliberately, knowing the conse-quences. Regardless of how he got captured, he is not morally obligated to remain in captivity for *any* period of time for the sake of permitting any number of potential people to come into actuality, so great is the margin by which one actual person's right to liberty outweighs whatever right to life even a hundred thousand potential people have. And it seems reasonable to conclude that the rights of a woman will outweigh by a similar margin whatever right to life a fetus may have by virtue of its potential personhood.

Thus, neither a fetus's resemblance to a person, nor its potential for becoming a person provides any basis whatever for the claim that it has any significant right to life. Consequently, a woman's right to protect her health, happiness, freedom, and even her life, by terminating an unwanted pregnancy, will always override whatever right to life it may be appropriate to ascribe to a fetus, even a fully developed one. And thus, in the absence of any overwhelming social need for every possible child, the laws which restrict the right to obtain an abortion, or limit the period of pregnancy during which an abortion may be performed, are a wholly unjustified violation of a woman's most basic moral and constitutional rights.

POSTSCRIPT ON INFANTICIDE

Since the publication of this article, many people have written to point out that my argument appears to justify not only abortion, but infanticide as well, for a newborn infant is not significantly more personlike than an advanced fetus, and consequently it would seem that if the destruction of the latter is permissible so too must be that of the former. Inasmuch as most people, regardless of how they feel about the morality of abortion, consider infanticide a form of murder, this might appear to represent a serious flaw in my argument.

Now, if I am right in holding that it is only people who have a full-fledged right to life, and who can be murdered, and if the criteria of personhood are as I have described them, then it obviously follows that killing a newborn infant isn't murder. It does *not* follow, however, that infanticide is permissible, for two reasons. In the first place, it would be wrong, at least in this country and in this period of history, and other things being equal, to kill a newborn infant, because even if its parents do not want it and would not suffer from its destruction, there are other people who would like to have it, and would, in all probability, be deprived of a great deal of pleasure by its destruction. Thus, infanticide is wrong for reasons analogous to those which make it wrong to wantonly destroy natural resources, or great works of art.

Secondly, most people, at least in this country, value infants and would much prefer that they be preserved, even if foster parents are not immediately available. Most of us would rather be taxed to support orphanages than allow unwanted infants to be destroyed. So long as there are people who want an infant preserved, and who are willing and able to provide the means of caring for it, under reasonably humane conditions, it is *ceteris paribus*, wrong to destroy it.

But, it might be replied, if this argument shows that infanticide is wrong, at least at this time and in this country, doesn't it also show that abortion is wrong? After all, many people value fetuses, are disturbed by their destruction, and would much prefer that they be preserved, even at some cost to themselves. Furthermore, as a potential source of pleasure to some foster family, a fetus is just as valuable as an infant. There is, however, a crucial difference between the two cases: so long as the fetus is unborn, its preservation, contrary to the wishes of the pregnant woman, violates her rights to freedom, happiness, and self-determination. Her rights override the rights of those who would like the fetus preserved, just as if someone's life or limb is threatened by a wild animal, his right to protect himself by destroying the animal overrides the rights of those who would prefer that the animal not be harmed.

The minute the infant is born, however, its preservation no longer violates any of its mother's rights, even if she wants it destroyed, because she is free to put it up for adoption. Consequently, while the moment of birth does not mark any sharp discontinuity in the degree to which an infant possesses the right to life, it does mark the end of its mother's right to determine its fate. Indeed, if abortion could be performed without killing the fetus, she would never possess the right to have the fetus destroyed, for the same reasons that she has no right to have an infant destroyed.

On the other hand, it follows from my argument that when an unwanted or defective infant is born into a society which cannot afford and/or is not willing to care for it, then its destruction is permissible. This conclusion will, no doubt, strike many people as heartless and immoral; but remember that the very existence of people who feel this way, and who are willing and able to provide care for unwanted infants, is reason enough to conclude that they should be preserved.

For Further Reflection

1. Has Warren successfully refuted Noonan's argument against abortion? Are there any aspects of Noonan's argument that she has not successfully answered?

2. Examine Warren's postscript on infanticide. Does Warren's analysis of the morality of abortion lead to the justification of infanticide? Does it lead to justification of killing the severely retarded, mentally ill, and senile?

3. Is there a middle ground between Noonan's conservatism and Warren's liberalism on abortion?

The Moderate Position:
Beyond the Personhood Argument   IX.66

JANE ENGLISH

Jane English (1947–1978) taught philosophy at the University of North Carolina, Chapel Hill, and was the author of several essays in applied ethics, including the essay that is included here.

English argues that the issue, of whether a fetus is a person, cannot be resolved, and that the very concept of personhood is not clear or decisive enough to bear the weight of a solution to the abortion debate. Advancing a moderate position, similar to that of F. W. Sumner, English argues that regardless of whether a fetus is a person, the principle of self-defense permits a woman to have an abortion in some cases, especially in the early stages of pregnancy. On the other hand, even if the fetus is not a person, it is too much like a baby in the later stages of pregnancy to permit an abortion—except to avoid significant injury or death.

Study Questions

1. Why does English think that both the conservative and liberal positions on abortion are "clearly mistaken"?
2. What does English think is the key issue in the abortion debate?
3. What is English's conclusion regarding criteria for personhood? How does she describe personhood?
4. Does English think it is sometimes permissible to kill an innocent person? If so, under what conditions? If not, why not?
5. How are some cases of pregnancy like being attacked by an innocent (hypnotized) person?
6. Even if the fetus is a person, would it sometimes, according to English, be permissible to have an abortion? Under what conditions?
7. What is the anti-abortionist's strongest argument?
8. What is English's judgment on Tooley's argument?

THE ABORTION DEBATE rages on. Yet the two most popular positions seem to be clearly mistaken. Conservatives maintain that a human life begins at conception and that therefore abortion must be wrong because it is murder. But not all killings of humans are murders. Most notably, self defense may justify even the killing of an innocent person.

Liberals, on the other hand, are just as mistaken in their argument that since a fetus does not become a person until birth, a woman may do whatever she pleases in and to her own body. First, you cannot do as you please with your own body if it affects other people adversely. Second, if a fetus is not a person, that does not imply that you can do to it anything you wish.

Reprinted from "Abortion and the Concept of a Person," Canadian Journal of Philosophy *vol. 5, 2 (October 1975) by permission. Footnotes deleted.*

Animals, for example, are not persons, yet to kill or torture them for no reason at all is wrong.

At the center of the storm has been the issue of just when it is between ovulation and adulthood that a person appears on the scene. Conservatives draw the line at conception, liberals at birth. In this paper I first examine our concept of a person and conclude that no single criterion can capture the concept of a person and no sharp line can be drawn. Next I argue that if a fetus is a person, abortion is still justifiable in many cases; and if a fetus is not a person, killing it is still wrong in many cases. To a large extent, these two solutions are in agreement. I conclude that our concept of a person cannot and need not bear the weight that the abortion controversy has thrust upon it.

I

The several factions in the abortion argument have drawn battle lines around various proposed criteria for determining what is and what is not a person. For example, Mary Anne Warren lists five features (capacities for reasoning, self-awareness, complex communication, etc.) as her criteria for personhood and argues for the permissibility of abortion because a fetus falls outside this concept. Baruch Brody uses brain waves. Michael Tooley picks having-a-concept-of-self as his criterion and concludes that infanticide and abortion are justifiable, while the killing of adult animals is not. On the other side, Paul Ramsey claims a certain gene structure is the defining characteristic. John Noonan prefers conceived-of-humans and presents counterexamples to various other candidate criteria. For instance, he argues against viability as the criterion because the newborn and infirm would then be non-persons, since they cannot live without the aid of others. He rejects any criterion that calls upon the sorts of sentiments a being can evoke in adults on the grounds that this would allow us to exclude other races as nonpersons if we could just view them sufficiently unsentimentally.

These approaches are typical: Foes of abortion propose sufficient conditions for personhood which fetuses satisfy, while friends of abortion counter with necessary conditions for personhood which fetuses lack. But these both presuppose that the concept of a person can be captured in a strait jacket of necessary and/or sufficient conditions. Rather, "person" is a cluster of features, of which rationality, having a self concept and being conceived of humans are only part.

What is typical of persons? Within our concept of a person we include, first, certain biological factors: descended from humans, having a certain genetic makeup, having a head, hands, arms, eyes, capable of locomotion, breathing, eating, sleeping. There are psychological factors: sentience, perception, having a concept of self and of one's own interests and desires, the ability to use tools, the ability to use language or symbol systems, the ability to joke, to be angry, to doubt. There are rationality factors: the ability to reason and draw conclusions, the ability to generalize and to learn from past experience, the ability to sacrifice present interests for greater gains in the future. There are social factors: the ability to work in groups and respond to peer pressures, the ability to recognize and consider as valuable the interests of others, seeing oneself as one among "other minds," the ability to sympathize, encourage, love, the ability to evoke from others the responses of sympathy, encouragement, love, the ability to work with others for mutual advantage. Then there are legal factors: being subject to the law and protected by it, having the ability to sue and enter contracts, being counted in the census, having a name and citizenship, the ability to own property, inherit, and so forth.

Now the point is not that this list is incomplete, or that you can find counter-instances to each of its points. People typically exhibit rationality, for instance, but someone who was irrational would not thereby fail to qualify as a person. On the other hand, something could exhibit the majority of these features and still fail to be a person, as an advanced robot might.

There is no single core of necessary and sufficient features which we can draw upon with the assurance that they constitute what really makes a person: there are only features that are more or less typical.

This is not to say that no necessary or sufficient conditions can be given. Being alive is a necessary condition for being a person, and being a U.S. Senator is sufficient. But rather than falling inside a sufficient condition or outside a necessary one, a fetus lies in the penumbra region where our concept of a person is not so simple. For this reason I think a conclusive answer to the question whether a fetus is a person is unattainable.

Here we might note a family of simple fallacies that proceed by stating a necessary condition for personhood and showing that a fetus has that characteristic. This is a form of the fallacy of affirming the consequent. For example, some have mistakenly reasoned from the premise that a fetus is human (after all, it is a human fetus rather than, say, a canine fetus), to the conclusion that it is *a* human. Adding an equivocation on "being," we get the fallacious argument that since a fetus is something both living and human, it is a human being.

Nonetheless, it does seem clear that a fetus has very few of the above family of characteristics, whereas a newborn baby exhibits a much larger proportion of them—and a two-year-old has even more. Note that one traditional anti-abortion argument has centered on pointing out the many ways in which a fetus resembles a baby. They emphasize its development ("It already has ten fingers . . .") without mentioning its dissimilarities to adults (it still has gills and a tail). They also try to evoke the sort of sympathy on our part that we only feel toward other persons ("Never to laugh . . . or feel the sunshine?") This all seems to be a relevant way to argue, since its purpose is to persuade us that a fetus satisfies so many of the important features on the list that it ought to be treated as a person. Also note that a fetus near the time of birth satisfies many more of these factors than a fetus in the early months of development.

This could provide reason for making distinctions among the different stages of pregnancy, as the U.S. Supreme Court has done.

Historically, the time at which a person has been said to come into existence has varied widely. Muslims date personhood from fourteen days after conception. Some medievals followed Aristotle in placing ensoulment at forty days after conception for a male fetus and eighty days for a female fetus. In European common law since the Seventeenth Century, abortion was considered the killing of a person only after quickening, the time when a pregnant woman first feels the fetus move on its own. Nor is this variety of opinions surprising. Biologically, a human being develops gradually. We shouldn't expect there to be any specific time or sharp dividing point when a person appears on the scene.

For these reasons I believe our concept of a person is not sharp or decisive enough to bear the weight of a solution to the abortion controversy. To use it to solve that problem is to clarify *obscurum per obscurius*.

II

Next let us consider what follows if a fetus is a person after all. Judith Jarvis Thomson's landmark article, "A Defense of Abortion," correctly points out that some additional argumentation is needed at this point in the conservative argument to bridge the gap between the premise that a fetus is an innocent person and the conclusion that killing it is always wrong. To arrive at this conclusion, we would need the additional premise that killing an innocent person is always wrong. But killing an innocent person is sometimes permissible, most notably in self defense. Some examples may help draw out our intuitions or ordinary judgments about self defense.

Suppose a mad scientist, for instance, hypnotized innocent people to jump out of the bushes and attack innocent passers-by with knives. If you are so attacked, we agree you have a right to kill the attacker in self defense, if killing him is the only way to protect your life or to save yourself from serious injury. It does not seem to matter here that the attacker is not malicious but himself an innocent pawn, for your killing of him is not done in a spirit of retribution but only in self defense.

How severe an injury may you inflict in self defense? In part this depends upon the severity of the injury to be avoided: you may not shoot someone merely to avoid having your clothes torn. This might lead one to the mistaken conclusion that the defense may only equal the threatened injury in severity; that to avoid death you may kill, but to avoid a black eye you may only inflict a black eye or the equivalent. Rather, our laws and customs seem to say that you may create an injury somewhat, but not enormously, greater than the injury to be avoided. To fend off an attack whose outcome would be as serious as rape, a severe beating or the loss of a finger, you may shoot; to avoid having your clothes torn, you may blacken an eye.

Aside from this, the injury you may inflict should only be the minimum necessary to deter or incapacitate the attacker. Even if you know he intends to kill you, you are not justified in shooting him if you could equally well save yourself by the simple expedient of running away. Self defense is for the purpose of avoiding harms rather than equalizing harms.

Some cases of pregnancy present a parallel situation. Though the fetus is itself innocent, it may pose a threat to the pregnant woman's well-being, life prospects or health, mental or physical. If the pregnancy presents a slight threat to her interests, it seems self defense cannot justify abortion. But if the threat is on a part with a serious beating or the loss of a finger, she may kill the fetus that poses such a threat, even if it is an innocent person. If a lesser harm to the fetus could have the same defensive effect, killing it would not be justified. It is unfortunate that the only way to free the woman from the pregnancy entails the death of the fetus (except in very late stages of pregnancy). Thus a self defense model supports Thomson's point

that the woman has a right only to be freed from fetus, not a right to demand its death.

The self defense model is most helpful when we take the pregnant woman's point of view. In the pre-Thomson literature, abortion is often framed as a question for a third party; do you, a doctor, have a right to choose between the life of the woman and that of the fetus? Some have claimed that if you were a passer-by who witnessed a struggle between the innocent hypnotized attacker and his equally innocent victim, you would have no reason to kill either in defense of the other. They have concluded that the self defense model implies that a woman may attempt to abort herself, but that a doctor should not assist her. I think the position of the third party is somewhat more complex. We do feel some inclination to intervene on behalf of the victim rather than the attacker, other things equal. But if both parties are innocent, other factors come into consideration. You would rush to the aid of your husband whether he was attacker or attackee. If a hypnotized famous violinist were attacking a skid row bum, we would try to save the individual who is of more value to society. These considerations would tend to support abortion in some cases.

But suppose you are a frail senior citizen who wishes to avoid being knifed by one of these innocent hypnotics, so you have hired a bodyguard to accompany you. If you are attacked, it is clear we believe that the bodyguard, acting as your agent, has a right to kill the attacker to save you from a serious beating. Your rights of self defense are transferred to your agent. I suggest that we should similarly view the doctor as the pregnant woman's agent in carrying out a defense she is physically incapable of accomplishing herself.

Thanks to modern technology, the cases are rare in which a pregnancy poses as clear a threat to a woman's bodily health as an attacker brandishing a switchblade. How does self defense fare when more subtle, complex and long-range harms are involved?

To consider a somewhat fanciful example, suppose you are a highly trained surgeon when you are kidnapped by the hypnotic attacker. He says he does not intend to harm you but to take you back to the mad scientist who, it turns out, plans to hypnotize you to have a permanent mental block against all your knowledge of medicine. This would automatically destroy your career which would in turn have a serious adverse impact on your family, your personal relationships and your happiness. It seems to me that if the only way you can avoid this outcome is to shoot the innocent attacker, you are justified in so doing. You are defending yourself from a drastic injury to your life prospects. I think it is no exaggeration to claim that unwanted pregnancies (most obviously among teenagers) often have such adverse life-long consequences as the surgeon's loss of livelihood.

Several parallels arise between various views on abortion and the self defense model. Let's suppose further that these hypnotized attackers only operate at night, so that it is well known that they can be avoided completely by the considerable inconvenience of never leaving your house after dark. One view is that since you could stay home at night, therefore if you go out and are selected by one of these hypnotized people, you have no right to defend yourself. This parallels the view that abstinence is the only acceptable way to avoid pregnancy. Others might hold that you ought to take along some defense such as Mace which will deter the hypnotized person without killing him, but that if this defense fails, you are obliged to submit to the resulting injury, no matter how severe it is. This parallels the view that contraception is all right but abortion is always wrong, even in cases of contraceptive failure.

A third view is that you may kill the hypnotized person only if he will actually kill you, but not if he will only injure you. This is like the position that abortion is permissible only if it is required to save a woman's life. Finally, we have the view that it is all right to kill the attacker, even if only to avoid a very slight inconvenience to yourself and even if you knowingly walked down the very street where all these incidents have been taking place without taking along any Mace or protective escort. If we assume that a fetus is a person, this is the analogue of the view that abortion is always justifiable, "on demand."

The self defense model allows us to see an important difference that exists between abortion and infanticide, even if a fetus is a person from conception. Many have argued that the only way to justify abortion without justifying infanticide would be to find some characteristic of personhood that is acquired at birth. Michael Tooley, for one, claims infanticide is justifiable because the really significant characteristics of person are acquired some time after birth. But all such approaches look to characteristics of the developing human and ignore the relation between the fetus and the woman. What if, after birth, the presence of an infant or the need to support it posed a grave threat to the woman's sanity or life prospects? She could escape this threat by the simple expedient of running away. So a solution that does not entail the death of the infant is available. Before birth, such solutions are not available because of the biological dependence of the fetus on the woman. Birth is the crucial point not because of any characteristics the fetus gains, but because after birth the woman can defend herself by a means less drastic than killing the infant. Hence self defense can be used to justify abortion without necessarily thereby justifying infanticide.

III

On the other hand, supposing a fetus is not after all a person, would abortion always be morally permissible? Some opponents of abortion seem worried that if a fetus is not a full-fledged person, then we are justified in treating it in any way at all. However, this does not follow. Non-persons do get some consideration in our moral code, though of course they do not have the same rights as persons have (and in general they do not have moral responsibilities), and though their interests may be overridden by the interests of persons. Still, we cannot just treat them in any way at all.

Treatment of animals is a case in point. It is wrong to torture dogs for fun or to kill wild birds for no reason at all. It is wrong Period, even though dogs and birds do not have the same rights persons do. However, few people think it is wrong to use dogs as experimental animals, causing them considerable suffering in some cases, provided that the resulting research will probably bring discoveries of great benefit to people. And most of us think it all right to kill birds for food or to protect our crops. People's rights are different from the consideration we give to animals, then, for it is wrong to experiment on people, even if others might later benefit a great deal as a result of their suffering. You might volunteer to be a subject, but this would be supererogatory; you certainly have a right to refuse to be a medical guinea pig.

But how do we decide what you may or may not do to non-persons? This is a difficult problem, one for which I believe no adequate account exists. You do not want to say, for instance, that torturing dogs is all right whenever the sum of its effects on people is good—when it doesn't warp the sensibilities of the torturer so much that he mistreats people. If that were the case, it would be all right to torture dogs if you did it in private, or if the torturer lived on a desert island or died soon afterward, so that his actions had no effect on people. This is an inadequate account, because whatever moral consideration animals get, it has to be indefeasible, too. It will have to be a general proscription of certain actions, not merely a weighing of the impact on people on a case-by-case basis.

Rather, we need to distinguish two levels on which consequences of actions can be taken into account in moral reasoning. The traditional objections to Utilitarianism focus on the fact that it operates solely on the first level, taking all the consequences into account in particular cases only. Thus Utilitarianism is open to "desert island" and "lifeboat" counterexamples because these cases are rigged to make the consequences of actions severely limited.

Rawls' theory could be described as a teleological sort of theory, but with teleology operating on a higher level. In choosing the principles to regulate society from the original position, his hypothetical choosers make their decision on the basis of the total consequences of various systems. Furthermore, they are constrained to choose a general set of rules which people can readily learn and apply. An ethical theory must operate by generating a set of sympathies and attitudes toward others which reinforces the functioning of that set of moral principles. Our prohibition against killing people operates by means of certain moral sentiments including sympathy, compassion and guilt. But if these attitudes are to form a coherent set, they carry us further: we tend to perform supererogatory actions, and we tend to feel similar compassion toward person-like non-persons.

It is crucial that psychological facts play a role here. Our psychological constitution makes it the case that for our ethical theory to work, it must prohibit certain treatment of non-persons which are significantly person-like. If our moral rules allowed people to treat some person-like non-persons in ways we do not want people to be treated, this would undermine the system of sympathies and attitudes that makes the ethical system work. For this reason, we would choose in the original position to make mistreatment of some sorts of animals wrong in general (not just wrong in the cases with public impact), even though animals are not themselves parties in the original position. Thus it makes sense that it is those animals whose appearance and behavior are most like those of people that get the most consideration in our moral scheme.

It is because of "coherence of attitudes," I think, that the similarity of a fetus to a baby is very significant. A fetus one week before birth is so much like a newborn baby in our psychological space that we cannot allow any cavalier treatment of the former while expecting full sympathy and nurturative support for the latter. Thus, I think that anti-abortion forces are indeed giving their strongest arguments when they point to the similarities between a fetus and a baby, and when they try to evoke our emotional attachment to and sympathy for the fetus. An early horror story from New York about nurses who were expected to alternate between caring for six-week premature infants and disposing of viable 24-week aborted fetuses is just that—a horror story. These beings are so much alike that no one can be asked to draw a distinction and treat them so very differently.

Remember, however, that in the early weeks after conception, a fetus is very much unlike a person. It is hard to develop these feelings for a set of genes which doesn't yet have a head, hands, beating heart, response to touch or the ability to move by itself. Thus it seems to me that the alleged "slippery slope" between conception and birth is not so very slippery. In the early stages of pregnancy, abortion can hardly be compared to murder for psychological reasons, but in the latest stages it is psychologically akin to murder.

Another source of similarity is the bodily continuity between fetus and adult. Bodies play a surprisingly central role in our attitudes toward persons. One has only to think of the philosophical literature on how far physical identity suffices for personal identity or Wittgenstein's remark that the best picture of the human soul is the human body. Even after death, when all agree the body is no longer a person, we still observe elaborate customs of respect for the human body; like people who torture dogs, necrophiliacs are not to be trusted with people. So it is appropriate that we show respect to a fetus as the body continuous with the body of a person. This is a degree of resemblance to persons that animals cannot rival.

Michael Tooley also utilizes a parallel with animals. He claims that it is always permissible to drown newborn kittens and draws conclusions about infanticide. But it is only permissible to drown kittens when their survival would cause some hardship. Perhaps it would be a burden to feed and house six more cats or to find other homes for them. The alternative of letting them starve produces even more suffering than the drowning. Since the kittens get their rights second-hand, so to speak, *via* the need for coherence in our attitudes, their interests are often

overridden by the interests of full-fledged persons. But if their survival would be no inconvenience to people at all, then it is wrong to drown them, *contra* Tooley.

Tooley's conclusions about abortion are wrong for the same reason. Even if a fetus is not a person, abortion is not always permissible, because of the resemblance of a fetus to a person. I agree with Thomson that it would be wrong for a woman who is seven months pregnant to have an abortion just to avoid having to postpone a trip to Europe. In the early months of pregnancy when the fetus hardly resembles a baby at all, then, abortion is permissible whenever it is in the interests of the pregnant woman or her family. The reasons would only need to outweigh the pain and inconvenience of the abortion itself. In the middle months, when the fetus comes to resemble a person, abortion would be justifiable only when the continuation of the pregnancy or the birth of the child would cause harms—physical, psychological, economic or social—to the woman. In the late months of pregnancy, even on our current assumption that a fetus is not a person, abortion seems to be wrong except to save a woman from significant injury or death.

The Supreme Court has recognized similar gradations in the alleged slippery slope stretching between conception and birth. To this point, the present paper has been a discussion of the moral status of abortion only, not its legal status. In view of the great physical, financial and sometimes psychological costs of abortion, perhaps the legal arrangements most compatible with the proposed moral solution would be the absence of restrictions, that is, so-called abortion "on demand."

So I conclude, first, that application of our concept of a person will not suffice to settle the abortion issue. After all, the biological development of a human being is gradual. Second, whether a fetus is a person or not, abortion is justifiable early in pregnancy to avoid modest harms and seldom justifiable late in pregnancy except to avoid significant injury or death.

For Further Reflection

1. Can we get beyond the personhood issue, as English proposes? Has she successfully shown that we don't need to resolve this issue in order to deal with the morality of abortion? Where do you agree or disagree with her?

2. English's view has been called moderate because she accepts most early stage abortions and rejects most later stage abortions. If so, how can this be reconciled with her proposal or, at least acceptance, of abortion "on demand"?

3. Does English's argument appeal too much to our emotions and too little to reason? For example, she says, "It is crucial that psychological facts play a role here. Our psychological constitution makes it the case that for our ethical theory to work, it must prohibit certain treatment of nonpersons which are significantly person-like." What does English mean? Is this an appeal to ignorance or to human irrationality or something else?

4. What is her "coherence of attitudes" argument? How much weight should such considerations be given in the abortion debate? Could my "coherence" structure be different from yours, and yours be different from other people's? Discuss the case of the New York nurses who were expected to alternate between caring for six-week premature infants and disposing of viable 24-week aborted fetuses. What bearing does this have on the question of the morality of abortion?

IX.B   Is the Death Penalty Morally Permissible?

What kind and what degree of punishment does public justice take as its principle and norm? None other than the principle of equality in the movement of the pointer of the scale of justice, the principle of not inclining to one side more than to the other. Thus any undeserved evil which you do to someone else among the people is an evil done to yourself. If you rob him, you rob yourself; if you slander him, you slander yourself; if you strike him, you strike yourself; and if you kill him, you kill yourself. (Immanuel Kant)

On August 15, 1990, Angel Diaz, age 19, was sentenced in the Bronx for the murder of an Israeli immigrant who had employed one of Diaz's friends. After strangling the man with a shoelace and stabbing him, Diaz and four friends donned Halloween masks to rob, beat, and gang-rape the man's wife and 16-year-old daughter. The women were then sexually tortured while the murdered man's 3-year-old daughter watched from her crib.

Angel Diaz already had been convicted of burglary four times before he was 16-years old. Diaz's lawyer, Paul Auerbach, said that Diaz was an honest boy forced by poverty to do bad things. Diaz was sentenced to prison for 38 and one-third years to life on 13 counts of murder, robbery, burglary, and conspiracy. His accomplice, Victor Sanchez, 21, who worked for the murdered man and planned the murder, had already been sentenced to 15 years to life.[1]

The National Center of Health Statistics has reported that the homicide rate for young men in the United States is 4 to 73 times the rate of other industrialized countries. In 1994, 23,330 murders were committed in the United States. Whereas killings per 100,000 by men 15 through 24 years old in 1987 was 0.3 in Austria and 0.5 in Japan, the figure was 21.9 in the United States and as high as 232 per 100,000 for blacks in some states. The nearest nation to the United States was Scotland, with a 5.0 homicide rate. In some central city areas the rate is 732 times that of men in Austria. In 1994, the rate was 37 per 100,000 men between the ages of 15 and 24.[2] In New York City there were more than 2,000 homicides in 1990. Black males in Harlem are said to have a lower life expectancy than males in Bangladesh. Escalating crime has caused an erosion in the quality of urban living. It is threatening the fabric of our social life.

What is to be done about crime? Improving social conditions, no doubt, is a large part of the answer. But people commit crimes even in good societies. So long as we hold people responsible for their actions, punishment will be a fitting response to crime, and among the modes of punishment to be considered is the death penalty for the most serious crimes.

We begin with Supreme Court Justice Thurgood Marshall's important dissenting opinion in *Gregg v. Georgia* in which he argued that the death penalty violated the Eighth and Fourteenth Ammendments prohibiting cruel and unusual punishments. We then turn to Burton Leiser's defense of the death penalty, and finally to Hugo Adam Bedau's rejection of the death penalty.

NOTES

1. "Jail for Crime that Shocked Even the Jaded," *New York Times* (August 16, 1990).
2. Statistics are from the National Center of Health Statistics and are available from the Center for Disease Control. The National Center for Injury Prevention and Control reports that in 1994 8,116 young people aged 15–24 were victims of homicide. This amounts to an average of 22 youth victims per day in the United States. This homicide rate is 10 times higher than Canada's, 15 times higher than Australia's, and 28 times higher than France's and Germany's. In 1994 in the United States 102,220 rapes and 618,950 robberies were reported.

The Death Penalty Is a Denial of Human Dignity IX.67

THURGOOD MARSHALL

Thurgood Marshall (1908–93), the first African American to be appointed to the United States Supreme Court, was the most outspoken opponent of capital punishment on the Court. He gained national prominence in his role as the counsel for the plaintiff in the landmark civil rights case, *Brown v. Board of Education* (1954).

The following is Justice Marshall's dissenting opinion in *Gregg v. Georgia* (1976), the Supreme Court's decision that capital punishment did not violate the Constitution. Marshall argued that capital punishment is excessive and that if the American people were fully informed as to the purposes of the death penalty, they would find it morally unacceptable. It is a violation of the Eighth Amendment, which forbids cruel and unusual punishment.

Study Questions

1. Does Justice Marshall believe the U.S. Constitution permits the death penalty?
2. Which amendment does he point to?
3. Does Marshall believe the American public has adequate information about the death penalty?
4. What are the two purposes that sustain the death penalty?
5. What does Marshall say about these two purposes?

IN *FURMAN V. GEORGIA* (1972) (concurring opinion), I set forth at some length my views on the basic issue presented to the Court in [this case]. The death penalty, I concluded, is a cruel and unusual punishment prohibited by the Eighth and Fourteenth Amendments. That continues to be my view.

I have no intention of retracing the "long and tedious journey" that led to my conclusion in *Furman*. My sole purposes here are to consider the suggestion that my conclusion in *Furman* has been undercut by developments since then, and briefly to evaluate the basis for my Brethren's holding that the extinction of life is a permissible form of punishment under the Cruel and Unusual Punishments Clause.

In *Furman* I concluded that the death penalty is constitutionally invalid for two reasons. First, the death penalty is excessive. And second, the American people, fully informed as to the purposes of the death penalty and its liabilities, would in my view reject it as morally unacceptable.

Since the decision in *Furman*, the legislatures of 35 states have enacted new statutes authorizing the imposition of the death sentence for certain crimes, and Congress has enacted a law providing the death penalty for air piracy resulting in death. I would be less than candid if I did not acknowledge that these developments have a significant bearing on a realistic assessment of the moral acceptability of the death penalty to the American people. But if the constitutionality of the death penalty turns, as I have urged, on the opinion of an *informed* citizenry, then even the enactment of new death statutes cannot be viewed as conclusive. In *Furman*, I observed that the American people are largely unaware of the information critical to a judgment on the morality of the death penalty, and concluded that if they were better informed they would consider it shocking, unjust, and unacceptable. A recent study, conducted after the enactment of the post-*Furman* statutes, has confirmed that the American people know little about the death penalty, and that the opinions of an informed public would differ significantly from those of a public unaware of the consequences and effects of the death penalty.

Even assuming, however, that the post-*Furman* enactment of statutes authorizing the death penalty renders the prediction of the views of an informed citizenry an uncertain basis for a constitutional decision, the enactment of those statutes has no bearing whatsoever on the conclusion that the death penalty is unconstitutional because it is excessive. An excessive penalty is invalid under the Cruel and

---

United States Supreme Court. 428 U.S. 153 (1976).

Unusual Punishments Clause "even though popular sentiment may favor" it. The inquiry here, then, is simply whether the death penalty is necessary to accomplish the legitimate legislative purposes in punishment, or whether a less severe penalty—life imprisonment—would do as well.

The two purposes that sustain the death penalty as nonexcessive in the Court's view are general deterrence and retribution. In *Furman*, I canvassed the relevant data on the deterrent effect of capital punishment. The state of knowledge at that point, after literally centuries of debate, was summarized as follows by a United Nations Committee:

> It is generally agreed between the retentionists and abolitionists, whatever their opinions about the validity of comparative studies of deterrence, that the data which now exist show no correlation between the existence of capital punishment and lower rates of capital crime.

The available evidence, I concluded in *Furman*, was convincing that "capital punishment is not necessary as a deterrent to crime in our society."
. . .

. . . The evidence I reviewed in *Furman* remains convincing, in my view, that "capital punishment is not necessary as a deterrent to crime in our society." The justification for the death penalty must be found elsewhere.

The other principal purpose said to be served by the death penalty is retribution. The notion that retribution can serve as a moral justification for the sanction of death finds credence in the opinion of my Brothers Stewart, Powell, and Stevens. . . . It is this notion that I find to be the most disturbing aspect of today's unfortunate [decision].

The concept of retribution is a multifaceted one, and any discussion of its role in the criminal law must be undertaken with caution. On one level, it can be said that the notion of retribution or reprobation is the basis of our insistence that only those who have broken the law be punished, and in this sense the notion is

quite obviously central to a just system of criminal sanctions. But our recognition that retribution plays a crucial role in determining who may be punished by no means requires approval of retribution as a general justification for punishment. It is the question whether retribution can provide a moral justification for punishment—in particular, capital punishment—that we must consider.

My Brothers Stewart, Powell, and Stevens offer the following explanation of the retributive justification for capital punishment:

> The instinct for retribution is part of the nature of man, and channeling that instinct in the administration of criminal justice serves an important purpose in promoting the stability of a society governed by law. When people begin to believe that organized society is unwilling or unable to impose upon criminal offenders the punishment they "deserve," then there are sown the seeds of anarchy—of self-help, vigilante justice, and lynch law.

This statement is wholly inadequate to justify the death penalty. As my Brother Brennan stated in *Furman*, "[t]here is no evidence whatever that utilization of imprisonment rather than death encourages private blood feuds and other disorders." It simply defies belief to suggest that the death penalty is necessary to prevent the American people from taking the law into their own hands.

In a related vein, it may be suggested that the expression of moral outrage through the imposition of the death penalty serves to reinforce basic moral values—that it marks some crimes as particularly offensive and therefore to be avoided. The argument is akin to a deterrence argument, but differs in that it contemplates the individual's shrinking from antisocial conduct, not because he fears punishment, but because he has been told in the strongest possible way that the conduct is wrong. This contention, like the previous one, provides no support for the death penalty. It is inconceivable that any individual concerned about conforming his conduct to what society says is "right" would fail to realize that murder is "wrong" if the penalty were simply life imprisonment.

The foregoing contentions—that society's expression of moral outrage through the imposition of the death penalty pre-empts the citizenry from taking the law into its own hands and reinforces moral values—are not retributive in the purest sense. They are essentially utilitarian in that they portray the death penalty as valuable because of its beneficial results. These justifications for the death penalty are inadequate because the penalty is, quite clearly I think, not necessary to the accomplishment of those results.

There remains for consideration, however, what might be termed the purely retributive justification for the death penalty—that the death penalty is appropriate, not because of its beneficial effect on society, but because the taking of the murderer's life is itself morally good. Some of the language of the opinion of my Brothers Stewart, Powell, and Stevens . . . appears positively to embrace this notion of retribution for its own sake as a justification for capital punishment. They state:

> [T]he decision that capital punishment may be the appropriate sanction in extreme cases is an expression of the community's belief that certain crimes are themselves so grievous an affront to humanity that the only adequate response may be the penalty of death.

They then quote with approval from Lord Justice Denning's remarks before the British Royal Commission on Capital Punishment:

> The truth is that some crimes are so outrageous that society insists on adequate punishment, because the wrong-doer deserves it, irrespective of whether it is a deterrent or not.

Of course, it may be that these statements are intended as no more than observations as to the popular demands that it is thought must be responded to in order to prevent anarchy. But the implication of the statements appears to me to be quite different—namely, that society's judgment that the murderer "deserves" death must be respected not simply because the preservation of order requires it, but because it is appropriate that society make the judgment and carry it out. It is this latter notion, in particular, that I consider to be fundamentally at odds with the Eighth Amendment. The mere fact that the community demands the murderer's life in return for the evil he has done cannot sustain the death penalty, for as Justices Stewart, Powell, and Stevens remind us, "the Eighth Amendment demands more than that a challenged punishment be acceptable to contemporary society." To be sustained under the Eighth Amendment, the death penalty must "compor[t] with the basic concept of human dignity at the core of the Amendment"; the objective in imposing it must be "[consistent] with our respect for the dignity of [other] men." Under these standards, the taking of life "because the wrongdoer deserves it" surely must fail, for such a punishment has as its very basis the total denial of the wrongdoer's dignity and worth.

The death penalty, unnecessary to promote the goal of deterrence or to further any legitimate notion of retribution, is an excessive penalty forbidden by the Eighth and Fourteenth Amendments. I respectfully dissent from the Court's judgment upholding the [sentence] of death imposed upon the [petitioner in this case].

For Further Reflection

1. What are Marshall's arguments against the death penalty? Do you think he is correct?
2. Do you agree with Marshall's statement that the American people, if fully informed, would find the death penalty morally unacceptable?

The Death Penalty Is Permissible   IX.68

BURTON LEISER

Burton Leiser is professor of philosophy at Pace University and the author of several books and articles in the areas of law, morality, and religion, among them *Liberty, Justice and Morals*, from which this selection is taken.

Leiser responds directly to Justice Marshall's claim that the death penalty constitutes a denial of the criminal's worth and dignity. Just the reverse, argues Leiser. The death penalty, based on retributivism, actually affirms the offender's dignity and worth, for it treats him or her as a fully responsible person. In the last part of the essay Leiser discusses the limits of the death penalty.

Study Questions

1. How did the residents of a midwestern town take the law into their own hands regarding a ferocious bully?
2. How is this incident relevant to the death penalty?
3. How does Leiser respond to Justice Marshall's dissent? (See Reading IX.67.)
4. Why, according to Leiser, isn't the death penalty "cruel and unusual"?
5. What does Leiser mean by *mens rea*?

RETRIBUTION

Vengeance and Vigilante Justice

IN HIS OPINION for the majority in *Gregg v. Georgia*, upholding the death penalty as constitutionally permissible, Justice Potter Stewart observed that capital punishment "is an expression of society's moral outrage at particularly offensive conduct," and that even though this function may be unappealing to many, "it is essential in an ordered society that asks its citizens to rely on legal processes rather than self-help to vindicate their wrongs." Without orderly means of imposing penalties upon offenders proportionate to what the aggrieved parties feel is deserved, society runs the risk of anarchy, vigilante justice, and lynch law. Even if retribution is not the dominant objective of the criminal law, he said, it is neither forbidden by the Constitution nor inconsistent with the dignity of men. Indeed, he went on, capital punishment "may be the appropriate sanction in extreme cases [as] an expression of the community's belief that certain crimes are themselves so grievous that the only adequate response may be the penalty of death." As Lord Justice Denning told the British Royal Commission on Capital Punishment, "Some crimes are so outrageous that society insists on capital punishment, because the wrong-doer deserves it, irrespective of whether it is a deterrent or not."

In a report on "vicious youth gangs" in Detroit, the *New York Times* quoted a black resident as saying, "If I know who steals or breaks

Reprinted from Liberty, Justice and Morals, *3rd ed. (New York: Macmillan Publishing Company, 1986) by permission.*

into my home, I'm going to get my gun. I'm going to hunt him. They can lock me up, but that's the only thing left. The police, they're not doing the job." Following another report on violent juvenile crime, a reader wrote to the *Times*, "Sudden death for a young man who does not want to surrender his wallet is cruel and unusual punishment. Why not let the punishment fit the crime, even if we have to amend the Constitution? The bleeding-heart mentality has caused too much bloodshed." And in a small town in the Midwest, after the residents concluded that the authorities would do nothing to relieve them of the violent behavior of a ferocious bully, a large group waylaid him and fatally shot him. Afterward, no one in the community could be found who was willing to cooperate with the authorities in their attempt to solve his murder. It is clear that their sense of justice was so outraged that they considered his death to be justifiable homicide, and not murder.

These sentiments are clearly consistent with those theories of government which declare that when people agree to lay down their rights to self-help, transferring their right to avenge themselves on those who harm them to their common sovereign (the government), the sovereign assumes the duty to see that justice is done. By conferring exclusive jurisdiction over criminal sanctions upon the government, the people prevent blood feuds from developing and bring order to the fixing of guilt and the exacting of retribution, which they would otherwise have done informally and summarily. As public frustration grows, as more and more innocent persons feel that they are direct or indirect victims of vicious criminals, and as more people become convinced that their demand for retribution will not be met by those into whose hands they placed the responsibility of exacting appropriate penalties from wrongdoers, the danger of vigilante justice grows. Thus, the move from orderly processes of exacting public retribution toward the arbitrary process of private vengeance gains greater momentum until it

is finally translated into action, as it was in that Midwestern town.

Retribution and Human Dignity.

In his dissent in *Gregg v. Georgia*, Justice Thurgood Marshall said that "it simply defies belief to suggest that the death penalty is necessary to prevent the American people from taking the law into their hands." He went on to assert that Lord Denning's contention that some crimes are so outrageous as to deserve the death penalty, regardless of its deterrent effects, is at odds with the Eighth Amendment. "The mere fact that the community demands the murderer's life for the evil he has done," he said, "cannot sustain the death penalty," for

> the Eighth Amendment demands more than that a challenged punishment be acceptable to contemporary society. To be sustained under the Eighth Amendment, the death penalty must [comport] with the basic concept of human dignity at the core of the Amendment; the objective in imposing it must be [consistent] with our respect for the dignity of [other] men. Under these standards, the taking of life "because the wrongdoer deserves it" surely must fail, for such a punishment has as its very basis the total denial of the wrongdoer's dignity and worth. The death penalty, unnecessary to promote the goal of deterrence or to further any legitimate notion of retribution, is an excessive penalty forbidden by the Eighth and Fourteenth Amendments.

Robert A. Pugsley has argued that the principle of retribution demands that the death penalty *not* be invoked. Capital punishment, he says, is symbolically the ultimate ostracization of an individual. It "emphatically transgresses the inviolability of the executed" and also "destroys those bonds of community which criminal punishment should strive to reaffirm." It is difficult, he says, to reconcile the "respect required for the individual's dignity and moral capacity," which he believes to be the essential point of retributivism, with the practice of execution. The executed criminal is not treated as a human being, but as an object to be discarded. Execution is dehumanizing. It is the "total negation of the moral worth of the person to be executed."

A more proper retributivist response, he says, may be derived from the following considerations:

> Even if [the convicted murderer] is sentenced to a life term without possibility of parole, he retains his membership in the community, and has had that status reaffirmed by the process of adjudication and punishment. His formal bond with the community *is* the punishment bond. It is that which signifies the community's recognition of him as a responsible moral agent and deserving of its respect, expressed of necessity through penalty and censure. He in turn accepts, if only tacitly, his punishment as justified; he acknowledges that he *ought* to feel guilty and suffer for his violative behavior. In the instance of the life term, particularly, there is this paradox: The community has "cared enough to give the very worst" punishment which, by abolishing the death penalty, it has permitted itself to impose.

As Justice Brennan put it in supporting the abolition of the death penalty, capital punishment treats members of the human race "as nonhumans, as objects to be toyed with and discarded." As such, it is inconsistent with the fundamental principle that "even the vilest criminal remains a human being possessed of common human dignity," whereas capital punishment is "uniquely degrading to human dignity."

CRUEL AND UNUSUAL PUNISHMENT

The Eighth Amendment, which proscribed cruel and unusual punishments, was not intended to outlaw capital punishment as such. This is particularly evident if one considers that the Fifth Amendment, written and adopted at the same time, provides that "no person shall be held to answer for a capital . . . crime, unless on a presentment or indictment of a Grand Jury," and that no person "shall be deprived of life, liberty, or property, without due process of law." It is evident, then, that with a grand jury indictment, and with

due process, a person may be deprived of his life, just as he may be deprived of his liberty or property. The cruel and unusual punishments that were banned by the Eighth Amendment were those that involved torture or a lingering death and those that were disproportionate to the offenses being punished. Later Courts have found, on the same basic principle, that *any* punishment for the mere status of being a drug addict is cruel and unusual, just as a single day in prison would be a cruel and unusual punishment for the "crime" of having a common cold.

The Court found that although the Eighth Amendment was dynamic, evolving over the years as public moral perceptions changed, capital punishment was not cruel and unusual as that term stands in the Constitution. As the liberal Chief Justice Earl Warren had once said, "the death penalty has been employed throughout our history, and, in a day when it is still widely accepted, it cannot be said to violate the constitutional concept of cruelty." Earlier Courts had found that that concept implied "something inhuman and barbarous, something more than the mere extinguishment of life," and that the suffering necessarily involved in any execution was not banned by the Eighth Amendment, though a cruel form of execution was. The Court noted that at least 35 state legislatures had enacted new statutes after *Furman*, providing for the death penalty, as had the Congress. It noted also that the people of California had amended their constitution, by referendum, so as to negate a decision by that state's highest court banning capital punishment. Juries, too, are a measure of public morality, and in March, 1976, more than 460 persons were subject to death sentences.

Arguing that the traditional justifications for capital punishment (deterrence and retribution) were sufficiently well founded, despite the reservations that some people have about them, to continue to play a role in penal policy, the Court concluded that the death penalty is not unreasonable, that it is consistent with contemporary moral standards, and that it is not a cruel and unusual punishment as that term is used in the Constitution. In view of the safeguards erected around defendants accused of capital offenses in Georgia and other states, the Court concluded that previous reservations about the death penalty being imposed in an arbitrary and capricious manner no longer applied and that it could therefore be imposed whenever similar safeguards existed.

THE LIMITS OF CAPITAL PUNISHMENT

The death penalty has historically been employed for such diverse offenses as murder, espionage, treason, kidnapping, rape, arson, robbery, burglary, and theft. Except for the most serious crimes, it is now agreed that lesser penalties are sufficient.

The distinction between first- and second-degree murder does not permit fine lines to be drawn between (for example) murder for hire and the killing of a husband by his jealous wife. Many murders committed in the United States are of a domestic nature—spouses or other close relatives becoming involved in angry scenes that end in homicide. Such crimes, usually committed in the heat of a momentary passion, seem inappropriate for the supreme penalty. Although they are premeditated in the legal sense (for it takes no more than an instant for a person to form the intent that is necessary for the legal test to be satisfied), there seems to be a great difference between such crimes and those committed out of a desire for personal gain or for political motives, between a crime committed in an instant of overwrought emotion and one carefully charted and planned in advance. It is reasonable, therefore, to suggest that the vast majority of murders not be regarded as capital crimes, because the penalty may be disproportionate to the crime committed.

Only the most heinous offenses against the state and against individual persons seem to deserve the ultimate penalty. If the claim that life is sacred has any meaning at all, it must be that no man may deliberately cause another to lose his life without some compelling justification.

Such a justification appears to exist when individuals or groups employ wanton violence against others in order to achieve their ends, whatever those ends might be. However appealing the cause, however noble the motives, the deliberate, systematic destruction of innocent human beings is one of the gravest crimes any person can commit and may justify the imposition of the harshest available penalty, consistent with the principles of humanity, decency, and compassion. Some penalties, such as prolonged torture, may in fact be worse than death, and may be deemed such even by the intended victims. Civilized societies reject them as being too barbarous and too cruel to the victims, and too dehumanizing to those who must carry them out.

Perpetrators of such crimes as genocide (the deliberate extermination of entire peoples, racial, religious, or ethnic groups) deserve a penalty no less severe than death on purely retributive grounds. Those who perpetrate major war crimes, crimes against peace, or crimes against humanity, deliberately and without justification plunging nations into violent conflicts that entail widespread bloodshed or causing needless suffering on a vast scale, deserve no less.

Because of the reckless manner in which they endanger the lives of innocent citizens and their clear intention to take human lives on a massive scale in order to achieve their ends, terrorists should be subject to the death penalty, on retributive grounds, on the ground that it serves as the ultimate form of incapacitation—guaranteeing that terrorists who are executed will never again deprive an innocent person of his life, and on the ground that no other penalty can reasonably be expected to serve as a deterrent to persons whose colleagues are likely to engage in further acts of terrorism in order to achieve their release from prison.

Major crimes against the peace, security, and integrity of the state constitute particularly heinous offenses, for they shake the very foundations upon which civilization rests and endanger the lives, the liberties, and the fundamental rights of all the people who depend upon the state for protection. Treason, espionage, and sabotage, particularly during times of great danger (as in time of war), ought to be punishable by death.

Murder for personal gain and murder committed in the course of the commission of a felony that is being committed for personal gain or out of a reckless disregard for the lives or fundamental rights and interests of potential victims ought to be punishable by death.

Murder committed by a person who is serving a life sentence ought to be punishable by death, both because of the enormity of the crime itself and because no other penalty is likely to deter such crimes.

Needless to say, if a person is so deranged as to be legally insane, neither death nor any other punishment is appropriate. The very concept of punishment entails the assumption that the person being punished had the capacity, at the time he committed the act for which he is being punished, to act or refrain from acting, and of behaving at least in a minimally rational way. A person who commits a homicide while insane has not, strictly speaking, committed a murder or, for that matter, any crime at all; for no crime *can* (logically or legally) be committed without *mens rea,* the *intention* or *will* to carry it out.

The mere fact, however, that a person has carried out a homicide in a particularly vile, wanton, or malicious way is not sufficient to establish that that person is insane, for such a fact is consistent with many other explanations (e.g., that the perpetrator, making shrewd and calculated judgments as to what would most likely enable him to succeed without being caught, concluded that it would be in his own best interests if the crime *appeared* to be the act of an insane person who happened to be in the neighborhood).

Bearing these caveats in mind, we may conclude that any murder (as opposed to a mere homicide) committed in a particularly vile, wanton, or malicious way ought to be punishable by death.

One of the principal justifications for the state's existence is the protection it offers those who come under its jurisdiction against violations of their fundamental rights. Those who are entrusted with the responsibility for carrying out the duties of administering the state's functions, enforcing its laws, and seeing that justice is done carry an onerous burden and are particularly likely to become the targets of hostile, malicious, or rebellious individuals or groups. Their special vulnerability entitles them to special protection. Hence, any person guilty of murdering a policeman, a fireman, a judge, a governor, a president, a lawmaker, or any other person holding a comparable position while that person is carrying out his official duties or because of the office he holds has struck at the very heart of government and thus at the foundations upon which the state and civilized society depend. The gravity of such a crime warrants imposition of the death penalty.

From the fact that some persons who bring about the deaths of fellow humans do so under conditions that just and humane men would consider sufficient to justify either complete exculpation or penalties less than death, it does not follow that all of them do. If guilt is clearly established beyond a reasonable doubt under circumstances that guarantee a reasonable opportunity for the defendant to confront his accusers, to cross-examine witnesses, to present his case with the assistance of professional counsel, and in general to enjoy the benefits of due process of law; if in addition he has been given the protection of laws that prevent the use of torture to extract confessions and is provided immunity against self-incrimination; if those who are authorized to pass judgment find there were no excusing or mitigating circumstances; if he is found to have committed a wanton, brutal, callous murder or some other crime that is subversive of the very foundations of an ordered society; and if, finally, the representatives of the people, exercising the people's sovereign authority have prescribed death as the penalty for that crime; then the judge and jury are fully justified in imposing that penalty, and the proper authorities are justified in carrying it out.

For Further Reflection

1. How does Leiser respond to Marshall's point that the death penalty is a denial of the wrongdoer's dignity and worth? Is his response cogent? Explain.

2. What are the moral limits of the use of the death penalty?

IX.69   No, the Death Penalty Is Not Morally Permissible

HUGO ADAM BEDAU

Hugo Adam Bedau is professor of philosophy at Tufts University and past president of the American League to Abolish Capital Punishment. He has been a leading spokesman for the abolitionist movement and is the editor of *The Death Penalty in America* (1982) and the author of *The Courts, the Constitution and Capital Punishment* (1977).

In this selection Bedau first draws an analogy between self-defense and the death penalty. Just as in defending ourselves we are to use no more force than is necessary to prevent harm, so in punishing criminals we are to use no more violence than is necessary to adequately punish the criminal. Bedau then argues that neither the deterrence nor the retributive argument for capital punishment is a good argument. He thinks that the literal application of the *lex talionis* is barbaric and that long-term imprisonment is adequate punishment.

Study Questions

1. What is the analogy between self-defense and capital punishment?
2. When does the law impose "a duty to retreat"?
3. According to Bedau, how much violence can justifiably be used to ward off aggression?
4. How does Bedau apply this idea of resentment to the issue of punishment for crime?
5. Does Bedau think that the threat of the death penalty deters would-be murderers better than the threat of long-term prison sentences does?
6. Would Bedau oppose the death penalty if there was good evidence that it did deter would-be murderers?
7. What are the two principles of retributive justice relevant to the death penalty controversy?
8. Why, according to Bedau, aren't we consistent in our application of the principle of retribution (the *lex talionis*)?
9. In what way does Bedau think that the application of the death penalty is biased? Why does this unfairness occur?

THE ANALOGY
WITH SELF-DEFENSE

CAPITAL PUNISHMENT, it is sometimes said, is to the body politic what self-defense is to the individual. If the latter is not morally wrong, how can the former be morally wrong? In order to assess the strength of this analogy, we need to inspect rather closely the morality of self-defense.

Except for the absolute pacifists, who believe it is morally wrong to use violence even to defend themselves or others from unprovoked and undeserved aggression, most of us believe that it is not morally wrong and may even be our moral duty to use violence to prevent aggression. The law has long granted persons the right to defend themselves against the unjust aggressions of others, even to the extent of killing a would-be assailant. It is very difficult to think of any convincing argument that would show it is never rational to risk the death of another in order to prevent death or grave injury to oneself or to others. Certainly self-interest dictates the legitimacy of self-defense. So does concern for the well-being of others. So also does justice. If it is unfair for one person to attempt violence on another, then it is hard to see why morality compels the victim to acquiesce in the attempt by another to hurt him or her, rather than to resist it, even if that resistance may involve injury to the assailant.

The foregoing account assumes that the person acting in self-defense is innocent of any provocation of the assailant. It also assumes that there is no alternative to victimization except resistance. In actual life, both assumptions—especially the second—are often false, because there may be a third alternative: escape, or removing oneself from the scene of danger and imminent aggression. Hence, the law imposes on us the so-called "duty to retreat." Before we use violence to resist aggression, we must try to get out of the way, lest unnecessary violence be used to resist aggression. Now suppose that unjust aggression is imminent, and there is no path open for escape. How much violence may justifiably be used to ward off aggression? The answer is: No more violence than is necessary to prevent the aggressive assault. Violence beyond that is unnecessary and therefore unjustified. We may restate the principle governing the use of violence in self-defense in terms of the use of "deadly force" by the police in the discharge of their duties. The rule is this: Use of deadly force is justified only to prevent loss of life in immediate jeopardy where a lesser use of force cannot reasonably be expected to save the life that is threatened.

In real life, violence in self-defense in excess of the minimum necessary to prevent aggression is often excusable. One cannot always tell what will suffice to deter or prevent becoming a victim, and the law looks with a certain tolerance upon the frightened and innocent would-be victim who turns upon a vicious assailant and inflicts a fatal injury even though a lesser injury would have been sufficient. What is not justified is deliberately using far more violence than is necessary to prevent becoming a victim. It is the deliberate, not the impulsive, use of violence that is relevant to the death-penalty controversy, since the death penalty is enacted into law and carried out in each case only after ample time to weigh alternatives. Notice that we are assuming that the act of self-defense is to protect one's person or that of a third party. The reasoning outlined here does not extend to the defense of one's property. Shooting a thief to prevent one's automobile from being stolen cannot be excused or justified in the way that shooting an assailant charging with a knife pointed at one's face can be. In terms of the concept of "deadly force," our criterion is that deadly force is never justified to prevent crimes against property or other violent crimes not immediately threatening the life of a person.

The rationale for self-defense as set out above illustrates two moral principles of great importance to our discussion. One is that if a life is to be risked, then it is better that it be the life of someone who is guilty (in our context, the initial assailant) rather than the life of someone who is not (the innocent potential victim). It is not fair to expect the innocent prospective victim to run the added risk of severe injury or death in order to avoid using violence in self-defense to the extent of possibly killing his assailant. It is only fair that the guilty aggressor run the risk.

The other principle is that taking life deliberately is not justified so long as there is any feasible alternative. One does not expect miracles, of course, but in theory, if shooting a burglar through the foot will stop the burglary and enable one to call the police for help, then there is no reason to shoot to kill. Likewise, if the burglar is unarmed, there is no reason to shoot at all. In actual life, of course, burglars are likely to be shot at by aroused householders because one does not know whether they are armed, and prudence may dictate the assumption that they are. Even so, although the burglar has no right to commit a felony against a person or a person's property, the attempt to do so does not give the chosen victim the right to respond in whatever way he or she pleases in retaliation, and then to excuse or justify such conduct on the ground that he or she was "only acting in self-defense." In these ways the law shows a tacit regard for the life of even a felon and discourages the use of unnecessary violence even by the innocent; morality can hardly do less.

THE DEATH PENALTY AS A CRIME DETERRENT

Determining whether the death penalty is an effective deterrent is even more difficult than determining its effectiveness as a crime preventive. In general, our knowledge about how penalties deter crimes and whether in fact they do— whom they deter, from which crimes, and under what conditions—is distressingly inexact. Most people nevertheless are convinced that punish-

ments do deter, and that the more severe a punishment is the better it will deter. For more than a generation, social scientists have studied the question of whether the death penalty is a deterrent and of whether it is a better deterrent than the alternative of imprisonment. Their verdict, while not unanimous, is fairly clear. Whatever may be true about the deterrence of lesser crimes by other penalties, the deterrence achieved by the death penalty for murder is not measurably greater than the deterrence achieved by long-term imprisonment. In the nature of the case, the evidence is quite indirect. No one can identify for certain any crimes that did not occur because the would-be offender was deterred by the threat of the death penalty and that would not have been deterred by a lesser threat. Likewise, no one can identify any crimes that did occur because the offender was not deterred by the threat of prison even though he would have been deterred by the threat of death. Nevertheless, such evidence as we have fails to show that the more severe penalty (death) is really a better deterrent than the less severe penalty (imprisonment) for such crimes as murder.

If the conclusion stated above is correct, and the death penalty and long-term imprisonment are equally effective (or ineffective) as deterrents to murder, then the argument for the death penalty on grounds of deterrence is seriously weakened. One of the moral principles identified earlier comes into play and requires us to reject the death penalty on moral grounds. This is the principle that unless there is a good reason for choosing a more rather than a less severe punishment for a crime, the less severe penalty is to be preferred. This principle obviously commends itself to anyone who values human life and who concedes that, all other things being equal, less pain and suffering is always better than more. Human life is valued in part to the degree that it is free of pain, suffering, misery, and frustration, and in particular that it is free of such experiences when they serve no purpose. If the death penalty is not a more effective deterrent than imprisonment, then its greater severity than imprisonment is gratuitous, purposeless suffering and deprivation.

A COST/BENEFIT ANALYSIS OF THE DEATH PENALTY

A full study of the costs and benefits involved in the practice of capital punishment would not be confined solely to the question of whether it is a better deterrent or preventive of murder than imprisonment. Any thoroughgoing utilitarian approach to the death-penalty controversy would need to examine carefully other costs and benefits as well, because maximizing the balance of social benefits over social costs is the sole criterion of right and wrong according to utilitarianism. Let us consider, therefore, some of the other costs and benefits to be calculated. Clinical psychologists have presented evidence to suggest that the death penalty actually incites some persons of unstable mind to murder others, either because they are afraid to take their own lives and hope that society will punish them for murder by putting them to death, or because they fancy that they, too, are killing with justification, analogous to the justified killing involved in capital punishment. If such evidence is sound, capital punishment can serve as a counterpreventive or an incitement to murder, and these incited murders become part of its social cost. Imprisonment, however, has not been known to incite any murders or other crimes of violence in a comparable fashion. (A possible exception might be found in the imprisonment of terrorists, which has inspired other terrorists to take hostages as part of a scheme to force the authorities to release their imprisoned comrades.) The risks of executing the innocent are also part of the social cost. The historical record is replete with innocent persons indicted, convicted, sentenced, and occasionally legally executed for crimes they did not commit, not to mention the guilty persons unfairly convicted, sentenced to death, and executed on the strength of perjured testimony, fraudulent evidence, subornation of jurors, and other violations of the civil rights and liberties of the accused. Nor is this all. The high costs of a capital trial, of the inevitable appeals, the costly methods of custody most prisons adopt for convicts on "death row," are among the straightforward economic costs that the death penalty incurs. No scientifically valid cost/benefit analysis of capital punishment has ever been conducted, and it is impossible to predict exactly what such a study would show. Nevertheless, based on such evidence as we do have, it is quite possible that a study of this sort would favor abolition of all death penalties rather than their retention.

WHAT IF EXECUTIONS DID DETER?

From the moral point of view, it is quite important to determine what one should think about capital punishment if the evidence clearly showed that the death penalty is a distinctly superior method of social defense by comparison with less severe alternatives. Kantian moralists, as we have seen, would have no use for such knowledge, because their entire case for the morality of the death penalty rests on the way it is thought to provide just retribution, not on the way it is thought to provide social defense. For a utilitarian, however, such knowledge would be conclusive. Those who follow Locke's reasoning would also be gratified, because they defend the morality of the death penalty both on the ground that it is retributively just and on the ground that it provides needed social defense.

What about the opponents of the death penalty, however? To oppose the death penalty in the face of incontestable evidence that it is an effective method of social defense seems to violate the moral principle that where grave risks are to be run, it is better that they be run by the guilty than by the innocent. Consider in this connection an imaginary world in which by executing a murderer the victim is invariably restored to life, whole and intact, as though the murder had never occurred. In such a miraculous world, it is hard to see how anyone could oppose the death penalty on moral grounds. Why shouldn't a murderer die if that will infallibly bring the victim back to life? What could possibly be morally wrong with taking the murderer's life under such conditions? It would turn the death penalty into an instrument of perfect restitution, and it would give a new and better meaning to *lex talionis,* "a life for a life." The whole idea is fanciful, of course, but it shows better than anything else how opposition to the death penalty cannot be both moral and wholly unconditional. If opposition to the death penalty is to be morally responsible, then it must be conceded that there are conditions (however unlikely) under which that opposition should cease.

But even if the death penalty were known to be a uniquely effective social defense, we could still imagine conditions under which it would be reasonable to oppose it. Suppose that in addition to being a slightly better preventive and deterrent than imprisonment, executions also have a slight incitive effect (so that for every ten murders an execution prevents or deters, it also incites another murder). Suppose also that the administration of criminal justice in capital cases is inefficient, unequal, and tends to secure convictions of murderers who least "deserve" to be sentenced to death (including some death sentences and a few executions of the innocent). Under such conditions, it would still be reasonable to oppose the death penalty, because on the facts supposed more (or not fewer) innocent lives are being threatened and lost by using the death penalty than would be risked by abolishing it. It is important to remember throughout our evaluation of the deterrence controversy that we cannot ever apply the principle that advises us to risk the lives of the guilty in order to save the lives of the innocent. Instead, the most we can do is weigh the risk for the general public against the execution of those who are *found* guilty by an imperfect system of criminal justice. These hypothetical factual assumptions illustrate the contingencies upon which the morality of opposition to the death penalty rests. And not only the morality

of opposition; the morality of any defense of the death penalty rests on the same contingencies. This should help us understand why, in resolving the morality of capital punishment one way or the other, it is so important to know, as well as we can, whether the death penalty really does deter, prevent, or incite crime, whether the innocent really are ever executed, and whether any of these things are likely to occur in the future.

HOW MANY GUILTY LIVES IS ONE INNOCENT LIFE WORTH?

The great unanswered question that utilitarians must face concerns the level of social defense that executions should be expected to achieve before it is justifiable to carry them out. Consider three possible situations: (1) At the level of a hundred executions per year, each additional execution of a convicted murderer reduces the number of murder victims by ten. (2) Executing every convicted murderer reduces the number of murders to 5,000 victims annually, whereas executing only one out of ten reduces the number to 5,001. (3) Executing every convicted murderer reduces the murder rate no more than does executing one in a hundred and no more than a random pattern of executions does.

Many people contemplating situation (1) would regard this as a reasonable trade-off: The execution of each further guilty person saves the lives of ten innocent ones. (In fact, situation (1) or something like it may be taken as a description of what most of those who defend the death penalty on grounds of social defense believe is true.) But suppose that, instead of saving 10 lives, the number dropped to 0.5, i.e., one victim avoided for each two additional executions. Would that be a reasonable price to pay? We are on the road toward the situation described in situation (2), where a drastic 90 percent reduction in the number of persons executed causes the level of social defense to drop by only 0.0002 percent. Would it be worth it to execute so many more murderers at the cost of such a slight decrease in social defense? How many guilty lives is one innocent life worth? In situation (3), of course, there is no basis for executing all convicted murderers, since there is no gain in social defense to show for each additional murderer executed after the first out of each hundred murderers has been executed. How, then, should we determine which out of each hundred convicted murderers is the unlucky one to be put to death?

It may be possible, under a complete and thoroughgoing cost/benefit analysis of the death penalty, to answer such questions. But an appeal merely to the moral principle that if lives are to be risked then let it be the lives of the guilty rather than the lives of the innocent will not suffice.... Nor will it suffice to agree that society deserves all the crime prevention and deterrence it can get by inflicting severe punishments. These principles are consistent with too many different policies. They are too vague by themselves to resolve the choice on grounds of social defense when confronted with hypothetical situations like those proposed above.

Since no adequate cost/benefit analysis of the death penalty exists, there is no way to resolve these questions from this standpoint at the present time. Moreover, it can be argued that we cannot have such an analysis without already establishing in some way or other the relative value of innocent lives versus guilty lives. Far from being a product of a cost/benefit analysis, this comparative evaluation of lives would have to be brought into any such analysis. Without it, no cost/benefit analysis can get off the ground. Finally, it must be noted that we have no knowledge at present that begins to approximate anything like the situation described above in (1), whereas it appears from the evidence we do have that we achieve about the same deterrent and preventive effects whether we punish murder by death or by imprisonment. Therefore, something like the situation in (2) or in (3) may be correct. If so, this

shows that the choice between the two policies of capital punishment and life imprisonment for murder will probably have to be made on some basis other than social defense; on that basis the two policies are equivalent and therefore equally acceptable.

CAPITAL PUNISHMENT AND RETRIBUTIVE JUSTICE

. . . There are two leading principles of retributive justice relevant to the capital-punishment controversy. One is the principle that crimes should be punished. The other is the principle that the severity of a punishment should be proportional to the gravity of the offense. (A corollary to the latter principle is the judgment that nothing so fits the crime of murder as the punishment of death.) Although these principles do not seem to stem from any concern over the worth, value, dignity, or rights of persons, they are moral principles of recognized weight and no discussion of the morality of capital punishment would be complete without them. Leaving aside all questions of social defense, how strong a case for capital punishment can be made on the basis of these principles? How reliable and persuasive are these principles themselves?

CRIME MUST BE PUNISHED

Given [a general rationale for punishment], there cannot be any dispute over this principle. In embracing it, of course, we are not automatically making a fetish of "law and order," in the sense that we would be if we thought that the most important single thing society can do with its resources is to punish crimes. In addition, this principle is not likely to be in dispute between proponents and opponents of the death penalty. Only those who completely oppose punishment for murder and other erstwhile capital crimes would appear to disregard this principle. Even defenders of the death penalty must admit that putting a convicted murderer in prison for years is a punishment of that criminal. The principle that crime must be punished is neutral to our controversy, because both sides acknowledge it and comply with it.

It is the other principle of retributive justice that seems to be a decisive one. Under the principle of retaliation, *lex talionis*, it must always have seemed that murderers ought to be put to death. Proponents of the death penalty, with rare exceptions, have insisted on this point, and it seems that even opponents of the death penalty must give it grudging assent. The strategy for opponents of the death penalty is to show either (a) that this principle is not really a principle of justice after all, or (b) that although it is, other principles outweigh or cancel its dictates. As we shall see, both these objections have merit.

IS MURDER ALONE TO BE PUNISHED BY DEATH?

Let us recall, first, that not even the Biblical world limited the death penalty to the punishment of murder. Many other nonhomicidal crimes also carried this penalty (e.g., kidnapping, witchcraft, cursing one's parents). In our own recent history, persons have been executed for aggravated assault, rape, kidnapping, armed robbery, sabotage, and espionage. It is not possible to defend any of these executions (not to mention some of the more bizarre capital statutes, like the one in Georgia that used to provide an optional death penalty for desecration of a grave) on grounds of just retribution. This entails that either such executions are not justified or that they are justified on some ground other than retribution. In actual practice, few if any defenders of the death penalty have ever been willing to rest their case entirely on the moral principle of just retribution as formulated in terms of "a life for a life." Kant seems to have been a conspicuous exception. Most defenders of the death penalty have implied by their willingness to use executions

to defend limb and property, as well as life, that they did not place much value on the lives of criminals when compared to the value of both lives and things belonging to innocent citizens.

ARE ALL MURDERS TO BE PUNISHED BY DEATH?

Our society for several centuries has endeavored to confine the death penalty to some criminal homicides. Even Kant took a casual attitude toward a mother's killing of her illegitimate child. ("A child born into the world outside marriage is outside the law . . . , and consequently it is also outside the protection of the law.")[1] In our society, the development nearly 200 years ago of the distinction between first- and second-degree murder was an attempt to narrow the class of criminal homicides deserving of the death penalty. Yet those dead owing to manslaughter, or to any kind of unintentional, accidental, unpremeditated, unavoidable, unmalicious killing are just as dead as the victims of the most ghastly murder. Both the law in practice and moral reflection show how difficult it is to identify all and only the criminal homicides that are appropriately punished by death (assuming that any are). Individual judges and juries differ in the conclusions they reach. The history of capital punishment for homicides reveals continual efforts, uniformly unsuccessful, to identify before the fact those homicides for which the slayer should die. Benjamin Cardozo, a justice of the United States Supreme Court fifty years ago, said of the distinction between degrees of murder that it was

> . . . so obscure that no jury hearing it for the first time can fairly be expected to assimilate and understand it. I am not at all sure that I understand it myself after trying to apply it for many years and after diligent study of what has been written in the books. Upon the basis of this fine distinction with its obscure and mystifying psychology, scores of men have gone to their death.[2]

Similar skepticism has been registered on the reliability and rationality of death-penalty statutes that give the trial court the discretion to sentence to prison or to death. As Justice John Marshall Harlan of the Supreme Court observed a decade ago,

> Those who have come to grips with the hard task of actually attempting to draft means of channeling capital sentencing discretion have confirmed the lesson taught by history. . . . To identify before the fact those characteristics of criminal homicide and their perpetrators which call for the death penalty, and to express these characteristics in language which can be fairly understood and applied by the sentencing authority, appear to be tasks which are beyond present human ability.[3]

The abstract principle that the punishment of death best fits the crime of murder turns out to be extremely difficult to interpret and apply.

If we look at the matter from the standpoint of the actual practice of criminal justice, we can only conclude that "a life for a life" plays little or no role whatever. Plea bargaining (by means of which one of the persons involved in a crime agrees to accept a lesser sentence in exchange for testifying against the others to enable the prosecutor to get them all convicted), even where murder is concerned, is widespread. Studies of criminal justice reveal that what the courts (trial or appellate) decide on a given day is first-degree murder suitably punished by death in a given jurisdiction could just as well be decided in a neighboring jurisdiction on another day either as second-degree murder or as first-degree murder but without the death penalty. The factors that influence prosecutors in determining the charge under which they will prosecute go far beyond the simple principle of "a life for a life." Nor can it be objected that these facts show that our society does not care about justice. To put it succinctly, either justice in punishment does not consist of retribution, because there are other principles of justice; or there are other moral considerations besides justice that must be honored; or retributive justice is not adequately expressed in the idea of "a life for a life."

IS DEATH SUFFICIENTLY RETRIBUTIVE?

Given the reality of horrible and vicious crimes, one must consider whether there is not a quality of unthinking arbitrariness in advocating capital punishment for murder as the retributively just punishment. Why does death in the electric chair or the gas chamber or before a firing squad or on a gallows meet the requirements of retributive justice? When one thinks of the savage, brutal, wanton character of so many murders, how can retributive justice be served by anything less than equally savage methods of execution for the murderer? From a retributive point of view, the oft-heard exclamation, "Death is too good for him!" has a certain truth. Yet few defenders of the death penalty are willing to embrace this consequence of their own doctrine.

The reason they do not and should not is that, if they did, they would be stooping to the methods and thus to the squalor of the murderer. Where criminals set the limits of just methods of punishment, as they will do if we attempt to give exact and literal implementation to *lex talionis*, society will find itself descending to the cruelties and savagery that criminals employ. But society would be deliberately authorizing such acts, in the cool light of reason, and not (as is often true of vicious criminals) impulsively or in hatred and anger or with an insane or unbalanced mind. Moral restraints, in short, prohibit us from trying to make executions perfectly retributive. Once we grant the role of these restraints, the principle of "a life for a life" itself has been qualified and no longer suffices to justify the execution of murderers.

Other considerations take us in a different direction. Few murders, outside television and movie scripts, involve anything like an execution. An execution, after all, begins with a solemn pronouncement of the death sentence from a judge, is followed by long detention in maximum security awaiting the date of execution, various appeals, perhaps a final sanity hearing, and then "the last mile" to the execution chamber itself. As the French writer Albert Camus remarked,

> For there to be an equivalence, the death penalty would have to punish a criminal who had warned his victim of the date at which he would inflict a horrible death on him and who, from that moment onward, had confined him at his mercy for months. Such a monster is not encountered in private life.[4]

DIFFERENTIAL SEVERITY DOES NOT REQUIRE EXECUTIONS

What, then, emerges from our examination of retributive justice and the death penalty? If retributive justice is thought to consist in *lex talionis*, all one can say is that this principle has never exercised more than a crude and indirect effect on the actual punishments meted out. Other principles interfere with a literal and single-minded application of this one. Some murders seem improperly punished by death at all; other murders would require methods of execution too horrible to inflict; in still other cases any possible execution is too deliberate and monstrous given the nature of the motivation culminating in the murder. Proponents of the death penalty rarely confine themselves to reliance on this principle of just retribution and nothing else, since they rarely confine themselves to supporting the death penalty only for all murders.

But retributive justice need not be thought to consist of *lex talionis*. One may reject that principle as too crude and still embrace the retributive principle that the severity of punishments should be graded according to the gravity of the offense. Even though one need not claim that life imprisonment (or any kind of punishment other than death) "fits" the crime of murder, one can claim that this punishment is the proper one for murder. To do this, the

schedule of punishments accepted by society must be arranged so that this mode of imprisonment is the most severe penalty used. Opponents of the death penalty need not reject this principle of retributive justice, even though they must reject a literal *lex talionis*.

EQUAL JUSTICE AND CAPITAL PUNISHMENT

During the past generation, the strongest practical objection to the death penalty has been the inequities with which it has been applied. As Supreme Court Justice William O. Douglas once observed, "One searches our chronicles in vain for the execution of any member of the affluent strata of this society."[5] One does not search our chronicles in vain for the crime of murder committed by the affluent. Every study of the death penalty for rape has confirmed that black male rapists (especially where the victim is a white female) are far more likely to be sentenced to death (and executed) than white male rapists. Half of all those under death sentence during 1976 and 1977 were black, and nearly half of all those executed since 1930 were black. All the sociological evidence points to the conclusion that the death penalty is the poor man's justice; as the current street saying has it, "Those without the capital get the punishment."

Let us suppose that the factual basis for such a criticism is sound. What follows for the morality of capital punishment? Many defenders of the death penalty have been quick to point out that since there is nothing intrinsic about the crime of murder or rape that dictates that only the poor or racial-minority males will commit it, and since there is nothing overtly racist about the statutes that authorize the death penalty for murder or rape, it is hardly a fault in the idea of capital punishment if in practice it falls with unfair impact on the poor and the black. There is, in short, nothing in the death penalty that requires it to be applied unfairly and with arbitrary or discriminatory results. It is at worst a fault in the system of administering criminal justice (and some, who dispute the facts cited above, would deny even this).

Presumably, both proponents and opponents of capital punishment would concede that it is a fundamental dictate of justice that a punishment should not be unfairly—inequitably or unevenly—enforced and applied. They should also be able to agree that when the punishment in question is the extremely severe one of death, then the requirement to be fair in using such a punishment becomes even more stringent. Thus, there should be no dispute in the death penalty controversy over these principles of justice. The dispute begins as soon as one attempts to connect these principles with the actual use of this punishment.

In this country, many critics of the death penalty have argued, we would long ago have got rid of it entirely if it had been a condition of its use that it be applied equally and fairly. In the words of the attorneys who argued against the death penalty in the Supreme Court during 1972, "It is a freakish aberration, a random extreme act of violence, visibly arbitrary and discriminatory—a penalty reserved for unusual application because, if it were usually used, it would affront universally shared standards of public decency."[6] It is difficult to dispute this judgment, when one considers that there have been in the United States during the past fifty years about half a million criminal homicides but only about 4,000 executions (all but 50 of which were of men).

We can look at these statistics in another way to illustrate the same point. If we could be assured that the 4,000 persons executed were the worst of the worst, repeated offenders without exception, the most dangerous murderers in captivity—the ones who had killed more than once and were likely to kill again, and the least likely to be confined in prison without imminent danger to other inmates and the staff—then one might accept half a million murders and a few thousand executions with a sense that

rough justice had been done. But the truth is otherwise. Persons are sentenced to death and executed not because they have been found to be uncontrollably violent, hopelessly poor parole and release risks, or for other reasons. Instead, they are executed for entirely different reasons. They have a poor defense at trial; they have no funds to bring sympathetic witnesses to court; they are immigrants or strangers in the community where they were tried; the prosecuting attorney wants the publicity that goes with "sending a killer to the chair"; they have inexperienced or overworked counsel at trial; there are no funds for an appeal or for a transcript of the trial record; they are members of a despised racial minority. In short, the actual study of why particular persons have been sentenced to death and executed does not show any careful winnowing of the worst from the bad. It shows that the executed were usually the unlucky victims of prejudice and discrimination, the losers in an arbitrary lottery that could just as well have spared them as killed them, the victims of the disadvantages that almost always go with poverty. A system like this does not enhance respect for human life; it cheapens and degrades it. However heinous murder and other crimes are, the system of capital punishment does not compensate for or erase those crimes. It only tends to add new injuries of its own to the catalogue of our inhumanity to each other.

NOTES

1. Immanuel Kant, *The Metaphysical Elements of Justice* (1797), tr. John Ladd, p. 106.

2. Benjamin Cardozo, "What Medicine Can Do for Law" (1928), reprinted in Margaret E. Hall, ed., *Selected Writings of Benjamin Nathan Cardozo* (1947), p. 204.

3. *McGautha v. California*, 402 U.S. 183 (1971), at p. 204.

4. Albert Camus, *Resistance, Rebellion, and Death* (1961), p. 199.

5. *Furman v. Georgia*, 408 U.S. 238 (1972), at pp. 251–252.

6. NAACP Legal Defense and Educational Fund, Brief for Petitioner in *Aikens v. California*, O.T. 1971, No. 68–5027, reprinted in Philip English Mackey, ed., *Voices Against Death: American Opposition to Capital Punishment*, 1787–1975 (1975), p. 288.

For Further Reflection

1. Is the death penalty "cruel and unusual punishment," thus meriting prohibition under the Eighth Amendment?
2. Do you agree with Bedau that the death penalty "only tends to add new injuries of its own to the catalogue of our inhumanity to each other"?
3. Do you think that long-term imprisonment is an adequate punishment for first-degree murder? Some people think that long-term imprisonment is worse punishment than execution. Do you agree? Explain.

IX.C   Do Animals Have Rights?

Every minute of the day, 24 hours a day, 100 animals are killed in laboratories in the United States. Fifty million animals used in experiments are put to death each year. Some die during testing of industrial and cosmetic products, some are killed after being force fed or after being tested for pharmaceutical drugs. Product testing on animals is required by government before the products are allowed for use by human beings.

Legal requirements that animals be anesthetized are circumvented in many experiments. Recently, at a major university, baboons were strapped down in boxlike vises and had specially designed helmets cemented to their skulls. Then a pneumatic device delivered calibrated blows to the helmet to determine its strength. The blows continued until the baboon's skull was fractured and the animal was brain damaged. Dogs are driven insane with electric shocks so that scientists can study the effects of insanity. Cats are deprived of sleep until they die. Primates have been restrained for months in steel chairs allowing no movement, and elephants have been given LSD to study aggression. Legs have been cut off mice to study how they walk on the stumps, and polar bears have been drowned in vats of crude oil to study the effect of oil spills in polar regions.

Kittens have been blinded, castrated, and rendered deaf so researchers could see what effect these incapacities would have on their sexual development. Civet cats are placed in small cages in dark rooms where the temperature is 110° F and confined there until they die. The musk that is scraped from their genitals once a day for as long as they can survive makes the scent of perfume last a bit longer after each application.

Neither is all well down on the farm. Factory farming with high-tech machinery has replaced free-range agriculture. Farmer McDonald doesn't visit his hens in barns to pick an egg from the comfortable nest. Now, as soon as chicks are hatched, they are placed in small cages. Between five and nine chickens are pressed together in cages about 18 inches by 10 inches where they cannot move around, with thin wire-mesh floors that hurt their feet. They are painfully debeaked so that they cannot attack each other in these unnatural quarters. In other chicken factories, the chickens are hung by their feet from conveyer belts that transport them through automatic throat-slicing machines. Three billion chickens are killed in the United States each year. Likewise, pigs and veal calves are kept in pens so small they cannot move or turn around and develop muscles. They are separated from their mothers so they cannot be suckled and are fed a diet low in iron so they will produce very tender meat.

Do animals have rights? Given the practices just described, do we have a responsibility to improve our behavior toward the animal kingdom? No one disagrees that we should not cause animals *unnecessary* suffering, but those who defend animal factories and animal experimentation argue that human need justifies these practices. On the other side of the controversy, animal rights advocates argue that animals should be accorded equal consideration with humans—that their specific needs should be taken seriously. If this were done, we would become vegetarians, cease to use leather, and cease all (or almost all) animal experimentation.

In our first reading, Peter Singer, the torchbearer of animal liberation, argues that animals should be treated with equal consideration as human beings. Singer says that if a nonhuman and a human are suffering, and we have only enough painkiller for one, it is not clear who should get the painkiller.

Carl Cohen argues in our second reading that the idea of rights does not apply to animals since "rights" is a concept appropriate only to members of the moral community and animals cannot make moral decisions. Humans are of far greater value than animals. Cohen readily admits that gratuitous suffering should be prohibited, but animal experimentation is needed to ameliorate human suffering, and, as such, it is justified.

The Case for Animal Liberation   IX.70

PETER SINGER

Peter Singer is a member of the philosophy department at Princeton University. His book, *Animal Liberation* (1975), from which this selection is taken, is one of the most influential books ever written on the subject and inaugurated the contemporary animal rights movement. Singer argues that animal liberation today is analogous to racial and gender justice. Just as people once thought it incredible that women should be treated as equal to men, or blacks as equal to whites, so now "speciesists" mock the idea that all animals should be given equal consideration. Singer defines "speciesism" as the prejudice (unjustified bias) that favors one's own species over every other. That which equalizes all sentient beings is our ability to suffer. In that, we and animals are equal and deserve equal respect.

Study Questions

1. What is the relationship between the women's rights movement, the civil rights movement, and the animal rights movement?
2. How does Singer define "speciesism"?
3. What is the basis of equality in humans and nonhumans?
4. Does equal consideration mean that we should treat animals exactly as we treat humans?
5. What changes would have to be made in our behavior if we took animal rights seriously?

THIS [VIEWPOINT] IS about the tyranny of human over nonhuman animals. This tyranny has caused and today is still causing an amount of pain and suffering that can only be compared with that which resulted from the centuries of tyranny by white humans over black humans. The struggle against this tyranny is a struggle as important as any of the moral and social issues that have been fought over in recent years.

Most readers will take what they have just read to be a wild exaggeration. Five years ago I myself would have laughed at the statements I have now written in complete seriousness. Five years ago I did not know what I know today.

. . .

CHANGING PREJUDICIAL ATTITUDES

A liberation movement demands an expansion of our moral horizons. Practices that were previously regarded as natural and inevitable come to be seen as the result of an unjustifiable prejudice. Who can say with any confidence that none of his or her attitudes and practices can legitimately be questioned? If we wish to avoid being numbered among the oppressors, we must be prepared to rethink all our attitudes to other groups, including the most fundamental. . . .

I believe that our present attitudes are based on a long history of prejudice and arbitrary discrimination. I argue that there can be no reason—except the selfish desire to preserve the privileges of the exploiting group—for refusing to extend the basic principle of equality of consideration to members of other species. I ask you to recognize that your attitudes to members of other species are a form of prejudice no less objectionable than prejudice about a person's race or sex. . . .

"Animal Liberation" may sound more like a parody of other liberation movements than a serious objective. The idea of "The Rights of Animals" actually was once used to parody the case for women's rights. When Mary Wollstonecraft, a forerunner of today's feminists, published her *Vindication of the Rights of Women* in 1792, her views were widely regarded as absurd, and before long an anonymous publication appeared entitled *A Vindication of the Rights of Brutes*. The author of this satirical work (now known to have been Thomas Taylor, a distinguished Cambridge philosopher) tried to refute Mary Wollstonecraft's arguments by showing that they could be carried one stage further. If the argument for equality was sound when applied to women, why should it not be applied to dogs, cats, and horses? The reasoning seemed to hold for these "brutes" too; yet to hold that brutes had rights was manifestly absurd; therefore the reasoning by which this conclusion had been reached must be unsound, and if unsound when applied to brutes, it must also be unsound when applied to women, since the very same arguments had been used in each case. . . .

One way in which we might reply is by saying that the case for equality between men and

Reprinted by permission of the author from Animal Liberation *(New York Review of Books, 1975).*

women cannot validly be extended to nonhuman animals. Women have a right to vote, for instance, because they are just as capable of making rational decisions about the future as men are; dogs, on the other hand, are incapable of understanding the significance of voting, so they cannot have the right to vote. There are many other obvious ways in which men and women resemble each other closely, while humans and animals differ greatly. So, it might be said, men and women are similar beings and should have similar rights, while humans and nonhumans are different and should not have equal rights.

EQUAL CONSIDERATION OF RIGHTS

The reasoning behind this reply to Taylor's analogy is correct up to a point, but it does not go far enough. There *are* important differences between humans and other animals, and these differences must give rise to *some* differences in the rights that each has. Recognizing this obvious fact, however, is no barrier to the case for extending the basic principle of equality to nonhuman animals. The differences that exist between men and women are equally undeniable, and the supporters of Women's Liberation are aware that these differences may give rise to different rights. Many feminists hold that women have the right to an abortion on request. It does not follow that since these same feminists are campaigning for equality between men and women they must support the right of men to have abortions too. Since a man cannot have an abortion, it is meaningless to talk of his right to have one. Since a dog can't vote, it is meaningless to talk of its right to vote. There is no reason why either Women's Liberation or Animal Liberation should get involved in such nonsense. The extension of the basic principle of equality from one group to another does not imply that we must treat both groups in exactly the same way, or grant exactly the same rights to both groups. Whether we should do so will depend on the nature of the members of the two groups. The basic principle of equality does not require equal or identical *treatment;* it requires equal *consideration.* Equal consideration for different beings may lead to different treatment and different rights. . . .

THE BASIS OF EQUALITY

Although, it may be said, humans differ as individuals there are no differences between the races and sexes *as such.* From the mere fact that a person is black or a woman we cannot infer anything about that person's intellectual or moral capacities. This, it may be said, is why racism and sexism are wrong. The white racist claims that whites are superior to blacks, but this is false—although there are differences among individuals, some blacks are superior to some whites in all of the capacities and abilities that could conceivably be relevant. The opponent of sexism would say the same: a person's sex is no guide to his or her abilities, and this is why it is unjustifiable to discriminate on the basis of sex. . . .

It is an implication of this principle of equality that our concern for others and our readiness to consider their interests ought not to depend on what they are like or on what abilities they may possess. Precisely what this concern or consideration requires us to do may vary according to the characteristics of those affected by what we do: concern for the well-being of a child growing up in America would require that we teach him to read; concern for the well-being of a pig may require no more than that we leave him alone with other pigs in a place where there is adequate food and room to run freely. But the basic element—the taking into account of the interests of the being, whatever those interests may be—must, according to the principle of equality, be extended to all beings, black or white, masculine or feminine, human or nonhuman. . . .

When in the 1850s the call for women's rights was raised in the United States, a remarkable black feminist named Sojourner Truth [spoke] . . . at a feminist convention:

They talk about this thing in the head; what do they call it? ["Intellect," whispered someone near by.] That's it. What's that got to do with women's rights or Negroes' rights? If my cup won't hold but a pint and yours holds a quart, wouldn't you be mean not to let me have my little half-measure full?

It is in accordance with this principle that the attitude that we may call "speciesism," by analogy with racism, must also be condemned. Speciesism—the word is not an attractive one, but I can think of no better term—is a prejudice or attitude of bias toward the interest of members of one's own species and against those members of other species. . . .

Many philosophers and other writers have proposed the principle of equal consideration of interests, in some form or other, as a basic moral principle; but not many of them have recognized that this principle applies to members of other species as well as to our own. Jeremy Bentham was one of the few who did realize this. In a forward-looking passage written at a time when black slaves had been freed by the French but in the British minions were still being treated in the way we now treat animals, Bentham wrote:

The day *may* come when the rest of the animal creation may acquire those rights which never could have been withholden from them but by the hand of tyranny. The French have already discovered that the blackness of the skin is no reason why a human being should be abandoned without redress to the caprice of a tormentor. It may one day come to be recognized that the number of the legs, the villosity of the skin, or the termination of the *os sacrum* are reasons equally insufficient for abandoning a sensitive being to the same fate. What else is it that should trace the insuperable line? Is it the faculty of reason, or perhaps the faculty of discourse? But a full-grown horse or dog is beyond comparison a more rational, as well as a more conversable animal, than an infant of a day or week or even a month, old. But suppose they were otherwise, what would it avail. The question is not, Can they *reason?* nor Can they *talk?* but, *Can they suffer?*

In this passage Bentham points to the capacity for suffering as the vital characteristic that gives a being the right to equal consideration. The capacity for suffering—or more strictly, for suffering and/or enjoyment or happiness—is not just another characteristic like the capacity for language or higher mathematics. Bentham is not saying that those who try to mark "the insuperable line" that determines whether the interests of a being should be considered happen to have chosen the wrong characteristic. By saying that we must consider the interests of all beings with the capacity for suffering or enjoyment Bentham does not arbitrarily exclude from consideration any interests at all—as those who draw the line with reference to the possession of reason or language do. The capacity for suffering and enjoyment is *a prerequisite for having interests at all,* a condition that must be satisfied before we can speak of interests in a meaningful way. It would be nonsense to say that it was not in the interests of a stone to be kicked along the road by a schoolboy. A stone does not have interests because it cannot suffer. Nothing that we can do to it could possibly make any difference to its welfare. A mouse, on the other hand, does have an interest in not being kicked along the road, because it will suffer if it is.

NO EXCUSE FOR IGNORING SUFFERING

If a being suffers there can be no moral justification for refusing to take that suffering into consideration. No matter what the nature of the being, the principle of equality requires that its suffering be counted equally with the like suffering—in so far as rough comparisons can be made—of any other being. If a being is not capable of suffering, or of experiencing enjoyment or happiness, there is nothing to be taken into account. So the limit of sentience (using the term as a convenient if not strictly accurate shorthand for the capacity to suffer and/or experience enjoyment) is the only defensible boundary of concern for the interests of others. To mark this boundary by some other characteristic like intelligence or rationality would be to mark it in an arbitrary manner. Why not choose some other characteristic, like skin color?

The racist violates the principle of equality by giving greater weight to the interests of members of his own race when there is a clash between their interests and the interests of those of another race. The sexist violates the principle of equality by favoring the interests of his own sex. Similarly the speciesist allows the interests of his own species to override the greater interests of members of other species. The pattern is identical in each case.

For Further Reflection

1. Has Singer convinced you that animals have rights equal to humans not to suffer needlessly? If Singer is correct, how should we change our social practices?

2. What are the broader implications of Singer's proposal? How far should we go with equal treatment of all animals? Should we kill bacteria or call the exterminator when termites are making a meal of our house? Does his theory lead to a reverence for all life in the manner of Albert Schweitzer?

Albert Schweitzer (1875–1965), the missionary doctor and Nobel Peace Prize winner, combined a Christian and animist view in advocating what he called "Reverence for Life."

I am life which wills to live, and I exist in the midst of life which wills to live. . . . A living world—and life view, informing all the facts of life, gushes forth from it continually, as from an eternal spring. A mystically ethical oneness with existence grows forth from it unceasingly. . . . Ethics thus consists in this, that I experience the necessity of practising the same reverence for life toward all will-to-live, as toward my own. Therein I have already the needed fundamental principle of morality. It is *good* to maintain and cherish life; it is evil to destroy and to check life. A man is really ethical only when he obeys the constraint laid on him to help all life which he is able to succour, and when he goes out of his way to avoid injuring anything living. He does not ask how far this or that life deserves sympathy as valuable in itself, nor how far it is capable of feeling. To him life as such is sacred. . . . He tears no leaf from its tree, breaks off no flower, and is careful not to crush any insect as he walks. If he works by lamplight on a summer evening, he prefers to keep the window shut and to breathe stifling air, rather than to see insect after insect fall on his table with singed and sinking wings.

If he goes out into the street after a rainstorm and sees a worm which has strayed there, he reflects that it will certainly dry up in the sunshine, if it does not quickly regain the damp soil into which it can creep, and so he helps it back from the deadly paving stones into the lush grass. Should he pass by an insect which has fallen into a pool, he spares the time to reach it a leaf or stalk on which it may clamber and save itself.

Ethics is, in its unqualified form, extended responsibility with regard to everything that has life.

How do you react to this passage? Is it consistent with Singer's idea of liberation? If the ideas are not exactly the same, where do they differ? What do you think of the reverence for life principle?

IX.71   The Case Against Animal Rights

CARL COHEN

Carl Cohen is a professor at the University of Michigan. Cohen argues that while humans have a duty to treat animals humanely, animals cannot have rights. The idea of rights does not apply to animals since "rights" is a concept appropriate only to members of the moral community and animals cannot make moral decisions. Humans are of far greater value than animals, and the result of not using animals for medical experimentation would be greater human suffering.

Study Questions

1. Why don't animals have rights? What does one need to have in order to have moral rights?
2. What are some philosophical views on the attributes necessary for moral capability?
3. What does Kant say that makes humans members of the moral community?
4. Why does Cohen defend speciesism?
5. What are the "absurd consequences" of the animal rights position?

USING ANIMALS AS RESEARCH subjects in medical investigations is widely condemned on two grounds: first, because it wrongly violates the *rights* of animals, and second, because it wrongly imposes on sentient creatures much avoidable *suffering*. Neither of these arguments is sound. The first relies on a mistaken understanding of rights; the second relies on a mistaken calculation of consequences. Both deserve definitive dismissal.

WHY ANIMALS HAVE NO RIGHTS

A right, properly understood, is a claim, or potential claim, that one party may exercise against another. The target against whom such a claim may be registered can be a single person, a group, a community, or (perhaps) all human-

kind. The content of rights claims also varies greatly: repayment of loans, nondiscrimination by employers, noninterference by the state, and so on. To comprehend any genuine right fully, therefore, we must know *who* holds the right, *against whom* it is held, and *to what* it is a right.

Alternative sources of rights add complexity. Some rights are grounded in constitution and law (e.g., the right of an accused to trial by jury); some rights are moral but give no legal claims (e.g., my right to your keeping the promise you gave me); and some rights (e.g., against theft or assault) are rooted both in morals and in law.

The differing targets, contents, and sources of rights, and their inevitable conflict, together weave a tangled web. Notwithstanding all such complications, this much is clear about rights in general: they are in every case claims, or potential claims, within a community of moral agents.

Reprinted from The New England Journal of Medicine *vol. 315, pp. 864–870 by permission of the editor.*

Rights arise, and can be intelligibly defended, only among beings who actually do, or can, make moral claims against one another. Whatever else rights may be, therefore, they are necessarily human; their possessors are persons, human beings.

The attributes of human beings from which this moral capability arises have been described variously by philosophers, both ancient and modern: the inner consciousness of a free will (Saint Augustine); the grasp, by human reason, of the binding character of moral law (Saint Thomas Aquinas); the self-conscious participation of human beings in an objective ethical order (G. W. F. Hegel); human membership in an organic moral community (F. H. Bradley); the development of the human self through the consciousness of other moral selves (G. H. Mead); and the underivative, intuitive cognition of the rightness of an action (H. A. Prichard). Most influential has been Immanuel Kant's emphasis on the universal human possession of a uniquely moral will and the autonomy its use entails. Humans confront choices that are purely moral; humans—but certainly not dogs or mice—lay down moral laws, for others and for themselves. Human beings are self-legislative, morally *autonomous.*

Animals (that is, nonhuman animals, the ordinary sense of that word) lack this capacity for free moral judgment. They are not beings of a kind capable of exercising or responding to moral claims. Animals therefore have no rights, and they can have none. This is the core of the argument about the alleged rights of animals. The holders of rights must have the capacity to comprehend rules of duty, governing all including themselves. In applying such rules, the holders of rights must recognize possible conflicts between what is in their own interest and what is just. Only in a community of beings capable of self-restricting moral judgments can the concept of a right be correctly invoked.

Humans have such moral capacities. They are in this sense self-legislative, are members of communities governed by moral rules, and do possess rights. Animals do not have such moral capacities. They are not morally self-legislative, cannot possibly be members of a truly moral community, and therefore cannot possess rights. In conducting research on animal subjects, therefore, we do not violate their rights, because they have none to violate. . . .

Genuinely moral acts have an internal as well as an external dimension. Thus, in law, an act can be criminal only when the guilty deed, the *actus reus,* is done with a guilty mind, *mens rea.* No animal can ever commit a crime; bringing animals to criminal trial is the mark of primitive ignorance. The claims of moral rights are similarly inapplicable to them. Does a lion have a right to eat a baby zebra? Does a baby zebra have a right not to be eaten? Such questions, mistakenly invoking the concept of right where it does not belong, do not make good sense. Those who condemn biomedical research because it violates "animal rights" commit the same blunder.

IN DEFENSE OF SPECIESISM

Abandoning reliance on animal rights, some critics resort instead to animal sentience—their feelings of pain and distress. We ought to desist from the imposition of pain insofar as we can. Since all or nearly all experimentation on animals does impose pain and could be readily forgone, say these critics, it should be stopped. The ends sought may be worthy, but those ends do not justify imposing agonies on humans, and by animals the agonies are felt no less. The laboratory use of animals (these critics conclude) must therefore be ended—or at least very sharply curtailed.

Argument of this variety is essentially utilitarian, often expressly so; it is based on the calculation of the net product, in pains and pleasures, resulting from experiments on animals. Jeremy Bentham, comparing horses and dogs with other sentient creatures, is thus commonly quoted: "The question is not, Can they reason? nor Can they talk? but, Can they suffer?"

BIOMEDICAL RESEARCH MUST STILL PROCEED

Animals certainly can suffer and surely ought not to be made to suffer needlessly. But in inferring, from these uncontroversial premises, that biomedical research causing animal distress is largely (or wholly) wrong, the critic commits two serious errors. The first error is the assumption, often explicitly defended, that all sentient animals have equal moral standing. Between a dog and a human being, according to this view, there is no moral difference; hence the pains suffered by dogs must be weighed no differently from the pains suffered by humans. To deny such equality, according to this critic, is to give unjust preference to one species over another; it is "speciesism." The most influential statement of this moral equality of species was made by Peter Singer:

> The racist violates the principle of equality by giving greater weight to the interests of members of his own race when there is a clash between their interests and the interests of those of another race. The sexist violates the principle of equality by favoring the interests of his own sex. Similarly the speciesist allows the interests of his own species to override the greater interests of members of other species. The pattern is identical in each case.

This argument is worse than unsound; it is atrocious. It draws an offensive moral conclusion from a deliberately devised verbal parallelism that is utterly specious. Racism has no rational ground whatever. Differing degrees of respect or concern for humans for no other reason than that they are members of different races is an injustice totally without foundation in the nature of the races themselves. Racists, even if acting on the basis of mistaken factual beliefs, do grave moral wrong precisely because there is no morally relevant distinction among the races. The supposition of such differences has led to outright horror. The same is true of the sexes, neither sex being entitled by right to greater respect or concern than the other. No dispute here.

Between species of animate life, however—between (for example) humans on the one hand and cats or rats on the other—the morally relevant differences are enormous, and almost universally appreciated. Humans engage in moral reflection; humans are morally autonomous; humans are members of moral communities, recognizing just claims against their own interest. Human beings do have rights; theirs is a moral status very different from that of cats or rats.

SPECIESISM IS NECESSARY

I am a speciesist. Speciesism is not merely plausible; it is essential for right conduct, because those who will not make the morally relevant distinctions among species are almost certain, in consequence, to misapprehend their true obligations. The analogy between speciesism and racism is insidious. Every sensitive moral judgment requires that the differing natures of the beings to whom obligations are owed be considered. If all forms of animate life—or vertebrate animal life—must be treated equally, and if therefore in evaluating a research program the pains of a rodent count equally with the pains of a human, we are forced to conclude (1) that neither humans nor rodents possess rights, or (2) that rodents possess all the rights that humans possess. Both alternatives are absurd. Yet one or the other must be swallowed if the moral equality of all species is to be defended. . . .

Those who claim to base their objection to the use of animals in biomedical research on their reckoning of the net pleasures and pains produced make a second error, equally grave. Even if it were true—as it is surely not—that the pains of all animate beings must be counted equally, a cogent utilitarian calculation requires that we weigh all the consequences of the use, and of the nonuse, of animals in laboratory research. Critics relying (however mistakenly) on animal rights may claim to ignore the beneficial results of such research, rights being trump cards to which interest and advantage must give away. But an argument that is explicitly framed in terms of interest and benefit for all over the long run must attend also to the disadvanta- geous consequences of not using animals in re- search, and to all the achievements attained and attainable only through their use. The sum of the benefits of their use is utterly beyond quan- tification. The elimination of horrible disease, the increase of longevity, the avoidance of great pain, the saving of lives, and the improvement of the quality of lives (for humans and for animals) achieved through research using animals is so in- calculably great that the argument of these crit- ics, systematically pursued, establishes not their conclusion but its reverse: to refrain from using animals in biomedical research is, on utilitarian ground, morally wrong.

When balancing the pleasures and pains re- sulting from the use of animals in research, we must not fail to place on the scales the terrible pains that would have resulted, would be suf- fered now, and would long continue had ani- mals not been used. Every disease eliminated, every vaccine developed, every method of pain relief devised, every surgical procedure in- vented, every prosthetic device implanted—in- deed, virtually every modern medical therapy is due, in part or in whole, to experimentation using animals. Nor may we ignore, in the bal- ancing process, the predictable gains in human (and animal) well-being that are probably achievable in the future but that will not be achieved if the decision is made now to desist from such research or to curtail it. . . .

THE ABSURD CONSEQUENCES OF ANIMAL RIGHTS

Finally, inconsistency between the profession and the practice of many who oppose research using animals deserves comment. This frankly *ad hominem* observation aims chiefly to show that a coherent position rejecting the use of ani- mals in medical research imposes costs so high as to be intolerable even to the critics themselves.

One cannot coherently object to the killing of animals in biomedical investigations while con- tinuing to eat them. Anesthetics and thoughtful animal husbandry render the level of actual ani- mal distress in the laboratory generally lower than that in the abattoir. So long as death and discomfort do not substantially differ in the two contexts, the consistent objector must not only refrain from all eating of animals but also protest as vehemently against others eating them as against others experimenting on them. No less vigorously must the critic object to the wearing of animal hides in coats and shoes, to employ- ment in any industrial enterprise that uses animal parts, and to any commercial development that will cause death or distress to animals. . . .

Scrupulous vegetarianism, in matters of food, clothing, shelter, commerce, and recreation, and in all other spheres, is the only fully coherent po- sition the critic may adopt. At great human cost, the lives of fish and crustaceans must also be protected, with equal vigor, if speciesism has been forsworn. A very few consistent critics adopt this position. It is the *reductio ad absur- dum* of the rejection of moral distinctions be- tween animals and human beings.

For Further Reflection

1. Compare Cohen's argument against animal rights with Singer's argument for animal rights. Which, in your opinion, is closer to the truth? Explain.

2. Examine Cohen's "absurd consequences." How absurd do you think they really are?

3. Cohen doesn't address the problem of suffering caused by factory farming. Given his assumptions, how might he respond to the facts itemized in the introduction to this section? How do you react to them?

IX.D   Is Affirmative Action Morally Justified?

Hardly a week goes by that the subject of Affirmative Action does not come up. Whether in the form of preferential hiring, nontraditional casting, quotas, "goals and time tables," minority scholarships, race-norming, reverse discrimination, or employment of members of underutilized groups, the issue confronts us as a terribly perplexing problem. Affirmative action was one of the issues that divided the Democratic and Republican parties during the 1996 election, the Democrats supporting it ("Mend it, don't end it") and the Republicans opposing it ("affirmative action is reverse racism"). During a general election (November 7, 1996) California voters by a 55 percent to 45 percent vote approved Proposition 209 (called the "California Civil Rights Initiative") which made it illegal to discriminate on the basis of race or gender, hence ending Affirmative Action in California. The Supreme Court recently refused to rule on the appeal, thus leaving it to the individual states to decide how they will deal with this issue. Both sides have reorganized for a renewed battle.

After a long legacy of egregious, unjust racial discrimination, the forces of civil justice came to a head during the decade of 1954–1964. In the 1954 U.S. Supreme Court decision, *Brown v. Board of Education*, racial segregation was declared inherently and unjustly discriminatory, a violation of the constitutional right to equal protection. In 1964 Congress passed the Civil Rights Act, which banned all forms of racial discrimination.

> Title VII, Section 703(a) Civil Rights Act of 1964: It shall be an unlawful practice for an employer — (1) to fail or refuse to hire or to discharge any individual or otherwise to discriminate against any individual with respect to his compensation, terms, conditions, or privileges of employment, because of such individual's race, color, sex, or national origin; or
>
> (2) to limit, segregate, or classify his employees or applicants for employment in any way which would deprive or tend to deprive any individual of employment opportunities or otherwise adversely affect his status as an employee because of such individual's race, color, religion, sex, or national origin. {42 U.S.C. 2000e–2(a).}
>
> . . . Nothing contained in this title shall be interpreted to require any employer . . . to grant preferential treatment to any individual or to any group . . . on account of an imbalance which may exist with respect to the total numbers or percentage of persons of any race . . . employed by any employer . . . in comparison with the total or percentage of persons of such race . . . in any community, State, section, or other area, or in the available work force in any community, State, section, or other area. {42 U.S.C. 2000e - 2(j)}

The Civil Rights Act of 1964 espouses a meritocratic philosophy, calling for equal opportunity and prohibiting reverse discrimination as just another form of prejudice. The Voting Rights Act (1965) was passed, and Jim Crow laws throughout the South were overturned. Schools were integrated and public accommodations opened to all. Branch Rickey's promotion of Jackie Robinson from the minor leagues in 1947 to play for the Brooklyn Dodgers was seen as the paradigm case of this kind of equal opportunity—the successful recruiting of a deserving person.

But it was soon noticed that the elimination of discriminatory laws was not producing the fully integrated society that leaders of the civil rights movement had envisioned. Eager to improve the situation, in 1965 President Johnson went beyond equal opportunity to Affirmative Action. He issued the famous Executive Order 11246 in which the Department of Labor was enjoined to issue government contracts with construction companies on the basis of race. That is, it would engage in reverse discrimination to make up for the evils of the past. He explained the act in terms of the shackled runner analogy:

> Imagine a hundred yard dash in which one of the two runners has his legs shackled together. He has progressed 10 yards, while the unshackled runner has gone 50 yards. How do they rectify the situation? Do they merely remove the shackles and allow the race to proceed? Then they could say that "equal opportunity" now prevailed. But one of the runners would still be forty yards ahead of the other. Would it not be the better part of justice to allow the previously shackled runner to make-up the forty yard gap; or to start the race all over again? That would be affirmative action towards equality. (President Lyndon Johnson in 1965, inaugurating the Affirmative Action Policy of Executive Order 11246).

In 1967 President Johnson issued Executive Order 11375 extending Affirmative Action (henceforth "AA") to women. Note here that AA originates in the executive branch of government. Until the Kennedy-Hawkins Civil Rights Act of 1990, AA policy was never put to a vote or passed by Congress. Gradually, the benefits of AA were extended to Hispanics, native Americans, Asians, and handicapped people. The policy has been with us in one form or another ever since.

I. DEFINITIONS

First let me define my terms:

Discrimination is simply judging one thing to differ from another on the basis of some criterion. "Discrimination" is essentially a good quality, having reference to our ability to make distinctions. As rational and moral agents we need to make proper distinctions. To be rational is to discriminate between good and bad arguments, and to think morally is to discriminate between reasons based on valid principles and those based on invalid ones. What needs to be distinguished is the difference between rational and moral discrimination, on the one hand, and irrational and immoral discrimination, on the other hand.

Prejudice is a discrimination based on irrelevant grounds. It might simply be an attitude that never surfaces in action, or it can cause prejudicial actions. A prejudicial discrimination in action is immoral if it denies someone a fair deal. So discrimination on the basis of race or sex, where these are not relevant for job performance, is unfair. Likewise, one can act prejudicially in applying a relevant criterion on insufficient grounds, as where I apply the criterion of being a hard worker but then assume, on insufficient evidence, that the Black man who applies for the job is not a hard worker.

There is a difference between *prejudice* and *bias*. Bias signifies a tendency towards one thing rather than another where the evidence is incomplete or based on nonmoral factors. For example, you might have a bias towards blondes and I towards red-heads. But prejudice is an attitude (or action) where unfairness is present—where one *should* know or do better, as in the case where I give people jobs simply because they are red-heads. Bias implies ignorance or incomplete knowledge, whereas prejudice is deeper, involving a moral failure—usually a failure to pay attention to the evidence. But note that calling people racist or sexist without good evidence is also an act of prejudice.

Equal Opportunity is offering everyone a fair chance at the best positions that society has at its disposal. Only native aptitude and effort should be decisive in the outcome, not factors of race, sex or special favors.

Affirmative Action is the effort to rectify past injustice as well as to produce a situation closer to the ideal of equal opportunity by special policies. Put this way, it is Janus-faced or ambiguous, having both a backward-looking and a forward-looking feature. The backward-looking feature is its attempt to correct and compensate for past injustice. This aspect of Affirmative Action is strictly deontological. The forward-looking feature is its implicit ideal of a society free from prejudice, where one's race or gender is irrelevant to basic opportunities. This is both deontological and utilitarian: deontological in that it aims at treating people according to their merits or needs; utilitarian in that a society perceived as fair will be a happier society.

When we look at a social problem from a backward-looking perspective we need to determine who has committed or benefited from a wrongful or prejudicial act and to determine who deserves compensation for that act.

When we look at a social problem from a forward-looking perspective we need to determine what a just society (one free from prejudice) would look like and how to obtain that kind of society. The forward-looking aspect of Affirmative Action is paradoxically race-conscious, since it uses race to bring about a society which is not race-conscious, which is color-blind (in the morally relevant sense of this term).

In our first reading Albert Mosley sets forth both backward looking (compensatory) and forward looking arguments in favor of Affirmative Action. He meets several objections to his position. In the second article, I offer eight arguments why I think strong Affirmative Action is morally wrong.

IX.72   The Case for Affirmative Action

ALBERT MOSLEY

Albert Mosley is professor of philosophy at Smith College. In this essay from his book (with Nicholas Capaldi) *Affirmative Action: Social Justice or Unfair Preference?* (1997), he argues that governments have *prima facie* moral obligations to recompense groups and individuals for liabilities they have incurred. He develops a backward-looking argument of restitution to those unjustly oppressed as well as a forward-looking argument that aims at rectifying any ongoing injustice.

Study Questions

1. What is Mosley's basic *Backward Looking* justification of Affirmative Action?
2. Does Mosley think Affirmative Action involves mainly promoting equal opportunity or does it also involve reparations?
3. How does Judith Jarvis Thomson, whom Mosley quotes, support Affirmative Action?
4. Does Mosley think that the resentment White males feel at being passed over in favor of Affirmative Action candidates is justified?
5. Does Mosley believe that we should work for equal results in employment?
6. Does Mosley believe that compensation belongs to groups as well as individuals? If so, why?
7. What is Mosley's forward-looking justification of Affirmative Action?
8. How does he deal with Scalia and Posner's charge that the members of minority groups who receive preferential treatment will often be those who have not been the victims of discrimination, while the nonminority people who are excluded from preferences are often neither the culprits nor beneficiaries of discrimination?
9. Does Mosley think that race, sex and social background are morally irrelevant?
10. How does Mosley conclude his essay?

THERE ARE MANY INTERESTS that governments pursue—maximization of social production; equitable distribution of rights, opportunities, and services; social safety and cohesion; restitution—and those interests may conflict in various situations. In particular, governments as well as their constituents have a *prima facie* obligation to satisfy the liabilities they incur. One such liability derives from past and present unjust exclusionary acts depriving minorities and women of opportunities and amenities made available to other groups.

[BACKWARD-LOOKING JUSTIFICATION OF AFFIRMATIVE ACTION]

"Backward looking" arguments defend affirmative action as a matter of *corrective justice,* where paradigmatically the harm doer is to make restitution to the harmed so as to put the harmed in the position the harmed most likely would have occupied had the harm not occurred. An important part of making restitution is the acknowledgment it provides that the actions causing injury were unjust and such actions will be curtailed and corrected. In this regard Bernard Boxill writes:

> Without the acknowledgment of error, the injurer implies that the injured has been treated in a manner that befits him. . . . In such a case, even if the unjust party repairs the damage he has caused.. nothing can be demanded on legal or moral grounds, and the repairs made are gratuitous. . . . Justice requires that we acknowledge that this treatment of others can be required of us; thus, where an unjust injury has occurred, the injurer reaffirms his belief in the other's equality by conceding that repair can be demanded of him, and the injured rejects the

Reprinted by permission of Rowman & Littlefield Publishers and the author. Footnotes have been deleted.

allegation of his inferiority . . . by demanding reparation.

This view is based on the idea that restitution is a basic moral principle that creates obligations that are just as strong as the obligations to maximize wealth and distribute it fairly. If x has deprived y of opportunities y had a right not to be deprived of in this manner, then x is obligated to return y to the position y would have occupied had x not intervened; x has this obligation irrespective of other obligations x may have. This can be illustrated another way as follows: Suppose y is deprived of t by x and we determine retroactively that y had a right to t. Then x has an obligation to return t to y or provide y with something else of equal value to t. In other words, x has an obligation to correct his or her effect on y, and restore y's losses.

A slightly different case illustrates a further point. Suppose x deprives y of the use of y's car for a day without y's consent and suppose further that x's use of the car produces $100 while y's use of the car would have produced only $50. In so far as an act is justified if it increases social utility, x is justified in having taken y's car. At most, x need only provide y with the value ($50) that y would have received if x had not taken the car. If y would not have used the car at all, presumably x would owe y only the depreciated value of the car resulting from its extra use. But though x increases social utility, x also deprives y of the exclusive use of y's private property. And to the extent that we consider the right of exclusive use important, it is wrong for x to profit from benefits that derive from x's enrichment through a violation of y's rights.

A further application of this principle involves the case where x is not a person but an entity, like a government or a business. If y was unjustly deprived of employment when firm F hired z instead of y because z was White and y Black, then y has a right to be made whole, that is, brought to the position he/she would have achieved had that deprivation not occurred. Typically, this involves giving y a position at least as good as the one he/she would have acquired originally and

issuing back pay in the amount that y would have received had he/she been hired at the time of the initial attempt.

Most critics of preferential treatment acknowledge the applicability of principles of restitution to individuals in specific instances of discrimination. The strongest case is where y was as or more qualified than z in the initial competition, but the position was given to z because y was Black and z was White. Subsequently, y may not be as qualified for an equivalent position as some new candidate z', but is given preference because of the past act of discrimination by F that deprived y of the position he or she otherwise would have received.

Some critics have suggested that, in such cases, z' is being treated unfairly. For z', as the most qualified applicant, has a right not to be excluded from the position in question purely on the basis of race; and y has a right to restitution for having unjustly been denied the position in the past. But the dilemma is one in appearance only. For having unjustly excluded y in the past, the current position that z' has applied for is not one that F is free to offer to the public. It is a position that is already owed to y, and is not available for open competition. Judith Jarvis Thompson makes a similar point:

> Suppose two candidates [A and B] for a civil service job have equally good test scores, but there is only one job available. We could decide between them by coin-tossing. But in fact we do allow for declaring for A straightway, where A is a veteran, and B is not. It may be that B is a non-veteran through no fault of his. . . . Yet the fact is that B is not a veteran and A is. On the assumption that the veteran has served his country, the country owes him something. And it is plain that giving him preference is not an unjust way in which part of that debt of gratitude can be paid.

In a similar way, individual Blacks who have suffered from acts of unjust discrimination are owed something by the perpetrator(s) of such acts, and this debt takes precedence over the perpetrator's right to use his or her options to hire the most qualified person for the position in question.

Many White males have developed expectations about the likelihood of their being selected for educational, employment, and entrepreneurial opportunities that are realistic only because of the general exclusion of women and non-Whites as competitors for such positions. Individuals enjoying inflated odds of obtaining such opportunities because of racist and sexist practices are recipients of an "unjust enrichment."

Redistributing opportunities would clearly curtail benefits that many have come to expect. And given the frustration of their traditional expectations, it is understandable that they would feel resentment. But blocking traditional expectations is not unjust if those expectations conflict with the equally important moral duties of restitution and just distribution. It is a question, not of "is," but of "ought": not "Do those with decreased opportunities as a result of affirmative action feel resentment?" but "Should those with decreased opportunities as a result of affirmative action feel resentment?"

White males who are affected by such redistributions may be innocent in the sense that they have not practiced overt acts of racial discrimination, have developed reasonable expectations based on the status quo, and have exerted efforts that, given the status quo, would normally have resulted in their achieving certain rewards. Their life plans and interests are thus thwarted despite their having met all of the standards "normally" required for the achievement of their goals. Clearly, disappointment is not unnatural or irrational. Nonetheless, the resentment is not sufficiently justified if the competing moral claims of restitution and fair distribution have equal or even greater weight.

Since Title VII protects bona fide seniority plans, it forces the burden of rectification to be borne by Whites who are entering the labor force rather than Whites who are the direct beneficiaries of past discriminatory practices. Given this limitation placed on affirmative action remedies, the burden of social restitution may, in many cases, be borne by those who were not directly involved in past discriminatory practices. But it is generally not true that those burdened have not benefited at all from past discriminatory practices. For the latent effects of acts of invidious racial discrimination have plausibly bolstered and encouraged the efforts of Whites in roughly the same proportion as it inhibited and discouraged the efforts of Blacks. Such considerations are also applicable to cases where F discriminated against y in favor of z, but the make-whole remedy involves providing compensation to y' rather than y. This suggests that y' is an *undeserving beneficiary* of the preferential treatment meant to compensate for the unjust discrimination against y, just as z' above appeared to be the innocent victim forced to bear the burden that z benefited from. Many critics have argued that this misappropriation of benefits and burdens demonstrates the unfairness of compensation to groups rather than individuals. But it is important that the context and rationale for such remedies be appreciated.

In cases of "egregious" racial discrimination, not only is it true that F discriminated against a particular Black person y, but F's discrimination advertised a general disposition to discriminate against another Black person who might seek such positions. The specific effect of F's unjust discrimination was that y was refused a position he or she would otherwise have received. The latent (or dispositional) effect of F's unjust discrimination was that many Blacks who otherwise would have sought such positions were discouraged from doing so. Thus, even if the specific y actually discriminated against can no longer be compensated, F has an obligation to take affirmative action to communicate to Blacks as a group that such positions are indeed open to them. After being found in violation of laws prohibiting racial discrimination, many agencies have disclaimed further discrimination while in fact continuing to do so. In such cases, the courts have required the discriminating agencies to actually hire and/or promote Blacks who may not be as qualified as some current White applicants until Blacks approach the proportion in F's labor force they in all likelihood would have achieved had F's unjust discriminatory acts not deterred them.

Of course, what this proportion would have been is a matter of speculation. It may have been less than the proportion of Blacks available in the relevant labor pool from which applicants are drawn if factors other than racial discrimination act to depress the merit of such applicants. This point is made again and again by critics. Some, such as Thomas Sowell, argue that cultural factors often mitigate against Blacks meriting representation in a particular labor force in proportion to their presence in the pool of candidates looking for jobs or seeking promotions. Others, such as Michael Levin, argue that cognitive deficits limit Blacks from being hired and promoted at a rate proportionate to their presence in the relevant labor pool. What such critics reject is the assumption that, were it not for pervasive discrimination and overexploitation, Blacks would be equally represented in the positions in question. What is scarcely considered is the possibility that, were it not for racist exclusions, Blacks might be over rather than under represented in competitive positions.

Establishing Blacks' presence at a level commensurate with their proportion in the relevant labor market need not be seen as an attempt to actualize some valid prediction. Rather, given the impossibility of determining what level of representation Blacks would have achieved were it not for racist discrimination, the assumption of proportional representation is the only *fair* assumption to make. This is not to argue that Blacks should be maintained in such positions, but their contrived exclusion merits an equally contrived rectification.

Racist acts excluding Blacks affected particular individuals, but were directed at affecting the behavior of the group of all those similar to the victim. Likewise, the benefits of affirmative action policies should not be conceived as limited in their effects to the specific individuals receiving them. Rather, those benefits should be conceived as extending to all those identified with the recipient, sending the message that opportunities are indeed available to qualified Black candidates who would have been excluded in the past.

Reflecting the view of many critics of preferential treatment, Robert Fullinwider writes:

> Surely the most harmed by past employment discrimination are those Black men and women over fifty years of age who were denied an adequate education, kept out of the unions, legally excluded from many jobs, who have lived in poverty or close to it, and whose income-producing days are nearly at an end. Preferential hiring programs will have virtually no effect on these people at all. Thus, preferential hiring will tend not to benefit those most deserving of compensation.

Because of the failure to appreciate the latent effects of discriminatory acts, this conclusion is flawed in two important respects. First, it limits the effect of specific acts of discrimination to the specific individuals involved. But the effect on the individual that is the specific object of a racist exclusion is not the only effect of that act, and may not be the effect that is most injurious or long term. For an invidious act affects not only y, but also y's family and friends. And it may well be that the greatest injury is, not to y, but to those who are deprived of sharing not only the specific benefits denied y, but also the motivation to seek (as y did) educational and employment opportunities they believe they would be excluded from (as y was).

Second, the conclusion that "preferential hiring will tend not to benefit those most deserving of compensation" fails to appreciate the extent that helping one member of a group may contribute indirectly to helping other members of that group. Clearly, admitting y' to medical school to compensate for not having admitted y in the past may nonetheless benefit y by increasing y's chance of obtaining medical services that otherwise might not be available.

We should conceive of the purpose of preferential treatment as being to benefit, not only the specific individuals directly affected by past racist acts, but also those counterfactually indicated in such acts. Affirmative action communicates not only to the specific Blacks and Whites involved in a particular episode, but to all Blacks and Whites that invidious racial discrimination is no longer the order of the day. Unless this is recognized, the purpose of preferential treatment will not be understood . . .

There are many factors that influence individual prospective employers in choosing between candidates: the way they dress, their posture and demeanor, their choice of cologne, hairstyle, personal relationship to the employer and many if not most may be totally irrelevant to the person's ability to perform the job in question. But it is not always immoral to choose a candidate based on factors irrelevant to their ability to perform, as in the case of hiring a person because he or she is a close relative. In any case, it would be impossible to identify all such factors and legislate against them.

Civil rights legislation prohibits using factors that historically have been used systematically to exclude certain groups of individuals from opportunities generally available to members of other groups. Thus, the disabled have systematically been excluded relative to the physically normal, women excluded relative to men, Blacks excluded relative to Whites, Muslims and Jews excluded relative to Christians, and so on.

We can expect many individuals equal with respect to their productive capacity to have been treated unequally by the market because of random factors that influence the choices of decision makers for available opportunities. Within both excluded and preferred groups, there will be some who are better off than others, based on random factors that have influenced their economic destiny. But it is only at the level of the group that systematic as opposed to random factors can be distinguished. Economist Lester Thurow estimates that "70 to 80 percent of the variance in individual earnings is caused by factors that are not within the control of even perfect governmental economic policies," and he concludes: "The economy will treat different individuals unequally no matter what we do. Only groups can be treated equally."

Because of a history of racist exclusion from educational, employment, and investment opportunities, Blacks generally have a lower ratio of relevant job-related skills and attitudes than Whites. Eliminating racism would do nothing to eliminate this deficit in human capital, which in itself is sufficient to ground a continuing prejudice against Blacks.

As Owen Fiss has argued, preferential treatment for a disadvantaged group provides members of that group with positions of power, prestige, and influence that they would otherwise not attain in the near future. Such positions empower both the individuals awarded those positions as well as the group they identify with and are identified with by others. Individuals awarded such positions serve as models that others within their group may aspire to, and (more often than not) provide the group with a source of defense and advocacy that improves the status of the group.

Fiss acknowledges, as many critics have stressed, that preferential treatment might encourage claims that Blacks do not have the ability to make it on their own, thereby perpetuating the myth of Black inferiority. But I do not see this as a serious problem. For the assumption of Black inferiority is used to explain both why Blacks do not occupy prestigious positions when they are in fact absent from such positions and why they do occupy them when they are in fact present in such positions. The assumption of Black inferiority exists with either option, and Blacks who do occupy positions they would likely not occupy but for affirmative action are not losing credibility they otherwise might have. On the other hand, Blacks who do occupy such positions and perform at or above expectation do gain a credibility they otherwise would not have.

An enduring legacy of racism (and sexism) is the presumption that Blacks (and women) are generally less competent and undeserving of nonmenial opportunities. Thus, the issue is not whether Blacks will be considered incompetent, but whether the effects of that assumption will continue. "The ethical issue is whether the position of perpetual subordination is going to be brought to an end for our disadvantaged groups, and if so, at what speed and at what cost." . . .

I believe that government perpetrates the injuries of slavery—and segregation if it initiates no effort to correct for those injuries. Refusing to act when action is called for can be as great a source of injury as inappropriate intervention. It does no good to cite a statute of limitations, since demands for restitution have been made continuously since slavery was abolished. The Freedmen's Bureau was initially conceived as a means of providing freed slaves with the education and capital necessary to make them at least self-sufficient. But these amenities were withdrawn in favor of a system that perpetuated the subordination of freed slaves through political exclusion, inadequate educational facilities, job reservations, and housing segregation . . .

In response to the claim that Blacks are owed restitution for the injuries suffered under slavery, segregation, and other racially exclusionary practices, some critics have objected that contemporary Whites should not be required to accept responsibility for something they had no choice in. Whatever benefits they may have received, they had no choice in receiving. And since a person or party can be held morally responsible only for something that they could have done or avoided doing, it is unjust to require restitution from those least responsible for the injuries inflicted by segregation and racism. As one critic puts it, "it is morally absurd to penalize [someone] for an evil that he could not have prevented."

But the morally relevant issue is not whether the beneficiaries of unjust acts are responsible for the unjust acts, but whether the beneficiaries sincerely attempt to make restitution for their continuing enrichment from such acts. Certainly, contemporary Whites are not responsible for many of the current injuries suffered by Blacks. But they are responsible for continuing to profit from benefits that derive from such injuries. Continuing to benefit from acts of injustice creates a liability to make restitution for them, at least to the degree of relinquishing the undeserved benefits.

Another objection to preferential treatment as a form of restitution derives from the principle, central to corrective justice, that those most responsible for harm should bear the primary cost of restitution and those most harmed should receive the greatest share of the restitution. However, while older Whites are most likely to be responsible for the injuries of racism, it is young Whites seeking educational and employment positions who are forced to bear the primary cost of restitution. Likewise, while it is older Blacks with the least education and training who bear the greatest injuries from the legacy of slavery and segregation, it is young Blacks with the highest qualifications who are the beneficiaries of preferential treatment.

But again, there is little need to quibble with the fact that older White workers are the direct beneficiaries of past racist exclusions, and are now granted a strong measure of protection by seniority systems in recognition of their subsequent investment of time, energy, and effort in those positions. But young Whites are the indirect beneficiaries of past racist acts and the direct beneficiaries of current ones. Institutional racism gives young Whites a decided advantage over young Blacks because they have generally received better educational and entrepreneurial opportunities, and because they are less subject to stigmatized stereotypes.

Prior to affirmative action, Blacks were penalized in direct proportion to their level of qualification. Those with higher levels of qualifications were typically subjected to greater prejudice and higher rates of exclusion from opportunities to develop and profit from those qualifications. Among Blacks harmed most by racism would thus be individuals with maximum potential who were prevented by racist exclusions from developing that potential into even minimal qualifications. However, the fact that preferential treatment does not reach Blacks who have been most harmed by racism is no criticism for helping those less harmed. One does not condemn aspirin as a remedy for headaches because it does not also remedy migraines. . . .

FORWARD-LOOKING JUSTIFICATIONS OF AFFIRMATIVE ACTION

While Loury defends a form of reparation for Blacks but rejects preferential treatment, others have defended preferential treatment but denied that it should be viewed as a form of reparation. This latter group rejects "backward looking" justifications of affirmative action and defends it instead on "forward-looking" grounds that include distributive justice, minimizing subordination, and maximizing social utility.

Thus, Ronald Fiscus argues that backward-looking arguments have distorted the proper justification for affirmative action policies. Backward-looking arguments depend on the paradigm of traditional tort cases, where a specific individual x has deprived another individual y of a specific good t through an identifiable act a, and x is required to restore y to the position y would have had, had a not occurred. But typically, preferential treatment requires that x' (rather than x) restore y' (instead of y) with a good t' that y' supposedly would have achieved had y not been deprived of t by x. The displacement of perpetrator (x' for x) and victim (y' for y) gives rise to the problem of (1) White males who are innocent of acts having caused harm nonetheless being forced to provide restitution for such acts; and (2) Blacks who were not directly harmed by those acts nonetheless becoming the principal beneficiaries of restitution for those acts.

For many, the backward-looking justification for affirmative action makes it seem that innocent White males are forced to bear the principle burden for correcting the wrongs of the past, and that the least harmed Blacks are the undeserving beneficiaries of their unjust sacrifice. This is clearly the sense expressed in Justice Scalia's opposition to affirmative action:

> My father came to this country when he was a teenager. Not only had he never profited from the sweat of any Black man's brow, I don't think he had ever seen a Black man. There are, of course man's White ethnic groups that came

to this country in great numbers relatively late in its history—Italians, Jews, Poles—who not only took no part in, and derived no profit from, the major historic suppression of the currently acknowledged minority groups, but were, in fact, themselves the object of discrimination by the dominant Anglo-Saxon majority. To be sure, in relatively recent years some or all of these groups have been the beneficiaries of discrimination against Blacks, or have themselves practiced discrimination, but to compare their racial debt . . . with that of those who plied the slave trade, and who maintained a formal caste system for many years thereafter, is to confuse a mountain with a molehill. Yet curiously enough, we find that in the system of restorative justice established by the Wisdoms and the Powells and the Whites, it is precisely these groups that do most of the restoring. It is they who, to a disproportionate degree, are the competitors with the urban Blacks and Hispanics for jobs, housing, education.

Similarly Judge Richard Posner writes:

> The members of the minority group who receive preferential treatment will often be those who have not been the victims of discrimination while the nonminority people excluded because of preferences are unlikely to have perpetrated, or to have in any demonstrable sense benefited from, the discrimination.

Fiscus argues that the backward-looking argument reinforces the perception that preferential treatment is unfair to innocent White males, and so long as this is the case, both the courts and the public are likely to oppose strong affirmative action policies such as quotas, set-asides, and other preferential treatment policies.

In contrast, Fiscus recommends that preferential treatment be justified in terms of distributive justice, which as a matter of equal protection, "requires that individuals be awarded the positions, advantages, or benefits they would have been awarded under fair conditions," that is, conditions under which racist exclusion would not have precluded Blacks from attaining "their deserved proportion of the society's important benefits." Conversely, "distributive justice also holds that individuals or groups may not claim positions, advantages, or benefits that they would not have been awarded under fair conditions." These conditions jointly prohibit White males from claiming an unreasonable share of social benefits and protects White males from having to bear an unreasonable share of the redistributive burden.

Fiscus takes the position that any deviation between Blacks and Whites from strict proportionality in the distribution of current goods is evidence of racism. Thus, if Blacks were 20 percent of a particular population but held no positions in the police or fire departments, that is indicative of past and present racial discrimination. While discrimination exists with respect to many characteristics other than race (i.e., height and attractiveness), the Fourteenth Amendment prohibits such in the case of race. As such, deviations in the distribution of goods with respect to groups defined by race are subject to legal review, unlike deviations in the distribution of goods with respect to groups defined by attractiveness.

Because the Equal Protection Clause of the Fourteenth Amendment protects citizens from statistical discrimination on the basis of race, the use of race as the principal reason for excluding certain citizens from benefits made available to other citizens is a violation of that person's constitutional rights. This was one basis for Bakke's suit against the UC Davis medical school's 16 percent minority set-aside for medical school admission. There were eighty-four seats out of the one hundred admission slots that he was eligible to fill, and he was excluded from competing for the other sixteen slots because of his race. On the basis of the standard criteria (GPA, MCAT scores, etc.), Bakke argued that he would have been admitted before any of the Black applicants admitted under the minority set-aside. He therefore claimed that he was being excluded from the additional places available because he was White.

Currently, Blacks have approximately 3.25 times fewer physicians than would be expected given their numbers in the population. Native Americans have 7 times fewer physicians than what would have been expected if intelligent, well-trained, and motivated Native Americans had tried to become physicians at the same rate as did European Americans.

For Fiscus, the underrepresentation of African and Native Americans among physicians and the maldistribution of medical resources to minority communities is clearly the effect of generations of racist exclusions. Because of stereotypes portraying them as the product of cognitive deficiencies, unstable families, bad habits, and inadequate educations, Blacks and Native Americans seeking to obtain educational, employment, and investment opportunities have traditionally been perceived to be less prepared than their White competitors. Not only are qualified members of the oppressed group harmed by this prejudice, but even more harmed are the many who would have been qualified but for injuries induced by racial prejudice.

For Fiscus, individuals of different races would have been as equally distributed in the social body as the molecules of a gas in a container and he identifies the belief in the inherent equality of races with the Equal Protection Clause of the Fourteenth Amendment. In a world without racism, minorities would be represented among the top one hundred medical school applicants at UC Davis in the same proportion as they were in the general population. Accordingly, because Bakke did not score among the top eighty-four Whites, he would not have qualified for admission. Thus, he had no right to the position he was contesting, and indeed if he were given such a position in lieu of awarding it to a minority, Bakke would be much like a person who had received stolen goods. "Individuals who have not personally harmed minorities may nevertheless be prevented from reaping the benefits of the harm inflicted by the society at large."

Justice O'Connor has voiced skepticism toward the assumption that members of different races would "gravitate with mathematical exactitude to each employer or union absent unlawful discrimination." She considers it sheer speculation as to "how many minority students would have been admitted to the medical school at Davis absent past discrimination in educational opportunities." I likewise consider it speculative to assume that races would be represented in every area in proportion to their proportion of the general population. But because it is impossible to reasonably predict what that distribution would have been absent racial discrimination, it is not mere speculation but morally fair practice to assume that it would have been the same as the proportion in the general population. Given the fact of legally sanctioned invidious racism against Blacks in U.S. history, the burden of proof should not be on the oppressed group to prove that it would be represented at a level proportionate to its presence in the general population. Rather, the burden of proof should be on the majority to show why its overrepresentation among the most well off is not the result of unfair competition imposed by racism. We are morally obligated to assume proportional representation until there are more plausible reasons than racism for assuming otherwise.

Like Fiscus, I believe that races are equal, but that need not imply that they are identical in all relevant respects. Belief in racial equality requires us to acknowledge that racial differences, if they exist, should be allowed opportunities for cultivation free of racist restrictions. Only when opportunities are openly available can natural distributions based on natural differences be determined. In a situation not skewed by racism, Blacks might be more concentrated in certain areas and less concentrated in others. But to accept as the norm that they would be concentrated in the lower echelons of most areas, if represented at all, is racist. Because of the universality of prejudice against Blacks, gross disparities in proportional representation should alert us to the probability that it is caused by racist restrictions rather than racialist differences or personal preferences.

Thus, it should be the responsibility of the Alabama Department of Public Safety to show why no Blacks were members of its highway patrol as of 1970, even though Blacks were 25 percent of the relevant workforce in Alabama. It

should be the responsibility of the company and the union to explain why there were no Blacks with seniority in the union at the Kaiser plant in Louisiana, although Blacks made up 39 percent of the surrounding population. Likewise, it should be the responsibility of the union to explain why no Blacks had been admitted to the Sheet Metal Workers' Union in New York City although minorities were 29 percent of the available workforce. If no alternative explanations are more plausible, then the assumption that the disparity in representation is the result of racism should stand.

The question should not be whether White males are innocent or guilty of racism or sexism, but whether they have a right to inflated odds of obtaining benefits relative to minorities and women. A White male is innocent only up to the point where he takes advantage of "a benefit he would not qualify for without the accumulated effects of racism. At that point he becomes an accomplice in, and a beneficiary of, society's racism. He becomes the recipient of stolen goods."

While Justice Scalia dismisses the racism that may have been practiced on Italians, Irish, and other immigrant groups as insignificant compared to the racism practiced under slavery, it is plausible that racism after slavery was more instrumental in creating the situation that affirmative action was meant to relieve than racism during slavery.

While many European immigrant groups were no more literate than Blacks who were already in America, they were nonetheless granted state support in acquiring property (the Homestead Acts, the FHA, urban renewal), education (the Morrill Act, segregated schools), and jobs (NLRB and governmental support for racist unions) that Blacks were denied. Unions, municipalities, and lending institutions used legally sanctioned means to exclude Blacks from employment, educational, and investment opportunities made available to European immigrants. While union members benefited from government interventions in the labor Market as a result of legislation such as the Wagner Act, the National Apprenticeship Act, and the Davis-Bacon

Act, they actively practiced nepotism and ethnic preferences in the award of jobs and training. . . .

In aiming at proportionality, not as a natural outcome but as a condition necessary to determine natural outcomes, the rights of innocent White males are not being sacrificed for the greater good of increasing the participation of minorities and women. The good of a more diverse society should not be conceived of as justifying the sacrifice of a "randomly chosen" subset of White males currently seeking educational, employment, and entrepreneurial opportunities. Rather, White males are being forced to relinquish benefits that are ill gotten, benefits they would likely not have received in a racially fair world. . . .

A central question in the debate over affirmative action is the extent to which racial classifications are important in accomplishing the goal of relieving the subordinate status of minorities and women. Given the aim of improving safety in transportation, classifying people in terms of their race is rationally irrelevant, while classifying them in terms of their driving competency, visual acuity, and maturity is essential. On the other hand, given the aim of improving health care in Black neighborhoods, classifying applicants for medical school in terms of their race is, in addition to their academic and clinical abilities, a very relevant factor.

To illustrate, African Americans, Hispanics, and Native Americans make up 22 percent of the population but represent only 10 percent of entering medical students and 7 percent of practicing physicians. A number of studies have shown that underrepresented minority physicians are more likely than their majority counterparts to care for poor patients and patients of similar ethnicity. Indeed, "each ethnic group of patients was more likely to be cared for by a physician of their own ethnic background than by a physician of another ethnic background." This suggests that sociocultural factors such as language, physical identity, personal background, and experiences are relevant factors in determining the kinds of

communities in which a physician will establish a practice. If this is the case, then the race of a medical school applicant would be an important factor in providing medical services to certain underrepresented communities. Thus, while there might be some purposes for which race is irrelevant, there might be other purposes in which race is important (though perhaps not necessary) for achieving the end in view. The remedy targets Blacks as a group because racially discriminatory practices were directed against Blacks as a group.

Some argue that characteristics such as race, sex, and social background are morally irrelevant because an individual has no choice as to whether such attributes shall attach to him or her. But an individual has no choice about whether he or she will be born with a high IQ or not. Yet, we do not advocate eliminating intellectual potential as a criteria for receiving scarce educational opportunities. Individuals with high IQ are valued because we believe that such individuals play an important role in increasing aggregate wealth. To the extent that we want our society to be a productive one, we allocate special places to such individuals.

A similar rationale holds in the case of race. To the extent that we want our society to be not only productive, but also just, to that extent is it important to demonstrate a concern for those who face decreased opportunities because of racism. Preferential treatment programs are meant to offset the disadvantages imposed by racism so that Blacks are not forced to bear the principal costs of that error.

It is commonly objected that proportionate representation achieved in this manner is artificial. But barriers that exclude Blacks from educational, employment, and entrepreneurial opportunities impose and maintain an artificial underrepresentation. To condemn policies meant to correct for racial barriers as themselves erecting barriers is to ignore the difference between action and reaction, cause and effect, aggression and self-defense. Even a critic of affirmative action such as Robert Fullinwider admits that "If equal opportunity is looked at as some kind of equilibrium, then we can see nothing amiss about tampering with a situation that has got into disequilibrium. We add and subtract weights here and there until equilibrium is restored." Clearly, granting preferential treatment to individuals who suffer the present burdens of discrimination is exactly the kind of tampering that is appropriate.

CONCLUSION

Racism was directed against Blacks whether they were talented, average, or mediocre, and attenuating the effects of racism requires distributing remedies similarly. Affirmative action policies compensate for the harms of racism (overt and institutional) through antidiscrimination laws and preferential policies. Prohibiting the benign use of race as a factor in the award of educational, employment and business opportunities would eliminate compensation for past and present racism and reinforce the moral validity of the status quo, with Blacks overrepresented among the least well off and underrepresented among the most well off.

It has become popular to use affirmative action as a scapegoat for the increased vulnerability of the White working class. But it should be recognized that the civil rights revolution (in general) and affirmative action (in particular) has been beneficial, not just to Blacks, but also to Whites (e.g., women, the disabled, the elderly) who otherwise would be substantially more vulnerable than they are now.

Affirmative action is directed toward empowering those groups that have been adversely affected by past and present exclusionary practices. Initiatives to abolish preferential treatment would inflict a grave injustice on African Americans, for they signal a reluctance to acknowledge that the plight of African Americans is the result of institutional practices that require institutional responses.

For Further Reflection

1. Analyze Mosley's arguments. How strong or weak are they? Do minorities, especially Blacks, deserve compensation from the government for past injustice? Explain your answer.

2. Consider Mosley's argument for equal results; that is that justice demands roughly equal representation of minorities in the different types of employment. Does he make a strong case for his views?

3. What is Mosley's attitude toward well-qualified White males who may themselves be innocent of harming Black but are passed by Affirmative Action candidates? How strong are his arguments?

4. There are many ways in which the phrase "Affirmative Action" is used. For example, during the last Presidential race, General Colin Powell went on record as supporting it. Analyze his statement. What does he mean by Affirmative Action?

Equal right and equal opportunity, however, mean just that. They do not mean preferential treatment. Preferences, no matter how well intended, ultimately breed resentment among the nonpreferred. And preferential treatment demeans the achievement that minority Americans win by their own efforts. The present debate over affirmative action has a lot to do with definitions. If affirmative action means programs that provide equal opportunity, then I am all for it. If it leads to preferential treatment or helps those who no longer need help, I *am* opposed. I benefited from equal opportunity and affirmative action in the Army, but I was not shown preference. The Army, as a matter of fairness, made sure that performance would be the only measure of advancement. When equal performance does not result in equal advancement, then something is wrong with the system, and our leaders have an obligation to fix. it. If a history of discrimination has made it difficult for certain Americans to meet standards, it is only fair to provide temporary means to help them catch up and compete on equal terms. Affirmative action in the best sense promotes equal consideration, not reverse discrimination. Discrimination "for" one group means, inevitably, discrimination "against" another; and all discrimination is offensive.

Colin Powell, *My American Journey* (with Joseph E. Persico).
New York: Ballantine Books, 1995.

IX.73   The Case Against Affirmative Action

LOUIS P. POJMAN

Louis P. Pojman is professor of philosophy at the U.S. Military Academy. He was a civil rights activist in the 1960s before becoming a philosopher. This essay sets forth eight arguments against *Strong Affirmative Action*, which is defined as *preferential treatment*, discriminating in favor of members of underrepresented groups which have been treated unjustly in the past, against innocent people. This is distinguished from *Weak Affirmative Action*, which simply seeks to promote equal opportunity to the goods and offices of a society. The essay argues against *Strong Affirmative Action*, attempting to show that two wrongs don't make a right. This form of *Affirmative Action*, as it is applied against *White males*, is both *racist* and *sexist*.

Study Questions

1. What is the difference between Weak Affirmative Action and Strong Affirmative Action?
2. Why doesn't Pojman think the *Need for Role Models* is a good reason for Affirmative Action?
3. How does the *Compensation Argument* work? What is Pojman's criticism of it?
4. What does Pojman say about the argument for compensation from those who innocently benefited from past injustice?
5. What is the *Equal Results Argument,* and why doesn't Pojman think it supports Affirmative Action?
6. Why do some philosophers hold that no one deserves his talents? How does this affect the idea of Affirmative Action?
7. Why does Pojman think that Affirmative Action encourages mediocrity and incompetence?
8. What is the *Argument from Merit*? How does it affect the idea of Affirmative Action?
9. Why does Professor Derrick Bell think that Supreme Court Judge Clarence Thomas "doesn't think black"? Is there such a thing as Black thinking? as White thinking?
10. What is Pojman's conclusion about Affirmative Action?

AFFIRMATIVE ACTION HAS BECOME one of the most heated moral issues of our time. It might be the most complex. Consider, it juxtaposes *backward-looking* considerations (past injustice) with *forward-looking* ones (producing a society of equal opportunity); it creates a requirement to include people on the basis of their race and gender; it focuses political, economic, legal, and, above all, moral considerations onto a single issue. It paradoxically advocates preferential treatment in the name of nonpreferential treatment. Its proposals often depend on taking a position on the nature/nurture debate, itself one of the most controversial issues of our day. Is it any wonder, then, that society is divided over this issue? Or that good people can honestly differ? Nevertheless, philosophical reason should help us lower the temperature, while bringing more daylight to this issue. This is what I shall attempt to do in defending equal opportunity against preferential treatment, what I call *Strong Affirmative Action.*

Let us agree that despite the evidences of a booming economy, the poor are suffering grievously, with children being born into desperate material and psychological poverty; for them the ideal of "equal opportunity for all" is a cruel joke. Many feel that the federal government has abandoned its guarantee to provide the minimum necessities for each American, so that the pace of this tragedy seems to be worsening daily. In addition to this, African-Americans have a legacy of slavery and unjust discrimination to contend with, and other minorities have also suffered from injustice. Women have their own peculiar history of being treated unequally in relevant ways. What is the answer to these national problems? Is it increased welfare? more job training? more support for education? required licensing of parents to have children? negative income tax? more support for families or for mothers with small children? All of these have merit and should be part of the national de-

bate. But, my thesis is that however tragic the situation might be (and we might disagree on just how tragic it is), one policy is *not* a legitimate part of the solution and that is *reverse, unjust discrimination* against young, white males. Strong Affirmative Action, which implicitly advocates reverse discrimination, although no doubt well intentioned, is morally heinous, asserting—by implication—that *two wrongs make a right.*

The *Two Wrongs Make a Right* Thesis goes like this: Because *some* Whites once enslaved some Blacks, the descendants of those slaves (some of whom might now enjoy high incomes and social status) have a right to opportunities and offices over better qualified Whites who had nothing to do with either slavery or the oppression of Blacks (and who might even have suffered hardship comparable to that of poor Blacks). In addition, Strong Affirmative Action creates a new Hierarchy of the Oppressed: Blacks get primary preferential treatment, women second, Native Americans third, Hispanics fourth, Handicapped fifth, and Asians sixth and so on until White males, no matter how needy or well qualified, must accept the left-overs. Naturally, combinations of oppressed classes (for example, a one-eyed, Black, Hispanic female) trump all single classifications. The equal protection clause of the Fourteenth Amendment becomes reinterpreted as "Equal protection for all equals, but some equals are more equal than others."

Before analyzing arguments concerning Affirmative Action, I must define my terms.

By *Weak Affirmative Action* I mean policies that will increase the opportunities of disadvantaged people to attain social goods and offices. It includes such things as dismantling segregated institutions, widespread advertisement to groups not previously represented in certain privileged positions, special scholarships for the disadvantaged classes (for example, the poor, regardless of race or gender), and even using di-

This article is reprinted from The International Journal of Applied Philosophy *vol 12. (1998) by permission. It has been slightly revised for this book.*

versity or underrepresentation of groups with a history of past discrimination as a tie breaker when candidates for these goods and offices are relatively equal. The goal of *Weak Affirmative Action* is equal opportunity to compete, not equal results. We seek to provide each citizen regardless of race or gender a fair chance to the most favored positions in society. There is no more moral requirement to guarantee that 12 percent of professors are Black than to guarantee that 85 percent of the players in the National Basketball Association are White.

By *Strong Affirmative Action* I mean preferential treatment on the basis of race, ethnicity, or gender (or some other morally irrelevant criterion), discriminating in favor of underrepresented groups against overrepresented groups, aiming at roughly equal results. *Strong Affirmative Action is reverse discrimination*. It says it is right to do wrong to correct a wrong. This is the policy currently being promoted under the name of *Affirmative Action*, so I will use that term or "AA" for short throughout this essay to stand for this version of affirmative action. I will not argue for or against the principle of *Weak Affirmative Action*. Indeed, I think it has some moral weight. *Strong Affirmative Action* has none, or so I will argue.

This essay concentrates on AA policies regarding race, but the arguments can be extended to cover ethnicity and gender. I think that if a case for Affirmative Action can be made, it will be as a corrective to racial oppression. I will examine eight arguments regarding AA. The first five will be *negative*, attempting to show that the best arguments for Affirmative Action fail. The last three will be *positive* arguments for policies opposing Affirmative Action:

I. A CRITIQUE OF ARGUMENTS FOR AFFIRMATIVE ACTION

1. The Need for Role Models

This argument is straightforward. We all need role models, and it helps to know that others like us can be successful. We learn and are encouraged to strive for excellence by emulating our heroes and "our kind of people" who have succeeded.

In the first place it's not clear that role models of one's own racial or sexual type are necessary (let alone sufficient) for success. One of my heroes was Gandhi, an Indian Hindu, another was my grade school science teacher, Miss DeVoe, and another was Martin Luther King, behind whom I marched in Civil Rights demonstrations. More important than having role models of one's "own type" is having genuinely good people, of whatever race or gender, to emulate. Our common humanity should be a sufficient basis for us to see the possibility of success in people of virtue and merit. To yield to the demand, however tempting it might be, for "role-models-just-like-us" is to treat people like means not ends. It is to elevate morally irrelevant particularity over relevant traits, such as ability and integrity. We don't need people exactly like us to find inspiration. As Steve Allen once quipped, "If I had to follow a role model exactly, I would have become a nun."

Furthermore, even if it is of some help to people with low self-esteem to gain encouragement from seeing others of their particular kind in successful positions, it is doubtful whether this is a sufficient reason to justify preferential hiring or reverse discrimination. What good is a role model who is inferior to other professors or physicians or business personnel? The best way to create role models is to promote people because they are the best qualified for the job. It is the violation of this fact that is largely responsible for the widespread whisper in the medical field (at least in New York), "Never go to a Black physician under 40" (referring to the fact that AA has affected the medical system during the past 20 years). Fight the feeling how I will, I cannot help wondering on seeing a Black or woman in a position of honor, "Is she in this position because she merits it or because of Affirmative Action?" Where Affirmative Action is the policy, the "figment of pigment" creates a stigma of undeservedness, whether or not it is deserved.[1]

Finally, entertain this thought experiment. Suppose we discovered that tall handsome white males somehow made the best role models for the most people, especially poor people. Suppose even large numbers of minority people somehow found inspiration in their sight. Would we be justified in hiring tall handsome white males over better qualified short Hispanic women, who were deemed less role-model worthy?[2]

2. *The Compensation Argument*

The argument goes like this: Blacks have been wronged and severely harmed by Whites. Therefore White society should compensate Blacks for the injury caused them. Reverse discrimination in preferential hiring, contracts, and scholarships is a fitting way to compensate for the past wrongs.[3]

This argument actually involves a distorted notion of compensation. Normally, we think of compensation as owed by a specific person A to another person B whom A has wronged in a specific way C. For example, if I have stolen your car and used it for a period of time to make business profits that would have gone to you, it is not enough that I return your car. I must pay you an amount reflecting your loss and my ability to pay. If I have made $5,000 and only have $10,000 in assets, it would not be possible for you to collect $20,000 in damages—even though that is the amount of loss you have incurred.

Sometimes compensation is extended to groups of people who have been unjustly harmed by the greater society. For example, the United States government has compensated the Japanese-Americans who were interred during the Second World War, and the West German government has paid reparations to the survivors of Nazi concentration camps. But here a specific people have been identified who were wronged in an identifiable way by the government of the nation in question.

On the face of it, demands by Blacks for compensation do not fit the usual pattern. Southern States with Jim Crow laws could be accused of unjustly harming Blacks, but it is hard to see that the United States government was involved in

doing so. Much of the harm done to Blacks was the result of private discrimination, not state action. So the Germany–United States analogy doesn't hold. Furthermore, it is not clear that all Blacks were harmed in the same way or whether some were *unjustly* harmed or harmed more than poor Whites and others (for example, short people). Finally, even if identifiable Blacks were harmed by identifiable social practices, it is not clear that most forms of Affirmative Action are appropriate to restore the situation. The usual practice of a financial payment seems more appropriate than giving a high level job to someone unqualified or only minimally qualified, who, speculatively, might have been better qualified had he or she not been subject to racial discrimination. If John is the star tailback of our college team with a promising professional future, and I accidentally (but culpably) drive my pick-up truck over his legs, and so cripple him, John may be due compensation, but he is not due the tailback spot on the football team.

Still, there might be something intuitively compelling about compensating members of an oppressed group who are minimally qualified. Suppose that the Hatfields and the McCoys are enemy clans, and some youths from the Hatfields go over and steal diamonds and gold from the McCoys, distributing it within the Hatfield economy. Even though we do not know which Hatfield youths did the stealing, we would want to restore the wealth, as far as possible, to the McCoys. One way might be to tax the Hatfields, but another might be to give preferential treatment for scholarships and training programs and hiring to the McCoys.

This is perhaps the strongest argument for Affirmative Action, and it might well justify some weaker versions of AA, but it is doubtful whether it is sufficient to justify strong versions with quotas and goals and time tables in skilled positions. There are at least two reasons for this. First, we have no way of knowing how many people of any given group would have achieved some given level of competence had the world been different. This is especially relevant if my objections to the Equal Results Argument (#5 below) are correct. Second, the normal criterion of competence is a strong *prima facie* consideration when the most important positions are at stake. There are three reasons for this: (1) treating people according to their merits respects them as persons, as ends in themselves, rather than as means to social ends (if we believe that individuals possess a dignity that deserves to be respected, then we ought to treat that individual on the basis of his or her merits, not as a mere instrument for social policy); (2) society has given people expectations that if they attain certain levels of excellence they will be awarded appropriately; and (3) filling the most important positions with the best qualified is the best way to ensure efficiency in job-related areas and in society in general. These reasons are not absolutes. They can be overridden.[4] But there is a strong presumption in their favor, so that a burden of proof rests with those who would override them.

At this point we get into the problem of whether innocent non-Blacks should have to pay a penalty for the preferential hiring of Blacks. We turn to that argument.

3. The Argument for Compensation from Those who Innocently Benefited from Past Injustice

Young White males as innocent beneficiaries of unjust discrimination against Blacks and women have no grounds for complaint when society seeks to level the tilted field. They might be innocent of oppressing Blacks, other minorities, and women, but they have unjustly benefited from that oppression or discrimination. So it is perfectly proper that less qualified women and Blacks be hired before them.

The operative principle is this: He who knowingly and willingly benefits from a wrong must help pay for the wrong. Judith Jarvis Thomson puts it this way. "Many [White males] have been direct beneficiaries of policies which have downgraded Blacks and women . . . and even those who did not directly benefit . . . had, at any rate,

the advantage in the competition which comes of the confidence in one's full membership [in the community], and of one's right being recognized as a matter of course."[5] That is, White males obtain advantages in self respect and self-confidence deriving from a racist and sexist system that denies these to Blacks and women.

Here is my response to this argument: As I noted in the previous section, compensation is normally individual and specific. If A harms B regarding x, B has a right to compensation from A regarding x. If A steals B's car and wrecks it, A has an obligation to compensate B for the stolen car, but A's son has no obligation to compensate B. Furthermore, if A dies or disappears, B has no moral right to claim that society compensate him for the stolen car—though if A has insurance, B can make such a claim to the insurance company. Sometimes a wrong cannot be compensated, and we just have to make the best of an imperfect world.

Suppose my parents, divining that I would grow up to have an unsurpassable desire to be a basketball player, bought an expensive growth hormone for me. Unfortunately, a neighbor stole it and gave it to little Michael, who gained the extra 13 inches—my 13 inches—and shot up to an enviable 6 feet 6 inches. Michael, better known as Michael Jordan, would have been a runt like me but for his luck. As it is, he profited from the injustice and excelled in basketball, as I would have done had I had my proper dose.

Do I have a right to the millions of dollars that Jordan made as a professional basketball player—the unjustly innocent beneficiary of my growth hormone? I have a right to something from the neighbor who stole the hormone, and it might be kind of Jordan to give me free tickets to the Bull's basketball games and remember me in his will. But, as far as I can see, he does not *owe* me anything, either legally or morally.

Suppose further that Michael Jordan and I are in high school together and we are both qualified to play basketball, only he is far better than I. Do I deserve to start in his position because I would have been as good as he is had someone not cheated me as a child? Again, I think not. But if being the lucky beneficiary of wrong-doing does not entail that Jordan (or the coach) owes me anything regarding basketball, why should it be a reason to engage in preferential hiring in academic positions or highly coveted jobs? If minimal qualifications are not adequate to override excellence in basketball, even when the minimality is a consequence of wrongdoing, why should they be adequate in other areas?

4. The Diversity Argument

It is important that we learn to live in a pluralistic world, learning to get along with those of other races, conditions, and cultures, so we should have schools and employment situations as fully integrated as possible. In a shrinking world we need to appreciate each other's culture and specific way of looking at life. Diversity is an important symbol and educative device. Thus, proponents of AA argue, preferential treatment is warranted to perform this role in society.

Once again, there is some truth in these concerns. Diversity of ideas challenges us to scrutinize our own values and beliefs, and diverse customs have aesthetic and moral value, helping us to appreciate the novelty and beauty in life. Diversity can expand our moral horizons. But, again, although we can admit the value of diversity, it hardly seems adequate to override the moral requirement to treat each person with equal respect. *Diversity for diversity's sake is moral promiscuity,* since it obfuscates rational distinctions, undermines treating individuals as ends, treating them, instead as mere means (to the goals of social engineering), and, furthermore, unless those hired are highly qualified, the diversity factor threatens to become a fetish. At least at the higher levels of business and the professions, *competence* far outweighs considerations of diversity. I do not care whether the group of surgeons operating on me reflect racial or gender balance, but I do care that they are highly qualified. Neither do most football or basketball fans care whether their team reflects ethnic and gender diversity, but demand the best combination of players available. And likewise with airplane pilots, military leaders, business executives, and, may I say it, teachers and university professors. One need not be a White male to teach, let alone, appreciate Shakespeare, nor need one be Black to teach, let alone appreciate, Alice Walker's *Color Purple.*

There might be times when diversity seems to be "crucial" to the well-being of a diverse community, such as for a police force. Suppose that White policemen tend overreact to young Black males, and the latter group distrust White policemen. Hiring more less qualified Black policemen, who would relate better to these youth, can have overall utilitarian value. But such a move, although we might make it as a lesser evil, could have serious consequences in allowing the demographic prejudices to dictate social policy. A better strategy would be to hire the best police, that is, those who can perform in disciplined, intelligent manner, regardless of their race. A White policeman must be able to arrest a Black burglar, even as a Black policeman must be able to arrest a White rapist. The quality of the police man or woman, not their race or gender is what counts.

On the other hand, if a Black policeman, though lacking some of the formal skills of the White policeman, really is able to do a better job in the Black community, this might constitute a case of merit, not Affirmative Action. As Stephen Kershnar points out, this is similar to the legitimacy of hiring Chinese men to act as undercover agents in Chinatown.[6]

5. The Equal Results Argument

Some philosophers and social scientists hold that human nature is roughly identical, so that on a fair playing field the same proportion from every race and ethnic group and both genders would attain to the highest positions in every area of endeavor. It would follow that any inequality of results itself is evidence for inequality of opportunity.

History is important when considering governmental rules like Test 21 because low scores by Blacks can be traced in large measure to the legacy of slavery and racism: segregation, poor schooling, exclusion from trade unions, malnutrition, and poverty have all played their roles. Unless one assumes that Blacks are naturally less able to pass the test, the conclusion must be that the results are themselves socially and legally constructed, not a mere given for which law and society can claim no responsibility.

The conclusion seems to be that genuine equality eventually requires equal results. Obviously Blacks have been treated unequally throughout U.S. history, and just as obviously the economic and psychological effects of that inequality linger to this day, showing up in lower income and poorer performance in school and on tests than Whites achieve. Because we have no reason to believe that differences in performance can be explained by factors other than history, equal results are a good benchmark by which to measure progress made toward genuine equality (John Arthur, *The Unfinished Constitution* (Belmont, CA: Wadsworth Publishing, 1990), p. 238.).

Albert G. Mosley develops a similar argument. "Establishing Blacks' presence at a level commensurate with their proportion in the relevant labor market need not be seen as an attempt to actualize some valid prediction. Rather, given the impossibility of determining what level of representation Blacks would have achieved were it not for racial discrimination, the assumption of proportional representation is the only *fair* assumption to make. This is not to argue that Blacks should be maintained in such positions, but their contrived exclusion merits equally contrived rectification."[7] The result of a just society should be equal numbers in proportion to each group in the work force.

However, Arthur and Mosley fail even to consider studies that suggest that there are innate differences between races, sexes, and groups. If there are genetic differences in intelligence, temperament, and other qualities within families, why should we not expect such differences between racial groups and the two genders? Why should the evidence for this be completely discounted?

Mosley's reasoning is as follows: Since we don't know for certain whether groups proportionately differ in talent, we should presume that they are equal in every respect. So we should presume that if we were living in a just society, there would be roughly proportionate representation in every field (for example, equal representation of doctors, lawyers, professors, carpenters, air-plane pilots, basketball players, and criminals). Hence, it is only fair—productive of justice—to aim at proportionate representation in these fields.

But the logic is flawed. Under a situation of ignorance we should not presume equality or inequality of representation—but conclude that we *don't know* what the results would be in a just society. Ignorance doesn't favor equal group representation any more than it favors unequal group representation. It is neutral between them.

Consider this analogy. Suppose that you were the owner of a National Basketball Association team. Suppose that I and other frustrated White basketball players bring a class-action suit against you and all the other team owners, claiming that you have subtly and systematically discriminated against White and Asian basketball players who make up less than 20 percent of the NBA players. You reply that you and the other owners are just responding to individual merit. We respond that the discrimination is a function of deep prejudice against White athletes, especially basketball players, who are discouraged in every way from competing on fair terms with Blacks who dominate the NBA. You would probably wish that the matter of unequal results was not brought up in the first place, but once it has been, would you not be in your rights to defend yourself by producing evidence, showing that *average* physiological differences exist between Blacks and Whites and Asians, so that we should not presume unjust discrimination?

Similarly, the proponents of the Doctrine of Equal Results open the door to a debate over average ability in ethnic, racial, and gender groups. The proponent of equal or fair opportunity would just as soon down-play this feature in favor of judging people as individuals by their merit (hard though that might be). But if the proponent of AA insists on the Equal Results Thesis, we are obliged to examine the Equal Abilities Thesis, on which it is based—the thesis that various ethnic and gender groups all have the same distribution of talent on the relevant characteristic. Regarding cognitive skills, we must consult the best evidence we have on average group differences. We need to compare average IQ scores, SAT scores, standard personality testing, success in academic and professional areas and the like. If the evidence shows that group differences are nonexistent, the AA proponent might win, but if the evidence turns out to be against the Equal Abilities Thesis, the AA proponent loses. Consider for a start that the average White and Asian scores 195 points higher on the SAT tests and that on virtually all IQ tests for the past seven or eight decades—the average Black IQ is 85 compared with the average White and Asian IQ at over 100—or that males and females differ significantly on cognitive ability tests.[8] Note, we are speaking about statistical averages. There are brilliant and retarded people in each group.

When such statistics are discussed many people feel uncomfortable and want to drop the subject. Perhaps these statistics are misleading, but then we need to look carefully at the total evidence. The proponent of equal opportunity urges us to get beyond racial and gender criteria in assignment of offices and opportunities and treat each person, not as an *average* white or Black or female or male, but as a *person* judged on his or her own merits.

Justice Powell spoke wisely, when in the *Bakke* case (1978) he rejected the *disparate impact thesis*, namely, that unequal results are strong evidence for unequal justice. Addressing the minority opinion that held the disparate impact thesis, he wrote:

> The [minority] would require as a justification for a program . . . only two findings: (1) that there has been some form of discrimination against the preferred minority groups "by society at large" . . . and (2) that "there is reason to believe" that the disparate impact [unequal results] is the "product" of such discrimination.
>
> The breadth of this hypothesis is unprecedented in our constitutional system. The first step is easily taken . . . The second step, however, involves a speculative leap: but for this discrimination by society at large, Bakke "would have failed to qualify for admission" because Negro applicants . . . would have made better scores. *Not one word in the record supports this conclusion* . . . [It] offers no standard for courts to use in applying a presumption of causation to other racial or ethnic classifications.
>
> There is no principled basis for deciding which groups would merit "heightened judicial solicitude" and which would not. . . . This kind of variable sociological and political analysis necessary to produce such rankings simply does not lie within the judicial competence . . . isolated segments of our vast government structures are not competent to make those decisions at least in the absence of legislative mandates and legislatively determined criteria.[9]

Furthermore, on the logic of Mosley and company, we should take aggressive AA against Asians and Jews because they are overrepresented in science, technology, and medicine, and we should presume that Asians and Jews are no more talented than average. So that each group receives its fair share, we should ensure that 12 percent of the philosophers in the United States are Black, reduce the percentage of Jews from an estimated 15 percent to 2 percent—thus firing about 1,300 Jewish philosophers. The fact that Asians are producing 50 percent of Ph.D.s in science and math in this country and Blacks less than 1 percent clearly shows, on this reasoning, that we are providing special secret advantages to Asians. By this logic, we should reduce the quota of Blacks in the NBA to 12 percent.

But why does society have to enter into this results game in the first place? Why do we have to decide whether all difference is environmental or genetic? Perhaps we should simply admit that we lack sufficient evidence to pronounce on these issues with any certainty—but if so, should we not be more modest in insisting on equal results? Here's a thought experiment. Take two families of different racial groups, Green and Blue. The Greens decide to have only two children, to spend all their resources on them, and to give them the best possible education. The two Green kids respond well and end up with achievement test scores in the 99th percentile. The Blues fail to practice family planning and have 15 children. They can only afford 2 children, but lack of ability or whatever prevents them from keeping their family size down. Now they need help for their large family. Why does society have to step in and help them? Society did not force them to have 15 children. Suppose that the achievement test scores of the 15 children fall below the 25th percentile. They cannot compete with the Greens. But now enters AA. It says that it is society's fault that the Blue children are not as able as the Greens and that the Greens must pay extra taxes to enable the Blues to compete. No restraints are put on the Blues regarding family size. This seems unfair to the Greens. Should the Green children be made to bear responsibility for the consequences of the Blues' voluntary behavior?[10]

My point is simply that philosophers like Arthur and Mosley need to cast their net wider and recognize that demographics and childbearing and childrearing practices are crucial factors in achievement. People have to take some responsibility for their actions. The equal results argument (or axiom) misses a greater part of the picture.

We have considered five arguments for Affirmative Action and have found no compelling case for Strong AA and only one plausible argument (a version of the compensation argument) for Weak AA. We must now turn to the arguments against Affirmative Action to see whether they fare any better.

II. ARGUMENTS AGAINST AFFIRMATIVE ACTION

6. Affirmative Action Requires Discrimination Against a Different Group

Weak AA weakly discriminates against new minorities, mostly innocent young White males, and Strong Affirmative Action strongly discriminates against these new minorities. As I argued in I. 4, this discrimination is unwarranted, since, even if some compensation to Blacks were indicated, it would be unfair to make innocent White males bear the whole brunt of the payments. Recently I had this experience. I knew a brilliant philosopher, with outstanding publications in first level journals, who was having difficulty getting a tenure-track position. For the first time in my life I offered to make a phone call on his behalf to a university to which he had applied. When I got the Chair of the Search Committee, he offered that the committee was under instructions from the Administration to hire a woman or a Black. They had one of each on their short-list, so they weren't even considering the applications of White males. At my urging he retrieved my friend's file, and said, "This fellow looks far superior to the two candidates we're interviewing, but there's nothing I can do about it." Cases like this come to my attention regularly. In fact, it is poor White youth who become the new pariahs on the job market. The children of the wealthy have little trouble getting into the best private grammar schools and, on the basis of superior early education, into the best universities, graduate schools, and managerial and professional positions. Affirmative Action simply shifts injustice, setting Blacks, Hispanics, Native Americans, Asians, and women against young White males, especially ethnic and poor White males. It makes no more sense to discriminate in favor of a rich Black or female who had the opportunity of the best family and education available against a poor White, than it does to discriminate in favor of White males against Blacks or women. It does little to rectify the goal of providing equal opportunity to all.

At the end of his essay supporting Affirmative Action, Albert Mosley points out that other groups besides Blacks have been benefited by AA, "women, the disabled, the elderly."[11] He's correct in including the elderly, for through powerful lobbies, such as the AARP, they do get special benefits, including Medicare, and can sue on the grounds of being discriminated against because of *Agism*, prejudice against older people. Might this not be a reason to reconsider Affirmative Action? Consider the sheer rough percentages of those who qualify for AA programs.

The elderly can sue on the grounds of Agism, receive entitlements in terms of Social Security and Medicare, and have the AARP lobbying on their behalf. Recently, it has been proposed that homosexuals be included in oppressed groups deserving Affirmative Action.[12] At Northeastern University in 1996 the faculty governing body voted to grant homosexuals Affirmative Action status at this university. How many more percentage points would this add? Several authors have advocated putting all poor people on the list.[13] And if we took handicaps seriously would we not add ugly people, obese people, and, especially, short people, for which there is ample evidence of discrimination? How about left-handed people (about 9 percent of the population)—they can't play short-stop or third base and have to put up with a right-handedly biased world. The only group not the list is that of White males. Are they, especially healthy, middle class young White males, becoming the new "oppressed class"? Should we add them to our list?

Respect for persons entails that we treat each person as an end in him or herself, not simply as a means to be used for social purposes. What is wrong about discrimination against Blacks is that it fails to treat Black people as individuals, judging them by their skin color, rather than their merit. What is wrong about discrimination against women is that it fails to treat them as individuals, judging them by their gender, rather than their merit. What is equally wrong about *Affirmative Action* is that it fails to treat White males with dignity as individuals, judging them by *both their race and gender*, instead of by their merit. *Current Strong Affirmative Action is both racist and sexist.*

Group	Percentage in Population
1. Women	52
2. Blacks	12
3. Hispanics	9
4. Native Americans	2
5. Asians	4
6. Physically & Mentally Disabled	10
7. Welfare recipients	6
8. The Elderly	25
	(est. Adults over 60)
9. Italians (in New York City)	3
Totals	123

Table 1

7. Affirmative Action Encourages Mediocrity and Incompetence

A few years ago Reverend Jesse Jackson joined protesters at Harvard Law School in demanding that the Law School faculty hire Black women. Jackson dismissed Dean of the Law School Robert C. Clark's standard of choosing the best qualified person for the job as "Cultural anemia." "We cannot just define who is qualified in the most narrow vertical academic terms," he said. "Most people in the world are yellow, brown, black, poor, non-Christian and don't speak English, and they can't wait for some White males with archaic rules to appraise them."[14] It might be noted that if Jackson is correct about the depth of cultural decadence at Harvard, Blacks might be well advised to form and support their own more vital law schools and leave places like Harvard to their archaism.

Bernard Davis, the nationally renown biochemist at Harvard Medical School, objected that black medical students at Harvard were being allowed to graduate without passing their final medial exam. When one student repeatedly failed but was nevertheless given his medical degree, Davis protested. He was ordered by the administration to keep quiet about it. When Davis revealed the story to the Harvard newspaper, he was stunned to find that not only was his news unwelcome, but he was branded as a traitor by the majority of faculty and students. Isolated from the faculty, he finally issued a public apology for his "offense."

At several universities, the administration has forced departments to hire members of minorities even when far superior candidates were available. Shortly after obtaining my Ph.D. in the late 1970s I was mistakenly identified as a black philosopher (I had a civil rights record and was once a Black studies major) and was flown to a major university, only to be rejected for a more qualified candidate when it discovered that I was White.

Stories of the bad effects of Affirmative Action abound. The philosopher Sidney Hook writes, "At one Ivy League university, representatives of the Regional HEW[15] demanded an explanation of why there were no women or minority students in the Graduate Department of Religious Studies. They were told that a reading of knowledge of Hebrew and Greek was presupposed. Whereupon the representatives of HEW advised orally: 'Then end those old fashioned programs that require irrelevant languages. And start up programs on relevant things which minority group students can study without learning languages.'"[16]

Here is the HEW Revised Order No. 4, requiring colleges to devise plans to recruit and hire members of minority groups and women, "to reject male (white) and nonminority applicants who might have better credentials than female and minority applicants so long as the latter have qualifications *better than the least qualified member presently employed by a department*."[17]

Furthermore, no test may be given to candidates unless it is *proved* to be relevant to the job.

No standard or criteria which have, by intent or effect, worked to exclude women or minorities as a class can be utilized, unless the institution can demonstrate the necessity of such standard to the performance of the job in question.

Whenever a validity study is called for . . . the user should include . . . an investigation of suitable alternative selection procedures and suitable alternative methods of using the selection procedure which have as little adverse impact as possible. . . . Whenever the user is shown an alternative selection procedure with evidence of less adverse impact and substantial evidence of validity for the same job in similar circumstances, the user should investigate it to determine the appropriateness of using or validating it in accord with these guidelines.[18]

At the same time Americans are wondering why standards in our country are falling, and the Japanese and Koreans are getting ahead. Affirmative Action with its twin idols—Sufficiency of Qualification and Diversity—is the enemy of excellence. I will develop this thought in the next section.

8. An Argument from the Principle of Merit

Traditionally, we have believed that the highest positions in society should be awarded to those who are best qualified. The Koran states, "A ruler who appoints any man to an office, when there is in his dominion another man better qualified for it, sins against God and against the State." Rewarding excellence both seems just to the individuals in the competition and makes for efficiency. Note that one of the most successful acts of racial integration, the Brooklyn Dodger's recruitment of Jackie Robinson in the late 40s, was done in just this way—according to merit. If Robinson had been brought into the major league as a mediocre player or had batted .200 he would have been scorned and sent back to the minors where he belonged.

Merit is not an absolute value, but there are strong *prima facie* reasons for awarding positions on that basis, and it should enjoy a weighty presumption in our social practices.

In a celebrated article Ronald Dworkin says "Bakke had no case" because society did not owe Bakke anything. That might be, but then why does society owe anyone anything? Dworkin puts the matter in terms of Utility, but if that is the case, society might owe Bakke a place at the University of California, Davis, for it seems a reasonable rule-utilitarian principle that achievement should be rewarded in society. We generally want the best to have the best positions, the best qualified candidate to win the political office, the most brilliant and competent scientist to be chosen for the most challenging research project, the best qualified pilots to become commercial pilots, only the best soldiers to become generals. Only when little is at stake do we weaken the standards and content ourselves with sufficiency (rather than excellence)—there are plenty of jobs where "sufficiency" rather than excellence is required. Perhaps we have even come to feel that medicine or law or university professorships are so routine that they can be performed by minimally qualified people—in which case AA has a place.

Note! No one is calling for quotas or proportional representation of *underutilized* groups in the National Basketball Association where Blacks make up 80 percent of the players. But, surely, if merit and merit alone reigns in sports, should it not be valued at least as much in education and industry?

The case for meritocracy has two pillars. One pillar is a deontological argument that holds that we ought to treat people as ends and not merely means. By giving people what they deserve as *individuals,* rather than as members of *groups* we show respect for their inherent worth. If you and I take a test, and you get 95 percent of the answers correct, and I only get 50 percent correct, it would be unfair to you for both of us to receive the same grade, say an A, and even more unfair to give me a higher grade, A+, than your B+. Although I have heard cases where teachers have been instructed to "race norm" in grading (giving Blacks and Hispanics higher grades for the same numerical scores as Whites get), most proponents of AA stop short of advocating such a practice. But isn't race-norming just a logical extension of preferential treatment in admissions? If teachers shouldn't do it, why should administrators?

The second pillar for meritocracy is utilitarian. In the end, we will be better off by honoring excellence. We want the best leaders, teachers, policemen, physicians, generals, lawyers, and airplane pilots that we can possibly produce in society. So our program should be to promote equal opportunity, as much as is feasible in a free market economy, and reward people according to their individual merit.[19]

CONCLUSION

Let me sum up my discussion. The goal of the Civil Rights movement and of moral people everywhere has been justice for all, including equal opportunity. The question is how best to get there. Civil Rights legislation removed the unjust legal barriers, opening the way towards equal opportunity, but it did not tackle the deeper causes that produce differential results. Weak Affirmative Action aims at encouraging minorities to strive for excellence in all areas of life, without unduly jeopardizing the rights of majorities. The problem of Weak Affirmative Action is that it easily slides into Strong Affirmative Action where quotas, "goals and time-tables," "equal results,"—in a word—*reverse discrimination*— prevail and are forced onto groups, thus promoting mediocrity, inefficiency, and resentment. Furthermore, AA aims at the higher levels of society—universities and skilled jobs, but if we want to improve our society, the best way to do it is to concentrate on families, children, early education, and the like, so all are prepared to avail themselves of opportunity. Affirmative Action, on the one hand, is too much, too soon and on the other hand, too little, too late.

In addition to the arguments I have offered, Affirmative Action, rather than uniting people of good will in the common cause of justice, tends to balkanize us into segregation-thinking. Professor Derrick Bell of Harvard Law School recently said that the African American Supreme Court Judge Clarence Thomas, in his opposition to Affirmative Action "doesn't think black."[20] Does

Bell really claim that there is a standard and proper "Black" (and presumably a White) way of thinking? Ideologues like Bell, whether radical Blacks like himself, or Nazi's who advocate "think Aryan," both represent the same thing: cynicism about rational debate, the very antithesis of the quest for impartial truth and justice. People who believe in reason to resolve our differences will oppose this kind of balkanization of the races.

Martin Luther said that humanity is like a man mounting a horse who always tends to fall off on the other side of the horse. This seems to be the case with Affirmative Action. Attempting to redress the discriminatory iniquities of our history, our well-intentioned social engineers now engage in new forms of discriminatory iniquity and thereby think that they have successfully mounted the horse of racial harmony. They have only fallen off on the other side of the issue.[21]

NOTES

1. This argument is related to *The Need of Breaking Stereotypes Argument*. Society might simply need to know that there are talented Blacks and women, so that it does not automatically assign them lesser respect or status. The right response is that hiring less qualified people is neither fair to those better qualified who are passed over nor an effective way to remove inaccurate stereotypes. If high competence is accepted as the criterion for hiring, then it is unjust to override it for purposes of social engineering. Furthermore, if Blacks and women are known to hold high positions simply because of reverse discrimination, they will still lack the respect due those of their rank.

2. Stephen Kershnar suggested this point to me.

3. For a good discussion of this argument see B. Boxill, "The Morality of Reparation" in *Social Theory and Practice* 2:1 (1972) and Albert G. Mosley in his and Nicholas Capaldi, *Affirmative Action: Social Justice or Unfair Preference?* (Rowman and Littlefield, 1996), p. 23–27 (reprinted in this volume).

4. Merit sometimes can be justifiably overridden by need, as when parents choose to spend extra earnings on special education for their disabled child rather than for their gifted child. Sometimes we override

merit for utilitarian purposes. For example, suppose you are the best short stop on a baseball team but are also the best catcher. You'd rather play short stop, but the manager decides to put you at catcher because, although your friend can do an adequate job at short, no one else is adequate at catcher. It's permissible for you to be assigned the job of catcher. Probably, some expression of appreciation would be due you.

5. Judith Jarvis Thomson, "Preferential Hiring" in Marshall Cohen, Thomas Nagel, and Thomas Scanlon eds., *Equality and Preferential Treatment* (Princeton: Princeton University Press, 1977).

6. Stephen Kershnar pointed this out in written comments (Dec. 22, 1997).

7. See Mosley, op. cit., p. 28 and Bernard Boxill *Blacks and Social Justice* (Rowman & Littlefield, 1984), whom Mosley quotes in his article, and who also defends this position.

8. The results of average GRE, LSAT, MCAT scores show similar patterns or significant average racial difference. The Black scholar Glenn Loury notes, "In 1990 black high school seniors from families with annual incomes of $70,000 or more scored an average of 855 on the SAT, compared with average scores of 855 and 879 respectively for Asian-American and White seniors whose families had incomes between $10,000 and 20,000 per year." Larry Hedges and Amy Nowell, "Sex Differences in Mental Test Scores, Variability, and Numbers of High-Scoring Individuals" *Science* vol. 269 (July 1995), pp. 41–45. See Phillip E. Vernon's summary of the literature in *Intelligence: Heredity and Environment* (New York, 1979), Yves Christen, "Sex Differences in the Human Brain" in Nicholas Davidson (ed.) *Gender Sanity* (Rowman & Littlefield, 1989) and T. Bouchard, et al., "Sources of Human Psychological Differences: The Minnesota Studies of Twins Reared Apart" *Science* vol 250 (1990); Richard Herrnstein and Charles Murray, The Bell Curve (New York: Free Press, 1994); and Michael E. Levin, *Why Race Matters* (Westport, CT: Praeger, 1997) for support for the thesis of racial and gender differences. Although these matters are controversial, the evidence for average differences must be carefully considered before we accept the equal outcomes thesis. See also Arianna Stassinopoulos, *The Female Woman* (Davis-Poynter, 1973) p. 28f for corroboration of this thesis.

9. Powell, 1978, 2751, note #36, *Supreme Court Reporter*, 98A. Italics added. Alan Bakke sued the University of California at Davis Medical school be-

cause it rejected him in favor of 16 Black candidates who had lower scores.

10. Iddo Landau, "Are You Entitled to Affirmative Action" (*Applied Philosophy* vol. 11 (Winter/ Spring 1997) and Richard Kahlenberg "Class Not Race" (*The New Republic* April 3, 1995) advocate affirmative action on the basis of class or low income, not race or gender. I think this is an improvement, depending on how it is implemented, but it ignores family responsibility.

11. Albert Mosley, op. cit., p. 53.

12. J. Sartorelli, "The Nature of Affirmative Action, Anti-Gay Oppression, and the Alleviation of Enduring Harm" *International Journal of Applied Philosophy* (vol. 11. No. 2, 1997).

13. For example, Iddo Landau, "Are You Entitled to Affirmative Action?" *International Journal of Applied Philosophy* (vol. 11. No. 2, 1997) and Richard Kahlenberg "Class Not Race" (*The New Republic* April 3, 1995).

14. *New York Times*, May 10, 1990.

15. HEW stands for the Federal Department of "Health, Education & Welfare."

16. Quoted by Nicholas Capaldi, *Out of Order: Affirmative Action and the Crisis of Doctrinaire Liberalism* (Buffalo, NY: Prometheus, 1985).

17. Quoted in John Bunzel, "Minority Faculty Hiring: Problems and Prospects," *American Scholar* 59 (1990), p. 39. I'm curious about how one was supposed to identify the "least qualified."

18. Capaldi, Ibid. Michael Levin begins his book *Feminism and Freedom* (Transaction Press: 1987) with federal court case *Beckman v NYFD* in which 88 women who failed the New York City Fire Department's entrance exam in 1977 filed a class-action sex discrimination suit. The court found that the physical strength component of the test was not job-related, and thus a violation of Title VII of the Civil Rights Act, and ordered the city to hire 49 of the women. It further ordered the fire department to devise a special, less-demanding physical strength exam for women. Following EEOC guidelines, if the passing rate for women is less than 80 percent that of the passing rate of men, the test is presumed invalid.

19. For further discussion of this point, see my "Equality and Desert" *Philosophy* 72 (1997) and the version of this essay in *The International Journal of Applied Ethics* (1998).

20. See L. Gordon Crovitz, "Borking Begins, but Mudballs Bounce Off Judge Thomas," *The Wall Street Journal*, July 17, 1991. Have you noticed the irony in this mudslinging at Judge Thomas? The same Blacks and Whites who oppose Judge Thomas, as not the best person for the job, are themselves the strongest proponents of Affirmative Action, which embraces the tenet that minimally qualified Blacks and women should get jobs over White males.

21. Some of the material in this essay appeared in "The Moral Status of Affirmative Action" *Public Affairs Quarterly*, vol 6:2 (1992). I have not had space to consider all the objections to my position or discuss the issue of freedom of association that, I think, should be given much scope in private but not in public institutions. Barbara Bergmann (*In Defense of Affirmative Action* [New York: Basic Books, 1996, p. 122–125]) and others argue that we already offering preferential treatment for athletes and veterans, especially in university admissions, so, being consistent, we should provide it for women and minorities. My answer is that I am against giving athletic scholarships, and I regard scholarships to veterans as a part of a contractual relationship, a reward for service to one's country. But I distinguish entrance programs from actual employment. I don't think that veterans should be afforded special privilege in hiring practices, unless it be as a tie breaker.

I should also mention that my arguments from merit and respect apply more specifically to public institutions than private ones, where issues of property rights and freedom of association carry more weight.

My gratitude to Wallace Matson, Bill Shaw, Stephen Kershnar, Jim Landesman, and Elliot Cohen for comments on earlier versions of this essay.

For Further Reflection

1. Analyze the differences between Weak and Strong Affirmative Action. Do you think the distinction is plausible? Is there a better way to distinguish different types of Affirmative Action?

2. Examine Pojman's eight arguments. Which seem the strongest and which the weakest?

3. Does Pojman overstate the case that Affirmative Action is racist and sexist? Is there a difference in the intent of racism and sexism versus the intent of Affirmative Action? If so, how significant is this from a moral point of view?

4. Examine Derrick Bell's claim at the end of this article where he claims that Supreme Court Judge Clarence Thomas "doesn't think black"? Do you agree with Bell? Should people of different racial and ethnic groups reason differently or is reason impartial between race, ethnicity, and gender?

5. Compare Mosley and Pojman's articles. How do their arguments differ? Who has made the better case?

6. What do you think about Affirmative Action? Explain your views.

Suggestions for Further Reading

Boxill, Bernard. *Blacks & Social Justice.* Lanham, MD: Rowman & Littlefield, 1992.

Beckwith, Frank, and Todd Jones, eds. *Affirmative Action.* Amherst, NY: Prometheus, 1997.

Bergmann, Barbara R. *In Defense of Affirmative Action.* New York: Basic Books, 1996.

Cahn, Steven M., ed. *The Affirmative Action Debate.* New York: Routledge, 1995.

Carter, Stephen. *Reflections of an Affirmative Action Baby.* New York: Basic Books, 1993.

Cohen, Carl. *Naked Racial Preference.* New York: Madison Books, 1995.

Cohen, Marshall, Thomas Nagel and Thomas Scanlon, eds. *Equality and Preferential Treatment.* Princeton: Princeton University Press, 1977. Contains important essays by Ronald Dworkin, Thomas Nagel, Robert Simon, George Sher and Judith Jarvis Thomson.

D'Souza, Dinesh. *The End of Racism.* New York: Free Press, 1995.

Ezorsky, Gertrude. *Racism and Justice.* Ithaca, NY: Cornell University Press, 1991.

Levin, Michael. *Why Race Matters.* West Port, CT: Praeger, 1997.

Mosley, Albert G. and Nicholas Capaldi. *Affirmative Action: Social Justice or Unfair Preference?* Lanham, MD: Rowman & Littlefield, 1997.

Sadler, A. E. ed. *Affirmative Action.* San Diego, CA: Greenhaven Press, 1996.

Sowell, Thomas. *Race and Culture: A World View.* New York: Basic Books, 1993.

Steele, Shelby. *The Content of Our Character.* New York: St. Martin's Press, 1990.

Thernstron, Stephan and Abigail Thernstrom. *America in Black and White: One Nation, Indivisible.* New York: Simon & Schuster, 1997.

Wasserstrom, Richard. "On Racism and Sexism" in *Today's Moral Problems,* ed. Richard Wasserstrom. 3rd ed. New York: Macmillan, 1985.

Appendix

How to Read and Write a Philosophy Paper

Nothing worthwhile was ever accomplished without great difficulty.

PLATO, *The Republic*

Just about everyone who comes to philosophy—usually in college—feels a sinking sensation in his or her stomach when first encountering this very strange material, involving a different sort of style and method from anything else they have ever dealt with. It was certainly my first reaction as a student. Lured by questions such as "Is there a God? What can I truly know? What is the meaning of life? How shall I live my life?" I began to read philosophy on my own. My first book was Bertrand Russell's *History of Western Philosophy,* which is much more than a history of the subject, being also Russell's own analysis and evaluation of major themes in the history of Western philosophy. Although it is not a terribly difficult text, most of the ideas and arguments were new to me. Since he opposed many of the beliefs that I had been brought up with, I felt angry with him. But since he seemed to argue so persuasively, my anger gave way to confusion and then to a sense of defeat and despair. Yet I felt compelled to go on with this "forbidden fruit," finishing Russell's long work and going on to read Plato's *Republic,* René Descartes' *Meditations,* David Hume's *Dialogues on Natural Religion,* selected writings of Immanuel Kant, William James' *Will to Believe,* and finally contemporary readings by Antony Flew, R. M. Hare, John Hick, and Ludwig Wittgenstein. Gradually, I became aware that on every issue on which I disagreed with Hume or Russell, Kant or Hick, someone else had a plausible counterargument. Eventually, I struggled to the place where I could see weaknesses in arguments (sometimes in the arguments of those figures with whom I had agreed) and finally I came to the point where I could write out arguments of my own. The pain of the process slowly gave way to joy—almost addictive joy, let me warn you—so that I decided to go to graduate school to get an advanced degree in philosophy.

As I mentioned earlier, it was a gnawing worry about fundamental questions of existence that drew me to philosophy. Is there a God? What can I know for sure? Do I have a soul that will live forever? Am I truly free, or simply determined by my heredity and environment? What is it to live a moral life? If you have asked these questions and

Reprinted from Louis P. Pojman, Introduction to Philosophy: Classical and Contemporary Readings *(Belmont, CA: Wadsworth, 1991).*

pondered alternative responses, most of the essays in this book will make sense to you. But if you haven't spent a lot of time thinking about this sort of subject matter, you might ask yourself whether or not these questions are important, and you might outline your own present responses to them. For unless you've asked the questions, the proposed answers can sound like only one end of a telephone conversation.

This textbook is meant to suggest responses to stimulate you to work out your own position on the questions addressed herein. This text, offering readings on alternative sides of each issue, along with a teacher to serve as a guide—and, I hope, some fellow students with whom to discuss the material—should challenge you to begin to work out your own philosophy of life.

However, neither the textbook nor the teacher will be sufficient to save you from a sense of disorientation and uncertainty in reading and writing about philosophy, so let me offer a few tips from my experience as a student and as a teacher of philosophy.

Suggestions on Reading a Philosophy Text

The styles and methods of philosophy are different from other subjects with which you have been acquainted since grammar school: English, history, psychology, and science. Of course, there are many methods, and some writings—for example, those of the existentialists: Søren Kierkegaard, Friedrich Nietzsche, Albert Camus, and Jean-Paul Sartre—do resemble what we encounter in literature more than more typical essays in philosophical analysis. In some ways philosophy resembles mathematics because it usually strives to develop a deductive argument much like a mathematical proof, only the premises of the argument are usually in need of a lot of discussion and objections need to be considered. Sometimes I think of arguing about a philosophical problem as a kind of legal reasoning before a civil court. Each side presents its evidence and gives reasons for accepting its conclusion rather than the opponent's. For example, suppose you believe in freedom of the will and I believe in determinism. We each set forth the best reasons we have for accepting our respective conclusions. The difference between philosophical argument and the court case is that we are also the jury. We can change our minds on hearing the evidence and even change sides by hearing our opponent make a persuasive case.

Suggestions on Writing a Philosophy Paper

Talking about philosophy and writing philosophy are excellent ways to improve your understanding of the content and process of the subject as well as to improve your philosophical reasoning skill. Writing an essay on a philosophical issue focuses your mind and forces you to concentrate on the essential arguments connected with the

issue. The process is hard, but it's amazing how much progress one can make—some faster than others, but in my experience some of those who have the hardest time at first end up doing the deepest, most thorough work.

First, identify a *problem* you want to shed light on or solve or a *thesis* you want to defend. Be sure that you have read at least a few good articles on different sides of the issue and can put the arguments in your own words.

Now you are ready to begin to write. Here are some suggestions that might help you.

1. Identify the problem you want to analyze. For example, you might want to show that W.T. Stace (in Part V) has put forth an unsound argument for the thesis that free will and determinism are compatible.

2. As clearly as possible, state the problem and what you intend to show (for example, "I intend to analyze Stace's argument for compatibilism and show that he has misconstrued the issue. His argument for compatibilism is unsound.").

3. Set forth your argument in logical order, supporting your own premises with reasons. It might help to illustrate your points with examples or to point out counterexamples to the opposing points of view.

4. Consider alternative points of view from your own and objections to your position. Try to meet these charges and to show why your position is more plausible.

5. End your paper with a summary and a conclusion: Review your argument and show its implications for other issues.

6. You will probably need to write at least two drafts before you have a working copy. It helps to have another philosophy student go over the preliminary draft before you write a final draft. Make sure that your argument is well constructed and that your paper as a whole is coherent.

7. Regarding style, write *clearly*, in an active voice, put other people's ideas in your own words as much as possible, and give credit in the text and in bibliographic notes wherever you have used someone else's idea or quoted someone.

8. Include a bibliography at the end of your paper, listing all the sources you used for your paper.

When you have a serious problem, do not hesitate to contact your teacher. That is what he or she is there for: to help you make progress in doing philosophical reasoning.

Good luck and I hope you come to enjoy the philosophical quest for truth and wisdom as much as I have.

Glossary

Abduction   A form of nondeductive reasoning. Sometimes it is referred to as inference to the best explanation in which the proponent argues that this explanation beats all its rivals as a plausible account of the events in question.

Absolute   A moral absolute is a principle that is universally binding. It can never be overridden by another principle. Utilitarianism is a type of system that has only one ethical absolute principle: Do that action which maximizes utility. Kant's system has several absolutes, whereas other deontological systems may have only a few broad absolutes, such as "Never cause unnecessary harm." Sometimes *ethical absolutism* refers to the notion that there is only one correct answer to every moral problem. Diametrically opposed to ethical absolutism is ethical relativism (see also *relativism*), which says that the validity of ethical principles is dependent on social acceptance. Between these polar opposites is ethical objectivism (see *objectivism*, following).

Ad hoc   A proposition added to a theory to save it from being considered logically impossible or implausible. As *ad hoc*, the proposition itself may have little or no support itself, but simply serve to stave off rejection of the original theory.

Affirmative Action   The attempt to correct for past injustice by increasing opportunities for disadvantaged groups. *Weak Affirmative Action* does this by promoting greater equal opportunity *for all, including paying increased attention to the causes of disadvantage. Strong Affirmative Action* goes beyond providing equal opportunity and institutes preferential treatment, which includes reverse discrimination against people who belong to groups that were previously privileged.

Agnosticism   The view that we do not know whether God exists. It is contrasted with theism, the belief in God, and atheism, the belief that there is no such being.

Anthropomorphism   From the Greek "form of humanity," it is the tendency to see the divine as having human properties. David Hume (in Reading II.8) accuses theists of viewing God as a super-human being, rather than as something infinitely beyond humanity.

A posteriori   From the Latin "the later." Knowledge that is obtained only from experience, such as sense perceptions or pain sensations, is a posteriori.

A priori   From the Latin "preceding." Knowledge that is not based on sense experience but is innate or known simply by the meaning of words or definitions is a priori. Hume limited the term to "relations of ideas," referring to analytic truths and mathematics.

Aretaic ethics   (Greek, *arete*, virtue)   The theory, first presented by Aristotle, that the basis of ethical assessment is character. Rather than seeing the heart of ethics in actions or duties, it focuses on the character and dispositions of the agent. Whereas *deontological* and *teleological* ethical systems emphasize *doing*, aretaic or virtue ethics emphasize *being*, being a certain type of person who will no doubt manifest his or her being in appropriate actions. See Part VI.

Atheism   The view that there is no such being as God (see *agnosticism* and *theism*).

Bourgeoisie   In Marxism the bourgeoisie are the capitalists, who own the means of production, the machines and factories, and thus control the lives of the workers, the proletariat.

Categorical imperative   The categorical imperative commands actions which are necessary of themselves without reference to other ends. This is contrasted with *hypothetical imperative* (see following), which commands actions not for their own sakes but for some other good. For Kant, moral duties command categorically. They represent the injunctions of reason, which endows them with universal validity and objective necessity.

Coherence theory of knowledge   The theory that all knowledge or justified beliefs derive from inferential relations between beliefs, forming a web of belief. Its main rival is *Foundationalism*.

Coherence theory of truth   The theory of truth which holds that the truth of a proposition is decided by its cohering with other propositions in an Ultimate System of Reality. Individual propositions may possess degrees of truth to the extent that they diverge from the complete System.

Communism   The political-economic philosophy developed in its most famous form by Karl Marx and Friedrich Engels in the nineteenth century, which holds to (1) economic determinism—that the way a society produces its wealth determines all else; and (2) the notion of a class struggle in which the working class will eventually overthrow the bourgeoisie and establish a proletariat dictatorship.

Compatibilism   The view that an act may be entirely determined and yet be free in the sense that it was done voluntarily and not under external coercion. Stace represents this position in Reading V.41. It is sometimes referred to as "soft determinism."

Contingent   A proposition is contingent if its denial is logically possible. Its denial is not contradictory. A being is contingent if it is not logically necessary.

Contradiction   When one statement denies another, both of which cannot be true. For example, "God exists" and "God does not exist."

Correspondence theory of truth   The theory that a *proposition* is true just in case it corresponds with the facts or states of affairs in reality. The theory goes back to Plato and, especially, Aristotle, who said, "To say of what is that it is not, or of what is not that it is, is false, while to say of what is that it is, or of what is not that it is not, is true."

Deductive argument   An argument is a sound deductive argument if it follows a valid form and has true premises. In that case, the truth of its conclusion is guaranteed. A deductive argument is valid (but not necessarily sound) if it follows an approved form that would guarantee the truth of the conclusion if the premises were true.

Deism   The view that God exists but takes no interest in human affairs. He wound up the world as a clock and then left it to run itself down.

Deontological ethics   Deontological (from the Greek *deon*, which means "duty") ethical systems see certain features in the moral act itself as having intrinsic value. These are contrasted with *teleological ethics* (see following), which see the ultimate criterion of morality in some nonmoral value that results from actions. For example, for the deontologist there is something right about truth-telling even when it might cause pain or harm, and there is something wrong about lying even when it might produce good consequences. See Part VI.

Determinism   The theory that every event and state of affairs in the world, including human actions, is caused. There are two versions of determinism: hard determinism, which states that because every event is caused, no one is responsible for his or her actions, and soft determinism, or *compatibilism*, which states that rational creatures can still be held accountable for their actions insofar as they acted voluntarily.

Disjunctive syllogism (DS)   The logical form of denying the disjunct: Either *P* or *Q*, but not-*P*, therefore *Q*.

Dualism or **dualistic interactionism**   The view that there are two types of substances or realities in conscious beings—mind and matter—and that these interact with one another, the body producing mental events and the mind leading to physical action.

Egoism   There are two types of egoism. Psychological egoism is a *descriptive* theory about human motivation which holds that people always act to satisfy their perceived best interest. Ethical egoism is a *prescriptive* or normative theory about how people *ought* to act. They ought to act according to their perceived best interests. See Part VI.B.

Emergentism   The emergent property view says that in nature the whole is often greater than the sum of its parts. Nature exhibits a hierarchy of systems—subatomic particles, atoms, molecules, cells, organs, and organisms. Each whole manifests properties that its parts lack. For example, water has the property wetness, which its parts, H_2O molecules, lack. Likewise, the mind is a whole, which has the property of consciousness, which its individual parts lack. This view is related to *epiphenomenalism* (see following). See Part IV.B.

Empiricism   The school of philosophy which asserts that the source of all knowledge is experience. John Locke stated that our minds were like blank slates (*tabula rasa*) on which experience writes her messages. There are no innate ideas. Empiricism is contrasted with rationalism, which holds that there are innate ideas so that the mind can discover important metaphysical truth through reason alone. In our readings, Hume and Russell are empiricists.

Epiphenomenalism   A version of dualism which holds that bodily events cause mental events, but mental events do not cause bodily events. The action is one way only, from body to mind.

Epistemology   The study of the nature, origin, and validity of knowledge and belief. See Part III.

Existentialism   The philosophical method that studies human existence from the inside of the subject's experience rather than the outside. It takes a first-person or subjective approach to the ultimate questions rather than a third-person or objective approach. Examples of this view are found in our readings by Jean-Paul Sartre and Albert Camus.

Foundationalism   A theory of knowledge according to which (1) some beliefs are basic, known or justified non-inferentially and (2) these basic beliefs provide the foundations for all other justified beliefs. Its main rival is the *Coherence Theory of Knowledge*.

Hedonic (Greek *hedone*, pleasure)   Possessing pleasurable or painful quality. Sometimes *hedon* is used to stand for a quantity of pleasure.

Hedonism   Psychological hedonism is the theory that motivation is to be explained exclusively in terms of desire for pleasure and aversion from pain. Ethical hedonism is the theory that pleasure is the only intrinsic positive value and pain or "unpleasant consciousness" the only thing which has negative intrinsic value or intrinsic disvalue. All other values are derived from these two. See Part VIII.

Hedonistic paradox   This is the apparent contradiction arising from the doctrine that pleasure is the only thing worth seeking and the fact that whenever one seeks pleasure, it is not found. Pleasure normally arises as as accompaniment of satisfaction of desire whenever one reaches one's goal.

Heteronomy of the will   This is Kant's term for the determination of the will on nonrational grounds. It is contrasted with *autonomy of the will*, where the will is guided by reason.

Hypothetical imperative   Hypothetical imperatives command actions because they are useful for the attainment of some end which one may or may not desire to obtain. Ethicists who view moral duties to be dependent on consequences would view moral principles as hypothetical imperatives. They have the form: If you want *X*, do action *A* (for example, if you want to live in peace, do all in your power to prevent violence). This is contrasted with the *categorical imperative* (above).

Indeterminism   The view that some events are uncaused. Some versions state that some events are uncaused because they happen by chance. Others hold the minimal thesis that some events or states of being (for example, the self) are uncaused, so that free will is consistent with the position. This view is contrasted with *determinism* (above).

Inductive argument   An argument in which the premises support the truth of the conclusion but do not guarantee it (as a valid deductive argument would).

Innate ideas   The theory that appears in Descartes (Reading III.18) that states that all humans are born with certain knowledge.

Intentionality   The view that consciousness is always *about* or *of* something. One never finds mere consciousness existing all by itself. Mental states have objects. I have a belief *about* the president, a thought *of* getting a good grade, a desire *for* friendship.

Intuitionism   This is the ethical theory that the good or the right thing to do can be known directly via the intuition. G.E. Moore is an intuitionist about the good, defining it as a simple, unanalyzable property.

Lex talionis   Literally, the law of the claw. The theory of retaliation, stemming from the biblical passage (Exod. 21:23f), which says that the punishment for a crime shall be "a life for a life, an eye for an eye, a tooth for a tooth, hand for hand, foot for foot, burning for burning, wound for wound, stripe for stripe."

Libertarianism   The metaphysical theory that humans have free will in the sense that given the same antecedent conditions, one can do otherwise. That is, the self is undetermined by causes and is itself the determining cause of action. This view is represented by William James and Richard Taylor in Reading 42. Contrasted with *compatibilism* and *determinism* (see earlier). Political Libertarianism, on the other hand, holds that citizens should be free to do as they wish, so long as they are not violating the rights of others.

Metaphysics ("Beyond physics")   The study of ultimate reality, that which is not readily accessible through ordinary empirical experience. Metaphysics includes within its domain such topics as free will, causality, the nature of matter, immortality, and the existence of God.

Modus ponens (MP)   The logical form of affirming the antecedent in a conditional or hypothetical proposition. For example, If *P* then *Q, P*, therefore *Q*.

Modus tollens (MT)   The logical form of denying the consequent of a conditional or hypothetical proposition. For example, If *P* then *Q*, not-*Q*, therefore not-*P*.

Monism   The theory that reality is all of one substance, rather than two or more. Examples are materialist monism, which holds that matter is the single substance that makes up all there is, and idealism, which holds that all reality is spiritual or made up of ideas. Lucretius, Democritus, Bertrand Russell, and Richard Taylor all hold to materialistic monism. Spinoza, Berkeley, and Hinduism are examples of proponents of idealism.

Naturalism   The theory that ethical terms are defined through factual terms in that ethical terms refer to natural properties. Ethical hedonism is one version of ethical naturalism, for it states that the good which is the basis of all ethical judgment refers to the experience of pleasure. Other naturalists like Geoffrey Warnock speak of the content of morality in terms of promoting human flourishing or ameliorating the human predicament.

Natural theology   The view that knowledge of God can be obtained through the use of reason. Strong versions hold that we can prove the existence of God. It is contrasted with revealed theology, which holds that all knowledge of God must come from a revelation of God.

Necessary truth   One that cannot be false, such as analytic propositions (for example, "All bachelors are male").

Noncognitivism   This is the theory that ethical judgments have no truth value but express attitudes or prescriptions.

Objectivism   This is the view that moral principles have objective validity whether or not people recognize them as such; that is, moral rightness or wrongness does not depend on social approval but on independent considerations. Objectivism differs from absolutism in that it allows that all or many of its principles are overridable in given situations. See Part VI.

Objectivity   The view that reason can make impartial judgments; that there is "inter-subjectively accessible knowledge, by definition truly independent of anyone's biases, traditions, wishes, or other influences" (Levin, Reading III.26).

Occam's Razor   Sometimes called "the principle of parsimony." Named after William of Occam (1290–1349), this states that "entities are not to be multiplied beyond necessity." The razor metaphor connotes that useless or unnecessary material should be cut away from any explanation and the simplest hypothesis accepted.

Pantheism   The view that God is everything and everything is God.

Physicalism   The view that everything (or every substance) in the universe is physical and subject to the laws of science. Related to the mind / body problem. The physicalist says that even our mental states are physical states. We have no separate soul or mind.

Pragmatism   The theory set forth by C.S. Peirce and William James that interprets the meaning of a statement in terms of its practical consequences. They usually go on to say, as James does in Reading III.24, that a proposition is true or false according to its results.

Prima facie   The Latin word that means "at first glance." It signifies an initial status of an idea or principle. In ethics, beginning with W.D. Ross, it stands for a duty that has a presumption in its favor but may be overridden by another duty. *Prima facie* duties are contrasted with *actual duties* or *all-things-considered duties*.

Proposition   A sentence or statement that must either be true or false. Every statement that "states" how the world is is a proposition. Questions and imperatives are not propositions. "Would you open the door" and "Please, open the door," are not propositions, but "The door is open" is since it claims to describe a situation.

Rationalism   Certain truths are knowable *a priori*, through reflection about those truths. That is, refection alone without empirical observation can yield knowledge of reality. Its main rival is *Empiricism*.

Reductio ad absurdum   (RAA) The logical form of showing that if one accepts a certain proposition as true, he or she would have to accept a contradiction as true, which is irrational.

Reflective Equilibrium   A process of deciding on moral and political correctness through adjusting one's moral principles with one's intuitions.

We begin with our considered moral judgments (those which survive critical scrutiny) and via reflection adjust them to our deepest moral principles, which themselves get altered in this process, until we reach a coherent system. The idea was first described by Nelson Goodman and figures prominently in John Rawls' Theory of Justice.

Relativism   There are two main types of relativism, cultural and ethical. Cultural relativism is a descriptive thesis, stating that there is enormous variety of moral beliefs across cultures. It is neutral as to whether this is the way things ought to be. Ethical relativism, on the other hand, is an evaluative thesis which holds that the truth of a moral judgment depends on whether a culture recognizes the principle in question. See Readings VI.43 and 44.

Retributivism   The view on punishment that the criminal (or moral offender) deserves to be punished in proportion to the seriousness of the offense. Kant held this view. See Part IX.B.

Skepticism   The view that we can have no knowledge. Universal skepticism holds that we cannot know anything at all, whereas local, or particular, skepticism holds that there are important realms in which we are ignorant (e.g., Hume regarding metaphysics).

Speciesism   The view first put forth by Peter Singer (Reading IX.70) that just as one may have a prejudice in favor of one's own race, one may have a prejudice in favor of one's own species.

Supererogatory(from the Latin *supererogatus*—beyond the call of duty)   A supererogatory act is one that is not required by moral principles but contains enormous value. Supererogatory acts are those that are beyond the call of duty, such as risking one's life to save a stranger. Although most moral systems allow for the possibility of supererogatory acts, some theories (most versions of classical utilitarianism) deny that there can be such acts.

Teleological ethics   Teleological ethical theories place the ultimate criterion of morality in some nonmoral value (for example, happiness or welfare) that results from acts. Whereas *deontological* ethical theories (above) ascribe intrinsic value to features of the acts themselves, teleological theories see only instrumental value in the acts but intrinsic value in the consequences of those acts. Both ethical egoism and utilitarianism are teleological theories. See Part VI.

Theism   The belief that a personal God exists and is providentially involved in human affairs. It is to be contrasted with atheism, which believes that no such being exists, and deism, which holds that God exists but he is not providentially concerned with human affairs.

Theodicy   This view holds that evil can be explained in the light of an overall plan of God and that, rightly understood, this world is the best of all possible worlds. John Hick holds to a version of this doctrine in Reading II.12.

Universalizability   This principle, found explicitly in Kant's and R.M. Hare's philosophy and implicitly in most ethicists' work, states that if some act is right (or wrong) for one person in a situation, it is right (or wrong) for any relevantly similar person in that kind of a situation. It is a principle of consistency, which aims to eliminate irrelevant considerations from ethical assessment.

Utilitarianism   The theory that the right action is that which maximizes utility. Sometimes utility is defined in terms of *pleasure* (Jeremy Bentham), *happiness* (J.S. Mill), *ideals* (G.E. Moore and H. Rashdall), or *interests* (R.B. Perry). Its motto, which characterizes one version of utilitarianism, is "the greatest happiness for the greatest number." Utilitarians further divide into *act* and *rule* utilitarians. Act utilitarians hold that the right act in a situation is that which results (or is most likely to result) in the best consequences, whereas rule utilitarians hold that the right act is that which conforms to the set of rules which in turn will result in the best consequences (relative to other sets of rules). (See Reading VI.50.)